WITHDRAWN

THE
MACMILLAN
TREASURY
OF
RELEVANT
QUOTATIONS

THE
MACMILLAN
TREASURY
OF
RELEVANT
QUOTATIONS

THE

MACMILLAN

TREASURY

OF

RELEVANT

QUOTATIONS

Edward F. Murphy

M

First published 1979 and
reprinted 1980 by
THE MACMILLAN PRESS LTD London and Basingstoke

Companies and representatives throughout the world

ISBN 0 333 30038 6

ACKNOWLEDGMENTS

Grateful acknowledgment is made to the following for permission to reprint selections included in this book:

HARRY N. ABRAMS, INC. for The Face of Violence by J. Bronowski. GEORGE ALLEN & UNWIN LTD. for The Joys of Forgetting by Odell Shepard; Thus Spake Zarathustra by Friedrich Nietzsche. ARNO PRESS, INC. for Art and Reality: Ways of the Creative Process by Joyce Cary; Over the Bent World edited by Sr. Mary Louise, S.L.; What America Means to Me and Other Poems and Prayers by Francis Cardinal Spellman. ASSOCIATED BOOK PUBLISHERS LTD. for The Blue Lion by Robert Lynd; 365 Days and One More, by E.V. Lucas. THE ATLANTIC MONTHLY PRESS for The Letters of William James edited by Henry James. A.S. BARNES & COMPANY, INC. for Mark Twain at Your Fingertips edited by Caroline Thomas Harnsberger. BASIC BOOKS, INC. for The Letters of Sigmund Freud selected and edited by Ernst L. Freud, translated by Tania and James Stern, © 1960 by Sigmund Freud Copyrights Ltd. London. BEACON PRESS for The Pursuit of Loneliness by Philip Slater, revised edition, copyright 1970, 1976 by Philip E. Slater. BERNER & GUTLIN (ATTORNEYS) for Mince Pie by Christopher Morley. Visva-Bharati for Letters to a Friend by Rabindranath Tagore. BLACK SPARROW PRESS for "A Poet Recognizing the Echo of the Voice," copyright 1970 by Diäne Wakoski, reprinted from The Magellanic Clouds. BOBBS-MERRILL COMPANY, INC. for Journey for Myself by Colette, copyright 1972. THE BODLEY HEAD for The Bodley Head Scott Fitzgerald, Volume III. GEORGES BORCHARDT, INC. for Pretexts by André Gide. JAMES BROWN ASSOCIATES for Selected Poems and Letters of Emily Dickinson edited by Robert N. Linscott. CAMBRIDGE UNIVERSITY PRESS for On Education by Sir Richard Livingstone; Art and Reality by Joyce Cary. CHATTO AND WINDUS LTD. and THE OWEN ESTATE for "All Sounds Have Been as Music" from The Collected Poems of Wilfred Owen edited by C. Day Lewis, copyright The Owen Estate and Chatto and Windus Ltd.; Gift From the Sea by Anne Morrow Lindbergh; The Right Place by C.E. Montague, copyright Mrs. Rose Elton and Chatto and Windus Ltd. CLARKE, IRWIN AND CO. LTD. for The Table Talk of Samuel Marchbanks by Robertson Davies, copyright 1949 by Clarke Irwin and Co. Ltd. CONSTABLE PUBLISHERS for The Journal of Katherine Mansfield by Katherine Mansfield. COWARD, McCANN & GEOGHEGAN, INC. for The American Male by Myron Brenton, copyright 1966 by Myron Brenton. THOMAS Y. CROWELL CO., INC. for Are You Sure You Love Me? by Lois Wyse; Any Number Can Play by Clifton Fadiman. CROWN PUBLISHERS, INC. for Ideas and Opinions by Alfred Einstein, copyright 1954. CURTIS BROWN LTD. for A Churchill Reader: The Wit and Wisdom of Sir Winston Churchill edited by Colin Coote, copyright 1954 by Colin Coote. DODD, MEAD & COMPANY, INC. for The Diary of Alice James edited by Leon Edel, reprinted by permission of Dodd, Mead & Company, Inc., copyright 1934 by Dodd, Mead & Company, Inc. copyright renewed 1962 by Anna R. Burr, copyright 1964 by Leon Edel. DOUBLEDAY PUBLISHING COMPANY for Selected Poems and Letters of Emily Dickinson edited by Robert N. Linscott; Pieces of Hate and Other Enthusiasms by Heywood Broun; The Craft of Poetry edited by William Packard; The Diary of a Young Girl by Anne Frank; The Friendly Road by David Grayson; Either/Or, two volumes by Sören Kierkegaard; The Almost Perfect State by Don Marquis; Inward Ho by Christopher Morley; Mince Pie by Christopher Morley; Supertalk by Digby Diehl; Dear Theo: The Autobiography of Vincent Van Gogh by Irving Stone. E.P. DUTTON & CO., INC. for Visions and Tasks by Phillips Brooks; The Private Papers of Henry Ryecroft by George Gissing; The Oracle by Baltasar Gracian, translated by L.B. Walton; Letters to His Son W.B. Yeats and Others by J.B. Yeats edited by Joseph Hone. EDITIONS GALLIMARD for The Temptation to Exist by E.M. Cioran, copyright 1956. FARRAR, STRAUS & GIROUX, INC. for On the Contrary by Mary McCarthy; The Selected Letters of Anton Chekov edited by Lillian Hellman; "To the Lacedemonians" from Collected Poems 1919-1976 by Allen Tate, copyright 1952, 1953, 1970, 1977 by Allen Tate; "Pilgrim" by Daniel Sargent from Incident in Silver: A Book of Lyrics by A.M. Sullivan, copyright 1950 by A.M. Sullivan, copyright renewed 1978 by A.M. Sullivan. THE FOLEY AGENCY for The American Male by Myron Brenton. SIGMUND FREUD COPYRIGHTS LTD. for The Letters of Sigmund Freud edited by Ernst L. Freud. HAMISH HAMILTON LTD. for Resistance, Rebellion and Death by Albert Camus, translated by Justin O'Brien,

Norell, Louise Nevelson, et al., *Bulletin,* November 1968. UNIVERSITY OF MINNESOTA PRESS for *Memoirs and Letters* by Oscar W. Firkins, copyright 1934 by the University of Minnesota Press, Minneapolis. WILLIAM MORROW AND COMPANY, INC. for "The December of My Springs" and "The Women Gather" from *The Women and the Men* by Nikki Giovanni, copyright © 1970, 1974, 1975 by Nikki Giovanni. NEW DIRECTIONS PUBLISHING CORP. for *The Crack-Up* by F. Scott Fitzgerald, copyright 1934, 1936 by Esquire Inc. copyright 1945 by New Directions Publishing Corporation, reprinted by permission of New Directions Publishing Corporation; *The Air-Conditioned Nightmare* by Henry Miller, copyright 1945 by New Directions Publishing Corporation; *The Books in My Life* by Henry Miller, copyright © 1969 by New Directions Publishing Corporation; *The Cosmological Eye* by Henry Miller, copyright 1939 by New Directions Publishing Corporation; "All Sounds Have Been as Music" from *Collected Poems* by Wilfred Owen, copyright © by Chatto and Windus Ltd., 1946, 1963. THE NEW YORK TIMES for sixty quotations, copyright 1977 by The New York Times Company, reprinted by permission. W.W. NORTON & CO., INC. for *The Literature of Gossip* by Elizabeth Drew; *Man's Search for Himself* by Rollo May; *The Meaning of Culture* by John Cowper Powys; *Letters of Rainer Maria Rilke* translated by Jane Bannard Greene and M.D. Herter; *Letters to a Young Poet* by Rainer Maria Rilke, translated by Reginald Snell; *Wisdom* edited by James Nelson; *Wisdom for Our Time* edited by James Nelson. OXFORD UNIVERSITY PRESS for *Last Pages From a Journal* by Mark Rutherford (William Hale White); *The Complete Poetical Works of Thomas Hood,* "A Serenade" by Thomas Hood, edited by Walter Jerrold; *The Poems of Gerard Manley Hopkins,* 4th edition edited by W.H. Gardner and N.H. MacKenzie (1947); *The Marriage of Heaven and Hell* by William Blake, edited by Sir Geoffrey Keynes. PENGUIN BOOKS LTD. for *The Politics of Experience* by R.D. Laing; pages 11, 12, 24, 47, 48, 50, 61, 64, 65, 79, 110, copyright © 1967 by R.D. Laing, reprinted by permission of Penguin Books Ltd.; *Selected Essays* by D.H. Lawrence. PHILOSOPHICAL LIBRARY INC. for *De Profundis* by Oscar Wilde. PRINCETON UNIVERSITY PRESS for *Psychological Reflections: An Anthology From the Writing of C.G. Jung* by C.G. Jung, edited by Jolande Jacobi and R.F.C. Hull, Bollingen Series XXXI, copyright 1953 by Princeton University Press, reprinted by permission of Princeton University Press, new edition copyright © 1970 by Princeton University Press; *Either/Or,* 2 volumes by Sören Kierkegaard. G.P. PUTNAM'S SONS for *Gravity and Grace*\by\Simone Weil, copyright 1952 by G.P. Putnam's Sons; *Waiting For God* by Simone Weil, copyright 1951 by G.P. Putnam's Sons. QUADRANGLE BOOKS, INC./THE NEW YORK TIMES BOOK CO. for *The Temptation to Exist* by E.M. Cioran, translated by Richard Howard, copyright © 1956 by Librairie Gallimard, English translation 1968 by Quadrangle Books, Inc., reprinted by permission of Quadrangle Books, Inc./The New York Times Book Co. RANDOM HOUSE, INC. (PANTHEON BOOKS) for *Gift From the Sea* by Anne Morrow Lindbergh, copyright © by Anne Morrow Lindbergh, reprinted by permission of Pantheon Books, a division of Random House, Inc.; *Prophetic Voices: Ideas and Words on Revolution* edited by Ned O'Gorman, copyright © 1969 by Random House, Inc., reprinted by permission of the publisher; *Collected Poems* by W.H. Auden, edited by Edward Mendelson, copyright 1934 and renewed 1962 by W.H. Auden; "Elegy for a Dead Soldier" from *Selected Poems* by Karl Shapiro; *Notebooks 1935–1942* by Albert Camus, translated by Philip Thody, copyright 1963 by Hamish Hamilton Ltd. and Alfred A. Knopf, Inc., reprinted by permission of the publisher; *Resistance, Rebellion and Death,* by Albert Camus, translated by Justin O'Brien, copyright © 1960 by Alfred A. Knopf, Inc., reprinted by permission of the publisher; *The Journals of André Gide* by André Gide, 2 volumes, copyright 1947, 1948, 1949, 1951, © 1956 by Alfred A. Knopf, Inc., reprinted by permission of the publisher; *Markings* by Dag Hammarskjold, translated by Leif Sjoberg and W.H. Auden, copyright © 1964 by Alfred A. Knopf, Inc. and Faber and Faber Ltd., reprinted by permission of the publisher; *Assorted Articles* by D.H. Lawrence, copyright 1940 by Alfred A. Knopf, Inc., reprinted by permission of the publisher; *Selected Poems* by Langston Hughes, copyright © 1959 by Langston Hughes, reprinted by permission of Alfred A. Knopf, Inc. REAL PEOPLE PRESS for *Notes to Myself* by Hugh Prather. ROUTLEDGE & KEEGAN PAUL LTD. for *Psychological Reflections: An Anthology* by C.G. Jung, edited by Jolande Jacobi and R.F.C. Hull, Bollingen Series XXXI, copyright 1953. SCHOCKEN BOOKS, INC. for *The Diaries of Franz Kafka 1914–1923* edited by Max Brod, copyright © 1949 by Schocken Books, Inc., copyright renewed © 1976 by Schocken Books, Inc. CHARLES SCRIBNER'S SONS for *The Letters of Thomas Wolfe* edited by Elizabeth Nowell, copyright 1956 by Edward C. Aswell; *Of Time and the River* by Thomas Wolfe, copyright © 1935 by Charles Scribner's Sons, copyright © 1956 by Edward C. Aswell; *What America Means to Me and Other Poems and Prayers* by Francis Cardinal Spellman. MARTIN SECKER & WARBURG LTD. for *The Diaries of Franz Kafka 1914–1923* edited by Max Brod; *The Journals of André Gide* translated by Justin O'Brien. THE SEED CENTER for *The Lazy Man's Guide to Enlightenment* by Thaddeus Golas. Simon & Schuster for *The Business of Life* by William Feather, copyright © 1949, 1976 by William Feather, reprinted by permission of Simon & Schuster, a Division of Gulf + Western Corporation; *What We Live By* by Abbe Ernest Dimnet, copyright © 1932, 1959 by the Fiduciary Trust Company of New York, reprinted by permission of Simon & Schuster; *Love or Perish* by Dr. Smiley Blanton, copyright © 1955, 1956 by Dr. Smiley Blanton, reprinted by permission of Simon & Schuster; *Journeys* by Richard Lewis, copyright © 1969 by Richard Lewis, reprinted by permission of Simon & Schuster; *Miracles* by Richard Lewis, copyright © 1966 by Richard Lewis, reprinted by permission of Simon & Schuster. THE SOCIETY OF AUTHORS for *Selected Essays* by Havelock Ellis, copyright by the Society of Authors as the literary representative of the Estate of Havelock

Ellis; *Southward Ho! and Other Essays* by Holbrook Jackson, copyright The Society of Authors as the literary representative of the Estate of Holbrook Jackson; *Biography* by John Masefield, copyright the Society of Authors as the literary representative of the Estate of John Masefield; *Poems* by John Masefield, copyright 1912, renewed 1940 by John Masefield. VANGUARD PRESS for *Edith Sitwell: Selected Letters (1919–1964)* edited by John Lehmann and Derek Parker, letters copyright 1970 by Francis Sitwell, editorial matter copyright 1970 by John Lehmann and Derek Parker. THE VIKING PRESS, INC., PUBLISHERS for *A Certain World: A Commonplace Book* by W.H. Auden, copyright © 1970 by W.H. Auden, reprinted by permission of The Viking Press; *Close-Up* by John Gruen, copyright © 1967, 1968 by John Gruen, copyright © 1963, 1964, 1965, 1966, 1967 by *New York Herald Tribune Inc.; A Psychiatrist's World* by Dr. Karl Menninger, copyright © 1959 by Karl Menninger; *Open Secrets* by Barbaralee Diamonstein, copyright © 1970, 1972 by Barbaralee Diamonstein; *Writers at Work/The Paris Review Interviews* edited by Malcolm Cowley, copyright © 1958 by *Paris Review; Writers at Work/The Paris Review Interviews, Third Series* edited by George Plimpton, copyright © 1967 by *Paris Review Inc.; Selected Letters of D.H. Lawrence* edited by Diana Trilling. A.P. WATT & SONS for *Autobiography* by W.B. Yeats; *Letters on Poetry from W.B. Yeats to Dorothy Wellesley* by W.B. Yeats, permission of the Macmillan Co. of London and Basingstoke, M.B. Yeats and Miss Anne Yeats. WESLEYAN UNIVERSITY PRESS for *The Complete Poems of W.H. Davies,* copyright © 1963 by Jonathan Cape Ltd., Reprinted by permission of Wesleyan University Press. WILLIAM FREDERICK PRESS for *The Answering Radiance* by Lydia B. Atkinson.

ABILITY

It is always pleasant to be urged to do something on the ground that one can do it well.

GEORGE SANTAYANA,
The Letters of George Santayana

I get quiet joy from the observation of anyone who does his job well.

WILLIAM FEATHER,
The Business of Life

A man must not deny his manifest abilities, for that is to evade his obligations.

ROBERT LOUIS STEVENSON,
The Treasure of Franchard

Behind an able man there are always other able men.

CHINESE PROVERB

Great ability develops and reveals itself increasingly with every new assignment.

BALTASAR GRACIAN,
The Oracle

Those who believe in our ability do more than stimulate us. They create for us an atmosphere in which it becomes easier to succeed.

JOHN LANCASTER SPALDING,
Aphorisms and Reflections

I don't think thinking about a situation does much good. One knows by instinct what one can do.

A. C. BENSON,
*Excerpts from the Letters
of Dr. A. C. Benson to M. E. A.*

No man's abilities are so remarkably shining as not to stand in need of a proper opportunity, a patron, and even the praises of a friend to recommend them to the notice of the world.

PLINY

We may judge a man's ability by three things: by what he has done (including the impression he has made on others), by what he himself appears to believe he can do, by our own dramatic imagination, based on his immediate personality, of what he might do. If these do not agree it

is prudent to observe him further.

CHARLES HORTON COOLEY,
Life and the Student

ABNEGATION

Every affirmation ends up in abnegation. Everything you renounce in yourself will take on life. Everything that strives to affirm itself negates itself; everything that renounces itself affirms itself.

ANDRÉ GIDE,
Pretexts

ABNORMALITY

In the degree to which I have been privileged to know the intimate secrets of hearts, I ever more realize how great a part is played in the lives of men and women by some little concealed germ of abnormality.

For the most part they are occupied in the task of stifling and crushing those germs, treating them like weeds in their gardens. There is another and better way, even though more difficult and more perilous. Instead of trying to suppress the weeds that can never be killed, they may be cultivated into useful or beautiful flowers. For it is impossible to conceive any impulse in a human heart which cannot be transformed into Truth or into Beauty or into Love.

HAVELOCK ELLIS,
Impressions and Comments

ABORTION

Abortion is a step beyond Contraception. They both control or interfere with Birth. I don't see how anyone who favors Contraception or considers it permissible can object to Abortion.

DR. OSCAR FASKER

A live fetus is, in effect, a pre-infant as a child is a pre-adult. Thus, killing a pre-infant is, like killing any human, homicide.

LAURIE TILSIN, R.N.

Whatever your views concerning suicide may be, would you help anyone to commit suicide? Whatever your views concerning abortion may be, would you help anyone to commit abortion? Think about it.

REV. J.R. REINEST

ABSENCE

Morning without you is dwindled dawn.

EMILY DICKINSON,
Selected Poems and Letters of Emily Dickinson

Take warning from all those times when, on meeting again, we feel ashamed because we realize we had accepted the false simplification which absence permits, its obliteration of all those characteristics which, when we meet face to face, force themselves upon even the blindest.

DAG HAMMARSKJÖLD,
Markings

When you're away, I'm restless, lonely,
Wretched, bored, dejected; only
Here's the rub my darling dear,
I feel the same when you are near.

SAMUEL HOFFENSTEIN,
"When You're Away,"
Poems in Praise of Practically Nothing

No one speaks of us in our presence as he does in our absence.

BLAISE PASCAL,
Pensées

Absence abates a moderate passion and intensifies a great one—as the wind blows out a candle but fans fire into flame.

LA ROCHEFOUCAULD,
Maxims

Where you used to be, there is a hole in the world, which I find myself constantly walking around in the day-time, and falling into at night. I miss you like hell.

EDNA ST. VINCENT MILLAY,
Letters of Edna St. Vincent Millay

The absent are always at fault.

SPANISH PROVERB

ABSURD

There is only one truth, steadfast, healing, salutary, and that is the absurd.

ANDREW SALMON,
quoted in *The Third Rose*
by John Malcolm Brinnin

Why shouldn't things be largely absurd, futile, and transitory? They are so, and we are so, and they and we go very well together.

GEORGE SANTAYANA,
The Letters of George Santayana

Talking about things that are understandable only weighs down the mind and falsifies the memory, but the absurd excites the mind and makes the memory work.

ALFRED JARRY,
quoted in *The Third Rose*
by John Malcolm Brinnin

My impression is that if I try to find the meaning of my own experience it leads me, nearly always, in directions regarded as absurd.

CARL R. ROGERS,
On Becoming a Person

Everything is funny; the greatest earnestness is funny; even tragedy is funny. And I think what I try to do in my plays is to get this recognizable reality of the absurdity of what we do and how we behave and how we speak.

HAROLD PINTER,
The Theatre of the Absurd by Martin Esslin

ACADEMIC (*See* SCHOLAR)

ACCEPTANCE

We cannot change anything unless we accept it. Condemnation does not liberate, it oppresses.

C. G. JUNG,
Psychological Reflections,
edited by Jolande Jacobi and R. F. Hull

Almost any event will put on a new face when received with cheerful acceptance,

and no questions asked.
ANONYMOUS (HENRY S. HASKINS),
Meditations in Wall Street

Welcome everything that comes to you, but do not long for anything else.
ANDRÉ GIDE,
The Fruits of the Earth

I have accepted all and I am free. The inner chains are broken as well as those outside.
C.-F. RAMUZ,
The Life of Samuel Belet

The spirit of rejection finds its support in the consciousness of separateness; the spirit of acceptance finds its base in the consciousness of unity.
RABINDRANATH TAGORE,
Letters to a Friend

I wish they would only take me as I am.
VINCENT VAN GOGH,
*Dear Theo:
An Autobiography of Vincent Van Gogh*

I don't know whether I am getting very wise or very silly, but the only comment I seem to be able to make about anything is, "All is well," or "So be it." . . . There is no such thing as a definite conclusion. Everything must be followed by a question mark. All I can do is act according to my deepest instinct, and be whatever I must be, crazy or ribald or sad or compassionate or loving or indifferent. That is all anybody can do.
KATHERINE BUTLER HATHAWAY,
The Journals and Letters of the Little Locksmith

ACCOMPLISHMENT

There is probably not a single man or woman, who, mostly from self-interest, it is true, but it might also have been from a superior motive, has not overcome powerful obstacles and accomplished things extremely difficult to undertake.
ERNEST DIMNET,
What We Live By

Accomplishment makes cavil absurd.
JOHN LANCASTER SPALDING,
Things of the Mind

We accomplish little except as we get into a current which will bear us without great effort. This may be a current prepared by institutions, or it may be one which we have created in our own character by sustained endeavor.
CHARLES HORTON COOLEY,
Life and the Student

ACHIEVEMENT

Take it for granted that the greater your achievement the more genuine will be the surprise of your friends and neighbors.
JOSEPH FARRELL,
Lectures of a Certain Professor

Praise the ripe field not the green corn.
IRISH PROVERB

The reality which smashes every ideologue and his system is human nature, incessantly striving towards a personal achievement in a world which is essentially free and personal.
JOYCE CARY,
Art and Reality

If you want to hit a bird on the wing you must have all your will in focus, you must not be thinking about yourself, and, equally, you must not be thinking about your neighbor; you must be living in your eye on that bird. Every achievement is a bird on the wing.
OLIVER WENDELL HOLMES, JR.,
The Mind and Faith of Justice Holmes,
edited by Max Lerner

It is strange how the memory of a man may float to posterity on what he would have himself regarded as the most trifling of his works.
SIR WILLIAM OSLER,
*Aphorisms from His Bedside Teachings
and Writings*

What strange perversity is it that induces a man to set his heart on doing those things which he has not succeeded in and makes him slight those in which his achievement has been respectable.

GAMALIEL BRADFORD,
The Letters of Gamaliel Bradford

We must not waste life in devising means. It is better to plan less and do more.

WILLIAM ELLERY CHANNING,
Dr. Channing's Note-book

Everybody sets out to do something, and everybody does something, but no one does what he sets out to do.

GEORGE MOORE

If a great thing can be done at all, it can be done easily. But it is that kind of ease with which a tree blossoms after long years of gathering strength.

JOHN RUSKIN,
quoted in *The Author's Kalendar, 1920,*
compiled by Anna C. Woodford

Having once decided to achieve a certain task, achieve it at all costs of tedium and distaste. The gain in self-confidence of having accomplished a tiresome labour is immense.

ARNOLD BENNETT

ACQUAINTANCE

We need two kinds of aquaintances, one to complain to, while we boast to the others.

LOGAN PEARSALL SMITH,
All Trivia

We live in an eternal atmosphere of acquaintanceship, and acquaintanceship stands in the same relation to friendship that a flirtation does to a love affair—exciting but unsatisfying.

ALEC WAUGH,
On Doing What One Likes

Almost all men improve on acquaintance.

ANDRÉ MAUROIS,
The Art of Living

We like new acquaintances, not so much that we are wearied of our old friends, or that we enjoy change, but because of our disappointment at not being sufficiently admired by those who know us too well and because of a hope that people who know us less intimately may admire us more.

LA ROCHEFOUCAULD,
Maxims

As there are some flowers which you should smell but slightly to extract all that is pleasant in them ... so there are some men with whom a slight acquaintance is quite sufficient to draw out all that is agreeable; a more intimate one would be unsafe and unsatisfactory.

WALTER SAVAGE LANDOR,
quoted in *Between Friends,*
compiled by Warwick James

ACT

When I talked no one listened to me. But as soon as I acted I became persuasive, and I no longer find anyone incredulous.

GIOSUÈ BORSI,
A Soldier's Confidence with God

Our own acts are isolated and one act does not buy absolution for another.

W. B. YEATS,
Autobiography

I am no mere thinker, no mere creature of dreams and imagination. I stamp and post my letters; I buy new bootlaces and put them in my boots. And when I set out to get my hair cut, it is with the iron face of those men of empire and unconquerable will, those Caesars and Napoleons, whose footsteps shake the earth.

LOGAN PEARSALL SMITH,
More Trivia

You say that you'll act, if Mrs. S. and Mrs. B. will begin. If so, none of you will do anything. Have you never heard the story of the bewitched forest—how an evil spirit told all the trees that the first of them to blossom in the spring would be withered and destroyed, and how each of them waited for someone else to begin, and so the whole forest remained dark and dead for a thousand years?

J. A. SPENDER,
The Comments of Bagshot, Second Series

Make up your mind to act decidedly and take the consequences. No good is ever done in this world by hesitation.

THOMAS HENRY HUXLEY,
Aphorisms and Reflections

The fact is, that in everything we do we give up something, and attain something. In every act, therefore, there is really a double character present. In very many cases one side of it or the other may not be noticeable, but both are always present.

BERNARD BOSANQUET,
Some Suggestions in Ethics

Make the least ado about your greatest gifts. Be content to act, and leave the talking to others.

BALTASAR GRACIAN,
The Oracle

ACTION

That is the principal thing—not to remain with the dream, with the intention, with the being-in-the-mood, but always forcibly to convert it into all things.

RAINER MARIA RILKE,
Letters of Rainer Maria Rilke 1892–1910

We are weak in action by our best qualities; we are strong in action by will and a certain one-sidedness.

ERNEST RENAN,
quoted in *Elbert Hubbard's Scrap Book*

Only for his dreams is a man responsible—his actions are what he must do. Actions are a bastard race to which a man has not given his full paternity.

J. B. YEATS,
Letters to His Son, W. B. Yeats and Others

With all due respect for the cheering section the man who gets down on the field and tries to spill a few of the trick plays is doing a great deal more.

HEYWOOD BROUN,
Collected Edition of Heywood Broun

I have frequently experienced myself the mood in which I felt that all is vanity; I have emerged from it not by means of any philosophy, but owning to some impera-

tive necessity of action.

BERTRAND RUSSELL,
The Conquest of Happiness

I got the blues thinking of the future, so I left off and made some marmalade. It's amazing how it cheers one up to shred oranges or scrub the floor.

D. H. LAWRENCE,
Selected Letters of D. H. Lawrence

When I am idle and shiftless, my affairs become confused; when I work, I get results: not great results, but enough to encourage me in well-doing.

E. W. HOWE,
Preaching from the Audience

Action is consolatory. It is the enemy of thought and the friend of flattering illusions. Only in the conduct of our action can we find the sense of mastery over the Fates.

JOSEPH CONRAD,
Nostromo

We cannot seek or attain health, wealth, learning, justice or kindness in general. Action is always specific, concrete, individualized, unique.

JOHN DEWEY,
Reconstruction in Philosophy

Our life is composed greatly from dreams, from the unconscious, and they must be brought into connection with action. They must be woven together.

ANAÏS NIN,
The Diaries of Anaïs Nin, Vol. IV

Between eighteen and twenty, life is like an exchange where one buys stocks, not with money, but with actions. Most men buy nothing.

ANDRÉ MALRAUX,
quoted in *Julian Green: Diary 1928–1957*

Arouse yourself, gird your loins, put aside idleness, grasp the nettle, and do some hard work.

SAINT BERNARD OF CLAIRVAUX,
Letters

Any action whose reasons and explanations can all be contained in a few smooth practical sentences, and which arouses a unanimous chorus of approval from all the family and relations, may well be suspected of not being a living, deep-rooted action at all and scarcely worth pursuing.

KATHERINE BUTLER HATHAWAY,
The Journals and Letters of the Little Locksmith

Conditions are never just right. People who delay action until all factors are favorable are the kind who do nothing.

WILLIAM FEATHER,
The Business of Life

Something inherently mean in action! Even the creation of the universe disturbs my idea of the Almighty's greatness.

SAMUEL TAYLOR COLERIDGE,
quoted in *A Treasury of English Aphorisms,*
edited by Logan Pearsall Smith

The man of action is always unscrupulous; it is only the observer who has conscience.

GOETHE

And I would flee the grim inaction of
words
And the paralysis of wish and dream.
How can a man in love sit still and stare?

JESSICA POWERS,
"I Would Define My Love,"
The Place of Splendor

My experience of the world is that things left to themselves don't get right.

THOMAS HENRY HUXLEY,
Aphorisms and Reflections

Considering the chaos and disorder in the world—both outwardly and inwardly—seeing all this misery, starvation, war, hatred, brutality—many of us have asked what one can do.... One feels one must be committed.... When you commit yourself, you are committed to a part and therefore the part becomes important and that creates division. Whereas, when one is involved completely, totally with the whole problem of living, action is entirely different. Then action is not only inward, but also outward; it is in relationship with the whole problem of life.

J. KRISHNAMURTI,
You Are the World

You may know a tree by its fruit, but certainly not men and women by their actions.

JOHN OLIVER HOBBES,
Some Emotions and a Moral

Every man feels instinctively that all the beautiful sentiments in the world weigh less than a single lovely action.

JAMES RUSSELL LOWELL

You ask me why I do not write something.... I think one's feelings waste themselves in words, they ought all to be distilled into actions and into actions which bring results.

FLORENCE NIGHTINGALE,
Florence Nightingale,
by Cecil Woodham-Smith

The ultimate can only be expressed in conduct. Example moves the world more than doctrine. The great examplars are the poets of action, and it makes little difference whether they be forces for good or forces for evil.

HENRY MILLER,
The Cosmological Eye

Even if it doesn't work, there is something healthy and invigorating about direct action.

HENRY MILLER,
Remember to Remember

What you theoretically know, vividly realize.

FRANCIS THOMPSON,
"Shelley," *Works,* Vol. III

Out of action, action of any sort, there grows a peculiar, useful, everyday wisdom. Truth is rarely found by the idle. Nor is it the result of deep and long study. It is a sort of essence that is secreted from a concrete deed.

DR. FRANK CRANE,
"Habit," *Essays*

There are risks and costs to a program of action. But they are far less than the long-range risks and costs of comfortable inaction.

JOHN F. KENNEDY,
message to Americans for Democratic Action, May 12, 1961

He truly is a rare and marvellous work of heavenly grace, who when he comes into the din and tumult of the world can view things just as he calmly contemplated them in the distance, before the time of action came.

JOHN HENRY CARDINAL NEWMAN,
Oxford University Sermons

Personally, it interests me more to hear of actions than of motives ... of course *ordinary actions* of every day, that everyone knows, are not worth talking about, but action in difficult circumstances, in crisis, in moments of peril and emergency, in carrying out plans, in laying out work, in all these sometimes small but thrilling points of decision in our lives, I think it is immensely instructive and interesting to know what people *do* and *did* and *would do*.

JANET ERSKINE STUART,
*Life and Letters
of Janet Erskine Stuart*
by Maud Monahan

Things do not get better by being left alone. Unless they are adjusted, they explode with a shattering detonation.

SIR WINSTON CHURCHILL,
A Churchill Reader,
edited by Colin R. Coote

How, then, find the courage for action? By slipping a little into unconsciousness, spontaneity, instinct which holds one to the earth and dictates the relatively good and useful. ... By accepting the human condition more simply and candidly, by dreading troubles less, calculating less, hoping more.

HENRI FRÉDÉRIC AMIEL,
The Private Journal of Henri Frédéric Amiel

A man who goes through life without playing an active part is a failure. He may be a noble one; but his life is a real tragedy. To me there seems to be more and more truth in what I used to think the vulgar commonplaces of Philistia. The Philistines, to be sure, mouth their precepts with so little knowledge of their inner meaning that one may be forgiven for thinking them meaningless. But, just as

truly as ever, action is the ideal that we should keep before us—an active struggle with the life we are born to, a full sense of all its temptations, of all its earthly significance as well as its spiritual.

BARRETT WENDELL,
Barrett Wendell and His Letters
by M. A. DeWolfe Howe

Man looks forward to rest only to be delivered from toil and subjection; but he can find enjoyment in action alone, and cares for nothing else.

VAUVENARGUES,
Reflections and Maxims

ACTIVITY

We must forget what is behind. If we cease to originate, we are lost. We can only keep what we have, by new activity.

WILLIAM ELLERY CHANNING,
Dr. Channing's Note-book

The busier one is in a group of activities, the more acceptable an excuse one has for avoiding commitments on a deeper level elsewhere—commitments one feels less than adequate to handle.

MYRON BRENTON,
The American Male

ACTORS AND ACTING

Acting can work a peculiar magic on the actor. From my own experience, I know that it can cure you—at least for the length of a performance—of a whole variety of ailments. Migraine headaches, miserable colds, or toothaches will suddenly disappear as you're up there going through your paces.

BARBARA HARRIS,
Close-up by John Gruen

Acting is the most immediate art of all. The audience is either caught up entirely or not; it's now or nothing.

MICHAEL REDGRAVE,
Player: A Profile of an Art
by Lillian Ross and Helen Ross

Nothing helped me toward a conscientious

performance so much as a conscious interest in the royalties.

> HOWARD LINDSAY,
> *Actors on Acting,*
> edited by Toby Cole and Helen Chinoy

Let [the audience] see you are afraid of it, and it will snap at you; face it boldly, and it will eat out of your hand.

> GEORGE ARLISS,
> quoted in *Times and Tendencies*
> by Agnes Repplier

Stay away from the theatre as much as you can. Stay out of the theatrical world, out of its petty interests, its inbreeding tendencies.... Dwell in this artificial world, and you will know only the externals of acting.

> MINNIE MADDERN FISKE,
> Advice to Young Actors,
> in *Leading Ladies* by Barbara Marinacci

Security is knowing all your lines.

> CHARLIE BROWN,
> *Showcase* by Roy Newquist

I think the young actor who really wants to act will find a way—there's no advice you can really offer except to keep at it and seize every opportunity that comes along.

> SIR JOHN GIELGUD,
> *Showcase* by Roy Newquist

Working in films is a lazy man's existence compared to working in the theatre where, if you're a star, there is a terrible responsibility. You have to be always on top. You can't let down for a moment, or everybody lets down without knowing that he is doing it.

> ETHEL BARRYMORE,
> *Leading Ladies* by Barbara Marinacci

I like to think of the art of acting as an immediate reward and an immediate death. The greater the moment on the stage, the longer the mourning.

> ROD STEIGER,
> *Player: A Profile of an Art*
> by Lillian Ross and Helen Ross

Only a true actor with a deep-seated compulsion is going to stick out the struggle

that goes with being in the theater. It's brutal, it's worse than a Marine bootcamp, and they drop out by the thousands. But they have also been enriched by the experience they've had.

> HELEN HAYES,
> *Showcase* by Roy Newquist

I do not trust the printing press when I deliver my written words to it. How a dramatist can rely on the mouth of an actor!

> KARL KRAUS,
> *Karl Kraus* by Harry Zohn

Acting deals with very delicate emotions. It is not putting up a mask. Each time an actor acts he does not hide; he exposes himself.

> JEANNE MOREAU,
> *New York Times,* June 30, 1976

No good actor is ever wholly masculine: something, some vocal or physical trick, betrays his debt to womankind, the debt which every man owes, but which most of us, out of some primitive animosity, do our best to hide.

> KENNETH TYNAN,
> *He That Plays the King*

Only a great actor finds the difficulties of the actor's art infinite.

> ELLEN TERRY,
> *Actors on Acting,*
> edited by Toby Cole and Helen Chinoy

There's life for an actor in the characters he plays. Being another character is more interesting than being yourself. It's a great pleasure to me.... It's such a beautiful physical escape. I enjoy the transformation of personality.

> SIR JOHN GIELGUD,
> *Player: A Profile of an Art*
> by Lillian Ross and Helen Ross

Actors sometimes—not always but sometimes—prefer to bore the audience for three hours rather than amuse it for five minutes.

> LUCIEN GUITRY,
> *Actors on Acting,*
> edited by Toby Cole and Helen Chinoy

At some time or other in their careers actors are most notoriously abused. I personally keep no scrapbook since the majority of the reading matter therein would be unendurable.

ORSON WELLES,
quoted in *He That Plays the King*
by Kenneth Tynan

Despite the pettiness, the egomania, and the persecution complexes of stagefolk, they are more amusing, more generous, and more stimulating than any other professional group.

RICHARD MANEY,
Fanfare

In every actor you'll find something of the missionary—the feeling that he must get his message across to *everybody*.

JULIE HARRIS,
Talks to Young Actors

The actor should make you forget the existence of author and director, and even forget the actor.

PAUL SCOFIELD,
Player: A Profile of an Art
by Lillian Ross and Helen Ross

An actor formerly was supposed to be a good-looking man, with a handsome figure, beautiful movements, and a noble diction. These attributes are no longer necessary for a stage career; indeed, in America they are a positive handicap. A good-looking young man who moves well and speaks well is becoming almost unemployable in American "legit" theatre; his best hope today is to look for work in musical comedy. Or posing for advertisements.

MARY MCCARTHY,
On the Contrary

What the actor does has a very short life, no overwhelming importance; and compared to most of the other arts I think we are of little significance.

HUME CRONYN,
Showcase by Roy Newquist

We can telegraph and telephone and wire pictures across the ocean; we can fly over it. But the way to the human being next to us is still as far as the stars. The actor takes us on this way.

MAX REINHARDT,
Actors on Acting,
edited by Toby Cole and Helen Chinoy

You've got to find in an actor a man who will not be too proud to scavenge the tiniest little bit of human circumstance; observe it, find it, use it some time or other.

SIR LAURENCE OLIVIER,
quoted in *Talks to Young Actors*
by Julie Harris

Sacrificial as they are, many people in the theater are not sacrificial enough. Who hasn't heard of the young actor who works all night at Riker's so he can sit all day at Walgreen's and wish there were repertory theaters where he could perform with permanence.

HERBERT BLAU,
The Impossible Theater

Just as the painter who merely sets down the image of an apple that looks like one is not an artist, so the actor who merely "imitates" the surface impression that we might gather from a perusal of the play's text—an actor who does not create a life beyond what was there before he assumed his role—belies the art of the theatre.

HAROLD CLURMAN,
Lies Like Truth

As an actress, what I've had has been an instinct for being somebody else, just as some women have an instinct for doing their own hair. I've never had an instinct for doing my own hair, and I have no instinct about clothes. But I knew I had the acting instinct.

KATHARINE CORNELL,
Player: A Profile of an Art
by Lillian Ross and Helen Ross

On [Sarah Bernhardt's] initial visit to America, when the crowds went wild over her, one reporter exclaimed, "Why, New York didn't give Dom Pedro of Brazil such an ovation!" Sarah serenely announced, "Yes, but he was only an emperor."

Quoted in *Madam Sarah*
by Cornelia Otis Skinner

It exasperates me to be unable to do anything without being accused of eccentricity. I had great fun going up in a balloon, but now I dare not do so. I assure you that I have never skinned dogs or burned cats. And I regret that I cannot prove that I am a natural blonde. . . .

SARAH BERNHARDT,
quoted in *The Gilded Age*
by Henry Knepler

Actresses will happen in the best-regulated families.

OLIVER HERFORD

Women who play dominating parts become unhappy in their private lives. Women tend, more than men, to *become* the part.

SIR JOHN GIELGUD,
Player: A Profile of an Art
by Lillian Ross and Helen Ross

It had been drilled into us that when an audience pays to see a performance, it is entitled to the best performance you can give. Nothing in your personal life must interfere, neither fatigue, illness, nor anxiety—not even joy.

LILLIAN GISH,
The Movies, Mr. Griffith and Me

Why is it that women of the stage are generally more alluring than women in private life? Because they have about them the plaything air.

GEORGE JEAN NATHAN,
"Women as Playthings,"
Man Against Woman,
edited by Charles Neider

I used to sneak off to the theater as a child. . . . I sat there in the dark and watched all these people in the light on the stage. I got so excited. I thought that I was not destined to be in the dark; my vocation was to be in the light, to live in that extraordinary dimension and escape that darkness that most people have to live in.

JEANNE MOREAU,
New York Times, June 30, 1976

Beauty is not all-important as an asset. . . . I cannot for the moment recall a single great actress who is a beauty. At least not in the popularly accepted idea of what constitutes beauty.

LAURETTE TAYLOR,
Actors on Acting,
edited by Toby Cole and Helen Chinoy

I wish I had a beautiful face. For a woman of the theater, it is a wondrous possession. A beautiful woman can climb so easily. An unattractive one has to work doubly hard to offset her lack of facial charm.

JUDITH ANDERSON,
Actors on Acting,
edited by Toby Cole and Helen Chinoy

I hate the word professional. That's the dry rot of every place because a person can never be professional until he gets a chance to become professional.

ELLEN STEWART,
Behind the Scenes,
edited by Joseph F. McCrindle

Actors spend years and years being treated like dirt. They're constantly in a state of debasement, making the rounds of casting directors and having to look happy and great. I made the rounds for years, but I wasn't good at it. But then *nobody* is. You need a very strong stomach. You need a sense of the business as a whole, so that you don't get lacerated every time somebody tells you you're lousy. You need strength, and no matter how strong you get, you always need to get stronger.

MAUREEN STAPLETON,
Player: A Profile of an Art
by Lillian Ross and Helen Ross

You're never too old to play St. Joan. You're only too young.

DAME SYBIL THORNDIKE,
quoted in *Talks to Young Actors*
by Julie Harris

I can't for the life of me see what nudity has to do with good acting. But perhaps if I were younger, I would feel differently.

JULIE HARRIS,
Talks to Young Actors

ADAPT

They are wondering how to *be adapted*.
They should first know how to *be*.

HENRI DE LUBAC,
Paradoxes

On the one side, people never fit in perfectly with ourselves; and, on the other
hand, we ourselves are practically always
largely to blame when that's the case.

ROBERT HUGH BENSON,
*Spiritual Letters of Monsignor
R. Hugh Benson
to One of His Converts*

Be ever soft and pliable like a reed, not
hard and unbending like a cedar.

TALMUD

If you want to slip into a round hole, you
must make a ball of yourself.

GEORGE ELIOT,
The Mill on the Floss

Man is not a machine in the sense that he
can consistently maintain the same output
of work. He can only meet the demands of
outer necessity in an ideal way if he is also
adapted to his own inner world, that is to
say, if he is in harmony with himself. Conversely, he can only adapt to his inner
world and achieve unity with himself
when he is adapted to the environmental
conditions.

C. G. JUNG,
Psychological Reflections,
edited by Jolande Jacobi and R. F. Hull

ADMINISTRATOR

The man of narrower mind is often the
better administrator.

JOSEPH RICKABY,
An Old Man's Jottings

That mobilizing of the mind to meet and
sway the minds of other men, involved in
the conduct of affairs, blunts a sense of
fine truth. The administrator is the death
of the artist.

CHARLES HORTON COOLEY,
Life and the Student

ADMIRATION

The time of my life that I consider to have
been wasted, from the intellectual point of
view, was the time when I tried, in a spirit
of dumb loyalty, to admire all the things
that were said to be admirable.

A. C. BENSON,
From a College Window

Admiration warms and exalts. The lover is
made happier by his love than the object
of his affection.

RALPH WALDO EMERSON,
Journals of Ralph Waldo Emerson

By law of Nature, no man can admire, for
no man can understand, that of which he
has no echo in himself.

FRANCIS THOMPSON,
Works, Vol. III

There is nothing more becoming than
genuine admiration, and it shares this
with love, that it does not become contemptible though misplaced.

ROBERT LOUIS STEVENSON,
The Amateur Emigrant

We may admire what we cannot share;
reverence what we do not imitate.

WALTER BAGEHOT,
Literary Studies, Vol. III

They who admire us give us purer pleasure than they who love us, for they are
less exacting.

JOHN LANCASTER SPALDING,
Glimpses of Truth

Let every man be respected as an individual and no man idolized. It is an irony
of fate that I myself have been the recipient of excessive admiration and reverence
from my fellow-beings, through no fault,
and no merit of my own.

ALBERT EINSTEIN,
Ideas and Opinions

It is almost impossible to find those who
admire us lacking in taste.

J. PETIT-SENN,
Conceits and Caprices

We always admire the other fellow more after we have tried to do his job.

WILLIAM FEATHER,
quoted in *Ladies' Home Journal*,
September 1949

All that man is capable of admiring is possible with God.

SIMONE WEIL,
Waiting for God

The worth of admiration is, after all, in proportion to the value of the thing admired,—a circumstance overlooked by the people who talk much pleasant nonsense about sympathy, and the courage of our emotions, and the open and generous mind.

AGNES REPPLIER,

Americans and Others

I never knew a man so mean that I was not willing he should admire me.

E. W. HOWE,
Country Town Sayings

You write me that a "blind admiration" is not at all flattering. I could answer you, with the pride of Hell and the impudence of a person damned, that such is precisely the admiration for which I thirst. I have never desired any other, and when I myself have happened to admire someone, I admired as generously as I could, without glancing back, without reservation; drawing myself aside, forgetting myself entirely, especially when I knew the one I admired was a poor man wonderfully deprived of his wages, a captive in dark places.

LEON BLOY,
Leon Bloy: Pilgrim of the Absolute,
edited by Raissa Maritain

No, amid all the fruitless turmoil and miscarriage of the world, if there be one thing steadfast and of favorable omen, one thing to make optimism distrust its own obscure distrust, it is the rooted instinct in men to admire what is better and more beautiful than themselves.

JAMES RUSSELL LOWELL

We must become cheerful, ready to receive things much greater than ourselves.... We must, in one word, be capable of admiration.

DOM ANSCAR VONIER,
The Art of Christ

ADOLESCENCE

We do not tolerate in our adolescents a firm sense of their own identity, or the impassioned, if transitory commitments through which different identities can be tried and accepted or rejected. We are deathly afraid that they will get a record that will count against them in later life; as, indeed, they will: school counselors compile it continuously and record strong commitment as an aberration.

EDGAR Z. FRIEDENBERG,
The Dignity of Youth and Other Atavisms

Adults who do not like and respect adolescents—and this includes a large proportion of those who make a career of working with them—are badly frightened by the increasingly democratic relationships between adolescents and adults that are coming to prevail in our society.

EDGAR Z. FRIEDENBERG,
The Vanishing Adolescent

In no order of things is adolescence the time of the simple life.

JANET ERSKINE STUART,
Life and Letters of Janet Erskine Stuart
by Maud Monahan

As for boys and girls, it is one of the sorriest of mistakes to talk down to them: almost always your lad of fifteen thinks more simply, more fundamentally than you do; and what he accepts as good coin is not facts or precepts, but feelings and convictions.

DAVID GRAYSON,
The Friendly Road

What I like in my adolescents is that they have not yet hardened. We all confuse hardening and strength. Strength we must achieve, but not callousness.

ANAÏS NIN,
The Diaries of Anaïs Nin, Vol. IV

What the teen-agers hunger for is a sense of dedication, and they have a way of reaching out for it, even in the most unlikely places, with the same gusto with which they will raid the icebox.

MAX LERNER,
The Unfinished Country

Fifteen is really medieval and pioneer and nothing is clear and nothing is sure, and nothing is safe and nothing is come and nothing is gone but it all might be.

GERTRUDE STEIN,
Gertrude Stein: Her Life and Her Work
by Elizabeth Sprigge

ADOPTION

When you adopt a child, an idea, or a life-style, you accept a responsibility. You have to nurture the child, you have to further and spread the idea, you have to conform to the life-style you have chosen.

NATHAN P. WANZIG

ADORATION

Annihilation of this swarm of petty invading cares by adoration! They possess and distract, not by their inherent strength but through the absence of a dominant power.

MARK RUTHERFORD,
Last Pages from a Journal

Man is most truly himself, as the Eastern Church well knows, not when he toils but when he adores. And we are learning more and more that all innocent joy in life may be a form of adoration.

VIDA P. SCUDDER,
The Privilege of Age

It is magnificent to be clothed like the lilies of the field . . . but the supreme glory is to be nothingness in adoration.

SØREN KIERKEGAARD,
quoted in *Rectitude* by Antonin Sertillanges

If we would understand Divine things, we must cultivate an attitude of humble adoration. Who does not begin by kneeling down, runs every possible risk.

ERNEST HELLO,
Life, Science, and Art

When I look at those beautiful and mysterious apparitions we call people, I like to think of their adoration for one another; how they listen for one another's voices, and love to gaze in the enchanted mirrors of each other's eyes.

LOGAN PEARSALL SMITH,
Afterthoughts

ADULT

It is necessary for the health of the individual that, having been during his childhood a mere passive particle in a rotating system, he should, as an adult, himself become the centre of a new system.

C. G. JUNG,
Psychological Reflections,
edited by Jolande Jacobi and R. F. Hull

Considering the increased perplexities of life, the fragmentary nature of our knowledge, the accidentalness of adult existence, the unavoidable errors we make, the situation of the adult is by no means as different from that of the child as it is generally assumed. Every adult is in need of help, of warmth, of protection, in many ways differing and yet in many ways similar to the needs of the child.

ERICH FROMM,
The Sane Society

ADVANTAGE

Next to knowing when to seize an opportunity, the most important thing in life is to know when to forego an advantage.

BENJAMIN DISRAELI,
quoted in *Elbert Hubbard's Scrap Book*

ADVENTURE

The most beautiful adventures are not those we go to seek.

ROBERT LOUIS STEVENSON,
An Inland Voyage

It is because we are not humble enough in the presence of the divine daily fact, that adventure knocks so rarely at our door. A thousand times I have had to learn this truth ... and I suppose I shall have to learn it a thousand times more.

DAVID GRAYSON,
The Friendly Road

Dunkirk was so absorbing that for days we could think of nothing else. An acquaintance of Hubert's took his motor-boat there and says it was the finest weekend he ever had in his life. He came back with the boat riddled with shot.

EVELYN UNDERHILL,
The Letters of Evelyn Underhill

What is it that pulls me away from what others call happiness, home and loved ones, why does my love for them not hold me down, root me? Games. Adventures. The unknown.

ANAÏS NIN,
The Diaries of Anaïs Nin, Vol. II

Adventures are to the adventurous.

BENJAMIN DISRAELI,
Coningsby

ADVERSARY

Treating your adversary with respect is striking soft in battle.

SAMUEL JOHNSON

In dealing with a foolish or stubborn adversary remember your own mood constitutes half the force opposing you.

AUSTIN O'MALLEY,
Keystones of Thought

ADVERSITY

Adversity not only draws people together but brings forth that beautiful inward friendship, just as the cold winter forms ice-figures on the window-panes which the warmth of the sun effaces.

SØREN KIERKEGAARD,
The Journals of Søren Kierkegaard

All sorts of spiritual gifts come through privations, if they are accepted.

JANET ERSKINE STUART,
Life and Letters of Janet Erskine Stuart
by Maud Monahan

When it comes to a knockdown struggle with adversity, it is a question of how many last gasps we can gasp.

ANONYMOUS (HENRY S. HASKINS),
Meditations in Wall Street

In prosperous times I have sometimes felt my fancy and powers of language fail, but adversity is to me at least a tonic and a bracer; the fountain is awakened from its innermost recesses, as if the spirit of affliction had troubled it in his passage.

SIR WALTER SCOTT,
Sir Walter Scott's Journal (1825-1832)

Adversity is the state in which a man most easily becomes acquainted with himself, being especially free from admirers then.

SAMUEL JOHNSON

By trying we can easily learn to endure adversity. Another man's, I mean.

MARK TWAIN,
Following the Equator

ADVERTISING

Advertising may be described as the science of arresting the human intelligence long enough to get money from it.

STEPHEN LEACOCK

Living in an age of advertisement, we are perpetually disillusioned. The perfect life is spread before us every day, but it changes and withers at a touch.

J. B. PRIESTLEY,
All About Ourselves and Other Essays

It is far easier to write ten passably effective Sonnets, good enough to take in the not too inquiring critic, than one effective advertisement that will take in a few thousand of the uncritical buying public.

ALDOUS HUXLEY,
On the Margin

If we define pornography as any message from any communication medium that is intended to arouse sexual excitement, then it is clear that most advertisements are covertly pornographic.

PHILIP SLATER,
The Pursuit of Loneliness

A good advertising man is a first-class pragmatist. If he has any basic theorem at all, it is that most advertising is an intrusion upon the time and attention of people; a justifiable one but an intrusion nonetheless. The reader has bought the magazine for something other than the ads. . . . Therefore the copywriters undertake to stop him in spite of himself.

ALBERT LYND,
The Amazing Advertising Business

The philosophy behind much advertising is based on the old observation that every man is really two men—the man he is and the man he wants to be.

WILLIAM FEATHER,
The Business of Life

Doing business without advertising is like winking at a girl in the dark. You know what you are doing, but nobody else does.

STEUART HENDERSON BRITT,
quoted in the New York *Herald-Tribune*,
October 30, 1956

Have you ever considered what anxious thought, what consummate knowledge of human nature, what dearly-bought experiences go into the making of an advertisement?

WILLIAM J. LOCKE,
Septimus

The thing, however, that repels us in these advertisements is their naïve falsity to life. Who are these advertising men kidding . . . ? Between the tired, sad, gentle faces of the subway riders and the grinning Holy Families of the Ad-Mass, there exists no possibility of even a wishful identification.

MARY MCCARTHY,
On the Contrary

Why, I ask, isn't it possible that advertising as a whole is a fantastic fraud, presenting an image of America taken seriously by no one, least of all by the advertising men who create it?

DAVID RIESMAN,
The Lonely Crowd

The aggregate effect of advertising is to bring about wide sharing of tastes. The actual social function of advertising is *not* to mold taste in any particular way, nor to debase it. . . . It does not matter what people want to buy as long as they want to buy enough of the same thing to make mass production possible. Advertising helps to unify taste, to de-individualize it and thus to make mass . production possible.

ERNEST VAN DEN HAAG,
Man Alone,
edited by Eric Josephson
and Mary Josephson

Many a small thing has been made large by the right kind of advertising.

MARK TWAIN,
A Connecticut Yankee in King Arthur's Court

ADVICE

The advice of the elders to young men is very apt to be as unreal as a list of the hundred best books.

OLIVER WENDELL HOLMES, JR.,
The Mind and Faith of Justice Holmes,
edited by Max Lerner

Whenever my advice is followed I confess that I always feel oppressed with a great burden of responsibility, and I can never be confident, and always await the outcome with anxiety.

SAINT BERNARD OF CLAIRVAUX,
Letters

I never had a man come to me for advice yet, but what I soon discovered that he thought more of his own opinion than he did of mine.

JOSH BILLINGS,
His Works Complete

All of us, at certain moments of our lives, need to take advice and to receive help from other people.

ALEXIS CARREL,
Reflections on Life

It is well enough, when one is talking to a friend, to hedge in an odd word by way of counsel now and then; but there is something mighty irksome in its staring upon one in a letter, where one ought to see only kind words and friendly remembrances.

MARY LAMB,
The Letters of Charles and Mary Lamb

I agree with every word you write, and I can prove this in no better way than by taking your advice from beginning to end.

ELLEN GLASGOW,
Letters of Ellen Glasgow

As far as other human beings are concerned it is always best to leave people mentally and morally alone while you lavish whatever generous impulses you have in making their bodies comfortable. The more money you give to people the better; and the less advice.

JOHN COWPER POWYS,
The Meaning of Culture

No one wants advice—only corroboration.

JOHN STEINBECK,
The Winter of Our Discontent

Although we act on the best advice, yet, so uncertain is the future, the results are often contrary.

FRANCESCO GUICCIARDINI,
Counsels and Reflections

Please give me some good advice in your next letter. I promise not to follow it.

EDNA ST. VINCENT MILLAY,
Letters of Edna St. Vincent Millay

Many a man wins glory for prudence by seeking advice, then seeking advice as to what advice would be best to take, and finally following appetite.

AUSTIN O'MALLEY,
Keystones of Thought

Do not offer advice which has not been seasoned by your own performance.

ANONYMOUS (HENRY S. HASKINS),
Meditations in Wall Street

There is little serenity comparable to the serenity of the inexperienced giving advice to the experienced.

ANONYMOUS (HENRY S. HASKINS),
Meditations in Wall Street

Advice is like snow; the softer it falls, the longer it dwells upon, and the deeper it sinks into the mind.

SAMUEL TAYLOR COLERIDGE

Teeth placed before the tongue give good advice.

ITALIAN PROVERB

Not to judge for one's neighbor, not to advise even for a friend, but rather to present grounds of judgment and advice, is often the wisest rule of personal influence.

CHAUNCEY WRIGHT,
Letters of Chauncey Wright

Sometimes I give myself admirable advice, but I am incapable of taking it.

Lady Mary Wortley Montagu,
*The Complete Letters of
Lady Mary Wortley Montagu*

I might have saved myself much distraction if I had been less shy about asking advice. I did not understand that people rather like to give it and can often think better for others than for themselves.

CHARLES HORTON COOLEY,
Life and the Student

Men of much depth of mind can bear a great deal of counsel; for it does not easily deface their own character, nor render their purposes indistinct.

SIR ARTHUR HELPS,
Essays Written in the Intervals of Business

The best advisers, helpers, friends, always are those not who tell us how to act in special cases, but who give us, out of themselves, the ardent spirit and desire to act right, and leave us then, even through many blunders, to find out what our own form of right action is.

PHILLIPS BROOKS,
Visions and Tasks

The true secret of giving advice is, after you have honestly given it, to be perfectly indifferent whether it is taken or not, and never persist in trying to set people right.

HANNAH WHITALL SMITH,
Philadelphia Quaker
by Logan Pearsall Smith

He who builds according to every man's advice will have a crooked house.

DANISH PROVERB

AFFECTION

A neurotic person may have a feeling of terror when he approaches the realization that some genuine fondness is being offered to him.

KAREN HORNEY,
The Neurotic Personality of Our Time

Praise is well, compliment is well, but affection—that is the last and final and most precious reward that any man can win.

MARK TWAIN,
Mark Twain at Your Fingertips,
edited by Caroline T. Harnsberger

A woman is not so grateful for affection as she is anxious to show others how much someone is devoted to her, and a great many men are equally self-seeking.

JOHN OLIVER HOBBES,
The Herb-Moon

There is a monotony in the affections, which people living together or, as we do now, very frequently seeing each other, are apt to give in to: a sort of indifference in the expression of kindness for each other, which demands that we should sometimes call to our aid the trickery of surprise.

CHARLES LAMB,
The Letters of Charles and Mary Lamb

AFFLUENT

The rich get richer and the poor get poorer.

ANDREW CARNEGIE

You are affluent when you buy what you want, do what you wish and don't give a thought to what it costs.

J. P. MORGAN

Affluence means Influence.

JACK LONDON

AFRAID (*See* FEAR)

AFRICA

Africa is called the Dark Continent not only because most of its inhabitants are dark (black) but chiefly because it is unknown and the light of the world is not on it.

CECIL RHODES

AGE

Nothing ages a man like living always with the same woman.

NORMAN DOUGLAS,
An Almanac

There is more felicity on the far side of baldness than young men can possibly imagine.

LOGAN PEARSALL SMITH,
All Trivia

There are women who reach a perfect time of life, when the face will never again be as good, the body never as graceful or as powerful.

LILLIAN HELLMAN,
Pentimento

I find that a man is as old as his work. If his work keeps him moving forward, he will look forward with the work.

WILLIAM ERNEST HOCKING (at 86),
Wisdom for Our Time,
edited by James Nelson

You make me chuckle when you say that you are no longer young, that you have turned 24. A man is or may be young to after 60, and not old before 80.

OLIVER WENDELL HOLMES, JR.,
The Mind and Faith of Justice Holmes,
edited by Max Lerner

What is it that attracts me to the young? When I am with mature people I feel their rigidities, their tight crystallizations. They have become, at least in my eyes, like the statues of the famous. Achieved. Final.

ANAÏS NIN,
The Diaries of Anaïs Nin, Vol. IV

I sometimes think we all die at twenty-five and after that are nothing but walking corpses, with gramophones inside.

GEORGE SANTAYANA,
The Letters of George Santayana

The fact remains that unless one hopes that tomorrow will be more exciting than today, and that next week will be more exciting still, it's rather futile to go on living after fifty, especially in this torn world.

SIR JOHN GIELGUD,
Showcase by Roy Newquist

The fear of ageing, a commonplace neurosis, does not usually wait for age and spares neither sex.

COLETTE,
Journey for Myself

At times it seems that I am living my life backward, and that at the approach of old age my real youth will begin. My soul was born covered with wrinkles—wrinkles that my ancestors and parents most assiduously put there and that I had the greatest trouble removing, in some cases.

ANDRÉ GIDE,
Pretexts

As we grow older . . . we discover that the lives of most human beings are worthless except in so far as they contribute to the enrichment and emancipation of the spirit. . . . No one over thirty-five is worth meeting who has not something to teach us,—something more than we could learn by ourselves, from a book.

CYRIL CONNOLLY,
The Unquiet Grave

It seems a token and habit of older age to feel very deeply the charm there is in every display of life: I love it yearly more and more—in the antics and questions of children, in the roaming of a baby's surprised eyes, in the sparrows (now as I write) cracking seeds on the balcony . . . in the white shimmer of apple-blossom I saw yesterday at Clamart, and in the garden there in the dusk, when we walked under the chestnuts.

STEPHEN MACKENNA,
Journal and Letters of Stephen Mackenna

The whole business of marshaling one's energies becomes more and more important as one grows older.

HUME CRONYN,
Showcase by Roy Newquist

A young man of twenty-five is the Lord of life. The very age itself is, for him, the symbol of his mastery. . . . Like an ignorant fighter, for he has never been beaten, he is exultant in the assurance of his knowledge and his power.

THOMAS WOLFE,
The Web and the Rock

I agree with R. L. Stevenson in holding that the right human life is to take our fill of all the activities and pleasures proper to each age. In that way man need have no regrets. But so many of us warped human beings invert the order of life, are never young, and so are never wholesomely middle-aged or old.

JOHN ADDINGTON SYMONDS,
*Letters and Papers of
John Addington Symonds*

Years and sins are always more than owned.

ITALIAN PROVERB

Difference of age never made much difference to me at any moment of my life, nor does it now. That is to say it would not, but for the increasing age-consciousness that has crept upon us since I myself was a young person. During my visits to the U.S.A. I began to feel more and more parked into a round where we had to keep turning with our contemporaries like Paolo and Francesca in their circle of Dante's Inferno, seldom meeting the older and never the young. Indeed, we never saw the children of our best friends at their own table, and scarcely knew them by sight.

BERNARD BERENSON,
Rumor and Reflection

'Tis a maxim with me to be as young as long as I can: there is nothing can pay one for that invaluable ignorance which is the companion of youth; those sanguine groundless hopes, and that lively vanity, which makes all the happiness of life. To my extreme mortification I grow wiser every day.

LADY MARY WORTLEY MONTAGU,
*The Complete Letters of
Lady Mary Wortley Montagu*

Long life is the right mode for some people and not for others—just as some people write books in ten volumes and others epigrams in two lines—and the two works may be of exactly equal value.

FREDERICK GOODYEAR,
Letters and Remains

There must be a day or two in a man's life when he is the precise age for something important.

FRANKLIN P. ADAMS,
Nods and Becks

No man is ever old enough to know better.

HOLBROOK JACKSON,
Ladies' Home Journal, January 1950

To say that a man is thirty, fifty, or seventy tells you very little more about him than if you were only told his name. The name, however, might convey nothing to you, whereas the age would induce you from force of habit to make an estimate of him which might prove entirely false.

ARTHUR PONSONBY,
Casual Observations

A woman's always younger than a man of equal years.

ELIZABETH BARRETT BROWNING,
Aurora Leigh

To grow older is a new venture in itself.

GOETHE

AGE, MIDDLE

Forty,—sombre anniversary to the hedonist—in seekers after truth like Buddha, Mahomet, Mencius, St. Ignatius, the turning-point of their lives.

CYRIL CONNOLLY,
The Unquiet Grave

The real sadness of fifty is not that you change so much but that you change so little. . . . My only birthday resolution is to change some of my habits every year, even if for the worse.

MAX LERNER,
The Unfinished Country

At middle age the soul should be opening up like a rose, not closing up like a cabbage.

JOHN ANDREW HOLMES,
Wisdom in Small Doses

Whatever happens, please believe you can never lose your beauty or any bit of your quality. That was a terrible phrase you used, "degrading loss of beauty and youth." I must say I feel it in myself sometimes, but I think it's only that one sinks sometimes and then rises again. It isn't anything permanent. There are days of oldness, and then one gets young again.

KATHERINE BUTLER HATHAWAY,
*The Journals and Letters
of the Little Locksmith*

Setting a good example for your children takes all the fun out of middle age.

WILLIAM FEATHER,
The Business of Life

The nearer we approach to the middle of life, and the better we have succeeded in entrenching ourselves in our personal standpoints and social positions, the more it appears as if we had discovered the right course and the right ideals and principles of behaviour. . . . We wholly overlook the essential fact that the achievements which society rewards are won at the cost of diminution of personality. Many—far too many—aspects of life which should also have been experienced lie in the lumber-room among dusty memories. Sometimes, even, they are glowing coals under grey ashes.

C. G. JUNG,
Psychological Reflections,
edited by Jolande Jacobi and R. F. Hull

The transition from morning to afternoon is a revaluation of earlier values. There comes the necessity of examining into the value of the opposites of our previous ideals, of becoming aware of the error in our former convictions, of recognizing the falsehood in what had been before the truth, and of feeling how much resistance and even hostility lay in that which we had till now accepted as love.

C. G. Jung,
Psychological Reflections,
edited by Jolande Jacobi and R. F. Hull

An energetic middle life is, I think, the only safe precursor of a vitally happy old age.

Vida D. Scudder,
The Privilege of Age

Middle life brings such interest, as we see unfold gradually the destinies of our friends, and they take the stamp given by the end.

Alice James,
The Diary of Alice James

For is it not possible that middle-age can be looked upon as a period of second flowering, second growth, even a kind of second adolescence... The signs that presage growth, so similar, it seems to me, to those in early adolescence: discontent, restlessness, doubt, despair, longing, are interpreted falsely as signs of decay. In youth one does not as often misinterpret the signs; one accepts them, quite rightly, as growing pains. One takes them seriously, listens to them, follows where they lead.

Anne Morrow Lindbergh,
Gift from the Sea

In middle age we are apt to reach the horrifying conclusion that all sorrow, all pain, all passionate regret and loss and bitter disillusionment are self-made.

Kathleen Norris,
Hands Full of Living

Few women, I fear, have had such reason as I have to think the long sad years of youth were worth living for the sake of middle age.

George Eliot,
Diary

Of middle age the best that can be said is that a middle-aged person has likely learned how to have a little fun in spite of his troubles.

Don Marquis,
The Almost Perfect State

This is one of the great problems of the age, the problem of how to keep the middle-aged young. It is an individual problem, but it is much more than that, for it affects social and political life at every point. For the purposes of that life the middle-aged are more important than the young; they occupy inevitably most of the key posts and directing positions in national life; and they have the experience of human nature and affairs which are indispensable for practical business and which youth in the nature of things cannot have. It would be disastrous if men were physically old in their fifties, as they used to be, but it is an even greater loss if most of them lose their intellectual and spiritual energy by that age.

Sir Richard Livingstone,
On Education

Hostility to youth is the worst vice of the middle-aged.

J. A. Spender,
The Comments of Bagshot, Second Series

AGE, OLD

When we are old, we may sometimes enlighten, but we can no longer persuade.

Madame Swetchine,
The Writings of Madame Swetchine

Let me advise thee not to talk of thyself as being *old*. There *is* something in Mind Cure, after all, and, if thee continually talks of thyself as being old, thee may perhaps bring on some of the infirmities of age. At least I would not risk it if I were thee.

Hannah Whitall Smith,
Philadelphia Quaker
by Logan Pearsall Smith

I believe that one has to be seventy before one is full of courage. The young are always half-hearted.

D. H. Lawrence,
Selected Letters of D. H. Lawrence

To have lived long does not necessarily imply the gathering of much wisdom and experience. A man who has pedaled twenty-five thousand miles on a stationary bicycle has not circled the globe. He has only garnered weariness.

PAUL ELDRIDGE,
Horns of Glass

Within I do not find wrinkles and used heart, but unspent youth.

RALPH WALDO EMERSON (at 61),
Journals of Ralph Waldo Emerson

No one frankly admits the foul offence of being nearer sixty than fifty, but no one over ninety can resist boasting of it.

JOHN AYSCOUGH,
Levia-Pondera

The tragedy of old age is not that one is old, but that one is young.

OSCAR WILDE,
The Picture of Dorian Gray

The dangerous and pitiful deterioration of later life is not the product of the aging process, but of a stagnant and inert period of maturity.

DR. MARTIN GUMPERT,
The Harvest Years by Janet H. Baird

Religion often gets credit for curing rascals when old age is the real medicine.

AUSTIN O'MALLEY,
Keystones of Thought

I agree that the last years of life are the best, if one is a philosopher.

GEORGE SANTAYANA,
The Letters of George Santayana

Older people may insist that they have earned love as a reward for past deeds. But others rarely acknowledge the debt even if it exists, and we doom ourselves to bitterness and neglect if we expect automatic payment.

DR. SMILEY BLANTON,
Love or Perish

When a man grows old, wisdom will not keep him alive. He will repeat the wisdom previously acquired. He is petrified. But emotion will preserve him. He should be careful to feed passion.

MARK RUTHERFORD,
Last Pages from a Journal

The care of the old is a vocation as delicate and difficult as the care of the young.

JAMES DOUGLAS,
Down Shoe Lane

I must not forget to tell you of the death of a fellow of Trinity College aged 97. His funeral was attended by a brother of 99. The latter was much distressed and said he had always told his junior that theological research was not ·compatible with longevity. "God," he solemnly told Rutherford, "does not mean us to pry into these matters." After the funeral the old man went back to Trinity and solemnly drank his half-bottle of port. He was asked his prescription for health and said with great fervour, "Never deny yourself anything." He explained that he had never married as he had found fidelity restrictive as a young man. "I was once engaged, when I was forty," he said, "and I found it gave me very serious constipation. So I broke off the engagement and the lady quite understood." He was very anxious not to be thought past the age of flirtation.

HAROLD J. LASKI,
Holmes-Laski Letters, Vol. II

To grow old is more difficult than to die, for it costs less to renounce a good once and for all, and all at once, than to renew the sacrifice every day in some detail. To endure one's decay, to accept the diminution of oneself, is a rarer and more bitter virtue than to brave death.

HENRI FRÉDÉRIC AMIEL,
The Private Journal of Henri Frédéric Amiel

It is the ugliness of old age I hate. Being old is not bad if you keep away from mirrors, but broken-down feet, bent knees, peering eyes, rheumatic knuckles, withered skin, these are *ugly,* hard to tolerate with patience.

EMILY CARR,
Revelations: Diaries of Women,
edited by Mary Jane Moffat
and Charlotte Painter

To forge a fixed and arbitrary rule in terms of years as the limit of a man's usefulness or human service, would only be to behead a large portion of the world's intellectual and moral leadership and thereby to impoverish mankind.

NICHOLAS MURRAY BUTLER,
in a speech
given at Columbia University,
June 1, 1937

If you have only two or three things that you can enjoy, and they are things which time and decay may remove from you, what are you going to do in old age?

HENRY WARD BEECHER,
quoted in *Ladies' Home Journal*,
January 1944

What I wouldn't give to be 70 again!

OLIVER WENDELL HOLMES, JR.
(at 92, after seeing a pretty girl)

I seem to be all right now. I stoop but I haven't lumbago. The doctor said little processes like icicles had grown from my spine and there was nothing to do but grin and bear it. Don't you wish you had icicles growing from your vertebrae?

OLIVER WENDELL HOLMES, JR.,
Holmes-Pollock Letters, Vol. II

Grandmother, about 80, is visiting in the East and sends home things she has bought for her house. "I don't suppose I shall live forever," she says, "but while I do live I don't see why I shouldn't live as if I expected to."

CHARLES HORTON COOLEY,
Life and the Student

We can't reach old age by another man's road. My habits protect my life, but they would assassinate you.

MARK TWAIN,
Mark Twain at Your Fingertips,
edited by Caroline T. Harnsberger

I have often noticed that a kindly, placid good-humor is the companion of longevity, and, I suspect, frequently the leading cause of it.

SIR WALTER SCOTT,
Sir Walter Scott's Journal (1825-1832)

Don't try to convert the elderly person: circumvent him.

HOLBROOK JACKSON,
Platitudes in the Making

A human being would certainly not grow to be seventy or eighty years old if his longevity had no meaning for the species to which he belongs. The afternoon of human life must also have a significance of its own and cannot be merely a pitiful appendage to life's morning.

C. G. JUNG,
Psychological Reflections,
edited by Jolande Jacobi and R. F. Hull

Old age seems, anyhow, such a queer cavernous place, full of dim shapes and unaccountable shadows, that we have got to go into for a final adventure. It seems a much heavier business to behave oneself in it than in any of the jobs of youth, which are really of the nature of grand larks.

C. E. MONTAGUE,
C. E. Montague: A Memoir by Oliver Elton

As we grow old, time surrounds us by those who love us, instead of those we love.

J. PETIT-SENN,
Conceits and Caprices

There is no greater error of age than to suppose that it can recover the enjoyment of youth by possessing itself of what youth only can enjoy.

SIR HENRY TAYLOR,
Notes from Life

Solitude is ill-suited to old age, and the course of circumstances tends too often to leave the old in solitude.

SIR HENRY TAYLOR,
Notes from Life

We cannot do a great deal for the older person without at the same time doing a great deal for society. One is a reflex of the other.

LAWRENCE K. FRANK,
New Goals for Old Age,
edited by George Lawton

We are not making sufficient demands upon older people. What they want is not idleness and freedom, but an opportunity to do something with their lives that will make them significant.

LAWRENCE K. FRANK,
New Goals for Old Age,
edited by George Lawton

Between the years of ninety-two and a hundred and two, we shall be the ribald, useless, drunken, outcast person we have always wished to be. We shall have a long white beard and long white hair; we shall not walk at all, but recline in a wheel chair and bellow for alcoholic beverages; in the winter we shall sit before the fire with our feet in a bucket of hot water, a decanter of corn whisky near at hand, and write ribald songs against organized society; strapped to one arm of our chair will be a forty-five calibre revolver, and we shall shoot out the lights when we want to go to sleep, instead of turning them off; when we want air, we shall throw a silver candlestick through the front window and be damned to it; we shall address public meetings (to which we have been invited because of our wisdom) in a vain of jocund malice. . . . We shall know that the Almost Perfect State is here when the kind of old age each person wants is possible to him. Of course, all of you may not want the kind we want . . . some of you may prefer prunes and morality to the bitter end.

DON MARQUIS,
The Almost Perfect State

When one has reached 81 one likes to sit back and let the world turn by itself, without trying to push it.

SEAN O'CASEY,
New York Times, September 25, 1960

If by the time we're sixty we haven't learned what a knot of paradox and contradiction life is, and how exquisitely the good and the bad are mingled in every action we take, and what a compromising hostess Our Lady of Truth is, we haven't grown old to much purpose.

JOHN COWPER POWYS,
The Art of Growing Old

Old people, sometimes, are the ones who become young, know, are aware, act, believe, and are gay. And get things done.

LE CORBUSIER,
When the Cathedrals Were White

Old age has its pleasures, which, though

different, are not less than the pleasures of youth.

W. SOMERSET MAUGHAM,
The Summing Up

Older people are neglected and left to get along as best they can. . . . If it is important to give the human animal a good start in life, it is just as important to see that he makes a good finish. We should be as much interested in actual fulfillment as in setting the stage for the realization of possibilities.

GEORGE E. LAWTON,
New Goals for Old Age,
edited by George Lawton

No one thinks he looks as old as he is.

E. W. HOWE,
Country Town Sayings

Most people say that as you get old, you have to give up things. I think you get old because you give up things.

SENATOR THEODORE F. GREEN (at 87)

To see a young couple loving each other is no wonder; but to see an old couple loving each other is the best sight of all.

WILLIAM MAKEPEACE THACKERAY,
quoted in *Fiery Grains,*
edited by H. R. L. Sheppard
and H. P. Marshall

AGE (TIME PERIOD)

Every age has a keyhole to which its eye is pasted.

MARY McCARTHY,
On the Contrary

We are children of our age, but children who can never know their mother.

LOGAN PEARSALL SMITH,
Afterthoughts

One is always of his age, and especially he who least appears so.

SAINTE-BEUVE

Every age has a blind eye and sees nothing wrong in practices and institutions which its successors view with just horror.

SIR RICHARD LIVINGSTONE,
On Education

In every age, even in the most enlightened, there is what may justly be called the spirit of the time—a kind of atmosphere that will pass away, but which, while it lasts, deceives everybody as to importance and even the truth of the dominant opinions.

JOSEPH JOUBERT,
Pensées

To dislike the age in which you live is not inhuman, though it is probably impolitic, and unlikely to help you in being of service to it.

JOHN AYSCOUGH,
Levia-Pondera

Men of the very highest distinction are dependent upon their times. Not all of them have lived in the age which they deserved; and, many, even though they did so, failed to take advantage of it.

BALTASAR GRACIAN,
The Oracle

The fact is insufficiently observed, and almost never acted upon, that human beings are still ancient, medieval, and modern; for it is a gross error to suppose that all the individuals belonging to these several classifications have been accurately distributed into their respective niches of time. ... The fact is that most of us are astray in time; and when you consider how the centuries have been stirred and beaten together to make that hasty pudding which we call modernity, it is no wonder.

ODELL SHEPARD,
The Joys of Forgetting

AGGRESSION

Apart from its obvious use for self-protection against enemies, aggression provides an indispensable dynamo of energy for almost every kind of human work. The hunter kills, the woodsman chops, the cook roasts, the surgeon cuts, the lawyer prosecutes: these tasks all involve outright destruction to a greater or lesser degree. Indeed, virtually every trade or profession of civilized life entails the constant use of aggressive energy in the service of beneficent ends.

DR. SMILEY BLANTON,
Love or Perish

The truth is often a terrible weapon of aggression. It is possible to lie, and even to murder, with the truth.

ALFRED ADLER,
Problems of Neurosis

We do not know how many important behavior patterns of man include aggression as a motivating factor, but I believe it occurs in a great many. What is certain is that, with the elimination of aggression ... the tackling of a task or problem, the self-respect without which everything that a man does from morning till evening, from the morning shave to the sublimest artistic or scientific creations, would all lose impetus; everything associated with ambition, ranking order, and countless other equally indispensable behavior patterns would probably also disappear from human life.

KONRAD LORENZ,
On Aggression

AGONY (*See* also PAIN)

On the outskirts of every agony sits some observant fellow who points.

VIRGINIA WOOLF,
The Waves

AGREEABLE

To be agreeable, all that is necessary is to take an interest in other persons and in other things, to recognize that other people as a rule are much like oneself, and thankfully to admit that diversity is a glorious feature of life.

FRANK SWINNERTON,
Tokefield Papers

The greatest mistake is trying to be more agreeable than you can be.

WALTER BAGEHOT

I do not want people to be very agreeable as it saves me the trouble of liking them a great deal.

JANE AUSTEN,
quoted in *Ladies of Literature*
by Laura L. Hinkley

AGREEMENT

Nodding the head does not row the boat.
IRISH PROVERB

What a misfortune it would be ... if we could only work happily with those who saw things as we do.

JANET ERSKINE STUART,
Life and Letters of Janet Erskine Stuart,
by Maud Monahan

Agreement is easy when there is question of things for which we do not care.

JOHN LANCASTER SPALDING,
Glimpses of Truth

AGRICULTURE (See FARMING)

AIM

To profess to have an aim and then to neglect the means of its execution is self-delusion of the most dangerous sort.

JOHN DEWEY,
Reconstruction in Philosophy

To me the supreme aim is an act of faith and reason to make one rejoice in the midst of tragedy. An impossible aim; yet I think it true that nothing can injure us.

W. B. YEATS,
*Letters on Poetry
from W. B. Yeats to Dorothy Wellesley*

It is a good plan to aim a little higher than your target so as to make your shot sure, but not so high that you overshoot the mark.

BALTASAR GRACIAN,
The Oracle

AIR

The air vibrates with equal facility to the thunder and to the squeak of a mouse; invites man with provoking indifference to total indolence and to immortal actions.

RALPH WALDO EMERSON,
Journals of Ralph Waldo Emerson

Fresh air and innocence are good if you don't take too much of them—but I always remember that most of the achievements and pleasures of life are in bad air.

OLIVER WENDELL HOLMES, JR.,
Holmes-Laski Letters, Vol. I

Today is a goblet day. The whole heavens have been mingled with exquisite skill to a delicious flavor, and the crystal cup put to every lip. Breathing is like ethereal drinking. It is a luxury simply to exist.

HENRY WARD BEECHER,
Eyes and Ears

ALCOHOLIC (See DRINKING EXCESS, LIQUOR)

ALIENATION

No man can begin to think, feel or act now except from the starting point of his or her own alienation.

R. D. LAING,
The Politics of Experience

Alienation as our present destiny is achieved only by outrageous violence perpetrated by human beings on human beings.

R. D. LAING,
The Politics of Experience

Alienation as we find it in modern society is almost total; it pervades the relationship of man to his work, to the things he consumes, to the state, to his fellow man, and to himself.

ERICH FROMM,
The Sane Society

By alienation is meant a mode of experience in which the person experiences himself as an alien. He has become, one might say, estranged from himself. He does not experience himself as the center of his world, as the creator of his own acts—but his acts and their consequences have become his masters, whom he obeys, or whom he may even worship. The alienated person is out of touch with himself as he is out of touch with any other person.

ERICH FROMM,
The Sane Society

ALIMONY

Judges, as a class, display, in the matter of arranging alimony, that reckless generosity which is found only in men who are giving away somebody else's cash.

P. G. WODEHOUSE,
Louder and Funnier

ALONE

Alone, alone, oh! We have been warned about solitary vices. Have solitary pleasures ever been adequately praised? Do many people know that they exist?

JESSAMYN WEST,
Hide and Seek

The prohibition against solitude is forever. A Carry Nation rises in every person when he thinks he sees someone sneaking off to be alone. It is not easy to be solitary unless you are also born ruthless. Every solitary repudiates someone.

JESSAMYN WEST,
Hide and Seek

You go to see an older friend to tell him everything. Or, at least, something which is stifling you. But he is in a hurry. You talk about everything and about nothing at all. The time to speak has gone. And here I am, more alone and empty than before.

ALBERT CAMUS,
Notebooks 1935–1942

It is not good to be alone, even in Paradise.

YIDDISH PROVERB

Man can will nothing unless he has first understood that he must count on no one but himself; that he is alone, abandoned on earth in the midst of his infinite responsibilities, without help, with no other aim than the one he sets himself, with no other

destiny than the one he forges for himself on this earth.

JEAN PAUL SARTRE

In the ages since Adam's marriage, it has been good for some men to be alone, and for some women also.

GEORGE ELIOT,
Felix Holt

The deepest need of man is the need to overcome his separateness, to leave the prison of his aloneness.

ERICH FROMM,
The Art of Loving

In fact, we have developed a phobia of being alone; we prefer the most trivial and even obnoxious company, the most meaningless activities, to being alone with ourselves; we seem to be frightened at the prospect of facing ourselves. Is it because we feel we would be such bad company? I think the fear of being alone with ourselves is rather a feeling of embarrassment, bordering sometimes on terror at seeing a person at once so well known and so strange; we are afraid and run away.

ERICH FROMM,
Man for Himself

The timidity of the child or the savage is entirely reasonable; they are alarmed at this world because this world is a very alarming place. They dislike being alone because it is verily and indeed an awful idea to be alone.

G. K. CHESTERTON,
Tremendous Trifles

Anything, everything, little or big becomes an adventure when the right person shares it. Nothing, nothing, nothing is worthwhile when we have to do it all alone.

KATHLEEN NORRIS,
Hands Full of Living

Alone is a good way to go to a fight or the races, because you have more time to look around you, and you can always get all the conversation you can use anyway.

A. J. LIEBLING,
The Sweet Science

You may talk all you please of the misfortune of being "old and alone," but I tell you that approaches not one degree the misfortune of being young and alone.

THOMAS WOLFE,
Thomas Wolfe by Andrew Turnbull

Man was formed for society, and is neither capable of living alone, nor has the courage to do it.

SIR WILLIAM BLACKSTONE,
Commentaries on the Laws of England

When you become used to never being alone, you may consider yourself Americanized.

ANDRÉ MAUROIS

I intend to go there every day. It is entertaining and distracting. One can also be gloriously alone there in all that crowd.

SIGMUND FREUD,
The Letters of Sigmund Freud

In spite of language, in spite of intelligence and intuition and sympathy, one can never really communicate anything to anybody. The essential substance of every thought and feeling remains incommunicable, locked up in the impenetrable strong-room of the individual soul and body. Our life is a sentence of perpetual solitary confinement.

ALDOUS HUXLEY,
Collected Essays

A man who lives by himself and for himself is apt to be corrupted by the company he keeps.

CHARLES PARKHURST,
quoted in *Ladies' Home Journal,* May 1947

I am truly a "lone traveler" and have never belonged to my country, my home, my friends, or even my immediate family, with my whole heart; in the face of all these ties, I have never lost a sense of distance and a need for solitude—feelings which increase with the years. One becomes sharply aware, but without regret, of the limits of mutual understanding and consonance with other people.

ALBERT EINSTEIN,
Ideas and Opinions

No man can cut out new paths in company. He does that alone.

OLIVER WENDELL HOLMES, JR.,
The Mind and Faith of Justice Holmes,
edited by Max Lerner

I am here alone for the first time in weeks, to take up my "real" life again at last. That is what is strange—that friends, even passionate love, are not my real life unless there is time alone in which to explore and to discover what is happening or has happened.

MAY SARTON,
Journal of a Solitude

ALTRUISM

A large part of altruism, even when it is perfectly honest, is grounded upon the fact that it is uncomfortable to have unhappy people about one.

H. L. MENCKEN,
A Mencken Chrestomathy

AMATEUR

Amateurs are always short.

WALTER HAGEN

Amateur is a term used to indicate an inferior performer – but that is not true in the world of tennis.

WILLIAM T. TILDEN

AMBITION

Ambition sets up external standards; by ambition the rebel angels fell and so do the artists.

J. B. YEATS,
Letters to His Son, W. B. Yeats and Others

As long as I can remember, I've been absolutely hagridden with ambition. I think that if I could wish to have anything in the world it would be to be free of that ambition.

TALLULAH BANKHEAD,
Miss Tallulah Bankhead by Lee Israel

It is the ambition to seem that is distracting. The ambition to become, finding gradual but secure realization, brings neither despair nor elation.

CHARLES HORTON COOLEY,
Life and the Student

Children, you must remember something. A man without ambition is dead. A man with ambition but no love is dead. A man with ambition and love for his blessings here on earth is ever so alive. Having been alive, it won't be hard in the end to lie down and rest.

PEARL BAILEY,
Talking to Myself

There are no persons capable of stooping so low as those who desire to rise in the world.

LADY MARGUERITE BLESSINGTON

Every ambitious man is a captive and every covetous one a pauper.

ARAB PROVERB

A proud ambition cares little for popularity. He will not seek it. He will hardly bend to receive it. A vain ambition courts it by every act, and spreads every sail to catch the least breath of popular applause.

HENRY CARDINAL MANNING,
Pastime Papers

Keep away from people who try to belittle your ambitions. Small people always do that, but the really great make you feel that you, too, can become great.

MARK TWAIN

But the moment you turn a corner you see another straight stretch ahead and there comes some further challenge to your ambition.

OLIVER WENDELL HOLMES, JR.,
Holmes-Pollock Letters, Vol. II

I don't understand ambition for an office. The only one that I feel is to believe when the end comes, for till then it is always in doubt, that one has touched the superlative. No outsider can give you that, although the judgment of the competent, of course, helps to confidence—or at least to hope.

OLIVER WENDELL HOLMES, JR.,
Holmes-Pollock Letters, Vol. II

Ambition is the grand enemy of all peace.

JOHN COWPER POWYS,
The Meaning of Culture

There is no eel so small but it hopes to become a whale.

GERMAN PROVERB

AMENITIES

We must probe to the depths of our civilization before we can understand and deplore the limitations which make it difficult for us to approach one another with mental ease and security. We have yet to learn that the amenities of life stand for its responsibilities, and translate them into action. They express externally the fundamental relations which ought to exist between men.

AGNES REPPLIER,
Americans and Others

AMERICA

France was a land, England was a people, but America, having about it still that quality of the idea, was harder to utter—it was the graves at Shiloh and the tired, drawn, nervous faces of its great men, and the country boys dying in the Argonne for a phrase that was empty before their bodies withered. It was a willingness of the heart.

F. SCOTT FITZGERALD,
The Crack-up

In America an hour is forty minutes.

GERMAN PROVERB

I love America more than any other country in this world, and, exactly for this reason, I insist on the right to criticize her perpetually.

JAMES BALDWIN,
Notes of a Native Son

The strongest argument for the un-materialistic character of American life is the fact that we tolerate conditions that are, from a materialistic point of view, intolerable. What the foreigner finds most objectionable in American life is its lack of basic comfort. No nation with any sense of material well-being would endure the food we eat, the cramped apartments we live in, the noise, the traffic, the crowded subways and buses. American life, in large cities, at any rate, is a perpetual assault on the senses and the nerves; it is out of asceticism, out of unworldliness, precisely, that we bear it.

MARY McCARTHY,
On the Contrary

Snobbishness is particularly tenacious in America because it is so hard in a changing society to have clear claims to unassailable distinction.

IRWIN EDMAN,
The Uses of Philosophy,
edited by Charles Frankel

America is not only big and rich, it is mysterious; and its capacity for the humorous or ironical concealment of its interests matches that of the legendary inscrutable Chinese.

DAVID RIESMAN,
The Lonely Crowd

I was [in America] constantly being introduced to eminent persons by people who were quite unmistakably superior to these notables, and most modestly unaware of it.

JOHN AYSCOUGH,
First Impressions in America

There is one thing that America knows well, and that she teaches as a great and precious lesson to those who come into contact with her amazing adventure: that is the value and dignity of the man of common humanity, the value and dignity of the people.

JACQUES MARITAIN,
Christianity and Democracy

The thing I like most are the names of all

the states of the United States. They make music and they are poetry, you do not have to recite them all but you just have to say any one two three four or five of them and you will see they make music and they make poetry.

GERTRUDE STEIN,
Wars I Have Seen

I do not know why but Arkansas touched me particularly, anything touches me particularly now that is American. There is something in this native land business and you cannot get away from it, in peace time you do not seem to notice it much particularly when you live in foreign parts but when there is a war and you are all alone and completely cut off from knowing about your country well then there it is, your native land is your native land, it certainly is.

GERTRUDE STEIN,
Wars I Have Seen

It is, I believe, the destiny of America to produce the first of a new species of man.

WYNDHAM LEWIS,
America and Cosmic Man

In American society everyone contrives to wear a happy expression and to disguise the impersonality of social relations by greeting the stranger, as though he, and he alone, were the only one expected.

RAYMOND ARON,
As Others See Us, edited by Franz M. Joseph

America is the child society *par excellence,* and possibly the only one ever politically arrived at. It is the society of all rights and no obligations, the society of deliberate wreckage and waste, the only society that ever raised gangsterism to the status of myth, and murder to the status of tragedy or politics.

KARL SHAPIRO,
To Abolish Children and Other Essays

America is full of a violent desire to learn.
LE CORBUSIER,
When the Cathedrals Were White

My greatest problem here, in a polemic-loving America, is my dislike of polemics, of belligerence, of battle. Even intellectually, I do not like wrestling matches, I do not like talk marathons. I do not like arguments, or struggles to convert others. I seek harmony. If it is not there, I move away.

ANAÏS NIN,
The Diaries of Anaïs Nin, Vol. IV

The shell is America's most active contribution to the formation of character. A tough hide. Grow it early.

ANAÏS NIN,
The Diaries of Anaïs Nin, Vol. IV

There may have been a time when America by a show of great strength could bend many critical world situations to its will. If that power existed, it was of short duration. Certainly it does not exist today.

WILLIAM O. DOUGLAS,
America Challenged

The problem of justice for the Negro has gnawed on the national conscience ever since this nation was founded. It is, in an important sense, *the* American problem. If any problem is especially and peculiarly ours, with roots in our history and scars in our memory, this is it.

No other modern problem touches more profoundly the values we profess to cherish. And history has handed our generation the task of solving it.

JOHN W. GARDNER,
No Easy Victories, edited by Helen Rowan

I'd like a country in which there was a maximum of opportunity for any individual to discover his talents and develop his capacities—discover his fullest self and by so doing learn to respect other selves a little. Man is interesting in his differences.

ROBERT PENN WARREN,
Writers at Work,
edited by Malcolm Cowley

The true map of human geography in America is impossible to make. It would be a gigantic electrical tableau in which were luminously represented all the highways and the flow of their vehicles, all the rivers, lakes, and canals and the flow of their ships, all the railways and the flow of their trains, all the telephone and telegraph networks and the flow of their messages, all airlines and the flow of their planes, all networks of radio and television and the flow of their waves. The enormous web would be of blinding incandescence, a sort of vast furnace.

RAYMOND L. BRUCKBERGER,
One Sky to Share

I wonder whether the feverish ebb and flow of energy that makes up our lives here is human or only trans-Atlantic. Calm, steady, regular, healthy, normal progress from day to day seems almost out of the question. Temperance in life is a virtue almost unknown. Over-action and crushing reaction seem the rule.

BARRETT WENDELL,
Barrett Wendell and His Letters
by M. A. DeWolfe Howe

I do not think white America is committed to granting equality to the American Negro . . . . this is a passionately racist country; it will continue to be so in the foreseeable future.

SUSAN SONTAG,
Styles of a Radical Will

What I *crave* most is some wild American country. It is a curious organic-feeling need. One's social relations with European landscape are entirely different, everything being so fenced or planted that you can't lie down and sprawl.

WILLIAM JAMES,
The Letters of William James, Vol. II

What a tide of homesickness swept me under for the moment! What a longing to see a shaft of sunshine shimmering through the pines, breathe in the resinous air, and throw my withered body down upon my mother earth, bury my face in the coarse grass, worshipping all that the ugly, raw emptiness of the blessed land stands for,—the embodiment of a huge chance for hemmed-in humanity; its flexible conditions stretching and lending themselves to all sizes of man; pallid and naked of necessity; undraped by the illusions and mystery of a moss-grown, cobwebby past, but overflowing with a divine good-humour and benignancy, a helping hand for the faltering, and indulgent thought for the discredited, a heart of hope for every outcast of tradition.

ALICE JAMES,
The Diary of Alice James

I do like having the big, unbroken spaces round me. There is something savage, unbreakable in the spirit of the place out here—the Indians drumming and yelling at our camp-fire at evening. But they'll be wiped out too, I expect—schools and education will finish them.

D. H. LAWRENCE,
Selected Letters of D. H. Lawrence

"No," said Whitman. "Keep out of mansions. A mansion may be heaven on earth, but you might as well be dead. Strictly avoid mansions. The soul is herself when she is going on foot down the open road."

This is Whitman's essential message. The heroic message of the American future. It is the inspiration of thousands of Americans today, the best souls of today, men and women. And it is a message that only in America can be fully understood, finally accepted.

D. H. LAWRENCE,
Studies in Classic American Literature

I shall use the words America and democracy as convertible terms.

WALT WHITMAN,
Democratic Vistas

I say that democracy can never prove itself beyond cavil, until it founds and luxuriantly grows its own forms of art, poems, schools, theology, displacing all that exists, or that has been produced anywhere in the past, under opposite influences.

WALT WHITMAN,
Democratic Vistas

A man builds a house in England with the expectation of living in it and leaving it to

his children; while we shed our houses in America as easily as a snail does his shell.

HARRIET BEECHER STOWE,
quoted in *Harriet Beecher Stowe*
by Catherine Gilbertson

And perhaps you may guess why I love to stay here abroad, and mainly in Italy—it is because people are kind to me, I feel kindness round me, good-will, and love. And I have come to think of my own country as lacking in kindness; at home people are indifferent or absorbed or silent; it is like death, when it is not like killing.

GEORGE E. WOODBERRY,
Selected Letters of George Edward Woodberry

Depend upon it, it is a mistake sometimes to have been too well brought up, it prevents you realising that in America everything hitherto respected including your politeness and reticence is *quite out of date*. Every day of my life, I meet with some fresh surprise. People will do and say anything, and except for a few things like the multiplication table, nothing is sacred.

J. B. YEATS,
Letters to His Son, W. B. Yeats and Others

One is a distincter man if he can root himself somewhere and grow with the neighborhood; he gains in depth, significance, flavor, absorbs a local tradition and spirit, sees himself as part of a continuing whole. If this is no longer possible to our shifting life perhaps we can make America itself a neighborhood and absorb that.

CHARLES HORTON COOLEY,
Life and the Student

A hot young satyr in pursuit of nymphs is not nearly so common a symbol of American vice as a cold old party in pursuit of dollars, and sin in this country has been always said to be rather calculating than impulsive.

FRANK MOORE COLBY,
The Colby Essays, Vol. 1

Perhaps this is our strange and haunting paradox here in America—that we are fixed and certain only when we are in movement.

THOMAS WOLFE,
You Can't Go Home Again

I got into the car and lit out to drift for a time. I had a grand ride, over mountains and rivers and out onto the prairies, crossed the Cumberland, Tennessee, Ohio, Mississippi and Missouri Rivers. It rained, the wind blew and the sun shone. Again I got in love with America. What a land! O, Charles, if we can but begin to love it and treat it decently some day! It is so violent and huge and gorgeous and rich and willing to be loved, like a great, fine wench.

SHERWOOD ANDERSON,
Letters of Sherwood Anderson

Of nothing are you allowed to get the real odor or savour. Everything is sterilized and wrapped in cellophane. The only odor which is recognized and admitted as an odor is halitosis, and of this all Americans live in mortal dread.

HENRY MILLER,
The Air-Conditioned Nightmare

I am frequently surprised by references to bodily violence which are tabooed in Europe. Even gentle refined women over here smile approvingly when the narrator comes to, "Well, I took off my coat. ..." There is a philosophy behind this attitude.

ERNEST DIMNET,
My New World

It is veneer, rouge, aestheticism, art museums, new theaters, etc. that make America impotent. The good things are football, kindness, and jazz bands.

GEORGE SANTAYANA,
The Letters of George Santayana

In temper America is docile and not at all tyrannical; it has not predetermined its career, and its merciless momentum is a passive resultant .... Any tremulous thought or playful experiment anywhere may be a first symptom of great changes, and may seem to precipitate the cataract in a new direction.

GEORGE SANTAYANA,
Character and Opinion in the United States

Even what is best in American life is compulsory—the idealism, the zeal, the beautiful happy unison of its great moments. You must wave, you must cheer, you must push with the irresistible crowd; otherwise you will feel like a traitor.

GEORGE SANTAYANA,
Character and Opinion in the United States

We would like to see an America where the welfare of every citizen is the concern of all ... which makes full use of its great capacities to advance the welfare of all— not a welfare state—but a state with meaningful compassion for those whose welfare has been undermined.

JOHN F. KENNEDY,
speech in Chicago, April 28, 1961

AMERICAN

No country's population travels farther and faster. After the war, more veterans of this than any other nation chose to start their new lives in places other than the home town they had dreamed of in the front lines. To many Americans, then, while there is "no place like home," it is important that you should be able to take it with you or find its facsimile a thousand miles away. Those with the best places to stay in probably travel most.

ERIK H. ERIKSON,
Childhood and Society

For a nation which has an almost evil reputation for bustle, bustle, bustle, and rush, rush, rush, we spend an enormous amount of time standing around in line in front of windows, just waiting.

ROBERT BENCHLEY,
Benchley—or Else!

"Ah, the Americans are sly and clever," said Tan, whereupon the Americans present broke out in uncontrolled laughter. The interpreter explained to Tan that the Americans themselves never thought of themselves as either sly or clever.

BERNARD B. FALL,
Last Reflections on a War

In spite of his rude, gross nature, this early Western man was an idealist withal. He dreamed dreams and beheld visions.

FREDERICK JACKSON TURNER,
The Frontier in American History

Where, in the past, men have reached out beyond the temporal world to a fulfilling experience, viewing it as the goal of the human endeavor, in the American aim, the search has also been for experiential fulfillment, but within the historical process itself.

ROBERT C. POLLOCK,
American Philosophy and the Future,
edited by Michael Novak

There's no country I've been to where people, when you come into a room and sit down with them, so often ask you, "What do you do?" And, being American, many's the time I've almost asked that question, then realized it's good for my soul not to know. For a while! Just to let the evening wear on and see what I think of this person without knowing what he does and how successful he is, or what a failure. We're *ranking* everybody every minute of the day.

ARTHUR MILLER,
Writers at Work, Third Series,
edited by George Plimpton

In talking with [Henry James] about the extraordinary adaptability of the American to new circumstances he said: "He hasn't to cease being something else first; and then he is used all his life to seeing people become anything, in the course of five minutes."

ALICE JAMES,
The Diary of Alice James

For Americans war is almost all of the time a nuisance, and military skill is a luxury like Mah-Jongg. But when the issue is brought home to them, war becomes as important, for the necessary period, as business or sport. And it is hard to decide which is likely to be the more ominous for the Axis—an American decision that this is sport, or that it is business.

D. W. BROGAN,
The American Character

Someone we didn't know asked how it was that everything goes so well with the Americans, though they swear at every second word.

FRANZ KAFKA,
The Diaries of Franz Kafka 1914–1923

After all, this is a nation that, except for a hard core of winos at the bottom, and a hard crust of aristocrats at the top, has been gloriously middle class for two decades, as far as the breezeways stretch. There is no telling how many millions of American women of the new era know exactly what Ingrid Bergman meant when she said she loved playing opposite Cary Grant in "Notorious" (1946): "I didn't have to take my shoes off in the love scenes."

TOM WOLFE,
*The Kandy-Kolored
Tangerine-Flake Streamline Baby*

It is a curious fact that you can give an American man some kind of a ball and he will be thoroughly content.

JUDSON P. PHILIPS,
Hold 'Em, Girls!

I thought I was almost the only American who had had always that feeling of exile, of being not only in a strange country but on a strange planet.

ELLEN GLASGOW,
Letters of Ellen Glasgow

In the American metaphysic, reality is always material reality, hard, resistant, unformed, impenetrable, and unpleasant. And that mind alone is felt to be trustworthy which most resembles this reality by most nearly reproducing the sensations it affords.

LIONEL TRILLING,
The Liberal Imagination

The standardized American is largely a myth created not least by Americans themselves.

IRWIN EDMAN,
The Uses of Philosophy,
edited by Charles Frankel

And there is in us all the dark conscience of our murder of the primeval forests—of something in their depth which is a depth in us; of our refusal of their value, of our disdain of the red man who was the spirit of those forests and who is yet, beneath the layers of law and memory, the spirit of ourselves. For our root is the red man; our true building must rise from recognition of his base in our heart: and our denial of this is a disease within us.

WALDO FRANK,
The Rediscovery of America

The American lives even more for his goals, for the future, than the European. Life for him is always becoming, never being.

ALBERT EINSTEIN,
Ideas and Opinions

Passivity and not aggressiveness is the dominant trait of the American character.

MARY MCCARTHY,
On the Contrary

The openness of the American situation creates the pity and the terror; status is not protection; life for the European is a career; for the American, it is a hazard.

MARY MCCARTHY,
On the Contrary

The actual God of many Americans, perhaps of most, is simply the current of American life, which is large and hopeful enough to employ all the idealism they have.

CHARLES HORTON COOLEY,
Life and the Student

Americans are abstract. They are disconnected. They have a relation, but it is to everywhere, to everybody, and to always.

THORNTON WILDER,
Atlantic Monthly, July 1952

To this day many an American is breaking his life on an excessive demand for the perfect, the absolute, and the boundless in realms where it is accorded to few—in love and friendship for example. The doctrines of moderation and the golden mean . . . do not flourish here, save as counsels of despair.

THORNTON WILDER,
Atlantic Monthly, August 1952

Surely, moreover, a splendid ignorance about sexual happiness characterizes American husbands and wives; at least, so one must conclude from the eagerness with which Americans purchase "how to" books. Can there ever have been a race that advertised it more and enjoyed it less?

MICHAEL NOVAK,
Prophetic Voices,
edited by Ned O'Gorman

Ask any American what we shall do to be saved, and, if he speak his mind, he will probably bid us educate our fellow men.

BARRETT WENDELL,
The Privileged Classes

The typical successful American businessman was born in the country where he worked like hell so he could live in the city, where he worked like hell so he could live in the country.

DON MARQUIS

Americans have a profound tendency to feel like outsiders—they wonder where the action is and wander about in search of it (this puts an enormous burden on celebrities, who are supposed to know, but in fact feel just as doubtful as everyone else). Americans have created a society in which they are automatically nobodies, since no one has any stable place or enduring connection. The village idiot of earlier times was less a "nobody" in this sense than the mobile junior executive or academic. An American has to "make a place for himself" because he does not have one.

PHILIP SLATER,
The Pursuit of Loneliness

Nothing seems too abstract or highly specialized for the Americans to want to have it explained . . . . This people want to know—everything; and in the only possible manner of such an enterprise, easily, simply, preferably by pictures. I hope they will never be snubbed or scared out of it.

WILLIAM BOLITHO,
Camera Obscura

If we were to attempt to construct an "average American" we would necessarily put together an effigy which would have the common qualities of all Americans, but would have the eccentricities, peculiarities, and unique qualities of no American. It would, like the sociologist's statistical high-school student, approximate everyone and resemble no one.

BEN SHAHN,
The Shape of Content

No American worth his salt should go looking around for a root.

WYNDHAM LEWIS,
America and Cosmic Man

We Americans, with our terrific emphasis on youth, action, and material success, certainly tend to belittle the afternoon of life and even to pretend it never comes. We push the clock back and try to prolong the morning, over-reaching and over-straining ourselves in the unnatural effort. ... In our breathless attempts we often miss the flowering that waits for afternoon.

ANNE MORROW LINDBERGH,
Gift from the Sea

No sensible person relishes the immature aspects of our optimism, but if we lose that optimism we will surely be a less spirited people, a less magnanimous people and an immeasurably less venturesome people. Zest and generosity will disappear from our national style. And our impact on the world may well disappear along with them.

JOHN W. GARDNER,
No Easy Victories,
edited by Helen Rowan

Comfort isn't enough. Ingenious diversions aren't enough. "Having enough of everything" isn't enough. If they were, the large number of Americans who have been able to indulge their whims on a scale unprecedented in history would be deliriously happy. They would be telling one another of their unparalleled serenity and bliss instead of trading tranquilizer prescriptions.

JOHN W. GARDNER,
No Easy Victories,
edited by Helen Rowan

I am still very much of an American. That is to say, naive, optimistic, gullible. ... Like it or not, I am a product of this land of plenty, a believer in super-abundance, a believer in miracles.

HENRY MILLER,
A Devil in Paradise

It is also true—and this is a curious paradox about America—that these same men who stand upon the corner and wait around on Sunday afternoons for nothing are filled at the same time with an almost quenchless hope, an almost boundless optimism, an almost indestructible belief that something is bound to turn up, something is sure to happen.

THOMAS WOLFE,
You Can't Go Home Again

They are not men, they are not women, they are Americans.

PABLO PICASSO,
quoted in *The Third Rose*
by John Malcolm Brinnin

The dream of the American male is for a female who has an essential languor which is not laziness, who is unaccompanied except by himself, and who does not let him down. He desires a beautiful, but comprehensible creature who does not destroy a perfect situation by forming a complete sentence.

E. B. WHITE,
The Second Tree from the Corner

[The American woman] is unpredictable, not from a calculated charm, but because she really does not know what to do with her inner self.

PEARL BUCK,
Of Men and Women

American women generally do not want freedom. Amazing, terrifying that this is so; and yet one is constrained to believe it true.

PEARL BUCK,
Of Men and Women

They will let you have your black theory of the universe if you like; but they will insist on your enjoying the new clubhouse in the meantime; and, somehow or other, they succeed in making you enjoy it.

ALFRED NOYES,
New Essays and American Impressions

I believe that for a great majority of our people, preadolescence is the nearest that they come to untroubled human life—that from then on the stresses of life distort them to inferior caricatures of what they might have been.

HARRY STACK SULLIVAN,
Conceptions of Modern Psychiatry

In their actual life Americans are not only a non-intellectual but an anti-intellectual people. The charm of the American as a new human type, his rough-and-ready pragmatism, his spontaneity and openness to experience are true of him only because he is unreflective by nature.

WILLIAM BARRETT,
Irrational Man

Americans cherish their *wanderlust* and constantly look forward to changes. I hear them frequently using the words—hateful to them—"stale" or "in a rut."

ERNEST DIMNET,
My New World

They are interested in ideas, keenly so, but you see them at once transforming your ideas into their ideal and ready to champion them, to devote their energies to them as soon as they cease to be purely intellectual. In a minute your thoughts become part of the American's personality and add to the tenseness of his will. You were a mirror; he is a force.

ERNEST DIMNET,
My New World

For all its sophistication the American mind retains the essential quality of the savage mind: it is vulnerable, capturable, manipulable. Perhaps there is something about the American continent itself, with its vast, still virgin stretch, which makes this quality appropriate.

MAX LERNER,
The Unfinished Country

I think lots of men die of their wives and thousands of women die of their husbands. But not an American. Here, if there is a little trouble over a hand glass or a tooth brush, they shake hands and part, unless of course, there is a lot of money, when the lawyers take a hand.

J. B. YEATS,
Letters to His Son,
W. B. Yeats and Others

The Americans *never* walk. In winter too cold and in summer too hot.

J. B. YEATS,
Letters to His Son,
W. B. Yeats and Others

Enjoyment seems to me—if it be enjoyment at all—to *begin* in the senses—that is, in the concrete—and then crown itself in the affection and in the spirit; the richer the concrete the richer afterwards the abstract. These Americans are making huge efforts to get away from the concrete and live in the abstract. This is their plan for living the higher life, and nothing comes of it except a delirious activity.

J. B. YEATS,
Letters to His Son,
W. B. Yeats and Others

The American appears to prefer a constrained attitude—his feet above his head—to a vigorous exertion of his muscles with his feet on the ground; and when he moves he prefers to fly, getting over the ground and the movement as expeditiously as possible. He may, with his instincts and nerves, ultimately develop wings, like a bat, and rest, hanging entirely by his heels, like that nervous animal—a near relation, by the way, zoologically, to the human species.

CHAUNCEY WRIGHT,
Letters of Chauncey Wright

To watch an American on a beach or crowding into a subway, or buying a theater ticket, or sitting at home with his radio on, tells you something about one aspect of the American character: the capacity to withstand a great deal of outside interference, so to speak; a willing acceptance of frenzy which, though it's never self-conscious, amounts to a willingness to let other people have and assert their own lively, and even offensive, character. They are a tough race in this.

ALISTAIR COOKE,
One Man's America

There is something about prosperity, the hunger for it, the pretense in all these middle-class Americans, that makes the soul sick.

SHERWOOD ANDERSON,
The Letters of Sherwood Anderson

Primarily the difficulty with all of us is that, being Americans, we in some way got a wrong start in life. The notion of success in affairs, in love, in our daily life is so ingrained that it is almost impossible to shake it off.

SHERWOOD ANDERSON,
The Letters of Sherwood Anderson

Americans take their coats off anywhere and anywhen, and somehow it strikes the visitor as the most symbolic thing about them.

RUPERT BROOKE,
Letters from America

Many American men dislike women because they were dominated by them throughout childhood and early youth. . . . The earliest recollections of the American boy, perhaps, are of holding up his hand in school and saying to a woman teacher, "Miss Bessie, may I be excused?"

DAVID L. COHN,
Love in America

American women, I believe, weary of men whose emotional content is no greater than that of a boy. They want to be loved by men. They long for that experience which they have not had in their evolution on this soil.

DAVID L. COHN,
Love in America

I would dare say that *Walden* and *Huckleberry Finn* are the two books that reflect most deeply and most clearly the basic tensions involved in being an American.

CLIFTON FADIMAN,
Any Number Can Play

All his life [the American] jumps into the train after it has started and jumps out before it has stopped; and he never once gets left behind, or breaks a leg.

GEORGE SANTAYANA,
Character and Opinion in the United States

The American talks about money, because that is the symbol and measure he has at hand for success, intelligence, and power; but as to money itself he makes, loses, spends, and gives it away with a very light heart.

GEORGE SANTAYANA,
Character and Opinion in the United States

His instinct is to think well of everybody, and to wish everybody well, but in a spirit of rough comradeship, expecting every man to stand on his own legs and to be helpful in his turn. When he has given his neighbor a chance he thinks he has done enough for him; but he feels it is an absolute duty to do that. It will take some hammering to drive a coddling socialism into America.

GEORGE SANTAYANA,
The Letters of George Santayana

Most men—this is less true of the ladies—in America lose their youth and their liberty at 25: they are thereafter what a German philosopher named Jaspers pretends that we all are: our situation personified.

GEORGE SANTAYANA,
The Letters of George Santayana

Every true American likes to think in terms of thousands and millions. The word "million" is probably the most pleasure-giving vocable in the language.

AGNES REPPLIER,
Times and Tendencies

It would be hard to say when or why the American mind acquired the conviction that the lonely farmhouse or the sacrosanct village was the proper breeding-place for great Americans.

AGNES REPPLIER,
Times and Tendencies

An active man or woman stopping to think in the morning may well be appalled at the variety of his or her life. The ubiquity of the modern American subconsciousness is something unique. We wish to know everything there is to know.

ROBERT GRANT,
The Art of Living

An American is either a Jew, or an anti-Semite, unless he is both at the same time.

JEAN-PAUL SARTRE,
Altona, Vol. I

I have seen many American women who look like queens, but I have never seen an American man who looks like a king.

COUNT HERMANN KEYSERLING,
Ladies' Home Journal, October 1946

The signs of friendship, of love, are a necessity for the American. He is insatiable in his demands for them, for any occasion on which they are withheld raises the gnawing doubt that maybe one is not lovable, not a success. . . . The emotional egalitarianism of America demands that all relationships shall bear some resemblance to those of love and friendship.

GEOFFREY GORER,
The American People

One always feels that Americans do not feel entirely at home on their own soil, and that they are still on it as guests. . . . The first time I walked up Fifth Avenue I still thought that all the people had come from the country for the day. I had the same impression in all American cities.

RAYMOND L. BRUCKBERGER,
One Sky to Share

I think that the reason why we Americans seem to be so addicted to trying to get rich suddenly is merely because the *opportunity* to make promising efforts in that direction has offered itself to us with a frequency out of all proportion to the European experience.

MARK TWAIN,
Mark Twain at Your Fingertips,
edited by Caroline T. Harnsberger

An American will tinker with anything he can put his hands on. But how rarely can he be persuaded to tinker with an abstract idea.

LELAND STOWE,
They Shall Not Sleep

But then Americans are always boasting about bribery and corruption, as if it was their own special invention, and as if nobody else had any.

BRENDAN BEHAN,
Evergreen Review, Vol. V, No. 18

Whatever Americans *talk* about, they are always thinking of themselves.

JOHN AYSCOUGH,
First Impressions in America

The fact is that Americans never seem to me to be real people at all. . . . As individuals, they never achieve any kind of reality for me. . . . When the American party, at which I was the only English guest, broke up the other night, I really doubted whether the others went anywhere at all, and imagined them merely crumpling up, vanishing into space, as soon as the door was closed upon them.

J. B. PRIESTLEY,
All About Ourselves and Other Essays

An American is brought up with the huge burning phrases of great revolutionaries . . . forever ringing in his ears. To forget them, to act against their hope and faith in men, is to take an axe to his own roots. There is in the American mind, just because it *is* an American mind, an idealism that cannot be quenched, a small voice of conscience that all the hokum in the world cannot drown.

J. B. PRIESTLEY,
'47 Magazine of the Year,
October 1947

We are castigating ourselves for lack of courage, of energy, of ability to venture and to do. But these things are our excellences—and our vices by excess. Unwillingness to sit still, to think, restiveness at critical discrimination as wasting time which might be spent in "doing something," desire to lay hold of short cuts to results—these are our weaknesses.

> JOHN DEWEY,
> *Characters and Events,* Vol. II

I have been seeing a lot of Americans lately, and they all seem to have that kind of fervour which means aiding and not hindering life.

> ROBERT HUGH BENSON,
> *The Life of Monsignor Robert Hugh Benson,*
> Vol. II,
> edited by C. C. Martindale

AMUSE

We never respect those who amuse us, however we may smile at their comic powers.

> LADY MARGUERITE BLESSINGTON,
> *Desultory Thoughts and Reflections*

AMUSEMENT

There is no position in the world more wearisome than that of a man inwardly indifferent to the amusement in which he is trying to take part.

> PHILIP G. HAMERTON,
> *The Intellectual Life*

The more seriously one takes an amusement, the more amusing it becomes.

> A. C. BENSON,
> *From a College Window*

Personally, I think competition always a more or less disagreeable thing. I dislike it in real life, and I do not see why it should be introduced into one's amusements. If it amuses me to do a thing, I do not very much care whether I do it better than another person.

> A. C. BENSON,
> *From a College Window*

ANALOGY

Though analogy is often misleading, it is the least misleading thing we have.

> SAMUEL BUTLER,
> *Samuel Butler's Notebooks*

There is no worse enemy of thought than the demon of analogy.

"A freshly shaved field. . . ."
What is more tiresome than that mania of certain writers who cannot see an object without thinking at once of another?

> ANDRÉ GIDE,
> *Pretexts*

ANCESTOR

One of the odd things about ancestors, even if they are no older than grandfathers, is that we can scarcely help feeling that, compared to them, we are degenerate.

> ROBERT LYND,
> *The Peal of Bells*

ANGEL

I said in my lecture that if some angel without a carnal body appeared to me and assured me that he was perfectly happy on prayer and music, I should congratulate him, but shouldn't care to imitate him.

> GEORGE SANTAYANA,
> *The Letters of George Santayana*

An angel can illumine the thought and mind of man by strengthening the power of vision, and by bringing within his reach some truth which the angel himself contemplates.

> SAINT THOMAS AQUINAS,
> *The Bliss of the Way,*
> compiled by Cecily Hallack

"Angel" is the only word in the language which never can be worn out. No other word would exist under the pitiless use made of it by lovers.

> VICTOR HUGO,
> *Les Miserables*

Every man contemplates an angel in his future self.

> RALPH WALDO EMERSON,
> *Journals of Ralph Waldo Emerson*

To wish to act like angels while we are still in this world is nothing but folly.

> SAINT TERESA OF AVILA,
> *Saint Teresa in Her Writings*
> by the Abbé Rodolphe Hoornaert

All the angels we know anything about are men.

JOHN OLIVER HOBBES,
Some Emotions and a Moral

ANGER

One privilege of being associated with people whom a person loves is that of being angry with them.

ARTHUR T. JERSILD,
Educational Psychology,
edited by Charles E. Skinner

Anger is an expensive luxury in which only men of a certain income can indulge.

GEORGE WILLIAM CURTIS,
Prue and I

A good indignation brings out all one's powers.

RALPH WALDO EMERSON,
Journals of Ralph Waldo Emerson

Anger and jealousy can no more bear to lose sight of their objects than love.

GEORGE ELIOT,
The Mill on the Floss

A man out of temper does not wait for proofs before feeling toward all things, animate and inanimate, as if they were in a conspiracy against him, but at once thrashes his horse or kicks his dog in consequence.

GEORGE ELIOT,
The Mill on the Floss

There was never an angry man that thought his anger unjust.

SAINT FRANCIS DE SALES,
Introduction to the Devout Life

I know of no more disagreeable sensation than to be left feeling generally angry without anybody in particular to be angry at.

FRANK MOORE COLBY,
The Colby Essays, Vol. 1

If you are patient in one moment of anger, you will escape a hundred days of sorrow.

CHINESE PROVERB

Every normal man must be tempted at times, to spit on his hands, hoist the black flag, and begin slitting throats.

H. L. MENCKEN,
Prejudices, First Series

The whole condemnation of anger rests on our failure to make proper use of it or on the inadequate or mistaken causes for it. There is no defence for the man who loses his temper with the furniture after barking his shin on a chair. But there is still less defence for the man who passes quietly on when he sees a child ill-treated.

ARTHUR PONSONBY,
Casual Observations

Anger is not only inevitable, it is necessary. Its absence means indifference, the most disastrous of all human failings.

ARTHUR PONSONBY,
Casual Observations

There is nothing more galling to angry people than the coolness of those on whom they wish to vent their spleen.

ALEXANDRE DUMAS

Truthfully, he who doesn't know anger doesn't know anything. He doesn't know the immediate.

HENRY MICHAUX,
Selected Writings of Henry Michaux

But on the whole, my impression is that temper is considered the worst trait in the society of the glad hand. It is felt as an internal menace to one's cooperative attitudes.

DAVID RIESMAN,
The Lonely Crowd

The world needs anger. The world often continues to allow evil because it isn't angry enough.

BEDE JARRETT,
The House of Gold

A man who is liable to grow angry is almost always a man of deep affections.

ERNEST HELLO,
Life, Science, and Art

People say, I believe, that in anger a person says things that are a caricature of the truth; but in that caricature you can find truth about yourself that you could never find any other way.

KATHARINE BUTLER HATHAWAY,
The Journals and Letters of the Little Locksmith

Anger would break the whole world to pieces if it could.

FREDERICK W. FABER,
Notes on Doctrinal and Spiritual Subjects,
Vol. II

Bad temper is sometimes shot by its own explosion to an altitude where only good temper can breathe.

ANONYMOUS (HENRY S. HASKINS),
Meditations in Wall Street

Hate is a kind of "passive suffering," but indignation is a kind of joy.

W. B. YEATS,
Letters of W. B. Yeats

One should not lose one's temper unless one is certain of getting more and more angry to the end.

W. B. YEATS,
W. B. Yeats Memoirs,
edited by Denis Donaghue

If we are deprived of our just due, we naturally experience emotions of anger.

DR. SMILEY BLANTON,
Love or Perish

ANIMAL

The way most people "like animals" is very insulting to them. They look down upon them from the height of "superior intelligence." When I feel for a moment a "superior being," I remember the hawk's optic nerve and compare it with my own. Or I compare my powers of scent with those of the dog, or my nerve telegraphy with that of the cat, or my strength with that of almost any animal.

ALGERNON S. LOGAN,
Vistas from the Stream, Vol. II

Animals are such agreeable friends—they ask no questions, they pass no criticisms.

GEORGE ELIOT,
Mr. Gilfil's Love-Story

It is an engaging problem in ethics whether, if you have been lent a cottage, you have the right to feed the mice.

ROBERT LYND,
The Peal of Bells

Out in the wilds I have learned to beware of abrupt movements. The creatures with which you are dealing there are shy and watchful, they have a talent for evading you when you least expect it. No domestic animal can be as still as a wild animal. The civilized people have lost the aptitude of stillness, and must take lessons in silence from the wild before they are accepted by it.

ISAK DINESEN,
Out of Africa

She lies on the hay and I lie on her. The rain drips off the roof while the rain pours outside she's warm and I like just lying there talking to her softly. It's only a small shed about four feet high and we're both squashed together but it's nice just how I like to feel.

SUSAN STREET,
Age 12, New Zealand,
"My Goat Tinker Bell,"
*Journeys: Prose by Children
of the English-Speaking World,*
collected by Richard Lewis

What harshness is needed, I asked myself, to lose the trust of animals? Refinements of torture are vain and never exile an animal long from us. A kindly gesture bestowed by us on an animal arouses prodigies of understanding and gratitude.

COLETTE,
Journey for Myself

I am driven to the conclusion that my sense of kinship with animals is greater than most people feel. It amuses me to talk to animals in a sort of jargon I have invented for them; and it seems to me that it amuses them to be talked to, and they respond to the tone of the conversation, though its intellectual content may to some extent escape them.

GEORGE BERNARD SHAW,
Preface, *Killing for Sport*

It is one of the ironies of nature that few animals are more unsteady on their legs than centipedes.

FREDERICK GOODYEAR,
Letters and Remains

Sheep of all animals in the world express two things: the natural subject of civilization and culture, and the equality of acceptance, of bowing to necessity. Anyone who has killed as many sheep as I have will know this last quality well. Even when the knife is at its throat the sheep does not struggle: it makes no sound while its throat is being cut. It accepts death as no other animal on earth.

LAURENS VAN DER POST,
The Heart of the Hunter

Of course I agree that animals too are involved in the Fall and await redemption and transfiguration. (Do you remember Luther looking up from Romans viii. 21 and saying to his dog, "Thou too shalt have a little golden tail"?) And man is no doubt offered the chance of being the mediator of that redemption. But not by taming, surely? Rather by loving and reverencing the creatures enough to leave them free. When my cat goes off on her own occasions I'm sure she goes with God—but I do not feel so sure of her theological position when she is sitting on the best chair before the drawing-room fire.

EVELYN UNDERHILL,
The Letters of Evelyn Underhill

It is just like man's vanity and impertinence to call an animal dumb because it is dumb to his dull perceptions.

MARK TWAIN,
Mark Twain at Your Fingertips,
edited by Caroline T. Harnsberger

I saw a moving sight the other morning before breakfast.... The young man of the house had shot a little wolf called a coyote in the early morning. The heroic little animal lay on the ground, with his big furry ears, and his clean white teeth, and his jolly cheerful little body, but his brave little life was gone. It made me think how brave all these living things are.

Here little coyote was, without any clothes or house or books or anything, with nothing but his own naked self to pay his way with, and risking his life so cheerfully—and losing it—just to see if he could pick up a meal near the hotel. He was doing his coyote-business like a hero, and you must do your boy-business, and I my man-business bravely too, or else we won't be worth as much as that little coyote. Your mother can find a picture of him in those green books of animals, and I want you to copy it.

WILLIAM JAMES,
The Letters of William James, Vol. II

In the country sometimes I go about looking at horses and cattle. They eat grass, make love, work when they have to, bear their young. I am sick with envy of them.

SHERWOOD ANDERSON,
Letters of Sherwood Anderson

I consider the tiger is a *being,* a created being. If you kill all tigers still the tiger-soul continues. . . . But the point is I don't *want* the tiger superseded. Oh, may each she-tigress have seventy-seven whelps. And may they all grow in strength and shine in stripes like day and night, and may each one eat at least seventy miserable featherless human birds, and lick red chops of gusto after it.

D. H. LAWRENCE,
Selected Letters of D. H. Lawrence

I think I could turn and live with
    animals,
    they're so placid and self-contained,
I stand and look at them long and long.

WALT WHITMAN,
"Song of Myself," *Leaves of Grass*

The simplicity, the integrity, the one thing at a time, of a good animal's eyes is a great beauty, and is apt to cause us to exaggerate our sense of their expressiveness.

ALICE MEYNELL,
The Children

Presently a fox barks away up the next mountain, and I imagine I can almost see him sitting there, in his furs, upon the illuminated surface, and looking down in my direction. As I listen, one answers him from behind the woods in the valley. What a wild winter sound, wild and weird, up among the ghostly hills! Since the wolf has ceased to howl upon these mountains, and the panther to scream, there is nothing to be compared with it. So wild! I get up in the middle of the night to hear it. It is refreshing to the ear, and one delights to know that such wild creatures are among us.

JOHN BURROUGHS,
Nature's Diary

Individual man, shielded by civilization against the elementary dangers of life, is ordinarily free of the need to maintain a primitive state of alertness. Yet the ways of the animal world still hold a strange fascination for us, and men periodically feel compelled to return to the exposed life of the forest and the sea. Something buried deep within us responds to the fierce concentration of the flying seagull as it darts its piercing eyes over the expanse of water in ceaseless search of food. We identify easily with the startled deer as it raises its head above the brush to listen with agonized intentness for the approach of some stealthy aggressor. The intensity with which these creatures use their sensory mechanism seems to recall a mode of existence we once shared and would strive to recapture, if only for a moment.

DR. SMILEY BLANTON,
Love or Perish

ANNIVERSARY

Men hold the anniversaries of their birth, of their marriage, of the birth of their firstborn, and they hold—although they spread no feast, and ask no friends to assist—many another anniversary besides. On many a day in every year does a man remember what took place on that selfsame day in some former year, and chews the sweet or bitter herb of memory, as the case may be.

ALEXANDER SMITH,
Dreamthorp

I don't know what you think about anniversaries. I like them, being always minded to drink my cup of life to the bottom, and take my chance of the sweets and bitters.

THOMAS HENRY HUXLEY,
Aphorisms and Reflections

ANNOYANCE

It is easy to stand a pain, but difficult to stand an itch; it is easy to bear the bitter taste, but difficult to bear the sour taste.

CHANG CH'AO,
quoted in *The Importance of Living*
by Lin Yutang

Many commit a great fault who are annoyed at having been annoyed, vexed at having been vexed.

SAINT FRANCIS DE SALES,
Spiritual Maxims

Of the innumerable small annoyances that fret and harass us, a few only would be discharged by any obvious increment of income.

ALEC WAUGH,
On Doing What One Likes

To get annoyed will only serve to encourage the meddlesome.

BALTASAR GRACIAN,
The Oracle

ANSWER

People of many kinds ask questions, but few and rare people listen to answers. Why?

JANET ERSKINE STUART,
Life and Letters of Janet Erskine Stuart
by Maud Monahan

It is a good answer which knows when to stop.

ITALIAN PROVERB

He who has the final answers can no longer speak to the other, breaking off genuine communication for the sake of what he believes in.

KARL JASPERS,
quoted in
Styles of Radical Will by Susan Sontag

The brevity of a pointed answer to a question worth our while gives us artistic pleasure.

ERNEST DIMNET,
What We Live By

"But why don't you look at it more positively?" I would exclaim ... "Why don't you let us help you free yourself? There are no limits to what one person can do for another, is that not so?"

Of course he had an answer to that. His great failing was that he had an answer for everything.

HENRY MILLER,
A Devil in Paradise

ANTICIPATE

Things almost always turn out otherwise than one anticipates.

MAURICE HULST,
The Way of the Heart

ANTIQUE (*See* AGE, COLLECTING)

ANTI-SEMITISM

Anti-Semitism is a horrible disease from which nobody is immune, and it has a kind of evil fascination that makes an enlightened person draw near the source of infection, supposedly in a scientific spirit, but really to sniff the vapors and dally with the possibility.

MARY McCARTHY,
On the Contrary

Anti-Semitism ... is the most horrible slap in the face suffered in the ever-continuing Passion of Our Lord.

LEON BLOY,
quoted in *Ransoming the Time*
by Jacques Maritain

ANXIETY

What does your anxiety do? It does not empty tomorrow of its sorrow; but oh! it empties today of its strength.

JAN MACLAREN,
quoted in *The Author's Kalendar, 1920*
compiled by Anna C. Woodford

One cannot remove anxiety by arguing it away.

PAUL TILLICH,
The Courage to Be

Anxiety is love's greatest killer. It makes others feel as you might when a drowning man holds on to you. You want to save him, but you know he will strangle you with his panic.

ANAÏS NIN,
The Diaries of Anaïs Nin, Vol. IV

No good work is ever done while the heart is hot and anxious and fretted.

OLIVE SCHREINER,
The Letters of Olive Schreiner

There is then a whole to living, mostly everybody has for this an anxious feeling, some have not any such anxious feeling to the whole of them, many have the anxious feeling in every minute of their living, every minute is a whole to them in an anxious feeling which each minute ends (in) them. ...

Anxious feeling can be in some as always an ending to them, it can be in some as always a beginning in them of living, there are some who have it in them as their own way of living.

GERTRUDE STEIN,
Gertrude Stein: Her Life and Her Work
by Elizabeth Sprigge

It is well to remind ourselves that anxiety signifies a conflict, and so long as a conflict is going on, a constructive solution is possible.

ROLLO MAY,
Man's Search for Himself

This bewilderment—this confusion as to who we are and what we should do—is the most painful thing about anxiety. But the positive and hopeful side is that just as anxiety destroys our self-awareness, so awareness of ourselves can destroy anxiety.

That is to say, the stronger our consciousness of ourselves, the more we can take a stand against and overcome anxiety.

ROLLO MAY,
Man's Search for Himself

APHORISM

Someone who can write aphorisms should not fritter away his time in essays.

KARL KRAUS,
Karl Kraus by Harry Zohn

It's the danger of the aphorism that it states too much in trying to be small.

GEORGE DOUGLAS,
The House with the Green Shutters

An aphorism is true where it has fixed the impression of a genuine experience.

F. H. BRADLEY

We endeavor to stuff the universe into the gullet of an aphorism.

PAUL ELDRIDGE,
Horns of Glass

Exclusive of abstract sciences, the largest and worthiest portion of our knowledge consists in aphorisms, and the greatest of men is but an aphorism.

SAMUEL TAYLOR COLERIDGE,
Aids to Reflection

A pensée is best when strongly felt and wholly spontaneous and of the moment, with the individuality and naïve detail that such thoughts have, yet not without some large outlook. It should be between the thinker and God; whatever suggests another audience impairs it.

CHARLES HORTON COOLEY,
Life and the Student

The aphorism affords at least one test by which you can judge a writer. The Greeks loved to embed gnomic wisdom of this kind in their literature, and there are few great writers who have not contributed to the small stack of the great aphorisms in their language.

ROBERT LYND,
Solomon in All His Glory

It is a difficult enterprise, a delicate undertaking, to write "thoughts." What a well-informed mind, what a fertile imagination, what a just and profound feeling of things, what a happy style, is requisite to attain even mediocrity therein.

JOSEPH ROUX,
Meditations of a Parish Priest

It is my ambition to say in ten sentences what other men say in whole books—what other men do *not* say in whole books.

FRIEDRICH NIETZSCHE,
The Twilight of the Idols

APPEARANCE

The tragedy of our time is that we are so eye centered, so appearance besotted.

JESSAMYN WEST,
Love Is Not What You Think

As always the appearance is precisely the opposite of the reality; my ostensible life is the reverse of my fundamental aspiration.

HENRI FRÉDÉRIC AMIEL,
Private Journal of Henri Frédéric Amiel

I am sure that nothing has such a decisive influence upon a man's course as his personal appearance, and not so much his appearance as his belief in its attractiveness or unattractiveness.

LEO TOLSTOY,
quoted in *The Note Books of a Woman Alone*,
edited by M. G. Ostle

To appear rich, we become poor.

LADY MARGUERITE BLESSINGTON,
Desultory Thoughts and Reflections

There are some people who state that the exterior, sex, or physique of another person is indifferent to them, that they care only for the communion of mind with mind; but these people need not detain us. There are some statements that no one ever thinks of believing, however often they are made.

G. K. CHESTERTON,
The Defendant

With nice appearance people want to be deceived.

GERMAN PROVERB

No man—or so it seems to me—at least until he has passed all his life before a mirror, or as a portrait painter, can have a very exact idea of his own appearance.

GEORGE SAND,
quoted in *Men in Epigram,*
compiled by Frederick W. Morton

It is all to the good that insignificant-looking persons should do great things, but human nature will ever resent it. We are such determined idealists, we have such a passion for symmetry, that our first wish will always be that handsome does and handsome is shall be one.

E. V. LUCAS,
365 Days and One More

Some men become proud and insolent because they ride a fine horse, wear a feather in their hat, or are dressed in a fine suit of clothes. Who does not see the folly of this? For if there be any glory in such things, the glory belongs to the horse, the bird, and the tailor.

SAINT FRANCIS DE SALES,
Introduction to the Devout Life

It is only shallow people who do not judge by appearances. The mystery of the world is the visible, not the invisible.

OSCAR WILDE,
quoted in *Against Interpretation*
by Susan Sontag

All of us have a maternal side, but it is not so obvious in our appearance. We pride ourselves in not even looking like wives, but more like mistresses. The *femme fatale* is our ideal in appearance.

ANAÏS NIN,
The Diaries of Anaïs Nin, Vol. IV

Things do not pass for what they are, but for what they seem. Most things are judged by their jackets.

BALTASAR GRACIAN,
The Oracle

The world is the dupe of appearances, and recognizes nothing without them. In the world's eyes there is no pain but it is accompanied by tears, no piety without practice, no want without tatters and rags.

Of a truth, hypocrites treat the world as it deserves.

DIANE DE POITIERS

We must try to love without imagining. To love the appearance in its nakedness without interpretation. What we love then is truly God.

SIMONE WEIL,
Gravity and Grace

APPLAUSE

He who seeks only for applause from without has all his happiness in another's keeping.

OLIVER GOLDSMITH,
quoted in *Ladies' Home Journal,*
December 1949

Much venom has been spit out in overly loud huzzas.

ANONYMOUS (HENRY S. HASKINS),
Meditations in Wall Street

The applause of a single human being is of great consequence.

SAMUEL JOHNSON,
Life of Johnson by James Boswell

Applause is the beginning of abuse.

JAPANESE PROVERB

APPRECIATION

Only a just appreciation of things will enable us to possess them in tranquility, or console ourselves for their loss.

MADAME SWETCHINE,
The Writings of Madame Swetchine

It is painful to be told that anything is very fine, and not to be able to feel that it is fine—something like being blind, when people talk of the sky.

GEORGE ELIOT

How much, what infinite leisure it requires, as of a lifetime, to appreciate a single phenomenon! You must camp down beside it as for life, having reached your land of promise, and give yourself wholly to it. It must stand for the whole world to you, symbolical of all things.

HENRY DAVID THOREAU,
Journal

A poor life this if, full of care,
We have no time to stand and stare.

> WILLIAM HENRY DAVIES,
> "Leisure,"
> *The Collected Poems of William H. Davies*

I now perceive one immense omission in my *Psychology*—the deepest principle of Human Nature is the *craving to be appreciated.*

> WILLIAM JAMES,
> *The Letters of William James,* Vol. II

The aim of life is appreciation; there is no sense in not appreciating things; and there is no sense in having more of them if you have less appreciation of them.

> G. K. CHESTERTON,
> *Autobiography*

I think we talk a deal of nonsense about getting a lot out of life, meaning a hundred different things very few of which we can really appreciate. Life must surely be like books and people. One should know a few of them very well.

> ROBERT SPEAIGHT,
> *The Unbroken Heart*

The man who desires to improve a human being must begin by appreciating him.

> ROMANO GUARDINI,
> *The Church and the Catholic*

The victory always remains with those who admire, rather than with those who deride, and the power of appreciating is worth any amount of the power of despising.

> A. C. BENSON,
> *From a College Window*

Most men do discern a dividing line between appreciation and gush, and feel vaguely uncomfortable when that line is passed.

> FRANK MOORE COLBY,
> *The Colby Essays,* Vol. 1

It would be idle to deny that a word of praise, a word of thanks, sometimes a word of criticism, have been powerful factors in the lives of men of genius. We know how profoundly Lord Byron was affected by the letter of a consumptive girl written simply and soberly, signed with initials only, seeking no notice and giving no address; but saying in a few candid words that the writer wished before she died to thank the poet for the rapture his poems had given her.

> AGNES REPPLIER,
> *Americans and Others*

APPROVAL

Be careful not to enter the world with any need to seduce, charm, conquer what you do not really want only for the sake of approval. This is what causes the frozen moment before people, and cuts all naturalness and trust.

> OTTO RANK,
> quoted in *The Diaries of Anais Nin,* Vol. IV

ARCHITECTURE

Architecture is a sort of oratory of power by means of forms.

> FRIEDRICH NIETZSCHE,
> *Twilight of the Idols*

The duty of the artist is to strain against the bonds of the existing style . . . and only this procedure makes the development of architecture possible.

> PHILIP JOHNSON,
> *Conversations with Artists*
> by Selden Rodman

Perhaps the blank faceless abstract quality of our modern architecture is a reflection of the anxiety we feel before the void, a kind of visual static which emanates from the psyche of us all, as if we do not know which way to go.

> NORMAN MAILER,
> *Cannibals and Christians*

We all see more of architecture than of any other art. Every street is a gallery of architects' work, and in most streets, whatever their age, there is good work and bad. Through these amusing shows many of us walk unperceivingly all our days, like illiterates in a library, so richly does the fashionable education provide us with blind sides.

C. E. MONTAGUE,
The Right Place

Architecture, of all the arts, is the one which acts the most slowly, but the most surely, on the soul.

ERNEST DIMNET,
What We Live By

What the modern architect has really done is to revolt against forms of construction which have become so conventional, so conceptualised, that they are like the dead phrases which no poet can use again, clichés like the ambient air, the silver stream, the vasty deep, the trackless wild. These have become conceptual forms, standard decorations, pieces of fustian, which actually hide the original intuition, true and powerful, of air, sea, and desert.

JOYCE CARY,
Art and Reality

ARGUMENT

How beggarly arguments appear before a defiant deed!

WALT WHITMAN,
"Song of the Broad-Axe," *Leaves of Grass*

What renders the least flicker of an argument so profitless, so sterilizing, is that the minds of both the disputants are turned towards something quite different from either's authentic inner truth.

JOHN COWPER POWYS,
The Meaning of Culture

When we quarrel, O then we wish we had always kept our appetites in rein, that we might speak so coolly and majestically from the unquestionable heights of character.

RALPH WALDO EMERSON,
Journals of Ralph Waldo Emerson

Men are conquered only by love and kindness, by quiet, discreet example, which does not humiliate them and does not constrain them to give in. They dislike to be attacked by the man who has no other desire but to overcome them.

GIOSUÈ BORSI,
A Soldier's Confidences with God

To state one argument is not necessarily to be deaf to all others.

ROBERT LOUIS STEVENSON,
An Apology for Idlers

Most of the arguments to which I am a party fall somewhat short of being impressive, owing to the fact that neither I nor my opponent knows what we are talking about.

ROBERT BENCHLEY,
Benchley—or Else!

The same arguments which we deem forcible as applied to others, seem feeble to us when turned against ourselves.

JOSEPH ROUX,
Meditations of a Parish Priest

Nothing will ruin an interesting intelligent argument more quickly than the arrival of a pretty girl.

WILLIAM FEATHER,
The Business of Life

Never argue; repeat your assertion.

ROBERT OWEN

If you try to set forth in a catalogue what will be the exact settlement of an affair you will find that the moment you leave the area of pious platitude you will descend into the arena of heated controversy.

SIR WINSTON CHURCHILL

There is no sense in having an argument with a man so stupid he doesn't know you have the better of him.

JOHN W. RAPER,
What This World Needs

You cannot argue with your neighbor, except on the admission for the moment that he is as wise as you, although you may by no means believe it.

OLIVER WENDELL HOLMES, JR.,
The Mind and Faith of Justice Holmes,
edited by Max Lerner

I am sorry you found my last note so cross-grained. It is my fate that, somebody having made a statement, I contradict it, thinking that the argument is just beginning, while my correspondent or interlocutor is apt to take the line that "if that's the way you answer me it's no good talking to you."

FREDERICK GOODYEAR,
Letters and Remains

When someone tries to argue with you, say, "You are nothing if not accurate, and you are not accurate." Then escape from the room.

CHRISTOPHER MORLEY,
Mince Pie

There is no greater mistake than the hasty conclusion that opinions are worthless because they are badly argued.

THOMAS HENRY HUXLEY,
Natural Rights and Political Rights

ARMY (*See* BATTLE, WAR)

ART

I feel that art has something to do with the achievement of stillness in the midst of chaos. A stillness which characterizes prayer, too, and the eye of the storm. I think that art has something to do with an arrest of attention in the midst of distraction.

SAUL BELLOW,
Writers at Work, Third Series,
edited by George Plimpton

Without freedom, no art; art lives only on the restraints it imposes on itself, and dies of all others.

ALBERT CAMUS,
Resistance, Rebellion, and Death

I believe that any art communicates what you're in the mood to receive. If you're at the Met and are in the mood for an Egyptian wall painting, it communicates a lot; if you're not, it says nothing. The same

goes for a Titian. Art is nothing. A little bit of nothing.

LARRY RIVERS,
Conversations with Artists by Selden Rodman

Well, for my part, I believe that art is the only form of activity in which man, as man, shows himself to be a true individual who is capable of going beyond the animal state. Art is an outlet toward regions which are not ruled by time and space.

MARCEL DUCHAMP,
Wisdom, edited by James Nelson

God is so very much, and so essentially an artist that there must be something wrong with those who despise art, even when they are pious and believe.

THEODOR HAECKER,
Journal in the Night

Time extracts various values from a painter's work. When these values are exhausted the pictures are forgotten, and the more a picture has to give, the greater it is.

HENRI MATISSE,
Notebooks

A work of art must carry in itself its complete significance and impose it upon the beholder even before he can identify the subject-matter.

HENRI MATISSE,
Notebooks

One must not walk around a statue any more then around a painting, because one does not walk around a shape in order to conceive the impression of it.

MEDARO ROSSO,
Artists on Art,
edited by Robert Goldwater
and Marco Treves

Abstract painting is abstract. It confronts you. There was a reviewer a while back who wrote that my pictures didn't have any beginning or end. He didn't mean it as a compliment, but it was. It was a fine compliment.

JACKSON POLLOCK,
quoted in *Up Against the Fourth Wall*
by John Lahr

The arts are an even better barometer of what is happening in our world than the stock market or the debates in Congress.

HENDRIK WILLEM VAN LOON,
The Arts

In every school it is taught: Never leave stale flowers in a vase. Throw them away! So it should be taught: Never leave stale pictures on the wall. Burn them! The value of a picture lies in the aesthetic emotion it brings, exactly as if it were a flower. The aesthetic emotion dead, the picture is a piece of ugly litter.

D. H. LAWRENCE,
Assorted Articles

I believe that in modern work the spectator has to bring with him more than half the emotion. To most people who look at a mobile, it's no more than a series of flat objects that move. To a few, though, it may be poetry.

ALEXANDER CALDER,
Conversations with Artists by Selden Rodman

In the end, works of art are the only media of complete and unhindered communication between man and man that can occur in a world full of gulfs and walls that limit community of experience.

JOHN DEWEY,
Art as Experience

The problem of the relation of art and morals is too often treated as if the problem existed only on the side of art. It is virtually assumed that morals are satisfactory in idea if not in fact, and that the only question is whether and in what ways art should conform to a moral system already developed.

JOHN DEWEY,
Art as Experience

The most immoral and disgraceful and dangerous thing that anybody can do in the arts is knowingly to feed back to the public its own ignorance and cheap tastes.

EDMUND WILSON,
Memoirs of Hecate County

Art, to a certain extent and at a given moment, is a force which blows the roof off the cave where we crouch imprisoned.

ERNEST HELLO,
Life, Science, and Art

The stacking together of the paintings of the great masters in museums is a catastrophe, and a collection of a hundred good intellects produces collectively one idiot.

C. G. JUNG,
Psychological Reflections,
edited by Jolande Jacobi and R. F. Hull

What was any art but an effort to make a sheath, a mould in which to imprison for a moment the shining, elusive element which is life itself?

WILLA CATHER,
The Song of the Lark

The artistic tendency is not expansive but contractive. And art is the apotheosis of solitude.

HUGH KENNER,
The Stoic Comedians

The violent reactions against modern art in collectivist (Nazi, Communist) as well as conformist (American democratic) groups show that they feel seriously threatened by it. But one does not feel spiritually threatened by something which is not an element of oneself.

PAUL TILLICH,
The Courage to Be

The preoccupation with self-expression is probably no more appropriate to the world of art than it is to the world of surgery. That doesn't mean I would reduce self-expression in surgery to zero, because, indeed, I'm sure that the really great surgeons operate on the edge of intuition. But the tremendous, rigorous constraints in surgery—those are what are important in any art.

CHARLES EAMES,
Supertalk by Digby Diehl

I remember being handed a score composed by Mozart at the age of eleven. What could I say? I felt like de Kooning, who was asked to comment on a certain abstract painting, and answered in the negative. He was then told it was the work of a celebrated monkey. "That's different. For a monkey, it's terrific."

IGOR STRAVINSKY,
"Conversations with Stravinsky,"
London Magazine, March 1967

In art, all who have done something other than their predecessors have merited the epithet of revolutionary; and it is they alone who are masters.

PAUL GAUGUIN,
Gauguin by Henri Perruchot

In painting one must search rather for suggestion than for description, as is done in music. Sometimes people accuse me of being incomprehensible only because they look for an explicative side to my pictures which is not there.

PAUL GAUGUIN,
Artists on Art,
edited by Robert Goldwater
and Marco Treves

Sadistic excess attempts to reach roughly and by harshness what art reaches by fineness.

PERCY WYNDHAM LEWIS,
The Art of Being Ruled

Whoever absorbs a work of art into himself goes through the same process as the artist who produced it—only he reverses the order of the process and increases its speed.

FRIEDRICH HEBBEL,
quoted in *The Poet's Work* by John Holmes

There is a great saying that Art is all that cannot be suppressed.

LOUIS DANZ,
Dynamic Dissonance

There are a hundred thousand men born to live and die who will not be as valuable to the world as one canvas.

SHERWOOD ANDERSON,
Letters of Sherwood Anderson

I myself know enough to know that, in the field of painting, in all the plastic arts, for example, I know little or nothing about a work of art until I have seen it many times.

I have to let the thing live in itself a long time before my eyes. It is a fact that a work of art has a life as definite as your wife, your mistress, your friend, your brother.

And just as important too.

SHERWOOD ANDERSON,
Letters of Sherwood Anderson

The public lies far outside consciousness of what is going on among artists. The public is both more stupid and purer, better at bottom perhaps.

SHERWOOD ANDERSON,
Letters of Sherwood Anderson

Poetry gets a good deal of neglect. That's probably good for it. It's the same with all the arts. They get a good deal of neglect—adversity. Nobody knows just how much is good for the arts.

ROBERT FROST,
Wisdom, edited by James Nelson

All these imbecile bourgeois who ceaselessly utter the words: immoral, immorality, morality in art and other idiotic phrases, make me think of Louise Villedieu, the five-franc whore, who, having accompanied me one day to the Louvre, where she had never been before, began blushing and covering her face with her hands. And as we stood before the immortal statues and pictures she kept plucking me by the sleeve and asking how they could exhibit such indecencies in public.

CHARLES BAUDELAIRE,
Intimate Journals

The essence of all beautiful art, all great art, is gratitude.

FRIEDRICH NIETZSCHE

Works of art can wait: indeed, they do nothing but that and do it passionately.

RAINER MARIA RILKE,
Letters of Rainer Maria Rilke 1892–1910

Works of art are of an infinite loneliness and with nothing so little to be reached as with criticism. Only love can grasp and hold and fairly judge them.

RAINER MARIA RILKE,
Letters to a Young Poet

A work of art is good if it has sprung from necessity. In this nature of its origin lies its judgment. There is no other.

RAINER MARIA RILKE,
Letters to a Young Poet

Artistic experience lies so incredibly close to that of sex, to its pain and desire, that the two manifestations are indeed but different forms of one and the same yearning and delight.

RAINER MARIA RILKE,
Letters to a Young Poet

Probably the history of most of the abortive efforts at art is the history of wilful men who could not abandon their cause, but continued to worry it as a dog worries a bone, expecting to perform by fingers and rules what can come by magic only.

JOHN CROWE RANSOM,
quoted in *Inward Ho*
by Christopher Morley

A work of art has no importance whatever to society. It is only important to the individual.

VLADIMIR NABOKOV,
Strong Opinions

The practice of pitting works of art against each other, an intellectual activity, is at the opposite pole from the mood of relaxation which alone makes contemplation possible. To the Asiatic's thinking an art collection ... is as preposterous as would be a concert in which one listened to a programme of ill-assorted pieces following in unbroken succession.

ANDRÉ MALRAUX,
The Voices of Silence

Our feeling for a work of art is rarely independent of the place it occupies in art history.

ANDRÉ MALRAUX,
The Voices of Silence

By the mere fact of its birth every great art modifies that that arose before it; after Van Gogh Rembrandt has never been quite the same as he was after Delacroix.

ANDRÉ MALRAUX,
The Voices of Silence

What folly to admire in art anything whose original we should not admire.

BLAISE PASCAL

Men have valued art, ever since there has been any art, for its own sake; yet always they have cast about for irrelevant reasons why they should value it; and, even now, though we have discovered that it is to be valued for its own sake, we are puzzled by that discovery, and still often fail to think of art in terms of itself. There remains a conflict between our actual experience of art and our thought about that experience, which we can ignore only by a conscious and painful effort; the moment we are off our guard, we begin to think in the old terms.

A. CLUTTON-BROCK,
Essays on Life

There is nothing in life so much exaggerated as the importance of art. If it were all wiped off the surface of the earth tomorrow, the world would scarcely miss it.

RICHARD LE GALLIENNE,
Prose Fancies

Art should not only express those forces which are dominant in life and action, it must also reveal those minor chords of the spirit whose music is often drowned by the insistent iteration of the major notes of existence, yet which is so necessary to the full symphony of life.

EDWARD HOWARD GRIGGS,
A Book of Meditations

It constantly happens that the arts influence one another, that they intermingle, or that, as a result of their natural evolution, they overflow their boundaries and invade the domains of neighboring arts. Now it is music that would become painting, now painting that would become music.

ROMAIN ROLLAND,
Great Essays by Nobel Prize Winners,
edited by Leo Hamalian
and Edmond L. Volpe

Nature and art, being two different things, cannot be the same thing. Through art we express our conception of what nature is not.

PABLO PICASSO,
Artists on Art,
edited by Robert Goldwater
and Marco Treves

To me there is no past or future in art. If a work of art cannot live always in the present it must not be considered at all.

PABLO PICASSO,
Artists on Art,
edited by Robert Goldwater
and Marco Treves

In my opinion to search means nothing in painting. To find is the thing.

PABLO PICASSO,
Artists on Art,
edited by Robert Goldwater
and Marco Treves

Everyone wants to understand art. Why not try to understand the song of a bird? Why does one love the night, flowers, everything around one, without trying to understand them? But in the case of a painting people have to understand. ... People who try to explain pictures are usually barking up the wrong tree.

PABLO PICASSO,
Artists on Art,
edited by Robert Goldwater
and Marco Treves

Appreciation of art is a moral erection; otherwise mere dilettantism.

JEAN COCTEAU,
Writers at Work, Third Series,
edited by George Plimpton

The worst that can happen to a work of art is to have no fault found with it so that its author is not obliged to take up an attitude of opposition.

JEAN COCTEAU,
Writers at Work, Third Series,
edited by George Plimpton

Art when really understood is the province of every human being. It is simply a question of doing things, anything, well. It is not an outside, extra thing.

ROBERT HENRI,
The Art Spirit

It is harder to *see* than it is to express. The whole value of art rests in the artist's ability to see well into what is before him.

ROBERT HENRI,
The Art Spirit

The man who has honesty, integrity, the love of inquiry, the desire to see beyond, is ready to appreciate good art. He needs no one to give him an art education; he is already qualified.

ROBERT HENRI,
The Art Spirit

Art disenchants; and this is a great merit. It teaches how little of what might be, is; how far beneath our capabilities we ourselves are content to remain.

JOHN LANCASTER SPALDING,
Essays and Reviews

A work of art has an author and yet, when it is perfect, it has something which is essentially anonymous about it.

SIMONE WEIL,
Gravity and Grace

The only portraits in which one believes are portraits where there is very little of the sitter and a very great deal of the artist.

OSCAR WILDE,
The Decay of Lying

In art, good intentions are not of the smallest value. All bad art is the result of good intentions.

OSCAR WILDE,
De Profundis

Art has taken on new life for us because of the mural decorations in the Radio City Music Hall. The point is, some of the art treasures are in the men's rooms, and some are in the ladies' rooms. Thus, half of the art works must remain forever unseen by half the population. This is an advance aesthetically. The quality of unattainability is the quintessence of beauty.

E. B. WHITE,
Every Day Is Saturday

I often wish that we had a more beautiful word than "art" for so beautiful a thing; it is in itself a snappish, explosive word, like the cry of an angry animal; and it has, too, to bear the sad burden of its own misuse by affected people.

A. C. BENSON,
From a College Window

The people who stand most stubbornly in the way of progress in any art are generally the very people who know most about it.

DEEMS TAYLOR

Criticism is powerless to reach art. Art proceeds itself in a region quite beyond the reach of other expression save itself.

JOHN JAY CHAPMAN,
Memories and Milestones

In a beautiful city an art gallery would be superfluous. In an ugly one it is a narcotic.

HOLBROOK JACKSON,
Platitudes in the Making

We are prone to talk as if some place, or some work of art, that is famous for its beauty were always the same thing, a certain fixed treasure to which anybody can go at any time, and in any state of himself, and still find it there. But many things must have happened in the inside of yourself before even the most celebrated of these cynosures can make much difference to you—and you are the only person for whom you can ever know for certain how much the difference amounts to. . . . "Silly old washerwoman, she and her brat," I have heard a very good fellow say at sight of the Sistine Madonna. Here the collaborators, my friend and Raphael, seem to have hardly succeeded at all.

C. E. MONTAGUE,
The Right Place

We are all heirs to the loveliness of the visible world, but only by process of art can we be inducted into possession of this large estate.

C. E. MONTAGUE,
A Writer's Notes on His Trade

This is the thing that I don't think you can come back to often enough; the tremendous importance of art to make one realize in the gravel of one's gizzard what otherwise might become simply an abstraction in the head.

ARCHIBALD MACLEISH,
*The Dialogues of Archibald MacLeish
and Mark Van Doren*

When a thing needs no imaginative effort to get hold of it, it's not a work of art.

WILLIAM J. LOCKE

All my life I have found that regarding works of art and brooding over artists and their ways is not only delightful in itself but enlarges and renews my spirit and way of thinking. I hardly know why; it is partly the relief and release that comes from thinking of man as a maker of beauty, and of myself, even, as possibly a sharer in this. One gets a fresh sense of life.

CHARLES HORTON COOLEY,
Life and the Student

Real art has the capacity to make us nervous. By reducing the work of art to its content and then interpreting *that,* one tames the work of art. Interpretation makes art manageable, conformable.

SUSAN SONTAG,
Against Interpretation

And there can be no art, no cry to the brain, unless there is violence. The hard thing is to do violence in the neatly right degree: you must tap your man's skull but not crack it: you must wake him but not daze him: he is to be made to hear, he is not to be deafened.

STEPHEN MACKENNA,
Journal and Letters of Stephen Mackenna

Hardly anyone knows that the secret of beautiful work lies to a great extent in truth and sincere sentiment. Smartness, as they call it here—the word is so much used . . . is that what must save art?

VINCENT VAN GOGH,
*Dear Theo:
An Autobiography of Vincent Van Gogh*

The truth is that sincerity in art is not an affair of will, of a moral choice between honesty and dishonesty. It is mainly an affair of talent.

ALDOUS HUXLEY,
Essays New and Old

If it were not for the intellectual snobs who pay—in solid cash—the tribute which philistinism owes to culture, the arts would perish with their starving practitioners. Let us thank heaven for hypocrisy.

ALDOUS HUXLEY,
Jesting Pilate

Sex is almost as completely private a matter as death, and a work of art which powerfully expresses the truth about either of them is very painful to the respectable figure we imagine ourselves to be.

ALDOUS HUXLEY,
Collected Essays

Other things being equal, the work of art which in its own way "says" more about the universe will be better than the work of art which says less.

ALDOUS HUXLEY,
Collected Essays

The good thing about a work of art is that it tells all sorts of things to different spectators, of none of which things the artist ever knew a word.

WILLIAM JAMES,
The Thought and Character of William James, Vol. II,
by Ralph Barton Perry

It has become obvious that art itself in America is without what might be called a natural environment. Art and artists often exist in a public climate that is either indifferent or hostile to their profession.

BEN SHAHN,
The Shape of Content

Art is only a means to life, to the life more abundant. It merely points the way, something which is overlooked not only by the public, but very often by the artist himself. In becoming an end it defeats itself.

HENRY MILLER,
The Wisdom of the Heart

Art almost always has its ingredient of impudence, its flouting of established authority, so that it may substitute its own authority, and its own enlightenment.

BEN SHAHN,
The Shape of Content

Does Man love Art? Man visits Art, but squirms.
Art hurts. Art urges voyages—
and it is easier to stay at home,
the nice beer ready.

GWENDOLYN BROOKS,
"The Chicago Picasso," *On Being Black*,
edited by Charles T. Davis
and Daniel Walden

A life passed among pictures makes not a painter—else the policeman in the National Gallery might assert himself. As well allege that he who lives in a library must needs be a poet.

JAMES A. MCNEILL WHISTLER,
Artists on Art,
edited by Robert Goldwater
and Marco Treves

Art is limited to the infinite, and beginning there cannot progress.

JAMES A. MCNEILL WHISTLER,
Artists on Art,
edited by Robert Goldwater
and Marco Treves

Art flourishes when there is a sense of adventure, a sense of nothing having been done before, of complete freedom to experiment; but when caution comes in you get repetition, and repetition is the death of art.

ALFRED NORTH WHITEHEAD,
Dialogues of Alfred North Whitehead

ARTIST

One of the dangers of the American artist is that he finds himself almost exclusively thrown in with persons more or less in the arts. He lives among them, eats among them, quarrels with them, marries them.

THORNTON WILDER,
Writers at Work,
edited by Malcolm Cowley

The artist appeals to that part of our being which is not dependent on wisdom; to that in us which is a gift and not an acquisition—and, therefore, more permanently enduring. He speaks to our capacity for delight and wonder, to the sense of mystery surrounding our lives; to our sense of pity, of beauty and of pain; to the latent feeling of fellowship with all creation.

> JOSEPH CONRAD,
> quoted in *Wisdom and Beauty from Conrad,*
> compiled by M. Harriet Capes

Debauchery is useful to the artist as a form of spiritual exercise—also because it enables him to resist more serious temptations.

> JOHN PEALE BISHOP,
> *The Collected Essays of John Peale Bishop*

The failure of the artist must strike close to the identity and potency of the man.

> BERNARD DE VOTO

Every good painter invents a new way of painting.

> ALDOUS HUXLEY,
> *Collected Essays*

The artist does not draw what he sees, but what he must make others see. Only when he no longer knows what he is doing does the painter do good things.

> EDGAR DEGAS,
> *Artists on Art,*
> edited by Robert Goldwater
> and Marco Treves

It would seem that in art, as in diet, as in the spiritual life, the same rules of elimination apply: the more one can do without, the better, and to the court of the only ruler of princes, the artist as the saint, should come empty handed.

> ANNE FREEMANTLE,
> *Desert Calling*

A painter told me that nobody could draw a tree without in some sort becoming a tree.

> RALPH WALDO EMERSON,
> "History," *Essays*

Artistic temperament is like a king with vigor and unlimited opportunity. You shake the structure to pieces by playing with it.

> F. SCOTT FITZGERALD,
> *The Crack-up*

An artist cannot fail; it is a success to be one.

> CHARLES HORTON COOLEY,
> *Life and the Student*

To desire to be an artist is to desire to be a complete man, in respect to some one function, to realize yourself utterly. A man is a poor thing who is content not to be an artist.

> CHARLES HORTON COOLEY,
> *Life and the Student*

There are few outsiders who have any dream of the difficulties an artist has to meet in the mere putting on of his paint.

> ROBERT HENRI,
> *The Art Spirit*

I don't believe any real artist cares whether what he does is "art" or not. Who, after all, knows what is art? I think the real artists are too busy with just being and growing and acting (on canvas or however) like themselves, to worry about the end. This end is what it will be. The object is intense living, fulfillment, the great happiness in creation.

> ROBERT HENRI,
> *The Art Spirit*

The man who has something very definite to say and tries to force the medium to say it will learn how to draw.

> ROBERT HENRI,
> *The Art Spirit*

When the artist is alive in any person, whatever his kind of work may be, he becomes an inventive, searching, daring, self-expressing creature. He becomes interesting to other people. He disturbs, upsets, enlightens, and he opens ways for a better understanding. Where those who are not artists are trying to close the book, he opens it, shows there are still more pages possible.

> ROBERT HENRI,
> *The Art Spirit*

I breathe painting; I never cease thinking about it. And when I paint, I never really know what I will paint. I look at the many colors before me. I look at my blank canvas. Then, I try to seek an equilibrium. . . .

I try to apply colors like words that shape poems, like notes that shape music.

JOAN MIRÓ,
Close-up by John Gruen

All great artists are preoccupied, as if by nature, with reality. They assume, from the beginning, that it is their task to reveal a truth about some permanent and fundamental real.

JOYCE CARY,
Art and Reality

It is out of their limitations that men create beauty, and the new and lovely things that have been given to the world have been very often but the result of the conflict of the artist with his shortcomings.

W. SOMERSET MAUGHAM,
The Gentleman in the Parlour

Painting is a blind man's profession. He paints not what he sees, but what he feels, what he tells himself about what he has seen.

PABLO PICASSO,
Journals by Jean Cocteau

The artist . . . must pass judgment only on what he understands; his circle is as limited as that of any other specialist—this I repeat and on this I always insist.

ANTON CHEKHOV,
The Selected Letters of Anton Chekhov

An artist may make a success or a failure of his work. He may make a success or a failure of his life. But if he can tell himself that, finally, as a result of his long effort, he has ceased or decreased the various forms of bondage weighing upon men, then in a sense he is justified and, to some extent, he can forgive himself.

ALBERT CAMUS,
Resistance, Rebellion, and Death

All intellectual work is the same,—the artist feeds the public on his own bleeding insides.

WILLIAM JAMES,
The Thought and Character of William James,
Vol. II,
by Ralph Barton Perry

It needs a certain purity of spirit to be an artist, of any sort. . . . An artist may be a profligate and, from the social point of view, a scoundrel. But if he can paint a nude woman, or a couple of apples, so that they are a living image, then he was pure in spirit, and, for the time being, his was the kingdom of heaven.

D. H. LAWRENCE,
Assorted Articles

With a small temperament one can be very much of a painter. One can do good things without being very much of a harmonist or a colorist. It is sufficient to have a sense of art—and this sense is doubtless the horror of the bourgeois. Therefore institutions, pensions, honors can only be made for cretins, rogues, and rascals. Do not be an art critic, but paint; therein lies salvation.

PAUL CÉZANNE,
Artists on Art, edited by Robert Goldwater
and Marco Treves

The only thing that is really difficult is to prove what one believes. So I am going on with my researches. . . . I am continually making observations from nature, and I feel that I am making some slight progress. I should like to have you here with me, for my solitude always oppresses me a little; but I am old, ill, and I have sworn to die painting.

PAUL CÉZANNE,
(letter to his son)

How people ever lose themselves who are not artists I do not know. Perhaps they, some of them, do it in love.

SHERWOOD ANDERSON,
Letters of Sherwood Anderson

I shall keep at painting. It is a doorway out of much that is disordered in myself.

SHERWOOD ANDERSON,
Letters of Sherwood Anderson

Not many of our painters have much straight sensual joy in life—in fruits, hills, women's bodies, skies, rivers, etc. Most of them, I think, get painting too much up into their heads to ever paint really well.

SHERWOOD ANDERSON,
Letters of Sherwood Anderson

Any writer, I suppose, feels that the world into which he was born is nothing less than a conspiracy against the cultivation of his talent—which attitude certainly has a great deal to support it. On the other hand, it is only because the world looks on his talent with such a frightening indifference that the artist is compelled to make his talent important.

JAMES BALDWIN,
Notes of a Native Son

That thrill of creation which we experience when we see a masterpiece is not unlike the feeling of the artist who created it; such a work is a fragment of the world which he has annexed and which belongs to him alone.

ANDRÉ MALRAUX,
The Voices of Silence

Artists do not save the world. They practice art.

ARCHIBALD MACLEISH,
The Irresponsibles

I suppose one ought to be indifferent to praise or blame, and yet the artist faced with indifference is always cut to the quick.

JACOB EPSTEIN

Painters are especial sufferers from the visits of talkative people who know little or nothing of the art they talk about, and yet who have quite influence enough to disturb the painter's mind by proving to him that his noblest thoughts are surest to be misunderstood.

PHILIP G. HAMERTON,
The Intellectual Life

If the subject of a painting sells, paint that subject again. After all, it's like jazz—if you play a tune, and it goes right, you try for it again the next time.

LARRY RIVERS,
Close-up by John Gruen

To lay off for a while, which is not too difficult, to ponder over, to think on, to vision, what I have done, am doing, am to do, what I have seen, am seeing, am to see, in, of, and on this world about me in which I am living, that impels the doing of my do—that's more difficult.

JOHN MARIN,
Artists on Art,
edited by Robert Goldwater
and Marco Treves

One thing about artists is that most of them agree in thinking that nothing important can be said about art. Another is that almost without exception they love to talk about it.

SELDEN RODMAN,
Conversations with Artists

An original artist *cannot* copy. So he has only to copy in order to be original.

JEAN COCTEAU

In feeling his way an artist may open a secret door and never discover that behind this door a whole world lay concealed.

JEAN COCTEAU

The work of every creator is autobiography, even if he does not know it or wish it, even if his work is "abstract." It is why you cannot redo your work.

JEAN COCTEAU,
Writers at Work, Third Series,
edited by George Plimpton

An artist cannot speak about his art any more than a plant can discuss horticulture.

JEAN COCTEAU,
quoted in *Newsweek,* May 16, 1955

It is the artist's task to fuse, to bring together the human and the animal in man, to make an imaginative synthesis of what society has dismembered.

ISAAC ROSENFELD,
An Age of Enormity

Nearly always the mark of that era in which an artist is young will in some way lie upon his work, however far he may advance into the future.

CONSTANCE ROURKE,
American Humor

It is very pretty, however, to see how much better he draws his wife than any other model. When he was merely in love with her he used to exaggerate all the faults of her face and think them beauties, but now that he's married he just draws her rightly, and so much more tenderly than other women that all his harshness and eccentricity vanish whenever she sits.

JOHN RUSKIN,
Letters of John Ruskin to Charles Eliot Norton

Artists are proverbially kind. They are the only people, socially superior to the working classes, who possess the virtues of the working classes.

ERNEST DIMNET,
What We Live By

Artists hate the enlightened amateur, unless he buys.

ERNEST DIMNET,
What We Live By

Or was it that he had persuaded himself that it were better to retain his own mistakes than to accept any suggestions, even if they were improvements? A view of art for which a great deal may be said when the artist has arrived at maturity of thought and expression, but a very dangerous one when the artist is but a beginner.

GEORGE MOORE,
Hail and Farewell, Vol. I

Natanson reports to me these sentences of Maillol:
"A model! A model; what the hell would I do with a model? When I need to verify something, I go and find my wife in the kitchen; I lift up her chemise; and I have the marble."

ANDRÉ GIDE,
The Journals of André Gide, Vol. I

I will maintain that the artist needs this: a special world of which he alone has the key. It is not enough that he should bring *one* new thing; although that is already an achievement; but rather that everything in him should be or seem new, seen through a powerful coloring idiosyncrasy.

I have discovered too, and this is very important, that he must have a personal manner of joking, his own sense of humor.

ANDRÉ GIDE,
The Journals of André Gide

There is only one difference between a madman and me. I am not mad.

SALVADOR DALI,
The American, July 1956

I don't think that an artist should bother about his audience. His best audience is the person he sees in his shaving mirror every morning. I think that the audience an artist imagines, when he imagines that kind of thing, is a room filled with people wearing his own mask.

VLADIMIR NABOKOV,
Strong Opinions

True artists are the antennae of nature. Coming nature casts its artists before it.

A. R. ORAGE,
Essays and Aphorisms

When I am *in* my painting, I'm not aware of what I'm doing. It is only after a sort of "get acquainted" period that I see what I have been about. I have no fears about making changes, destroying the image, etc. because the painting has a life of its own. I try to let it come through. It is only when I lose contact with the painting that the result is a mess.

JACKSON POLLOCK,
Close-up by John Gruen

The preference for certain subjects in any art is a sign of compact between the artist and society.

W. B. YEATS,
W. B. Yeats Memoirs,
edited by Denis Donaghue

When we speak of the artistic temperament we are usually referring to the sum qualities which hinder the artist in producing.

ARTHUR SCHNITZLER,
Work and Echo

It may sound paradoxical, but Kafka, Mondrian and Webern have never been influential. It's their imitators that are influential. That's what gives every artist his real prestige . . . his imitators.

IGOR STRAVINSKY,
"Conversations with Stravinsky,"
London Magazine, March 1967

All people in this world are made to "give evidence" or to signify something. Perhaps it can be said that as artists some are made only to show what surface light does to color—and we call the people who practice this very limited but perfectly valid work Impressionists. Still others may be here only to reveal the possibilities of the color blue.

SISTER MAGDALEN MARY,
Conversations with Artists
by Selden Rodman

I so often think how insane it would have been, how destructive for him, if Van Gogh had had to share the uniqueness of his vision with anyone, had had to examine the motives with someone, before he had made his pictures out of them, those existences that justify him with their whole soul, that answer for him, that swear to his reality.

RAINER MARIA RILKE,
Letters of Rainer Maria Rilke 1892–1910

In artistic work one needs nothing so much as conscience: it is the sole standard.

RAINER MARIA RILKE,
Letters of Rainer Maria Rilke 1892–1910

Being an artist means, not reckoning and counting, but ripening like the tree which does not force its sap and stands confident in the storms of spring without the fear that after them may come no summer. It does come. But it comes only to the patient, who are there as though eternity lay before them, so unconcernedly still and wide.

RAINER MARIA RILKE,
Letters to a Young Poet

It is the artist's part to love life and show it is beautiful. Without him we might well doubt the fact.

ANATOLE FRANCE,
quoted in *As the Poet Says,*
compiled by Benjamin Musser

The quality that above all deserves the greatest glory in art—and by that word we must include all creations of the mind—is courage. . . . To plan, dream, and imagine fine works is a pleasant occupation to be sure. . . . But to produce, to bring to birth, to bring up the infant work with labor, to put it to bed full-fed with milk, to take it up again every morning with inexhaustible maternal love, to lick it clean, to dress it a hundred times in lovely garments that it tears up again and again; never to be discouraged by the convulsions of this mad life, and to make of it a living masterpiece that speaks to all eyes in sculpture, or to all minds in literature, to all memories in painting, to all hearts in music— that is the task of execution.

HONORÉ DE BALZAC,
Cousin Bette

You see—to me—life and work are two things indivisible. It's only by being true to life that I can be true to art. And to be true to life is to be *good, sincere, simple, honest.*

KATHERINE MANSFIELD,
The Journal of Katherine Mansfield

Friendliness and benevolence toward life make up the artist's fundamental instinct.

THOMAS MANN,
quoted in *The Book of Marriage,*
edited by Count Hermann Keyserling

A sheet of paper so shocks me that as soon as it is on the easel I am forced to scrawl on it with charcoal or pencil, or anything else, and this process gives it life.

ODILON REDON,
Artists on Art, edited by Robert Goldwater
and Marco Treves

A painter is not intellectual when, having painted a nude woman, he leaves in our minds the idea that she is going to get dressed again right away.

ODILON REDON,
Artists on Art, edited by Robert Goldwater
and Marco Treves

The only health for the artist is the constant practice of his craft.

HENRY JAMES,
quoted in *Henry James' Stories*
of Writers and Artists by F. O. Matthiessen

The ideal artist is he who know everything, feels everything, experiences everything, and retains his experience in a spirit of wonder and feeds upon it with creative lust.

GEORGE BELLOWS,
Artists on Art,
edited by Robert Goldwater
and Marco Treves

The young artist has to observe in his own way and keep it an absolute secret from those around him until he can work it into his own books.

SIR OSBERT SITWELL,
Wisdom, edited by James Nelson

Any living situation in which an artist finds material pertinent to his own temper is a proper situation for art.

BEN SHAHN,
The Shape of Content

I believe that if it were left to artists to choose their own labels most would choose none. For most artists have expended a great deal of energy in scrambling out of classes and categories and pigeon-holes, aspiring toward some state of perfect freedom which unfortunately neither human limitations nor the laws allow—not to mention the critics.

BEN SHAHN,
The Shape of Content

The artistic temperament—whatever may be its disadvantages—always ensures its possessor against two evil things, namely the fear of man and the love of money.

E. T. FOWLER,
quoted in *Canon Charles Kingsley*
by Una Pope-Hennessy

The notion of making money by popular work, and then retiring to do good work on the proceeds, is the most familiar of all the devil's traps for artists.

LOGAN PEARSALL SMITH

I like *live* art. A painting is just too passive. The artist can never really feel what contact, if any, has been made between the spectator and the painting. I want to give the spectator a far more active role. I want him as part of my work.

ROBERT RAUSCHENBERG,
Close-up by John Gruen

Too many of the artists of Wales spend too much time about the position of the artist in Wales. There is only one position for an artist anywhere: and that is, upright.

DYLAN THOMAS,
quoted in *New Statesman,*
December 18, 1964

The creative life is often a groping, a terrible stumbling until the artist finds himself doing what his subconscious has demanded all along.

ANDREW TURNBULL,
Thomas Wolfe

An artist must be a reactionary. He has to stand out against the tenor of the age and not go flopping along; he must offer some little opposition.

EVELYN WAUGH,
Writers at Work, Third Series,
edited by George Plimpton

I prefer to think how arms, legs, and head are attached to the body than whether I myself am or am not more or less an artist.

VINCENT VAN GOGH,
Dear Theo:
An Autobiography of Vincent Van Gogh

The great artists are all contemporaries.

LIONEL JOHNSON

To say to the painter, that Nature is to be taken as she is, is to say to the player, that he may sit on the piano.

JAMES A. MCNEILL WHISTLER,
Artists on Art,
edited by Robert Goldwater
and Marco Treves

The artist is the opposite of the politically-minded individual, the opposite of the reformer, the opposite of the idealist. The artist does not tinker with the universe: he recreates it out of his own experience and understanding of life. He knows that the transformation must proceed from within outward, not vice versa. The world problem becomes the problem of the Self.

HENRY MILLER,
The Cosmological Eye

What every great artist is manifesting in his work is a desire to lead a richer life; his work itself is only a description, an intimation, as it were, of those possibilities. The worst sin that can be committed against the artist is to take him at his word, to see in his work a fulfillment instead of a horizon.

HENRY MILLER,
The Cosmological Eye

Some of the sharpest traders we know are artists, and some of the best salesmen are writers.

E. B. WHITE,
Every Day Is Saturday

The artist does us an immense service when he tells us to stop treating things as means and utilities for a moment and to look at them and love their beauty.

GERALD VANN,
The Heart of Man

I hope you take things easy. *I failed because I worked too hard.* I let myself be driven by that foul witch, an uneasy conscience, which is only another name for *Fear*—who is the demon of all life, and the great source of almost all its crimes and criminals. Since I came to New York I have taken things easily, *never worked at any thing a moment longer than I was interested in it,* that is the secret—*never interest yourself in anything you don't care about.* This is not the rule for conduct, but it's the rule for art, and for artists in their work.

J. B. YEATS,
Letters to His Son, W. B. Yeats and Others

I also think that a painter or poet should be all on fire with his motive whether it be an impression or an emotion, and *then work with cold logic and resolute purpose,* till he has created his work of art—the work of art completed, all the fire will be *in it* forever—all the fire with which he first started and then apparently forgot; and it is so in the achievements of practical life.

J. B. YEATS,
Letters to His Son, W. B. Yeats and Others

I came to the conclusion that the only sincerity in a practical world is that of the artist. Hence the eternal dispute between them and the rulers of the world. If we speak at all, we must say what we believe otherwise our tongue is palsied. For which reason, artists, in the world's history, *have, when they have been wise, always kept themselves apart.*

J. B. YEATS,
Letters to His Son, W. B. Yeats and Others

It is not, I think, often enough realized that the basis of the successful artistic temperament is a certain hardness combined with great superficial sensitiveness. . . . It is this hardness which has so often made artists such excellent men of business, so alert to strike favorable bargains.

A. C. BENSON,
From a College Window

Bad artists always admire each other's work. They call it being large-minded and free from prejudice. But a truly great artist cannot conceive of life being shown, or beauty fashioned, under any conditions other than those he has selected.

OSCAR WILDE,
The Critic as Artist

ASCETICISM

Each man . . . must discover his own asceticism. He must unite with whatever truth he is pursuing and willingly pay the price of union. And if he is pursuing many things he must find that needle-point of identity where they are one.

ROBERT SPEAIGHT,
The Unbroken Heart

You have never seen the world if you have not realized that an element of asceticism lies at the foundation of life. You may expel it with the fork of reason or of self-enjoyment, but being part of Nature herself it must ever return. All the art of living lies in a fine mingling of letting go and holding in.

HAVELOCK ELLIS,
Selected Essays

Asceticism . . . is essentially the asserting of the body, not its negation.

ANSCAR VONIER,
The Human Soul

I suppose it will have to be recognized . . . that [asceticism] is a basic thing in human nature, and as ineradicable in its way as the other equally necessary instinct towards Pleasure. To put it another way, perhaps the ordinary Hedonism makes a mistake in failing to recognize . . . the pleasure which lies in the denial of pleasure. In order to enjoy life one must be a master of life—for to be a slave to its inconsistencies can only mean torment; and in order to enjoy the senses one must be master of *them*.

EDWARD CARPENTER,
Love's Coming of Age

The ascetic is an artist; he selects and controls his human nature in order that it may be, according to a certain plan, harmonious and beautiful. It is only in the extreme that his becomes a narrow and futile art, a mere refuge for timid spirits.

CHARLES HORTON COOLEY,
Life and the Student

We can only reach the delicate truth of mysticism through the commonplace sincerities of asceticism.

FREDERICK W. FABER,
Spiritual Conferences

ASK

To ask is no sin and to be refused is no calamity.

RUSSIAN PROVERB

I ask of people more than they can give me. It is useless to maintain the contrary. But what a mistake and what despair.

ALBERT CAMUS,
Notebooks 1935–1942

This is too busy a world for us to stop to wonder whether a man wants what he does not ask for; too many are clamouring loudly for what we cannot give.

WILLIAM J. LOCKE,
The White Dove

Know how to ask. There is nothing more difficult for some people nor, for others, easier.

BALTASAR GRACIAN,
The Oracle

Many things are lost for want of asking.

ENGLISH PROVERB

ASPIRATION

The individual aspiration is always defeated of its perfect fruition and expression, but it is never lost; it passes somehow into the conglomerate being of the race.

DON MARQUIS,
The Almost Perfect State

Little by little, in the long run, aspirations *can* realize themselves. Work for that. We must count it our wealth.

RUTH BENEDICT,
An Anthropologist at Work
by Margaret Mead

ASTROLOGY

Astrology is an interesting social phenomenon, idiotic as anything to be taken seriously.

ELIZABETH JANEWAY,
Open Secrets by Barbaralee Diamonstein

The science of astrology has not perhaps the importance today that it had in the time of the ancient Egyptians or of the Chaldeans, but it is certain that our psychic life is under the influence of the planets, and if parents understood this they would study the stars in the creation of more beautiful children.

ISADORA DUNCAN,
My Life

How much luckier than all the rest of mankind are the astrologers who, if they tell one truth among a hundred lies, obtain so much credit that even their lies are believed. . . . This is due to the inquisitive nature of men, who, desiring to know the future, and lacking other means of information, will run after any one who promises to enlighten them.

FRANCESCO GUICCIARDINI,
Counsels and Reflections

ATTACHMENT

Attachment is a manufacturer of illusions and whoever wants reality ought to be detached.

SIMONE WEIL,
Gravity and Grace

We do not attach ourselves lastingly to anything that has not cost us care, labor, or longing.

HONORÉ DE BALZAC

ATTACK

This I will advise you to, which is, never to attack whole bodies of any kind—individuals forgive sometimes; but bodies and societies never do.

LORD CHESTERFIELD

It is dangerous to attack a man from whom you have taken away all other means of escape except his arms.

MONTAIGNE

Your not having given offence or just cause for quarrelling is no reason to think yourself immune from attack.

FRANCESCO GUICCIARDINI,
Counsels and Reflections

ATTENTION

Attention is a hard thing to get from men.

FRANCIS A. BAKER,
Sermons

What deserves your attention most is the last thing to get it.

EPICTETUS

The one serviceable, safe, certain, remunerative, attainable quality in every study and every pursuit is the quality of attention.

CHARLES DICKENS,
quoted in *The Ambassador of Christ*
by James Cardinal Gibbons

In our periods of fervour, we get a glimpse of what it is like to have real lucidity. . . . We get near to supreme liberty, which consists in the power of being attentive to everything, and changing the sort of attention we give each thing according to the nature of the thing itself, and seeing each so well for what it is that each takes its place in the order of reality, and the soul bears down upon it, as the bee upon the flower, for the good it can yield.

P. R. RÉGAMEY,
Poverty

In the intellectual order, the virtue of humility is nothing more nor less than the power of attention.

SIMONE WEIL,
Gravity and Grace

The authentic and pure values, truth, beauty, and goodness, in the activity of a human being are the result of one and the same act, a certain application of the full attention to the object.

SIMONE WEIL,
Gravity and Grace

Something in our soul has a far more violent repugnance for true attention than the flesh has for bodily fatigue. This something is much more closely connected with evil than is the flesh. That is why every time we really concentrate our attention, we destroy the evil in ourselves. If we concentrate with this intention, a quarter of an hour of attention is better than a great many good works.

SIMONE WEIL,
Waiting for God

ATTITUDE

It all depends on how we look at things,

and not on how they are in themselves.

C. G. JUNG,
Modern Man in Search of a Soul

Things are in their essence what we choose to make them. A thing is, according to the mode in which one looks at it. "Where others," says Blake, "see but the dawn coming over the hill, I see the sons of God shouting for joy."

OSCAR WILDE,
De Profundis

It seems to me probable that any one who has a series of intolerable positions to put up with must have been responsible for them to some extent:—not that it was simply "their fault"—I don't mean that—but that they have contributed to it by unpatience, or intolerance, or brusqueness— or some provocation.

ROBERT HUGH BENSON,
Spiritual Letters of Monsignor R. Hugh Benson to One of His Converts

A stiff attitude is one of the phenomena of rigor mortis.

ANONYMOUS (HENRY S. HASKINS),
Meditations in Wall Street

There are in life as many aspects as attitudes towards it; and aspects change with attitudes. At present we see life, generally speaking, in only a passive aspect because we bring only a passive attitude to bear upon it. Could we change our attitude, we should not only see life differently, but life itself would come to *be* different. Life would undergo a change of appearance because we ourselves had undergone a change in attitude.

KATHERINE MANSFIELD,
Essays and Aphorisms by A. R. Orage

Our attitudes toward the other sex correspond to our general approach toward life—toward any problem with which life confronts us.

DR. RUDOLF DREIKURS,
The Challenge of Marriage

I have sometimes a queer mystical feeling as regards the attitude of people in general. . . . Just as there are physical diseases, so there are diseases of feeling. In a little town like this I feel that on some days everyone goes about hating everyone else. Then something happens and good feeling comes back. I think the whole of mankind must be like that.

SHERWOOD ANDERSON,
Letters of Sherwood Anderson

We awaken in others the same attitude of mind we hold toward them.

ELBERT HUBBARD,
quoted in *The Author's Kalendar, 1921,*
compiled by Anna C. Woodford

Try, for a moment, to become interested in everything that is being said and done; act, in imagination, with those who act, and feel with those who feel; in a word, give your sympathy its widest expansion: as though at the touch of a fairy wand you will see the flimsiest of objects assume importance, and a gloomy hue spread over everything. Now step aside, look upon life as a disinterested spectator: many a drama will turn into a comedy.

HENRI BERGSON,
Laughter

AUTHOR (*See* WRITERS AND WRITING)

AUTHORITY

Authority without wisdom is like a heavy ax without an edge, fitter to bruise than polish.

ANNE BRADSTREET,
Meditations Divine and Moral

Much talk is especially injurious for one in authority.

WALTER ELLIOTT,
The Spiritual Life

There's very few men that can bear authority if they haven't been born with the shoulders for it. If you gave a man a nose who never had one, he would be blowing it all day.

JOHN OLIVER HOBBES,
A Study in Temptations

One thing that has become clear more than any other in this psychological age is that many of the emotional problems of the adult stem from a childhood inability to establish consistent and, on the whole, good-willed feelings toward those in authority over him.

BONARO OVERSTREET,
Understanding Fear in Ourselves and Others

The weaker a man in authority ... the stronger his insistence that all his privileges be acknowledged.

AUSTIN O'MALLEY,
Keystones of Thought

When you are saying something which doesn't seem to mean much, you must say it with a great deal of authority.

VIRGIL THOMPSON,
Ladies' Home Journal, October 1944

I don't like authority, at least I don't like other people's authority.

A. C. BENSON,
Excerpts from the Letters of Dr. A. C. Benson to M. E. A.

AUTOBIOGRAPHY

Just as there is nothing between the admirable omelette and the intolerable, so with autobiography.

HILAIRE BELLOC,
A Conversation with a Cat

Autobiography is an unrivalled vehicle for telling the truth about other people.

PHILIP GUEDALLA

I am sure that those of us who understand and care for them would not lose the personal records of men's souls for any consideration, and it certainly profits us to read them, whatever disadvantage there may be to them in writing them.

GAMALIEL BRADFORD,
The Letters of Gamaliel Bradford

No woman has ever told the whole truth of her life. The autobiographies of most famous women are a series of accounts of the outward existence, of petty details and anecdotes which give no realisation of their real life. For the great moments of joy or agony they remain strangely silent.

ISADORA DUNCAN,
My Life

Autobiographies are the most difficult things to write correctly, for there is nothing that a man knows less about than himself.

JOSH BILLINGS

AUTOMOBILE

Take it for granted that nobody, not even a genius, can guarantee that your car won't fall apart five minutes after he's examined it. A car is even more delicate than a Swiss watch. And a lot more diabolical, if you know what I mean.

HENRY MILLER,
The Air-Conditioned Nightmare

Rubbing elbows with a man will reveal several things about him you never before realized. The same is true of rubbing fenders.

THELMA DOSS,
New York Times, August 16, 1953

Rush Hour: That hour when traffic is almost at a standstill.

J. B. MORTON,
Morton's Folly

Warning: When a motor vehicle is traveling so fast that it cannot pull up quickly enough to avoid knocking down a pedestrian, the horn is blown. This is called a warning.

J. B. MORTON,
Morton's Folly

The freedom that the automobile has given the average American is a good thing, even though it may take him a long time to learn how to use it.

ELMER DAVIS,
America as Americans See It

I think life is excruciatingly funny. People traveling every day on the tube and doing things which are a means to an end but become ends in themselves, like buying cars to get about at weekends, and spending every weekend cleaning them.

N. F. SIMPSON,
quoted in the *London Daily Mail*,
February 25, 1960

When I was a boy I dreamed that I sat always at the wheel of a magnificent Stutz—in those days the Stutz was the stamp of the romantic life—a Stutz as low as a snake and as red as an Indiana barn. But in point of fact, the best I could manage was the intermittent use of the family car.

F. SCOTT FITZGERALD,
The Crack-up

Nothing's ever said about the lives the average driver saves during a little spin around town.

KIN HUBBARD,
Abe Martin on Things in General

If one drives a car with the help of one's mind, one can go only in the lowest gear. The mind cannot keep pace with all the movements necessary for developing a greater speed. To drive at full speed, especially in the streets of a large town, while steering with the help of one's mind is absolutely impossible for the ordinary man.

GEORGES GURDJIEFF,
In Search of the Miraculous
by P. D. Ouspensky

What's wrong with [this sentence]:
The automobilist came to a full stop to let a pedestrian cross safely and smilingly called out: "That's all right: I'm in no hurry"?

H. I. PHILLIPS,
On White or Rye

Unhappiness is being trapped on a rainy highway with a slow-moving truck in front of you and a fast-moving truck coming up behind you.

OGDEN NASH,
The Old Dog Barks Backwards

I have always considered that the substitu-tion of the internal combustion machine for the horse marked a very gloomy milestone in the progress of mankind.

SIR WINSTON CHURCHILL,
A Churchill Reader,
edited by Colin R. Coote

America's love affair with the automobile is not over, it has matured into a marriage.

JAMES M. ROCHE,
New York Times, April 4, 1971

Men who are indifferent to what they wear, and not terribly concerned with what they eat, as long as they do eat, will make absurd sacrifices to possess an automobile. A sociologist once noted that the first topic of conversation among American men was not sex, not politics, not money, but the automobile.

KEN W. PURDY,
Ken Purdy's Book of Automobiles

The young men I have known who were most crazy about automobile-driving were, to begin with, the least interested in traveling. The pleasure is no longer that of seeing the country or even of quickly reaching a certain place, where nothing really attracts them; but simply that of going fast. And though one enjoys thereby sensations just as deeply inartistic or anti-artistic as those of mountain-climbing, it must be admitted that they are intense and indomitable.

ANDRÉ GIDE,
The Journals of André Gide, Vol. I

As the horsepower in modern automobiles steadily rises, the congestion of traffic steadily lowers the average possible speed of your car. This is known as Progress.

SYDNEY J. HARRIS,
Strictly Personal

Last year I was watching the cars by my house. They were slippin' around just like tails swishin' on cats.

BRIAN HOBAN,
age 7, United States, *Journeys: Prose by Children of the English-Speaking World*,
collected by Richard Lewis

In India it is regarded as a good idea to

dart in front of an oncoming car, for the car is sure to kill the evil spirits who are pursuing you, and all the rest of your life you will have good luck.

ROBERTSON DAVIES,
The Table Talk of Samuel Marchbanks

I am sitting in my own car.... It goes at terrific speed. It climbs mountains. The makers of cars understand the feeling that gives me. You see it constantly implied in the advertisements. I am to be made to feel superior to my fellows. Do I accept that feeling as real? Do I take the power in the car to be my own power? ... Every claim I make, every feeling I have, of power that is not my own, that is merely bought, is a cheating of the inner me.

SHERWOOD ANDERSON,
Perhaps Women

AUTUMN

Then summer fades and passes, and October comes. Will smell smoke then, and feel an unsuspected sharpness, a thrill of nervous, swift elation, a sense of sadness and departure.

THOMAS WOLFE,
You Can't Go Home Again

And the great winds howl and swoop across the land: they make a distant roaring in great trees, and boys in bed will stir in ecstasy, thinking of demons and vast swoopings through the earth. All through the night there is the clean, the bitter rain of acorns, and the chestnut burrs are plopping to the ground.

THOMAS WOLFE,
Of Time and the River

One drifting yellow leaf on a windowsill can be a city dweller's fall, pungent and melancholy as any hillside in New England.

E. B. WHITE,
Every Day Is Saturday

The day not merely bright, but radiant, full of glory.... I have to pause and regard the day as one presses a rose to his

nose; all the maple trees in the valley burning.

JOHN BURROUGHS,
The Heart of Burroughs' Journals

Now is the time of the illuminated woods ... every leaf glows like a tiny lamp; one walks through their lighted halls with a curious enjoyment.

JOHN BURROUGHS,
The Heart of Burroughs' Journals

I love the fall. I love it because of the smells that you speak of; and also because things are dying, things that you don't have to take care of any more, and the grass stops growing.

MARK VAN DOREN,
*The Dialogues of
Archibald MacLeish and Mark Van Doren*

Doesn't it seem as if autumn were the real creator, more creative then spring, which all at once *is,* more creative, when it comes with its will to change and destroys the much too finished, much too satisfied, indeed almost bourgeois-comfortable picture of summer?

RAINER MARIA RILKE,
Letters of Rainer Maria Rilke 1892-1910

By the middle of the month most of the trees will be stripped bare and the ground below each tree will be covered with leaves, in crumpled flat heaps of colour, like the petticoat out of which a woman has stepped at bedtime.

CLARE LEIGHTON,
Four Hedges

In such a season, golden, spacious, but already whispering of the end, there will often come to a man a certain solemn mood, a vein of not unpleasing melancholy, and for a little while he will see all life moving to a grave measure, an adagio for strings.

J. B. PRIESTLEY,
All About Ourselves and Other Essays

The autumn always gets me badly, as it breaks into colours. I want to go south, where there is no autumn, where the cold doesn't crouch over one like a snow-leopard waiting to pounce.

D. H. LAWRENCE,
Selected Letters of D. H. Lawrence

Fallen leaves lying on the grass in November bring more happiness than the daffodils.

CYRIL CONNOLLY,
The Unquiet Grave

The morns are meeker than they were,
The nuts are getting brown;
The berry's cheek is plumper,
The rose is out of town.

The maple wears a gayer scarf,
The field a scarlet gown.
Lest I should be old-fashioned,
I'll put a trinket on.

EMILY DICKINSON,
Selected Poems and Letters of Emily Dickinson

AWAKE

Awakening begins when a man realizes that he is going nowhere and does not know where to go.

GEORGES GURDJIEFF,
In Search of the Miraculous
by P. D. Ouspensky

Everyone is familiar with the phenomenon of feeling more or less alive on different days. Everyone knows on any given day that there are energies slumbering in him which the incitements of the day do not call forth, but which he might display if these were greater.... Compared with what we ought to be, we are only half awake.

WILLIAM JAMES,
"The Energies of Men,"
Essays on Faith and Morals

It is delightful to feel that one is wide awake and intelligent. A little self-consciousness here is not offensive.

JOHN LANCASTER SPALDING,
Thoughts and Theories of Life and Education

People would rather sleep their way through life than stay awake for it.

EDWARD ALBEE,
Behind the Scenes,
edited by Joseph F. McCrindle

AWARENESS

Primarily however it is based upon the discovery in psychotherapy, that as the individual becomes more open to, more aware of, all aspects of his experience, he is increasingly likely to act in a manner we would term socialized. If he can be aware of his hostile impulses, but also of his desire for friendship and acceptance; aware of the expectations of his culture, but equally aware of his own purposes; aware of his selfish desires, but aware also of tender and sensitive concern for another; then he behaves in a fashion which is harmonious, integrated, constructive.

CARL R. ROGERS,
On Becoming a Person

Some men go through a forest and see no firewood.

ENGLISH PROVERB

Perhaps too I have made some further progress in observing, as everything overwhelms me so; but, I keep thinking, how old one must become in order really sufficiently to marvel, to remain nowhere behind the world; how much one still undervalues, overlooks, misconstrues.

RAINER MARIA RILKE,
Letters of Rainer Maria Rilke 1892-1910

To remain unaware of what we propose to do, never helps us to live.

JOSIAH ROYCE,
The Problem of Christianity

It is a very rare matter when any of us at any time in life sees things as they are at the moment. This happens at times ... that we become aware of what is going on about us and of the infinite great worlds of force, of feeling and of idea in which we live, and in the midst of which we have always been living. These worlds are really in progress all the time; and the difference between one man and another, or the difference in the same man at different times, is the difference in his *awareness* of what is happening.

JOHN JAY CHAPMAN,
Memories and Milestones

It has seemed to me sometimes as though I could see men hardening before my eyes, drawing in a feeler here, walling up an opening there. Naming things! Objects fall into categories for them and wear little sure channels in the brain. . . . Life solidifies itself in words. And finally how everything wearies them and that is old age!

Is not the prime struggle of life to keep the mind plastic? To see and feel and hear things newly? To accept nothing as settled; to defend the eternal right of the questioner? To reject every conclusion of yesterday before the surer observations of today?—is that not the best life we know?

DAVID GRAYSON,
Adventures in Friendship

AWE

The tremor of awe is the best in man.

GOETHE,
quoted in *The Journals of André Gide*, Vol. I

It is strange what positive awe people seem to have of each other. They are so near and yet so far.

JOSEPH FARRELL,
Lectures of a Certain Professor

BABY

I see the sleeping babe, nestling the
    breast of its mother;
The sleeping mother and babe-hushed,
I study them long and long.

WALT WHITMAN,
"Mother and Babe," *Leaves of Grass*

For our part we have never understood the fear of some parents about babies getting mixed up in the hospital. What difference does it make so long as you get a good one?

HEYWOOD BROUN,
Pieces of Hate

Lullaby, o lullaby!
    Thus I heard a father cry,
Lullaby, o lullaby!
    The brat will never shut an eye;
Hither come, some power divine!
    Close his lids or open mine.

THOMAS HOOD,
"A Serenade,"
The Complete Poetical Works of Thomas Hood

A child is helpless in inverse ratio to his age. He is at the zenith of his powers while he is an infant in arms. What on earth is more powerful than a very young baby?

ALINE KILMER,
Hunting a Hair Shirt

Baby: an alimentary canal with a loud voice at one end and no responsibility at the other.

ELIZABETH I. ADAMSON,
quoted in *The Treasury of Modern Humor*
by Martha Lupton

Women say . . . that if men had to have babies there soon would be no babies in the world. . . . I have sometimes wished that some clever man would actually have a baby in a new, labour-saving way; then all men could take it up, and one of the oldest taunts in the world would be stilled forever.

ROBERTSON DAVIES,
The Table Talk of Samuel Marchbanks

Everyone on earth knows I am going to have a baby—not that I look so enormous, and I dress carefully, but I suppose everyone has read the story (it's come out over and over again) and my coats and scarves tell the rest. Such solicitous care I have never had. Chairs pulled out for me, things picked up for me, milk offered me, an arm offered for high steps, etc., etc., questions as to my health, information about obstetricians, etc. At first it bothered me; now I think it rather a relief—

sometimes very funny and sometimes very nice.

ANNE MORROW LINDBERGH,
Hours of Gold, Hours of Lead

We got ... from Father ... a letter ... announcing to us that we had given birth to a nephew. So the third generation of the James family is in full swing! We are uncles, grandmothers, aunts, etc., all drawing subsistence as such from that one wormlike being in Wisconsin.

WILLIAM JAMES,
The Thought and Character of William James,
Vol. II, by Ralph Barton Perry

My point is that no matter what the ordinary person says ... no matter who it is that speaks, or what superlatives are employed, no baby is admired sufficiently to please the mother.

E.V. LUCAS

Myself have seen and known even a baby envious; it could not speak, yet it turned pale and looked bitterly on its foster-brother. Who knows not this? Mothers and nurses tell you that they allay these things by I know not what remedies.

SAINT AUGUSTINE,
Confessions

She ventured slowly down that shadowed lane,
Now bright with wonder and now dark with pain ...
The trembling thread of life stretched taut and thin,
But softly then, new radiance filtered in.

LYDIA B. ATKINSON,
"Birth," *The Answering Radiance*

Last night my child was born—a very strong boy, with large black eyes.... If you ever become a father, I think the strangest and strongest sensation of your life will be hearing for the first time the thin cry of your own child. For a moment you have the strange feeling of being double; but there is something more, quite impossible to analyze—perhaps the echo in a man's heart of all the sensations felt by all the fathers and mothers of his race at a similar instant in the past. It is a very tender, but also a very ghostly feeling.

LAFCADIO HEARN,
Lafcadio Hearn: Life and Letters, Vol. 2,
edited by Elizabeth Bisland

When one becomes a father, then first one becomes a son. Standing by the crib of one's own baby, with that world-old pang of compassion and protectiveness toward this so little creature that has all its course to run, the heart flies back in yearning and gratitude to those who felt just so towards one's self. Then for the first time one understands the homely succession of sacrifices and pains by which life is transmitted and fostered down the stumbling generations of men.

CHRISTOPHER MORLEY,
Mince Pie

BACHELOR

A bachelor is a man who never makes the same mistake once.

ED WYNN,
Ladies' Home Journal, January 1942

It's the bachelor who thinks he's safe who comes down with the worst wallop.

COLLINSON OWEN,
New York Times, February 24, 1952

I can think of nothing marriage could give me, but I can think of many things it could take away from me.

GEORGE JEAN NATHAN,
"Women as Playthings"
Man Against Woman,
edited by Charles Neider

The bachelor's admired freedom is often a yoke, for the freer a man is to himself, the greater slave he often is to the whims of others.

GEORGE JEAN NATHAN

The infinite, deep, warm, saving happiness of sitting beside the cradle of one's child opposite its mother.

There is in it also something of this feeling: matters no longer rest with you, unless you wish it so. In contrast, this feeling of those who have no children: it perpetually rests with you, whether you will or no, every moment to the end, every nerve-wracking moment, it perpetually rests with you, and without result. Sisyphus was a bachelor.

FRANZ KAFKA,
The Diaries of Franz Kafka 1914-1923

A man without a wife is like a man in winter without a fur hat.

RUSSIAN PROVERB

I have had sympathy enough with my married griefs, but when it came to the perplexing torments of my single life—not a fellow mourner could I find.

DONALD G. MITCHELL,
quoted in *Marriage in Epigram,*
compiled by Frederick W. Morton

BALANCE

In every person, even in such as appear most reckless, there is an inherent desire to attain balance.

JAKOB WASSERMAN,
The Book of Marriage,
edited by Count Hermann Keyserling

BALLET (*See* DANCING)

BARBARITY

Barbarous acts are rarely committed out of the blue. . . . Step by step, a society becomes accustomed to accept, with less and less moral outrage and with greater and greater indifference to legitimacy, the successive blows.

DANIEL BELL,
The Radical Right

BASEBALL

I became a good pitcher when I stopped trying to make them miss the ball and started trying to make them hit it.

SANDY KOUFAX,
quoted in *A Thinking Man's
Guide to Baseball* by Leonard Koppet

Two hours is about as long as an American can wait for the close of a baseball game—or anything else, for that matter.

A. G. SPALDING,
quoted in the *New York Times,*
April 9, 1950

It ain't nothin' till I call it.

BILL KLEM,
quoted in *You Can't Beat the Hours*
by Mel Allen and Ed Fitzgerald

There is no trick to catching a ball in the open field, no matter how far it is hit, as long as it stays in the air long enough. The test of an outfielder's skill comes when he has to go against the fence to make a catch.

JOE DiMAGGIO,
quoted in *Mostly Baseball* by Tom Meany

The phrase "off with the crack of the bat," while romantic, is really meaningless, since the outfielder should be in motion long before he hears the sound of the ball meeting the bat.

JOE DiMAGGIO,
The Second Fireside Book of Baseball,
edited by Charles Einstein

All winter long I am one for whom the
  bell is tolling;
I can arouse no interest in basketball,
  indoor fly casting or bowling;
The sports pages are strictly no soap,
And until the cry of Play Ball! I simply
  mope.

OGDEN NASH,
Sports Illustrated, April 15, 1957

A baseball game is twice as much fun if you're seeing it on the company's time.

WILLIAM FEATHER,
The Business of Life

Sometimes I hit him like I used to hit Koufax, and that's like drinking coffee with a fork. Did you ever try that?

WILLIE STARGELL on Steve Carlton,
quoted in *Baseball Illustrated*, 1975

Fans don't boo nobodies.

REGGIE JACKSON,
quoted in *Baseball Illustrated*, 1975

It's not hard. When I'm not hittin', I don't
hit nobody. But when I'm hittin', I hit
anybody!

WILLIE MAYS,
quoted in *You Can't Beat the Hours*
by Mel Allen and Ed Fitzgerald

Whenever you have a tight situation and
there's a close pitch, the umpire gets a
squawk no matter how he calls it. You
wonder why men want to take a job in
which they get so much abuse.

RED BARBER,
World Series broadcast, October 6, 1952

From the start catching appealed to me as
a chance to be in the thick of the game
continuously. I never had to be lonely behind the plate where I could talk to the
hitters. I also learned that by engaging
them in conversation I could sometimes
distract them.

ROY CAMPANELLA,
It's Good to Be Alive

There is excitement in the game, but little
beauty except in the long-limbed
"pitcher," whose duty it is to hurl the ball
rather further than the length of a cricket-
pitch, as bewilderingly as possible. In his
efforts to combine speed, mystery, and
curve, he gets into attitudes of a very novel
and fantastic, but quite obvious beauty.

RUPERT BROOKE,
Letters from America

Any minute, any day, some players may
break a long-standing record. That's one
of the fascinations about the game—the
unexpected surprises.

CONNIE MACK,
My 66 Years in the Big Leagues

The faces of a baseball crowd are gay,
happy, ecstatic, sad, glum, disgusted. . . .
They vary tremendously from person to
person, but they have a common denominator: a detailed and constantly
growing knowledge of the game.

ROBERT W. CREAMER,
Sports Illustrated, April 15, 1957

The small boy does not know that the best
third baseman in baseball is human: that
he fights with his wife, worries about bills
and occasionally swears at the bat boy. All
the small boy knows is that the third baseman is his hero, and a hero always does
the right thing.

ROBERT W. CREAMER,
The Second Fireside Book of Baseball,
edited by Charles Einstein

Baseball's clock ticks inwardly and silently, and a man absorbed in a ball game
is caught in a slow, green place of removal
and concentration and in a tension that is
screwed up slowly and ever more tightly
with each pitcher's windup and with the
almost imperceptible forward lean and little half-step with which the fielders accompany each pitch. Whatever the pace
of the particular baseball game we are
watching, whatever its outcome, it holds
us in its own continuum and mercifully
releases us from our own.

ROGER ANGELL,
The Summer Game

Baseball gives you every chance to be
great. Then it puts every pressure on you
to prove that you haven't got what it
takes. It never takes away the chance, and
it never eases up on the pressure.

JOE GARAGIOLA,
Baseball Is a Funny Game

Hell, if the game was half as complicated
as some of these writers make out it is, a
lot of us boys from the farm would never
have been able to make a living at it.

BUCKY WALTERS,
quoted in *You Can't Beat the Hours*
by Mel Allen and Ed Fitzgerald

To survive in the minors today, a player
must use rose-colored glasses as standard

equipment. It is the sort of apprenticeship served only by dedicated men—a youth in a seminary, an overworked intern, a rural schoolteacher. You must trust to your reward being in the future—or in the hereafter. It certainly is not in the present.

TOM MEANY,
There've Been Some Changes

When you come right down to it, the baseball owners are really little boys with big wallets.

HAROLD PARROTT,
The Lords of Baseball

Last year, more Americans went to symphonies than went to baseball games. This may be viewed as an alarming statistic, but I think that both baseball and the country will endure.

JOHN F. KENNEDY,
The Kennedy Wit, edited by Bill Adler

Although he is a bad fielder he is also a very poor hitter.

RING LARDNER,
quoted in *The American Treasury,* edited by Clifton Fadiman and Charles Van Doren

They say you can't do it, but sometimes it doesn't always work.

CASEY STENGEL
quoted in *The American Treasury,* edited by Clifton Fadiman and Charles Van Doren

They say you can't do it, but sometimes it doesn't always work.

CASEY STENGEL,
quoted in *A Thinking Man's Guide to Baseball* by Leonard Koppet

When we *are* getting some hits we aren't getting them when we have somebody on the bases. It's very aggravating. But maybe it's better to see them left there than not getting them on at all. If they keep getting on you got to figure one of these days they'll be getting home. Or it could be one of these years, you know.

CASEY STENGEL,
quoted in *Casey Stengel* by Frank Graham, Jr.

A baseball fan has the digestive apparatus of a billy goat. He can—and does—devour any set of diamond statistics with insatiable appetite and then nuzzle hungrily for more.

ARTHUR DALEY

The comprehensibility of baseball is in sharp contrast with so much of the serious news of the day.... It is a self-enclosed world of competition and action in which the emotions can have free play without the consequences being dangerous.

JAMES T. FARRELL,
My Baseball Diary

But I'll tell you this—I made up my mind a long time ago not to get too excited, no matter which way the crowd goes. I get paid for playing left field and for hitting that baseball. I am not a participant in a popularity contest.

TED WILLIAMS,
Saturday Evening Post, April 10, 1954

One of the chief duties of the fan is to engage in arguments with the man behind him. This department of the game has been allowed to run down fearfully.

ROBERT BENCHLEY,
The Baseball Reader,
edited by Ralph S. Graber

Catching a fly ball is a pleasure but knowing what to do with it after you catch it is a business.

TOMMY HENRICH,
quoted in the *New York Times,*
November 5, 1976

Just hold them for a few innings, fellas. I'll think of something.

CHARLIE DRESSEN,
quoted in *You Can't Beat the Hours*
by Mel Allen and Ed Fitzgerald

In its beauty and design that vision of the soaring stands, the pattern of forty thousand empetalled faces, the velvet and unalterable geometry of the playing field, and the small lean figures of the players, set there, lonely, tense and waiting in their places, bright, desperate, solitary atoms encircled by that huge wall of faces, is incredible.

THOMAS WOLFE,
Of Time and the River

Let me get a good grip on the bat, as if I wanted to leave my finger-prints on the wood: let me swing with a quick snap which comes from a powerful wrist, and, if I've gotten back of the ball it sure will travel.

JIMMY FOXX,
quoted in *Famous American Athletes of Today,*
Fourth Series, by Charles H. L. Johnston

All I can tell 'em is pick a good one and sock it. I get back to the dugout and they ask me what it was I hit and I tell 'em I don't know except it looked good.

BABE RUTH,
quoted in *The American Treasury,* edited by
Clifton Fadiman and Charles Van Doren

I didn't mean to hit the umpire with the dirt, but I did mean to hit that bastard in the stands. If I make a home run every time I bat, they think I'm all right. If I don't, they think they can call me anything they like.

BABE RUTH,
quoted in *Babe* by Robert W. Creamer

A man ought to get all he can earn. A man who knows he's making money for other people ought to get some of the profit he brings in. Don't make any difference if it's baseball or a bank or a vaudeville show. It's business, I tell you. There ain't no sentiment to it. Forget that stuff.

BABE RUTH,
quoted in *Babe* by Robert W. Creamer

Every great batter works on the theory that the pitcher is more afraid of him than he is of the pitcher.

TY COBB,
quoted in *The Tiger Wore Spikes*
by John McCallum

You would be amazed how many important outs you can get by working the count down to where the hitter is sure you're going to throw to his weakness, and then throw to his power instead.

WHITEY FORD,
The Second Fireside Book of Baseball,
edited by Charles Einstein

The true fan is not only violently partisan, but very noisy, and an expert at offering advice to the home team, sometimes in not very polite terms. I used to amuse myself with wondering what would happen if a group of fans of this order would turn up at a tennis match or a golf meet.

W. R. BURNETT,
The Roar of the Crowd

No game in the world is as tidy and dramatically neat as baseball, with cause and effect, crime and punishment, motive and result, so cleanly defined.

PAUL GALLICO,
quoted in *The Baseball Reader,*
edited by Ralph S. Graber

The romance between intellectuals and the game of baseball is, for the most part, one-sided to the point of absurdity. A large percentage of intelligent Americans evaluate the four hundred men who play major baseball as awesomely gifted demigods. A large percentage of the muscular four hundred rate intellectuals several notches below umpires.

ROGER KAHN,
The Second Fireside Book of Baseball,
edited by Charles Einstein

It is better to throw a theoretically poorer pitch wholeheartedly, than to throw the so-called right pitch with a feeling of doubt—doubt that it's right, or doubt that you can make it behave well at that moment. You've got to feel sure you're doing the right thing—sure that you *want* to throw the pitch that you're going to throw.

SANDY KOUFAX,
quoted in *A Thinking Man's
Guide to Baseball* by Leonard Koppet

BASKETBALL

I put the most pressure on myself because of my ambitions to be the best basketball player ever. What happens around me can't put any more pressure on me than that.

JULIUS ERVING,
quoted in *The Legend of Dr. J*
by Marty Bell

I'm just the utility man. I do a little of everything. All right—sometimes I do a *lot* of everything.

JULIUS ERVING,
Sports Illustrated, May 17, 1976

The thing about him is that you know he is going to get to the basket, you just never know how.

BOBBY JONES on Julius Erving,
Sports Illustrated, May 17, 1976

The cooperation in basketball is remarkable because the flow of action always includes a role for creative spontaneity; the potential for variation is unlimited. Players improvise constantly. The unity they form is not achieved at the expense of individual imagination.

BILL BRADLEY,
Life on the Run

Nothing there but basketball, a game which won't be fit for people until they set the basket umbilicus-high and return the giraffes to the zoo.

OGDEN NASH,
The Old Dog Barks Backwards

You never want to give anyone the opinion you've given up. I figure if I keep coming back at them, even though we're about to lose, it might have a good effect in the future.

JOHN HAVLICEK,
quoted in *That Championship Feeling*
by Joe Fitzgerald

If I were given a change of life, I'd like to see how it would be to live as a mere six-footer.

WILT CHAMBERLAIN,
quoted in *Basketball's Lonely Heroes*
by Merv Harris

My remarks were strong, but not abusive. I said the call was stupid, and it was.

RED AUERBACH,
quoted in *Basketball's Greatest Stars*
by Al Hirschberg

Everyone's always talking about guys who are good passers, but they never talk about guys who are good receivers. It's as important in basketball as it is in football.

RICK BARRY,
Confessions of a Basketball Gypsy

The players make the coach. The coach who thinks his coaching is more important than his talent is an idiot.

JOE LAPCHICK,
quoted in *Basketball's Greatest Stars*
by Al Hirschberg

It has been basketball which has shown the most conspicuous explosion of black talent.

JAMES MICHENER,
Sports in America

There's no way you can have consistent success without players. *No one* can win without material. But not everyone can win *with* material.

JOHN WOODEN,
quoted in *The Wizard of Westwood*
by Dwight Chapin and Jeff Prugh

I've always been able to lose myself in the games, to concentrate on the play. ... If you're worried about the crowd, if you hear what the fans yell, if you're thinking about how you look or what you're going to do after the game, it's bound to take a lot away from your performance.

JERRY WEST,
Mr. Clutch

I don't look for excuses when we lose, and I don't buy excuses when we win.

DAVE COWENS,
quoted in *That Championship Feeling*
by Joe Fitzgerald

There isn't a basketball player alive who doesn't register anything from simple annoyance to wild-eyed rage when a foul is called on him, even if it's a palpable foul and one that he knows he's committed.

BOB COUSY,
Basketball Is My Life

If we win you will have a lot of free time; if we lose you belong to me.

RED HOLZMAN,
quoted in *Life on the Run* by Bill Bradley

The game's over, the season's over, and it's

like death—you can't change it. You can't go out and say, add up the score again.

RED HOLZMAN,
about losing the NBA playoffs,
New York Times, April 20, 1971

BATTLE

A revealing light is thrown on this subject through the studies by Medical Corps psychiatrists of the combat fatigue cases in the European Theater. They found that fear of killing, rather than fear of being killed, was the most common cause of battle failure, and that fear of failure ran a strong second.

S. L. A. MARSHALL,
Men Against Fire

The good company has no place for the officer who would rather be right than be loved, for the time will quickly come when he walks alone, and in battle no man may succeed in solitude.

S. L. A. MARSHALL,
Men Against Fire

Men who have been in battle know from first-hand experience that when the chips are down, a man fights to help the man next to him, just as a company fights to keep pace with its flanks. Things have to be that simple.

S. L. A. MARSHALL,
Men Against Fire

In the conduct of military operations, great illusions are born out of a poverty of information coupled with a wealth of confidence that the enemy in any case is unequal to the task of promoting a decisive change in events.

S. L. A. MARSHALL,
The River and the Gauntlet

Battle—between man and man, tribe and tribe, village, city, state and nation—regarded by the unthinking as the abnormal or aberrant in human behavior, has been, historically, the norm.

HANSON W. BALDWIN,
Battles Lost and Won

It is quite a characteristic of modern battles that all misfortunes and losses which take place in the course of them can be retrieved by fresh forces, because the arrangement of the modern battle order and the way in which troops are brought into action permit their use in almost any place and in any situation.

KARL VON CLAUSEWITZ,
On War

The Battle of Britain is about to begin.... The whole fury and might of the enemy must very soon be turned on us. Hitler knows that he will have to break us in this island or lose the war.... Let us therefore brace ourselves to our duties, and so bear ourselves that, if the British Empire and its Commonwealth, last for a thousand years, man will say, "This was their finest hour."

SIR WINSTON CHURCHILL,
quoted in *Battles Lost and Won*
by Hanson W. Baldwin

In combat, life is short, nasty and brutish. The issues of national policy which brought him into war are irrelevant to the combat soldier; he is concerned with his literal life chances.

CHARLES S. MOSKOS, JR.,
"A Sociologist Appraises the G. I.,"
War: An Anthology, edited by Edward
Huberman and Elizabeth Huberman

They were learning the reality of war, these youngsters, getting face to face with the sickening realization that men get killed uselessly because their generals are stupid, so that desperate encounters where the last drop of courage has been given serve the country not at all and make a patriot look a fool.

BRUCE CATTON,
Mr. Lincoln's Army

Few people remembered that Tuesday was the anniversary of the Battle of Waterloo, another occasion when disaster trod very close on the heels of this country, and when it seemed impossible that the

British squares could stand up to the assault of the greatest military machine in the world, led by the greatest commander. "Hard pounding, this, gentlemen," said Wellington to his staff at one stage of that battle. "Let's see who will pound the longest." "Don't worry, lidy," one of the strawberry-barrow proprietors said, on Tuesday to a stout and apprehensive matron, " 'e'll find us an 'ard nut to crack and no mistike."

MOLLY PANTER-DOWNES,
"Letter from London," June 22, 1940,
The New Yorker Book of War Pieces

Battle is far less frightening than those who have never been in it are apt to think. All this bull about thinking of your mother, and your sweetheart, and your wives (who should also be your sweethearts) is emphasized by writers who describe battles not as they are but as writers who have never heard a hostile shot or missed a meal think they are.

GEORGE S. PATTON,
quoted in *Patton: Ordeal and Triumph*
by Ladislas Farago

Battle is the most magnificent competition in which a human being can indulge. It brings out all that is best; it removes all that is base.

GEORGE S. PATTON,
quoted in *Patton: Ordeal and Triumph*
by Ladislas Farago

The aim of military training is not just to prepare men for battle, but to make them long for it.

LOUIS SIMPSON,
War: An Anthology,
edited by Edward Huberman
and Elizabeth Huberman

The excitement and confusion of battle always breeds conflicts on numbers, distances, hits and misses, the time things happened.

WALTER LORD,
Incredible Victory

After a battle is over people talk a lot about how decisions were methodically reached, but actually there's always a hell of a lot of groping around.

REAR ADMIRAL FRANK JACK FLETCHER,
quoted in *Incredible Victory*
by Walter Lord

I am trying to remember how I reacted to the whole thing. My first feeling when the deafening barrage went up from the whole convoy, dominated by the great bangs of the naval guns, and the planes swooped over us, and the blue sky was dotted with hundreds of little circular black and white clouds—my first feeling was one of surprise—the surprise of being right in the midst of a naval battle. After that, the dominating feeling was not of fear, but excitement.... It was all sensationally *new*.

ALEXANDER WERTH,
The Year of Stalingrad

Mobile warfare in the desert has often and rightly been compared with a battle at sea—where it is equally wrong to attack piecemeal and leave half a fleet in port during the battle.

FIELD MARSHAL ERWIN ROMMEL,
quoted in *The Taste of Courage,*
edited by Desmond Flower
and James Reeves

Gentlemen. Marines have never lost a battle. This Brigade will not be the first to establish such a precedent.

BRIGADIER GENERAL EDWARD CRAIG,
during battle for Pusan, Korea,
quoted in *Conflict* by Robert Leckie

I am heartened that the Marine Brigade will move against the Naktong salient tomorrow. They are faced with impossible odds, and I have no valid reason to substantiate it, but I have a feeling they will halt the enemy.

I realize my expression of hope is unsound, but these Marines have the swagger, confidence and hardness that must have been in Stonewall Jackson's Army of the Shenandoah. They remind me of the Coldstreams at Dunkerque. Upon this thin line of reasoning, I cling to the hope of victory.

A British Military Observer In Korea,
quoted in *The New Breed: The Story of
the U.S. Marines in Korea* by Andrew Geer

I heard of a high British officer who went
over the battlefield just after the action
was over. American boys were still lying
dead in their foxholes, their rifles still
grasped in firing position in their dead
hands. And the veteran English soldier remarked time and time again, in a sort of
hushed eulogy spoken only to himself,
"Brave men. Brave men!"

Ernie Pyle,
Here Is Your War

If only the battle for Moscow had started
fourteen days earlier, the city would have
now been in our hands. Or even if the
rains had held off for fourteen days. If—
if—if.

Heinrich Haape,
quoted in *The Taste of Courage,*
edited by Desmond Flower
and James Reeves

Retreat? We're coming out of here as a
Marine Division. We're bringing our
equipment . . . our wounded . . . our dead.
Retreat, hell! We're just fighting in another direction.

Major General Oliver Prince Smith,
before withdrawal from
Changjin Reservoir in Korea, quoted in
This Is War! by David Douglas Duncan

They asked no quarter and they gave
none. They died hard—those savage men—
not gently like a stricken dove folding its
wings in peaceful passing, but like a
wounded wolf at bay, with lips curled
back in sneering menace, and always a
nerveless hand reaching for that long
sharp machete knife which long ago they
had substituted for the bayonet. And
around their necks, as we buried them,
would be a thread of dirty string with its
dangling crucifix. They were filthy, and
they were lousy, and they stank. And I
loved them.

General Douglas MacArthur,
Reminiscences

They wish to hell they were someplace
else, and they wish to hell they would get
relief. They wish to hell the mud was dry
and they wish to hell their coffee was hot.
They want to go home. But they stay in
their wet holes and fight, and then they
climb out and crawl through minefields
and fight some more.

Bill Mauldin,
Up Front

To a soldier in a hole, nothing is bigger or
more vital to him than the war which is
going on in the immediate vicinity of his
hole. If nothing is happening to him, and
he is able to relax that day, then it is a
good war, no matter what is going on
elsewhere.

Bill Mauldin,
Up Front

Underneath this wooden cross there lies
A Christian killed in battle. You who
  read,
Remember that this stranger died in
  pain;
And passing here, if you can lift your
  eyes
Upon a peace kept by a human creed,
Know that one soldier has not died in
  vain.

Karl Shapiro,
"Elegy for a Dead Soldier,"
V-Letter and Other Poems

There *was* an afternoon for one Marine,
and he spent it carefully learning to light
and keep alive the warmth of a peasant's
charcoal brazier, upon which he heated a
single can of beans and a canteen cup of
coffee. And that was victory. The freedom
to sprawl loosely upon a city street, heat
his coffee and eat a can of beans . . . with
no enemy bullets forcing him to toss the
can aside while diving behind another
wall for momentary survival.

David Douglas Duncan,
This Is War!

BEARD

The beard, like a strong tree, should be
allowed to grow to its maturity unrestrained except for a slight pruning. The

trimmed beard, fashioned into curious spikes, is simply a form of inexcusable vanity.

FELIX RIESENBERG,
The Rough Log

If you think that to grow a beard is to acquire wisdom, a goat is at once a complete Plato.

LUCIAN,
On Magical Whiskers

It would be worth some statistician's while to go through the great names of English literature and compare the amount of genius that has gone bearded with the amount of genius that has been clean-shaven. The beardless, I fancy, would be in a numerical majority, but we can estimate the weight of genius on the other side when we remember that Chaucer, Shakespeare, Bacon, Spenser, Dickens, Carlyle, Ruskin, Browning, Tennyson, Swinburne, Meredith, Morris and Mr. Shaw have all worn beards, while Matthew Arnold wore whiskers.

ROBERT LYND,
Solomon in All His Glory

The great ages of prose are the ages in which men shave. The great ages of poetry are those in which they allow their beards to grow.

ROBERT LYND,
Solomon in all His Glory

What would Jupiter be without a beard? Who would countenance a shaved Christ?

JAMES WARD,
Defence of the Beard

Too many whiskers will spoil the broth.

FRANK RICHARDSON,
quoted in *Concerning Beards*
by Edwin V. Mitchell

One of the greatest risks in wearing a beard, particularly in the old days, seems to have been that it made an excellent handle by which one's enemy could seize one.

EDWIN V. MITCHELL,
Concerning Beards

Three hairs from a king's beard stuck in the wax seal of a document gave extraor-dinary solemnity to the instrument, and the pledging of one's beard for the performance of some act was once not uncommon, a beard being considered security of the highest order. Money was frequently raised in this way. But it is to be feared that bankers would look askance if such collateral was offered for a loan today.

EDWIN V. MITCHELL,
Concerning Beards

When a resolute young fellow steps up to the great bully, the world, and takes him boldly by the beard, he is often surprised to find it comes off in his hand, and that it was only tied on to scare away timid adventurers.

OLIVER WENDELL HOLMES,
Elsie Venner

He that hath a beard is more than a youth, and he that hath no beard is less than a man.

SHAKESPEARE,
Much Ado About Nothing

That ornamental excrement which grow-eth beneath the chin.

THOMAS FULLER,
Worthies of England

It always seemed to me that men wore their beards, like they wear their neckties, for show. I always remember Lewis for saying his beard was part of him.

D. H. LAWRENCE,
Kangaroo

BEAUTY

I would like to ask you to think some time—try to imagine working for the pure love of making something beautiful—something that can't be sold or used to help sell anything else, but that is simply a communication between man and man, a bond of understanding and human enlightenment.

HART CRANE,
The Letters of Hart Crane

Beauty is a fruit which we look at without trying to seize it.

SIMONE WEIL,
Gravity and Grace

On the other hand a sense of beauty, although mutilated, distorted, and soiled, remains rooted in the heart of men as a powerful incentive. It is present in all the preoccupations of secular life. If it were made true and pure, it would sweep all secular life in a body to the feet of God.

SIMONE WEIL,
Waiting for God

The most beautiful things in the world are those from which all excess weight has been removed.

HENRY FORD,
quoted in *Success*
by Robert E. Shafer and Verlene C. Bernd

When we speak of beauty, we're speaking of something we're more or less indifferent to.

EDITH HAMILTON,
Wisdom for Our Time,
edited by James Nelson

We are so blind
To all the realm of real, so numb to
  feeling
Anything but the ache inside the breast,
It takes a miracle to make the healing
Miracle of beauty manifest.

ALFRED BARRETT,
"Inspiration," *Mint by Night*

Anyone who keeps the ability to see beauty never grows old.

FRANZ KAFKA

Do you notice how busy people always like ugliness? It has for them the actuality of a stench. It takes prolonged effort, and prolonged leisure to enjoy beauty.

J. B. YEATS,
Letters to His Son, W. B. Yeats and Others

A little faith, some insight, and perhaps a great deal of expectation and hope, are all that we ever need in order to pierce the apparently sordid crust of things and to come at the beauty that lies always within them. Where have we ever found actual and invincible dullness except in ourselves, and what has ever seemed to us hopelessly sordid unless we were so?

ODELL SHEPARD,
The Joys of Forgetting

The passion excited by beauty is nearer to a species of melancholy than to jollity and mirth.

EDMUND BURKE,
The Sublime and the Beautiful

An air of robustness and strength is very prejudicial to beauty. An appearance of delicacy, and even of fragility, is almost essential to it.

EDMUND BURKE,
The Sublime and the Beautiful

All beauty implies completeness.

ERNEST HELLO,
Life, Science, and Art

Man nor king can see unmoved the coming of a wind-filled sail, the coming of a lovely lady, the coming of a horse in speed.

JAMES STEPHENS,
In the Land of Youth

I hate that aesthetic game of the eye and the mind, played by these connoisseurs, these mandarins who "appreciate" beauty. What *is* beauty, anyway? There's no such thing. I never "appreciate," any more than I "like." I love or I hate.

PABLO PICASSO,
Life with Picasso
by Françoise Gilot and Carlton Lake

It is the beautiful bird which gets caged.

CHINESE PROVERB

It is the test of beauty and vitality that a beholder refuses to acquiesce at first glance. There is a conflict to be undergone.

NORMAN DOUGLAS,
An Almanac

Learn to foster an ardent imagination; so shall you descry beauty which others passed unheeded.

NORMAN DOUGLAS,
An Almanac

We live only to discover beauty. All else is a form of waiting.

KAHLIL GIBRAN,
Sand and Foam

When you reach the heart of life you shall

find beauty in all things, even in the eyes that are blind to beauty.

> KAHLIL GIBRAN,
> *Sand and Foam*

A beautiful thing, whatsoever it be, cannot exist without fertilising all about it through admiration, challenge, contradiction, provocation, or through consequence.

> PAUL CLAUDEL,
> *Ways and Crossways*

I know that I have worn my soul to rags and fretted my spirit to desolation, endeavoring to keep some slight track of the hurrying intellectual world about me, and I begin to know that it is a mistake. Beauty is with us always in spite of all the pedants. Beauty is sure, even in its infinite fleetingness and intangibility.

> GAMALIEL BRADFORD,
> *The Letters of Gamaliel Bradford*

A man who has never enjoyed beautiful things in the company of a woman whom he loved has not experienced to the full the magic power of which such things are capable.

> BERTRAND RUSSELL,
> *The Conquest of Happiness*

The beautiful is less what one sees than what one dreams.

> BELGIAN PROVERB

No *thing* is beautiful. But all things await the sensitive and imaginative mind that may be aroused to pleasurable emotion at the sight of them. This is beauty.

> ROBERT HENRI,
> *The Art Spirit*

There is nothing which has such absolute self-contained loveliness that we can say of it that it would be lovely everywhere and always. Put it into certain surroundings, throw certain lights upon it and it would seem ugly.

> PHILLIPS BROOKS,
> *Visions and Tasks*

Beauty is an *experience,* nothing else. It is not a fixed pattern or an arrangement of features. It is something *felt,* a glow or a communicated sense of fineness. What ails us is that our sense of beauty is so bruised and blunted, we miss all the best.

> D. H. LAWRENCE,
> *Assorted Articles*

Things are not done beautifully. The beauty is an integral part of their being done.

> ROBERT HENRI,
> *The Art Spirit*

Now sex and beauty are one thing, like flame and fire. If you hate sex you hate beauty. If you love *living* beauty, you have a reverence for sex. Of course you can love old, dead beauty and hate sex. But to love living beauty you must have a reverence for sex.

> D. H. LAWRENCE,
> *Assorted Articles*

I love the beauty of life intensely; columbine flowers, for example, the way they dangle, or the delicate way a young girl sits and wonders, or the rage with which a man turns and kicks a fool dog that suddenly attacks him—beautiful that, the swift fierce turn and lunge of a kick, then the quivering pause for the next attack; or even the slightly silly glow that comes over some men as they are getting tipsy—it still is a glow, beautiful; or the swift look a woman fetches me when she would really like me to go off with her, but she is troubled; or the real compassion I saw a woman express for a man who slipped and wrenched his foot: life, the beauty, the beauty of life!

> D. H. LAWRENCE,
> *Assorted Articles*

The human soul needs actual beauty even more than bread.

> D. H. LAWRENCE,
> *Selected Essays*

The esthetic sense is very close to the religious; beauty has a great educative power.

> ALEXIS CARREL,
> *Reflections on Life*

Beauty does not season soup.

POLISH PROVERB

What a strange power the perception of beauty is! It seems to ebb and flow like some secret tide, independent alike of health and disease, of joy or sorrow.

A. C. BENSON,
From a College Window

There are days when it seems impossible to be thrilled by anything, when a perverse dreariness holds the mind; and then all of a sudden the gentle and wistful mood flows back, and the world is full of beauty to the brim.

A. C. BENSON,
From a College Window

I feel more and more that the instinct for beauty (spiritual and moral as well as natural) is the most trustworthy of all instincts, and the surest sign of the nearness of God.

A. C. BENSON,
Excerpts from the Letters of Dr. A. C. Benson to M. E. A.

I think the only way of making people feel the presence of beauty and love is that one should create it, so to speak—strike a match and light a fire.

A. C. BENSON,
Excerpts from the Letters of Dr. A. C. Benson to M. E. A.

The necessity of rejecting and destroying some things that are beautiful is the deepest curse of existence.

GEORGE SANTAYANA,
Character and Opinion in the United States

What I care for is the beautiful itself and the vision of the beautiful, in so far as they manage to exist, or to be suggested: and this frail, intermittent, but actual realization of the beautiful I call the spiritual sphere. All life is, intrinsically, a part of it; but horribly interrupted and perturbed.

GEORGE SANTAYANA,
The Letters of George Santayana

I don't often trouble now to describe corn-fields and groups of harvesting women in loose blues and reds, and little staring yellow frocked girls. But that's not my eyes' fault: coming back the other evening from Charleston, again all my nerves stood upright, flushed, electrified (what's the word?) with the sheer beauty—beauty astounding and super-abounding. So that one almost resents it, not being capable of catching it all and holding it all at the moment.

VIRGINIA WOOLF,
A Writer's Diary

If you lack beauty, you live this beauty out in the other. But it is the same with ugliness.

ANAÏS NIN,
The Diaries of Anaïs Nin, Vol. IV

After all, I suppose that all ugliness passes, and beauty endures, excepting of the skin.

EDITH SITWELL,
Edith Sitwell: Selected Letters 1916-1964

In the case of exceptionally sensitive—often also particularly gifted—people, contact with beauty becomes an hourly necessity to which everything else is sacrificed.

ERNEST DIMNET,
What We Live By

In a certain sense there is more in the tremulously faint and far reflection of a thing than there is in the thing itself. The dog who preferred the reflection of his bone in the water to the bone itself, though from a practical point of view he made a lamentable mistake, was aesthetically justified. No "orb," as Tennyson said, is a "perfect star" while we walk therein. Aloofness is essential to the beatific vision. If we entered its portals heaven would no longer be heaven.

HAVELOCK ELLIS,
Selected Essays

If we were charged so much a head for sunsets, if God sent round a drum before the hawthorn came in flower, what a work should we make about their beauty.

ROBERT LOUIS STEVENSON,
An Inland Voyage

Our minds not only rationalize but hedonize. They tend to work over their content until it is joyous as well as consistent. Thus we are likely to mould almost anything to beauty if we have time to cherish and brood over it. If we do not do so with our age it is because we are restless and unripe, not because the age is incapable of beauty.

CHARLES HORTON COOLEY,
Life and the Student

What worth has beauty if it is not seen?

ITALIAN PROVERB

If the path be beautiful, let us not ask where it leads.

ANATOLE FRANCE

I don't think then of all the misery, but of the beauty that still remains. This is one of the things that Mummy and I are so entirely different about. Her counsel when one feels melancholy is "Think of all the misery in the world and be thankful that you are not sharing in it!" My advice is: "Go outside, to the fields, enjoy nature and the sunshine, go out and try to recapture happiness in yourself and in God. Think of all the beauty that's still left in and around you and be happy!"

ANNE FRANK,
Anne Frank: The Diary of a Young Girl

After a lovely day out of doors by myself I saw that a single act of admiration is of little use. We must live with beauty, without any straining effort to admire, quietly attentive, absorbent, until by degrees the beauty becomes one with us and alters our blood.

MARK RUTHERFORD,
Last Pages from a Journal

The assumption is commonly made, or implied, that in the presence of some reputedly beautiful thing there is one right way of feeling, or thinking, and that there are many wrong ways. The opposite is the truth. No wrong way exists, so long as it is a vehement personal way of somebody's own. The only way you can fail, as a spectator of nature or art, is to say things, and try to believe them, just because some aesthetic pundit or critical mandarin has said them before. That way humbug lies, and boredom too.

C. E. MONTAGUE,
The Right Place

I have just been for a little walk by myself and it seemed to me I could never have really noticed apple-blossom before, it is so extraordinarily lovely. There's a curious reaming look about it, like foaming cream or some sort of light puffy chiffon on a beautiful dress. I was feeling lonely and the beauty of it made me feel lonelier. There's something about beautiful days and beautiful places and things that seem to act on any sad feelings of one's own as a hollow dome acts on music—and makes it enormously more resonant, and makes it possess one more completely.

C. E. MONTAGUE,
C. E. Montague: A Memoir by Oliver Elton

One cannot appreciate beauty on the run. When I can be motionless long enough, there is no limit I have ever reached to the revelations in an opening bud.

VIDA D. SCUDDER,
The Privilege of Age

It's only now that I am beginning to see again and to recognise again the beauty of the world. Take the swallows today, their flutter-flutter, their velvet-forked tails, their transparent wings that are like the fins of fishes. The little dark head and the breast golden in the light. Then the beauty of the garden, and the beauty of raked paths. . . . Then, the silence.

KATHERINE MANSFIELD,
The Journal of Katherine Mansfield

Exuberance is Beauty.

WILLIAM BLAKE,
The Marriage of Heaven and Hell

There's the Istra itself, its water sluggish and dark green, its winding banks overgrown with willows. You can't swim there. You just look and look and feel a tightening of the throat from so much quiet beauty, and it would be good to cry, as if a friend you hadn't seen in a long time suddenly appears and you put your head on his shoulder and weep for joy.

SVETLANA ALLILUYEVA,
Twenty Letters to a Friend

Why am I unsatisfied,
I for whom the pensive night
Binds her cloudy hair with light,
I for whom all beauty burns
Like incense in a million urns?
Oh, beauty, are you not enough?
Why am I crying after love?

SARA TEASDALE,
"Spring Night,"
Collected Poems of Sara Teasdale

Why do we seek this lurking beauty in skies, in poems, in drawings? Ah! because there we are safe, there we neither sicken nor die. I think we fly to Beauty as an asylum from the terrors of finite nature. We are made immortal by the kiss, by the contemplation of beauty.

RALPH WALDO EMERSON,
Journals of Ralph Waldo Emerson

The hours when the mind is absorbed by beauty are the only hours when we really live.

RICHARD JEFFERIES,
Pageant of Summer

BEAUTY, FEMALE

A woman is truly beautiful only when she is naked and she knows it.

ANDRÉ COURRÈGES
Fashion, Art, and Beauty,
The Metropolitan Museum of Art Bulletin,
November 1967

Women have become liberated little by little through thought, work, and clothes. I cannot imagine that they will ever turn back. Perhaps they will continue to suffer occasionally to be beautiful, but more than ever they seek to be both beautiful and free.

ANDRÉ COURRÈGES,
Fashion, Art, and Beauty,
The Metropolitan Museum of Art Bulletin,
November 1967

I think that most of the beauty of women evaporates when they achieve domestic happiness at the price of their independence.

CYRIL CONNOLLY,
The Unquiet Grave

Some fall in love with women who are rich, aristocratic or stupid. I am attracted by those who mysteriously hold out a promise of the integrity which I have lost; unsubdued daughters of Isis, beautiful as night, tumultuous as the moon-stirred Atlantic.

CYRIL CONNOLLY,
The Unquiet Grave

The average girl would rather have beauty than brains because she knows the average man can see much better than he can think.

ANONYMOUS,
Ladies' Home Journal, April 1947

Is there anywhere
a man
who
will not punish us
for our beauty?

He is the one
we all search for,
chanting names for exotic oceans of the
    moon.

DIANE WAKOSKI,
"A Poet Recognizing the
Echo of the Voice," *The Magellanic Clouds*

A very beautiful woman hardly ever leaves a clearcut impression of features and shape in the memory. Usually there remains only an aura, a living color.

WILLIAM BOLITHO,
Camera Obscura

Of course the sexual element in the pleasure of the sight of perfect beauty is very small, or, if you like, very much out of consciousness. These excellences are, as they have always been, for the class who have the task of power, whether grim barbarian conquerors, or hereditary oligarchs, or fat, amusing stock brokers. No poet has ever owned a peerless beauty any more than he has owned a Kohinoor.

WILLIAM BOLITHO,
(after seeing the Ziegfeld Follies)
Camera Obscura

Beauty and chastity are always quarreling.

SPANISH PROVERB

The plainest person can look beautiful, can *be* beautiful. It only needs the fire of sex to rise delicately to change an ugly face to a lovely one. That is really sex appeal: the communicating of a sense of beauty.

D. H. LAWRENCE,
Assorted Articles

Having painted thousands of women, I do not undervalue physical beauty; but without certain feminine qualities of spirit such beauty is a grass-cheap thing.... Flesh uninhabited by spirit tends to deteriorate with appalling rapidity.

JAMES MONTGOMERY FLAGG,
quoted in *Ladies' Home Journal,*
March 1947

A woman without the vanity which delights in her power of attracting would be by that very fact without power to attract.

COVENTRY PATMORE,
Religio, Poetae, Etc.

Beauty in a woman is, of course, a form of genius and like other forms of genius it is instinct with danger for those who possess it and for those who fall within its aura.

DAVID L. COHN,
Love in America

A woman who cannot be ugly is not beautiful.

KARL KRAUS

My love is dark as yours is fair,
 Yet lovelier I hold her
Than listless maids with pallid hair,
 And blood that's thin and colder.

COUNTEE CULLEN,
"A Song of Praise," *On These I Stand*

What beautiful woman delights us by her look of character? That shows itself when

beauty is gone, being the creation of habit, the bare stalk when the flower of spring has withered.

WILLIAM BUTLER YEATS,
Autobiography

Tough and durable youthfulness is a product of the temperate zone, the modern beauty parlour and the culture of the abdomen. Some of our professional beauties are almost everlasting.... But here, near the Equator, it is still, as in Malherbe's day it was with us, a matter of roses.

ALDOUS HUXLEY,
Beyond the Mexique Bay

A woman's beauty is one of her great missions.

RICHARD LE GALLIENNE,
Prose Fancies

In years to come I often thought what the course of my life would have been if I had been homely, or a man. The attention of men is, to say the least, a marvellous distraction; and loving one can seem more important than anything else—at least for a while. The narcissus in woman goes to the pool too often for reassurance, when the reflection should lie secure in the deep recess of self.

MARYA MANNES,
Out of My Time

Female beauty is an important Minor Sacrament which cannot be received too often; I am not at all sure that neglect of it does not constitute a sin of some kind.

ROBERTSON DAVIES,
The Table Talk of Samuel Marchbanks

It is generally a feminine eye that first detects the moral deficiencies hidden under the "dear deceit" of beauty.

GEORGE ELIOT,
Adam Bede

She is grace itself.... That is what a woman ought to be. She ought to produce the effect of exquisite music.

GEORGE ELIOT,
quoted in *Women's Thoughts for Women,*
compiled by Rose Porter

Beauty is a good letter of introduction.
GERMAN PROVERB

Zest is the secret of all beauty. There is no beauty that is attractive without zest.
CHRISTIAN DIOR,
Ladies' Home Journal, April 1956

I really didn't like "Picnic" after the first reading, yet something about it attracted me. There was something Inge was saying about pretty girls that hit home. It was that most people treat pretty girls as pretty girls and nothing else—as though nothing could be wrong if a girl was pretty, so she had no right to be miserable.
JANICE RULE,
Player: A Profile of an Art
by Lillian Ross and Helen Ross

Most females will forgive a liberty, rather than a slight; and if any woman were to hang a man for stealing her picture, although it were set in gold, it would be a new case in law; but if he carried off the setting and left the portrait, I would not answer for his safety.
CHARLES CALEB COLTON,
Lacon

Everybody could be beautiful, really, but most women present themselves so awkwardly. Women should set themselves forth attractively but innocently, like a cat. A cat is never a presentation, but an innocent happening.
ALWIN NIKOLAIS,
Fashion, Art, and Beauty,
The Metropolitan Museum of Art Bulletin,
November 1967

One drop of wine is enough to redden an entire glass of water; the entrance of a prettier woman than themselves is enough to tinge with some ill-humor a whole party of pretty women—particularly when there is but one man present in the company.
VICTOR HUGO,
Notre Dame de Paris

You are beautiful and faded
Like an old opera tune
Played upon a harpsichord.
AMY LOWELL,
"A Lady" *The Complete Works of Amy Lowell*

I do but aver that the beautiful woman, widely and wisely likened to the flowers, which are inaccessibly more beautiful, must not, for her own sake, be likened to the always accessible child.
ALICE MEYNELL,
The Children

A beautiful and seductive head, a woman's head, I mean, makes one dream, but in a confused fashion, at once of pleasure and of sadness; conveys an idea of melancholy, of lassitude, even of satiety—a contradictory impression, or an ardour, that is to say, and a desire for life together with a bitterness which flows back upon them as if from a sense of deprivation and hopelessness.
CHARLES BAUDELAIRE,
Intimate Journals

If you are a miracle of beauty, you can't help it. That is why you are so immensely applauded for it.
JOHN AYSCOUGH,
Levia-Pondera

To be so beautiful, so alluring, that the man forgets all else and simply loves, that is what every woman wants, and whoever denies it is in error, or wilfully lying.
GEORG GRODDECK,
The Book of the It

I know a man who, when he saw a woman of striking beauty, praised the Creator for her. The sight of her lit within him the love of God.
SAINT JOHN CLIMACHUS,
quoted in *The New Christian Year,*
chosen by Charles Williams

Won't you come into the garden? I would like my roses to see you.
RICHARD BRINSLEY SHERIDAN

Have you ever watched a woman take a bath? They do it ever so slowly, almost in slow motion. They observe themselves as though they were works of art. They linger and pause, and they move as if in a trance. Beautiful! Beautiful and fascinating!
RICHARD LINDER,
Close-up by John Gruen

Beauty in distress is much the most affecting beauty.

EDMUND BURKE,
The Sublime and the Beautiful

The saying that beauty is but skin deep is but a skin deep saying.

JOHN RUSKIN,
Personal Beauty

BEER

It is said that beer drinkers are slow, and a little stupid; that they have an ox-like placidity not quite favourable to any brilliant intellectual display. But there are times when this placidity is what the labouring brain most needs. After the agitations of too active thinking there is safety in a tankard of ale. The wine drinkers are agile, but they are excitable; the beer drinkers are heavy, but in their heaviness there is peace.

PHILIP G. HAMERTON,
The Intellectual Life

For the poor, beer is a necessity, as tobacco is very nearly a necessity; it is only for people sufficiently rich and fashionable to be faddists that either is really a luxury.

G. K. CHESTERTON,
All I Survey

Beer is acceptable very late at night at the end of a party. It has many valuable functions but I cannot help thinking that it has been a little over-praised in the immediate past by poets of the school of Chesterton and Belloc. It is a fine honest staple rather than a theme for poetry.

EVELYN WAUGH,
Wine in Peace and War

A bar or a tavern is a place where you can buy a glass of draught beer for fifteen cents. Unfortunately, these are the very places that are most corrupted by TV. No more real talking! No more real drinking! The end of an era!

MIKE MORIARITY,
proprietor, Moriarity's Bar and Grill,
The New Yorker, July 16, 1960

BEGINNING

"We must do something" is the unanimous refrain. "You begin" is the deadening refrain.

WALTER DWIGHT,
The Saving Sense

Nothing, of course, begins at the time you think it did.

LILLIAN HELLMAN,
An Unfinished Woman

The beginning and the end reach out their hands to each other.

CHINESE PROVERB

All beginnings are somewhat strange; but we must have patience, and, little by little, we shall find things, which at first were obscure, becoming clear.

SAINT VINCENT DE PAUL,
St. Vincent de Paul by J. B. Boudignan

God always gives a greater blessing to humble beginnings than to those that start with a chiming of bells.

SAINT VINCENT DE PAUL,
Life and Works, Vol. 3

Things can be easily settled at the outset, but not so later on.

BALTASAR GRACIAN,
The Oracle

There is no such thing as a long piece of work, except one that you dare not start.

CHARLES BAUDELAIRE,
Intimate Journals

He who is outside the door has already a good part of his journey behind him.

DUTCH PROVERB

BEGUN

A thing that has not been begun cannot be finished.

ROBERT HENRI,
The Art Spirit

For a web begun God sends thread.

ITALIAN PROVERB

Can anything be sadder than work left

unfinished? Yes; work never begun.
CHRISTINA ROSSETTI

There is an old saying "well begun is half done"—'tis a bad one. I would use instead—Not begun at all till half done.
JOHN KEATS,
The Selected Letters of John Keats

BEING

What I am I am, and say not. Being is the great explainer. In the attempt to explain, shall I plane away all the spines, till it is no thistle, but a cornstalk?
HENRY DAVID THOREAU,
Journal

It is only when life is overwrought with the tyranny of doing that we miss the joy of being; and it is only the consciousness of being that makes us capable of any worthy action.
HOLBROOK JACKSON,
Southward Ho! and Other Essays

One who loves being in general, will necessarily value good will to being in general, wherever he sees it.
JONATHAN EDWARDS,
The Nature of True Virtue

BELIEF

Men to a great extent believe what they want to—although I see in that no basis for a philosophy that tells us what we should want to want.
OLIVER WENDELL HOLMES, JR.,
The Mind and Faith of Justice Holmes,
edited by Max Lerner

He that will believe only what he can fully comprehend must have a very long head or a very short creed.
C. C. COLTON

Once we are in the habit of filtering what we want to believe through a sieve, disbelief after disbelief splashes back in our face.
ANONYMOUS (HENRY S. HASKINS),
Meditations in Wall Street

What distinguishes the majority of men from the few is their inability to act according to their beliefs.
HENRY MILLER,
The Cosmological Eye

All things are possible to one who believes.
SAINT BERNARD OF CLAIRVAUX,
Letters

A man can believe a considerable deal of rubbish, and yet go about his daily work in a rational and cheerful manner.
NORMAN DOUGLAS,
An Almanac

We are all tattooed in our cradles with the beliefs of our tribes; the record may seem superficial, but it is indelible.
OLIVER WENDELL HOLMES,
quoted in *Life and Letters of Oliver Wendell Holmes* Vol. I, by John T. Morse, Jr.

The moment we want to believe something, we suddenly see all the arguments for it, and become blind to the arguments against it.
GEORGE BERNARD SHAW,
The Intelligent Woman's Guide to Socialism and Capitalism

Ye say, ye believe in Zarathustra? But of what account is Zarathustra! Ye are my believers: but of what account are all believers!

Ye had not sought yourselves: then did ye find me. So do all believers; therefore all belief is of so little account.

Now do I bid you lose me and find yourselves; and only when ye have all denied me, will I return unto you.
FRIEDRICH NIETZSCHE,
Thus Spake Zarathustra

It is often said it is no matter what a man believes if he is only sincere. But let a man sincerely believe that seed planted without ploughing is as good with; that January is as favorable for seed sowing as April; and that cockle seed will produce as good harvest as wheat, and is it so?
HENRY WARD BEECHER

Again, as to the difficulty of detecting and expressing the real reasons on which we believe, let this be considered,—how very differently an argument strikes the mind at one time and another, according to its particular state, or the accident of the moment. At one time it is weak and unmeaning,—at another, it is nothing short of demonstration. We take up a book at one time, and see nothing in it; at another, it is full of weighty remarks and precious thoughts. Sometimes a statement is axiomatic,—sometimes we are at a loss to see what can be said for it.

JOHN HENRY CARDINAL NEWMAN,
Oxford University Sermons

Two things are equally inept. One is to forget that human nature must have something upon which to rest; the other is to fancy that one's own preferred foundation-stones are the only things that will bring stability and security to others.

JOHN DEWEY,
Characters and Events, Vol. II

A man's verbal creed may have no real relation with the creed on which he acts. It is a very rare mind that believes what it does, and does what it actually believes. But only in such a mind are thought, feeling, and action really one.

A. R. ORAGE,
Essays and Aphorisms

Reason may introduce a belief to us but she seldom stays with it. The moment it is ours we become partisans and she has little or nothing to do with its defence.

MARK RUTHERFORD,
Last Pages from a Journal

We ought to struggle earnestly to increase our beliefs. Every addition to them is an extension of life, both in breadth and depth.

MARK RUTHERFORD,
Last Pages from a Journal

It is the belief men *betray* and not that which they *parade* which has to be studied.

CHARLES SANDERS PEIRCE,
Collected Papers of Charles Sanders Peirce,
Vol. V

Doubt is an uneasy and dissatisfied state from which we struggle to free ourselves and pass into the state of belief; while the latter is a calm and satisfactory state which we do not wish to avoid, or to change to a belief in anything else. On the contrary, we cling tenaciously, not merely to believing, but to believing just what we do believe.

CHARLES SANDERS PEIRCE,
Collected Papers of Charles Sanders Peirce,
Vol. V

Few really believe. The most only believe that they believe or even make believe.

JOHN LANCASTER SPALDING,
Thoughts and Theories of Life and Education

The great mischief, the one which destroys our moral existence and threatens the integrity of our mind and our character, is not that we should deceive ourselves and love an uncertain truth, but that we should remain constant to one in which we no longer wholly believe.

MAURICE MAETERLINCK

BELLS

The fire-bells are oftener now, almost, than the church-bells. Thoreau would wonder which did the most harm.

EMILY DICKINSON,
Selected Poems and Letters of Emily Dickinson

That cheap piece of tinkling brass which the farmer hangs about his cow's neck has been more to me than the tons of metal which are swung in the belfry.

HENRY DAVID THOREAU,
Journal

No music in the world is more beautiful than the ringing of church bells heard from a distance over an open country.

LLEWELYN POWYS,
Book of Days of Llewelyn Powys

The bell-rope that gathers God at dawn. . . .

HART CRANE,
"The Broken Tower," *Collected Poems*

BELONGING

To associate with other like-minded people in small purposeful groups is for the
great majority of men and women a
source of profound psychological satisfaction. Exclusiveness will add to the pleasure
of being several; and secrecy will intensify
it almost to ecstasy.

ALDOUS HUXLEY,
Beyond the Mexique Bay

BENEVOLENCE

Love of benevolence is that affection or
propensity of the heart to any being,
which causes it to incline to its well-being,
or disposes it to desire and take pleasure in
its happiness.

JONATHAN EDWARDS,
The Nature of True Virtue

Opportunities of doing good, though
abundant, and obvious enough, are not
exactly fitted to our hands; we must be
alert in preparing ourselves for them. Benevolence requires method and activity in
its exercise.

SIR ARTHUR HELPS,
Essays Written in the Intervals of Business

Man is certainly a benevolent animal. A.
never sees B. in distress without thinking
C. ought to relieve him directly.

SYDNEY SMITH

BEST

Everything keeps its best nature only by
being put to its best use.

PHILLIPS BROOKS,
Visions and Tasks

What the best minds see to be no longer
tenable, will little by little lose its hold on
the multitude also.

JOHN LANCASTER SPALDING,
Thoughts and Theories of Life and Education

The best of everything is the only individual of that thing. We should ignore the
rest.

LOUISE IMOGEN GUINEY,
Goose-Quill Papers

The best we can do for each other is to
remove unnecessary obstacles, and the
worst—to weaken any of the motives
which urge us to strive.

MRS. BERNARD BOSANQUET

Foolish people try to stop my mouth by
saying: Well, do your best; at any rate you
can do your best! Which is just about the
last thing in the world which I *can* do;
common sense itself tells me *that*. I may do
well, or I may do better, but to do my best
must be the hardest thing of all.

DANIEL CONSIDINE,
*The Virtues of the
Divine Child and Other Papers*

BIBLE

The New Testament is the Thesaurus of
sacred wisdom compared to which there is
no book or monument that deserves to be
named.

JOHN JAY CHAPMAN,
Memories and Milestones

Such as it is, the Gospel is enough for me.
As soon as I face it again, everything again
becomes luminous for me. Man's explanation only darkens it.

ANDRÉ GIDE,
Pretexts

I have not read much of anything else
lately except the gospel according to St.
John, which I found an entirely different
thing from what I used to find it. The
popular interpretation of Christianity
makes me sick.

EDWIN ARLINGTON ROBINSON,
Untriangulated Stars

It is worth while to have a *storm* of abuse
once in a while, for *one* reason to read the
Psalms—they are a radiant field of glory
that never shines unless the night shuts in.

HARRIET BEECHER STOWE,
Harriet Beecher Stowe
by Catherine Gilbertson

I was reading the Bible in many different
languages, and I saw that it cannot really
be translated, the real meaning cannot be

given in another language. It is only in Hebrew that you feel the full meaning of it—all the associations which a different word has.

DAVID BEN-GURION,
Wisdom, edited by James Nelson

I have found in it words for my inmost thoughts, songs for my joy, utterance for my hidden griefs, and pleadings for my shame and feebleness.

SAMUEL TAYLOR COLERIDGE,
quoted in *A Diary for the Thankful-Hearted*,
compiled by Mary Hodgkin

Opened the Bible. The unjust Judges. Confirmed in my own opinion, or at least in an opinion that I have already encountered in myself. But otherwise there is no significance to this, I am never visibly guided in such things, the pages of the Bible don't flutter in my presence.

FRANZ KAFKA,
The Diaries of Franz Kafka 1914-1923

Strange, after having passed the whole of my life in gliding about the dancing floors of philosophy, and abandoning myself to all the orgies of the intellect, and dallying with systems without ever being satisfied— I have suddenly arrived at the same point of view as Uncle Tom, taking my stand on the Bible and kneeling beside my black brother in prayer in the same act of devotion.

HEINRICH HEINE,
quoted in *The Writing Art,* selected by
Bertha W. Smith and Virginia C. Lincoln

Thousands have gone to heaven who have never read one page of the Bible.

FRANCIS A. BAKER,
Sermons

By the reading of Scripture I am so renewed that all nature seems renewed around me and with me. The sky seems to be a pure, a cooler blue, the trees a deeper green, light is sharper on the outlines of the forest and the hills and the whole world is charged with the glory of God and I feel fire and music in the earth under my feet.

THOMAS MERTON,
The Sign of Jonas

The Holy Bible is an abyss. It is impossible to explain how profound it is, impossible to explain how simple it is.

ERNEST HELLO,
Life, Science, and Art

The words of the Gospels, repeated to a child, a workman or a peasant, do not surprise him in the least. Nothing is told with a view to effect. Not a word in the Gospels is intended to startle.

ERNEST HELLO,
Life, Science, and Art

The whole Bible, from its first page to its last, is full of the assertion of the fundamental necessity of vitality; that the first thing which a man needs in order to live well, is to live.

PHILLIPS BROOKS,
Visions and Tasks

You can learn more about human nature by reading the Bible than by living in New York.

WILLIAM LYON PHELPS,
quoted in the *New York Times,*
October 19, 1952

At Christmas I managed to get hold of a Greek Testament, and every morning, after I had cleaned my cell and polished my tins, I read a little of the Gospels, a dozen verses taken by chance anywhere. It is a delightful way of opening the day. Every one, even in a turbulent, ill-disciplined life, should do the same. Endless repetition, in and out of season, has spoiled for us the freshness, the naïveté, the simple romantic charm of the Gospels. We hear them read far too often and far too badly, and all repetition is anti-spiritual. When one returns to the Greek, it is like going into a garden of lilies out of some narrow and dark house.

OSCAR WILDE,
De Profundis

Everybody reading the Bible I suppose is pulled up by an uneasy feeling that morality never elsewhere came holding out so many gifts. It is a ceaseless bribery: Keep the Sabbath and your days will be long in the land; Be chaste and you will become a woman of three cows; Serve God and He will serve you. It seems to me that England and America owe to their Bible reading their curiously commercial virtue: Celtic nations, in their vices as in their virtues, are less calculating, more instinctive, because they have not had this century-long training in the cash-down system of morality.

STEPHEN MACKENNA,
Journal and Letters of Stephen Mackenna

BIGOT (*See also* TOLERANCE)

I cannot tolerate bigots. They are all so obstinate, so opinionated.

JOSEPH MCCARTHY

BILLS (*See also* COST)

What can you say about bills? Curse them if you will, but pay you must.

GEORGE SANDERS

Pay cash and let the credit go.

JOHN WANAMAKER

BIOGRAPHY

You might compose a more accurate biography by recording the biographee's minor pleasures than by recording his major experiences.

CLIFTON FADIMAN,
Any Number Can Play

The writing of a biography is no facile task; it is the strenuous achievement of a lifetime, only to be accomplished in the face of endless obstacles and unspeakable prejudice.

HAVELOCK ELLIS,
Selected Essays

I have never read the life of any important person without discovering that he knew more and could do more than I could ever hope to know or do in half a dozen lifetimes.

J. B. PRIESTLEY,
All About Ourselves and Other Essays

What I learned first, and most lastingly, is that whoever would tell the truth about any man must be, in the literal sense, his apologist.... I mean that the first and perhaps the only duty of an honest biographer is, so far as may be, to set forth the man of whom he writes as that man saw himself, and to explain him on his own terms. Then judgment may best be left to those who read.

M. A. DEWOLFE HOWE,
Barrett Wendell and His Letters

One of the most arrogant undertakings, to my mind, is to write the biography of a man which pretends to go beyond external facts, and give the inmost motives. One of the most mendacious is autobiography.

THEODOR HAECKER,
Journal in the Night

On the trail of another man, the biographer must put up with finding himself at every turn: any biography uneasily shelters an autobiography within it.

PAUL MURRAY KENDALL,
The Art of Biography

What a man leaves behind him after he dies is a mess of paper: birth certificate, school grades, diary, letters, check stubs, laundry lists. ... This paper trail, extending from his entrance to his exit, is what the biographer tries to tread—after he has sorted it out, that is.

PAUL MURRAY KENDALL,
The Art of Biography

The biographer must be a sort of bifurcated animal, digger and dreamer; for biography is an impossible amalgam: half rainbow, half stone.

PAUL MURRAY KENDALL,
The Art of Biography

Edward Fitzgerald said that he wished we had more biographies of obscure persons. How often I have myself wished to ask simple, silent, deferential people, such as stationmasters, butlers, gardeners, what they make of it all! Yet one cannot do it, and even if one could, ten to one they would not or could not tell you.

A. C. BENSON,
From a College Window

Men's characters come to us from their graves. For life is dazzling and complex: we cannot grasp it, we never understand the heart-in-action. But when the heart has stopped beating forever we turn to the lamp and the manuscript. Some artist pulls aside a curtain and shows us the man. He becomes better known to posterity than he was to his intimate friends.

JOHN JAY CHAPMAN,
Memories and Milestones

The biographer's responsibility is large. He assays the role of a god, for in his hands the dead can be brought to life and granted a measure of immortality. He should, at least, then, seek to emulate the more reliable divinities in his zeal for truth, his tolerance of human frailty, and his love for mankind.

JOHN A. GARRATY,
The Nature of Biography

BIRDS

No bird sits a tree more proudly than a pigeon. It looks as though placed there by the Lord.

KATHERINE MANSFIELD,
The Journal of Katherine Mansfield

It is astonishing how violently a big branch shakes when a silly little bird has left it. I expect the bird knows it and feels immensely arrogant.

KATHERINE MANSFIELD,
The Journal of Katherine Mansfield

Birds in general are stupid, in the sense of being little able to meet unforeseen emergencies; but their lives are often emotional, and their emotions are richly and finely expressed.

JULIAN HUXLEY,
Essays of a Biologist

When a nightingale sits up all night singing to his wife, and singing very well, too, you can't make me believe that aesthetic values of a very high order are not present.

ALFRED NORTH WHITEHEAD,
Dialogues of Alfred North Whitehead

You rise early in the morning and go outdoors to make a before-breakfast circuit of the house and snuff the garden air ingrained with gold. But though you think yourself taking the day by the prime, it is already old to the birds.

CHRISTOPHER MORLEY,
Inward Ho

I find penguins at present the only comfort in life. One feels everything in the world so sympathetically ridiculous; one can't be angry when one looks at a penguin.

JOHN RUSKIN,
Letters of John Ruskin to Charles Eliot Norton,
Vol. I

If I shouldn't be alive
When the robins come,
Give the one in red cravat
A memorial crumb.

EMILY DICKINSON,
Selected Poems and Letters of Emily Dickinson

God made all flying things
Eagle and albatross,
With tapered body and spread of
 outstretched wings
To hang against the sunset like a cross.

ALFRED BARRETT,
"Bird of God," *Mint by Night*

I watch, in the morning when I wake up, a thrush on the wall opposite the window— not a thrush, a blackbird—and he sings opening his beak. . . . He looks so remote, so buried in primeval silence, standing there on the wall, and bethinking himself, then opening his beak to make strange, strong sounds. He seems as if his singing were a sort of talking to himself, or of thinking aloud his strongest thoughts. I wish I was a blackbird, like him. I hate men.

D. H. LAWRENCE,
Selected Letters of D. H. Lawrence

There is nothing in which the birds differ more from man than the way in which they can build and yet leave a landscape as it was before.

ROBERT LYND,
The Blue Lion

You know that if I were reincarnated, I'd want to come back as a buzzard. Nothing hates him or envies him or wants him or needs him. He is never bothered or in danger, and he can eat anything.

WILLIAM FAULKNER,
Writers at Work,
edited by Malcolm Cowley

When seagulls flash up from the water with every wing at full stretch there is no deliberation; it is as if each bird saw a sweeping arc before it followed its individual way faithfully. The unerring judgment of the grand curve when the wings are so near and yet never collide, the speed of descent, are pure poetry.

MARY WEBB,
The Spring of Joy

At no time of the year does the fellowship of the birds afford me keener enjoyment than in the dead of winter. In June one may see them everywhere . . . but in January the sight of a single brown creeper is sufficient to brighten the day, and the twittering of half a dozen goldfinches is like the music of angels.

BRADFORD TORREY,
A Rambler's Release

It seems so impossible to understand the emotional life of a bird. How, in the extreme terrors of its existence, can it sing so happily? There is no hint of fear in the song of any bird, nor does terror mar the beauty of its life. It seems able to live entirely in the moment, isolating its joys and fears.

CLARE LEIGHTON,
Four Hedges

In order to see birds it is necessary to become a part of the silence. One has to sit still like a mystic and wait. One soon learns that fussing, instead of achieving things, merely prevents things from happening.

ROBERT LYND,
Solomon in All His Glory

Sparrows are sociable, like a crowd of children begging from a tourist. They may be greedy . . . but their vices are the vices of creatures that love the company of their kind.

ROBERT LYND,
Solomon in All His Glory

I sat on a hillside in the woods late in the day amid the pines and hemlocks, and heard the soft, elusive spring call of the little owl—a curious musical undertone hardly separable from the silence; a bell, muffled in feathers tolling in the twilight of the woods and discernible only to the most alert ear. But it was the voice of spring.

JOHN BURROUGHS,
Riverby

How exciting is the gradual arrival of the birds in their summer plumage! To watch it is like sitting at the window on Easter Sunday to observe the new bonnets.

THOMAS WENTWORTH HIGGINSON,
The Procession of Flowers

Our nights are days to the owls. While we sleep under domestic quilts they are wide awake flying by hedgerows or over waste places where the poppies appear black in the moonlight, cognisant of the slightest stir, of the faintest shadow, even stooping for a beetle. And something of the strange inhumanity of unnoticed ditches, of unfrequented outhouse corners, has got into the round physiognomy of an owl, so eldritch, and at the same time so sagacious, like an old woman who is both a witch and a midwife.

LLEWELYN POWYS,
Earth Memories

Just after sundown I see a large flock of wild geese in a perfect harrow cleaving their way toward the northeast, with Napoleonic tactics splitting the forces of winter.

HENRY DAVID THOREAU,
Early Spring in Massachusetts

The tit is as gay as a wild beast. It is meticulous in the manner of those model housekeepers who fly into a rage if there is a stain on the parquet: the threshold of her nest does not bear a trace of white droppings. Fierce? How pretty she is when she kills! The worm snatched, she finishes it off with repeated blows and cuts it up with an executioner's fairness. Fierce, yes, no more and no less than innumerable lovers.

COLETTE,
Journey for Myself

Short lives have all these wild things, but there are innumerable flocks of them always alive; they must die, then, in innumerable flocks. And yet they keep the millions of the dead out of sight.

ALICE MEYNELL,
The Colour of Life

BIRTH *(See BABY, BIRTHDAY, CHILDREN)*

BIRTHDAY

My birthday was a good one, being at home again, and the day was properly diversified with flowers and a call or two, a letter or two, and a telegram or two, etc.—just what a birthday ought to be.

GEORGE E. WOODBERRY,
Selected Letters of George Edward Woodberry

Most of us can remember a time when a birthday—especially if it was one's own—brightened the world as if a second sun had risen.

ROBERT LYND,
The Peal of Bells

It is lovely, when I forget all birthdays, including my own, to find that somebody remembers me.

ELLEN GLASGOW,
Letters of Ellen Glasgow

BITTERNESS

Bitterness does not help oneself or weigh with others.

A. C. BENSON,
Excerpts from the Letters of Dr. A. C. Benson to M. E. A.

If you are bitter at heart, sugar in the mouth will not help you.

YIDDISH PROVERB

Every experience, however bitter, has its lesson, and to focus one's attention on the lesson helps one overcome the bitterness.

EDWARD HOWARD GRIGGS,
A Book of Meditations

My donkey is dead; let no more grass grow.

GREEK PROVERB

Taking the bitter with the sweet would be a different affair if the whole mixture did not immediately turn bitter when the bitter is added.

ANONYMOUS (HENRY S. HASKINS),
Meditations in Wall Street

BLACK *(See also COLOR, DARKNESS)*

Black is beautiful.

ANONYMOUS

BLAME

Whatever you blame, that you have done yourself.

GEORG GRODDECK,
quoted in *The Unquiet Grave* by Cyril Connolly

There can be no doubt that the average man blames much more than he praises.

ARNOLD BENNETT,
The Arnold Bennett Calendar, compiled by Frank Bennett

He who wants to blame sometimes finds the sugar sour.

GERMAN PROVERB

BOASTING

It's not the hen that cackles the loudest that lays the biggest egg.

SCOTCH PROVERB

They who constantly speak of the great things they will accomplish are like sterile women planning magnificent careers for their progeny.

PAUL ELDRIDGE,
Horns of Glass

A man should never boast of his courage, nor a woman of her virtue, lest their doing so should be the cause of calling their possession of them into question.

LADY MARGUERITE BLESSINGTON,
Desultory Thoughts and Reflections

Boasting is not courage.

AFRICAN PROVERB

BODY

We have so many words for states of the mind, and so few for the states of the body.

JEANNE MOREAU,
New York Times, June 30, 1976

Who can in practice separate his view of body and spirit? For example, what a friend would he be to us who should treat us ill, or deny us food, or imprison us; and say, after all, that it was our body he ill-treated, and not our soul?

JOHN HENRY CARDINAL NEWMAN,
Parochial and Plain Sermons, Vol. II

Talking about our bodies is a complex and difficult matter. We are so used to covering them up, to referring to them obliquely with slang terms or in a borrowed language, to hiding even infants' sex membership under blue and pink ribbons. It is difficult to become aware of those things about us which have been, and will always be, patterned by our own particular modesties and reticences.

MARGARET MEAD,
Male and Female

The body is a big sagacity, a plurality with one sense, a war and a peace, a flock and a shepherd.

FRIEDRICH NIETZSCHE,
Thus Spake Zarathustra

I hope you are more comfy and freer from pain. Sometimes I think the resurrection

of the body, unless much improved in construction, a mistake!

EVELYN UNDERHILL,
The Letters of Evelyn Underhill

Bless your body always. Speak no word of condemnation about it.

REBECCA BEARD,
Everyman's Search

The body remembers past pleasures and on being made aware of them, floods the mind with sweetness.

CYRIL CONNOLLY,
The Unquiet Grave

The body is an instrument which only gives off music when it is used as a body. Always an orchestra, and just as music traverses walls, so sensuality traverses the body and reaches up to ecstasy.

ANAÏS NIN,
The Diaries of Anaïs Nin, Vol. II

Language which does not acknowledge the body cannot acknowledge life.

JOHN LAHR,
Up Against the Fourth Wall

Our own physical body possesses a wisdom which we who inhabit the body lack. We give it orders which make no sense.

HENRY MILLER,
A Devil in Paradise

Why should I care what part of my body I reveal. . . . Is not all body and soul an instrument through which the artist expresses his inner message of beauty?

ISADORA DUNCAN,
quoted in *Charmers and Cranks*
by Ishbel Ross

Every human body has its optimum weight and contour, which only health and efficiency can establish. Whenever we treat women's bodies as aesthetic objects without function we deform them and their owners. Whether the curves imposed are the ebullient arabesques of the tit-queen or the attentuated coils of art nouveau, they are deformations of the dynamic, individual body, and limitations of the possibilities of being female.

GERMAINE GREER,
The Female Eunuch

When the life of the party wants to express the idea of a pretty woman in mime, he undulates his two hands in the air and leers expressively. The notion of a curve is so closely connected to sexual semantics that some people cannot resist sniggering at road signs. The most popular image of the female despite the exigencies of the clothing trade is all boobs and buttocks, a hallucinating sequence of parabolae and bulges.

GERMAINE GREER,
The Female Eunuch

Grace is to the body what clear thinking is to the mind.

LA ROCHEFOUCAULD,
Maxims

The word arse is as much god as the word face. It must be so, otherwise you cut off your god at the waist.

D. H. LAWRENCE,
D. H. Lawrence: Selected Literary Criticism,
edited by Anthony Beal

The blood also thinks inside a man, darkly and ponderously. It thinks in desires and revulsions, and it makes strange conclusions.

D. H. LAWRENCE,
Selected Essays

Hurt my tooth at breakfast. I look in the glass. Am conscious of the humiliating sorriness of my earthly tabernacle, and of the sad fact that the best of parents could do no better for me.... Why should a man's mind have been thrown into such close, sad, sensational, inexplicable relations with such a precarious object as his body?

THOMAS HARDY,
"Later Years of Hardy," *Bookman's Pleasure,*
compiled by Holbrook Jackson

Today, as never before, one must *love* the body, must be gently patient with it:
Daintied o'er with dear devices
Which He loveth, for He grew.

FRANCIS THOMPSON,
Works, Vol. III

The body is the mystery we know nothing of; it works its own will and goes its own way, like a cat or a god; as far as we know or have power over it, its joy springs from the secrets of its own dark life, it dies by its own calendar, and when we most think we are ruling it, it is obeying the order itself first gave. If we doctor it, we are but giving it the food it asked for, we don't know why; if they cut into it for us, it must be trimmed only so far and no farther—an inch more and something very strange comes upon us. It gives itself its own laws, and we obey them and it: the mystery is the body: it is the stranger: we can only gape at it when it stands in our doorway, and do our best to keep it in good humour, the awesome, powerful, venerable stranger.

STEPHEN MACKENNA,
Journal and Letters of Stephen Mackenna

A man's height gives him a different outlook on his environment and so changes his character.

W. SOMERSET MAUGHAM,
The Summing Up

The old ceremonial gestures of the human body are necessary to the health of the human soul: the gesture that pledged the guest in the goblet; that strewed the flowers upon the grave; that drew the sword for the salute or set up the candle before the shrine. In that sense a man can actually think with his muscles; he can pray with his muscles; he can love with his muscles and lament with his muscles.

G. K. CHESTERTON,
All Is Grist

The body and soul are one for the purpose of all real evolution, and regrettable is any term suggestive of divorce between them.

JOHN GALSWORTHY,
Castles in Spain and Other Screeds

I believe in the flesh and the appetites;
Seeing, hearing, feeling, are miracles and each part and tag of me is a miracle.

WALT WHITMAN,
"Song of Myself," *Leaves of Grass*

One reason, maybe, why Americans die so young—in middle age—especially in cities, is because they do not know their own bodies. They force themselves to live and do things without any psychic acquaintance with their bodies. Their instinct is deaf to the language of the body, which would tell them how to live if they would listen to it—they are absolute strangers to their own bodies, shy and self-conscious about them.

KATHARINE BUTLER HATHAWAY,
*The Journals and Letters
of the Little Locksmith*

Our efforts to disguise the animal within are more or less futile. We are born as animals and so we remain. Eventually we learn that even the idealized, deanimalized woman of our dreams has bowel and bladder functions and monthly catamenia. The processes of digestion, copulation, defecation, urination, sweating, getting old and dying remain primitive. So a psychological division, a social ambivalence, takes place between gusto and refinement. This is a critical inner struggle of man, because, as I have said, heartiness of appetite is the basis of health, mental and physical, and whatever injuries desire and satisfaction leads to illness and melancholy.

ABRAHAM MEYERSON,
Speaking of Man

The man who is so painstakingly cautious about doing his own body no harm seldom does anything for anyone else.

E. V. LUCAS,
365 Days and One More

No message comes through our senses but is full of worship—the taste of brown bread and red wine, the smell of a field of dazzling charlock, the sight of swallows sweeping back and forth over the tilted roof of a barn, the cool fair flesh of a young girl's body, the liquid song of a blackbird in the white twilight of the longest day.

LLEWELYN POWYS,
Earth Memories

The ability to be aware of one's body has a great importance all through life. It is a curious fact that most adults have so lost physical awareness that they are unable to tell how their leg feels if you should ask them, or their ankle, or their middle finger or any other part of the body. In our society the awareness of the different parts of the body is generally limited to some borderline schizophrenics, and other sophisticated people who have come under the influence of yoga or other Eastern exercises.

ROLLO MAY,
Man's Search for Himself

Far from distrusting the temporal delights that come through the body, we should abandon ourselves to them with confidence. The way of the senses is the way of life. It is the people with their hands in the till and their eyes on heaven who ruin existence. . . . Without doubt half the ethical rules they din into our ears are designed to keep us at work.

LLEWELYN POWYS,
Earth Memories

There is nothing so humiliating as to know what a controlling influence the intestines have on the thoughts and ways of men.

JOHN LANCASTER SPALDING,
Glimpses of Truth

BOOKS

The art of reading is in great part that of acquiring a better understanding of life from one's encounter with it in a book.

ANDRÉ MAUROIS,
The Art of Living

I do not know that I am happiest when alone; but this I am sure of, that I never am long in the society even of her I love . . . without a yearning for the company of my lamp and my utterly confused and tumbled over library.

LORD BYRON,
quoted in *The Literature of Gossip*
by Elizabeth Drew

There is a good saying to the effect that when a new book appears one should read an old one. As an author I would not recommend too strict an adherence to this saying.

SIR WINSTON CHURCHILL,
A Churchill Reader, edited by Colin R. Coote

I have been among my books all day, and they have confused and overpowered me with doubts and questions which start in books but are rarely answered there.

HAMILTON WRIGHT MABIE,
My Study Fire

Only one hour in the normal day is more pleasurable than the hour spent in bed with a book before going to sleep, and that is the hour spent in bed with a book after being called in the morning.

ROSE MACAULAY,
A Casual Commentary

Certain books come to meet one, as do people.

ELIZABETH BOWEN,
Vogue, September 15, 1955

I love some of my printed books as much as anyone can. Just the same, my heart beats faster at a book of blank pages than it does at any book filled with printing.

RUTH BENEDICT,
An Anthropologist at Work
by Margaret Mead

A book is like a garden carried in the pocket.

CHINESE PROVERB

When you reread a classic you do not see more in the book than you did before; you see more in *you* than was there before.

CLIFTON FADIMAN,
Any Number Can Play

The harmonies of bound books are like the flowers of the field.

HILAIRE BELLOC,
The Silence of the Sea

There is, I fancy, a kind of book which certainly influences the world directly, and, it may be truly said, is an original cause to the effect it creates. It is not the book which merely expresses what its audience was already feeling in a confused fashion, nor the book which fires enthusiasm by rhetoric; but the book which tells clearly the discovery of some truth, giving positive evidence for same.

HILAIRE BELLOC,
A Conversation with an Angel

There are two motives for reading a book: one, that you enjoy it; the other, that you can boast about it.

BERTRAND RUSSELL,
The Conquest of Happiness

When you take up a book you must swallow it at one mouthful. That is the only way to know it in its entirety.

GUSTAVE FLAUBERT,
quoted in *The Writing Art,* selected by
Bertha W. Smith and Virginia C. Lincoln

A book is a friend; a good book is a good friend. It will talk to you when you want it to talk, and it will keep still when you want it to keep still—and there are not many friends who know enough to do that.

LYMAN ABBOTT,
quoted in *Thoughts That Inspire,* Vol. II,
compiled by George H. Knox

Those whom books will hurt will not be proof against events. If some books are deemed most baneful and their sale forbid, how, then, with deadlier facts, not dreams of doting men? Events, not books, should be forbid.

HERMAN MELVILLE,
The Piazza Tales

People feel no obligation to buy books. It isn't their fault. Art seems cheap to them, because almost always it is cheap. . . . People stick any kind of stuff together between covers and throw it at them.

SHERWOOD ANDERSON,
Letters of Sherwood Anderson

The pleasure of all reading is doubled when one lives with another who shares the same books.

KATHERINE MANSFIELD
The Letters of Katherine Mansfield

There are some books of which scores of copies are bought for one which is read, and others which have dozens of readers for every copy sold.

JOHN AYSCOUGH,
Levia-Pondera

You are not allowed to think of the Torah in the toilet, and for this reason you may read worldly books there. A very pious man in Prague, a certain K., knew a great deal of the worldly sciences, he had studied them all in the toilet.

FRANZ KAFKA,
The Diaries of Franz Kafka 1914–1923

There are books one needs maturity to enjoy just as there are books an adult can come on too late to savor.

PHYLLIS MCGINLEY,
The Province of the Heart

I judge always, a great deal, by the general aspect of a page, as to whether it is, so to speak, luminous or not.

ROBERT HUGH BENSON,
quoted in *The Life of Monsignor Robert Hugh Benson*, Vol. II, edited by C. C. Martindale

The world of books is, in fact, the Grand Alsatia, to which all the hunted ones of the herded tribes of man can flee away and be at rest.

JOHN COWPER POWYS,
The Meaning of Culture

Perhaps the most wonderful of all thoughts . . . are the thoughts that come to us when we have been reading some particularly thrilling book and then stop for a second to observe the shadows on the hills, or to look out upon the lights of the streets, or to gaze down at the sea.

JOHN COWPER POWYS,
The Meaning of Culture

What a sense of superiority it gives one to escape reading some book which everyone else is reading.

ALICE JAMES,
The Diary of Alice James

A book, like a person, has its fortunes with one; it is lucky or unlucky in the precise moment of its falling in our way, and often by some happy accident counts with us for something more than its independent value.

WALTER PATER,
Marius the Epicurean

One always tends to overpraise a long book, because one has got through it.

E. M. FORSTER,
Abinger Harvest

People compare books with other books, not with experience.

GEORGE SANTAYANA,
The Letters of George Santayana

A book is a part of life, a manifestation of life, just as much as a tree or a horse or a star. It obeys its own rhythms, its own laws, whether it be a novel, a play, or a diary. The deep, hidden rhythm of life is always there—that of the pulse, the heart beat.

HENRY MILLER,
The Cosmological Eye

Until it is kindled by a spirit as flamingly alive as the one which gave it birth a book is dead to us.

HENRY MILLER,
The Books in My Life

Have you not noticed, after many heartaches and disillusionments, that in recommending a book to a friend the less said the better? The moment you praise a book too highly you awaken resistance in your listener.

HENRY MILLER,
The Books in My Life

Real bibliophiles do not put their books on shelves for people to look at or handle. They have no desire to show off their darlings, or to amaze people with their possessions. They keep their prized books hidden away in a secret spot to which they resort stealthily, like a Caliph visiting his harem, or a church elder sneaking into a bar. To be a book collector is to combine the worst characteristics of a dope-fiend with those of a miser.

ROBERTSON DAVIES,
The Table Talk of Samuel Marchbanks

Finishing a good book is like leaving a good friend.

WILLIAM FEATHER,
The Business of Life

Books are delightful society. If you go into a room filled with books, even without taking them down from their shelves, they seem to speak to you, to welcome you.

WILLIAM E. GLADSTONE,
quoted in *The Book of Common Joys*
by Mary L. Pendered

If I read a book that impresses me, I have to take myself firmly in hand, before I mix with other people; otherwise they would think my mind rather queer.

ANNE FRANK,
Anne Frank: The Diary of a Young Girl

No one ever reads a book. He reads himself through books, either to discover or to control himself. And the most objective books are the most deceptive.

ROMAIN ROLLAND,
Journey Within

The greatest book is not the one whose message engraves itself on the brain ... but the one whose vital impact opens up other viewpoints, and from writer to reader spreads the fire that is fed by the various essences, until it becomes a vast conflagration leaping from forest to forest.

ROMAIN ROLLAND,
Journey Within

The central theme of the novel is that they were glad to see each other.

GERTRUDE STEIN,
quoted in *The Third Rose*
by John Malcolm Brinnin

I think it is good of those who have read, and have cared for what they have read, to write and tell the author, who knows little of what her work is doing, once it has gone out into the world.

EVELYN UNDERHILL,
The Letters of Evelyn Underhill

There are some knightly souls who even go so far as to make their visits to bookshops a kind of chivalrous errantry at large.

They go in not because they need any certain volume but because they feel that there may be some book that needs them.

CHRISTOPHER MORLEY,
Pipefuls

Of making many books there is no end, and one often wishes that all save the greatest were consigned to oblivion. For that matter, in a sense they are.

VIDA D. SCUDDER,
The Privilege of Age

Books are not made for furniture, but there is nothing else that so beautifully furnishes a house.

HENRY WARD BEECHER,
Eyes and Ears

To spend several days in a friend's house, and hunger for something to read, while you are treading on costly carpets, and sitting upon luxurious chairs, and sleeping upon down, is as if one were bribing your body for the sake of cheating your mind.

HENRY WARD BEECHER,
Eyes and Ears

A lover of books also wants to possess them, but above and beyond this material desire for ownership he makes them his own, incorporates their content into his spiritual body.

OSWALD SCHWARZ,
The Psychology of Sex

Honest books are not impudently certain of all things. ... They are not written for the side of us that talks but for the silent side that keeps wondering at the lies we tell.

FRANK MOORE COLBY,
The Colby Essays, Vol. 1

There are certain literary sets in which the book is an instrument of torture. I⸢ you have not read it, you are made ⸜ feel unspeakably abject, for the book you have not read is always the one book in the world that you should have read.

FRANK MOORE COLBY,
The Colby Essays, Vol. 1

If we had read all those books, with whose

titles in histories of European literature we have grown so familiar, we should have had no time to live, and should, therefore, knowing nothing of life, be in no position to judge them rightly.

ALEC WAUGH,
On Doing What One Likes

There is no worse robber than a bad book.
ITALIAN PROVERB

There are books which I love to see on the shelf. I feel that virtue goes out of them, but I should think it undue familiarity to read them.

SAMUEL MCCHORD CROTHERS,
The Gentle Reader

I would not call any one a gentle reader who does not now and then take up a dull book and enjoy it in the spirit in which it was written.

SAMUEL MCCHORD CROTHERS,
The Gentle Reader

I read prodigiously. The Widener Library has crumpled under my attack. Ten, twelve, fifteen books a day are nothing.

THOMAS WOLFE,
The Letters of Thomas Wolfe

Remorse for the brevity of a book is a rare emotion. . . .
    Had I tried before reading your gift to thank you, it had perhaps been possible, but I waited, and now it disables my lips.

EMILY DICKINSON,
Selected Poems and Letters of Emily Dickinson

There is no quite good book without a good morality, but the world is wide, and so are morals.

ROBERT LOUIS STEVENSON,
"A Gossip on a Novel of Dumas's,"
Memories and Portraits

What's a book? Everything or nothing. The eye that sees it is all.

RALPH WALDO EMERSON,
Journals of Ralph Waldo Emerson

The book that alarms one man, threatening the disorganization of society, is heard by one of higher principle with no more emotion than the cheeping of a mouse in the wall.

RALPH WALDO EMERSON,
Journals of Ralph Waldo Emerson

Quite early in the history of medicine the doctors found out that a man could digest his food best if he ate it with pleasure among cheerful friends. So it is with books. You may devour them by the thousand, swiftly and grimly, and yet remain the lean soul that you were. The only mental food that will turn to new tissue within you, and build itself into your mind, is that which you eat with a good surge of joy and surprise that anything so exciting should ever have been written.

C. E. MONTAGUE,
A Writer's Notes on His Trade

And I must read a little Ibsen to compare with Euripides—Racine with Sophocles—perhaps Marlowe with Aeschylus. Sounds very learned; but really might amuse me; and if it doesn't, no need to go on.

VIRGINIA WOOLF,
A Writer's Diary

A book is good, bad or medium for me, and I usually don't know the reasons why. Years later, I will often think the good was not as good as I once thought, but on the record, my inability to know the why, my rather lumpish incoherent acceptance or rejection, has often been less mistaken than those who care more or know more of what literature is made.

LILLIAN HELLMAN,
An Unfinished Woman

There are, in actual fact, men who talk like books. Happily, however, there are also books that talk like men.

THEODOR HAECKER,
Journal in the Night

The public which reads, in any sense of the word worth considering, is very, very small; the public which would feel no lack if all book-printing ceased tomorrow, is enormous.

GEORGE GISSING,
The Private Papers of Henry Ryecroft

Just the knowledge that a good book is waiting one at the end of a long day makes that day happier.

KATHLEEN NORRIS,
Hands Full of Living

Often while reading a book one feels that the author would have preferred to paint rather than to write; one can sense the pleasure he derives from describing a landscape or a person, as if he were painting what he is saying, because deep in his heart he would have preferred to use brushes and colors.

PABLO PICASSO,
quoted in *The Third Rose*
by John Malcolm Brinnin

A book worthy of the name always belongs to its period on account of the spirit that quickens it.

JULIAN GREEN,
Julian Green: Diary 1928–1957

Of many books it may be said that they are nothing but the echoes of echoing echoes.

HENRY VAN DYKE,
The School of Life

To find one's home in space one may travel, but if a man is looking for his true habitat in time he must have books—and the right ones.

ODELL SHEPARD,
The Joys of Forgetting

Readers may be separated, roughly, into three zones: torrid, temperate, and frigid. It is notorious that many of the infelicities of literary intercourse are due merely to mismatings, as of a polar person with an equatorial book, or vice versa.

ODELL SHEPARD,
The Joys of Forgetting

For myself, public libraries possess a special horror, as of lonely wastes and dragon-haunted fens. The stillness and the heavy air, the feeling of restriction and surveillance, the mute presence of these other readers, "all silent and all damned," combine to set up a nervous irritation

fatal to quiet study.

KENNETH GRAHAME,
Pagan Papers

In book-buying you not infrequently condone an extravagance by the reflection that this particular purchase will be a good investment, sordidly considered: that you are not squandering income but sinking capital. But you know all the time that you are lying.

KENNETH GRAHAME,
Pagan Papers

In the pathetic companionship of books lived Southey, long after their beauty was shut out from him, passing his trembling hand up and down their ranks, and taking comfort in the certainty that they had not forsaken him.

LOUISE IMOGEN GUINEY,
Goose-Quill Papers

Lively books, read with lively interest, leave strong and living recollections.... The good sense of a busy public has practically discovered that what is read easily is recollected easily, and that what is read with difficulty is remembered with more.

WALTER BAGEHOT,
Literary Studies, Vol. I

Books, I say, are truly alchemical agents; for they, more than other of man's creations, have the power of transforming something common (meaning you and me as we are most of the time) into something precious (meaning you and me as God meant us to be).

LAWRENCE CLARK POWELL,
The Alchemy of Books

There are books which should be praised quickly before they are finished being talked about.

J. PETIT-SENN,
Conceits and Caprices

I have always read *in* books rather than *through* them and always with more profit from the books I read *in* than the books I read *through;* for when I set out to read *through* a book I always felt that I had a task before me, but when I read *in* a book it was the page or the paragraph that I wanted, and which left its impression and became a part of my intellectual furniture.

OLIVER WENDELL HOLMES,
Life and Letters of Oliver Wendell Holmes,
Vol. I, by John T. Morse, Jr.

It is the great books that last—like the Greek marbles they know no change—and they about make up all my little shelf nowadays; when you grow old they give up their body and spirit like old wines, believe me.

GEORGE E. WOODBERRY,
Selected Letters of George Edward Woodberry

I wish I had a book this minute to dally with for an hour—and the worst is there are dozens around me that I want to read if I could only think what they were. I never read Plato's *Laws*. . . . The day of judgment grows nearer—and though not necessary, it would be becoming to have read that.

OLIVER WENDELL HOLMES, JR.,
Holmes-Laski Letters, Vol. I

I am thinking now of reading *Moby Dick*. . . . I am trying to feel unscrupulous and to read it for amusement but it comes very hard.

OLIVER WENDELL HOLMES, JR.,
Holmes-Pollock Letters, Vol. II

Age increases my conviction that one cannot afford to give much time to the classics. Some time, yes. But one needs to enlarge and enrich one's view of life and the universe. The ideas of the classics, so far as living, are our commonplaces. It is the modern books that give us the latest and most profound conceptions. It seems to me rather a lazy makeshift to mumble over the familiar.

OLIVER WENDELL HOLMES, JR.,
The Mind and Faith of Justice Holmes,
edited by Max Lerner

Edwards, Book Collector, desired his coffin to be made out of some of the strong shelves of his library.

CHARLES LAMB,
Scrapbook

If I borrow a book, I cannot abstain from reading it without a pricking of conscience every time I see it and I cannot help seeing it every time I am looking for something else.

ROBERT LYND,
The Blue Lion

Perhaps the book means even more to me on account of my not having read it. At present it is not an achievement but a hope, a perpetual promise. After all, to have read a book is to have vulgarised it. It is to have exchanged Samarkand for Southend—the unknown for the known.

ROBERT LYND,
Solomon in All His Glory

Why is it that we get so little out of books, that we remain the same whatever we read? It is because we obstinately carry ourselves into them; we read ourselves and not the authors. Any little thing which agrees with our beliefs or prejudices we seize, and the rest we neglect. We should make it a rule to settle on that which is most difficult and that from which we most differ.

MARK RUTHERFORD,
Last Pages from a Journal

The power to give oneself up graciously to a book is the wealthiest habit, I imagine, that one can acquire.

CHAUNCEY WRIGHT,
Letters of Chauncey Wright

It is with books as with men,—it is easiest to acquaint oneself with those least worth knowing.

JOHN LANCASTER SPALDING,
Things of the Mind

The books that one reads in the impressionable years, and therefore absorbs and remembers, are always so much better and more exciting than life.

E. V. LUCAS,
365 Days and One More

I wish now that you [John Dewey] would make a collection of your scattered articles. . . . It is only books that tell. They seem to have a penetrating power which the same content in the shape of scattered articles wholly lacks. But the articles prepare buyers for the books.

WILLIAM JAMES,
The Thought and Character of William James
by Ralph Barton Perry

As a rule reading fiction is as hard to me as trying to hit a target by hurling feathers at it. I need *resistance,* to cerebrate!

WILLIAM JAMES,
quoted in *The Third Rose*
by John Malcolm Brinnin

The ideal world would be that in which there should be at least one lover for each woman. In the higher life of books the ideal is similar. No book should be brought into the world, which is not sure of love and lodging on some comfortable shelf.

RICHARD LE GALLIENNE,
Prose Fancies

Sir, the fact that a book is in a public library brings no comfort. Books are the one element in which I am personally and nakedly acquisitive. If it weren't for the law I would steal them. If it weren't for my purse I would buy them.

HAROLD J. LASKI,
Holmes-Laski Letters, Vol. I

Then yesterday, McIlwain and I went down to Oxford and had a great time book-hunting all day. I can't say we made any epoch-making discoveries, though we seem to have spent eight or ten pounds between us; but we had that peculiar thrill which comes from going into a room redolent with the faint mustiness of old calf and feeling that almost any volume may turn out a treasure.

HAROLD J. LASKI,
Holmes-Laski Letters, Vol. II

It is evident that to extract the essential soul and flavor of certain books one should endeavour to read them in the exact surroundings in which they were conceived, or in surroundings as nearly similar as may be; for the clear air, the sky, the water are, as it were, mixed with the writ-er's mind and woven into the very stuff of his imaginings. . . . Herrick should be read in a Devon lane in the time of violets. . . . Rabelais must be read among the rich lands of the Chionnais in Touraine, on the edge of a white road with cornfields and vineyards on either side. But let there be a farmyard near, with a ripe and aromatic muck-heap in it, the scent of which must be borne to you on the wind; and let there be also loud bursts of rustic laughter and a bottle of Chinon.

D. B. WYNDHAM LEWIS,
On Straw and Other Conceits

I fancy that I am going to discover my moral and intellectual welfare, rest and internal satisfaction of mind, the truth I seek, in every book that I scan and consult; as though these things were not within me, down in the very depths of my being, where with sustained and penetrating glance, I should look for them.

MAINE DE BIRAN,
quoted in *Essays Miscellaneous*
by Brother Azarias

What is it that makes most books unsatisfying? Is it not lack of character, of reality? A certain opportunism, aiming at the market rather than at the truth? The writers seem too much applicants for favor. They offer, for the most part, not solid individual contributions but voices in a chorus, each taking the key from the rest but striving to be a little louder or clearer or sharper or in some way consciously distinct, so as to be sure of being heard.

CHARLES HORTON COOLEY,
Life and the Student

BORE

Bores are good too. They may help you to a good indignation, if not to a sympathy.

RALPH WALDO EMERSON,
Journals of Ralph Waldo Emerson

It is as cruel to bore a child as to beat him.

GEORGE B. LEONARD,
Education and Ecstasy

What a bore it is, waking up in the morning always the same person.

H. P. SMITH,
quoted in *Fiery Grains*
by H. L. R. Sheppard and H. P. Marshall

Some ingenuity may be required to free yourself from a bore in the street. Words may be of no avail. A glance at your watch, accompanied by a sharp hiss of surprise, may bring release; or, if you are desperate, call a taxi. Even this, however, is risky, as he may ask, "Which way are you going?"

ARTHUR PONSONBY,
Casual Observations

I have kept clear of bores all my life long by judiciously pulling out my watch, when the boring stage was reached, and saying, "I am afraid I shall have to go to my work," or "I am afraid I must go out," or something. This gets you a character for being hard at work, and people are impressed rather than annoyed.

HANNAH WHITALL SMITH
Philadelphia Quaker
by Logan Pearsall Smith

Few people are bores at all times and places, and indeed one might venture on the charitable axiom: that when people bore us we are pretty sure to be boring them at the same time.

RICHARD LE GALLIENNE,
Prose Fancies

To be born for each other is, obviously, to be lovers. Well, not to be born for each other is to be bores.

RICHARD LE GALLIENNE,
Prose Fancies

We all denounce bores, but, while we do so, let us remember that there is nobody who isn't a bore to somebody.

J. A. SPENDER,
The Comments of Bagshot, Second Series

Every improvement in communication makes the bore more terrible. Nowadays he can get himself published as easily as at one time he could get himself invited out to dinner.

FRANK MOORE COLBY,
The Colby Essays, Vol. 1

A bore was trying to make small talk with James McNeill Whistler, the painter. "You know, Mr. Whistler, I passed by your house the other day," he said.

"Thank you," replied Whistler, "thank you very much."

ANONYMOUS,
Ladies' Home Journal, July 1941

BOREDOM

Boredom is a vital problem for the moralist, since at least half the sins of mankind are caused by the fear of it.

BERTRAND RUSSELL,
The Conquest of Happiness

A man would die, though he were neither valiant nor miserable, only upon a weariness to do the same thing oft over and over.

FRANCIS BACON,
Essays

I do not get my ideas from people on the street. If you look at faces on the street, what do you see? Nothing. Just boredom.

MARCEL MARCEAU,
New York Times, May 4, 1973

There is a time for play and a time for work, a time for creation and a time for lying fallow. And there is a time, glorious too in its own way, when one scarcely exists, when one is a complete void. I mean—when boredom seems the very stuff of life.

HENRY MILLER,
The Books in My Life

Boredom is the bitter fruit of too much routine or none at all.

BRENDAN FRANCIS

One can be bored until boredom becomes the most sublime of all emotions.

LOGAN PEARSALL SMITH,
Afterthoughts

Nobody is bored when he is trying to

make something that is beautiful, or to discover something that is true.

WILLIAM RALPH INGE,
Our Present Discontents

In the ancient recipe, the three antidotes for dulness or boredom are sleep, drink, and travel. It is rather feeble. From sleep you wake up, from drink you become sober, and from travel you come home again. And then where are you? No, the two sovereign remedies for dulness are love or a crusade.

D. H. LAWRENCE,
Assorted Articles

Now the great and fatal fruit of our civilisation, which is a civilisation based on knowledge, and hostile to experience, is boredom. All our wonderful education and learning is producing a grand sum-total of boredom. Modern people are inwardly thoroughly bored. Do as they may, they are bored.

D. H. LAWRENCE,
Assorted Articles

The war between being and nothingness is the underlying illness of the twentieth century. Boredom slays more of existence than war.

NORMAN MAILER,
Writers at Work, Third Series,
edited by George Plimpton

Over-excitement and boredom are states of mind which I equally shun, the first by never allowing myself to get over-excited, and the second by never allowing myself to feel bored. In whatever company I find myself I hold forth affably and agreeably to the company assembled. When other people begin talking I go away.

E. V. KNOX,
Gorgeous Times

Boredom is useful to me when I notice it and think: Oh, I'm bored—there must be something else I want to be doing. In this way boredom acts as an initiator of originality by pushing me into new activities or new thoughts.

HUGH PRATHER,
Notes to Myself

One of the worst forms of mental suffering is boredom, not knowing what to do with oneself and one's life. Even if man had no monetary, or any other reward, he would be eager to spend his energy in some meaningful way because he could not stand the boredom which inactivity produces.

ERICH FROMM,
The Sane Society

It is a characteristic of our big-city organizational society, that there's an agitated boredom that goes through everything. This looks like activity. Men are doing all kinds of things—except when you study what they're doing, they're performing avoidances of all kinds.

DR. RALPH GREENSON,
quoted in *The American Male*
by Myron Brenton

Indiscriminate work is a very uncertain remedy against *ennui*. The one sure means of dealing with it is to care for someone else, to do something kind and good.

THEODOR HAECKER,
Journal in the Night

We look wishfully to emergencies, to eventful revolutionary times from the desert of our ennui, and think how easy to have taken our part when the drum was rolling and the house was burning over our heads.

RALPH WALDO EMERSON,
Journals of Ralph Waldo Emerson

As for ennui and that sort of thing—the worm that never dies—I notice that it leaves me as soon as I am doing something that has got to be done—and comes on when I am in search of a job.

JOHN JAY CHAPMAN,
John Jay Chapman and His Letters
by M. A. DeWolfe Howe

BOSTON

There is about Boston a certain reminiscent and classical tone, suggesting an authenticity and piety which few other

American cities possess.

E. B. WHITE,
Every Day Is Saturday

Dear old Boston, what an unlovely place it is!

GEORGE SANTAYANA,
The Letters of George Santayana

I could not hear of a liberated Boston lady going to bed with an unconventional Boston gentleman, without thinking: "Oh, hell! They've thought it all out!" I could not imagine bed with a liberated Boston lady anyway.

THOMAS WOLFE,
The Letters of Thomas Wolfe

BOXING

Unless you've been in the ring when the noise is for you, there's no way you'll ever know what it's like.

SUGAR RAY ROBINSON,
Sugar Ray

When going into the ring I have always had it in mind that I would be the conqueror. That has always been my disposition.

JOHN L. SULLIVAN,
quoted in <i>The World Heavyweight
Boxing Championship
by John P. McCallum

O the joy of the strong-brawn'd fighter, towering in the arena in perfect condition, conscious of power, thirsting to meet his opponent.

WALT WHITMAN,
"A Song of Joys," <i>Leaves of Grass</i></div>

One day I learned that a punch comes from the leg. Then I just sent my fist up with a thrust from my right thigh. After that they went out in one blow.

GEORGES CARPENTIER,
quoted in the <i>New York Times,</i>
April 25, 1976

Few lapses of self-control are punished as immediately and severely as loss of temper during a boxing bout.

KONRAD LORENZ,
On Aggression

You can knock a man down with a blow to the jaw, but he'll get up fighting. Hit him hard enough and often enough in the mid-section and he'll go down for keeps.

JACK DEMPSEY,
quoted in <i>The Jack Dempsey Story</i>
by Gene Schoor

He goes down on one knee by the ropes. This was it. The whole world was screaming, "Come on, Rocky! Come on, Rocky!" All my life those three words were the sweetest music.

ROCKY GRAZIANO,
Somebody Up There Likes Me

He [Joe Louis] was a big lean copper spring, tightened and retightened through weeks of training until he was one pregnant package of coiled venom.

BOB CONSIDINE,
quoted in "<i>. . . And a Credit to His Race</i>"
by Gerald Astor

As they stand isolated in the chalky glare from the arc lights, the smoky darkness which frames them makes a picture out of them which has something of the quality of a Michelangelo. . . . They might stand immobile for one tense moment, each trying to sum up his opponent, to read his mind. In that moment they are superb statuary. . . . They are Greek athletes you are gazing on, molded in bronze to last for all time.

LOUIS GOLDING,
The Fireside Book of Boxing,
edited by W. C. Heinz

BOYS AND BOYHOOD

Never be surprised when you shake a cherry tree if a boy drops out of it; never be disturbed when you think yourself in complete solitude if you discover a boy peering out at you from a fence corner.

DAVID GRAYSON,
The Friendly Road

Now there is an animal in creation of no great general merit; but it has the eye of a hawk for affectation. It is called "a boy."

CHARLES READE,
The Cloister and the Hearth

It is sad to think that a human boy, like the morning star, full of life and joy, may be stricken down by death, and all his hilarity stifled in the grave; but to my mind it is even more melancholy to think that he may live to grow up, and be hard, and worldly, and ungenerous as any of the rest of us.

CHARLES B. FAIRBANKS,
My Unknown Chum

Boys are Erewhonians: they think that misfortune is disgraceful and must be concealed at all costs.

GEORGE ORWELL,
A Collection of Essays

It is impossible for the average boy to grow up and use the remarkable capacities that are in every boy, unless the world is for him and makes sense. And a society makes sense when it understands that its chief wealth *is* these capacities.

PAUL GOODMAN,
Growing Up Absurd

Quarrels among boys are harmless, and have more of a pleasant than a bitter character about them. And if boys quickly come to quarrel one with the other, they are easily calmed down again, and quickly come together with even greater friendliness.

SAINT AMBROSE,
Select Works and Letters

Little boys may be an intolerable nuisance; but when they are not there we regret them, we find ourselves homesick for their very intolerableness.

ALDOUS HUXLEY,
Beyond the Mexique Bay

Little boys are odd, tiresome creatures in many ways, with savage instincts; and I suppose many fathers feel that, if they are to maintain their authority, they must be a little distant and inscrutable. A boy goes for sympathy and companionship to his mother and sisters, not often to his father.

A. C. BENSON,
From a College Window

I remember seeing a picture of an old man

addressing a small boy. "How old are you?" "Well, if you go by what Mama says, I'm five. But if you go by the fun I've had, I'm most a hundred."

WILLIAM LYON PHELPS,
Essays on Things

Parents who have inner, often unconscious doubts about their own strength tend to demand that their children be especially courageous, independent and aggressive; they may buy the son boxing gloves, push him into competitive groups at an early age, and in other ways insist that the child be the "man" they inwardly feel they are not. . . . But as no child will develop courage by being overprotected, so no child will develop it by being pushed.

ROLLO MAY,
Man's Search for Himself

A fairly bright boy is far more intelligent and far better company than the average adult.

J. B. S. HALDANE,
quoted in the *New York Times,*
June 13, 1948

Every time a boy shows his hands, someone suggests that he wash them.

E. W. HOWE,
Country Town Sayings

Boys have their soft and gentle moods too. You would suppose by the morning racket that nothing could be more foreign to their nature than romance and vague sadness. . . . But boys have hours of great sinking and sadness, when kindness and fondness are peculiarly needful to them.

HENRY WARD BEECHER,
Eyes and Ears

Every boy wants someone older than himself to whom he may go in moods of confidence and yearning. The neglect of this child's want by grown people . . . is a fertile source of suffering.

HENRY WARD BEECHER,
Eyes and Ears

Not long ago, a little boy of my close acquaintance, only eighteen months old, and of a rare zest and energy, was given a saffron crocus-bud by his mother. His delight was boundless. He took it carefully in his small fist and so fell asleep with it unharmed. When she looked in on him later in the evening, it had come into bloom.

WALTER DE LA MARE,
Love

One of the ideas most difficult for parents and educators to accept is that the "good" child is often more in need of help and attention than the "naughty" child. Because of his aggressiveness the bad boy, so-called, is the object of a great deal of concern and counsel while the good lad receives praise or else is overlooked entirely.

DR. KARL MENNINGER,
A Psychiatrist's World

Boys and their pastimes are swayed by periodic forces inscrutable to man: so that tops and marbles reappear in their due season, regular like the sun and moon; and the harmless art of knucklebones has seen the fall of the Roman Empire and the rise of the United States.

ROBERT LOUIS STEVENSON,
Across the Plains

Every genuine boy is a rebel and an anarch. If he were allowed to develop according to his own instincts, his own inclinations, society would undergo such a radical transformation as to make the adult revolutionary cower and cringe. His would probably not be a comfortable or benevolent pattern of organization, but it would reflect justice, splendor and integrity. It would accelerate the vital pulse of life, abet and augment life. And what could be more terrifying to adults than such a prospect?

HENRY MILLER,
The Books in My Life

While the girl has prepared herself for child care through doll play, we still frown on boys doing the same. . . . We thus expect boys to accept a role in child rearing later in life for which they have never prepared themselves through childish play. On the contrary, the type of play which is encouraged for boys conditions many of them to be unable, as parents, to take care of their children in infancy without emotional conflict.

BRUNO BETTELHEIM,
American Journal of Orthopsychiatry,
January 1952

Whatever good there is in small boys is usually based upon their admiration for girls of their own age.

ARTHUR BRISBANE,
The Book of Today

All through my boyhood I had a profound conviction that I was no good, that I was wasting my time, wrecking my talents, behaving with monstrous folly and wickedness and ingratitude—and all this, it seemed, was inescapable, because I lived among laws which were absolute, like the law of gravity, but which it was not possible for me to keep.

GEORGE ORWELL,
A Collection of Essays

Boyhood is a most complex and incomprehensible thing. Even when one has been through it, one does not understand what it was. A man can never quite understand a boy, even when he has been the boy.

G. K. CHESTERTON,
Autobiography

BRAINS

I shall never respect my brains until I pick a few gold coins from them.

THOMAS WOLFE,
The Letters of Thomas Wolfe

In the matter of its own special activities the brain is usually undisciplined and unreliable. We never know what it will do next.

ARNOLD BENNETT,
The Arnold Bennett Calendar,
compiled by Frank Bennett

Many complain of their looks, but none of their brains.

YIDDISH PROVERB

It is impossible to live without brains, either one's own, or borrowed.

BALTASAR GRACIAN,
The Oracle

BREASTS

From the Cabaret aux Fleurs we went to the Boule Blanche. Mr. W. was very red after a month of hunting in Scotland. When the Negro hostess bent over to serve his drink, he stared at her so intensely that she simply pulled her breast out of her dress and offered it to him. His face was wonderful to see. If he had been riding one of his thoroughbreds, he would have fallen off.

ANAÏS NIN,
The Diaries of Anaïs Nin, Vol. II

The most highly prized curve of all is that of the bosom. . . . The degree of attention which breasts receive, combined with the confusion about what the breast fetishists actually want, makes women unduly anxious about them. They can never be just right; they must always be too small, too big, the wrong shape, too flabby. The characteristics of the mammary stereotype are impossible to emulate because they are falsely simulated, but they must be faked somehow or other. Reality is either gross or scrawny.

GERMAINE GREER,
The Female Eunuch

How do you like them? Like a pear, a lemon, *à la Montgolfiere,* half an apple, or a canteloup? Go on, choose, don't be embarrassed. You thought they didn't exist any longer, that they were all over with, absolutely done for. . . . If you don't mind, Madame, let's bring things up to date. They exist, and persist, however criticized and persecuted they may be.

COLETTE,
Journey for Myself

BREEDING

Good breeding consists in concealing how much we think of ourselves and how little we think of the other person.

MARK TWAIN,
Mark Twain at Your Fingertips,
edited by Caroline T. Harnsberger

There is no nonsense of merit about high birth; if you have got it you may not deserve it, and though you deserve it never so much you cannot attain it by your deserving it if it happens to be wanting. And that is precisely why it is really esteemed.

JOHN AYSCOUGH,
Levia-Pondera

Good breeding is the art of making everybody satisfied with themselves and pleased with you.

JOSH BILLINGS,
His Works Complete

BREVITY

In all men of real intelligence we find the tendency to express themselves briefly, to say speedily what is to be said.

GEORG C. LICHTENBERG,
The Lichtenberg Reader

It is nothing short of genius that uses one word when twenty will say the same thing.

DAVID GRAYSON,
The Friendly Road

BRIDGE

Bridge is a social but not a very sociable game—that is, if you take it seriously, as most bridge players do.

RUTH MILLS TEAGUE,
Ladies' Home Journal, January 1947

When the human passions are ebbing, bridge takes their place.

ANNE SHAW,
But Such Is Life

Bridge I regard as only one degree better than absolutely vacuous conversation, which is certainly the most fatiguing thing in the world.

A. C. BENSON,
From a College Window

BROTHER (*See* BROTHERHOOD, FAMILY)

BROTHERHOOD

We are beginning to discover that our problem is worldwide, and no one people of the earth can work out its salvation by detaching itself from others. Either we shall be saved together or drawn together into destruction.

RABINDRANATH TAGORE,
Letters to a Friend

I think there is a sort of background of agreement among all men, especially those of the same generation, although publicists often obscure rather than represent it, being taken up with party controversies or special causes.

GEORGE SANTAYANA,
The Letters of George Santayana

We need to neutralize the aggressions that well up within us—often, strangely enough, against those who have the most in common with us. To understand all is to forgive all, and to know one another well enough should not be to hate one another the more but to love one another the more.

DR. KARL MENNINGER,
A Psychiatrist's World

We live in a time when there dawns upon us a realization that the people living on the other side of the mountain are not made up exclusively of red-headed devils responsible for all the evil on this side of the mountain.

C. G. JUNG,
Psychological Reflections,
edited by Jolande Jacobi and R. F. Hull

Brotherhood is not so wild a dream as those, who profit by postponing it, pretend.

ERIC SEVAREID,
Not So Wild a Dream

To feel that others equally with ourselves are members of the human race is the most difficult of arts. The idea of equality,

as an idea, is easy to accept, but it is hard to translate into an emotion.

JOHN ERSKINE,
The Complete Life

Only when man succeeds in developing his reason and love further than he has done so far, only when he can build a world based on human solidarity and justice, only when he can feel rooted in the experience of universal brotherliness, will he have found a new, human form of rootedness, will he have transformed his world into a true, human home.

ERICH FROMM,
The Sane Society

I believe that if we really want human brotherhood to spread and increase until it makes life safe and sane, we must also be certain that there is no one true faith or path by which it may spread.

ADLAI E. STEVENSON,
This I Believe, edited by
Edward P. Morgan

What I inveigh against is a cursed spirit of intolerance, conceived in distrust and bred in ignorance, that makes the mental attitude perennially antagonistic, even bitterly antagonistic, to everything foreign, that subordinates everywhere the race to the nation, forgetting the higher claims of brotherhood.

SIR WILLIAM OSLER,
*Aphorisms from His Bedside Teachings
and Writings*

The brotherhood of man is evoked by particular men according to their circumstances. But it seldom extends to all man. In the name of our freedom and our brotherhood we are prepared to blow up the other half of the world, and to be blown up in turn.

R. D. LAING,
The Politics of Experience

Every victory of man over man has in itself a taste of defeat, a flavour of death; there is no essential difference between the various human groups, creatures whose bones and brains and members are the same; and every damage we do there is a form of mutilation, as if the fingers of the left hand were to be cut off by the right; there is no pleasure in it, nor any deep sense of achievement or of peace.

FREYA STARK,
Traveller's Quest, edited by M. A. Michael

Over chaotic roads, led by a nostalgia for unity, men battle each other in the darkness, driven against each other by the thought that they wish to have only brothers on earth. They have forgotten they are brothers. This luminous truth has been hidden from their eyes.

JULES-GÉRARD CARDINAL SALIÈGE,
Who Shall Bear the Flame?

What we are witnessing in our day, if we have eyes not only to see things, but to see into the heart of things, is not social disintegration, but a radical new reintegration of humanity, a profound change in the social evolution of man, a change not free, of course, from dangers—for there is no progress without danger—but one of boundless and immeasurable potentialities.

RABBI ABBA HILLEL SILVER,
What Brotherhood Means to Me

And I remember my father's words. "If you wish them to be brothers, have them build a tower. But if you would have them hate each other, throw them corn."

ANTONE DE SAINT-EXUPÉRY,
The Wisdom of the Saints

BUDDHA (*See* GOD)

BUDGET

A budget tells us what we can't afford, but it doesn't keep us from buying it.

WILLIAM FEATHER,
The Business of Life

BULLFIGHTING

Bull fighting is not a sport. It was never supposed to be. It is a tragedy. A very great tragedy. The tragedy is the death of the bull.

ERNEST HEMINGWAY,
Byline: Ernest Hemingway,
edited by William White

Bull fighting is an exceedingly dangerous occupation. . . . It is a good deal like Grand Opera for the really great matadors except they run the chance of being killed every time they cannot hit high C.

ERNEST HEMINGWAY,
Byline: Ernest Hemingway,
edited by William White

BURDEN

To carry one's own carefully wrapped-up burden with the nonchalance of the day— Nature forgot to make endowment for that; it is something, then, to be worked out wholly by oneself.

SUSAN GLASPELL,
quoted in *The Bliss of the Way,*
compiled by Cecily Hallack

And when we sweat, then do people say to us: "Yea, life is hard to bear!"

But man himself only is hard to bear! The reason thereof is that he carrieth too many extraneous things on his shoulders. Like the camel he kneeleth down, and letteth himself be well laden.

Especially the strong load-bearing man in whom reverence resideth. Too many *extraneous* heavy words and worths loadeth he upon himself—then seemeth life to him a desert!

FREDERICK NIETZSCHE,
Thus Spake Zarathustra

BUREAUCRAT

An official man is always an official man, and he has a wild belief in the value of reports.

SIR ARTHUR HELPS,
Conversation in a Railway Carriage

BUSINESS

In my business hours I avoid fatigue. I do this by not doing too much work—the only trustworthy recipe.

E. V. KNOX,
Gorgeous Times

Commerce is, in its very essence, *satanic.* Commerce is return of the loan, a loan in which there is the understanding: *give me more than I give you.*

CHARLES BAUDELAIRE,
Intimate Journals

Probably some other races, such as the Jews and Arabs, make individually better merchants, more shrewd, patient, and loving of their art. Englishmen and Americans often seem to miss or force opportunities, to play for quick returns, or to settle down into ponderous corporations; for successful men they are not particularly observant, constant, or economical.

GEORGE SANTAYANA,
Character and Opinion in the United States

The amount of prudence and sagacity needful for the successful transaction of business depends comparatively little on the scale of operation. Sometimes, indeed, the larger the scale the easier the task.

SIR HENRY TAYLOR,
Notes from Life

Life is all of one piece. Men err when they think they can be inhuman exploiters in their business life, and loving husbands and fathers at home. For achievement without love is a cold and tight-lipped murderer of human happiness everywhere.

DR. SMILEY BLANTON,
Love or Perish

BUSY

Many people who pretend to be very busy have the least to do.

BALTASAR GRACIAN,
The Oracle

The busy part of mankind will furnish the contemplative with the materials of speculation to the end of time.

SAMUEL JOHNSON,
quoted in *A Treasury of English Aphorisms,*
edited by Logan Pearsall Smith

Who does not know men, inaccessible to truth or kindliness, who are always so busy that they never have a minute either to do good or to ask themselves whether their work is not harmful. The most cruel men—your Neros and Peter the Greats—were constantly occupied.

LEO TOLSTOY,
quoted in *The Second Book of He and She,*
edited by James Moffatt

There are many busybodies without real purpose who rise at four in the morning to drive a nail at noon.

J. PETIT-SENN,
Conceits and Caprices

BUT

"But" is a fence over which few leap.

GERMAN PROVERB

"But" knows nothing of amenity or social deference. It is a contentious word and a contumacious one, delighting in mere oppugnancy, a verbal stick thrust among the spokes of the conversational wheel.

ODELL SHEPARD,
The Joys of Forgetting

BUTTOCKS

Buttock fetishism is comparatively rare in our culture. . . . Girls are often self-conscious about their behinds, draping themselves in long capes and tunics, but it is more often because they are too abundant in that region than otherwise.

GERMAINE GREER,
The Female Eunuch

CALAMITY

We are more disturbed by a calamity which threatens us than by one which has befallen us.

JOHN LANCASTER SPALDING,
Thoughts and Theories of Life and Education

You may regret calamities if you can thereby help the sufferer, but if you cannot, mind your own business.

RALPH WALDO EMERSON,
Journals of Ralph Waldo Emerson

Your own calamity is more useful to you than another's triumph.

BULGARIAN PROVERB

What quarrel, what harshness, what unbelief in each other can subsist in the presence of a great calamity, when all the artificial vesture of our life is gone, and we are all one with each other in primitive mortal needs?

GEORGE ELIOT,
The Mill on the Floss

CALIFORNIA

Every California girl has lost at least one ovary and none of them has read *Madame Bovary*.

F. SCOTT FITZGERALD,
The Crack-up

I am struck in California by the deep and almost religious affection which people have for nature, and by the sensitiveness they show to its influences; not merely poetically, but also athletically, because they like to live as nature lives. It is a relief from business and the genteel tradition.

GEORGE SANTAYANA,
The Letters of George Santayana

California is a wonderful place to live—if you're an orange.

FRED ALLEN

All Californians travel toward water: toward the sea; once toward the rivers; now toward the rivers impounded and called lakes; toward snow, which is frozen water. And even when Californians head toward the desert, they do so more to marvel at the presence of swimming pools and fountains than to play in the sand.

JESSAMYN WEST,
Hide and Seek

CALMNESS

Sometimes we are clarified and calmed healthily, as we never were before in our lives, not by an opiate, but by some unconscious obedience to the all-just laws, so that we become like a still lake of purest crystal and without an effort our depths are revealed to ourselves. All the world goes by us and is reflected in our deeps.

HENRY DAVID THOREAU,
Journal

CAMPING (*See* VACATION)

CANADA

Geography has made us neighbors. History has made us friends. Economics has made us partners and necessity has made us allies. Those whom nature has so joined together, let no man put asunder.

JOHN F. KENNEDY,
New York Times, May 18, 1961

CANDOR

If one says what he thinks, the other too says what he thinks.

CHARLES PÉGUY,
God Speaks

The art of life is to show your hand. There is no diplomacy like candor. You may lose by it now and then, but it will be a loss well gained if you do. Nothing is so boring as having to keep up a deception.

E. V. LUCAS,
365 Days and One More

The inadequacy of the human language, the inaccuracy of the human mind, the havoc wrought in social life, by any such attempt, the ruptures of friendship, the stabs to love, the injury to commerce, the death to political life—all these make any noticeable degree of truth-telling either impossible or undesirable or both.

ROSE MACAULAY,
A Casual Commentary

It sometimes happens that one must get rid of a busybody, whose questions are like a fishhook cast into one's vitals. Well, then, give an evasive answer; say something that politely means: Mind your own business. That is real truth-telling, for it candidly reveals your thoughts, though they are not the thoughts your meddlesome friend wants you to reveal.

> WALTER ELLIOTT,
> *The Spiritual Life*

Candor is always a double-edged sword; it may heal or it may separate.

> DR. WILHELM STEKEL,
> *Marriage at the Crossroads*

Rude speech is martial music, after rank upon rank of soft phrases have passed in review.

> ANONYMOUS (HENRY S. HASKINS),
> *Meditations in Wall Street*

He who speaks the truth must have one foot in the stirrup.

> ARMENIAN PROVERB

I propose to speak my mind. I cannot believe you would wish me to say what I did not think, or think what I did not say. Nothing is to be gained by concealment or equivocation. If you find my conclusions unpalatable, you are not without resource. You have only to assure yourselves that I am totally mistaken, which may, indeed, very likely be the truth. And—who knows?—I may learn wisdom, and come to think differently.

> W. MACNEILE DIXON,
> *The Human Situation*

A man that would call everything by its right name would hardly pass the streets without being knocked down as a common enemy.

> LORD HALIFAX,
> quoted in *Ladies' Home Journal*,
> October 1948

CAPABILITY

So few men have the courage to question themselves in order to ascertain what they are really capable of becoming. And so few have the will to become it.

> DÉSIRÉ JOSEPH CARDINAL MERCIER,
> *The Life of Cardinal Mercier*
> by John A. Gade

To feel inwardly the greatest that one is capable of doing is really the first consciousness of what it is one's duty to do.

> JEAN MARIE GUYUA,
> quoted in *On Shame and the Search for Identity*
> by Helen Merrell Lynd

Everything that enlarges the sphere of human powers, that shows man he could do what he thought he could not do, is valuable.

> SAMUEL JOHNSON,
> *Life of Johnson* by James Boswell

Capability of being greater and capability of being less travel together in the same man; when either prevails, the other bides its time.

> ANONYMOUS (HENRY S. HASKINS),
> *Meditations in Wall Street*

CAPACITY

We must make the choices that enable us to fulfill the deepest capacities of our real selves.

> THOMAS MERTON,
> *No Man Is an Island*

The little cup that is made to hold so much can hold so much and no more, though all the purple vats of Burgundy be filled with wine to the brim, and the treaders stand knee-deep in the gathered grapes of the stony vineyards of Spain.

> OSCAR WILDE,
> *De Profundis*

The truth is that all of us attain the greatest success and happiness possible in this life whenever we use our native capacities to their fullest extent.

> DR. SMILEY BLANTON,
> *Love or Perish*

Values are the development of capacities. It takes the whole system of values to draw out the whole capacity of man; it takes the whole capacity of man to be the basis of a perfect system of values. If in any community there are underdeveloped capacities, so far the system of values is straitened and obstructed.

> BERNARD BOSANQUET,
> *Some Suggestions in Ethics*

The mystery of man's being, the un-awakened capacities in him, we are not half aware of. A few of the race, the prophets, sages, and poets, give us a glimpse of his high destiny.

ISAAC T. HECKER,
quoted in *Life of Father Hecker*
by Walter Eliot

Many of our troubles arise from faculties unused.

A. C. BENSON,
Excerpts from the Letters of
Dr. A. C. Benson to M. E. A.

If love is faith in the divine capacities, then the great work is to bring them out.

WILLIAM ELLERY CHANNING,
Dr. Channing's Note-book

When a man's capacity is fully engaged, he is really living, even though it be but for a day.

JOSEPH H. ODELL,
Unmailed Letters

Your nature feels its own mysterious capacities too much to believe for a moment it can be nothing different from what it is. It crowds and presses for an outlet.

PHILLIPS BROOKS

CARE

I do not care for anything. I do not care to ride, for the exercise is too violent. I do not care to walk, walking is too strenuous. I do not care to lie down, for I should either have to remain lying, and I do not care to do that, or I should have to get up again, and I do not care to do that either. *Summa summarum:* I do not care at all.

SØREN KIERKEGAARD,
Either/Or, Vol. I

Care is no cure, but rather corrosive,
For things that are not to be remedied.

SHAKESPEARE,
Henry VI, Part 1, Act III, Scene 3

What is done for those whom one cares about becomes a matter of one's personal pleasure, hard to express, perhaps, but surely, deeply felt.

BARRETT WENDELL,
Barrett Wendell and His Letters
by M. A. DeWolfe Howe

Christianity has taught us to care. Caring is the greatest thing—caring matters most. My faith is not enough—it comes and goes. I have it about some things and not about others. So we make up and supplement each other. We give and others give to us.

BARON FRIEDRICH VON HÜGEL,
Letters from Baron
Friedrich Von Hügel to a Niece

Each of us is a being in himself and a being in society, each of us needs to understand himself and understand others, take care of others and be taken care of himself.

HANIEL LONG,
A Letter to St. Augustine

Many of our cares are but a morbid way of looking at our privileges.

SIR WALTER SCOTT

CAREER

Every calling is great when greatly pursued.

OLIVER WENDELL HOLMES, JR.,
The Mind and Faith of Justice Holmes,
edited by Max Lerner

A man with a career can have no time to waste upon his wife and friends; he has to devote it wholly to his enemies.

JOHN OLIVER HOBBES

It is the very wantonness of folly for a man to search out the frets and burdens of his calling and give his mind every day to a consideration of them. They belong to human life. They are inevitable. Brooding only gives them strength.

HENRY WARD BEECHER,
Eyes and Ears

Whenever it is in any way possible, every boy and girl should choose as his life work some occupation which he should like to do anyhow, even if he did not need the money.

WILLIAM LYON PHELPS,
Essays on Things

CARICATURE

All caricature need not be unkind; it may be tender, or even sublime. The distortion, the single emphasis, the extreme simplification may reveal a soul which rhetoric and self-love had hidden in a false rationality. The absurd is the naked truth, the pathetic appeal of sheer fact, attempting to come into existence, like a featherless chick peeping out of its eggshell.

GEORGE SANTAYANA,
Obiter Scripta

CASANOVA

A "self-made" man, if ever there was one, Casanova is not revered by those who worship self-help.

HAVELOCK ELLIS,
Selected Essays

A man of finer moral fibre could scarcely have loved so many women; a man of coarser fibre could never have left so many women happy.

HAVELOCK ELLIS,
Selected Essays

CAT

Cruel, but composed and bland,
  Dumb, inscrutable and grand,
So Tiberius might have sat
  Had Tiberius been a cat.

MATTHEW ARNOLD,
"Atossa," *Poems One Line and Longer,*
edited by William Cole

It is easy to understand why the rabble dislike cats. A cat is beautiful; it suggests ideas of luxury, cleanliness, voluptuous pleasures ... etc.

CHARLES BAUDELAIRE,
Intimate Journals

Drowsing, they take the noble attitude
Of a great sphinx, who, in a desert land,
Sleeps always, dreaming dreams that
  have no end.

CHARLES BAUDELAIRE,
The Cat, compiled by Agnes Repplier

A cat can be trusted to purr when she is pleased, which is more than can be said for human beings.

WILLIAM RALPH INGE,
Rustic Moralist

No man has ever dared to manifest his boredom so insolently as does a Siamese tomcat, when he yawns in the face of his amorously importunate wife. No man has ever dared to proclaim his illicit amours so frankly as this same tom caterwauling on the tiles.

ALDOUS HUXLEY,
Collected Essays

I saw the most beautiful cat today. It was sitting by the side of the road, its two front feet neatly and graciously together. Then it gravely swished around its tail to completely and snugly encircle itself. It was so *fit* and beautifully neat, that gesture, and so self-satisfied—so complacent.

ANNE MORROW LINDBERGH,
Bring Me a Unicorn

You remember my ideal cat has always a huge rat in its mouth, just going out of sight—though going out of sight in itself has a peculiar pleasure.

EMILY DICKINSON,
*Selected Poems and Letters of
Emily Dickinson*

We tie bright ribbons around their necks, and occasionally little tinkling bells, and we affect to think that they are as sweet and vapid as the coy name "kitty" by which we call them would imply. It is a curious illusion. For, purring beside our fireplaces and pattering along our back fences, we have got a wild beast as uncowed and uncorrupted as any under heaven.

ALAN DEVOE,
Plain and Fancy Cats, edited
by John Beecroft

The things which a man gives him are not so precious or essential that he will trade them for his birth-right, which is the right to be himself—a furred four-footed being of ancient lineage, loving silence and a-loneness and the night, and esteeming the smell of rat's blood above any possible human excellence.

ALAN DEVOE,
Plain and Fancy Cats,
edited by John Beecroft

Who can tell what just criticisms Murr the cat may be passing on us beings of wider speculation?

GEORGE ELIOT,
Middlemarch

Silently licking his gold-white paw,
Oh gorgeous Celestino, for
God made lovely things, yet
Our lovely cat surpasses them all;
The gold, the iron, the waterfall,
The nut, the peach, apple, granite
Are lovely things to look at, yet,
Our lovely cat surpasses them all.

JOHN GITTINGS,
age 8, England, "A Cat," *Miracles: Poems by Children of the English-speaking World,*
collected by Richard Lewis

No favor can win gratitude from a cat.

LA FONTAINE,
quoted in *The Cat,*
compiled by Agnes Repplier

God made the cat in order that man might have the pleasure of caressing the tiger.

FERNAND MÉRY,
Her Majesty the Cat

Are cats lazy? Well, more power to them if they are. Which one of us has not entertained the dream of doing just as he likes, when and how he likes, and as much as he likes?

FERNAND MÉRY,
Her Majesty the Cat

I can rarely remember having passed a cat in the street without stopping to speak to it.

BRUCE MARSHALL,
Thoughts of My Cats

Cats are admirable company. I am very fond of dogs, too; but their sphere is the field. In the house they do not understand that repose of manner which is the soul of breeding. The cat's manners or rather manner seems to have been perfected by generations, nay centuries, of familiar intercourse with the great and cultivated of the earth.

ALGERNON S. LOGAN,
Vistas from the Stream, Vol. II

You loved me when the fire was warm,
But, now I stretch a fondling arm,
You eye me and depart.
Cold eyes, sleek skin, and velvet paws,
You win my indolent applause,
You do not win my heart.

A. C. BENSON,
The Cat, compiled by Agnes Repplier

A cat cares for you only as a source of food, security and a place in the sun. Her high self-sufficiency is her charm.

CHARLES HORTON COOLEY,
Life and the Student

I will admit to feeling exceedingly proud when any cat has singled me out for notice; for, of course, every cat is really the most beautiful woman in the room. That is part of their deadly fascination.

E. V. LUCAS,
365 Days and One More

People with insufficient personalities are fond of cats. These people adore being ignored.

HENRY MORGAN,
quoted in *The Cat-Hater's Handbook*
by William Cole

Cats have a curious effect on people. They seem to excite more extreme sentiments than any other animals. There are people who cannot remain in the room with a cat—who feel instinctively the presence of a cat even though they do not actually see it. On the other hand, there are people who, whatever they may be doing, will at once get up and fondle a cat immediately they see it.

ARTHUR PONSONBY,
Casual Observations

God save all here, barrin' the cat.
OLD IRISH SALUTATION

The vanity of man revolts from the serene indifference of the cat.
AGNES REPPLIER,
Americans and Others

All cats and kittens, whether royal Persians or of the lowliest estate, resent patronage, jocoseness (which they rightly hold to be in bad taste), and demonstrative affection—those lavish embraces which lack delicacy and reserve.
AGNES REPPLIER,
Americans and Others

Cats make exquisite photographs. . . . They don't keep bouncing at you to be kissed just as you get the lens adjusted.
GLADYS TABER,
Ladies' Home Journal, October 1941

Now a cat will not take an excursion merely because a man wants a walking companion. Walking is a human habit into which dogs readily fall but it is a distasteful form of exercise to a cat unless he has a purpose in view.
CARL VAN VECHTEN,
Plain and Fancy Cats,
edited by John Beecroft

If a dog jumps up into your lap, it is because he is fond of you; but if a cat does the same thing, it is because your lap is warmer.
ALFRED NORTH WHITEHEAD,
Dialogues of Alfred North Whitehead

A cat licking herself solves most of the problems of infection. We wash too much and finally it kills us.
WILLIAM CARLOS WILLIAMS,
Selected Essays

I have just been given a very engaging Persian kitten, named after St. Philip Neri (who was very sound on cats) and his opinion is that *I* have been given to *him.*
EVELYN UNDERHILL,
The Letters of Evelyn Underhill

I shall never forget the indulgence with which Dr. Johnson treated Hodge, his cat, for whom he himself used to go out and buy oysters, lest the servants, having that trouble, should take a dislike to the poor creature.
JAMES BOSWELL,
The Cat, compiled by Agnes Repplier

The great charm of cats is their rampant egotism, their devil-may-care attitude toward responsibility, their disinclination to earn an honest dollar. In a continent which screams neurotically about cooperation and the Golden Rule, cats are disdainful of everything but their own immediate interests and they contrive to be so suave and delightful about it that they even receive the apotheosis of a National Week.
ROBERTSON DAVIES,
The Table Talk of Samuel Marchbanks

All cats are possessed of a proud spirit, and the surest way to forfeit the esteem of a cat is to treat him as an inferior being.
MICHAEL JOSEPH,
quoted in Ladies' Home Journal,
April 1947

Bathsheba! to whom none ever said scat—
No worthier cat
Ever sat on a mat,
Or caught a rat.
Requiescat!
JOHN GREENLEAF WHITTIER,
"For a Little Girl Mourning
Her Favorite Cat,"
Poems One Line and Longer,
edited by William Cole

CATASTROPHE (*See* CALAMITY)

CATHOLICISM

Oh, why has the Church failed, but because it talks of sin and not of love?
LIONEL JOHNSON,
Some Winchester Letters of Lionel Johnson

The Church is a holy thing: full of error and whitewash, and dead men's bones, and potential love!
LIONEL JOHNSON,
Some Winchester Letters of Lionel Johnson

As long as Catholicism lasts, it will feel the need for reform, for a more perfect assimilation of its actuality to the ideal which illumines its path.

KARL ADAM,
The Spirit of Catholicism

All the formulas, all the precautions of orthodoxy, all the scruples of literal conformity, all barriers, in a word, are powerless to safeguard the purity of the faith. If the spirit should be lacking, dogma becomes no more than a myth and the Church no more than a party.

HENRI DE LUBAC,
Paradoxes

For all in common she prays, for all in common she works, in the temptations of all she is tried.

SAINT AMBROSE,
Select Works and Letters

If you say that the history of the Church is a long succession of scandals, you are telling the truth, though if that is all you say, you are distorting the truth.

GERALD VANN,
The Heart of Man

All roads still lead to Rome and unless you place yourself there you will never be in the heart of the world or see it in the right perspective. To be a Protestant is to be cross-eyed.

GEORGE SANTAYANA,
The Letters of George Santayana

Christ lives on in the Church, but Christ crucified. One might almost venture to say that the defects of the Church are His Cross.

ROMANO GUARDINI,
The Church and the Catholic

Catholicism, which is as genuinely human as Christ Himself is human, is the religion for all those who know that the springs of mirth and holy laughter lie deeper than the sources of the world's tears.

CORNELIUS CLIFFORD,
Introibo

And the counterpart to the *grand tragic*

irony (Dante) of which I speak is the *grand humanist gaiety* and ribaldry—coarse, if you please, almost to the point of obscenity, but essentially wholesome—of the Catholic middle ages (Chaucer). How puny, how miserably puny and anaemic, modern Catholicism, at least in our expression and realization of it, is in danger of becoming, has become!

RUSSELL WILBUR,
Essays and Verses

Catholicism is successful in producing rather a fine type of woman, but it is not so happy with the men. The men have a need to shake off something which the Church hangs on them, and unless they do, they are ineffective as thinkers.

ALFRED NORTH WHITEHEAD,
Dialogues of Alfred North Whitehead

True Catholicity is commensurate with the wants of the human mind; but persons are often to be found who are surprised that they cannot persuade all men to follow them, and cannot destroy dissent, by preaching a portion of the Divine system, instead of the whole of it.

JOHN HENRY CARDINAL NEWMAN,
Oxford University Sermons

I have felt for a long time—in fact ever since I knew and loved Christ, and I still feel—that the Church is the total Revolution.

JULES-GÉRARD CARDINAL SALIÈGE,
Who Shall Bear the Flame?

CAUSE

By nature, and apart from some cause to which we are loyal, each of us is but a mass of caprices, a chaos of distracting passions, a longing for happiness that is never fulfilled, a seeking for success which never attains its goal.

JOSIAH ROYCE,
*William James and
Other Essays on the Philosophy of Life*

Willing endurance of suffering and grief is the price that you have to pay for conscious fidelity to any cause that is vast enough to be worthy of the loyalty of a lifetime.

JOSIAH ROYCE,
*William James and
Other Essays on the Philosophy of Life*

A bad cause requires many words.

GERMAN PROVERB

The whole method of judging a cause by the actions and words of the worst type of person you can find among its supporters is too cheap—I believe I've done it sometimes in politics, but I vow I won't any more—it's tempting because it's so easy.

C. E. MONTAGUE,
C. E. Montague: A Memoir by Oliver Elton

We are all ready to be savage in *some* cause. The difference between a good man and a bad one is the choice of the cause.

WILLIAM JAMES,
The Letters of William James, Vol. II

The man who does not go down to underlying causes will never get at the heart of evil.

HENRI DE LUBAC,
Paradoxes

There is something strange in the modern mind, by which a material cause always seems more like a real cause.

G. K. CHESTERTON,
All I Survey

The causes I am inclined to think are there all along, and the events which we see, and which look like freaks of chance, are only the last steps in long lines of causation.

ALFRED NORTH WHITEHEAD,
Dialogues of Alfred North Whitehead

CAUTION

Of all forms of caution, caution in love is perhaps the most fatal to true happiness.

BERTRAND RUSSELL,
The Conquest of Happiness

The whole world is burdened with young fogies. Old men with ossified minds are easily dealt with. But men who look young, act young, and everlastingly harp on the fact that they are young, but who nevertheless think and act with a degree of caution that would be excessive in their grandfathers, are the curses of the world.

ROBERTSON DAVIES,
The Table Talk of Samuel Marchbanks

There are those who are so scrupulously afraid of doing wrong that they seldom venture to do anything.

VAUVENARGUES

CENSORSHIP

To suppress the freedom of the arts is not only to cut off knowledge of the actual movements of human feeling but also, and more disastrously, contact with the realities of life. For those contacts can be renewed only by the continually new intuition of the artist.

JOYCE CARY,
Art and Reality

I never heard of anyone who was really literate or who ever really loved books who wanted to suppress any of them. Censors only read a book with great difficulty, moving their lips as they puzzle out each syllable, when somebody tells them that the book is unfit to read.

ROBERTSON DAVIES,
The Table Talk of Samuel Marchbanks

With the abolition of censorship, anything goes now. As a result we get the worst, artistically speaking, in all the media. That's the sad part of it. But the situation won't last forever.

HENRY MILLER,
Supertalk by Digby Diehl

The censor-moron does not really hate anything but the living and growing human consciousness.

D. H. LAWRENCE,
Selected Letters of D. H. Lawrence

Boston, having found Dreiser's book obscene, must be fairly full of corrupt minds. The book was published quite a time ago, and obscene literature is known to corrupt the mind. Although we sympathize with Boston in her hour of corruption, it is our opinion that the defense in the trial should have demanded that the prosecution produce at least one case of a corrupted mind as evidence. We'd like to have heard the prosecuting attorney, examining the witness: "Now, Mr. Gwimby, you say you were in Boston on the afternoon of Tuesday the twenty-sixth. In what condition was your mind?"

E. B. WHITE,
Every Day Is Saturday

Censors are necessary, increasingly necessary, if America is to avoid having a vital literature.

DON MARQUIS,
A Book of Prefaces

In some respects the life of a censor is more exhilarating than that of an emperor. The best the emperor can do is to snip off the heads of men and women, who are mere mortals. The censor can decapitate ideas which but for him might have lived forever.

HEYWOOD BROUN,
Pieces of Hate

Where there is official censorship it is a sign that speech is serious. Where there is none, it is pretty certain that the official spokesmen have all the loud-speakers.

PAUL GOODMAN,
Growing Up Absurd

In American society we have perfected a remarkable form of censorship: to allow everyone to have his political right to say what he believes, but to swamp his little boat with literally thousands of millions of newspapers, mass-circulation magazines, best-selling books, broadcasts and public pronouncements that disregard what he says and give the official way of looking at things. Usually there is no conspiracy to do this; it is simply that what he says is not what people are talking about, it is not newsworthy.

PAUL GOODMAN,
Growing Up Absurd

CEREMONY

All our ceremonies, our observances are for the weak who are cowards before the bare thrust of feeling. How we have hung the impertinent panoply of our funeral arrangements over the bleak tragedy of death! And joy too. What are our weddings, from the religious pomp to the irrelevant presents and the confetti, but presumptuous distractions from the proud mating of urgent love?

RUTH BENEDICT,
An Anthropologist at Work
by Margaret Mead

When I think of Etiquette and Funerals, when I consider the euphemisms and rites and conventions and various costumes with which we invest the acts of our animal existence; when I bear in mind how elegantly we eat our victuals, and remember the series of ablutions and preparations and salutations and exclamations and manipulations I went through when I dined out last evening, I reflect what creatures we are of ceremony; how elaborate, how pompous and polite a simian Species.

LOGAN PEARSALL SMITH,
More Trivia

CERTAINTY

Certainty is a good even when it confirms a fear. When it relieves one it is trebly welcome.

OSCAR W. FIRKINS,
Oscar Firkins: Memoirs and Letters,
edited by Ina Ten Eyck

The demand for certainty is a sign of weakness, and if we persist in it, induces paralysis. The successful man is he who when he sees that no further certainty is attainable, promptly decides on the most probable side, as if he were completely sure it was right.

MARK RUTHERFORD,
"Principles," *The Deliverance of Mark Rutherford*

Certitude is not the test of certainty. We

have been cock-sure of many things that were not so.

OLIVER WENDELL HOLMES, JR.,
The Mind and Faith of Justice Holmes,
edited by Max Lerner

Love of certainty is a demand for guarantees in advance of action.

JOHN DEWEY,
Human Nature and Conduct

I have lived in this world just long enough to look carefully the second time into things that I am most certain of the first time.

JOSH BILLINGS,
His Works Complete

CHANGE

Our being is continually undergoing and entering upon changes that are perhaps of no less intensity than the new ... that death brings with it. And just as at a certain point in that most striking of changes we must leave each other altogether, so we must, strictly speaking, at every moment give each other up and let each other go and not hold each other back.

RAINER MARIA RILKE,
Letters of Rainer Maria Rilke 1892–1910

Any change, even a change for the better, is always accompanied by drawbacks and discomforts.

ARNOLD BENNETT,
The Arnold Bennet Calendar,
compiled by Frank Bennett

Change *not the mass* but change the fabric of your own soul and your own visions, and you change all.

VACHEL LINDSAY,
quoted in *The Unadjusted Man*
by Peter Viereck

I have examined myself thoroughly and come to the conclusion that I don't need to change much.

SIGMUND FREUD,
The Letters of Sigmund Freud

A person needs at intervals to separate himself from family and companions and go to new places. He must go without his familiars in order to be open to influences, to change.

KATHARINE BUTLER HATHAWAY,
*The Journals and Letters
of the Little Locksmith*

We are chameleons, and our partialities and prejudices change place with an easy and blessed facility, and we are soon wonted to the change and happy in it.

MARK TWAIN,
Mark Twain at Your Fingertips,
edited by Caroline T. Harnsberger

Our fathers valued change for the sake of its results; we value it in the act.

ALICE MEYNELL,
The Children

The voice of forest water in the night, a woman's laughter in the dark, the clean, hard rattle of raked gravel, the cricketing stitch of midday in hot meadows, the delicate web of children's voices in the bright air—these things will never change.

THOMAS WOLFE,
You Can't Go Home Again

There are people who not only strive to remain static themselves, but strive to keep everything else so, and weep like Heraclitus to find that nothing ever stands still to be studied, understood, and described. Their grievance against the world is that it insists upon changing at every moment and destroying all their categories. Who that has lived at all has not sympathized with them at one time or another? And yet their position is almost laughably hopeless.

ODELL SHEPARD,
The Joys of Forgetting

The hardest thing for me is the sense of impermanence. All passes; nothing returns.

ELLEN GLASGOW,
Letters of Ellen Glasgow

Curious how our philosophies and emotional attitudes change! Every once in a while someone speaks to me about "mellowing" and I never know whether this is a compliment or an insult.

DR. KARL MENNINGER,
A Psychiatrist's World

Our days are a kaleidoscope. Every instant a change takes place in the contents. New harmonies, new contrasts, new combinations of every sort. Nothing ever happens twice alike. The most familiar people stand each moment in some new relation to each other, to their work, to surrounding objects. The most tranquil house, with the most serene inhabitants, living upon the utmost regularity of system, is yet exemplifying infinite diversities.

HENRY WARD BEECHER,
Eyes and Ears

New and stirrring things are belittled, because if they are not belittled the humiliating question arises, "Why then are you not taking part in them?"

H. G. WELLS,
The World of William Chissold

None of us knows what the next change is going to be, what unexpected opportunity is just around the corner, waiting a few months or a few years to change all the tenor of our lives.

KATHLEEN NORRIS,
Hands Full of Living

Just when I think I have learned the way to live, life changes and I am left the same. The more things change the more I am the same. ... I am what I started with, and when it is all over I will be all that is left of me.

HUGH PRATHER,
Notes to Myself

In all change, well looked into, the germinal good out-vails the apparent ill.

FRANCIS THOMPSON,
Works, Vol. III

We live in a moment of history where change is so speeded up that we begin to see the present only when it is already disappearing.

R. D. LAING,
The Politics of Experience

Alter your manner of life ten times if you wish.

LLEWELYN POWYS,
Book of Days

It may be mere sentimentalism, but there are some of us who can never see an old way of doing things passing without regret. It is as though we should like to see change permitted only in unimportant things, like sanitation and politics.

ROBERT LYND,
The Blue Lion

If one is going to change things, one has to make a fuss and catch the eye of the world.

ELIZABETH JANEWAY,
Open Secrets by Barbaralee Diamonstein

It is precisely in those elements of society which seem most fundamental and free from change, like work and property, that a great deal of transformation, growth and new relations are not only possible, but are real and accomplished facts. ... We must therefore take account of this changeable nature of things and of human institutions, and prepare for them with enlightened foresight and in complete resignation.

POPE PIUS XI,
quoted in *The Christian in a Changing World*
by Joseph Fitzsimmons

We all know how Adam said to Eve: "My dear, we live in a period of transition."

VIDA D. SCUDDER,
The Privilege of Age

It is only in romances that people undergo a sudden metamorphosis. In real life, even after the most terrible experiences, the main character remains exactly the same.

ISADORA DUNCAN,
My Life

Very often a change of self is needed more than a change of scene.

A. C. BENSON,
*Excerpts from the Letters of
Dr. A. C. Benson to M. E. A.*

Readjusting is a painful process, but most of us need it at one time or another.

A. C. BENSON,
Excerpts from the Letters of
Dr. A. C. Benson to M. E. A.

The physical as a symbol of the spiritual world. The people who keep old rags, old useless objects, who hoard, accumulate: are they also hoarders and keepers of old ideas, useless information, lovers of the past only, even in its form of detritus? I have the opposite obsession. In order to change skins, evolve into new cycles, I feel one has to learn to discard. If one changes internally, one should not continue to live with the same objects. They reflect one's mind and psyche of yesterday. I throw away what has no dynamic, living use.

ANAÏS NIN,
The Diaries of Anaïs Nin, Vol. IV

When people shake their heads because we are living in a restless age, ask them how they would like to live in a stationary one and do without change.

GEORGE BERNARD SHAW,
The Intelligent Woman's
Guide to Socialism and Capitalism

Actual social change is never so great as is apparent change. Ways of belief, of expectation, of judgment and attendant emotional dispositions of like and dislike, are not easily modified after they have once taken place. Political and legal institutions may be altered, even abolished; but the bulk of popular thought which has been shaped to their pattern persists.

JOHN DEWEY,
Human Nature and Conduct

Since changes are going on any way, the great thing is to learn enough about them so that we will be able to lay hold of them and turn them in the direction of our desires. Conditions and events are neither to be fled from nor passively acquiesced in; they are to be utilized and directed.

JOHN DEWEY,
Reconstruction in Philosophy

If you want to make enemies, try to change something. You know why it is: to do things today exactly the way you did them yesterday saves thinking.

WOODROW WILSON,
Woodrow Wilson Selections for Today,
edited by Arthur Bernon Tourtellot

Men are not so weak as you think. ... They can always leave anybody or any place without a pang—if they find another person or another place they like better. If they feel pricks and scruples it is merely because they cannot make up their mind that the change will be absolutely to their advantage.

JOHN OLIVER HOBBES,
The Herb-Moon

To change and to improve are two different things.

GERMAN PROVERB

The healthy being craves an occasional wildness, a jolt from normality, a sharpening of the edge of appetite, his own little festival of the Saturnalia, a brief excursion from his way of life.

ROBERT MacIVER,
Man Alone, edited by Eric Josephson
and Mary Josephson

CHAOS

Punctual, commonplace, keeping all appointments, as I go my round in the obvious world, a bit of Chaos and old Night seems to linger on inside me; a dark bewilderment of mind, a nebulous sea of speculation, a looming of shadowy universes out of nothing, and their collapse, as in a dream.

LOGAN PEARSALL SMITH,
More Trivia

CHARACTER

A man's character never changes radically from youth to old age. What happens is that circumstances bring out characteristics which had not been obvious to the superficial observer.

HESKETH PEARSON,
Dickens

There are people who are good because nothing evil occurs to them, and others who are good because they conquer their evil thoughts. I had reckoned you to the former class. No doubt it is my fault that you have lost your guilelessness. It doesn't matter greatly; whoever has much contact with life must lose it, and in place of it build up a character.

SIGMUND FREUD,
quoted in *The Life and Work of Sigmund Freud,* Vol. I, by Ernest Jones

I do not judge men by anything they can do. Their greatest deed is the impression they make on me. Some serene, inactive men can do everything. Talent only indicates a depth of character in some direction.

HENRY DAVID THOREAU,
Journal

I forgot that every little action of the common day makes or unmakes character, and that therefore what one has done in the secret chamber one has some day to cry aloud on the house-tops.

OSCAR WILDE,
De Profundis

Character is not only a compound of extremely various qualities, but the qualities themselves vary from year to year, even from hour to hour. The Spaniard will wisely say of a man, "He was brave *that* day." We are all at war with ourselves; if an "individual" meant one literally "undivided," no such creature would exist.

F. L. LUCAS,
Style

I begin to find that too good a character is inconvenient.

SIR WALTER SCOTT,
Sir Walter Scott's Journal (1825-1832)

If you hear that a mountain has moved, believe; but if you hear that a man has changed his character, believe it not.

MOHAMMEDAN PROVERB

The Saints see men through the golden haze of their own goodness; and too nice a discrimination of the characters of others is a sign that you are not too nice a character yourself.

LOGAN PEARSALL SMITH,
Afterthoughts

Only this much is certain,—all men and all nations have a character, and that character, when once taken, is, I do not say unchangeable . . . but the least changeable thing in this ever-varying and changeful world.

WALTER BAGEHOT,
Literary Studies, Vol. III

Some people strengthen the society just by being the kind of people they are.

JOHN W. GARDNER,
No Easy Victories,
edited by Helen Rowan

I have often thought that the best way to define a man's character would be to seek out the particular mental or moral attitude in which, when it came upon him, he felt himself most deeply and intensely active and alive. At such moments there is a voice inside which speaks and says: *"This is the real me!"*

WILLIAM JAMES

We have refused to acknowledge that the disintegration of character is the beginning, not the end, of defeat, or that this weakening moral fibre is first revealed in the quick or slow decline of human relationships, and in the abrupt conversion to a triumphant materialism.

ELLEN GLASGOW,
A Certain Measure

If a man has character, he also has his typical experience, which always recurs.

FRIEDRICH NIETZSCHE,
Beyond Good and Evil

When a man thinks he is reading the character of another, he is often unconsciously betraying his own; and this is especially the case with those persons whose knowledge of the world is of such sort that it results in extreme distrust of men.

JOSEPH FARRELL,
Lectures of a Certain Professor

The most fugitive word or deed, the mere air of doing a thing, the intimated purpose, expresses character, and the remote results of character are civil history and events that shake or settle the world. If you act, you show character; if you sit still, you show it; if you sleep.

RALPH WALDO EMERSON,
Journals of Ralph Waldo Emerson

With a character both proud and timid, one never amounts to anything.

JOSEPH ROUX,
Meditations of a Parish Priest

CHARITY

Charity should link us together by the very thing which divides or distinguishes us.

ANTONIN G. SERTILLANGES,
Rectitude

Charity that is always beginning at home stays there.

AUSTIN O'MALLEY,
Keystones of Thought

CHARM

It seems to me that great personal charm only belongs to people who are self-contained or when they are so. They only can say and do the *spontaneous* and the *unsuspected*.

J. B. YEATS,
Letters to His Son, W. B. Yeats and Others

Every charming thing gains in a measure from a background of barrenness.

ROBERT LYND,
Solomon in All His Glory

You know what charm is: a way of getting the answer yes without having asked any clear question.

ALBERT CAMUS,
The Fall

If a person has charm he never loses it; and charm never fatigues. The words and acts of a person with charm are constant

delights. Old age does not change one in this respect.

ANDRÉ MAUROIS,
The Art of Living

It is always good to know, if only in passing, charming human beings. It refreshes one like flowers, and woods, and clear brooks.

GEORGE ELIOT

CHAUVINISM

The unattractive thing about chauvinism is not so much the aversion to other nations, but the love of one's own.

KARL KRAUS,
Karl Kraus by Harry Zohn

CHEERFULNESS

Early morning cheerfulness can be extremely obnoxious.

WILLIAM FEATHER,
The Business of Life

My poor Goody, depending on cheerful looks of *mine* for thy cheerfulness. How I love thee, it is not probable that thou or any mortal will know. But cheerful looks, when the heart feels slowly dying in floods of confusion and obstruction, are not the things I have to give.

THOMAS CARLYLE,
to his wife, quoted in
The Literature of Gossip by Elizabeth Drew

If you do not drive in sleet to the woods, singing, you have to drive crying.

CZECH PROVERB

Thank heaven for what happiness you have, and after thinking a moment or two that you suffer in common with all mankind hold it not a sin to regain your cheerfulness.

JOHN KEATS,
The Selected Letters of John Keats

CHESS

It is impossible to win gracefully at chess.

No man has yet said "Mate!" in a voice which failed to sound to his opponent bitter, boastful and malicious.

A. A. MILNE,
Not That It Matters

When you play a game of chess, it is like designing something or constructing some mechanism of some kind by which you win or lose. The competitive side of it has no importance. The thing itself is very, very plastic. That is probably what attracted me to the game.

MARCEL DUCHAMP,
Wisdom, edited by James Nelson

It is a game too troublesome for some men's braines, too testy full of anxiety, all out as bad as study; besides, it is a cholericke game, and very offensive to him that looseth the Mate. *William* the Conquerour in his younger years, playing at chesse with the Prince of France, . . . losing a Mate, knocked the Chessboard about his pate, which was a cause afterward of much enmity between them.

ROBERT BURTON,
The Anatomy of Melancholy

CHILDHOOD

Indeed, now that I come to think of it, I never really feel grown-up at all. Perhaps this is because childhood, catching our imagination when it is fresh and tender, never lets go of us.

J. B. PRIESTLEY,
All About Ourselves and Other Essays

Before one went to school, almost every new human being one met seemed a stimulant; that is to say, if they took any notice of the small.

MAURICE BARING,
Lost Lectures

The barb in the arrow of childhood's suffering is this—its intense loneliness, its intense ignorance.

OLIVE SCHREINER,
The Story of an African Farm

Childhood is the world of miracle and wonder: as if creation rose, bathed in light, out of the darkness, utterly new and fresh and astonishing. The end of childhood is when things cease to astonish us. When the world seems familiar, when one has got used to existence, one has become an adult.

EUGÈNE IONESCO,
Fragments of a Journal

To children childhood holds no particular advantage.

KATHLEEN NORRIS,
Hands Full of Living

In those days we had the savage's happy faculty of creating an object of worship out of almost any chance stick or stone. . . . Our toys were almost idols. There was a glamour upon them such as we do not find in the more splendid possessions of our later years, as though a special light fell on them through some window of our hearts that is now blocked up forever.

ODELL SHEPARD,
The Joys of Forgetting

One can love a child, perhaps, more deeply than one can love another adult, but it is rash to assume that the child feels any love in return. Looking back on my own childhood . . . I do not believe that I ever felt love for any mature person, except my mother, and even her I did not trust, in the sense that shyness made me conceal most of my real feelings from her. Love, the spontaneous, unqualified emotion of love was something I could only feel for people who were young.

GEORGE ORWELL,
A Collection of Essays

Not to expose your true feelings to an adult seems to be instinctive from the age of seven or eight onwards.

GEORGE ORWELL,
A Collection of Essays

The child thinks of growing old as an almost obscene calamity, which for some mysterious reason will never happen to itself. All who have passed the age of thirty are joyless grotesques, endlessly fussing about things of no importance and staying alive without, so far as the child can see, having anything to live for. Only child life is real life.

GEORGE ORWELL,
A Collection of Essays

The pleasures of childhood should in the main be such as the child extracts from his environment by means of some effort and inventiveness.

BERTRAND RUSSELL,
The Conquest of Happiness

When I look back on the friendships of childhood they do not seem to differ in either quality or intensity from those of grown-up years. ... We loved the flowers and the hills. We loved the sunsets and the birds and the beasts. We loved one another. And will anyone tell me that we did not love those things as much as we have learned to love them since?

ERIC GILL,
Autobiography

I believe there are few whose whole view of life has not been affected by the stern or kindly influences of their early childhood, which threw them in upon themselves in timidity and reserve, or drew them out in genial confidence and sympathy with their fellow creatures.

BASIL W. MATURIN,
Laws of the Spiritual Life

Child desires are eternal and seldom yield to the lapse of time.

DR. WILHELM STEKHEL,
Marriage at the Crossroads

Have you ever felt like nobody?
Just a tiny speck of air.
When everyone's around you,
And you are just not there.

KAREN CRAWFORD,
age 9, United States
Miracles: Poems by Children of the English-speaking World, collected by Richard Lewis

Grown ups are no fun. They never have time to do things with you. ... If I could change grown ups I would make them do nothing but play with you. But everyone knows that you can't do that.

ANONYMOUS FIFTH GRADER,
"I Am a Lone Boy,"
compiled by Edward F. Murphy,
New York Times, December 5, 1965

I like and don't like people cause the grownups are mean as a mean fearce dog. In a sort of a way grownups don't understand you. You want a sertain dress, and if your parents don't like it you don't get it. It's the same thing with everything.

ANONYMOUS FIFTH GRADER,
"I Am a Lone Boy,"
compiled by Edward F. Murphy,
New York Times, December 5, 1965

I am stupit in the class and I will be a good angel and I will listen to the teacher. I am a lone boy.

ANONYMOUS FIFTH GRADER,
"I Am a Lone Boy,"
compiled by Edward F. Murphy,
New York Times, December 5, 1965

The adult on the verge of death may be permitted a return to childhood, as is the Japanese *kamikaze* flier who is given toys to play with.

MARGARET MEAD,
Childhood in Contemporary Cultures, edited by Margaret Mead and Martha Wolfenstein

Where the child in British films easily finds among the adults around him someone to idolize and it then behooves the adult to deserve this trust, the child in American films longs for an ideal man to appear from afar.... A stranger must come from afar, the child must journey away from home, or visions of a remote past must be conjured up to provide the missing hero.

MARTHA WOLFENSTEIN,
Childhood in Contemporary Cultures, edited by Margaret Mead and Martha Wolfenstein

The illusions of childhood are necessary experiences: a child should not be denied a balloon because an adult knows that sooner or later it will burst.

MARCELENE COX,
Ladies' Home Journal, September 1948

The little world of childhood with its familiar surroundings is a model of the greater world. The more intensively the family has shaped its character upon the child, the more it will tend to feel and see its earlier miniature world again in the bigger world of adult life.

C. G. JUNG,
Psychological Reflections,
edited by Jolande Jacobi and R. F. Hull

Two things are terrible in childhood: helplessness (being in other people's power) and apprehension—the apprehension that something is being concealed from us because it was too bad to be told.

ELIZABETH BOWEN,
Collected Impressions

There is in most men's minds a secret instinct of reverence and affection towards the days of their childhood. They cannot help sighing with regret and tenderness when they think of it.

SAINT AILRED OF RIEVAULX,
Christian Friendship

Childhood is only the beautiful and happy time in contemplation and retrospect: to the child it is full of deep sorrows, the meaning of which is unknown.

GEORGE ELIOT,
George Eliot's Family Life and Letters,
Vol. I, by Arthur Paterson

Grown people were always on the edge of telling you something valuable and then withdrawing it, a form of bully-teasing.

LILLIAN HELLMAN,
Pentimento

Childhood is less clear to me than to many people: when it ended I turned my face away from it for no reason that I know about, certainly without the usual reason of unhappy memories. For many years that worried me, but then I discovered that the tales of former children are seldom to be trusted. Some people supply too many past victories or pleasures with which to comfort themselves, and other people cling to pains, real and imagined, to excuse what they have become.

LILLIAN HELLMAN,
Pentimento

Children must eventually train their own children, and any impoverishment of their impulse life, for the sake of avoiding friction, must be considered a possible liability affecting more than one lifetime. Generations will depend on the ability of every procreating individual to face his children with the feeling that he was able to save some vital enthusiasm from the conflicts of his childhood.

ERIK H. ERIKSON,
Childhood and Society

And the portrait of my father is quite terrific. Of my mother I can only say that her physical beauty was far greater than that of the Richmond portrait in the book. But my life as a child and a girl was a squalid *hell:* it was no question of "misunderstanding" or severity or anything of that kind. There was something very seriously wrong, and I bore the whole brunt.

EDITH SITWELL,
Edith Sitwell: Selected Letters 1916–1964

Life is strangely suspicious and impatient of youth and candour and innocence and *naïvete.* Hardly does it perceive these exquisite qualities to exist than it rubs away their bloom with a rough finger. How often one longs for an arrested progress—for a little girl to go on being a little girl a little longer; for the perpetual kitten of our dreams! But no; the Creator is not that kind of artist.

E. V. LUCAS,
365 Days and One More

One of the unwritten laws of contemporary morality, the strictest and best respected of all requires adults to avoid any reference, above all any humorous reference, to sexual matters in the presence of children. This notion was entirely foreign to the society of old.

PHILIPPE ARIÈS,
Centuries of Childhood

CHILDREN

Viewing the child solely as an immature person is a way of escaping confronting him.

CLARK MOUSTAKAS,
Creativity and Conformity

One of the most obvious facts about grownups to a child, is that they have forgotten what it is like to be a child.

RANDALL JARRELL,
The Third Book of Criticism

If there is anything that we wish to change in the child, we should first examine it and see whether it is not something that could better be changed in ourselves.

C. G. JUNG,
Psychological Reflections,
edited by Jolande Jacobi and R. F. Hull

Whenever a child lies you will always find a severe parent. A lie would have no sense unless the truth were felt to be dangerous.

ALFRED ADLER,
quoted in the *New York Times,*
June 19, 1949

The finest inheritance you can give to a child is to allow it to make its own way, completely on its own feet.

ISADORA DUNCAN,
My Life

People murder a child when they tell it to keep out of the dirt. In dirt is life.

GEORGE WASHINGTON CARVER,
quoted in *Famous American Negroes*
by Langston Hughes

The healthy human child will keep
Away from home, except to sleep.
Were it not for the common cold,
Our young we never would behold.

OGDEN NASH,
You Can't Get There from Here

We call a child's mind "small" simply by habit; perhaps it is larger than ours, for it can take in almost anything without effort.

CHRISTOPHER MORLEY,
Mince Pie

It is ominous for the future of a child when the discipline he receives is based on the emotional needs of the disciplinarian rather than on any consideration of the child's own needs.

GORDON W. ALLPORT,
Prejudice in Modern Perspective

The only form of action open to a child is to break something or strike someone, its

mother or another child; it cannot cause things to happen in the world.

MARY MCCARTHY,
On the Contrary

The discontented child cries for toasted snow.

ARAB PROVERB

There is a theory that since the child will be obliged in later life to do many things that he does not want to do, he might as well learn how while he is young. The difficulty here seems to be that learning to do one kind of a thing that you do not want to do does not guarantee your readiness to do other kinds of unpleasant things. That art cannot be taught. Each situation of compulsion, unless the spirit is completely broken, will have its own peculiar quality of bitterness, and no guarantee against it can be inculcated.

RANDOLPH BOURNE,
Youth and Life

Punch had a picture of a very small child in the bedroom of his uncle at an early hour of the morning, asking: "Uncle John, what do you do when you feel too well?"

CECILY HALLACK,
The Bliss of the Way

In order not to influence a child, one must be careful not to be that child's parent or grandparent.

DON MARQUIS,
The Almost Perfect State

If a child shows himself incorrigible, he should be decently and quietly beheaded at the age of twelve, lest he grow to maturity, marry, and perpetuate his kind.

DON MARQUIS,
The Almost Perfect State

The parents exist to teach the child, but also they must learn what the child has to teach them; and the child has a very great deal to teach them.

ARNOLD BENNETT,
How to Make the Best of Life

There never was a child so lovely but his mother was glad to get him asleep.

RALPH WALDO EMERSON,
Journals of Ralph Waldo Emerson

Reasoning with a child is fine, if you can reach the child's reason without destroying your own.

JOHN MASON BROWN,
quoted in the *New York Times,*
June 19, 1955

Peter, who is a thoughtful child, wants everything clear right from the beginning. "Where did it all come from? All this? Who made it all?" And since his serious mind digests so carefully everything that he is given, it seems unforgiveable laziness to put him off with nonsense. So I took a deep breath and tried to make a version of Darwin for the Very Young. How serious and absurd parents must look from the outside.

NAN FAIRBROTHER,
An English Year

Time always seems long to the child who is waiting—for Christmas, for next summer, for becoming a grownup: long also when he surrenders his whole soul to each moment of a happy day.

DAG HAMMARSKJÖLD,
Markings

The scars left from the child's defeat in the fight against irrational authority are to be found at the bottom of every neurosis.

ERICH FROMM,
Man for Himself

The "good" child may be frightened, and insecure, wanting only to please his parents by submitting to their will, while the "bad" child may have a will of his own and genuine interests but ones which do not please the parents.

ERICH FROMM,
Man for Himself

Every child senses, with all the horse sense that's in him, that any parent is angry inside when children misbehave, and they dread more the anger that is rarely or never expressed openly, wondering how awful it might be.

DR. BENJAMIN SPOCK,
Ladies' Home Journal, April 1955

For a person in rugged health who is not particularly dressed up and does not want to write a letter or read the newspaper, we can imagine few diversions more enjoyable than to have a child turned loose upon him.

HEYWOOD BROUN,
Pieces of Hate

What a horrible thing that was, as a child, being conscious that we ought to admire people who were good, when all one cared about was whether they were kind.

A. C. BENSON,
*Excerpts from the Letters of
Dr. A. C. Benson to M. E. A.*

The disparity between the child's place in an inexorable routine of physical law and his place in the hearts of his parents is one of the things that impress me most painfully in life.

OSCAR W. FIRKINS,
Oscar Firkins: Memoirs and Letters,
edited by Ina Ten Eyck

I need not say that The Child is always discussed as if he were a monster of immense size, vast complexity, and strange and startling novelty.

G. K. CHESTERTON,
All I Survey

The real child does not confuse fact and fiction.... To him no two things could possibly be more totally contrary than playing at robbers and stealing sweets.

G. K. CHESTERTON,
Autobiography

His life, as the lives of others, is full of vain and tedious questionings. "Where have you been? Whom did you meet? What did they say? Are you back already?" The best answer is another question. "Why do you want to know?"

ROSE MACAULAY,
A Casual Commentary

A child has a way of extracting from each parent precisely those elements he most needs; and this usually comes about best in their special moments of solitary companionship; it is then that he has a chance to break into the special twoness of the parents.

LEWIS MUMFORD,
Green Memories

If ever there was a son who felt as deeply as I the heart-warming intimacy of filial affection, never was there a child more conscious of the barrier of years that separated me from my elders. And it is necessary to add, I had no desire to cross the barrier, for that over-ripe world had no attraction for me. The instinct of the child who rebels against touching his lips to a hairy or wrinkled cheek, and who wipes his own after being kissed, is for the most part healthy.

ROMAIN ROLLAND,
Journey Within

Innocence is the child, and forgetfulness, a new beginning, a game, a self-rolling wheel, a first movement, a holy Yea.

FRIEDRICH NIETZSCHE,
Thus Spake Zarathustra

A child enters your home and makes so much noise for twenty years that you can hardly stand it: then departs leaving the house so silent that you think you will go mad.

JOHN ANDREW HOLMES,
Wisdom in Small Doses

The purpose of the child is to live, to feel the mysterious presence of life in every limb, and in so far as he does this he is happy. But the purpose of the adult has become a febrile pursuit of the symbols of life. Real life fills him with dread and success in his endeavour is his undoing.

HOLBROOK JACKSON,
Southward Ho! and Other Essays

Never teach your child to be cunning for you may be certain that you will be one of the first victims of his shrewdness.

JOSH BILLINGS

I have seen infants who, at the age of only two months, had already developed real neuroses because of the way they had been handled by their mothers and fathers. The infants had absorbed their parents' anxieties like a blotter.

DR. SMILEY BLANTON,
Love or Perish

No one who has ever brought up a child can doubt for a moment that love is literally the life-giving fluid of human existence.

DR. SMILEY BLANTON,
Love or Perish

Curiosity about the vital details of life and birth stems from the deepest core of the child's mind, and is the source of all his later search for knowledge. Yet questions and actions designed to obtain information about these basic matters are precisely the ones that are likely to arouse the strongest adult antagonism.

DR. SMILEY BLANTON,
Love or Perish

When you are dealing with a child, keep all your wits about you, and sit on the floor.

AUSTIN O'MALLEY,
Keystones of Thought

To talk to a child, to fascinate him, is much more difficult than to win an electoral victory. But it is also more rewarding.

COLETTE,
Journey for Myself

A child may be a mass of egoism and rebelliousness, but it has not accumulated experience to give it confidence in its own judgments. On the whole it will accept what it is told, and it will believe in the most fantastic way in the knowledge and power of the adults surrounding it.

GEORGE ORWELL,
A Collection of Essays

A child's mind is unconsciously autonomous, its way of observation boldly individual, its expression eagerly original. "Lamps o' beauty, lamps o' beauty," I have heard a small child crooning to itself as it watched some blown daffodils swinging in the twilight. Another, on first noticing a mounting lark, said, "Look—two wings tied together and a little bit of stick, which is its beak!" That is how the undespoiled see and describe, the delighted perception rushing straight into live speech that cares for no canons and yet shirks no flight. But presently this wild gusto and grace are tabooed by the joint efforts of elder comrades and of the many second-rate minds to be found among teachers. ... He has been turned, for life, into a member of a set, a creature of dim vision and savourless speech and nervous conformities.

C. E. Montague,
The Right Place

A child which appears reasonably happy may actually be suffering horrors which it cannot or will not reveal. It lives in a sort of alien under-water world which we can only penetrate by memory or divination. Our chief clue is the fact that we were once children ourselves, and many people appear to forget the atmosphere of their own childhood almost entirely.

George Orwell,
A Collection of Essays

We speak indulgently of childish make-believe, childish fancy. Bret Harte was nearer the truth when he maintained that "the dominant expression of a child is gravity." The cold fact is that few of us have the energy to be serious at their pitch.

Walter de la Mare,
Pleasures and Speculations

We call their faith, even in ourselves, credulity; and are grown perhaps so accustomed to life's mysteries that we blanch at their candour. "I am afraid you cannot understand it, dear," exclaimed a long-suffering mother, at the end of her resources. "O yes, I can very well," was her little boy's reply, "if only you would not explain."

Walter de la Mare,
Pleasures and Speculations

I do not love him because he is good, but because he is my little child.

Rabindranath Tagore

Of all the things I dislike, there is nothing so abhorrent to me as a spoilt child. I have pinched several, and never had the slightest qualm of conscience afterwards; and though I am a man of peace, I hope to pinch many more before I die.

H. L. R. Sheppard,
Fiery Grains by H. L. R. Sheppard
and H. P. Marshall

The child is surrounded by so much authority, so much school, so mugh dignity, so much law, that it would have to break down under the weight of all these restraints if it were not saved from such a fate by meeting with a friend.

Dr. Wilhelm Stekhel,
The Depths of the Soul

There may be finer pleasures than that of a child who has stayed away from church or from school, but there was one child who would not have believed you if you had told him so.

Robert Lynd,
The Blue Lion

The child, if it were a philosopher, might say to us: "You laugh at me because I am so absorbed in make-believe, but you do not laugh at yourselves, though you are equally absorbed in make-believe. You, no more than I, have found the key to what is permanent, but live seriously in a world of playthings."

Robert Lynd,
The Peal of Bells

Sometimes when you meet your relatives you think you're a lollipop.

Paul Uhlir,
age 13, United States, *Journeys: Prose by
Children of the English-speaking World,*
collected by Richard Lewis

It has been said that to enter Heaven, a man must become as a little child; I am inclined to think that, lastingly to enjoy any Heaven yet invented, he must remain one.

F. L. Lucas,
The Greatest Problem and Other Essays

Smothering a child by anxious concern

over every detail of his life, robbing him of all opportunities to express himself naturally and to discover the world for himself, rebuking his early efforts to explore and direct his dawning sexuality, may be more crippling than beatings and curses.

DR. KARL MENNINGER,
A Psychiatrist's World

To cease to be loved is for the child practically synonymous with ceasing to live.

DR. KARL MENNINGER,
A Psychiatrist's World

The very calmness that grownups seem to bring with them into the fear-crowded darkness of a child's bedroom too often consists only in a hopeless insulation and imperviousness on their part, making them seem so superior and panic-proof that the child is driven to conceal from them all the really queer and terrible things he thinks and feels.

KATHARINE BUTLER HATHAWAY,
The Little Locksmith

The most turbulent, the most restless child, has, in the midst of all his faults, something true, ingenuous, and natural, which is of infinite value, and merits every respect.

FÉLIX A. DUPANLOUP,
The Child

Even the happiest child has moments when he wishes his parents were dead.

ALLAN FROMME,
New York Times, October 2, 1960

A great deal, of course, of that spiritual and perpetual joy that children bring to us is just this power of seeing the world as a new thing, as pure intuition, and so renewing for us the freshness of all life. But they always lose this power of original expression as soon as they begin their education.

JOYCE CARY,
Art and Reality

For children is there any happiness which is not also noise?

FREDERICK W. FABER,
Spiritual Conferences

It's a waste of time to read books on child psychology written by adults unless we are willing to check every page by what children know about the psychology of parents.

JOHN ERSKINE,
The Complete Life

The bringing up of children as a conspiracy on the part of adults: We lure them from their unconstrained rompings into our narrow dwellings by pretenses in which we perhaps believe, but not in the sense we pretend.

FRANZ KAFKA,
The Diaries of Franz Kafka 1914–1923

Parents who expect gratitude from their children (there are even some who insist on it) are like usurers who gladly risk their capital if only they receive interest.

FRANZ KAFKA,
The Diaries of Franz Kafka 1914–1923

There ought not to be any doubt that children should be fed on fairy-tales as their souls' most natural food.

HAVELOCK ELLIS,
Selected Essays

If there were no schools to take the children away from home part of the time, the insane asylums would be filled with mothers.

E. W. HOWE,
Country Town Sayings

It is difficult to give children a sense of security unless you have it yourself. If you have it, they catch it from you.

DR. WILLIAM C. MENNINGER,
Self-Understanding

Children are cunning enough behind their innocent faces, though prudent might be a kinder word to describe them.

NAN FAIRBROTHER,
An English Year

Here are the children all among us, and yet we often talk to one another, as if nobody under twenty had anything to do with the great things which are of such unspeakable importance after we have come of age.

PHILLIPS BROOKS,
Visions and Tasks

I do not believe that children should have to pay for the shortcomings and inequities of the society into which they are born. I do not think that children should have to pay for the real or supposed sins of their parents. And I think it would be short-sighted of a society to produce, by its neglect, a group of future citizens very likely to be unproductive and characterized by bitterness and alienation.

JOHN W. GARDNER,
No Easy Virtues, edited by Helen Rowan

Most of what we object to as misconduct in children is a natural rebellion against the intrusion of an unimaginative adult despotism in their lives.

FLOYD DELL,
Were You Ever a Child?

It is a grim old world, and I think one has need of children to keep one's faith clear and one's hope bright. One cannot think too evilly of a world in which one's sons and daughters are to live. For their sake one must try not only to make it better but to think it good.

OSCAR W. FIRKINS,
Oscar Firkins: Memoirs and Letters,
edited by Ina Ten Eyck

Children have an unerring instinct for knowing when they are being patronized. They go immediately on the defensive against head-patting adults who treat them like strange beings.

ART LINKLETTER,
Coronet, August 1955

Why does a boy or girl, when teasing someone, so often *sing* taunts and challenges and the like? Think of it, and you will recognize the fact. Is it a relic of savage usage? What is the instinct involved? The matter connects itself clearly with the strange fact that song and rhythm are among the earliest expressions of man.

GEORGE GISSING,
Commonplace Book

The hearts of small children are delicate organs. A cruel beginning in this world can twist them into curious shapes.

CARSON MCCULLERS,
The Member of the Wedding

I think the passion many people affect for children is merely a fashionable pose. I have a notion that children are all the better for not being burdened with too much parental love.

W. SOMERSET MAUGHAM,
The Gentleman in the Parlour

If children knew, oh, if they only knew their power! It is something absolutely glorious in its immensity. But they do not even see it dimly until it is gone forever.

ALINE KILMER,
Hunting a Hair Shirt

Children are not necessarily lovers of children. They do not gape at their own innocence, or marvel at imaginations as natural to them as spectacles on an elderly nose, or sit cherubically smiling at themselves amid their trailing clouds of glory. They dwell and flourish in their own natures, praeternaturally practical and crafty pygmies in the world of dull and tyrannical giants into which it has pleased God to call them.

WALTER DE LA MARE,
Pleasures and Speculations

They are contemplatives, solitaries, fakirs, who sink again and again out of the noise and fever of existence into a waking vision. We can approach them only by way of intuition and remembrance, only by becoming even as one of them.

WALTER DE LA MARE,
Pleasures and Speculations

I am serious about wishing I had children, beautiful children. I wouldn't care for the other variety.

TALLULAH BANKHEAD,
quoted in *Miss Tallulah Bankhead*
by Lee Israel

Children are born optimists, and we slowly educate them out of their heresy.

LOUISE IMOGEN GUINEY,
Goose-Quill Papers

Few, perhaps, are the children who, after the expiration of some months or years, would sincerely rejoice in the resurrection of their parents.

EDWARD GIBBON,
quoted in *A Peck of Trouble,*
collected by Daniel George

If your basic attitude is one of loving kindness, you may yell at children and even cuff them around a bit without doing any real harm.

DR. SMILEY BLANTON,
Love or Perish

When children sound silly, you will always find that it is in imitation of their elders.

ERNEST DIMNET,
What We Live By

It is quite obvious that children are more beautiful than adults. Out of any ten children, seven or eight are delightful; where as out of ten men . . .

FRANÇOISE MALLET-JORIS,
A Letter to Myself

The Home must go. . . . The question will, of course, be asked: How can you bring up children satisfactorily without a Home?

To which we rejoin: How can you bring them up satisfactorily anyhow?

DON MARQUIS,
The Almost Perfect State

Children, not knowing that they are having an easy time, have a good many hard times.

DON MARQUIS,
The Almost Perfect State

We assume a certain air of holiness when we go to deal with our children, and appeal at that moment to a principle to which we do not appeal at other times. Of course, we do not succeed: the child feels the fraud.

RALPH WALDO EMERSON,
Journals of Ralph Waldo Emerson

I discovered when I had a child of my own that I had become a biased observer of small children. Instead of looking at them with affectionate but nonpartisan eyes, I saw each of them as older or younger, bigger or smaller, more or less graceful, intelligent, or skilled than my own child. This troubled me. I felt that I had learned a great deal about mothers by being one, but that I had become in some way a less objective observer of children.

MARGARET MEAD,
Blackberry Winter

Children are remarkable for their intelligence and ardor, for their curiosity, their intolerance of shams, the clarity and ruthlessness of their vision.

ALDOUS HUXLEY,
Collected Essays

One must ask children and birds how cherries and strawberries taste.

GOETHE

A sparkling house is a fine thing if the children aren't robbed of their luster in keeping it that way.

MARCELENE COX,
Ladies' Home Journal, November 1945

It might as well be admitted that children irritate us; and this means that we are no longer capable of entering into their kingdom. We revenge ourselves by teaching them all sorts of worthless knowledge.

HOLBROOK JACKSON,
Southward Ho! and Other Essays

God help all the children as they move into a time of life they do not understand and must struggle through with precepts they have picked from the garbage can of older people, clinging with the passion of the lost to odds and ends that will mess them up for all time, or hating the trash so much they will waste their future on the hatred.

LILLIAN HELLMAN,
Pentimento

We should not make light of the troubles of children. They are worse than ours, because we can see the end of our trouble and they can never see any end.

WILLIAM MIDDLETON,
quoted in *Autobiography* by W. B. Yeats

There are no graves that grow so green as the graves of children. ... If no pang is sharper than parting with a beloved child, no recollection clears itself so naturally and perhaps I might say so early, of all but what is lovely to dwell upon.

OLIVER WENDELL HOLMES,
Life and Letters of Oliver Wendell Holmes,
Vol. I, by John T. Morse, Jr.

Children, as creatures of delight, are of comparatively recent discovery. ... It was left for Blake first to see that the child was not merely the young man but a separate creature, filled with fugitive and exquisite charm.

E. V. LUCAS,
365 Days and One More

All children talk with integrity up to about the age of five, when they fall victim to the influences of the adult world and mass entertainment. It is then that they begin, all unconsciously, to become plausible actors. The product of this process is known as maturity, or you and me.

CLIFTON FADIMAN,
Any Number Can Play

As we read the school reports upon our children, we realize with a sense of relief that can rise to delight that—thank Heaven—nobody is reporting in this fashion upon us.

J. B. PRIESTLEY,
Delight

People with bad consciences always fear the judgment of children.

MARY McCARTHY,
On the Contrary

We can't give our children the future, strive though we may to make it secure. But we can give them the present.

KATHLEEN NORRIS,
Hands Full of Living

"To become as little children." Everyone bows his head in silence when this utterance is repeated. But no one truly believes it. And parents will always be the last to believe.

HENRY MILLER,
The Books in My Life

This business of being out for a walk, coming across something of fascinating interest and then being dragged away from it by a yell from the schoolmaster, like a dog jerked onwards by the leash, is an important feature of school life and helps to build up the conviction, so strong in many children, that the things you want most to do are always unattainable.

GEORGE ORWELL,
A Collection of Essays

As far back as I can remember I was saddened by the amount of misery I saw in the world around me. Youth's unqualified *joie de vivre* I never really knew, and I believe that to be the case with many children, even though they appear outwardly merry and quite free from care.

ALBERT SCHWEITZER,
Memoirs of My Childhood and Youth

I was once present when an old mother, who had brought up a large family of children with eminent success, was asked by a young one what she would recommend in the case of some children who were too anxiously educated, and her reply was—"I think, my dear, a little wholesome neglect."

SIR HENRY TAYLOR,
Notes from Life

Many a small drama is played within the hearts of children. They suffer at being excluded from the too close intimacy of their parents.

ROMAIN ROLLAND,
Journey Within

Love means that the adult be genuinely concerned with the evolution of the true nature of the child. Children are not able to respond to a love which tries to fashion them according to the concept of an adult, no matter how good the latter's intention may be.

DR. GOTTHARD BOOTH,
quoted in *Love or Perish*
by Dr. Smiley Blanton

And of course children are wonderful and charming creatures. I've had Ann in talking about the white seal and wanting me to read to her. And how Karin manages to be so aloof I can't think. There's a quality in their minds to me very adorable; to be alone with them, and see them day by day would be an extraordinary experience. They have what no grown up has—that directness—chatter, chatter, chatter, on Ann goes, in a kind of world of her own, with its seals and dogs; happy because she's going to have cocoa tonight, and go blackberrying tomorrow. The walls of her mind all hung round with such bright vivid things, and she doesn't see what we see.

VIRGINIA WOOLF,
A Writer's Diary

Nature makes boys and girls lovely to look upon so they can be tolerated until they acquire some sense.

WILLIAM LYON PHELPS,
Essays on Things

For we like children who are a little afraid of us, docile, deferential children, though not, of course, if they are so obviously afraid that they threaten our image of ourselves as kind, lovable people whom there is no reason to fear. We find ideal the kind of "good" children who are just enough afraid of us to do everything we want, without making us feel that fear of us is what is making them do it.

JOHN HOLT,
How Children Fail

Even when we do not create children's fears, when they come to us with fears ready-made and built-in, we use these fears as handles to manipulate them and get them to do what we want.

JOHN HOLT,
How Children Fail

Play is not for every hour of the day, or for any hour taken at random. There is a tide in the affairs of children. Civilization is cruel in sending them off to bed at the most stimulating time of dusk.

ALICE MEYNELL,
The Children

I wonder if we who have grown up will ever know on this side of the grave how much we owe to children, who seem, but only seem, to owe us so much.

FRANCIS C. KELLEY,
*The Epistles of Father Timothy
to His Parishioners*

You never knew anything about your children—but living with them sometimes gave you the illusion that you did. Separation was in some ways a truer condition.

WILFRED SHEED,
Max Jamison

We of this self-conscious, incredulous generation, sentimentalize our children, analyse our children, think we are endowed with a special capacity to sympathize and identify ourselves with children. And the result is that we are not more childlike, but our children are less childlike.

FRANCIS THOMPSON,
Works, Vol. III

Children are on a different plane, belong to a generation and way of feeling properly their own; there is seldom complete understanding between them and their parents, so that affection here suffers from some strain and uncertainty, all the more painful the greater the affection is.

GEORGE SANTAYANA,
The Letters of George Santayana

There are some of us who in after years say to Fate, "Now deal us your hardest blow, give us what you will; but let us never again suffer as we suffered when we were children."

OLIVE SCHREINER,
The Story of an African Farm

The moment children begin to handle money they meet the world on an adult basis. The indulgences to which they are accustomed cease. Pleading eyes do not impress confectioners and men who sell tickets. The stern laws of economics make no exception for children.

WILLIAM FEATHER,
The Business of Life

Normally, children learn to gauge rather accurately from the tone of the parent's voice how seriously to take his threats. Of course, they sometimes misjudge and pay the penalty.

LOUIS KAPLAN,
*Mental Health
and Human Relations in Education*

Children who have things their own way may even feel that their parents do not love them since they do not care what they do.

LOUIS KAPLAN,
*Mental Health
and Human Relations in Education*

I do not believe in a child world. It is a fantasy world. I believe the child should be taught from the very first that the whole world is his world, that adult and child share one world, that all generations are needed.

PEARL BUCK,
To My Daughters, with Love

CHIVALRY (*See* COUNTRY, GENEROSITY, KINDNESS)

CHOICE

He who hunts two hares leaves one and loses the other.

JAPANESE PROVERB

I think that our power of conscious origination is where free will comes in. . . . We are continually choosing between the good and the less good, whether aware of it or not.

ALFRED NORTH WHITEHEAD,
Dialogues of Alfred North Whitehead

I think there is choice possible to us at any moment, as long as we live. But there is no sacrifice. There is a choice, and the rest falls away. Second choice does not exist. Beware of those who talk about sacrifice.

MURIEL RUKEYSER,
The Life of Poetry

The choice between life and death is ever-recurrent. In varying forms it appears whenever a new adaptation is needed or a new potential is ready to be born.

FRANCES G. WICKES,
The Inner World of Choice

In practical life, when confronted with one of its diverging grand highways, I was incapable of any decision whatever. I wanted to go both ways; I wanted to go all ways. I never could find the reason for a choice, and I rarely made one.

MAX EASTMAN,
Enjoyment of Living

Choice of attention—to pay attention to *this* and ignore *that*—is to the inner life what choice of action is to the outer. In both cases, a man is responsible for his choice and must accept the consequences, whatever they may be.

W. H. AUDEN,
A Certain World

We choose our joys and sorrows long before we experience them.

KAHLIL GIBRAN,
Sand and Foam

As you emphasize your life, you must localize and define it. The more truly and earnestly you come to do anything, the more clearly you will see that you cannot do everything. He who is truly good must be good for something. To be good for everything is to be good for nothing.

PHILLIPS BROOKS,
Visions and Tasks

When you have to make a choice and don't make it, that is in itself a choice.

WILLIAM JAMES

The demands of modern living are so exacting that men and women everywhere must exercise deliberate selection to live wisely.

ROBERT GRANT,
The Art of Living

CHRIST

We can hardly think of Jesus Christ without thinking of the sparrows, the grass, fig-trees, sheep.

VINCENT MCNABB,
God's Way of Mercy

Christ, like all fascinating personalities, had the power of not merely saying beautiful things himself, but of making other people say beautiful things to him.

OSCAR WILDE,
De Profundis

His morality is all sympathy, just what morality should be.

OSCAR WILDE,
De Profundis

He realised in the entire sphere of human relations that imaginative sympathy which in the sphere of Art is the sole secret of creation. He understood the leprosy of the leper, the darkness of the blind, the fierce misery of those who live for pleasure, the strange poverty of the rich.

OSCAR WILDE,
De Profundis

There was something that He hid from all men when He went up a mountain to pray. There was something He covered constantly by abrupt silence or impetuous isolation. There was some one thing that was too great for God to show us when He walked upon our earth; and I have sometimes fancied that it was His mirth.

G. K. CHESTERTON,
Orthodoxy

No one ever made more trouble than the "gentle Jesus meek and mild."

JAMES M. GILLIS,
This Our Day

Christ came when all things were growing old. He made them new.

SAINT AUGUSTINE,
Sermons

Theologians who are in danger of losing the sense of a living God, under the pressure of abstractions, might profitably meditate upon the eternal significance of the Second Person of the Blessed Trinity en-joying a good bowel movement among the Judean hills.

BRENDAN FRANCIS

As Gregory of Nyssa pictures it, He entered paradise bringing with Him His bride, Humanity, whom He had just wedded on the Cross.

JEAN DANIELOU,
The Salvation of the Nations

He simply wanted to be loved, nothing more. Of course, there are those who love him, even among Christians. But they are not numerous.

ALBERT CAMUS,
The Fall

He was born deserted, He lived alone, He died a lonely criminal's death; and if we want a proof that He felt it, we have it, first, in His frequent cries of pain, and second, in the eager way He grasped at and rewarded every mark of companionship offered Him.

ALBAN GOODIER,
The School of Love

I am amazed by the sayings of Christ. They seem truer than anything I have ever read. And they certainly turn the world upside down.

KATHARINE BUTLER HATHAWAY,
The Journals and Letters
of the Little Locksmith

It is wonderful never to have read or known anything about the teachings of Christ until you have found that in spite of your proud intellect and your worldly experience and your artistic insight you are defeated and helpless. Then they do seem like the flowers of spring—for freshness and miraculous beauty and so much more besides.

KATHARINE BUTLER HATHAWAY,
The Journals and Letters
of the Little Locksmith

No man took His life; He laid it down of Himself.

ROBERT HUGH BENSON,
Spiritual Letters of Monsignor R. Hugh Benson
to One of His Converts

When criticism has done its worst, the words and acts of Our Lord which remain are, *not* those of "a good and heroic man," but of one deliberately claiming unique authority and insight, and conscious of a unique destiny.

EVELYN UNDERHILL,
The Letters of Evelyn Underhill

CHRISTIAN AND CHRISTIANITY

The main business of a Christian soul is to go through the world turning its water into wine.

ANDREW LANG,
quoted in *The Bliss of the Way,*
compiled by Cecily Hallack

A mind attentive to the wants of others, which avoids everything calculated to give them pain, which is generous, which does not keep silence out of touchiness or pride, that mind is the mind of a Christian, and is the joy of everyone who comes in contact with it.

JEAN BAPTISTE LACORDAIRE,
Letters to Young Men,
edited by Count de Montalembert

Some Christians are like candles that have been lit once and then put away in a cupboard to be eaten up by mice.

HENRY VAN DYKE,
The Friendly Year

A strong Christian is not part of a system, a creature of habit. He is a revolutionary, in the good sense of the word. He revolts against all injustices, but especially against those which do not affect himself.

JULES-GÉRARD CARDINAL SALIÈGE,
Who Shall Bear the Flame?

Those who reject Christian beliefs, cannot count on keeping Christian morals.

SIR RICHARD LIVINGSTONE,
On Education

The Christian whose life is all sadness, and whose only hope lies beyond the grave may ... be sure that there is something amiss in his life or in his method.

BASIL W. MATURIN,
Laws of the Spiritual Life

Human nature,—not any one party,—yes, the very nature of the processes of growth themselves, and not any particular form of religious or of moral error, must be viewed as the source of the principal tragedies of the history of all the Christian ideals.

JOSIAH ROYCE,
The Problem of Christianity

The most remarkable feature with regard to the situation of the Christian heritage today is that its custody has to a considerable degree passed over into the keeping of secularized groups and forces.

AMOS N. WILDER,
Modern Poetry and the Christian Tradition

Christianity gave Eros poison to drink. Eros did not die of it, to be sure, but degenerated into Vice.

FRIEDRICH NIETZSCHE,
Genealogy of Morals

The charge that Christianity inculcates a "slave morality" of submission might well be thought ironical in view of the pugnacity of historical Christians. Indeed a doctrine that teaches men to control their merely personal passions may well make them more willing and formidable contestants for causes.

CHARLES HORTON COOLEY,
Life and the Student

Nothing is more depressing and more illogical than aggressive Christianity.

GERALD VANN,
The Heart of Man

Nowadays, the world is full of tame Christians; in consequence, the churches are empty of life, if not of people.

PHILIP RIEFF,
The Triumph of the Therapeutic

Christianity has need of thought that it may come to the consciousness of its real self.

ALBERT SCHWEITZER,
Out of My Life and Thought

Christianity, above all, consoles; but there are naturally happy souls who do not need consolation. Consequently Christianity begins by making such souls unhappy, for otherwise it would have no power over them.

ANDRÉ GIDE,
The Journals of André Gide, Vol. I

And if, in the bottom of Pandora's box Christianity were to be found, my word! I should not be too surprised.

ANDRÉ GIDE,
Pretexts

Christianity does mean getting down to actual ordinary life as the medium of the Incarnation, doesn't it, and our lessons in that get sterner, not more elegant as time goes on?

EVELYN UNDERHILL,
The Letters of Evelyn Underhill

Authentic Christianity never destroys what is good. It makes it grow, transfigures it and enriches itself from it.

CLAIRE HUTCHET BISHOP,
France Alive

My experience is that Christianity dispels more mystery than it involves. With Christianity it is twilight in the world; without it, night.

MADAME SWETCHINE,
The Writings of Madame Swetchine

When I look at a number of particular phenomena in the Christian life it seems to me that Christianity, instead of giving men strength—yes, that compared to the pagans such individuals are bereft of their manhood by Christianity and are as geldings to the stallion.

SØREN KIERKEGAARD,
The Journals, quoted in
A Kierkegaard Anthology,
edited by Robert Bretall

Christianity is not an object that we can hold in our hand: it is a mystery before which we are always ignorant and uninitiated.

HENRI DE LUBAC,
Paradoxes

Defenders of Christianity naturally select as reasons for belief, not the highest, the truest, the most sacred, the most intimately persuasive, but such as best admit of being exhibited in argument; and these are commonly not the real reasons in the case of religious men.

JOHN HENRY CARDINAL NEWMAN,
Oxford University Sermons

The promise of Christianity is as yet but half fulfilled. All that has been done yet in all the Christian centuries is only the sketch and prelude of what is yet to be done.

PHILLIPS BROOKS,
Visions and Tasks

Christianity is a heroism. People seem sometimes to think it is a dear darling, not-to-be-grumpy, not-to-be-impatient, not-to-be-violent life; a sort or wishy-washy sentimental affair. Stuff and nonsense! Christianity is not that. Christianity is an immense warning; a tremendous heroism.

BARON FRIEDRICH VON HÜGEL,
*Letters from Baron Friedrich Von Hügel
to a Niece*

It is not easy to take the principles of Christianity and to deduce how a Christian should behave in a concrete case in order to be, without any doubt, a Christian. For Christianity is not a philosophical problem composed of lifeless abstract principles. It is, on the contrary, of its very principles that every individual can always be under the living providence of the living God in every particular case—and then there is nothing to deduce, for God is freedom.

THEODOR HAECKER,
Journal in the Night

There may well be many aspects of Christianity that we have not yet discovered and that we shall not discover until Christianity has been refracted through every facet of the prism of human civilization.

JEAN DANIELOU,
The Salvation of the Nations

Christianity is a religion of motives—ways of acting and reasons for acting, more than actions.

FREDERICK W. FABER,
*Notes on Doctrinal
and Spiritual Subjects,* Vol. II

In one fundamental sense ... it seems to me that Christianity alone attacks the seat of evil in the kind of world we have been considering, and has a solvent for the intellectual predicaments which arise in such a world. It addresses itself precisely to that crust of self-righteousness which, by the nature of its teaching, it has to dissolve before it can do anything else with a man. The more human beings are lacking in imagination, the more incapable men are of any profound kind of self-analysis, the more we shall find that their self-righteousness hardens, so that it is just the thick-skinned who are more sure of being right than anybody else.

HERBERT BUTTERFIELD,
Christianity and History

At this time ... the renewal of Christianity depends solely on accepting the Incarnation in all its fulness. For without the realization of God's love for the world, we can love neither the world nor God.

ALAN W. WATTS,
Behold the Spirit

CHRISTMAS

The things we do at Christmas are touched with a certain extravagance, as beautiful, in some of its aspects, as the extravagance of Nature in June.

ROBERT COLLYER,
quoted in *A Year of Sunshine,*
selected by Kate Sanborn

I find it difficult to believe in Father Christmas. If he is the jolly old gentleman he is always said to be, why doesn't he behave as such? How is it that the presents go so often to the wrong people?

A. A. MILNE,
Not That It Matters

At Ambergate my sister had sent a motor-car for us—so we were at Ripley in time for turkey and Christmas pudding. My God, what masses of food here, turkey, large tongues, long wall of roast loin of pork, pork-pies, sausages, mince-pies, dark cakes covered with almonds, cheese-cakes,

lemon-tarts, jellies, endless masses of food, with whisky, gin, port wine, burgundy, muscatel. It seems incredible. We played charades—the old people of 67 playing away harder than the young ones—and lit the Christmas tree, and drank healths, and sang and roared—Lord above. If only one hadn't all the while a sense that next week would be the same dreariness as before. What a good party we might have had, had we really felt free of the world.

D. H. LAWRENCE,
The Selected Letters of D. H. Lawrence,
edited by Diana Trilling

What do people mean by sending you a dozen Christmas cards during the festive season, and not deigning to send you three lines by way of a letter during the rest of the year?

J. ASHBY-STERRY,
Cucumber Chronicles

How I wish we might be together these two Christmas days—I should so love to see you in the studio again. I have been working hard lately, just because of that Christmas sentiment, and because feeling is not enough: one must express it in one's work.

VINCENT VAN GOGH,
Dear Theo:
An Autobiography of Vincent Van Gogh

The Christmas season has come to mean the period when the public plays Santa Claus to the merchants.

JOHN ANDREW HOLMES,
Wisdom in Small Doses

All through November and December we watch it drawing nearer; we see the shop windows begin to glow with red and green and lively colors; we note the altered demeanor of bellboys and janitors as the Date flows quietly toward us; we pass through the haggard perplexity of "Only Four Days More" when we suddenly realize it is too late to make our shopping list the display of lucid affectionate reasoning we had contemplated, and clutch wildly at grotesque tokens—and then (sweetest of all) comes the quiet calmness of Christmas Eve.

CHRISTOPHER MORLEY,
Mince Pie

We'll bet that folks who spell Christmas "Xmas" leave their greeting cards unsealed so they'll go cheaper.

KIN HUBBARD,
Abe Martin on Things in General

Christmas has come and gone, and I—to speak selfishly—am glad of it. The season always gives me the blues in spite of myself, though I manage to get a good deal of pleasure from thinking of the multitudes of happy kids in various parts of the world.

EDWIN ARLINGTON ROBINSON,
Untriangulated Stars

Our children await Christmas presents like politicians getting election returns; there's the Uncle Fred precinct and the Aunt Ruth district still to come in.

MARCELENE COX,
Ladies' Home Journal, December 1950

The holidays are welcome to me partly because they are such rallying points for the affections which get so much thrust aside in the business and preoccupations of daily life.

GEORGE E. WOODBERRY,
Selected Letters of George Edward Woodberry

So much, indeed, is there to be said for and against any view about giving presents, that it is safer not to think about it, but to buy your presents first, and afterwards to consider what, if anything, you will do with them. After all, if you decide in the end not to give them to anyone, you can always keep them.

ROSE MACAULAY,
A Casual Commentary

A Christmas day, to be perfect, should be clear and cold, with holly branches in berry, a blazing fire, a dinner with mince pies, and games and forfeits in the evening. You cannot have it in perfection if you are very fine and fashionable. A

Christmas evening should, if possible, finish with music. It carries off the excitement without abruptness, and sheds a repose over the conclusion of the enjoyment.

LEIGH HUNT,
quoted in *A Year of Sunshine,*
selected by Kate Sanborn

Christmas morning i
got up before the others and
ran
naked across the plank
floor into the front
room to see grandmama
sewing a new
button on my last year
ragdoll.

CAROL FREEMAN,
"Christmas morning i," in *Black Fire,*
edited by LeRoi Jones and Roy Neal

I never could see why people were so happy about Dickens' *A Christmas Carol* because I never had any confidence that Scrooge was going to be different the next day.

DR. KARL MENNINGER,
A Psychiatrist's World

I had a stocking this year, full of sweets and cigars and mouth-organs and cherry brandy.

DYLAN THOMAS,
Letters to Vernon Watkins

I do hope your Christmas has had a little touch of Eternity in among the rush and pitter patter and all. It always seems such a mixing of this world and the next—but that after all is the idea!

EVELYN UNDERHILL,
The Letters of Evelyn Underhill

Was there ever a wider and more loving conspiracy than that which keeps the venerable figure of Santa Claus from slipping away, with all the other oldtime myths, into the forsaken wonderland of the past?

HAMILTON WRIGHT MABIE,
My Study Fire

One doesn't forget the rounded wonder in the eyes of a boy as he comes bursting upstairs on Christmas morning and finds the two-wheeler or the fire truck of which for weeks he scarcely dared dream.

MAX LERNER,
The Unfinished Country

I was glad to get a letter instead of a Christmas card. A Christams card is a rather innutritious thing.

OSCAR W. FIRKINS,
Oscar Firkins: Memoirs and Letters,
edited by Ina Ten Eyck

Were I a philosopher, I should write a philosophy of toys, showing that nothing else in life need to be taken seriously, and that Christmas Day in the company of children is one of the few occasions on which men become entirely alive.

ROBERT LYND,
The Peal of Bells

Christmas too is come which always puts a rattle into my morning scull. It is a visiting, unquiet, un-Quakerish season. I get more and more in love with solitude, and proportionately hampered with company.

CHARLES LAMB,
The Works of Charles and Mary Lamb, Vol. VI

The first rule in buying Christmas presents is to select something shiny. If the chosen object is of leather, the leather must look as if it had been well greased; if of silver, it must gleam with the light that never was on sea or land. This is because the wariest person will often mistake shininess for expensiveness.

P. G. WODEHOUSE,
Louder and Funnier

It is certainly very singular, that, every year as Christmas comes round, we do not seem to be celebrating a past event, so much as taking part in scenes that are actually present.

MOTHER FRANCIS RAPHAEL,
quoted in *A Memoir of Mother Francis Raphael* by Bertrand Wilberforce

It must be allowed that the regular recurrence of annual festivals among the same individuals has, as life advances, something in it that is melancholy. We meet on such occasions like the survivors of some perilous expedition, wounded and weakened ourselves, and looking through the diminished ranks of those who remain, while we think of those who are no more.

SIR WALTER SCOTT,
Sir Walter Scott's Journal (1825-1832)

CHURCH

·Churches in cities are the most wonderful solitudes.

THOMAS MERTON,
The Sign of Jonas

Those who are content with the church are just those who have not imagination enough to be Christians.

CHARLES HORTON COOLEY,
Life and the Student

Nowhere does the unpredictable, the unusual excite such confusion as in that settled institution—the church.

DAVID GRAYSON,
The Friendly Road

Why must all the churches be closed at night? How often has the wanderer groaned in front of those closed doors?

PAUL CLAUDEL,
Ways and Crossways

The great door sighs. It opens, and a child
Enters the church and kneels in the front pew.
The Maker of the Universe has smiled:
He made the church for this one interview.

DANIEL SARGENT,
"The Village Church," *God's Ambuscade*

For the true Church ... is still a sort of ideal challenge to the faithful, rather than an already finished institution,—a call upon men for a heavenly quest, rather than a present possession of humanity. "Create me,"—this is the word that the Church, viewed as an idea, addresses to mankind.

JOSIAH ROYCE,
The Problem of Christianity

CIGAR

A thing that has always baffled me about women is that they will saturate themselves with a pint of perfume, a pound of sachet powder, an evil-smelling lip rouge, a peculiar-smelling hair ointment and a half-dozen varieties of body oils, and then they have the effrontery to complain of the aroma of a fine dollar cigar.

GROUCHO MARX,
Ladies' Home Journal, November 1943

For my part I had rather smoke one cigar than hear two sermons.

ROBERT G. INGERSOLL,
Letters of Robert G. Ingersoll

The cigar, which is, in caricatures, the symbol of the ruthless plutocrat, the oppressor of the poor, in Churchill's mouth expresses a hundred admirable and popular qualities, such as vitality, love of life, defiance of popular opinion, independence of mind, together with all sorts of fine shades in allusion, according to the personal idea.

JOYCE CARY,
Art and Reality

CIRCUMSTANCES

We easily persuade ourselves that were circumstances more favorable we should be better and happier. It may be so, but the mood is weak and foolish.

JOHN LANCASTER SPALDING,
Opportunity and Other Essays

I believe that in every circumstance I have been able to see rather clearly the most advantageous course I could follow, which is very rarely the one I did follow.

ANDRÉ GIDE,
Pretexts

Do you know the times when one seems to stick fast in circumstances like the fly in the jam-pot? It can't be helped, and I suppose the best thing to do is to lay in a good store of jam!

A. C. BENSON,
Excerpts from the Letters of Dr. A. C. Benson to M. E. A.

Man's highest merit always is, as much as possible, to rule external circumstances and as little as possible to let himself be ruled by them.

GOETHE

Do not wait for ideal circumstances; they will never come; nor for the best opportunities.

JANET ERSKINE STUART,
Life and Letters of Janet Erskine Stuart
by Maud Monahan

No prudence in conduct, no wisdom or foresight can effect anything, for the most trivial circumstances will upset the deepest plan of the wisest mind.

RICHARD JEFFERIES,
The Story of My Heart

CITY

In the city you have neither heaven nor hell. You merely have smog overhead and pavement beneath your feet.

WILLIAM ERNEST HOCKING,
Wisdom for Our Time,
edited by James Nelson

Cities, like cats, will reveal themselves at night.

RUPERT BROOKE,
Letters from America

A wary eavesdropper can always surprise the secret of a city, through chance scraps of conversation, or by spying from a window, or by coming suddenly round corners.

RUPERT BROOKE
quoted in *Rupert Brooke:
A Reappraisal and Selection*

Lovers of the town have been content, for the most part, to say they loved it. They do not brag about its uplifting qualities. They have none of the infernal smugness which makes the lover of the country insupportable.

AGNES REPPLIER,
Times and Tendencies

With all history to contradict us, it is hardly worthwhile to speak of city life as entailing "spiritual loss," because it is out of touch with Nature. It is in touch with humanity, and humanity is Nature's heaviest asset.

AGNES REPPLIER,
Times and Tendencies

To most people the vision of a great city is that of streets, parks, rivers, bridges, and endless bustling crowds in the open under the sky. But the idea which most weighs on me as I sit here alone is that of a vast unexplored interior, with a million forms of hidden life.

J. A. SPENDER,
The Comments of Bagshot, Second Series

There is no solitude in the world like that of the big city.

KATHLEEN NORRIS,
Hands Full of Living

Father, a thousand tiny lights break
   through
The great grey darkness of the city night
And are as candles lit before Thy Shrine.

FRANCIS CARDINAL SPELLMAN,
*What America Means to Me
and Other Poems and Prayers*

Certainly when one contemplates the general condition of mental life in a large city, it seems as though it needed an inhuman obstinacy to avoid being sucked down by the vortex of vulgar sensationalism that seethes around us at every moment.

JOHN COWPER POWYS,
The Meaning of Culture

The plain fact is that most cities are not organized to cope with their problems. Their haphazard growth has brought such rampant administrative disorder that good government is scarcely possible.

JOHN W. GARDNER,
No Easy Victories, edited by Helen Rowan

In the slums of our great cities today boys and girls who could easily be brought to the full use of their powers are left stunted, inarticulate and angry.

JOHN W. GARDNER,
No Easy Victories, edited by Helen Rowan

All great industrial cities have surroundings stranger than anything in the moon.

WILLIAM BOLITHO,
Camera Obscura

When I was a child the streets of any city were full of street vendors and street entertainers of every kind, and of the latter the Italian organ-grinder with his monkey was one of the most endearing. Today, officialdom seems to have banished them all, and the only persons who still earn their living on the streets are prostitutes and dope peddlers.

W. H. AUDEN,
A Certain World

Let everything—almost everything—change with a will, in any city that you love. People gush and moan too much about the loss of ancient buildings of no special note—"landmarks" and "links with the past." In towns, as in human bodies, the only state of health is one of rapid wasting and repair.

C. E. MONTAGUE,
The Right Place

Big cities are monstrous organisms, where, like the microbes of all maladies, those of the mind multiply rapidly. New-comers, if they do not succumb at once ... must undergo a long and painful period to acclimatize their blood to these poisons.

ROMAIN ROLLAND,
Journey Within

Noise is manufactured in the city, just as goods are manufactured. The city is the place where noise is kept in stock, completely detached from the object from which it came.

MAX PICARD,
quoted in *A Certain World* by W. H. Auden

There are natures that go to the streams of life in great cities as the hart goes to the waterbrooks.

PHILIP G. HAMERTON,
The Intellectual Life

Before opening the front door I paused, for a moment of profound consideration.

Dim-lit, shadowy, full of menace and unimaginable chances, stretched all around my door the many-peopled streets. i could hear, ominous and muffled, the tides of multitudinous traffic, sounding along their ways. Was I equipped for the navigation of those waters, armed and ready to venture out into that dangerous world again?

Gloves? Money? Cigarettes? Matches? Yes; and I had an umbrella for its tempests, and a latchkey for my safe return.

LOGAN PEARSALL SMITH,
More Trivia

There is a lot of provincialism about New York or Chicago or London, at least about the typical inhabitant of those cities. When one is holding entirely aloof, coolly and calmly looking on from a distance, one sometimes catches the spirit of the great, hurrying, whirling throng better than if one is driven tumultuously in the midst of it.

GAMALIEL BRADFORD,
The Letters of Gamaliel Bradford

No city should be too large for a man to walk out of in a morning.

CYRIL CONNOLLY,
The Unquiet Grave

The town is new every day.

ESTONIAN PROVERB

In a great city men jostle one another in the street who live in spheres of thought and feeling as widely apart as though they dwelt in separate planets.

JOHN LANCASTER SPALDING,
Lectures and Discourses

Is it possible for the mind to conceive all the pain and suffering that lie pent within a great city? It is my belief that if a man succeeded in realizing it, the weight of it would crush him to earth.

ANATOLE FRANCE

As long as people live under humiliating conditions, they are going to be bitter and brutal. Architecture is only part of the problem of cities. Conceivably we could have a great city of mediocre buildings. It might be a happy place in which to live.

And you might have a beautiful city that is not a happy city.

ALLAN TEMKO,
The City, a pamphlet published by the Center for the Study of Democratic Institutions

If we got rid of all cars, if someone put them all in a huge crate and dumped them into the ocean, the relief would be magnificent. Of course, we would be left with our sprawling civilization and the problems of communication. How would we do it? Well, I think we would have to rebuild our cities.

ALLAN TEMKO,
The City, a pamphlet published by the Center for the Study of Democratic Institutions

The city is the flower of civilization. It gives to men the means to make their lives expressive. It offers a field of battle, and it could be made a livable place if its sons would stay and fight for it, instead of running away.

ANONYMOUS,
quoted in *Times and Tendencies* by Agnes Repplier

Yes, large towns are the absolute devil! Oh, how glad I shall be to get away—the difficulty to work is really appalling—one gets no distraction. By distraction I mean the sky and the grass and trees and little birds. I absolutely pine for the country.... I could kiss the grass.

KATHERINE MANSFIELD,
Katherine Mansfield Memories of LM

A large city cannot be experientially known; its life is too manifold for any individual to be able to participate in it.

ALDOUS HUXLEY,
Beyond the Mexique Bay

CIVILIZATION

The most fundamental of divisions is that between the intellect, which can only do its work by saying continually "thou fool," and the religious genius which makes all equal. That is why we have discovered that the mountain top and the monastery are necessary to civilisation. Civilisation dies of all those things that feed the soul, and both die if the Remnant refuses the wilderness.

W. B. YEATS,
Autobiography

Every civilization is, among other things, an arrangement for domesticating the passions and setting them to do useful work.

ALDOUS HUXLEY,
Collected Essays

Because I see so many weak ones trodden down, I greatly doubt the sincerity of much that is called progress and civilization. I do believe in civilization, but only in the kind that is founded on real humanity. That which costs human life I think cruel, and I do not respect it.

VINCENT VAN GOGH,
Dear Theo:
An Autobiography of Vincent Van Gogh

Civilization does not lie in a greater or lesser degree of refinement, but in an awareness shared by a whole people. And this awareness is never refined. It is even quite simple and straightforward.

ALBERT CAMUS,
Notebooks 1935–1942

With civilizations, as with individuals, the outer face is often merely the explosion resulting from the accumulated inner tension, the signs of which were plentifully present, though none of the persons concerned chose to heed them.

WILLIAM BARRETT,
Irrational Man

In youth one marvels that man remains at so low a stage of civilization; in later life one marvels that he has got so far.

GEORGE GISSING,
Commonplace Book

Civilization is drugs, alcohol, engines of war, prostitution, machines and machine slaves, low wages, bad food, bad taste, prisons, reformatories, lunatic asylums, divorce, perversion, brutal sports, suicides, infanticide, cinema, quackery, demagogy, strikes, lockouts, revolutions, putsches, col-onization, electric chairs, guillotines, sabotage, floods, famine, disease, gangsters, money barons, horse racing, fashion shows, poodle dogs, chow dogs, Siamese cats, condoms, pessaries, syphilis, gonorrhea, insanity, neuroses, etc., etc.

HENRY MILLER,
The Cosmological Eye

I say civilization, but in reality I mean a *few men*, a few great, extraordinary individuals whose spiritual development has so far outstripped that of the ordinary man that they remain unique and exert over the great majority of men a tyranny which is to all intents and purposes obsessive. The cold, steril crystallization of the truths which they have perceived and acted upon forms the framework of what is called civilization.

HENRY MILLER,
The Cosmological Eye

Private property being individualism, and its abolition being socialism, the two are correlative and must yield to each other just as rapidly as experience and necessity dictate. Civilization is a growth both ways—an intensification of private property in certain ways, an abolition of it in others.

HENRY DEMAREST LLOYD,
Man, The Social Creator,
edited by J. Addams and A. Withington

When it is said that we are too much occupied with the means of living to live, I answer that the chief worth of civilization is just that it makes the means of living more complex; that it calls for great and combined intellectual efforts, instead of simple, uncoordinated ones, in order that the crowd may be fed and clothed and housed and moved from place to place. Because more complex and intense intellectual efforts mean a fuller and richer life. They mean more life. Life is an end in itself, and the only question as to whether it is worth living is whether you have enough of it.

OLIVER WENDELL HOLMES, JR.,
The Mind and Faith of Justice Holmes,
edited by Max Lerner

CIVILIZED

The civilized are those who get more out of life than the uncivilized, and for this the uncivilized have not forgiven them.

CYRIL CONNOLLY,
The Unquiet Grave

CLASS

Every class is unfit to govern.

LORD ACTON,
quoted in *A Certain World* by W. H. Auden

It is since coming back from America that I ask myself seriously: Why is there so little contact between myself and the people whom I know? Why has the contact no vital meaning? . . .

The answer, as far as I can see, has something to do with class. Class makes gulfs, across which all the best human flow is lost. It is not exactly the triumph of the middle classes that has made the deadness, but the triumph of the middle-class *thing*.

D. H. LAWRENCE,
Assorted Articles

CLEANLINESS

I am always scared and ill at ease when I enter a house in which there are no ash trays. The room is apt to be too clean and orderly, the cushions are apt to be in their right places and the people are apt to be correct and unemotional. And immediately I am put on my best behavior, which means the same thing as the most uncomfortable behavior.

LIN YUTANG,
The Importance of Living

Cleanliness, said some sage man, is next to Godliness. It may be; but how it came to sit so very near is the marvel. Methinks some of the more human virtues might have put in for a place before it.

CHARLES LAMB,
"Saturday Night"

A man may have strong humanitarian and democratic principles; but if he happens to have been brought up as a bath-taking, shirt-changing lover of fresh air, he will have to overcome certain physical repugnances before he can bring himself to put those principles into practice to the extent, at any rate, of associating freely with men and women whose habits are different from his own. It is a deplorable fact; but it is there.

ALDOUS HUXLEY,
Collected Essays

With many people, women especially, bacilli have taken the place of spirits. Microbes for them are the personification of evil. They live in terror of germs and practise elaborate antiseptic rites in order to counteract their influence. . . . One is reminded irresistibly of the ritual washings and fumigations, the incessant preoccupation with unclean foods, unlucky days, and inauspicious places, so common among all the primitive peoples.

ALDOUS HUXLEY,
"The Substitutes for Religion,"
Proper Studies

If men cannot live on bread alone, still less can they do so on disinfectant.

ALFRED NORTH WHITEHEAD,
quoted in *The Unadjusted Man*
by Peter Viereck

Is it necessary to be so clean? People come out to see me at my place; oh, yes they certainly want to see the chrysanthemums and all the dogwood flowers. They take a short walk and come back and sit in the house. "Oh, I haven't got the right shoes." So what? If you walk on the leaves in the woods you get dust on your shoes. What is the psychology of that?

DR. KARL MENNINGER,
A Psychiatrist's World

I am no passionate admirer of the gospel of salvation by hygiene. So many things that the world holds precious have been developed under the most unhygienic conditions. Revolutions for the liberation of mankind have been plotted in unsanitary cellars and dungeons. Religions have taken root and prospered in catacombs. Great poems have been written in stuffy garrets. . . . It is not by accident that children, said to be the most beautiful thing in the world, are so inordinately fond of dust.

SIMEON STRUNSKY,
The Patient Observer

For a lifetime I had bathed with becoming regularity, and thought the world would come to an end unless I changed my socks every day. But in Africa I sometimes went without a bath for two months, and I went two weeks at a time without even changing my socks. Oddly enough, it didn't seem to make much difference.

ERNIE PYLE,
Here Is Your War

CLERGY

It may be that only men who have no intense, personal, passionate life of their own drift into the ministry, and again, it may be that the ministerial habit itself tends to foster such impersonality, to crush out all the intense, riving, tearing impulses that make the essence of the lives of most of us.

GAMALIEL BRADFORD,
The Letters of Gamaliel Bradford

It is a queer priest's pig that dies of starvation.

AUSTIN O'MALLEY,
Keystones of Thought

It is the best part of a man, I sometimes think, that revolts most against his being a minister. His good revolts from official goodness.

RALPH WALDO EMERSON,
Journals of Ralph Waldo Emerson

Heaven may be for the laity, but this world is certainly for the clergy.

GEORGE MOORE,
Epigrams of George Moore

The people may admire him for the eloquence of his sermons, but they will love him for the eloquence of his beneficent acts.

JAMES CARDINAL GIBBONS,
The Ambassador of Christ

Had an interesting lunch sitting next to the Archbishop (of Canterbury) on Wed. He ... told me a tale of an utterly lonely, poverty-stricken (minister) in an utterly irresponsive village, with an ill wife and no servants, who rang his own Church bell daily, said his offices and made his meditation and never lost heart; and then added quietly, "*That* is the true evidence of the Supernatural." Nice, don't you think?

EVELYN UNDERHILL,
The Letters of Evelyn Underhill

The higher clergy are far more sensitive to their own dignity than God's, and very justly so, since it is quite possible to be disrespectful to an ecclesiastic, while it is absolutely impossible *really* to think of God without awe mingled with love.

CHARLES SANDERS PEIRCE,
Collected Papers of Charles Sanders Peirce,
Vol. VI

The minister, priest, or rabbi is not to be regarded necessarily as one to whom religion has meant much; he is one for whom the expounding or administering of religion has meant much.

DR. KARL A. MENNINGER,
The Human Mind

Of all the professions the ecclesiastical one is that which most decidedly and most constantly affects the judgment of persons and opinions. It is peculiarly difficult for a clergyman to attain disinterestedness in his thinking, to accept truth just as it may happen to present itself, without passionately desiring that one doctrine may turn out to be strong in evidence and another unsupported.

PHILIP G. HAMERTON,
The Intellectual Life

It is not a priest's business to impose his own ideas, but to aid the workings of grace.

ABBÉ HUVELIN,
Some Spiritual Guides of the Seventeenth Century

Have you ever known well an old priest of the Catholic faith? He will make almost ribald remarks about Mother Church sometimes, but if you take that to mean he hasn't real love and devotion to her, you make a great mistake.

SHERWOOD ANDERSON,
Letters of Sherwood Anderson

The furnace of purification for the priest in the active ministry is charity for other men.

THOMAS MERTON,
The Sign of Jonas

A poor thing was dying, a London butterfly, broken on the wheel. They used her and cast her aside. She was now dying—hardly out of her teens. She had been drugging, trying to keep herself up to the level of that life. I was called in. She was conscious but speechless. There was no hope, poor child. I had infinite pity for her in my soul. She was a ruin, burnt, while others rejoiced. They used her and threw her aside, as a sucked orange. I was almost tempted to hate my fellow-men. . . .

She didn't want a priest. But I was sent by the Shepherd. I didn't care two straws whether she wanted me or didn't. God wanted her.

VINCENT MCNABB,
God's Way of Mercy

CLEVERNESS

A little touch of cleverness is not bad, and let us not have too much simplicity.

SAINT TERESA OF AVILA,
Saint Teresa in Her Writings
by the Abbé Rodolphe Hoornaert

Clever people seem not to feel the natural pleasure of bewilderment, and are always answering questions when the chief relish of life is to go on asking them.

FRANK MOORE COLBY,
The Colby Essays, Vol. 1

CLIMATE (*See* WEATHER)

CLOTHES

No matter how low their necks are cut, or how high their skirts get, we'll always have to take chances on their real dispositions.

KIN HUBBARD,
quoted in the *New York Times,*
August 30, 1953

No man can possibly realize how women are influenced by the clothes they wear. Put even the plainest woman into a beautiful dress and unconsciously she will try to live up to it.

LADY DUFF-GORDON,
quoted in *Ladies' Home Journal,* June 1944

Dress is at all times a frivolous distinction, and excessive solicitude about it often destroys its own aim.

JANE AUSTEN,
Northanger Abbey

For my part I delight in women when they go into a conference huddle over new clothes. They seem to me then most themselves and the furthest removed from my sex. They are at such times completely in their own world. They are half children, half witches.

J. B. PRIESTLEY,
Delight

Wearing clothes properly seems to me to be a full-time job, and as I happen to have a great many other, more important or more amusing things to do, I cheerfully bag and sag and look as if I had slept in my suits.

J. B. PRIESTLEY,
All About Ourselves and Other Essays

Always be well dressed, even when begging.

HINDU PROVERB

Women want to wear what they do because of what goes on in their heads. Their size and shape has practically nothing to do with the problem of dressing them.

ELIZABETH HAWES

A man can wear a hat for years without being oppressed by its shabbiness of usage and humiliated by its greasy comfort.

JAMES DOUGLAS,
Down Shoe Lane

We may not like the new mode the very first time that we see it; we may pity before we endure; but we end by embracing it.

KATHERINE FULLERTON GEROULD,
Modes and Morals

When virility is at its height, the female seeks defence in her draperies. When virility is at a low ebb the female exposes herself to attract the reluctant male.

ARTHUR PONSONBY,
Casual Observations

Pure style in clothes is as intimidating as pure style in anything else.

ELIZABETH BOWEN,
Collected Impressions

On the subject of dress almost no one, for one reason or another, feels truly indifferent: if their own clothes do not concern them, somebody else's do.

ELIZABETH BOWEN,
Collected Impressions

Clothes never remain a question of pure aesthetics; far too much personal feeling is involved in them. They play such an intimate part in the delicate business of getting oneself across that it seems impossible to discuss them, for long, objectively.

ELIZABETH BOWEN,
Collected Impressions

It is about as stupid to let your clothes betray that you know you are ugly as to have them proclaim that you know you are beautiful.

EDITH WHARTON,
quoted in the *New York Times,*
November 30, 1952

Almost any woman can dress well enough to attract the admiration of a man; it is the test of a well-dressed woman that she can attract the admiration of other women.

ROBERT LYND,
Solomon in All His Glory

Certainly, women would have a poor time of it if they had to depend on men for intelligent appreciation of their clothes. Men are influenced by women's clothes as they are influenced by the architecture of churches, but the influence in both cases is hypnotic; it does not awaken the observation and intelligence, but overwhelms them.

ROBERT LYND,
Solomon in All His Glory

There is one thing certain about a well-dressed woman: she has taken trouble. And to take trouble is to strengthen character.

ROBERT LYND,
quoted in *Ladies' Home Journal*

Tonight, as I was getting my hair done in the House Beauty Parlor, I was sitting under a hair dryer next to Louise Day Hicks, and the first thing she said to me was, "What are you going to wear tomorrow? Long or short?"

BELLA S. ABZUG,
Bella!

The average man knows nothing about fashions except the effect they have on him and that, for no reason he can grasp, they are always changing.

JOHN MASON BROWN,
Vogue, November 15, 1956

On Whit Monday I saw an English lower class crowd taking their holiday, and at Ascot I saw a higher class crowd doing the same, and I confess the principal difference between them seemed to be only and altogether in their *dress.* I wonder if Carlyle is right, and if we all went unclothed, whether we would all be on an absolute equality?

HANNAH WHITALL SMITH,
Philadelphia Quaker
by Logan Pearsall Smith

I confess it does seem to be a dreadful waste of time and money, and, worse still, of brains and of temper too, to turn your mortal frame into a dressmaker's block, and I cannot help thinking it must be

deteriorating to the character. Do assert thy independence and cut loose from it all.
HANNAH WHITALL SMITH,
Philadelphia Quaker
by Logan Pearsall Smith

What a man most enjoys about a woman's clothes are his fantasies of how she would look without them.
BRENDAN FRANCIS

You must either dress badly or spend more money than you wish to—in most cases more than you have got. It is a simple alternative, and every woman must make up her own mind which she intends to adopt. Many women adopt both.
ROSE MACAULAY,
A Casual Commentary

Almost every man looks more so in a belted trench coat.
SYDNEY J. HARRIS,
Strictly Personal

It must have been some hideous style in vogue at the time that prompted the poet to declare that lovely woman unadorned is adorned the most.
OLIVER BELL BUNCE,
Bachelor Bluff

I look at my overcoat and my hat hanging in the hall with reassurance; for although I go out of doors with one individuality today, when yesterday I had quite another, yet my clothes keep my various selves buttoned up together, and enable all these otherwise irreconcilable aggregates of psychological phenomena to pass themselves off as one person.
LOGAN PEARSALL SMITH,
More Trivia

When a woman wears a low-cut gown what does she expect you to do: look or not look?
WILLIAM FEATHER,
The Business of Life

No, I don't mind wearing other people's things,—I had five roommates last year at Vassar—because if they are things I like I always feel myself into them until I forget

that they actually "belong" to anybody at all.
EDNA ST. VINCENT MILLAY,
Letters of Edna St. Vincent Millay

All women's dresses, in every age and country, are merely variations on the eternal struggle between the admitted desire to dress and the unadmitted desire to undress.
LIN YUTANG,
quoted in *Ladies' Home Journal*,
November 1945

You may clothe part of the people all the time or all of the people part of the time, but you cannot force all the people to wear all their clothes all the time.
DON MARQUIS,
The Almost Perfect State

Not enough attention is paid to the negative side of fashion. Great effort is exerted to make people look smart, but somebody should face the fact that a lot of people never will be smart, and that they should be given some assistance in maintaining their fascinating dowdiness.
ROBERTSON DAVIES,
The Table Talk of Samuel Marchbanks

Being "well-dressed" is not a question of having expensive clothes or the "right" clothes—I don't care if you're wearing rags—but they must suit you.
LOUISE NEVELSON,
Fashion, Art, and Beauty,
The Metropolitan Museum of Art Bulletin,
November 1967

Today, elegance lies really within the nature of the person, rather than with what they could possibly wear. In a sense, this has always been true, but it's never been challenged. . . . Today, someone can put on a T-shirt and be extremely elegant, because there's an elegance in that human being.
RUDI GERNREICH,
Supertalk by Digby Diehl

Levi's will become the ultimate classic of any kind of pant. They're just totally utilitarian. They cannot be erased. Levi's are the most ultimate kind of garment in existence.

RUDI GERNREICH,
Supertalk by Digby Diehl

Even a little bikini feels like being fully dressed when you're used to swimming naked.

RUDI GERNREICH,
Supertalk by Digby Diehl

The history of the world is largely the history of dress. It is the most illuminating of records, and tells its tale with a candour and completeness which no chronicle can surpass.

AGNES REPPLIER,
Americans and Others

Men, since they ceased to covet beautiful clothes for themselves, have wasted much valuable time in counselling and censuring women.

AGNES REPPLIER,
Americans and Others

It is color that kills the clothes of the average woman. She runs to bright spots that take the eye away from her face and hair. She ceases to be woman clothed and becomes a mere piece of clothing womaned.

H. L. MENCKEN,
Prejudices, Second Series

Up to the time I was twenty-nine . . . I was too shabby for any woman to tolerate me. . . . Then I got a job to do and bought a suit of clothes with the proceeds. A lady immediately invited me to tea, threw her arms around me, and said she adored me.

GEORGE BERNARD SHAW

A woman otherwise quite subdued may suddenly appear in a hat that is all ablaze with feeling—no doubt imprisoned passion's single mad escape—and you sometimes meet a hat, infuriate hat, hardly venturing to look at the rabid face beneath, yet find there a countenance of great serenity. The riot of emotion had passed off in the hat, leaving the soul at peace.

FRANK MOORE COLBY,
The Colby Essays, Vol. 2

I have found that there is an intimate connection between the character of women and the fancy that makes them choose a particular material.

PROSPER MÉRIMÉE,
quoted in *Woman in Epigram,*
compiled by Frederick W. Morton

If the function of art is to bring joy through harmony, color, and form, perhaps we can, after all, by dressing a woman to feel younger and to participate fully in life, bring her joy comparable to that she experiences in contemplating a painting.

ANDRÉ COURRÈGES,
Fashion, Art, and Beauty,
The Metropolitan Museum of Art Bulletin,
November 1967

Like a bird she seems to wear gay plumage unconsciously, as if it grew upon her.

HENRY WARD BEECHER,
Eyes and Ears

CLOUD

Clouds today—great archangel wings across the sky.

ANNE MORROW LINDBERGH,
Bring Me a Unicorn

Spring and autumn are inconsiderable events in a landscape compared with the shadows of a cloud.

ALICE MEYNELL,
The Colour of Life

One cloud is sufficient to eclipse a whole sun.

BALTASAR GRACIAN,
The Oracle

CLUB

It is natural for men to belong to a club, as it is natural for other men who do not belong to a club to call it a clique.

> G. K. Chesterton,
> *All I Survey*

COFFEE

Nothing'll make a father swear before the children quicker than a cup of poor coffee.

> Kin Hubbard,
> *Abe Martin on Things in General*

No coffee can be good in the mouth that does not first send a sweet offering of odor to the nostrils.

> Henry Ward Beecher,
> *Eyes and Ears*

A cup of coffee—real coffee—home-browned, home-ground, home-made, that comes to you dark as a hazel-eye, but changes to a golden bronze as you temper it with cream that never cheated, but was real cream from its birth, thick, tenderly yellow, perfectly sweet, neither lumpy nor frothing on the Java: such a cup of coffee is a match for twenty blue devils, and will exorcise them all.

> Henry Ward Beecher,
> *Eyes and Ears*

The best proof that tea or coffee are favourable to intellectual expression is that all nations use one or the other as aids to conversation.

> Philip G. Hamerton,
> *The Intellectual Life*

In Europe the most obstreperous nations are those most addicted to coffee.... We rightly speak of a storm in a teacup as the tiniest disturbance in the world, but out of a coffee-cup come hurricanes.

> Robert Lynd,
> *The Blue Lion*

COLD

I hate red eyes and blowing of noses.

> Sir Walter Scott,
> *Sir Walter Scott's Journal (1825-1832)*

At night to supper, though with little com-fort, I find myself both head and breast in great pain, and what troubles me most my right ear is almost deaf. It is a cold, which God Almighty in justice did give me while I sat lewdly sporting with Mrs. Lane the other day with the broken window in my neck.

> Samuel Pepys,
> *Diary of Samuel Pepys*

Why is it that men who can go through severe accidents, air raids and any other major crisis always seem to think they are at death's door when they have a simple head cold?

> Shirley Booth,
> quoted in *Ladies' Home Journal,*
> November 1943

Contentment preserves me from catching a cold. Has a woman who *knew* she was well dressed ever caught cold?—No, not even when she had scarcely a rag to her back.

> Friedrich Nietzsche,
> *Twilight of the Idols*

Very few people go to the doctor when they have a cold. They go to the theatre instead.

> W. Boyd Gatewood,
> quoted in *Ladies' Home Journal,*
> October 1942

COLLECTING

To collect anything, no matter what, is the healthy human impulse of man and boy, and the longer and harder the search, the greater the joy of acquisition.

> Agnes Repplier,
> *Times and Tendencies*

I am glad you are collecting flowers, it is a sign of freshness to collect.

> A. C. Benson,
> *Excerpts from the Letters of*
> *Dr. A. C. Benson to M. E. A.*

If you had the collector's temperament you would know that to give away anything is nearly an impossibility, and to give away anything without regretting it is quite an impossibility.

E. V. LUCAS,
365 Days and One More

We know that every collector is an unconscious Don Juan who has transferred his passion from an erotic to a non-erotic sphere. But we also know that the passion with which the collected objects are loved emanates from the erotic domain.

DR. WILHELM STEKHEL,
The Depths of the Soul

COLLECTIVE

Collective man has become paramount, and his authority simply consists of the weight of the masses. No wonder that we have a feeling of impending disaster, as if an avalanche had broken loose which no mortal power is capable of holding up. Collective man is threatening to suffocate the individual who is absolutely indispensable, for it is on his sense of responsibility that every human achievement is ultimately founded.

C. G. JUNG,
Psychological Reflections,
edited by Jolande Jacobi and R. F. Hull

COLOR

Green is the fresh emblem of well-founded hopes. In blue the spirit can wander, but in green it can rest.

MARY WEBB,
The Spring of Joy

Red has been praised for its nobility of the colour of life. But the true colour of life is not red. Red is the colour of violence, or of life broken open, edited, and published.

ALICE MEYNELL,
The Colour of Life

The rich blue of the unattainable flower of the sky drew my soul to it, and there it rested, for pure colour is rest of heart.

RICHARD JEFFERIES,
The Story of My Heart

Color is a sort of food; every spot of color is a drop of wine to the heart.

RICHARD JEFFERIES,
quoted in *American Catholic Quarterly Review,*
January 1914

Familiarity breeds indifference. We have seen too much pure, bright color at Woolworth's to find it intrinsically transporting.

ALDOUS HUXLEY,
Heaven and Hell

To the Arabians ... blue was the most expressive of all colors. Blue—the color of the very material heavens which hold the stars in place. Blue—in the mystery of which dwells the very finite infinite.

LOUIS DANZ,
Dynamic Dissonance

Red, being the most corporeal of colors, best expresses the Greek concept of immediateness—bodily presence.

LOUIS DANZ,
Dynamic Dissonance

Pink is the color of romance, and a friend tells me that the girl with a pink dress at the party is the one who is selected for each dance.

ALFRED CARL HOTTES,
Garden Facts and Fancies

In *Kaleidoscope* (1956) I colored the dancers' hands and faces so that the figures wouldn't look decapitated. What interested me most was that as I watched one of my dancers painting one side of her face blue and the other side green, I really saw her for the first time. She was much more beautiful than I had thought.

ALWIN NIKOLAIS,
Fashion, Art, and Beauty,
The Metropolitan Museum of Art Bulletin,
November 1967

Colour is inward and alive. Indeed the men of science tell us that it is an intense vibration, almost a quick pulsation of life. The colour we see in nature—the burning hues of the poppy and the gorse, even the quiet shades of the heather and the primrose are alive. Not even the Alps in all the majesty of their outline are as one of the harebells on their slopes.

VINCENT MCNABB,
The Wayside

Pink acts like benzedrine on most males' jaded chivalry.

WILLIAM E. RICHARDSON,
quoted in the *New York Times,*
August 30, 1953

Probably the most joyous moment in the whole history of painting was the moment when the incipient impressionists discovered light, and with it, colour.

D. H. LAWRENCE,
Selected Essays

It is comparatively easy to achieve a certain unity in a picture by allowing one colour to dominate or by muting all the colours. Matisse did neither. He clashed his colours together like cymbals and the effect was like a lullaby.

JOHN BERGER,
Toward Reality

COMBAT (*See* BATTLE, WAR)

COMFORT

Certain it is that the divinest comfort is lodged in humanity itself, for we could do but little with a God's comforting; but our eyes would have to be a shade more seeing, our ears more receptive, our tongues savour more completely the taste of a fruit, we would need to have a more vigorous sense of smell and to be more present in spirit when we touch and are touched and less forgetful, if we were to extract from our most immediate experiences those consolations which are more compelling, more overmastering, and more true than all the suffering that can ever shake us.

RAINER MARIA RILKE,
Selected Letters of Rainer Maria Rilke
1902–1926

Comfort, like health, may be impaired by being too anxiously cared for.

SIR HENRY TAYLOR,
Notes from Life

Comfort is the great social tranquilizer.

PHILIP RIEFF,
The Triumph of the Therapeutic

We often find comfort in telling what is painful in actual experience.

SAINT BASIL,
Letters and Select Works

The power comfort has over me, my powerlessness without it. I know no one in whom both are so great. Consequently, everything I build is insubstantial, unstable; the maid who forgets to bring me my warm water in the morning overturns my world.

FRANZ KAFKA,
The Diaries of Franz Kafka 1914–1923

COMIC

To produce the whole of its effect . . . the comic demands something like a momentary anesthesia of the heart. Its appeal is to the intelligence, pure and simple.

HENRI BERGSON,
Laughter

Only the solemn things are ever comic.

BEDE JARRETT,
The House of Gold

The test of a real comedian is whether you laugh at him before he opens his mouth.

GEORGE JEAN NATHAN,
The World of George Jean Nathan,
edited by Charles Angoff

COMMERCE

The aim of commerce is not to sell what is best for people or even what they really need, but simply to sell: its final standard is successful sale.

SIR RICHARD LIVINGSTONE.
On Education

The commercial aspect of things is really more deeply seated in all of us than we quite dare allow ourselves to realize. I constantly myself have men come to me, men who I think love me too, and say: "Now, Anderson, you could write a novel or a play that would make money. Why don't you do it and thus make money enough to be a free man? Afterward you could of course do your real work."

One is, you see, to make a mess on the very floor of the temple wherein he worships.

SHERWOOD ANDERSON,
Letters of Sherwood Anderson

COMMITMENT

It is all very well to talk of being unhurt, keeping yourself clear, triumphant; it can't be. It isn't true. To give your faith, that is the risk.

KATHARINE BUTLER HATHAWAY,
*The Journals and Letters
of the Little Locksmith*

I am inclined to suppose that you ought to fight against being dreamy and taking life too easily. I am sure it is always right to throw oneself, heart and soul, into everything one does.

DOM JOHN CHAPMAN,
The Spiritual Letters of Dom John Chapman

The profundity of a spiritual act is in direct proportion to its author's commitment.

HENRI DE LUBAC,
Paradoxes

COMMITTEE

I hate being placed on committees. They are always having meetings at which half are absent and the rest late.

OLIVER WENDELL HOLMES,
Life and Letters of Oliver Wendell Holmes,
Vol. I, by John T. Morse, Jr.

I find it very useful to be a member of plenty of committees; I can point to the list whenever I am asked to do anything

which might involve real work, and ask how I can be expected to shoulder any new duties?

ROBERTSON DAVIES,
The Table Talk of Samuel Marchbanks

We always carry out by committee anything in which any one of us alone would be too reasonable to persist.

FRANK MOORE COLBY,
The Colby Essays, Vol. 1

COMMONPLACE

Most of us find it difficult to recognize the greatness and wonder of things too familiar to us. As the prophet is not without honor (save in his own country) so it is also with phenomena.

CHARLES SANDERS PEIRCE,
Collected Papers of Charles Sanders Peirce,
Vol. V

Curious how little impression experience too familiar makes upon men's minds, how little attention is paid to it. With an oversecure, not to say ridiculous, contempt, I bethink me, are we despising everyday experience, we specialists and half the world besides.

CHARLES SANDERS PEIRCE,
Collected Papers of Charles Sanders Peirce,
Vol. VI

To fear nothing and despise nothing—especially the commonplace.

JOHN PEALE BISHOP,
The Collected Essays of John Peale Bishop

We are indeed sponges to absorb the commonplace; but if one has character the commonplace will nourish that too and take its form. Great men have no better food than the rest of us, and often less of it.

CHARLES HORTON COOLEY,
Life and the Student

Human beings in the lump and mass learn to be tolerant, unselfish, and kind to each other. But their story never gets into the newspapers or the novels or the plays or the pictures. There is no drama in homespun loyalty and homespun love. But these things outlive and outlast all other things. They are the splendour and radiance and glory of the commonplace.

JAMES DOUGLAS,
Down Shoe Lane

No matter through what realms of the fantastic you may travel, you arrive inevitably at the commonplace.

WILLIAM J. LOCKE,
The Marvels of Marcus Ordeyne

You can't put a great soul into a commonplace person. Commonplace persons have commonplace souls.

D. H. LAWRENCE,
Selected Essays

And so you may be most vastly important to yourself. Which is the private aim of all men. The hero had it openly. The commonplace person has it inside himself, though outwardly he says: Of course I'm no better than anybody else! His very asserting it shows he doesn't think it for a second.

D. H. LAWRENCE,
Selected Essays

Familiarity is an almost insuperable obstacle to giving a lofty message. No good comes out of Nazareth, and Nazareth is always the place where we live. ... It is to the remote we look for a revelation, while all the time it would speak to us from the eyes of those who are near us and would voice itself through the commonplace world in which we live.

EDWARD HOWARD GRIGGS,
A Book of Meditations

If you will cling to Nature, to the simple in Nature, to the little things that hardly any one sees, and that can so unexpectedly become big and beyond measuring; if you have this love of inconsiderable things and seek quite humbly as a ministrant to win the confidence of what seems poor: then everything will become easier, more coherent and somehow more conciliatory for you, not in your intellect, perhaps, which

lags behind astonished, but in your inmost consciousness, waking and cognizance.

RAINER MARIA RILKE,
Letters to a Young Poet

There are no short cuts to Heaven, only the ordinary way of ordinary things.

VINCENT MCNABB,
God's Way of Mercy

COMMON SENSE

The mere intellect is perverse; it takes all sides, maintains all paradoxes, and comes to understanding only when it listens to the whisperings of common sense.

JOHN LANCASTER SPALDING,
Things of the Mind

There is no greater panacea for every kind of folly than common sense.

BALTASAR GRACIAN,
The Oracle

Common sense, however logical and sound, is after all only one human attitude among many others; and like everything human it may have its limitations—or *negative* side.

WILLIAM BARRETT,
Irrational Man

COMMUNICATION

I feel that instead of any inability to communicate there is a deliberate evasion of communication. Communication itself between people is so frightening that rather than do that there is a continual crosstalk, a continual talking about other things, rather than what is at the root of their relationship.

HAROLD PINTER,
quoted in *The Theatre of the Absurd*
by Martin Esslin

Communication in every form is so much a part of man as man in the very depth of his being, that it must always remain possible and one can never know how far it will go.

KARL JASPERS,
The Perennial Scope of Philosophy

There is no pleasure to me without communication; there is not so much as a sprightly thought comes into my mind but I grieve that I have no one to tell it to.

> MONTAIGNE,
> *Essays*

The fact that we are I don't know how many millions of people, yet communication, complete communication, is completely impossible between two of these people, is to me one of the biggest tragic things in the world. When I was a young boy I was afraid of it. I would almost scream because of it. It gave me such a sensation of solitude, of loneliness.

> GEORGES SIMENON,
> *Writers at Work,*
> edited by Malcolm Cowley

There are men who would quickly love each other if once they were to speak to each other; for when they spoke they would discover that their souls ... had only been separated by phantoms and diabolic delusions.

> ERNEST HELLO,
> *Life, Science, and Art*

COMMUNION

The natural impulse of my being, from my earliest recollection, was—not to observe others—but to flow into them.

> ROMAIN ROLLAND,
> *Journey Within*

Always seek communion. It is the most precious thing men possess. In this respect, the symbol of the religions is indeed full of majesty. Where there is communion there is something that is more than human, there is surely something divine.

> GEORGES DUHAMEL,
> *The Heart's Domain*

Like the glow-worm; dowdy, minute, passive, yet full of mystery to the poet, and passionate significance to its fellows; so everything and everybody eternally radiate their dim light for those who care to seek. The strawberry hidden under the last leaf cries, "Pick me"; the forgotten book, in the forgotten book shop, screams to be discovered. The old house hidden in the hollow agitates itself violently at the approach of its pre-destined admirer. Dead authors cry "Read me"; dead friends cry, "Remember me"; dead ancestors cry, "Unearth me"; dead places, "Revisit me": and sympathetic spirits, living and dead, are trying continually to enter into communion.

> CYRIL CONNOLLY,
> *The Unquiet Grave*

COMMUNISM

Radio talks, pamphlets, pious aspirations are not going to defeat Communism—the only answer to it is a just social order.

> JOSEPH FITZSIMMONS,
> *The Christian in a Changing World*

We must help the new countries rise to a level from which their people can laugh at Communism.

> JOHN F. KENNEDY,
> *This Week,* January 15, 1961

COMMUNITY

The community stagnates without the impulse of the individual. The impulse dies away without the sympathy of the community.

> WILLIAM JAMES,
> *The Will to Believe*

The individual, if left alone from birth, would remain primitive and beastlike in his thoughts and feelings to a degree that we can hardly conceive. The individual is what he is and has the significance that he has not so much in virtue of his individuality, but rather as a member of a great human community, which directs his material and spiritual existence from the cradle to the grave.

> ALBERT EINSTEIN,
> *Ideas and Opinions*

Man, the social being, naturally, and in one sense helplessly, depends on his communities. Sundered from them, he has neither worth nor wit, but wanders in waste places, and, when he returns finds the lonely house of his individual life empty, swept, and garnished.

JOSIAH ROYCE,
The Problem of Christianity, Vol. II

The individual self is conscious of enrichment not only by the experience of real things, but also by the community, which expands its self-consciousness into a consciousness of communal self. By direct sympathy, what belongs to another becomes mine own, and what belongs to me becomes his.

ROMANO GUARDINI,
The Church and the Catholic

COMMUTER

Most commuters are as untalkative as native Vermonters. You have your paper, and he has his. I remember a short story about a commuter who used to admire the girl who took the same train as his for twelve years, but never picked her up.

MAX LERNER,
The Unfinished Country

COMPANION (See ACQUAINTANCE, FRIEND)

COMPARISON

Comparison is the expedient of those who cannot reach the heart of things compared.

GEORGE SANTAYANA,
Character and Opinion in the United States

When a camel is at the foot of a mountain then judge of his height.

HINDU PROVERB

Comparisons of one's lot with others' teaches us nothing and enfeebles the will.

THORNTON WILDER,
Writers at Work,
edited by Malcolm Cowley

We are creatures of comparisons, because we are finite. We can only learn values or estimate truths by comparing them with others. We honor one thing by despising another. We can hardly do justice to a thing without first doing an injustice to something else.

FREDERICK W. FABER,
Bethlehem

COMPASSION

The bowels of compassion: a wonderful old phrase. They ought to be kept open.

NORMAN DOUGLAS,
An Almanac

If you think of your fellow creatures, then you only want to cry, you could really cry the whole day long. The only thing to do is to pray that God will perform a miracle and save some of them. And I hope that I am doing that enough!

ANNE FRANK,
Anne Frank: The Diary of a Young Girl

When individual fear or apathy passes by the unfortunate, life is of no account.

HANIEL LONG,
A Letter to St. Augustine

True humanity consists not in a squeamish ear; it consists not in starting or shrinking at tales of misery, but in a disposition of heart to relieve it.

CHARLES J. FOX

COMPENSATION

There is no mathematical law of compensation. ... Now it more than makes up for the evil, again there is no compensation at all. Much depends upon your attitude, as confident or otherwise, and upon what energy you have to assimilate or transform the hurt.

CHARLES HORTON COOLEY,
Life and the Student

All loss is gain. Since I have become so near-sighted I see no dust or squalor, and therefore conceive of myself as living in splendor.

ALICE JAMES,
The Diary of Alice James

COMPETITION

The more modern nations detest each other the more meekly they follow each other; for all competition is in its nature only a furious plagiarism.

G. K. CHESTERTON,
Charles Dickens

Our social fabric militates against relation. Competitiveness pervades everything we do and is taught from the time we are small children. Work and play are conceived of as contest and race. . . . We seize on the half-truth that competition forces everyone to do his best (*half*-truth, because his best is by no means always the best in human terms) and completely ignore what this does to human meeting. Our fundamental stance is not to respond to others, but to outdo them, vie with them, beat them.

GEORGE W. MORGAN,
Prophetic Voices, edited by Ned O'Gorman

COMPLAINT

Complaint always brings discredit in its train: it serves rather to stimulate the audacity of the hostile than to prompt the compassionate to console you.

BALTASAR GRACIAN,
The Oracle

Obtain from yourself all that makes complaining useless. No longer implore from others what you yourself can obtain.

ANDRÉ GIDE,
The Fruits of the Earth

To ourselves it is always good to make the best of a bad case; but in persuading others it is good to admit the worst in that which is the subject of their complaints.

FREDERICK W. FABER,
Spiritual Conferences

The one who complains the loudest is generally he who contributes the least.

A. G. SERTILLANGES,
Rectitude

True, it is most painful not to meet the kindness and affection you feel you have

deserved and have a right to expect from others; but it is a mistake to complain of it, for it is of no use. You cannot extort friendship with a cocked pistol.

SYDNEY SMITH,
Sayings

Learn to accept in silence the minor aggravations, cultivate the gift of taciturnity, and consume your own smoke with an extra draft of hard work, so that those about you may not be annoyed with the dust and soot of your complaints.

SIR WILLIAM OSLER,
quoted in *Life of Sir William Osler,*
Vol. I, by Harvey Cushing

Complain to one who can help you.

YUGOSLAV PROVERB

I think that the insane desire one has sometimes to bang and kick grumblers and peevish persons, is a Divine instinct.

ROBERT HUGH BENSON,
quoted in *The Life of Monsignor
Robert Hugh Benson,*
edited by C. C. Martindale

We mourn the transitory things and fret under the yoke of the immutable ones.

PAUL ELDRIDGE,
Horns of Glass

COMPLETE

Complete persons are exceptions. It is true that an overwhelming majority of educated people are fragmentary personalities and have a lot of substitutes instead of the genuine goods.

C. G. JUNG,
Psychological Reflections,
edited by Jolande Jacobi and R. F. Hull

Nothing is done while something re· ıains to be done. To finish is the mark ɔf the master.

HENRI FRÉDÉRIC AMIEL,
The Private Journal of Henri Frédéric Amiel

The complete character is that which is in communion with most sides of life—which sees, hears and feels most—which has for its fellows the sympathy of understanding, for nature the love that is without entire comprehension, and for the mystery beyond them the inexhaustible desire which surely prophesies fulfillment somewhere.

MARY WEBB,
The Spring of Joy

Some men never attain completeness: there is always something lacking in them; others develop slowly.

BALTASAR GRACIAN,
The Oracle

COMPLIMENT

Nothing makes people so worthy of compliments as occasionally receiving them. One is more delightful for being told one is delightful—just as one is more angry for being told one is angry.

KATHERINE FULLERTON GEROULD,
quoted in *Reader's Digest,* April 1935

Attention is a tacit and continual compliment.

MADAME SWETCHINE,
The Writings of Madame Swetchine

In vain do people say good things of us, for we think so many more.

J. PETIT-SENN,
Conceits and Caprices

Everybody knows how to utter a complaint, but few can express a graceful compliment.

WILLIAM FEATHER,
The Business of Life

To compliment often implies an assumption of superiority in the complimenter. It is, in fact, a subtle detraction.

HENRY DAVID THOREAU,
Journal

To pay compliments to the woman we love is the first way of caressing her. A compliment is like kissing through a veil.

VICTOR HUGO,
Les Miserables

The compliment that helps us on our way is not the one that is shut up in the mind, but the one that is spoken out.

MARK TWAIN,
Mark Twain at Your Fingertips,
edited by Caroline T. Harnsberger

Nothing is so silly as the expression of a man who is being complimented.

ANDRÉ GIDE,
The Journals of André Gide, Vol. I

K. has the most estimable habit of paying one compliments. . . . I make it a rule always to believe the compliments implicitly for five minutes, and to simmer gently for twenty more; that ensures a solid gain of twenty-five minutes out of twenty-four hours, in which one is in peace and charity of all mankind.

ALICE JAMES,
The Diary of Alice James

CONCENTRATION

One of the most important factors—not only in military matters, but in life as a whole—is the power of execution, the ability to direct one's whole energies towards the fulfillment of a particular task.

FIELD MARSHAL ERWIN ROMMEL,
The Rommel Papers

I must take my old way, and write myself into good-humor with my task. It is only when I dally with what I am about, look back, and aside, instead of keeping my eyes straight forward, that I feel these cold sinkings of the heart. All men I suppose do, more or less. They are like the sensations of a sailor when the ship is cleared for action, and all are at their places—gloomy enough; but the first broadside puts all to rights.

SIR WALTER SCOTT,
Sir Walter Scott's Journal (1825-1832)

If you would be Pope, you must think of nothing else.

SPANISH PROVERB

For him who has no concentration, there is no tranquility.

BHAGAVAD GITA

In me always (living as I have among men) there has been the sense of a persistent outcry of little distracting voices. Now it is as though the voices had begun to shout madly and meaninglessly. We will have to write and think and try to believe in beauty and innocence in the midst of the most terrible clutter.

SHERWOOD ANDERSON,
Letters of Sherwood Anderson

The difference in men does not lie in the size of their heads, nor in the perfection of their bodies, but in this one sublime ability of concentration—to throw the weight with the blow, live an eternity in an hour—"This one thing I do!"

ELBERT HUBBARD,
The Philosophy of Elbert Hubbard

The real essence of work is concentrated energy ... people who really have that in a superior degree by nature, are independent of the forms and habits and artifices by which less able and active people are kept up to their labors.

WALTER BAGEHOT,
Literary Studies

I am ready to believe ... that in single-heartedness and little childhood is the way to Salvation: it is not meant that children by their innocence are near to heaven, but that all good is gained by those whose thought and life are kept pointed close to one main thing, not scattered abroad upon a thousand.

STEPHEN MACKENNA,
Journal and Letters of Stephen MacKenna

CONCEPT

The concept, the label, is perpetually hiding from us all the nature of the real. . . . It is a narrow little house which becomes a prison to those who can't get out of it.

JOYCE CARY,
Art and Reality

CONCLUSION

Keep knowledge at nurse as long as possible; cherish its grounds, reasons, and ques-

tions; draw conclusions only when necessity of decision compels.

CHAUNCEY WRIGHT,
Letters of Chauncey Wright

In literature, in art, in life, I think that the only conclusions worth coming to are one's own conclusions. If they march with the verdict of the connoisseurs, so much the better for the connoisseurs; if they do not so march, so much the better for oneself.

A. C. BENSON,
From a College Window

Conclusions are usually consolidated guesses.

ANONYMOUS (HENRY S. HASKINS),
Meditations in Wall Street

The open mind never acts; when we have done our utmost to arrive at a reasonable conclusion, we still, when we can reason and investigate no more, must close our minds for the moment with a snap, and act dogmatically on our conclusions.

GEORGE BERNARD SHAW,
Preface, *Androcles and the Lion*

CONDOLENCES

There is a good deal of curiosity generally mingled with the haste of condolences.

VICTOR HUGO

Words seem very poor things at such a time of trouble as yours and yet they are all one can use to tell of one's sympathy.

BASIL W. MATURIN,
Father Maturin by Maisie Ward

One hesitates to invade the privacy of grief; one feels so clearly that the reverent thing is silence. The best words mean so little; yet so strangely compounded is human nature that the very words which, in their coming, vex us and mock us with their inadequacy are missed sometimes when they fail to come. Friends are needed, like other insufficient things, in hours of destitution, and they must be content with the pitiful crumb they can offer to the needs of famine.

OSCAR W. FIRKINS,
Oscar Firkins: Memoirs and Letters,
edited by Ina Ten Eyck

CONDUCT

It may be a good working guide to conduct might be framed on this ideal of living to the fullest here and now: it is likely that the soul seeking admission among the bodiless immortals in another world would be elected at once on the strength of having kept itself from death in days here below.

STEPHEN MACKENNA,
Journal and Letters of Stephen Mackenna

I am a firm believer in the theory that the strongest motive, whether we are conscious of it or not, rules our conduct.

ELLEN GLASGOW,
Letters of Ellen Glasgow

I don't never have any trouble in regulating my own conduct, but to keep other folks' straight is what bothers me.

JOSH BILLINGS,
His Works Complete

I do not know why it is that such a number of people try to make up for the virtue of their conduct by the viciousness of their beliefs.

ROBERT LYND,
The Blue Lion

There is an infinity of modes of conduct which appear ridiculous, the secret reasons of which are wise and sound.

LA ROCHEFOUCAULD,
Maxims

The ultimate test for us of what a truth means is the conduct it dictates or inspires.

WILLIAM JAMES

CONFERENCE

No grand idea was ever born in a conference, but a lot of foolish ideas have died there.

F. SCOTT FITZGERALD,
The Crack-up

CONFESSION

That which you confess today, you will perceive tomorrow.

COVENTRY PATMORE,
The Rod, the Root, and the Flower

Before confessing, be perfectly certain that you do not wish to be forgiven.

KATHERINE MANSFIELD,
quoted in *Katherine Mansfield*
by Antony Alpers

It is because sympathy is but a living again through our own past in a new form, that confession often prompts a response of confession.

GEORGE ELIOT,
Scenes from Clerical Life

CONFIDENCE

Do continue to believe that with your feeling and your work you are taking part in the *greatest;* the more strongly you cultivate in yourself this belief, the more will reality and the world go forth from it.

RAINER MARIA RILKE,
Letters of Rainer Maria Rilke 1892–1910

I admire the assurance and confidence everyone has in himself, whereas there is hardly anything I am sure I know or that I dare give my word I can do.

MONTAIGNE,
Essays

It is best in the theatre to act with confidence no matter how little right you have to it.

LILLIAN HELLMAN,
Pentimento

The confidence which we have in ourselves gives birth to much of that which we have in others.

LA ROCHEFOUCAULD,
Maxims

Confidence as an outgoing act is directness and courage in meeting the facts of life, trusting them to bring instruction and support to a developing self.

JOHN DEWEY,
Human Nature and Conduct

CONFIDING

How very sad it is to have a confiding nature, one's hopes and feelings are quite at the mercy of all who come along; and how very desirable to be a stolid individual, whose hopes and aspirations are safe in one's waistcoat pocket, and that a pocket indeed, and one not to be picked.

EMILY DICKINSON,
Letters of Emily Dickinson

CONFLICT

If we are to be participants in our particular phase of history, we cannot remain unaware of the dimensions of contemporary conflicts. Paradoxically, I believe that we could live less painfully with the almost overwhelming conflicts of the present, and find more of ourselves in the midst of them, if instead of protecting ourselves from them, we allowed ourselves to realize more fully their immense difficulty.

HELEN MERRELL LYND,
On Shame and the Search for Identity

All men have in them an instinct for conflict: at least, all healthy men.

HILAIRE BELLOC,
The Silence of the Sea

The stirring up of conflict is a Luciferian quality in the true sense of the word. Conflict creates the fire of affects and emotions, and like every fire it has two aspects: that of burning and that of giving light.

C. G. JUNG,
Psychological Reflections,
edited by Jolande Jacobi and R. F. Hull

No doubt there are other important things in life besides conflict, but there are not many other things so inevitably interesting. The very saints interest us most when we think of them as engaged in a conflict with the Devil.

ROBERT LYND,
The Blue Lion

When one ceases from conflict, whether because he has won, because he has lost, or

because he cares no more for the game, the virtue passes out of him.

CHARLES HORTON COOLEY,
Life and the Student

CONFORMITY

'Tis better to be trampled out by asses' hoofs than be the thing the asses' mind approves.

JOHN MASEFIELD,
quoted in *Linotype's Shining Lines,*
December 1937

Many things that come into the world are not looked into. The individual says "My crowd doesn't run that way." I say, don't run with crowds.

ROBERT HENRI,
The Art Spirit

We are half ruined by conformity; but we should be wholly ruined without it.

CHARLES DUDLEY WARNER,
My Summer in a Garden

What is it about us, the public, and what is it about conformity itself that causes us all to require it of our neighbors and of our artists and then, with consummate fickleness, to forget those who fall into line and eternally celebrate those who do not?

BEN SHAHN,
The Shape of Content

We would know mankind better if we were not so anxious to resemble one another.

GOETHE

Like all men who are fundamentally of the group, of the herd, he was incapable of taking a strong stand with the inevitable loneliness that is implied.

F. SCOTT FITZGERALD,
The Crack-up

The idea that men are created free and equal is both true and misleading: men are created different; they lose their social freedom and their individual autonomy in seeking to become like each other.

DAVID RIESMAN,
The Lonely Crowd

Conformity is the ape of harmony.

RALPH WALDO EMERSON,
Journals of Ralph Waldo Emerson

There is truth in the high opinion that in so far as a man conforms, he ceases to exist.

MAX EASTMAN,
quoted in *As the Poet Says,*
compiled by Benjamin Musser

Since keeping in step with our fellows is almost as necessary to us as eating, it takes more heroism than an ordinary person can muster to tear himself away from any crowd marching shoulder to shoulder, no matter where it is going.

DOROTHY CANFIELD FISHER,
Harper's Magazine, December 1932

Men have long begun to suspect that civilization's repression of our primitive impulses has somehow warped what are potentially the most productive forces in human nature. We are increasingly disturbed by the thought that society's passion for obedience and conformity may have overreached itself, causing us to lose in individual happiness perhaps as much as we have gained in group security.

DR. SMILEY BLANTON,
Love or Perish

Our society cannot have it both ways: to maintain a conformist and ignoble system *and* to have skillful and spirited men to man that system.

PAUL GOODMAN,
Growing Up Absurd

We see people quitting their own perceptions, and with specious promise of good to themselves being carried along by the common stream. All the while there abides in them the power which made them. And if so it be that they turn their reverence to this power instead of to the herd-instinct which permeates and actuates the masses, they are rewarded by impulses and instincts and cumulative inspiration which individualizes them and leads them forward to a special destiny. Nothing is truer than this, yet nothing is less generally accepted, believed, and turned to profitable account.

ANONYMOUS (HENRY S. HASKINS),
Meditations in Wall Street

For one man who thanks God that he is not as other men there are a thousand to offer thanks that they are as other men, sufficiently as others to escape attention.

JOHN DEWEY,
Human Nature and Conduct

I spent much of the morning walking in the Park, and going to the Queene's chapell, where I staid and saw their masse, till a man came and bid me go out or kneel down: so I did go out.

SAMUEL PEPYS,
Diary of Samuel Pepys

It is one of the ironic and yet pathetic aspects of our competitive life that with each step up the ladder of success, the regimentation of the individual and his family becomes more intense and coercive. The goal of competitive striving is to be allowed to submit to these exactions and find fulfillment only in doing as faithfully as possible what others in one's competitive class are doing.

LAWRENCE K. FRANK,
Society as the Patient

I am a believer and a conformist. Anyone can revolt; it is more difficult silently to obey our own interior promptings, and to spend our lives finding sincere and fitting means of expression for our temperaments and our gifts—if we have any.

GEORGES ROUAULT,
quoted in *Artists on Art,*
edited by Robert Goldwater
and Marco Treves

Individualism is a fatal poison. But individuality is the salt of common life. You may have to live in a crowd, but you do not have to live like it, nor subsist on its food. You may have your own orchard. You may drink at a hidden spring. Be yourself if you would serve others.

HENRY VAN DYKE,
The School of Life

CONFUSION

I once told Fordie [Ford Madox Ford] that if he were placed naked and alone in a room without furniture, I would come back and find total confusion.

EZRA POUND,
quoted in *The Working Novelist*
by V. S. Pritchett

I live from one tentative conclusion to the next, thinking each one is final. The only thing I know for sure is that I am confused.

HUGH PRATHER,
Notes to Myself

Try and find your deepest issue in every confusion, and abide by that.

D. H. LAWRENCE,
Selected Essays

Study any confusion and you find it is peace in an early stage.

ANONYMOUS (HENRY S. HASKINS),
Meditations in Wall Street

CONNOISSEUR (See AUTHORITY, KNOWLEDGE)

CONSCIENCE

When a man is content with the testimony of his own conscience, he does not care to shine with the light of another's praise.

SAINT BERNARD OF CLAIRVAUX,
Letters

Some good must come by clinging to the right. Conscience is a man's compass, and though the needle sometimes deviates, though one perceives irregularities in directing one's course by it, still one must try to follow its direction.

VINCENT VAN GOGH,
*Dear Theo:
An Autobiography of Vincent Van Gogh*

It was Clémenceau, I think, who said that when a man has character it's usually bad. True; and when one has a conscience, it's usually a bad one.

EUGÈNE IONESCO,
Fragments of a Journal

The mind is fearless so long as there is no reproach of conscience. When that comes, come breakage and bondage and a host of terrors.

LOUISE IMOGEN GUINEY,
Goose-Quill Papers

Conscience gets a lot of credit that belongs to cold feet.

ANONYMOUS,
quoted in *Ladies' Home Journal,*
March 1947

Conscience is the name which the orthodox give to their prejudices.

JOHN OLIVER HOBBES,
A Bundle of Life

To most men, conscience is an occasional, almost an external voice.

WALTER BAGEHOT,
Literary Studies, Vol. III

The more productively one lives, the stronger is one's conscience, and, in turn, the more it furthers one's productiveness. The less productively one lives, the weaker becomes one's conscience; the paradoxical—and tragic—situation of man is that his conscience is weakest when he needs it most.

ERICH FROMM,
Man for Himself

Your conscience is what your mother told you before you were six years old.

DR. G. BROCK CHISHOLM,
quoted in *Ladies' Home Journal,*
October 1949

Conscience implies a relation between the soul and a something exterior, and that, moreover, superior to itself; a relation to an excellence which it does not possess, and to a tribunal over which it has no power.

JOHN HENRY CARDINAL NEWMAN,
Oxford University Sermons

CONSCIENTIOUS

Conscientious men are, almost everywhere, less encouraged than tolerated.

JOSEPH ROUX,
Meditations of a Parish Priest

CONSCIOUSNESS

We can only be said to be alive in those moments when our hearts are conscious of our treasures.

THORNTON WILDER,
The Woman of Andros

As you open your awareness, life will improve of itself, you won't even have to try. It's a beautiful paradox; the more you open your consciousness, the fewer unpleasant events intrude themselves into your awareness.

THADDEUS GOLAS,
The Lazy Man's Guide to Enlightenment

Enlightenment is any experience of expanding our consciousness beyond its present limits. We could also say that perfect enlightenment is realizing that we have no limits at all, and that the entire universe is alive.

THADDEUS GOLAS,
The Lazy Man's Guide to Enlightenment

Watch your consciousness as much as you like, it will always be passing through some new phase which is never for two seconds identical.

ERNEST DIMNET,
What We Live By

The justification of consciousness is the having of it.

JOSIAH ROYCE,
The Spirit of Modern Philosophy

We must not force ourselves to be too conscious, even of God—our spirit cannot bear it. Depression comes very often from repletion. Our subconscious nature must have sufficient time to store up what our conscious nature requires.

RABINDRANATH TAGORE,
Letters to a Friend

If I were asked to make a graph of my mental life it would not be a curve. It would be a mad succession of zigzags, dartings hither and thither, leaps upward and plunges downward, like a fever chart. This stranger that I steer behaves oddly and queerly. I cannot explain his behaviour.

JAMES DOUGLAS,
Down Shoe Lane

For it is very possible that even without being conscious of having something one has it in himself and even in a form more effective than if he knew it. . . . Consciousness seems to obscure the actions it perceives, and only when they occur without it are they purer, more effective, more vital.

PLOTINUS,
quoted in *The Ways of the Will*
by Leslie H. Farber

What is man's great privilege, his exceptional experience? Consciousness and again consciousness, and it is in a passionate imaginative consciousness our true rewards are to be won.

LLEWELYN POWYS,
Now That the Gods Are Dead

If a man understands that he is asleep and if he wishes to awake, then everything that helps him to awake will be *good* and everything that hinders him, everything that prolongs his sleep, will be *evil*.

GEORGES GURDJIEFF,
quoted in *In Search of the Miraculous*
by P. D. Ouspensky

You will then see that you can think, feel, act, speak, work *without being conscious of it.* And if you learn to see in yourselves the moments of consciousness and the long periods of mechanicalness, you will as infallibly see in other people when they are conscious of what they are doing and when they are not.

GEORGES GURDJIEFF,
quoted in *In Search of the Miraculous*
by P. D. Ouspensky

Consciousness is a very superficial thing.

GEORGE SANTAYANA,
The Letters of George Santayana,

The latch-key which opens into the chambers of my inner consciousness fits, as I have sufficient reason to believe, the private apartments of a good many other people's thoughts. The longer we live the more we find that we are like other persons. When I meet with any facts in my own mental experience, I feel almost sure that I shall find them repeated or anticipated in the writings or conversation of others.

OLIVER WENDELL HOLMES,
quoted in *Priestly Practice*
by Arthur Barry O'Neill

The more I explore the systems of ratiocination by which men try to make their souls at home in this brute world, the more surely I come back to a categorical assertion of the value of conscious life as the premise of wisdom. It is the only valid meeting place of mind with nature, the only religion which does not play tricks with fact.

MAX EASTMAN,
Enjoyment of Living

Becoming conscious is of course a sacrilege against nature, it is as though you had robbed the unconscious of something.

C. G. JUNG,
quoted in *The Inner World of Choice*
by Frances G. Wickes

Mental endeavour (the process of consciousness in general) requires of man such a strenuous effort that under any circumstances he prefers simplicity, although it may not even be real. But if it is not real, then he becomes its slave.

C. G. JUNG,
quoted in *The Book of Marriage,*
edited by Count Hermann Keyserling

O miserable ratio of the transmissions to the unuttered and only half-apprehended broodings! This is so of everyone. Consider, then, that huge world of undivulged thought, that great sea of inward fancy, exultation, yearning, in which conscious and communicated life is a mere sprinkle of atolls.

CHRISTOPHER MORLEY,
Inward Ho

The worm in the apple of human existence is consciousness. It steals over the face of life like an intruder. Seen through the mirror everything becomes the background of the ego. The seers, the mystics, the visionaries smash this mirror again and again. They restore man to the pri-

mordial flux, they put him back in the stream like a fisherman emptying his net.

HENRY MILLER,
The Books in My Life

How to become conscious? ... It means that you will suffer still more—that's the first thing to realize. But you won't be dead, you won't be indifferent.... You will want to understand everything, even the disagreeable things. You will want to accept more and more—even what seems hostile, evil, threatening.

HENRY MILLER,
The Air-Conditioned Nightmare

CONSEQUENCES

How little can we foresee the consequences either of wise or unwise action, of virtue or of malice. Without this measureless and perpetual uncertainty, the drama of human life would be destroyed.

SIR WINSTON CHURCHILL,
The Gathering Storm, Vol. I

Every serious-minded person knows that a large part of the effort required in moral discipline consists in the courage needed to acknowledge the unpleasant consequences of one's past and present acts.

JOHN DEWEY,
Reconstruction in Philosophy

Our forecast of consequences is always subject ... to the bias of impulse and habit. We see what we want to see, we obscure what is unfavorable to a cherished, probably unavowed wish. We dwell upon favouring circumstances till they become weighted with reinforcing considerations. We don't give opposing consequences half a chance to develop.

JOHN DEWEY,
Human Nature and Conduct

Results are what you expect, and consequences are what you get.

SCHOOLGIRL DEFINITION,
quoted in *Ladies' Home Journal,*
January 1942

No matter how excellently a man's soul

may be inclined to the performance of a good action, in ninety cases out of a hundred he is driven away by dread of the consequences.

WILLIAM J. LOCKE,
Simon the Jester

Logical consequences are the scarecrows of fools and the beacons of wise men.

THOMAS HENRY HUXLEY,
Aphorisms and Reflections

CONSERVATIVE

The man for whom the law exists—the man of forms, the conservative—is a tame man.

HENRY DAVID THOREAU,
Journal

The most dangerous demagogues are the clever conservatives who despise the people.

J. A. SPENDER,
The Comments of Bagshot, Second Series

Whether a conservative fellow has any sense or not, he gets the benefit of the doubt.

KIN HUBBARD,
Abe Martin on Things in General

Conservatives, like embalmers, would keep intact the forms from which the vital principle has fled.

JOHN LANCASTER SPALDING,
Aphorisms and Reflections

CONSIDERATION

To be civilized is to be incapable of giving unnecessary offence, it is to have some quality of consideration for all who cross our path.

AGNES REPPLIER,
Americans and Others

What is more beautiful than considerateness for others, when we ourselves are unhappy?

FREDERICK W. FABER,
Spiritual Conferences

CONSISTENCY

Consistency is a jewel; and, as in the case of other jewels, we may marvel at the price that some people will pay for it.

GEORGE SANTAYANA,
Character and Opinion in the United States

I will believe in anything rather than in any man's consistency.

MONTAIGNE,
Essays

Too much consistency is as bad for the mind as for the body. Consistency is contrary to nature, contrary to life. The only completely consistent people are the dead.

ALDOUS HUXLEY,
Collected Essays

Consistency is a verbal criterion, which cannot be applied to the phenomena of life. Taken together, the various activities of a single individual may "make no sense," and yet be perfectly compatible with biological survival, social success and personal happiness.

ALDOUS HUXLEY,
Collected Essays

One must expect inconsistency. Every moment conditions are different, and therefore we are; every moment we are older, and there is less of life to live, and the thought can lead to odd impulses.

E. V. LUCAS,
365 Days and One More

CONSOLATION

I can understand the things that afflict mankind, but I often marvel at those which console it.

MADAME SWETCHINE,
The Writings of Madame Swetchine

Do not be greedy of consolation. I never got anything that way. Suffering teaches: life teaches.

BARON FRIEDRICH VON HÜGEL,
Letters from Baron Friedrich von Hügel to a Niece

Nobody can have the consolations of religion or philosophy unless he has first experienced their desolations.

ALDOUS HUXLEY,
Collected Essays

There are few things more consoling to men than the mere finding that other men have felt as they feel.

FREDERICK W. FABER,
Spiritual Conferences

The experience of centuries teaches us that men need consoling first, instructing afterwards.

ERNEST HELLO,
Life, Science, and Art

Consolation and light will often come, not by seeking for them directly, but by just putting ourselves straight. Intellectual trouble may disappear by simply doing our duty.

MARK RUTHERFORD,
Last Pages from a Journal

Great consolation may grow out of the smallest saying.

SWISS-GERMAN PROVERB

CONSUMER (*See also* PEOPLE)

Consumer? Why use that word? We're all consumers. Say people, or the public.

PROFESSOR JAXON KNOX

The Public be damned.

CORNELIUS VANDERBILT

CONTEMPLATION

The peace of the contemplative is at once the most beautiful and the most fruitful act of man.

STEPHEN MACKENNA,
Journal and Letters of Stephen Mackenna

Contemplatives are not useful, they are only indispensable.

ERNEST DIMNET,
What We Live By

By how much a man shall reserve himself to a contemplative life, by so much will he need a more constant and watchful self-regulation in the conduct of it; and by so much, also, will the task of self-regulation be difficult and severe. The regimen of external circumstance and of obligations contracted to others is an aid which only a strong man can dispense with in the ordering of his days and hours.

SIR HENRY TAYLOR,
Notes from Life

Half at least of all morality is negative and consists in keeping out of mischief. . . . The one-sided contemplative leaves undone many things that he ought to do; but to make up for it, he refrains from doing a host of things he ought not to do.

ALDOUS HUXLEY,
The Doors of Perception

The mind of the sage in repose becomes the mirror of the universe, the speculum of all creation.

CHUANG TZU,
quoted in *The Unquiet Grave*
by Cyril Connolly

For not, surely, by deliberate effort of thought does a man grow wise. The truths of life are not discovered by us. At moments unforeseen, some gracious influence descends upon the soul, touching it to an emotion which, we know not how, the mind transmutes into thought. This can happen only in a calm of the senses, a surrender of the whole being to passionless contemplation. I understand, now, the intellectual mood of the quietist.

GEORGE GISSING,
The Private Papers of Henry Ryecroft

In asking one's self what rating he shall put on the life of shut-in contemplation, one has to admit its intellectual poverty—I mean just poverty, not weakness—and its own unrest. It seems to me that devotees claim peace and secureness for a life that is in fact almost as agitated and unsettled as that of the world. The truth is there is no peace or safety anywhere except at the cost of stagnation. When life is not a battlefield it is a cemetery.

OSCAR W. FIRKINS,
Oscar Firkins: Memoirs and Letters,
edited by Ina Ten Eyck

CONTEMPT

It seems natural to affect contempt for what we lack, whether it be beauty or knowledge or money or virtue.

JOHN LANCASTER SPALDING,
Aphorisms and Reflections

Whatever you hold in contempt is your jailer.

BRENDAN FRANCIS

Indeed, what good comes of bullying and bluster and contempt, even if directed against our own selves?

DANIEL CONSIDINE,
The Virtues of the Divine Child

There are some tortoise-like carapaces against which contempt ceases to be a pleasure.

CHARLES BAUDELAIRE,
Intimate Journals

Contempt is the contrary of attention.

SIMONE WEIL,
Waiting for God

Most forms of contempt are unwise; but one of them seems to us peculiarly ridiculous—contempt for the age one lives in.

HENRY JAMES,
French Poets and Novelists

Unconscious envy is the sidelong look of your contempt.

FRIEDRICH NIETZSCHE,
Thus Spake Zarathustra

What is the greatest thing you can experience? It is the hour of great contempt. The hour in which even your happiness becomes loathsome to you, and also your reason and virtue.

FRIEDRICH NIETZSCHE,
Thus Spake Zarathustra

So remarkably perverse is the nature of man that he despises whoever courts him, and admires whoever will not bend before him.

PLATO,
quoted in *A Book of Days*
by Winifred Gordon

CONTENTMENT

To *feel* that one has a *place* in life solves half the problem of contentment.

GEORGE E. WOODBERRY,
Selected Letters of George Edward Woodberry

Those who face that which is actually before them, unburdened by the past, undistracted by the future, these are they who live, who make the best use of their lives; these are those who have found the secret of contentment.

ALBAN GOODIER,
The School of Love

Yes, there is a Nirvanah; it is in leading your sheep to a green pasture, and in putting your child to sleep, and in writing the last line of your poem.

KAHLIL GIBRAN,
Sand and Foam

Contentment, and indeed usefulness, comes as the infallible result of great acceptances, great humilities—of not trying to make ourselves this or that (to conform to some dramatized version of ourselves), but of surrendering ourselves to the fullness of life—of letting life flow through us.

DAVID GRAYSON,
Adventures in Friendship

Better a handful of dry dates and content therewith than to own the Gate of Peacocks and be kicked in the eye by a broody camel.

ARAB PROVERB

But she paid the normal penalty of contentment. She was aware—painfully sometimes—of a further experience, which must, she felt sure, be the end of living.

ROBERT SPEAIGHT,
The Unbroken Heart

If all were gentle and contented as sheep, all would be as feeble and helpless.

JOHN LANCASTER SPALDING,
Aphorisms and Reflections

To be content with little is difficult; to be content with much, impossible.

OLD PROVERB

CONTRADICTION

Trust only those who have the courage to contradict you with respect, and who value your character more than your favor.

FRANÇOIS DE FENELON,
Reflections and Meditations

The root of happiness is never to contradict any one and never to agree with any one. For if you contradict people, they will try to convince you; and if you agree with them, they will enlarge upon their views until they say something you will feel bound to contradict.

CHRISTOPHER MORLEY,
Mince Pie

The spirit of contradiction renders a man unendurable to everyone.

FÉLIX A. DUPANLOUP,
The Child

Do I contradict myself?
Very well, then, I contradict myself,
I am large, I contain multitudes.

WALT WHITMAN,
"Song of Myself" *Leaves of Grass*

The human soul is hospitable, and will entertain conflicting sentiments and contradictory opinions with much impartiality.

GEORGE ELIOT,
Romola

Is there anyone who has not, at some given moment, recognized in himself a hive of contradictions—between his word and his deed, his will and his work, his life and his principles?

HENRIK IBSEN

Contradiction is the salt which keeps truth from corruption.

JOHN LANCASTER SPALDING,
Means and Ends of Education

CONTROVERSY

Half the controversies in the world are verbal ones; and could they be brought to a plain issue, they would be brought to a prompt termination.

JOHN HENRY CARDINAL NEWMAN,
Oxford University Sermons

When men understand each other's meaning, they see, for the most part, that controversy is either superfluous or hopeless.

JOHN HENRY CARDINAL NEWMAN,
Oxford University Sermons

As a fact—a mere fact of history—nearly everything we hold to be truth, save what comes immediately from the evidence of our senses, has been established by controversy.

HILAIRE BELLOC,
The Silence of the Sea

Controversy equalizes fools and wise men in the same way—*and the fools know it.*

OLIVER WENDELL HOLMES

Controversy, for the most part, disfigures the question it seeks to elucidate.

FREDERICK W. FABER,
*Notes on Doctrinal
and Spiritual Subjects,* Vol. II

CONVENTION

It saves trouble to be conventional, for you're not always explaining things.

MYRTLE REED,
Old Rose and Silver

Conventionality is the adoration which both vice and virtue offer up to worldliness.

SIR ARTHUR HELPS,
Companions of My Solitude

CONVERSATION

I presume one forgets how unsophisticated, childlike, crude, life remains outside an artist class. Talk of food, of hunting, anecdotes. No real talk at all. One wonders how life goes on and on, men and women not caring much for anything in particular.

SHERWOOD ANDERSON,
Letters of Sherwood Anderson

Some people profess to feel that love means understanding some other person finally and completely. That sounds to me like pretty dull business. In such a state how can two people converse? Each knows before hand just what the other is going to say.

HEYWOOD BROUN,
Sitting on the World

All serious conversations gravitate towards philosophy.

ERNEST DIMNET,
What We Live By

What happens to all our "good talks" with those we love, and how can we hope to remember the tiniest fragment of them, with the warmth and affection in those voices, the gentle kindliness in those eyes? But it is these that would reveal us; it is there that we are to be found.

JULIAN GREEN,
Personal Record

The time to stop talking is when the other person nods his head affirmatively but says nothing.

ANONYMOUS (HENRY S. HASKINS),
Meditation in Wall Street

Civilized people can talk about anything. For them no subject is taboo.

CLIVE BELL,
Civilization, An Essay

Remember this—if you shut your mouth you have your choice.

F. SCOTT FITZGERALD,
The Crack-up

I take the conversational side of a number of people, almost everyone sooner or later has a perfectly determined rhythm in everything they do. It is not so much the words they speak, as the sense of the sound that they produce. That impression is what I have tried to set down.

GERTRUDE STEIN,
quoted in *The Third Rose*
by John Malcolm Brinnin

I say all men are best at their ease when they are talking shop. It is because they then have most material to hand, and because they are dealing with the thing which, if they will confess it, most occupies their mind.

HILAIRE BELLOC,
A Conversation with a Cat

The moment a man talks to his fellows he begins to lie.

HILAIRE BELLOC,
The Silence of the Sea

Conversation is possible, of course, between two people, but it can't be much of an art unless there are at least three.

JOHN ERSKINE,
The Complete Life

Only if we can restrain ourselves is conversation possible. Good talk rises upon much self-discipline.

JOHN ERSKINE,
The Complete Life

The mark of good conversation is that every member of the company takes part in it, and that all discuss the same theme.

JOHN ERSKINE,
The Complete Life

There is an essential truth about conversation, which is due to its fluid non-conclusiveness. Talk leaves every question open: and every question really is open.

JOHN JAY CHAPMAN,
Memories and Milestones

The most important things to say are those which often I did not think necessary for me to say—because they seemed to me too obvious.

ANDRÉ GIDE,
The Journals of André Gide, Vol. II

[(Paul Claudel)] talks endlessly; someone else's thought does not stop him for an instant; even a cannon could not divert him. ... He waits politely until you have finished your sentence, then resumes where he had stopped, at the very word, as if you had said nothing.

ANDRÉ GIDE,
The Journals of André Gide, Vol. II

I do not like talking casually to people—it does not interest me—and most of them are unwilling to talk at all seriously.

ANNE MORROW LINDBERGH,
Bring Me a Unicorn

When it comes to analysing the pleasures of life, the privilege of approving and disapproving in conversation must be ranked high.

E. V. LUCAS,
365 Days and One More

Take heed that in your talk you never heedlessly say what, being repeated to others, may cause them offence. For often at unlooked-for times and in unforeseen ways sayings of this sort will do you much hurt.

FRANCESCO GUICCIARDINI,
Counsels and Reflections

Good conversation unrolls itself like the spring or like the dawn.

W. B. YEATS,
Autobiography

I felt it shelter to speak to you.

EMILY DICKINSON,
Letters of Emily Dickinson

Women will gossip, often entertainingly, though quite uselessly. Men will speculate, often dully, and just as uselessly. But conversation can rarely be created out of gossip, however brilliant, whereas there's always a thin chance of creating it out of speculation, however crude.

CLIFTON FADIMAN,
Any Number Can Play

Barbarians "speak with naked hearts together": we have polite conversation.

LOUISE IMOGEN GUINEY,
Goose-Quill Papers

In truth we talk only to ourselves, but sometimes we talk loud enough that others may hear us.

KAHLIL GIBRAN,
Sand and Foam

Men will never talk to women with that rough frankness which they use between themselves. Conversation between the sexes will always be partially insincere.

PHILIP G. HAMERTON,
The Intellectual Life

The two best subjects for conversation are talking shop and making love.

PHYLLIS BOTTOME,
quoted in *Ladies' Home Journal,*
December 1942

Women love personal talk, and their care is to know, not what men think about, but what they feel.

SIR ARTHUR HELPS,
Companions of My Solitude

It is so easy to be full of conversation, of amusement, when you are dealing with people whom you far more seldom meet; but at home, to be alive, to be amusing, to be full of new subjects for conversation— that is a demand upon human nature to which human nature with growing feebleness responds.

BEDE JARRETT,
The House of Gold

Good talk rises out of happy situations, and social occasions do not often produce these, even when the company has been carefully selected with that hope.

DESMOND MACCARTHY,
Experience

After three days without reading, talk becomes flavorless.

CHINESE PROVERB

Actually, in life, conversation is more often likely to be an attempt at deliberate evasion, deliberate confusion, rather than communication. We're all cheats and liars, really.

JAMES JONES,
Writers at Work, Third Series,
edited by George Plimpton

We talk far too much. We should talk less and draw more. I personally should like to renounce speech altogether and, like organic Nature, communicate everything I have to say in sketches.

GOETHE,
quoted in *The Doors of Perception*
by Aldous Huxley

I am a firm believer in letting guests start off on commonplaces till they have shaken down and got the temperature of the room. Even the weather, or the climate, is an unfailingly good topic.

ALFRED NORTH WHITEHEAD,
Dialogues of Alfred North Whitehead

Would you call it a conversation if the other person is silent and, to keep up the appearance of a conversation, you try to substitute for him, and so imitate him, and so parody him, and so parody yourself?

FRANZ KAFKA,
The Diaries of Franz Kafka 1914–1923

We are made for conversation with our kind. When we are not urged into talk by the necessities of mutual dependence and assistance, we are brought to it by an inner push: communicate and share in the communications of others we must. Solitary confinement is the last term in the prison house of man, and speech with our fellows is the beginning of any liberation from the jail of necessity.

JOHN DEWEY,
Characters and Events, Vol. I

The introspective tendency of our Puritan ancestry is a commonplace. But the intellectual generation characteristic of today is even more introspective. Only its introspection is collective: we want to know what is the matter with us, not just with me; with America, not with the soul. Perhaps our fundamental trouble is lack of conversation. We do so much and say so little. Or our saying is so much of it just a little more doing rather than a conversation.

JOHN DEWEY,
Characters and Events, Vol. I

We had been talking as old friends should talk, about nothing, about everything.

LILLIAN HELLMAN,
An Unfinished Woman

I agree with Bob Barlow who said that apart from theology and sex there is really nothing to talk about.

HAROLD J. LASKI,
Holmes-Laski Letters, Vol. I

One day a few weeks ago, as I was coming in from Long Island on the train, . . . I sat down beside a young man, because there were only single seats,—and I have told you I always pick a man under those circumstances, because if they talk to you it is either interesting & you are glad they did, or rude & you can shut them up,—but women always talk & you can't do a thing about it.

EDNA ST. VINCENT MILLAY,
Letters of Edna St. Vincent Millay

No one is exempt from talking nonsense; the misfortune is to do it solemnly.

MONTAIGNE,
Essays

What great delight it is to see the ones we love and then to have speech with them.

VINCENT MCNABB,
God's Way of Mercy

The moment that one can talk about things, that moment they become bearable, and one sees them in the right light.

A. C. BENSON,
Excerpts from the Letters of Dr. A. C. Benson to M. E. A.

After a lively talk one is apt to remember far better what one has oneself contributed to the discussion than what other people have said.

A. C. BENSON,
From a College Window

It always happens in life that the man—or woman—with whom we would like to talk is at the next table. Those who really have something to say to each other so seldom have a chance of saying it.

RICHARD LE GALLIENNE,
Prose Fancies

A man may forgive many wrongs, but he cannot easily forgive anyone who makes it plain that his conversation is tedious.

ROBERT LYND,
The Blue Lion

Taken absolutely, without regard to the inferior conversation that fills up the whole world, even the most admirable conversation now seems to me like a dissipation. . . . And how guilty one feels! I always used to believe it came from a regret that one had given oneself out to someone not quite fine, mature; but no, it comes simply from the fact that giving oneself out is a sin, is music, is surrender. At bottom one must lock oneself up before one's best words and go into solitude. For the word must become flesh. That is the world's secret!

RAINER MARIA RILKE,
Letters of Rainer Maria Rilke 1892–1910

The unluckiest insolvent in the world is the man whose expenditure of speech is too great for his income of ideas.

CHRISTOPHER MORLEY,
Inward Ho

In days of hurry and complication, in the incessant pressure of human problems that thrust our days behind us, does one never dream of a way of life in which talk would be honored and exalted to its proper place in the sun?

CHRISTOPHER MORLEY,
Mince Pie

Don't keep jingling in the course of your conversation any intellectual money you may have.

JOSEPH FARRELL,
Lectures of a Certain Professor

The clever man when he converses, will think less of what he is saying than of the person with whom he is speaking; for then he is sure to say nothing which he will afterwards regret; he is sure not to lay himself open, not to commit an indiscretion. But his conversation will never be particularly interesting.

ARTHUR SCHOPENHAUER,
The Art of Controversy

I think men perish sometimes from sheer untalked conversation. For lack of a creative listener they gradually fill up with unexpressed emotion. Presently this emotion begins to ferment, and finally . . . they blow up, burst, disappear in thin air.

DAVID GRAYSON,
The Friendly Road

Talk with almost any man for half an hour, and you will find that his conversa-

tion, like an old-fashioned song, has a regularly recurrent chorus.

DAVID GRAYSON,
The Friendly Road

The marvellous thing about good conversation is that it brings to birth so many half-realized thoughts of our own—besides sowing the seeds of innumerable other thought-plants.

DAVID GRAYSON,
The Friendly Road

Ultimately the bond of all companionship, whether in marriage or in friendship, is conversation.

OSCAR WILDE,
De Profundis

After all, the only proper intoxication is conversation.

OSCAR WILDE

Though conversing face to face, their hearts have a thousand miles between them.

CHINESE PROVERB

We do contrive wonderfully in conversation to keep each other off our minds, and most of it is now done turtle-wise, with the mind snug inside its egotistic carapace, whereon the patter of a friend's talk is as rain on the roof. Talk moves mostly in parallels, and few minds ever meet, and even if they do they seem to part with equal enthusiasm.

FRANK MOORE COLBY,
The Colby Essays, Vol. 1

In America conversation is a game played with rules differing from England's. It is not tennis, in which you return the other fellow's service, but golf, in which you go on hitting your own ball. It might be defined as a tyranny of anecdote tempered by interruption.

RAYMOND MORTIMER,
quoted in *Reader's Digest,* April 1935

Talking to you is only thinking to myself—made easier.

JOHN OLIVER HOBBES,
The Sinner's Comedy

Small talk is like the air that shatters the stalactites into dust again. I do not participate. I wait. I laugh. I am aware that shallowness disintegrates the deeper undercurrents everyone seeks. The underground rivers of dreams, of deeper and deeper selves running underneath.

My reward is that I am often taken into those realms, and I find a far more fascinating personage.

ANAÏS NIN,
The Diaries of Anaïs Nin, Vol. III

Somehow I find talk very unsatisfactory. I never say the things I meant to say and am overwhelmed afterwards with the things I should have said and could not.

GAMALIEL BRADFORD,
The Letters of Gamaliel Bradford

When I write letters, my soul seems to flow out of me with astonishing ease. But when I try to talk, words desert me, and I only stammer and mumble, so that I have come to be utterly distrustful of the boasted charms of conversation. Do you ever get any that doesn't disappoint? Do you find rich, profitable talkers? Do you find that speech kindles the spirit and makes words and thoughts really fly back and forth with ever-enhanced exhilaration till it seems as if one soul touched another and bred love and beauty and power in it? Rarely, rarely, I have had such moments; but they are so rare and I have paid for them with such oceans of boredom.

GAMALIEL BRADFORD,
The Letters of Gamaliel Bradford

It is a long time since I have indulged in any serious talk. Except for tedious old men (and women) it takes youth to be really serious. What talks we used to have when we were young—we boys of my college days!

GEORGE E. WOODBERRY,
Selected Letters of George Edward Woodberry

I talk half the time to find out my own thoughts, as a school-boy turns his pockets inside out to see what is in them. One brings to light all sorts of personal property he had forgotten in his inventory.

OLIVER WENDELL HOLMES,
Life and Letters of Oliver Wendell Holmes,
Vol. I, by John T. Morse, Jr.

Certain it is that scandal is good brisk talk, whereas praise of one's neighbour is by no means lively hearing. An acquaintance grilled, scored, devilled, and served with mustard and cayenne pepper excites the appetite; whereas a slice of cold friend with currant jelly is but a sickly, unrelishing meat.

WILLIAM MAKEPEACE THACKERAY,
"Roundabout Papers" in *The Second Book of He and She,* edited by James Moffatt

There is nothing so good to the heart as well agreed conversation, when you know that your companion will answer to your thought as the anvil meets the hammer, ringing sound to merry stroke; better than wine, better than sleep, like love itself—for love is agreement of thought.

RICHARD JEFFERIES,
Nature Diaries and Notebooks

What a strange scene if the surge of conversation could suddenly ebb like the tide, and show us the real state of people's minds.

SIR WALTER SCOTT,
Sir Walter Scott's Journal (1825-1832)

I believe that, unless you know people well, your ideas are more elemental talking to females than males, especially young females. One's whole interest to start with is whether one is going to fall in love with them or not.

FREDERICK GOODYEAR,
Letters and Remains

Never try to say something remarkable. It is sure to be wrong.

MARK RUTHERFORD,
Last Pages from a Journal

True talk is founded as deep as love in the constitution of our being, and is a thing to relish with all our energy while yet we have it—and to be grateful for forever.

ROBERT LOUIS STEVENSON,
"Talk and Talkers," *Memories and Portraits*

Conclusions, indeed, are not often reached by talk any more than by private thinking. That is not the profit—the profit is in the exercise, and above all in the experience.

ROBERT LOUIS STEVENSON,
"Talk and Talkers," *Memories and Portraits*

One way to prevent conversation from being boring is to say the wrong thing.

FRANK SHEED,
lecture to the Outer Circle,
Columbia University, May 28, 1950

Modest egotism is the salt of conversation. You do not want too much of it; but if it is altogether omitted, everything tastes flat.

HENRY VAN DYKE,
The Friendly Year

CONVICTION

Every conviction was a whim at birth.

HEYWOOD BROUN,
Collected Edition of Heywood Broun

The hallmark of courage in our age of conformity is the capacity to stand on one's convictions—not obstinately or defiantly (these are gestures of defensiveness not courage) nor as a gesture of retaliation, but simply because these are what one believes.

ROLLO MAY,
Man's Search for Himself

The worth of every conviction consists precisely in the steadfastness with which it is held.

JANE ADDAMS,
quoted in *Jane Addams Speaks*,
compiled by Leonard S. Kenworthy

There are men and women—not many—who have the happy art of making their most fervent convictions endurable.

AGNES REPPLIER,
Americans and Others

We should know what our convictions are, and stand for them. Upon one's own philosophy, conscious or unconscious, depends one's ultimate interpretation of facts. Therefore it is wise to be as clear as possible about one's subjective principles. As the man is, so will be his ultimate truth.

C. G. JUNG,
Psychological Reflections,
edited by Jolande Jacobi and R. F. Hull

The man who knows, often finds himself at great disadvantage in the presence of fact-gatherers and persons who opine. His attitude is necessarily affirmative, and often, to the great scandal and contempt of his adversaries, simply affirmative.

COVENTRY PATMORE,
Religio, Poetae, Etc.

Opinions have their upsets and all is well. But once a cataclysm takes place among a man's convictions, the outcome is more than well—it is a supreme experience.

ANONYMOUS (HENRY S. HASKINS),
Meditations in Wall Street

As life goes on we discover that certain thoughts sustain us in defeat, or give us victory, whether over ourselves or others, and it is these thoughts, tested by passion, that we call convictions.

W. B. YEATS,
Autobiography

How eternally amazed or amused one is at the convictions of one's neighbors—imperturbably admitting reciprocity.

OLIVER WENDELL HOLMES, JR.,
Holmes-Pollock Letters, Vol. II

When convictions are inseparable from interests, arguments against them are futile.

JOHN LANCASTER SPALDING,
Thoughts and Theories of Life and Education

It is a great help to us to hear our own convictions uttered outside of us. A man believes more, is more conscious of his belief, his belief becomes more distinct, more serviceable, when he hears it from another's lips.

FRANCIS A. BAKER,
Sermons

A wise conviction is like light.

SIR ARTHUR HELPS,
Companions of My Solitude

I think it is better to be one-sided than no-sided.

A. C. BENSON,
*Excerpts from the Letters of
Dr. A. C. Benson to M. E. A.*

I look with a queer mixture of envy and disdain at the attachment of other men to their convictions. They remind me of those horses going round and round the same post, but it is just those horses who do the constructive work.

OSCAR W. FIRKINS,
Oscar Firkins: Memoirs and Letters,
edited by Ina Ten Eyck

If you maintain very strongly that something is true, the mediocre say you are conceited.

ERNEST HELLO,
quoted in *The Bliss of the Way*,
compiled by Cecily Hallack

COOKS AND COOKING

Men make better cooks than women because they put so much more feeling into it.

MYRTLE REED,
The Spinster Book

It is sheer foolhardiness to be arrogant to a cook.

AGNES REPPLIER,
Americans and Others

The true cook is the perfect blend, the only perfect blend, of artist and philosopher. He knows his worth: he holds in his palm the happiness of mankind, the welfare of generations yet unborn.

NORMAN DOUGLAS,
An Almanac

Once learnt, this business of cooking was to prove an ever growing burden. It scarcely bears thinking about, the time and labor that man and womankind has devoted to the preparation of dishes that are to melt and vanish in a moment like smoke or a dream, like a shadow, and as a post that hastes by, and the air closes behind them, and afterwards no sign where they went is to be found.

ROSE MACAULAY,
Personal Pleasures

You *have* to please men with cookery, or they will be worse than bears with sore heads.

HANNAH WHITALL SMITH,
Philadelphia Quaker
by Logan Pearsall Smith

And now with some pleasure I find that it's seven; and must cook dinner. Haddock and sausage meat. I think it is true that one gains a certain hold on sausage and haddock by writing them down.

VIRGINIA WOOLF,
A Writer's Diary

Be content to remember that those who can make omelettes properly can do nothing else.

HILAIRE BELLOC,
A Conversation with a Cat

There is no spectacle on earth more appealing than that of a beautiful woman in the act of cooking dinner for someone she loves.

THOMAS WOLFE,
The Web and the Rock

To a large extent we can let others do our cooking for us . . . but unless we too know how to cook, those who prepare our food will prepare it any way they like and we must take what we get.

JOHN ERSKINE,
The Complete Life

All cooking is a matter of time. In general, the more time the better.

JOHN ERSKINE,
The Complete Life

What is literature compared with cooking? The one is shadow, the other is substance.

E. V. LUCAS,
365 Days and One More

COOPERATION

As we come to see how many sources there are for events we have less confidence in any one scheme of betterment, any one person, class, race or nation; but more in what all can do by team-work in a common spirit.

CHARLES HORTON COOLEY,
Life and the Student

Three helping one another will do as much as six men singly.

SPANISH PROVERB

Certainly absolute freedom would be more beautiful if we were birds or poets; but cooperation and a loving sacrifice of part of ourselves—are beautiful too, if we are men living together.

GEORGE SANTAYANA,
Character and Opinion in the United States

CORRUPTION (*See* CRIME)

COST

If we are willing to give up nothing, we must expect nothing. . . . *Nothing for nothing.* The longer I live the more I feel that to be nature's inexorable law. We get nothing in this poor old world but the cash has to be laid down first.

OLIVE SCHREINER,
The Letters of Olive Schreiner

There is no such thing as cheapness in the universe. Everything costs its own cost, and one of our best virtues is a just desire to pay it.

JOHN RUSKIN,
*Letters of
John Ruskin to Charles Eliot Norton*

The cost of a thing is the amount of what I will call life which is required to pay for it, immediately or in the long run.

HENRY DAVID THOREAU,
Walden

COUNTRY

Our first parents lived in the country, and they promptly committed the only sin they were given a chance to commit.

AGNES REPPLIER,
Times and Tendencies

There is a vast deal of make-believe in the carefully nurtured sentiment for country life, and the barefoot boy, and the mountain girl.

AGNES REPPLIER,
Times and Tendencies

Nothing marks the change from the city to the country so much as the absence of grinding noises. The country is never silent. But its sounds are separate, distinct, and, as it were, articulate.

HENRY WARD BEECHER,
Eyes and Ears

Perhaps at bottom I'm . . . a country man. The warm earth feeling gets me hardest. It's land love, ground love.

SHERWOOD ANDERSON,
Letters of Sherwood Anderson

There is such a lack of conversational opportunities here. It is the real limitation to country town life.

SHERWOOD ANDERSON,
Letters of Sherwood Anderson

Some men come in among the hills for a swift hour or two on their way elsewhere, and are filled to overflowing with the beauty of the scene. Others live in it all their lives, and are as blind to its beauties as the mole in its catacomb.

VINCENT MCNABB,
The Wayside

The solitude is not so irksome as one might think—if we are cut off from good society, we are also delivered from bad.

JANE WELSH CARLYLE,
quoted in *Necessary Evil* by
Laurence and Elisabeth Hanson

The way to look at the country is to look at the same bit over and over again. There is a field above me which I am just beginning to understand after having paced it a hundred times. Not by a tourist can the country be known.

MARK RUTHERFORD,
Last Pages from a Journal

In dreams I am in Fleet Market, but I wake and cry to sleep again. ... O let no native Londoner imagine that health, and rest, and innocent occupation ... can make the country anything better than altogether odious and detestable.

CHARLES LAMB,
quoted in *The Literature of Gossip*
by Elizabeth Drew

Two things militate against pleasurable walking in the country. First there is nothing to look at but trees and grass and an occasional cow. ... Second, the people who live in the country firmly believe that anybody who walks in the country is either too poor to own a car, or has just had a flat tire and is employing a secondary and highly undesirable means of locomotion to obtain help for his damaged vehicle.

JEROME WEIDMAN,
Back Talk

No man, I suspect, ever lived long in the country without being bitten by meteorological ambitions. He likes to be hotter and colder, to have been more deeply snowed up, to have more trees and larger blown down than his neighbors.

JAMES RUSSELL LOWELL,
quoted in *A Certain World* by W. H. Auden

A little country town, with its inflexible social conditions, its petty sayings and jealousies, its obstinate mistrust of all that is strange and its crude gossip about all that it cannot comprehend ... may be as complicated and as hard to live in as great Babylon itself.

HENRY VAN DYKE,
The School of Life

Perhaps what I shall carry away from this prolonged visit to England more than anything else will be a love for the fields and the country air; it was one of the dreadful lacks in our education that we had nothing of that, and I feel it now as a permanent incapacity and disadvantage; the last six weeks of Paris and London have made me feel the change, for already I miss the country, and feel the oppression of pavements and walls, and the need of space and silence. Oxford last summer was a paradise in that respect, and I shall never forget my long solitary walks about that lovely region.

GEORGE SANTAYANA,
The Letters of George Santayana

COURAGE

Every act of courage is a manifestation of the ground of being, however questionable the content of the act may be.

PAUL TILLICH,
The Courage to Be

My dear thing, it all comes back, as everything always does, simply to personal pluck. It's only a question, no matter when or where, of having enough.

HENRY JAMES,
The Awkward Age

What is more mortifying than to feel that you have missed the plum for want of courage to shake the tree?

LOGAN PEARSALL SMITH,
Afterthoughts

The highest courage is not to be found in the instinctive acts of men who risk their lives to save a friend or slay a foe; the physical fearlessness of a moment or an hour is not to be compared with immolation of months or years for the sake of wisdom or art.

JOSEPH H. ODELL,
Unmailed Letters

Two-thirds of help is to give courage.

IRISH PROVERB

What would life be if we had no courage to attempt anything?

VINCENT VAN GOGH,
Dear Theo:
An Autobiography of Vincent Van Gogh

Courage is the basic virtue for everyone so long as he continues to grow, to move ahead.

ROLLO MAY,
Man's Search for Himself

Courage is required not only in a person's occasional crucial decision for his own freedom, but in the little hour-to-hour decisions which place the bricks in the structure of his building of himself into a person who acts with freedom and responsibility.

ROLLO MAY,
Man's Search for Himself

We learn courageous action by going forward whenever fear urges us back. A little boy was asked how he learned to skate. "Oh, by getting up every time I fell down," he answered.

DAVID SEABURY,
How to Worry Successfully

Courage is sustained ... by calling up anew the vision of the goal.

A. G. SERTILLANGES,
The Intellectual Life

Courage lies in the wanting to know, which solves nothing, but which has within itself all solutions.

FRANÇOISE MALLET-JORIS,
A Letter to Myself

Courage does not consist in calculation, but in fighting against chances.

JOHN HENRY CARDINAL NEWMAN,
Oxford University Sermons

Bon courage Rodin says to me sometimes, for no apparent reason, when we part in the evening, even when we have been talking of very good things; he knows how necessary that is, every day, when one is young.

RAINER MARIA RILKE,
Letters of Rainer Maria Rilke 1892–1910

We must assume our existence as *broadly* as we in any way can; everything, even the unheard-of,.must be possible in it. That is at bottom the only courage that is demanded of us: to have courage for the most extraordinary, the most singular and the most unexplicable that we may encounter.

RAINER MARIA RILKE,
Letters to a Young Poet

Many women miss their greatest chance of happiness through a want of courage in the decisive moments of their lives.

WINIFRED GORDON,
A Book of Days

The great virtue in life is real courage, that knows how to face facts and live beyond them.

D. H. LAWRENCE,
Selected Letters of D. H. Lawrence, edited by Diana Trilling

The highest courage is to dare to appear to be what one is.

JOHN LANCASTER SPALDING,
Glimpses of Truth

It needs courage to throw oneself forward; but it needs not less to hold oneself back.

DÉSIRÉ JOSEPH CARDINAL MERCIER,
quoted in *The Life of Cardinal Mercier* by John A. Gade

It is contrary to human nature to court privations. We know that the saints did court them, and valued them as avenues to grace. ... We ourselves are not hunting assiduously for hardships; but which one of us has not summoned up courage enough to laugh in the face of disaster?

AGNES REPPLIER,
Americans and Others

Great things are done more through courage than through wisdom.

GERMAN PROVERB

Courage is the best slayer,—courage which *attacketh:* for in every attack there is the sound of triumph.

FRIEDRICH NIETZSCHE,
Thus Spake Zarathustra

Very often submission to the will of God and humility are but a mantle thrown over the cowardice and pusillanimity which we experience at the moment when we ought to face our destiny with courage.

FRIEDRICH NIETZSCHE,
quoted in *The Life of Friedrich Nietzsche* by Daniel Halévy

Courage is as often the outcome of despair as of hope; in the one case we have nothing to lose, in the other everything to gain.

DIANE DE POITIERS,
quoted in *A Book of Days*
by Winifred Gordon

It requires moral courage to grieve; it requires religious courage to rejoice.

SØREN KIERKEGAARD,
The Journals of Søren Kierkegaard

When it comes to the pinch, human beings are heroic.

GEORGE ORWELL,
A Collection of Essays

Courage, in the final analysis, is nothing but an affirmative answer to the shocks of existence, which must be borne for the actualization of one's own nature.

DR. KURT GOLDSTEIN,
quoted in *Man's Search for Himself*
by Rollo May

As long as human terror exists, as long as men fear suffering and darkness and death, they will turn to anyone who can profess to give them relief; and relief, too, will come; for the essence of courage is, for many timid hearts, the dependence upon a stronger will.

A. C. BENSON,
From a College Window

But courage which goes against military expediency is stupidity, or, if it is insisted upon by a commander, irresponsibility.

FIELD MARSHAL ERWIN ROMMEL,
The Rommel Papers

No one has yet computed how many imaginary triumphs are silently celebrated by people each year to keep up their courage.

ANONYMOUS (HENRY S. HASKINS),
Meditations in Wall Street

Courage is not merely *one* of the virtues but the form of every virtue at the testing point, which means at the point of highest reality.

C. S. LEWIS,
quoted in *The Unquiet Grave*
by Cyril Connolly

There is a courage of happiness as well as a courage of sorrow.

MAURICE MAETERLINCK

A woman who is courageous has to conceal the fact if she wishes conventional men to like her. The man who is courageous in any matter except physical danger is also thought ill of.

BERTRAND RUSSELL,
The Conquest of Happiness

COURTESY

Custom is a mutable thing; yet we readily recognize the permanence of certain social values. Graciousness and courtesy are never old-fashioned.

EMILY POST,
Etiquette: The Blue Book of Social Usage

The habit of courtesy, when once acquired, is almost impossible to get rid of.

ROBERT LYND,
Solomon in All His Glory

Politeness, deeply searched, is but savagery. Instinctively we neither ask it nor use it in our dealings with our nearest; the easier manner that rules within the household may be a lurking danger to peace and lasting good-will, but it is the seal and token of a friendly union to which savage domineering and savage placation are alike strangers.

STEPHEN MACKENNA,
Journal and Letters of Stephen Mackenna

The courteous learns his courtesy from the discourteous.

TURKISH PROVERB

There are people who balk at small civilities on account of their manifest insincerity. ... It is better and more logical to accept all the polite phraseology which facilitates intercourse, and contributes to the sweetness of life. If we discarded the formal falsehoods which are the currency of conversation, we should not be one step nearer the vital things of truth.

AGNES REPPLIER,
Americans and Others

Genuine courtesy is a splinter from the true cross.

JOHN ANDREW HOLMES,
Wisdom in Small Doses

Cultivated manners are admirable, yet there is a sudden touch of inborn grace that goes beyond them all.

HENRY VAN DYKE,
The Friendly Year

The cobra will bite you whether you call it cobra or Mr. Cobra.

INDIAN PROVERB

Politeness gives only that it may receive. ... It measures and graduates its civilities, and exacts at least as much attention as it bestows, and is always apprehensive of being slighted or undervalued.

JEAN NICHOLAS GROU,
The Characteristics of True Devotion

If you think I shall like Miss [Gertrude] Stein, I am sure to do so. And even if I shouldn't like her, I should still be polite, because I was so unfortunate as to be born that way. I can be rude as anybody if I am prepared; but it takes me at least twenty-four hours to make ready.

ELLEN GLASGOW,
Letters of Ellen Glasgow

Courtesies are equally the language of frozen and melted hearts.

ANONYMOUS (HENRY S. HASKINS),
Meditations in Wall Street

It is incredible what a difference it makes to one's feelings towards the whole human race when one is treated with politeness and kindness in buses, trains, trams, subways, ferries, stores, ships and streets.

JOHN COWPER POWYS,
The Meaning of Culture

COURTSHIP

Courtships are sometimes the least smooth where there is on one side the most passion. A man who is quite competent to what is called "flirtation" under ordinary circumstances, will find himself dis-

qualified for it if deeply in love. And yet it may be by those sort of advances that he would have the best chance of making his way.

SIR HENRY TAYLOR,
Notes from Life

She delighted in hearing men talk of their own work, and that is the most fatal way of bringing a man to your feet.

RUDYARD KIPLING,
quoted in the *New York Times*,
February 24, 1952

In my callow youth, I was badly scratched several times before I learned that if there is one thing no girl wants to be called it is wholesome.

ROBERTSON DAVIES,
The Table Talk of Samuel Marchbanks

COWARDICE

To say a person is a coward has no more meaning than to say he is lazy: it simply tells us that some vital potentiality is unrealized or blocked.

ROLLO MAY,
Man's Search for Himself

One of the great disadvantages of being a coward is that one is constantly having to eat things that one does not wish to eat.

ROBERT LYND,
The Blue Lion

In their hearts they want simply one thing most of all: that no one hurt them. Thus do they anticipate every one's wishes and do well unto every one.

That, however, is *cowardice,* though it be called "virtue."

FRIEDRICH NIETZSCHE,
Thus Spake Zarathustra

CREATION

You know ... that a blank wall is an appalling thing to look at. The wall of a museum—a canvas—a piece of film—or a guy sitting in front of a typewriter. Then, you start out to do something—that vague thing called creation. The beginning strikes awe within you.

EDWARD STEICHEN,
Wisdom, edited by James Nelson

Millions of men have lived to fight, build palaces and boundaries, shape destinies and societies; but the compelling force of all times has been the force of originality and creation profoundly affecting the roots of the human spirit.

ANSEL ADAMS,
Photographers on Photography,
edited by Nathan Lyons

Creating—that is the great salvation from suffering and life's alleviation. But for the creator to appear, suffering itself is needed, and much transformation.

FRIEDRICH NIETZSCHE,
Thus Spake Zarathustra

Constantly and incorrigibly we forget how much harder it is to create, even with mediocre results, than to criticize.

F. L. LUCAS,
Style

CREATIVITY

Creative life is characterized by spontaneous mutability: it brings forth unknown issues, impossible to preconceive.

D. H. LAWRENCE,
Selected Essays

Joy is but the sign that creative emotion is fulfilling its purpose.

CHARLES DU BOS,
What Is Literature?

The thing that makes a creative person is to be creative and that is all there is to it.

EDWARD ALBEE,
Behind the Scenes,
edited by Joseph F. McCrindle

Without creative personalities able to think and judge independently, the upward development of society is as unthinkable as the development of the individual personality without the nourishing soil of the community.

ALBERT EINSTEIN,
Ideas and Opinions

The very essence of the creative is its novelty, and hence we have no standard by which to judge it.

CARL R. ROGERS,
On Becoming a Person

One man may be discovering a way of relieving pain, while another is devising a new and more subtle torture for political prisoners. Both these actions seem to me creative, even though their social value is very different.

CARL R. ROGERS,
On Becoming a Person

The only barrier I admit is that between the artist and the noncreative—or between the creative, I should say, and the noncreative. I have always cultivated the company of the beautiful and the sensitive and have found great pleasure in it. But I have always avoided the dull and the pretentious, and sought refuge with the simple.

SIR OSBERT SITWELL,
Wisdom, edited by James Nelson

No man has the right to dictate what other men should perceive, create or produce, but all should be encouraged to reveal themselves, their perceptions and emotions, and to build confidence in the creative spirit.

ANSEL ADAMS,
Photographers on Photography,
edited by Nathan Lyons

When the creative urge seizes one—at least, such is my experience—one becomes creative in all directions at once.

HENRY MILLER,
The Books in My Life

Every individual who is not creative has a negative, narrow, exclusive taste and succeeds in depriving creative being of its energy and life.

GOETHE,
quoted in *The Intellectual Life*
by A. G. Sertillanges

Creativity requires the freedom to consider "unthinkable" alternatives, to doubt the worth of cherished practices.

Every organization, every society is under the spell of assumptions so familiar that they are never questioned—least of all by those most intimately involved.

JOHN W. GARDNER,
No Easy Victories, edited by Helen Rowan

Creative powers may go with an intellect not, in other ways, very bright. . . . In the human world, nightingales can be geese.

F. L. LUCAS,
The Greatest Problem and Other Essays

When a man has a relation with a woman who is to him *femme inspiratrice,* he gains from the relationship the inspiration to create. To him his creation is the child of his love for the woman.

M. ESTHER HARDING,
The Way of All Women

Life never stops. The torment of men will be eternal, unless the function of creating and acting and changing, living intensely through each day, be considered an eternal joy.

LE CORBUSIER,
When the Cathedrals Were White

The value of the creative faculty derives from the fact that that faculty is the primary mark of man. To deprive man of its exercise is to reduce him to subhumanity.

ERIC GILL,
quoted in *Modern Christian Revolutionaries*
by Donald Attwater

The deepest experience of the creator is feminine, for it is experience of receiving and bearing.

RAINER MARIA RILKE,
Letters of Rainer Maria Rilke 1892–1910

But to make, to make is the thing. And once something is there, ten or twelve things are there, sixty or seventy little records about one, all made now out of this, now out of that impulse, then one has already won a piece of ground on which one can stand upright. Then one no longer loses oneself.

RAINER MARIA RILKE,
Letters of Rainer Maria Rilke 1892–1910

There is in us a lyric germ or nucleus

which deserves respect; it bids a man ponder or create; and in this dim corner of himself he can take refuge and find consolations which the society of his fellow-creatures does not provide.

NORMAN DOUGLAS,
An Almanac

The mainspring of creativity appears to be the same tendency which we discover so deeply as the curative force in psychotherapy—*man's tendency to actualize himself, to become his potentialities.* By this I mean the directional trend which is evident in all organic and human life—the urge to expand, extend, develop, mature—the tendency to express and activate all the capacities of the organism, or the self.

CARL R. ROGERS,
On Becoming a Person

The artistic impulse, a man's honest endeavor, when, no matter how, but of his best, with the means at his command, he tries not to parade himself but to *respond,* to answer a word by a word, a question by an act, and the Creator by a creation, cannot remain isolated, and it produces, whether its author knows or not, around him all manner of constructive consequences and propositions.

PAUL CLAUDEL,
Ways and Crossways

God is in the world, or nowhere, creating continually in us and around us. . . . Insofar as man partakes of this creative process does he partake of the divine, of God, and that participation is his immortality, reducing the question of whether his individuality survives death of the body to the estate of an irrelevancy. His true destiny as cocreator in the universe is his dignity and his grandeur.

ALFRED NORTH WHITEHEAD,
Dialogues of Alfred North Whitehead

Creativity . . . always involves a solemn compact between one's self and others or between one's self and the raw materials of nature and life. It is a pure form of self-other relatedness. However different, strange, and unordinary one's way may appear to others, when it is a genuine self-living and growing, it is also authentically related.

CLARK MOUSTAKAS,
Creativity and Conformity

One sits down first; one thinks afterwards.
JEAN COCTEAU

If a created being has no rights which his Creator is bound to respect, there is an end to all moral relations between them.
OLIVER WENDELL HOLMES,
Life and Letters of Oliver Wendell Holmes,
Vol. I, by John T. Morse, Jr.

CREDO

I have grown to believe that the one thing worth aiming at is simplicity of heart and life; that one's relations with others should be direct and not diplomatic; that power leaves a bitter taste in the mouth; that meanness, and hardness, and coldness are the unforgivable sins; that conventionality is the mother of dreariness; that pleasure exists not in virtue of material conditions, but in the joyful heart; that the world is a very interesting and beautiful place; that congenial labour is the secret of happiness; and many other things which seem, as I write them down, to be dull and trite commonplaces, but are for me the bright jewels which I have found beside the way.

A. C. BENSON,
From a College Window

CREED

Our real creed consists in the things we do. A man's real creed is his habits.
DR. FRANK CRANE,
Essays

CRIME

The study of crime begins with the knowledge of oneself. All that you despise, all that you loathe, all that you reject, all that

you condemn and seek to convert by punishment springs from you.

HENRY MILLER,
The Air-Conditioned Nightmare

No radical change on the plane of history is possible without crime.
COUNT HERMANN KEYSERLING,
The Book of Marriage

The real significance of crime is in its being a breach of faith with the community of mankind.
JOSEPH CONRAD,
Lord Jim

Crime is either another name of need or an aspect of a disease.
KAHLIL GIBRAN,
Sand and Foam

We are all criminals—it's a matter of degree. Crime is as human as being charitable. Of course, we must have tribal laws. But crime ... crime is like art, and the artist has always understood the criminal. The fear of the criminal is the same as the fear of the artist: both are terrified of exposure. It's basic to their nature.
RICHARD LINDNER,
quoted in *Close-up* by John Gruen

CRITICISM

The critic creates nothing, he only points out. But his pointing may show you powers that were indeed always there, and that were even effective, but that, once afresh seen, suggest to active passion a thousand devices whereby the world is revolutionized.
JOSIAH ROYCE,
The Spirit of Modern Philosophy

To see with one's own eyes, to feel and judge without succumbing to the suggestive power of the fashion of the day, to be able to express what one has seen and felt in a trim sentence or even in a cunningly wrought word—is that not glorious?
ALBERT EINSTEIN,
Ideas and Opinions

We must have passed through life unob-servantly, if we have never perceived that a man is very much himself what he thinks of others.

FREDERICK W. FABER,
Spiritual Conferences

To criticise is to neither praise or de-nounce, but to *get nearer your subject*.

J. B. YEATS,
Letters to His Son, W. B. Yeats and Others

Censure pardons the ravens but rebukes the doves.

LATIN PROVERB

One of the cheats of the critical tempera-ment is the belief that when its possessor is bored there is always some external reason to account for it. The critical person sel-dom admits that his ennui may be merely his own mind's little domestic tragedy.

FRANK MOORE COLBY,
The Colby Essays, Vol. 2

Criticism is asserted superiority.

HENRY CARDINAL MANNING,
Pastime Papers

It is by admiration and not by criticism that we live, and the main purpose of criti-cism should be to point out something to admire which we should not have noticed.

MARK RUTHERFORD,
More Pages from a Journal

It is salutary to train oneself to be no more affected by censure than by praise.

W. SOMERSET MAUGHAM,
The Summing Up

There is no virtue in being uncritical; nor is it a habit to which the young are given. But criticism is only the burying beetle that gets rid of what is dead, and, since the world lives by creative and constructive forces, and not by negation and destruc-tion, it is better to grow up in the com-pany of prophets than of critics.

SIR RICHARD LIVINGSTONE,
On Education

When a man tells you what people are saying about you, tell him what people are saying about him; that will immediately take his mind off your troubles.

E. W. HOWE,
quoted in *Ladies' Home Journal,*
February 1949

One should never criticize his own work except in a fresh and hopeful mood. The self-criticism of a tired mind is suicide.

CHARLES HORTON COOLEY,
Life and the Student

I hate being asked to criticize what I can-not praise.

GERARD MANLEY HOPKINS,
A Hopkins Reader, edited by John Pick

I like criticism, but it must be my way.

MARK TWAIN,
Mark Twain's Autobiography

We resent all criticism which denies us anything that lies in our line of advance.

RALPH WALDO EMERSON,
Journals of Ralph Waldo Emerson

CRITICISM, LITERARY

As a rule, the aesthetic preference is either something inexplicable or it is so cor-rupted by non-aesthetic motives as to make one wonder whether the whole of literary criticism is not a huge network of humbug.

GEORGE ORWELL,
A Collection of Essays

People may say that there is nothing for our critics to do, that all our contempo-rary works are meaningless and inferior. But that is a narrow view. Life must be observed not only on the plus side, but also on the minus. The conviction in itself that the eighties have not produced a sin-gle worthwhile writer may serve as mate-rial for five volumes.

ANTON CHEKHOV,
The Selected Letters of Anton Chekhov

Of all fatiguing, futile, empty trades, the worst, I suppose, is writing about writing.

HILAIRE BELLOC,
The Silence of the Sea

Critics are always linking writers to "schools." If they couldn't link people to schools, they'd die.

WILLIAM STYRON,
Writers at Work,
edited by Malcolm Cowley

Literary criticism is constantly attempting a very absurd thing—the explanation of passionate utterance by utterance that is unimpassioned: it is like trying to paint a sunset in lamp-black.

JOHN DAVIDSON,
Sentences and Paragraphs

The critics will say as always that literature is decaying. From the time of the first critic up to now they have said nothing else.

SIR OSBERT SITWELL,
Wisdom, edited by James Nelson

A critic knows more than the author he criticises, or just as much, or at least somewhat less.

HENRY CARDINAL MANNING,
About Critics

A critic has no right to the narrowness which is the frequent prerogative of the creative artist. He has to have a wide outlook or he has not anything at all.

E. M. FORSTER,
Aspects of the Novel

More than once, I have tried ... to shut myself within a system, in order that I might preach at my ease. ... And yet always something spontaneous and unexpected, out of the fulness and universality of life, arose to give the lie to my knowledge, that childish old maid, the deplorable daughter of Utopia. I could change or extend my criterion as much as I wanted, always it was too slow to catch up with the infinite variety of man.

JOHN PEALE BISHOP,
The Collected Essays of John Peale Bishop

O ye critics, will nothing melt ye?

SIR WALTER SCOTT,
Sir Walter Scott's Journal (1825-1832)

Critics and detectives are naturally suspicious. They scent allegories and bombs where there are no such abominations. It is difficult to convince them of our innocence.

RABINDRANATH TAGORE,
Letters to a Friend

I don't see how anyone has a right to resent criticism, if they write for the public. As well put yourself in a shopwindow, and think it hard that people don't admire your goods.

MOTHER FRANCIS RAPHAEL,
quoted in
A Memoir of Mother Francis Raphael
by Bertrand Wilberforce

How much more flattering it is to see a critic, out of malice or spite, force himself to disparagement than, out of cliqueness, to indulgence.

ANDRÉ GIDE,
Pretexts

Of course I like to be praised, or rather understood. But I am neither pained nor surprised if critics do not like my books, and they are welcome to say what they feel about them. I greatly believe in Dr. Johnson's dictum, that no one was ever written down except by himself.

A. C. BENSON,
*Excerpts from the Letters of
Dr. A. C. Benson to M. E. A.*

I got a glimpse into the uses of a certain kind of criticism this past summer at a writers' conference—into how the avocation of assessing the failures of better men can be turned into a comfortable livelihood, providing you back it up with a Ph.D. I saw how it was possible to gain a chair of literature on no qualifications other than persistence in nipping the heels of Hemingway, Faulkner, and Steinbeck. I know, of course, that there are true critics, one or two. For the rest all I can say is, "Deal around me."

NELSON ALGREN,
Writers at Work,
edited by Malcolm Cowley

Again and again I have been attacked for

looseness, lack of beauty in my prose, and the one attacking me used, as the vehicle of attack, prose I would have been ashamed to write.

SHERWOOD ANDERSON,
Letters of Sherwood Anderson

Why need every honest poet be suspected of leading a quadruple life? Sometimes the second or third meaning is less interesting than the first, and the only really difficult thing about a poem is the critic's explanation of it.

FRANK MOORE COLBY,
The Colby Essays, Vol. 2

I can imagine nothing more distressing to a critic than to have a writer see accurately into his own work.

NORMAN MAILER,
Writers at Work, Third Series,
edited by George Plimpton

If the critics are not less than the authors they criticise, they will at once burst into equal authorship. And being less than the authors they criticise, they must diminish these authors. For no critic can admit anything bigger than himself. And we are all, therefore, no bigger than our little critics.

D. H. LAWRENCE,
Selected Letters of D. H. Lawrence

Criticism in our day has become largely the making of finer and finer discriminations.

CLIFTON FADIMAN,
Any Number Can Play

O that word "constructive"! How, in the name of the mystery of genius, can criticism be anything else than an idolatry, a worship, a metamorphosis, a love affair!

JOHN COWPER POWYS,
Visions and Revisions

I read a good deal of criticism, but only as a vice, not so good as reading science fiction, rather better than reading mystery stories. But I do admire the confidence of our nobler critics. They've got it made, and they know it.

GORE VIDAL,
Behind the Scenes,
edited by Joseph F. McCrindle

I am wrong, perhaps, but I *never* read anything concerning my work. ... I (personally) feel that criticism is a letter to the public which the author, since it is not directed to him, does not have to open and read.

RAINER MARIA RILKE,
Letters of Rainer Maria Rilke 1892–1910

CROWD

The pleasure of being in crowds is a mysterious expression of sensual joy in the multiplication of Number.

CHARLES BAUDELAIRE,
Intimate Journals

The desert has its holiness of silence, the crowd its holiness of conversation.

WALTER ELLIOTT,
The Spiritual Life

I can't bear the thought of human beings except when I think of beauty or intelligence or rare and cloistral goodness in them—and one cannot think of these lovely things shining in a crowd.

STEPHEN MACKENNA,
Journal and Letters of Stephen Mackenna

Is there any theory, philosophy, or creed, is there any system or culture, any formulated method able to meet and satisfy each separate item of this agitated pool of human life? By which they may be guided, by which hope, by which look forward? ... Can any creed, philosophy, system, or culture endure the test and remain unmolten in this fierce focus of human life?

RICHARD JEFFERIES
(inspired by watching the crowd passing by London's Royal Exchange),
The Story of My Heart

In this age of crowds in which I have determined to be a solitary, perhaps the greatest sin would be to lament the presence of people on the threshold of my solitude.

THOMAS MERTON,
The Sign of Jonas

They move on with that beautiful optimism of an American crowd which has been trained in the belief that there is always plenty of room ahead.

SIMEON STRUNSKY,
The Patient Observer

A crowd, whether it be a dangerous mob, or an amiably joyous gathering at a picnic is not a community. It has a mind, but no institutions, no organization, no coherent unity, no history, no traditions.

JOSIAH ROYCE,
The Problem of Christianity, Vol. II

Any expression of feeling by a great multitude of men must have in it a large measure of unreality. It cannot help exaggerating itself simply because of the cumulative effect of emotion upon the crowd mind.

RABINDRANATH TAGORE,
Letters to a Friend

People speak of the sadness of being in a crowd and knowing no one. There is something pleasurable in it too.

SIR ARTHUR HELPS,
Companions of My Solitude

I imagine that people are divided into those who, if they see a crowd of human beings in a field, have a desire to join them, and those who, at the same sight, long to fly swiftly to the uttermost ends of the earth.

A. C. BENSON,
From a College Window

If ... people crowd together and form a mob, then the dynamics of the collective man are set free—beasts or demons which lie dormant in every person till he is part of a mob. Man in the crowd is unconsciously lowered to an inferior moral and intellectual level, to that level which is always there, below the threshold of consciousness, ready to break forth as soon as it is stimulated through the formation of a crowd.

C. G. JUNG,
Psychological Reflections,
edited by Jolande Jacobi and R. F. Hull

CRUELTY

The impulse to cruelty is, in many people, almost as violent as the impulse to sexual love—almost as violent and much more mischievous. Early training can fix principles and inspire a theoretical disgust. But, given free play, a sudden impulse can undo in a minute the work of years.

ALDOUS HUXLEY,
Beyond the Mexique Bay

I often wonder why any very atrociously cruel conduct is called inhuman; it seems to me that sort of thing is about as human as anything one can think of.

ALGERNON S. LOGAN,
Vistas from the Stream, Vol. II

I wonder to myself, times, if it was fair, clear weather on Golgotha when Mary looked up at the cross, and whether there was some small bird singing, and the bees busy in the clover. Ah! I think it was glass-clear weather, and bright. For no bitter lacked in that cup, and surely one of the bitterest things is to see the cruelty of man on some fair morning with blessing in it.

MARY WEBB,
Precious Bane

If I could believe that the present preoccupation with violence and obscenity springs, either in literature or in life, from compassion for suffering and a noble rage against social injustice, I should willingly offer thanks to any god ever invented, not excepting that strange deity worshipped by the Marquis de Sade.

ELLEN GLASGOW,
Letters of Ellen Glasgow

Experience has taught me that the only cruelties people condemn are those with which they do not happen to be familiar.

ELLEN GLASGOW,
Letters of Ellen Glasgow

CULTURE

There are moments when one is more ashamed of what is called culture than anyone can ever be of ignorance.

E. V. Lucas,
365 Days and One More

Culture without natural human goodness has an extremely disconcerting effect. There is something weird and terrifying about it. Indeed its effect upon the imagination of our race is summed up in the popular image of Nero fiddling while Rome burned.

John Cowper Powys,
The Meaning of Culture

Our idea of a cultured person is a person who doesn't want to live in a community of cultured persons.

E. B. White,
Every Day Is Saturday

There is no culture in the hearts of people unless the very utensils in the kitchen are beautiful.

William Butler Yeats,
quoted in *Ladies' Home Journal,*
June 1942

The blossom of a cultivated cherry tree is quite as uncompounded, and direct, and indivisibly "blossom" as that of the wild cherry. "Culture" does not destroy immediacy and directness, but enriches, ennobles, and beautifies it. Indeed the immediacy *as such* is more plainly revealed.

Theodor Haecker,
Journal in the Night

The failure to touch the common mind, upon which our cultivated people appear to pride themselves, is not, as they imagine, a sign of their superiority, but rather a clear proof of the inadequacy of their ideal. Culture invariably dies, unless refreshed by the common intelligence, and before it dies it very frequently becomes corrupt.

J. A. Spender,
The Comments of Bagshot, Second Series

Inevitably, the culture within which we live shapes and limits our imaginations, and by permitting us to do and think and feel in certain ways makes it increasingly

unlikely or impossible that we should do or think or feel in ways that are contradictory or tangential to it.

Margaret Mead,
Male and Female

CURE (See HELP)

CURIOSITY

A sense of curiosity is nature's original school of education.

Dr. Smiley Blanton,
Love or Perish

Every man ought to be inquisitive through every hour of his great adventure down to the day when he shall no longer cast a shadow in the sun. For if he dies without a question in his heart, what excuse is there for his continuance?

Frank Moore Colby,
The Colby Essays, Vol. 1

Curiosity is the same in all people—the vulgar stare and the refined peek through a crack.

Josh Billings,
His Works Complete

Consciously and unconsciously we are all intensely curious about each other, whether or not that curiosity is but the prelude to interest in self, as I believe it is, and in a way all profoundly interesting literature is in the nature of gossip.

Holbrook Jackson,
Southward Ho! and Other Essays

A man should live if only to satisfy his curiosity.

Yiddish Proverb

The days on which one has been most inquisitive are among the days on which one has been happiest.

Robert Lynd,
The Blue Lion

There are two sorts of curiosity—the momentary and the permanent. The momentary is concerned with the odd appearance on the surface of things. The permanent is attracted by the amazing and consecutive life that flows on beneath the surface of things.

ROBERT LYND,
Solomon in All His Glory

CURSE (*See* EVIL, SWEAR)

DANCING

I feel that classic ballet with its rigid discipline is a very very narrow medium—it doesn't have a wide or deep range of expressiveness. It can be very beautiful, I enjoy seeing it, but I think of it as decorative and relatively superficial, among the art forms.

DENISE LEVERTOV,
The Craft of Poetry,
edited by William Packard

Actually, I have rarely seen modern dance that seemed to reach the kind of depth and subtlety and have the range of language arts or music.

DENISE LEVERTOV,
The Craft of Poetry,
edited by William Packard

One should dance because the soul dances. Indeed, when one thinks of it, what are any real things but dances? I mean the only realities—moments of joy, acts of pleasure, deeds of kindness. Even the long silences, the deep quietness of serene souls, are dances; that is why they seem so motionless. When the top dances most perfectly it seems most still; just as the apparently still earth is dancing round itself and round the sun; just as the stars dance in the night.

HOLBROOK JACKSON,
Southward Ho! and Other Essays

Dancing is the loftiest, the most moving, the most beautiful of the arts because it is no mere translation or abstraction from life; it is life itself.

HAVELOCK ELLIS,
The Dance of Life

All there is to be said for work as opposed to dancing is that it is so much easier.

HEYWOOD BROUN,
Pieces of Hate

It is only in the dance that one gives thorough employment to this body of ours, this minister of beauty.... In sport we divide our homage; in dancing we worship but one god.

JOSEPH W. BEACH,
Meek Americans

It is a pity that dancing is so often degraded by the intrusion of extraneous considerations, social and humanitarian: must I propitiate this powerful lady by inviting her to dance? Should I take pity on this fading wallflower and stick her in my buttonhole? Nothing should be allowed to interfere with the choice of partners on purely aesthetic grounds.

JOSEPH W. BEACH,
Meek Americans

When seeing films of savage ritual dances I envy their intense precision and preoccupation.

JOANNA FIELD,
A Life of One's Own

He who cannot dance puts the blame on the floor.

HINDU PROVERB

Every day I count wasted in which there has been no dancing.

FRIEDRICH NIETZSCHE,
quoted in *The Dance of Life*
by Havelock Ellis

Sometimes I think that dancing, like youth, is wasted on the young.

MAX LERNER,
The Unfinished Country

DANGER

The sense of danger is never, perhaps, so fully apprehended as when the danger has been overcome.

SIR ARTHUR HELPS,
Essays Written in the Intervals of Business

We have short memories for the many dangerous storms before which we have sailed without taking harm.

> ANONYMOUS (HENRY S. HASKINS),
> *Meditations in Wall Street*

People never believe in volcanoes until the lava actually overtakes them.

> GEORGE SANTAYANA,
> *The Letters of George Santayana*

The fascination of danger is at the bottom of all great passions.

> ANATOLE FRANCE,
> *The Anatole France Calendar,*
> selected by A. S. Rappoport

The peril of the hour moved the British to tremendous exertions, just as always in a moment of extreme danger things can be done which had previously been thought impossible. Mortal danger is an effective antidote for fixed ideas.

> FIELD MARSHAL ERWIN ROMMEL,
> *The Rommel Papers*

DARE (See RISK)

DARKNESS

It is one thing to be blind, and another to be in darkness.

> COVENTRY PATMORE,
> *The Rod, the Root, and the Flower*

To see one's darkness proves the presence of a great light.

> RAOUL PLUS,
> *Living with God*

The darkness surrounding us might somewhat light up if we would first practice using the light we have on the place we are.

> ANONYMOUS (HENRY S. HASKINS),
> *Meditations in Wall Street*

DAWN

However early you get up you cannot hasten the dawn.

> SPANISH PROVERB

The dawn at my window ever causes a desire for longer thought, the recognition of the light at the moment of waking kindles afresh the wish for a broad day of the mind.

> RICHARD JEFFERIES,
> *The Story of My Heart*

Every dawn signs a new contract with existence.

> HENRI FRÉDÉRIC AMIEL,
> *The Private Journal of Henri Frédéric Amiel*

Dawn-wind in tree-tops is a thrilling murmur and stir: it gives the feeling that something is going to happen; that feeling of half-blissful, half-terrified expectancy which is the summit of life.

> CHRISTOPHER MORLEY,
> *Inward Ho*

And we shall sit in reverie till the dawn
Peers up the slope and flaunts his gold
  cockade.

> A. M. SULLIVAN,
> "The Trysting,"
> *Incident in Silver: A Book of Lyrics*

I am delighted to find that poets and painters are discovering that the break of day is not joyous, but, rather, awful. . . . The morn seems to come in so mournfully.

> SIR ARTHUR HELPS,
> *Conversation in a Railway Carriage*

DAY

They deem me mad because I will not sell my days for gold; and I deem them mad because they think my days have a price.

> KAHLIL GIBRAN,
> *Sand and Foam*

Men can bear all things except good days.

> DUTCH PROVERB

To sensible men, every day is a day of reckoning.

> JOHN W. GARDNER,
> *No Easy Victories,* edited by Helen Rowan

A day's endless when you're young, whereas when you grow old it's very soon over. When you're retired, a day's a flash,

when you're a kid it's very slow.
LOUIS-FERDINAND CÉLINE,
Writers at Work, Third Series,
edited by George Plimpton

"Old times" never come back—and I suppose it's just as well. What comes back is a new morning every day in the year, and that's better.
GEORGE E. WOODBERRY,
Selected Letters of George Edward Woodberry

If we only knew the real value of a day, nothing would contribute more to put us in possession of ourselves. . . . Once a man fully realizes that he can mould only the day he has, or if other days, only through it, he will begin both to take things easily and to do them well, and these two have a closer connection than most people seem to imagine.
JOSEPH FARRELL,
Lectures of a Certain Professor

DAYDREAMS

Day-dreams are the gaseous decomposition of true purpose.
ANONYMOUS (HENRY S. HASKINS),
Meditations in Wall Street

How many of our daydreams would darken into nightmares if there seemed any danger of their coming true!
LOGAN PEARSALL SMITH,
Afterthoughts

Without long, lovely moments spent in day-dreams life becomes an iron-ribbed, sterile puffing machine.
JOHN COWPER POWYS,
The Meaning of Culture

DEATH

Life being what it is in our world, the onset of death is often the first taste a man gets of freedom. At last the imagination can come into its own, and as a man yields to it his emotions take on a surprising depth and intensity.
ISAAC ROSENFELD,
An Age of Enormity

The dying man has probably lost during the course of life things more important than what he is about to lose by dying.
FRIEDRICH NIETZSCHE,
The Dawn of Day

If even dying is to be made a social function, then, please, grant me the favor of sneaking out on tiptoe without disturbing the party.
DAG HAMMARSKJÖLD,
Markings

When I was analyzing I observed clearly that the fear of death was in proportion to not-living. The less a person was in life, the greater the fear. By being alive I mean living out of all the cells, all the parts of one's self. The cells which are denied become atrophied, like a dead arm, and infect the rest of the body. People living deeply have no fear of death.
ANAÏS NIN,
The Diaries of Anaïs Nin, Vol. II

Few men ever drop dead from overwork, but many quietly curl up and die because of undersatisfaction.
SYDNEY J. HARRIS,
Strictly Personal

As I follow some insignificant mortal along the pavement, I am always led to reflect that he, even he, will at some moment be the very centre of the interest of humanity, viz: at the moment of his death.
GEORGE GISSING,
Commonplace Book

The wildest sorrow that comes at the thought of death is, I think, "Ages will pass over and no one ever again look on that nobleness or that beauty." What is this but to pity the living and to praise the dead?
W. B. YEATS,
Autobiography

Two or three have died within the last two twelve months, and so many parts of me have been numbed. One sees a picture, reads an anecdote, starts a casual fancy, and thinks to tell of it to this person in preference to every other—the person is gone whom it would have peculiarly suited. It won't do for *another*. Every departure destroys a class of sympathies.

CHARLES LAMB,
The Letters of Charles and Mary Lamb

The dead don't die. They look on and help.

D. H. LAWRENCE,
Selected Letters of D. H. Lawrence

What is there astonishing in the death of a mortal? But we are grieved at his dying before his time. Are we sure that this was not his time? We do not know how to pick and choose what is good for our souls, or how to fix the limits of the life of man.

SAINT BASIL,
Letters and Select Works

For me, you only had the right to die when you had a good tale to tell. To enter in, you tell your story and pass on.

LOUIS-FERDINAND CÉLINE,
Writers at Work, Third Series,
edited by George Plimpton

The event of death is always astounding; our philosophy never reaches, never possesses it; we are always at the beginning of our catechism; always the definition is yet to be made. What is death?

RALPH WALDO EMERSON,
Journal of Ralph Waldo Emerson

There is a kind of contempt of the landscape felt by him who has just lost by death a dear friend. The sky is less grand as it sets down over less worth in the population.

RALPH WALDO EMERSON,
"Nature," *Essays*

My father died a difficult and terrible death. It was the first and only time I had seen somebody die. God grants an easy death only to the just.

SVETLANA ALLILUYEVA,
(daughter of Joseph Stalin),
Twenty Letters to a Friend

A protracted illness *seems* to prepare one for the end, though when it comes, even after months of illness, it always seems sudden and terrible. I think death is always terrible, even in what is looked upon as its most peaceful and calmest forms.

BASIL W. MATURIN,
quoted in *Father Maturin* by Maisie Ward

After all, it's the daily round of life with all the little things that make it up from morning to evening and the intimate companionship that is woven more and more closely year by year—it's this that is broken in upon, and whatever else we look forward to in the other world, it will not be *this*—and you must sometimes wonder if Heaven itself can make up for the joy of life, with all its disappointments and troubles, in this dear old earth.

BASIL W. MATURIN,
quoted in *Father Maturin* by Maisie Ward

One always dies too soon—or too late. And yet one's whole life is complete at that moment, with a line drawn neatly under it, ready for the summing up.

JEAN-PAUL SARTRE,
No Exit

It is odd, is it not, to picture all these millions of human beings, sweating, swearing, fighting, cheating, loving, and all waiting for death—if they only stopped to think of it. And if they did, all the fighting and loving would stop, or would go on very half-heartedly, so it is just as well they do not.

GAMALIEL BRADFORD,
The Letters of Gamaliel Bradford

The dead can live only with the exact intensity and quality imparted to them by the living.

JOSEPH CONRAD,
Under Western Eyes

It is death which gives gambling and heroism their true meaning.

ALBERT CAMUS,
Notebooks 1935–1942

Perhaps the best tribute you can pay some one who dies is to share his belief in life by putting your life ahead of his death.

MAX LERNER,
The Unfinished Country

Since the death instinct exists in the heart of everything that lives, since we suffer from trying to repress it, since everything that lives longs for rest, let us unfasten the ties that bind us to life, let us cultivate our death wish, let us develop it, water it like a plant, let it grow unhindered. Suffering and fear are born from the repression of the death wish.

EUGÈNE IONESCO,
Fragments of a Journal

The world so quickly readjusts itself after any loss, that the return of the departed would nearly always throw it, even the circle most interested, into confusion.

CHARLES DUDLEY WARNER,
Backlog Studies

You never realize death until you realize love.

KATHARINE BUTLER HATHAWAY,
*The Journals and Letters
of the Little Locksmith*

I have always had a haunting distrust and fear of comfort and warmth because they seem to me a coating, a crust which quickly makes one dull to the reality of *real* things—like death. It seems to me that the true proportion of realities is that which one must see in the hour of death. If I could only constantly keep that proportion in my mind, I think life would be much greater.

KATHARINE BUTLER HATHAWAY,
*The Journals and Letters
of the Little Locksmith*

Men seldom see any misery in life so great as to outweigh the misery of leaving it.

PHILLIPS BROOKS,
Visions and Tasks

Once I give form to my thought, I must free myself from it. For the time being, it seems to me that I want absolute freedom to create new forms for new ideas. I am sure physical death has the same meaning for us—the creative impulse of our soul must have new forms for its realization. Death can continue to dwell in the same sepulchre, but life must unceasingly out-

grow its dwelling-place; otherwise the form gets the upper hand and becomes a prison.

RABINDRANATH TAGORE,
Letters to a Friend

It astonishes me to observe how irritated moderns become, not so much at the thought as at the mention of death. That's one thing they don't quite know how to take. I don't mean that we should be "brave." That stinks. But it is equally asinine to pretend to ignore it.

WILLIAM CARLOS WILLIAMS,
*Selected Letters of
William Carlos Williams*

The dark background which death supplies brings out the tender colors of life in all their purity.

GEORGE SANTAYANA,
Soliloquies in England

I feel so much the *continual* death of everything and everybody, and have so learned to reconcile myself to it, that the final and official end loses most of its impressiveness.

GEORGE SANTAYANA,
The Letters of George Santayana

Have pity upon every man, Lord in that hour when he has finished his task and stands before Thee like a child whose hands are being examined.

PAUL CLAUDEL,
quoted in *The Soul Afire*,
compiled by H. Reinhold

Men do not live any longer than they wish to.

ELBERT HUBBARD,
The Philosophy of Elbert Hubbard

In time, I hope and believe the anguish with you will be covered over. That is the only way to express it. It is like new skin covering a wound. That doesn't mean that one forgets the people who have gone away.

EDITH SITWELL,
Edith Sitwell: Selected Letters 1916–1964

You may have heard before this of the death of my wife, which not only takes away a half of my life but gives me notice. She was of the same age as I and at 88 the end is due. I may work on for a year or two, but I cannot hope to add much to what I have done. I am too sceptical to think that it matters much, but too conscious of the mystery of the universe to say that it or anything else does not. I bow my head, I think serenely, and say as I told someone the other day, O Cosmos—Now lettest thou thy ganglion dissolve in peace.

OLIVER WENDELL HOLMES, JR.,
The Mind and Faith of Justice Holmes,
edited by Max Lerner

Only think of Mrs. Holder's being dead! Poor woman, she has done the only thing in the world she could possibly do to make one cease to abuse her.

JANE AUSTEN,
quoted in *Ladies of Literature*
by Laura L. Hinkley

DECEPTION

The wolf will hire himself out very cheaply as a shepherd.

RUSSIAN PROVERB

I have met with many that would deceive; who would be deceived, no one.

SAINT AUGUSTINE,
Confessions

Consider the life of an ordinary private person, and what havoc complete truth would work in it. Directly we enter into contact with our fellows, deceit begins.

ROSE MACAULAY,
A Casual Commentary

One sprinkles the most sugar where the tart is burnt.

DUTCH PROVERB

Human beings seem to have an almost unlimited capacity to deceive themselves, and to deceive themselves into taking their own lies for truth.

R. D. LAING,
The Politics of Experience

No one likes to be deceived, and everyone is more or less in dread of it. But only too

often this dread deceives man and robs him of valuable things and experiences.

THEODOR HAECKER,
Journal in the Night

We get together and talk, and say we think and feel and believe in such a way, and yet what we really think and feel and believe we never say at all.

THOMAS WOLFE,
Of Time and the River

The abomination of desolation is not a burned town, nor a country wasted by war, but the discovery that the man who has moved you is an enthusiast upon calculation.

RALPH WALDO EMERSON,
Journals of Ralph Waldo Emerson

To be duped is not always the result of stupidity, but sometimes of virtue.

BALTASAR GRACIAN,
The Oracle

Deceiving someone for his own good is a responsibility which should be shouldered only by the gods.

ANONYMOUS (HENRY S. HASKINS),
Meditations in Wall Street

If you are not a saint, and sometimes even if you are, it is necessary to deceive one's fellow-creatures in many important matters.

JOHN COWPER POWYS,
The Meaning of Culture

DECISION

When making a decision of minor importance, I have always found it advantageous to consider all the pros and cons. In vital matters, however, such as the choice of a mate or a profession, the decision should come from the unconscious, from somewhere within ourselves. In the important decisions of personal life, we should be governed, I think, by the deep inner needs of our nature.

SIGMUND FREUD,
quoted in *Listening with the Third Ear*
by Dr. Theodor Reik

No man, who has not sat in the assemblies of men, can know the light, odd, and uncertain ways in which decisions are often arrived at by these bodies.

SIR ARTHUR HELPS,
Essays Written in Intervals of Business

A weak man has doubts before a decision: a strong man has them afterwards.

KARL KRAUS,
Karl Kraus by Harry Zohn

In 40 hours I shall be in battle, with little information, and on the spur of the moment will have to make most momentous decisions. But I believe that one's spirit enlarges with responsibility and that, with God's help, I shall make them and make them right.

GEORGE S. PATTON,
quoted in *Patton: Ordeal and Triumph*
by Ladislas Farago

The person's act of choosing itself throws a new element into the picture. The configuration is changed, if ever so slightly; someone has thrown his weight on one side or the other. This is the creative and the dynamic element in decision.

ROLLO MAY,
Man's Search for Himself

One's mind has a way of making itself up in the background, and it suddenly becomes clear what one means to do.

A. C. BENSON,
*Excerpts from the Letters of
Dr. A. C. Benson to M. E. A.*

It is no small part of the tactics of life to form the habit of making decisions when your spirit is fresh, as in the forenoon, and ignoring midnight apprehensions. To let dark moods lead is like choosing cowards to command armies.

CHARLES HORTON COOLEY,
Life and the Student

Some persons are very decisive when it comes to avoiding decisions.

BRENDAN FRANCIS

Once the *what* is decided, the *how* always follows. We must not make the *how* an excuse for not facing and accepting the *what*.

PEARL BUCK,
To My Daughters, with Love

But decisions, particularly important ones, have always made me sleepy, perhaps because I know that I will have to make them by instinct, and thinking things out is only what other people tell me I should do.

LILLIAN HELLMAN,
Pentimento

Each time we make a decision it is determined by the good or evil forces, respectively, which are dominant.

ERICH FROMM,
Man for Himself

Now who is to decide between "Let it be" and "Force it"?

KATHERINE MANSFIELD,
The Journal of Katherine Mansfield

Then and there I invented this rule for myself to be applied to every decision I might have to make in the future. I would sort out all the arguments and see which belonged to fear and which to creativeness, and other things being equal I would make the decision which had the larger number of creative reasons on its side. I think it must be a rule something like this that makes jonquils and crocuses come pushing through the cold mud.

KATHARINE BUTLER HATHAWAY,
*The Journals and Letters
of the Little Locksmith*

Continually one faces the horrible matter of making decisions: whether to make a luncheon date, whether to get one's hair cut ... which letters to answer, etc., etc. The solution (we honestly believe) is, as far as possible, to avoid conscious rational decisions and choices: simply to do what you find yourself doing; to float in the great current of life with as little friction as possible; to allow things to settle themselves, as indeed they do with the most infallible certainty.

CHRISTOPHER MORLEY,
Inward Ho

Most of the things we decide are not what we know to be best. We say yes, merely because we are driven into a corner and must say something.

DR. FRANK CRANE,
Essays

DEED

Every thought I have imprisoned in expression I must free by my deeds.

KAHLIL GIBRAN,
Sand and Foam

They will be hushed by a good deed who laugh at a wise speech.

FRENCH PROVERB

Deeds done, when viewed in themselves and not simply as means to ends, are also to be regarded as things made.

ERIC GILL,
quoted in *Modern Christian Revolutionaries*
by Donald Attwater

There's many a deed smells sweet at night that stinks in the heat of the sun.

JOHN BARTH,
The Sot-Weed Factor

Our deeds act upon us as much as we act upon them.

GEORGE ELIOT,
quoted in *The Journals of André Gide*

DEFENSES

We build up our defenses slowly, brick by brick, cementing them with our fear and anguish; and then, when they are no longer needed, we cannot bear to tear them down. We have leaned on them too long. Our lives have been shaped to fit them, psychic muscles have stiffened against them, emotions have learned to flow under them, our vocabulary has entwined itself around them until they are almost hidden from us.

LILLIAN SMITH,
The Journey

DEFICIENCY

With all our virtuous efforts to help our associates we often serve them best by those deficiencies for which they have to compensate.

CHARLES HORTON COOLEY,
Life and the Student

DEFINITION

For the most part we do not first see, and then define, we define first and then see. In the great blooming, buzzing confusion of the outer world we pick out what our culture has already defined for us, and we tend to perceive that which we have picked out in the form stereotyped for us by our culture.

WALTER LIPPMANN,
Public Opinion

Men who are given to defining too much inevitably run themselves into confusion in dealing with the vague concepts of common sense.

CHARLES SANDERS PEIRCE,
Collected Papers of Charles Sanders Peirce,
Vol. VI

Few of us pause for definition even in our most serious discussions, and when we do we are amazed, not that there is so much bitter misunderstanding and acrimony in life, but that there is so little.

JOSEPH H. ODELL,
Unmailed Letters

DELAY

It is a delaying world, boast as they like of its speed.

GEORGE E. WOODBERRY,
Selected Letters of George Edward Woodberry

Delay is a bitter tonic, but it increases the appetite.

AUSTIN O'MALLEY,
Keystones of Thought

That's a wise delay which makes the road safe.

SPANISH PROVERB

DELIGHT

Technology is preparing a world in which we may be learners all life long. In this world delight will not be a luxury but a necessity.

GEORGE B. LEONARD,
Education and Ecstasy

To give delight is hallowed—perhaps the toil of angels, whose avocations are concealed.

EMILY DICKINSON,
Selected Poems and Letters of Emily Dickinson

Nothing remains with man unless it is insinuated with some delight.

COVENTRY PATMORE,
The Rod, the Root, and the Flower

DEMOCRACY

The truth of the matter is that the ultimate development of the common man's democracy is in the direction of a police state—burn the books; put the artist in prison; prevent him telling the truth. The common man must be flattered—not told the truth.

SIR OSBERT SITWELL,
Wisdom, edited by James Nelson

The democratic philosophy of man and society has faith in the resources and the vocation of human nature.

JACQUES MARITAIN,
Christianity and Democracy

Democracy always makes for materialism, because the only kind of equality that you can guarantee to a whole people is, broadly speaking, physical.

KATHERINE FULLERTON GEROULD,
Modes and Morals

The duty of a democracy is to know then what it knows now.

E. B. WHITE,
One Man's Meat

A democracy can be distinguished, if its citizens are distinguishable; if each has an area of choice in which he really chooses. To keep that area of choice as large as possible is the real function of freedom.

G. K. CHESTERTON,
All Is Grist

The democratic conscience recoils before anything that savours of privilege; and lest it should concede an immediate privilege to any pursuit or person, it reduces all things as far as possible to the common denominator of quantity.

GEORGE SANTAYANA,
Character and Opinion in the United States

I get my most hopeful impressions of democracy from intelligent hardworking men, from farmers, teachers, impecunious students, from almost any source except the more opulent commercial and professional classes.

CHARLES HORTON COOLEY,
Life and the Student

There is, let me assure you, nothing more egocentrical than an embattled democracy. It soon becomes the victim of its own war propaganda. It then tends to attach to its own cause an absolute value which distorts its own vision on everything else. Its enemy becomes the embodiment of all evil. Its own side, on the other hand, is the center of all virtue.

GEORGE F. KENNAN,
Russia and the West under Lenin and Stalin

DEPENDENCE

The dependence on irrational authority results in a weakening of the will in the dependent person and, at the same time, whatever tends to paralyze the will makes for an increase in dependence. Thus a vicious circle is formed.

ERICH FROMM,
Man for Himself

From someone else's cart you have to get off halfway.

POLISH PROVERB

Human solidarity is a more evident and certain fact than personal responsibility or even individual liberty. Our dependence outweighs our independence, for we are independent only in our desire, while we are dependent on our health, on nature, on society, on everything in us and outside us. The circle of our liberty is only a point.

HENRI FRÉDÉRIC AMIEL,
The Private Journal of Henri Frédéric Amiel

Do not depend upon others: there is no grace, no help to be had from the outside.

BUDDHA

DEPRESSION

Many an attack of depression is nothing but the expression of regret at having to be virtuous.

DR. WILHELM STEKHEL,
The Depths of the Soul

In moods of heavy despondency, one feels as if it would be delightful to sink down in some quiet spot, and lie there forever, letting the soil gradually accumulate and form a little hillock over us, and the grass and perhaps flowers gather over it. At such times, death is too much of an event to be wished for;—we have not the spirits to encounter it; but choose to pass out of existence in this sluggish way.

NATHANIEL HAWTHORNE,
The American Notebooks

I have been fighting the powers of darkness lately. Still they prevail with me. But I have more or less got my head out of the inferno, my body will follow later. How one has to struggle, really, to overcome this accursed blackness. It would do me so much good if I could kill a few people.

D. H. LAWRENCE,
Selected Letters of D. H. Lawrence

I can enjoy feeling melancholy, and there is a good deal of satisfaction about being thoroughly miserable; but nobody likes a fit of the blues. Nevertheless, everybody has them; notwithstanding which, nobody can tell why. There is no accounting for them. You are just as likely to have one on the day you have come into a large fortune as on the day after you have left your new silk umbrella in the train.

JEROME K. JEROME,
The Idle Thoughts of an Idle Fellow

The value of solitude—one of its values—is, of course, that there is nothing to *cushion* against attacks from within, just as there is nothing to help balance at times of particular stress of depression. A few moments of desultory conversation . . . may calm an inner storm. But the storm, painful as it is, might have had some truth in it. So sometimes one has simply to endure a period of depression for what it may hold of illumination if one can live through it, attentive to what it exposes or demands.

MAY SARTON,
Journal of a Solitude

DESIRE

It is the thing that is most remote from the world in which we ourselves live that attracts us most. We are under the spell always of what is distant from us. It is not in our nature to desire passionately what is near at hand.

ALEC WAUGH,
On Doing What One Likes

Our desires attract supporting reasons as a magnet the iron filings.

W. MACNEILE DIXON,
The Human Situation

Man never has what he wants, because what he wants is *everything*.

C.-F. RAMUZ,
What Is Man?

It is by that which he longs for, that every man knows and apprehends the quality with which he has to serve God.

MARTIN BUBER,
Hasidism

Believe me, of all the people in the world those who want the most are those who have the most.

DAVID GRAYSON,
The Friendly Road

If we go down into ourselves we find that we possess exactly what we desire.

SIMONE WEIL,
Gravity and Grace

All our desires are contradictory.... I want the person I love to love me. If, however, he is totally devoted to me he does not exist any longer and I cease to love him. And as long as he is not totally devoted to me I do not love him.

SIMONE WEIL,
Gravity and Grace

A man can do what he wants, but not want what he wants.

ARTHUR SCHOPENHAUER,
quoted in *Ideas and Opinions*
by Albert Einstein

The central fire is desire, and all the powers of our being are given us to see, to fight for, and to win the object of our desire. Quench that fire and man turns to ashes.

BASIL W. MATURIN,
Laws of the Spiritual Life

A desire is real when the possibility of satisfaction exists for the individual who entertains it and the existence of such a possibility depends, first, on his present historical and social situation—a desire for a Cadillac which may be real for a prosperous American businessman would be fantastic for a Chinese peasant—and, secondly, on his natural endowment as an individual—for a girl with one eye to desire to be kept by a millionaire would be fantastic, for a girl with two beautiful ones it may not.

W. H. AUDEN,
The Dyer's Hand and Other Essays

He who likes cherries soon learns to climb.

GERMAN PROVERB

If men could regard the events of their own lives with more open minds, they would frequently discover that they did not really desire the things they failed to obtain.

ANDRÉ MAUROIS,
The Art of Living

It's weak and despicable to go on wanting things and not trying to get them.

JOANNA FIELD,
A Life of One's Own

It's rather nice to think of oneself as a sailor bending over the map of one's mind and deciding where to go and how to go. The great thing to remember is we can do whatever we wish to do provided our wish is strong enough. But the tremendous effort needed—one doesn't always want to make it—does one? And all that cutting down the jungle and bush clearing even after one has landed anywhere—it's tiring. Yes I agree. But what else can be done? What's the alternative? What do you want *most* to do? That's what I have to keep asking myself, in face of difficulties.

KATHERINE MANSFIELD,
quoted in *Katherine Mansfield Memories of LM*

The more wild and incredible your desire the more willing and prompt God is in fulfilling it, if you will have it so.

COVENTRY PATMORE,
The Rod, The Root, and the Flower

To drink is a small matter. To be thirsty is everything.

GEORGES DUHAMEL,
The Heart's Domain

The real way of living is to answer to one's wants. Not "I want to light up with my intelligence as many things as possible," but "For the living of my full flame—I want that liberty, I want that woman, I want that pound of peaches, I want to go to sleep, I want to go to the pub and have a good time, I want to look a beastly swell today, I want to kiss that girl, I want to insult that man." Instead of that, all these wants ... are utterly ignored, and we talk about some sort of ideas.

D. H. LAWRENCE,
Selected Letters of D. H. Lawrence,
edited by Diana Trilling

We can only know that from the unknown, profound desires enter in upon us, and that the fulfilling of these desires is the fulfilling of creation. We know that the rose comes to blossom. We know that we are incipient with blossom. It is our business to go as we are impelled, with faith and pure spontaneous morality, knowing that the rose blossoms, and taking that knowledge for sufficient.

D. H. LAWRENCE,
Selected Essays

For whereas the mind works in possibilities, the intuitions work in actualities, and what you *intuitively* desire, that is possible to you. Whereas what you mentally or "consciously" desire is nine times out of ten impossible: hitch your wagon to a star, and you'll just stay where you are.

D. H. LAWRENCE,
Selected Essays

Want a thing long enough, and you don't.

CHINESE PROVERB

I do not know that I ever desired anything earnestly in my life but 'twas denied me; I am many times afraid to wish a thing, merely lest my fortune should take that occasion to use me ill.

DOROTHY OSBORNE,
quoted in *The Literature of Gossip*
by Elizabeth Drew

I can tell you at any rate how to get what you want. You've just got to keep a thing in view and go for it and never let your eyes wander to right or left or up or down. And looking back is fatal—the truest thing in Scripture is about Lot's wife.

WILLIAM J. LOCKE,
Septimus

One should want *only one thing* and want it constantly. Then one is sure of getting it. But I desire everything and consequently get nothing. Each time I discover, and too late, that one thing had come to me while I was running after another.

ANDRÉ GIDE,
The Journals of André Gide, Vol. I

Long only for what you have.

ANDRÉ GIDE,
The Fruits of the Earth

The trouble is that really wanting things is so rare. It's a lukewarm world.

E. V. LUCAS,
365 Days and One More

What you can't get is just what suits you.

FRENCH PROVERB

I felt a continual sensation of craving for something, I didn't know what. It was so continual that it seemed an inherent part of life to be hungry, to feel a perpetual irritation of desire—never to be able to rest in contentment and peace. I suppose that craving was the work of the mysterious little instinct that continually seeks a balanced ratio of experience, seeks to make a work of art out of one's life. It was this craving that was the driving force behind everything I did ... so that one's whole life shall be as far as possible a complete fulfillment of one's capacity for living.

KATHARINE BUTLER HATHAWAY,
*The Journals and Letters
of the Little Locksmith*

When you want something you are at war with it.

ROBERT SPEAIGHT,
The Unbroken Heart

Have the courage of your desire.

GEORGE GISSING,
The Private Papers of Henry Ryecroft

A man's notion that he has this or that quality, seems to be almost always the stirring of that something really there: perhaps it may be true also that the desire of something to be within him is the sign, not yet clearly read, that the something is there, though deep-down, crusted over and not yet wholly able to shine out in the unmistakable brightness of the idea itself. Desire would be as it were the dim life of the thing of which idea was the clearer full life: from the desire of the thing to the idea of the real presence of the thing is not a great step: from the idea of the real presence of the thing to the use and enjoyment of the thing is hardly a step at all. Herein is much magic.

STEPHEN MACKENNA,
Journal and Letters of Stephen Mackenna

DESPAIR

If you are convinced of your despair, you must either act as if you did hope after all—or kill yourself. Suffering gives no rights.

ALBERT CAMUS,
Notebooks 1935–1942

Nothing makes me more pessimistic than the obligation not to be pessimistic. I feel that every message of despair is the statement of a situation from which everybody must freely try to find a way out.

EUGÈNE IONESCO,
quoted in *The Theatre of the Absurd*
by Martin Esslin

Despair lames most people, but it wakes others fully up.

WILLIAM JAMES,
"The Energies of Men,"
Essays on Faith and Morals

People who are in despair always make a mistake when they hang themselves; the next day often brings the unknown.

HENRI FRÉDÉRIC AMIEL,
The Private Journal of Henri Frédéric Amiel

We are all very near despair. The sheathing that floats us over its waves is compounded of hope, faith in the unexplainable worth and sure issue of its effort, and the deep, subconscious content which comes from the exercise of our powers.

OLIVER WENDELL HOLMES, JR.,
The Mind and Faith of Justice Holmes,
edited by Max Lerner

The final expression of an absolute despair would be: it has always been so, and it will always be so.

THEODOR HAECKER,
Journal in the Night

I once counselled a man in despair to do what I myself did in similar circumstances: to live for short terms. Come, I said to myself at that time, at any rate you can bear it for a quarter of an hour!

THEODOR HAECKER,
Journal in the Night

Despair is vinegar from the wine of hope.

AUSTIN O'MALLEY,
Keystones of Thought

Utter despair, impossible to pull myself together; only when I have become satisfied with my sufferings can I stop.

FRANZ KAFKA,
The Diaries of Franz Kafka 1914–1923

What's the good being hopeless, so long as one has a hobnailed boot to kick with?

D. H. LAWRENCE,
Selected Letters of D. H. Lawrence

I can't tell if a straw ever saved a drowning man, but I know that a mere glance is enough to make despair pause. For in truth we who are creatures of impulse are not creatures of despair.

JOSEPH CONRAD,
Chance

DESPISE

There are many things we despise, that we may not have to despise ourselves.

VAUVENARGUES,
Reflections and Maxims

I love the great despisers, because they are the great adorers, and arrows of longing for the other shore.

FRIEDRICH NIETZSCHE,
Thus Spake Zarathustra

Throughout Life, our worst weaknesses and meannesses are usually committed for the sake of the people whom we most despise.

CHARLES DICKENS,
Great Expectations

DESPOT

The universe is not friendly to despots, and they all perish sooner or later. It may be objected that the contemporaries of these personages have also perished. Such is indeed the fact.

DON MARQUIS,
The Almost Perfect State

DESTINY

To accomplish our destiny, it is not enough merely to guard prudently against road accidents. We must also cover before nightfall the distance assigned to each of us.

ALEXIS CARREL,
Reflections on Life

No matter what we have come through, or how many perils we have safely passed, or how imperfect and jagged—in some places perhaps irreparably—our life has been, we cannot in our heart of hearts imagine how it could have been different. As we look back on it, it slips in behind us in orderly array, and, with all its mistakes, acquires a sort of eternal fitness, and even, at times, of poetic glamour.

RANDOLPH BOURNE,
Youth and Life

Every man has his own destiny: the only imperative is to follow it, to accept it, no matter where it leads him.

HENRY MILLER,
The Wisdom of the Heart

How amusing it is to see the fixed mosaic of one's little destiny being filled out by tiny blocks of events,—the enchainment of minute consequences with the illusion of choice weathering it all!

ALICE JAMES,
The Diary of Alice James

We are not permitted to choose the frame of our destiny. But what we put into it is ours.

DAG HAMMARSKJÖLD,
Markings

Man wins destiny only through ties: not through coercive ties imposed on him as an impotent creature of great forces that lie without; but by ties freely comprehended which he makes his own. Such ties hold his life together, so that it is not frittered away but becomes the actuality of his possible existence.

KARL JASPERS,
Man in the Modern Age

On the face of it, one would think that we must needs all complete our destinies, merely by the simple process of living out our lives to the end.

ROSE MACAULAY,
A Casual Commentary

The appointed thing comes at the appointed time in the appointed way.

MYRTLE REED,
Master of the Vineyard

One meets his destiny often in the road he takes to avoid it.

FRENCH PROVERB

Men reach the higher or lower places to which they attain (above or below their ambition) without intention and upon the drift of a tide. No doubt the man who exercises judgment and will in critical turnings goes further (upwards or *downwards*) than the man who does not. He will have a longer run of good or evil fortune than a less skilful or a less determined one; but he knows no more than the weakest what he is to arrive at.

HILAIRE BELLOC,
A Conversation with a Cat

And when man faces destiny, destiny ends and man comes into his own.

ANDRÉ MALRAUX,
The Voices of Silence

We have already had to re-think so many of our conceptions of motion, we will also gradually learn to realize that that which we call destiny goes forth from within people, not from without into them.

RAINER MARIA RILKE,
Letters to a Young Poet

As there is design and symmetry in nature, I believe there is also design and symmetry in human experience if we will learn to yield ourselves to our destinies.

KATHARINE BUTLER HATHAWAY,
The Journals and Letters of the Little Locksmith

Lots of folks confuse bad management with destiny.

KIN HUBBARD

The masochist takes everything as destiny. The sadist loves to play destiny.

> OTTO WEININGER,
> quoted in *The Mind and Death of a Genius*
> by David Abrahamsen

But you can catch yourself entertaining habitually certain types of ideas and setting others aside; and that, I think, is where our personal destinies are largely decided.

> ALFRED NORTH WHITEHEAD,
> *Dialogues of Alfred North Whitehead*

We are like pigs at the teats of Destiny, and must spend much time in kneading and rooting for one full draught.

> JOHN BURROUGHS,
> *The Heart of Burroughs' Journals*

Our restless feet take us from place to place on the chase after benefits which, if they are intended for us, choose to do all the chasing.

> ANONYMOUS (HENRY S. HASKINS),
> *Meditations in Wall Street*

DESTROY

Were a miracle to produce in our woods some astounding orchid, a thousand hands would stretch out to tear it up, to destroy it. If the bluebird happens to fly past, every gun is sighted; and then people are amazed that it is rare!

> ANDRÉ GIDE,
> *The Journals of André Gide,* Vol. I

Tidied all my papers. Tore up and ruthlessly destroyed much. This is always a great satisfaction.

> KATHERINE MANSFIELD,
> *The Journal of Katherine Mansfield*

That man can destroy life is just as miraculous a feat as that he can create it, for life is *the* miracle, the inexplicable. In the act of destruction, man sets himself above life; he transcends himself as a creature. Thus, the ultimate choice for man, inasmuch as he is driven to transcend himself, is to create or to destroy, to love or to hate.

> ERICH FROMM,
> *The Sane Society*

DEVIL

And when I saw my devil, I found him serious, thorough, profound, solemn: he was the spirit of gravity—through him all things fall.

> FRIEDRICH NIETZSCHE,
> *Thus Spake Zarathustra*

The devil appeared to St. Bridget, and she asked him: "What is your name?" "Coldness itself."

> ABBÉ HUVELIN,
> *Some Spiritual Guides*
> *of the Seventeenth Century*

It must not be supposed that the Devil only tempts men of genius. Doubtless, he despises imbeciles, but he does not disdain their cooperation. Quite the reverse; it is upon them that he builds his greatest hopes.

> CHARLES BAUDELAIRE,
> *Intimate Journals*

Francis Thompson said that the devil doesn't know how to sing, only how to howl.

> VINCENT MCNABB,
> *God's Way of Mercy*

Satan stands for nothing but simple will, wilfullness, or personality. It was not for a cause he revolted.

> MARK RUTHERFORD,
> *Last Pages from a Journal*

If evil is caused by the flesh, how explain the wickedness of the Devil who has no flesh?

> SAINT AUGUSTINE,
> *The City of God*

Would you see the devil? Look in the mirror.

> A. R. ORAGE,
> *Essays and Aphorisms*

There are so many intellectual and moral angels battling for rationalism, good citizenship, and pure spirituality; so many and such eminent ones, so very vocal and authoritative! The poor devil in man needs all the support and advocacy he can get. The artist is his natural champion. When an artist deserts to the side of the angels, it is the most odious of treasons.

ALDOUS HUXLEY,
Collected Essays

I am not surprised at the idea of the devil being always at our elbows. Those who invented him no doubt could not conceive how men could be so atrocious to one another, without the intervention of a fiend.

HORACE WALPOLE,
quoted in *The Literature of Gossip*
by Elizabeth Drew

An old lady in church was seen to bow whenever the name of Satan was mentioned. One day the minister met her and asked why she did so.

"Well," she replied, "politeness costs nothing—and you never know."

ANONYMOUS,
quoted in *Ladies' Home Journal*,
March 1944

The Devil, having nothing else to do,
Went off to tempt My Lady Poltagrue.
My Lady, tempted by a private whim,
To his extreme annoyance, tempted him.

HILAIRE BELLOC,
"Our Lady Poltagrue, A Public Peril,"
Cautionary Verses

I met the Devil last night. It was exactly three minutes past midnight. He said: "After all, what does it matter whether you write it or not? Why not go to bed?"

CHRISTOPHER MORLEY,
Inward Ho

I do not know a description of a devil in literature which does not leave one with some sense of sympathy. Milton's devils are admirable; Dante's devils stir our pity; Goethe's devil makes us feel what a good thing has been wasted. Human nature seems incapable of imagining that which

is wholly bad, just because it is not wholly bad itself.

ALBAN GOODIER,
The School of Love

DIARY

I suppose this is the reason why diaries are so rarely kept nowadays—that nothing ever happens to anybody.

A. A. MILNE,
Not That It Matters

I suspect that a good many diaries record adventures of the mind and soul for lack of stirring adventures to the body. If they cannot say, "Attacked by a lion in Bond Street today," they can at least say, "Attacked by doubt in St. Paul's Cathedral."

A. A. MILNE,
Not That It Matters

I've kept journals at many times in my life starting from when I was about thirteen or fourteen. But it's boring and contrived to keep a journal every day. Better to write as the mood strikes.

ERICA JONG,
quoted in *The Craft of Poetry*,
edited by William Packard

Recently I began reading my old diaries. Back to before the war. Gradually I became very depressed. The reason for that is probably that I wrote only when there were obstacles and halts to the flow of life, seldom when everything was smooth and even. . . . I distinctly felt what a half-truth a diary presents.

KÄTHE KOLLWITZ,
Revelations: Diaries of Women, edited by
Mary Jane Moffat and Charlotte Painter

Diaries are written for various reasons. Sometimes they are meant to be a terse record of one's daily waking hours. Sometimes they are an unconscious relief from the day's tensions. There it is on paper, you say, plainly to be read, so it couldn't have been so unendurable.

EDNA FERBER,
A Kind of Magic

Yes, there is no doubt that paper is patient and as I don't intend to show this cardboard-covered notebook, bearing the proud name of "diary," to anyone, unless I find a real friend, boy or girl, probably nobody cares. And now I come to the root of the matter, the reason for my starting a diary: it is that I have no such real friend.

ANNE FRANK,
Anne Frank: The Diary of a Young Girl

Oh, so many things bubble up inside me as I lie in bed, having to put up with people I'm fed up with, who always misinterpret my intentions. That's why in the end I always come back to my diary. That is where I start and finish because Kitty [her diary] is always patient. I'll promise her that I shall persevere in spite of everything, and find my own way through it all, and swallow my tears.

ANNE FRANK,
Anne Frank: The Diary of a Young Girl

A diary need not be a dreary chronicle of one's movements; it should aim rather at giving a salient account of some particular episode, a walk, a book, a conversation.

A. C. BENSON,
From a College Window

Why has my motley diary no jokes? Because it is a soliloquy and every man is grave alone.

RALPH WALDO EMERSON,
Journals of Ralph Waldo Emerson

Most people are conscious sometimes of strange and beautiful fancies swimming before their eyes: the pen is the wand to arrest, and the journal is the mirror to detain and fix them.

R. A. WILLMOTT,
A Journal of Summertime

My diaries were written primarily, I think, not to preserve the experience but to savor it, to make it even more real, more visible and palpable, than in actual life. For in our family an experience was not finished, unless written down or shared with another.

ANNE MORROW LINDBERGH,
Bring Me a Unicorn

What good is this journal? I cling to these pages as to something fixed among so many fugitive things. I oblige myself to write anything whatever in them just so I do it regularly every day.

ANDRÉ GIDE,
The Journals of André Gide, Vol. I

I think that if I get into the habit of writing a bit about what happens, or rather doesn't happen, I may lose a little of the sense of isolation and desolation which abides with me.

ALICE JAMES,
The Diary of Alice James

One great use of keeping such a record as this is that one learns what blank things most of one's days are: reading, talking, eating, writing without interest or emotion, the days go by, blank: and it is life that passes: days make life, and if the days are blank—it is terrible. The only good thing in life is to have a vivid mental activity and some human love to warm it: all the rest is cold as fuel without fire. I believe it is a moral duty to think and to love; because it is a duty to live, and these are life.

STEPHEN MACKENNA,
Journal and Letters of Stephen Mackenna

I got out this diary and read, as one always reads one's own writing, with a kind of guilty intensity.

VIRGINIA WOOLF,
A Writer's Diary

Should you wish to make sure that your birthday will be celebrated three hundred years hence, your best course undoubtedly is to keep a diary. Only first be certain that you have the courage to lock your genius in a private book and the humour to gloat over a fame that will be yours in the grave. For the good diarist writes either for himself alone or for a posterity so distant that it can safely hear every secret and justly weigh every motive.

VIRGINIA WOOLF,
The Common Reader

DICTATOR

There is an interesting resemblance in the speeches of dictators, no matter what country they may hail from or what language they may speak.

EDNA FERBER,
A Kind of Magic

The essence of modern dictatorship is the combination of one-dimensional, flat thinking with power and terror.

THEODOR HAECKER,
Journal in the Night

DICTIONARY

I rarely look at a dictionary, which after all is merely somebody's estimate of polite usage, a matter on which one can form one's own opinion.

OLIVER WENDELL HOLMES, JR.,
Holmes–Pollock Letters, Vol. II

What single book would one choose to be cast away with on a desert island? My choice would be a Webster's Unabridged, that great mother of books, that matrix from which one man delivers *Finnegan's Wake,* another *A Shropshire Lad.* What a glorious prospect—to be alone on an island, with an opportunity to sit back against a banana tree, and read all the way from aardvark to zymurgy!

LAWRENCE CLARK POWELL,
The Alchemy of Books

Nothing in language is immutably fixed: the best writers are constantly changing it. Absolute government by dictionary would mean the arrest of this healthy process of change and growth.

C. E. MONTAGUE,
quoted in *C. E. Montague: A Memoir*
by Oliver Elton

From the actual use I have made of my dictionary I have got little but sorrow. Many excellent words are ruined by too definite a knowledge of their meaning.

ALINE KILMER,
Hunting a Hair Shirt

DIET

In the matter of diet—I have been persistently strict in sticking to the things which didn't agree with me until one or the other of us got the best of it.

MARK TWAIN,
Mark Twain at Your Fingertips,
edited by Caroline T. Harnsberger

Obesity is a mental state, a disease brought on by boredom and disappointment; greed, like the love of comfort, is a kind of fear. The one way to get thin is to re-establish a purpose in life.

CYRIL CONNOLLY,
The Unquiet Grave

It is possible to be so busy going on or off a diet that there isn't time left to enjoy life. Once people ate everything set before them, and had the courage to digest it too.

MARCELENE COX,
Ladies' Home Journal, March 1942

DIFFERENCE

It is futile to linger endlessly over differences; the fruitful research is to look for points of contact.

A. G. SERTILLANGES,
The Intellectual Life

In God's eyes the differences of social position, of intellect, of culture, of cleanliness, of dress, which different men exhibit, and all the other rarities and exceptions on which they so fantastically pin their pride, must be so small as practically quite to vanish; and all that should remain is the common fact that here we are, a countless multitude of vessels of life, each of us pent in to peculiar difficulties, with which we must severally struggle by using whatever of fortitude and goodness we can summon up.

WILLIAM JAMES,
"What Makes a Life Significant?"
Talks to Teachers

If we all pulled in one direction, the world would keel over.

YIDDISH PROVERB

DIFFERENT

Whatever helps us to visualize things as different from what our intellectual sleepiness shows them to be ought to be gladly welcomed.

ERNEST DIMNET,
What We Live By

Commandment No. 1 of any truly civilized society is this: Let people be different.

DAVID GRAYSON,
The Countryman's Year

What we mostly wish in life is to become one day different from what we have been.

ANATOLE FRANCE,
The Anatole France Calendar,
selected by A. S. Rappoport

DIFFICULTY

Can it be that man is essentially a being who loves to conquer difficulties? The creature whose function is to solve problems?

GORHAM MUNSON,
The Writer's Workshop

A man's worst difficulties begin when he is able to do what he likes.

THOMAS HENRY HUXLEY,
Aphorisms and Reflections

Settle one difficulty, and you keep a hundred others away.

CHINESE PROVERB

In this age, which believes that there is a short cut to everything, the greatest lesson to be learned is that the most difficult way is, in the long run, the easiest.

HENRY MILLER,
The Books in My Life

Providence has hidden a charm in difficult undertakings which is appreciated only by those who dare to grapple with them.

MADAME SWETCHINE,
The Writings of Madame Swetchine

We see those surmount, by dint of some egotism or infatuation, obstacles from which the prudent recoil.

RALPH WALDO EMERSON,
"Considerations by the Way,"
Conduct of Life

Some men storm imaginary Alps all their lives, and die in the foothills cursing difficulties which do not exist.

E. W. HOWE,
Success Easier Than Failure

Be of good courage, all is before you, and time passed in the difficult is never lost.

RAINER MARIA RILKE,
Letters of Rainer Maria Rilke 1892–1910

May life open up to you, door by door; may you find in yourself the ability to trust it, and the courage to give to the difficult most confidence of all.

RAINER MARIA RILKE,
Letters of Rainer Maria Rilke 1892–1910

The man who most vividly realizes a difficulty is the man most likely to overcome it.

JOSEPH FARRELL,
Lectures of a Certain Professor

Conquering any difficulty always gives one a secret joy, for it means pushing back a boundary-line and adding to one's liberty.

HENRI FRÉDÉRIC AMIEL,
The Private Journal of Henri Frédéric Amiel

Most of the fear that spoils our life comes from attacking difficulties before we get to them.

DR. FRANK CRANE,
Essays

When you encounter difficulties and contradictions, do not try to break them, but bend them with gentleness and time.

SAINT FRANCIS DE SALES,
Spiritual Meditations

It is wonderful sometimes how difficulties don't so much disappear, but assume their right proportions in a different scene.

A. C. BENSON,
*Excerpts from the Letters of
Dr. A. C. Benson to M. E. A.*

Difficulties increase the nearer one comes to the goal.

GOETHE

DIGNITY

A man who stands on his dignity is on a precarious perch; the only base broad enough to stand on is your humanity, which no one can knock you off without committing a crime against everyone else as well.

SYDNEY J. HARRIS,
Strictly Personal

When people begin to ignore human dignity, it will not be long before they begin to ignore human rights.

G. K. CHESTERTON,
All Is Grist

DILETTANTISM

Dilettantism, as we all know, is the nonserious dabbling within a presumably serious field by persons who are ill-equipped—and actually do not even want—to meet even the minimum standards of that field, or study, or practice.

BEN SHAHN,
The Shape of Content

DIPLOMACY

Let us never negotiate out of fear. But let us never fear to negotiate.

JOHN F. KENNEDY,
Inaugural Address, January 20, 1961

Consultation does not always, regardless of how long it may go on, does not always provide unanimity at the end of the consultation. But there is a more precise understanding of those areas where there is agreement and there is a more precise understanding of the reasons for positions which may be taken on which there is no agreement.

JOHN F. KENNEDY,
Paris news conference, June 2, 1961

Diplomacy is a game of chess in which the nations are checkmated.

KARL KRAUS,
Karl Kraus by Harry Zohn

The chief drawback of diplomatic life is that diplomats are inclined, instead of making friends with the natives of the country to which they are accredited, to live in a small circle entirely among themselves.

MAURICE BARING,
Lost Lectures

DISAGREEMENT

A disagreement may be the shortest cut between two minds.

KAHLIL GIBRAN,
Sand and Foam

There are things in which it is desirable forever to disagree: The meaning of life, the proper way to boil an egg, choosing a wife, which of Shakespeare's plays is the best, and the real reason for disliking Jones and admiring a sunset.

FRANK MOORE COLBY,
The Colby Essays, Vol. 2

Disagreement shakes us out of our slumbers and forces us to see our own point of view through contrast with another person who does not share it.

R. D. LAING,
The Politics of Experience

The reason why people so often disagree in discussion is that they say what they do not think. The things we think are not those which cause differences.

MARK RUTHERFORD,
Last Pages from a Journal

Make sure to be in with your equals if you're going to fall out with your superiors.

YIDDISH PROVERB

DISAPPOINTMENT

It is an iron universe. When the spears go

into you, rejoice. The iron gets into your blood that way.

DON MARQUIS,
The Almost Perfect State

Disappointments should be cremated, not embalmed.

ANONYMOUS (HENRY S. HASKINS),
Meditations in Wall Street

I had a friend, a most intimate friend, who told me in early life that it was a good tip to expect the worst, for thus one would receive no disappointment. I did not follow his advice; but I watched him living by that same doctrine, and I discovered him to be at last abominably disappointed.

HILAIRE BELLOC,
A Conversation with an Angel

From the first years to which my memory stretches, I have been a disappointed woman. When, with my brothers, I reached forth after sources of knowledge, I was reproved with "It isn't fit for you; it doesn't belong to women." ... In education, in marriage, in religion, in everything, disappointment is the lot of woman. It shall be the business of my life to deepen this disappointment in every woman's heart until she bows down to it no longer.

LUCY STONE,
quoted in *The Feminine Mystique*
by Betty Friedan

When the heart drops into the boots, there is often an unholy tendency to tread upon someone's toes or to kick defenseless shins.

WALTER DWIGHT,
The Saving Sense

DISCIPLE

No being is prosier than the uninspired disciple of the mystic. All that is stimulating—all the glorious vision—has melted away.

CHAUNCEY WRIGHT,
Letters of Chauncey Wright

Nothing is more embarrassing than disci-

ples. I have done what I could do to discourage them. ... I have always sought to encourage each in his own path and should not like to attract anyone to me.

ANDRÉ GIDE,
Pretexts

DISCIPLINE

Love preserves life and health; discipline or training, which is often merely rationalized hate, if it does not destroy them, commonly distorts their shape to fit the mold of an already misshapen culture.

DR. CHARLES BERG,
Deep Analysis

I find that in the long run the effect of an external artificial discipline on me is bad, as it merely clashes with my internal discipline. The latter may be imperfect, and I am aware that you take up the attitude that it doesn't exist and that I am an irresponsible person; but you can't have two disciplines anyway. Both may be good, but they are bound to clash and weaken each other.

FREDERICK GOODYEAR,
Letters and Remains

DISILLUSIONMENT

Disillusionment in living is the finding out nobody agrees with you not only those that are and were fighting with you.

GERTRUDE STEIN,
quoted in *Gertrude Stein: Her Life and Her Work* by Elizabeth Sprigge

DIVORCE (*See also* MARRIAGE)

The worst reconciliation is better than the best divorce.

CERVANTES

It's a toss-up between marriage and divorce. They're both right and wrong now and then, but mostly right.

NAT GOODWIN

DOCTOR (See also HEALTH, ILLNESS, PAIN, PSYCHIATRY)

Doctors are the guardians of our bodies, as priests, ministers and rabbis are the guardians of our souls. Doctors try to keep us from the heaven or hell that the priests, ministers and rabbis promise.

DR. OSCAR FASKER

Doctors make the worst patients.

ANONYMOUS

There is one advantage of being poor—a doctor will cure you faster.

KIN HUBBARD

Doctors know only what you tell them.

DON HAROLD

DOG

When a dog occasionally wants to hang out the "Do not disturb" sign, as all of us do now and then, he is regarded as a traitor to his species.

RAMONA C. ALBERT,
Living Your Dog's Life

Since dogs are relatively unimportant in the adult world, it is probably foolish to grieve when they go. But most people do grieve, inconsolably, for a time, and feel restless, lonely, and poor.

BROOKS ATKINSON,
quoted in Cold Noses and Warm Hearts

Wanted: a dog that neither barks nor bites, eats broken glass and shits diamonds.

GOETHE,
quoted in A Certain World by W. H. Auden

If dogs could talk, perhaps we would find it as hard to get along with them as we do with people.

KAREL CAPEK,
Intimate Things

Of course what he most intensely dreams of is being taken out on walks, and the more you are able to indulge him the more will he adore you and the more all the latent beauty of his nature will come out.

HENRY JAMES, (on his dog Max),
quoted in A Dog at All Things,
compiled by Agnes Lauchlan

Fido and Rover are partaking of a mystery of which, further up on the table, Cézanne and Beethoven are participants also.

REBECCA WEST,
The Strange Necessity

Doubtless, the modern carrier pigeon does everything but carry, and the pointer has even forgotten how to point. It is the same with dogs: fidgety and fussy man is producing all manner of abortions for the show ring which are a pain and grief to look upon.

EDEN PHILLPOTTS,
A Year with Bisshe-Bantam

A well-trained, well-treated sheep dog is more of a dog than a wild one, just as a stray, terrified by ill-usage, or a spoilt lap dog has had its "dogginess" debased.

W. H. AUDEN,
A Certain World

In regard to the transference of love, all I possess at present is concentrated on Victor, one of my dogs. I breakfast with him sitting opposite to me, his fine, large head resting on the table. Let us love dogs; let us love only dogs! Men and cats are unworthy creatures.

MARIE BASHKIRTSEFF,
Revelations: Diaries of Women, edited by
Mary Jane Moffat and Charlotte Painter

Not the least hard thing to bear when they go from us, these quiet friends, is that they carry away with them so many years of our own lives.

JOHN GALSWORTHY,
Memories

Dogs are so evidently intended by God to be our companions, protectors, and in many ways, examples.

BERTRAND WILBERFORCE,
The Life and Letters of
Father Bertrand Wilberforce by H. M. Capes

The infatuated little beast dances round him [Thomas Carlyle] on its hind legs as I ought to do and can't; and he feels flattered and surprised by such unwonted capers to his honour and glory.

JANE CARLYLE,
quoted in *The Literature of Gossip*
by Elizabeth Drew

I marvel that such
Small ribs as these
Can cage such vast
Desire to please.

OGDEN NASH,
"Please Pass the Biscuit," *Family Reunion*

At night my wife and I did fall out about the dog's being put down in the cellar, which I had a mind to have done because of his fouling the house, and I would have my will; and so we went to bed and lay all night in a quarrel.

SAMUEL PEPYS,
Diary of Samuel Pepys

Most dogs bark pointlessly, even if someone is just walking by in the distance; but some, perhaps not the best watchdogs, yet rational creatures, quietly walk up to a stranger, sniff at him, and bark only if they smell something suspicious.

FRANZ KAFKA,
The Diaries of Franz Kafka 1914–1923

We are alone, absolutely alone on this chance planet: and, amid all the forms of life that surround us, not one, excepting the dog has made an alliance with us.

MAURICE MAETERLINCK,
My Dog

And I am simply delighted that you have a Springer spaniel. That is the perfect final touch to our friendship. Do you know there is always a barrier between me and any man or woman who does not like dogs.

ELLEN GLASGOW,
Letters of Ellen Glasgow

The devotion of the dog has been greatly exaggerated. What a dog really wants is excitement. He is easily bored, cannot amuse himself, and therefore demands entertainment. The dog's ideal is a life of active uselessness.

WILLIAM LYON PHELPS,
Of Cats and Men,
compiled by Frances E. Clarke

To a man the greatest blessing is individual liberty, to a dog is the last word in despair.

WILLIAM LYON PHELPS,
Of Cats and Men,
compiled by Frances E. Clarke

The dog is a Yes-animal, very popular with people who can't afford to keep a Yes-man.

ROBERTSON DAVIES,
The Table Talk of Samuel Marchbanks

Dachshunds are ideal dogs for small children, as they are already stretched and pulled to such a length that the child cannot do much harm one way or the other.

ROBERT BENCHLEY,
quoted in *Cold Noses and Warm Hearts*

Things that upset a terrier may pass virtually unnoticed by the Great Dane.

DR. SMILEY BLANTON,
Love or Perish

When did any dog turn up his nose at a smell. . . .Times are, indeed, when smelliness pure and simple, quantity rather than quality, just the ineffable affluence of Nature's bounty to the nose, seems to ravish one of these great lovers almost clean off the earth.

C. E. MONTAGUE,
The Right Place

A dog, more than any other creature, it seems to me, gets interested in one subject, theme, or object, in life, and pursues it with a fixity of purpose which would be inspiring to Man if it weren't so troublesome.

E. B. WHITE,
One Man's Meat

Take our dogs and ourselves, connected as we are by a tie more intimate than most ties in this world; and yet, outside of that tie of friendly fondness, how insensible, each of us, to all that makes life significant for the other!—we to the rapture of bones under hedges, or smells of trees and lampposts, they to the delights of literature and art.

WILLIAM JAMES,
Talks to Teachers

I think my dog is very clever, and I'm teaching him to sing. I just play my mouth organ, and he begins to howl. My mother thinks he does it because he does not like the noise, but I know, and I am sure he does too, that he sings because he loves noise, just as I do.

ELIZABETH MARY WATSON,
age 13, England, *Journeys: Prose by Children of the English-speaking World,*
collected by Richard Lewis

A dog is a lion in his own lane.

HINDU PROVERB

In the streets of New York between seven and nine in the morning you will see the slow procession of dog and owner proceeding from street to tree to hydrant to trashbasket. They are apartment dogs. They are taken out twice a day, and, while it is a cliche, it is truly amazing how owner and dog resemble each other. They grow to walk alike, have the same set of head.

JOHN STEINBECK,
quoted in *Cold Noses and Warm Hearts*

Among passionate lovers of animals, particularly dog-lovers, there is a special category of unhappy people who, through bitter experience, have lost faith in mankind and seek refuge with animals.

KONRAD Z. LORENZ,
Man Meets Dog

I think that the great popularity enjoyed by some comical breeds of dogs is attributable to a large extent to our longing for gaiety.

KONRAD Z. LORENZ,
Man Meets Dog

DOGMA

Dogma is the anatomy of thought. As scientists tell you, even a bad doctrine is better than none at all. You can test it, differ from it, your mind has something to bite on. You need the rock to plan the lighthouse.

JOYCE CARY,
Art and Reality

Life is a rose that withers in the iron fist of dogma.

GEORGE MOORE,
Epigrams of George Moore

It is the rigid dogma that destroys truth; and, please notice, my emphasis is not on the dogma but on the rigidity. When men say of any question, "This is all there is to be known or said of the subject; investigation ends here," that is death.

ALFRED NORTH WHITEHEAD,
Dialogues of Alfred North Whitehead

There is no doubt that humanity is held apart by dogmas and statements of truth, by attempts to define truth. Humanity is drawn together by warm-hearted conduct. And yet the conduct we approve often rests upon dogmas which we do not approve. The dogmas then are as important as the conduct.

JOHN JAY CHAPMAN,
Memories and Milestones

What we have to eliminate just here is the popular literary notion that the dogmas of the Church are negligible but that its ritual and poetry are supremely important. If we have psychological insight at all, we must have the wit to see that this ritual and this poetry ultimately depend upon someone somewhere having faith in the importance of the dogma. These faithful ones may be very few in number, but it is their faith in the truth of the doctrine, and not any vague emotional feelings that we may have as to the beauty of the doctrine, that keeps the thing alive.

JOHN COWPER POWYS,
The Meaning of Culture

DOING

Nothing is harder than to make people think about what they're going to *do*.
ANDRÉ MALRAUX,
Man's Fate

If a thing is worth doing, it is worth doing badly.
G. K. CHESTERTON,
What Is Wrong with the World

Don't force yourself to do anything, yet don't feel unhappy that you force yourself, or that if you were to do anything, you would have to force yourself. And if you don't force yourself, don't hanker after the possibilities of being forced.
FRANZ KAFKA,
The Diaries of Franz Kafka 1914–1923

There are two patron saints to whom I have a tremendous devotion: a sheet of paper and a lead pencil. Mark down at least once a day everything you do and every time you do it. It will not make you proud to see all you do; but it will humble you by showing you all you don't do.
WILLIAM DOYLE,
A Year's Thoughts

What we love to do we find time to do.
JOHN LANCASTER SPALDING,
Aphorisms and Reflections

It is an undeniable law of nature, that by faithfully doing the thing which we see proper to be done, we come to see more keenly next time what is proper to be done; and by not doing it, we lose altogether the power of discerning it.
WILLIAM HALE WHITE,
Religion and Art of William Hale White
by Wilfred Stone

The step from knowing to doing is rarely taken, because the preliminary step is rarely taken from knowing to feeling.
JOSEPH FARRELL,
Lectures of a Certain Professor

If I had my life to lead over, I presume I would still be a writer, but I am sure I would give my first attention to learning how to do things directly with my hands. Nothing gives quite the satisfaction that doing things brings.
SHERWOOD ANDERSON,
Letters of Sherwood Anderson

It is a profoundly erroneous truism, repeated by all copy-books and by eminent people when they are making speeches, that we should cultivate the habit of thinking what we are doing. The precise opposite is the case. Civilization advances by extending the number of important operations which we can perform without thinking about them.
ALFRED NORTH WHITEHEAD,
quoted in *A Certain World*
by W. H. Auden

The shortest answer is doing.
ENGLISH PROVERB

DOLLS

In boys and girls alike, and in more of their elders, perhaps, than we suspect, the affection for dolls is chiefly an aspect of the social sense and an example of the pleasure we all take in projecting our own personalities and in controlling the lives of others.
ODELL SHEPARD,
The Joys of Forgetting

DOUBT

Our doubts are traitors,
And make us lose the good we oft might win
By fearing to attempt.
SHAKESPEARE,
Measure for Measure, Act I, Scene 5

When in doubt, risk it.
HOLBROOK JACKSON,
Platitudes in the Making

There is an increasing number of people to whom everything they are doing seems futile. They are still under the spell of the slogans which preach faith in the secular paradise of success and glamour. But doubt, the fertile condition of all progress, has begun to beset them and has made them ready to ask what their real self-interest as human beings is.

ERICH FROMM,
Man for Himself

The doubt of an earnest, thoughtful, patient and laborious mind is worthy of respect. In such doubt there may be found indeed more faith than in half the creeds.

JOHN LANCASTER SPALDING,
Means and Ends of Education

People who dislike doubt often get into worse trouble by committing themselves to an immature and untenable decision.

CHARLES HORTON COOLEY,
Life and the Student

When unhappy, one doubts everything; when happy, one doubts nothing.

JOSEPH ROUX,
Meditations of a Parish Priest

In doubts about one's life, one's work, one's method, one's principles, one's practice, there is always *living*. It is a sign of not being dead, to doubt and be discomfortable.

JOHN ADDINGTON SYMONDS,
Letters and Papers of John Addington Symonds

For I kept my heart from assenting to anything, fearing to fall headlong; but by hanging in suspense I was the worse killed.

SAINT AUGUSTINE,
Confessions

To have doubted one's own first principles is the mark of a civilized man.

OLIVER WENDELL HOLMES, JR.,
The Mind and Faith of Justice Holmes,
edited by Max Lerner

Your doubt may be a good quality if you *train it*. It must become *knowing*, it must become critical. Ask it, whenever it wants to spoil something for you, *why* something is ugly, demand proof from it, test it, and you will perhaps find it perplexed and embarrassed, or perhaps up in arms. But don't give in, insist on arguments, and act

this way, watchful and consistent, every single time, and the day will arrive when from a destroyer it will become one of your best workers—perhaps the cleverest of all that are building at your life.

RAINER MARIA RILKE,
Letters to a Young Poet

When our affairs are succeeding beyond expectation, when we are being benefited by our foresight and contrivance, and apparently are becoming a considerable person, a mean little thought bares its teeth and says: "Watch yourself! This is not going to last."

ANONYMOUS (HENRY S. HASKINS),
Meditations in Wall Street

Many and many a philosopher seems to think that taking a piece of paper and writing down "I doubt that" is doubting it, or that it is a thing he can do in a minute as soon as he decides what he wants to doubt. . . .Well, I guess not; for genuine doubt does not talk of *beginning* with doubting. The pragmatist knows that doubt is an art which has to be acquired with difficulty; and his genuine doubts will go much further than those of any Cartesian.

CHARLES SANDERS PEIRCE,
Collected Papers of Charles Sanders Peirce,
Vol. VI

DREAMS

One of the most adventurous things left us is to go to bed. For no one can lay a hand on our dreams.

E. V. LUCAS,
365 Days and One More

Do ye know the terror of him who falleth asleep?—To the very toes he is terrified, because the ground giveth way under him, and the dream beginneth.

FRIEDRICH NIETZSCHE,
Thus Spake Zarathustra

Almost impossible to sleep; plagued by dreams, as if they were being scratched on me, a stubborn material.

FRANZ KAFKA,
The Diaries of Franz Kafka 1914–1923

The pleasure of the true dreamer does not lie in the substance of the dream, but in this: that there things happen without any interference from his side, and altogether outside his control.

ISAK DINESEN,
Out of Africa

A dream which is not understood is like a letter which is not opened.

TALMUD

I am interested in the effect dreams may have upon our lives. I do not care much about what my living does to my dreams, but I would like to know how my dreaming shapes (if it does) my life.

JESSAMYN WEST,
Hide and Seek

A dream grants what one covets when awake.

GERMAN PROVERB

Anyone can escape into sleep, we are all geniuses when we dream, the butcher's the poet's equal there.

E. M. CIORAN,
The Temptation to Exist

For we have in the dream forsaken our allegiance to the organizing, controlling and rectifying forces of the world, the Universal Conscience. We have sworn fealty to the wild, incalculable, creative forces, the Imagination of the Universe.

ISAK DINESEN,
Shadows on the Grass

Recall the old story of the rather refined young man who preferred sex dreams to visiting brothels because he met a much nicer type of girl that way.

VIVIAN MERCIER,
Perspectives on Pornography,
edited by Douglas A. Hughes

Dreams are expressions not only of conflicts and repressed desires, but also of previous knowledge that one has learned, possibly many years before, and thinks he has forgotten. Even the unskilled person, if he takes the attitude that what his dreams tell him is not simply to be rejected as silly, may get occasional useful guidance from his dreams. And the person who has become skillful in the understanding of what he is saying to himself in his dreams can get from them, from time to time, marvelously valuable hints and insights into solutions to his problems.

ROLLO MAY,
Man's Search for Himself

All through the ages ... people have regarded their dreams as sources of wisdom, guidance and insight. But most of us today think of our dreams as odd episodes, as foreign as some strange ceremonial dance in Tibet. This results in the cutting off of an exceedingly great and significant portion of the self. We are then no longer able to use much of the wisdom and power of the unconscious.

ROLLO MAY,
Man's Search for Himself

We all dream; we do not understand our dreams, yet we act as if nothing strange goes on in our sleep minds, strange at least by comparison with the logical, purposeful doings of our minds when we are awake.

ERICH FROMM,
The Forgotten Language

There is no "as if" in the dream. The dream is present, real experience, so much so indeed, that it suggests two questions: What is reality? How do we know that what we dream is unreal and what we experience in our waking life is real? A Chinese poet has expressed this aptly: "I dreamt last night that I was a butterfly and now I don't know whether I am a man who dreamt he was a butterfly, or perhaps a butterfly who dreams now he is a man."

ERICH FROMM,
The Forgotten Language

And what else is one to believe, if not what dreams tell one; they are the expression of one's innermost thoughts. To say that when you dream you are not conscious is to speak loosely; one is only conscious, only lucid in dream.

EUGÈNE IONESCO,
Fragments of a Journal

Throw your dream into space like a kite, and you do not know what it will bring back, a new life, a new friend, a new love, a new country.

ANAÏS NIN,
The Diaries of Anaïs Nin, Vol. IV

Dreams pass into the reality of action. From the action stems the dream again; and this interdependence produces the highest form of living.

ANAÏS NIN,
The Diaries of Anaïs Nin, Vol. IV

He who would interpret a dream must himself be, so to speak, on a level with the dream, for in no single thing can one ever hope to see beyond what one is oneself.

C. G. JUNG,
Psychological Reflections,
edited by Jolande Jacobi and R. F. Hull

Within each one of us there is another whom we do not know. He speaks to us in dreams and tells us how differently *he* sees us from how *we* see ourselves. When we find ourselves in an insolubly difficult situation, this stranger in us can sometimes show us a light which is more suited than anything else to change our attitude fundamentally, namely just that attitude which has led us into the difficult situation.

C. G. JUNG,
Psychological Reflections,
edited by Jolande Jacobi and R. F. Hull

That's the reason many dreamers fail— they're not willing to come down out of the clouds and get to work at the things that turn their stomachs.

SUSAN GLASPELL,
quoted in *The Bliss of the Way,*
compiled by Cecily Hallack

An individual who is intensely interested in some particular task is pursued by the necessity of solving this problem even at

night. Some people do not sleep at all and constantly follow their problem while awake, others sleep but busy themselves with their plans in their dreams.

ALFRED ADLER,
Understanding Human Nature

Reality can destroy the dream, why shouldn't the dream destroy reality?

GEORGE MOORE,
The George Moore Calendar,
selected by Margaret Gough

Dreams, according to Freud, are the royal road to the unconscious. That remains true. But unfortunately it is a road that is easily lost if there is not full knowledge of all the territory around it.

KAREN HORNEY,
Self-Analysis

DRINKING

One more drink and I'd be under the host.

DOROTHY PARKER,
You Might As Well Live

They speak of my drinking, but never think of my thirst.

SCOTTISH PROVERB

Drink helps us to penetrate the veil; it gives us glimpses of the Magi of creation where they sit weaving their spells and sowing their seeds of incantation to the flowing mind.

DON MARQUIS,
The Almost Perfect State

He who drinks a little too much drinks much too much.

GERMAN PROVERB

For a bad hangover take the juice of two quarts of whisky.

EDDIE CONDON,
quoted in *Jam Session,*
edited by Ralph J. Gleason

It is one of the strange American changes in custom that the drunks of my day often hit each other, but never in the kind of bar fight that so often happens now with knives. In those days somebody hit somebody, and when that was finished one of them offered his hand and it would have been unheard of to refuse.

LILLIAN HELLMAN,
Pentimento

I hope you are not one of those people who get drunk on the idea of alcohol (blessed word). It is really very curious that people get more muddled in their heads by thinking about intoxicants than by drinking them.

FREDÉRICK GOODYEAR,
Letters and Remains

Take the drink for the thirst that is yet to come.

IRISH PROVERB

The sway of alcohol over mankind is unquestionably due to its power to stimulate the mystic faculties of human nature, usually crushed to earth by the cold facts and dry criticisms of the sober hour.

WILLIAM JAMES,
quoted in the *New York Times*,
February 29, 1948

Let's get out of these wet clothes and into a dry martini.

ROBERT BENCHLEY,
quoted in *George S. Kaufman*
by Howard Teichmann

There never seems to be any trouble brewing around a bar until a woman puts that high heel over the brass rail. Don't ask me why, but somehow women at bars seem to create trouble among men.

HUMPHREY BOGART,
quoted in *Ladies' Home Journal*, July 1947

We are accepting into our friendship (but not our theatre) the man we put out. Higgins said to my wife, "I cannot quarrel with the man. I like the way he looks at a glass of porter. He gives it a long look, a delicate look, as though he noticed its colour and the light on it."

W. B. YEATS,
*Letters on Poetry
from W. B. Yeats to Dorothy Wellesley*

One reason I don't drink is that I want to

know when I am having a good time.

LADY ASTOR,
quoted in *Reader's Digest,* November 1960

Put a man in a room where he can play dominoes, read newspapers, and have what he considers good talk; and you will observe that he will not drink as fast or as deep, or as strongly as he otherwise would. In short there would be other things to amuse him besides drinking: and what does he drink for, but to amuse himself, and to forget troubles of every kind?

SIR ARTHUR HELPS,
Organization in Daily Life

DRUGS

Anything that can be done chemically can be done in other ways—that is, if we have sufficient knowledge of the processes involved.

WILLIAM BURROUGHS,
Writers at Work, Third Series,
edited by George Plimpton

The drug propaganda is entirely evangelistic: take acid and you will be saved is the same message as Jesus Saves. . . . Legalization of the drugs would remove the thrill. . . .

KARL SHAPIRO,
To Abolish Children and Other Essays

One's condition on marijuana is always existential. One can feel the importance of each moment and how it is changing one. One feels one's being, one becomes aware of the enormous apparatus of nothingness—the hum of a hi-fi set, the emptiness of a pointless interruption, one becomes aware of the war between each of us, how the nothingness in each of us seeks to attack the being of others, how our being in turn in attacked by the nothingness in others.

NORMAN MAILER,
Writers at Work, Third Series,
edited by George Plimpton

While drugs do offer relief from anxiety, their more important task is to offer the illusion of healing the split between the

will and its refractory object. The resulting feeling of wholeness—no matter how
willfull the drugged state may appear to
an outsider—there seems to be, briefly and
subjectively, a responsible and vigorous
will. This is the reason, I believe, that the
addictive possibilities of our age are so
enormous.

> LESLIE H. FARBER,
> *The Ways of the Will*

DULLNESS

Evil and ugliness are the same thing, and
dullness is the mother of both.

> SIR OSBERT SITWELL,
> *Wisdom*, edited by James Nelson

Nothing fatigues like dullness: from the
weariness it begets there is no escape.

> JOHN LANCASTER SPALDING,
> *Opportunity and other Essays*

There's a freemasonry among the dull by
which they recognize and are sociable
with the dull, as surely as a correspondent
tact in men of genius.

> RALPH WALDO EMERSON,
> *Journals of Ralph Waldo Emerson*

DUTY

A sense of duty is useful in work, but
offensive in personal relations. People wish
to be liked, not endured with patient
resignation.

> BERTRAND RUSSELL,
> *The Conquest of Happiness*

We need to restore the full meaning of
that old word, duty. It is the other side of
rights.

> PEARL BUCK,
> *To My Daughters, with Love*

Do what you can to do what you ought,
and leave hoping and fearing alone.

> THOMAS HENRY HUXLEY,
> *Aphorisms and Reflections*

What a fearful object a long-neglected
duty gets to be.

> CHAUNCEY WRIGHT,
> *Letters of Chauncey Wright*

When a stupid man is doing something he
is ashamed of, he always declares that it is
his duty.

> GEORGE BERNARD SHAW,
> *Caesar and Cleopatra*

We must recognize that our real duty is
always found running in the direction of
our worthiest desires. No duty that runs
roughshod over the personality can have a
legitimate claim upon us.

> RANDOLPH BOURNE,
> *Youth and Life*

To most men duty means something unpleasant which the other fellow ought to
do.

> GEORGE HORACE LORIMER,
> quoted in *The Author's Kalendar 1909*,
> compiled by Anna C. Woodford

People are complaining almost everywhere that the sense of duty is disappearing. How could it be otherwise since no
one cares any more about his rights? Only
he who is uncompromising as to his rights
maintains the sense of duty.

> ALBERT CAMUS,
> *Resistance, Rebellion, and Death*

Duty does not have to be dull. Love can
make it beautiful and fill it with life.

> THOMAS MERTON,
> *The Sign of Jonas*

The best security for people doing their
duty is, that they should not know anything else to do.

> WALTER BAGEHOT,
> *Literary Studies*, Vol. III

The association of duty and claptrap is
what really dehumanizes man.

> THEODOR HAECKER,
> *Journal in the Night*

Good and beautiful things may easily be
spoilt by suggestions of rights and duties.

> A. C. BENSON,
> *Excerpts from the Letters of
> Dr. A. C. Benson to M. E. A.*

The path of duty lies in what is near at
hand, but men seek for it in what is
remote.

> JAPANESE PROVERB

EARNESTNESS

When a man's in earnest he doesn't think of opportunities and occasions.

JOHN OLIVER HOBBES,
Some Emotions and a Moral

Every one in earnest *is* narrow.

ROBERT HUGH BENSON,
Sermon Notes

Nothing great can come without entire sincerity of purpose and of life. Given this, and one may pass through the fire of mistakes and yet grow on into life; but without earnestness life means nothing.

EDWARD HOWARD GRIGGS,
A Book of Meditations

It is undoubtedly true that it is the more thoughtful and earnest people who feel most keenly the mysteries and difficulties which beset them on all sides.

BASIL W. MATURIN,
Laws of the Spiritual Life

EARTH

That we are bound to the earth does not mean that we cannot grow; on the contrary, it is the *sine qua non* of growth. No noble, well-grown tree ever disowned its dark roots, for it grows not only upwards but downwards as well.

C. G. JUNG,
Psychological Reflections,
edited by Jolande Jacobi and R. F. Hull

The earth is a Paradise, the only one we will ever know. We will realize it the moment we open our eyes. We don't have to make it a Paradise—it *is* one. We have only to make ourselves fit to inhabit it.

HENRY MILLER,
The Air-Conditioned Nightmare

When I realize how invigorating contact with the earth may sometimes be, I find myself wondering how humanity ever consented to come so far away from the jungle.

ELLEN GLASGOW,
Letters of Ellen Glasgow

Remain true to the earth, my brethren, with the power of your virtue! Let your bestowing love and your knowledge be devoted to the meaning of the earth! Thus do I pray and conjure you.

Let it not fly away from the earthly and beat against eternal walls with its wings! Ah, there hath always been so much flown away virtue!

FRIEDRICH NIETZSCHE,
Thus Spake Zarathustra

What you cannot find on earth is not worth seeking.

NORMAN DOUGLAS,
An Almanac

We are tied and bound to the people and things of earth by manifold claims and duties which we cannot neglect, except at the peril of losing our appetite for heavenly things.

BASIL W. MATURIN,
Laws of the Spiritual Life

EAT (*See* COOKING, FOOD)

ECCENTRIC

The art of life is to be thought odd. Everything will then be permitted to you. The best way to be thought odd is to return a cheque now and then on a conscientious scruple.

E. V. LUCAS,
365 Days and One More

Men and women one of these days will have the courage to be eccentric. They will do as they like—just as the great ones have always done. The word eccentric is a term of reproach and mild contempt and amusement today, because we live under a system which hates real originality.

HOLBROOK JACKSON,
Southward Ho! and Other Essays

Once we call a man a "crank", it is certain that we are prepared to dislike him, whereas, unless we are raging pretorians of convention, we feel a sort of tenderness for the eccentric.

J. B. PRIESTLEY,
All About Ourselves and Other Essays

Call it oddity, eccentricity, humour, or what you please, it is evident that the special flavour of mind or manner, which, independently of fortune, station, or profession, sets a man apart from his fellows, and which gives the charm of picturesqueness to society is fast disappearing from amongst us. A man may count the odd people of his acquaintance on his fingers; and it is observable that these odd people are generally well stricken in years. They belong more to the past generation than to the present. Our young men are terribly alike.

ALEXANDER SMITH,
Dreamthorp

ECONOMICS

No less than war or statecraft, the history of economics has its heroic ages.

ALDOUS HUXLEY,
Collected Essays

One of the difficulties of economics is that it is too easy to explain after a particular event has happened, why it should have happened; and too easy to explain before it happens, why it should not happen.

M. G. KENDALL,
London University,
quoted in *Montreal Star,* December 19, 1960

Instead of doing anything about economics the moralists fulminate against the murder of unborn children and the selfishness of modern young people (in the practice of birth prevention). As somebody said: "The drains are smelling—let's have a day of intercession." And as another said: "The economic depression is a good thing—it is sent to try us."

ERIC GILL,
Modern Christian Revolutionaries
by Donald Attwater

ECSTASY

The ecstasy of religion, the ecstasy of art, and the ecstasy of love are the only things worth thinking about or experiencing.

DON MARQUIS,
The Almost Perfect State

But do, for God's sake, mistrust and beware of these states of exaltation and ecstasy. They send you, anyone, swaying so far beyond the centre of gravity in one direction, there is the inevitable swing back with greater velocity in the other direction, and in the end you exceed the limits of your own soul's elasticity, and go smash, like a tower that has swung too far.

Besides, there is no real truth in ecstasy. All vital truth contains the memory of all that for which it is not true. Ecstasy achieves itself by virtue of exclusion; and in making any passionate exclusion, one has already put one's right hand in the hand of the lie.

D. H. LAWRENCE,
Selected Letters of D. H. Lawrence

There is an ecstasy such that the immense strain of it is sometimes relaxed by a flood of tears, along with which one's steps either rush or involuntarily lag, alternately. There is the feeling that one is completely out of hand, with the very distinct consciousness of an endless number of fine thrills and quiverings to the very toes.

FRIEDRICH NIETZSCHE,
quoted in *Education and Ecstasy*
by George B. Leonard

EDITOR

Editors are unaccountable in their judgments.

GEORGE E. WOODBERRY,
Selected Letters of George Edward Woodberry

On the whole, I have found editors friendly and pleasant, but unpredictable and uncertain and occasionally embarrassing in their desperation. So seldom do they get what they think they want that they tend to become incoherent in their insistent repetition of their needs. A writer does well to listen to them, but not too often, and not for too long.

JEROME WEIDMAN,
Back Talk

An editor of any degree of experience becomes incapable of complete agreement with anyone, and he reads the dictionary so much that he always knows more nasty names for any particular offence than the man who has committed it.

ROBERTSON DAVIES,
The Table Talk of Samuel Marchbanks

The editor of a magazine should be, above all, versatile. He need not necessarily be deep.

THOMAS O'HAGAN,
Chats by the Fireside

The average editor cannot escape feeling that telling a writer to do something is almost the same thing as performing it himself.

HEYWOOD BROUN,
Pieces of Hate

An editor would classify "What we want is humor" as a piece of cooperation on his part. It seems to him a perfect division of labor. After all, nothing remains for the author to do except to write.

HEYWOOD BROUN,
Pieces of Hate

There is a public which swallows, apparently, anything it gets, and never says what it does want, because it doesn't know. So editors have no resource but to pander to their own morbid taste, hoping that it may also be the taste of others.

ROSE MACAULAY,
A Casual Commentary

The job of editor in a publishing house is the dullest, hardest, most exciting, exasperating and rewarding of perhaps any job in the world.

JOHN HALL WHEELOCK,
Editor to Author

Writing for the magazines sounds a delightful occupation, but literally it means nothing without the cooperation of the editors of the magazines, and it is this cooperation which is so difficult to secure.

A. A. MILNE,
Not That It Matters

EDUCATION

I behaved in school like a half-wild animal who comes up to the common trough to get food, but sneaks off with it to his own den where he has gamier morsels of his own and his own ways of devouring them.

MAX EASTMAN,
Enjoyment of Living

I wonder whether if I had had an education I should have been more or less a fool than I am.

ALICE JAMES,
The Diary of Alice James

One might say that the American trend of education is to reduce the senses almost to nil.

ISADORA DUNCAN,
My Life

What is really important in education is not that the child learns this and that, but that the mind is matured, that energy is aroused.

SØREN KIERKEGAARD,
Either/Or, Vol. II

I miss in American life the tonic quality of Oxford where men sit down to examine great things greatly. It is so worth while to say frankly to the crowd that some people can't do other people's work; that merely by education John Smith won't become Adam Smith. But I doubt whether the argument looks convincing to most people.

HAROLD J. LASKI,
Holmes-Laski Letters, Vol. I

It doesn't make much difference what you study, as long as you don't like it.

FINLEY PETER DUNNE

Much education today is monumentally ineffective. All too often we are giving young people cut flowers when we should be teaching them to grow their own plants.

JOHN W. GARDNER,
No Easy Victories, edited by Helen Rowan

I am entirely certain that twenty years from now we will look back at education as it is practiced in most schools today and wonder that we could have tolerated anything so primitive.

JOHN W. GARDNER,
No Easy Victories, edited by Helen Rowan

The atmosphere of libraries, lecture rooms and laboratories is dangerous to those who shut themselves up in them too long. It separates us from reality like a fog.

ALEXIS CARREL,
Reflections on Life

Education is a thing of which only the few are capable; teach as you will, only a small percentage will profit by your most zealous energy.

GEORGE GISSING,
The Private Papers of Henry Ryecroft

It is one of the great pleasures of a student's life to buy a heap of books at the beginning of the autumn. Here, he fancies, are all the secrets.

ROBERT LYND,
Solomon in All His Glory

One certainly would not for anything have missed one's student days. To mix with other students is an education in itself. It is to come into touch with ideas that are "living creatures having hands and feet."

ROBERT LYND,
Solomon in All His Glory

The chief wonder of education is that it does not ruin everybody concerned in it, teachers and taught.

HENRY ADAMS,
The Education of Henry Adams

The carefully fostered theory that schoolwork can be made easy and enjoyable

breaks down as soon as anything, however trivial, has to be learned.

AGNES REPPLIER,
Americans and Others

It is impossible to withhold education from the receptive mind, as it is impossible to force it upon the unreasoning.

AGNES REPPLIER,
Times and Tendencies

It is because of our unassailable enthusiasm, our profound reverence for education, that we habitually demand of it the impossible. The teacher is expected to perform a choice and varied series of miracles.

AGNES REPPLIER,
Times and Tendencies

In the traditional method, the child must say something that he has merely learned. There is all the difference in the world between having something to say and having to say something.

JOHN DEWEY,
Dewey on Education, Selections

It is our American habit if we find the foundations of our educational structure unsatisfactory to add another story or wing. We find it easier to add a new study or course or kind of school than to reorganize existing conditions so as to meet the need.

JOHN DEWEY,
Characters and Events, Vol. II

So far, we do not seem appalled at the prospect of exactly the same kind of education being applied to all the school children from the Atlantic to the Pacific, but there is an uneasiness in the air, a realization that the individual is growing less easy to find; an idea, perhaps, of what standardization might become when the units are not machines, but human beings.

EDITH HAMILTON,
quoted in *Edith Hamilton*
by Doris Fielding Reid

A wise system of education will at least teach us how little man yet knows, how much he has still to learn.

SIR JOHN LUBBOCK,
The Pleasures of Life

If we succeed in giving the love of learning, the learning itself is sure to follow.

SIR JOHN LUBBOCK,
The Pleasures of Life

It is in fact nothing short of a miracle that the modern methods of instruction have not yet entirely strangled the holy curiosity of inquiry.... It is a very grave mistake to think that the enjoyment of seeing and searching can be promoted by means of coercion and a sense of duty.

ALBERT EINSTEIN,
quoted in *Education and Ecstasy*
by George B. Leonard

Education is a matter of holding a balance between discipline and laxity, between over-solicitude and neglect, between spartanism and indulgence, between attachment and independence: that is true in one's self-development and true in the relations of parent and teacher, too. There is no single prescribed path for creating this equilibrium; and the right measure for one moment will be the wrong measure for the next.

LEWIS MUMFORD,
Green Memories

It is because modern education is so seldom inspired by a great hope that it so seldom achieves a great result. The wish to preserve the past rather than the hope of creating the future dominates the minds of those who control the teaching of the young.

BERTRAND RUSSELL,
"Education," *Selected Papers*

If our methods and techniques and the long formation which our educators impose on themselves do not culminate in making man a little more free and in arousing in him the élan of love, all these things are not worth one hour of trouble.

ANDRÉ GODIN,
Thought, December 1950

Children are notoriously curious about everything—everything except . . . the things people want them to know. It then remains for us to refrain from forcing any kind of knowledge upon them, and they will be curious about everything.

FLOYD DELL,
Were You Ever a Child?

There is no human reason why a child should not admire and emulate his teacher's ability to do sums, rather than the village bum's ability to whittle sticks and smoke cigarettes; the reason why the child doesn't is plain enough—the bum has put himself on an equality with him and the teacher has not.

FLOYD DELL,
Were You Ever a Child?

Theories are more common than achievements in the history of education.

SIR RICHARD LIVINGSTONE,
On Education

Examinations are harmless when the examinee is indifferent to their result, but as soon as they matter, they begin to distort his attitude to education and to conceal its purpose. The more depends on them, the worse their effect.

SIR RICHARD LIVINGSTONE,
On Education

If the school sends out children with a desire for knowledge and some idea of how to acquire and use it, it will have done its work.

SIR RICHARD LIVINGSTONE,
On Education

Whatever educates us merely for its own use, without regard to us as living beings, whatever takes us for granted, degrades and impoverishes us. It does not matter that we are told it is for our own good.

HANIEL LONG,
A Letter to St. Augustine

Education bewildered me with knowledge and facts in which I was only mildly interested.

CHARLES CHAPLIN,
My Autobiography

I suppose other things may be more exciting to others, but to me undoubtedly when I was at school the really completely exciting thing was diagramming sentences and that has been to me ... the one thing that has been completely exciting and completely completing. I like the feeling the everlasting feeling of sentences as they diagram themselves.

GERTRUDE STEIN,
quoted in *The Third Rose*
by John Malcolm Brinnin

Educational writers are always blaming subjects instead of men, looking for some galvanic theme or method which when applied by a man without any gift for teaching to a mind without any capacity for learning will somehow produce intellectual results.

FRANK MOORE COLBY,
The Colby Essays, Vol. 2

The forcing of Latin, geometry, and algebra in a certain kind of manner into a certain kind of head is not education; it is persecution.

FRANK MOORE COLBY,
The Colby Essays, Vol. 2

Academic questions are interlopers in a world where so few of the real ones have been answered.

ANONYMOUS (HENRY S. HASKINS),
Meditations in Wall Street

The great difficulty in education is to get experience out of idea.

GEORGE SANTAYANA,
The Life of Reason

I was at Eton, yes, for four or five years. I didn't like it, and I have been blamed for putting in *Who's Who* that I obtained my education in the holidays from Eton.

SIR OSBERT SITWELL,
Wisdom, edited by James Nelson

Life is full of untapped sources of pleasure. Education should train us to discover and exploit them.

NORMAN DOUGLAS,
An Almanac

Before letters were invented, or books were, or governesses discovered, the neighbours' children, the outdoor life, the fists and the wrestling sinews, the old games,— the oldest things in the world,—the bare hill and clear river—these were education. And now, though Xenophon and sums be come, these are and remain.

WALTER BAGEHOT,
Literary Studies, Vol. III

The course of my education was broken by a series of accidents, and in the end that is not a misfortune; for in those years one has not really the ability to *choose* one's education, which later makes the winnowing of knowledge and truth so precious.

RAINER MARIA RILKE,
Letters of Rainer Maria Rilke 1892–1910

It is hard to get far enough away from the canvas to take any general view of such a subject as education. Education means everything.

JOHN JAY CHAPMAN,
Memories and Milestones

True goodness lies not in the negation of badness, but in the mastery of it. It is the miracle that turns the tumult of chaos into the dance of beauty. True education is that power of miracle, that ideal of creation.

RABINDRANATH TAGORE,
Letters to a Friend

No one can look back on his schooldays and say with truth that they were altogether unhappy.

GEORGE ORWELL,
A Collection of Essays

I believe that the testing of the student's achievements in order to see if he meets some criterion held by the teacher, is directly contrary to the implications of therapy for significant learning.

CARL R. ROGERS.
On Becoming a Person

If we value independence, if we are disturbed by the growing conformity of knowledge, of values, of attitudes, which our present system induces, then we may wish to set up conditions of learning which make for uniqueness, for self-direction, and for self-initiated learning.

CARL R. ROGERS,
On Becoming a Person

Modern education, from the viewpoint of the psychiatrist, does not aim to free the child from all inhibitions or to lift all repressions, but to allow him a natural development which will bring him to emotional as well as intellectual maturity.

DR. KARL A. MENNINGER,
The Human Mind

The teaching profession should hang its official head at the way the superior child has been neglected.

DR. KARL A. MENNINGER,
The Human Mind

A young man who is not a radical about something is a pretty poor risk for education.

JACQUES BARZUN,
Teacher in America

Young people at universities study to achieve knowledge and not to learn a trade. We must all learn how to support ourselves, but we must also learn how to live. We need a lot of engineers in the modern world, but we do not want a world of modern engineers.

SIR WINSTON CHURCHILL,
A Churchill Reader,
edited by Colin R. Coote

University education cannot be handed out complete like a cake on a tray. It has to be fought for, intrigued for, conspired for, lied for, and sometimes simply stolen. If it had not, it would scarcely be education.

ARNOLD BENNETT,
How to Make the Best of Life

All education is a continuous dialogue—questions and answers that pursue every problem to the horizon. That is the essence of academic freedom.

WILLIAM O. DOUGLAS,
Wisdom, October 1956

What is learned in high school, or for that matter anywhere at all, depends far less on what is taught than on what one actually experiences in the place.

EDGAR Z. FRIEDENBERG,
The Dignity of Youth and Other Atavisms

Teaching youngsters isn't much like making steel ... and essential as good technique is, I don't think education is basically a technological problem. It is a problem of drawing out of each youngster the best he has to give and of helping him to see the world he is involved in clearly enough to become himself—among other people—in it, while teaching him the skills he will need in the process.

EDGAR Z. FRIEDENBERG,
The Dignity of Youth and Other Atavisms

I consider it a monstrous presumption that university lecturers should think themselves competent to go on talking year after year to young men, students, while holding themselves aloof from the opportunity of learning from eager youth, which is one of the most valuable things on earth

ALFRED NORTH WHITEHEAD,
Dialogues of Alfred North Whitehead

From the very beginning of his education, the child should experience the joy of discovery.

ALFRED NORTH WHITEHEAD,
The Aims of Education

All practical teachers know that education is a patient process of the mastery of details, minute by minute, hour by hour, day by day.

ALFRED NORTH WHITEHEAD,
The Aims of Education

When one considers in its length and in its breadth the importance of this question of the education of a nation's young, the broken lives, the defeated hopes, the national failures, which result from the frivolous inertia with which it is treated, it is difficult to restrain within oneself a savage rage. In the conditions of modern life the rule is absolute, the race which does not value trained intelligence is doomed. Not all your heroism, not all your social charm, not all your wit, not all your victories on land or at sea, can move back the finger of fate. Today we maintain ourselves. Tomorrow science will have moved forward yet one more step, and there will be no appeal from the judgment which will then be pronounced on the uneducated.

ALFRED NORTH WHITEHEAD,
The Aims of Education

Unfortunately, we are inclined to talk of man as it would be desirable for him to be rather than as he really is. . . . True education can proceed only from naked reality, not from any ideal illusion about man, however attractive.

C. G. JUNG,
Psychological Reflections,
edited by Jolande Jacobi and R. F. Hull

Sometimes I relax the children with eyes closed to dream. When they awake I hear these dreams. The violence of those has to be heard to be believed. A lot of it is violence against me—which they tell me cheerfully enough. I come out very badly. My house has been burnt down, bombs fall on me, I'm shot with all makes of guns and handed over to the gorilla. Presumably it's the authority and discipline which I represent.

SYLVIA ASHTON-WARNER,
Teacher

No time is too long spent talking to a child to find out his key words, the key that unlocks himself, for in them is the secret of reading, the realisation that words can have intense meaning. Words having no emotional significance to him, no instinctive meaning, could be an imposition, doing him more harm than not teaching him at all. They may teach him that words mean nothing and that reading is undesirable.

SYLVIA ASHTON-WARNER,
Teacher

It was a formidable criticism when a student said, "They do not know I am here." In fact no teacher or official does, in most cases, become aware of the student as a human whole; he is known only by detached and artificial functions.

CHARLES HORTON COOLEY,
Life and the Student

We now spend a good deal more on drink and smoke than we spend on education. This, of course, is not surprising. The urge to escape from selfhood and the environment is in almost everyone almost all the time. The urge to do something for the young is strong only in parents, and in them only for the few years during which their children go to school.

ALDOUS HUXLEY,
The Doors of Perception

Literary or scientific, liberal or specialist, all our education is predominantly verbal and therefore fails to accomplish what it is supposed to do. Instead of transforming children into fully developed adults, it turns out students of the natural sciences who are completely unaware of Nature as the primary fact of experience, it inflicts upon the world students of the humanities who know nothing of humanity, their own or anyone else's.

ALDOUS HUXLEY,
The Doors of Perception

There is always money for, there are always doctorates in, the learned foolery of research into what, for scholars, is the all-important problem: Who influenced whom to say what when? Even in this age of technology the verbal humanities are honored. The non-verbal humanities, the arts of being directly aware of the given facts of our existence, are almost completely ignored.

ALDOUS HUXLEY,
The Doors of Perception

I was a modest, good-humored boy; it is Oxford that has made me insufferable.

SIR MAX BEERBOHM

It was never learning I associated with that school: only the necessity to succeed, to get ahead of the others in the daily struggle to "make a good impression" on our teachers. . . . The white, cool, thinly ruled record book sat over us from their desks all day long, and had remorselessly entered into it each day . . . our attendance, our conduct, our "effort," our merits and demerits; and to the last possible decimal point in calculation, our standing in an unending series of "tests"—surprise tests, daily tests, weekly tests, formal midterm tests, final tests. They never stopped trying to dig out of us whatever small morsel of fact we had managed to get down the night before. We had to prove that we were really alert, ready for anything, always in the race.

ALFRED KAZIN,
A Walker in the City

No use to shout at them to pay attention. . . . If the situations, the materials, the problems before a child do not interest him, his attention will slip off to what does interest him, and no amount of exhortation or threats will bring it back.

JOHN HOLT,
How Children Fail

Nowhere is our obsession with timetables more needless and foolish than in reading. We make much too much of the difficulties of learning to read. Teachers may say, "But reading must be difficult, or so many children wouldn't have trouble with it." I say it is *because* we assume that it is so difficult that so many children have trouble with it. Our anxieties, our fears, and the ridiculous things we do to "simplify" what is simple enough already, *cause* most of the trouble.

JOHN HOLT,
How Children Learn

The common stock of intellectual enjoyment should not be difficult of access because of the economic position of him who would approach it.

JANE ADDAMS,
quoted in *Jane Addams Speaks,*
compiled by Leonard S. Kenworthy

The association only with men of one's own class, such as the organization of college life today fosters, is simply fatal to any broad understanding of life. The refusal to make the acquaintance while in

college of as many as possible original, self-dependent personalities, regardless of race and social status, is morally suicidal.

RANDOLPH BOURNE,
Youth and Life

What a shallow culture, after all, is that of one's first education. Superimpose a second education upon this first one and again a third one upon the second. Break up the soil of your mind by ploughing it more than once and in different directions.

ALPHONSE GRATRY,
The Well-Springs

It is hard to convince a high-school student that he will encounter a lot of problems more difficult than those of algebra and geometry.

E. W. HOWE,
Country Town Sayings

Our progress as a nation can be no swifter than our progress in education. . . . The human mind is our fundamental resource.

JOHN F. KENNEDY,
Message to Congress, Febuary 20, 1961

Let us think of education as the means of developing our greatest abilities, because in each of us there is a private hope and dream which, fulfilled, can be translated into benefit for everyone and greater strength for our nation.

JOHN F. KENNEDY,
designating American Education Week,
New York Times, July 30, 1961

A classroom, any classroom, is an awesome place of shadows and shifting colors, a place of unacknowledged desires and powers, a magic place. Its inhabitants are tamed. After years of unnecessary repetition, they will be able to perform their tricks—reading, writing, arithmetic and their more complex derivatives. But they are tamed only in the manner of a cage full of jungle cats. Let the right set of circumstances arise, the classroom will explode.

GEORGE B. LEONARD,
Education and Ecstasy

The psychological realities which affect human beings most profoundly are rather simple and can be grasped at an early age. Affection knows no grade level. Fear is as much fear in the fourth grade as it is in college. The little child knows what it is to have his feelings hurt, to be sad, to be disappointed, to feel the disapproval of others, and to feel disapproval of self, with much the same basic psychological meanings as are experienced by the postgraduate student.

ARTHUR T. JERSILD,
In Search of Self

The great desideratum of human education is to make all men aware that they are gods in the making, and that they can all walk upon water if they will.

DON MARQUIS,
The Almost Perfect State

One chief aim of any true system of education must be to impart to the individual the courage to play the game against any and all odds, the nerve to walk into the ambushes of existence, the hardness to face the most despicable truth about himself and not let it daunt him permanently; it must armour him with an ultimate carelessness.

DON MARQUIS,
The Almost Perfect State

There is a grave defect in the school where the playground suggests happy, and the classroom disagreeable thoughts.

JOHN LANCASTER SPALDING,
Aphorisms and Reflections

Observant anthropologists have suggested that the basic values of the early grades are a stylized version of the feminine role in the society, cautious rather than daring, governed by a ladylike politeness.

JEROME S. BRUNER,
Toward a Theory of Instruction

The goals of integration and quality education must be sought together; they are interdependent. One is not possible without the other.

KENNETH B. CLARK,
Dark Ghetto

It is an ironic and tragic inversion of the purpose of education that Negro children in ghetto schools tend to lose ground in I.Q. as they proceed through the schools and to fall further and further behind the standard for their grade level in academic performance. The schools are presently damaging the children they exist to help.

KENNETH B. CLARK,
Dark Ghetto

Children who are treated as if they are uneducable almost invariably become uneducable.

KENNETH B. CLARK,
Dark Ghetto

The homework habit is disgraceful. Children loathe homework, and that is enough to condemn it.

A. S. NEILL,
Summerhill

The fact is, our process of universal education is today so uncouth, so psychologically barbaric, that it is the most terrible menace to the existence of our race. We seize hold of our children, and by parrot-compulsion we force into them a set of mental tricks. By unnatural and unhealthy compulsion we force them into a certain amount of cerebral activity. And then, after a few years, with a certain number of windmills in their heads, we turn them loose, like so many inferior Don Quixotes, to make a mess of life.

D. H. LAWRENCE,
Fantasia of the Unconscious

And this is the way to educate children: the instinctive way of mothers. There should be no effort made to teach children to think, to have ideas. Only to lift them and urge them into dynamic activity. The voice of dynamic sound, not the words of understanding. Damn understanding. Gestures, and touch, and expression of the face, not theory. Never have ideas about children—and never have ideas *for* them.

D. H. LAWRENCE,
Fantasia of the Unconscious

It is not possible to spend any prolonged period visiting public school classrooms without being appalled by the mutilation visible everywhere—mutilation of spontaneity, of joy in learning, of pleasure in creating, of sense of self.

CHARLES E. SILBERMAN,
Crisis in the Classroom

No one who examines classroom life carefully can fail to be astounded by the proportion of the students' time that is taken up just in waiting.

CHARLES E. SILBERMAN,
Crisis in the Classroom

Unless one has taught ... it is hard to imagine the extent of the demands made on a teacher's attention.

CHARLES E. SILBERMAN,
Crisis in the Classroom

What the school wants first from any child, whatever the psychologists say, is that he gets his work done—if only because children who don't work tend to employ their spare time by making mischief.

MARTIN MAYER,
The Schools

But there is one blanket statement which can be safely made about the world's schools: the teachers talk too much.

MARTIN MAYER,
The Schools

Much that occurs in the education of the child is and always will be incomprehensible to the fully formed adult. If ever all is known about the schools, there will remain a large element of mystery.

MARTIN MAYER,
The Schools

EFFORT

The work will teach you how to do it.
ESTONIAN PROVERB

Few things are impossible of themselves; application to make them succeed fails us more often than the means.

LA ROCHEFOUCAULD,
Maxims

The trite objects of human efforts—possessions, outward success, luxury—have al-

ways seemed to me contemptible.
ALBERT EINSTEIN,
Ideas and Opinions

All effort is in the last analysis sustained by faith that it is worth making.

ORDWAY TEAD,
The Art of Leadership

No one knows what is in him till he tries, and many would never try if they were not forced to.

BASIL W. MATURIN,
Laws of the Spiritual Life

Pray to God, but keep rowing to the shore.
RUSSIAN PROVERB

If experience went for anything, we should all come to a stand-still; for there is nothing so discouraging as effort.

CHARLES DUDLEY WARNER,
Backlog Studies

As I wrote many years ago, the mode in which the inevitable comes to pass is through effort. Consciously or unconsciously we all strive to make the kind of a world we like.

OLIVER WENDELL HOLMES, JR.,
The Mind and Faith of Justice Holmes,
edited by Max Lerner

One is daily annoyed by some little corner that needs clearing up and when by accident one at last is stirred to do the needful, one wonders that one should have stood the annoyance so long when such a little effort would have done away with it. Moral: When in doubt, do it.

OLIVER WENDELL HOLMES, JR.,
Holmes-Laski Letters, Vol. I

We strain hardest for things which are almost but not quite within our reach.

FREDERICK W. FABER,
Spiritual Conferences

It isn't so much a man's eminence of elementary faculties that pulls him through. They may be rare, and he do nothing. It is the steam pressure to the square inch behind that moves the machine.

WILLIAM JAMES,
The Letters of William James, Vol. II

The hope that our labors shall at last lead us to rest and the tranquil enjoyment of life, is an incentive to effort, and therefore good, though delusive, since active minds are incapable of repose and the tranquil enjoyment of life.

JOHN LANCASTER SPALDING,
Thoughts and Theories of Life and Education

EGO

"The ego is hateful," you say. Not mine. I should have liked it in another; should I be hard to please simply because it is mine? On what worse ego might I not have fallen?

ANDRÉ GIDE,
The Journals of André Gide, Vol. I

The burden of the absolute ego is the chief agony of life.

WALDO FRANK,
The Re-discovery of America

What's wrong with this egotism? If a man doesn't delight in himself and the force in him and feel that he and it are wonders, how is all life to become important to him? The interest in the lives of others, the high evaluation of these lives, what are they but the overflow of the interest he finds in himself, the value he attributes to his own being?

SHERWOOD ANDERSON,
Memoirs

What I chiefly desire for you is a genuine, full-blooded egoism which shall force you for a time to consider the thing that concerns you as the only thing of any consequence and everything else as non-existent. Now don't take this wish as something brutal in my nature! There is no way you can benefit society more than by coining the metal that you know is yourself.

HENRIK IBSEN,
Letters of Henrik Ibsen

How the *I* pervades all things!

WILLIAM ELLERY CHANNING,
Dr. Channing's Note-book

You will commonly find most egotism in reserved people.

JOSEPH FARRELL,
Lectures of a Certain Professor

After all, the wonder is, in this mysterious world, not that there is so much egotism abroad, but that there is so little! Considering the narrow space, the little cage of bones and skin, in which our spirit is confined, like a fluttering bird, it often astonishes me to find how much of how many people's thoughts is not given to themselves, but to their work, their friends, their families.

A. C. BENSON,
From a College Window

Egotism is the natural temptation of all those whose individuality is strong; the man of intense desires, of acute perceptions, of vigorous preferences, of eager temperament, is in danger of trying to construct his life too seduously on his own lines; and yet these are the very people who help other people most, and in whom the hope of the race lives. Meek, humble, timid persons, who accept things as they are, who tread in beaten paths, who are easily persuaded, who are cautious, prudent, and submissive, leave things very much as they find them.

A. C. BENSON,
From a College Window

The worst egotism is not individual, but corporate. . . . Those who as individuals are kindly or even generous lose conscience and grow hard and unrelenting when there is a question of their party or their clique; and thus what is called patriotism, or what is called religious zeal, had led men to commit the most atrocious crimes.

JOHN LANCASTER SPALDING
Opportunity and Other Essays

Self answers to self, and we love a congenial egotist. We love him because by sympathy we can and do expand our spirit to the measure of his.

CHARLES HORTON COOLEY,
Life and the Student

The truth is that egotists ... are people whose selves are conscious, social and expressive, and for that reason likely to be more human and less ruthless than those that have never come out into the common life. If a man lacks a streak of kindly egotism, beware of him.

CHARLES HORTON COOLEY,
Life and the Student

[Vachel] Lindsay's vigor and exuberant health and buoyancy are splendid and infectious and all his egotism amounts to is a rich and joyous instinct of imparting to everybody at all times and places the abounding sweep and sway of his own wide interest in life and work. That is not the egotism which hurts anyone. In fact, it is the glorious force that accomplishes all the great things of life. The egotism that really hurts is the slow and subtle kind that lives for itself inwardly, is too proud to flaunt itself before the world, but nurses its own morbid obsession in silence and solitude.

GAMALIEL BRADFORD,
The Letters of Gamaliel Bradford

HAVELOCK ELLIS

You are the first human being who has been perfect rest to me.

OLIVE SCHREINER,
The Letters of Olive Schreiner

ELOQUENCE

Eloquence is a republican art, as conversation is an aristocratic one.

GEORGE SANTAYANA,
Character and Opinion in the United States

He need not search his pockets for words.

RUSSIAN PROVERB

True eloquence foregoes eloquence.

ANDRÉ GIDE,
Pretexts

I notice once more how unsuitable real passion is to eloquence.

ANDRÉ GIDE,
The Journals of André Gide, Vol. I

In perfect eloquence, the hearer would lose the sense of dualism, of hearing from another; would cease to distinguish between the orator and himself.

RALPH WALDO EMERSON,
Journals of Ralph Waldo Emerson

RALPH WALDO EMERSON

There is something in that splendid serenity of Emerson that gives me courage.

THOMAS WOLFE,
The Letters of Thomas Wolfe

There are times, indeed, when one is inclined to regard Emerson's whole work as a hymn to intelligence, a paean to the all-creating, all-disturbing power of thought.

JOHN DEWEY,
Characters and Events, Vol. I

I am not acquainted with any writer ... whose movement of thought is more compact and unified, nor one who combines more adequately diversity of intellectual attack with concentration of form and effect. . . .

JOHN DEWEY,
Characters and Events, Vol. I

Never in my life have I met anyone who did not agree that Emerson is an inspiring writer. One may not accept his thought in toto, but one comes away from a reading of him purified, so to say, and exalted. He takes you to the heights, he gives you wings. He is daring, very daring. In our day he would be muzzled, I am certain.

HENRY MILLER,
The Books in My Life

The only fire-brand of my youth that burns to me as brightly as ever is Emerson.

OLIVER WENDELL HOLMES, JR. (at 89)

A vivid but fragmentary writer, like Emerson, influences us more than we are aware of. The thought takes root, but as there is nothing to trace it by we forget where it came from. You may find him in much of what is essential in Nietzsche, Bergson, William James, and John Dewey.

CHARLES HORTON COOLEY,
Life and the Student

No prose-writer of his time had such resources of imagery essentially poetic in nature as Emerson. . . .His understanding played about a thought like lightning about a vane. It suggested numberless analogies, an endless sequence of associated ideas, countless aspects, shifting facets of expression; and it were much if he should not set down a poor three or four of them. We, hard-pushed for our one pauper phrase, may call it excess in him: to Emerson, doubtless, it was austerity.

FRANCIS THOMPSON,
Works, Vol. III

With Emerson dead, it seems folly to be alive.

JOHN BURROUGHS,
The Heart of John Burroughs' Journals

EMOTION

My emotions flowered in me like a divine revelation.

ANDRÉ GIDE,
The Fruits of the Earth

Each of us makes his own weather, determines the color of the skies in the emotional universe which he inhabits.

FULTON J. SHEEN,
Way to Happiness

Yet, it would be easy to lead a bearable life, were we not always looking for clear-cut, excessive and exclusive emotions, while the only practicable feelings are the complex and the grey.

GUSTAVE FLAUBERT,
Letters of Gustave Flaubert

It is always one of the tragedies of any relationship, even between people sensitive to each other's moods, that the moments of emotion so rarely coincide.

NAN FAIRBROTHER,
An English Year

It is true that if we abandon ourselves unreservedly to our emotional impulses, we often render ourselves incapable of doing any work.

ANDRÉ MAUROIS,
The Art of Living

We think we can have our emotions for nothing. We cannot. Even the finest and the most self-sacrificing emotions have to be paid for. Strangely enough, that is what makes them fine. . . . As soon as we have to pay for an emotion we shall know its quality and be better for such knowledge.

OSCAR WILDE,
De Profundis

A trembling in the bones may carry a more convincing testimony than the dry documented deductions of the brain.

LLEWELYN POWYS,
Book of Days of Llewelyn Powys

Just as nature bears us ill-will, as it were, if we possess a secret to which mankind has not attained, so also has she a grudge against us if we withhold our emotions from our fellowmen. Nature decidedly abhors a vacuum in this respect, in the long run nothing is more unbearable than a tepid harmony in personal relations brought about by withholding emotion.

C. G. JUNG,
Modern Man in Search of a Soul

But are not this struggle and even the mistakes one may make better, and do they not develop us more, than if we kept systematically away from emotions? The latter is, in my belief, what makes many so-called strong spirits in reality but weaklings.

VINCENT VAN GOGH,
*Dear Theo:
An Autobiography of Vincent Van Gogh*

Cherish your emotions and never undervalue them.

ROBERT HENRI,
The Art Spirit

It may well be that the audience that emphasizes an emotional quality of a performer, such as sincerity, escapes from the need for emotional response to the performance itself. Though the listener likes a star who, as the teen-ager says, can "send me," he does not want to go very far.

DAVID RIESMAN,
The Lonely Crowd

Pure are all emotions that gather you together and lift you up; impure is that emotion which seizes only *one* side of your being and so distorts you. Everything that you can think in the face of your childhood, is right. Everything that makes *more* of you than you have heretofore in your best hours been, is right. Every enhancement is good if it is in your *whole* blood, if it is not intoxication, not turbidity, but joy, which one can see clear to the bottom.

RAINER MARIA RILKE,
Letters to a Young Poet

One of the effects of safe and civilised life is an immense oversensitiveness which makes all the primary emotions seem somewhat disgusting. Generosity is as painful as meanness, gratitude as hateful as ingratitude.

GEORGE ORWELL,
A Collection of Essays

Emotion is important because it is the one thing everybody has an abundance of, and in this respect we most resemble the animal kingdom. But emotion itself is a reservoir of inchoate violence. The triumph is to use it, temper it, transmute it. Isn't that triumph the difference between the beast and the man, the madman and the artist?

JUNE WAYNE,
Conversations with Artists
by Selden Rodman

The secret of our emotions never lies in the bare object, but in its subtle relations to our own past: no wonder the secret escapes the unsympathizing observer, who might as well put on his spectacles to discern odors.

GEORGE ELIOT,
Romola

The search for excitement . . . is a desperate attempt to escape from the prevalent deadness, a frenzied desire to *feel*. And just as a man who is dying of thirst will drink even polluted water, so one who is dying from lack of emotion will do anything to regain it. No wonder the manifestations of emotion we see today so frequently take the forms of infantilism or violence.

GEORGE W. MORGAN,
Prophetic Voices, edited by Ned O'Gorman

No emotional crisis is wholly the product of outward circumstances. These may precipitate it. But what turns an objective situation into a subjectively critical one is the interpretation the individual puts upon it—the meaning it has in his emotional economy; the way it affects his self-image.

BONARO OVERSTREET,
Understanding Fear in Ourselves and Others

To give vent now and then to his feelings, whether of pleasure or discontent, is a great ease to a man's heart.

FRANCESCO GUICCIARDINI,
Counsels and Reflections

It is terribly amusing how many different climates of feeling one can go through in a day.

ANNE MORROW LINDBERGH,
Bring Me a Unicorn

The only hard facts, one learns to see as one gets older, are the facts of feeling. Emotion and sentiment are, after all, incomparably more solid than statistics. So that when one wanders back in memory through the field of life one has traversed, as I have, in diligent search of hard facts, one comes back bearing in one's arms a sheaf of feelings. They after all are the only facts hard enough to endure as long as life itself endures.

HAVELOCK ELLIS,
Selected Essays

Formulate your feelings as well as your thoughts.

A. R. ORAGE,
Essays and Aphorisms

It is so many years before one can believe enough in what one feels even to know what the feeling is.

W. B. YEATS,
Autobiography

The most important part of man's existence, that part where he most truly lives and is aware of living, lies entirely within the domain of personal feeling.

JOYCE CARY,
Art and Reality

Seeing's believing, but feeling is God's own truth.   IRISH PROVERB

Analysis, synthesis, reasoning, abstraction, and experience, wishing to take counsel together, begin by banishing sentiment, which carries away the light when it departs, and leaves them in darkness.
JOSEPH ROUX,
Meditations of a Parish Priest

I wonder whether you can tell me why it is that people always try so hard to hide their real feelings? How is it that I always behave quite differently from what I should in other people's company?

Why do we trust one another so little? I know there must be a reason but still I sometimes think it's horrible that you find you can never really confide in people, even in those nearest you.
ANNE FRANK,
Anne Frank: The Diary of a Young Girl

There is a depth in the human psyche at which all feelings are one, and the disparagement of any contaminates and constricts all.
PHILIP SLATER,
The Pursuit of Loneliness

We nurse a fiction that people love to cover up their feelings; but I have learned that if the feeling is real and deep they love far better to find a way to uncover it.
DAVID GRAYSON,
The Friendly Road

The way to kill any feeling is to insist on it, harp on it, exaggerate it. Insist on loving humanity, and sure as fate you'll come to hate everybody. Because, of course, if you insist on loving humanity, then you insist that it shall be lovable: which half the time it isn't. In the same way, insist on loving your husband, and you won't be able to help hating him secretly. Because of course nobody is *always* lovable. . . . The result of forcing any feeling is the death of that feeling, and the substitution of some sort of opposite.
D. H. LAWRENCE,
Selected Essays

The one thing men have not learned to do is to stick up for their own instinctive feelings, against the things they are taught.
D. H. LAWRENCE,
Assorted Articles

Some people *dare* not feel fully—all life must be a long self-repression.
OLIVE SCHREINER,
The Letters of Olive Schreiner

EMOTIONS (*See also* ANGER, HATE, LOVE)

ENCOURAGEMENT

There is nothing better than the encouragement of a good friend.
KATHARINE BUTLER HATHAWAY,
*The Journals and Letters
of the Little Locksmith*

To give a generous hope to a man of his own nature, is to enrich him immeasurably.
WILLIAM ELLERY CHANNING,
Dr. Channing's Note-book

There is a point with me in matters of any size when I must absolutely have encouragement as much as crops rain; afterwards I am independent.
GERARD MANLEY HOPKINS,
quoted in "Emily Dickinson"
by Thornton Wilder,
Atlantic Monthly, November 1952

ENDURANCE

He that can't endure the bad, will not live to see the good.
YIDDISH PROVERB

There remain times when one can only endure. One lives on, one doesn't die, and the only thing that one can do, is to fill one's mind and time as far as possible with the concerns of other people. It doesn't bring immediate peace, but it brings the dawn nearer.
A. C. BENSON,
*Excerpts from the Letters of
Dr. A. C. Benson to M. E. A.*

There is no such thing as a situation so intolerable that human beings must necessarily rise up against it. People can bear anything, and the longer it exists the more placidly they will bear it.

PHILIP SLATER,
The Pursuit of Loneliness

One can go a long way after one is tired.

FRENCH PROVERB

ENEMY

I owe much to my friends; but, all things considered, it strikes me that I owe even more to my enemies. The real person springs to life under a sting, even better than under a caress.

ANDRÉ GIDE,
Pretexts

"Love your enemies," if you can do it, is shrewd practice. It saves you from the wear and tear of evil passions, while your opposition will be all the more effective for being good-natured.

CHARLES HORTON COOLEY,
Life and the Student

No enemy is stronger than one who does not know he is beaten.

J. MIDDLETON MURRY,
Pencillings

Often we attack and make ourselves enemies, to conceal that we are vulnerable.

FRIEDRICH NIETZSCHE,
Thus Spake Zarathustra

All enemies, except those fighting for the strictly limited food supply of a given territory, may be described as artificial enemies.

ALDOUS HUXLEY,
Beyond the Mexique Bay

Some of us bring out all our heavy artillery to meet an enemy that could be disposed of with a pea-shooter.

JANET ERSKINE STUART,
Life and Letters of Janet Erskine Stuart
by Maud Monahan

If you have no enemies, you are apt to be in the same predicament in regard to friends.

ELBERT HUBBARD,
A Thousand and One Epigrams

When we are in the mood to be effective, we know that our enemies cannot keep us from placing ourselves at the center of their attention and of their interest. They prefer us to themselves, they take our affairs to heart. In our turn we are concerned with them. . . . They save us, belong to us—they are our own.

E. M. CIORAN,
The Temptation to Exist

ENERGY, POWER, STRENGTH

Life begets life. Energy creates energy. It is by spending oneself that one becomes rich.

SARAH BERNHARDT,
quoted in *Madam Sarah*
by Cornelia Otis Skinner

Hell is full of the talented but Heaven of the energetic.

SAINT JANE FRANCIS DE CHANTAL,
quoted in *The Splendour of the Saints*
by W. J. Roche

The greater the contrast, the greater is the potential. Great energy only comes from a correspondingly great tension between opposites.

C. G. JUNG,
Psychological Reflections,
edited by Jolande Jacobi and R. F. Hull

There are certain days when one seems to have the strength of some gigantic and prehistoric monster. It has been so with me today. . . .

All day my mind has reached out and out. I have thought of everyone and everything. Minute little happenings in the lives of many people have been revealed to me. Today, had I a dozen hands, I could write a dozen tales, strange wonderful tales, all at one time.

SHERWOOD ANDERSON,
Letters of Sherwood Anderson

A man should be *felt*. He always is when

he has a self-subsistent energy.
WILLIAM ELLERY CHANNING,
Dr. Channing's Note-book

It is notorious that a single successful effort of moral volition, such as saying "no" to some habitual temptation, or performing some courageous act, will launch a man on a higher level of energy for days and weeks, will give him a new range of power.
WILLIAM JAMES,
"The Energies of Men,"
Essays on Faith and Morals

ENGLAND AND THE ENGLISH

England's reputation in the world rests largely on our poetic aptitudes and our political capacity.
HAVELOCK ELLIS,
Selected Essays

A turn of the road brought us into Roman Italy. That is really the most delightful thing about England. You never know—could never guess—what is waiting for you round the corner. Eccentric aristocrats have worked their wills on this island for centuries, with the result that anything may happen in it.
J. B. PRIESTLEY,
All About Ourselves and Other Essays

England is the only country where they understand liberty, and there consequently no one cares about justice.
J. B. YEATS,
Letters to His Son, W. B. Yeats and Others

To say truth, there is no part of the world where our sex is treated with so much contempt as in England.
LADY MARY WORTLEY MONTAGU,
quoted in *The Literature of Gossip*
by Elizabeth Drew

For my part nothing is comparable to the ruined abbeys of Yorkshire, and no churches ever built by man approach the English cathedrals in sublimity and beauty.
ELLEN GLASGOW,
Letters of Ellen Glasgow

That is why I love England. It is so little, and so full, and so old.
ROBERT SPEAIGHT,
The Unbroken Heart

England is not . . . the best possible world but it is the best actual country, and a great rest after America.
GEORGE SANTAYANA,
The Letters of George Santayana

In England it is a very dangerous handicap to have a sense of humor.
E. V. LUCAS,
365 Days and One More

I am glad not to be coming to England just yet. It is funny how I dread my native land. But here it is so free. The tightness of England is horrid.
D. H. LAWRENCE,
Selected Letters of D. H. Lawrence

The real tragedy of England, as I see it, is the tragedy of ugliness. The country is so lovely: the man-made England is so vile.
D. H. LAWRENCE,
Selected Essays

England always seems to me like a man swimming with his clothes on his head.
HENRY JAMES,
The James Family by F. O. Matthiessen

If it is good to have one foot in England, it is still better, or at least as good, to have the other out of it.
HENRY JAMES,
The James Family by F. O. Matthiessen

As I said, it makes one impatient at times; and one finds oneself wondering whether England can afford forever, when her rivals are living by the light of pure rationality to so great an extent, to go blundering thus unsystematically along, and trusting to mere luck to help her to find what is good, a fragment at a time. It's a queer mystery.
WILLIAM JAMES,
The James Family by F. O. Matthiessen

Contrary to popular belief, English women do not wear tweed nightgowns.
HERMIONE GINGOLD,
Saturday Review, April 16, 1955

How fast and how loud foreigners talk! It is a gift; the British cannot talk so loud or so fast. They have too many centuries of fog in their throats.

ROSE MACAULAY,
Personal Pleasures

No Englishman could pass for an American.

HEYWOOD BROUN,
Pieces of Hate

The close presence of the sea feeds the Englishman's restlessness. She takes possession of his heart like some capricious mistress.

ALEXANDER SMITH,
Dreamthorp

As long as the Englishman was powerful, he was detested, feared; now, he is understood; soon, he will be loved. . . . He is no longer a nightmare for anyone. Excess, delirium—he protects himself against these, sees them only as an aberration, or an impoliteness. What a contrast between his former excesses and the prudence he invokes now! Only at the price of great abdications does a nation become *normal*.

E. M. CIORAN,
The Temptation to Exist

The average Englishman does not see why a stranger should accost him with jocosity—many Englishmen do not see why a stranger should accost them at all.

WILLIAM LYON PHELPS,
Essays on Things

The English are cautious socially. We hesitate to enter upon new friendships. Our island is too small. We live in such proximity to one another that we are on our guard against committing ourselves to a relationship that may prove awkward.

ALEC WAUGH,
Traveller's Quest, edited by M. A. Michael

I suppose that there is no nation in the world which has so little capacity for doing nothing gracefully, and enjoying it, as the English.

A. C. BENSON,
From a College Window

And you do admire a little overmuch English detachment. It often is mere indifference and lack of life.

D. H. LAWRENCE,
Selected Letters of D. H. Lawrence

Curiously, I like England again, now I am up in my own regions. It braces me up: and there seems a queer, odd sort of potentiality in the people, especially the common people. One feels in them some odd, unaccustomed sort of plasm twinkling and nascent. They are not finished. And they have a funny sort of purity and gentleness, and at the same time, unbreakableness, that attracts one.

D. H. LAWRENCE,
Selected Letters of D. H. Lawrence

The English possess too many agreeable traits to permit them to be as much disliked as they think and hope they are.

AGNES REPPLIER,
Americans and Others

Two Englishmen, having climbed the Matterhorn, were regarding the wonderful view that stretched before them.

"Not half bad!" commented one of them.

"No," replied the other, "but you needn't rave about it like a love-struck poet!"

ANONYMOUS,
quoted in *The Wayside Book,*
edited by Heather White

As for our love of gardens, it is the last refuge of art in the minds and souls of many Englishmen: if we did not care for gardens, I hardly know what in the way of beauty we should care for.

SIR ARTHUR HELPS,
Companions of My Solitude

It is not only in war and politics that the English favour the habit of muddling through. They do it in life, where it is even more dangerous.

SIR RICHARD LIVINGSTONE,
On Education

The English can be explained by their Anglo-Saxon heritage and the influence of the Methodists. But I prefer to explain them in terms of tea, roast beef, and rain. A people is first of all what it eats, drinks, and gets pelted with.

PIERRE DANINOS,
The Secret of Major Thompson

The British people are good all through. You can test them as you would put a bucket into the sea and always find it salt.

SIR WINSTON CHURCHILL,
A Churchill Reader,
edited by Colin R. Coote

In nothing more is the English genius for domesticity more notably declared than in the institution of this festival—almost one may call it so—of afternoon tea. . . . The mere chink of cups and saucers tunes the mind to happy repose.

GEORGE GISSING,
The Private Papers of Henry Ryecroft

ENJOYMENT

Everybody knows how to weep, but it takes a fine texture of mind to know thoroughly how to enjoy the bright and happy things of life.

OLIVER BELL BUNCE,
Bachelor Bluff

Not what we have, but what we enjoy, constitutes our abundance.

J. PETIT-SENN,
Conceits and Caprices

It matters very little whether a man is discontented in the name of pessimism or progress, if his discontent does in fact paralyse his power of appreciating what he has got. The real difficulty of man is not to enjoy lamp-posts or landscapes, not to enjoy dandelions or chops; but to enjoy enjoyment.

G. K. CHESTERTON,
Autobiography

The business of life is to enjoy oneself; everything else is a mockery.

NORMAN DOUGLAS,
An Almanac

Nobody who looks as though he enjoyed life is ever called distinguished, though he is a man in a million.

ROBERTSON DAVIES,
The Table Talk of Samuel Marchbanks

Just as a petty vice may be more revealing than a large, unavoidably public weakness, so some trivial enjoyment, particularly if it be confessed only to oneself, may prove the Ariadne's thread leading to a man's center.

CLIFTON FADIMAN,
Any Number Can Play

The man who thoroughly enjoys what he reads or does, or even what he says, or simply what he dreams or imagines, profits to the full. The man who *seeks* to profit, through one form of discipline or another, deceives himself.

HENRY MILLER,
The Books in My Life

Thought of the determination to enjoy. We see it in all nature, from the leaf on the tree to the titled lady at the ball. . . . It is achieved, of a sort, under superhuman difficulties. Like pent-up water it will find a chink of possibility somewhere. Even the most oppressed of men and animals find it, so that out of a thousand there is hardly one who has not a sun of some sort for his soul.

THOMAS HARDY,
quoted in *The Early Life of Thomas Hardy*
by Florence Emil Hardy

The goal of all civilization, all religious thought, and all that sort of thing is simply to have a Good Time. But man gets so solemn over the process that he forgets the end.

DON MARQUIS,
The Almost Perfect State

Certainly it is important to do things that provide enjoyment. But fun cannot be the end that shapes man's life. If all is "enjoyed," one will not know true joy.

GEORGE W. MORGAN,
Prophetic Voices, edited by Ned O'Gorman

Verily, I have done this and that for the afflicted: but something better did I always seem to do when I had learned to enjoy myself better. . . .

And when we learn better to enjoy ourselves, then do we unlearn best to give pain unto others, and to contrive pain.

FRIEDRICH NIETZSCHE,
Thus Spake Zarathustra

What we enjoy most is activity that is pleasant in itself and also hopeful for the future, as building a garage for one's car, preparing a garden, assorting notes for a book. There is a glamour on such things. What ends in the moment, like savory food, or games, or even beauty or passion, seems, when the mind rests upon it, to baulk our human nature a little. We need to live *for* something to discipline and enhance the present by a larger aim.

CHARLES HORTON COOLEY,
Life and the Student

The practice of self-denial is good: it may be learnt. More difficult than self-denial is enjoyment, rejoicing in that which ought to delight us. This perhaps may be partly learnt, but not without severest discipline.

MARK RUTHERFORD,
Last Pages from a Journal

ENLIGHTENMENT

There is nothing you need to do first in order to be enlightened.

THADDEUS GOLAS,
The Lazy Man's Guide to Enlightenment

Enlightenment doesn't care how you get there.

THADDEUS GOLAS,
The Lazy Man's Guide to Enlightenment

ENTHUSIASM

The enthusiastic, to those who are not, are always something of a trial.

ALBAN GOODIER,
The School of Love

Enthusiasm finds the opportunities, and energy makes the most of them.

ANONYMOUS (HENRY S. HASKINS),
Meditations in Wall Street

There is no aloofness so forlorn as our aloofness from an uncontagious enthusiasm, and there is no hostility so sharp as that aroused by a fervour which fails of response.

AGNES REPPLIER,
Americans and Others

Like simplicity and candour, and other much-commended qualities, enthusiasm is charming until we meet it face to face, and cannot escape from its charm.

AGNES REPPLIER,
Americans and Others

No one . . . needs to be told that enthusiasm for one's end operates to lessen the disagreeableness of his patient working toward attainment of it.

THOMAS EAKINS,
quoted in *Artists on Art,*
edited by Robert Goldwater
and Marco Treves

The world belongs to the Enthusiast who keeps cool.

WILLIAM MCFEE,
Casuals of the Sea

ENVIRONMENT

Unless man can make new and original adaptations to his environment as rapidly as his science can change the environment, our culture will perish.

CARL R. ROGERS,
On Becoming a Person

Slowly the wasters and despoilers are impoverishing our land, our nature, and our beauty, so that there will not be one beach, one hill, one lane, one meadow, one forest free from the debris of man and the stigma of his improvidence.

MARYA MANNES,
Man Alone, edited by Eric Josephson
and Mary Josephson

After all anybody is as their land and air is. Anybody is as the sky is low or high, the air heavy or clear and anybody is as there is wind or no wind there. It is that which makes them and the arts they make and the work they do and the way they eat and the way they drink and the way they learn and everything.

GERTRUDE STEIN,
"What Are Masterpieces,"
Gertrude Stein: Her Life and Her Work
by Elizabeth Sprigge

All the declarations of independence in the world will not render anybody really independent. You may disregard your environment, you cannot escape it; and your disregard of it will bring you moral impoverishment and some day unpleasant surprises.

GEORGE SANTAYANA,
Character and Opinion in the United States

People often complain of their environment: it is dull, colorless, or even hostile; and it never occurs to them to enliven it or rectify it rather than just endure it. A lamp doesn't complain because it must shine at night.

ANTONIN G. SERTILLANGES,
Rectitude

In the working of silver or drilling of turquoise the Indians had exhaustless patience. . . . But their conception of decoration did not extend to the landscape. . . . It was as if the great country were asleep, and they wished to carry on their lives without awakening it; or as if the spirits of earth and air and water were things not to antagonize and arouse. . . . The land and all that it bore they treated with consideration; not attempting to improve it, they never desecrated it.

WILLA CATHER,
Death Comes For the Archbishop

ENVY

The heaven of the envied is hell for the envious.

BALTASAR GRACIAN,
The Oracle

The envious man does not only die once but as many times as the person he envies lives to hear the voice of praise.

BALTASAR GRACIAN,
The Oracle

It is not given to the children of men to be philosophers without envy. Lookers-on can hardly bear the spectacle of the great world.

WALTER BAGEHOT,
Literary Studies

Envy eats nothing but its own heart.

GERMAN PROVERB

Show me what a man envies the least in others and I will show you what he has got the most of himself.

JOSH BILLINGS,
His Works Complete

The envious man does not always insult others, sometimes he never insults them at all, but he speaks depreciatingly of that which is above him.

ERNEST HELLO,
Life, Science, and Art

Beggars do not envy millionaires, though of course they will envy other beggars who are more successful.

BERTRAND RUSSELL,
The Conquest of Happiness

Other people's eggs have two yolks.

BULGARIAN PROVERB

It is a sickening thing to think how many angry and evil passions the mere name of admitted excellence brings into full activity.

SIR WALTER SCOTT,
Sir Walter Scott's Journal (1825-1832)

Whoever has freed himself from envy and bitterness may begin to try to see things as they are.

JOHN LANCASTER SPALDING,
Means and Ends of Education

If envy were a fever, all the world would be ill.

DANISH PROVERB

EPIGRAM

Anyone can tell the truth, but only very few of us can make epigrams.
W. SOMERSET MAUGHAM,
A Writer's Notebook

I don't see how an epigram, being a bolt from the blue, with no introduction or cue, ever gets itself writ.
WILLIAM JAMES,
The Letters of William James, Vol. II

The most ardent love is rather epigrammatic than lyrical.
COVENTRY PATMORE,
The Rod, the Root, and the Flower

The highest and deepest thoughts do not "voluntary move harmonious numbers," but rather run to grotesque epigram and doggerel.
COVENTRY PATMORE,
The Rod, the Root, and the Flower

Epigram and truth are rarely commensurate. Truth has to be somewhat chiselled, as it were, before it will fit into an epigram.
JOSEPH FARRELL,
Lectures of a Certain Professor

Somewhere in the world there is an epigram for every dilemma.
HENDRIK WILLEM VAN LOON,
Tolerance

A ten-word epigram to be accurate needs a ten-page footnote, yet what it lacks in accuracy it makes up in nimbleness.
JOHN ANDREW HOLMES,
Wisdom in Small Doses

Epigrams are worth little for guidance to the perplexed, and less for comfort to the wounded.
HENRY VAN DYKE,
The Friendly Year

EQUALITY

Before God and the bus driver we are all equal.
GERMAN PROVERB

In life there is really no great or small thing. All things are of equal value and of equal size.
OSCAR WILDE,
De Profundis

One must begin with the *equality* of men. Then indeed one can and must go on to speak of the inequality of men. The reverse order is full of dangers, and leads in practice to frightful catastrophes.
THEODOR HAECKER,
Journal in the Night

There is no merit in equality, unless it be equality with the best.
JOHN LANCASTER SPALDING,
Thoughts and Theories of Life and Education

Whatever advantages may have arisen, in the past, out of the existence of a specially favored and highly privileged aristocracy, it is clear to me that today no argument can stand that supports unequal opportunity or any intrinsic disqualification for sharing in the whole of life.
MARGARET MEAD,
Blackberry Winter

When there were no human rights, the exceptional individual had them. That was inhuman. Then equality was created by taking the human rights away from the exceptional individual.
KARL KRAUS,
Karl Kraus by Harry Zohn

He who treats as equals those who are far below him in strength really makes them a gift of the quality of human beings, of which fate has deprived them. . . .
SIMONE WEIL,
Waiting for God

Respect for the personality of others, a strong sense of the dignity and intrinsic worth of each person, realization that all men are similar and on an equal footing in more ways than they are different—all this is essentially a religious and democratic outlook in the best and deepest sense.
ORDWAY TEAD,
The Art of Leadership

ERROR

There is something to be said for every error, but whatever may be said for it, the most important thing to be said about it is that it is erroneous.

G. K. CHESTERTON,
All Is Grist

The error of one moment becomes the sorrow of a whole life.

CHINESE PROVERB

The error which we hold inquiringly, striving to find what element of fact there be in it, is worth more to us than the truth which we accept mechanically and retain with indifference.

JOHN LANCASTER SPALDING,
Thoughts and Theories of Life and Education

The most considerable difference I note among men is not in their readiness to fall into error, but in their readiness to acknowledge these inevitable lapses.

THOMAS HENRY HUXLEY,
Aphorisms and Reflections

Error is always in a hurry.

ENGLISH PROVERB

Error is just as important a condition of life as truth.

C. G. JUNG,
Psychological Reflections,
edited by Jolande Jacobi and R. F. Hull

ESSAY

A good essay must have this permanent quality about it; it must draw its curtain round us, but it must be a curtain that shuts us in not out.

VIRGINIA WOOLF,
The Common Reader, First Series

I am not sure that there ought not to be a second version of every essay, in which the writer could say some of the things he intended to say when he sat down to write the first one.

ROBERT LYND,
The Blue Lion

ETIQUETTE (*See* COURTESY)

EVENT

I find that seeing extraordinary events does not in the least spoil one's enjoyment of ordinary ones or of quite eventless times. The big events and experiences seem like a kind of cake that somehow makes bread eat better than ever after it.

C. E. MONTAGUE,
C. E. Montague: A Memoir by Oliver Elton

A dire event needs a crowd to endow it with reality; it is the murmuring, nudging people, the peering heads, the avid eyes that give it drama; without these, it is insignificant, and might be part of a dream.

ELSPETH HUXLEY,
The Flame Trees of Thika

I do not ask of God that He should change anything in events, but that He should change me in regard to things, so that I might have the power to create my own universe about me, to govern my dreams, instead of enduring them.

GÉRARD DE NERVAL,
quoted in *The Poet's Work* by John Holmes

Yet even the eyewitness does not bring back a naïve picture of the scene. For experience seems to show that he himself brings something to the scene which he later takes away from it, that oftener than not what he imagines to be the account of an event is really a transfiguration of it.

WALTER LIPPMANN,
Public Opinion

Events solve the great problems, and our discussions and contentions are but the foam that crests the wave.

JOHN LANCASTER SPALDING,
Things of the Mind

EVIL

It is tempting to deny the existence of evil since denying it obviates the need to fight it.

ALEXIS CARREL,
Reflections on Life

Evil does not exist; once you have crossed the threshold, all is good. Once in another

world, you must hold your tongue.
FRANZ KAFKA,
Diaries of Franz Kafka 1914–1923

Why is pettiness always ahead and so active; and why is magnanimity so stupid and slow? In short, what is the origin of evil?
CHAUNCEY WRIGHT,
Letters of Chauncey Wright

Non-resistance to evil which takes the form of paying no attention to it is a way of promoting it.
JOHN DEWEY,
Human Nature and Conduct

Never let yourselves do evil that good may come. If you do, you hinder the coming of the real, the perfect good in its due time.
PHILLIPS BROOKS,
Visions and Tasks

And day and night, over and over, the soldiers came. They looted, they beat us, they raped us women whenever they caught us. From time to time there was a Russian who was friendly, and even slipped us a piece of bread. Perhaps there are many more such among them than I know. But I have never seen as clearly how contagious evil is.
ANONYMOUS,
quoted in *The Flight in the Winter*
by Jürgen Thorwald

One does evil enough when one does nothing good.
GERMAN PROVERB

It is so easy and so much more satisfactory to our pride to transfer the source of evil from ourselves to things outside of us; to say we were defiled, instead of, what is nearer the truth, we ourselves defiled what was otherwise clean.
BASIL W. MATURIN,
Laws of the Spiritual Life

I can't bring myself, as so many men seem able to do, to blink the evil out of sight, and gloss it over. It's as real as the good, and if it is denied, good must be denied too. It must be accepted and hated and resisted while there's breath in our bodies.
WILLIAM JAMES,
The Thought and Character of William James
by Ralph Barton Perry

The notion of evil and its cure is the best criterion of the profundity of a religious teaching.
HENRI FRÉDÉRIC AMIEL,
The Private Journal of Henri Frédéric Amiel

When there is a choice of two evils, most men take both.
AUSTIN O'MALLEY,
Keystones of Thought

We who live beneath a sky still streaked with the smoke of crematoriums, have paid a high price to find out that evil is really evil.
FRANÇOIS MAURIAC,
"An Author and His Work,"
Great Essays by Nobel Prize Winners,
edited by Leo Hamalian
and Edmond L. Volpe

The darkened mind, the callous heart, the paralytic will—these are the root evils.
JOHN LANCASTER SPALDING,
Opportunity and Other Essays

Like a boil is the evil deed; it itcheth and irritateth and breaketh forth—it speaketh honorably.
"Behold, I am disease," saith the evil deed: that is its honorableness.
FRIEDRICH NIETZSCHE,
Thus Spake Zarathustra

The first impulse of men in the presence of evil is to resist and try to abolish it; but when evil is seen to be ineradicable in the world, their next impulse is to elude it in their own persons, so recasting their habits as to be strengthened against it and to lay up their chief treasures beyond its reach.
GEORGE SANTAYANA,
Obiter Scripta

One man's despicable evil is another man's delightful good.
BRENDAN FRANCIS

Just as a very little fresh water is blown away by a storm of wind and dust, in like manner the good deeds, that we think we do in this life, are overwhelmed by the multitude of evils.
SAINT BASIL,
Letters and Select Works

There is in all the evil I see about me some latent germ of good; and it is the good that fructifies the most after all—even though it bear what seems but sorry fruit.
BARRETT WENDELL,
Barrett Wendell and His Letters
by M. A. DeWolfe Howe

Were I to cry out against what is evil and say nothing about what is good, I would prove myself a mere backbiter and not a reformer, one who would rather carp at evil than remedy it.
SAINT BERNARD OF CLAIRVAUX,
Letters

Everything evil is revenge.
OTTO WEININGER,
quoted in *The Mind and Death of a Genius*
by David Abrahamsen

All that is evil in man is the result of a lack of consciousness.
OTTO WEININGER,
quoted in *The Mind and Death of a Genius*
by David Abrahamsen

Every minute you are thinking of evil, you might have been thinking of good instead. Refuse to pander to a morbid interest in your own misdeeds. Pick yourself up, be sorry, shake yourself, and go on again.
EVELYN UNDERHILL,
The Letters of Evelyn Underhill

The belief in evil spirits, though still common, is probably less widespread than it was, but the human tendency to hypostasize its sense of values is still as strong as ever. Evil spirits being out of fashion, it must therefore find expression in other beliefs.
ALDOUS HUXLEY,
"The Substitutes for Religion,"
Proper Studies

What we think the greatest evils in our minute lives often bring to us the greatest blessings. It may be so with nations.
JOHN JAY CHAPMAN,
Memories and Milestones

I much prefer absolute silence about things which with the best will I do not understand, to the semi, forced explanations that leave a bitter taste in my mind. It is so easy to say God permits evil—and what evil!—in order to bring good out of it. I confess that while I understand that, it has never *entirely* satisfied me. And so I prefer to be silent in the abyss of my ignorance, and to pray.
THEODOR HAECKER,
Journal in the Night

The greater part of our evils are not real but imaginary.
SAINT FRANCIS DE SALES,
Saint Francis de Sales in His Letters

EXAMPLE

Not the cry, but the flight of the wild duck, leads the flock to fly and follow.
CHINESE PROVERB

I have preached to you by example; but example is really no maxim since cases are different.
GEORGE SANTAYANA,
The Letters of George Santayana

One does not improve through argument but through example; one does not touch except through emotion; one does not hope to excite love except through love. Be what you wish to make others become. Make yourself, not your words, a sermon.
HENRI FRÉDÉRIC AMIEL,
The Private Journal of Henri Frédéric Amiel

A man is fortunate if he encounters living examples of vice, as well as of virtue, to inspire him.
BRENDAN FRANCIS

Few things are harder to put up with than the annoyance of a good example.
MARK TWAIN,
Pudd'nhead Wilson

I heard many discourses which were good for the soul, but I could not discover in the case of any one of the teachers that his life was worthy of his words.
SAINT BASIL,
Letters and Select Works

The man who is called a good example is

no more an example than an old-fashioned milepost is. Both show the direction
to take, but neither shows you how you
are going to get to your destination or how
fit you are for the journey.

ANONYMOUS (HENRY S. HASKINS),
Meditations in Wall Street

A good example is like a bell that calls
many to church.

DANISH PROVERB

It is most misleading to judge by examples; for unless these be in all respects par-
allel, they are of no force, the least
diversity in the circumstances giving rise
to the widest divergence in conclusions.

FRANCESCO GUICCIARDINI,
Counsels and Reflections

It is a safer thing any time to follow a
man's advice rather than his example.

JOSH BILLINGS,
His Works Complete

EXCELLENCE

To be faithful to your instincts and impulses that carry you in the direction of
the excellence you most desire and value—
surely that is to lead the noble life.

GEORGE E. WOODBERRY,
Selected Letters of George Edward Woodberry

If I had given you any parting advice it
would I think all have been comprised in
this one sentence *to live up always to the best
and highest you know.*

HANNAH WHITALL SMITH,
quoted in *Philadelphia Quaker*
by Logan Pearsall Smith

One of the rarest things that a man ever
does is to do the best he can.

JOSH BILLINGS,
His Works Complete

Hit the ball over the fence and you can
take your time going around the bases.

JOHN W. RAPER,
What This World Needs

Knowledge of the first-rate gives direction,
purpose and drive: direction, because it

shows what is good as well as what is bad;
purpose, because it reveals an ideal to pursue; drive, because an ideal stirs to action.

SIR RICHARD LIVINGSTONE,
On Education

Real excellence and humility are not incompatible one with the other, on the contrary they are twin sisters.

JEAN BAPTISTE LACORDAIRE,
Letters to Young Men,
edited by Count de Montalembert

Before the gates of excellence the high
gods have placed sweat; long is the road
thereto and rough and steep at first; but
when the heights are reached, then there is
ease, though grievously hard in the
winning.

HESIOD,
Works and Days

I am inclined to think that is one of the
permanent tragedies in life that the finer
quality doesn't prevail over the next less
fine.

ALFRED NORTH WHITEHEAD,
Dialogues of Alfred North Whitehead

If you wish to make people stare by doing
better than others, why, make them stare
till they stare their eyes out.

SAMUEL JOHNSON

Those who attain any excellence, commonly spend life in one pursuit; for excellence is not often granted upon easier
terms.

SAMUEL JOHNSON

Everything superlatively good has always
been quantitatively small, and scarce.

BALTASAR GRACIAN,
The Oracle

The artistic sense of perfection in work is
another much-to-be-desired quality to be
cultivated. No matter how trifling the
matter on hand, do it with a feeling that it
demands the best that is in you, and when
done look it over with a critical eye, not
sparing a strict judgment of yourself.

SIR WILLIAM OSLER,
*Aphorisms from His Bedside Teachings
and Writings*

There ought to be so many who are excellent, there are so few.

> JANET ERSKINE STUART,
> *Life and Letters of Janet Erskine Stuart*
> by Maud Monahan

To aim at the best and to remain essentially ourselves is one and the same thing.

> JANET ERSKINE STUART,
> *Life and Letters of Janet Erskine Stuart*
> by Maud Monahan

EXCESS

If we say but little it is easy to add, but having said too much it is hard to withdraw and never can it be done so quickly as to hinder the harm of our excess.

> SAINT FRANCIS DE SALES,
> *Saint Francis de Sales in His Letters*

Almost all human affairs are tedious. Everything is too long. Visits, dinners, concerts, plays, speeches, pleadings, essays, sermons, are too long. Pleasure and business labour equally under this defect, or, as I should rather say, this fatal superabundance.

> SIR ARTHUR HELPS,
> *Companions of My Solitude*

When a thing is not worth overdoing, leave it alone!

> ANONYMOUS (HENRY S. HASKINS),
> *Meditations in Wall Street*

Nothing so tires me as seeing too many fine things at once.

> JEAN BAPTISTE LACORDAIRE,
> *Letters to Young Men,*
> edited by Count de Montalembert

Something is always born of excess: great art was born of great terrors, great loneliness, great inhibitions, instabilities, and it always balances them.

> ANAÏS NIN,
> *The Diaries of Anaïs Nin,* Vol. IV

Too far east is west.

> ENGLISH PROVERB

EXCITEMENT

Man lives by habit indeed, but what he lives for is thrills and excitement.

> WILLIAM JAMES

There are occasions in a man's existence when he must make something happen, must fling a splash of colour into his life, or some part of him, perhaps the boy in him, will perish, flying broken before the grey armies of age, timidity, or boredom.

> J. B. PRIESTLEY,
> *All About Ourselves and Other Essays*

The happiest excitement in life is to be convinced that one is fighting for all one is worth on behalf of some clearly seen and deeply felt good, and against some greatly scorned evil.

> RUTH BENEDICT,
> *An Anthropologist at Work*
> by Margaret Mead

As we go on in life, we find we cannot afford excitement, and we learn to be parsimonious in our emotions.

> SIR ARTHUR HELPS,
> *Companions of My Solitude*

EXECUTIVE

An executive: A man who can make quick decisions and is sometimes right.

> ELBERT HUBBARD,
> *A Thousand and One Epigrams*

By shifting papers about my desk, writing my initials on things, talking to my colleagues about things which they already know, fumbling in books of reference, making notes about things which are already decided, and staring out of the window while tapping my teeth with a pencil, I can successfully counterfeit a man doing a heavy day's work. . . . I am, in short, an executive.

> ROBERTSON DAVIES,
> *The Table Talk of Samuel Marchbanks*

EXERCISE

I have never taken any exercise, except for

sleeping and resting, and I never intend to take any. Exercise is loathsome.

MARK TWAIN,
Mark Twain at Your Fingertips
edited by Caroline T. Harnsberger

Those who do not find time for exercise will have to find time for illness.

OLD PROVERB

If the desire for exercise is strong, I throw aside all other engagements, whether they be those of society or business, and take it. Little good can come of regular exercise which reduces life to a monotonous machine. On the other hand, when the call of the wild comes to me, wherever I may happen to be it is my practice to follow it.

E. V. KNOX,
Gorgeous Times

Any workout which does not involve a certain minimum of danger or responsibility does not improve the body—it just wears it out.

NORMAN MAILER,
Writers at Work, Third Series,
edited by George Plimpton

The trouble with so many of the physical-culture devotees is that they tire out the soul in trying to serve it. I am inclined to believe that the beneficent effects of the regular quarter-hour's exercise before breakfast, is more than offset by the mental wear and tear in getting out of bed fifteen minutes earlier than one otherwise would.

SIMEON STRUNSKY,
The Patient Observer

EXHAUSTION (*See* WEAKNESS)

EXISTENCE

How very much of one piece is what befalls us, in what a relationship one thing stands to another, has given birth to itself and grows up and is brought up to itself, and we in reality have only to *exist,* but simply, but ardently, as the earth exists, assenting to the years, light and dark and altogether in space, not desiring to be at rest in anything save in the net of influences and forces in which the stars feel themselves secure.

RAINER MARIA RILKE,
Letters of Rainer Maria Rilke 1892–1910

In our ordinary hours we use things for some purpose, forgetting the pure fact that they exist.

PAUL CLAUDEL,
quoted in *Introduction to Paul Claudel*
by Mary Ryan

Every existing thing is equally upheld in its existence by God's creative love. The friends of God should love him to the point of merging their love into his with regard to all things here below.

SIMONE WEIL,
Waiting for God

The more unintelligent a man is, the less mysterious existence seems to him.

ARTHUR SCHOPENHAUER

This thing which we call existence; is it not something which has its roots far down below in the dark, and its branches stretching out into the immensity above, which we among the branches cannot see? Not a chance jumble; a living thing, a *One.* The thought gives us intense satisfaction, we cannot tell why.

OLIVE SCHREINER,
The Story of an African Farm

To know any man is not merely to be sure of his existence, but to have some conception of what his existence signifies, and what it is for.

PHILLIPS BROOKS,
Visions and Tasks

Of no individual thing one can "say" *what it is.* Our very first comprehension implies this. We comprehend that the understanding never gets to the bottom of things.

THEODOR HAECKER,
Journal in the Night

The greatest happiness of existence is Thinking; or, to be a little more precise, that mixture of Thinking and Feeling that constitutes an agreeable awareness of living without too definite intention of doing anything about it.

CHRISTOPHER MORLEY,
Inward Ho

EXPECTATION

Verily—happiness is only anticipating possibilities, denying impossibilities. Life is filled up with dreams of the future.

DR. WILHELM STEKHEL,
The Depths of the Soul

The quality of our expectations determines the quality of our action.

ANDRÉ GODIN,
Thought, December 1950

Talk about the joys of the unexpected, can they compare with the joys of the expected, of finding everything delightfully and completely what you knew it was going to be?

ELIZABETH BIBESCO,
Balloons

Our expectation of what the human animal can learn, can do, can be remains remarkably low and timorous.

GEORGE B. LEONARD,
Education and Ecstasy

Men expect too much, do too little.

ALLEN TATE,
"To the Lacedemonians," *Poems*

As subjects, we all live in suspense, from day to day, from hour to hour; in other words, we are the hero of our own story. We cannot believe that it is finished, that we are "finished," even though we may be so; we expect another chapter, another installment, tomorrow or next week.

MARY MCCARTHY,
On the Contrary

For the rest, just leave me to my expectation, which is so great that it cannot be disappointed. Where one expects something big, it is not upon this or that that one counts, one cannot count or counsel at all; for it is a matter of the unexpected, the unforseeable.

RAINER MARIA RILKE,
Letters of Rainer Maria Rilke 1892–1910

It is a common observation that those who dwell continually upon their expectations are apt to become oblivious to the requirements of their actual situation.

CHARLES SANDERS PEIRCE,
Collected Papers of Charles Sanders Peirce,
Vol. V

Men have a trick of coming up to what is expected of them, good or bad.

JACOB RIIS,
quoted in *The Author's Kalendar,* 1911,
compiled by Anna C. Woodford

I was surprised this morning when I reflected how large a stake I had in what was uncertain, in that for which I could but hope, and how little I live in that of which I am assured. The wise man should reverse the order.

MARK RUTHERFORD,
Last Pages from a Journal

Emotion is apt to be so unterribly unjust— and many people have been wounded for not being what they never professed to be.

A. C. BENSON,
*Excerpts from the Letters of
Dr. A. C. Benson to M. E. A.*

Mother's notion (and also mine)—that a figure stands in our van with arm uplifted, to knock us back from any pleasant prospect that we indulge in as probable.

THOMAS HARDY,
Thomas Hardy's Notebooks

You've got the hiccup from the bread and butter you never ate.

IRISH PROVERB

Never, I think, was man born to be, more than myself, a Waiter: I am like the Princes of Greece round Penelope, a ten years' Wooer: I am always in my mind waiting for some bell to ring that never rings, for some wonderful thing to happen that never happens. I try to show myself that luck follows work as harvest comes by ploughing: deep down I have never believed it; I cannot believe it; I cannot make myself believe it.

STEPHEN MACKENNA,
Journal and Letters of Stephen Mackenna

There is one illusion that has much to do with most of our happiness, and still more to do with most of our unhappiness. It may be told in a word. We expect too much.

JOSEPH FARRELL,
Lectures of a Certain Professor

As a man gets wiser, he expects less, and probably gets more than he expects.

JOSEPH FARRELL,
Lectures of a Certain Professor

EXPERIENCE

You cannot acquire experience by making experiments. You cannot create experience. You must undergo it.

ALBERT CAMUS,
Notebooks 1935–1942

Experience teaches only the teachable.

ALDOUS HUXLEY,
Collected Essays

Being true to one's own experience is the central requirement in the continued existence of a real self.

CLARK MOUSTAKAS,
Creativity and Conformity

And, you know ... experience is a dim lamp which only lights the one who bears it ... and incommunicable.

LOUIS-FERDINAND CÉLINE,
Writers at Work, Third Series,
edited by George Plimpton

Ordinarily one learns from experience the necessity of modifying our wishful thinking to conform to the realities of existence; to change from thinking on the basis of the *pleasure principle* to thinking on the basis of the *reality principle,* as Freud put it.

DR. KARL A. MENNINGER,
The Human Mind

What one has not experienced, one will never understand in print.

ISADORA DUNCAN,
My Life

All well-brought-up people are afraid of having any experience which seems to them uncharacteristic of themselves as they imagine themselves to be. Yet this is the only kind of experience that is really alive and can lead them anywhere worth going. New, strange, uncharacteristic experience, coming at the needed moment, is sometimes as necessary in a person's life as a plow in a field.

KATHARINE BUTLER HATHAWAY,
*The Journals and Letters
of the Little Locksmith*

It seems to me frightfully silly to want to look untouched by experience when one is not touched.

KATHARINE BUTLER HATHAWAY,
*The Journals and Letters
of the Little Locksmith*

It is a great temptation to people who have mind and imagination to substitute the *idea* of the thing for the *experience* of the thing itself.

KATHARINE BUTLER HATHAWAY,
*The Journals and Letters
of the Little Locksmith*

As experience widens, one begins to see how much upon a level all human things are.

JOSEPH FARRELL,
Lectures of a Certain Professor

We have to initiate ourselves into the essential nature of our body, our mind and our environment; to make contact with concrete reality.... Only from the data of observation and experience can we derive any notion of how to fit ourselves into the scheme of things.

ALEXIS CARREL,
Reflections on Life

Nothing which has entered into our experience is ever lost.

WILLIAM ELLERY CHANNING,
Dr. Channing's Note-book

There is something in our minds which expects all experience to have a direct effect upon conduct. Whatever happens to us is, we assume, a command or a stimulus to do something; we connect it with our future, and judge it by its effect upon that future.... It is only in afterthought that we connect our experience with our future at all.

A. CLUTTON-BROCK,
Essays on Life

We cannot afford to forget any experience, even the most painful.

DAG HAMMARSKJÖLD,
Markings

Among the many advantages of experience, one of the most valuable is that we come to know the range of our own powers, and if we are wise we keep contentedly within them.

PHILIP G. HAMERTON,
The Intellectual Life

What ephemerae we all are, to be sure: experience leaves no permanent furrow, but, like writing on sand, is washed out by every advancing ripple of changing circumstances.

ALICE JAMES,
The Diary of Alice James

Experience seems to be like the shining of a bright lantern. It suddenly makes clear in the mind what was already there, perhaps, but dim.

WALTER DE LA MARE,
Come Hither

Contempt for experience has had a tragic revenge in experience; it has cultivated disregard for fact and this disregard has been paid for in failure, sorrow and war.

JOHN DEWEY,
Reconstruction in Philosophy

The inevitable shallowness that goes with people who have learned everything from experience.

F. SCOTT FITZGERALD,
The Crack-up

Experience of life ... led me to reject experience altogether. As well might the horse believe that the road the bridle forces it to traverse every day encircles the earth as I believe in experience.

RICHARD JEFFERIES,
The Story of My Heart

Dreadful experiences raise the question whether he who experiences them is not something dreadful also.

FRIEDRICH NIETZSCHE,
Beyond Good and Evil

To reach something good it is very useful to have gone astray, and thus acquire experience.

SAINT TERESA OF AVILA,
Saint Teresa in Her Writings
by the Abbé Rodolphe Hoornaert

In a person who is open to experience each stimulus is freely relayed through the nervous system, without being distorted by any process of defensiveness.

CARL R. ROGERS,
On Becoming a Person

This whole train of experiencing, and the meanings that I have thus far discovered in it, seem to have launched me on a process which is both fascinating and at times a little frightening. *It seems to mean letting my experience carry me on, in a direction which appears to me forward, towards goals that I can but dimly define, as I try to understand at least the current meaning of that experience.* The sensation is that of floating with a complex stream of experience, with the fascinating possibility of trying to comprehend its ever changing complexity.

CARL R. ROGERS,
On Becoming a Person

Our experience is composed rather of illusions lost than of wisdom acquired.

JOSEPH ROUX,
Meditations of a Parish Priest

If you can learn from hard knocks, you can also learn from soft touches.

CAROLYN KENMORE,
Mannequin: My Life as a Model

Nothing that does not originate in an experience can become an experience for others.

DR. THEODOR REIK,
Listening with the Third Ear

[William] James reckons that the tribulations with which scientific theories have beset our present age are not to be compared with the glory that perchance shall be, if only we open our eyes to what experience itself has to reveal to us.

JOSIAH ROYCE,
William James and Other Essays
on the Philosophy of Life

We are strangely wooed to our experiences, but once there, one has to hold on firmly and confront what comes.

A. C. BENSON,
Excerpts from the Letters of
Dr. A. C. Benson to M. E. A.

There is nothing so easy to learn as experience and nothing so hard to apply.

JOSH BILLINGS,
His Works Complete

Experience is a grindstone and it is lucky for us if we get brightened by it—not ground.

JOSH BILLINGS,
His Works Complete

It is strange how one's soul passes through great experiences and one plods on in the same round, and no one notices any difference or imagines what one has been through.

BASIL W. MATURIN,
quoted in *Father Maturin* by Maisie Ward

Many people, most people, live in the present and think it a waste to resuscitate the past. But the real waste is to leave untouched the store of experience which a human life is bound to accumulate.

ERNEST DIMNET,
What We Live By

No amount of speculation takes the place of experience.

CHARLES SANDERS PEIRCE,
Collected Papers of Charles Sanders Peirce,
Vol. I

Experience does not teach us that every enthusiasm is absurd. From it we learn simply to wait for results, not from high-sounding words, but from hard work and great courage.

ANDRÉ MAUROIS,
The Art of Living

All the best part of experience consists in discovering that perfectly trite pieces of observation are shiningly and exhilaratingly true.

C. E. MONTAGUE,
The Right Place

Some of our deepest experiences forfeit their validity and influence because we haven't the courage to record them. The mere act of reciting them or writing them gives an objective reality which they would lose if retained as secrets.

JOSEPH H. ODELL,
Unmailed Letters

See a great fire, how the flames pass from shape into shape, lambent and aspirant flames, poised or waving, some open like fully-blown tulips and some pursed to a point like shut daisies, but all vanishing as soon as formed and none recurring just as it was. All experience burns away like that.

C. E. MONTAGUE,
The Right Place

An enormous part of our mature experience . . . cannot be expressed in words.

ALFRED NORTH WHITEHEAD,
Dialogues of Alfred North Whitehead

Experiences are savings which a miser puts aside. Wisdom is an inheritance which a wastrel cannot exhaust.

KARL KRAUS,
Karl Kraus by Harry Zohn

Don't seek experience; you'll get enough of it if you'll just let nature take its course.

WILLIAM FEATHER,
The Business of Life

What little I have learned
Has added to my lack,
For the road has always turned
And never once led back.

A. M. SULLIVAN,
"Pilgrim," *Incident in Silver: A Book of Lyrics*

Half, maybe more, of the delight of experiencing is to know *what* you are experiencing.

JESSAMYN WEST,
Hide and Seek

Doubt and despair, like hope, are born in the imagination—some say, in the digestion. Experience is simply an unprincipled witness who will give evidence on either side.

> ROBERT LYND,
> *The Blue Lion*

Experience is what you get looking for something else.

> MARY PETTIBONE POOLE,
> *Ladies' Home Journal,* March 1942

The years teach much which the days never knew.

> RALPH WALDO EMERSON,
> "Experience," *Essays*

Few people even scratch the surface, much less exhaust the contemplation of their own experience.

> RANDOLPH BOURNE,
> *Youth and Life*

For the weakness of experience is that it so soon gets stereotyped; without new situations and crises it becomes so conventional as to be practically unconscious. Very few people get any really new experience after they are twenty-five, unless there is a real change of environment. Most older men live only in the experience of their youthful years.

> RANDOLPH BOURNE,
> *Youth and Life*

What a strange narrowness of mind now is that, to think the things we have not known are better than the things we have known.

> SAMUEL JOHNSON

In all experience there is the consciousness of something which lies deeper than experience.

> JOHN LANCASTER SPALDING,
> *Aphorisms and Reflections*

Experience is always experience of oneself: it cannot, therefore, make others wise.

> JOHN LANCASTER SPALDING,
> *Aphorisms and Reflections*

EXPERIMENT

Do not be too timid and squeamish about your actions. All life is an experiment. The more experiments you make the better.

> RALPH WALDO EMERSON,
> *Journals of Ralph Waldo Emerson*

There is always more chance of hitting upon something valuable when you aren't too sure what you want to hit upon.

> ALFRED NORTH WHITEHEAD,
> *Dialogues of Alfred North Whitehead*

To those who are alive, every action, every thought, is in the nature of an experiment. Thought and deed go hand in hand, the twin instruments of those who recognise that a great deal more of life has yet to be revealed to man than the most visionary of men have yet imagined. We have, as yet, only touched the veriest hem of life's garment.

> HOLBROOK JACKSON,
> *Southward Ho! and Other Essays*

But though we are fixed, each of us, in a largely unconscious life-attitude, we can borrow a little daring from the experimental, gymnastic attitude. We can try a new step here, a little leap there.

> GORHAM MUNSON,
> *The Writer's Workshop*

People who really experiment with themselves find out that all the old things are true.

> F. SCOTT FITZGERALD,
> *The Crack-up*

EXPLANATION

You should avoid making yourself too clear even in your explanations.

> BALTASAR GRACIAN,
> *The Oracle*

When you don't know much about a subject you are explaining, compliment the person you are explaining to on knowing all about it and he will think that you do, too.

> DON MARQUIS,
> *The Almost Perfect State*

No explanation ever explains the necessity of making one.

> ELBERT HUBBARD,
> *The Philosophy of Elbert Hubbard*

Whenever one says anything, one wants to explain that one sees the other side.

> OLIVER WENDELL HOLMES, JR.,
> *Holmes-Laski Letters,* Vol. I

Where one cannot understand without words, no amount of explanation will make things clear.

> MYRTLE REED,
> *The Master's Violin*

I am the master of everything I can explain.

> THEODOR HAECKER,
> *Journal in the Night*

Explanations grow under our hands, in spite of our effort at compression.

> JOHN HENRY CARDINAL NEWMAN,
> *Oxford University Sermons*

I am the enemy of long explanations; they deceive either the maker or the hearer, generally both.

> GOETHE

EXPRESSION

We should not forget all those who lived without expressing themselves. They may have possessed part of the secret we are still seeking.

> MAURICE MAETERLINCK,
> *The Great Beyond*

Even when you elect to be absolutely honest it is difficult. Expression seems such a natural, God-given thing—and yet it's not either. It's a lifelong struggle to find yourself.

> HENRY MILLER,
> *Lawrence Durrell and Henry Miller,*
> *A Private Correspondence*

It is better not to express what one means than to express what one does not mean.

> KARL KRAUS,
> *Karl Kraus* by Harry Zohn

One can and should say everything—if one knows how to say it.

> ANATOLE FRANCE,
> *The Anatole France Calendar,*
> selected by A. S. Rappoport

Have you ever noticed the two types of mind described by Fénelon, the mind which can express things almost without having seen and felt, and the mind which sees and feels but cannot express itself, at all events not yet?

> ALPHONSE GRATRY,
> *The Well-Springs*

All over-expression, whether by journalists, poets, novelists, or clergymen, is bad for the language, bad for the mind; and by over-expression I mean the use of words running beyond the sincere feeling of writer or speaker or beyond what the event will sanely carry.

> JOHN GALSWORTHY,
> *Castles in Spain and Other Screeds*

It may be that what is uttered is never what is innermost—that it must cease to be innermost before it can be uttered.

> JOHN LANCASTER SPALDING,
> *Aphorisms and Reflections*

However vital the truth, if there is a flaw in the expression, someone will stamp it more authentically and make it his own.

> JOHN LANCASTER SPALDING,
> *Thoughts and Theories of Life and Education*

The act counts less than the echo produced by the act. And here is where expression comes in—expression which is poetry, whether in words, color, line, volume or sound. For the truth is that, if it is the act alone which counts at the moment, what is said about the act determines its future. The act, if you like, belongs to history and is passive in the face of history; but what is said of the act creates its own legend by which it goes on living in a continual, everlasting action of its own.

> C.-F. RAMUZ,
> *What is Man?*

Misunderstanding may occur not only through wrong or excessive expressions of feeling, but through repression and failure to express. Think how tongue-tied we often are in expressing our true feelings. I was once told by my mother that her own mother, though she had a fairly happy married life, thought that her husband did not love her deeply because he rarely spoke of it. He was a non-conformist minister, deeply religious and very restrained. There has come into my possession an old diary of his, found after his death, and in one passage he refers to his wife and his deep love for her, and then he adds the words, "Lord save me from idolatry"; but his wife read this only after his death.

CHARLES W. VALENTINE,
Psychology and Mental Health

EYES

I have always felt a mixed reverence and fear of human creatures, so that I have sometimes even been afraid to look into the eyes of strangers; they seemed to me gates into chambers where intimate and terrible secrets lie bare.

HAVELOCK ELLIS,
My Life

To meet at all, one must open one's eyes to another; and there is no true conversation, no matter how many words are spoken, unless the eye, unveiled and listening, opens itself to the other.

JESSAMYN WEST,
Love Is Not What You Think

I asked Margot if she thought I was very ugly. She said that I was quite attractive and that I had nice eyes. Rather vague, don't you think?

ANNE FRANK,
Anne Frank: The Diary of a Young Girl

It's queer to think of all the people in the world, and how troubled they are when they look each other straight in the eyes.

CHRISTOPHER MORLEY,
Thunder on the Left

Now, it is perfectly possible to be on tolerably intimate terms with a person for a long time and yet to be quite unable to recall the colour of his or her eyes.

G. K. CHESTERTON,
All I Survey

The richness and rightness of our spiritual vision depend largely upon the keenness and careful use of our eyes.

CHARLES-DAMIAN BOULOGNE,
My Friends the Senses

Love comes in at the eye.

W. B. YEATS,
quoted in *The Right Place*
by C. E. Montague

A woman's eyes are for me very important. I look at them often and then I think so many things that I were only a head, I should prefer that girls were only eyes.

GEORG C. LICHTENBERG,
quoted in *Frailty Thy Name*,
compiled by Paul Guermonprez

It annoys many when I talk about blue eyes but any man who ever amounted to a damn in history had them.

ARTHUR BRISBANE

FACE

To look at her face is like being shone upon by a ray of the sun.

NATHANIEL HAWTHORNE,
The American Notebooks

After a certain degree of prettiness, one pretty girl is as pretty as another.

F. SCOTT FITZGERALD,
The Crack-up

What effect does the sudden sight of an extraordinarily beautiful person have upon you? I mean the very *first*. Is it not an effect of sadness? Analyze it; and perhaps you will find yourself involuntarily thinking of *death*.

LAFCADIO HEARN,
Lafcadio Hearn: Life and Letters, Vol. 2,
edited by Elizabeth Bisland

Part of the reason for the ugliness of adults, in a child's eyes, is that the child is usually looking upwards, and few faces are at their best when seen from below.

GEORGE ORWELL,
A Collection of Essays

Policemen and firemen have action faces.

ANONYMOUS 7-YEAR-OLD SCHOOLBOY,
quoted in the *New York Times*,
July 6, 1952

As an adolescent I had a quicker eye, I fear, for ugliness than for beauty. On shopping trips to Los Angeles I saw faces so gross, so cruel, so vindictive, so unloving, my own heart withered.

JESSAMYN WEST,
Hide and Seek

There are people who think that everything one does with a serious face is sensible.

GEORG C. LICHTENBERG,
The Lichtenberg Reader

I admire beautiful people, and I am strongly attracted by distinguished ugliness. It is the blank faces, empty of charm, distinction, beauty or meaning of any kind, which arouse my dislike.

ROBERTSON DAVIES,
The Table Talk of Samuel Marchbanks

Plainness has its peculiar temptations quite as much as beauty.

GEORGE ELIOT,
quoted in *Women's Thoughts for Women,*
compiled by Rose Porter

The painter does not copy the expression a face may have shown, he divines and paints the expression the face must have shown had the man fully revealed himself.

EDWARD HOWARD GRIGGS,
A Book of Meditations

These eye-encounters in the street, little touches of love-liking; faces that ask, as they pass, "Are you my new lover?" Shall I one day in Park Lane or Oxford Street perhaps—see the unknown Face I dread and look for?

LOGAN PEARSALL SMITH,
More Trivia

I see few faces that express a clearly achieved character. Is our time a bad artist?

CHARLES HORTON COOLEY,
Life and the Student

Only by returning to life in the city does one rediscover the unbelievable complexity, excitement, and beauty of the human face. There are faces in the country, of course, but they are widely spaced like filling stations.

JEROME WEIDMAN,
Back Talk

Happy the man who never puts on a face, but receives every visitor with that countenance he has on.

RALPH WALDO EMERSON,
Journals of Ralph Waldo Emerson

But the loveliest face in all the world will not please you if you see it suddenly, eye to eye, at a distance of half an inch from your own.

MAX BEERBOHM,
Zuleika Dobson

One needs a certain time to realize that the faces in the Italian primitives are those one meets daily in the street. This is because we have lost the habit of seeing what is really important in a face. We no longer look at our contemporaries, and select only what is useful to our aims (in every sense of the word).

ALBERT CAMUS,
Notebooks 1935–1942

Somehow, people with nice faces inspire me with much more confidence than those who I am assured have beautiful minds. One can see their faces—that makes so much difference.

E. F. BENSON

I think much of the most beautiful of Chinese lanthorns, your face. I found some Irish story once of men who threshed by the light of a lock of hair, but that was a more mundane light.

W. B. YEATS,
Letters on Poetry
from W. B. Yeats to Dorothy Wellesley

What beautiful woman delights us by her look of character? That shows itself when beauty is gone, being the creation of habit; it's the stalk that remains after the flowers of spring have withered. Beauty consumes character with what Patmore calls "the integrity of fire."

W. B. YEATS,
W. B. Yeats Memoir,
edited by Denis Donaghue

Do you think it odd that I talk all the time about everybody's being beautiful or handsome? It was a different age—people really were good-looking then. Just look at the old Russian revolutionaries. They all had marvelous faces, eyes that were full of expression, firm lips and high, intellectual foreheads. There were no doubts, no skepticism, no meanness in their faces.

SVETLANA ALLILUYEVA,
Twenty Letters to a Friend

Any survey of a lovely face is, or should be, followed by a "fall," even though it be a fall no more dangerous than that of a worker bee into a flower.

WALTER DE LA MARE,
Love

You have such a nice look on your face when I look at it. I admire it very much. . . . Who else should I think of but you. When I've had enough of work I always take a break to think of you.

JOHN KYRIAKIS,
age 7, United States,
Journeys: Prose by Children of the English-speaking World,
collected by Richard Lewis

Every human face is a very special door to Paradise, which cannot possibly be confused with any other, and through which there will never enter but one soul.

LEON BLOY,
quoted in *God and Man,*
compiled by Victor Gollancz

There is no such thing as complete blankness, however much outward appearances may seem to indicate it.

ARTHUR PONSONBY,
Casual Observations

Men who have been famous for their looks have never been famous for anything else.

ARTHUR PONSONBY,
Casual Observations

Through the years, a man peoples a space with images of provinces, kingdoms, mountains, bays, ships, islands, fishes, rooms, tools, stars, horses and people. Shortly before his death, he discovers that the patient labyrinth of lines traces the image of his own face.

JORGE LUIS BORGES

Why is a woman lovely, if ever, in her twenties? It is the time when sex rises softly to her face, as a rose to the top of a rose bush.

D. H. LAWRENCE,
Assorted Articles

A sweet face is a page of sadness to a man over thirty—the raw material of a corpse.

THOMAS HARDY,
Thomas Hardy's Notebooks

That girl in the omnibus had one of those faces of marvellous beauty which are seen casually in the streets but never among one's friends. It was perfect in its softened classicality—a Greek face translated into English. Moreover she was fair, and her hair pale chestnut. Where do these women come from? Who marries them? Who knows them?

THOMAS HARDY,
quoted in *The Early Life of Thomas Hardy*
by Florence Emil Hardy

Grown-ups exhibit their faces as if they had earned them, as if they were a private possession with which they could do what they pleased. It seems, however, the child did not even know that it bore a face. . . . When, in time of great need, the face of the adult does not know where to turn, there is the face of the child ready to receive it.

MAX PICARD,
quoted in *Love,*
edited by Walter de la Mare

There is no greater wonder than the way the face of a young woman fits in a man's mind and stays there, and he could never tell you why; it just seems it was the thing he wanted.

ROBERT LOUIS STEVENSON,
Catriona

Some persons continue to see in the face they have lived with for ten years, or twenty, or thirty, the same face they saw when they met it first; the insensible graduation of change being to them almost as conservative as if the face had been embalmed.

> SIR HENRY TAYLOR,
> *Notes from Life*

This face is a dog's snout sniffing for garbage,
Snakes nest in that mouth, I hear the sibilant threat.

> WALT WHITMAN,
> "Faces," *Leaves of Grass*

This face is flavor'd fruit ready for eating.

> WALT WHITMAN,
> "Faces," *Leaves of Grass*

And now we come to the greatest discovery ever for the Female Face. . . . All I can say is, that though it looks more repellent when put on the face than anything you can conceive,—it is made partly of the blood of the lamb, and one looks like a cannibal—one comes out looking *at least* fifteen years younger. I have easily *never* seen anything to touch the effect. . . . One looks like the young dawn.

> EDITH SITWELL,
> *Edith Sitwell: Selected Letters 1916-1964*

FACT

The trouble with facts is that there are so many of them.

> SAMUEL McCHORD CROTHERS,
> *The Gentle Reader*

I hate facts. I always say the chief end of man is to form general propositions—adding that no general proposition is worth a damn.

> OLIVER WENDELL HOLMES, JR.
> *The Mind and Faith of Justice Holmes,*
> edited by Max Lerner

All that life offers any man from which to start his thinking or striving is a fact. And if this universe is one universe, if it is so far thinkable that you can pass in reason from one part of it to another, it does not matter very much what that fact is. For every fact leads to every other by the path of air.

Only men do not yet see how, always.

> OLIVER WENDELL HOLMES, JR.,
> *The Mind and Faith of Justice Holmes,*
> edited by Max Lerner

You must see the infinite, i.e., the universal in your particular or it is only gossip.

> OLIVER WENDELL HOLMES, JR.,
> *Holmes-Laski Letters,* Vol. II

The truth seems to be that it is impossible to lay the ghost of a fact. You can face it or shirk it—and I have come across a man or two who could wink at their familiar shades.

> JOSEPH CONRAD,
> *Lord Jim*

There are no facts, only interpretations.

> FRIEDRICH NIETZSCHE,
> quoted in *Against Interpretation*
> by Susan Sontag

One of the most untruthful things possible, you know, is a collection of facts, because they can be made to appear so many different ways.

> DR. KARL MENNINGER,
> *A Psychiatrist's World*

I believe in general in a dualism between facts and the ideas of those facts in human heads.

> GEORGE SANTAYANA,
> *The Letters of George Santayana*

All solid facts were originally mist.

> ANONYMOUS (HENRY S. HASKINS),
> *Meditations in Wall Street*

If a man will take his place before almost any fact and scrounge down into it, he will come upon something not adequately known.

> CHARLES HORTON COOLEY,
> *Life and the Student*

To treat your facts with imagination is one thing, to imagine your facts is another.

> JOHN BURROUGHS,
> *The Heart of Burroughs' Journals*

The sense of relief and freedom which always followed when I managed to bring myself to ask, "What are the facts?" instead of, "What shall I do?" was like waking up from one of those tiresome dreams in which one is continually involved in futile efforts, such as trying to pack and catch a train and everything goes wrong.

JOANNA FIELD,
A Life of One's Own

Facts are carpet-tacks under the pneumatic tires of theory.

AUSTIN O'MALLEY,
Keystones of Thought

Let us take things as we find them: let us not attempt to distort them into what they are not. True philosophy deals with facts. We cannot make facts. All our wishing cannot change them. We must use them.

JOHN HENRY CARDINAL NEWMAN,
Oxford University Sermons

In the spider-web of facts, many a truth is strangled.

PAUL ELDRIDGE,
Horns of Glass

FAD (*See* FASHION, FOLLY)

FAILURE

Doing is overrated, and success undesirable, but the bitterness of Failure even more so.

CYRIL CONNOLLY,
The Unquiet Grave

The psychotherapist learns little or nothing from his successes. They mainly confirm him in his mistakes, while his failures, on the other hand, are priceless experiences in that they not only open up the way to a deeper truth, but force him to change his views and methods.

C. G. JUNG,
Modern Man in Search of a Soul

My own errors, my looseness, my constant experiment—and failure is the only decent thing about me, man. I would like you to understand that, man.

I would like you to comprehend freely that what is to be got at to make the air sweet, the ground good under the feet, can only be got at by failure, trial, again and again and again failure.

SHERWOOD ANDERSON,
Letters of Sherwood Anderson

We are perhaps too prone to get our ideas and standards of worth from the successful, without reflecting that the interpretations of life which patriotic legend, copybook philosophy, and the sayings of the wealthy give us, are pitifully inadequate for those who fall behind in the race.

RANDOLPH BOURNE,
Youth and Life

I suppose that there is no one who had failed but knows that at least he need not have failed as badly as he did, and can see in looking back, calls and opportunities to which if he had corresponded the results would have been very different.

BASIL W. MATURIN,
Laws of the Spiritual Life

One may be very merciful in one's judgments on those who fail in some ways, and very unmerciful on those who fail in others.

BASIL W. MATURIN,
Laws of the Spiritual Life

Half the failures in life arise from pulling in one's horse as he is leaping.

J. C. AND A. W. HARE,
Guesses at Truth

Is it age, or was it always my nature, to take a bad time, block out the good times, until any success became an accident and failure seemed the only truth?

LILLIAN HELLMAN,
An Unfinished Woman

Perhaps the only real failure is that implying waste—a conscious and flagrant nonuse or misuse of ability. If one paints barns when he might paint Madonnas, because immediate gain is better than deferred fortune . . . or if, scorning ideals, one surrenders himself meekly to custom while possessing the ability to create precedents and force issues—these I might call failure.

JOSEPH H. ODELL,
Unmailed Letters

When we can begin to take our failures non-seriously, it means we are ceasing to be afraid of them. It is of immense importance to learn to laugh at ourselves.

KATHERINE MANSFIELD,
The Journal of Katherine Mansfield

The fear of failure is a realistic one because, in general, the chances of failing are much greater than those of succeeding and because failures in a competitive society entail a realistic frustration of needs. They mean not only economic insecurity, but also loss of prestige and all kinds of emotional frustration.

KAREN HORNEY,
The Neurotic Personality of Our Time

Many a man ends in failure because he forces himself to explain to himself in advance just what it is he is going to do to win success.

ANONYMOUS (HENRY S. HASKINS),
Meditations in Wall Street

The gain isn't counted to the recluse and inactive that, having nothing to measure themselves by and never being tested by failure, they simmer and soak perpetually in conscious complacency.

ALICE JAMES,
The Diary of Alice James

We fail far more often by timidity than by over-daring.

DAVID GRAYSON,
The Friendly Road

One of the reasons mature people stop learning is that they become less and less willing to risk failure.

JOHN W. GARDNER,
No Easy Victories, edited by Helen Rowan

Failure sometimes enlarges the spirit. You have to fall back upon humanity and God.

CHARLES HORTON COOLEY,
Life and the Student

Incompetence has one other advantage. Not only does it reduce what others expect and demand of you, it reduces what you expect or even hope for yourself. When you set out to fail, one thing is certain—you can't be disappointed. As the old saying goes, you can't fall out of bed when you sleep on the floor.

JOHN HOLT,
How Children Fail

Children who depend heavily on adult approval may decide that, if they can't have total success, their next-best bet is to have total failure. Perhaps, in using the giving and withholding of approval as a way of making children do what we want, we are helping to make these deliberate failers.

JOHN HOLT,
How Children Fail

Persistent failure of one sort and another—job-failure among them—is, we have come to recognize, a not infrequent device for self-punishment.

BONARO OVERSTREET,
Understanding Fear in Ourselves and Others

The man who fails because he aims astray or because he does not aim at all is to be found everywhere.

FRANK SWINNERTON,
The Tokefield Papers

Dividing people into successes and failures means looking upon human nature from the narrow, preconceived point of view. . . . Are you a failure or not? Am I? Napoleon? Your servant Vasili? Where is the criterion? One must be God to be able to distinguish successes from failures and not make mistakes.

ANTON CHEKHOV,
The Selected Letters of Anton Chekhov

Failure at a task may be the result of having tackled it at the wrong time. Therefore, wisdom decrees that we try it again at what may prove to be precisely the right moment.

BRENDAN FRANCIS

FAITH

We must have infinite faith in each other. If we have not, we must never let it leak out that we have not.

HENRY DAVID THOREAU,
Journal

Religious faith, indeed, relates to that which is above us, but it must arise from that which is within us.

JOSIAH ROYCE,
William James and Other Essays on the Philosophy of Life

Things unseen have a light of their own.

RAOUL PLUS,
Living with God

No faith today can be so certain as to call doubt madness. It is in fact the mark of all genuine faith that while the affirmative choice is made, the struggle toward it is great and uneven, and the adversary is not slighted. All the rest is complacence.

ISAAC ROSENFELD,
An Age of Enormity

It is by believing in roses that one brings them to bloom.

FRENCH PROVERB

Faith . . . acts promptly and boldly on the occasion, on slender evidence, as if guessing and reaching forward to the truth, amid darkness or confusion.

JOHN HENRY CARDINAL NEWMAN,
Oxford University Sermons

Great is his faith who does believe his eyes.

COVENTRY PATMORE,
The Rod, the Root, and the Flower

There is a moral faith which is a virtue—faith in a friend for example. Is there not an intellectual faith which is a virtue, which holds fast when proof fails? I believe there is such an intellectual faith and that it is a sign of strength.

MARK RUTHERFORD,
Last Pages from a Journal

A person consists of his faith. Whatever is his faith, even so is he.

HINDU PROVERB

It is faith and not reason which impels men to action. . . . Intelligence is content to point out the road but never drives us along it.

ALEXIS CARREL,
Reflections on Life

A man's faith can go down to zero without being shaken by doubt.

HENRI DE LUBAC,
Paradoxes

Faith is the sturdiest, the most manly of the virtues. It lies behind our pluckiest, blindest, most heartbreaking strivings. It is the virtue of the storm, just as happiness is the virtue of the sunshine. It is a mistake to feel that it has to do only with the future: faith in the present too has the weight of all authority behind it.

RUTH BENEDICT,
An Anthropologist at Work
by Margaret Mead

All our language is personal; we cannot hand our faith to one another. This has always been true. Even in the Middle Ages when faith was theoretically uniform it was always practically individual.

JOHN JAY CHAPMAN,
Memories and Milestones

It was the central excitement of one's life that one had to take every article—even God Himself—on faith.

ROBERT SPEAIGHT,
The Unbroken Heart

The great act of faith is when a man decides he is not God.

OLIVER WENDELL HOLMES, JR.,
The Mind and Faith of Justice Holmes,
edited by Max Lerner

But then I remembered the faith that I partly have expressed, faith in a universe not measured by our fears, a universe that has thought and more than thought inside of it, and as I gazed, after the sunset and above the electric lights there shone the stars.

OLIVER WENDELL HOLMES, JR.,
The Mind and Faith of Justice Holmes,
edited by Max Lerner

It is a fact of human nature that men can live and die by the help of a sort of faith that goes without a single dogma or definition.

WILLIAM JAMES,
The Will to Believe

If you can't have faith in what is held up to you for faith, you must find things to believe in yourself, for a life without faith in something is too narrow a space to live.

GEORGE E. WOODBERRY,
Selected Letters of George Edward Woodberry

Your faith is what you believe, not what you know.

JOHN LANCASTER SPALDING,
Means and Ends of Education

FAME

In these days a man is nobody unless his biography is kept so far posted up that it may be ready for the national breakfast table on the morning after his demise.

ANTHONY TROLLOPE,
Doctor Thorne

All men desire fame. I have never known a single exception to that rule, and I doubt if anyone else has.

HILAIRE BELLOC,
The Silence of the Sea

Something in his nature never got over things, never accepted his sudden rise to fame, because all the steps weren't there.

F. SCOTT FITZGERALD,
The Crack-up

If you acquire fame, people begin putting you outside themselves. You are something special. Who wants to be that?

SHERWOOD ANDERSON,
Letters of Sherwood Anderson

The fame of this world vanishes like smoke. That is true enough. But this, too, must be realised, and made real. That is to say, a man must acquire and possess this fame and *then* recognize that it is nothing and leaves his soul empty. Only then is the saying true.

THEODOR HAECKER,
Journal in the Night

The more inward a man's greatness, in proportion to the external show of it, the more substantial, and therefore lasting, his fame.

JOHN AYSCOUGH,
Levia-Pondera

It is a mark of many famous people that they cannot part with their brightest hour: what worked once must always work.

LILLIAN HELLMAN,
Pentimento

Whoe'er among his fellows wins a name
Soon learns that Envy is the price of
    Fame.

ARTHUR BARRY O'NEILL,
"The Price of Fame," *Between the Whiles*

Fame! What a vain word, and what a vain recompense! Since I have known the simple life of the Pacific, I think only of withdrawing myself far from men, and in consequence far from fame: as soon as possible, I shall go and bury my talent among the savages and no more will be heard of me.

PAUL GAUGUIN,
quoted in *Gauguin* by Henri Perruchot

Young man anywhere, in whom something stirs that makes you tremble, profit by the fact that no one knows you! And if they contradict you who hold you of no account, and if they abandon you entirely with whom you go about, and if they would destroy you because of your precious thoughts—what is this obvious danger, which holds you concentrated within yourself, compared to the later, subtle enmity of fame which leaves you harmless by scattering your forces?

RAINER MARIA RILKE,
The Journey of My Other Self

However much gloomy moralists may mock at fame and glory, they are good things not to be disdained by Christians.

P. R. RÉGAMEY,
Poverty

A man comes to be famous because he has the matter of fame within him. To seek for, to hunt after fame, is a vain endeavour.

GOETHE

I am surprised that in my later life I should have become so experienced in taking degrees when as a schoolboy I was so bad at passing examinations. In fact, one might almost say that no one ever passed so few examinations and received so many degrees.

SIR WINSTON CHURCHILL,
A Churchill Reader,
edited by Colin R. Coote

FAMILIARITY

I like familiarity. In me it does not breed contempt. Only more familiarity.

GERTRUDE STEIN,
quoted in *Reader's Digest,* April 1935

When you are accustomed to anything, you are estranged from it.

GEORGE CABOT LODGE,
quoted in *The American Treasury,*
edited by Clifton Fadiman
and Charles Van Doren

People love to recognize, not venture. The former is so much more comfortable and self-flattering.

JEAN COCTEAU,
Writers at Work, Third Series,
edited by George Plimpton

Familiarity causes us to see things according to our prejudices, and the result is that we do not see things as they are.

JAMES MAHONEY,
The Music of Life

The other day I heard about a little boy who was spending the night at his aunt's and complained about the fact that she had turned out the light. "What is the matter with you, Tommy?" asked the aunt. "You sleep in the dark at home, don't you?" "Yes, Auntie," replied the boy, "but it is my own dark."

DR. THEODOR REIK,
Listening with the Third Ear

FAMILY

Fond as we are of our loved ones, there comes at times during their absence an unexplainable peace.

ANNE SHAW,
But Such Is Life

It is only in home-relations that people are true enough to each other,—and show what human nature is, the beauty of it, the divinity of it. We are otherwise all on our guard against each other.

LAFCADIO HEARN,
Lafcadio Hearn: Life and Letters,
edited by Elizabeth Bisland

Where does the family start? It starts with a young man falling in love with a girl—no superior alternative has yet been found.

SIR WINSTON CHURCHILL,
A Churchill Reader,
edited by Colin R. Coote

Every large family has its angel and its demon.

JOSEPH ROUX,
Meditations of a Parish Priest

Family quarrels are bitter things. They don't go according to any rules. They're not like aches or wounds; they're more like splits in the skin that won't heal because there's not enough material.

F. SCOTT FITZGERALD,
The Crack-up

Surface togetherness—the-family-that-plays-together-stays-together kind of thing—serves a desirable end when it isn't carried to absurd extremes. But when it becomes an end in itself, it definitely turns into a specious form of personal communication.

MYRON BRENTON,
The American Male

Of late years, the family has got hold of man, and begun to destroy him. When a man is clutched by his family, his deeper social instincts and intuitions are all thwarted, he becomes a negative thing.

D. H. LAWRENCE,
Assorted Articles

There is no group so uncongenial as an uncongenial family.

RANDOLPH BOURNE,
Youth and Life

There's plenty of peace in any home where the family don't make the mistake of trying to get together.

KIN HUBBARD,
Abe Martin's Barbed Wire

In every dispute between parent and child, both cannot be right, but they may be, and usually are, both wrong. It is this situation which gives family life its peculiar hysterical charm.

ISAAC ROSENFELD,
An Age of Enormity

So much of what is best in us is bound up in our love of family, that it remains the measure of our stability because it measures our sense of loyalty. All other pacts of love or fear derive from it and are modeled upon it.

HANIEL LONG,
A Letter to St. Augustine

Each family, however modest its origin, possesses its own particular tale of the past—a tale which can bewitch us with as great a sense of insistent romance as can ever the traditions of kings.

LLEWELYN POWYS,
Earth Memories

It is pleasant to have the family grow, too; in the chances of this world, the more the merrier is the best motto; I have always a little uneasiness when there is only one child. It is too much to stake so much love singly. I suppose the same argument would lead to polygamy, but you know it's dangerous to press even the best logic to the extremity of wisdom. One gets into trouble so.

GEORGE E. WOODBERRY,
Selected Letters of George Edward Woodberry

Without a family, man, alone in. the world, trembles with the cold.

ANDRÉ MAUROIS,
The Art of Living

The levelling influence of mediocrity and the denial of the supreme importance of the mind's development account for many revolts against family life.

ANDRÉ MAUROIS,
The Art of Living

A friend loves you for your intelligence, a mistress for your charm, but your family's love is unreasoning; you were born into it and are of its flesh and blood. Nevertheless it can irritate you more than any group of people in the world.

ANDRÉ MAUROIS,
The Art of Living

One would think that near relations, who live constantly together, and always have done so, must be pretty well acquainted with one another's characters. They are nearly in the dark about it. Familiarity confounds all traits of distinction: interest and prejudice take away the power of judging.

WILLIAM HAZLITT,
quoted in *The Book of Friendship,*
arranged by Arthur Ransome

Among the various forms of domestic tyranny none occupies a more distinguished place than the tyranny of the weak over the strong.

SIR ARTHUR HELPS,
Companions of My Solitude

The human being cannot live too long in the infantile environment, that is, in the bosom of his family, without serious danger to his psychic health. Life demands from him independence, and he who fails to answer the stern call through childish laziness and timidity is threatened with a neurosis.

C. G, JUNG,
Psychological Reflections,
edited by Jolande Jacobi and R. F. Hull

I don't believe there is any such thing as an ideal social unit. The nuclear family is not large enough to give sufficient variation of experience to children, and should be supplemented. But it does form a solid base of concern and affection where it is integrated into a wider community of kinship.

ELIZABETH JANEWAY,
Open Secrets by Barbaralee Diamonstein

One thing is certain, that as much fine humanity is wrecked by family restrictions as by the very passion that seeks to break through these barriers.

RICARDA HUCH,
The Book of Marriage,
edited by Count Hermann Keyserling

The lack of emotional security of our American young people is due, I believe, to their isolation from the large family unit. No two people—no mere father and mother—as I have often said, are enough to provide emotional security for a child. He needs to feel himself one in a world of kinfolk, persons of variety in age and temperament, and yet allied to himself by an indissoluble bond which he cannot break if he would, for nature has welded him into it before he was born.

PEARL BUCK,
To My Daughters, with Love

Men say to us, "There is this problem of the family. How are we to preserve it? It seems to be dissolving before our eyes." That has been true perhaps always and everywhere. Everywhere good things have seemed to be going. Yet everywhere they are merely struggling to their new birth.

BEDE JARRETT,
The House of Gold

FANATIC

Fanatics in power and the funnel of a tornado have this in common—the narrow path in which they move is marked by violence and destruction.

OSCAR OSTLUND,
Nature Magazine, October 1950

History teaches us that no one feels so disgustingly cèrtain of victory, or is so unteachably sure, and immune to reason, as the fanatic, and that no one is so absolutely certain of ultimate defeat.

THEODOR HAECKER,
Journal in the Night

Hitler's hand rustled across the map.

"I always hear figures," he said in a low, shaky voice. Suddenly he spoke more firmly. "I hear nothing about the inner strength of the troops. All that is needed is

fanatical faith. Our movement has shown"—he now shouted—"our movement has shown that faith moves mountains. If your soldiers are filled with fanatical faith they will stand their ground, they will win this battle on which hinges the fate of Germany.... The one thing that counts today is who has the stronger faith, who can outlast the other. And it is going to be me, and every soldier on the Oder must know that, and must believe it fanatically."

JÜRGEN THORWALD,
The Flight in the Winter

Fanatics seldom laugh. They never laugh at themselves.

JAMES GILLIS,
In This Our Day

The downright fanatic is nearer to the heart of things than the cool and slippery disputant.

E. H. CHAPIN

We wonder at the growth of fanatical movements, but it is more necessary that an idea should be active and communicable than that it should be reasonable. Or rather whatever releases activity along lines of desire will commonly appear reasonable. And any such movement gives the participant a sense of importance that the saner world may refuse.

CHARLES HORTON COOLEY,
Life and the Student

FANTASY

It is far harder to kill a phantom than a reality.

VIRGINIA WOOLF,
Virginia Woolf by Monique Nathan

The true nature of things, truth itself, can be revealed to us only by fantasy, which is more realistic than all the realisms.

EUGÈNE IONESCO,
quoted in *The Theatre of the Absurd*
by Martin Esslin

Fantasy is revealing; it is a method of cognition: everything that is imagined is true;

nothing is true if it is not imagined.

EUGÈNE IONESCO,
quoted in *The Theatre of the Absurd*
by Martin Esslin

All prisoners engaged in a great deal of daydreaming. Both individual and group daydreams were wildly wish-fulfilling and a favorite pastime if the general emotional climate was not too depressed. . . .

In their daydreams they were certain to emerge as prominent leaders of the future, but they were less certain they would continue to live with their wives and children, or to be able to resume their roles as husbands and fathers. Partly these fantasies were an effort to deny their utter dejection, and partly a confession of the feeling that only high public office could help them to regain standing with their families, or win back their own good opinion of themselves.

BRUNO BETTELHEIM,
The Informed Heart

FARMING

I sometimes fancy that I enjoy ploughing and mowing more when other people are engaged in them than if I were working myself. Sweat away, my hearties, I say; I am in the shade of this tree watching you, and enjoying the scene amazingly.

HENRY WARD BEECHER,
Eyes and Ears

The wisest men, in the bulk, are the men who have tilled the earth and whose fathers have tilled it before them, and the least wise, without a doubt, are those who miss the meaning of that august sequence in human affairs.

HILAIRE BELLOC,
The Silence of the Sea

I live in the country. I have no other home. I am impressed with certain things about farmers. One of them is their destructiveness. One of them is their total lack of the appreciation of the beautiful—in the main. There are exceptions. Some of them have an exquisite, sensitive perception of the beautiful which they did not learn in school.

DR. KARL MENNINGER,
A Psychiatrist's World

Husbandry has in our time been glorified in eloquence which for the most part is vain, endeavouring as it does, to prove a falsity—that the agricultural life is, in itself, favourable to gentle emotions, to sweet thoughtfulness, and to all the human virtues. Agriculture is one of the most exhausting forms of toil, and, in itself, by no means conducive to spiritual development.

GEORGE GISSING,
The Private Papers of Henry Ryecroft

FASHION

No woman can look as well out of fashion as in it.

MARK TWAIN,
Mark Twain at Your Fingertips,
edited by Caroline T. Harnsberger

Fashion is a game of hide-and-seek, played between seduction and modesty, with moves so rapid by that, from one minute to another, no one can tell which, or who, is "It."

JAMES LAVER,
Fashion, Art, and Beauty,
The Metropolitan Museum of Art Bulletin,
November 1967

The woman who dresses well draws her husband from another woman's door.

SPANISH PROVERB

Most people in the fashion industry are convinced that women no longer want to look alike. They want to look different in the latest way.

MOLLY IVINS,
New York Times, August 15, 1976

The trouble is, once one has managed to achieve a style that indicates one's status group and expresses one's personality, then a whole herd of Bloomingdale's rack-slappers comes along and copies it, and then one has to start all over.

MOLLY IVINS,
New York Times, August 15, 1976

He who goes against the fashion is himself its slave.

LOGAN PEARSALL SMITH,
quoted in *The Poet's Work* by John Holmes

Each new fashion is novel for a time, and in novelty the easiest satisfaction of vanity is to be attained. It calls for no gifts of mind or person, neither cleverness nor loveliness is required: an empty head can display the most outrageously new sort of hat quite as conspicuously as one filled with all the wisdom of Solomon.

JOHN AYSCOUGH,
Levi-Pondera

The trouble about the fashions is, there are too many going on at once, and you can't follow them all. Sometimes, I think I will give them all up, and just be dowdy.

ROSE MACAULAY,
Personal Pleasures

A man of eighty has outlived probably three new schools of painting, two of architecture and poetry, a hundred in dress.

JOYCE CARY,
Art and Reality

Fashion is as profound and critical a part of the social life of man as sex, and is made up of the same ambivalent mixture of irresistible urges and inevitable taboos.

RENE KONIG,
The Restless Image: A Sociology of Fashion

We smile at the women who are eagerly following the fashions in dress while we are as eagerly following the fashions in thought.

AUSTIN O'MALLEY,
Keystones of Thought

Being "well dressed" is not a question of having expensive clothes or the "right" clothes—I don't care if you're wearing rags—but they must suit you.

LOUISE NEVELSON,
Fashion, Art, and Beauty,
Metropolitan Museum of Art Bulletin,
November 1967

If a woman's young and pretty, I think you can see her good looks all the better for being plainly dressed.

GEORGE ELIOT,
Adam Bede

The caprices of fashion do more than illustrate a woman's capacity or incapacity for selection. They mirror her inward refinements, and symbolize those feminine virtues and vanities which are so closely akin as to be occasionally indistinguishable.

AGNES REPPLIER,
Americans and Others

My idea of chic is that everyone in the world would have the same dress and the chicest woman would be whoever could do the best thing with it.

NORMAN NORELL,
Fashion, Art, and Beauty,
Metropolitan Museum of Art Bulletin,
November 1967

As for fashion, yes, I think short skirts are fine. Why not? They suit the times. I'm tired of all this talk about bad legs. After all, there are a lot of ugly faces hanging out.

NORMAN NORELL,
Fashion, Art, and Beauty,
The Metropolitan Museum of Art Bulletin,
November 1967

Why do fashions in clothes change? Because, really, we ourselves change, in the slow metamorphosis of time. If we imagine ourselves now in the clothes we wore six years ago, we shall see that it is impossible. We are, in some way, different persons now, and our clothes express our different personality.

D. H. LAWRENCE,
Assorted Articles

It is time that we treated life as a joke again, as they did in the really great periods like the Renaissance. Then the young men swaggered down the street with one leg bright red, one leg bright yellow, doublet of puce velvet and yellow feather in silk cap.... If a dozen men would stroll down the Strand and Piccadilly tomorrow, wearing tight scarlet trousers fitting the leg, gay little orange-brown jackets and bright green hats, then the revolution against dullness which we need so much would have begun.

D. H. LAWRENCE,
Assorted Articles

Woman is fine for her own satisfaction alone; man only knows man's insensibility to a new gown.

JANE AUSTEN,
quoted in *Woman in Epigram,*
compiled by Frederick W. Morton

FATE

One of the many lessons that one learns in prison is, that things are what they are and will be what they will be.

OSCAR WILDE,
De Profundis

Fate determines many things, no matter how we struggle.

OTTO WEININGER,
quoted in *The Mind and Death of a Genius*
by David Abrahamsen

"To be master of one's fate" is a crude expression which needs first of all to be interpreted in order to yield its truth. How should I be master of something which as a rule is not in my hands?

THEODOR HAECKER,
Journal in the Night

We talk about fate as if it were something visited upon us; we forget that we create our fate every day we live. And by fate I mean the woes that beset us, which are merely the effects of causes which are not nearly as mysterious as we pretend. Most of the ills we suffer from are directly traceable to our own behaviour.

HENRY MILLER,
A Devil in Paradise

It is to be remarked that a good many people are born curiously unfitted for the fate waiting them on this earth.

JOSEPH CONRAD,
Chance

What an imaginative culture must do in dealing with others is to acquire the habit of regarding everyone except oneself as under the absolute domination of fate in all their ways and words and feelings, while at the same time one recognizes that all one's own ways and words and feelings are under the control of one's own free will.

JOHN COWPER POWYS,
The Meaning of Culture

To guess a man's fate is comparatively easy: to perceive its necessity, its why and wherefore, is given only to the man himself, and then after much seeking and through a mist.

JOHN OLIVER HOBBES,
The Sinner's Comedy

There's much to be said for challenging fate instead of ducking behind it.

DIANA TRILLING,
Selected Letters of D. H. Lawrence,
edited by Diana Trilling

I was thinking of my patients, and how the worst moment for them was when they discovered they were masters of their own fate. It was not a matter of bad or good luck. When they could no longer blame fate, they were in despair.

ANAÏS NIN,
The Diaries of Anaïs Nin, Vol. II

I have always believed that all things depended upon Fortune, and nothing upon ourselves.

LORD BYRON,
quoted in *The Literature of Gossip,*
by Elizabeth Drew

Let us always remember that nothing befalls us that is not of the nature of ourselves. . . . And whether you climb up the mountain or go down the hill to the valley, whether you journey to the end of the world or merely walk round your house, none but yourself shall you meet on the highway of fate.

MAURICE MAETERLINCK

FATHER

You have to dig deep to bury your Daddy.

GYPSY PROVERB

I could not point to any need in childhood as strong as that for a father's protection.

SIGMUND FREUD,
Civilization and Its Discontents

The birth of my son took place on September 6, 1912, in a private hospital on 46th Street. It was a dark and confused rather than a joyful event to me. It wears the same quality in memory as my youthful attempts to pray, a disturbed and earnest but unsuccessful striving after the appropriate emotion.

MAX EASTMAN,
Enjoyment of Living

Men derive more genuine undutiful amusement and companionship from youngsters than do women.

HILDA COLE ESPY,
Ladies' Home Journal, October 1946

This thought lately, that as a little child I had been defeated by my father and because of ambition have never been able to quit the battlefield all these years despite the perpetual defeats I suffer.

FRANZ KAFKA,
The Diaries of Franz Kafka 1914-1923

If a man smiles at home somebody is sure to ask him for money.

WILLIAM FEATHER,
The Business of Life

You hear it said that fathers want their sons to be what they feel they cannot themselves be, but I tell you it also works the other way. A boy wants something very special from his father.

SHERWOOD ANDERSON,
Memoirs

What the father hath hid cometh out in the son; and oft have I found in the son the father's revealed secret.

FRIEDRICH NIETZSCHE,
Thus Spake Zarathustra

I never could dance around you, my father. No one ever danced around you. As soon as I left you, my father, the whole world swung into a symphony.

ANAÏS NIN,
The Diaries of Anaïs Nin, Vol. II

Children want to feel instinctively that their father is behind them as solid as a mountain, but, like a mountain, is something to look up to.

DOROTHY THOMPSON,
Ladies' Home Journal, June 1956

I had not known my father very well. We had got on badly, partly because we shared, in our different fashions, the vice of stubborn pride. When he was dead I realized that I had hardly ever spoken to him. When he had been dead a long time I began to wish I had. It seems to be typical of life in America, where opportunities, real and fancied, are thicker than anywhere else on the globe, that the second generation has no time to talk to the first.

JAMES BALDWIN,
Notes of a Native Son

My daddy doesn't work, he just goes to the office; but sometimes he does errands on the way home.

ANONYMOUS,
Ladies' Home Journal, November 1946

To be sure, working—that is, earning a living—is one aspect of fathering. It's one means that the father has of extending protection to his family. But it's *just* one. If he concentrates on this to the exclusion of other aspects, it becomes not a form of fathering, but an escape.

MYRON BRENTON,
The American Male

I have sometimes thought that a thoroughly judicious father is one of the rarest creatures to be met with.

SIR ARTHUR HELPS,
Companions of My Solitude

To show a child what has once delighted you, to find the child's delight added to your own, so that there is now a double delight seen in the glow of trust and affection, this is happiness.

J. B. PRIESTLEY,
Delight

There are to us no ties at all just in being a father. A son is distinctly an acquired taste. It's the practice of parenthood that makes you feel that, after all, there may be something in it.

HEYWOOD BROUN,
Pieces of Hate

Only a person extraordinarily satisfied with himself can derive pleasure if this child in his house is a little person who gives him back nothing but a reflection. You want a new story and not the old one, which wasn't particularly satisfactory in the first place.

HEYWOOD BROUN,
Pieces of Hate

Presently, I noticed that Jacquelin was getting tired. . . . "Do you want me to carry you?" I asked. "Yes, Henry, please carry me, I'm so tired," she said putting out her arms. I lifted her up and placed her little arms around my neck. . . . Once I had carried my own child this way. . . . How can one say no to a child? How can one be anything but a slave to one's own flesh and blood?

HENRY MILLER,
The Air-Conditioned Nightmare

It is no new observation, I believe, that a lover in most cases has no rival so much to be feared as the father.

CHARLES LAMB,
quoted in *To Be a Father,*
edited by Alvin Schwartz

It is easier for a father to have children than for children to have a real father.

POPE JOHN XXIII,
Reader's Digest, November 1960

The need for a father is as crucial as the need for a son, and the search of each for the other—through all the days of one's life—exempts no one. Happy the man who finds both.

MAX LERNER,
The Unfinished Country

I always found my daughters' beaux
Invisible as the emperor's clothes,
And I could hear of them no more
Than the slamming of an auto door.
My chicks would then slip up to roost;
They were, I finally deduced,

Concealing tactfully, pro tem,
Not boys from me but me from them.

OGDEN NASH,
You Can't Get There from Here

I'm not jealous of Margot [her sister], never have been. I don't envy her good looks or her beauty. It is only that I long for Daddy's real love: not only as his child, but for me—Anne, myself.

ANNE FRANK,
Anne Frank: The Diary of a Young Girl

There has been a succession of women's revolutions in America. But watch out for the revolt of the father, if he should get fed up with feeding others, and get bored with being used, and lay down his tools, and walk off to consult his soul.

MAX LERNER,
The Unfinished Country

The kind of man who thinks that helping with the dishes is beneath him will also think that helping with the baby is beneath him, and then he certainly is not going to be a very successful father.

ELEANOR ROOSEVELT,
Ladies' Home Journal, December 1944

The bitterest "fact" of all is, that I had believed Papa to have loved me more than he obviously does: but I never regret knowledge—I mean I never would *unknow* anything—even were it the taste of apples by the Dead Sea—and this must be accepted like the rest.

ELIZABETH BARRETT BROWNING,
quoted in *Ladies of Literature*
by Laura L. Hinkley

Happy is the child whose father acquits himself with credit in the presence of its friends.

ROBERT LYND,
The Blue Lion

Happy is the father whose child finds his attempts to amuse it amusing.

ROBERT LYND,
The Peal of Bells

There is no good father, that's the rule. Don't lay the blame on men but on the bond of paternity, which is rotten. To beget children, nothing better; to *have* them, what iniquity!

JEAN-PAUL SARTRE,
The Words

Boys and girls need chances to be around their father, to be enjoyed by him and if possible to do things with him. Better to play 15 minutes enjoyably and then say, "Now I'm going to read my paper" than to spend all day at the zoo crossly.

DR. BENJAMIN SPOCK,
Ladies' Home Journal, June 1960

You don't write to your little papa. I think you've forgotten him. How is your health? You're not sick, are you? What are you up to? Have you seen Lyolka? How are your dolls? I thought I'd be getting an order from you soon, but no. Too bad. You're hurting your little papa's feelings. Never mind. I kiss you. I am waiting to hear from you.

JOSEF STALIN,
quoted in *Twenty Letters to a Friend*
by Svetlana Alliluyeva

The years lived by our father before he begot us have upon them a wonder that cannot easily be matched. Just as we feel ourselves half participant in the experiences of our children, so in some dim way do we share in those adventures of this mortal who not so long ago moved over the face of the earth like a god to call us up from the deep.

LLEWELYN POWYS,
Earth Memories

Our three young children are all in Switzerland, the older boy in Munich, and my wife and I are like middle-aged omnibus-horses let loose in a pasture. The first time we have had a holiday together for 15 years; I feel like a barrel without hoops!

WILLIAM JAMES,
The Letters of William James, Vol. I

We think of a father as an old, or at least a middle-aged man. The astounding truth is that most fathers are young men, and that

they make their greatest sacrifices in their youth. I never meet a young man in a public park on Sunday morning wheeling his first baby in a perambulator without feeling an ache of reverence.

JAMES DOUGLAS,
Down Shoe Lane

The father in praising his son extols himself.

CHINESE PROVERB

This is going to be fairly short; to have father's character done complete in it; and mother's; and St. Ives. and childhood; and all the usual things I try to put in—life, death, etc. But the centre is father's character, sitting in a boat, reciting "We perished, each alone," while he crushes a dying mackerel.

VIRGINIA WOOLF,
A Writer's Diary

If you've never seen a real, fully developed look of disgust, just tell your son how you conducted yourself when you were a boy.

KIN HUBBARD,
Abe Martin on Things in General

Thanks for the sweet things you said about my little boy. . . . No man can possibly know what life means, what the world means, what anything means, until he has a child and loves it. And then the whole universe changes and nothing will ever again seem exactly as it seemed before.

LAFCADIO HEARN,
Lafcadio Hearn: Life and Letters, Vol. 2,
edited by Elizabeth Bisland

As my mother had divorced my father when I was a baby in arms, I had never seen him. Once, when I asked one of my aunts whether I ever had a father, she replied, "Your father was a demon who ruined your mother's life." After that I always imagined him as a demon in a picture book, with horns and tail, and when other children at school spoke of their fathers, I kept silent.

ISADORA DUNCAN,
My Life

The father is the guest in the house.

BULGARIAN PROVERB

When a father is indulgent, he is more indulgent than a mother. Little ones treat their mother as the authority of rule, and their father as the authority of dispensation.

FREDERICK W. FABER,
Bethlehem

There is something ultimate in a father's love, something that cannot fail, something to be believed against the whole world. We almost attribute practical omnipotence to our father in the days of our childhood.

FREDERICK W. FABER,
Bethlehem

Father and son are natural enemies and each is happier and more secure in keeping it that way.

JOHN STEINBECK,
quoted in *To Be a Father,*
edited by Alvin Schwartz

In spite of the great difference between the Roman paterfamilias, whose family was his property, and the modern father, the feeling that children are brought into the world to satisfy the parents and compensate them for the disappointments of their own lives is still widespread.

ERICH FROMM,
Man for Himself

One word of command from me is obeyed by millions ... but I cannot get my three daughters, Pamela, Felicity and Joan, to come down to breakfast on time.

VISCOUNT ARCHIBALD WAVELL,
Ladies' Home Journal, November 1945

Once an angry man dragged his father along the ground through his own orchard. "Stop!" cried the groaning old man at last, "Stop! I did not drag my father beyond this tree."

GERTRUDE STEIN,
The Making of Americans

Don't be a lion in your own house.

CZECH PROVERB

My maddening old father is in Italy; and has sent through a message to say that if we cannot send money through to him by December, he will be starving. What an end and climax to a life in which one has been a constant nuisance to one's offspring! Of course Osbert is asking the authorities here what he can do, and what they advise ... but still!

EDITH SITWELL,
Edith Sitwell: Selected Letters 1916-1964

"Yes, they are good boys," I once heard a kind father say. "I talk to them very much, but do not like to beat my children—the world will beat them." It was a beautiful thought, though not elegantly expressed.

ELIHU BURRITT

My father and I were always on the most distant terms when I was a boy—a sort of armed neutrality, so to speak. At irregular intervals this neutrality was broken, and suffering ensued; but I will be candid enough to say that the breaking and suffering were always divided with strict impartiality between us—which is to say, my father did the breaking and I did the suffering.

MARK TWAIN,
quoted in *Mark Twain at Your Fingertips,*
edited by Caroline T. Harnsberger

A man wants to protect his son, wants to teach him the things he, the father, has learned or thinks he has learned. But it's exactly that which a child resents. He wants to know but he wants to know on his own—and the longer the paternal influence lasts the harder it is to break down and the more two individuals who should have much in common are pushed apart. Only a sudden enforced break can get through that one.

WILLIAM CARLOS WILLIAMS,
Selected Letters of William Carlos Williams

I passed through a terrible scourging when last at my father's. I cannot tell you how deep the iron entered my soul. I never felt more deeply the degradation of my sex. To think that all in me of which my father would have felt a proper pride had I been a man, is deeply mortifying to him because I am a woman.

ELIZABETH CADY STANTON,
quoted in *Prudery and Passion*
by Milton Rugoff

Pat went down quietly to his father and sat beside him on the steps, huddling close to the great arched back, the huge hairy arms of him.—And oh, the pain to reach, to touch, to know him, this giant of a man, his father, puffing contentedly on the battered pipe. They sat the two thus silently until the paleness in the sky bled slowly into the dusk, till yellow-gold spatters of light flicked on across the valley.

MICHAEL O'MALLEY,
Miners Hill

It is a delight above all delights to see one's children turn out—as ours have done—all that the heart covets in children; and my delight is so full that I sometimes fancy my heart will have to burst for its own relief.

HENRY JAMES, SR.,
quoted in *The James Family*
by F. O. Matthiessen

FAULT

If the best man's faults were written on his forehead, it would make him pull his hat over his eyes.

GAELIC PROVERB

Ask yourself what your predominant fault is: you have discovered, in a misguided but clearly identified state, your greatest resource.

ANTONIN G. SERTILLANGES,
Rectitude

Happy people rarely correct their faults.

LA ROCHEFOUCAULD,
Maxims

Take your faults with a matter-of-factness that would seem to you almost brutal. Pay no more attention to your moods than a

reasonable person with serious duties on hand, pays to the weather.

JANET ERSKINE STUART,
Life and Letters of Janet Erskine Stuart
by Maud Monahan

When, for unconscious reasons, we develop fear and dislike of someone or something, it is a psychological necessity for us to justify such feelings in order to save our face. Faults found with the feared or disliked person, even when they contain a modicum of truth, can be recognized quite frequently as mirror images of our own faults and feelings.

DR. KARL A. MENNINGER,
The Human Mind

When God wishes a man well, He gives him insight into his faults.

MOHAMMEDAN PROVERB

Men strengthen each other in their faults. Those who are alike associate together, repeat the things which all believe, defend and stimulate their common faults of disposition, and each one receives from the others a reflection of his own egotism.

HENRY WARD BEECHER,
Eyes and Ears

I read biographies, and wish in vain, that there were more lives of imperfect people, or at least more said about men's faults and failures.

A. C. BENSON,
*Excerpts from the Letters of
Dr. A. C. Benson to M. E. A.*

There is only one way of getting rid of one's faults and that is to acquire the habits contradictory to them.

ERNEST DIMNET,
What We Live By

The most frequent mistake is to imagine that one is more natural by letting other people see one's faults than by letting them see one's qualities.

ERNEST DIMNET,
What We Live By

I refuse to live out my flaws. I bury them and condemn them and deny them. Unable to manifest themselves, they inhabit others. In others I accept uncombed hair, a hole in the shoes, a not-too-clean dress, temper, lies, cowardices, treacheries, jealousies. Allowing others to become mad for you, allowing others to complain for you. The guilt involved in this secret participation leads to responsibility for others' lives.

ANAÏS NIN,
The Diaries of Anaïs Nin, Vol. IV

Wink at small faults, for you have great ones yourself.

SCOTTISH PROVERB

People who have no faults are terrible; there is no way of taking advantage of them.

ANATOLE FRANCE,
The Crime of Sylvestre Bonnard

They came to tell your faults to me,
They named them over one by one;
I laughed aloud when they were done,
I knew them all so well before;—
Oh, they were blind, too blind to see
Your faults had made me love you more.

SARA TEASDALE,
"Faults," *Collected Poems of Sara Teasdale*

All wrong translations, all absurdities in geometry problems, all clumsiness of style, and all faulty connection of ideas in compositions and essays, all such things are due to the fact that thought has seized upon some idea too hastily, and being thus prematurely blocked, is not open to the truth. The cause is always that we have wanted to be too active; we have wanted to carry out a search. This can be proved every time, for every fault, if we trace it to its roots. There is no better exercise than such a tracing down of our faults, for this truth is one to be believed only when we have experienced it hundreds and thousands of times. This is the way it is with all essential truths.

SIMONE WEIL,
Waiting for God

Make peace with men and quarrel with your faults.

RUSSIAN PROVERB

We like to find fault ourselves; but we are never attracted to another man who finds fault. It is the last refuge of our good humor that we like to have a monopoly of censure.

FREDERICK W. FABER,
Spiritual Conferences

It is better to run the risk of falling into faults in a course which leads us to act with effect and energy, than to loiter out our days without blame and without use.

EDMUND BURKE,
quoted in *America,* April 4, 1956

In spite of the pain that our friends' faults cause us, we keep up a fantastic pretence of blindness in order that we may remain tolerable to each other. That is why we have to talk behind people's backs. There is no other chance of talking freely.

ROBERT LYND,
The Peal of Bells

It is commonly thought that men most easily condone to themselves their own faults, but it is not always so; and some men who have been "their own worst enemies" find it almost impossible to forgive themselves.

JOSEPH FARRELL,
Lectures of a Certain Professor

Who is so loud in denouncing a fault as he whose inner consciousness tells him that every moment he is on the verge of committing it?

JOSEPH FARRELL,
Lectures of a Certain Professor

He is great whose faults can be numbered.

HEBREW PROVERB

There are only two kinds of perfectly faultless men—the dead and the deadly.

HELEN ROWLAND,
A Guide to Men

Faults are thick where love is thin.

DANISH PROVERB

The business of finding fault is very easy, and that of doing better very difficult.

SAINT FRANCIS DE SALES,
Spiritual Maxims

FEAR

Proust has pointed out that the predisposition to love creates its own objects: is this not true of fear?

ELIZABETH BOWEN,
Collected Impressions

When people feel threatened and anxious they become more rigid, and when in doubt they tend to become dogmatic; and then they lose their own vitality. They use the remnants of traditional values to build a protective encasement and then shrink behind it; or they make an outright panicky retreat into the past.

ROLLO MAY,
Man's Search for Himself

Now there is nothing strange about fear: no matter in what guise it presents itself it is something with which we are all so familiar that when a man appears who is without it we are at once enslaved by him.

HENRY MILLER,
The Wisdom of the Heart

Fears are educated into us, and can, if we wish, be educated out.

DR. KARL A. MENNINGER,
The Human Mind

Fear is a fine spur, so is rage.

IRISH PROVERB

It is the disease you fear that strikes you: for every idea tends to materialize.

C.-F. RAMUZ,
What Is Man?

Fear is never a good counselor and victory over fear is the first spiritual duty of man.

NICHOLAS BERDYAEV,
Towards a New Epoch

Often in my life I have found that the one thing that can save is the thing which appears most to threaten. In peace and war I have found that frequently, naked and unashamed, one has to go down into what one most fears and in that process, from somewhere beyond all conscious expectation, comes a saving flicker of light and energy that, even if it does not produce the courage of a hero, at any rate enables a trembling mortal to take one step further.

LAURENS VAN DER POST,
The Lost World of the Kalahari

When we are afraid we ought not to occupy ourselves with endeavoring to prove that there is no danger but in strengthening ourselves to go on in spite of the danger.

MARK RUTHERFORD,
Last Pages from a Journal

Servile fear is no honor to God; for what father feels honored by his son's dread of the rod?

WALTER ELLIOTT,
The Spiritual Life

We all know individuals who make their lives the exact realization of what they are afraid of.

WALDO FRANK,
Re-discovery of America

Everybody is afraid for himself, and everybody thinks his neighbor's fears ridiculous, as they generally are.

J. A. SPENDER,
The Comments of Bagshot, Second Series

Every man, through fear, mugs his aspirations a dozen times a day.

BRENDAN FRANCIS

I wonder if you know General Grant, great, big, odd child; strange that he should have been a fighter. He was like a field. Nothing jarred him. He had a simple, childlike receipt for meeting life. "I am terribly afraid," he said, "but the other fellow is afraid too."

There is the wisdom of the ages in that simple comment.

SHERWOOD ANDERSON,
Letters of Sherwood Anderson

One has to take some action against fear when once it lays hold of one.

RAINER MARIA RILKE,
The Journal of My Other Self

Fear, true fear, is a savage frenzy. Of all the insanities of which we are capable, it is surely the most cruel. There is nought to equal its drive, and nought can survive its thrust.

GEORGES BERNANOS,
A Diary of My Times

All reigns of Terror are alike, all are of the same origin, you will not get me to distinguish between them. I have seen too much, I know men too well, and I am too old now. Fear disgusts me in everybody, and behind all the fine talk of those butchers, lies fear, and only fear. Massacres are due to fear, hate is but an alibi.

GEORGES BERNANOS,
A Diary of My Times

He who fears something gives it power over him.

MOORISH PROVERB

A man who is not afraid is not aggressive, a man who has no sense of fear of any kind is really a free, a peaceful man.

J. KRISHNAMURTI,
You Are the World

But one should not insult even one's fears.

D. H. LAWRENCE,
Selected Essays

Fear always remains. A man may destroy everything within himself, love and hate and belief, and even doubt; but as long as he clings to life he cannot destroy fear; the fear, subtle, indestructible, and terrible that pervades his being; that tinges his thoughts; that lurks in his heart; that watches on his lips the struggle of his last breath.

JOSEPH CONRAD,
"An Outpost of Progress," *Tales of Unrest*

One can be afraid only of life.

OTTO WEININGER,
quoted in *The Mind and Death of a Genius*
by David Abrahamsen

We do more to disarm those whom we fear than to oblige those whom we love.

J. PETIT-SENN,
Conceits and Caprices

Fear of life in one form or another is the great thing to exorcise; but it isn't reason that will ever do it. Impulse without reason is not enough, and reason without impulse is a poor makeshift.

WILLIAM JAMES,
The Letters of William James, Vol. II

How very little can be done under the spirit of fear! It is the very sentence pronounced upon the serpent: "Upon thy belly shalt thou go all the days of thy life."

FLORENCE NIGHTINGALE,
quoted in *The Bliss of the Way,*
compiled by Cecily Hallack

The wise man in the storm prays God, not for safety from danger, but for deliverance from fear. It is the storm within which endangers him, not the storm without.

RALPH WALDO EMERSON,
Journals of Ralph Waldo Emerson

Fear has a smell, as love does.

MARGARET ATWOOD,
Surfacing

Where there is no capacity to affirm another as a person *in his own right* there is no love. There is only masked fear.

BONARO OVERSTREET,
Understanding Fear in Ourselves and Others

Perhaps the most important thing we can undertake toward the reduction of fear is to make it easier for people to accept themselves; to like themselves.

BONARO OVERSTREET,
Understanding Fear in Ourselves and Others

One give-away symptom by which *fear disguised as goodness* shows itself not to be genuine goodness is its tendency to define virtue in negative rather than positive terms: in terms of *refraining from* rather than in terms of productive outreach; of resisting temptation rather than of affirming life.

BONARO OVERSTREET,
Understanding Fear in Ourselves and Others

I'd forgotten something else that he talked about. He said, "I don't know what fear is, except when I think of my own shortcomings. But I'm getting over that too."

ANNE FRANK,
Anne Frank: The Diary of a Young Girl

All the passions seek whatever nourishes them: fear loves the idea of danger.

JOSEPH JOUBERT,
Pensées

To relinquish a present good through apprehension of a future evil is in most instances unwise, unless the evil be very certain and near, or far exceed the good in degree. Otherwise, from a fear which may afterwards turn out groundless, you lost the good that lay within your grasp.

FRANCESCO GUICCIARDINI,
Counsels and Reflections

FIND

It is curious how long the childish delight of *finding* something, quite apart from its value, survives in one—but it does survive.

A. C. BENSON,
Excerpts from the Letters of Dr. A. C. Benson to M. E. A.

The special quality of the act of finding something, with its consequent exhilaration, is half unexpectedness and half separateness. There being no warning, and the article coming to you by chance, no one is to be thanked, no one to be owed anything. In short, you have achieved the greatest human triumph—you have got something for nothing.

E. V. LUCAS,
365 Days and One More

FIRE

Never neglect your fireplace. Much of the cheerfulness of life depends upon it. What makes a fire so pleasant is, I think, that it is a live thing in a dead room.

SYDNEY SMITH,
quoted in *Ladies' Home Journal*,
June 1947

Never in all my life have I made an attempt to light, rearrange or even poke a fire that some man hasn't leaped to his feet and with a "Let me do that" snatched the implements from my reluctant hands

and spoiled all my fun.... And what's worse, I have to thank him.

CORNELIA OTIS SKINNER,
Dithers and Jitters

I find one's room—one's own special den—never looks to such advantage as it does in the firelight. All its shortcomings are smoothed over, all the errors you may have made in color or arrangement are lost sight of, and everything gains in value by the sombre shadows and the fitful flutter of the flames.

J. ASHBY-STERRY,
Cucumber Chronicles

Fairylike, the fire rose in two branched flames like the golden antlers of some enchanted stag.

KATHERINE MANSFIELD,
The Journal of Katherine Mansfield

What a divine gift is fire. In the clearing up that I have nearly finished I have cut short a thousand hesitations and shut out many fool vistas of possible interest by burning odds and ends. Civilization is the process of reducing the infinite to the finite.

OLIVER WENDELL HOLMES, JR.,
Holmes-Pollock Letters, Vol. II

The next thing that came out of my pocket was a box of matches. Then I saw fire, which is stronger even than steel, the old, fierce female thing, the thing we all love, but dare not touch.

G. K. CHESTERTON,
Tremendous Trifles

In winter a fire is better than a muscat rose.

PERSIAN PROVERB

People who light fires on the slightest provocation are always the nicest. There's something comforting about fires.

JANE ENGLAND,
quoted in the *New York Times*,
September 26, 1948

I was at a fire the other night and heard a man say: "That corner stack is alight now quite nicely." People's sympathies seem generally to be with the fire so long as no one is in danger of being burned.

SAMUEL BUTLER,
Samuel Butler's Notebooks

Fire drives a thorn of memory in the heart.

THOMAS WOLFE,
Of Time and the River

What a friendly and companionable thing is a campfire! How generous and outright it is! It plays for you when you wish to be lively, and it glows for you when you wish to be reflective.

DAVID GRAYSON,
The Friendly Road

The fire had died down to a great coal pinned like a crimson rose to the dark earth.

LAURENS VAN DER POST,
The Lost World of the Kalahari

We human beings see things in the fire. To gaze into the glowing heat is to gaze into the light: the fire is our magic crystal. It helps us to see visions and to dream dreams. To put out the fire is to put out the light.

HOLBROOK JACKSON,
Southward Ho! and Other Essays

Now when the hearth burns with a rich glow and the chairs circle round the warmth, in the twilight when it seems a fault to light up, man harks back to his dim beginnings. His contented silence as he watches the embers form strange fantasies to fit his dreams; his sense of peace and comfort is charged with a thousand memories born out of the unfathomable past.

HOLBROOK JACKSON,
Southward Ho! and Other Essays

One can enjoy a wood fire worthily only when he warms his thoughts by it as well as his hands and feet.

ODELL SHEPARD,
quoted in the *New York Times,*
December 11, 1949

FISHING

A trout is a fish known mainly by hearsay.

It lives on anything not included in a fisherman's equipment.

H. I. PHILLIPS,
On White or Rye

A gentleman trying to get a fly out of the milk or a piece of cork out of his glass of wine often imagines himself to be irritated. Let him think for a moment of the patience of anglers sitting by dark pools, and let his soul be immediately irradiated with gratification and repose.

G. K. CHESTERTON,
All Things Considered

The attraction of angling for all the ages of man, from the cradle to the grave, lies in its uncertainty. 'Tis an affair of luck.

HENRY VAN DYKE,
Fisherman's Luck

The curious thing about fishing is you never want to go home. If you catch anything, you can't stop. If you don't catch anything, you hate to leave in case something might bite.

GLADYS TABER,
Ladies' Home Journal, July 1941

Someone just back of you while you are fishing is as bad as someone looking over your shoulder while you write a letter to your girl.

ERNEST HEMINGWAY,
By-Line: Ernest Hemingway,
edited by William White

If you are lucky, sooner or later there will be a swirl or a double swirl where the trout strikes and misses and strikes again, and then the old, deathless thrill of the plunge of the rod and the irregular plunging, circling, cutting up stream and shooting into the air fight the big trout puts up, no matter what country he may be in.

ERNEST HEMINGWAY,
By-Line: Ernest Hemingway,
edited by William White

Probably it was in that moment that all the bickerings and back-talk of husbands and wives originated; when Adam called to Eve to come and look at his First Fish while it was still silver and vivid in its living colors; and Eve answered she was busy.

CHRISTOPHER MORLEY,
Mince Pie

If you wish to be happy for an hour, get intoxicated.
If you wish to be happy for three days, get married.
If you wish to be happy for eight days, kill your pig and eat it.
If you wish to be happy forever, learn to fish.

CHINESE PROVERB,
New York State Conservationist,
June-July 1955

The charm of fishing is that it is the pursuit of what is elusive but attainable, a perpetual series of occasions for hope.

JOHN BUCHAN,
quoted in the *New York Times,*
April 15, 1951

It is not a fish until it is on the bank.

IRISH PROVERB

There is peculiar pleasure in catching a trout in a place where nobody thinks of looking for them, and at an hour when everybody believes they cannot be caught.

HENRY VAN DYKE,
quoted in the *New York Times,*
April 6, 1952

Our idea of fishing is to put all the exertion up to the fish. If they are ambitious we will catch them. If they are not, let them go about their business.

DON MARQUIS,
Prefaces

All Americans believe that they are born fishermen. For a man to admit a distaste for fishing would be like denouncing mother-love or hating moonlight.

JOHN STEINBECK,
Reader's Digest, December 1954

A beautiful stream to one man is just so much water in which he may possibly catch so many fish.

ARTHUR BRISBANE,
The Book of Today

If there is to be adequate chivalry in the pastime no man should be allowed a rod and line until he has first signed an agreement that every time he fails to pull a hooked fish out of the water he himself will accept and signalize defeat by jumping into the lake. The man gets the fish or the fish gets the man. I can see no other fair way.

HEYWOOD BROUN,
Sitting on the World

Bragging may not bring happiness, but no man having caught a large fish goes home through an alley.

ANONYMOUS,
Reader's Digest, February 1949

There is no use in your walking five miles to fish when you can depend on being just as unsuccessful near home.

MARK TWAIN

FLATTERY

In vain does flattery swell a little virtue to a mountain; self-love can swallow it like a mustard seed.

J. PETIT-SENN,
Conceits and Caprices

It is natural to despise those who court us, for they are beggars who need not beg.

JOHN LANCASTER SPALDING,
Aphorisms and Reflections

Flattery is the politeness of contempt.

JOHN LANCASTER SPALDING,
Aphorisms and Reflections

Would you continue to enjoy the sunshine of my smiles you must also abstain from flattery (at least of the *common sort*). ... I value one compliment to my judgment above twenty to my person (for the latter, my glass declares to me every morning, is totally unmerited, whereas I may be tempted to believe the former has some foundation).

JANE WELSH CARLYLE,
quoted in *Necessary Evil*
by Laurence and Elisabeth Hanson

Attention is a silent and perpetual flattery.
MADAME SWETCHINE,
The Writings of Madame Swetchine

It must be a rock-bound kind of person that remains unmoved when a pleasant warm gush of flattery is playing on him. The best of us suspend all critical self-examination at such a moment.
FRANK MOORE COLBY,
The Colby Essays, Vol. 2

The sweet inebriant only comes my way on occasion, and stays not long enough to obliviate that negligence which is man's normal earthly portion. I would that it were otherwise.
ROSE MACAULAY,
Personal Pleasures

Flattery is praise insincerely given for an interested purpose.
HENRY WARD BEECHER,
Eyes and Ears

Flattery must be pretty thick before anybody objects to it.
WILLIAM FEATHER,
The Business of Life

The very people who require you to court their favor despise a flatterer and surrender to a master.
A. G. SERTILLANGES,
The Intellectual Life

We should have very little pleasure were we never to flatter ourselves.
LA ROCHEFOUCAULD,
Maxims

Words really flattering are not those which we prepare but those which escape us unthinkingly.
NINON DE LENCLOS

FLOWERS

Flowers often grow more beautifully on dung-hills than in gardens that look beautifully kept.
SAINT FRANCIS DE SALES,
Saint Francis de Sales in His Letters

I have noticed the almost selfish passion for their flowers which old gardeners have, and their reluctance to part with a leaf or a blossom from their family. They love the flowers for themselves.
CHARLES DUDLEY WARNER,
Backlog Studies

When you look at a flower, at a color, without naming it, without like or dislike, without any screen between you and the thing you see as a flower, without the word, without thought, then the flower has an extraordinary color and beauty. But when you look at the flower through botanical knowledge, when you say: "This is a rose," you have already conditioned your response.
J. KRISHNAMURTI,
You Are the World

A house with daffodils in it is a house lit up, whether or no the sun be shining outside. Daffodils in a green bowl—and let it snow if it will.
A. A. MILNE,
Not That It Matters

When worshipers offer flowers at the altar, they are returning to the gods things which they know, or (if they are not visionaries) obscurely feel, to be indigenous to heaven.
ALDOUS HUXLEY,
Heaven and Hell

If there were nothing else to trouble us, the fate of the flowers would make us sad.
JOHN LANCASTER SPALDING,
Aphorisms and Reflections

If I had but two loaves of bread, I would sell one and buy hyacinths, for they would feed my soul.
THE KORAN

Flowers perish so fast that often we should scarcely value their lovely fragility except as the symbol and token of something quite as lovely and not so frail.
OSCAR W. FIRKINS,
Oscar Firkins: Memoirs and Letters,
edited by Ina Ten Eyck

The fairest thing in nature, a flower, still has its roots in earth and manure.

D. H. LAWRENCE,
D. H. Lawrence: Selected Literary Criticism,
edited by Anthony Beal

No wild flowers, however wild, are rebels.

ALICE MEYNELL,
The Colour of Life

Nobody sees a flower—really—it is so small—we haven't time—and to see takes time like to have a friend takes time.

GEORGIA O'KEEFFE,
Life, March 1, 1968

I've always hated artificial flowers unless they were just flagrantly and beautifully, sort of brassily, artificial. But the good imitations, the ones that you think are real until you get up to them, and then there's that awful dead plastic, are really vile. And the reason why I think they're so vile is because so much of the beauty of a flower is in its very perishableness. One doesn't want it to last forever and accumulate dust.

DENISE LEVERTOV,
The Craft of Poetry,
edited by William Packard

It gives one a sudden start in going down a barren, stony street, to see upon a narrow strip of grass, just within the iron fence, the radiant dandelion, shining in the grass, like a spark dropped from the sun.

HENRY WARD BEECHER,
Eyes and Ears

Flowers . . . have a mysterious and subtle influence upon the feelings, not unlike some strains of music. They relax the tenseness of the mind. They dissolve its rigor.

HENRY WARD BEECHER,
Eyes and Ears

For me huge flower masses hold no particular delight. Such effects could be created as easily by a house painter. An individual blossom, with its delicacies and magical personal distinction, affords me the greater pleasure.

EDEN PHILLPOTTS,
A Year with Bisshe-Bantam

Misshapen, black, unlovely to the sight,
O mute companion of the murky mole,
You must feel overjoyed to have a white
Imperious, dainty lily for a soul.

RICHARD KENDRELL MUNKITTRICK,
"A Bulb," *Poems One Line and Longer,*
edited by William Cole

You buy some flowers for your table;
You tend them tenderly as you're able;
You fetch them water from hither and thither—
What thanks do you get for it all? They wither.

SAMUEL HOFFENSTEIN,
Untitled, *Poems in Praise
of Practically Nothing*

Flowers are restful to look at. They have neither emotions nor conflicts.

SIGMUND FREUD,
quoted by Alfred Kazin in
the *New York Times,* May 5, 1956

The career of flowers differs from ours only in audibleness. I feel more reverence for these mute creatures whose suspense or transport may surpass our own.

EMILY DICKINSON,
Selected Poems and Letters of Emily Dickinson

I wish I could show you the hyacinths that embarrass us by their loveliness, though to cower before a flower is perhaps unwise, but beauty is often timidity—perhaps oftener pain.

EMILY DICKINSON,
Selected Poems and Letters of Emily Dickinson

It is so wrong to think of the beauty of flowers only when they are at their height of blooming; bud and half developed flower, fading blossom and seed pod are as lovely, and often more interesting.

CLARE LEIGHTON,
Four Hedges

We once had a lily here that bore *108* flowers on one stalk: it was photographed naturally for all the gardening papers. The bees came from miles and miles, and there were the most disgraceful Bacchanalian scenes: bees hardly able to find their way home.

EDITH SITWELL,
Edith Sitwell: Selected Letters 1916–1964

I once saw a botanist most tenderly re-
place a plant which he had inadvertently
uprooted, though we were on a bleak hillside in Tibet, where no human being was
likely to see the flower again.

> SIR FRANCIS YOUNGHUSBAND,
> quoted in the *New York Times,*
> March 7, 1948

I kept looking at the flowers in a vase near
me: lavender sweet peas, fragile winged
and yet so still, so perfectly poised, apart
and complete. . . . But flowers *always* have
it—poise, completion, fulfillment, perfection; I, only occasionally, like that moment. For that moment I and the sweet
peas had an understanding.

> ANNE MORROW LINDBERGH,
> *Bring Me a Unicorn*

Arranging a bowl of flowers in the morning can give a sense of quiet in a crowded
day—like writing a poem, or saying a
prayer.

> ANNE MORROW LINDBERGH,
> *Gift from the Sea*

It is nice to be a flower; but it is perhaps
better to be a man, if one can.

> ROMAIN ROLLAND,
> *Letters of Romain Rolland
> and Malwida von Meyserling*

There are many bees, small wild solitary
bees, that will take only the nectar of certain short-lived and local wildflowers. . . .
And often the flower must wait for this
one right consummation, out of a world of
flitting insect wings.

> DONALD CULROSS PEATTIE,
> *The Flowering Earth*

One sure way to lose another woman's
friendship is to try to improve her flower
arrangements.

> MARCELENE COX,
> *Ladies' Home Journal,* February 1948

I like to see flowers growing, but when
they are gathered they cease to please. I
never offer flowers to those I love; I never
wish to receive them from hands dear to
me.

> CHARLOTTE BRONTË,
> *Villette*

FOLLY

Folly will find a place even at the side of
princes. That was the thing symbolized by
great men's jesters.

> SIR ARTHUR HELPS,
> *Companions of My Solitude*

The more general the folly of mankind,
the more likely is the critic himself to
share it, especially as folly is a thing that
folly is prone to impute.

> GEORGE SANTAYANA,
> *Obiter Scripta*

Our wisdom, whether expressed in private
or in public belongs to the world, but our
folly belongs to those we love.

> G. K. CHESTERTON,
> quoted in *The Bliss of the Way,*
> compiled by Cecily Hallack

I believe more follies are committed out of
complaisance to the world, than in following our own inclinations.

> LADY MARY WORTLEY MONTAGU,
> *The Complete Letters of
> Lady Mary Wortley Montagu,* Vol. I

The follies which a man regrets the most,
in his life, are those which he didn't commit when he had the opportunity.

> HELEN ROWLAND,
> *A Guide to Men*

Leave each one his touch of folly; it helps
to lighten life's burden which, if he could
see himself as he is, might be too heavy to
carry.

> JOHN LANCASTER SPALDING,
> *Thoughts and Theories of Life and Education*

Much prudence does not always keep one
from committing follies, nor much sense
from thinking them, nor much wit from
uttering them.

> JOSEPH ROUX,
> *Meditations of a Parish Priest*

FOOD

More eating of corn bread would I'm sure
make a better foundation for an American
literature. The white bread we eat is to

corn bread what Hollywood will be to real American dramatic literature when it comes.

SHERWOOD ANDERSON,
Memoirs

Shall we never learn the worthlessness of other people's views of food?

There is no authoritative body of comment on food. Like all the deeper personal problems of life, you must face it alone.

FRANK MOORE COLBY,
The Colby Essays, Vol. 2

The best bill of fare I know of is a good appetite.

JOSH BILLINGS,
His Works Complete

You can put everything, and the more things the better, into salad, as into a conversation; but everything depends upon the skill of mixing.

CHARLES DUDLEY WARNER,
My Summer in a Garden

Talking of Pleasure, this moment I was writing with one hand and with the other holding to my Mouth a Nectarine—good God how fine. It went down soft, pulpy, slushy, oozy—all its delicious embodiment melted down my throat like a large Beautiful, strawberry. I shall certainly breed.

JOHN KEATS,
The Selected Letters of John Keats

Now and then it is a joy to have one's table red with wine and roses.

OSCAR WILDE,
De Profundis

A dog will carry his bone to a private nook and do his gnawing undisturbed, but civilized man wants companions who can talk, to nourish his mind as well as his body.

JOHN ERSKINE,
The Complete Life

Since hunger is the most primitive and permanent of human wants, men always eat, but since their wish not to be a mere animal is also profound, they have always attended with special care to the manners which conceal the fact that at the table we are animals feeding.

JOHN ERSKINE,
The Complete Life

If there were no such thing as eating, we should have to invent it to save man from despairing.

DR. WILHELM STEKHEL,
The Depths of the Soul

It is not a meaningless custom that we honor distinguished persons by dining them. By so doing we create a situation in which there is no superiority and in which we feel ourselves at one with the great man and on a level with him.

DR. WILHELM STEKHEL,
The Depths of the Soul

Food for all is a necessity. Food should not be a merchandise, to be bought and sold as jewels are bought and sold by those who have the money to buy. Food is a human necessity, like water and air, and it should be available.

PEARL BUCK,
To My Daughters, with Love

Taking food and drink is a great enjoyment for healthy people, and those who do not enjoy eating seldom have much capacity for enjoyment or usefulness of any act.

CHARLES W. ELIOT,
The Happy Life

The way one eats is the way one works.

CZECH PROVERB

What I say is that, if a man really likes potatoes, he must be a pretty decent sort of fellow.

A. A. MILNE,
Not That It Matters

Gave up spinach for Lent.

F. SCOTT FITZGERALD,
The Crack-up

Strange to see how a good dinner and feasting reconciles everybody.

SAMUEL PEPYS,
Diary of Samuel Pepys

One of the easiest forms of pretense to

break down is the pretense of enthusiasm for exotic foods. Just bring on the exotic foods.

ROBERT BENCHLEY,
Benchley—or Else!

Like everything else, meals are tiresome, but it is no use to make a fuss, because nothing else will be less tiresome.

BERTRAND RUSSELL,
The Conquest of Happiness

Although there were eight servants in the house, the food was always of the utmost simplicity, and even of what there was, if there was anything at all nice, I was not allowed to have it because it was not good for children to eat nice things. For instance, there would be rice pudding and apple tart. The grownups had the apple tart and I had the rice pudding.

BERTRAND RUSSELL,
Wisdom, edited by James Nelson

When God gives hard bread He gives sharp teeth.

GERMAN PROVERB

There are a lot of people who must have the table laid in the usual fashion or they will not enjoy the dinner.

CHRISTOPHER MORLEY,
Inward Ho

We are all dietetic sinners; only a small percent of what we eat nourishes us, the balance goes to waste and loss of energy.

SIR WILLIAM OSLER,
Aphorisms from His Bedside Teachings and Writings

An oyster, that marvel of delicacy, that concentration of sapid excellence, that mouthful before all other mouthfuls, who first had faith to believe it, and courage to execute? The exterior is not persuasive.

HENRY WARD BEECHER,
Eyes and Ears

There must be hundreds of unsung heroes and heroines who first tasted strange things growing—and think of the man who first ate a lobster. This staggers the imagination. I salute him every time I take my

nutcracker in hand and move the melted-butter pipkin closer.

GLADYS TABER,
Stillmeadow Daybook

When going to an eating house, go to one that is filled with customers.

CHINESE PROVERB

A big man is always accused of gluttony, whereas a wizened or osseous man can eat like a refugee at every meal, and no one ever notices his greed.

ROBERTSON DAVIES,
The Table Talk of Samuel Marchbanks

At a dinner party one should eat wisely but not too well, and talk well but not too wisely.

W. SOMERSET MAUGHAM,
A Writer's Notebook

There is poetry in a pork chop to a hungry man.

PHILIP GIBBS,
quoted in the *New York Times,*
August 26, 1951

When ordering lunch the big executives are just as indecisive as the rest of us.

WILLIAM FEATHER,
The Business of Life

The last man in the world whose opinion I would take on what to eat would be a doctor. It is far safer to consult a waiter, and not a bit more expensive.

ROBERT LYND,
Solomon in All His Glory

I declare that a meal prepared by a person who loves you will do more good than any average cooking, and on the other side of it a person who dislikes you is bound to get that dislike into your food, without intending to.

LUTHER BURBANK,
The Harvest of the Years

Walking from Danbury to Chelmsford (Sept. '87)
I came across excellent blackberries, & ate of them heartily. It was mid-day, & when I left the brambles, I found I had a suf-

ficient meal so that there was no need to go to an inn. Of a sudden it struck me as *an extraordinary thing.* Here had I satisfied my hunger, without payment, without indebtedness to any man. The vividness with which I felt that this was extraordinary seems to me a shrewd comment on a social state which practically denies a man's right to food unless he have money.

GEORGE GISSING,
Commonplace Book

A good meal makes a man feel more charitable toward the whole world than any sermon.

ARTHUR PENDENYS,
quoted in the *New York Times,*
November 22, 1953

Ever since Eve started it all by offering Adam the apple, woman's punishment has been to have to supply a man with food and then suffer the consequences when it disagrees with him.

HELEN ROWLAND,
A Guide to Men

Five muffins are enough for any man at any one meal, and the breast and wing of a chicken should suffice without attacking the fibrous legs. Very different, however, is the case of *pâté de fois gras,* sandwiches, oysters, and meringues. I cannot eat too many of these. I make it, therefore, my rule to consume very limited quantities of plain food in order to leave as much room as possible for delicacies.

E. V. KNOX,
Gorgeous Times

Grub first, then ethics.

BERTOLT BRECHT

When one has an honest appetite all food tastes good: shrimps Newburg with hot rolls and alligator pear salad, or black bread and sour cheese.

KATHLEEN NORRIS,
Hands Full of Living

The cost takes away the taste.

FRENCH PROVERB

Good taste in viands has been painfully

acquired; it is a sacred trust. Beware of gross feeders. They are a menace to their fellowcreatures. Will they not act, on occasion, even as they feed? Assuredly they will. Everybody acts as he feeds.

NORMAN DOUGLAS,
Alone

Eating without conversation is only stoking.

MARCELENE COX,
Ladies' Home Journal, June 1943

Another sad comestive truth is that the best foods are the products of infinite and wearying trouble. The trouble need not be taken by the consumer, but someone, ever since the Fall, has had to take it.

ROSE MACAULAY,
Personal Pleasures

Coleridge holds that a man cannot have a pure mind who refuses apple dumplings, I am not certain but he is right.

CHARLES LAMB,
quoted in the *New York Times,*
March 3, 1947

Since I saw you I have been in France, and have eaten frogs. The nicest little rabbity things you ever tasted. Do look about for them. Make Mrs. Clare pick off the hind quarters, boil them plain, with parsley and butter. The fore quarters are not so good. She may let them hop off by themselves.

CHARLES LAMB,
The Letters of Charles and Mary Lamb

A good dinner is not to be despised. It paves the way for all the virtues.

LOUISE IMOGEN GUINEY,
Goose-Quill Papers

He who cannot cut the bread evenly cannot get on well with people.

CZECH PROVERB

We can go to any restaurant at all and be made uncomfortable by the waiters, waiters seeming to be a breed gifted in making guests ill at ease. They are always older, wearier, and wiser than we are; and they have us at a disadvantage because we are sitting down and they are standing up. We should very much like to discover a restaurant where we would be allowed to stand up to our food, and the waiters be compelled to sit down, so we could lord it over them!

E. B. WHITE,
Every Day Is Saturday

In our opinion food should be sniffed lustily at table, both as a matter of precaution and as a matter of enjoyment, the sniffing of it to be regarded in the same light as the tasting of it.

E. B. WHITE,
Every Day Is Saturday

FOOL

If a fool be associated with a wise man all his life, he will perceive the truth as little as a spoon perceives the taste of truth.

CHINESE PROVERB

Looking back upon any period of our career, we can safely say: "What a fool I was!"

PAUL ELDRIDGE,
Horns of Glass

There is no fool who has not his own kind of sense.

IRISH PROVERB

It is as idle to range against man's fatuity as to hope that he will ever be less a fool.

GEORGE GISSING,
The Private Papers of Henry Ryecroft

Nothing looks so like a man of sense as a fool who holds his tongue.

GERMAN PROVERB

Do you think that the things people make fools of themselves about are any less real than the things they behave sensibly about? They are more true: they are the only things that are true.

GEORGE BERNARD SHAW,
Candida

Luck sometimes visits a fool, but never sits down with him.

GERMAN PROVERB

A fellow who is always declaring he's no fool usually has his suspicions.

WILSON MIZNER,
quoted in *Ladies' Home Journal,* May 1950

Nobody is more insufferable than a fool who happens to be right by chance.

SYDNEY J. HARRIS,
Strictly Personal

A woman never forgives anybody who tries to keep her from making a fool of herself over a man.

JOHN W. RAPER,
What This World Needs

Of the whole rabble of thieves, the fools are the worst: for they rob you of both time and peace of mind.

GOETHE,
quoted in the *New York Times,*
April 29, 1953

FOOTBALL

There is something in the swoop and shock of a hard tackle which stirs a racial memory and satisfies an ancient desire.

MAJOR FRANK CAVANAGH,
Inside Football

So many moves you can make, so many stunts. But the best philosophy is to simply keep hitting them with your best lick.

MERLIN OLSEN,
quoted in *A Thinking Man's Guide
to Pro Football* by Paul Zimmerman

In the end it's the defense that dictates your game. The defense tells you when to throw, where to throw and how to throw. The most important thing a quarterback has to learn is how to react to the defense.

SONNY JERGENSEN,
quoted in *Quarterbacks Have All the Fun*
by Dick Schaap

When a game is lost, or well on the way to being lost, the bench is quiet and the strong faces grow still and watchful. The only happiness for the proud ones is victory.

TEX MAULE,
The Pros by Robert Riger

Guards make your running game. If you don't have good guards, you can't run inside.

LARRY CSONKA,
quoted in the *New York Times,*
May 30, 1976

Among the most thankless tasks in the world is playing on the offensive line of a professional football team. The key blocks which pry a crack in the defense are almost always hidden in the hurly-burly at the line of scrimmage.

ANDY ROBUSTELLI,
Sports Illustrated Book of Football

You're a hero when you win and a bum when you lose. That's the game. They pay their money and they can boo if they feel like it.

JOHNNY UNITAS,
quoted in *Quarterbacks Have All the Fun*
by Dick Schaap

To watch a football game is to be in prolonged neurotic doubt as to what you're seeing. It's more like an emergency happening at a distance than a game.

JACQUES BARZUN,
God's Country and Mine

To me football is like a day off. I grew up picking cotton on my daddy's farm and nobody asked for your autograph or put your name in the paper for that.

LEE ROY JORDAN,
*The Complete Handbook
of Pro Football 1975*

Gentlemen, you are about to play football for Yale against Harvard. Never in your lives will you do anything so important.

T. A. D. JONES,
Esquire's Great Men and Moments in Sports

Never tell 'em how many letter men you've got coming back. Tell 'em how many you lost.

KNUTE ROCKNE,
quoted in *Football's Greatest Coaches*
by Edwin Pope

I think that I would still rather score a touchdown on a particular day than make love to the prettiest girl in the United States.

PAUL HORNUNG,
Football and the Single Man

Women will not be talking about football unless one of them is in love with a football player, and then suddenly you discover that they know everything that is to be known about it.

JEANNE MOREAU,
New York Times, June 30, 1976

If you want to be impressed with what a dumb amateur you are, with what trained, intelligent, and discriminating intellectuals the professionals are, sit in a hotel room with some coaches scouting a game, and hear what *they* have to say about the football game you thought you saw that afternoon.

RANDALL JARRELL,
Mademoiselle

They don't call the middle of the line The Pit for nothing. We really do get like animals in there. It is very hard in The Pit. No matter how it seems, no matter what the score shows, it's always hard.

MERLIN OLSEN,
quoted in *A Thinking Man's Guide
to Pro Football* by Paul Zimmerman

If lessons are learned in defeat, as they say, our team is really getting a great education.

MURRAY WARMATH,
quoted in *Sports Illustrated,*
November 3, 1958

Defense builds confidence in the quarterback. You go into a game and you are able to bide your time and program your ideas better because you know you are going to get the ball back.

Y. A. TITTLE,
Y. A. Tittle I Pass, My Story,
as told to Dan Smith

I won't mention the name of this particular team we were playing, but at half time we came in, pulled off our socks and began putting iodine on the teeth marks in our legs. Coach Bob Zuppke said, "I'll tell you one thing, if we ever play this team again, it'll be on a Friday."

RED GRANGE,
quoted in *Sports Illustrated*,
December 8, 1958

Often an All-American is made by a long run, a weak defense, and a poet in the pressbox.

BOB ZUPPKE,
quoted in *Football's Greatest Coaches*
by Edwin Pope

Politics is an astonishing profession. It has enabled me to go from being an obscure member of the junior varsity at Harvard to being an honorary member of the Football Hall of Fame.

JOHN F. KENNEDY,
The Kennedy Wit,
edited by Bill Adler

For every pass I caught in a game, I caught a thousand passes in practice.

DON HUTSON,
quoted in *Pro Football's Hall of Fame*
by Arthur Daley

I'm for the upperdog. I was for the underdog because I was one. Now I see the pressures that are on the upperdog. When you get to be an upperdog, you know the scratching and the clawing and the grabbing that everybody underneath does to knock you off your perch. The average fan cannot appreciate the pressure and the emotional peak you must reach each week to keep from getting knocked off your perch at the top.

BART STARR,
quoted in *Quarterbacks Have All the Fun*
by Dick Schaap

When I'm traveling, I ask farm boys how to get to a certain place. If they point with their finger I move on. If they pick up the plow and point with it, I stop and sell them on the University of Minnesota.

GIL DOBIE,
quoted in *Football's Greatest Coaches*
by Edwin Pope

It's pretty hard to describe how that feels, throwing a pass and seeing a man catch it and seeing him in the end zone and seeing the referee throw his arms up in the air, signaling a touchdown, signaling that you've done just what you set out to do. It's an incredible feeling. It's like your whole body is bursting with happiness.

JOE NAMATH,
I Can't Wait Until Tomorrow

What I do is take a look at who's getting off me. If I don't recognize the face right away I look at the number. That way I know who should have got him—who's not doing his job.

CHARLEY CONERLY,
quoted in *Quarterbacks Have All the Fun*
by Dick Schaap

I do know that if a boy wants to play football and for any reason you keep him from it, you will probably find that his character—or his temper, at least—will not improve.

ELEANOR ROOSEVELT,
Ladies' Home Journal, January 1942

When you do everything right and the ball is on target, you get what I think is the biggest thrill in football: you get to run with the ball.

RAY BERRY,
quoted in *Sports Illustrated Book of Football*

Pro football is like nuclear warfare. There are no winners, only survivors.

FRANK GIFFORD,
quoted in *Sports Illustrated*, July 4, 1960

Fewer than three touchdowns is not enough and more than five is rubbing it in.

JOCK SUTHERLAND,
quoted in *Football's Greatest Coaches*
by Edwin Pope

We think Tarkenton uses audibles when we're chasing him. Audibles like "Help!"

ROGER BROWN,
quoted in *A Thinking Man's Guide
to Pro Football* by Paul Zimmerman

A head coach is guided by this main objective: dig, claw, wheedle, coax that fanatical effort out of the players. You want them to play every Saturday as if they were planting the flag on Iwo Jima.

DARRELL ROYAL,
Darrell Royal Talks Football

He was the only man I ever saw who ran his own interference.

STEVE OWEN on Bronko Nagurski,
quoted in *Pro Football's Hall of Fame*
by Arthur Daley

The bonds uniting old football men are strong enough to conquer any other association. When recounting bygone games, telling over again of magnificent runs, the beautiful drop, how the game was lost and won, enthusiasm grows strong, the time slips by, and true football lore obliterates for the time all antagonisms and rivalry.

WALTER CAMP,
quoted in *Touchdown!*
by Amos Alonzo Stagg

Bulk, strength, grace and speed are so much lath and painted plaster if they are not backed up by football temperament, and imagination is the prime ingredient of that temperament—imagination to dramatize the conflict and one's own part in it, imagination to anticipate what and where the foe's next move will be, imagination to capitalize instantly on any break in the game.

AMOS ALONZO STAGG,
Touchdown!

When a person looks at a game of football, he tends to see a reflection of his own life. If it's mainly violence and getting ahead and winning at all costs, he'll tend to see that in the game. Or if life is mainly statistics and numbers and measurements, he'll tend to see that—many people have an incredible interest in football statistics. People look at the game and project their own reality onto it.

JOHN BRODIE,
quoted in *Quarterbacks Have All the Fun*
by Dick Schaap

There is a function of a quasi religious nature performed by a few experts but followed in spirit by the whole university world, serving indeed as a symbol to arouse in the students and in the alumni certain congregate and hieratic emotions. I refer, of course, to football.

CHARLES HORTON COOLEY,
Life and the Student

We brought up our rookies much different than they do now. During training camp, if we went to a tavern and a rookie came—well he just didn't *dare* come in. Rookies found their own joints.

BOBBY LANE,
quoted in *Quarterbacks Have All the Fun*
by Dick Schaap

Tackling is more natural than blocking. If a man is running down the street with everything you own, you won't let him get away. That's tackling.

VINCE LOMBARDI,
quoted in *A Thinking Man's Guide
to Pro Football* by Paul Zimmerman

FORGIVENESS

"Forgive and forget," we say, not for the alliteration alone, but because there is a real conviction. ... A naturally forgetful man cannot bear a grudge long, as King Darius knew when he commissioned a special slave to bawl in his ear three times a day: "Sire, remember the Athenians!"

ODELL SHEPARD,
The Joys of Forgetting

In every pardon there is love.

WELSH PROVERB

How could a man live at all if he did not grant absolution every night to himself and all his fellows!

GOETHE,
quoted in *Ladies' Home Journal,*
March 1946

Beware of the man who does not return your blow; he neither forgives you nor allows you to forgive yourself.

GEORGE BERNARD SHAW

It is so difficult to forgive God.

VINCENT MCNABB,
God's Way of Mercy

Lord, forgive them, for they know what they do!

KARL KRAUS,
Karl Kraus by Harry Zohn

Although we are outsiders I think we can agree that perhaps the greatest, most thrilling sentence that comes to us from ancient times is: Father forgive them; for they know not what they do. One who sees the inevitable everywhere has occasion to remember it pretty often.

OLIVER WENDELL HOLMES, JR.,
Holmes-Laski Letters, Vol. I

It is easier to forgive an enemy than a friend.

AUSTIN O'MALLEY,
Keystones of Thought

To ask that one's own higher self should forgive one's own trespasses is the hardest prayer to answer that we can ever offer up. . . . We cannot forgive others in any comprehensible sense unless we have first learnt how to forgive ourselves.

HAVELOCK ELLIS,
Selected Essays

The offender never forgives.

RUSSIAN PROVERB

If we are to love others as we love ourselves, then we must learn to love the little self which so often needs to be forgiven for doing the things we do not want to do and saying the things we do not want to say.

REBECCA BEARD,
Everyman's Search

Kind words will set right things which have got most intricately wrong. In reality an unforgiving heart is a rare monster. Most men get tired of the justest quarrels.

FREDERICK W. FABER,
Spiritual Conferences

FORTUNE

It is good fortune to be so placed that you *can* forget antagonism and see men as brothers. To have found your work and to see your way clear ahead is the main thing. If a man is living his life he should have no great difficulty in loving his neighbors.

CHARLES HORTON COOLEY,
Life and the Student

One never hugs one's good luck so affectionately as when listening to the relation of some horrible misfortune which has overtaken others.

ALEXANDER SMITH,
Dreamthorp

Our always poor and defective skill in controlling fortune is indeed a valuable part of our reasonableness, since it is the natural basis upon which a higher spiritual life may be built.

JOSIAH ROYCE,
William James and Other Essays on the Philosophy of Life

Alas, the doors of fortune do not open inward, so that by storming them one can force them open; but they open outward, and therefore nothing can be done.

SØREN KIERKEGAARD,
Either/Or, Vol. I

A man's fortune must first be changed from within.

CHINESE PROVERB

He who finds Fortune on his side should go briskly ahead, for she is wont to favor the bold.

BALTASAR GRACIAN,
The Oracle

Fortune rarely shows anyone to the door; her civility towards those who are arriving is matched by her rudeness towards those who are leaving.

BALTASAR GRACIAN,
The Oracle

The tendency would seem to be to hide good fortune as closely as possible, but trumpet the bad on every patient ear.

EDEN PHILLPOTTS,
A Year with Bisshe-Bantam

Fortune is like the market, where many times, if you can stay a little, the price will fall.

FRANCIS BACON,
Essays

FORTUNETELLER

I love the fortunetelling profession because its clients are all people who are at that stage in their lives when they want more of life than they are getting. Instead of asking just to be quietly spared any more experience, as most of them probably will sooner than they could possibly believe, they are at that stage when they are only too willing and eager to live at almost any price. They are all hungry and amorous and softhearted and pitifully vulnerable, just from carrying around with them day and night such a fantastic load of wishes. The old and secure and contented never bother with fortunetellers.

KATHARINE BUTLER HATHAWAY,
*The Journals and Letters
of the Little Locksmith*

FRANCE AND THE FRENCH

Thought about French women and their impudent confidence in the power of sex.

KATHERINE MANSFIELD,
The Journal of Katherine Mansfield

It may be the only country in the world where the rich are sometimes brilliant.

LILLIAN HELLMAN,
An Unfinished Woman

The hospitality of manners in France is not complemented by real hospitality of thought.

HENRI FRÉDÉRIC AMIEL,
The Private Journal of Henri Frédéric Amiel

The excitation of the French always remains at the same level, without acute rises or falls, and therefore the Frenchman until advanced senility sets in, is normally excited. In other words, the Frenchman doesn't have to waste his energy on inordinate excitement; he dispenses his strength with common sense, and that is why he never goes bankrupt.

ANTON CHEKHOV,
The Selected Letters of Anton Chekhov

It is a land of milk and honey, the best milk and the most perfumed honey, where all the good things of the earth overflow and are cooked to perfection.

WILLIAM BOLITHO,
Camera Obscura

The Frenchman is a farmyard animal, so well domesticated that he dares not jump over any fence. Witness his tastes in art and literature.

CHARLES BAUDELAIRE,
Intimate Journals

The smell of autumnal woods, as well as of coffee roasting in the towns, are among the few things that the French arrange better than we.

E. V. LUCAS,
365 Days and One More

In a French inn you may be as witty as you can, as intelligent as you can, but someone there will be more intelligent, more witty.

E. V. LUCAS,
365 Days and One More

Amusing that the typical figure of that country in so many people's imagination is a saucy girl with little or nothing on, whereas in reality it is an old woman in mourning.

E. V. LUCAS,
365 Days and One More

French people hate broken French worse than most of us hate broken English.

FRANK MOORE COLBY,
"Profession of a Gallows Maniac,"
The Margin of Hesitation

Somebody should write a book about the French people's passion for doing things in as complicated a way as possible.

KATHARINE BUTLER HATHAWAY,
*The Journals and Letters
of the Little Locksmith*

I like—I have heard a good judge say—to hear a Frenchman talk. He strikes a light, but what light he will strike it is impossible to predict.

WALTER BAGEHOT,
Literary Studies, Vol. III

The French never boast of the superiority of their ways. They simply never bring

them into comparison with other people's.
JOSEPH WARREN BEACH,
Meek Americans

I believe that lightheartedness, the ability to revert to youth, is the chief attraction of Frenchwomen.
MERRILL PANITT,
Ladies' Home Journal, September 1945

Whenever I hear French spoken as I approve, I find myself quietly falling in love.
E. R. BULWER-LYTTON,
Lucile, Vol. I

I could but remember ... the saying that a Frenchman wouldn't mind lying about the facts on occasion but would think himself dishonored if untrue to his beliefs—whereas an Englishman who wouldn't misstate facts would equivocate about his beliefs. I suspect there is truth in it and that it points to the French being on a higher plane *quo ad hoc*.
OLIVER WENDELL HOLMES, JR.,
Holmes-Laski Letters, Vol. I

FRANCIS OF ASSISI

The life of St. Francis was the true *Imitatio Christi*, a poem compared to which the book of that name is merely prose.
OSCAR WILDE,
De Profundis

Sweet St. Francis, would that he were
here again
He that in his catholic wholeness used to
call the very flowers
Sisters, Brothers—and the beasts—
whose pains are hardly less than ours.
ALFRED LORD TENNYSON

He brought asceticism from the cell into the fields, and became the monk of Nature.
HAVELOCK ELLIS,
Selected Essays

A contemporary St. Francis, one likes to believe, would delight in not flowers but football, not stars but subways, not clouds but computers, not trees but traffic jams.
BRENDAN FRANCIS

St. Francis was a lean and lively little man; thin as a thread and vibrant as a bowstring; and in his motions like an arrow from the bow.
G. K. CHESTERTON,
St. Thomas Aquinas

FRATERNITY

I remember one evening sitting with a lot of men in the Coffee House in New York—we had all been drinking, carousing—rather cheap actresses, magazine illustrators, popular painters, popular novelists. A pretty bad lot in general, sold out and all that, but suddenly I found myself saying to myself, "These are my people."
SHERWOOD ANDERSON,
Letters of Sherwood Anderson

FREEDOM

If we would have a living thing, we must give that thing some degree of liberty—even though liberty bring with it some risk. If we would debar all liberty and all risk, then we can have only the mummy and the dead husk of the thing.
EDWARD CARPENTER,
Love's Coming of Age

Freedom of action is all right when a powerful desire, a great passion, or an unflagging will directs it. But not this: having given an equal freedom of the city to all my desires, having welcomed them all with open arms, I now find that all of them at the same time claim the place of honor.
ANDRÉ GIDE,
The Journals of André Gide, Vol. I

Free, dost thou call thyself? Thy ruling thought would I hear of, and not that thou hast escaped from a yoke.
FRIEDRICH NIETZSCHE,
Thus Spake Zarathustra

It is better for a man to go wrong in freedom than to go right in chains.
THOMAS HENRY HUXLEY,
Aphorisms and Reflections

Today freedom has not many allies. I have been known to say that the real passion of the twentieth century was slavery.

ALBERT CAMUS,
Resistance, Rebellion and Death

Liberty is the way, and the only way, of perfectibility. Without liberty heavy industry can be perfected, but not justice or truth.

ALBERT CAMUS,
Resistance, Rebellion and Death

When one knows of what man is capable, for better and for worse, one also knows that it is not the human being who must be protected but the possibilities he has within him—in other words, his freedom. ... Freedom is nothing else but a chance to be better, whereas enslavement is a certainty of the worst.

ALBERT CAMUS,
Resistance, Rebellion and Death

The aim of art, the aim of a life can only be to increase the sum of freedom and responsibility to be found in every man and in the world. It cannot, under any circumstances, be to reduce or suppress that freedom, even temporarily.... No great work has ever been based on hatred and contempt. On the contrary, there is not a single true work of art that has not in the end added to the inner freedom of each person who has known and loved it.

ALBERT CAMUS,
Resistance, Rebellion and Death

Freedom is not a reward or a decoration that is celebrated with champagne. Nor yet a gift, a box of dainties designed to make you lick your chops. Oh, no! It's a chore, on the contrary, and a long-distance race, quite solitary and very exhausting.

ALBERT CAMUS,
The Fall

Caution is security. "Bold" is freedom—the breaking thing .... Freedom lies in being bold.

ROBERT FROST,
Wisdom, edited by James Nelson

I detest all restraint. I'd willingly wear a hair shirt, eat dry bread and drink only water and live in a cave, if only I was free, i.e., felt free. If there is no such thing as freedom, then it is the illusion of freedom which counts.

FREDERICK GOODYEAR,
Letters and Remains

I do not at all believe in human freedom in the philosophical sense. Everybody acts not only under external compulsion but also in accordance with inner necessity.

ALBERT EINSTEIN,
Ideas and Opinions

We all want to be terribly clever, we are all so sophisticated, intellectual, we read such a lot. The whole psychological history of mankind (not who was king and what kinds of wars there were and all the absurdity of nationalities) is within oneself. When you can read that in yourself you have understood. Then you are a light to yourself, then there is no authority, then you are actually free.

J. KRISHNAMURTI,
You Are the World

Everybody favors free speech in the slack moments when no axes are being ground.

HEYWOOD BROUN,
Collected Edition of Heywood Broun

There are only two kinds of freedom in the world: the freedom of the rich and powerful, and the freedom of the artist and the monk who renounces possessions.

ANAÏS NIN,
The Diaries of Anaïs Nin, Vol. III

Not easy to achieve freedom without chaos.

ANAÏS NIN,
The Diaries of Anaïs Nin, Vol. IV

To be entirely free, and at the same time entirely dominated by law, is the eternal paradox of human life that we realise at every moment.

OSCAR WILDE,
De Profundis

Political liberty is but one of the instruments of Freedom; it can never by anything more. Real Freedom begins deep down in the consciousness of the individual; it is the stuff of variation and growth, the fuel of life.

HOLBROOK JACKSON,
Southward Ho! and Other Essays

It requires something like religious valour to follow your inner consciousness to its last whim and eccentricity; for that is what Freedom means.

HOLBROOK JACKSON,
Southward Ho! and Other Essays

Believe me, if you have been shut up for a year and a half, it can get too much for you some days. In spite of all justice and thankfulness, you can't .crush your feelings. Cycling, dancing, whistling, looking out into the world, feeling young, to know that I'm free—that's what I long for; still, I mustn't show it, because I sometimes think if all eight of us began to pity ourselves, or went about with discontented faces, where would it lead us?

ANNE FRANK,
Anne Frank: The Diary of a Young Girl

There are those who question the future of the ideal of freedom. To them we answer that it has more than a future: it has eternity.

BENEDETTO CROCE,
"Of Liberty," *The Foreign Affairs Reader,*
edited by Hamilton Fish Armstrong

The most unfree souls go west, and shout of freedom. Men are freest when they are most unconscious of freedom. The shout is a rattling of chains, always was.

D. H. LAWRENCE,
Studies in Classic American Literature

Variation is a consequence of freedom, and the slight but radical diversity of souls in turn makes freedom requisite.

GEORGE SANTAYANA,
Character and Opinion in the United States

Even craving for power and possessions may be regarded as the love of a free life on a larger scale, for which more instruments and resources are needed.

GEORGE SANTAYANA,
Character and Opinion in the United States

A man is morally free when, in full possession of his living humanity, he judges the world, and judges other men, with uncompromising sincerity.

GEORGE SANTAYANA,
The Letters of George Santayana

To my unilluminated mind it seems impossible that mankind should all be free, in any full sense of this word. They cannot be free if they don't exist; they can't exist, if they don't eat; and they can't eat, if they don't work. But to have to work, even if not to overwork, at definite tasks, hours, and places, is not freedom. It is compulsion, and living willy-nilly in a once-determined groove.

GEORGE SANTAYANA,
The Letters of George Santayana

Persecution for the expression of opinions seems to me perfectly logical. If you have no doubt of your premises or your power and want a certain result with all your heart you naturally express your wishes in law and sweep away all opposition. . . . But when men have realized that time has upset many fighting faiths, they may come to believe even more than they believe the foundations of their own conduct that the ultimate good desired is better reached by free trade in ideas—that the best test of truth is the power of the thought to get itself accepted in the competition of the market, and that truth is the only ground upon which their wishes safely can be carried out.

OLIVER WENDELL HOLMES, JR.,
The Mind and Faith of Justice Holmes,
edited by Max Lerner

If there is any principle of the Constitution that more imperatively calls for attachment than any other it is the principle of free thought—not free thought for those who agree with us but freedom for the thought that we hate.

OLIVER WENDELL HOLMES, JR.,
The Mind and Faith of Justice Holmes,
edited by Max Lerner

Freedom of choice, freedom to pursue my vocation as man, freedom of thought, of expression, of worship, of the press, of teaching, freedom for all. All freedoms are inter-dependent. To destroy one is to destroy the others.

JULES-GERARD CARDINAL SALIÈGE,
Who Shall Bear the Flame?

In this century freedom has received more tributes than ever before. There has been public debate on every sort of freedom, economic, political, religious. Yet there has not been a corresponding increase in independence of mind.

E. J. OLIVER,
Coventry Patmore

We crave freedom, but freedom is never an end in itself; it is a means to be used for further aims. Its value lies in the extent to which it can assist the development of life. To possess freedom with no life for which to use it is but the bitterest farce. . . . Life never means complete freedom, and every action and relation is an added bond. Life is to be attained, not through a non-moral freedom of caprice, but through a glad welcoming and loyal fulfillment of every bond and obligation which comes in the daily path of life.

EDWARD HOWARD GRIGGS,
A Book of Meditations

Men instinctively desire to be free, and it is the wont of all of them never to rest contented with their condition, but always to be pushing forward from the point at which they find themselves.

FRANCESCO GUICCIARDINI,
Counsels and Reflections

How absurd men are! They never use the liberties they have, they demand those they do not have. They have freedom of thought, they demand freedom of speech.

SØREN KIERKEGAARD,
Either/Or, Vol. I

All men are frail. And especially must those who are freely loyal possess a certain freedom to become faithless if they choose. This evil is a condition of the highest good that the human world contains.

JOSIAH ROYCE,
The Problem of Christianity

The fundamental defect in the present state of democracy is the assumption that political and economic freedom can be achieved without first freeing the mind. Freedom of mind is not something that spontaneously happens. It is not achieved by the mere absence of obvious restraints. It is a product of constant unremitting nurture of right habits of observation and reflection.

JOHN DEWEY,
Characters and Events, Vol. II

It is awful to look into the mind of man and see how free we are, to what frightful excesses our vices may run under the whited wall of a respectable reputation. Outside, among your fellows, among strangers, you must preserve appearances, a hundred things you cannot do; but inside, the terrible freedom!

RALPH WALDO EMERSON,
Journals of Ralph Waldo Emerson

Man desires to be free, not in order to be spared tribulation—this is more liable to increase in proportion to the degree of self-determination attained—but in order to grow.

COUNT HERMANN KEYSERLING,
The Book of Marriage

Now, I do not tremble at the word "revolution." We believe in the progress of mankind. We believe in freedom, and we intend to be associated with it in the days to come.

JOHN F. KENNEDY,
quoted in the *New York Times,*
May 30, 1961

It requires greater courage to preserve inner freedom, to move on in one's inward journey into new realms, than to stand defiantly for outer freedom. It is often easier to play the martyr, as it is to be rash in battle.

ROLLO MAY,
Man's Search for Himself

Freedom is not an idol, or an end, but a prerequisite condition of human worth. Man needs a margin to move about in and try himself out and show what he is worth and attract grace.

CHARLES PÉGUY,
quoted in *Charles Péguy* by Daniel Halévy

Intuitively I've always been aware of the vitally important pact which a man has with himself, to be all things to himself, and to be identified with all things, to stand self-reliant, taking advantage of his haphazard connection with a planet, riding his luck, and following his bent with the tenacity of a hound. My first and greatest love affair was with this thing we call freedom, this lady of infinite allure, this dangerous and beautiful and sublime being who restores and supplies us all.

E. B. WHITE,
One Man's Meat

One day last October, I lay on sun-baked slopes in a mountain wood, looking up into delicate white birches, swaying with exquisite grace in a gentle wind. Silently the golden leaves detached themselves, and with soft erratic waverings floated down to the waiting earth. I watched them find the freedom toward which they had always strained, tugging at their restraining twigs whenever breezes blew. Liberty theirs at last—but liberty to die. For living freedom is that of the leaf tight fastened, with the sap of the tree of which it is a product and a part vibrating through it, controlling it, till it reaches its mature being, its perfect form. Here is experience, not theory.

VIDA D. SCUDDER

FRIEND

Things like sticking to old friends have really got bigger to me than anything else.

SHERWOOD ANDERSON,
Letters of Sherwood Anderson

I think one of the strangest things I feel is the necessity of keeping alive some personal touch with a few men about the country who have not grown too weary. ... Perhaps my touch has been too much with older men. The sense of life slips easily out of the grasp of Americans apparently.

All of which is but to say that my desire to keep touch with you is that I feel you alive. One likes this feeling of other men at work in other places. I like the figure of you walking in the path along the hill at the edge of Pittsburgh and noting the kind of terrain and the beauty of the black river bottoms and the smoke lying there—like the thought of dreams and impulses singing up in you.

SHERWOOD ANDERSON,
Letters of Sherwood Anderson

Do not protect yourself by a fence, but rather by your friends.

CZECH PROVERB

No medicine is more valuable, none more efficacious, none better suited to the cure of all our temporal ills than a friend, to whom we may turn for consolation in time of trouble, and with whom we may share our happiness in time of joy.

SAINT AILRED OF RIEVAULX,
Christian Friendship

Don't believe your friends when they ask you to be sincere with them. They merely hope you will encourage them in the good opinion they have of themselves by providing them with the additional assurance they will find in your promise of sincerity.

ALBERT CAMUS,
The Fall

When a friend is in trouble, don't annoy him by asking if there is anything you can do. Think up something appropriate and do it.

E. W. HOWE,
Country Town Sayings

Probably no man ever had a friend he did not dislike a little; we are all so constituted by nature than no one can possibly entirely approve of us.

E. W. HOWE,
The Indignations of E. W. Howe

A good friend can tell you what is the matter with you in a minute. He may not seem such a good friend after telling.

ARTHUR BRISBANE,
The Book of Today

If two friends ask you to be judge in a dispute, don't accept, because you will lose one friend; on the other hand, if two strangers come with the same request, accept, because you will gain one friend.

SAINT AUGUSTINE,
quoted in *Ladies' Home Journal,* April 1949

There is no man that imparteth his joys to his friends, but that he joyeth the more; and no man that imparteth his griefs to his friends, but he grieveth the less.

FRANCIS BACON,
Essays

There are moments in life when all that we can bear is the sense that our friend is near us; our wounds would wince at the touch of consoling words, that would reveal the depths of pain.

HONORÉ DE BALZAC,
Le Cousin Pons

If our friends' idealizations of us need the corrective of our own experience, it may be true also that our own sordid view of our lives needs the corrective of our friends' idealizations.

OSCAR W. FIRKINS,
Oscar Firkins: Memoirs and Letters,
edited by Ina Ten Eyck

It is in the thirties that we want friends. In the forties we know they won't save us any more than love did.

F. SCOTT FITZGERALD,
The Crack-up

Give and take makes good friends.

SCOTCH PROVERB

If I had to choose between betraying my country and betraying my friend, I hope I should have the guts to betray my country.

E. M. FORSTER,
quoted in *The Unquiet Grave*
by Cyril Connolly

Even from the best of human friends I must not ask for more than he can give.

ALBAN GOODIER,
The School of Love

I confess that, for myself, I never enter a new company without the hope that I may discover a friend, perhaps *the* friend, sitting there with an expectant smile. That hope survives a thousand disappointments.

A. C. BENSON,
The Beauty of Life,
compiled by Caroline Abbott Derby

The support to one's personality by friends. A part of one's self and a real foundation and existence.

KATHARINE BUTLER HATHAWAY,
*The Journals and Letters
of the Little Locksmith*

Nothing changes your opinion of a friend so surely as success—yours or his.

FRANKLIN P. JONES,
Saturday Evening Post, November 29, 1953

Really, one has some friends, and when one comes to think about it it is impossible to tell how one ever became friendly with them.

FRANÇOISE MALLET-JORIS,
A Letter to Myself

A man loves his friend the better if he does not know why he loves him.

ERNEST DIMNET,
What We Live By

Our faith in others betrayeth wherein we would fain have faith in ourselves. Our longing for a friend is our betrayer.

FRIEDRICH NIETZSCHE,
Thus Spake Zarathustra

Art thou pure air and solitude and bread and medicine to thy friend? Many a one cannot loosen his own fetters, but is nevertheless his friend's emancipator.

FRIEDRICH NIETZSCHE,
Thus Spake Zarathustra

There is nothing we like to see so much as the gleam of pleasure in a person's eye when he feels that we have sympathized with him, understood him, interested ourself in his welfare. At these moments something fine and spiritual passes between two friends. These moments are the moments worth living.

DON MARQUIS,
Prefaces

It is easier to visit friends than to live with them.

CHINESE PROVERB

The friends who fail you are always replaced by new ones who appear at the critical moment and from the most unexpected quarters.

HENRY MILLER,
The Books in My Life

The friend who understands you, creates you.

ROMAIN ROLLAND,
Journey Within

It should be part of our private ritual to devote a quarter of an hour every day to the enumeration of the good qualities of our friends. When we are not *active* we fall back idly upon defects, even of those whom we most love.

MARK RUTHERFORD,
Last Pages from a Journal

For what do my friends stand? Not for the clever things they say: I do not remember them half an hour after they are spoken. It is always the unspoken, the unconscious, which is their reality to me.

MARK RUTHERFORD,
Last Pages from a Journal

The love of our private friends is the only preparatory exercise for the love of all men.

JOHN HENRY CARDINAL NEWMAN,
Parochial and Plain Sermons, Vol. II

A pretext is never lacking to him who would break with a friend.

SAINT BERNARD OF CLAIRVAUX,
Letters

Many a person has held close, throughout their entire lives, two friends to him that always remained strange to one another, because one of them attracted by virtue of similarity, the other by virtue of difference.

EMIL LUDWIG,
Of Life and Love

For my part, I should like most candid friends to be anonymous. We should then all of us get the benefit of their inestimable advice, and they would be saved the painful necessity of making themselves odious.

J. A. SPENDER,
Men and Things

I like a highland friend who will stand by me, not only when I am in the right, but when I am a *little* in the wrong.

SIR WALTER SCOTT,
quoted in *Sir Walter Scott*
by Hesketh Pearson

An enemy can partly ruin a man, but it takes a good-natured injudicious friend to complete the thing and make it perfect.

MARK TWAIN,
Mark Twain at Your Fingertips,
edited by Caroline T. Harnsberger

Old friends are the great blessing of one's later years—half a word conveys one's meaning. They have memory of the same events and have the same mode of thinking.... I am lamenting my other self. Half is gone ... He is gone to whom I ran with every scrap of news I heard.

HORACE WALPOLE,
quoted in *The Literature of Gossip*
by Elizabeth Drew

None is so rich as to throw away a friend.

TURKISH PROVERB

We rejoice in the good fortune of our friends, always provided that it be not too dazzling or too undeserved.

RANDOLPH BOURNE,
Youth and Life

A man with few friends is only half-developed; there are whole sides of his nature which are locked up and have never been expressed. He cannot unlock them himself, he cannot even discover them; friends alone can stimulate him and open him.

RANDOLPH BOURNE,
Youth and Life

I am treating you as my friend, asking you to share my present *minuses* in the hope I can ask you to share my future *pluses*.

KATHERINE MANSFIELD,
Katherine Mansfield Memories of L M

There was a definite process by which one made people into friends, and it involved talking to them and listening to them for hours at a time.

REBECCA WEST,
The Thinking Reed

When our friends are alive, we see the good qualities they lack; dead, we remember only those they possessed.

J. PETIT-SENN,
Conceits and Caprices

Friends who are full of devotion when we need nothing remind me of pine trees which offer us shade in winter.

J. PETIT-SENN,
Conceits and Caprices

When one friend washes another both become clean.

DUTCH PROVERB

Two friends playing together. And love is when you like to play when he wants to and you may not want to.

DAVID WILSON,
age 7, United States, *Journeys: Prose by Children of the English-speaking World*, collected by Richard Lewis

One discovers a friend by chance, and cannot but feel regret that twenty or thirty years of life maybe have been spent without the least knowledge of him.

CHARLES DUDLEY WARNER,
Backlog Studies

Do not wish your friends much good fortune, if you do not want to lose them.

BALTASAR GRACIAN,
The Oracle

Prospective brides ought to be told that while a man will stand a great deal of criticism of himself from a woman, he will not accept criticism of his friends from her. The first is merely a reflection on his temperament, the second on his judgment, which is a much more vital area.

SYDNEY J. HARRIS,
Strictly Personal

There is no reason why a man should show his life to the world. The world does not understand things. But with people whose affection one desires to have it is different.

OSCAR WILDE,
De Profundis

How few of his friends' houses would a man choose to be at when he is sick.

SAMUEL JOHNSON,
Life of Johnson by James Boswell

Men only become friends by community of pleasures. He who cannot be softened into gaiety cannot easily be melted into kindness.

SAMUEL JOHNSON,
Life of Johnson by James Boswell

Who seeks a faultless friend remains friendless.

TURKISH PROVERB

A great man is no hero to his valet, they say; and the same thing is apt to be true of friends who are near—the great lines are not seen.

GEORGE E. WOODBERRY,
Selected Letters of George Edward Woodberry

To find a friend one must close one eye. To keep him—two.

NORMAN DOUGLAS,
An Almanac

The need for a friend surely is in direct relation to the need for confession.

DR. WILHELM STEKHEL,
The Depths of the Soul

In reality, we are still children. We want to find a playmate for our thoughts and feelings.

DR. WILHELM STEKHEL,
The Depths of the Soul

The success of any man with any woman is apt to displease even his best friends.

MADAME DE STAËL,
quoted in *Men in Epigram*,
compiled by Frederick W. Morton

My life seems to have become suddenly hollow, and I do not know what is hanging over me. I cannot even put the shadow that has fallen on me into words. At least into written words. I would give a great deal for a friend's voice.

JOHN ADDINGTON SYMONDS,
Letters and Papers of John Addington Symonds

I had Perucho [Valdemoro] here two days ago; by what he tells me, I have a really good friend in him. May God deliver me from him.

SAINT TERESA OF AVILA,
Saint Teresa in Her Writings
by the Abbé Rodolphe Hoornaert

Do not remove a fly from your friend's forehead with a hatchet.

CHINESE PROVERB

The tribulations of our best friends arouse sentiments in us which are not entirely unpleasant.

LA ROCHEFOUCAULD,
Maxims

Can you understand how cruelly I feel the want of friends who will believe in me a bit? People think that I'm a queer sort of fish that can write; that is all, and how I loathe it.

D. H. LAWRENCE,
Selected Letters of D. H. Lawrence,
edited by Diana Trilling

A friend is a poem.

PERSIAN PROVERB

Friend that sticketh closer than a brother ... eight years. Dashed bit of a slip of a girl ... eight weeks! And—where's your friend?

RUDYARD KIPLING,
The Story of the Gadsbys

Nothing wounds a friend like a want of confidence.

JEAN BAPTISTE LACORDAIRE,
Letters to Young Men,
edited by Count de Montalembert

I am learning to live close to the lives of my friends without ever seeing them. No miles of any measurement can separate your soul from mine.

JOHN MUIR,
Letters to a Friend:
Written to Mrs. Ezra C. Carr

If a man should importune me to give a reason why I loved my friend, I find it could not be otherwise expressed than by the answer, "Because he was he: and be-cause I was I."

MONTAIGNE,
Essays

Love me, please; I love you; I can bear to be your friend. So ask of me anything, and hurt me whenever you must; but never be "tolerant," or "kind." And never say to me again,—don't dare to say to me again—"Anyway, you can make a trial" of being friends with you! Because I can't do things in that way; I am not a tentative person. Whatever I do I give up my whole self to it.

EDNA ST. VINCENT MILLAY,
Letters of Edna St. Vincent Millay

If you want to make a dangerous man your friend, let him do you a favor.

LEWIS E. LAWES,
20,000 Years in Sing Sing

We call that person who has lost his father, an orphan; and a widower, that man who has lost his wife. And that man who has known that immense unhappiness of losing a friend, by what name do we call him? Here every language holds its peace in impotence.

JOSEPH ROUX,
Meditations of a Parish Priest

We are fonder of visiting our friends in health than in sickness. We judge less favourably of their characters, when any misfortune happens to them; and a lucky hit, either in business or reputation, improves even their personal appearance in our eyes.

WILLIAM HAZLITT,
quoted in *The Book of Friendship,*
arranged by Arthur Ransome

Pretty wife, old wine—many friends.

BULGARIAN PROVERB

Since there is nothing so well worth having as friends, never lose a chance to make them. For men are brought into constant contact with one another, and friends help and foes hinder at times and places where you least expect it.

FRANCESCO GUICCIARDINI,
Counsels and Reflections

I observed once to Goethe . . . that when a friend is with us we do not think the same of him as when he is away. He replied, "Yes! because the absent friend is yourself, and he exists only in your head; whereas the friend who is present has an individuality of his own, and moves according to laws of his own, which cannot always be in accordance with those which you form for yourself."

ARTHUR SCHOPENHAUER,
The Art of Controversy

Friends are lost by calling often and calling seldom.

SCOTCH PROVERB

FRIENDSHIP

I believe sexuality is the basis of all friendship.

JEAN COCTEAU,
Writers at Work, Third Series,
edited by George Plimpton

It takes time and a kind of power in oneself to know another just as it does to get anywhere in one of the crafts.

SHERWOOD ANDERSON,
Letters of Sherwood Anderson

The friendships which last are those wherein each friend respects the other's dignity to the point of not really wanting anything from him.

CYRIL CONNOLLY,
The Unquiet Grave

Friendship is honey—but don't eat it all.

MOROCCAN PROVERB

The reward of friendship is itself. The man who hopes for anything else does not understand what true friendship is.

SAINT AILRED OF RIEVAULX,
Christian Friendship

The fact probably is, that no one person can possibly combine all the elements supposed to make up what everyone means by friendship.

FRANCIS MARION CRAWFORD,
Katherine Lauderdale, Vol. I

Friendship needs no words—it is solitude delivered from the anguish of loneliness.

DAG HAMMARSKJÖLD,
Markings

Human beings are born into this little span of life of which the best thing is its friendships and intimacies, and soon their places will know them no more, and yet they leave their friendships and intimacies with no cultivation, to grow as they will by the roadside, expecting them to "keep" by force of mere inertia.

WILLIAM JAMES,
The Letters of William James, Vol. II

Many a friendship, long, loyal, and self-sacrificing, rested at first on no thicker a foundation than a kind word.

FREDERICK W. FABER,
Spiritual Conferences

Of course platonic friendship is possible—but only between husband and wife.

ANONYMOUS,
quoted in *Ladies' Home Journal,* April 1944

The art of friendship has been little cultivated in our society, a fact which is readily seen when we compare this relationship with the other personal relationships of our society—those of husband-wife, parent-child, and even teacher-pupil.

ROBERT J. HAVIGHURST,
Potentialities of Women in the Middle Years,
edited by Irma H. Gross

It seems to me that the one privilege of *friendship* is "to quench the fiery darts of the wicked," to make the best of friends, to encourage and believe in them, to hand on the pleasant things.

A. C. BENSON,
*Excerpts from the Letters of
Dr. A. C. Benson to M. E. A.*

Perhaps the most delightful friendships are those in which there is much agreement, much disputation, and yet more personal liking.

GEORGE ELIOT

Reckoning up is friendship's end.

IRISH PROVERB

Friendship will not stand the strain of very much good advice for very long.

ROBERT LYND,
The Peal of Bells

I always felt that the great high privilege, relief and comfort of friendship was that one had to explain nothing.

KATHERINE MANSFIELD,
quoted in *Katherine Mansfield*
by Antony Alpers

The truth is friendship is to me every bit as sacred and eternal as marriage.

KATHERINE MANSFIELD,
Katherine Mansfield
The Memories of L M

Like everyone else I feel the need of relations and friendship, of affection, of friendly intercourse, and I am not made of stone or iron, so I cannot miss these things without feeling, as does any other and intelligent man, a void and deep need. I tell you this to let you know how much good your visit has done me.

VINCENT VAN GOGH,
Dear Theo:
An Autobiography of Vincent Van Gogh

If friendship is not sheer utility, it is nonsense.

AUSTIN O'MALLEY,
Keystones of Thought

Good friendships are fragile things and require as much care as any other fragile and precious things.

RANDOLPH BOURNE,
Youth and Life

Our friends are chosen for us by some hidden law of sympathy, and not by our conscious wills.

RANDOLPH BOURNE,
Youth and Life

Keep the inner fires burning; it will be such happiness for me to feel their genial warmth when we next meet.

GEORGE SANTAYANA,
The Letters of George Santayana

Friends need not agree in *everything* or go *always* together, or have *no* comparable other friendship of the same intimacy. On the contrary, in friendship union is more about ideal things: and in that sense it is more ideal and less subject to trouble than marriage is.

GEORGE SANTAYANA,
The Letters of George Santayana

Friendship is not so warm as Eros and not so spiritual as Agape, but it is freer and more intellectual. It *chooses* in the friend the side with which it will sympathize, and it brings an unstipulated, independent contribution to that common interest.

GEORGE SANTAYANA,
The Letters of George Santayana

Friendship with oneself is all-important, because without it one cannot be friends with anyone else in the world.

ELEANOR ROOSEVELT,
Ladies' Home Journal, November 1944

'Tis the privilege of friendship to talk nonsense, and have her nonsense respected.

CHARLES LAMB,
The Letters of Charles and Mary Lamb, Vol. I

A man becomes like those whose society he loves.

HINDU PROVERB

The chain of friendship, however bright, does not stand the attrition of constant close contact.

SIR WALTER SCOTT,
Sir Walter Scott's Journal (1825–1832)

The wise man does not permit himself to set up even in his own mind any comparison of his friends. His friendship is capable of going to extremes with many people, evoked as it is by many qualities.

CHARLES DUDLEY WARNER,
Backlog Studies

I cannot concentrate all my friendship on any single one of my friends because no one is complete enough in himself. I pursue in them echoes, vague resemblances to bigger relationships.

ANAÏS NIN,
The Diaries of Anaïs Nin, Vol. IV

Friendship requires great communication between friends. Otherwise, it can neither be born nor exist.

SAINT FRANCIS DE SALES,
Introduction to the Devout Life

Friendship is an art, and very few persons are born with a natural gift for it.

KATHLEEN NORRIS,
Hands Full of Living

If we were all given by magic the power to read each other's thoughts, I suppose the first effect would be to dissolve all friendships.

BERTRAND RUSSELL,
quoted in *Ladies' Home Journal*

An old man, a superior of mine, once, in a moment of great trouble, came for refuge to my room and there burst into tears; that was a moment of happy agony, a moment of perfect friendship.

ALBAN GOODIER,
The School of Love

If one could be friendly with women, what a pleasure—the relationship so secret and private compared with relations with men.

VIRGINIA WOOLF,
A Writer's Diary

It is the steady and merciless increase of occupations, the augmented speed at which we are always trying to live, the crowding of each day with more work than it can profitably hold, which has cost us, among other good things, the undisturbed enjoyment of friends. Friendship takes time, and we have no time to give it.

AGNES REPPLIER,
In the Dozy Hours

When men are friendly even water is sweet.

CHINESE PROVERB

Affinities are rare. They come but a few times in a life. It is awful to risk losing one when it arrives.

FLORENCE H. WINTERBURN,
Vacation Hints

The holy passion of Friendship is of so sweet and steady and loyal and enduring a nature that it will last through a whole lifetime, if not asked to lend money.

MARK TWAIN,
Mark Twain at Your Fingertips,
edited by Caroline T. Harnsberger

I am a little singular in my thought of love and friendship. I must have first place or none. . . . I cannot bear a slight from those I love.

MARY WOLLSTONECRAFT,
quoted in *Mary Wollstonecraft*
by Eleanor Flexner

It is not what you give your friend, but what you are willing to give him, that determines the quality of friendship.

MARY DIXON THAYER,
Things to Live By

I hate the prostitution of the word friendship to signify modish and worldly alliances.

RALPH WALDO EMERSON,
"Friendship," *Essays: First Series*

It was such a joy to see thee. I wish I could tell how much thee is to my life. I always turn to thee as a sort of rest and often just think about thy face when I get troubled. I am not very good at saying all I feel, but deep down I do feel it all so much.

LADY HENRY SOMERSET,
quoted in *Philadelphia Quaker*
by Logan Pearsall Smith

I think, from some brief experience of the thing, that as friendships grow old, they seem to depend less on actual contacts and messages in order to maintain their soundness; the growth has got into the wood of the tree, and is there; and yet I am also quite sure that no friendship yields its true pleasure and nobility of nature without frequent communication, sympathy and service.

GEORGE E. WOODBERRY,
Selected Letters of George Edward Woodberry

Of all intellectual friendships, none are so beautiful as those which subsist between old and ripe men and their younger brethren in science, or literature, or art. It is by these private friendships, even more than by public performance, that the tradition of sound thinking and great doing is perpetuated from age to age.

> PHILIP G. HAMERTON,
> *The Intellectual Life*

Every man ought to be friends with a nun and a whore and while talking with them forget which is which.

> BRENDAN FRANCIS

FRUSTRATION

One of the sources of pride in being a human being is the ability to bear present frustrations in the interests of longer purposes.

> HELEN MERRELL LYND,
> *On Shame and the Search for Identity*

In my clinical experience, the greatest block to a person's development is his having to take on a way of life which is not rooted in his own powers.

> ROLLO MAY,
> *Man's Search for Himself*

Curious this having a passion for a fine thing and no way to live it out rightly!

> STEPHEN MACKENNA,
> *Journal and Letters of Stephen Mackenna*

Society expects man to be a passive social animal who believes like the People of the Field in *Jurgen* that "to do what you have always done" and "what is expected of you" are the twin rules of life. This, of course, is not true. The wanton crucifixion of impulses, the unnecessary blocking and frustration of the drives and urges, are an evil that reflects itself in sophistication, ennui and boredom, dissatisfaction, melancholy, fatigue, anxiety and neurosis.

> ABRAHAM MYERSON,
> *Speaking of Man*

Let the gods do it is back of a shocking number of frustrations.

> ANONYMOUS (HENRY S. HASKINS),
> *Meditations in Wall Street*

The moment that any life, however good, *stifles* you, you may be sure it isn't your real life.

> A.C. BENSON,
> *Excerpts from the Letters of Dr. A. C. Benson to M. E. A.*

FULFILLMENT

It is a sign of feeble character to seek for a shortcut to fulfillment through the favor of those whose interest lies in keeping it barred—the one path to fulfillment is the difficult path of suffering and self-sacrifice.

> RABINDRANATH TAGORE,
> *Letters to a Friend*

A man may fulfill the object of his existence by asking a question he cannot answer, and attempting a task he cannot achieve.

> OLIVER WENDELL HOLMES,
> *The Life and Letters of Oliver Wendell Holmes,*
> Vol. I, by John T. Morse, Jr.

The greatness of the work of the fulfiller, as compared with the work of the destroyer, is indicated by the faculties and qualities which it requires. Destruction calls for nothing but hatred and vigor. Fulfillment calls for sympathy, intelligence, patience and hope.

> PHILLIPS BROOKS,
> *Visions and Tasks*

You cannot stop a living thing capable of growth from tending to its fulness, any more than you can deny its existence.

> P. R. RÉGAMEY,
> *Poverty*

FUTURE

The habit of looking to the future and thinking that the whole meaning of the present lies in what it will bring forth is a pernicious one. There can be no value in the whole unless there is value in the parts.

> BERTRAND RUSSELL,
> *The Conquest of Happiness*

The greater part of our lives is spent in dreaming over the morrow, and when it comes, it, too, is consumed in the anticipation of a brighter morrow, and so the cheat is prolonged, even to the grave.

MARK RUTHERFORD,
The Deliverance of Mark Rutherford

It is a cheap generosity which promises the future in compensation for the present.

J. A. SPENDER,
The Comments of Bagshot, Second Series

The future is not in the past; it is in the future.

JEAN GUITTON,
Essay on Human Love

The most effective way to ensure the value of the future is to confront the present courageously and constructively.

ROLLO MAY,
Man's Search for Himself

If the future belongs to anybody it belongs to those to whom it has always belonged, to those, that is to say, too absorbed in living to feel the need for thought, and they will come, as the barbarians have always come, absorbed in the processes of life for their own sake, eating without asking if it is worthwhile to eat, begetting children without asking why they should beget them, and conquering without asking for what purpose they conquer.

JOSEPH WOOD KRUTCH,
The Modern Temper

The only light upon the future is faith.

THEODOR HAECKER,
Journal in the Night

Concern for the future is so new a thing in human history that we are hardly yet at home with the feeling. Perhaps, if we thought more about what was before us, we should come to know more about it.

RANDOLPH BOURNE,
Youth and Life

Very strange is this quality of our human nature which decrees that unless we feel a future before us we do not live completely in the present where we stand today.

PHILLIPS BROOKS,
Visions and Tasks

We can easily picture to ourselves a human nature which might have been so created so that it should never think about the future. . . . But that is not our human nature. It always must look forward. The thing which it hopes to become is already a power and decides the thing it is.

PHILLIPS BROOKS,
Visions and Tasks

Those who foresee the future and recognize it as tragic are often seized by a madness which forces them to commit the very acts which makes it certain that what they dread shall happen.

REBECCA WEST,
The Meaning of Treason

We grow in time to trust the future for our answers.

RUTH BENEDICT,
An Anthropologist at Work
by Margaret Mead

Most truly has the wise man said that of things future and contingent we can have no certain knowledge. Turn this over in your mind as you will, the longer you turn it over the more you will be satisfied of its truth.

FRANCESCO GUICCIARDINI,
Counsels and Reflections.

I do not pin my dreams for the future to my country or even to my race. I think it probable that civilization somehow will last as long as I care to look ahead—perhaps with smaller numbers, but perhaps also bred to greatness and splendor by science. I think it is not improbable that man, like the grub that prepares a chamber for the winged thing it never has seen but is to be—that man may have cosmic destinies that he does not understand. And so beyond the vision of battling races and an impoverished earth I catch a dreaming glimpse of peace.

OLIVER WENDELL HOLMES, JR.,
The Mind and Faith of Justice Holmes,
edited by Max Lerner

Strange, how her courage had revived with the sun! She saw now, as she had seen in the night, that life is never what one dreamed, that it is seldom what one desired; yet for the vital spirit and the eager mind, the future will always hold the search for buried treasure and the possibilities of high adventure.

ELLEN GLASGOW,
Barren Ground

GAMBLING

Any new system is worth trying when your luck is bad.

HEYWOOD BROUN,
Pieces of Hate

If you should play roulette, put twenty-five francs on for me just for luck.

ANTON CHEKHOV,
The Selected Letters of Anton Chekhov

A cunning gamester never plays the card which his adversary expects, and far less that which he desires.

BALTASAR GRACIAN,
The Oracle

If you must play, decide upon three things at the start: the rules of the game, the stakes, and the quitting time.

CHINESE PROVERB

The only people who can endure gambling are those who have a special neurosis on the subject . . . or people who have said "No" to the universe, who do not want to find out about things. If one has said "Yes" . . . time spent in a casino is time given to death, a foretaste of the hour when one's flesh will be diverted to the purposes of the worm and not of the will.

REBECCA WEST,
quoted in *Rebecca West: Artist and Thinker* by Peter Wolfe

Playing stud poker at the National Press Club was what hardened my character.

GEORGE S. KAUFMAN,
quoted in *George S. Kaufman* by Howard Teichman

Gambling and superstition go hand in hand, and both result from the inexpug-nable human instinct to escape from the rational.

J. A. SPENDER,
quoted in the *New York Times*,
October 7, 1951

Nine gamblers could not feed a single rooster.

YUGOSLAV PROVERB

There is enough energy wasted in poker to make a hundred thousand successful men every year.

ARTHUR BRISBANE,
The Book of Today

Betting and gambling would lose half their attractiveness, did they not deceive us with the fancy that there may be an element of personal merit in our winnings. Our reason may protest, but our self-love is credulous.

ROBERT LYND,
The Peal of Bells

For the wholesome-minded person, with a keen sense of life and a broad sympathy with its interests, there is ever a fascination in watching the chances of a gaming table. Fortune seems to come down and give a private exhibition of her wheel. The great universe seems to stand still for a while, and only this microcosm to be subjected to its chances.

WILLIAM J. LOCKE,
A Study in Shadows

GAME

It may be that all games are silly. But, then, so are human beings.

ROBERT LYND,
Solomon in All His Glory

But games always cover something deep and intense, else there would be no excitement in them, no pleasure, no power to stir us.

ANTOINE DE SAINT-EXUPÉRY,
Airman's Odyssey

In a game where the players are equally matched it is a great advantage to have the first move.

BALTASAR GRACIAN,
The Oracle

I think games are significant in people's lives because in a game everything is clearly defined. You've got the rules and a given period of time in which to play; you've got boundaries and a beginning and an end. And whether you win, lose, or draw, at least something is sure. But life ain't like that at all. So I think people invent and play games in order to kid themselves, at least for a time, into thinking that *life* is a game; in order to forget that at the end of life there is nothing but a big blank wall.

JAMES JONES,
Writers at Work, Third Series,
edited by George Plimpton

Almost any game with any ball is a good game.

ROBERT LYND,
The Peal of Bells

Onlookers have a clearer view of the game than the players.

SIR RICHARD LIVINGSTONE,
On Education

GARDENS AND GARDENING

A modest garden contains, for those who know how to look and to wait, more instruction than a library.

HENRI FRÉDÉRIC AMIEL,
The Private Journal of Henri Frédéric Amiel

Last night, there came a frost, which has done great damage to my garden. . . . It is sad that Nature will play such tricks with us poor mortals, inviting us with sunny smiles to confide in her, and then, when we are entirely within her power, striking us to the heart.

NATHANIEL HAWTHORNE,
The American Notebooks

A garden without its statue is like a sentence without its verb.

JOSEPH W. BEACH,
Meek Americans

It is good to be alone in a garden at dawn or dark so that all its shy presences may haunt you and possess you in a reverie of suspended thought.

JAMES DOUGLAS,
Down Shoe Lane

This is a darling little garden when one can get out of one's shell and look at it. But what does it profit a man to look at anything if he is not *free?* Unless one is free to offer oneself up wholly and solely to the pansy—one receives nothing. It's promiscuous love instead of a living relationship—a dead thing.

KATHERINE MANSFIELD,
*Katherine Mansfield
The Memories of L M*

I think that if ever a mortal heard the voice of God it would be in a garden at the cool of the day.

F. FRANKFORT MOORE,
A Garden of Peace

What is a weed? I have heard it said that there are sixty definitions. For me, a weed is a plant out of place.

DONALD CULROSS PEATTIE,
The Flowering Earth

It is a consoling thought that gardens and their laws of birth and death endure, while political crises and panaceas appear only to vanish.

VIDA D. SCUDDER,
The Privilege of Age

I do not like gardening, nor am I particularly interested in gardens—in country gardens, that is to say. A town garden is a very different thing. It breaks up the bricks and mortar and provides a refuge from them for the town dweller.

SHEILA KAYE-SMITH,
Kitchen Fugue

I hate to be reminded of the passage of time, and in a garden of flowers one can never escape from it. It is one of the charms of a garden of grass and evergreens, that there for a while one is allowed to hug the illusion that time tarries.

E. V. LUCAS,
365 Days and One More

Is the fancy too far brought, that this love for gardens is a reminiscence haunting the race of that remote time when but two persons existed—a gardener named Adam, and a gardener's wife called Eve?

ALEXANDER SMITH,
Dreamthorp

A garden is an awful responsibility. You never know what you may be aiding to grow in it.

CHARLES DUDLEY WARNER,
My Summer in a Garden

One should learn also to enjoy the neighbor's garden, however small; the roses straggling over the fence, the scent of lilacs drifting across the road.

HENRY VAN DYKE,
The School of Life

Weather means more when you have a garden. There's nothing like listening to a shower and thinking how it is soaking in and around your lettuce and green beans.

MARCELENE COX,
Ladies' Home Journal, September 1944

Try to keep a garden beautiful to yourself alone and see what happens—the neighbor, hurrying by to catch his train of mornings, will stop to snatch a glint of joy from the iris purpling by your doorstep. The motorist will throw on brakes and back downhill just to see those Oriental poppies massed against the wall.

Nature is always on the side of the public.

RICHARDSON WRIGHT,
Truly Rural

One of the most delightful things about a garden is the anticipation it provides.

W. E. JOHNS,
The Passing Show

How could sour cherries, or half-ripe strawberries, or wet rosebuds, even if they do come from one's own garden, reward a man for the loss of the ease and the serene conscience of one who sings merrily in the streets, and cares not whether worms burrow, whether suns burn, whether birds steal, whether winds overturn, whether droughts destroy, whether floods drown, whether gardens flourish or not?

OLIVER BELL BUNCE,
Bachelor Bluff

Gardening has compensations out of all proportion to its goals. It is creation in the pure sense.

PHYLLIS MCGINLEY,
The Province of the Heart

The trouble with gardening is that it does not remain an avocation. It becomes an obsession.

PHYLLIS MCGINLEY,
The Province of the Heart

The love of flowers is really the best teacher of how to grow and understand them.

MAX SCHLING,
Everyman's Garden

But each spring ... a gardening instinct, sure as the sap rising in the trees, stirs within us. We look about and decide to tame another little bit of ground.

LEWIS GANNETT,
Crown Hill

All gardeners know better than other gardeners.

CHINESE PROVERB

After his death the gardener does not become a butterfly, intoxicated by the perfumes of the flowers, but a garden worm tasting all the dark, nitrogenous, and spicy delights of the soil.

KAREL CAPEK,
The Gardener's Year

To a gardener there is nothing more exasperating than a hose that just isn't long enough.

CECIL ROBERTS,
quoted in the *New York Times,*
May 13, 1951

I have taken to gardening a little, not a very inspiring business, though the strange debris of life which one turns up interests me.

A. C. BENSON,
*Excerpts from the Letters of
Dr. A. C. Benson to M. E. A.*

We ought to be custodians, not owners; it should be our privilege to help the living things in our garden. A really good man should want to tend a garden, even if it is not his own; this is the decisive test.

CLARE LEIGHTON,
Four Hedges

It is a greater act of faith to plant a bulb than to plant a tree. . . . It needs a great fling of imagination to see in these wizened, colourless shapes the subtle curves of the iris reticulata or the tight locks of the hyacinth. At the time of bulb planting one most nearly approaches the state of mind of the mystic.

CLARE LEIGHTON,
Four Hedges

When you have done your best for a flower, and it fails, you have some reason to be aggrieved.

FRANK SWINNERTON,
Tokefield Papers

The truth is, I have a brown thumb. Every green thing I touch withers.

ROBERTSON DAVIES,
The Table Talk of Samuel Marchbanks

The man who has planted a garden feels that he has done something for the good of the whole world.

CHARLES DUDLEY WARNER,
My Summer in a Garden

The more one gardens, the more one learns; and the more one learns, the more one realizes how little one knows. I suppose the whole of life is like that: the endless complications, the endless difficulties, the endless fight against one thing or another, whether it be green-fly on the roses or the complexity of personal relationships.

V. SACKVILLE-WEST,
A Joy of Gardening

Green are the lawns of country places, and the blooms are abundant. Yet we've wondered often if the dweller in peaceful blooming suburb experiences the grand passion that fires the man with a city back-garden.

E. B. WHITE,
Every Day Is Saturday

We have descended into the garden and caught.300 slugs. How I love the mixture of the beautiful and the squalid in gardening. It makes it so lifelike.

EVELYN UNDERHILL,
The Letters of Evelyn Underhill

Gardening should really be done in blinders. Its distractions are tempting and persistent, and only by stern exercise of will do I ever finish one job without being lured off to another.

RICHARDSON WRIGHT,
The Gardener's Bed-Book

The best way to get real enjoyment out of the garden is to put on a wide straw hat, dress in thin loose-fitting clothes, hold a little trowel in one hand and a cool drink in the other, and tell the man where to dig.

CHARLES BARR,
quoted in the *New York Times,*
July 11, 1948

GENERATION

At no point is one generation more likely to differ from the next than about where the line of reserve ought to be drawn. It is this, by-the-by, that often makes communication between children and parents so difficult; they are shy or frank about different things.

DESMOND MACCARTHY,
The Listener, January 1935

So long as there is life in the world, each generation will react against its predecessor, correct it, go beyond it. The house that accommodates the fathers never quite suits the children.

SIR RICHARD LIVINGSTONE,
On Education

Each generation has a different language, and can't learn what former generations knew until it has been translated into their words.

KATHARINE BUTLER HATHAWAY,
The Journals and Letters of the Little Locksmith

Our hope in the future generations is due less to the confidence we have in them than to the habit of placing our burdens upon the shoulders of others.

PAUL ELDRIDGE,
Horns of Glass

Each generation is a secret society, and has incommunicable enthusiasms, tastes and interests which are a mystery both to its predecessors and to posterity.

JOHN JAY CHAPMAN,
Memories and Milestones

GENEROSITY

Generosity is not in giving me that which I need more than you do, but it is in giving me that which you need more than I do.

KAHLIL GIBRAN,
Sand and Foam

How delightful is the company of generous people, who overlook trifles and keep their minds instinctively fixed on whatever is good and positive in the world about them.

VAN WYCK BROOKS,
A Chilmark Miscellany

No one is so generous as he who has nothing to give.

FRENCH PROVERB

It is always pleasant to be generous, though very vexatious to pay debts.

RALPH WALDO EMERSON

Giving money is a very good criterion, in a way, of a person's mental health. Generous people are rarely mentally ill people.

DR. KARL MENNINGER,
A Psychiatrist's World

When the hand ceases to scatter, the mouth ceases to praise.

IRISH PROVERB

Lots of people think they're charitable if they give away their old clothes and things they don't want.

MYRTLE REED,
Old Rose and Silver

The return we reap from generous actions is not always evident.

FRANCESCO GUICCIARDINI,
Counsels and Reflections

I am convinced that the majority of people would be generous from selfish motives, if they had the opportunity.

CHARLES DUDLEY WARNER,
My Summer in a Garden

Open your eyes and look for some man, or some work for the sake of men, which needs a little time, a little friendship, a little sympathy, a little sociability, a little human toil. . . . Who can reckon up all the ways in which that priceless fund of impulse, man, is capable of exploitation! He is needed in every nook and corner. Therefore search and see if there is not some place where you may invest your humanity.

ALBERT SCHWEITZER,
The Philosophy of Civilization

GENIUS

There are dancing motes or elements in genius which are impossible to pin down. One can only note their action, marvel at what they leave behind.

ELIZABETH BOWEN,
Collected Impressions

Genius, by its very intensity, decrees a special path of fire for its vivid power.

PHILLIPS BROOKS,
Visions and Tasks

Clear military inspirations never occur to shopkeepers and farmers, as bright ideas about checkmates occur only to persons who have studied chess. The prosaic business, then, of the man of genius is to accumulate that preparatory knowledge without which his genius can never be available, and he can do work of this kind as regularly as he likes.

PHILIP G. HAMERTON,
The Intellectual Life

Surely youth and genius hand in hand were the most beautiful sight in the world.

HENRY JAMES,
Roderick Hudson

With talent, you do what you like. With genius, you do what you can.

JEAN INGRES,
quoted in *Julian Green: Diary 1928–1957*

A man of genius should be like a growing boy, who is never, never, and never will be grown up. He must have a new style and new methods, not for fashion's sake, but because he has outgrown the old ways.

J. B. YEATS,
Letters to His Son, W. B. Yeats and Others

Let the minor genius go his light way and enjoy his life—the great nature cannot so live, he is never really in holiday mood, even though he often plucks flowers by the wayside and ties them into knots and garlands like little children and lads out on a sunny morning.

J. B. YEATS,
Letters to His Son, W. B. Yeats and Others

Have you noticed that when we talk of a man of genius, one tries to explain his failure? When one talks of a man of talent, we try to account for his success.

J. B. YEATS,
Letters to His Son, W. B. Yeats and Others

In every man of genius a new strange force is brought into the world.

HAVELOCK ELLIS,
Selected Essays

Mediocrity? Nature abhors it; shuns it. The flower that droops, the animal that drops, the bird that falls, the man who surrenders—Nature passes them by. The beautiful flower is the normal flower. Genius is the full stature of the normal man. He is the flower of mankind.

LOUIS DANZ,
Dynamic Dissonance

The whole notion of genius needs to be reassessed, needs perhaps to · be deglamorized somewhat. For genius is certainly much more a matter of degree than of kind. The genius so-called is only that one who discerns the pattern of things within the confusion of details a little sooner than the average man.

BEN SHAHN,
The Shape of Content

It is a sign of real genius that it remains unspoiled by success.

MARTIN ESSLIN,
The Theatre of the Absurd

The highest endowments do not create—they only discover. All transcendent genius has the power to make us know this as utter truth. Shakespeare, Beethoven—it is inconceivable that they have *fashioned* the works of their lives; they only saw and heard the universe that is opaque and dumb to us.

RUTH BENEDICT,
An Anthropologist at Work
by Margaret Mead

But the genius, as with the birds, discovers within himself that which never need be sought. "I do not seek, I find," Picasso says, and before him, Cézanne spoke, "I am the primitive of my way."

LOUIS DANZ,
Dynamic Dissonance

Genius must.

LOUIS DANZ,
Dynamic Dissonance

When genius seems to work disregarding rule, we may be sure that it has assimilated to itself whatever is best in every rule.

LOUISE IMOGEN GUINEY,
Goose-Quill Papers

Genius is the ability to put into effect what is in your mind.

F. SCOTT FITZGERALD,
The Crack-up

Genius goes around the world in its youth incessantly apologizing for having large feet. What wonder that later in life it should be inclined to raise those feet too swiftly to fools and bores.

F. SCOTT FITZGERALD,
The Crack-up

Genius can do much, but even genius falls short of the actuality of a single human life.

HAMILTON WRIGHT MABIE,
My Study Fire

The world is always ready to receive talent with open arms. Very often it does not know what to do with genius.

OLIVER WENDELL HOLMES,
The Autocrat of the Breakfast-Table

When a country produces a man of genius he never is what it wants or believes it wants; he is always unlike its idea of itself.

W. B. YEATS,
Autobiography

I know now that revelation is from the self, but from that age-long memoried self, that shapes the elaborate shell of the mollusc and the child in the womb, that teaches the birds to make their nest; and that genius is a crisis that joins that buried self for certain moments to our trivial daily mind.

W. B. YEATS,
Autobiography

A genius is the man in whom you are least likely to find the power of attending to anything insipid or distasteful in itself. He breaks his engagements, leaves his letters unanswered, neglects his family duties incorrigibly, because he is powerless to turn his attention down and back from those more interesting trains of imagery with which his genius constantly occupies his mind.

WILLIAM JAMES,
Talks to Teachers

Institutions and genius are in the nature of things antithetical, and if a man of genius is found living contentedly in a university it is peculiarly creditable to both.

CHARLES HORTON COOLEY,
Life and the Student

My notion is that there are offices to be discharged by talent for the relief of genius: meaning that one has the play side; the gift when it is mere gift, unapplied gift; and the gift when it is serious, going to business. And one relieves the other.

VIRGINIA WOOLF,
A Writer's Diary

To the eye which is not congenial, the fresh manifestation of genius in almost any kind has something in it alarming and revolting; and it is welcomed with an "Ugh, ugh! the horrid thing! It's alive!"

COVENTRY PATMORE,
Religio, Poetae, Etc.

Indeed, it is difficult to say how far an absolute moral courage in acknowledging intuitions may not be of the very nature of genius: and whether it might not be described as a sort of interior sanctity which dares to see and to confess to itself that it sees, though its vision should place it in a minority of one.

COVENTRY PATMORE,
Religio, Poetae, Etc.

Genius, no doubt, has to live, with a will, the life of its own epoch.

C. E. MONTAGUE,
A Writer's Notes on His Trade

I've lived long enough to see a lot of genius that never got a chance. I believe, in fact, that genius, meaning by that an original creative power, is both much more common than we suppose and much more fragile. It is certainly more fragile than talent. For talent belongs to the capable and intelligent who understand their own powers and know how to manage them. Genius is sensitive and impressionable.

JOYCE CARY,
Art and Reality

All the men of genius that we have ever heard of have triumphed over adverse circumstances, but that is no reason for supposing that there were not innumerable others who succumbed in youth.

BERTRAND RUSSELL,
The Conquest of Happiness

The essential definition of a genius, I think, is that he is a man who not only knows the laws of things, but experiences them in himself with self-evident certainty. This experience of pure being transcends even love.

OSWALD SCHWARZ,
The Psychology of Sex

It is funny this thing of being a genius, there is no reason for it, there is no reason that it should be you and should not have been him, no reason at all that it should have been you, no reason at all.

GERTRUDE STEIN,
quoted in *The Third Rose*
by John Malcolm Brinnin

If there is genius, the thing is a marvellous intuition, little dependent on observation.

THOMAS WOLFE,
The Letters of Thomas Wolfe

If genius is profuse, never ending—stuck in the middle of a work is—the wrong track. Genius is the track, seen. Once seen it is impossible to keep it from it. The superficial definitions, such as "genius is industry, genius is hard work," etc. are nonsense. It is to see the track, smell it out, to know it inevitable—sense sticking out all round feeling, feeling, seeing—hearing, touching. The rest is pure gravity (the earth pull).

WILLIAM CARLOS WILLIAMS,
Selected Essays

Genius might well be defined as the ability to make a platitude sound as though it were an original remark.

L. B. WALTON,
Introduction, *The Oracle*
by Baltasar Gracian

Men of genius are not only equally fit but much fitter for the business of the world than dunces, providing always they will give their talents fair play by curbing them with application.

SIR WALTER SCOTT,
Sir Walter Scott's Journal (1825-1832)

Genius makes its way with so much difficulty, because this lower world is in the hands of two omnipotences,—that of the wicked and that of the fools.

JOSEPH ROUX,
Meditations of a Parish Priest

Great things are done by devotion to one idea; there is one class of geniuses, who would never be what they are, could they grasp a second.

JOHN HENRY CARDINAL NEWMAN,
Historical Sketches, Vol. III

Genius not only hears more sounds in the rushing tumult of life, but selects more harmonious strains from the din.

RADOSLAV A. TSANOFF,
The Ways of Genius

GENTLEMAN

A gentleman never heard a story before.

AUSTIN O'MALLEY,
Keystones of Thought

The thousand and one gentlemen whom I meet, I meet despairingly, and but to part from them, for I am not cheered by the hope of any rudeness from them. . . . Your gentlemen, they are all alike.

HENRY DAVID THOREAU,
Journal

He makes light of favours while he does them, and seems to be receiving when he is conferring.

JOHN HENRY CARDINAL NEWMAN,
The Idea of a University

Those who seek to impress upon us that they are gentlemen will usually be found mistaken.

EDEN PHILLPOTTS,
A Year with Bisshe-Bantam

A gentleman is a man whose principal ideas are not connected with his personal needs and his personal success.

W. B. YEATS,
Autobiography

What is it to be a gentleman? The first to thank and the last to complain.

SERBIAN PROVERB

The quality of a gentleman is so very fine a thing that it seems to me one should not be at all hasty in concluding that one possesses it.

GERARD MANLEY HOPKINS,
A Hopkins Reader, edited by John Pick

GIFT

What brings joy to the heart is not so much the friend's gift as the friend's love.

SAINT AILRED OF RIEVAULX,
Christian Friendship

Givers have things too much their own way and receive too delicate consideration. They are bolstered up by a belief that they can do no wrong. Yet they can fill a man's house with abominations and secret misery.

FRANK MOORE COLBY,
The Colby Essays, Vol. 2

One should, I think, always give children money, for they will spend it for themselves far more profitably than we can ever spend it for them.

ROSE MACAULAY,
A Casual Commentary

Lack of deserts is no reason for refusing a gift.

ERIC GILL,
Autobiography

How painful to give a gift to any person of sensibility, or of equality! It is next worse to receiving one.

RALPH WALDO EMERSON,
Journals of Ralph Waldo Emerson

It is a dangerous thing to accept gifts: for two days after come requests.

HENRY CARDINAL MANNING,
Pastime Papers

It is so often that men do not recognise the magical gifts of the gods when they are presented to them under circumstances that are easy of access or purchase.

MAURICE BARING,
Lost Lectures

He that gives me small gifts would have me live.

ENGLISH PROVERB

In my experience we are apt to forget with desolating selfishness the gifts, but retain a bright memory of the things we paid for.

EDEN PHILLPOTTS,
A Year with Bisshe-Bantam

What's your rule for purchasing a present? Mine is would I like it? Who knows what anyone else likes, but if I like it, that at least is something.

RUTH GORDON,
Myself Among Others

What was the least expected is the more highly esteemed.

BALTASAR GRACIAN,
The Oracle

To receive a present handsomely and in a right spirit, even when you have none to give in return, is to give one in return.

LEIGH HUNT,
quoted in *Ladies' Home Journal,* April 1950

The excellence of a gift lies in its appropriateness rather than in its value.

CHARLES DUDLEY WARNER,
Backlog Studies

In choosing presents people should remember that the whole point of a present is that it is an extra.

E. V. LUCAS,
365 Days and One More

Wedding-presents are but a form of loan, which you are expected to pay back, with compound interest at 50 percent, in "hospitality," "entertainment," and your still more precious time.

RICHARD LE GALLIENNE,
Prose Fancies

GIVING

Complete possession is proved only by giving. All you are unable to give possesses you.

ANDRÉ GIDE,
Pretexts

What is called generosity is usually only the vanity of giving; we enjoy the vanity more than the thing given.

LA ROCHEFOUCAULD,
Maxims

It is indeed misery if I stretch an empty hand to men and receive nothing; but it is hopelessness if I stretch a full hand and find none to receive.

KAHLIL GIBRAN,
Sand and Foam

A hundred times a day I remind myself that my inner and outer life are based on the labors of other men, living and dead, and that I must exert myself in order to give in the same measure as I have received and am still receiving.

ALBERT EINSTEIN,
Ideas and Opinions

It is a good maxim to ask of no one more than he can give without inconvenience to himself.

W. SOMERSET MAUGHAM,
A Writer's Notebook

It is a dangerous illusion to believe that one can publish without receiving, write without reading, talk without listening, produce without feeding oneself, to give of oneself without recovering one's strength.

CHARLES PÉGUY,
Basic Verities

To give quickly is a great virtue.

HINDU PROVERB

Never give beyond the possibility of return.

BALTASAR GRACIAN,
The Oracle

The unbirthday present demands the nicest of care. . . . It is the only kind to which the golden rule of present-giving imperatively applies—the golden rule which insists that you must never give to another that which you would not rather keep for yourself, nothing that does not cost you a pang to part from.

E. V. LUCAS,
365 Days and One More

The more one gives, the more one has to give—like milk in the breast.

ANNE MORROW LINDBERGH,
Gift from the Sea

To try to benefit others, and yet not to have enough of oneself to give others, is a poor affair.

RABINDRANATH TAGORE,
Letters to a Friend

Many look with one eye at what they give and with seven at what they receive.

GERMAN PROVERB

He who has the rare courage to face himself, and permits others to look into his mistakes as well as his successes, turn them over in the palm and study them, is the prince of givers.

HANIEL LONG,
A Letter to St. Augustine

Giving is not at all interesting; but receiving is, there is no doubt about it, delightful.

ROSE MACAULAY,
A Casual Commentary

It is the special hardship of women that it is their destiny to make gifts, and that the quality of their giving is decided by . . . those who do the taking.

REBECCA WEST,
quoted in *Rebecca West:
Artist and Thinker* by Peter Wolfe

He who gives to me teaches me to give.

DANISH PROVERB

We must not only give what we *have;* we must also give what we *are.*

DESIRÉ JOSEPH CARDINAL MERCIER,
quoted in *The Life of Cardinal Mercier*
by John A. Gade

Giving is the highest expression of potency. In the very act of giving, I experience my strength, my wealth, my power . . . . I experience myself as overflowing, spending, alive, hence as joyous.

ERICH FROMM,
The Art of Loving

In the sphere of material things giving

means being rich. Not he who *has* much is rich, but he who *gives* much. The hoarder who is anxiously worried about losing something is, psychologically speaking, the poor, impoverished man, regardless of how much he has.

> ERICH FROMM,
> *The Art of Loving*

Is devotion to others a cover for the hungers and the needs of the self, of which one is ashamed? I was always ashamed to take. So I gave. It was not a virtue. It was a disguise.

> ANAÏS NIN,
> *The Diaries of Anaïs Nin,* Vol. IV

There is only one reason for living, and that is to give what we have to others; to expend upon others the strength we have in ourselves without it recoiling upon us and becoming like a malady.

> C.-F. RAMUZ,
> *The Life of Samuel Belet*

Sometimes a man imagines that he will lose himself if he gives himself, and keep himself if he hides himself. But the contrary takes place with terrible exactitude.

> ERNEST HELLO,
> *Life, Science, and Art*

The golden rule is a false guide in giving. Observe the motto about putting yourself in his place, but in applying this don't project all your peculiar whims into people whom they cannot fit.

> FRANK MOORE COLBY,
> *The Colby Essays,* Vol. 2

There persists in my nature a great, almost passionate inclination toward every kind of giving: I have known, since childhood, no more tumultuous joy than to keep back nothing and to begin the giving away with the dearest. I know that this is more a kind of instability and almost sentimental pleasure-seeking and no kindness whatsoever. For to turn it into a virtue, I must acquire the power to gather together all my giving in the one thing, the difficult, the laborious: in work.

> RAINER MARIA RILKE,
> *Letters of Rainer Maria Rilke 1892-1910*

I *shall* be glad if thy bag and the down quilt make thy bed more comfortable. And they have helped me to find such a nice thing about God that I had never thought of before, and it was this—that if I enjoyed giving things to my children a thousand times more than keeping them for myself, so of course must He.

> HANNAH WHITALL SMITH,
> *Philadelphia Quaker*
> by Logan Pearsall Smith

We are rich only through what we give, and poor only through what we refuse.

> MADAME SWETCHINE,
> *The Writings of Madame Swetchine*

When the giver comes, the gate opens by itself.

> GERMAN PROVERB

GOD

They say that God is everywhere, and yet we always think of Him as somewhat of a recluse.

> EMILY DICKINSON,
> quoted in *Ladies' Home Journal,*
> March 1947

If God lived on earth, people would break his windows.

> YIDDISH PROVERB

God does not die on the day when we cease to believe in a personal deity.

> DAG HAMMARSKJÖLD,
> *Markings*

On the bookshelf of life, God is a useful work of reference, always at hand but seldom consulted.

> DAG HAMMARSKJÖLD,
> *Markings*

Sheer joy is his, and this demands companionship.

> SAINT THOMAS AQUINAS,
> *Theological Texts*

The name of God should no longer come from the mouth of man. This word that has been so long degraded by usage no longer means anything. . . .To use the word God is more than sloth, it is a refusal to think, a kind of short cut, a hideous shorthand.

ARTHUR ADAMOV,
The Endless Humiliation

God's a good man.

ENGLISH PROVERB

I cannot conceive of a God who rewards and punishes his creatures, or has a will of the kind that we experience in ourselves.

ALBERT EINSTEIN,
Ideas and Opinions

If you want to find God, stop looking for Him.

BRENDAN FRANCIS

Even in the midst of the lowest pleasures, the most abandoned voluptuary is still seeking God; nay more, as far as regards what is positive in his acts, that is to say all that makes them an analogue of the true Love, it is God Himself who, in him and for him, seeks Himself.

ETIENNE GILSON,
The Spirit of Medieval Philosophy

Thou hast put salt in our mouths that we may thirst for Thee.

SAINT AUGUSTINE,
Confessions

Many years ago, when Harry was five or thereabouts, William undertook to explain to him the nature of God, and hearing that he was everywhere, asked whether he was the chair or the table. "Oh, no! God isn't a thing; He is everywhere about us; He pervades." "Oh, then, he is a skunk." How would the word "pervade" suggest anything else to an American child?

ALICE JAMES,
The Diary of Alice James

The people I love best, I love for their spiritual quality, for it shows me God somehow, and I hunger for him even when I am least positive of his being underneath us all.

ELLEN GLASGOW,
Letters of Ellen Glasgow

Father in Heaven, when the thought of Thee wakes in our hearts, let it not awaken like a frightened bird that flies about in dismay, but like a child waking from its sleep with a heavenly smile.

SØREN KIERKEGAARD,
quoted in *A Diary of Readings*
by John Baillie

God has more than He has given away.

CZECH PROVERB

Imagine an artist whose inspiration was ceaseless and continually followed by realization. A Shakespeare or a Beethoven constantly at his best. All we can do to form an idea of God's personality should be in that direction, removing limitations all the time. That is prayer and that is adoration!

ERNEST DIMNET,
What We Live By

The theologians of all ages and races have formed an image of God after their own fancies, and nothing could be more improbable than that He resembles in the least particular their conceptions of Him.

W. MacNEILE DIXON,
The Human Situation

Though most men allow that there is a God, yet in their ordinary view of things, his being is not apt to come into the account, and to have the influence and effect of a real existence, as it is with other beings which they see, and are conversant with by their external senses.

JONATHAN EDWARDS,
The Nature of True Virtue

In making up the character of God, the old theologians failed to mention that He is of infinite cheerfulness. The omission has caused the world much tribulation.

MICHAEL MONAHAN,
Palms of Papyrus

God is a busy worker, but He loves help.

BASQUE PROVERB

"I love God, father," she said haughtily. He took a quick look at her in the light of the candle burning on the floor—the hard

old raisin eyes under the black shawl—
another of the pious—like himself.

"How do you know? Loving God isn't
any different from loving a man—or a
child. It's wanting to be with Him, to be
near Him." He made a hopeless gesture
with his hands. "It's wanting to protect
Him from yourself."

GRAHAM GREENE,
The Power and the Glory

Whether he be named St. Paul, Luther, or
Calvin, I see him as beclouding the whole
truth of God.

ANDRÉ GIDE,
The Journals of André Gide, Vol. I

A clear understanding of God makes one
want to follow the direction of things, the
direction of oneself.

ANDRÉ GIDE,
The Journals of André Gide, Vol. I

She must not snatch the management of
the world out of God's hands. In practical
details she found herself apt to give the
Divine Will directions. "I MUST remember God is not my private secretary," she
wrote on an odd scrap of paper.

CECIL WOODHAM-SMITH,
Florence Nightingale

A devout rustic told me that it beat him
now and again to know what the Lord was
up to. "If 'twas a human," he said, "you'd
rush to put the man right."

EDEN PHILLPOTTS,
A Year with Bisshe-Bantam

I believe more and more that God must
not be judged on this earth. It is one of his
sketches that has turned out badly.

VINCENT VAN GOGH,
quoted in *The Rebel* by Albert Camus

But I always think that the best way to
know God is to love many things.

VINCENT VAN GOGH,
Dear Theo:
An Autobiography of Vincent Van Gogh

It always strikes me, and it is very peculiar, that when we see the image of indescribable and unutterable desolation—of

loneliness, of poverty and misery, the end
of all things, or their extreme—then rises in
our mind the thought of God.

VINCENT VAN GOGH,
Dear Theo:
An Autobiography of Vincent Van Gogh

Of all the things and all the happenings
that proclaim God's will to the world, only
very few are capable of being interpreted
by men. And of these few, fewer still find a
capable interpreter.

THOMAS MERTON,
No Man Is an Island

This is what gives Him the greatest glory—
the achieving of great things through the
weakest and most improbable means.

THOMAS MERTON,
The Sign of Jonas

What we on earth call God is a little tribal
god who has made an awful mess.

WILLIAM BURROUGHS,
Writers at Work, Third Series,
edited by George Plimpton

You think about people, but God thinks
about you.

LEO TOLSTOY,
Last Diaries

How important the concept of God is, and
how instead of valuing what has been
given us, we with light hearts spurn it
because of absurdities that have been attached to it.

LEO TOLSTOY,
Last Diaries

I don't know why it is that the religious
never ascribe commonsense to God.

W. SOMERSET MAUGHAM,
A Writer's Notebook

He would make all plain, if He could; He
gives us what we need; and when we at
last awake we shall be satisfied.

A. C. BENSON,
From a College Window

Why, only the other day Boris and I we
spent the whole day talking about this,
talking about the "living word." It comes

forth with the breath, just the simple act of opening the mouth, and *being with God*, to be sure. Max understands it too, in this way. That the facts are nothing. Behind the facts there must be the man, and *the man must be with God*, must talk like God Almighty.

HENRY MILLER,
The Cosmological Eye

Is it not certain that the Creator yawns in earthquake and thunder and other popular displays, but toils in rounding the delicate spiral of a shell?

W. B. YEATS,
Autobiography

As to God, open your eyes—and your heart, which is also a perceptive organ—and you see him.

CHARLES SANDERS PEIRCE,
Collected Papers of Charles Sanders Peirce,
Vol. VI

In general, God is perpetually creating us, that is developing our real manhood, our spiritual reality. Like a good teacher, He is engaged in detaching us from a false dependence upon Him.

CHARLES SANDERS PEIRCE,
Collected Papers of Charles Sanders Peirce,
Vol. VI

God forbid that I should measure the immensity of God's love by the narrow limits of my own capacity for faith and hope.

SAINT BERNARD OF CLAIRVAUX,
Letters

God is really only another artist. He invented the giraffe, the elephant and the cat. He has no real style, He just goes on trying other things.

PABLO PICASSO,
quoted in *Life with Picasso*
by Françoise Gilot and Carlton Lake

It is difficult to believe in God, not because He is so far off, but because He is so near.

MARK RUTHERFORD,
Last Pages from a Journal

God often visits us, but most of the time we are not at home.

JOSEPH ROUX,
Meditations of a Parish Priest

God's comings are not striking in appearance. He comes noiselessly. He is afraid, as it were, to startle us.

RAOUL PLUS,
Living with God

This sentence expresses my Theology in a few words: "It is enough to know that God's responsibility is irrevocable, and His resources limitless."

HANNAH WHITALL SMITH,
Philadelphia Quaker
by Logan Pearsall Smith

The Infinite fascinates us and we call it God, but in reality God is the Finite. The Infinite as Infinite is nothing.

MARK RUTHERFORD,
Last Pages from a Journal

It is not my business to think about myself. My business is to think about God. It is for God to think about me.

SIMONE WEIL,
Waiting for God

There are times when thinking of God separates us from him.

SIMONE WEIL,
Waiting for God

Why should I wish to see God better than
this day?
I see something of God each hour of the
twenty-four, and each moment then,
In the faces of men and women I see
God, and in my own face in the glass,
I find letters from God dropt in the
street, and every one is sign'd by God's
name,
And I leave them where they are, for I
know that wheresoe'er I go,
Others will punctually come for ever
and ever.

WALT WHITMAN,
"Song of Myself," *Leaves of Grass*

Silent and amazed even when a little
boy,
I remember I heard the preacher every
Sunday put God in his statements,
As contending against some being or
influence.

WALT WHITMAN,
"A Child's Amaze," *Leaves of Grass*

I need God to take me by force, because if death, doing away with the shield of the flesh, were to put me face to face with him, I should run away.

SIMONE WEIL,
Gravity and Grace

Fear God, yes, but don't be afraid of Him.

J. A. SPENDER,
The Comments of Bagshot, Second Series

It is a mistake to suppose that God is only, or even chiefly, concerned with religion.

WILLIAM TEMPLE
(Archbishop of Canterbury),
quoted in *In Search of Serenity*
by R. V. C. Bodley

Whatever your conception of God may be, believe Him to be your Friend.

DR. FRANK CRANE,
Essays

You have lost the knack of drawing strength from God: and vain strivings after communion of the *solitude à deux* sort will do nothing for you at this point. Seek contact with Him now in the goodness and splendour which is in other people, in *all* people, for those who have the art to find it.

EVELYN UNDERHILL,
The Letters of Evelyn Underhill

It would be terrible if God were not the God of the exception too.

THEODOR HAECKER,
Journal in the Night

God in whose image we are made,
Let me not be afraid,
To trace thy likeness in what best we are.

COVENTRY PATMORE,
quoted in *The Bliss of the Way,*
compiled by Cecily Hallack

GOLF

Golf is so popular simply because it is the best game in the world at which to be bad.

A. A. MILNE,
Not That It Matters

It is true that my predecessor did not object as I do to pictures of one's golfing skill in action. But neither, on the other hand, did he ever bean a Secret Service man.

JOHN F. KENNEDY,
The Kennedy Wit, edited by Bill Adler

Playing the game I have learned the meaning of humility. It has given me an understanding of the futility of human effort.

ABBA EBAN,
quoted in *Eighteen Holes in My Head*
by Milton Gross

If I were a man I wouldn't have half a dozen Tom Collinses before going out to play golf, then let profanity substitute for proficiency on the golf course.

PATTY BERG,
Ladies' Home Journal, February 1945

It seems that the most reticent of men on other subjects no sooner takes to golf than eloquence descends upon him.

JOHN HOGBEN,
quoted in *On the Green*
by Samuel J. Looker

A golf spectator is satisfied when he gets to see, at least a few times during the course of his long day, a ball struck with consummate power and amazing control; a ball sent soaring from a standing start, then floating to earth and stopping within a prescribed swatch of lawn. It is an awesome sensation, not unlike watching a rocket launch.

AL BARKOW,
Golf's Golden Grind

If a woman can walk, she can play golf.

LOUISE SUGGS,
Secrets of the Golfing Greats,
compiled by Tom Scott

In a gin'ral way, all I can say about it is that it's a kind iv game iv ball that ye play with ye'er own worst inimy, which is ye'ersilf.

FINLEY PETER DUNNE,
quoted in *Golf's Golden Grind* by Al Barkow
At Random through the Green,
compiled by John Stobbs

I'm playing like Tarzan—and scoring like Jane.

CHI CHI RODRIGUEZ,
quoted in *The Masters* by Dick Schaap

The least thing upset him on the links. He missed short putts because of the uproar of butterflies in the adjoining meadow.

P. G. WODEHOUSE,
At Random through the Green, compiled by John Stobbs

Every great golfer has learned to think positively, to assume the success and not the failure of a shot, to disregard misfortune and to accept disaster, and never to indulge the futility of remorse and blame. These are the hardest lessons of all.

PAT WARD-THOMAS,
quoted in *At Random through the Green,* compiled by John Stobbs

I'll be honest about it. I want to win more than [Bobby] Jones. That's what you play for, to separate yourself from the crowd.

JACK NICKLAUS,
quoted in *Sports Illustrated,* March 8, 1971

Golfers are the greatest worriers in the world of sports. . . . In fast-action sports, like football, baseball, basketball, or tennis, there is little time to worry compared to the time a golfer has on his hands between shots.

BILLY CASPER,
Secrets of the Golfing Greats, compiled by Tom Scott

It is nothing new or original to say that golf is played one stroke at a time. But it took me many years to realize it.

BOBBY JONES,
At Random through the Green, compiled by John Stobbs

GOOD

In the quiet hours when we are alone with ourselves and there is nobody to tell us what fine fellows we are, we come sometimes upon a weak moment in which we wonder, not how much money we are earning, nor how famous we are becoming, but what good we are doing.

A. A. MILNE,
Not That It Matters

Those people work more wisely who seek to achieve good in their own small corner of the world and then leave the leaven to leaven the whole lump, than those who are forever thinking that life is vain unless one can act through the central government, carry legislation, achieve political power and do big things.

HERBERT BUTTERFIELD,
Christianity and History

I know what things are good: Friendship and work and conversation. These I shall have.

RUPERT BROOKE,
quoted in *Linotype's Shining Lines,* October 1937

We are sometimes so occupied with being good angels that we neglect to be good men and women.

SAINT FRANCIS DE SALES,
Saint Francis de Sales in His Letters

If we shall take the good we find, asking no questions, we shall have heaping measures.

RALPH WALDO EMERSON,
"Experience," *Essays*

On the whole, human beings want to be good, but not too good, and not quite all the time.

GEORGE ORWELL,
A Collection of Essays

Philosophers and clergymen are always discussing why we should be good as if any one doubted that he ought to be.

G. M. TREVELYAN,
Clio, a Muse and Other Essays

To call Good Evil is the great sin—the sin of the Puritan and Philistine. To call Evil Good is comparatively venial.

COVENTRY PATMORE,
The Rod, the Root, and the Flower

True goods are peacefully desired, sought without eagerness, possessed without elation, and postponed without regret.

COVENTRY PATMORE,
The Rod, the Root, and the Flower

Better one good thing that is than two good things that were.

IRISH PROVERB

The pity of it is that generally the man with a good wife or the woman with a good husband or the children with good parents discover too late the goodness they overlooked while it was in full bloom.

JAMES DOUGLAS,
Down Shoe Lane

An act of goodness, the least act of true goodness, is indeed the best proof of the existence of God.

JACQUES MARITAIN,
Approaches to God

People are accustomed to think that good and evil must be the same for everyone, and, above all, that good and evil exist for everyone. In reality, however, good and evil exist only for a few, for those who have an aim and pursue that aim. Then what hinders the pursuit of that aim is evil and what helps is good.

GEORGES GURDJIEFF,
In Search of the Miraculous
by P. D. Ouspensky

Anyone who proposes to do good must not expect people to roll stones out of his way, but must accept his lot calmly if they even roll a few more upon it.

ALBERT SCHWEITZER,
Out of My Life and Thought

How sick one gets of being "good," how much I should respect myself if I could burst out and make every one wretched for 24 hours; embody selfishness.

ALICE JAMES,
The Diary of Alice James

If we accept the common usage of words, nothing can be more readily disproved than the old saw, "You can't keep a good man down." Most human societies have been beautifully organized to keep good men down.

JOHN W. GARDNER,
No Easy Victories edited by Helen Rowan

The good we think that we voluntarily perform we could not help doing if we tried.

ANONYMOUS (HENRY S. HASKINS),
Meditations in Wall Street

A sure way for me to have a disastrous experience is to do something because "it will be good for me."   HUGH PRATHER,
Notes to Myself

The good we secure for ourselves is precarious and uncertain ... until it is secured for all of us and incorporated into our common life.

JANE ADDAMS,
Jane Addams Speaks,
compiled by Leonard S. Kenworthy

Men in the mass are never moved to act jointly except through prejudice and when stirred by passion. Thus even the most praiseworthy purposes are always adulterated and sometimes distorted. In spite of this a great deal of good is accomplished, if not at once, yet in the course of time; if not directly, then indirectly.

GOETHE,
Wisdom and Experience

GOSSIP

Who brings a tale takes two away.

IRISH PROVERB

Surely it is better to tell the truth behind people's backs than never to tell it at all.

ROBERT LYND,
The Peal of Bells

Young people do not perceive at once that the giver of wounds is the enemy and the quoted tattle merely the arrow.

F. SCOTT FITZGERALD
The Crack-up

I am grateful that my worst offenses have not been found out. We all complain about gossip, but gossip is merciful to all of us in that it does not know all.

E. W. HOWE,
Preaching from the Audience

Truly unexpected tidings make both ears tingle.

SAINT BASIL,
Letters and Select Works

Why is it that in all ages small towns and remote villages have fostered little malignities of all kinds? The true answer is, that people will backbite one another to any extent rather than not be amused. Nay, so strong is this desire for something to go on that may break the monotony of life, that people, not otherwise ill-natured, are pleased with the misfortune of their neighbors, solely because it gives something to think of, something to talk about.

SIR ARTHUR HELPS,
Companions of My Solitude

If you want to get the most out of life why the thing is to be a gossiper by day and a gossipee by night.

OGDEN NASH,
Ogden Nash Pocket Book

Gossiping isn't just a woman's monopoly. Look at the male gossip columnists and the masculine maligning that goes on in barbershops. Gossip is part of human nature—not just a feminine characteristic.

BIDU SAYAO,
Ladies' Home Journal, February 1945

A man who is much talked about is always attractive. One feels there must be something in him, after all.

OSCAR WILDE,
The Importance of Being Earnest

GOVERNMENT

My experience in government is that when things are non-controversial, beautifully coordinated and all the rest, it must be that there is not much going on.

JOHN F. KENNEDY,
The Kennedy Wit, edited by Bill Adler

All real government is what may be called a Pentegerontamphitrapezy, i.e. five (more or less) old (more or less) gentlemen (more or less) sitting round a table.

JOSEPH RICKABY,
An Old Man's Jottings

If the gods should hand down to mortals, as mortals now are, a perfect system, it would be all bunged up and skewed twistways inside of ten years.

DON MARQUIS,
The Almost Perfect State

Even a fool can govern if nothing happens.

GERMAN PROVERB

When one is in office one has no idea how damnable things can feel to the ordinary rank and file of the public.

SIR WINSTON CHURCHILL,
A Churchill Reader,
edited by Colin R. Coote

Sometimes we wonder whether what the state really needs is the ripe wisdom of vigorous old men. It is possible that what the state needs is the foolish but lovable ideals of extreme youth.

E. B. WHITE,
Every Day Is Saturday

Life is a great and noble game between the citizen and the government. The government nearly always scores, but the citizen should not thereby be discouraged. Even if he always loses the game, it is in his power to inflict a considerable amount of annoyance on the victors.

ROSE MACAULAY,
A Casual Commentary

GRANDPARENTS

It is as grandmothers that our mothers come into the fullness of their grace. When a man's mother holds his child in her gladdened arms he is aware of the roundness of life's cycle; of the mystic harmony of life's ways.

CHRISTOPHER MORLEY,
Mince Pie

Once your children are grown up and have children of their own, the problems are theirs, and the less the older generation interferes the better.

ELEANOR ROOSEVELT,
Ladies' Home Journal, January 1946

So many things we love are you, I can't seem to explain except by little things, but flowers and beautiful handmade things—small stitches. So much of our reading and thinking—so many sweet customs and so much of our ... well, our religion. It is all *you.* I hadn't realized it before. This is so vague but do you see a little, dear Grandma? I want to thank you.

ANNE MORROW LINDBERGH,
Bring Me a Unicorn

Grandparents are frequently more congenial with their grandchildren than with their children. An old man, having retired from active life, regains the gaiety and irresponsibility of childhood. He is ready to play. . . . He cannot run with his son, but he can totter with his grandson. Our first and last steps have the same rhythm; our first and last walks are similarly limited.

ANDRÉ MAUROIS,
The Art of Living

As I do not live in an age when rustling black skirts billow about me, and I do not carry an ebony stick to strike the floor in sharp rebuke, as this is denied me, I rap out a sentence in my note book and feel better. If a grandmother wants to put her foot down, the only safe place to do it in these days is in a note book.

FLORIDA SCOTT-MAXWELL,
Revelations: Diaries of Women,
edited by Mary Jane Moffat
and Charlotte Painter

The closest friends I have made all through life have been people who also grew up close to a loved and loving grandmother or grandfather.

MARGARET MEAD,
Blackberry Winter

If becoming a grandmother was only a matter of choice I should advise every one of you straight way to become one. There is no fun for old people like it!

HANNAH WHITALL SMITH,
Philadelphia Quaker
by Logan Pearsall Smith

GRATITUDE

I have never yet found . . . that ill-will dies in debt, or what is called gratitude distresses herself by frequent payments.

SIR WALTER SCOTT,
Sir Walter Scott's Journal (1825-1832)

Joy untouched by thankfulness is always suspect.

THEODOR HAECKER,
Journal in the Night

Who does not thank for little will not thank for much.

ESTONIAN PROVERB

Be thankful f'r what ye have not, Hinnissy,—'tis the only safe rule.

FINLEY PETER DUNNE,
quoted in the *New York Times,*
November 21, 1948

It is not always possible to show gratitude by a gift, for there are many obligations which cannot be liquidated by money. Nobody can live without being laden with debts of the soul.

JAMES DOUGLAS,
Down Shoe Lane

One finds little ingratitude so long as one is in a position to grant favors.

FRENCH PROVERB

I cannot understand why I feel so embarrassed when being thanked. When thanks are at all profuse I get flustered, begin to wriggle and twist so that to cut things short I get rude.

BERNARD BERENSON,
Rumor and Reflection

The greatest number of grateful persons will be found in the ranks of the geniuses. . . . One who has so much to give need not be ashamed to have accepted something. And more especially as he knows with certainty that in life everyone must accept.

DR. WILHELM STEKHEL,
The Depths of the Soul

Gratitude sits awkwardly upon me: it produces a gasping incoherence—you will understand.

LIONEL JOHNSON,
Some Winchester Letters of Lionel Johnson

It is of grace not of ourselves that we lead civilized lives. There is sound sense in the old pagan notion that gratitude is the root of all virtue. Loyalty to whatever in the established environment makes a life of excellence possible is the beginning of all progress.

JOHN DEWEY,
Human Nature and Conduct

We should spend as much time in thanking God for His benefits as we do in asking Him for them.

SAINT VINCENT DE PAUL,
quoted in *St. Vincent de Paul*
by J. B. Boudignan

People like to spread abroad the services received at the hands of the great, less from gratitude than ostentation.

J. PETIT-SENN,
Conceits and Caprices

The obligation of gratitude may easily become a trap, and the young are often caught and maimed in it.

ERIC GILL,
Autobiography

We have all known ingratitude, ungrateful we have never been.

DIANE DE POITIERS,
quoted in *A Book of Days*
by Winifred Gordon

GREATNESS

All great men are gifted with intuition. They know without reasoning or analysis, what they need to know.

ALEXIS CARREL,
Reflections on Life

That which is great has more existence, and is further removed from nothing than that which is little. . . . An archangel must be supposed to have more existence, and to be every way further removed from nonentity, than a worm.

JONATHAN EDWARDS,
The Nature of True Virtue

All great gifts are one-sided and pretty well exclude the others.

THEODOR HAECKER,
Journal in the Night

Let us cease to wonder what they, the great, the illustrious ones, are doing in the beyond. Know that they are still singing hymns of praise. Here on earth they may have been practicing. *There* they are perfecting their song.

HENRY MILLER,
The Books in My life

If we are intended for great ends, we are called to great hazards.

JOHN HENRY CARDINAL NEWMAN,
Oxford University Sermons

It seems to me that any human individuality that has strongly aroused the love and hatred of men must be far too complex for absolute condemnation or absolute approval.

HAVELOCK ELLIS,
Selected Essays

It is a consolation to many—I have seen it so stated in a respectable review—that Nietzsche went mad. No doubt also it was once a consolation to many that Socrates was poisoned, that Jesus was crucified, that Bruno was burnt. But hemlock and the cross and the stake proved sorry weapons against the might of ideas even in those days, and there is no reason to suppose that a doctor's certificate will be more effectual in our own.

HAVELOCK ELLIS,
Selected Essays

Every life has a theme, and the theme of the great life raises questions, to answer which one must advance the actual frontiers of knowledge.

ISAAC ROSENFELD,
An Age of Enormity

We see from experience that nearly all those who help another to become great, grow in time to be little loved by him.

FRANCESCO GUICCIARDINI,
Counsels and Reflections

There is not a single man who has not had great moments, has not risen to rare occasions.

ERNEST DIMNET,
What We Live By

It is difficult to achieve greatness of mind or character where our responsibility is diminutive and fragmentary, where our whole life occupies and affects an extremely limited area.

RABINDRANATH TAGORE,
Letters to a Friend

It has often seemed to me that something great has only to be *thought* in order to exist indestructibly!

RAINER MARIA RILKE,
Letters of Rainer Maria Rilke 1892–1910

Altogether it will be found that a quiet life is characteristic of great men, and that their pleasures have not been of the sort that would look exciting to the outward eye.

BERTRAND RUSSELL,
The Conquest of Happiness

I don't believe an artist, or any man, ever had great thoughts he dared not utter. The people who daren't utter great thoughts are not the people who have them.

MAARTEN MAARTENS,
The Letters of Maarten Maartens

There are no great men save the poet, the priest, and the soldier.
The man who sings, the man who offers up sacrifice, and the man who sacrifices himself.
The rest are born for the whip.

CHARLES BAUDELAIRE,
Intimate Journals

Nations only produce great men in spite of themselves. Thus the great man is the conqueror of his whole nation.

CHARLES BAUDELAIRE,
Intimate Journals

Great men cling to the truth as if their hearts had teeth.

LOUIS DANZ,
Dynamic Dissonance

I have concerned myself very little with the individual great men whom you mention. Nor have I taken too much interest in the whole species. It has always seemed to me that ruthlessness and arrogant self-confidence constitute the indispensable condition for what, when it succeeds, strikes us as greatness; and I also believe that one ought to differentiate between greatness of achievement and greatness of personality.

SIGMUND FREUD,
The Letters of Sigmund Freud

Greatness is, however, too often anything but happiness, though not à dull, depressing misery. It is often a tumult in which the heavens are at war with each other.

CHAUNCEY WRIGHT,
Letters of Chauncey Wright

Doubtless one reason why the great men of the past seem so great to us is because all other voices are silent, theirs alone are heard. All the hum and roar and gabble and racket of those days are gone, hushed, dead, and the few voices that reach us seem to fill the world of that time.

JOHN BURROUGHS,
The Heart of Burroughs' Journals

There is no doubt that one of the most unpleasant kinds of falsehood is that of showing us nothing but the full-face view and bust of great men.

FRANÇOISE MALLET-JORIS,
A Letter to Myself

We all go to our graves unknown, worlds of unsuspected greatness.

FREDERICK W. FABER,
Spiritual Conferences

The world on the whole and in the mass is neither very strong-minded nor very hard-hearted, and it gradually modifies the ideas of great men to its own likeness; anthropomorphism is as active in biography and history as it is in theology.

JOHN DAVIDSON,
Sentences and Paragraphs

How impossible it is to predict which of two young men has the main talent—which of them will end by establishing himself and forcing his times to accept him. The greatest talent of all is a talent for life; and this often lies hidden under a mound of golden inertia, or of frivolity and incompetence, and is brought to the surface by those slow upheavals which run through the world and bring the slow men to the top. When I look at a row of little boys I often wonder which one of them it is who is hiddenly in touch with the enduring powers of the world, and how they will each look forty years later. There seems to exist no key to these enigmas. The dunces of genius and the real dunces look very much alike; and the boys of brilliant promise cannot be prophetically classified.

JOHN JAY CHAPMAN,
Memories and Milestones

We are very near to greatness: one step and we are safe: can we not take the leap?

RALPH WALDO EMERSON,
Journals of Ralph Waldo Emerson

A great man who succeeded in being what little men desired him to be, would have only one drawback—that of being like them.

ERNEST HELLO,
Life, Science, and Art

It is most idle to take a man apart from the circumstances which, in fact, were his.... A great man represents a great ganglion in the nerves of society, or, to vary the figure, a strategic point in the campaign of history, and part of his greatness consists in his being *there*.

OLIVER WENDELL HOLMES, JR.,
The Mind and Faith of Justice Holmes,
edited by Max Lerner

Great passions are for the great of soul, and great events can be seen only by those who are on a level with them.

OSCAR WILDE,
De Profundis

We are always glad when a great man reassures us of his humanity by possessing a few peculiarities.

ANDRÉ MAUROIS,
The Art of Living

The surrounding social conditions for a great age have to be present, but much, if not all, depends on the chance of there being a powerful personality to set it going.... Much depends on the chance production of a great man whose powers are adapted to the needs of his age. He voices those needs.

ALFRED NORTH WHITEHEAD,
Dialogues of Alfred North Whitehead

To get really into a subject takes more energy than "nothing too much," and a man has to ignore much to get on with something. A certain element of excess seems to be a necessary element in all greatness.

ALFRED NORTH WHITEHEAD,
Dialogues of Alfred North Whitehead

And then there is the incentive of any great figure doing good work. It sets off a lot of others.

ALFRED NORTH WHITEHEAD,
Dialogues of Alfred North Whitehead

It is no sign of intellectual greatness to hold other men cheaply. A great intellect takes for granted that other men are more or less like itself.

HENRY CARDINAL MANNING,
Pastime Papers

I think the wisest men—and often the greatest—have come to their powers of great service somewhat by accident and the place they found themselves in; but one condition of their power in the end was they had the habit of doing little things day by day, and always as well as they could, and so their greatness came on them almost unobserved. They didn't think about greatness, but grew up to it.

GEORGE E. WOODBERRY,
Selected Letters of George Edward Woodberry

GREED (See DESIRE)

GRIEF (See SADNESS, SORROW)

GROWTH

If we dropped our stratagems for six

months, our growing-pains would become so acute that we could hardly walk.

ANONYMOUS (HENRY S. HASKINS),
Meditations in Wall Street

The rung of a ladder was never meant to rest upon, but only to hold a man's foot long enough to enable him to put the other somewhat higher.

THOMAS HENRY HUXLEY,
Life and Letters of Thomas Huxley

I do only want to advise you to keep growing quietly and seriously throughout your development; you cannot disturb it more rudely than by looking outward and expecting from outside replies to questions that only your inmost feeling in your quietest hours can perhaps answer.

RAINER MARIA RILKE,
Letters to a Young Poet

I am learning to see. I do not know why it is, but everything penetrates more deeply within me, and no longer stops at the place, where until now, it always used to finish.

RAINER MARIA RILKE,
The Journal of My Other Self

The poles by great beans overleapt
  Were not o'erun in sudden flight,
But they, while all the squashes slept,
  Were sneaking upward through the night.

DON MARQUIS,
The Almost Perfect State

The desire to grow, the right to live and to blossom is stronger than filial love and consideration . . . terrible conflict.

KATHARINE BUTLER HATHAWAY,
*The Journals and Letters
of the Little Locksmith*

People evolving—they are supposed to evolve when young and up to middle life, then one is just as evolutionary but external forces against it grow stronger and stronger because one's life has become more intricately attached to other lives, and evolving is liable to disrupt others. Therefor one hesitates—see all those older

people soggy . . . tragic ones whose forward-going movement has been destroyed.

KATHARINE BUTLER HATHAWAY,
*The Journals and Letters
of the Little Locksmith*

My aim is to bring about a psychic state in which my patient begins to experiment with his own nature—a state of fluidity, change and growth, in which there is no longer anything eternally fixed and hopelessly petrified.

C. G. JUNG,
Modern Man in Search of a Soul

Every forward step we take we leave some phantom of ourselves behind.

JOHN LANCASTER SPALDING,
Aphorisms and Reflections

When we blindly adopt a religion, a political system, a literary dogma, we become automatons. We cease to grow.

ANAÏS NIN,
The Diaries of Anaïs Nin, Vol. IV

We do not grow absolutely, chronologically. We grow sometimes in one dimension, and not in another, unevenly. We grow partially. We are relative. We are mature in one realm, childish in another. The past, present, and future mingle and pull us backward, forward, or fix us in the present. We are made up of layers, cells, constellations.

ANAÏS NIN,
The Diaries of Anaïs Nin, Vol. IV

Then after the axiom that happiness is the chief end of man, the next truth of natural ethics is that the chief way to be happy is to grow.

MAX EASTMAN,
Enjoyment of Living

There was that law of life, so cruel and so just, that one must grow or else pay more for remaining the same.

NORMAN MAILER,
The Deer Park

What grows makes no noise.

GERMAN PROVERB

In this world, things that are naturally destined to endure for a long time, are the slowest in reaching maturity.

SAINT VINCENT DE PAUL,
St. Vincent de Paul by J. B. Boudignan

It is my thesis that the core of the problem for women today is not sexual but a problem of identity—a stunting or evasion of growth that is perpetuated by the feminine mystique. It is my thesis that as the Victorian culture did not permit women to accept or gratify their basic sexual needs, our culture does not permit women to accept or gratify their basic need to grow and fulfill their potentialities as human beings, a need which is not solely defined by their sexual role.

BETTY FRIEDAN,
The Feminine Mystique

Be not afraid of going slowly, be afraid only of standing still.

CHINESE PROVERB

Every human being on this earth is born with a tragedy, and it isn't original sin. He's born with the tragedy that he has to grow up. That he has to leave the nest, the security, and go out to do battle. He has to lose everything that is lovely and fight for a new loveliness of his own making, and it's a tragedy. A lot of people don't have the courage to do it.

HELEN HAYES,
Showcase by Roy Newquist

Beauty, truth, power, God, all these come without searching, without effort. The struggle is not for these; the struggle is deeper than that. The struggle is to synchronize the potential being with the actual being, to make a fruitful liaison between the man of yesterday and the man of tomorrow. It is the process of growth which is painful, but unavoidable. We either grow or we die, and to die while alive is a thousand times worse than to "shuffle off this mortal coil."

HENRY MILLER,
The Cosmological Eye

To teach a man how he may learn to grow

independently, and for himself, is perhaps the greatest service that one man can do another.

BENJAMIN JOWETT

GUEST

A guest should be permitted to graze, as it were, in the pastures of his host's kindness, left even to his own devices, like a rational being, and handsomely neglected.

LOUISE IMOGEN GUINEY,
Goose-Quill Papers

History was made in our household recently; a guest used a guest towel.

MARCELENE COX,
Ladies' Home Journal, September 1943

With guests I am conscious of myself as a solid, but as soon as they have gone I expand into a gas again. And a gas can have more delight than a solid.

J. B. PRIESTLEY,
Delight

I always feel that I have two duties to perform with a parting guest: one, to see that he doesn't forget anything that is his; the other, to see that he doesn't take anything that is mine.

ALFRED NORTH WHITEHEAD,
Dialogues of Alfred North Whitehead

A guest is really good or bad because of the host or hostess who makes being a guest an easy or a difficult task.

ELEANOR ROOSEVELT,
Ladies' Home Journal, January 1947

To be a really good guest and at ease under alien roofs it is necessary, I suspect, to have no home ties of one's own; certainly to have no very tyrannical habits.

E. V. LUCAS,
365 Days and One More

Staying with people consists in your not having your way, and their not having theirs.

MAARTEN MAARTENS,
quoted in *A Book of Days*
by Winifred Gordon

I remember grandpa Whitall used to say, "Short visits make long friends," and I believe he was right in most cases. I have always found that long visits seemed to exhaust my powers of affection. Not of course in the case of relatives who are congenial, but of outside friends, let them be ever so congenial. There *is* something in blood that helps you to put up with things.

HANNAH WHITALL SMITH,
Philadelphia Quaker
by Logan Pearsall Smith

It is bad manners to contradict a guest. You must never insult people in your own house—always go to theirs.

MYRTLE REED,
The Book of Clever Beasts

A sign in each guest room, giving the hours of meals, political and religious preferences of the family, general views on exercise, etc., etc., with a blank for the guest to fill out stating his own views, would make it possible to visit (or entertain) with a sense of security thus far unknown upon our planet.

ROBERT BENCHLEY,
quoted in *Ladies' Home Journal,*
March 1943

The most charming visitor may linger one day too long. The best time to go is when everybody's asking you to stay.

ELIZA C. HALL,
quoted in *The Author's Kalendar, 1915,*
compiled by Anna C. Woodford

It's what the guests say as they swing out of the driveway that counts.

ANONYMOUS,
quoted in the *New York Times,*
August 3, 1947

HABIT

Habit and routine have an unbelievable power to waste and destroy.

HENRI DE LUBAC,
Paradoxes

A very slight change in our habits is sufficient to destroy our sense of our daily reality, and the reality of the world about us; the moment we pass out of our habits we lose all sense of permanency and routine.

GEORGE MOORE,
Epigrams of George Moore

Beware of your habits. The better they are the more surely will they be your undoing.

HOLBROOK JACKSON,
Platitudes in the Making

A laxity due to decadence of old habits cannot be corrected by exhortations to restore old habits in their former rigidity. Even though it were abstractly desirable it is impossible. And it is not desirable because the inflexibility of old habits is precisely the chief cause of their decay and disintegration.

JOHN DEWEY,
Human Nature and Conduct

What we have grown accustomed to seems good enough, and they who fall into ways and ruts find it natural to walk therein to the end.

JOHN LANCASTER SPALDING,
Glimpses of Truth

Habits are safer than rules; you don't have to watch them. And you don't have to keep them either. They keep you.

DR. FRANK CRANE,
Essays

Every grown-up man consists wholly of habits, although he is often unaware of it and even denies having any habits at all.

GEORGES GURDJIEFF,
In Search of the Miraculous
by P. D. Ouspensky

The man who interferes with another's habits has the worst one.

ANONYMOUS (HENRY S. HASKINS),
Meditations in Wall Street

HAND

We read in this hand how it hath healed a bitter wound; and in that, how it hath locked the door against a cry.

LOUISE IMOGEN GUINEY,
Goose-Quill Papers

Ordinarily we think of the human hand as a delicate and wonderfully skilled instrument. A study of its structure and mode of operation, however, reveals that it is actually a modified kind of talon. Despite evolutionary development, the human hand still remains essentially what it was in primitive times—an aggressive mechanism designed to seize and grasp, to rip and scratch, to squeeze, push and strike.

DR. SMILEY BLANTON,
Love or Perish

I cannot look at the *hands* of a toiling man or woman without feeling deeply wretched. To compare my own with them, shames me.

GEORGE GISSING,
Commonplace Book

The hand will not reach for what the heart does not long for.

WELSH PROVERB

I hate the giving of the hand unless the whole man accompanies it.

RALPH WALDO EMERSON,
Journals of Ralph Waldo Emerson

HAPPINESS

Until we are once happy, the longing for happiness must be, I suppose, the preoccupation of life.

RUTH BENEDICT,
An Anthropologist at Work
by Margaret Mead

There is a time when a man distinguishes the idea of felicity from the idea of wealth; it is the beginning of wisdom.

RALPH WALDO EMERSON,
Journals of Ralph Waldo Emerson

Two happy days are seldom brothers.

BULGARIAN PROVERB

Felicity, felicity—how shall I say it?—is quaffed out of a golden cup in every latitude: the flavour is with you—with you alone, and you can make it as intoxicating as you please.

JOSEPH CONRAD,
Lord Jim

The truth is, most of us believe in trying to make other people happy only if they can be happy in ways which we can approve.

ROBERT LYND,
Life's Little Oddities

Why is it that so many people are afraid to admit they are happy? . . . If everything is going as well as could possibly be expected and you ask them how they are, they say, "Can't complain."

WILLIAM LYON PHELPS,
Essays on Things

At times the sight of a mountain of felicity will not raise a man's spirits; at other times, if his foot trips over a molehill, he will cry out in ecstasy at the goodness of life.

J. B. PRIESTLEY,
All About Ourselves and Other Essays

When a man is happy he does not hear the clock strike.

GERMAN PROVERB

Do not worry; eat three square meals a day; say your prayers; be courteous to your creditors; keep your digestion good; exercise, go slow and easy. Maybe there are other things your special case requires to make you happy, but my friend, these I reckon will give you a good lift.

ABRAHAM LINCOLN,
quoted in *The Author's Kalendar, 1916,*
compiled by Anna C. Woodford

True happiness, we are told, consists in getting out of one's self, but the point is not only to get out—you must stay out; and to stay out you must have some absorbing errand.

HENRY JAMES,
Roderick Hudson

Human nature is very perverse, and we only care to hear of another's happiness when we are the givers of it.

GEORGE MOORE,
Epigrams of George Moore

No doubt there are some prudent persons who cleave to the paradoxical conviction that to pursue happiness is only to lose it, since it can be captured only by *not* pursuing it. Yet this, after all, is only a subtler method of pursuit—an attack in flank, instead of in front.

F. L. LUCAS,
The Greatest Problem and Other Essays

The happiness of most people we know is not ruined by great catastrophes or fatal errors, but by the repetition of slowly destructive little things.

ERNEST DIMNET,
What We Live By

Men are made for happiness, and anyone who is completely happy has a right to say to himself: "I am doing God's will on earth."

ANTON CHEKHOV,
quoted in *The Bliss of the Way,*
compiled by Cecily Hallack

Men are often able to agree on what virtue to dispense with as non-essential to happiness, but each person clings to a favorite vice.

DON MARQUIS,
The Almost Perfect State

Fate often puts all the material for happiness and prosperity into a man's hands just to see how miserable he can make himself with them.

DON MARQUIS

A happiness that is sought for ourselves alone can never be found: for a happiness that is diminished by being shared is not big enough to make us happy.

THOMAS MERTON,
No Man Is an Island

Happiness puts on as many shapes as discontent, and there is nothing odder than the satisfactions of one's neighbor.

PHYLLIS MCGINLEY,
The Province of the Heart

The heat of the day is spent in reading or working, and about six or seven o'clock I walk out into a common that lies hard by the house, where a great many young wenches keep sheep and cows and sit in the shade singing of [sic] ballads. . . . I talk to them, and find they want nothing to make them the happiest people in the world but the knowledge that they are so.

DOROTHY OSBORNE,
quoted in *The Literature of Gossip*
by Elizabeth Drew

Give me twelve hours of work on *one* occupation for happiness.

WILLIAM JAMES,
The Thought and Character of
William James, Vol. II,
by Ralph Barton Perry

It is difficult to describe happiness and impossible to dramatise it. Nobody will listen to an account of other people's bliss. For a hundred people who read the "Inferno" and "Purgatorio" of Dante's *Divine Comedy,* there is surely but one who penetrates to, and sustains a passage through, the "Paradiso."

RICHARD CHURCH,
Over the Bridge

The happy man would have faces round him; a sad face is a reproach to him for his happiness.

A. A. MILNE,
Not That It Matters

Happiness is not a horse; you cannot harness it.

RUSSIAN PROVERB

I . . . have always had a strong and shameless interest in having a good time. I have felt that something was profoundly the matter, and that desperate measures should be taken, if I was not happy.

MAX EASTMAN,
Enjoyment of Living

For the last year I have been happy for the first time in my life—happy not in the outward shadow part of me, but in my soul which is clear and radiant out of a long darkness.

ELLEN GLASGOW,
Letters of Ellen Glasgow

The conventional notions of happiness cannot possibly be taken seriously by anyone whose intellectual or moral development has progressed beyond that of a three-week-old puppy.

JOHN W. GARDNER,
No Easy Victories, edited by Helen Rowan

Just as a cautious businessman avoids investing all his capital in one concern, so wisdom would probably admonish us also not to anticipate all our happiness from one quarter alone.

SIGMUND FREUD,
Civilization and Its Discontents

We must not seek happiness in peace, but in conflict.

PAUL CLAUDEL,
quoted in *The Journals of André Gide,* Vol. I

We fall short when we ascribe all modes of happiness to walking in paths of rectitude. There are joys which only tramps and thieves know.

ANONYMOUS (HENRY S. HASKINS),
Meditations in Wall Street

I think that all happiness depends on the energy to assume the mask of some other self; that all joyous or creative life is a rebirth as something not oneself, something which has no memory and is created in a moment and perpetually renewed.

W. B. YEATS,
Autobiography

I believe in the possibility of happiness, if one cultivates intuition and outlives the grosser passions, including optimism.

GEORGE SANTAYANA,
The Letters of George Santayana

We should not set our hearts ... on a material possession of anything, but our happiness should be made to lie in this, that whatever we possess for a time should reveal the ideal good to us and make us better in ourselves.

GEORGE SANTAYANA,
quoted in *Love Is Not What You Think*
by Jessamyn West

There are many happy men who cannot bear to be alone with their happiness, for man has even more need of help in joy than in sorrow.

GEORGES DUHAMEL,
The Heart's Domain

I have never looked upon ease and happi-

ness as ideals in themselves—this ethical basis I call the ideal of the pigsty.

ALBERT EINSTEIN,
Ideas and Opinions

I have come to know happy individuals, by the way, who are happy only because they are whole. Even the lowliest, provided he is whole, can be happy and in his own way perfect.

GOETHE,
Wisdom and Experience

Happiness is a great love and much serving.

OLIVE SCHREINER,
quoted in *A Diary for the Thankful-Hearted,*
compiled by Mary Hodgkin

Good heavens, of what uncostly material is our earthly happiness composed—if we only knew it. What incomes have we not had from a flower, and how unfailing are the dividends of the seasons!

JAMES RUSSELL LOWELL,
Letters

Not to call a thing good a day longer or a day earlier than it seems good to us is the only way to remain really happy.

FRIEDRICH NIETZSCHE

On the whole I really don't believe it is important to be happy in the sense in which people expect it, but I can so infinitely understand this laborious happiness which lies in arousing by some determined work powers that themselves begin to work upon one.

RAINER MARIA RILKE,
Letters of Rainer Maria Rilke 1892–1910

Happiness is a wine of the rarest vintage, and seems insipid to a vulgar taste.

LOGAN PEARSALL SMITH,
Afterthoughts

Happiness is not a matter of events; it depends upon the tides of the mind.

ALICE MEYNELL,
Prose and Poetry

Nobody shall say of me that I have not known perfect happiness, but few could put their finger on the moment, or say what made it. Even I myself, stirring occasionally in the pool of content, could only say But this is all I want; could not think of anything better; and had only my half superstitious feeling at the Gods who must when they have created happiness, grudge it. Not if you get it in unexpected ways, though.

> VIRGINIA WOOLF,
> *A Writer's Diary*

When one is happy there is no time to be fatigued; being happy engrosses the whole attention.

> E. F. BENSON,
> quoted in *The Author's Kalendar, 1915,*
> compiled by Anna C. Woodford

We follow happiness whenever we see it, even to our own destruction, following it we seem, because of our sympathy, to possess it.

> J. B. YEATS,
> *Letters to His Son, W. B. Yeats and Others*

We haven't time to be ourselves. All we have time for is happiness.

> ALBERT CAMUS,
> *Notebooks 1935–1942*

Happiness would be to be alone at the seaside and then be left in peace. And to eat very little; yes. Almost nothing. A candle. I wouldn't live with electricity and things. A candle! A candle, and then I'd read the newspaper.

> LOUIS-FERDINAND CÉLINE,
> *Writers at Work,* Third Series,
> edited by George Plimpton

Very few people can stand conditions of life that are too happy; the great majority become stultified by them. Life is only felt to be real when it is creatively active. Thus people who appear to outsiders to be exceptionally happy, because of their freedom from care, are as a rule the least satisfied.

> COUNT HERMANN KEYSERLING,
> *The Book of Marriage*

When a happy moment, complete and rounded as a pearl, falls into the tossing ocean of life, it is never wholly lost.

> AGNES REPPLIER,
> *Points of View*

One man I know is happy only when he is playing bridge, but as he plays bridge morning, noon and night he is always happy.

> HUGH WALPOLE,
> *Roman Fountain*

Happiness comes, I know, from within a man—from some curious *adjustment* to life. The happiest people I have known in this world have been the Saints—and, after these, the men and women who get immediate and conscious enjoyment from little things.

> HUGH WALPOLE,
> *Roman Fountain*

The happiness that is genuinely satisfying is accompanied by the fullest exercise of our faculties, and the fullest realization of the world in which we live.

> BERTRAND RUSSELL,
> *The Conquest of Happiness*

Fundamental happiness depends more than anything else upon what may be called a friendly interest in persons and things.

> BERTRAND RUSSELL,
> *The Conquest of Happiness*

If there were in the world today any large number of people who desired their own happiness more than they desired the unhappiness of others, we could have a paradise in a few years.

> BERTRAND RUSSELL,
> quoted in the *New York Times,*
> May 18, 1961

The secret of happiness (and therefore of success) is to be in harmony with existence, to be always calm, always lucid, always willing "to be joined to the universe without being more conscious of it than an idiot," to let each wave of life wash us a little farther up the shore.

> CYRIL CONNOLLY,
> *The Unquiet Grave*

The happiness which is lacking makes one think even the happiness one has unbearable.

JOSEPH ROUX,
Meditations of a Parish Priest

I know well that happiness is in little things,—if anywhere,—but it is essentially within one, and being within, *seems* to fasten on little things. When I have been unhappy, I have heard an opera from end to end, and it seemed the shreiking of winds; when I am happy, a sparrow's chirp is delicious to me. But it is not the chirp that makes me happy, but I that make *it* sweet.

JOHN RUSKIN,
*Letters of John Ruskin
to Charles Eliot Norton,* Vol. I

Most people are prompt enough to appreciate the conditions under which other people ought to be happy.

JOSEPH FARRELL,
Lectures of a Certain Professor

Why should we refuse the happiness this hour gives us, because some other hour might take it away?

JOHN OLIVER HOBBES,
A Bundle of Life

Not many things are certain in our own haphazard world, but there is at least one thing about which there is little doubt, that is that those who seek happiness miss it, and those who discuss it, lack it.

HOLBROOK JACKSON,
Southward Ho! and Other Essays

Suspicion of happiness is in our blood.

E. V. LUCAS,
365 Days and One More

Happiness will never be any greater than the idea we have of it.

MAURICE MAETERLINCK,
The Great Beyond

We are more interested in making others believe we are happy than in trying to be happy ourselves.

LA ROCHEFOUCAULD,
Maxims

HATE

I find just as much profit in cultivating my hates as my loves.

ANDRÉ GIDE,
The Journals of André Gide, Vol. I

The important thing is not to let oneself be poisoned. Now, hatred poisons.

ANDRÉ GIDE,
The Journals of André Gide, Vol. I

What we hate, and how intensely, is the true touchstone of our mettle.

PAUL ELDRIDGE,
Horns of Glass

We shall always discover reasons, which we shall proclaim inevitable and divinely ordained, for hating one another.

PAUL ELDRIDGE,
Horns of Glass

Hate . . . has what lust entirely lacks—persistence and continuity: the persistence and continuity of purposive spirit.

ALDOUS HUXLEY,
Beyond the Mexique Bay

Whenever there is hatred between two people there is bond or brotherhood of some kind.

OSCAR WILDE,
De Profundis

I feel that a careful study of the particular effects of civilization upon women and the way in which it deprives them of instinctual gratifications is important in understanding why we grow up so much more prone to hate than to love.

DR. KARL MENNINGER,
Love Against Hate

It would be a rather serious error if the child did not *learn* to hate certain things. The real fact seems to be that he does not *learn* to hate; he comes into the world equipped with it, for better or for worse, and then he learns to use it, wisely or unwisely according to his experiences.

DR. KARL MENNINGER,
Love Against Hate

The rage of the southern poor white

against the Negro suspected of some dereliction is referable to the hate he feels inwardly at having been, like the Negro, unwanted. The same is perhaps true in the case of Germans and Jews and in many other situations which give the opportunity for the expression of hatred in the denial of the feeling of being rejected.

DR. KARL MENNINGER,
Love Against Hate

Many of the disasters of life which are blamed on Fate, heredity, misfortune, or the machinations of foes can be traced to this unconscious destructive force within ourselves.

DR. KARL MENNINGER,
A Psychiatrist's World

I don't agree that love gives the best insight. Hate gives a much better, I think, when hate keeps its head.

MAARTEN MAARTENS,
The Letters of Maarten Maartens

It is possible that emotion is an avocation and in ways beyond the senses alters events, creating good or evil luck. Certain individuals who hate much seem to be followed by violent events outside their control. . . . It is possible to explain it by saying that hatred brings certain associations and causes a tendency to violent action. But there are times when there seems to be more than this—an actual stream of ill-luck.

W. B. YEATS,
W. B. Yeats Memoirs,
edited by Denis Donaghue

Hate is able to provoke disorders, to ruin a social organization, to cast a country into a period of bloody revolutions; but it produces nothing.

GEORGES SOREL

The woman who cannot hate like a bitch afire, and express it, cannot love like a tigress, or a kitten.

BRENDAN FRANCIS

When you visualized a man or a woman carefully, you could always begin to feel pity. . . . That was a quality God's image carried with it. . . . When you saw the lines at the corners of the eyes, the shape of the mouth, how the hair grew, it was impossible to hate. Hate was just a failure of imagination.

GRAHAM GREENE,
The Power and The Glory

Man is a hating rather than a loving animal.

REBECCA WEST,
quoted in *Rebecca West: Artist and Thinker*
by Peter Wolfe

We never get to love by hate, least of all by self-hatred.

BASIL W. MATURIN,
quoted in *Father Maturin* by Maisie Ward

A vast number of attachments subsist on the common hatred of a third person.

MADAME SWETCHINE,
The Writings of Madame Swetchine

The time comes when every one of us has to abandon the illusory anticipation with which in our youth we regarded our fellow-men, and when we realize how much hardship and suffering we have been caused in life through their ill-will.

SIGMUND FREUD,
Civilization and Its Discontents

I imagine one of the reasons people cling to their hates so stubbornly is because they sense, once hate is gone, that they will be forced to deal with pain.

JAMES BALDWIN,
Notes of a Native Son

For this is the true name of hate: it is neither pursuit nor reproach nor fury—it is separation.

ERNEST HELLO,
Life, Science, and Art

The person who is afraid of love constantly reacts against it with hatred. In new surroundings he acts as though he were in the old surroundings of his early life. He eternally puts his new wine into old bottles. His behavior may be completely unsuitable to the present, but his real self is smothered by this compulsive necessity to act as though the present were the past.

> DR. SMILEY BLANTON,
> *Love or Perish*

Psychiatrists today ... see the irrational hostility that people everywhere vent upon one another as chiefly *projected self-hate.*

> BONARO OVERSTREET,
> *Understanding Fear in Ourselves and Others*

Hate must make a man productive. Otherwise one might as well love.

> KARL KRAUS,
> *Karl Kraus* by Harry Zohn

There is no hate without fear. Hate is crystallized fear, fear's dividend, fear objectivized. We hate what we fear and so where hate is, fear is lurking. Thus we hate what threatens our person, our liberty, our privacy, our income, popularity, vanity and our dreams and plans for ourselves. If we can isolate this element in what we hate we may learn to cease from hating.

> CYRIL CONNOLLY,
> *The Unquiet Grave*

There is a community of hatred. Hatred floods your mind with the idea of the one you hate. Your thought reflects his, and you act in his spirit.... If you wish to be like your enemy, to be wholly his, open your mind and hate him.

> CHARLES HORTON COOLEY,
> *Life and the Student*

HEALTH

A man too busy to take care of his health is like a mechanic too busy to take care of his tools.

> SPANISH PROVERB

Be careful to preserve your health. It is a trick of the devil, which he employs to deceive good souls, to incite them to do more than they are able, in order that they may no longer be able to do anything.

> SAINT VINCENT DE PAUL,
> quoted in *St. Vincent de Paul*
> by J. B. Boudignan

When a man loses his health, then he first begins to take good care of it.

> JOSH BILLINGS,
> *His Works Complete*

Must be out-of-doors enough to get experience of wholesome reality, as a ballast to thought and sentiment. Health requires this relaxation, this aimless life.

> HENRY DAVID THOREAU,
> *Journal*

A man needs a purpose for real health.

> SHERWOOD ANDERSON,
> *Letters of Sherwood Anderson*

The cult of physical health is simply absurd nowadays. Health has a relative value, like other things. That value is very low, if your health is to be used by somebody else for his benefit.

Again, doctor's health is only a special kind and takes no account of the mental activity of the patient which may be stimulated by a different physical state.

> FREDERICK GOODYEAR,
> *Letters and Remains*

Do the best you can, without straining yourself too much and too continuously, and leave the rest to God. If you strain yourself too much you'll have to ask God to patch you up. And for all you know, patching you up may take time that it was planned to use some other way.

> DON MARQUIS,
> *The Almost Perfect State*

He who has health has hope; and he who has hope has everything.

> ARAB PROVERB

It is true that I am carrying out various methods of treatment recommended by doctors and dentists in the hope of dying in the remote future in perfect health.

> GEORGE SANTAYANA,
> *The Letters of George Santayana*

Health of body and mind is a great blessing, if we can bear it.

> JOHN HENRY CARDINAL NEWMAN,
> *Parochial and Plain Sermons,* Vol. I

All sorts of bodily diseases are produced by half-used minds.

GEORGE BERNARD SHAW,
On the Rocks

HEART

Nowhere are there more hiding places than in the heart.

GERMAN PROVERB

The secret of the heart—a thing personal and intimate—being expressed, stated perhaps with diffidence, turns out to be the great lamp of truth, an axis on which human life turns, and has ever turned.

JOHN JAY CHAPMAN,
Memories and Milestones

Even inanimate objects do not speak to the heart, if the heart has nothing to say.

C.-F. RAMUZ,
What Is Man?

We pay tribute to all those to whom we open our hearts.

BALTASAR GRACIAN,
The Oracle

Life had taught her one great lesson, and when one door of her heart was closed, she opened another as quickly as possible.

MYRTLE REED,
Old Rose and Silver

A lion Lurks in everyone's heart; awake him not.

BULGARIAN PROVERB

When the heart is crowded, it has most room; when empty, it can find place for no new guest.

AUSTIN O'MALLEY,
Keystones of Thought

The logic of the heart is usually better than the logic of the head, and the consistency of sympathy is superior as a rule for life to the consistency of the intellect.

RANDOLPH BOURNE,
Youth and Life

One should hold fast one's heart; for when one letteth it go, how quickly doth one's head run away!

FRIEDRICH NIETZSCHE,
Thus Spake Zarathustra

I understand the ties that are between us too well to talk about the heart—that pump!
It lies between the brain-box and the penis,
and when these masters stir that slave will jump.

JAMES SIMMONS,
"The Summing Up,"
Poems One Line and Longer,
edited by William Cole

What a number of the dead we carry in our hearts. Each of us bears his cemetery within.

GUSTAVE FLAUBERT,
Letters of Gustave Flaubert

Always there remain portions of our heart into which no one is able to enter, invite them as we may.

MARY DIXON THAYER,
Things to Live By

There are no little events with the heart. It magnifies everything; it places in the same scales the fall of an empire and the dropping of a woman's glove, and almost always the glove weighs more than the empire.

HONORÉ DE BALZAC

Yet if, putting aside for a moment all convention and custom, one will look quietly within himself, he will perceive that there are most distinct and inviolable inner forces, binding him by different ties to different people, and with different and inevitable results according to the quality and nature of the affection bestowed—that there is in fact in that world of the heart a kind of cosmical harmony and variety, and an order almost astronomical.

EDWARD CARPENTER,
Love's Coming of Age

No pleasure or success in life quite meets the capacity of our hearts. We take in our good things with enthusiasm, and think ourselves happy and satisfied; but after-

ward, when the froth and foam have sub-
sided, we discover that the goblet is not
more than half-filled with the golden liquid that was poured into it.

LOUISE IMOGEN GUINEY,
Goose-Quill Papers

A man's heart gets cold if he does not keep
it warm by living in it; and a censorious
man is one who ordinarily lives out of his
own heart.

FREDERICK W. FABER,
Spiritual Conferences

HEAVEN

When you first learn to love hell, you will
be in heaven.

THADDEUS GOLAS,
The Lazy Man's Guide to Enlightenment

The last thing I should expect to meet in
heaven would be a dead level of intellect
and taste. I admire the notion of some of
the theologians that each individual angel
is a distinct species in himself.

JOSEPH FARRELL,
Lectures of a Certain Professor

Heaven and hell are relative and *essentially
prospective;* by the time we get to either we
begin to see that each of them has its other
side.

GEORGE SANTAYANA,
Letters of George Santayana

I have an idea heaven will be both absolutely happy and absolutely dark, to protect us from the blaze of God.

EVELYN UNDERHILL,
The Letters of Evelyn Underhill

A genteel Philadelphia lady once crisply
remarked that there were no marriages in
Heaven because "Women were there no
doubt in plenty; but not a man whom any
woman would have."

AGNES REPPLIER,
Americans and Others

Heaven, hell, the worlds are within us.
Man is the great abyss.

HENRI FRÉDÉRIC AMIEL,
The Private Journal of Henri Frédéric Amiel

Do our eyes indeed close forever on the
beauty of earth when they open on the
beauty of Heaven? I think not so; ... I
believe that in Heaven is earth.

FRANCIS THOMPSON,
Works, Vol. III

To be excited and at the same time satisfied; to desire and possess—that has been
described somewhere as the wise man's
ideal of heaven. And certainly one might
search a long time for a better definition.

ALEC WAUGH,
On Doing What One Likes

He who looks only at heaven may easily
break his nose on earth.

CZECH PROVERB

Perhaps the chief interest of Heavens lies
in the light they throw on the mentalities
of the men who conceived them—on their
pugnacity, their indolence, their sensuality, or their servility. As for streets of gold,
gates of pearl, foundations of chalcedony
and sardonyx, some may find them too
like the garish pipe-dream of some too-
simple oil-magnate from the Middle West.

F. L. LUCAS,
The Greatest Problem and Other Essays

They have a poor idea of the Deity, and
the rewards which are destined for the just
made perfect, who can only adopt the literal sense of an eternal concert—a never-
ending Birthday Ode.... I cannot help
thinking that a life of active benevolence is
more consistent with my ideas than an
eternity of music.

SIR WALTER SCOTT,
Sir Walter Scott's Journal (1825-1832)

HELL (*See* EVIL)

HELP

I want to help you, but I know how hard
it is to help anybody at any time—only I
think that the sense that some one else
cares always helps because it is the sense of
love.

GEORGE E. WOODBERRY,
Selected Letters of George Edward Woodberry

Help your brother's boat across, and your own will reach the shore.

HINDU PROVERB

It seems sometimes as if one were powerless to do any more from within to overcome troubles, and that help must come from without.

A. C. BENSON,
Excerpts from the Letters of Dr. A. C. Benson to M. E. A.

People seldom refuse help, if one offers it in the right way.

A. C. BENSON,
Excerpts from the Letters, of Dr. A. C. Benson to M. E. A.

People who won't help others in trouble "because they got into trouble through their own fault," would probably not throw a lifeline to a drowning man until they learned whether he fell in through his own fault or not.

SYDNEY J. HARRIS,
Strictly Personal

It is one of the beautiful compensations of this life that no one can sincerely try to help another without helping himself.

CHARLES DUDLEY WARNER,
Backlog Studies

We all of us need assistance. Those who sustain others themselves want to be sustained.

MAURICE HULST,
The Way of the Heart

Something that has puzzled me all my life is why, when I am in special need of help, the good deed is usually done by somebody on whom I have no claim.

WILLIAM FEATHER,
The Business of Life

Mistrust your zeal for doing good to others.

ABBÉ HUVELIN,
Some Spiritual Guides of the Seventeenth Century

To help all created things, that is the measure of our responsibility; to be helped by all, that is the measure of our hope.

GERALD VANN,
The Heart of Man

There are people in life, and there are many of them, whom you will have to help as long as they live. They will never be able to stand alone.

SIR WILLIAM OSLER,
A Way of Life

The best we can do for one another is to exchange our thoughts freely; and that, after all, is about all.

JAMES FROUDE

HERO

As you get older it is harder to have heroes, but it is sort of necessary.

ERNEST HEMINGWAY,
quoted in *Portrait of Hemingway*
by Lillian Ross

Oh, mother-in-law, you are nice and old, and understand, as the first maiden understood, that a man must be more than nice and good, and that heroes are worth more than saints.

D. H. LAWRENCE,
Selected Letters of D. H. Lawrence

The opportunities for heroism are limited in this kind of world: the most people can do is sometimes not to be as weak as they've been at other times.

ANGUS WILSON,
Writers at Work,
edited by Malcolm Cowley

Heroic action is essentially an operation of health, of good humor, of joy, even of gayety, almost of banter; an act, an operation of ease, of bounty, of readiness, of dexterity, of fecundity.... Without any tension, without any rigidity. Without sweat.

CHARLES PÉGUY,
Men and Saints

The ordinary man is involved in action, the hero acts. An immense difference.

HENRY MILLER,
The Books in My Life

For high and dangerous action teaches us to believe as right beyond dispute things for which our doubting minds are slow to find words of proof. Out of heroism grows faith in the worth of heroism. The proof comes later, and even may never come.

OLIVER WENDELL HOLMES, JR.,
The Mind and Faith of Justice Holmes,
edited by Max Lerner

To be a hero, one must give an order to oneself.

SIMONE WEIL,
Notebooks, Vol. I

What a hero one can be without moving a finger!

HENRY DAVID THOREAU,
Journal

The political or spiritual hero will always be the one who, when others crumbled, stood firm till a new order built itself around him; who showed a way out and beyond where others could only see written "no thoroughfare."

WILLIAM JAMES,
Collected Essays and Reviews

No hero without a wound.

BULGARIAN PROVERB

In some ways, heroism can be the highest assertion of individuality. It was therefore contrary to Gestapo ideology to allow a prisoner to gain prominence by heroic action. Since all prisoners were exposed to severe mistreatment, those who died because of it, though perhaps martyrs to political or religious convictions, were not considered heroes by other prisoners. Only those who suffered for their efforts to protect other prisoners were accepted as heroes.

BRUNO BETTELHEIM,
The Informed Heart

Too much has been said of the heroes of history—the strong men, the troublesome men; too little of the amiable, the kindly, and the tolerant.

STEPHEN LEACOCK,
Essays and Literary Studies

HISTORY

History is much decried; it is a tissue of errors, we are told no doubt correctly; and

rival historians expose each other's blunders with gratification. Yet the worst historian has a clearer view of the period he studies than the best of us can hope to form of that in which we live.

ROBERT LOUIS STEVENSON,
quoted in *The Writing Art,* selected by Bertha W. Smith and Virginia C. Lincoln

The real history does not get written, because it is not in people's brains but in their nerves and vitals.

ALFRED NORTH WHITEHEAD,
Dialogues of Alfred North Whitehead

Perhaps one of the most prolific sources of error in contemporary thinking rises precisely from the popular habit of lifting history out of its proper context and bending it to the values of another age and day. In this way history is never allowed to be itself.

LAURENS VAN DER POST,
The Lost World of the Kalahari

History never looks like history when you are living through it. It always looks confusing and messy, and it always feels uncomfortable.

JOHN W. GARDNER,
No Easy Victories, edited by Helen Rowan

Indeed, history's amphitheatre has always contained the martyr and the lion. The former relied on eternal consolations and the latter on raw historical meat.

ALBERT CAMUS,
Resistance, Rebellion, and Death

History unfolds itself by strange and unpredictable paths. We have little control over the future; and none at all over the past.

SIR WINSTON CHURCHILL,
A Churchill Reader,
edited by Colin R. Coote

Working upon us all the while in the darker regions of our nature—in defiance of the power over us of the particular age into which we are born—is always a furtive predilection for some historic era against all the others.

JOHN COWPER POWYS,
The Meaning of Culture

I hold the view that the greatest changes in human history are to be traced back to internal causal conditions, and that they are founded upon internal psychological necessity. For it often seems that external conditions serve merely as occasions on which a new attitude long in preparation becomes manifest.

C. G. JUNG,
Psychological Reflections,
edited by Jolande Jacobi and R. F. Hull

As an antidote to the War I now read history. Histories of Poland, Russia, Austria, Italy, France. One gets a sense of the long line of events. The present sinks into nothingness.

SHERWOOD ANDERSON,
Letters of Sherwood Anderson

Our ignorance of history causes us to slander our own times.

GUSTAVE FLAUBERT,
quoted in *In Search of Serenity*
by R. V. C. Bodley

We have constantly to check ourselves in reading history with the remembrance that, to the actors in the drama, events appeared very different from the way they appear to us. We know what they were doing far better than they knew themselves.

RANDOLPH BOURNE,
Youth and Life

In my old age I have about come to believe that the whole of written history is miscreated and flawed by these discrepancies in the two ideals systems: the one of how we would all like to believe humanity might be, but only the privileged can afford to believe it; and the one of how we all really know humanity in fact is, but none of us wants to believe it.

JAMES JONES,
WW II

It would seem as though the great movements of history arose like those sudden broad waves heaving out of the deep sea in calm weather, and rolling forth incomprehensibly under no wind.

HILAIRE BELLOC,
A Conversation with an Angel

Perhaps history is a thing that would stop happening if God held His breath, or could be imagined as turning away to think of something else.

HERBERT BUTTERFIELD,
Christianity and History

I have always been convinced that individual and collective crimes are closely linked; and in my capacity of journalist I have only tried to make clear that the day to day horrors of our political history are no more than the visible consequences of the invisible history unfolding in the secrecy of the human heart.

FRANÇOIS MAURIAC,
"An Author and His Work," *Great Essays*
by Nobel Prize Winners, edited by
Leo Hamalian and Edmond L. Volpe

The historical is *not* just another thread in the psyche. Actually the latter is historical through and through. In no one of its moments does it have the full courage to act and commit itself unless it is convinced that the world is committed in the direction it would itself take.

WILLIAM F. LYNCH,
Thought, Spring 1951

One of the deepest impulses in man is the impulse to record,—to scratch a drawing on a tusk or keep a diary, to collect sagas and heap cairns. This instinct as to the enduring value of the past is, one might say, the very basis of civilization.

JOHN JAY CHAPMAN,
Memories and Milestones

It is not the neutrals or the lukewarms who make history.

ADOLF HITLER,
speech, Berlin, April 23, 1933

The history of the past is the story of all the truths that man has released.

ANDRÉ GIDE,
The Journals of André Gide, Vol. I

For me, in fact, the mark of the historic is the nonchalance with which it picks up an individual and deposits him in a trend, like a house playfully moved by a tornado.

MARY MCCARTHY,
On the Contrary

History that should be a left hand to us, as of a violinist, we bind up with prejudice, warping it to suit our fears as Chinese women do their feet.

WILLIAM CARLOS WILLIAMS,
quoted in *The Tragedy of American Diplomacy*
by William A. Williams

History may be viewed as a process of pushing back walls of inevitability, of turning what have been thought to be inescapable limitations into human possibilities.

HELEN MERRELL LYND,
On Shame and the Search for Identity

All that the historians give us are little oases in the desert of time, and we linger fondly in these, forgetting the vast tracks between one and another that were trodden by the weary generations of men.

J. A. SPENDER,
The Comments of Bagshot, Second Series

Our historic imagination is at best slightly developed. We generalise and idealise the past egregiously. We set up little toys to stand as symbols for centuries and the complicated lives of countless individuals.

JOHN DEWEY,
Characters and Events, Vol. II

HOAX (*See* DECEPTION)

HOBBY

No man is really happy or safe without a hobby, and it makes precious little difference what the outside interest may be ... anything will do as long as he straddles a hobby and rides it hard.

SIR WILLIAM OSLER,
*Aphorisms from His Bedside Teachings
and Writings*

A hobby is the result of a distorted view of things. It is putting a planet in the place of the sun.

JOHN LANCASTER SPALDING,
Aphorisms and Reflections

HOLIDAY (*See* ANNIVERSARY, CEREMONY, CHRISTMAS, RELIGION, VACATION)

HOME

Better be kind at home than burn incense in a far place.

CHINESE PROVERB

It takes patience to appreciate domestic bliss; volatile spirits prefer unhappiness.

GEORGE SANTAYANA,
The Life of Reason, Vol. II

No matter how much a man likes his own home, a week or so by himself in a hotel room can be pretty nice, every year or so.

JOHN MCNULTY,
The World of John McNulty

The first thing in one's home is comfort; let beauty of detail be added if one has the means, the patience, the eye.

GEORGE GISSING,
The Private Papers of Henry Ryecroft

Some furniture may satisfy us for a lifetime. Some may be quite unsuitable after ten years. But certain it is that the cushions and curtains and pictures will begin to stale after a couple of years .... Dead and dull permanency in the home, dreary sameness, is a form of inertia, and very harmful to the modern nature, which is in a state of flux, sensitive to its surroundings for more than we really know.

D. H. LAWRENCE,
Assorted Articles

One's own surroundings mean so much to one, when one is feeling miserable.

EDITH SITWELL,
Edith Sitwell: Selected Letters 1916-1964

Many of us live publicly with featureless public puppets, images of the small public abstractions. It is when we pass our own private gate, and open our own secret door, that we step into the land of the giants.

G. K. CHESTERTON,
Charles Dickens

HOMOSEXUALITY

Among many of my gay friends, no precept, no matter how dearly held, is allowed to rest unchallenged. No new thought, no matter how absurd it may seem to be, fails to receive its day in court. Whether one discusses politics or medicine, philosophy or literature, no matter how far removed from the field of sex, the homosexual brings a mind that is unusually questioning and skeptical.

DONALD CORY,
"From Handicap to Strength," *Man Alone,*
edited by Eric Josephson
and Mary Josephson

If the need for affection is concentrated on the same sex, this may be one of the determining factors in latent or manifest homosexuality. The need for affection may be directed toward the same sex if the way to the other sex is barred by too much anxiety. Needless to say, this anxiety need not be manifest, but may be concealed by a feeling of disgust or disinterest concerning the opposite sex.

KAREN HORNEY,
The Neurotic Personality of Our Time

It's a lot more difficult to march out of the closet than to march for peace. It can cost you your job or your career.

JIM OWLES,
president of the Gay Activist Alliance,
quoted in the *New York Times,*
June 27, 1971

The whole idea of homosexual experience in a man's life is so much more written about, only because women's homosexuality isn't taken seriously. Even when they do think about it, men think a woman homosexual could be turned around by a good night in bed with a man. It's not threatening, because they assume there couldn't be true love between two women.

GLORIA STEINEM,
Supertalk by Digby Diehl

Human relations are possible between homosexuals just as between a man and a woman. Homosexuals can love, give, elevate others and elevate themselves. It's surely better to get into bed with a boy friend than to go traveling in Nazi Germany when France has been defeated and strangled.

JEAN-PAUL SARTRE,
quoted in *The Manufacture of Madness*
by Dr. Thomas S. Szasz

It's easier to be accepted in our society as a murderer than as a homosexual.

ABBY MANN,
quoted in *The Manufacture of Madness*
by Dr. Thomas S. Szasz

To the heterosexual man, who is *secure* in his own feelings of sexuality, the homosexual, whether male or female, offers no more threat than a flower in bloom. He welcomes all sexuality that is in blossom.

BRENDAN FRANCIS

Homosexuality would certainly be an easier subject to describe and to analyze if it were confined to the people who practice it.

C. A. TRIPP,
The Homosexual Matrix

Certainly there is less homosexuality in our society than there would be if taboos against it did not exist. But the same kinds of taboos also dampen heterosexuality, often to the extent of making homosexual choices seem the least violational.

C. A. TRIPP,
The Homosexual Matrix

HONESTY (*See* TRUTH)

HOPE

As it is our nature to be more moved by hope than fear, the example of one whom we see abundantly rewarded cheers and encourages us far more than the sight of many who have not been well treated disquiets us.

FRANCESCO GUICCIARDINI,
Counsels and Reflections

A hope, if it is not big enough, can poison much more thoroughly than most despairs, for hope is more essentially an irritant than a soporific.

WILLIAM BOLITHO,
Camera Obscura

No cause is hopeless. . . . Things have a way of bringing about their antitheses, of surprising us radically.

JOYCE CAROL OATES,
Open Secrets by Barbaralee Diamonstein

If I were another person observing myself and the course of my life, I should be compelled to say that it must all end unavailingly, be consumed in incessant doubt, creative only in its self-torment. But, an interested party, I go on hoping.

FRANZ KAFKA,
The Diaries of Franz Kafka 1914–1923

Insoluble problem: Am I broken? Am I in decline? Almost all the signs speak for it (coldness, apathy, state of my nerves, distractedness, incompetence on the job, headaches, insomnia): almost nothing but hope speaks against it.

FRANZ KAFKA,
The Diaries of Franz Kafka 1914–1923

Hope is a thing with feathers
That perches in the soul,
And sings the tune without the words
And never stops at all.

EMILY DICKINSON,
Selected Poems and Letters of Emily Dickinson

Hope is a bad thing. It means that you are not what you want to be. It means that part of you is dead, if not *all* of you. It means that you entertain illusions. It's a sort of spiritual clap, I should say.

HENRY MILLER,
The Cosmological Eye

The mind which renounces, once and forever, a futile hope, has its compensations in ever-growing calm.

GEORGE GISSING,
The Private Papers of Henry Ryecroft

Ersatz hope can puff you up and blind you to reality. You then subsist on a diet of fat hopes, sparse deeds, and bitter fruit.

BRENDAN FRANCIS

Hope must feel that the human breast is amazingly tolerant.

ANONYMOUS (HENRY S. HASKINS),
Meditations in Wall Street

Hope is the first thing to take some sort of action.

VINCENT MCNABB,
God's Way of Mercy

Everything is all stirred up here at home and I am living on hope and faith, which, by the way, make a pretty good diet when the mind will receive them.

EDWIN ARLINGTON ROBINSON,
Untriangulated Stars

He rose up in his dying bed
and asked for a fish.
His wife looked it up in her dream book
and played it.

LANGSTON HUGHES,
"Hope," *Selected Poems of Langston Hughes*

Memory and hope constantly incite us to the extensions of the self which play so large a part in our daily life.

JOSIAH ROYCE,
The Problem of Christianity, Vol. II

HORSERACING

I like horses to pick the bit up. When they wanna run, they run. Y'know. You gotta try to get 'em to pick the bit up and do their own thing.

STEVE CAUTHEN,
quoted in the *New York Times,*
February 20, 1977

They're ungrateful. They don't appreciate. They think everybody's trying to steal and pull horses. They don't understand that, y'know, that's not the way it is. If you run four or five races, they want you to do it every day. Even if you're on four or five bums.

STEVE CAUTHEN (on racing fans),
quoted in the *New York Times,*
February 20, 1977

Millions of words are written annually, purporting to tell how to beat the races, whereas the best possible advice on the subject is found in the three monosyllables: "Do not try."

DAN PARKER,
The ABC of Horse Racing

Perseverance, courage, acumen, increasing vigilance, hard work and application are all required of the man who would win money at the races. He should also have some capital in easily marketable securities.

HEYWOOD BROUN,
Pieces of Hate

In choosing the winner of a horse race, a good guess may beat all the skill and all the special knowledge in the world.

ROBERT LYND,
The Peal of Bells

Horses don't run any better for me than anybody else; I just find out how they want to be ridden.

WILLIE HARTACK,
quoted in *Life,* January 16, 1956

Never back the horses you admire most, for the horses you admire most never win races.

J. A. SPENDER,
Men and Things

The people who think they can wind up ahead of the races are everybody who has ever won a bet.

OGDEN NASH,
Ogden Nash Pocket Book

In betting on races, there are two elements that are never lacking: hope as hope, and an incomplete recollection of the past.

E. V. LUCAS,
quoted in the *New York Times,*
October 7, 1951

I attribute a great part of my longevity to spending my spare evenings in spotting tomorrow's winners, either on the strength of the photographs of the horses or of the sound of their names.

E. V. KNOX,
Gorgeous Times

No jockey likes to be booed and I'm no exception, but we all learn to take it with fairly good grace.

EDDIE ARCARO,
I Ride to Win

It is beautiful to watch a fine horse gallop, the long stride, the rush of the wind as he passes—my heart beats quicker to the thud of the hoofs and I feel his strength. Gladly would I have the strength of the Tartar stallion roaming the wild steppe; that very strength, what vehemence of soul-thought would accompany it.

RICHARD JEFFERIES,
The Story of My Heart

HOUSE

Old houses, I thought, do not belong to people ever, not really, people belong to them.

GLADYS TABER,
Stillmeadow Daybook

Unless one decorates one's house for oneself alone, best leave it bare, for other people are wall-eyed.

D. H. LAWRENCE,
Selected Letters of D. H. Lawrence,
edited by Diana Trilling

The fingers of the housewife do more than a yoke of oxen.

GERMAN PROVERB

When the body of Lord Mohun [killed in a duel] was carried home, bleeding, to his house, Lady Mohun was very angry, because it was "flung upon the best bed."

NATHANIEL HAWTHORNE,
The American Notebooks

Why should I enjoy housecleaning? There is just too much of it. However, I never feel sorry for myself, just wonder why I don't make better arrangements. I am a natural-born slut and have learned to live with myself.

IMOGEN CUNNINGHAM,
Open Secrets by Barbaralee Diamonstein

When you dwell in a house you dislike,

you will look out of a window a deal more than those that are content with their dwelling.

MARY WEBB,
Precious Bane

Of all hateful occupations, housekeeping is to my mind the most hateful.

HANNAH WHITALL SMITH,
Philadelphia Quaker
by Logan Pearsall Smith

The house does not rest upon the ground, but upon a woman.

MEXICAN PROVERB

At the worst, a house unkept cannot be so distressing as a life unlived.

ROSE MACAULAY,
A Casual Commentary

Human nature is rarely so amusing as when trying to get a house off its hands. Women at this task can be untruthful enough, but their untruth lacks the infusion of candour which a skilful male liar can introduce.

E. V. LUCAS,
365 Days and One More

In the sacred precinct of that dwelling where the despotic woman wields the sceptre of fierce neatness, one treads as if he carried his life in his hands.

HENRY WARD BEECHER,
Eyes and Ears

When the lamps in the house are lighted it is like the flowering of lotus on the lake.

CHINESE PROVERB

To a woman the house is life militant; to a man it is life in repose.

OLIVER BELL BUNCE,
Bachelor Bluff

I happen to like household chores, and resent them only when performing them makes it difficult for me to fulfill my professional duties.

KAY BOYLE,
Open Secrets by Barbaralee Diamonstein

Houses are always the liveliest and all that sort of thing when the woman isn't one of those awfully good housekeepers.

JOHN OLIVER HOBBES,
Some Emotions and a Moral

Do you think it is only a little thing to possess a house from which lovely things can be seen?

SAINT TERESA OF AVILA,
Saint Teresa in Her Writings
by the Abbé Rodolphe Hoornaert

The dust comes secretly day after day,
Lies on my ledge and dulls my shining
   things.
But O this dust I shall drive away
   Is flowers and kings,
Is Solomon's temple, poets, Nineveh.

VIOLA MEYNELL,
"Dusting," quoted in *The Week-End Book*,
edited by Vera Mendel
and Francis Meynell

Staying in the house breeds a sort of insanity always. Every house is, in this sense, a hospital.

HENRY DAVID THOREAU,
Journal

HUMAN NATURE

No man really knows about other human beings. The best he can do is to suppose that they are like himself.

JOHN STEINBECK,
The Winter of Our Discontent

The essence of being human is that one does not seek perfection, that one *is* sometimes willing to commit sins for the sake of loyalty, that one does not push asceticism to the point where it makes friendly intercourse impossible, and that one is prepared in the end to be defeated and broken up by life, which is the inevitable price of fastening one's love upon other human individuals.

GEORGE ORWELL,
A Collection of Essays

I object to anything that divides the two sexes. My main point is this: human development has now reached a point at which sexual difference has become a thing of altogether minor importance. We make too much of it; we are men and women in the second place, human beings in the first.

OLIVE SCHREINER,
The Letters of Olive Schreiner

When you know what men are capable of you marvel neither at their sublimity nor their baseness. There are no limits in either direction apparently.

HENRY MILLER,
The Air-Conditioned Nightmare

A sublime faith in human imbecility has seldom led those who cherish it astray.

HAVELOCK ELLIS,
Selected Essays

We are odd compounds full of explosive material to which circumstances may at any time apply a spark, with results undreamed of even by those who thought they knew us best.

JOSEPH FARRELL,
Lectures of a Certain Professor

We are all more average than we think.

GORHAM MUNSON,
The Writer's Workshop

There are no watertight compartments in our inmost nature.

ALEXIS CARREL,
Reflections on Life

I have lived to see it as almost impossible to believe people worse than they are; and so will you.

SIR PETER OSBORNE,
quoted in *The Literature of Gossip*
by Elizabeth Drew

Everybody thinks of others as being excessively human, with all the frailties and crotchets appertaining to that curious condition. But each of us also seems to regard himself as existing on a detached plane of observation, exempt (save in moments of vivid crisis) from the strange whims of humanity en masse.

CHRISTOPHER MORLEY,
Pipefuls

People talk of fundamentals and superlatives and then make some changes of detail.

OLIVER WENDELL HOLMES, JR.,
Holmes-Laski Letters, Vol. I

We were made to be human beings here, and when people try to be anything else, they generally get into some sort of scrapes.

HANNAH WHITHALL SMITH,
Philadelphia Quaker
by Logan Pearsall Smith

It must be terrible to have to live among people and not like human nature.

WILLIAM FEATHER,
The Business of Life

How man thorns of human nature—hard, sharp, lifeless protuberances that tear and wound us, narrow prejudices, bristling conceits that repel and disgust us—are arrested developments, calcified tendencies, buds of promise that should have lifted a branch up into the sunny day with fruit and flowers to delight the heart of men, but now all grown hard, petrified, for want of culture and a congenial soil and climate.

JOHN BURROUGHS,
The Heart of Burroughs' Journals

The strictly logical mind is usually if not always at fault in its valuations of that defiantly illogical thing known as human nature.

OSCAR W. FIRKINS,
Oscar Firkins: Memoirs and Letters
edited by Ina Ten Eyck

We are all *potentially* such sick men. The sanest and best of us are of one clay with lunatics and prison-inmates. And whenever we feel this, such a sense of the vanity of our voluntary career comes over us, that all our morality appears as a plaster hiding a sore it can never cure, and all our well-doing as the hollowest substitute for that *well-being* that our lives ought to be grounded in, but alas! are not.

WILLIAM JAMES,
The Thought and Character of William James
by Ralph Barton Perry

It is part of human nature to think wise things and do ridiculous ones.

ANATOLE FRANCE

When I hear a traveller dogmatizing about the character of the native—how he loves being beaten, despises those that are kind to him, admires those that oppress him—I say to myself that, though I have no idea what kind of man the native may be, I am sure he is not this kind of man. *Never accept from anyone an account of a man which inverts human nature.*

J. A. SPENDER,
The Comments of Bagshot, Second Series

There's nought so queer as folk.

ENGLISH PROVERB

"The nature of man is his whole nature," said Pascal. I accept that position. To strip the human being, for example, of all his attributes save his logical or calculating powers is an unwarrantable mutilation. Nature made him what he is. You cannot pick and choose. Nature is asserting herself in him, and you must take account not of one or two, but of all her assertions.

W. MACNEILE DIXON,
The Human Situation

If, as I grow older and older, I think less of human nature, I also think better of it than I did, in many ways; it is inscrutable, I guess, full of amazing surprises, undreamed of depths of tranquil loyalties and sweet memories that seem to have "shoots of everlastingness" in them—and all this in the strangest places.

GEORGE E. WOODBERRY,
Selected Letters of George Edward Woodberry

There is scarcely a blow in after life comparable to that first sad intimation (perhaps in early youth), that human nature is not what we thought it, not the thing of our dreams; little else than a tissue of frailties woven together.

LOUISE IMOGEN GUINEY,
Goose-Quill Papers

HUMANITY

We cannot escape each other, no matter how wide or how erratic our divigations. All passions, all struggles, all hopes, all despairs, are human in common.

GAMALIEL BRADFORD,
The Letters of Gamaliel Bradford

The chief obstacle to the progress of the human race is the human race.

DON MARQUIS,
The Almost Perfect State

Take upon yourself as much humanity as possible. That is the correct formula.

ANDRÉ GIDE,
The Journals of André Gide, Vol. I

A man may be wrong; so may a generation; but humanity does not make mistakes.

ANDRÉ MAUROIS,
The Art of Living

In all ages the prophets and moralists have upbraided and denounced their fellow creatures. I desire to be excused their honorable company. I will sit on no jury for the arraignment of the human species.

W. MACNEILE DIXON,
The Human Situation

I have, in common with yourself, a desire to leave the world a little more human than if I had not lived; for a true humanity is, I believe, our nearest approach to Divinity, while we work out our atmospheric apprenticeship on the surface of this second-class planet.

OLIVER WENDELL HOLMES,
Life and Letters of Oliver Wendell Holmes,
Vol. I, by John T. Morse, Jr.

You know the theory of some learned divine, that the human race goes mad at times and, of course, like other mad people, does not suspect its madness.

SIR ARTHUR HELPS,
Conversation in a Railway Carriage

Are not those who nurse their egos on contempt of humanity—"the herd in the slime" and that sort of thing—hurt spirits who compensate in this way for a sense of inequality to life? They may have remarkable powers, like Nietzsche, but are never robust and sane. They lack, especially, a sense of humor.

CHARLES HORTON COOLEY,
Life and the Student

Whenever there is lost the consciousness that every man is an object of concern for us just because he is a man, civilization and morals are shaken, and the advance to fully developed inhumanity is only a question of time.

ALBERT SCHWEITZER,
quoted in *Man and God,*
compiled by Victor Gollancz

HUMILITY

Humility does not consist in an ignorance of truth. If a man is above the average height of men, he cannot help knowing it.

HENRY CARDINAL MANNING,
Pastime Papers

When will you be humble enough not to be afraid of anyone thinking this or that of you, even if it be something good?

MAURICE HULST,
The Way of the Heart

Only the man with true pride in his capacities as a human being can have a significant humility; only the truly humble in apprehending the immensity of the universe and the world beyond himself can have a significant pride—a sense of his own identity.

HELEN MERRELL LYND,
On Shame and the Search for Identity

I would be subdued before my friends, and thank them for subduing me; but among multitudes of men I have no feel of stooping; I hate the idea of humility to them.

JOHN KEATS,
The Selected Letters of John Keats

To the truly humble man the ordinary ways and customs and habits of men are not a matter for conflict.

THOMAS MERTON,
Seeds of Contemplation

Humility is the portion of every true man and of every true artist. As to the pomp, the ceremony, and the retinue with which great men and great artists have surrounded themselves from time to time, it is only a sort of "swagger" whereby poor mortals would persuade themselves that they are as the immortal gods. In every king's household and in every great man's retinue is some "honest" counsellor who does not admire, some Horatio or Kent who just because they do not admire may be taken for friends and lovers.

J. B. YEATS,
Letters to His Son, W. B. Yeats and Others

We do not acquire humility. There is humility in us—only we humiliate ourselves before false gods.

SIMONE WEIL

The boughs that bear most hang lowest.

ENGLISH PROVERB

And, though at present my friends may find it a hard thing to believe, it is true none the less, that for them living in freedom and idleness and comfort it is more easy to learn the lessons of humility than it is for me, who begin the day by going down on my knees and washing the floor of my cell. For prison life with its endless privations and restrictions makes one rebellious. ... And he who is in a state of rebellion cannot receive grace, to use the phrase of which the Church is so fond—so rightly fond, I dare say—for in life as in art the mood of rebellion closes up the channels of the soul, and shuts out the airs of heaven.

OSCAR WILDE,
De Profundis

Nothing so entrances a man of words as to imagine himself in a situation in which words are powerless. It is this which keeps him humble. Men of action, I notice, are rarely humble, even in situations where action of any kind is a great mistake, and masterly inaction is called for.

ROBERTSON DAVIES,
The Table Talk of Samuel Marchbanks

There is a sort of docility of mind, a knowledge of our own impotence, that is very near to the threshold of intellectual vision and to the threshold of religious feeling. Whenever a man has this sentiment very strongly, people almost always give him credit for being somehow a religious person—even if the man protests he is not interested in religion. It seems to be true that great intellects are almost always filled with this sense of not quite understanding what truth is, of being powerless and ignorant.

JOHN JAY CHAPMAN,
Memories and Milestones

Instead of wasting energy in being disgusted with yourself, *accept* your own failures, and just say to God, "Well, in spite of all I may say or fancy, this is what I am really like—so please help my weakness." This, not self-disgust, is the real and fruitful humility.

EVELYN UNDERHILL,
The Letters of Evelyn Underhill

HUMOR

The essence of humour is that it should be unexpected, that it should embody an element of surprise, that it should startle us out of that reasonable gravity which, after all, must be our habitual frame of mind.

AGNES REPPLIER,
Americans and Others

Humor distorts nothing, and only false gods are laughed off their earthly pedestals.

AGNES REPPLIER,
Points of View

It should be clear to any student who might be considering a career of humor that after he has written his arm off, for funnier or for worse, even his best friend will still ask: "When are you going to do something really important?"

E. B. WHITE,
Every Day Is Saturday

Humor is perhaps a sense of intellectual perspective: an awareness that some things are really important, others not; and that the two kinds are most oddly jumbled in everyday affairs.

CHRISTOPHER MORLEY,
Inward Ho

Anything which can be made funny must have at its heart some tragic implications.

DR. KARL MENNINGER,
A Psychiatrist's World

A woman without humor is an annoyance; she is as the touch of wet velvet, or a mouse nibbling in the night. She is as a cigar whose wrapper is torn, and the air leaketh therein; nothing can mend her.

GELETT BURGESS,
The Maxims of Methuselah

To be wildly enthusiastic, or deadly serious—both are wrong. Both pass. One must keep ever present a sense of humour. It depends entirely on yourself how much you see or hear or understand. But the sense of humour I have found of use in every single occasion of my life.

KATHERINE MANSFIELD,
The Journal of Katherine Mansfield

Whom the gods would make bigots, they first deprive of humor.

JAMES M. GILLIS,
This Our Day

There is of course something wrong with a man who is only partly humorous, or is only humorous at times, for humor ought to be a yeast, working through the whole of a man and his bearing.

THEODOR HAECKER,
Journal in the Night

I once asked Edwin Arlington Robinson if he did not think his sense of humor had lengthened his life. "I think," he replied, "my life has lengthened my sense of humor."

DANIEL GREGORY MASON,
Music in My Time,
quoted in *Reader's Digest,* April 1942

Humor is not a postscript or an incidental afterthought; it is a serious and weighty part of the world's economy. One feels increasingly the height of the faculty in which it arises, the nobility of the things associated with it, and the greatness of the services it renders.

OSCAR W. FIRKINS,
Oscar Firkins: Memoirs and Letters,
edited by Ina Ten Eyck

One may have learned to enjoy the sublime, the beautiful, the useful, the orderly, but he has missed something if he has not also learned to enjoy the incongruous, the illusive, and the unexpected. Artistic sensibility finds its satisfaction only in the perfect. Humor is the frank enjoyment of the imperfect. Its objects are not so high,—but there is more of them.

SAMUEL MCCHORD CROTHERS,
The Gentle Reader

Any man will admit, if need be, that his sight is not good, or that he cannot swim, or shoots badly with a rifle, but to touch upon his sense of humor is to give him a mortal affront.

STEPHEN LEACOCK,
The Leacock Roundabout

HUNTING

No sportsman wants to kill the fox or the pheasant as I want to kill him when I see him doing it.

GEORGE BERNARD SHAW,
quoted in *Killing for Sport,*
edited by Henry S. Salt

When you have shot one bird flying you have shot all birds flying, they are all different and they fly different ways but the sensation is the same and the last one is as good as the first.

ERNEST HEMINGWAY,
"Fathers and Sons,"
The Short Stories of Ernest Hemingway

Shooting gives me a good feeling. A lot of it is being together and friendly instead of feeling you are in some place where everybody hates you and wishes you ill. It is

faster than baseball, and you are out on one strike.

ERNEST HEMINGWAY,
quoted in *Portrait of Hemingway*
by Lillian Ross

How anyone can profess to find animal life interesting and yet take delight in reducing the wonder of any animal to a bloody mass of fur or feathers is beyond my comprehension.

JOSEPH WOOD KRUTCH,
Saturday Review, August 17, 1957

Man is still a hunter, still a simple searcher after meat for his growling belly, still a provider for his helpless mate and cubs. . . . *Bringing home the bacon* is the modern equivalent of banging a curly behemoth over the head with a big sharp rock.

ROBERT C. RUARK,
Horn of the Hunter

Killing by itself is not the hunter's object. The very people who shudder most over the cruelty of the hunter are apt to forget that slaughter, in the grimmest sense of the word, is a process that they entrust daily to the butcher, and that unlike the game in the forest, even the dumbest creatures in the slaughterhouse know what lies in store for them. Hunting is an occupation in which the incidents are as much a part of the object as the final result: everything about it, from the kind of clothes worn to the manner of the weapon used, enhances, in some degree, the hunter's pleasure.

LEWIS MUMFORD,
Green Memories

A wounded deer leaps highest,
I've heard the hunter tell;
'Tis but the ecstasy of death,
And then the brake is still.

EMILY DICKINSON,
Selected Poems and Letters of Emily Dickinson

We shoot [geese and ducks] because they are so gamey, such good sports. As in war, it is the brave that die first in this game. They die for their beauty, they die because

they are wild and freedom-loving.
DONALD CULROSS PEATTIE,
1937 Essay Annual,
edited by Erich A. Walter

HURRY

Nothing can be more useful to a man than a determination not to be hurried.
HENRY DAVID THOREAU,
Journal

One of the odd things about being in a hurry is that it seems so fiercely important when you yourself are the hurrier and so comically ludicrous when it is someone else.
CHRISTOPHER MORLEY,
Pipefuls

He is invariably in a hurry. Being in a hurry is one of the tributes he pays to life.
ELIZABETH BIBESCO,
Balloons

The greatest pleasure of all is to realize that there is no hurry, and to escape from this universal folly of rushing at full speed to a place that is no better than the place one is at already.
ROBERT LYND,
Solomon in All His Glory

Nobody running at full speed has either a head or a heart.
W. B. YEATS,
Autobiography

HURT

Everyone makes a greater effort to hurt other people than to help himself.
ALEXIS CARREL,
Reflections on Life

HUSBAND

It is nothing—they are only thrashing my husband.
PORTUGUESE PROVERB

Marriage is not harmed by seducers but by cowardly husbands.
SØREN KIERKEGAARD,
Either/Or, Vol. II

A woman seldom comes out of a sullen spell until she's sure her husband has suffered as much as she thinks he should.
WILLIAM FEATHER,
The Business of Life

The true index of a man's character is the health of his wife.
CYRIL CONNOLLY,
The Unquiet Grave

It is hardly possible to estimate how many marriages fail to prosper or are actually ruined because the man lacks any inkling of the art of love.
COUNT HERMANN KEYSERLING,
The Book of Marriage

The majority of husbands remind me of an orangutan trying to play the violin.
HONORÉ DE BALZAC,
The Physiology of Marriage

There was the halt, the wistfulness about the ensuing year, which is like autumn in a man's life. His wife was casting him off, half regretfully, but relentlessly; casting him off and turning now for love and life to the children. Henceforward he was more or less a husk. And he half acquiesced, as so many men do, yielding their place to their children.
D. H. LAWRENCE,
Sons and Lovers

Changing husbands is only changing troubles.
KATHLEEN NORRIS,
Hands Full of Living

Husbands who have the courage to be tender enjoy marriages that mellow through the years.
BRENDAN FRANCIS

All any woman asks of her husband is that he love her and obey her commandments.
JOHN W. RAPER,
What This World Needs

I know many married men; I even know a few happily married men; but I don't know one who wouldn't fall down the first open coal-hole running after the first pretty girl who gave him a wink.

GEORGE JEAN NATHAN,
"Women as Playthings,"
Man Against Woman,
edited by Charles Neider

It is really asking too much of a woman to expect her to bring up a husband and her children too.

LILLIAN BELL,
quoted in *Ladies' Home Journal,* April 1944

A simple enough pleasure, surely, to have breakfast alone with one's husband, but how seldom married people in the midst of life achieve it.

ANNE MORROW LINDBERGH,
Gift from the Sea

A husband should not insult his wife publicly, at parties. He should insult her in the privacy of the home.

JAMES THURBER,
Thurber Country

And the woman must realise that the man is a boy always, and will take his pleasures always as a boy. He must have his own circle of fellow-men. That is his way of pleasure. That is how he escapes. Sports, games, recreation—he is a boy again; living a boy's memories even to old age.

BEDE JARRETT,
The House of Gold

To keep your marriage brimming,
With love in the loving cup,
Whenever you're wrong, admit it;
Whenever you're right, shut up.

OGDEN NASH,
"A Word to Husbands," *Poems of One Line
and Longer,* edited by William Cole

Before marriage, a man declares that he would lay down his life to serve you; after marriage, he won't even lay down his newspaper to talk to you.

HELEN ROWLAND,
A Guide to Men

There is a vast difference between the savage and the civilized man, but it is never

apparent to their wives until after breakfast.

HELEN ROWLAND,
A Guide to Men

Of the same leaven are those wives who, when their husbands are gone a journey, must have a letter every post upon pain of fits and hystericks; and a day must be fixed for their return home without the least allowance for business, or sickness, or accidents, or weather: upon which I can only say that in my observation, those ladies, who are apt to make the greatest clutter on such occasions, would liberally have paid a messenger for bringing them news, that their husbands had broken their necks on the road.

JONATHAN SWIFT,
"A Letter to a Very Young Lady
on Her Marriage" quoted in *Made on
Earth,* edited by Hugh Kingsmill

IDEA

Ideas, when vended in a book, carry with them a kind of dignity and certainty which awe many into implicit belief.

BRONSON ALCOTT,
The Journals of Bronson Alcott

No matter what you attempt, if an idea is not yet mature you will not be able to realize it. ... Unless I have the inner incorruptible conviction: *this is the solution,* I do *nothing.* Not even if the whole Party tries to drive me into action.

ADOLF HITLER,
quoted in *Hitler: A Study in Tyranny*
by Alan Bullock

If we could see man surrounded by his incarnate ideas, alive, howling, innumerable, and not allowing him to do what he wants, to go where he wants, in a word to be his own master, we would be horrified.

MAURICE MAETERLINCK,
The Great Beyond

An idea isn't responsible for the people who believe in it.

DON MARQUIS,
quoted in *Ladies' Home Journal,* June 1941

What matters is not the idea a man holds, but the depth at which he holds it.

EZRA POUND

To conceive ideas is exhilarating, but it is only safe when you conceive so many that you ascribe no undue consequence to them and can take them for what they are worth. People who conceive few find it very difficult not to regard them with inordinate respect.

W. SOMERSET MAUGHAM,
The Summing Up

New ideas are not only the enemies of old ones; they also appear often in an extremely unacceptable form.

C. G. JUNG,
Psychological Reflections,
edited by Jolande Jacobi and R. F. Hull

I do not worry when I lose sight of a budding idea. I am sure to find it growing cheerfully next time I work in that corner of the garden. Any thought that you can lose is not truly yours.

But a certain order of expression should be caught on the fly: it does not always return.

CHARLES HORTON COOLEY,
Life and the Student

I am interested in the shape of ideas even if I do not believe in them. There is a wonderful sentence in Augustine ... "Do not despair: one of the thieves was saved; do not presume: one of the thieves was damned." That sentence had a wonderful shape. It is the shape that matters.

SAMUEL BECKETT,
quoted in *Up Against the Fourth Wall*
by John Lahr

You are never quite at ease about a new idea born in your mind, for you do not know in what storms of contradiction it may involve you.

JEAN GUIBERT,
On Kindness

The ideas of the average decently informed person are so warped, and out of perspective, and ignorant, and entirely perverse and wrong and crude, on nearly every mortal subject, that the task of discussing anything with him seriously and fully and to the end is simply appalling.

ARNOLD BENNETT,
quoted in *Ladies' Home Journal,*
February 1942

One thing that ideas do is to contradict other ideas and keep us from believing them.

WILLIAM JAMES,
"The Energies of Men,"
Essays on Faith and Morals

As soon as an idea is accepted it is time to reject it.

HOLBROOK JACKSON,
Platitudes in the Making

The difference between a man who faces death for the sake of an idea and an imitator who goes in search of martyrdom is that whilst the former expresses his idea most fully in death it is the strange feeling of bitterness which comes from failure that the latter really enjoys; the former rejoices in his victory, the latter in his suffering.

SØREN KIERKEGAARD,
The Journals of Søren Kierkegaard

The very idea that there is another idea is something gained.

RICHARD JEFFERIES,
The Story of My Heart

Except by illustrations drawn from familiar things, there is no way of indicating a new idea.

RICHARD JEFFERIES,
The Story of My Heart

The other day when I was speaking at the Arts Club someone asked me what life I would recommend to young Irishmen, the thought of my whole speech if it were logical should have led up to. I was glad I was able to reply, "I do not know, though I have thought much about it." Who does not distrust complete ideas?

W. B. YEATS,
Autobiography

I know little about history, politics, literature, art, science, philosophy, religion, etc. I know only what I have seized through experience. I put no trust in the men who explain life to us in terms of history, economics, art, etc. They are the fellows who bugger us up, juggling their abstract ideas.

HENRY MILLER,
The Cosmological Eye

Man is ready to die for an idea, provided that idea is not quite clear to him.

PAUL ELDRIDGE,
Horns of Glass

The limits of thought are not so much set from outside, by the fullness or poverty of experiences that meet the mind, as from within, by the power of conception, the wealth of formulative notions with which the mind meets experience. Most new discoveries are suddenly-seen things that were always there. A new idea is a light that illuminates presences which simply had no form for us before the light fell on them.

SUSAN K. LANGER,
Philosophy in a New Key

Great ideas have such radiant strength. They cross space and time like avalanches: they carry along with them whatever they touch. They are the only riches that one shares without ever dividing them.

GEORGES DUHAMEL,
The Heart's Domain

There are ideas language is too gross for, and shape too arbitrary, which come to us and have a definite influence upon us; and yet we cannot fasten on the filmy things and make them visible and distinct to ourselves, much less to others.

GEORGE MEREDITH,
The Ordeal of Richard Feverel

The life of some men, and those not the least eminent among divines and philosophers, has centered in the development of one idea; nay, perhaps has been too short for the process.

JOHN HENRY CARDINAL NEWMAN,
Oxford University Sermons

Ideas often flash across our minds more

complete than we could make them after much labor.

LA ROCHEFOUCAULD,
Maxims

Hang ideas. They are tramps, vagabonds, knocking at the back door of your mind, each taking a little of your substance, each carrying away some crumb of that belief in a few simple notions you must cling to if you want to live decently and would like to die easy.

JOSEPH CONRAD,
Lord Jim

The greatest ideas seem meagre enough when they have passed through the sieve of petty minds.

HENRI DE LUBAC,
The New Man

Psychologists speak of the association of ideas. It is a pleasant thought, but it is, in reality, difficult to induce ideas to associate in a neighborly way.

SAMUEL McCHORD CROTHERS,
The Gentle Reader

It's no good to seize hold of the idea against its will; it then seems so surly that you wonder what attracted you in it. The preferred idea comes only when there is no other idea in its place. Hence you can invoke it by thinking of nothing else.

ANDRÉ GIDE,
The Journals of André Gide, Vol. I

An idea isn't worth much until a man is found who has the energy and ability to make it work.

WILLIAM FEATHER,
The Business of Life

A new and valid idea is worth more than a regiment and fewer men can furnish the former than can command the latter.

OLIVER WENDELL HOLMES, JR.,
The Mind and Faith of Justice Holmes,
edited by Max Lerner

One might almost venture on the paradox that by the time a proposition becomes generally articulate it ceases to be true—because things change about as fast as they are realized.

OLIVER WENDELL HOLMES, JR.,
The Mind and Faith of Justice Holmes,
edited by Max Lerner

To an imagination of any scope the most far-reaching form of power is not money, it is the command of ideas.

OLIVER WENDELL HOLMES, JR.,
The Mind and Faith of Justice Holmes,
edited by Max Lerner

The power of vested interests is usually exaggerated when compared with the gradual encroachment of ideas. . . . Indeed the world is ruled by little else. . . . Madmen in authority, who hear voices in the air, are distilling their frenzy from some academic scribbler of a few years back.

JOHN MAYNARD KEYNES,
quoted in *The Unadjusted Man*
by Peter Viereck

Ideas have a trick of taking to themselves some of the glamour of the time when they were first conceived. A man who suddenly struck out a new theory about the Reformation while walking through the fields with his first love would be loth to let it go and would probably defend it for years on quite illogical grounds.

J. B. PRIESTLEY,
All About Ourselves and Other Essays

Ideas won't keep. Something must be done about them. The idea must constantly be seen in some new aspect. Some element of novelty must be brought into it freshly from time to time; and when that stops, it dies. The meaning of life is adventure.

ALFRED NORTH WHITEHEAD,
Dialogues of Alfred North Whitehead

Whenever I hear, as I sometimes do, one of my colleagues say that there are no ideas which cannot be expressed clearly in simple language, I think, "Then your ideas must be very superficial."

ALFRED NORTH WHITEHEAD,
Dialogues of Alfred North Whitehead

I was always singularly feeble in laying hold of an idea. . . . But, nevertheless, ideas would frequently lay hold of *me* with such relentless tenacity that I was passive in their grasp.

MARK RUTHERFORD,
The Autobiography of Mark Rutherford

IDEAL

When they come down from their Ivory Towers, Idealists are very apt to walk straight into the gutter.

LOGAN PEARSALL SMITH,
Afterthoughts

Nothing is so easy to fool as impulse and no one is deceived so readily as a person under strong emotion. Hence the idealism of man is easily brought to nought.

JOHN DEWEY,
Human Nature and Conduct

If we put an absurdly high ideal before us, it ceases to be an ideal at all, because we have no idea of acting upon it.

FREDERICK W. FABER,
Spiritual Conferences

I thought what an awful thing is idealism when reality is so marvellous.

JOANNA FIELD,
A Life of One's Own

It would be a sad thing indeed if one's ideal was never to go beyond one's own infirmities.

SIR ARTHUR HELPS,
Companions of My Solitude

The spirit of a great ideal may be immortal; its ultimate victory, as we may venture to maintain, may be predetermined by the very nature of things; but that fact does not save such an ideal from the fires of the purgatory of time.

JOSIAH ROYCE,
The Problem of Christianity

Idealism increases in direct proportion to one's distance from the problem.

JOHN GALSWORTHY

Those in whose minds the reality of the ideal is not clear, and love for the ideal is not strong, try to find their compensation in the success of the work; and they are therefore ready for all kinds of compromise.

RABINDRANATH TAGORE,
Letters to a Friend

The test of an ideal or rather of an idealist, is the power to hold to it and get one's inspiration from it under difficulties. When one is comfortable and well off, it is easy to talk high.

OLIVER WENDELL HOLMES, JR.,
The Mind and Faith of Justice Holmes,
edited by Max Lerner

An ideal is often but a flaming vision of reality.

JOSEPH CONRAD,
Chance

IDLENESS

Loafing needs no explanation and is its own excuse.

CHRISTOPHER MORLEY,
Mince Pie

Work is a dull thing; you cannot get away from that. The only agreeable existence is one of idleness, and that is not, unfortunately, always compatible with continuing to exist at all.

ROSE MACAULAY,
A Casual Commentary

Alas! The hours we waste in work
   And similar inconsequence,
Friends, I beg you do not shirk
   Your daily task of indolence.

DON MARQUIS,
The Almost Perfect State

How beautiful it is to do nothing, and then rest afterward.

SPANISH PROVERB

To be idle requires a strong sense of personal identity.

ROBERT LOUIS STEVENSON,
quoted in *Man's Search for Himself*
by Rollo May

The men who do anything worth doing

are just the men it is easiest to catch doing nothing.

HOLBROOK JACKSON,
Southward Ho! and Other Essays

Idleness is not doing nothing. Idleness is *being free to do anything.*

FLOYD DELL,
Were You Ever a Child?

Weariness has no pain equal to being all rested up with nothing to do.

ANONYMOUS (HENRY S. HASKINS),
Meditations in Wall Street

IGNORANCE

A man with little learning is like the frog who thinks its puddle a great sea.

BURMESE PROVERB

It is necessary to fathom one's ignorance on one subject in order to discover how little one knows on other subjects.

J. A. SPENDER,
The Comments of Bagshot, Second Series

I myself know the sense of strain that comes when one speaks to ignorant or, still worse, half-ignorant men. There is a perpetual temptation not merely to over-simplification but to exaggeration, for all ignorant thought is exaggerated thought.

W. B. YEATS,
Autobiography

A young levite once remarked to his professor: "God can dispense with my learning." "Yes," was the reply, "but He has still less need of your ignorance."

JAMES CARDINAL GIBBONS,
The Ambassador of Christ

In all types of activity it is important to know how to stop before what you do not know and not to think that you know what you do not know.

LEO TOLSTOY,
Last Diaries

How exactly proportioned to a man's ignorance of the subject is the noise he makes about it at a public meeting.

SIR ARTHUR HELPS,
Companions of My Solitude

The pleasures of ignorance are as great, in their way, as the pleasures of knowledge.

ALDOUS HUXLEY,
Collected Essays

After all, there are two aspects of ignorance, one of peace as well as one of torment. I have always sought the first; but the tantalizing goddess persists in showing me the second.

GAMALIEL BRADFORD,
The Letters of Gamaliel Bradford

Men are qualified for their work by knowledge, but they are also negatively qualified for it by their ignorance. ... If we have any kind of efficiency, very much of it is owing to our narrowness, which is favourable to a powerful individuality.

PHILIP G. HAMERTON,
The Intellectual Life

ILLNESS

Many are sick because they have not the heart to be well.

JOHN LANCASTER SPALDING,
Thoughts and Theories of Life and Education

The healthy can endure invalids only when the latter are quiet and motionless. Let them but cough or scratch, and sympathy flies out the window.

ROBERTSON DAVIES,
The Table Talk of Samuel Marchbanks

I do think illness, if not too painful, unseals the mental eye, and renders the talents more acute, in the study of the fine arts at least.

SIR WALTER SCOTT,
Sir Walter Scott's Journal (1825-1832)

Fifty per cent or more of the people who go to doctors to be healed of their sicknesses are suffering from neuroses. Most of them can be helped, many of them cured. Many others would not under any circumstances dare to permit themselves to be cured. They live only by the grace of their symptoms.

DR. KARL A. MENNINGER,
The Human Mind

One pleasant little thing about a sickbed is that from its hardships one's daily burdens come to look like pleasures; one never dreamed that they could look so cheerful.

OSCAR W. FIRKINS,
Oscar Firkins: Memoirs and Letters,
edited by Ina Ten Eyck

How well I should be if it were not for all these people shouting that I am ill!

ANDRÉ GIDE,
Pretexts

I believe that there are certain doors that only illness can open. There is a certain state of health that does not allow us to understand everything; and perhaps illness shuts us off from certain truths; but health shuts us off just as effectively from others, or turns us away from them so that we are not concerned with them.

ANDRÉ GIDE,
The Journals of André Gide, Vol. II

You ask me, do I feel things very much?—and I do. And that's why I too am ill. The hurts, and the bitterness sink in, however much one may reject them with one's spirit. They sink in and there they lie, inside one, wasting one. What is the matter with us is primarily chagrin. Then the microbes pounce. One ought to be tough and selfish: and one is never tough enough, and never selfish in the proper self-preserving way. Then one is laid low.

D. H. LAWRENCE,
Selected Letters of D. H. Lawrence,
edited by Diana Trilling

Men make use of their illnesses at least as much as they are made use of by them.

ALDOUS HUXLEY,
Collected Essays

The virtue of a medicine probably lies to a considerable extent in the will to get well with which one purchases it.

ROBERT LYND,
The Peal of Bells

Since I have heard that you are beginning to grow stronger and better it has lifted a positive weight of anxiety from my mind. Do keep it up, my friend, there is so much in the power of will—I mean in really wishing to grow well—and then you are so much of interest and pleasure to us all.

ELLEN GLASGOW,
Letters of Ellen Glasgow

IMAGINATION

But how entirely I live in my imagination; how completely depend upon spurts of thought, coming as I walk, as I sit; things churning up in my mind and so making a perpetual pageant, which is to be my happiness.

VIRGINIA WOOLF,
A Writer's Diary

Imagination and fiction make up more than three quarters of our real life. Rare indeed are the true contacts with good and evil.

SIMONE WEIL,
Gravity and Grace

By logic and reason we die hourly; by imagination we live.

J. B. YEATS,
Letters to His Son, W. B. Yeats and Others

Without imagination—and of the kind that creates—there is no love, whether it be love of a girl or love of a country or love of one's friend or even of children, and of our wives.

J. B. YEATS,
Letters to His Son, W. B. Yeats and Others

Imagination does not often get away itself without breaking some rule or other or paying in some way or other.

SYLVIA ASHTON-WARNER,
Teacher

Imagination grows by exercise and contrary to common belief is more powerful in the mature than in the young.

W. SOMERSET MAUGHAM,
The Summing Up

If the imagination goes, reality goes with it—the reality of man above all. If the imagination goes, then the madmen, who have no imagination, will return, and they will put us all, a hank of hair and a rag of bones, back in Dachau and Buchenwald.

WILLIAM F. LYNCH,
"The Imagination," *Prophetic Voices,*
edited by Ned O'Gorman

All the works of man have their origin in creative fantasy. What right have we then to depreciate imagination?

C. G. JUNG,
Modern Man in Search of a Soul

Variety of imagination—what is that but fatal, in the world of affairs, unless so disciplined as not to be distinguished from monotony?

HENRY JAMES,
The Golden Bowl

What is it that we ask of our ideal audience? It is imagination. And is not all our writing a profession of belief in the powers of the imagination?

KATHERINE MANSFIELD,
Katherine Mansfield by Antony Alpers

Evil comes to us men of imagination wearing as its mask all the virtues. I have known, certainly, more men destroyed by the desire to have wife and child and to keep them in comfort than I have seen destroyed by harlots and drink.

W. B. YEATS,
W. B. Yeats Memoirs,
edited by Denis Donaghue

It's queer the way the imagination, having exhausted one field, turns for rest and re-invigoration to another.

ELLEN GLASGOW,
Letters of Ellen Glasgow

You have to pay dearly for being an imaginative person. You see a great deal and feel a great deal, but there is ugliness to see and feel as well as beauty, and in yourself as well as in others.

I fancy what you have to try to learn is to give as little time as possible to self-pity. That seems to spoil most imaginative men. They are a bit more sensitive than others. They exaggerate the consequences.

SHERWOOD ANDERSON,
Letters of Sherwood Anderson

Always be on guard against your imagination. How many lions it creates in our paths, and so easily! And we suffer so much if we do not turn a deaf ear to its tales and suggestions.

GEORGE PORTER,
The Letters of the Late Father George Porter, S.J.

The imagination must be fed constantly by external nature. . . . The most imaginative men always study the hardest, and are the most thirsty for new knowledge.

JOHN RUSKIN,
quoted in *The Writing Art*, selected by Bertha W. Smith and Virginia C. Lincoln

All one's inventions are true, you can be sure of that. . . . No doubt my poor *Bovary* is suffering and weeping in twenty French villages at this very moment.

GUSTAVE FLAUBERT,
Letters of Gustave Flaubert

Without imagination of the one kind or the other, mortal existence is indeed a dreary and prosaic business. . . . Illumined by the imagination, our life—whatever its defeats and despairs—is a never-ending, unforeseen strangeness and adventure and mystery.

WALTER DE LA MARE,
Pleasures and Speculations

IMITATION

Each of us is in fact what he is almost exclusively by virtue of his imitativeness.

WILLIAM JAMES,
Talks to Teachers

Imitation may be the sincerest flattery, but imitation never produces the deepest resemblance. The man who imitates is concerned with that which is outward; but kinship of spirit is inward.

HENRY VAN DYKE,
The Friendly Year

When people are free to do as they please, they usually imitate each other.

ERIC HOFFER,
The Passionate State of Mind

One dog barks at something, and a hundred bark at the sound.

CHINESE PROVERB

We are disposed to imitate what we least understand. . . . The amiable man whom everyone likes no one imitates. . . . What we understand we understand. We imitate the inscrutable.

J. B. YEATS,
Letters to His Son, W. B. Yeats and Others

Imitation can acquire pretty much everything but the power which created the thing imitated.

ANONYMOUS (HENRY S. HASKINS),
Meditations in Wall Street

Imitation is a necessity of human nature. . . . Most of the things we do, we do for no better reason than that our fathers have done them or that our neighbors do them, and the same is true of a larger part than we suspect of what we think.

OLIVER WENDELL HOLMES, JR.
The Mind and Faith of Justice Holmes,
edited by Max Lerner

The ass went seeking for horns and lost his ears.

ARAB PROVERB

The world is full of people who think they know what they really do not know—other people have had their convictions and beliefs and feelings for them.

THOMAS WOLFE,
The Web and the Rock

IMMORTALITY

And how little to have gained from the experience of life, if one's thoughts are lingering still upon personal fulfillments, and not rooted in the knowledge that the great immortalities, Love, Goodness, and Truth, include all others; and one need pray for no lesser survivals.

ALICE JAMES,
The Diary of Alice James

Even immortality is not certain to be able to work all on its lone—it is just as well to give it what help you can. The Egyptian embalmers and pyramid-builders felt that.

FREDERICK GOODYEAR,
Letters and Remains

I do not even find in myself any great curiosity as to whether my soul is immortal or not.

REBECCA WEST,
This I Believe,
edited by Edward P. Morgan

For a great part of our life we are merely animal or quite dead: immortality in another sphere does not seem so certainly a boon as would be immortality during our present life.

STEPHEN MACKENNA,
Journal and Letters of Stephen Mackenna

The belief in immortality rests not very much on the hope of going on. Few of us want to do that, but we would like very much to begin again.

HEYWOOD BROUN,
Pieces of Hate

Having learned to see the person as inseparable from an organic social life I could not imagine him as living on unless that lived on also: if the individual soul abides society must abide too.

CHARLES HORTON COOLEY,
Life and the Student

I suppose that everyone of us hopes secretly for immortality; to leave, I mean, a name behind him that will live forever in this world, whatever he may be doing, himself, in the next.

A. A. MILNE,
By Way of Introduction

Immortality. I notice that as soon as writers broach this question they begin to quote. I hate quotations. Tell me what you know.

RALPH WALDO EMERSON,
Journals of Ralph Waldo Emerson

Those who live in the Lord never see each other for the last time.

GERMAN PROVERB

Without love immortality would be frightful and horrible.

THEODOR HAECKER,
Journal in the Night

Happily, society comprises not only the living but the dead, and the great dead still live in our midst. We can contemplate them and listen to them at will.

ALEXIS CARREL,
Reflections on Life

To do the best one can, without thinking of any reward, acquiescent at last if the essential stuff we are made of is thrown back into the central cauldrons to be used again in new processes of creation—this also is to identify one's self with splendour and with deity. And for all any of us know, this may be the sort of unselfishness ultimately demanded of us.

DON MARQUIS,
The Almost Perfect State

IMPERFECTION

All action is involved in imperfection, like fire in smoke.

BHAGAVAD-GITA

We have to begin to love the imperfect for the beautiful things it contains, and that takes discipline. The alternative is to mistake the imperfect for the perfect, which to my mind is a much sadder fate.

GEORGE SANTAYANA,
The Letters of George Santayana

I cling to my imperfection as the very essence of my being.

ANATOLE FRANCE,
The Anatole France Calendar,
selected by A. S. Rappoport

One of the best exercises of meekness we can perform is never to fret at our own imperfections.

SAINT FRANCIS DE SALES,
Introduction to the Devout Life

It is very singular that we recognize all the bodily defects that unfit a man for military service, and all the intellectual ones that limit his range of thought, but always talk at him as if all his moral powers were perfect.

OLIVER WENDELL HOLMES,
Life and Letters of Oliver Wendell Holmes,
Vol. I, by John T. Morse, Jr.

Only the person who is allowed to make mistakes and go on respecting himself can avoid the pitfalls of perfectionism. ... To carry the matter further, only the person who is allowed to fail, and size up the reason for failure, and try again—without having to divert his energies into breast-beating self-contempt—can generously allow other people to be the limited humans they are.

BONARO OVERSTREET,
Understanding Fear in Ourselves and Others

IMPOSSIBLE

It looks impossible till you do it, and then you find it is possible.

EVELYN UNDERHILL,
The Letters of Evelyn Underhill

It is always the impossible that happens.

FRENCH PROVERB

An impossibility does not disturb us until its accomplishment shows what fools we were.

ANONYMOUS (HENRY S. HASKINS),
Meditations in Wall Street

IMPRESSION

Nothing is truer to experience or more wholesome to recognize than that the impression we make comes from what we are, in inmost desire and habit, and not from what we may try to seem to be. Our souls are not much hidden.

CHARLES HORTON COOLEY,
Life and the Student

A most curious and useful thing to realize is that one never knows the impression one is creating on other people.

ARNOLD BENNETT,
The Arnold Bennett Calendar,
compiled by Frank Bennett

IMPROVEMENT

Half a man's life is devoted to what he calls improvements, yet the original had some quality which is lost in the process.

E. B. WHITE,
One Man's Meat

To better my life—don't you think I eagerly desire it? I wish I were much better than I am. But just because I long for it, I am afraid of remedies that are worse than the evil itself.

VINCENT VAN GOGH,
Dear Theo:
An Autobiography of Vincent Van Gogh

I don't care what becomes of me so long as it's a change for the better.

WILLIAM FEATHER,
The Business of Life

Every human being has a right to all the means of improvement which society can afford.

WILLIAM ELLERY CHANNING,
Dr. Channing's Note-book

They act as if they supposed that to be very sanguine about the general improvement of mankind is a virtue that relieves them from taking trouble about any improvement in particular.

JOHN MORLEY,
Compromise

Never cease to be convinced that life might be better—your own and others'.

ANDRÉ GIDE,
The Fruits of the Earth

IMPULSE

There is implanted in everyone an impulse which drives the spirit to beat its wings like an imprisoned eagle in the cages of this earth until there is blood on its plumes.

FULTON J. SHEEN,
Way to Happiness

In the world in which we live men have learned to cover the nakedness of their souls no less than that of their bodies. In almost every act, and even thought, of our lives we are so clothed in rationalization and dissemblance that we can recognize but dimly the deep primal impulses that motivate us.

JAMES RAMSEY ULLMAN,
River of the Sun

Many a man gets weary of clamping down on his rough impulses, which if given occasional release would encourage the living of a life with salt in it in place of dust.

ANONYMOUS (HENRY S. HASKINS),
Meditations in Wall Street

One of the few reasons why so few of us ever act, instead of reacting, is because we are continually stifling our deepest impulses.

HENRY MILLER,
The Books in My Life

If there is any appalling and spiritually murderous sensation on earth, it is the knowledge that on a certain date or at a given time and place you have got to be somewhere doing some set, prescribed, definite thing. This winter we shall keep our horizon perfectly, absolutely, crystallinely open, ready every day for the scouring gales of impulse.

JOHN MISTLETOE,
"Journal, 1923," *A Book of Days,*
compiled by Christopher Morley

INDECISION

The indecisive are always open to signs. They solicit portents; seek guidelines in the sky; open Bibles to find prophetic verses. They even (I did once) walk down a row of books in a library, with eyes closed, and point to a title that will provide guidance. Eyes closed, I touched a book and found, when I opened my eyes, that I had chosen the perfect text for the indecisive: Frank Stockton's *Lady, or the Tiger.*

JESSAMYN WEST,
Hide and Seek

Nothing is so exhausting as indecision, and nothing is so futile.

BERTRAND RUSSELL,
The Conquest of Happiness

Our danger is not too few but too many opinions; not to be penned in a single belief but to be puzzled by innumerable alternatives; not a closed mind but an irresolute one; to drift unanchored from one station to another, from deeps to shallows, from safe water to the rocks; an incapacity to refuse the evil and choose the good.

SIR RICHARD LIVINGSTONE,
Education for a World Adrift

INDEPENDENCE

It's the man who dares to take, who is independent, not he who gives.

D. H. LAWRENCE,
Selected Letters of D. H. Lawrence,
edited by Diana Trilling

Some trees grow very tall and straight and large in the forest close to each other, but some must stand by themselves or they won't grow at all.

OLIVER WENDELL HOLMES,
Life and Letters of Oliver Wendell Holmes,
Vol. I, by John T. Morse, Jr.

There is a great deal of self-will in the world, but very little genuine independence of character.

FREDERICK W. FABER,
Spiritual Conferences

It is tragic how few people ever "possess their souls" before they die. "Nothing is more rare in any man," says Emerson, "than an act of his own." It is quite true. Most people are other people. Their thoughts are someone else's opinions, their lives a mimicry, their passions a quotation.

OSCAR WILDE,
De Profundis

While analyzing so many people I realized the constant need of a mother, or a father, or a god (the same thing) is really immaturity. It is a childish need, a human need, but so universal that I can see how it gave birth to all religions. Will we ever be able to look for this strength in ourselves. . . . Woman will be the last one on earth to learn independence, to find strength in herself.

ANAÏS NIN,
The Diaries of Anaïs Nin, Vol. II

A man *should be* an individual, but not independent. The very laws of Nature forbid independence, which have man in a thousand ways inevitably dependent on his fellows.

FRANCIS THOMPSON,
Works, Vol. III

Let us honour if we can
The vertical man
Though we value none
But the horizontal one.

W. H. AUDEN,
Poems

The beauty of independence, departure, actions that rely on themselves.

WALT WHITMAN,
"Song of the Broad-Axe," *Leaves of Grass*

INDIFFERENCE

Not to him who is offensive to us are we most unfair, but to him who doth not concern us at all.

FRIEDRICH NIETZSCHE,
Thus Spake Zarathustra

Most of us have no real loves and no real hatreds. Blessed is love, less blessed is hatred, but thrice accursed is that indifference which is neither one nor the other.

MARK RUTHERFORD,
The Deliverance of Mark Rutherford

By far the most dangerous foe we have to fight is *apathy*—indifference from whatever cause, not from a lack of knowledge, but from carelessness, from absorption in other pursuits, from a contempt bred of self-satisfaction.

SIR WILLIAM OSLER,
Aphorisms from His Bedside Teachings and Writings

INDIVIDUALISM

To you I am an illustration of a certain kind of Capricorn; to an analyst I'm something else; to a Marxist another kind of specimen, and so on. What's all that to *me?*

HENRY MILLER,
A Devil in Paradise

Let each one turn his gaze inward and regard himself with awe and wonder, with mystery and reverence; let each one promulgate his own laws, his own theories; let each one work his own influence, his own havoc, his own miracles. Let each one as an individual, assume the roles of artist, healer, prophet, priest, king, warrior, saint. No division of labor. Let us recombine the dispersed elements of our individuality. Let us reintegrate.

HENRY MILLER,
The Cosmological Eye

One succeeds by will power in losing the sense of one's individuality. It is not happiness, of course, but it is not suffering.

GUSTAVE FLAUBERT,
Letters of Gustave Flaubert

Individuality does not consist in the use of the very personal pronoun I; it consists in tone, in method, in attitude, in point of view, it consists in saying things in such a way that you will yourself be recognized as a force in saying them.

WOODROW WILSON,
quoted in *The Author's Kalendar, 1917,*
compiled by Anna C. Woodford

The true or absolute individuality of a person is always beyond scientific grasp and invariably much less significant in the person's living than he has been taught to believe.

HARRY STACK SULLIVAN,
Conceptions of Modern Psychiatry

The real man is a maze of a million notes: the label is all one note.

HILAIRE BELLOC,
A Conversation with an Angel

Birthday resolution: From now on specialize; never again make any concession to the ninety-nine per cent of you which is like everybody else at the expense of the one per cent which is unique. Never listen to the False Self talking.

CYRIL CONNOLLY,
The Unquiet Grave

There are no precedents: You are the first You that ever was.

CHRISTOPHER MORLEY,
Inward Ho

The way of salvation cannot lie in melting people down into a mass, but on the contrary in their separation and individuation.

THEODOR HAECKER,
Journal in the Night

I felt his cold eyes all over me, ignoring me. I wanted to get away from my body that he had touched—to leave it to him. To have one's individuality completely ignored is like being pushed quite out of life. Like being blown out as one blows out a light. I began to believe myself invisible.

EVELYN SCOTT,
Revelations: Diaries of Women, edited by Mary Jane Moffat and Charlotte Painter

Each individual thinks himself the center of the world. Nothing seems more important to us than our own existence.

ALEXIS CARREL,
Reflections on Life

Each human being is a more complex structure than any social system to which he belongs.

ALFRED NORTH WHITEHEAD,
Atlantic Monthly, March 1939

The individual man, since his separate existence is manifested only by ignorance and error, so far as he is anything apart from his fellows, and from what he and they are to be, is only a negation.

CHARLES SANDERS PEIRCE,
Collected Papers of Charles Sanders Peirce

Probably a crab would be filled with a sense of personal outrage if it could hear us class it without ado or apology as a crustacean, and thus dispose of it. "I am no such thing," it would say; "I am MYSELF, MYSELF alone."

WILLIAM JAMES,
The Varieties of Religious Experience

We talk much more about individualism and liberty than our ancestors. But as so often happens, when anything becomes conscious, the consciousness is compensatory for absence in practice.

JOHN DEWEY,
Characters and Events, Vol. I

In a psychological sense we live in a pool of thoughts, feelings, deeds which flow in and out of us, which become incorporated into our psyche, which organize our activity and energy. There is a veritable stream of feeling from man to man, so that the "illusion of individuality" reaches its height in the belief of an individual that he is separate from the rest of mankind; that his will is his own; that his thoughts, deeds, and feelings are *sui generis.*

ABRAHAM MEYERSON,
Speaking of Man

In a circle of friends, and in relation to close associates or competitors, there is no shortcut through, and no substitute for, an individualized understanding. Those whom we love and admire most are the men and women whose consciousness is peopled thickly with persons rather than with types, who know us rather than the classification into which we might fit.

WALTER LIPPMANN,
Public Opinion

It is after all our own individuality that hinders us from becoming aware of the individualities of others to their full extent.

GOETHE,
Wisdom and Experience

INDOLENCE

The right to laziness is one of the rights that sensible humanity will learn to consider as something self-evident. For the time being we are still in conflict with ourselves. We shun the truth. We look upon laziness as degrading. We still stand in too much awe of ourselves to be able to find the right measure. Our mothers' voices still ring in our ears: "Have you done your lessons?"

DR. WILHELM STEKHEL,
The Depths of the Soul

The need for laziness becomes overpowering in all of us from time to time. We long for a vacation. We want to recuperate from work. Well, there are a few sensible people. They go off into a corner somewhere and are as lazy as can be.

DR. WILHELM STEKHEL,
The Depths of the Soul

A lazy person, whatever the talents with which he starts out, will have condemned himself to second-rate thoughts, and to second-rate friends.

CYRIL CONNOLLY,
The Unquiet Grave

With ill humor it is just as with indolence, for it is a kind of indolence. Our nature leans very much that way, and yet, once we muster the strength to shake it off, work goes smoothly and we find a real delight in activity.

GOETHE,
Wisdom and Experience

There is a case, and a strong case, for that particular form of indolence that allows us to move through life knowing only what immediately concerns us.

ALEC WAUGH,
On Doing What One Likes

INDULGENCE

Our young contemporaries do not wish to suffer or grow pale; on the contrary, they have a most determined desire to grow pink and enjoy themselves. But too much enjoyment "blunts the fine point of seldom pleasure." Unrestrained indulgence kills not merely passion, but, in the end, even amusement.

ALDOUS HUXLEY,
Collected Essays

INFLUENCE

The influences we never speak of; the strongest ones, it so happens, are the secret ones. . . . We let ourselves be influenced by a woman or by those whom we want to please, whose regard or esteem we want to win.

ANDRÉ GIDE,
Pretexts

Human beings are not influenced by any-

thing to which they are not naturally disposed.

HESKETH PEARSON,
Dickens

He who goes with wolves learns to howl.

SPANISH PROVERB

I am often uncertain and almost blind where things, events, books, sciences are concerned. I only begin to see their worth, or worthlessness again when I look at the people whom they influence.

THEODOR HAECKER,
Journal in the Night

Only one man can say *convincingly* what may afterwards prove to have been said by thousands of others at the same time. The mystery of this capacity to impress and convince is not easy to explain rationally, yet this is by no means the same thing as saying that the grounds are unreasonable.

THEODOR HAECKER,
Journal in the Night

I cannot but believe that people's influence is in proportion to their power of abstract thinking; or at least that some very strong wave of force goes out from anyone who is excited by abstract ideas.

JOHN JAY CHAPMAN,
Memories and Milestones

We live at the mercy of a malevolent word. A sound, a mere disturbance of the air, sinks into our very soul sometimes.

JOSEPH CONRAD,
Chance

If I am not pleased with myself, but should wish to be other than I am, why should I think highly of the influences which have made me what I am?

JOHN LANCASTER SPALDING,
Means and Ends of Education

In the world are to be found the figures of those who have influenced me as reality; not the transient creatures who were mere acquaintances, but the enduring personalities who made me aware of myself. There no longer exists a pantheon, but there is a place set apart in the imagination for the remembrance of genuine human beings, of those whom we have to thank for being what they are.

KARL JASPERS,
Man in the Modern Age

We have to find our own way, I am sure of that; and I have a distrust of deflecting anyone from his own orbit. I believe in cooperation, not in influence.

A. C. BENSON,
Excerpts from the Letters of Dr. A. C. Benson to M. E. A.

On faraway influences: You were certain that others disapproved of your behavior without their having expressed their disapproval. In solitude you felt a quiet sense of well-being without having known why; some faraway person thought well of you, spoke well of you.

FRANZ KAFKA,
The Diaries of Franz Kafka 1914–1923

Let a man mean well for himself by all means. I for one shall never quarrel with him. But when he means well for *me,* and to fit, and, if it will not fit, as usually it will not, to force his meaning on my life, then I should wish to get as quickly as possible out of the sphere of his good intentions.

JOSEPH FARRELL,
Lectures of a Certain Professor

You can exert no influence if you are not susceptible to influence.

C. G. JUNG,
Modern Man in Search of a Soul

One of the things a man has to learn to fight most bitterly is the influence of those who love him.

SHERWOOD ANDERSON,
Letters of Sherwood Anderson

It is more difficult to turn a weak than a strong man. The weak man tempts us to continual efforts to change him, but we find in the end that we must leave him alone.

MARK RUTHERFORD,
Last Pages from a Journal

However brief may be the intercourse we have with a man, we always come away with it somewhat modified; we find we are a little greater than we were before, or a little less great, better or worse, exalted or diminished.

GEORGES DUHAMEL,
The Heart's Domain

It is certainly often sad and depressing when one tries to effect something in life by one's words and sees in the end that one has effected nothing; but that the person in question obstinately perseveres in his opinion; but on the other hand there is something great in the fact that the other person, and in same way, everyone, is a world unto himself, has his holy of holies into which no strange hand can penetrate.

SØREN KIERKEGAARD,
The Journals of Søren Kierkegaard

There seems to be no agent more effective than another person in bringing a world for oneself alive, or, by a glance, a gesture, or a remark, shriveling up the reality in which one is lodged.

ERVING GOFFMAN,
quoted in *The Politics of Experience* by R. D. Laing

INFORMATION

Ignorance is the curse of the age we live in. We talk about the dark ages. When was there one so dark as this? We have smothered ourselves, buried ourselves, in the vast heap of information which all of us have and none of us has.

GAMALIEL BRADFORD,
The Letters of Gamaliel Bradford

Information is not culture. In the mind of a truly educated man, facts are organized and they make up a living world in the image of the world of reality.

ANDRÉ MAUROIS,
The Art of Living

You get a great deal more light on the street than you do in the closet. You get a good deal more light by keeping your ears open among the rank and file of your fellow citizens than you do in any private conference whatever.

WOODROW WILSON,
Woodrow Wilson Selections for Today,
edited by Arthur Bernon Tourtellot

Reports in matters of this world are many, and our resources of mind for the discrimination of them very insufficient.

JOHN HENRY CARDINAL NEWMAN,
Oxford University Sermons

INNOCENCE

Innocence finds not nearly as much protection as guilt.

LA ROCHEFOUCAULD,
Maxims

It takes a sharp observer to tell innocence from assurance.

CHARLES DUDLEY WARNER,
Baddeck and That Sort of Thing

Innocence always calls mutely for protection, when we would be so much wiser to guard ourselves against it; innocence is like a dumb leper who has lost his bell, wandering the world, meaning no harm.

GRAHAM GREENE,
The Quiet American

Innocence comes in contact with evil and doesn't know it; it baffles temptation; it is protected where no one else is.

BASIL W. MATURIN,
Father Maturin by Maisie Ward

Man is prone to connect the idea of innocence with that of abstention. There are, however, abstentions which are crimes.

ERNEST HELLO,
Life, Science, and Art

What hope is there for innocence if it is not recognized?

SIMONE WEIL,
Gravity and Grace

INSIGHT

No deep insight into human minds is possible without unconscious comparisons with our own experiences.

DR. THEODOR REIK,
Listening with the Third Ear

The evidence in studies of creative people is that they get their important insights on those particular problems on which they have wrestled with perseverance and diligence, even though the insight itself may come at a moment of lull.

ROLLO MAY,
Man's Search for Himself

The larger the field of activity the personality has, the greater will be its insights into reality.

WILLIAM F. LYNCH,
Thought, September 1950

It is not easy to repent of anything that has given us truer insight.

JOHN LANCASTER SPALDING,
Glimpses of Truth

INSPIRATION

Something tells me needs only decent attention and confidence to tell us much more.

ANONYMOUS (HENRY S. HASKINS),
Meditations in Wall Street

We sing as we are bid. Our inspirations are very manageable and tame. Death and Sin have whispered in the ear of our wild horses and they have become drays and hacks.

RALPH WALDO EMERSON,
Journals of Ralph Waldo Emerson

There is no inspiration in the ideals of plenty and stability.

JOHN LANCASTER SPALDING,
Religion, Agnosticism, and Education

Inspirations never go in for long engagements; they demand immediate marriage to action.

BRENDAN FRANCIS

Inspiration always comes when a man wills it, but it does not always depart when he wishes.

CHARLES BAUDELAIRE,
Intimate Journals

You ask if inspiration can be lost; no, when creation has started (then it goes on like the child in the womb).

W. B. YEATS,
*Letters on Poetry
from W. B. Yeats to Dorothy Wellesley*

I am absolutely decided to shut myself up for a certain number of hours every day, and no matter where and under what exterior conditions ... for the sake of my work: whether it really comes now or whether I only make the appropriate gestures, unfilled. ... So I will kneel down and rise up, every day, alone in my room, and I will consider sacred what happened to me in it: even the not having come, even the disappointment, even the forsakenness. There is no poverty which would not be fullness if one took it seriously and worthily and did not make it into an exasperation and abandon it.

RAINER MARIA RILKE,
Letters of Rainer Maria Rilke 1892–1910

It is better to obey the mysterious direction, without any fuss, when it points to a new road, however strange that road may be. There is probably as much reason for it, if the truth were known, as for anything else.

H. M. TOMLINSON,
The Face of the Earth

INSTANCE

When one comes down to particular instances, everything becomes more complicated.

ALBERT CAMUS,
Notebooks 1935–1942

INSTINCT

Ideas pull the trigger, but instinct loads the gun.

DON MARQUIS,
The Almost Perfect State

Everyone was searching for a formula for survival in the sea of media in which we little fishes were swimming around. And the only formula that worked was no formula. Instinct—that's all you had to go on.

CAROLYN KENMORE,
Mannequin: My Life as a Model

It is only by following your deepest instinct that you can lead a rich life and if you let your fear of consequence prevent you from following your deepest instinct, then your life will be safe, expedient and thin.

KATHARINE BUTLER HATHAWAY,
*The Journals and Letters
of the Little Locksmith*

Here we are in this workaday world, little creatures, mere cells in a social organism itself a poor and little thing enough, and we must look to see what little and definite task our circumstances have set before our little strength to do. The performance of that task will require us to draw upon all our powers, reason included. And in the doing of it we should chiefly depend not upon that department of the soul which is most superficial and fallible—I mean our reason—but upon that department that is deep and sure—which is instinct.

CHARLES SANDERS PEIRCE,
Collected Papers of Charles Sanders Peirce

Few of us have vitality enough to make any of our instincts imperious.

GEORGE BERNARD SHAW

INSTITUTION

Too often the man who should be criticizing institutions spends his energy in criticizing those who would reform them.

JOHN DEWEY,
Human Nature and Conduct

Those political institutions are best which subtract as little as possible from a people's natural independence as the price of their protection.

JOHN HENRY CARDINAL NEWMAN,
Discussions and Arguments

We no longer pay much attention to the institution to which anyone belongs. We judge him rather on his personal merits;

what he thinks and what he is worth. That is the present tendency and it is a right one.

ABBÉ HENRI DE TOURVILLE,
Letters of Direction

Nothing but the daily sequence of events enables us to believe in our institutions. Why should distant men remit me money, or students assemble in my classroom? Think of almost anything that goes on and ask yourself whether it would have been credible if you had not seen it. I notice that when I am removed from usual conditions I begin to doubt their existence. No wonder that men thrown out of their rut lose their grip on life.

CHARLES HORTON COOLEY,
Life and the Student

INTELLECTUAL

An intellectual? Yes. And never deny it. An intellectual is someone whose mind watches itself. I am happy to be both halves, the watcher and the watched.

ALBERT CAMUS,
Notebooks 1935–1942

It is better for the intellectual not to talk all the time. To begin with, it would exhaust him, and, above all, it would keep him from thinking. He must create if he can, first and foremost, especially if his creation does not sidestep the problems of his time.

ALBERT CAMUS,
Resistance, Rebellion, and Death

If you are way ahead with your head you naturally are old-fashioned and regular in your daily life.

GERTRUDE STEIN,
quoted in *The Third Rose*
by John Malcolm Brinnin

But, of course only morons would ever think of themselves as intellectuals. That's why they all look so sad.

ELLEN GLASGOW,
Letters of Ellen Glasgow

I think that those of us who are what are called intellectuals make a terrible mistake in overvaluing the yen we have for the arts, books, etc. There is a sweet, fine quality in life that has nothing to do with this, and more and more I find myself valuing myself with those people.

SHERWOOD ANDERSON,
Letters of Sherwood Anderson

Intellectuals can tell themselves anything, sell themselves any bill of goods, which is why they were so often patsies for the ruling classes in nineteenth-century France and England, or twentieth-century Russia and America.

LILLIAN HELLMAN,
An Unfinished Woman

The intellectual *is* different from the ordinary man, but only in certain sections of his personality, and even then not all the time.

GEORGE ORWELL,
A Collection of Essays

One of the great tragedies of our time is the separation of the two, of the man of intelligence from the people. The whole vocation of the former is to give light to the people; but he will himself seldom find light in any other source.

WILLIAM F. LYNCH,
Thought, September 1950

INTELLIGENCE

It is a mistake to think that men are united by elemental affections. Our affections divide us. We strike roots in time and space, and fall in love with our locality, the customs and language in which we were brought up. Intelligence unites us with mankind, by leading us in sympathy to other times, other places, other customs; but first the prejudiced roots of affection must be pulled up.

JOHN ERSKINE,
*The Moral Obligation
to Be Intelligent and Other Essays*

Intelligence is not something possessed once for all. It is in constant process of forming, and its retention requires constant alertness in observing consequences, and open-minded will to learn and courage in readjustment.

JOHN DEWEY,
Reconstruction in Philosophy

True intelligence very readily conceives of an intelligence superior to its own; and this is why truly intelligent men are modest.

ANDRÉ GIDE,
Pretexts

The day when people began to write *intelligence* with a capital *I*, all was damn well lost. There is no such thing as Intelligence; one has intelligence of this or that. One must have intelligence only for what one is doing.

EDGAR DEGAS,
quoted in *The Journals of André Gide*, Vol. I

You speak of the need of a certain modicum of intelligence for justice. It seems to me that the whole scheme of salvation depends on having a required modicum of intelligence. People are born fools and damned for not being wiser.

OLIVER WENDELL HOLMES, JR.,
The Mind and Faith of Justice Holmes,
edited by Max Lerner

INTENTION

It is easy enough to endow the Matterhorn with another and less exalted meaning. The scale of 1:50,000 may be roughly the proportion in which fate fulfills our wishes, and in which we ourselves carry out our good intentions.

SIGMUND FREUD,
The Letters of Sigmund Freud

I have always found that the less we speak of our intentions, the more chance there is of realizing them.

JOHN RUSKIN,
quoted in *The Author's Kalendar, 1914*,
compiled by Anna C. Woodford

INTEREST

Interest is a good, though loose, measure

of wellbeing; in sickness everything is stupid for us but our pain.

OSCAR W. FIRKINS,
Oscar Firkins: Memoirs and Letters,
edited by Ina Ten Eyck

One idea of the devil . . . is to give people vital interests which are of no vital importance.

A. G. FRANCIS STANTON,
quoted in *The Bliss of the Way*,
compiled by Cecily Hallack

There is so little time for the discovery of all that we want to know about the things that really interest us. We cannot afford to waste it on the things that are only of casual concern for us, or in which we are interested only because other people have told us that we ought to be.

ALEC WAUGH,
On Doing What One Likes

Often we hear it said that people do well the things in which they are interested. This is not quite true. The correct statement is that we are interested in the things we do well.

WILLIAM FEATHER,
The Business of Life

I have known some quite good people who were unhappy, but never an *interested* person who was unhappy.

A. C. BENSON,
*Excerpts from the Letters of
Dr. A. C. Benson to M. E. A*

A great preservative against angry and mutinous thoughts, and all impatience and quarreling, is to have some great business and interest in your mind, which like a sponge shall suck up your attention and keep you from brooding over what displeases you.

JOSEPH RICKABY,
Waters That Go Softly

INTERRUPTION

The effectiveness of work increases according to geometrical progression if there are no interruptions.

ANDRÉ MAUROIS,
The Art of Living

Other people's interruptions of your work are relatively insignificant compared with the countless times you interrupt yourself.

BRENDAN FRANCIS

INTROSPECTION

Perhaps one should not think so much of oneself, though it is an interesting subject.

NORMAN DOUGLAS,
An Almanac

There are people who never speak of themselves, for fear of interrupting their own introspection.

MADAME SWETCHINE,
The Writings of Madame Swetchine

I have no heart to write—I *think* too much. One of my Italian friends used to say, "Tell me quick, or I shall *think*," as if that were the worst. Well, I know what he meant, now.

GEORGE E. WOODBERRY,
Selected Letters of George Edward Woodberry

Think of the world you carry within you, and call this thinking what you will; whether it be remembering your own childhood or yearning towards your own future—only be attentive to that which rises up in you and set it above everything that you observe about you. What happens in your innermost being is worthy of your whole love; you must somehow keep working at it and not lose too much time and too much courage in explaining your position to people.

RAINER MARIA RILKE,
Letters to a Young Poet

INTUITION

"I tell you these things, not because you know them not, but because you know them." All living instruction is nothing but corroboration of intuitive knowledge.

COVENTRY PATMORE,
The Rod, the Root, and the Flower

Some of the finest moral intuitions come to quite humble people. The visiting of

lofty ideas doesn't depend on formal schooling. Think of those Galilean peasants.

ALFRED NORTH WHITEHEAD,
Dialogues of Alfred North Whitehead

Modern man's besetting temptation is to sacrifice his direct perceptions and spontaneous feelings to his reasoned reflections; to prefer in all circumstances the verdict of his intellect to that of his immediate intuitions.

ALDOUS HUXLEY,
Do What You Will

Hence I pronounce this, that as old experience doth attain to something like prophetic strain, so all comely facility traces back to long pondering; intuitions are the reward of ancient gropings.

STEPHEN MACKENNA,
Journal and Letters of Stephen Mackenna

The mind can assert anything, and pretend it has proved it. My beliefs I test on my body, on my intuitional consciousness, and when I get a response there, then I accept.

D. H. LAWRENCE,
Selected Essays

Intuition comes very close to clairvoyance; it appears to be the extrasensory perception of reality.

ALEXIS CARREL,
Reflections on Life

IRELAND AND THE IRISH

We Irish are too poetical to be poets; we are a nation of brilliant failures, but we are the greatest talkers since the Greeks.

OSCAR WILDE,
quoted in *Autobiography* by W. B. Yeats

The more imagination, the less possibility of perceiving the spiritual light; hence the Irish are almost never mystics.

DOM JOHN CHAPMAN,
The Spiritual Letters of Dom John Chapman

You'll hear more wit, and better wit, in an Irish street row than would keep West-

minster Hall in humour for five weeks.
WALTER BAGEHOT,
Literary Studies, Vol. III

If [Adolf Hitler] conquers these islands, he will certainly add the Irish to the list, as several authorities have maintained that the Irish are the lost tribes of Israel.
GEORGE BERNARD SHAW,
quoted in *The Taste of Courage,* edited by Desmond Flower and James Reeves

You will acknowledge that we have not the collective mind in Ireland. The English reproach us with a lack of seriousness—that lack is the lack of the collective mind. Any day we prefer a ghost story or a fairy tale to the *Times* newspaper, aye, and to good books like Macaulay's history—doubtless, in time, and with much labour and sorrow and with the aid of the great reformers, we shall acquire this collective mind, and be as dull as the House of Commons and as serious as the Bank of England.
J. B. YEATS,
Letters to His Son, W. B. Yeats and Others

Ireland is a fruitful mother of genius, but a barren nurse.
JOHN BOYLE O'REILLY,
Watchwords

The Irish began to go to America the moment the door was opened. . . . So that America has always been a friend to the Irish people. And when I went over there—I never felt as if I were a foreigner at all.
SEAN O'CASEY,
Wisdom, edited by James Nelson

What Irish genius might have done, had it not beaten its wounded and bleeding wings against the iron bars of oppression, we know not.
THOMAS O'HAGAN,
Chats by the Fireside

Hatred as a basis of imagination, in ways one could explain even without magic, helps to dry up the nature and makes the sexual abstinence, so common among young men and women in Ireland, possi-

ble. This abstinence reacts in turn on the imagination, so that we get at last that strange eunuch-like tone and temper.
W. B. YEATS,
quoted in *W. B. Yeats Memoirs,*
edited by Denis Donaghue

In any event, solutions to problems in Ireland are never as simple as that. As Ed Murrow once said about Vietnam, anyone who isn't confused doesn't really understand the situation.
WALTER BRYAN,
The Improbable Irish

Everywhere in Irish prose there twinkles and peers the merry eye and laugh of a people who had little to laugh about in real life.
DIARMUID RUSSELL,
Introduction, *The Portable Irish Reader*

IRRESOLUTION

I am not far from thinking that in irresolution lies the secret of not growing old.
ANDRÉ GIDE,
The Counterfeiters

WILLIAM JAMES

There was, in spite of his playfulness, a deep sadness about James. You felt that he had just stepped out of this sadness in order to meet you, and was to go back into it the moment you left him.
JOHN JAY CHAPMAN,
Memories and Milestones

He could not help making the expression of his philosophy intelligible, because to him a philosophy that was merely technical and professional missed the point of philosophy: the illumination and enlargement of the human mind on the things that are its most vital concern.
JOHN DEWEY,
Characters and Events, Vol. I

William James shared the passions of liberalism. He belonged to the left, which, as they say in Spain, is the side of the heart, as the right is that of the liver; at any rate there was much blood and no gall in his philosophy.

GEORGE SANTAYANA,
Character and Opinion in the United States

His comprehension of men to the very core was most wonderful. Who, for example, could be of a nature so different from his than I? He so concrete, so living; I a mere table of contents, so abstract, a very snarl of twine. Yet in all my life I found scarce any soul that seemed to comprehend, naturally (not) my concepts, but the mainspring of my life better than he did. He was even greater (in the) practice than in the theory of psychology.

CHARLES SANDERS PEIRCE,
*Collected Papers of
Charles Sanders Peirce*, Vol. VI

JAZZ

Jazz music is to be played sweet, soft, plenty rhythm. When you have your plenty rhythm, with a plenty swing, it becomes beautiful.

JELLY ROLL MORTON,
quoted in *Jam Session,*
edited by Ralph J. Gleason

A jazz musician is a juggler who uses harmonies instead of oranges.

BENNY GREEN,
The Reluctant Art

It is curious how the jazzband has become a living image of American experience as it relates to a new type of community whose very survival depends on a widening range of individual spontaneity. How felicitously, too, it brings out the creative inwardness which is the life force of our society. For the jazz player is asserting his freedom from all that would hinder him from obeying a higher call; he seeks out a larger vision of life's possibilities and maintains in himself a vivid awareness of something indefinable and beyond his grasp.

ROBERT C. POLLOCK,
American Philosophy and the Future,
edited by Michael Novak

In jazz the audience is an essential participant. . . . The first challenge of a jazz performer is to unify the diverse response of an audience so that it becomes an entity.

DAVE BRUBECK,
quoted in *Jam Session,*
edited by Ralph J. Gleason

The memory of things gone is important to a jazz musician. I remember I once wrote a sixty-four-bar piece about a memory when I was a little boy in bed and heard a man whistling in the street outside, his footsteps echoing away.

DUKE ELLINGTON,
Hear Me Talkin' to Ya
by Nat Shapiro and Nat Hentoff

When you play music with a man you understand and who understands you, you preach to him with your horn and he answers back with his "Amen," never contradicting you. Your message and his message get together like pie and ice cream. When that happens, man, you know you've got a friend.

MEZZ MEZROW,
Really the Blues

Jazz to me is one of the inherent expressions of Negro life in America: the eternal tom-tom beating in the Negro soul—the tom-tom of revolt against weariness in a white world, a world of subway trains, and work, work, work; the tom-tom of joy and laughter, and pain swallowed in a smile.

LANGSTON HUGHES,
"The Negro Artist
and the Racial Mountain,"
On Being Black, edited by
Charles T. Davis and Daniel Walden

JEALOUSY

Jealousy would be far less torturous if we understood that love is a passion entirely unrelated to our merits.

PAUL ELDRIDGE,
Horns of Glass

As to the green-eyed monster jealousy . . . set on him at once and poison him with extra doses of kindness to the person whom he wants to turn you against.

GEORGE PORTER,
*The Letters of
the Late Father George Porter, S. J.*

Jealousy is the dragon in paradise; the hell of heaven; and the most bitter of the emotions because associated with the sweetest.

A. R. ORAGE,
Essays and Aphorisms

Women regard all other women as their competitors, whereas men as a rule only have this feeling towards other men in the same profession. Have you ever been so imprudent as to praise an artist to another artist? Have you ever praised a politician to another politician of the same party? Have you ever praised an Egyptologist to another Egyptologist? If you have, it is a hundred to one that you will have produced an explosion of jealousy?

BERTRAND RUSSELL,
The Conquest of Happiness

JEW

To be a Jew is a destiny.

VICKI BAUM,
And Life Goes On

There is, of course, no greater fallacy than the one about the stinginess of Jews. They are the most lavish and opulent race on earth.

THOMAS WOLFE,
The Web and the Rock

The greatest race—taking its vicissitudes and its achievements, its numbers and its glories—that ever existed.

JOHN BOYLE O'REILLY,
Watchwords

The anti-Semite is not afraid of the comparatively insignificant Jewish individual, but of his stereotype of *the* Jew, who is invested with all that is evil in himself. How dangerous his undesirable inner drives are, and how powerful, he knows only too well. An enumeration of the qualities which the SS, for instance, imputed to *the* Jew is some index of the qualities they tried to deny in themselves. Instead of fighting these qualities in themselves, they fought them by persecuting the Jews.

BRUNO BETTELHEIM,
The Informed Heart

JOY

We call "happiness" a certain set of circumstances that makes joy possible.

But we call joy that state of mind and emotions that needs nothing to feel happy.

ANDRÉ GIDE,
Pretexts

The more joy we have, the more nearly perfect we are.

BENEDICT DE SPINOZA,
Ethics

Joy is of the will which labours, which overcomes obstacles, which knows triumph.

W. B. YEATS,
Autobiography

Man is more himself, man is more manlike, when joy is the fundamental thing in him, and grief the superficial.

G. K. CHESTERTON,
Orthodoxy

I can wade grief,
Whole pools of it,—
I'm used to that.
But the least push of joy
Breaks up my feet,
And I tip—drunken.

EMILY DICKINSON,
Selected Poems and Letters of Emily Dickinson

Your readiest desire is your path to joy—even if it destroy you.

HOLBROOK JACKSON,
Platitudes in the Making

If all the people who have been hurt by the war were to exclude joy from their lives, it would be almost as if they had died. Men without joy seem like corpses.

KÄTHE KOLLWITZ,
Revelations: Diaries of Women, edited by
Mary Jane Moffat and Charlotte Painter

There are some people who have the quality of richness and joy in them and they communicate it to everything they touch. ... With such people it makes no difference if they are rich or poor: they are really always rich because they have such wealth and vital power within them that they give everything interest, dignity, and a warm color.

THOMAS WOLFE,
The Web and the Rock

Well, I suppose joy is a passion, and all passionate things are perhaps very close in nature to their opposites. Joy, pain, fear—there comes a point perhaps, where one no longer knows which is which.... What people call ecstasy is more like terror than it is like contentment, isn't it?

DENISE LEVERTOV,
The Craft of Poetry,
edited by William Packard

The miserable man may think well and express himself with great vehemence, but he cannot make beautiful things, for Aphrodite never rises from any but a tide of joy.

W. B. YEATS,
quoted in *The Poet's Work* by John Holmes

It is strange what a contempt men have for the joys that are offered them freely.

GEORGES DUHAMEL,
The Heart's Domain

One joy scatters a hundred griefs.

CHINESE PROVERB

Joy appears now in little things. The big themes remain tragic. But a leaf fluttered in through the window this morning, as if supported by the rays of the sun, a bird settled on the fire escape, joy in the taste of the coffee, joy accompanied me as I walked to the press. The secret of joy is the mastery of pain.

ANAÏS NIN,
The Diaries of Anaïs Nin, Vol. IV

There is a joy in the possibilities of any actual life, and a deeper joy that comes with a sense of sharing the whole and endless adventure of mankind.

IRWIN EDMAN,
The Uses of Philosophy,
edited by Charles Frankel

JUDGMENT

Never a sound judgment without charity. When man judges man, charity is less a bounty from our mercy than just allowance for the insensible leeway of human fallibility.

HERMAN MELVILLE,
The Confidence Man

In order to judge properly, one must get away somewhat from what one is judging, after having loved it. This is true of countries, of persons, and of oneself.

ANDRÉ GIDE,
Pretexts

It is not open to the cool bystander ... to set himself up as an impartial judge of events which would never have occurred had he outstretched a helping hand in time.

SIR WINSTON CHURCHILL,
A Churchill Reader,
edited by Colin R. Coote

The value and force of a man's judgment can be measured by his ability to think independently of his temperamental leanings.

ALGERNON S. LOGAN,
Vistas from the Stream

We are always giving things absolutely arbitrary characters. This thing is good, that thing is bad, we say; but badness or goodness, beauty or ugliness are not in things themselves, but in the ways those things relate themselves to us.

PHILLIPS BROOKS,
Visions and Tasks

When the judge is unjust he is no longer a judge but a transgressor.

GIOSUÈ BORSI,
A Soldier's Confidences with God

No man has yet lived long enough in this

world to doubt the infallibility of his own judgment.

JOSH BILLINGS,
His Works Complete

The most terrible thing is your own judgment.

ROBERT FROST,
Atlantic Monthly, January 1962

One can no more judge of a man by the actions of an hour than of the climate of a country by the temperature of a day.

J. PETIT-SENN,
Conceits and Caprices

When one observes oneself as one actually is, then either one is moved to despair because one considers oneself as hopeless, ugly, miserable; or one looks at oneself without any judgment. And to look at oneself without any judgment is of the greatest importance, because that is the only way you can understand yourself and know about yourself.

J. KRISHNAMURTI,
You Are the World

JUSTICE

No man suffers injustice without learning, vaguely but surely, what justice is.

ISAAC ROSENFELD,
An Age of Enormity

Whoever suffers from the malady of being unable to endure any injustice, must never look out of the window, but stay in his room with the door shut. He would also do well, perhaps, to throw away his mirror.

J. G. SEUME,
quoted in *A Certain World* by W. H. Auden

Distrust all those who talk much of their justice! Verily, in their souls not only honey is lacking.

FRIEDRICH NIETZSCHE,
Thus Spake Zarathustra

People who live in a narrow circle are kind, perhaps, but rarely just. Only an open and varied life educates us to share many points of view, and so to become capable of justice.

CHARLES HORTON COOLEY,
Life and the Student

Justice is what we get when the decision is in our favor.

JOHN W. RAPER,
What This World Needs

Justice. To be ever ready to admit that another person is something quite different from what we read when he is there (or when we think about him). Or rather, to read in him that he is certainly something different, perhaps something completely different from what we read in him.

SIMONE WEIL,
Gravity and Grace

Justice consists in seeing that no harm is done to men. Whenever a man cries inwardly, "Why am I being hurt?", harm is being done to him. He is often mistaken when he tries to define the harm, and why and by whom it is being inflicted upon him. But the cry itself is infallible.

SIMONE WEIL,
quoted in *A Certain World* by W. H. Auden

One must always be ready to change sides with justice, that fugitive from the winning camp.

SIMONE WEIL,
quoted in *The Unadjusted Man*
by Peter Viereck

The perfection of justice implies charity, because we have a right to be loved.

AUSTIN O'MALLEY,
Keystones of Thought

A community in which there is injustice must be full of pain and bad conscience in as far as its mind is active.

BERNARD BOSANQUET,
Some Suggestions in Ethics

Men are always invoking justice; and it is justice which should make them tremble.

MADAME SWETCHINE,
The Writings of Madame Swetchine

KINDNESS

One can pay back the loan of gold, but one dies forever in debt to those who are kind.

MALAYAN PROVERB

I have had that curiously *symbolical* and reassuring pleasure, of being entertained with overflowing and simple kindness by a family of totally unknown people—an adventure which always brings home to me the goodwill of the world.

A. C. BENSON,
*Excerpts from the Letters of
Dr. A. C. Benson to M. E. A.*

Is it not strange, Carrie, that in this world we cannot do really kind and Christlike things without getting into trouble? We may do a thing in a business way and it turns out a great success; but do the same thing as a kindness, and it is sure to make a muss somehow.

HANNAH WHITALL SMITH,
Philadelphia Quaker
by Logan Pearsall Smith

It is because a man feels that he is and ought to be free, that he hates to yield to force, but gives way easily to kindness.

JEAN GUIBERT,
On Kindness

A kind word is like a Spring day.

RUSSIAN PROVERB

True kindness presupposes the faculty of imagining as one's own the sufferings and joy of others. Without imagination, there can be weakness, theoretical or practical philanthropy, but not true kindness.

ANDRÉ GIDE,
Pretexts

There is a kind way of assisting our fellow-creatures which is enough to break their hearts while it saves their outer envelope.

JOSEPH CONRAD,
Chance

Kindness causes us to learn, and to forget, many things.

MADAME SWETCHINE,
The Writings of Madame Swetchine

My feeling is that there is nothing in life but refraining from hurting others, and comforting those that are sad.

OLIVE SCHREINER,
The Letters of Olive Schreiner

Kind thoughts are rarer than either kind words or kind deeds. They imply a great deal of thinking about others. This in itself is rare. But they also imply a great deal of thinking about others without the thoughts being criticisms. This is rarer still.

FREDERICK W. FABER,
Spiritual Conferences

Nobody is kind only to one person at once, but to many persons in one.

FREDERICK W. FABER,
Spiritual Conferences

Charity looks at the need and not at the cause.

GERMAN PROVERB

The milk of human kindness is less apt to turn sour if the vessel that holds it stands steady, cool, and separate, and is not too often uncorked.

GEORGE SANTAYANA,
Character and Opinion in the United States

I begin to think maybe the difference between occidentals and orientals is the curious quality of kindness, the "icy waters of forgiveness" that Douys speaks of in his book of culture—the Christian quality—never condemning utterly, saving the lost lamb—always giving another chance—something beyond self, beyond the brain.

KATHARINE BUTLER HATHAWAY,
*The Journals and Letters
of the Little Locksmith*

There is a sort of restless kindliness, imbecile and lowering to the human person: do not in an April shower run out to hold an umbrella over a bee.

STEPHEN MACKENNA,
Journal and Letters of Stephen Mackenna

By a sweet tongue and kindness, you can drag an elephant with a hair.

PERSIAN PROVERB

And when he thinks it out, the revolutionary may be surprised to discover that the main necessity on both sides of a revolution is *kindness,* which makes possible the most astonishing things. To treat one's neighbor as oneself is still the fundamental maxim for revolutions.

FREYA STARK,
Prophetic Voices, edited by Ned O'Gorman

KISS

The decision to kiss for the first time is the most crucial in any love story. It changes the relationship of two people much more strongly than even the final surrender; because this kiss already has within it that surrender.

EMIL LUDWIG,
Of Life and Love

When they kissed it seemed as if they did indeed imbibe each other, as if each were wine to the other's thirst.

ROBERT SPEAIGHT,
The Unbroken Heart

It takes a lot of experience for a girl to kiss like a beginner.

ANONYMOUS,
quoted in *Ladies' Home Journal,* April 1948

For though I know he loves me,
  Tonight my heart is sad;
His kiss was not so wonderful
  As all the dreams I had.

SARA TEASDALE,
"The Kiss," *Collected Poems of Sara Teasdale*

KNOWLEDGE

You can know more and more about one thing but you can never know everything about one thing: it's hopeless.

VLADIMIR NABOKOV,
Strong Opinions

It is easier to be impressed than to be instructed, and the public is very ready to believe that where there is noble language not without obscurity there must be profound knowledge.

GEORGE SANTAYANA,
The Sense of Beauty

It is the tragedy of the world that no one knows what he doesn't know—and the less a man knows, the more sure he is that he knows everything.

JOYCE CARY,
Art and Reality

The struggle for knowledge has a pleasure in it like that of wrestling with a fine woman.

LORD HALIFAX,
Political, Moral and Miscellaneous Reflections

No knowledge is so easily found as when it is needed.

ROBERT HENRI,
The Art Spirit

This is what knowledge really is. It is finding out something for oneself with pain, with joy, with exultancy, with labor, and with all the little ticking, breathing moments of our lives, until it is ours as that only is ours which is rooted in the structure of our lives.

THOMAS WOLFE,
The Web and the Rock

It is in the matter of knowledge that a man is most haunted with a sense of inevitable limitation.

JOSEPH FARRELL,
Lectures of a Certain Professor

We know ourselves, and yet even with all the efforts we make, we do not know ourselves. We know our fellow man, and yet we do not know him, because we are not a thing, and our fellow man is not a thing. The further we reach into the depths of our being, or someone else's being, the more the goal of knowledge eludes us.

ERICH FROMM,
The Art of Loving

Strength exists only as the opposite of weakness, and supreme knowledge of one subject presupposes as supreme an ignorance of others.

ALEC WAUGH,
On Doing What One Likes

If we would have new knowledge, we must get a whole world of new questions.

SUSAN K. LANGER,
Philosophy in a New Key

I am constantly amazed at how little painters know about painting, writers about writing, merchants about business, manufacturers about manufacturing. Most men just drift.

SHERWOOD ANDERSON,
Letters of Sherwood Anderson

To be master of any branch of knowledge, you must master those which lie next to it; and thus to know anything you must know all.

OLIVER WENDELL HOLMES, JR.,
The Mind and Faith of Justice Holmes,
edited by Max Lerner

Much of the most useful knowledge has to be buffeted into us.

JOHN LANCASTER SPALDING,
Aphorisms and Reflections

Too long we were taught that good will was the same as goodness. We now see that most evil is done by those who mean well. What we urgently want is knowledge—true perceptions of the working of each part on every other part in the common life of man.

CHARLES HORTON COOLEY,
Life and the Student

As soon as one begins to look deeply into any subject one realizes how very little is known, how very, very much is conjecture, hypothesis, surmise and speculation. . . . When it comes to vital instruction, almost everything that has been written for our edification can be junked.

HENRY MILLER,
The Books in My Life

All knowledge is sterile which does not lead to action and end in charity.

DESIREÉ JOSEPH CARDINAL MERCIER,
The Life of Cardinal Mercier
by John A. Gade

I believe one gets more sound ideas when thoughts arise from direct contact with things than when one looks at them with the set purpose of finding certain facts in them.

VINCENT VAN GOGH,
Dear Theo:
An Autobiography of Vincent Van Gogh

One day Soshi was walking on the bank of a river with a friend. "How delightfully the fishes are enjoying themselves in the water!" exclaimed Soshi. His friend then said to him: "You are not a fish; how do you know that the fishes are enjoying themselves?" "You are not myself," returned Soshi; "how do you know that I do not know that the fishes are enjoying themselves?"

OKAKURA KAZUKO,
"The Book of Tea," *A Book of Days,*
compiled by Christopher Morley

Knowledge brings doubts and exceptions and limitations which, though occasionally some aids to truth, are all hindrances to vigorous statement.

SIR ARTHUR HELPS,
Companions of My Solitude

Man does not want to know. When he knows very little he plays with the possibility of knowledge, but when he finds that the pieces he has been putting together are going to spell out the answer to the riddle he is frightened and he throws them in every direction; and another civilization falls.

REBECCA WEST,
quoted in *Rebecca West: Artist and Thinker*
by Peter Wolfe

LANGUAGE

Every legend . . . contains its residuum of truth, and the root function of language is to control the universe by describing it.

JAMES BALDWIN,
Notes of a Native Son

Language may die at the hands of the schoolmen: it is regenerated by the poets.

EMMANUEL MOUNIER,
Be Not Afraid

It is amazing how little of a foreign language you need if you have a passion for the thing written in it.

JOHN JAY CHAPMAN,
Learning and Other Essays

Language is the most imperfect and expensive means yet discovered for communicating thought.

WILLIAM JAMES,
The Thought and Character of William James,
Vol. II, by Ralph Barton Perry

My language is the common prostitute that I turn into a virgin.

KARL KRAUS,
Karl Kraus by Harry Zohn

All language is rhetorical, and even the senses are poets.

GEORGE SANTAYANA,
The Letters of George Santayana

It is an immense loss to have all robust and sustaining expletives refined away from one; at such moments of trial, refinement is a feeble reed to lean upon.

ALICE JAMES,
The Diary of Alice James

One of the best things ever said about language is the little remark of Luttrell that the finest evidence of the riches of the human spirit is that it should have created such a language as Greek and then let it die. And just so, real, live creatures are spinning the web of language all the time, making it as they use it, without the slightest regard to the formulas of professors or the precepts of pedants.

GAMALIEL BRADFORD,
The Letters of Gamaliel Bradford

We must learn how to handle words effectively; but at the same time we must preserve and, if necessary, intensify our ability to look at the world directly and not through that half opaque medium of concepts, which distorts every given fact into the all too familiar likeness of some generic label or explanatory abstraction.

ALDOUS HUXLEY,
The Doors of Perception

The limits of my language stand for the limits of my world.

LUDWIG WITTGENSTEIN,
quoted in *Karl Kraus* by Harry Zohn

It is a very difficult thing to discover and acquire the language of one's own thought. Each separate individual is very likely original in his thought. But between his thought and its fit expression the well-established common language stands like an enormous, impenetrable wall, like an all-devouring monster, like a steam-roller levelling everything down.

THEODOR HAECKER,
Journal in the Night

LATE

He who is late may gnaw the bones.

YUGOSLAV PROVERB

In spite of all our speeding it's still the fashion to be late.

KIN HUBBARD,
Abe Martin on Things in General

I have noticed that the people who are late are often so much jollier than the people who have to wait for them.

E. V. LUCAS,
365 Days and One More

People count up the faults of those who keep them waiting.

FRENCH PROVERB

LAUGHTER

You would hardly appreciate the comic if you felt yourself isolated from others. Laughter appears to stand in need of an echo.

HENRI BERGSON,
Laughter

It has been wisely said that we cannot really love anybody at whom we never laugh.

AGNES REPPLIER,
Americans and Others

There is always a secret irritation about a laugh in which we cannot join.

AGNES REPPLIER,
Points of View

Not by wrath, but by laughter, do we slay.

FRIEDRICH NIETZSCHE,
Thus Spake Zarathustra

He who has the courage to laugh is almost as much master of the world as he who is ready to die.

ITALIAN PROVERB

So long as there's a bit of a laugh going, things are all right. As soon as this infernal seriousness, like a greasy sea, heaves up, everything is lost.

D. H. LAWRENCE,
Selected Letters of D. H. Lawrence,
edited by Diana Trilling

Genuine laughter is the physical effect produced in the rational being by what suddenly strikes his immortal soul as being damned funny.

HILAIRE BELLOC,
A Conversation with an Angel

I wonder sometimes if any one learns to laugh—*really* laugh—much before he is forty.

DAVID GRAYSON,
The Friendly Road

Laughter with us is still suspect to this extent at least, that not yet do we without a shock think of God laughing.

A. CLUTTON-BROCK,
Essays on Life

To become conscious of what is horrifying and to laugh at it is to become master of that which is horrifying. . . . Laughter alone does not respect any taboo, laughter alone inhibits the creation of new anti-taboos; the comic alone is capable of giving us the strength to bear the tragedy of existence.

EUGÈNE IONESCO,
quoted in *The Theatre of the Absurd*
by Martin Esslin

A good laugh is a mighty good thing, and rather too scarce a good thing; the more's the pity.

HERMAN MELVILLE,
Moby Dick

In laughing whole-heartedly a man must attain a certain freedom from selfishness, a certain purity; and the greatest saints are the merriest-hearted people.

MARY WEBB,
Spring of Joy

The ultimate test of the laughing instinct is that a man should always be ready to laugh at himself.

GAMALIEL BRADFORD,
American Portraits

LAW

People say law but they mean wealth.

RALPH WALDO EMERSON,
Journals of Ralph Waldo Emerson

Laws are-re made to throuble people an' the more throuble they make th' longer they stay on th' stachoo book.

FINLEY PETER DUNNE,
Observations by Mr. Dooley

All sorts of substitute for wisdom are used by the world. When the court doesn't know, it consults precedent. The court that made the precedent guessed at it. Yesterday's guess, grown gray and wearing a big wig, becomes today's justice.

DR. FRANK CRANE,
Essays

Laws, like the spider's web, catch the fly and let the hawk go free.

SPANISH PROVERB

Now, the law is good but some of these judges just don't know how to handle it in court. They simply don't have the experience. There are an awful lot of "C" law students practicing law and sitting on the bench.

MELVIN BELLI,
Supertalk by Digby Diehl

No man can imagine, not Swift himself, things more shameful, absurd, and grotesque than the things which do take place daily in the law.

SIR ARTHUR HELPS,
Companions of My Solitude

There is something sickening in seeing poor devils drawn into great expense about trifles by interested attorneys. But too cheap access to litigation has its evils on the other hand, for the proneness of the lower class to gratify spite and revenge in this way would be a dreadful evil were

they able to endure the expense.
SIR WALTER SCOTT,
Sir Walter Scott's Journal (1825-1832)

He that goes to law holds a wolf by the tail.
ENGLISH PROVERB

Law and justice are not always the same. When they aren't, destroying the law may be the first step toward changing it.
GLORIA STEINEM,
Open Secrets by Barbaralee Diamonstein

Nothing is more destructive of respect for the government and the law of the land than passing laws which cannot be enforced.
ALBERT EINSTEIN,
Ideas and Opinions

Law itself is an iron compulsion whose very existence matures the criminal. And yet a state cannot endure without laws.
DR. WILHELM STEKHEL,
Marriage at the Crossroads

I have said to my brethren many times that I hate justice, which means that I know if a man begins to talk about that, for one reason or another he is shirking thinking in legal terms.
OLIVER WENDELL HOLMES, JR.,
The Mind and Faith of Justice Holmes,
edited by Max Lerner

The very considerations which judges most rarely mention, and always with an apology, are the secret root from which the law draws all the juices of life. I mean, of course, considerations of what is expedient for the community concerned.
OLIVER WENDELL HOLMES, JR.,
The Mind and Faith of Justice Holmes,
edited by Max Lerner

I have been mad with work. First, a stinker of a case that frightened me, and then, as 500 times before, gradually sank to the dimensions of a poodle, no longer diabolic except for the longwindedness and confused argument of counsel.
OLIVER WENDELL HOLMES, JR.,
Holmes-Laski Letters, Vol. I

When I talk of law I talk as a cynic. I don't care a damn if twenty professors tell me that a decision is not law if I know that the courts will enforce it.
OLIVER WENDELL HOLMES, JR.,
Holmes-Laski Letters, Vol. I

There is scarcely anything more important in the government of men than the exact— I will even say the pedantic—observance of the regular forms by which the guilt or innocence of accused persons is determined.
SIR WINSTON CHURCHILL,
A Churchill Reader,
edited by Colin R. Coote

When laws cease to have usefulness to society, they should be changed, not enforced. All one has to do is to think of the jimcrow laws of most states in the South not so many years ago to know what I mean.
CORETTA SCOTT KING,
Open Secrets by Barbaralee Diamonstein

There will be more flexibility about the legal system in the Almost Perfect State than there is in our own legal system. There will be, of course, a great many laws, but no person will be expected to obey a law that someone else has made if he can himself make a law on the spur of the moment that is a better law and more justly applicable to his own case.
DON MARQUIS,
The Almost Perfect State

There is no man so good, who, were he to submit all his thoughts and actions to the laws, would not deserve hanging ten times in his life.
MONTAIGNE,
Essays

Without it we cannot live; only with it can we insure the future which by right is ours. The best of man's hopes are enmeshed in its success; when it fails they must fail; the measure in which it can reconcile our passions, our wills, our conflicts, is the measure of our opportunity to find ourselves.
LEARNED HAND,
The Spirit of Liberty,
edited by Irving Dilliard

D. H. LAWRENCE

No other writer in the twentieth century, except Freud, has been subjected to so much abuse from so many otherwise intelligent people.

PHILIP RIEFF,
The Triumph of the Therapeutic

LAWYER

I am not so afraid of lawyers as I used to be. They are lambs in wolves' clothing.

EDNA ST. VINCENT MILLAY,
Letters of Edna St. Vincent Millay

A peasant between two lawyers is like a fish between two cats.

SPANISH PROVERB

Some lawyers love their work as passionately as artists do, others dislike it very heartily, most of them seem to take it as a simple business to be done for daily bread.

PHILIP G. HAMERTON,
The Intellectual Life

I see nothing wrong with giving Robert some legal experience as Attorney General before he goes out to practice law.

JOHN F. KENNEDY,
The Kennedy Wit, edited by Bill Adler

The training of lawyers is a training in logic. The processes of analogy, discrimination, and deduction are those in which they are most at home. The language of judicial decision is mainly the language of logic. And the logical method and form flatter that longing for certainty and for repose which is in every human mind. But certainty generally is illusion, and repose is not the destiny of man.

OLIVER WENDELL HOLMES, JR.,
The Mind and Faith of Justice Holmes,
edited by Max Lerner

To be sure, most lawyers today recognize that their most important work is done in the office, not in the courtroom; the elaborate masked ritual of the courtroom holds attraction only for the neophyte and layman.

DAVID RIESMAN,
Individualism Reconsidered

LEADERSHIP

Leadership should be born out of the understanding of the needs of those who would be affected by it.

MARIAN ANDERSON,
quoted in the *New York Times,*
July 22, 1951

No amount of study or learning will make a man a leader unless he has the natural qualities of one.

SIR ARCHIBALD WAVELL,
London Times, February 17, 1941

As I stand aloof and look
there is to me something profoundly
    affecting in large masses of
men following the lead of those who do
    not believe in men.

WALT WHITMAN,
"Thought," *Leaves of Grass*

The leader is a stimulus, but he is also a response.

EDWARD C. LINDEMAN,
Social Discovery

Different situations call for different leaders. When we say that someone is a leader, we don't mean that he is a leader in every group he belongs to.

KENNETH A. WELLS,
Guide to Good Leadership

To command is to serve, nothing more and nothing less.

ANDRÉ MALRAUX,
Man's Hope

The study of followership is an important avenue to understanding leadership. If a person will analyze his experiences and attitudes as a follower, he will obtain a new concept of leadership.

EMORY S. BOGARDUS,
Leaders and Leadership

The leader of genius must have the ability

to make different opponents appear as if they belonged to one category.

SIR ADOLF HITLER,
Mein Kampf

The art of leading, in operations large or small, is the art of dealing with humanity, of working diligently on behalf of men, of being sympathetic with them, but equally, of insisting that they make a square facing toward their own problems.

S. L. A. MARSHALL,
Men Against Fire

I am certainly not one of those who need to be prodded. In fact, if anything, I am the prod.

SIR WINSTON CHURCHILL,
A Churchill Reader,
edited by Colin R. Coote

There is no worse mistake in public leadership than to hold out false hopes soon to be swept away.

SIR WINSTON CHURCHILL,
A Churchill Reader,
edited by Colin R. Coote

If, in order to succeed in an enterprise, I were obliged to choose between fifty deer commanded by a lion, and fifty lions commanded by a deer, I should consider myself more certain of success with the first group than with the second.

SAINT VINCENT DE PAUL,
St. Vincent de Paul by J. B. Boudignon

The most important quality in a leader is that of being acknowledged as such. All leaders whose fitness is questioned are clearly lacking in force.

ANDRÉ MAUROIS,
The Art of Living

The most important quality in a leader is that of being acknowledged as such. All leaders whose fitness is questioned are clearly lacking in force.

ANDRÉ MAUROIS,
The Art of Living

Nothing so betrays the leader as reluctance to stand behind, defend and pay the price of the course of action he has chosen to follow. He must be willing squarely to shoulder the responsibility; and it is at this point that many people reveal deficiencies which debar them from real strength as leaders.

ORDWAY TEAD,
The Art of Leadership

In the simplest terms, a leader is one who knows where he wants to go, and gets up, and goes.

JOHN ERSKINE,
The Complete Life

In the case of political, and even of religious, leaders it is often very doubtful whether they have done more good or harm.

ALBERT EINSTEIN,
Ideas and Opinions

I don't like a kind man in power.... Nothing is so dangerous for the underdog as a good-natured man at the top.

CHARLES PÉGUY,
quoted in *Péguy* by Daniel Halévy

People think of leaders as men devoted to service, and by service they mean that these men serve their followers. . . . The real leader serves truth, not people.

J. B. YEATS,
Letters to His Son, W. B. Yeats and Others

The competent leader of men cares little for the interior niceties of other people's characters: he cares much—everything for the external uses to which they may be put.

WOODROW WILSON,
Leaders of Men

LEARNING

I have come to feel that the only learning which significantly influences behavior is self-discovered, self-appropriated learning.

CARL R. ROGERS,
On Becoming a Person

He who is afraid of asking is ashamed of learning.

DANISH PROVERB

If you want to know how to do a thing you must first have a complete desire to do that thing.

ROBERT HENRI,
The Art Spirit

Some minds learn most when they seem to learn least. A certain placid, unconscious, equable taking-in of knowledge suits them, and alone suits them.

WALTER BAGEHOT,
Literary Studies, Vol. I

Effective learning means arriving at new power, and the consciousness of new power is one of the most stimulating things in life.

JANET ERSKINE STUART,
Life and Letters of Janet Erskine Stuart
by Maud Monahan

It is not that I first learn and then act according to what I have learned, but learning is acting; the learning is not separate from acting. One is going to learn about fear or about what to do, how to live. But if you have a system that tells you how to live, or a method that says, "Live this way," then you are conforming to the method which is established by somebody else. Therefore you are not learning, you are conforming and acting according to a pattern, which is not action at all, it is just imitation.

J. KRISHNAMURTI,
You Are the World

Personally I am always ready to learn, although I do not always like being taught.

SIR WINSTON CHURCHILL,
A Churchill Reader,
edited by Colin R. Coote

Real study, real learning must, for the individual, be quite valueless or it loses its value.

STEPHEN LEACOCK,
Model Memoirs

I have learned silence from the talkative, toleration from the intolerant, and kindness from the unkind; yet strange, I am ungrateful to these teachers.

KAHLIL GIBRAN,
Sand and Foam

Once learning solidifies, all is over with it.

ALFRED NORTH WHITEHEAD,
Dialogues of Alfred North Whitehead

LEISURE

Leisure is time at personal risk.

A. M. SULLIVAN,
The Three-Dimensional Man

Leisure is indeed an affair of mood and atmosphere rather than simply of the clock. It is not a chronological occurrence but a spiritual state. It is unhurried pleasurable living among one's native enthusiasms.

IRWIN EDMAN,
The Uses of Philosophy,
edited by Charles Frankel

To be for one day entirely at leisure is to be for one day an immortal.

CHINESE PROVERB

Leisure, like its sister peace, is among those things which are internally felt rather than seen from the outside.

VERNON LEE,
Limbo and Other Essays

There is no country and no people who can look forward to the age of leisure and abundance without dread.

JOHN MAYNARD KEYNES,
quoted in *Life Against Death*
by Norman O. Brown

To those who sweat for their daily bread leisure is a longed-for sweet until they get it.

JOHN MAYNARD KEYNES,
quoted in *Life Against Death*
by Norman O. Brown

It is in his pleasure that a man really lives; it is from his leisure that he constructs the true fabric of self.

AGNES REPPLIER,
Essays in Idleness

Leisure is the curse of the poor in spirit.
NORMAN DOUGLAS,
An Almanac

The art of leisure lies, to me, in the power of absorbing without effort the spirit of one's surroundings; to look, without speculation, at the sky and sea; to become part of a green plain; to rejoice, with a tranquil mind, in the feast of colour in a bed of flowers.
DION CALTHROP,
The Charm of Gardens

Now, when so many have leisure, they have become detached from themselves, not merely from the earth. From all the widened horizons of our greater world a thousand voices call us to come near, to understand, and to enjoy, but our ears are not trained to hear them. The leisure is ours but not the skill to use it. So leisure becomes a void, and from the ensuing restlessness men take refuge in delusive excitations or fictitious visions, returning to their own earth no more.
ROBERT MACIVER,
Man Alone,
edited by Eric Josephson
and Mary Josephson

Leisure only means a chance to do other jobs that demand attention.
OLIVER WENDELL HOLMES, JR.,
Holmes-Pollock Letters, Vol. II

"Give me leisure," I cried, "and you will see what I shall do." The gods laughed. I got the leisure.
Long days of nothing to do. "Write, man." But what shall I write?
I am sitting on a hill in the country or walking in the streets of a town. I am in despair, such despair as you know.
Well, I argue with myself. "But, man, you do not have to write. Live."
But I have come to live by writing. I want beauty and meaning always at my fingertips, and there is no beauty or meaning anywhere in me.
SHERWOOD ANDERSON,
Letters of Sherwood Anderson

LETTER

An intention to write never turns into a letter. A letter must happen to one like a surprise, and one may not know where in the day there was room for it to come into being.
RAINER MARIA RILKE,
Letters of Rainer Maria Rilke·1892-1910

A grand letter from you yesterday was like a fragrant scent in a dismal world.
HAROLD J. LASKI,
Holmes-Laski Letters, Vol. II

Who writes love letters grows thin; who carries them, fat.
DUTCH PROVERB

The one good thing about not seeing you is that I can write you letters.
SVETLANA ALLILUYEVA,
Twenty Letters to a Friend

Well, your letter makes up for today's bad weather; within me the sun is shining from a blue sky, outside there is fog and drizzle.
SIGMUND FREUD,
The Letters of Sigmund Freud

I consider it a good rule for letter writing to leave unmentioned what the recipient already knows, and instead tell him something new.
SIGMUND FREUD,
The Letters of Sigmund Freud

A lifelong sustained correspondence, like a lifelong unbroken friendship or happy marriage, requires explaining: all the cards are stacked against it.
MAX LERNER,
The Mind and Faith of Justice Holmes,
edited by Max Lerner

I have noticed that letters are generally the outcome of being bored by everything else, so I always think, no letters, no boredom.
HANNAH WHITALL SMITH,
Philadelphia Quaker
by Logan Pearsall Smith

Letters have their power of speech which tongues do not possess. And therefore, when we meet, some part of our thoughts will remain unuttered for the want of a great space and silence between us.

RABINDRANATH TAGORE,
Letters to a Friend

The letter which merely answers another letter is no letter at all.

MARK VAN DOREN,
quoted in *Any Number Can Play*
by Clifton Fadiman

The true use of a letter is to let one know that one is remembered and valued.

JAMES RUSSELL LOWELL,
quoted in *Bookman's Pleasure,*
compiled by Holbrook Jackson

I am a poor letter writer because I have so many letters to write—this is the 16th today and the only one it was a pleasure to write.

W. B. YEATS,
Letters on Poetry
from W. B. Yeats to Dorothy Wellesley

Robert Graves wrote the other day to two people who sent him a letter of introduction "If you are the couple I saw on the beach yesterday afternoon, I don't want to know you."

W. B. YEATS,
Letters on Poetry
from W. B. Yeats to Dorothy Wellesley

A letter always feels to me like Immortality because it is the mind alone, without corporeal friend. Indebted in our talk to attitude and accent, there seems a spectral power in thought that walks alone.

EMILY DICKINSON,
Selected Poems and Letters of Emily Dickinson

It is so seldom that I get a letter which I enjoy as much as I enjoy my own.

FREDERICK GOODYEAR,
Letters and Remains

Writing to a pretty woman seems about as foolish as entering into correspondence with a Strassburg pie. Everything in this world should be enjoyed in its own way.

HEINRICH HEINE,
quoted in *Ladies' Home Journal,*
October 1942

If possible this letter is more disconnected and rambling than yours, but if it proves half as welcome I shall be satisfied.

EDWIN ARLINGTON ROBINSON,
Untriangulated Stars

I owe you money and I've got to write you. I take pleasure in it, too; in this one, at least. Don't be a fool and not answer. You'd cheat yourself of some good letters, perhaps some damned good letters, at another time.

THOMAS WOLFE,
The Letters of Thomas Wolfe

Let us consider letters—how they come at breakfast, and at night, with their yellow stamps and their green stamps, immortalized by the postmark—for to see one's own envelope on another table is to realize how soon deeds sever and become alien. Then at last the power of the mind to quit the body is manifest, and perhaps we fear or hate or wish annihilated this phantom of ourselves, lying on the table.

VIRGINIA WOOLF,
Jacob's Room

What I say in a letter is all a matter of chance. I don't write what I want to write, but something else.

J. B. YEATS,
Letters to His Son, W. B. Yeats and Others

We ought to write oftener, if only little notes. The frequency of the expression of affection is a very important thing in human life.

GEORGE E. WOODBERRY,
Selected Letters of George Edward Woodberry

Why it should be such an effort to write to the people one loves I cannot imagine. It's none at all to write to those who don't really count.

KATHERINE MANSFIELD,
The Journal of Katherine Mansfield

It does me good to write a letter which is not a response to a demand, a gratuitous letter, so to speak, which has accumulated in me like the waters of a reservoir.

HENRY MILLER,
The Books in My Life

You will find that out of a dozen people who like something in public improvements one will write a letter about it or say something about it. If they don't like something, eleven out of twelve will tell you that. That seems to be human nature.

ROBERT MOSES,
Wisdom for Our Time,
edited by James Nelson

Why is it that you can sometimes feel the reality of people more keenly through a letter than face to face? Is it because the letter is focused spirit while in conversation the dross of matter is too in evidence? The very body of the person is a barrier. One is distracted by outward things and loses the essence.

ANNE MORROW LINDBERGH,
Bring Me a Unicorn

Your letters are as good as a visit from somebody nice. I love people who can write reams and reams about themselves: it seems generous.

D. H. LAWRENCE,
Selected Letters of D. H. Lawrence

A good letter is an exercise of the ego, a modest letter writer a contradiction in terms.

CLIFTON FADIMAN,
Any Number Can Play

It takes two to write a letter as much as it takes two to make a quarrel.

ELIZABETH DREW,
The Literature of Gossip

LIE

It is the honest lies we tell—statements factually correct and essentially deceiving—which debauch our manhood and stunt our growth.

ANONYMOUS (HENRY S. HASKINS),
Meditations in Wall Street

One can be absolutely truthful and sincere even though admittedly the most outrageous liar. Fiction and invention are of the very fabric of life.

HENRY MILLER,
The Wisdom of the Heart

When men no longer have the least fear of saying something untrue, they very soon have no fear whatsoever of doing something unjust.

THEODOR HAECKER,
Journal in the Night

Better a lie that heals than a truth that wounds.

CZECH PROVERB

LIFE

People "died" all the time in their lives. Parts of them died when they made the wrong kinds of decisions—decisions against life. Sometimes they died bit by bit until finally they were just living corpses walking around. If you were perceptive you could see it in their eyes; the fire had gone out. . . . But you always knew when you made a decision against life. When you denied life you were warned. The cock crowed, always, somewhere inside of you. The door clicked and you were safe inside—safe and dead.

ANNE MORROW LINDBERGH,
The Steep Ascent

Life may be prodigious, enormous, morbidly distended, but never can it be quite full. I take "full" to mean full of energies, activities, deeds, emotions. Of course, it is always full of something, if only of inertia.

ROSE MACAULAY,
A Casual Commentary

Life is an onion which one peels crying.

FRENCH PROVERB

Being unready and ill-equipped is what you have to expect in life. It is the universal predicament. It is your lot as a human being to lack what it takes. Circumstances are seldom right. You never have the capacities, the strength, the wisdom, the virtue you ought to have. You must always do with less than you need in a situation vastly different from what you would have chosen as appropriate for your special endowments.

CHARLTON OGBURN, JR.,
The Marauders

There are positive motivations in the human spirit not born of fear and guilt and hate, but of life and love. The life instinct not only battles against the death instinct, it has an autonomy and purpose of its own.

DR. KARL MENNINGER,
A Psychiatrist's World

Those who cannot live fully often become destroyers of life.

ANAÏS NIN,
The Diaries of Anaïs Nin, Vol. IV

Well, I have found life an enjoyable, enchanting, active, and sometimes a terrifying experience, and I've enjoyed it completely. A lament in one ear, maybe, but always a song in the other. And to me life is simply an invitation to live.

SEAN O'CASEY,
Wisdom, edited by James Nelson

Is life so wretched? Isn't it rather your hands which are too small, your vision which is muddied? You are the one who must grow up.

DAG HAMMARSKJÖLD,
Markings

What we the living require is most of all each other. Progeny we must have, company, provender, friends, and even enemies. The whole long vital experiment on earth is symbiotic by chains of cause and relation past glib explaining.

It is not explained why there is for us all but one life, but it is plain that all life is one.

DONALD CULROSS PEATTIE,
The Flowering Earth

That daily life is really good one appreciates when one wakes from a horrible dream, or when one takes the first outing after a sickness. Why not realize it now?

WILLIAM LYON PHELPS,
Essays on Things

Mark how we realize the beauty and blessing of life itself only in rare, inexplicable moments, and then most keenly. It comes to us like a sudden blare of trumpets in the wind.

J. B. PRIESTLEY,
All About Ourselves and Other Essays

Life is like going through a girl's room; a rambling mess as far as you can see.

LAURIE FAURE,
age 12, United States, *Journeys: Prose by Children of the English-speaking World,* collected by Richard Lewis

Our whole life is spent in sketching an ineradicable portrait of ourselves.

ANDRÉ GIDE,
The Journals of André Gide

It's strange ... isn't it that I who have comparative health and strength to work and play and wander about the earth and make friends and enemies if I choose (who can hold also to a hardly bought philosophy even in tragic moments)—that I who have all these things should possess so little of the natural happy instinct for life that today at thirty-two, I could lie quietly down and give it up and pass on to one of the thousand lives I see beyond.

ELLEN GLASGOW,
Letters of Ellen Glasgow

This brings me to your question:—"Have you liked your life?" And I answer, not one day, not one hour, not one moment— or perhaps, *only one* hour and one day.

ELLEN GLASGOW,
Letters of Ellen Glasgow

My theory is to enjoy life, but the practice is against it.

CHARLES LAMB,
The Letters of Charles and Mary Lamb

If, after all, men cannot always make history have a meaning, they can always act so that their own lives have one.

ALBERT CAMUS,
Resistance, Rebellion, and Death

If you do everything you should do, and do not do anything you should not do, you will, according to the best available statistics, live exactly eighteen hours longer than you would otherwise.

DR. LOGAN CLENDENING,
quoted in *Ladies' Home Journal,*
March 1944

My life is absolutely meaningless. When I consider the different periods into which it falls, it seems like the word *Schnur* in the dictionary, which means in the first place a string, in the second a daughter-in-law. The only thing lacking is that the word *Schnur* should mean in the third place a camel, in the fourth, a dust-brush.

SØREN KIERKEGAARD,
Either/Or, Vol. I

Life has its own hidden forces which you can only discover by living.

P. R. RÉGAMEY,
Poverty

Try to keep your soul young and quivering right up to old age, and to imagine right up to the brink of death that life is only beginning. I think that is the only way to keep adding to one's talent, to one's affections, and one's inner happiness.

GEORGE SAND,
quoted in *The Writing Art,* selected by
Bertha Smith and Virginia C. Lincoln

In the deep of the night, lying on my back, I ask myself what life is and I see that I do not know; but I also see that it is a royal thing to be alive.

C.-F. RAMUZ,
What Is Man?

I know no way of going to the roots of life, except going to the roots of one's own life, secure in the confidence that the roots of all other lives are there, if you go deep enough.

GAMALIEL BRADFORD,
The Letters of Gamaliel Bradford

If you wish to live, you must first attend your own funeral.

KATHERINE MANSFIELD,
Katherine Mansfield by Antony Alpers

But warm, eager, living life—to be rooted in life—to learn, to desire, to know, to feel,

to think, to act. That is what I want. And nothing less. That is what I must try for.

KATHERINE MANSFIELD,
The Journal of Katherine Mansfield

Life is a dream, and it is well that it is so, or who could survive some of its experiences?

ISADORA DUNCAN,
My Life

This is the true joy in life, the being used for a purpose recognized by yourself as a mighty one; the being thoroughly worn out before you are thrown on the scrap heap; the being a force of Nature instead of a feverish little clod of ailment and grieving, complaining that the world will not devote itself to making you happy.

GEORGE BERNARD SHAW,
Preface, *Man and Superman*

There is much talk of the chaotic character of human life. It is, in fact, a tangled growth, but always sequent, always proceeding from roots, like the vines and brambles in the swamp. You may not be able to get through, you may be entangled, lost, destroyed, but the life itself is orderly—delicately, beautifully so, if you could stop to examine it.

CHARLES HORTON COOLEY,
Life and the Student

After all it is those who have a deep and real inner life who are best able to deal with the "irritating details of outer life."

EVELYN UNDERHILL,
The Letters of Evelyn Underhill

Our life is not entirely a life of responses to external stimuli; but rather a life determined to respond and seeking stimuli that will justify the response.

A. CLUTTON-BROCK,
Essays on Life

The boy and girl going hand in hand through a meadow; the mother washing her baby; the sweet simple things in life. We have almost lost track of them. On the one side, we overintellectualize everything; on the other hand, we are overmechanized. We can understand the danger of the atomic bomb, but the danger of our misunderstanding the meaning of life is much more serious.

EDWARD STEICHEN,
Wisdom, edited by James Nelson

Life is always at some turning point.

IRWIN EDMAN,
The Uses of Philosophy,
edited by Charles Frankel

Protection and security are only valuable if they do not cramp life excessively; and in the same way the superiority of consciousness is desirable only if it does not suppress and exclude too much of our existence. As always, life is a voyage between Scylla and Charybdis.

C. G. JUNG,
Psychological Reflections,
edited by Jolande Jacobi and R. F. Hull

You have striven so hard, and so long, to *compel* life. Can't you now slowly change, and let life slowly drift into you. Surely it is even a greater mystery and preoccupation even than willing, to let the invisible life steal into you and slowly possess you.

D. H. LAWRENCE,
Selected Letters of D. H. Lawrence,
edited by Diana Trilling

Well—life itself is life—even the magnificent frost-foliage on the window. While we live, let us live.

D. H. LAWRENCE,
Selected Letters of D. H. Lawrence
edited by Diana Trilling

Why do we live? Most of us need the very thing we never ask for. We talk about revolution as if it were peanuts. What we need is some frank thinking and a few revolutions in our own guts; to hell with most of the sons of bitches that I know and myself along with them if I don't take hold of myself and turn about when I need to—or go ahead further if that's the game.

WILLIAM CARLOS WILLIAMS,
Selected Letters of William Carlos Williams

I am impressed by the transitoriness of human life to such an extent that I am often saying a farewell—after dining with Roger for instance; or reckoning how many more times I shall see Nessa.

VIRGINIA WOOLF,
A Writer's Diary

Life is, soberly and accurately, the oddest affair; has in it the essence of reality. I used to feel this as a child—couldn't step across a puddle once, I remember, for thinking how strange—what am I? etc.

VIRGINIA WOOLF,
A Writer's Diary

How little one counts, I think: how little anyone counts; how fast and furious and masterly life is; and how all these thousands are swimming for dear life.

VIRGINIA WOOLF,
A Writer's Diary

When I think of all the books I have read, and of the wise words I have heard spoken, and of the anxiety I have given to parents and grandparents, and of the hopes that I have had, all life weighed in the scales of my own life seems to me a preparation for something that never happens.

W. B. YEATS,
Autobiography

LIGHT

There is more light than can be seen through the window.

RUSSIAN PROVERB

The idea of more light, more beauty, more love possesses an irresistible magic.

ERNEST DIMNET,
What We Live By

Why do we say that we are seeking light, when we have only the vaguest notion of what we mean by light? We make use of set expressions, imitate set ambitions, borrow set opinions, and make set acceptance of traditionary rubbish that has been dumped into our lives, and call this seeking light.

ANONYMOUS (HENRY S. HASKINS),
Meditations in Wall Street

Ah, that I were dark and nightly! How would I suck at the breasts of light!

FRIEDRICH NIETZSCHE,
Thus Spake Zarathustra

LIMIT

How often have I dreamed of a garden that never ended, of a street that continued indefinitely and led straight out of the world! As a child I sometimes felt angry at the idea of limits being imposed to space; a wall, a door, made me indignant.

JULIAN GREEN,
Julian Green: Diary 1928–1957

If one feels one's limits very intensely, one must burst.

FRANZ KAFKA,
The Diaries of Franz Kafka 1914–1923

Something out of Nothing requires humility and more humility, to accept limits and work within limits.

KATHARINE BUTLER HATHAWAY,
*The Journals and Letters
of the Little Locksmith*

LIMITATION

This is a world in which each of us knowing his limitations, knowing the evils of superficiality and the terrors of fatigue, will have to cling to what is close to him, to what he knows, to what he can do, to his friends and his tradition and his love, lest he be dissolved in a universal confusion and know nothing and love nothing.

J. ROBERT OPPENHEIMER,
quoted in *The Unadjusted Man*
by Peter Viereck

Every man, indeed, works with the limitations of his qualities, just as we all struggle beneath the weight of the superincumbent atmosphere; our defects are even a part of our qualities, and it would be foolish to quarrel with them.

HAVELOCK ELLIS,
Selected Essays

If you accept your limitations, you go beyond them.

BRENDAN FRANCIS

The only way to live is to make the limitations of one's life one's *choice;* one can be free, even in a cage, if one thinks of the bars as one's horizon—the world ends

somewhere for each of us!

A. C. BENSON,
*Excerpts from the Letters of
Dr. A. C. Benson to M. E. A.*

LIQUOR (*See also* DIET, DRINKING, EXCESS)

Brandy, whiskey—liquor generally—can be quite beneficial except that—like sugar, salt, and many other things—if taken in excess liquor can be very harmful.

L. ROSENSTIEL

The human intellect owes its superiority over that of the lower animals in great measure to the stimulus when alcohol has given to imagination.

SAMUEL BUTLER

*Drink a highball at nightfall and be good fellows
while you may—for tomorrow may bring sorrow,
so tonight let's all be gay.*

UNIVERSITY OF PENNSYLVANIA SONG

LISTENING

Then I want to sit and listen and have someone talk, tell me things—their life histories—books they have read, things they have done—new worlds! Not to say anything—to listen and listen and be taught.

ANNE MORROW LINDBERGH,
Bring Me a Unicorn

If you listen, really listen, you will hear people repeating themselves. You will hear their pleading nature or their attacking nature or their asserting nature. People who say that I repeat too much do not really listen; they cannot hear that every moment of life is full of repeating.

GERTRUDE STEIN,
quoted in "Gertrude Stein Makes Sense"
by Thornton Wilder,
'47 Magazine of the Year, October 1947

Sometimes it is a great joy just to listen to someone we love talking.

VINCENT MCNABB,
God's Way of Mercy

So when you are listening to somebody,

completely, attentively, then you are listening not only to the words, but also to the feeling of what is being conveyed, to the whole of it, not part of it.

J. KRISHNAMURTI,
You Are the World

A good listener tries to understand thoroughly what the other person is saying. In the end he may disagree sharply, but before he disagrees, he wants to know exactly what it is he is disagreeing with.

KENNETH A. WELLS,
Guide to Good Leadership

A man is already halfway in love with any woman who listens to him.

BRENDAN FRANCIS

We listen to every voice and to everybody but not ourselves. We are constantly exposed to the noise of opinions and ideas hammering at us from everywhere: motion pictures, newspapers, radio, idle chatter. If we had planned intentionally to prevent ourselves from ever listening to ourselves, we could have done no better.

ERICH FROMM,
Man for Himself

Listen to people talking just as a mere noise striking the ear. It is utterly different from what one fancies.

OLIVE SCHREINER,
The Letters of Olive Schreiner

One friend, one person who is truly understanding, who takes the trouble to listen to us as we consider our problem, can change our whole outlook on the world.

DR. ELTON MAYO,
quoted in "Someone to Talk To"
by Gretta Palmer,
Ladies' Home Journal,
May 1947

To talk to someone who does not listen is enough to tense the devil.

PEARL BAILEY,
Talking to Myself

I have suggested that listening requires something more than remaining mute while looking attentive—namely, it requires the ability to attend imaginatively to another's language. Actually, in listening we speak the other's words.

LESLIE H. FARBER,
The Ways of the Will

To be listened to is, generally speaking, a nearly unique experience for most people. It is enormously stimulating. . . . It is small wonder that people who have been demanding all their lives to be heard so often fall speechless when confronted with one who gravely agrees to lend an ear. Man clamors for the freedom to express himself, and for knowing that he counts. But once offered these conditions, he becomes frightened.

ROBERT C. MURPHY,
Psychotherapy Based on Human Longing

Difficult as it is really to listen to someone in affliction, it is just as difficult for him to know that compassion is listening to him.

SIMONE WEIL,
Waiting for God

LITERATURE

All literary men can tell people what they ought not to be; that is literature. But to tell them what they ought to do is—politics, and it would be mere impertinence for a literary man to suggest anything practical.

JOHN GALSWORTHY,
Castles in Spain and Other Screeds

I am always reading or thinking about reading, or I am writing, or thinking about it. . . . My consciousness is almost entirely given up to literature; in a sense, I belong to literature and have no permanent identity apart from it.

JOYCE CAROL OATES,
Open Secrets by Barbaralee Diamonstein

When I was a boy, people were already talking about fiction going downhill. In the years that have elapsed, almost everything has gone downhill, including the people who said it. But fiction remains at the top of the tree.

SIR OSBERT SITWELL,
Wisdom, edited by James Nelson

A Review only continues to have life in it so long as each issue annoys at least one fifth of its subscribers. Justice lies in seeing that this fifth is not always the same.

CHARLES PÉGUY,
quoted in *A Certain World* by W. H. Auden

To have nothing to say and to say it at all hazards, passes for much that is called achievement in literature.

MICHAEL MONAHAN,
Palms of Papyrus

Literature and fine arts (in modern times) have, for their own convenience, made man a much more emotional creature than he is, or than he *was,* at least, for very soon man began to conform to the image that he was offered of himself.

ANDRÉ GIDE,
The Journals of André Gide

I doubt if anything learnt at school is of more value than great literature learnt by heart.

SIR RICHARD LIVINGSTONE,
On Education

All literature, all art, best seller or worst, must be sincere, if it is to be successful. . . . Only a person with a Best Seller mind can write Best Sellers; and only someone with a mind like Shelley's can write *Prometheus Unbound.* The deliberate forger has little chance with his contemporaries and none at all with posterity.

ALDOUS HUXLEY,
Essays New and Old

In many of my stories and poems the central character is a literary man. Well, this means to say that I think that literature has not only enriched the world by giving it books but also by evolving a new type of man, the man of letters.

JORGE LUIS BORGES,
Conversations with Jorge Luis Borges
by Richard Burgin

I think of the world's literature as a kind of forest, I mean it's tangled and it entangles us but it's growing.

JORGE LUIS BORGES,
Conversations with Jorge Luis Borges
by Richard Burgin

LOGIC

People who lean on logic and philosophy and rational exposition end by starving the best part of the mind.

J. B. YEATS,
Letters to His Son, W. B. Yeats and Others

The fatal errors of life are not due to man's being unreasonable. An unreasonable moment may be one's finest. They are due to man's being logical.

OSCAR WILDE,
De Profundis

The very first lesson that we have a right to demand that logic shall teach us is, how to make our ideas clear; and a most important one it is, depreciated only by minds who stand in need of it.

CHARLES SANDERS PEIRCE,
Collected Papers of Charles Sanders Peirce

Few persons care to study logic, because everybody conceives himself to be proficient enough in the art of reasoning already. But I observe that this satisfaction is limited to one's own ratiocination, and does not extend to that of other men.

CHARLES SANDERS PEIRCE,
Collected Papers of Charles Sanders Peirce

Men may argue badly, but they reason well; that is, their professed grounds are no sufficient measures of their real ones.

JOHN HENRY CARDINAL NEWMAN,
Oxford University Sermons

We have noticed a disposition on the part of the human race always to take its logic with a chaser.

DON MARQUIS,
The Almost Perfect State

One truth does not displace another. Even apparently contradictory truths do not displace one another. Logic is far too coarse to make the subtle distinctions life demands.

D. H. LAWRENCE,
Selected Essays

I dream of new harmonies—a subtler, franker art of words, not rhetorical, not seeking to prove anything.

Oh, who will deliver my mind from the heavy chains of logic? My sincerest emotion is distorted as soon as I express it.

ANDRÉ GIDE,
The Fruits of the Earth

Logic never attracts men to the point of carrying them away.

ALEXIS CARREL,
Reflections on Life

LONDON

London is strangely elusive to the tourist. Indeed, I know of no place, save Paris, which eludes those who come to see her so effectively as London.

HOLBROOK JACKSON,
Southward Ho! and Other Essays

For nine-tenths of the year London life, with its noise and colour and animation, is like a story by Dostoieffsky. In August it's like a story by Turgenev, still and calm and deep.

ALEC WAUGH,
On Doing What One Likes

London . . . is a place full of fog, where bright ideas are always welcome, provided they come in under quota and fill out the proper form.

LEONARD FEENEY,
London Is a Place

London to most of us never becomes real at all; it is merely a dream, a phantasmagoria, a changing pattern of sight and sound, with little bits of reality here and there, like currants in a vague and enormous pudding.

J. B. PRIESTLEY,
All About Ourselves and Other Essays

There is something about an open fire, bread and butter sandwiches, very strong tea, yellow fog without and the cultural drawl of English voices which makes London very attractive and if I had been fascinated before, from that moment I loved it dearly.

ISADORA DUNCAN,
My Life

London seems to me like some hoary massive underworld, a hoary ponderous inferno. The traffic flows through the rigid grey streets like the rivers of hell through their banks of dry, rocky ash.

D. H. LAWRENCE,
Selected Letters of D. H. Lawrence

I'm not going to London again for years; its intelligentsia is so hurried in the head that nothing stays there; its glamour smells of goat; there's no difference between good and bad.

DYLAN THOMAS,
Letters to Vernon Watkins

The air seems dead in this quiet country, we're out of the stream. I must rush up to London to breathe.

GEORGE MEREDITH,
quoted in *The Charm of London*,
compiled by Alfred H. Hyatt

LONELINESS

Man is essentially alone and lonely, and from this isolation he cannot be saved by someone else but only by himself through the fact that he loves, that he belongs to another human being. This opening-up of ourselves is the great liberating function of love.

OSWALD SCHWARZ,
The Psychology of Sex

We have this sense of loneliness. Men are lonely and they struggle to overcome it. We don't try to overcome it. We know we are lonely in the major events of our bodies, of our lives.

JEANNE MOREAU,
quoted in the *New York Times*,
June 30, 1976

The loneliness of a man entirely surrounded by women and children surpasses even the loneliness of a man isolated in the middle of the Sahara.

ROBERT LYND,
The Blue Lion

Better be quarreling than lonesome.

IRISH PROVERB

We must always be more or less lonely, but sometimes it is given to spirit to touch spirit. . . . Then we understand and are understood.

JANET ERSKINE STUART,
Life and Letters of Janet Erskine Stuart
by Maud Monahan

Men love because they are afraid of themselves, afraid of the loneliness that lives in them, and need someone in whom they can lose themselves as smoke loses itself in the sky.

V. F. CALVERTON,
quoted in *Ladies' Home Journal*, April 1945

Man does not become lonely as a result of circumstances, he makes himself lonely.

DR. WILHELM STEKHEL,
Marriage at the Crossroads

Like all men who are fundamentally of the group, of the herd, he was incapable of taking a strong stand, with the inevitable loneliness that implied.

F. SCOTT FITZGERALD,
The Crack-up

Sometimes I think we Americans are the loneliest people in the world. To be sure, we hunger for the power of affection, the self-acceptance that gives life. It is the oldest and strongest hunger in the world. But hungering is not enough.

SHERWOOD ANDERSON,
Letters of Sherwood Anderson

The lives of men who have to live in our great cities are often tragically lonely. In many more ways than one, these dwellers in the hive are modern counterparts of Tantalus. They are starving to death in the midst of abundance. The crystal stream flows near their lips but falls away when they try to drink it. The vine, rich-weighted with its golden fruit, bends down, comes near, but springs back when they reach to touch it.

THOMAS WOLFE,
You Can't Go Home Again

Americans become unhappy and vicious because their preoccupation with amassing possessions obliterates their loneliness.

This is why production in America seems to be on such an endless upward spiral: every time we buy something we deepen our emotional deprivation and hence our need to buy something.

PHILIP SLATER,
The Pursuit of Loneliness

At the innermost core of all loneliness is a deep and powerful yearning for union with one's lost self.

BRENDAN FRANCIS

To one man, lonesomeness is the flight of the sick one; to another, it is the flight *from* the sick ones.

FRIEDRICH NIETZSCHE,
Thus Spake Zarathustra

Real loneliness consists not in being alone, but in being with the wrong person, in the suffocating darkness of a room in which no deep communication is possible.

SYDNEY J. HARRIS,
Strictly Personal

The evils that now and then wring a groan from my heart are ... not that I am a *single* woman and likely to remain a *single* woman—but because I am a *lonely* woman and likely to be *lonely*.

CHARLOTTE BRONTË,
quoted in *Ladies of Literature*
by Laura L. Hinkley

LOOKING BACK

There is a point at which everything becomes simple and there is no longer any question of choice, because all you have staked will be lost if you look back. Life's point of no return.

DAG HAMMARSKJÖLD,
Markings

When I look back at the three or four choices in my life which have been decisive, I find that, at the time I made them, I had very little sense of the seriousness of what I was doing and only later did I discover what had seemed an unimportant brook was, in fact, a Rubicon.

W. H. AUDEN,
The Dyer's Hand and Other Essays

LOVE

Perhaps men and women were born to love one another, simply and genuinely, rather than to this travesty that we call love. If we can stop destroying ourselves we may stop destroying others. We have to begin by admitting and even accepting our violence, rather than blindly destroying ourselves with it, and therewith we have to realize that we are as deeply afraid to live and to love as we are to die.

R. D. LAING,
The Politics of Experience

Life has taught us that love does not consist in gazing at each other but in looking outward together in the same direction.

ANTOINE DE SAINT-EXUPÉRY,
Airman's Odyssey

Love is the child of freedom, never that of domination.

ERICH FROMM,
The Art of Loving

In the divisions of love, there always abides the unity of him who loves.

JOHN DEWEY,
Characters and Events, VOL. I

But to love is quite another thing: it is to will an object for itself, to rejoice in its beauty and goodness for themselves, and without respect to anything other than itself.

ETIENNE GILSON,
The Spirit of Medieval Philosophy

We [women] learn it at last—that the one gift in our treasure house is love—love—love. If we may not give it, if no one looks into our eyes and asks our gift—we may indeed collect ourselves and offer our second-best to the world, and the world may applaud. But the vital principle is gone from our lives.

RUTH BENEDICT,
An Anthropologist at Work
by Margaret Mead

To love deeply in one direction makes us more loving in all others.

MADAME SWETCHINE,
The Writings of Madame Swetchine

No woman ever loved her husband for his intellect or his admirable principles—or friend his friend—*love is the instinctive movement of personality.*

J. B. YEATS,
Letters to His Son, W. B. Yeats and Others

Love does not express itself on command; it cannot be called out like a dog to its master—merely because one thinks he needs to see it. Love is autonomous; it obeys only itself.

ROBERT C. MURPHY,
Psychotherapy Based on Human Longing

We are never so defenceless against suffering as when we love, never so forlornly unhappy as when we have lost our love-object or its love.

SIGMUND FREUD,
Civilization and Its Discontents

A strong egotism is a protection against disease, but in the last resort we must begin to love in order that we may not fall ill, and must fall ill, if in consequence of frustration, we cannot love.

SIGMUND FREUD,
quoted in *Life Against Death*
by Norman O. Brown

Love is but the discovery of ourselves in others, and the delight in the recognition.

ALEXANDER SMITH,
Dreamthorp

Love that has been given to you is too sacred a thing to be talked of to anyone ... except just to the person who is like part of you and who will feel it as you do.

OLIVE SCHREINER,
Letters of Olive Schreiner

Love disregards manifest qualities and sees right through them down to the true essential value. Furthermore, love divines all the talents, the still dormant possibilities of the beloved, brings them to life, and thus increases his value.

OSWALD SCHWARZ,
The Psychology of Sex

We receive love—from our children as well as others—not in proportion to our de-

mands or sacrifices or needs, but roughly in proportion to our own capacity to love.
ROLLO MAY,
Man's Search for Himself

To be capable of giving and receiving mature love is as sound a criterion as we have for the fulfilled personality. But by that very token it is a goal gained only in proportion to how much one has fulfilled the prior condition of becoming a person in one's own right.
ROLLO MAY,
Man's Search for Himself

I am a lover who has not found his thing to love.
SHERWOOD ANDERSON,
Letters of Sherwood Anderson

Love which is all-inclusive seems to repel us.
HENRY MILLER,
The Books in My Life

You can love a person deeply and sincerely whom you do not like. You can like a person passionately whom you do not love.
ROBERT HUGH BENSON,
Spiritual Letters of Monsignor R. Hugh Benson to One of His Converts

When the satisfaction or security of another person becomes as significant to one as is one's own satisfaction or security, then the state of love exists. So far as I know, under no other circumstances is a state of love present, regardless of the popular usage of the word.
HARRY STACK SULLIVAN,
Conceptions of Modern Psychiatry

It is no doubt very tolerable finite or creaturely love to love one's own in another, to love another for his conformity to one's self: but nothing can be in more flagrant contrast with the creative Love, all whose tenderness *ex vi termini* must be reserved only for what intrinsically is most bitterly hostile and negative to itself.
HENRY JAMES, SR.,
quoted in the *Collected Papers of Charles Sanders Peirce*

Unfortunately, it is easy to imagine that anyone hates you, and hard to think any-

one loves you. But you must be bold to believe in love if you would be happy.
DR. FRANK CRANE,
Essays

We find rest in those we love, and we provide a resting place in ourselves for those who love us.
SAINT BERNARD OF CLAIRVAUX,
Letters

It is nice to feel the atmosphere of love round you once in a while, and nobody out of tune.
GEORGE E. WOODBERRY,
Selected Letters of George Edward Woodberry

To be loved for what one is, is the greatest exception. The great majority love in another only what they lend him, their own selves, their version of him.
GOETHE,
Wisdom and Experience

Whatever you are doing, love yourself for doing it. Whatever you are thinking, love yourself for thinking it.
THADDEUS GOLAS,
The Lazy Man's Guide to Enlightenment

Love it the way it is.
THADDEUS GOLAS,
The Lazy Man's Guide to Enlightenment

Love is never merely an amiable tolerance of whatever form human frailty and folly may take.
JOSIAH ROYCE,
The Problem of Christianity

There's so much of the child in me yet, and life to me means love just as it does to a child—love of many kinds and degrees, but each and all helping us on our way and bringing the journey's end a little nearer the knowledge of God.
ELLEN GLASGOW,
Letters of Ellen Glasgow

How have we the courage to wish to live, how can we make a movement to preserve ourselves from death, in a world where love is provoked by a lie and consists solely in the need of having our sufferings appeased by whatever being has made us suffer?

MARCEL PROUST,
quoted in *The Politics of Experience*
by R. D. Laing

Where love rules, there is no will to power; and where power predominates, there love is lacking. The one is the shadow of the other.

C. G. JUNG,
Psychological Reflections,
edited by Jolande Jacobi and R. F. Hull

The great tragedy of life is not that men perish, but that they cease to love.

W. SOMERSET MAUGHAM,
The Summing Up

I here and now, finally and forever, give up knowing anything about love, or wanting to know. I believe it doesn't exist, save as a word: a sort of wailing phoenix that is really the wind in the trees.

D. H. LAWRENCE,
Selected Letters of D. H. Lawrence

Love does not recognize the difference between peasant and mikado.

JAPANESE PROVERB

When you really want love you will find it waiting for you.

OSCAR WILDE,
De Profundis

This is the worst of life, that love does not give us common sense but is a sure way of losing it. We love people, and we say that we were going to do more for them than friendship, but it makes such fools of us that we do far less, indeed sometimes what we do could be mistaken for the work of hatred.

REBECCA WEST,
quoted in *Rebecca West: Artist and Thinker*
by Peter Wolfe

To an ordinary human being love means nothing if it does not mean loving some people more than others.

GEORGE ORWELL,
A Collection of Essays

Love, recognizing germs of loveliness in the hateful, gradually warms it into life, and makes it lovely.

CHARLES SANDERS PEIRCE,
Collected Papers of Charles Sanders Peirce

Who promised love should be happiness? Nature may have some other end.

MARK RUTHERFORD,
Last Pages from a Journal

some say we are responsible
for those we love
others know we are responsible
for those who love us

NIKKI GIOVANNI,
"The December of My Springs,"
The Women and the Men

LOVE: MAN AND WOMAN

A great many people fall in love with or feel attracted to a person who offers the least possibility of a harmonious union.

DR. RUDOLF DREIKURS,
The Challenge of Marriage

Men's insistence on being of service sometimes expresses less consideration than girls like to believe. Helping women, treating them, bestowing gifts—these things are done much more for the donor's sake, as assertions of his superiority.

DR. RUDOLF DREIKURS,
The Challenge of Marriage

I've never been able to work without a woman to love. Perhaps I'm cruel. They are earth and sky and warmth and light to me. I'm like an Irish peasant, taking potatoes out of the ground. I live by the woman loved. I take from her. I know damned well I don't give enough.

SHERWOOD ANDERSON,
Letters of Sherwood Anderson

There is one woman whom fate has destined for each of us. If we miss her, we are saved.

ANONYMOUS,
quoted in the *New York Times,*
May 9, 1948

Love is like butter, it goes well with bread.

YIDDISH PROVERB

I had discovered that Love might be a pastime as well as a tragedy. I gave myself to it with pagan innocence.

ISADORA DUNCAN,
My Life

To say that love is "an exchange of psychic energy" is to state a literal fact. The woman who scans the face of her lover anxiously when he is disturbed, and reaches out with a soothing hand to comfort him, is actually transmitting to him a healing force within her own nature. She is obeying the same kind of impulse that directs the heart to pump more blood to the wounded limb.

DR. SMILEY BLANTON,
Love or Perish

Lovers always think that other people have had their eyes put out.

SPANISH PROVERB

I think we had the chief of all love's joys
Only in knowing that we loved each
    other.

GEORGE ELIOT,
Spanish Gypsy

My last night alone in bed for many a day. It seems "putting off childish things" to have someone to love. Yet I was hoping together we might be more childlike, less oppressed with heavy cares and heavy experiences. It all feels very inevitable—like spring following winter.

JOANNA FIELD,
Revelations: Diaries of Women edited by
Mary Jane Moffat and Charlotte Painter

A woman would no doubt need a great deal of imagination to love a man for his virtue.

JOHN OLIVER HOBBES,
The Sinner's Comedy

When a woman likes to wait on a man, that settles it: she loves him.

E. W. HOWE,
Country Town Sayings

Against all the evidence of his senses the man in love declares that he and his beloved are one, and is prepared to behave

as if it were a fact.

SIGMUND FREUD,
Civilization and Its Discontents

It is the fate of sensual love to become extinguished when it is satisfied; for it to be able to last, it must . . . be mixed with purely tender components—with such, that is, as are inhibited in their aims.

SIGMUND FREUD,
Group Psychology and the Analysis of the Ego

How bold one gets when one is sure of being loved!

SIGMUND FREUD,
The Letters of Sigmund Freud

There is something terrible about two human beings who love each other and can find neither the means or the time to let the other know, who wait until some misfortune or disagreement extorts an affirmation of affection.

SIGMUND FREUD,
The Letters of Sigmund Freud

Most of us love from our need to love not because we find someone deserving.

NIKKI GIOVANNI,
"The Women Gather,"
The Women and the Men

Perhaps a great love is never returned.

DAG HAMMARSKJÖLD,
Markings

I have a stinking hangover and don't speak on the ride back, don't even think much except to tell myself how much jabber there is in the name of love.

LILLIAN HELLMAN,
An Unfinished Woman

Of all the realities whose values we ignore, in childish preoccupation with our feeble dreams, the human realities of companionship which each sex has to offer the other are among the richest. Despite all our romantic serenadings, men and women have only begun to discover each other.

FLOYD DELL,
Were You Ever a Child?

Getting along with men isn't what's truly important. The vital knowledge is how to get along with a man, one man.

PHYLLIS MCGINLEY,
The Province of the Heart

A woman does not want her love affairs talked about. Yet she wants everybody to know that someone loves her.

ANDRÉ MAUROIS,
quoted in *Ladies' Home Journal,* April 1942

For a time men will endure scenes of anger and jealousy from the women they deeply love. Some prefer agitated love affairs as they prefer rough seas to calm ones; but most of them are definitely peace-loving. They are easily won by good temper, simplicity and gentleness, especially if some mad woman has previously cured them of their taste for violence.

ANDRÉ MAUROIS,
The Art of Living

Love everywhere tends to magnify both its object and itself. It makes unreasonable claims as to its own strength, depth, duration, and intensity.

OSCAR W. FIRKINS,
Oscar Firkins: Memoirs and Letters,
edited by Ina Ten Eyck

The ability to make love frivolously is the chief characteristic which distinguishes human beings from beasts.

HEYWOOD BROUN,
quoted in *George S. Kaufman*
by Howard Teichman

The superficial character of human relationships leads many to hope that they can find depth and intensity of feeling in individual love. But love for one person and love for one's neighbor are indivisible; in any given culture, love relationships are only a more intense expression of the relatedness to man prevalent in that culture.

ERICH FROMM,
Man for Himself

Would you be happier if a woman swore to you that she would love you always?

ANATOLE FRANCE,
The Anatole France Calendar,
selected by A. S. Rappoport

The more you love someone the more he wants from you and the less you have to give since you've already given him your love.

NIKKI GIOVANNI,
Gemini

What is so withering to people's life-illusion and to their secret culture is ... the possessiveness of love. This possessiveness is something quite different from sex-attraction. It is a projection of that maternal or paternal cannibalism which desires to hug what belongs to it, even unto death.

JOHN COWPER POWYS,
The Meaning of Culture

Women have no favour or mercy for the silence their charms impose on us. Little are they aware of the devotion we are offering to them, in that state wherein the true lover is ever prone to fall, and which appears to them inattention, indifference or moroseness.

WALTER SAVAGE LANDOR,
Imaginary Conversations

Only by oneself, apart, can one consummate this seemingly most shared experience that love is.

RAINER MARIA RILKE,
Letters of Rainer Maria Rilke 1892–1910

There are a great many ways of proposing. All of them are good. In fact, experience teaches that unless you are very careless in the way you propose, you are in positive danger of being accepted.

FRANK RICHARDSON,
Love and All About It

One makes mistakes: that is life. But it is never quite a mistake to have loved.

ROMAIN ROLLAND,
Summer

She is the type of female whom males do not conquer with the brilliance of their plumage, nor with their suppleness, nor with their courage, but with their laments, whimpers and recitals of failure. This is a woman who loves men in their period of decline.

ANTON CHEKHOV,
The Selected Letters of Anton Chekhov

There are two great moments in a woman's life: when first she finds herself to be deeply in love with her man, and when she leaves him. . . . Women are different from men, and to break with the past and mangle their mate in the process fulfills a dark need of theirs.

CYRIL CONNOLLY,
The Unquiet Grave

With every woman, to love a man is to feel that she must positively know just where he is going as soon as he is out of her sight.

F. MARION CRAWFORD,
quoted in *Ladies' Home Journal,*
August 1944

He had learned tonight that love was not enough. There had to be a higher devotion than all the devotions of this fond imprisonment.

THOMAS WOLFE,
You Can't Go Home Again

As is usual with most lovers in the city, they were troubled by the lack of that essential need of love—a meeting place.

THOMAS WOLFE,
The Web and the Rock

In spite of all indignant protests to the contrary, the fact remains that love, its problems and its conflicts, is of fundamental importance in human life and, as careful inquiry consistently shows, is of far greater significance than the individual suspects.

C. G. JUNG,
Two Essays in Analytical Psychology

The wretched part of it is that we can't love frivolously if we mean it.

ANONYMOUS (HENRY S. HASKINS),
Meditations in Wall Street

I have an idea that in most relationships between a man and a woman one is the contained and one is the container; and this balance, once having been determined, can't ever be changed.

KATHARINE BUTLER HATHAWAY,
The Journals and Letters of the Little Locksmith

The hardships of living together. Forced upon us by strangeness, pity, lust, cowardice, vanity, and only deep down, perhaps, a thin little stream worthy of the name of love, impossible to seek out, flashing once in the moment of a moment.

FRANZ KAFKA,
The Diaries of Franz Kafka 1914–1923

The emotion, the ecstasy of love, we all want, but God spare us the responsibility.

JESSAMYN WEST,
Love Is Not What You Think

Everyone, naturally, wants love, but the real thing, when it arrives, is cruel, disconcerting, and frightening. One's partner refuses merely to be an object, a thing, an impersonal presence, and demands one's precious time, careful reflection, and emotional entanglement.

MICHAEL NOVAK,
Prophetic Voices, edited by Ned O'Gorman

Love is the desire to prostitute oneself. There is, indeed, no exalted pleasure which cannot be related to prostitution.

CHARLES BAUDELAIRE,
Intimate Journals

I think, when one loves, one's very sex passion becomes calm, a steady sort of force, instead of a storm.

D. H. LAWRENCE,
Selected Letters of D. H. Lawrence

A woman unsatisfied must have luxuries. But a woman who loves a man would sleep on a board.

D. H. LAWRENCE,
quoted in *Ladies' Home Journal,*
February 1949

this time i think i'll face love
with my heart instead of my glands
rather than hands clutching to satiate
my fingers will stroke to satisfy
i think it might be good
to decide rather than to need

NIKKI GIOVANNI,
"The December of My Springs,"
The Women and the Men

I suppose love is whatever breaks and bridges the terrible pathos of separateness of human beings from each other. It doesn't mean much, however, unless it exists between two people who are uniquely themselves.

MAX LERNER,
The Unfinished Country

LOYALTY

I have a good deal of respect for the old woman who, in time of war, started out with a poker when the enemy was approaching. She was asked what she could do with that, and she replied, "I can show them which side I am on."

DWIGHT L. MOODY,
quoted in *The Author's Kalendar, 1916,*
compiled by Anna C. Woodford

I know a woman who, whenever one of her intimates is attacked in her presence, merely states: "She is my friend," and refuses to say more.

ANDRÉ MAUROIS,
The Art of Living

When I meet a new person, I am on the lookout for signs of what he or she is loyal to. It is a preliminary clue to the sense of belonging, and hence of his or her humanity.

HANIEL LONG,
A Letter to St. Augustine

Loyalty means not that I *am* you, or that I *agree* with everything you say or that I believe you are always right. Loyalty means that I share a common ideal with you and that regardless of minor differences we fight for it, shoulder to shoulder, confident in one another's good faith, trust, constancy, and affection.

DR. KARL MENNINGER,
A Psychiatrist's World

LUCK

Give me, mother, luck at my birth, then throw me if you will on the rubbish heap.

BULGARIAN PROVERB

Luck, bad if not good, will always be with us. But it has a way of favoring the intelligent and showing its back to the stupid.

JOHN DEWEY,
Human Nature and Conduct

Most of us regard good luck as our right, and bad luck as a betrayal of that right.

WILLIAM FEATHER,
The Business of Life

It would seem that you don't be having any good luck until you believe there is no such thing as luck in it at all.

IRISH PROVERB

It is the dream of every Utopian to throw luck out of the world—the luck of birth, of brains, of beauty, of fate—to make all destinies equal. That is a dream that can't be realised. The world is inescapably shot through with luck, because it is also shot through with freedom.

JOYCE CARY,
Art and Reality

LUXURY (*See also* MONEY)

A luxury for one person may be a necessity for another.

H. GEORGE

Caviar is a luxury for the general, but may be a necessity for a particular gourmet.

TED SAUCIER

MACHINE

I guess you know that I have been one of the outstanding little protesters against the machine age.

However, it is here, and recently I have had a change of heart. I have been trying recently to go to machinery as a man might go to the mountains and to the forests and rivers.

SHERWOOD ANDERSON,
Letters of Sherwood Anderson

The God of this world is in the machine, not out of it.

GEORGE MEREDITH,
The Ordeal of Richard Feverel

The machine is lethal whenever it constrains man to its banalities, its repetitions, its primary dogmatism, no more and no less than ideas of our philosophers. But it can also be the mighty poetry of our own hands.

EMMANUEL MOUNIER,
Be Not Afraid

MADNESS

No, I do not wish to leave the world—I want to go into a madhouse and see whether the profundity of madness will not solve the riddle of life for me.

SØREN KIERKEGAARD,
The Journals of Søren Kierkegaard

Dream not, Coleridge, of having tasted all the grandeur and wildness of Fancy, till you have gone mad. All now seems to me vapid, comparatively so.

CHARLES LAMB,
The Letters of Charles and Mary Lamb

The human race consists of the dangerously insane and such as are not.

MARK TWAIN,
Mark Twain at Your Fingertips,
edited by Caroline T. Harnsberger

Should those about us agree to think us mad it would be difficult to keep faith in one's own sanity.

JOHN LANCASTER SPALDING,
Glimpses of Truth

Madness need not be all breakdown. It may also be breakthrough. It is potentially liberation and renewal as well as enslavement and existential death.

R. D. LAING,
The Politics of Experience

If you simply look at the phenomena—the bare data—then you don't see sanity or madness. The attribution of sanity or madness comes in as something superimposed upon the data. "Is this person crazy? Is this person mad?" I don't find that I get any mileage out of it. I'm often asked that question by people who seem to think that it's very important to them to decide who's crazy.

R. D. LAING,
Supertalk by Digby Diehl

Madness alone is entirely free from the commonplace. However terrible or twisted or invalid the visions of sick brains, each is individual and new.

WILLIAM BOLITHO,
Camera Obscura

It is not by confining one's neighbor that one is convinced of one's own sanity.

FEODOR DOSTOEVSKI,
The Diary of a Writer

MAN (HUMANITY)

Man is a whole, but a whole with an astounding capacity for living, simultaneously or successively, in watertight compartments. What happens here has little or no effect on what happens there.

ALDOUS HUXLEY,
Collected Essays

Our achievement, when we compare it with that of cows or elephants, is remarkable. They automatically make dung; we collect it, and turn it into fuel. It is not something to be depressed about; it is something to be proud of.

ALDOUS HUXLEY,
Collected Essays

Man is harder than rock and more fragile than an egg.

YUGOSLAV PROVERB

The collective impulses of mankind seem to me always baser than the individual hopes and desires.

A. C. BENSON,
*Excerpts from the Letters of
Dr. A. C. Benson to M. E. A.*

Man will become better only when you will make him see what he is like.

ANTON CHEKHOV,
quoted in *The Carillon*
by Lawrence W. Pearson

Man uses his intelligence less in the care of his own species than he does in his care of anything else he owns or governs.

ABRAHAM MEYERSON,
Speaking of Man

Nothing will prevent me from thinking that humanity might be more vigorous than it is, healthier, and consequently happier, and that we are responsible for almost all the ills from which we suffer.

ANDRÉ GIDE,
The Fruits of the Earth

The devotion to what men at their best may be, to what at their best they make of the world, constitutes a love that is nothing less than religious.

IRWIN EDMAN,
The Uses of Philosophy,
edited by Charles Frankel

I only mean that when one thinks coldly I see no reason for attributing to man a significance different in kind from that which belongs to a baboon or a grain of sand.

OLIVER WENDELL HOLMES, JR.,
Holmes-Pollock Letters, Vol. II

Ill-adapted for living an easy life, he is well adapted for living a difficult one. . . . Never is he more at home in this universe than when he finds himself "upon an engagement very difficult."

L. P. JACKS,
The Challenge of Life

When I inquire about the future of man, I must, if my questions are seriously meant, disregard all mere aspects, be they splendid or be they dispiriting, and thus dig down to the sources of the possible where man, equipped with the fullest attainable knowledge, strives to make his own future, and not merely to contemplate it.

KARL JASPERS,
Man in the Modern Age

Now man cannot live without some vision of himself. But still less can he live without a vision that is true to his inner experience and inner feeling.

D. H. LAWRENCE,
Assorted Articles

A thousand paths are there which have never yet been trodden; a thousand salubrities and hidden islands of life. Unexhausted and undiscovered is still man and man's world.

FRIEDRICH NIETZSCHE,
Thus Spake Zarathustra

Here, then, is man, this moth of time, this dupe of brevity and numbered hours, this travesty of waste and sterile action. Yet if the gods could come here to a desolate, deserted earth where only the ruin of man's cities remained, where only a few marks and carvings of his hand were legible upon his broken tablets, where only a wheel lay rusting in the desert sand, a cry would burst out of their hearts and they would say: "He lived, and he was here!"

THOMAS WOLFE,
You Can't Go Home Again

Man identifies himself with earth or the material. . . . Spirit is strange to him; he is afraid of ghosts.

HENRY DAVID THOREAU,
Journal

Strange inhabitants are we of a world so strange that at one moment the heart aches at its loveliness, and another aches at its miseries, so strange that when we think of death we are in love with life, when of life we are enamoured of death. What kind of beings are we in fact? Whatever we are, never forget that we are nature's children, her contradictions are ours, ours also her talents and graces.

W. MACNEILE DIXON,
The Human Situation

MAN (MALE)

Men are all the same. They always think that something they are going to get is better than what they have got.

JOHN OLIVER HOBBES,
The Herb-Moon

Men don't understand, as a rule, that women like to get used to them by degrees.

JOHN OLIVER HOBBES,
Some Emotions and a Moral

Indeed, I should say without reservation that men fear and hate women more than women fear and hate men. I think it is this rather than the male's superior strength that makes it possible for our civilization to be called "a man's world." It is not a

contest of strength; it is a contest of hate.
DR. KARL MENNINGER,
A Psychiatrist's World

Whether, as some psychologists believe, some women suffer from penis envy, I am not sure. I am quite certain, however, that all males without exception suffer from penis rivalry, and that this trait has now become a threat to the future existence of the human race.
W. H. AUDEN,
A Certain World

If you would understand men, study women.
FRENCH PROVERB

As for the idea—well, I was worn out with having men write what they know or don't know about the dangerous ages in women.
ELLEN GLASGOW,
Letters of Ellen Glasgow

It is a conviction of mine that refined and perfect domestic comfort is understood by men only.
OLIVER BELL BUNCE,
Bachelor Bluff

All I ask our brethren is that they will take their feet from off our necks and permit us to stand upright.
SARAH GRIMKE,
quoted in *Prudery and Passion*
by Milton Rugoff

I think it can be stated without denial that no man ever saw a man that he would be willing to marry if he were a woman.
GEORGE GIBBS,
How to Stay Married

It may be that to love one's neighbor is also a part of manhood, to suffer quietly for another as true a piece of bravery as to fell him for a careless word.
RICHARD LE GALLIENNE,
Prose Fancies

It takes a brave man to face a brave woman, and man's fear of woman's creative energy has never found an expression more clear than in the old German clamor, renewed by the Nazis, of *"Kinder,*

Kuchen and *Kirche"* for women.
PEARL BUCK,
To My Daughters, with Love

The great truth is that women actually like men, and men can never believe it.
ISABEL PATTERSON,
quoted in *Ladies' Home Journal,*
October 1944

The problems besetting men have many names. Call them boredom and restlessness and discontent and frustration. In some men they're intense and consistent. In the majority of men they're much more vague and sporadic. There's a feeling that the job, the wife, the sex, the kids, or the leisure time—in short, the good life—is . . . well . . . good, but not *that* good. Real fulfillment, one senses, is a long way around the corner.
MYRON BRENTON,
The American Male

It's fallacious to go in for a so-called masculine activity in order to arrive at a masculine attitude. The two just aren't synonymous, although it's characteristic of men caught in the masculinity trap to confuse activity with attitude.
MYRON BRENTON,
The American Male

Men are more conventional than women and much slower to change their ideas.
KATHLEEN NORRIS,
Hands Full of Living

The average man takes all the natural taste out of his food by covering it with ready-made sauces, and all the personality out of a woman by covering her with his ready-made ideals.
HELEN ROWLAND,
A Guide to Men

Every man wants a woman to appeal to his better side, his nobler instincts and his higher nature—and another woman to help him forget them.
HELEN ROWLAND,
A Guide to Men

When two men fight over a woman it's the fight they want, not the woman.
BRENDAN FRANCIS

The male has been taught that he is superior to women in nearly every way, and this is reinforced by the submissive tactics of many women in their desperate antics of flirtation and hunting; it would be a wonder if the average male did not come to believe that he was superior.

JOYCE CAROL OATES,
Open Secrets by Barbaralee Diamonstein

With some men, it would be quite a task to appear dumber.

(In response to, "Pretend to be dumber in the presence of a man?")

JOYCE CAROL OATES,
Open Secrets by Barbaralee Diamonstein

Men don't bite unless you know them very well indeed. If you have good teeth, too, why not be friendly?

G. M. WHITE,
Ladies' Home Journal, May 1949

There is a type of man for whom men have not the slightest use but whom women, for a while at any rate, find irresistibly attractive.

ALEC WAUGH,
On Doing What One Likes

A man who has nothing to do with women is always incomplete.

CYRIL CONNOLLY,
The Unquiet Grave

All men ... have the idea that they are always busy, and if they are not, a woman can soon persuade them that they are. Just say, "I don't see how you do it all," without saying what *all* is.

STEPHEN LEACOCK,
Last Years

Men are only animals anyway. They like to get out into the woods and growl round at night and feel something bite them.

STEPHEN LEACOCK,
The Leacock Roundabout

To satisfy his deeper social instincts and intuitions, a man must be able to get away from his family altogether, and foregather in the communion of men.

D. H. LAWRENCE,
Assorted Articles

When it comes to women, modern men are idiots. They don't know what they want, and so they never want, permanently, what they get. They want a cream cake that is at the same time ham and eggs and at the same time porridge. They are fools. If only women weren't bound by fate to play up to them.

D. H. LAWRENCE,
Selected Essays

A man can be a tramp, purposeless, and be happy. . . . I verily believe vast numbers of men would gladly drift away as wasters, if there were anywhere to drift to.

D. H. LAWRENCE,
Selected Essays

I like a man who can cry. My father cried. My brother Rusty cries.

JESSAMYN WEST,
Hide and Seek

Any man worthy of the name is only too willing to make a fool of himself for the sake of a woman.

FRANK RICHARDSON,
Love: And All About It

More than one woman has complained that all men want only one thing, and always the same.

OSWALD SCHWARZ,
The Psychology of Sex

Intellectual men are not less alive to the charms of women than other men are; indeed the greatest of them have always delighted in the society of women.

PHILIP G. HAMERTON,
The Intellectual Life

Having created a technological and social-structural juggernaut by which they are daily buffeted, men tend to use their wives as opiates to soften the impact of the forces they have set into motion against themselves.

PHILIP SLATER,
The Pursuit of Loneliness

Societies in which deprived mothers turn to their children for what they cannot obtain from adults tend to produce males who are vain, boastful, aggressive, and skittish toward women. Such males have great fear of losing self-control, of becoming dependent upon women, of weakness. They often huddle together in male gangs.

PHILIP SLATER,
The Pursuit of Loneliness

It is a marvelous thing to be physically a woman if only to know the marvels of a man.

MARYA MANNES,
Out of My Time

A woman I have heard, takes to herself a mate and reproduces her kind, and is thereby complete; with a woman completion, I believe, signifies multiplication. As to a man, I doubt if even multiplication completes him; possibly nothing completes him; possibly he remains an imperfect creature to the end.

ROSE MACAULAY,
A Casual Commentary

They are so obsessed by public affairs that they see the world as by moonlight, which shows the outlines of every object but not the details indicative of their nature.

REBECCA WEST,
quoted in *Rebecca West: Artist and Thinker* by Peter Wolfe

Our Aunts and Grandmothers allwaies tell us Men are a sort of Animals, that if ever they are constant 'tis only where they are ill us'd. Twas a kind of Paradox I could never believe. Experience has taught me the truth of it.

LADY MARY WORTLEY MONTAGU,
The Complete Letters of Lady Mary Wortley Montagu

I react against the plain, the one-dimensional men. . . . I meet them everywhere, prosaic, down-to-earth, always talking of politics, never for one moment in the world of music or pleasure, never free of the weight of daily problems, never joyous, never elated, made of either concrete and steel or like work horses, indifferent to their bodies, obsessed with power.

ANAÏS NIN,
The Diaries of Anaïs Nin, Vol. IV

Men build bridges and throw railroads across deserts, and yet they contend successfully that the job of sewing on a button is beyond them.

HEYWOOD BROUN,
Collected Edition of Heywood Broun

In hotel bedrooms I learnt to call people *toi,* and I learnt a vast, all-embracing kindness for men—men sweating or coughing, handsome or ugly, sunburnt or pale, who all smoked after they made love. The time of shady hotels with their creaking lifts and dangling wallpaper is past, but I have never forgotten that kindness.

FRANÇOISE MALLET-JORIS,
A Letter to Myself

At eleven-thirty on a rainy Thursday morning we counted the persons in the north hall of the reading-room in the Library. There were one hundred and seven men and fourteen women. Our conclusions, interesting, and well thought out, were: men are more scholarly, curious, persistent, indifferent to weather, romantic, earnest, intellectual, early-rising, conscientious, creative, sober, and unoccupied, than women. But we may be wrong.

E. B. WHITE,
Every Day Is Saturday

Men control the political scene—internationally as well as nationally. They make the wars, and make the treaties. They control international finance. They make and interpret most of the laws, many of them disadvantageous to women, poor people, blacks, American Indians, Puerto Ricans, etc. While there are outstanding exceptions in the case of individuals, the male domination in many areas has been singularly insensitive to the needs of the weak.

CORETTA SCOTT KING,
Open Secrets by Barbaralee Diamonstein

It is true, of course, that the increased activity of women in economic life tends to reduce the differences between male and female roles, but the cause of the alteration in these roles lies also in the decline of the ancient values and the unshackling and unmasking of a masculine hunger for emotional gratifications.

JULES HENRY,
Culture Against Man

The male stereotype makes masculinity not just a fact of biology but something that must be proved and re-proved, a continual quest for an ever-receding Holy Grail.

MARC FEIGEN FASTEAU,
The Male Machine

By and large men do prefer the company of other men, not only in their structured time but in the time they fill with optional, nonobligatory activity. They prefer to play games, drink, and talk, as well as work and fight together. Yet something is missing. Despite the time men spend together, their contact rarely goes beyond the external, a limitation which tends to make their friendships shallow and unsatisfying.

MARC FEIGEN FASTEAU,
The Male Machine

MARRIAGE

One should not think about it too much when marrying or taking pills.

DUTCH PROVERB

I shall half wish you unmarried (don't show this to Mrs. C) for one evening only, to have the pleasure of smoking with you and drinking egg-hot in some little smoky room in a pothouse, for I know not yet how I shall like you in a decent room and looking quite happy. My best love and respects to Sara notwithstanding.

CHARLES LAMB,
(to Samuel Taylor Coleridge),
quoted in *The Book of Friendship,*
arranged by Arthur Ransome

A marriage without conflicts is almost as inconceivable as a nation without crises.

ANDRÉ MAUROIS,
The Art of Living

In any case, as long as more male passion, roughly calculated, goes into watching pro football on television than into gently seducing the Mrs., and so long as the lady of the house secretly yearns for a tenderness she no longer seems to attract, the American ship of marriage sails near dangerous rocks.

MICHAEL NOVAK,
Prophetic Voices, edited by Ned O'Gorman

Just because a girl's married ain't no sign she hasn't loved and lost.

KIN HUBBARD,
Abe Martin on Things in General

If you're talkative and like to hold the center of the stage a lot, for goodness' sake have sense enough to marry a quiet girl who enjoys listening to you, if you can find one. A city girl who is used to noise would do in a pinch.

ANNE SHAW,
Brides Are Like New Shoes

In a successful marriage, there is no such thing as one's way. There is only the way of both, only the bumpy, dusty, difficult, but always mutual path.

PHYLLIS McGINLEY,
The Province of the Heart

For a male and female to live continuously together is ... biologically speaking, an extremely unnatural condition.

ROBERT BRIFFAULT,
quoted in *The Female Eunuch*
by Germaine Greer

Do not choose your wife at a dance, but in the field among the harvesters.

CZECH PROVERB

In a perfect union the man and the woman are like a strung bow. Who is to say whether the string bends the bow, or the bow tightens the string? Yet male bow and female string are in harmony with each other, and their arrow can be aimed. Unstrung the bow hangs aimless; the cord flaps idly.

CYRIL CONNOLLY,
The Unquiet Grave

The tragedy of modern marriage is that married couples no longer enjoy the support of society, although marr age, difficult at any time, requires every social sanction.

CYRIL CONNOLLY,
The Unquiet Grave

It is sad and wrong to be so dependent for the life of my life on any human being as I am on you; but I cannot by any force of logic cure myself at this date, when it has become second nature. If I have to lead another life in any of the planets, I shall take precious good care not to hang myself round any man's neck, either as a locket or a millstone.

JANE CARLYLE,
quoted in *The Literature of Gossip*
by Elizabeth Drew

Married couples: the man tries to shine before a third person. Immediately his wife says: "But you're just the same ..." and tries to bring him down, to make him share her mediocrity.

ALBERT CAMUS,
Notebooks 1935–1942

I have one case record of a man who claims he thought *he* was taking his wife to see the psychiatrist, not realizing until too late that his wife had made the arrangements.

ERVING GOFFMAN,
Asylums

Few men understand their wives. It is not fatal to enjoyment. People who are perfectly clear to each other are simply keeping things back.

FRANK MOORE COLBY,
The Colby Essays, Vol. 2

Women have one great advantage over men. It is commonly thought that if they marry they have done enough, and need career no further. If a man marries, on the other hand, public opinion is all against him if he takes this view.

ROSE MACAULAY,
A Casual Commentary

When the news of Napoleon's death came, before the King had been informed of it by his Ministers, Sir E. Nagle, anxious to communicate the welcome tidings, said to him, "Sir, your bitterest enemy is dead." "Is she, by God!" said the tender husband.

HENRY EDWARD FOX,
quoted in *A Peck of Trouble,*
edited by Daniel George

Most married couples conduct themselves as if each party were afraid that the other one could see that it was the weaker.

ALFRED ADLER,
The Book of Marriage,
edited by Count Hermann Keyserling

Marriage is menaced by disaster if people who wed look on themselves as martyrs. Unavoidably they will let the other feel this and cheat him out of his happy sentiments.

ALFRED ADLER,
The Book of Marriage,
edited by Count Hermann Keyserling

It is very difficult for the average person to realize that friction with his spouse is based not so much upon minor contemporary provocations as upon the earlier frustrations and resentments of his childhood.

DR. KARL MENNINGER,
A Psychiatrist's World

I see no marriages which sooner fail than those contracted on account of beauty and amorous desire.

MONTAIGNE,
Essays

Even the God of Calvin never judged anyone as harshly as married couples judged each other.

WILFRED SHEED,
Max Jamison

You called and said, "I won't be home,"
So I put the roast beef in the refrigerator.
And part of me went
In cold storage, too.

LOIS WYSE,
"7:15 P.M.," *Are You Sure You Love Me?*

I think a man and a woman should choose each other for life, for the simple reason that a long life with all its accidents is barely enough for a man and a woman to understand each other; and in this case to understand is to love. The man who understands one woman is qualified to understand pretty well everything.

J. B. YEATS,
Letters to His Son, W. B. Yeats and Others

A good marriage is one which allows for change and growth in the individuals and in the way they express their love.

PEARL BUCK,
To My Daughters, with Love

Everyone is deeply interested in maintaining the faults of his partner.

DR. RUDOLF DREIKURS,
The Challenge of Marriage

The complaints which anyone voices against his mate indicate exactly the qualities which stimulated attraction before marriage.

DR. RUDOLF DREIKURS,
The Challenge of Marriage

Only the strong of heart can be well married, since they do not turn to marriage to supply what no other human being can ever get from another—a sure sense of the fortress within himself.

MAX LERNER,
The Unfinished Country

The idea of imprisoning each woman alone in a small, self-contained, and architecturally isolating dwelling is a modern invention, dependent upon an advanced technology. In Moslem societies, for example, the wife may be a prisoner but she is at least not in solitary confinement. In our society the housewife may move about freely, but since she has nowhere to go and is not a part of anything anyway her prison needs no walls.

PHILIP SLATER,
The Pursuit of Loneliness

Unlived life is a destructive and irresistible force working quietly but relentlessly. The result is that the married woman begins to doubt marriage. The unmarried woman believes in it, because she desires marriage.

C. G. JUNG,
Psychological Reflections,
edited by Jolande Jacobi

In a society which really supported marriage the wife would be encouraged to go to the office and make love to her husband on the company's time and with its blessing.

BRENDAN FRANCIS

There's one consolation about matrimony. When you look around you can always see somebody who did worse.

WARREN H. GOLDSMITH,
quoted in *Ladies' Home Journal,*
November 1948

Methinks this birth-day of our married life is like a cape, which we now have doubled, and find a more infinite ocean of love stretching out before us. God bless us and keep us; for there is something more awful in happiness than in sorrow—the latter being earthly and finite, the former composed of the texture and substance of eternity, so that spirits still embodied may well tremble at it.

NATHANIEL HAWTHORNE,
The American Notebooks

It's a mistake to suppose that it is absolutely necessary to give up being in love directly you are married.

FRANK RICHARDSON,
Love: And All About It

It isn't silence you can cut with a knife any more, it's interchange of ideas. Intelligent discussion of practically everything is what is breaking up modern marriage, if anything is.

E. B. WHITE,
Every Day Is Saturday

If very many marriages could simply let themselves dissolve after a few years, the partners would suddenly become brighter, rosier, and younger.

PAUL GOODMAN,
Growing Up Absurd

Hegel said that the most moral approach to marriage brought first the determination to get married, and then affection following in its train, so that finally both were present. I read this with pleasure, for it was exactly so with me, and is doubtless very often the case.

THOMAS MANN,
The Book of Marriage,
edited by Count Hermann Keyserling

It is a matter of life and death for married people to interrupt each other's stories; for if they did not, they would burst.

LOGAN PEARSALL SMITH,
Afterthoughts

Nothing contrasts more sharply with the masculine image of self-confidence, rationality, and control than men's sulky, obtuse, and, often virtually, total dependence on their wives to articulate and deal with their own unhappy feelings, and their own insensitivity, fear, and passivity in helping their wives to deal with theirs.

MARC FEIGEN FASTEAU,
The Male Machine

Love, for too many people in our time, consists of sleeping with a seductive woman, one who is properly endowed with the right distribution of curves and conveniences, and one upon whom a permanent lien has been acquired through the institution of marriage.

ASHLEY MONTAGU,
The Natural Superiority of Women

There is in marriage an energy and impulse of joy that lasts as long as life and that survives all sorts of suffering and distress and weariness. The triumph of marriage over all its antagonists is almost inexplicable.

JAMES DOUGLAS,
Down Shoe Lane

If you marry, you will regret it; if you do not marry, you will also regret it.

SØREN KIERKEGAARD,
Either/Or, Vol. I

All that is good and commendable now existing would continue to exist if all marriage laws were repealed tomorrow. ... I have an inalienable constitutional and natural right to love whom I may, to love as long or as short a period as I can, to change that love every day if I please!

VICTORIA CLAFLIN WOODHULL,
quoted in *The Female Eunuch*
by Germaine Greer

All I meant was that I could never exult in a marriage. I never could assume as a matter of course that a woman should be congratulated on an engagement, as if her soul were saved thereby, that is to say by the bare fact of ceasing to be single.

WILLIAM HALE WHITE,
quoted in *Religion and Art
of William Hale White* by Wilfred Stone

A happy marriage is still the greatest treasure within the gift of fortune.

EDEN PHILLPOTTS,
A Year with Bisshe-Bantam

Because women are less privatized than they have traditionally been, marriage offers more for millions of people than ever before in its long history.

DAVID RIESMAN,
The Lonely Crowd

A man, proceeding from his known self, likes a woman because she is in sympathy with what he knows. He feels that he and she know one another. They marry. And then the fun begins.

D. H. LAWRENCE,
Assorted Articles

Monogamy is for those who are whole and clear, all in one stroke. But for those whose stroke is broken into two different directions, then there must be two fulfillments.

D. H. LAWRENCE,
Selected Letters of D. H. Lawrence

Moreover, the educative role does not affect only the offspring of love but also those who love each other. In addition to the external fertility of which we usually speak there is an inward fertility which brings it to pass that the first children of love are the parents themselves. The husband is the child of the wife; and perhaps, although less obviously, the reverse is true.

JEAN GUITTON,
Essay on Human Love

The attempt to separate the sensual currents of love from the tender or ideal aspects in marriage is at bottom an infantile illusion which cannot be maintained in adult life without serious damage to one's happiness and stability. ... From my experience, I believe at least one-fourth of all divorces stem from this source.

DR. SMILEY BLANTON,
Love or Perish

The "institution" of marriage is just formalizing an emotion, an attempt to make it seem permanent. The emotion will last or it won't last; nothing can guarantee it. But as society becomes more and more unstable, as traditions break up, there will have to be a small unit of faithfulness, at least one person upon whom another person can depend, or society may disintegrate into madness.

JOYCE CAROL OATES,
Open Secrets by Barbaralee Diamonstein

Honeymoons not seldom end worse than they began, and to recover from them may take quite a long time.

ARNOLD BENNETT,
How to Make the Best of Life

No matter how happily a woman may be married, it always pleases her to discover that there is a nice man who wishes that she were not.

H. L. MENCKEN,
A Mencken Chrestomathy

The man who has entered into a beautiful union is sure of at least one person to whom he can give the best that he possesses.

GEORGES DUHAMEL,
The Heart's Domain

As man is essentially a dynamic, aspiring, evolutionary being, marriage can bring fulfillment only inasmuch as it intensifies life. Wherever it causes diminution it fails in its purpose.

COUNT HERMANN KEYSERLING,
The Book of Marriage

But, once the realization is accepted, that even between the *closest* human beings infinite distances continue to exist, a wonderful living side by side can grow up, if they succeed in loving the distance between them which makes it possible for each to see the other whole and against a wide sky!

RAINER MARIA RILKE,
Letters of Rainer Maria Rilke 1892-1910

MATURITY

In psychological writings the definition of maturity has frequently been a rather negative one. ... According to this view, the emotionally mature person is able to keep a lid on his feelings. He can suffer in silence; he can bide his time in spite of present discomfort. He is not subject to swings in mood, he is not volatile. When he does express emotion he does so with moderation, decently, and in good order. He is not carried away by his feelings. ... Actually, in the writer's opinion, a person can live up to all of these prescriptions and still be an abjectly immature person, as well as a very cold fish.

ARTHUR T. JERSILD,
Educational Psychology,
edited by Charles E. Skinner

Inclinations to wastefulness ought, when a man is mature, to be replaced by a wish to concentrate and produce.

CHARLES BAUDELAIRE,
Intimate Journals

When we consider the maturation of the personality, we should recognize that maturation is a process of repeated giving up, relinquishing, rejecting of what has been painfully learned, in order to establish a new and replacing pattern, a new role, or to establish a new relationship more appropriate to enlarging capacities, experiences and opportunities.

LAWRENCE K. FRANK,
Potentialities of Women in the Middle Years,
edited by Irma H. Gross

MEAN

The devil is an optimist if he thinks he can

make people meaner.

KARL KRAUS,
Karl Kraus by Harry Zohn

Some men have a necessity to be mean, as if they were exercising a faculty which they had to partially neglect since childhood.

F. SCOTT FITZGERALD,
The Crack-up

MEANING

The least of things with a meaning is worth more in life than the greatest of things without it.

C. G. JUNG,
Psychological Reflections,
edited by Jolande Jacobi and R. F. Hull

What makes people despair is that they try to find a universal meaning to the whole of life, and then end up saying it is absurd, illogical, empty of meaning. . . . To seek a total unity is wrong. To give as much meaning to one's life as possible is right for me.

ANAÏS NIN,
The Diaries of Anaïs Nin, Vol. IV

The most pregnant passages of Scripture, of the wise ancients, and of great poets are those which seem to you to have no meaning or an absurd one.

COVENTRY PATMORE,
The Rod, the Root, and the Flower

MEANS

Using vile means to attain worthy ends makes the ends themselves vile.

ANTON CHEKHOV,
The Selected Letters of Anton Chekhov

It is a lucky means to an end which gets within hailing distance of the end.

ANONYMOUS (HENRY S. HASKINS),
Meditations in Wall Street

It is frequently simpler to ascertain by a consideration of the means whether an end is one which we ought to endeavour to compass. The means are nearer to us and may be more easily judged than the end.

MARK RUTHERFORD,
Last Pages from a Journal

It is a pitiful weakness to be resolved as to the end, and to remain irresolute as to the means.

JOHN LANCASTER SPALDING,
Aphorisms and Reflections

MEDIOCRITY

Mediocrity obtains more with application than superiority without it.

BALTASAR GRACIAN,
The Oracle

The majority of men find no difficulty in always being themselves, that means to say they are always their middling selves, and of course middling men. And nevertheless they are probably all created quite differently by their creator. When one sees them as children, one is convinced of the fact; when one sees them as grown ups, it is easy to be vexed and scandalized at the thought that God has created a very middling, not to say mediocre world.

THEODOR HAECKER,
Journal in the Night

The mediocre man, in his distrust of all that is great, maintains that he values good sense before everything. But he has not the remotest idea what good sense is. He merely understands by that expression the negation of all that is lofty.

ERNEST HELLO,
Life, Science, and Art

Over and over again mediocrity is promoted because real worth isn't to be found.

KATHLEEN NORRIS,
Hands Full of Living

Often we are more indulgent towards mediocrity than towards talent; for the first puts criticism to sleep while the latter arouses envy.

J. PETIT-SENN,
Conceits and Caprices

Minds of moderate calibre ordinarily condemn everything which is beyond their range.

LA ROCHEFOUCAULD,
Maxims

MEDITATION

I think what I am after is free meditation. I don't think anybody gets it when he's in anybody's company—only when his soul's alone. I do it when I wake up in the morning.

ROBERT FROST,
quoted in *The Poet's Work*
by John Holmes

Meditation is a contented but perfectly conscious dwelling of the mind on something likely to elevate our life.

ERNEST DIMNET,
What We Live By

The world is to the meditative man what the mulberry plant is to the silkworm.

ALEXANDER SMITH,
Dreamthorp

MEETING

There is always an awkward moment when people meet suddenly, even if they are friends.

ARTHUR PONSONBY,
Casual Observations

The meeting of two personalities is like the contact of two chemical substances: if there is any reaction, both are transformed.

C. G. JUNG,
Modern Man in Search of a Soul

There are some meetings in life so useful, so truly wonderful, that they seem like visible interventions of Providence.

ERNEST HELLO,
Life, Science, and Art

Why is it that when a man steps off the reservation, he bumps right into somebody he'd travel a hundred miles to avoid?

WILLIAM FEATHER,
The Business of Life

MEMORY

I think it is all a matter of love: the more you love a memory, the stronger and stranger it is.

VLADIMIR NABOKOV,
Strong Opinions

It is not the slow, the punctual sanded drip of the unnumbered days that we remember best, the ash of time; nor is it the huge monotone of the lost years, the unswerving schedules of the lost life and the well-known faces that we remember best. It is a face seen once and lost forever in a crowd, an eye that looked, a face that smiled and vanished on a passing train, it is a prescience of snow upon a certain night, the laughter of a woman in a summer street long years ago, it is the memory of a single moon seen at the pine's dark edge in old October—and all of our lives is written in the twisting of a leaf upon a bough, a door that opened, and a stone.

THOMAS WOLFE,
Of Time and the River

The memory has so little talent for photography. It likes to paint pictures. Experience is not laid away in it like a snapshot to be withdrawn at will but is returned to us as a portrait painted in our own psychic colors, its form and pattern structured on that of our life.

LILLIAN SMITH,
The Journey

Some memories are realities, and are better than anything that can ever happen to one again.

WILLA CATHER,
My Antonia

One of the most moving aspects of life is how long the deepest memories stay with us. It is as if individual memory is enclosed in a greater, which even in the night of our forgetfulness stands like an angel with folded wings ready, at the moment of acknowledged need, to guide us back to the lost spoor of our meanings.

LAURENS VAN DER POST,
The Lost World of the Kalahari

Our memories are card-indexes consulted, and then put back in disorder by authorities whom we do not control.

CYRIL CONNOLLY,
The Unquiet Grave

We do not know the true value of our moments until they have undergone the test of memory.

GEORGES DUHAMEL,
The Heart's Domain

Do not trust your memory; it is a net full of holes; the most beautiful prizes slip through it.

GEORGES DUHAMEL,
The Heart's Domain

The life that is lived wholly in memory is the most perfect conceivable, the satisfactions of memory are richer than reality, and have a security that no reality possesses.

SØREN KIERKEGAARD,
Either/Or, Vol. I

What was hard to bear is sweet to remember.

PORTUGUESE PROVERB

Memory is not just the imprint of the past upon us; it is the keeper of what is meaningful for our deepest hopes and fears.

ROLLO MAY,
Man's Search for Himself

A great memory is never made synonymous with wisdom, any more than a dictionary would be called a treatise.

JOHN HENRY CARDINAL NEWMAN,
Oxford University Sermons

Probably as a result of malnutrition, mental anguish, and ambivalence toward the outside world, prisoners tended to forget names, places and events of their past lives. Often they could not recall the names of their closest relatives, even while remembering insignificant details. It was as if their emotional ties to the past were breaking, as if the ordinary order of importance, of the connections of experiences, was no longer valid. Prisoners were quite upset about this loss of memory for things past, which added to their sense of frustration and incompetence.

BRUNO BETTELHEIM,
The Informed Heart

The charm, one might say the genius of memory, is that it is choosy, chancy, and temperamental: it rejects the edifying cathedral and indelibly photographs the small boy outside, chawing a hunk of melon in the dust.

ELIZABETH BOWEN,
Vogue, September 15, 1955

Things which have greatly concerned and bothered one should never be allowed to recur once they are in fact settled; they should be left alone, even in thought. Those who live predominantly in the realm of memory often offend against this law of prudence. Memories of this kind are as a rule very agreeable, once the real danger has been eliminated. They offer a sort of intellectual pleasure that weakens and unnerves the spiritual life.

THEODOR HAECKER,
Journal in the Night

It is all right for beasts to have no memories; but we poor humans have to be compensated.

WILLIAM BOLITHO,
Camera Obscura

As memory may be a paradise from which we cannot be driven, it may also be a hell from which we cannot escape.

JOHN LANCASTER SPALDING,
Aphorisms and Reflections

METAPHYSICS

Metaphysics is the only thoroughly emotional thing.

G. K. CHESTERTON,
Tremendous Trifles

I suppose I am doomed to pass through as many intellectual phases as are possible to this planet, but the truth remains that in the roughest place in my life, I was brought back to some kind of acceptance and reconciliation wholly through an interest in the most abstruse and transcendental metaphysics in existence which is that of the sacred books of the East.

ELLEN GLASGOW,
Letters of Ellen Glasgow

Metaphysicians are poets gone wrong.

NORMAN DOUGLAS,
An Almanac

The private life of man, in its humblest details, is the translation into action of the metaphysics he has adopted.

ERNEST HELLO,
Life, Science, and Art

A little metaphysical reading saves us, as nothing else can, from that slavish adherence to popular scientific catchwords which is so barbarous a fault in many clever moderns.

JOHN COWPER POWYS,
The Meaning of Culture

MIDDLE-CLASS

A society person who is enthusiastic about modern painting or Truman Capote is already half a traitor to his class. It is only middle-class people who, quite mistakenly, imagine that a lively pursuit of the latest in reading or painting will advance their status in the world.

MARY McCARTHY,
On the Contrary

I'm hopelessly middle-class. I have all the middle-class separation from things and people, and the middle-class introspection too. I stalk life; I'm not wed to it.

ROBERT SPEAIGHT,
The Unbroken Heart

How we are fooled by words. Bourgeois, bourgeoisism, how hateful in our Latin-Quarter days, however unLatin we be in heart and act. I always saw, however, that bourgeoisism is a hardened mysticism: nearly all the virtues of the bourgeois are true virtues of the poet too; the artist is deeper as well as saner for being the faithful husband of one wife and keeping healthy hours and temperate diet. The mischief is that the bourgeois too is fooled

by words: he lives his virtue (and judges others) by formula, not in the freedom of the children of the Light, and formulas are starched robes; forced upon a lovely figure, they will often make it look out of law and ugly.

STEPHEN MACKENNA,
Journal and Letters of Stephen Mackenna

I have already raised the question of whether our intellectual and literary culture is not too severe and derisive about the middle-class vice of anxiousness. . . .

I am inclined to think that we should form a union of the anxious ones, to defend our right to be anxious, our right to be tense, our right to aspirin and to our allergies.

DAVID RIESMAN,
Individualism Reconsidered

Poverty programs put very little money into the hands of the poor because middle-class hands are so much more gifted at grasping money—they know better where it is, how to apply for it, how to divert it, how to concentrate it. That is what being middle class means, just as a race means competition.

PHILIP SLATER,
The Pursuit of Loneliness

When men—particularly middle-class men—talk honestly about themselves and their lives, the twin themes expressed by this civil engineer frequently crop up: (1) a feeling of somehow being harried, being trapped, and (2) a nostalgia for the old days, at least for an idealized—if inaccurate—version of them.

MYRON BRENTON,
The American Male

We are in the Middle Depths when we . . .
. . . accept the values and first principles of others without question;
. . . are enchained by property and household appliances;
. . . fall into toils of unnecessary responsibility, and
. . . cannot imagine giving up certain comforts and safeguards.

ALAN HARRINGTON,
Life in the Crystal Palace

HENRY MILLER

I wrote for ten years in America without once having a manuscript accepted. I had to beg, borrow and steal to get by.

HENRY MILLER,
The Cosmological Eye

I went back to intuition and instinct when I turned to D. H. Lawrence, and then to Henry, who represents the non-rational. The very fact that he is all paradox and contraries, unresolved and without core, is like life itself.

ANAÏS NIN,
The Diaries of Anaïs Nin, Vol. II

I don't think he has read a pornographic book in his life. Pornography puts him to sleep, he has told me time and again.

ALFRED PERLES,
My Friend Henry Miller

Last week I went up to London to meet Henry Miller who is a dear, mad, mild man, bald and fifty, with great enthusiasms for commonplaces. Also Lawrence Durrell. We spent 2 days together, and I returned a convinced wreck.

DYLAN THOMAS,
Letters to Vernon Watkins

MIND

A small room in a tranquil college, daily walks and thoughtful talk, a little income and a few friends—these, and these only, suit a still and meditative mind.

WALTER BAGEHOT,
Literary Studies, Vol. III

The mind is the most capricious of insects—flitting, fluttering.

VIRGINIA WOOLF,
A Writer's Diary

One sees the mind is always demanding to be certain, to be secure, to be safe. A mind that is safe, secure, is a bourgeois mind, a shoddy mind. Yet that is what all of us want: to be completely safe.

J. KRISHNAMURTI,
You Are the World

To love with all one's mind is to detect, wherever they exist, the hunger and thirst of the intellect, and to fly to their relief. To love with all one's mind is to go to the assistance of the mind, wherever it lives, wherever it suffers.

ERNEST HELLO,
Life, Science, and Art

Our minds are like crows. They pick up everything that glitters, no matter how uncomfortable our nets get with all that metal in them.

THOMAS MERTON,
Seeds of Contemplation

The world of mind is a comfortable Wombland, a place to which we flee from the bewildering queerness and multiplicity of the actual world.

ALDOUS HUXLEY,
Collected Essays

Almighty God influences us and works in us, through our minds, not without them or in spite of them.

JOHN HENRY CARDINAL NEWMAN,
Oxford University Sermons

O the mind, mind has mountains; cliffs
of fall
Frightful, sheer, no-man-fathomed. Hold
them cheap
May who n'er hung there. . . .

GERARD MANLEY HOPKINS,
"Sonnet #41,"
Collected Poems of Gerard Manley Hopkins

Nothing in life is as good as the marriage of true minds between man and woman. As good? It is life itself.

PEARL BUCK,
To My Daughters, with Love

Experience offers proof on every hand that vigorous mental life may be but one side of a personality, of which the other is moral barbarism.

GEORGE GISSING,
The Private Papers of Henry Ryecroft

Such a cultivated mind doesn't really attract me, . . . the mind I love must still have wild places, a tangled orchard where dark damsons drop in the heavy grass, an overgrown little wood, the chance of a snake or two (real snakes), a pool that nobody's fathomed the depth of—and paths threaded with those little flowers planted by the mind. It must also have *real* hiding places, not artificial ones—not gazebos and mazes. And I have never yet met the cultivated mind that has not its shrubbery. I loathe and detest shrubberies.

KATHERINE MANSFIELD,
The Journal of Katherine Mansfield

Might we not say to the confused voices which sometimes arise from the depths of our being, "Ladies, be so kind as to speak only four at a time?"

MADAME SWETCHINE,
The Writings of Madame Swetchine

Hardly anybody, except perhaps the Greeks at their best, has realized the sweetness and glory of being a rational animal.

GEORGE SANTAYANA,
Character and Opinion in the United States

The mind has its own womb to which, baffled by speculation, it longs to return.

CYRIL CONNOLLY,
The Unquiet Grave

I am incurably convinced that the object of opening the mind, as of opening the mouth, is to shut it again on something solid.

G. K. CHESTERTON,
Autobiography

Few of us make the most of our minds. The body ceases to grow in a few years; but the mind, if we will let it, may grow almost as long as life lasts.

SIR JOHN LUBBOCK,
The Pleasures of Life

In studying the history of the human mind one is impressed again and again by the fact that the growth of the mind is the widening of the range of consciousness, and that each step forward has been a most painful and laborious achievement. One could almost say that nothing is more hateful to man than to give up even a particle of his unconsciousness. Ask those who have tried to introduce a new idea!

C. G. JUNG,
Psychological Reflections,
edited by Jolande Jacobi and R. F. Hull

If we live in the mind we live in a more real way with the absent and the dead, than with those who are under the same roof with us.

JOHN LANCASTER SPALDING,
Aphorisms and Reflections

There is an immense ocean over which the mind can sail, upon which the vessel of thought has not yet been launched.

RICHARD JEFFERIES,
The Story of My Heart

No mind, however loving, could bear to see plainly into all the recesses of another mind.

ARNOLD BENNETT,
How to Make the Best of Life

The discovery that the mind *can* regulate its thoughts, fostering some and dismissing others, is one of the most important stages in the art of self-culture. It is astonishing how little this art is practised among Westerners.

JOHN COWPER POWYS,
The Meaning of Culture

Modern philosophy has never been able quite to shake off the Cartesian idea of mind, as something that "resides"—such is the term—in the pineal gland. Everybody laughs at this nowadays, and yet everybody continues to think of mind in this same general way, as something within this person or that, belonging to him and correlative to the real world. A whole course of lectures would be required to expose this error. I can only hint that if you reflect upon it, without being dominated by preconceived ideas, you will soon begin to perceive that it is a very narrow idea of mind.

CHARLES SANDERS PEIRCE,
Collected Papers of Charles Sanders Peirce,
Vol. V

However brilliant a man's mind may be,

however fascinating an exploration for himself, it can never compare with the outside world in complexity and range and meaning. There is simply not enough in any single mind to be satisfying, we *must* see the world through it as well.

NAN FAIRBROTHER,
An English Year

The way the human mind ordinarily works, in apparent contempt of the logicians, is *conclusion first, premises afterwards.*

JOSEPH RICKABY,
An Old Man's Jottings

MINUTE

Every minute of life carries with it its miraculous value, and its face of eternal youth.

ALBERT CAMUS,
Notebooks 1935–1942

This minute that comes to me over the
    past decillions,
There is no better than it and now.

WALT WHITMAN,
"Starting from Paumanok," *Leaves of Grass*

MISERY

But even if there were no Communists, the wealthy white western minority of the world could not hope to prosper if most of the rest of mankind were foundering in hopeless poverty. Islands of plenty in a vast ocean of misery have never been a good recipe for commercial success.

BARBARA WARD,
Adventures of the Mind, Second Series

MISTAKE

Only he who does nothing makes a mistake.

FRENCH PROVERB

It was not in his nature to make the mistake of doing something when there was nothing to be done.

ROBERT SPEAIGHT,
The Unbroken Heart

If only one could have two lives: the first, in which to make one's mistakes, which seem as if they *had* to be made; and the second in which to profit by them.

D. H. LAWRENCE,
Selected Letters of D. H. Lawrence

If we do not always see our own mistakes and omissions we can always see those of our neighbors.

KATHLEEN NORRIS,
Hands Full of Living

I sometimes react to making a mistake as if I have betrayed myself. My fear of making a mistake seems to be based on the hidden assumption that I am potentially perfect and that if I can just be very careful I will not fall from heaven. But a "mistake" is a declaration of the way I *am,* a jolt to the way I intend, a reminder that I am not dealing with the facts. When I have *listened* to my mistakes I have grown.

HUGH PRATHER,
Notes to Myself

An error no wider than a hair will lead a hundred miles away from the goal.

GERMAN PROVERB

A man who has committed a mistake and doesn't correct it is committing another mistake.

CONFUCIUS

To be a victim of one's own mistakes is bad enough, but to be a victim of the other fellow's mistakes as well is too much.

HENRY MILLER,
The Air-Conditioned Nightmare

Mistakes fail in their mission of helping the person who blames them on the other fellow.

ANONYMOUS (HENRY S. HASKINS),
Meditations in Wall Street

MODEL

When crack photographers and great producers want to use you again and again, it means you've got it. No amount of bed hopping or crotch politics is any sub-

stitute. You've either got it or you haven't.
CAROLYN KENMORE,
Mannequin: My Life as a Model

Everybody has to see every one of your pores before they're ready to go. You might have a crease around your middle or a hickey on your shoulder. A whole committee of fat, bloated, ugly, deformed hairy freaks has to inspect you to make sure *you* are flawless.
CAROLYN KENMORE,
Mannequin: My Life as a Model

Among all the modernized aspects of the most luxurious of industries, the model, a vestige of voluptuous barbarianism, is like some plunder-laden prey. She is the object of unbridled regard, a living bait, the passive realization of an ideal. ... No other female occupation contains such potent impulses to moral disintegration as this one, applying as it does the outward signs of riches to a poor and beautiful girl.
COLETTE,
Journey for Myself

MODERN AGE

It is indeed difficult to define just who the "modern man" is, and what views he has to hold in order to be modern.
JOSIAH ROYCE,
The Problem of Christianity

The so-called selfishness of moderns is partly due to the tremendous amount of stimulation received. They are aroused and drawn into experience by theatres, books, automobiles, great cities. The current is quick and strong.
KATHARINE BUTLER HATHAWAY,
*The Journals and Letters
of the Little Locksmith*

I sometimes think of what future historians will say of us. A single sentence will suffice for modern man: he fornicated and read the papers.
ALBERT CAMUS,
The Fall

We are continually associating our ideas of a modern humanity with bustling movement, struggle and progress. But a more imposing feature of the human mass is passivity. Poets write of "a motion toiling through the gloom": you examine: it is not there.
THOMAS HARDY,
Thomas Hardy's Notebooks

There is an enormous amount of goodness and goodwill and right feeling and action in the modern world.
SIR RICHARD LIVINGSTONE,
On Education

It must be clearly understood that the mere fact of living in the present does not make a man modern, for in that case everyone at present alive would be so. He alone is modern who is fully conscious of the present.
C. G. JUNG,
Psychological Reflections,
edited by Jolande Jacobi and R. F. Hull

We differ from our forefathers not only in our responses but in our nonresponses. Our field of vision is in part defined by what we are blind to. What has died out in us, or is dying, sheds an eerie light on what is alive in us.
CLIFTON FADIMAN,
Any Number Can Play

The age has come when all artificial fences are breaking down. Only that will survive which is basically consistent with the universal; while that which seeks safety in the out-of-the-way hole of the special will perish. ...We may hug our holy aloofness from some imagined security of a corner, but the world will prove stronger than our corner, and it is our corner that will have to give way receding and pressing against its walls till they burst on all sides.
RABINDRANATH TAGORE,
Letters to a Friend

The present age, for all its cosmopolitan hustle, is curiously surburban in spirit.
NORMAN DOUGLAS,
An Almanac

We are living the events which for centuries to come will be minutely studied by scholars who will undoubtedly describe these days as probably the most exciting and creative in the history of mankind. But preoccupied with our daily chores, our worries and our personal hopes and ambitions, few of us are actually living in the present.

LAWRENCE K. FRANK,
Nature and Human Nature

We live lost in a spider's web of machinery, material and social, and don't know what we are living for or how we manage to live at all.

GEORGE SANTAYANA,
The Letters of George Santayana

Perhaps this is an age when men think bravely of the human spirit; for surely they have a strange lust to lay it bare.

CHRISTOPHER MORLEY,
Inward Ho

In a confused time there is a possibility of seeing life more largely than in any other, because no one tradition dominates thought and the need to choose opens our perspective.

CHARLES HORTON COOLEY,
Life and the Student

MOMENT

After all, any given moment has its value; it can be questioned in the light of after-events, but the moment remains.

F. SCOTT FITZGERALD,
The Crack-up

Sometimes I would almost rather have people take away years of my life than take away a moment.

PEARL BAILEY,
Talking to Myself

It may be life is only worthwhile at moments. Perhaps that is all we ought to expect.

SHERWOOD ANDERSON,
Letters of Sherwood Anderson

Seize from every moment its unique novelty and do not prepare your joys.

ANDRÉ GIDE,
The Fruits of the Earth

In order to be utterly happy the only thing necessary is to refrain from comparing this moment with other moments of the past—which I often did not fully enjoy because I was comparing them with other moments of the future.

ANDRÉ GIDE,
The Journals of André Gide, Vol. I

It is the privilege of living to be aware of a curtain's fold or the intonation of a human voice. To be acutely, agonizingly conscious of the moment that is always present and always passing.

MARYA MANNES,
Out of My Time

Because it is not lasting, let us not fall into the cynic's trap and call it an illusion. Duration is not a test of true or false. ... Validity need have no relation to time, to duration, to continuity. It is on another plane, judged by other standards. It relates to the actual moment in time and place.

ANNE MORROW LINDBERGH,
Gift from the Sea

Florence Farr once said to me, "If we could say to ourselves, with sincerity, 'this passing moment is as good as any I shall ever know,' we could die upon the instant, and be united to God."

W. B. YEATS,
Autobiography

One realm we have never conquered: the pure present. One great mystery of time is *terra incognita* to us: the instant. The most superb mystery we have hardly recognized: the immediate, instant self. The quick of all time is the instant. The quick of all the universe, of all creation, is the incarnate, carnal self.

D. H. LAWRENCE,
Selected Essays

There is a part of me that wants to write, a part that wants to theorize, a part that wants to sculpt, a part that wants to teach. ... To force myself into a single role, to decide to be just one thing in life, would kill off large parts of me. Rather, I recognize that I live now and only now, and I will do what I want to do *this* moment and not what I decided was best for me yesterday.

HUGH PRATHER,
Notes to Myself

MONDAY

I hate Monday. It is a crabbed, nasty, overcooked, strangled sort of day, all out of balance, like a fool trying to stand on one leg.

J. B. MORTON,
Morton's Folly

MONEY

A man who has money may be anxious, depressed, frustrated and unhappy, but one thing he's not—and that's broke.

BRENDAN FRANCIS

True, you can't take it with you, but then that's not the place where it comes in so handy.

BRENDAN FRANCIS

Real richness is in how you spend your money.

JACQUES LIPCHITZ,
Conversations with Artists
by Selden Rodman

If you have no money, be polite.

DANISH PROVERB

Being very rich as far as I am concerned is having a margin. The margin is being able to give.

MAY SARTON,
Journal of a Solitude

Money ruins life: I mean, to have to think of it, to take account of it, to know that it is there. Men apart from money, men in an army, men of an expedition of exploration, emerge to a new life. Money is gone.

STEPHEN LEACOCK,
Model Memoirs

Whenever you receive a letter from a creditor write fifty lines upon some extraterrestrial subject, and you will be saved.

CHARLES BAUDELAIRE,
Intimate Journals

Priorities are reflected in the things we spend money on. Far from being a dry accounting of bookkeepers, a nation's budget is full of moral implications; it tells what a society cares about and what it does not care about; it tells what its values are.

SENATOR J. W. FULBRIGHT,
quoted in *War: An Anthology,*
edited by Edward Huberman and
Elizabeth Huberman

When your fortune increases, the columns of your house appear to be crooked.

ARMENIAN PROVERB

There is a kind of shrewdness many men have that enables them to get money. It is the shrewdness of the fox after the chicken. A low order of mentality often goes with it.

SHERWOOD ANDERSON,
Letters of Sherwood Anderson

Selecting jobs for the pseudo independence that higher pay seems to offer, instead of for autonomous reasons—i.e., the job offering deepest satisfaction because it has intrinsic meaning for the person and adds to his self respect—is likewise due to neurotic tendencies, namely the unrecognised equation of money with true status. Here, too, the outer security (what money can buy) is accepted in lieu of inner security; the impersonal coin of exchange is given more relevance than the particular product of one's labor.

BRUNO BETTELHEIM,
The Informed Heart

Nothing is sadder than the consequences of having worldly standards without worldly means.

VAN WYCK BROOKS,
A Chilmark Miscellany

Novel: the man who realizes that one needs to be rich in order to live, who devotes himself completely to the acquisition of money, who succeeds, lives and dies *happy*.

ALBERT CAMUS,
Notebooks 1935–1942

I have a prejudice against people with money. I have known so many, and none have escaped the corruption of power. In this I am a purist. I love people motivated by love and not by power. If you have money and power, and are motivated by love, you give it all away.

ANAÏS NIN,
The Diaries of Anaïs Nin, Vol. IV

I'm opposed to millionaires, but it would be dangerous to offer me the position.

MARK TWAIN,
Mark Twain at Your Fingertips,
edited by Caroline T. Harnsberger

Bread sets free; but does not necessarily set free for good ends—that dear illusion of so many generous hearts. It sets a man free to choose: it often sets free for the bad, but man has a right to that choice and to that evil, without which he is no longer a man.

FRANÇOISE MALLET-JORIS,
A Letter to Myself

What I as a *human being* cannot do, in other words, what all my individual faculties cannot do, I can do by means of *money*. Hence money makes every one of these faculties into something which it is not in itself, i.e., turns it into its *opposite*.

KARL MARX,
"Literature and Art"
by Karl Marx and Frederick Engels,
Selections from Their Writings

My power is as great as is the power of money. The qualities of money are my— the possessor's—qualities and potentialities. What I *am* and *can do,* therefore, is by no means determined by my individuality. I *am* ugly, but I can buy the *most beautiful* woman. So I am not *ugly,* for the effect of *ugliness,* its repulsive power, is eliminated by money.

KARL MARX,
"Literature and Art"
by Karl Marx and Frederick Engels,
Selections from Their Writings

Without money one cannot go anywhere, not even to church.

CROATIAN PROVERB

One has tea out of doors but it's so exquisite. One's cup and saucer gleams and the lemon is new born and nobody *fusses.* That's the chief point of money. One can buy that complete freedom from *fuss.*

KATHERINE MANSFIELD,
quoted in *Katherine Mansfield
Memories of L M*

I must say I hate money but it's the lack of it I hate most.

KATHERINE MANSFIELD,
quoted in *Katherine Mansfield*
by Antony Alpers

We may not know when we're well off, but investment salesmen get on to it somehow.

KIN HUBBARD,
Abe Martin on Things in General

Maybe money is unreal for most of us, easier to give away than things we want.

LILLIAN HELLMAN,
An Unfinished Woman

Money is life. Not material life only. It touches the soul. Who steals our purse steals not trash, but our blood, time, muscle, nervous force, our power to help others, our future possibility of turning out creditable work.

DON MARQUIS,
Prefaces

The chief value of money lies in the fact that one lives in a world in which it is overestimated.

H. L. MENCKEN,
A Mencken Chrestomathy

If rich people could hire other people to die for them, the poor could make a wonderful living.

YIDDISH PROVERB

Happiness is the deferred fulfillment of a prehistoric wish. That is why wealth brings so little happiness; money is not an infantile wish.

SIGMUND FREUD,
quoted in *Life Against Death*
by Norman O. Brown

With money I'll throttle the beast-blind world between my fingers. Without it I am strapped; weakened; my life is a curse and a care.

THOMAS WOLFE,
The Letters of Thomas Wolfe

A broker is a man who runs your fortune into a shoestring.

ALEXANDER WOOLLCOTT,
quoted in *George S. Kaufman*
by Howard Teichman

The only people who claim that money is not important are people who have enough money so that they are relieved of the ugly burden of thinking about it.

JOYCE CAROL OATES,
Open Secrets by Barbaralee Diamonstein

Why doesn't someone write a poem on money? Nobody does anything but abuse it. There's hardly a good word for money to be found in literature. The poets and writers have been needy devils and thought to brave out their beggary by pretending to despise it. This shows what liars poets and literary men are. The chief cry of their hearts has never found its way into their books during the last three thousand years.

JOHN JAY CHAPMAN,
John Jay Chapman and His Letters
by M. A. DeWolfe Howe

It is money that we have not earned, the windfall, the magical bonus, that starts us capering.

J. B. PRIESTLEY,
Delight

Money does not make you happy but it quiets the nerves.

SEAN O'CASEY

Some folks seem to get the idea that they're worth a lot of money just because they have it.

SETH PARKER,
quoted in *Ladies' Home Journal*, May 1941

If we can imagine an unrepressed man—a man strong enough to live and therefore strong enough to die, and therefore what no man has ever been, an individual—such a man, having overcome guilt and anxiety, could have no money complex.

NORMAN O. BROWN,
Life Against Death

When the accumulation of wealth is no longer of high social importance, there will be great changes in the code of morals. . . . The love of money as a possession—as distinguished from the love of money as a means to the enjoyments and realities of life—will be recognized for what it is, a somewhat disgusting morbidity, one of those semi-criminal, semi-pathological propensities which one hands over with a shudder to the specialists in mental disease.

NORMAN O. BROWN,
Life Against Death

The self that saves feels himself thwarted at every turn by the self that spends, and the self that spends is irritated by the knowledge that the self that saves is constantly watching him and grudging him every penny in his fingers.

ROBERT LYND,
The Money-Box

Money is human happiness in the abstract: he, then, who is no longer capable of enjoying human happiness in the concrete devotes himself utterly to money.

ARTHUR SCHOPENHAUER,
quoted in *A Certain World*
by W. H. Auden

It cuts off from life, from vitality, from the alive sun and the alive earth, as *nothing* can. Nothing, not even the most fanatical dogmas of an iron-bound religion, can insulate us from the inrush of life and inspiration, as money can.

D. H. LAWRENCE,
Selected Essays

Money is time. With money I buy for cheerful use the hours which otherwise would not be mine; nay, which would make me their miserable bondsman.

GEORGE GISSING,
The Private Papers of Henry Ryecroft

MOOD

The truth dawns on me that all our "incomprehensible" moods are logical and that they must all have a secret psychic motivation.

DR. WILHELM STEKHEL,
The Depths of the Soul

There is no arguing with a mood; it can be changed by some fortunate event, or by a change in our bodily condition, but it cannot be changed by argument.

BERTRAND RUSSELL,
The Conquest of Happiness

We lose our best moods by hoarding them instead of turning them into action.

ANONYMOUS (HENRY S. HASKINS),
Meditations in Wall Street

Moods are incorrigibly lazy.

BRENDAN FRANCIS

We know that we are not always up to the level of our best mood, but we rigorously exact equality of mood from others.

JOSEPH FARRELL,
Lectures of a Certain Professor

Every state of mind, whether we are in society or alone, should be pressed to the last drop.

NORMAN DOUGLAS,
An Almanac

What are moods? Are they the grace and perfume of existence, or are they the uncertain shoals on which we run aground and perish? Are they to be cultivated as the finest flowers of existence, or are they to be rooted out as the weeds "that choke the true Word"? The Romanticists based their whole scheme of life on the ideal unfolding of moods; they treated them royally.

RUTH BENEDICT,
An Anthropologist at Work
by Margaret Mead

MOON

Tell me what you feel in your room when the full moon is shining in upon you and your lamp is dying out, and I will tell you how old you are, and I shall know if you are happy.

· HENRI FRÉDÉRIC AMIEL,
The Private Journal of Henri Frédéric Amiel

Emotional expression is infinitely rich and varied of form; the moonlight causes a Yankee butcher to say to his wife: "It's such a beautiful night I can't lie still another minute; I must go out and do some slaughtering."

ALICE JAMES,
The Diary of Alice James

Today we can no more predict what use mankind may make of the Moon than could Columbus have imagined the future of the continent he had discovered.

ARTHUR C. CLARKE,
The Exploration of Space

Surely she knows
If she is true to herself, the moon is
  nothing
But a circumambulating aphrodisiac
Divinely subsidised to provoke the world
Into a rising birthrate—.

CHRISTOPHER FRY,
quoted in *The Present Age
in British Literature* by David Daiches

The moon, first as an influence of fertility and later as a deity, has been considered throughout the ages to be in a peculiar relation to women. It is source and origin of their power to bear children, the goddess who keeps watch over them and all matters that primarily concern them. These beliefs are very widespread. They are to be found almost all the world over and persisting from remote times up to the present.

M. ESTHER HARDING,
Woman's Mysteries

MORALITY

Morals is not preaching, it is beauty of a rare kind.

ERNEST DIMNET,
What We Live By

It has always been found a terrible matter to war with the moral system of one's age; it will have its revenge, one way or another, from within or from without, whatever happens after.
HAVELOCK ELLIS,
Selected Essays

Anglo-Saxon morality takes such very good care that its prophecies of woe to the erring person shall find fulfillment.
GEORGE GISSING,
Commonplace Book

Our morality seems to me only a check on the ultimate domination of force, just as our politeness is a check on the impulse of every pig to put his feet in the trough.
OLIVER WENDELL HOLMES, JR.,
The Mind and Faith of Justice Holmes,
edited by Max Lerner

What offends me most in my compositions is the moral element in them. The repentant say never a brave word. Their resolves should be mumbled in silence. Strictly speaking, morality is not healthy.
HENRY DAVID THOREAU,
Journal

Too many moralists begin with a dislike of reality; a dislike of men as they are. They are free to dislike them, but not at the same time to be moralists.
CLARENCE DAY,
This Simian World

The moralist draws from his own when he paints the mind of others.
J. PETIT-SENN,
Conceits and Caprices

It is only on paper that one moralizes—just where one shouldn't.
RICHARD LE GALLIENNE,
Prose Fancies

What do people want nowadays? In any case they do not want moralizing lectures, for all that can be said in that direction most of them have known long ago.
C. G. JUNG,
Psychological Reflections,
edited by Jolande Jacobi and R. F. Hull

MORNING

The morning has gold in its mouth.
GERMAN PROVERB

You can get dressed much quicker in the morning if the night before when you are going to bed you take off your trousers and underdrawers at once, leaving the latter inside the former.
ROBERT BENCHLEY,
Inside Benchley

There will be something—anguish or
    elation—
That is peculiar to this day alone.
I rise from sleep and say: Hail to the
    morning!
Come down to me, my beautiful
    unknown.
JESSICA POWERS,
"Song at Daybreak," *The Place of Splendor*

I have always been delighted at the prospect of a new day, a fresh try, one more start, with perhaps a bit of magic waiting somewhere behind the morning.
J. B. PRIESTLEY,
Delight

Some people greet the morning with a smile, but it's more natural to protest its presence with sleepy sulkiness. "Who asked you to come again?" we feel like saying to it, as if it were a most unwelcome guest.
BRENDAN FRANCIS

MOTHER

My mother was dead for five years before I knew that I had loved her very much.
LILLIAN HELLMAN,
An Unfinished Woman

My mother is a pretty lady. I wish to kiss her all day but I have to go to school.
TANIA PRICE,
age 6, Australia, *Journeys: Prose by Children of the English-speaking World,*
collected by Richard Lewis

No matter how old a mother is she

watches her middle-aged children for signs of improvement.
FLORIDA SCOTT-MAXWELL,
Revelations: Diaries of Women, edited by Mary Jane Moffat and Charlotte Painter

An ounce of mother is worth a pound of clergy.
SPANISH PROVERB

As well as her love for her child then, there exists in every mother an aversion for the child. . . . If you recognize mother love, do you also recognize mother hate?
GEORG GRODDECK,
The Book of the It

A man who has been the indisputable favorite of his mother keeps for life the feeling of a conqueror, that confidence of success that often induces real success.
SIGMUND FREUD,
The Letters of Sigmund Freud

She leads away from aces and neglects to keep jump bids alive. But she is still my mother.
HEYWOOD BROUN,
Collected Edition of Heywood Broun

The concept of "Momism" is male nonsense. It is the refuge of a man seeking excuses for his own lack of virility.
PEARL BUCK,
To My Daughters, with Love

I can never forgive that woman . . . for I think I had naturally not a bad heart; but it has been so bent, twisted and trampled upon, that it has now become as hard as a Highlander's heel-piece.
LORD BYRON,
quoted in *The Literature of Gossip*
by Elizabeth Drew

Some people believe that every laborer is worthy of his hire—except a mother.
MARCELENE COX,
Ladies' Home Journal, June 1945

Motherhood is never honored by excessive talk about the heroics of pregnancy.
LEONARD FEENEY,
The Leonard Feeney Omnibus

Nobody can have the soul of me. My mother has had it, and nobody can have it again. Nobody can come into my very self again, and breathe me like an atmosphere.
D. H. LAWRENCE,
Selected Letters of D. H. Lawrence

—is expecting an infant. . . . I think she feels no woman ever had a child before, and she is the inventress of the human race: which no doubt is quite the right spirit.
D. H. LAWRENCE,
Selected Letters of D. H. Lawrence

The successful mother sets her children free and becomes more free herself in the process.
ROBERT J. HAVIGHURST,
Potentialities of Women in the Middle Years,
edited by Irma H. Gross

The mother cult is something that will set future generations roaring with laughter.
GUSTAVE FLAUBERT,
Letters of Gustave Flaubert

It is not that women have less impulse than men to be creative and productive. But through the ages having children, for women who wanted children, has been so satisfying that it has taken some special circumstances—spinsterhood, barrenness, or widowhood—to let women give their whole minds to other work.
MARGARET MEAD,
Blackberry Winter

No one but doctors and mothers know what it means to have interruptions.
KARL A. MENNINGER,
The Human Mind

My mother was a wit, but never a sentimental one. Once, when somebody in our house stepped on our cat's paw, she turned to the cat and said sternly, "I *told* you not to go around barefoot!"
ZERO MOSTEL,
Player: A Profile of an Art
by Lillian Ross and Helen Ross

In my generation, many of us knew that we did not want to be like our mothers, even when we loved them. We could not help but see their disappointment. . . . Strangely, many mothers who loved their daughters—and mine was one—did not want their daughters to grow up like them either. They knew we needed something more.

BETTY FRIEDAN,
The Feminine Mystique

Women are aristocrats, and it is always the mother who makes us feel that we belong to the better sort.

JOHN LANCASTER SPALDING,
Things of the Mind

Who has not watched a mother stroke her child's cheek or kiss her child *in a certain way,* and felt a nervous shudder at the possessive outrage done to a free solitary human soul?

JOHN COWPER POWYS,
The Meaning of Culture

A mother never realises that her children are no longer children.

HOLBROOK JACKSON,
Southward Ho! and Other Essays

I don't think that all good mothers have to bake and sew and make beds and wear percale bungalow aprons. Some of the finest never go into their kitchens at all; some of the most devoted are also some of the richest.

KATHLEEN NORRIS,
Hands Full of Living

Everybody knows that a good mother gives her children a feeling of trust and stability. She is their earth. She is the one they can count on for the things that matter most of all. She is their food and their bed and the extra blanket when it grows cold in the night; she is their warmth and their health and their shelter; she is the one they want to be near when they cry. She is the only person in the whole world or in a whole lifetime who can be these things to her children. There is no substitute for her. Somehow even her clothes feel different to her children's hands from anybody else's clothes. Only to touch her skirt or her sleeve makes a troubled child feel better.

KATHARINE BUTLER HATHAWAY,
*The Journals and Letters of
the Little Locksmith*

The child, in the decisive first years of his life, has the experience of his mother, as an all-enveloping, protective, nourishing power. Mother is food; she is love; she is warmth; she is earth. To be loved by her means to be alive, to be rooted, to be at home.

ERICH FROMM,
The Sane Society

It is odd how all men develop the notion, as they grow older, that their mothers were wonderful cooks. I have yet to meet a man who will admit that his mother was a kitchen assassin, and nearly poisoned him.

ROBERTSON DAVIES,
The Table Talk of Samuel Marchbanks

Why isn't more said about the sensuousness between mother and baby? Men paint it and seem to assume it—women don't even mention it among themselves. Either it is completely taken for granted or it isn't considered at all. It's more than a fringe benefit.

FRANCES KARLEN SANTAMARIA,
Revelations: Diaries of Women, edited by
Mary Jane Moffat and Charlotte Painter

In the eyes of its mother every beetle is a gazelle.

MOROCCAN PROVERB

The spectacle of the young mother devoting all her time and strength to her children and husband, and surrendering all other interests to the interests of the home, is usually considered inspiring and attractive, especially by the men. Not so attractive is she thirty years later, when, her family cares having lapsed and her children scattered, she is left high and dry in the world.

RANDOLPH BOURNE,
Youth and Life

Just had a big bust-up with Mummy for the umpteenth time. . . . Margot's and

Mummy's natures are completely strange to me. I can understand my friends better than my own mother—too bad!

ANNE FRANK,
Anne Frank: The Diary of a Young Girl

Mothers, at least American mothers, are a weird lot. Some sea-change seems to happen in a woman as soon as she becomes a mother. If she gives up enjoying sex with her boyfriend when she finally marries him and becomes a wife, she gives up even dreaming about it when she becomes a mother. All sorts of virtues claim her, and she claims them.

JAMES JONES,
WW II

I never had a mother. I suppose a mother is one to whom you hurry when you are troubled.

EMILY DICKINSON,
Letters of Emily Dickinson

Mother was the absolutely dominating force in all our lives. Even her mere existence in these last years, was a sort of centre around which we revolved, in thought if not in our actual movements. We shall be living henceforth in an essentially different world.

GEORGE SANTAYANA,
The Letters of George Santayana

My father was poor. . . . He thought that with the music there was very little to do, and he thought better to be a carpenter. He was thinking seriously of that for me, but my mother said to him, "This boy has a gift, and it is our duty to follow it." She was a wonderful woman.

PABLO CASALS,
Wisdom, edited by James Nelson

Mother is the dead heart of the family, spending father's earnings on consumer goods to enhance the environment in which he eats, sleeps, and watches television.

GERMAINE GREER,
The Female Eunuch

The home is her province and she is lonely there. She wants her family to spend time with her for her only significance is in relation to that almost fictitious group. She struggles to hold her children to her, imposing restrictions, waiting up for them, prying into their affairs. They withdraw more and more into non-communication and thinly veiled contempt.

GERMAINE GREER,
The Female Eunuch

A group of children can be more successfully civilized by one or two women who have voluntarily undertaken the work than they can be when divided and tyrannized over by a single woman who finds herself bored and imposed upon.

GERMAINE GREER,
The Female Eunuch

Why do we like war? Is it that all men would revenge themselves for their betrayal by their mothers and of their mothers, hitting out blindly to efface the memory of the triple expulsion—expulsion from the sovereignty of the womb, from the sanctuary of the breast, from the intoxication of the bed and lap?

CYRIL CONNOLLY,
The Unquiet Grave

MOUNTAIN

Looking from the mountain, I always think faster and freer and better, but about any thing rather than the landscape. It seems so much better to talk *from* the beauty than *of* it. Perhaps I don't properly appreciate it, but value it like meat and drink, the pure air and . . . my cigar, only for the excitement it gives.

CHAUNCEY WRIGHT,
Letters of Chauncey Wright

It is not by mass that mountains affect us: as mere bulges of earth they are as uninteresting as hippopotami. They need dilution to be effective, and their dilutents are sky and air and water.

OSCAR W. FIRKINS,
Oscar Firkins: Memoirs and Letters,
edited by Ina Ten Eyck

A man climbs because he needs to climb, because that is the way he is made. Rock and ice and wind and the great blue canopy of the sky are not all that he finds upon the mountain-tops. He discovers things about his own body and mind that he had almost forgotten in the day-to-day, year-to-year routine of living. He learns what his legs are for, what his lungs are for, what the wise men of old meant by "refreshment of the spirit."

JAMES RAMSEY ULLMAN,
High Conquest

You do not laugh when you look at the mountains, or when you look at the sea.

LAFCADIO HEARN,
Lafcadio Hearn: Life and Letters,
edited by Elizabeth Bisland

I expected to have been among the foothills drift long ago, but the mountains fairly seized me. . . . Had a glorious storm and a thousand sacred beauties that seemed yet more and more divine. . . . I was alone, and during the whole excursion, or period rather, was in a kind of calm, uncurable ecstasy. I am hopelessly and forever a mountaineer.

JOHN MUIR,
Letters to a Friend:
Written to Mrs. Ezra C. Carr

The mountain people are sweet. No books, little false education, real humbleness. It does so beat talking to pretentious half-artists. We may try to acquire a few acres and a cabin.

SHERWOOD ANDERSON,
Letters of Sherwood Anderson

Mountains, once looked upon by travellers as mere dangerous nuisances, the haunt of brigands, are now symbols of the sublime. . . . Obvious associations are with the whiteness of snow, virgin snow, meaning purity, chastity and so related with vestal virgins, nuns; height connected with aloofness; danger related to awe and to the most primitive feelings about gods, even the Christian God; remoteness connected with the transcendent.

JOYCE CARY,
Art and Reality

Whether a man's lust for big-breasted women is a hunger for mountains or his hunger for mountains is a lust for big-breasted women is a moot question.

BRENDAN FRANCIS

For overhead there is always the strange radiance of the mountains. . . .

And the ice and upper radiance of snow are brilliant with timeless immunity from the flux and the warmth of life. Overhead they transcend all life, all the soft, moist fire of the blood. So that a man must needs live under the radiance of his own negation.

D. H. LAWRENCE,
Selected Essays

MOVIES

There are all those movie houses
Over on Third Avenue
And they promise
Love and romance,
Easy answers and quick intrigue.
Don't the actors ever look at the people
Who look at them?

LOIS WYSE,
"Look at Me, Paul Newman,"
Are You Sure You Love Me?

If you're only a personality, without talent, and you're photographed right, you can look like an actor in the movies, but the beauty of humanness is always sacrificed for surface appearances.

ROD STEIGER,
Player: Profile of an Art
by Lillian Ross and Helen Ross

In good films, there is always a directness that entirely frees us from the itch to interpret.

SUSAN SONTAG,
Against Interpretation

Most horror movies are certainly that.

BRENDAN FRANCIS

Everyone criticizes the movies. Yet everyone seems to continue to go to them.

JAMES M. GILLIS,
This Our Day

If you give everything to acting, you are

embroiled in a constant fight for a bigger part, a better part. There is no time to live. You get old and you still want to be young. That is not life. A woman is a fool if she does not learn this.

SIMONE SIGNORET,
Player: Profile of an Art
by Lillian Ross and Helen Ross

But the fascinating thing about film is that it's an illusion. You see people pointing to the screen and saying, "That movie ..." That's not where the movie is, it's up in the projection booth, in the can. What they're pointing at is just shadows on the wall and projections of their own emotions.

PETER BOGDANOVICH,
Supertalk by Digby Diehl

Every film is launched like a squid in an obscuring cloud of spectacular publicity.

DUDLEY NICHOLS,
Introduction to the Art of the Movies
by Lewis Jacobs

MUSIC

It is better to make a piece of music than to perform one, better to perform one than to listen to one, better to listen to one than to misuse it as a means of distraction, entertainment, or acquisition of "culture."

JOHN CAGE,
Silence

There are certain things that grab people in a song; in the business we call them "hooks." You can't look for hooks when you're writing, they just happen to come about. You can recognize them only when they're done.

BURT BACHARACH,
Supertalk by Digby Diehl

God save me from a bad neighbor and a beginner on the fiddle.

ITALIAN PROVERB

It is not unjust to define amateur concerts by saying that the music performed at them seems to have been composed to make those who render it happy and drive

those who listen to despair.

ADOLPHE ADAM,
quoted in *The Music Lover's Miscellany*
by Eric Blom

A splendid brass band has just been playing a few pieces on the street, in the rain. It felt like velvet to one's inner being.

HENRI FRÉDÉRIC AMIEL,
The Private Journal of Henri Frédéric Amiel

I lost myself in a Schubert Quartet at the end of a Crowndale Road concert, partly by ceasing all striving to understand the music, partly by driving off intruding thoughts, partly by feeling the music coming up inside me, myself a hollow vessel filled with sound.

JOANNA FIELD,
A Life of One's Own

Music is a beautiful opiate, if you don't take it too seriously.

HENRY MILLER,
The Air-Conditioned Nightmare

The thought of the eternal efflorescence of music is a comforting one, and comes like a messenger of peace in the midst of universal disturbance.

ROMAIN ROLLAND,
Musicians of Former Days

I find that I never lose Bach. I don't know why I have always loved him so. Except that he is so pure, so relentless and incorruptible, like a principle of geometry.

EDNA ST. VINCENT MILLAY,
Letters of Edna St. Vincent Millay

The first response to any really strange music is laughter—the Javanese conceal well-bred smiles on hearing Beethoven, and we grin shamelessly at their love songs accompanied by nose-blown flutes.

JACQUES BARZUN,
Pleasures of Music

I am always thirsting for beautiful, beautiful, beautiful music. I wish I could make it. Perhaps there isn't any music on earth like what I picture to myself.

OLIVE SCHREINER,
The Letters of Olive Schreiner

I love my music because it is most important to love something in life; to be in love with something. If I were not in love with my music, what could I do? Nothing.

WANDA LANDOWSKA,
Wisdom, edited by James Nelson

Writing more and more to the sound of music, writing more and more like music. Sitting in my studio tonight, playing record after record, music a stimulant of the highest order, far more potent than wine.

ANAÏS NIN,
The Diaries of Anaïs Nin, Vol. II

Music is another lady that talks charmingly and says nothing.

AUSTIN O'MALLEY,
Keystones of Thought

What most people relish is hardly music; it is rather a drowsy revery relieved by nervous thrills.

GEORGE SANTAYANA,
quoted in *Pleasures of Music*
by Jacques Barzun

What is the Ninth Symphony compared to a pop tune played by a hurdy-gurdy and a memory!

KARL KRAUS,
Karl Kraus by Harry Zohn

Muzak pervades Las Vegas from the time you walk into the airport upon landing to the last time you leave the casinos. It is piped out to the swimming pool. It is in the drugstores. It is as if there were a communal fear that someone, somewhere in Las Vegas, was going to be left with a totally vacant minute on his hands.

TOM WOLFE,
*The Kandy-Kolored
Tangerine-Flake Streamline Baby*

I never fully understood the need for a "live" audience. My music, because of its extreme quietude, would be happiest with a dead one.

IGOR STRAVINSKY,
London Magazine, March 1967

When he was playing we admired him. He was somehow enlarged by the music; it sat upon him like a mantle and gave him a dignity that was not his own.

ROBERT SPEAIGHT,
The Unbroken Heart

Music finds its way where the rays of the sun cannot penetrate. My room is dark and dismal, a high wall almost excludes the light of day. The sounds must come from a neighboring yard; it is probably some wandering musician. . . . Carry me away then once more, O tones so rich and powerful, to the company of the maidens, to the pleasures of the dance.

SØREN KIERKEGAARD,
Either/Or, Vol. I

I wish the Government would put a tax on pianos for the incompetent.

EDITH SITWELL,
Edith Sitwell: Selected Letters 1916–1964

MYSTERY

Use and want make all life a commonplace thing. Our ordinary minds demand an ordinary world and feel at ease only when they have explained and taken for granted the mysteries among which we have been given so short a license to breathe.

LLEWELYN POWYS,
Earth Memories

The most beautiful experience we can have is the mysterious. It is the fundamental emotion which stands at the cradle of true art and true science.

ALBERT EINSTEIN,
Ideas and Opinions

As I make my slow pilgrimage through the world, a certain sense of beautiful mystery seems to gather and grow.

A. C. BENSON,
From a College Window

The mysterious is always attractive. People will always follow a veil.

BEDE JARRETT,
The House of Gold

The thought of the unknowable and the infinite becomes truly salutary only when it is the unexpected recompense of the intelligence that has given itself loyally and unreservedly to the study of the knowable and the finite. There is a notable difference between the mystery which comes before our ignorance and the mystery which comes after what we have learned.

MAURICE MAETERLINCK,
quoted in *Characters and Events,*
Vol. I, by John Dewey

MYSTICISM

The mystics are not only themselves an incarnation of beauty, but they reflect beauty on all who with understanding approach them.

HAVELOCK ELLIS,
Selected Essays

Mysticism and sex have been frequent associates because they are kindred.

OSCAR W. FIRKINS,
Oscar Firkins: Memoirs and Letters,
edited by Ina Ten Eyck

Only on the wings of mysticism can the spirit soar to its full height.

ALEXIS CARREL,
Reflections on Life

The worst danger of the mystic is a quest of spiritual privilege leading to aloofness from the common lot.

VIDA D. SCUDDER,
The Privilege of Age

Everything begins in mysticism and ends in politics.

CHARLES PÉGUY,
quoted in *God and Man,*
edited by Victor Gollancz

When critics reproach mysticism with expressing itself in the same terms as passionate love, they forget that it was love which began by plagiarizing mysticism, borrowing from it its fervor, its rapture, its ecstasies: in using the language of a passion it had transfigured, mysticism has only resumed possession of its own.

HENRI BERGSON,
The Two Sources of Morality and Religion

I do not think reading the mystics would hurt you myself. You say you must avoid books which deal with "feelings"—but the mystics don't deal with *feelings* but with *love* which is a very different thing. You have too many "feelings," but not nearly enough love.

EVELYN UNDERHILL,
The Letters of Evelyn Underhill

Any profound view of the world is mysticism, in that it brings men into a spiritual relation with the Infinite.

ALBERT SCHWEITZER,
Out of My Life and Thought

Beware the mystic when he materializes! That transmutation of thinking energy to practical ends is the most formidable thing in the world.

J. A. SPENDER,
The Comments of Bagshot, Second Series

The incommunicableness of the transport is the keynote of all mysticism. Mystical truth exists for the individual who had the transport, but for no one else.

WILLIAM JAMES,
The Varieties of Religious Experience

Possibly the mystic pure keeps silence.

JAMES O'MAHONY,
The Music of Life

NAME

I understand why one wants to know the names of what he loves. . . . Naming is a kind of possessing, of caressing and fondling.

JESSAMYN WEST,
Hide and Seek

Hoary idea, in any case, expecting a woman to surrender her name to her husband's in exchange for his. Why? Would any man submerge his identity and heritage to the woman he wed?

MARYA MANNES,
Out of My Time

There is something in one's name which seems so private to oneself that any mention of it by others brings for a moment a vague sense of discomfort, as if a liberty were threatened.

A. A. MILNE,
By Way of Introduction

Naming a child after someone who has died young is in some sense, I think, a promise that an interrupted pattern will, after all, be completed.

MARGARET MEAD,
Blackberry Winter

You would find it ridiculous if, when you asked someone his name, he replied, "My name is whatever you like to call it."

You would find such an answer ridiculous. And if he were to add, "I have whatever name you care to give me, and it is my real name," you would consider him mad. And yet that is what we must perhaps get accustomed to; indeterminacy become a positive fact, a positive element of knowledge.

PAUL VALÉRY,
quoted in *The Third Rose*
by John Malcolm Brinnin

This is unfortunately a world in which things find it difficult, frequently impossible, to live up to their names.

J. B. PRIESTLEY,
All About Ourselves and Other Essays

Each planet, each plant, each butterfly, each moth, each beetle, becomes doubly real to you when you know its name. Lucky indeed are those who from their earliest childhood have heard all these things named. This is no superficial pedantry. Deep in the oldest traditions of the human race dwells the secret of the magical power of names. . . . If one named a supernatural personage by his true name one did not conjure or invoke him in vain.

JOHN COWPER POWYS,
The Meaning of Culture

NATURE

My approach to photography is based on my belief in the vigor and values of the world of nature—in the aspects of gran-

deur and of the minutiae all about us. I believe in growing things, and in the things which have grown and died magnificently.

ANSEL ADAMS,
Photographers on Photography,
edited by Nathan Lyons

I laughed, as a child, when I was told of a Hindu sage who had the road swept in front of him lest, inadvertently, he should destroy the life crawling there. But I never see the quick-legged caterpillar going about his business across the garden-walk without remembering that long-dead Buddhist priest.

ERNEST DIMNET,
What We Live By

The love of nature is a passion for those in whom it once lodges. It can never be quenched. It cannot change. It is a furious, burning, physical greed, as well as a state of mystical exaltation. It will have its own.

MARY WEBB,
The House in Dormer Forest

Nature is material, but not materialistic; it issues in life, and breeds all sorts of warm passions and idle beauties.

GEORGE SANTAYANA,
Character and Opinion in the United States

No creature is fully itself till it is, like the dandelion, opened in bloom of pure relationship to the sun, the entire living cosmos.

D. H. LAWRENCE,
Selected Essays

The struggle for existence, [Nietzsche] said, is only an exception in nature; it is exuberance, an even reckless superfluity, which rules.

HAVELOCK ELLIS,
Selected Essays

These warm hills, rolling sensuous hills, full of milk. Some of them almost give a man an erection they are so voluptuously beautiful.

SHERWOOD ANDERSON,
Letters of Sherwood Anderson

This ground under our feet, how we Americans have been as whoremasters with it, treating the very fields, rivers, and hills as though they were whores.

The deep feminine thing in earth, it's waiting the male too, the lover.

SHERWOOD ANDERSON,
Letters of Sherwood Anderson

I do not believe that Nature has a heart; and I suspect that, like many another beauty, she has been credited with a heart because of her face.

FRANCIS THOMPSON,
Works, Vol. III

The losing of Paradise is enacted over and over again by the children of Adam and Eve. We clothe our souls with messages and doctrines and lose the touch of the great life in the naked breast of Nature.

RABINDRANATH TAGORE,
Letters to a Friend

There is undoubtedly a deep affinity, probably both psychic and chemical, between every individual human being and some particular type of landscape. It is well to find out as soon as possible what kind this is; and then to get as much of it as you can.

JOHN COWPER POWYS,
The Meaning of Culture

I have loved the feel of the green grass under my feet, and the sound of the running stream by my side, and the face of the fields has often comforted me more than the faces of men.

JOHN BURROUGHS,
quoted in *The Author's Kalendar, 1920,*
compiled by Anna C. Woodford

Nature is an excellent sedative. It pacifies, i.e., makes a man carefree. And being carefree is of the essence in this world.

ANTON CHEKHOV,
The Selected Letters of Anton Chekhov

I thought that nature was enough
  Till human nature came.

EMILY DICKINSON,
quoted in *Atlantic Monthly,* August 1952

When I realize how invigorating contact with the earth may sometimes be, I find myself wondering how humanity ever consented to come so far away from the jungle.

ELLEN GLASGOW,
Letters of Ellen Glasgow

What sublime thoughts filled my mind as I bent to the wind, and trudged through the gorse and heather? I will tell you. I was wondering how much money I shall make out of my next book.

Thus does nature keep us in touch with the great realities of existence.

J. B. MORTON,
Morton's Folly

There is nothing human in nature. The earth, though loved so dearly, would let me perish on the ground, and neither bring forth food nor water. Burning in the sky the great sun, of whose company I have been so fond, would merely burn on and make no motion to assist me.

RICHARD JEFFERIES,
The Story of My Heart

NECESSITY

Human creatures have a marvellous power of adapting themselves to necessity.

GEORGE GISSING,
The Private Papers of Henry Ryecroft

Great necessity elevates man, petty necessity casts him down.

GOETHE,
Wisdom and Experience

It is only necessity which makes people build upon one another.

ROBERT SPEAIGHT,
The Unbroken Heart

Necessity does the work of courage.

GEORGE ELIOT,
Romola

NEED

It is when we try to grapple with another man's infinite need that we perceive how incomprehensible, wavering, and misty are the beings that share with us the sight

of the stars and the warmth of the sun.
JOSEPH CONRAD,
Lord Jim

It is inevitable when one has a great need of something one finds it. What you need you attract like a lover.
GERTRUDE STEIN,
quoted in *Gertrude Stein: Her Life and Her Work* by Elizabeth Sprigge

He who encounters a man in need of something will divine the need if he loves the man.
ERNEST HELLO,
Life, Science, and Art

People do so often hate what they need.
FLORENCE H. WINTERBURN,
Vacation Hints

To be needed is one of the richest forms of moral and spiritual nourishment, and not to be needed is one of the most severe forms of psychic deprivation.
JOHN W. GARDNER,
No Easy Victories, edited by Helen Rowan

Everything comes to the man who does not need it.
FRENCH PROVERB

This is the discovery that each man must make for himself—the discovery that what he really stands in need of he cannot get for himself, but must wait till God gives it to him.
JOHN JAY CHAPMAN,
Memories and Milestones

How strange it is, that what seem to be the highest and deepest needs get no fulfillment!
A. C. BENSON,
Excerpts from the Letters of Dr. A. C. Benson to M. E. A.

It is all right your saying you do not need other people, but there are a lot of people who need you.
SHERWOOD ANDERSON,
Letters of Sherwood Anderson

I believe that we are always attracted to what we need most, an instinct leading us towards the persons who are to open new vistas in our lives and fill them with new knowledge.
HELEN ISWOLSKY,
Light Before Dusk

NEGLECT

The majority of men suffer from a sort of neglect, they suffer from not being possessed by anyone, from offering themselves in vain. Stretch out your hand and seize them.
GEORGES DUHAMEL,
The Heart's Domain

NEIGHBOR

If your neighbor is an early riser, you will become one.
ALBANIAN PROVERB

There are many who dare not kill themselves for fear of what the neighbors will say.
CYRIL CONNOLLY,
The Unquiet Grave

We have two girls next door with a gramophone and cars. The place is not the same. The girl is attractive though and for this reason I cannot be as splenetic as I wish to be. She hangs up on the line little silken meshes for supporting her little breasts which are as pleasantly shaped as any William pears on your garden wall.
LLEWELYN POWYS,
Letters

Mix with your neighbors, and you learn what's doing in your own house.
YIDDISH PROVERB

It would probably astound each of [us] beyond measure to be let into his neighbor's mind and to find how different the scenery there was from that of his own.
WILLIAM JAMES,
Principles of Psychology, Vol. I

Life goes on as usual here. I am not very pleased with my room; first, because the landlady finds fault, and secondly, I have discovered there is the thinnest partition between my room and the one next door, so that everything is overheard and sometimes I am forced to escape from the balalaika with which my neighbor amuses himself under my ear. Fortunately this has not happened very often. He is usually out and then the flat is quiet.

NIKOLAI LENIN,
The Letters of Lenin

Outwardly you may be on friendly terms with the people next door, but, if the truth were known, you do not think much of them. Their ways may be well enough, but they are not your ways. It is not hatred, far less envy; neither is it contempt exactly. Only you do not understand why they live as they do.

FRANK MOORE COLBY,
The Colby Essays, Vol. 2

God grant us no neighbor with two eyes.

ARAB PROVERB

The idea that one should know one's immediate neighbors has died out in large centers of population, but still lingers in small towns and in the country. It has become a foolish idea, since there is no need to be dependent upon immediate neighbors for society. More and more it becomes possible to choose our companions on account of congeniality rather than on account of mere propinquity.

BERTRAND RUSSELL,
The Conquest of Happiness

NEW ENGLAND

I wonder if anybody ever reached thirty-five in New England without wanting to kill himself.

BARRETT WENDELL,
Barrett Wendell and His Letters
by M. A. DeWolfe Howe

I was sometimes bewildered by our family of dissimilar, assorted selves—all under restraint. New England restraint never giving any experience or understanding of volatile nature ... embarrassed to show changes of mood—sensible.

KATHARINE BUTLER HATHAWAY,
*The Journals and Letters
of the Little Locksmith*

All well-brought-up New England boys who are specially intellectual or sensitive want to save the world.

GEORGE E. WOODBERRY,
Selected Letters of George Edward Woodberry

You are a New Englander and quieter about it, but every American has this exultant feeling at times—the way snow comes in New England and the way it spits against your window at night and the sounds of the world get numb ... and there was the train for Boston in the middle of it, black, warm, fast, and all around the lonely and tragic beauty of New England.

THOMAS WOLFE,
The Letters of Thomas Wolfe

NEWSPAPER

Ink-fresh papers, millions of them—ink-fresh with morning, orange juice, waffles, eggs and bacon, and cups of strong, hot coffee. How fine it is, here in America, at ink-fresh, coffee-fragrant morning, to read the paper!

THOMAS WOLFE,
You Can't Go Home Again

The making of a journalist: no ideas and the ability to express them.

KARL KRAUS,
Karl Kraus by Harry Zohn

A journalist is stimulated by a deadline. He writes worse when he has time.

KARL KRAUS,
Karl Kraus by Harry Zohn

Every journal, from the first line to the last, is nothing but a tissue of horrors. ... And it is with this loathsome appetizer that civilized man daily washes down his morning repast.

CHARLES BAUDELAIRE,
Intimate Journals

You should always believe all you read in newspapers, as this makes them more interesting.

ROSE MACAULAY,
A Casual Commentary

I would urge the newspaper world to try the experiment of leaving out most of what they at present publish, of publishing much of what they at present leave out, and see if the result is not accepted meekly by the public and consumed with unquestioning relish. For we are wonderfully tamed.

ROSE MACAULAY,
A Casual Commentary

But I got something out of working on a newspaper. I learned that I had to wind things up. I used to leave things half-written, you know. But things couldn't go in the paper unless they were rounded out.

ROBERT FROST,
Wisdom, edited by James Nelson

A free press can of course be good or bad, but, most certainly, without freedom it will never be anything but bad.

ALBERT CAMUS,
Resistance, Rebellion, and Death

One of the most valuable philosophical features of journalism is that it realizes the truth is not a solid but a liquid. It is not easy to tell the truth, nor is it always desirable.

CHRISTOPHER MORLEY,
Inward Ho

The newspaper ... knows nearly everything and guesses at the rest.... Without it, democratic government would be difficult and travelling in the subway quite impossible.

SIMEON STRUNSKY,
The Patient Observer

Let persons in a high station beware of defending themselves in the press, or responding to the challenges of those who have command of it....A controversy *with* the press *in* the press is the controversy of a fly with a spider.

SIR HENRY TAYLOR,
Notes from Life

People accuse journalism of being too personal; but to me it has always seemed far too impersonal. It is charged with tearing away the veils from private life; but it seems to me to be always dropping diaphanous but blinding veils between men and men.

G. K. CHESTERTON,
Tremendous Trifles

What is really the matter, with almost every paper, is that it is much too full of things suitable to the paper.

G. K. CHESTERTON,
Autobiography

Apropos of "journalese jargon" of which you speak I remember once saying: profanity is vitriol, slang is vinegar, but reporters' English is rancid butter.

OLIVER WENDELL HOLMES, JR.,
Holmes-Pollock Letters, Vol. II

Early in life I had noticed that no event is ever correctly reported in a newspaper.

GEORGE ORWELL,
A Collection of Essays

What a devil of a bore it must be to be the superior person!—those mental anaemics who never read about murders, divorces, or whatever the special squeamishness may be to which they pin their vanity—as grotesque as going to the play and boasting that you shut your eyes tight whenever the villain walks across.

ALICE JAMES,
The Diary of Alice James

For anyone who spends more than six weeks on a miraculously inviolate shore, with no sound but the battering of the angry sea, the faint, silky ripping of the calm tides, the mewing of the gulls and the plaintive note of the red-foot, reading the newspapers becomes astonishing. "An hour's delirium" is what we call the period after the arrival of the postman here.

COLETTE,
Journey for Myself

NEW YEAR

On the approach of a New Year, we, too, can believe in something better than experience has justified us in hoping for.

ROBERT LYND,
The Blue Lion

And now let us believe in a long year that is given to us, new, untouched, full of things that have never been, full of work that has never been done, full of tasks, claims, and demands; and let us see that we learn to take it without letting fall too much of what it has to bestow upon those who demand of it necessary, serious and great things.

RAINER MARIA RILKE,
Letters of Rainer Maria Rilke 1892–1910

A year has passed—another has commenced. These solemn divisions of time influence our feelings as they recur. Yet there is nothing in it, for every day in the year closes a twelvemonth as well as the 31st of December.

SIR WALTER SCOTT,
Sir Walter Scott's Journal (1825–1832)

NEW YORK

It is late. [Joan] Miró, and all of us, walk briskly toward Third Avenue. It has become even chillier. Miró breathes in the air. "Ah, what vitamins! This city is a tonic! This city is a doctor!"

JOHN GRUEN,
Close-up

I think you know that when an American stays away from New York too long something happens to him. Perhaps he becomes a little provincial, a little dead and afraid.

SHERWOOD ANDERSON,
Letters of Sherwood Anderson

Each man reads his own meaning into New York.

MEYER BERGER,
The Empire City,
edited by Alexander Klein

New York is the only real city-city.

TRUMAN CAPOTE,
Writers at Work,
edited by Malcolm Cowley

It is often said that New York is a city for only the very rich and the very poor. It is less often said that New York is also, at least for those of us who came there from somewhere else, a city for only the very young.

JOAN DIDION,
Slouching Towards Bethlehem

New York has a trip-hammer vitality which drives you insane with restlessness, if you have no inner stabilizer.

HENRY MILLER,
The Colossus of Maroussi

Across
The Harlem roof-tops
Moon is shining.
Night sky is blue
Stars are great drops
Of golden dew.

LANGSTON HUGHES,
"Harlem Night Song," *On City Streets,*
selected by Nancy Larrick

It wasn't until I got to New York that I became Kansan. Everyone there kept reminding me that they were Jewish or Irish, or whatever, so I kept reminding them that I was midwestern. Before I knew it, I actually began to *brag* about being from Kansas! I discovered that I had something a bit unique, but it was the nature of New York that forced me to claim my past.

WILLIAM INGE,
Behind the Scenes,
edited by Joseph F. McCrindle

Cut off as I am, it is inevitable that I should sometimes feel like a shadow walking in a shadowy world. When this happens I ask to be taken to New York City. Always I return home weary but I have the comforting certainty that mankind is real and I myself am not a dream.

HELEN KELLER,
The Empire City,
edited by Alexander Klein

I miss the animal buoyancy of New York, the animal vitality. I did not mind that it had no meaning and no depth.

ANAÏS NIN,
The Diaries of Anaïs Nin, Vol. II

I tell you, there were times when, as Mayor, I truly wanted to jump. You would look out over the city from some place high above it, and you would say to yourself, "Good Jesus, it's too much for me."

WILLIAM O'DWYER,
quoted in *Mayor Watching
and Other Pleasures* by Philip Hamburger

If, in New York, you arrive late for an appointment, say, "I took a taxi."

ANDRÉ MAUROIS,
quoted in the *New York Times,*
August 13, 1950

There are certainly numberless women of fashion who consider it perfectly natural to go miles down Fifth Avenue, or Madison Avenue, yet for whom a voyage of half a dozen blocks to east or west would be an adventure, almost a dangerous impairment of good breeding.

JULES ROMAINS,
quoted in *Mirror for Gotham* by Bayrd Still

New York is large, glamorous, easy-going, kindly and incurious—but above all it is a crucible—because it is large enough to be incurious.

FORD MADOX FORD,
New York Is Not America

The true New Yorker does not really seek information about the outside world. He feels that if anything is not in New York it is not likely to be interesting.

AUBREY MENEN,
Holiday, October 1959

If the planet grows cold, this city will nevertheless have been mankind's warmest moment.

PAUL MORAND,
New York

As a city, New York moves in the forefront of today's great trend of great cities toward neurosis. She is confused, self-pitying, helpless and dependent.

JOHN LARDNER,
New York Times, February 1, 1953

New York has more hermits than will be found in all the forests, mountains and deserts of the United States.

SIMEON STRUNSKY,
No Mean City

You only know what it's like to play around here if you've played somewhere else first. This is the city for an athlete.

Y. A. TITTLE,
Quarterbacks Have All the Fun,
edited by Dick Schaap

One belongs to New York instantly, one belongs to it as much in five minutes as in five years.

THOMAS WOLFE,
The Web and the Rock

FRIEDRICH NIETZSCHE

From first to last, wherever you open his books, you light on sayings that cut to the core of the questions that every modern thinking man must face.

HAVELOCK ELLIS,
Selected Essays

Rightly construed, this surging anarchism of his is a revolt against the doctrine which the supermen have imposed upon the world, and a call to the lowly and meek to assert their manhood against their oppressors; and it is a singular perversion which makes it the gospel and justification of the oppressor.

J. A. SPENDER,
The Comments of Bagshot, Second Series

When N. talked about the Will to Power, the last thing he meant was a pack of Germans going out in a herd to conquer the world. But the word goes in excellent, and comes out fleshly. As a matter of fact, N.'s religious teaching is just as much a natural development of Christianity as a denial of it.

FREDERICK GOODYEAR,
Letters and Remains

NIGHT

There is something strangely determinate and fatal about a single shot in the night. It is as if someone had cried a message to you in one word, and would not repeat it.

ISAK DINESEN,
Out of Africa

We sip sherry at leisure in front of a fire. We start supper and we talk. Evening is the time for conversation. Morning is for mental work. ... But evening is for sharing, for communication. Is it the uninterrupted dark expanse of the night after the bright segmented day, that frees us to each other? Or does the infinite space and infinite darkness dwarf and chill us, turning us to seek small human sparks?

ANNE MORROW LINDBERGH,
Gift from the Sea

That the hands of the sisters Death and
    Night incessantly
softly wash again, and ever again, this
    soil'd world.

WALT WHITMAN,
"Reconciliation," *Leaves of Grass*

Press close bare-bosom'd night—press
    close magnetic nourishing night!
Night of south winds—night of the large
    few stars!
Still nodding night—mad naked summer
    night.

WALT WHITMAN,
"Song of Myself," *Leaves of Grass*

Night is the mother of advice.

CORSICAN PROVERB

Night is the time of love, of strange thoughts, of dreams.

SHERWOOD ANDERSON,
Perhaps Women

O, sweep of stars over Harlem streets,
O, little breath of oblivion that is night,
    A city building
    To a mother's song.
    A city dreaming
    To a lullaby.
Reach up your hand, dark boy, and take
    a star.
Out of the little breath of oblivion
    That is night,
    Take just
    One star.

LANGSTON HUGHES,
"Stars," *Selected Poems of Langston Hughes*

Darkness closes two eyes—but darkness opens a thousand others within us. Those

unseen eyes are sometimes troublesome. Yes, night brings strange fears and longings.

LOUIS DANZ,
Dynamic Dissonance

O God, my God, the night has values that day has never dreamed of.

THOMAS MERTON,
The Sign of Jonas

Nevertheless it is the eve. Let us accept all inflows of vigor and real tenderness. And at dawn, armed with an eager impatience, we shall enter splendid towns.

ARTHUR RIMBAUD,
A Season in Hell

Longfellow was taking poetic license when he wrote, "The day is done, and the darkness Falls from the wings of Night." Night does not fall. It rises.

LORUS J. AND MARGERY J. MILNE,
The World of Night

Night, you are for a man more nourishing than bread and wine.

CHARLES PÉGUY,
God Speaks

They stood in silence for a moment, receiving, as a common sacrament, the grandeur and tranquillity of the night.

ROBERT SPEAIGHT,
The Unbroken Heart

NOISE

If thee could only settle down to noises as being part of the ordained order of things, they would not disturb thee. I hear no noises here at night at all when thee is not here, but, as soon as thee comes, I am so afraid of thy being disturbed, that I hear them all the time.

HANNAH WHITALL SMITH,
Philadelphia Quaker
by Logan Pearsall Smith

Police are called to prevent distraction by the joyous noises of laughter and song, but not to stop the harsh and abrasive roar of power saws, air hammers, power mowers, snow blowers, and other baneful machines.

PHILIP SLATER,
The Pursuit of Loneliness

Noise is the most impertinent of all forms of interruption. It is not only an interruption, but a disruption of thought. Of course, where there is nothing to interrupt, noise will not be so particularly painful.

ARTHUR SCHOPENHAUER,
quoted in *The Poet's Work* by John Holmes

At times I am inclined to believe that all this noise is a sign of failure, an elegy of despair. The discord of modern life ... is probably nothing more than the wailing of a lost multitude, of a people who have mislaid life's highway, and ... are calling pitiful and chimerical directions to each other.

HOLBROOK JACKSON,
Southward Ho! and Other Essays

NORMAL

Nothing sweeter than to drag oneself along behind events; and nothing more *reasonable*. But without a strong dose of madness, no initiative, no enterprise, no gesture. Reason: the rust of our vitality. ... We cannot be *normal* and *alive* at the same time.

E. M. CIORAN,
The Temptation to Exist

The condition of alienation, of being asleep, of being unconscious, of being out of one's mind, is the condition of the normal man.

Society highly values its normal man. It educates children to lose themselves and to become absurd, and thus to be normal.

Normal men have killed perhaps 100,-000,000 of their fellow normal men in the last fifty years.

R. D. LAING,
The Politics of Experience

Possibly the greatest crime we commit against each other is this daily show of "normality." I have countless *little* conversations with a variety of people, and the impression I get is that most men don't have problems. Even the complainer presents himself as a victim. He doesn't suggest that he is experiencing confusion. He is all right: it is circumstances which are bad.

HUGH PRATHER,
Notes to Myself

NUDE

Did you know I painted pictures last year—seven or eight big oils—nudes—some people very shocked—worse than my writing. But I think they're rather lovely and almost holy.

D. H. LAWRENCE,
Selected Letters of D. H. Lawrence

A young lady (I only met her once) told several of us at dinner that she and her husband and her friend and her husband lived in the woods naked—I asked, absolutely naked? and she answered, absolutely naked, and when I asked why she said it was so convenient for bathing in the lake!

J. B. YEATS,
Letters to His Son, W. B. Yeats and Others

No other subject is so indicative of the photographer's taste and talent as the nude.

PETER LACEY,
A History of the Nude in Photography

In literature as in the plastic arts and in life itself, the nude is nearer to virtue than the *décolleté*.

HAVELOCK ELLIS,
Selected Essays

If prudery (and the wantonness of which it is commonly the cloak or the accompaniment) be rampant, let there be naked bathing in parks. If sexual frigidity be rampant, let nakedness be restricted, for clothes are the best aphrodisiac. But prudes cannot decide who are wantons, nor can wantons decide who are prudes.

ERIC GILL,
It All Goes Together

Although the artist cannot construct a

beautiful nude by mathematical rules, any more than the musician can compose a beautiful fugue, he cannot ignore them. They must be lodged somewhere at the back of his mind or in the movements of his fingers. Ultimately he is as dependent on them as an architect.

KENNETH CLARK,
The Nude

When it reached the point when frontal nudity was acceptable in a number of major motion pictures which were reaching the same young audience we were reaching, I told them the time was right for *Playboy*. But with pubic hair, it's a complicated thing. Part of it is sexual, and part of it has to do with some people with a taste thing, not unlike underarm hair. Some people have just been raised in a society in which all graphic images of nude females have all been without hair and it disturbs them. But it's a childish thing which we hope we'll get society out of.

HUGH HEFNER,
Supertalk by Digby Diehl

Whenever we treat women's bodies as aesthetic objects without function we deform them and their owners.

GERMAINE GREER,
The Female Eunuch

OBLIGATION

An old lady said to me the other day that she had set too much value all her life on *positive obligation.* I am going to begin to practise a little *negative obligation,* and boldly say there are things I *can't* do.

A. C. BENSON,
*Excerpts from the Letters of
Dr. A. C. Benson to M. E. A.*

Nothing comes of a sortie you have got out of.

ANTOINE DE SAINT-EXUPÉRY,
Airman's Odyssey

We cannot hope to scale great moral heights by ignoring petty obligations.

AGNES REPPLIER,
Americans and Others

To be under obligations always oppresses us. We have the instinctive impulse to disregard them.

DR. WILHELM STEKHEL,
The Depths of the Soul

OBSERVATION

Every scene, even the commonest, is wonderful, if only one can detach oneself, casting off all memory of use and custom and behold it, as it were, for the first time.

ARNOLD BENNETT,
Journal, quoted in *Reader's Digest,*
February 1935

To linger in the observation of things other than the self implies a profound conviction of their worth.

CHARLES-DAMIAN BOULOGNE,
My Friends the Senses

There is no more difficult art to acquire than the art of observation, and for some men it is quite as difficult to record an observation in brief and plain language.

SIR WILLIAM OSLER,
*Aphorisms from His Bedside Teachings
and Writings*

You don't seem to know how observant I am. Do you remember how in our walk with Minna along the *Beethovengang* you kept going aside to pull up your stockings? It is bold of me to mention it, but I hope you don't mind.

SIGMUND FREUD,
quoted in *The Life and Work
of Sigmund Freud,* Vol. I, by Ernest Jones

We must learn how to handle words effectively; but at the same time we must preserve and, if necessary, intensify our ability to look at the world directly and not through that half opaque medium of concepts, which distorts every given fact into the all too familiar likeness of some generic label or explanatory abstraction.

ALDOUS HUXLEY,
The Doors of Perception

Method for understanding images, symbols, etc. Not to try to interpret them, but to look at them till the light suddenly dawns.

Generally speaking, a method for the exercise of the intelligence, which consists of looking.

SIMONE WEIL,
Gravity and Grace

The observation of others is coloured by our inability to observe ourselves impartially. We can never be impartial about anything until we can be impartial about our own organism.

A. R. ORAGE,
Essays and Aphorisms

OBSTACLE

Life is like walking along a crowded street—there always seem to be fewer obstacles to getting along on the opposite pavement—and yet, if one crosses over, matters are rarely mended.

THOMAS HENRY HUXLEY,
Aphorisms and Reflections

A man who is not to be deterred by obstacles needs a tongue and an arm.

ABBÉ HUVELIN,
Some Spiritual Guides of the Seventeenth Century

OCCULT (*See also* SPIRITUAL)

The Master would not discuss prodigies, prowess, lawlessness or the supernatural.

CONFUCIUS

OFFICIAL

Any official, whether a minister, a theatre manager or a newspaper editor, can sometimes be an estimable individual, but he is never a man of distinction. They are persons without personality, unoriginal, born for office, that is, for domestic service to the public.

CHARLES BAUDELAIRE,
Intimate Journals

Official dignity tends to increase in inverse ratio to the importance of the country in which the office is held.

ALDOUS HUXLEY,
Beyond the Mexique Bay

There is no subtler way of flattering a retired official than to criticise his successor in office.

J. A. SPENDER,
The Comments of Bagshot, Second Series

OPERA

You should remember the number of composers who were exiled because of their messages. . . . One could write a thesis on the subject of the opera form having attracted rebels.

MARC BLITZSTEIN,
Close-up by John Gruen

If the inhabitant of another planet should visit the earth, he would receive, on the whole, a truer notion of human life by attending an Italian opera than he would by reading Emerson's volumes. He would learn from the Italian opera that there were two sexes; and this, after all, is probably the fact with which the education of such a stranger ought to begin.

JOHN JAY CHAPMAN,
Emerson and Other Essays

I think my favorite opera of all is *Die Meistersinger*, and I have always thought that I would like to die to the strains of the last act but one of that. Lovely music, enchanting music.

W. SOMERSET MAUGHAM,
Wisdom for Our Time,
edited by James Nelson

There was a time when I heard eleven operas in a fortnight, an astonishing fit of debauchery this, which left me bankrupt and half-idiotic for a month.

J. B. PRIESTLEY,
All About Ourselves and Other Essays

I don't really believe in it. You know, how can people sing away their troubles? How can they all make love to each other singing? I can't quite believe it, but I like it and can appreciate the music. As a form, it's complete unto itself.

JOSÉ QUINTERO,
Behind the Scenes,
edited by Joseph F. McCrindle

There is a childlike, unsophisticated quality about opera which commands respect in this wicked world. All that hooting and hollering because somebody has pinched somebody else's girl, or killed the wrong man, or sold his soul to the devil! These are commonplaces in daily life ... and it is astonishing to hear them treated with so much noisy consideration.

ROBERTSON DAVIES,
The Table Talk of Samuel Marchbanks

OPINION

In all matters of opinion our adversaries are insane.

MARK TWAIN,
Mark Twain at Your Fingertips,
edited by Caroline T. Harnsberger

But it is just when opinions universally prevail and we have added lip service to their authority that we become sometimes most keenly conscious that we do not believe a word that we are saying.

VIRGINIA WOOLF,
The Common Reader, First Series

Lidian says that the only sin which people never forgive in each other is a difference of opinion.

RALPH WALDO EMERSON,
Journals of Ralph Waldo Emerson

Opinion is that exercise of the human will which helps us to make a decision without information.

JOHN ERSKINE,
The Complete Life

I see no impropriety ... in suggesting the isolated reflection that with effervescing opinions, as with the not yet forgotten champagnes, the quickest way to let them get flat is to let them get exposed to the air.

OLIVER WENDELL HOLMES, JR.,
The Mind and Faith of Justice Holmes,
edited by Max Lerner

I am a little surprised to find how commonly people suppose that when one is unable to accept their opinions one is therefore necessarily hostile to them.

HAVELOCK ELLIS,
quoted in *Ladies' Home Journal,* May 1947

If we knew where opinion ended and fact began, we should have discovered, I suppose, the absolute.

ALEC WAUGH,
On Doing What One Likes

People often seem to take me for someone else; they talk to me as if I were a person of earnest views and unalterable convictions. "What is your opinion of Democracy?" they ask. "Are you in favor of the Channel Tunnel?" "Do you believe in existence after Death?"

I assume a thoughtful attitude, and by means of grave looks and evasive answers, I conceal—or at least I hope I conceal—my discreditable secret.

LOGAN PEARSALL SMITH,
More Trivia

I want to find someone on the earth so intelligent that he welcomes opinions which he condemns.

JOHN JAY CHAPMAN,
John Jay Chapman and His Letters
by M. A. DeWolfe Howe

All empty souls tend to extreme opinion. It is only in those who have built up a rich world of memories and habits of thought that extreme opinions affront the sense of probability. Propositions, for instance, which set all the truth upon one side can only enter rich minds to dislocate and strain, if they can enter at all, and sooner or later the mind expels them by instinct.

W. B. YEATS,
Autobiography

It is probable that a given opinion, as held by several individuals, even when of the most congenial views, is as distinct from itself as are their faces.

JOHN HENRY CARDINAL NEWMAN,
Oxford University Sermons

Most often people seek in life occasions for persisting in their opinions rather than for educating themselves. Each of us looks for justification in the event. The rest, which runs counter to that opinion, is over-looked. . . . It seems as if the mind enjoys nothing more than sinking deeper into error.

ANDRÉ GIDE,
Pretexts

There is no greater mistake than the hasty conclusion that opinions are worthless because they are badly argued.

THOMAS HENRY HUXLEY,
Aphorisms and Reflections

OPPORTUNITY

Dawn does not come twice to awaken a man.

ARAB PROVERB

Heavens, how many opportunities and examples for becoming something,—and over against them, how much laziness, distraction, and half-will on our side. A lament, a lament—.

RAINER MARIA RILKE,
Letters of Rainer Maria Rilke 1892–1910

One can present people with opportunities. One cannot make them equal to them.

ROSAMOND LEHMANN,
The Ballad and the Source

He who refuses to embrace an unique opportunity loses the prize as surely as if he had failed.

WILLIAM JAMES,
The Will to Believe

Seize the opportunity by the beard, for it is bald behind.

BULGARIAN PROVERB

Half the pleasures of life consists of opportunities one has neglected.

OLIVER WENDELL HOLMES, JR.,
quoted in *Ladies' Home Journal,*
October 1941

Fortune does not stoop often to take any one up. Favorable opportunities will not happen precisely in the way that you have imagined. Nothing does.

SIR ARTHUR HELPS,
Companions of My Solitude

In the scene with Warren driving at night with Betty near Beverly—in summing it up, say how it was a lost opportunity, because of my fear and shyness, because of caution. This opportunity became failure to learn something wonderful . . . something about the mystery of attraction, of intimacy—of love—the essential thing which is always near, always possible, except for self-imposed barriers.

KATHARINE BUTLER HATHAWAY,
*The Journals and Letters
of the Little Locksmith*

For the highest task of intelligence is to grasp and recognize genuine opportunity, possibility.

JOHN DEWEY,
Human Nature and Conduct

OPPOSITE

He who always sails the seas loves dry land; he who is eternally absorbed in prose passionately pines for poetry.

ANTON CHEKHOV,
The Selected Letters of Anton Chekhov

OPTIMISM

An optimist is a man who starts a cross-word puzzle with a fountain pen.

ANONYMOUS,
Ladies' Home Journal, June 1942

Nothing is more dangerous than ill-founded optimism; in the end it can produce only despair.

HENRI DE LUBAC,
The New Man

To the question whether I am a pessimist or an optimist, I answer that my knowledge is pessimistic, but my willing and hoping are optimistic.

ALBERT SCHWEITZER,
Out of My Life and Thought

The man who feels that he must be hopeful and cheerful to get along ignores the careers of some pretty successful misanthropes.

ANONYMOUS (HENRY S. HASKINS),
Meditations in Wall Street

There is only one optimist. He has been here since man has been on this earth, and that is "man" himself. If we hadn't had such a magnificent optimism to carry us through all these things, we wouldn't be here. We have survived everything, and we have only survived it on our optimism.

EDWARD STEICHEN,
Wisdom, edited by James Nelson

The men who are for ever slapping one on the back and saying that everything will come right are bad enough, but more intolerable are those persons who will persist in slapping humanity itself on the back and regarding all life with an unchanging grin of approval. . . . Stupidity, downright insensitiveness, is the secret of such optimism, which fits as much as it can of life into its bright little boxes and blandly ignores the rest.

J. B. PRIESTLEY,
All About Ourselves and Other Essays

When I said you were an optimist, I didn't mean that you took too rosy a view of matters of fact, but that you were full of the zest of life and confident about the value and the success of what you undertook—a sentiment which is healthy and natural in any energetic person, and characteristic (for obvious good reasons) of America.

GEORGE SANTAYANA,
The Letters of George Santayana

ORATOR

The least effect of the oration is on the orator; yet it is something; a faint recoil; a kicking of the gun.

RALPH WALDO EMERSON,
Journals of Ralph Waldo Emerson

I always think a great orator convinces us not by force of reasoning, but because he is *visibly enjoying the beliefs which he wants us to accept.*

J. B. YEATS,
Letters to His Son, W. B. Yeats and Others

"One evening," Hamish relates, "Hitler went to a cinema where Kellermann's *Tunnel* was being shown. In this piece an agitator appears who rouses the masses by his speeches. Hitler almost went crazy. The impression it made on him was so strong that for days afterwards he spoke of nothing except the power of the spoken word."

ALAN BULLOCK,
Hitler: A Study in Tyranny

Let us have a reason for beginning, and let our end be within due limits. For a speech that is wearisome only stirs up anger.

SAINT AMBROSE,
Select Works and Letters

O the orator's joys!
To inflate the chest, to roll the thunder of
   the voice out from the ribs and throat,
To make the people rage, weep, hate,
   desire, with yourself,
To lead America—to quell America with
   a great tongue.

WALT WHITMAN,
"A Song of Joys," *Leaves of Grass*

I do not object to people looking at their watches when I am speaking—but I strongly object when they start shaking them to make certain they are still going.

LORD BIRKETT,
quoted in the *New York Times*,
November 13, 1960

Among the superstitions of America, please mention the admiration and ambition of public speaking. I have assured several *savant*-struck ladies that enthusiasm in speech is very apt to be proportioned to crudeness in ideas.

CHAUNCEY WRIGHT,
Letters of Chauncey Wright

There must be something wrong with after-dinner speaking because it is notoriously the lowest form of American oratory. . . . The trouble, we think, is that dinner guests are much too friendly. It is the custom that the man at the speakers' table may not be heckled. He is privileged and privilege has made him dull.

HEYWOOD BROUN,
Pieces of Hate

Intelligent men do not as a rule assume, in talking with us privately, that all wisdom and virtue are with them. They agree with us in some points, and they try to understand our point of view. But in addressing us collectively they will show the most shocking cynicism as to what we can understand. Many a thought will be held back because it is supposed to be too big for us. . . .The truth is, the public can stand from any man the best there is in him.

FRANK MOORE COLBY,
The Colby Essays, Vol. 2

ORDER

Put things into their places, and they will put you in your place.

ARAB PROVERB

From a little distance one can perceive an order in what at the time seemed confusion.

F. SCOTT FITZGERALD,
The Crack-up

ORGANIZATION

Our admiration of our great organizations would soon dwindle were we to become aware of the other side of the wonder, namely the tremendous heaping up and accentuation of all that is primitive in man and the unavoidable disintegration of his individuality in favour of that monstrosity which every great organization, on its nether side, is.

C. G. JUNG,
Psychological Reflections,
edited by Jolande Jacobi and R. F. Hull

The intangible duty of making things run smoothly is apt to be thankless, because people don't realise how much time and trouble it takes and believe it is the result of a natural and effortless unction.

A. C. BENSON,
*Excerpts from the Letters of
Dr. A. C. Benson to M. E. A.*

Organization can't be beaten without organization.

HEYWOOD BROUN,
Collected Edition of Heywood Broun

Whereas man made his peace with nature very largely as an individual—as a farmer, a hunter, a fisherman, a sailor—he makes his peace with technology through social organization. The technology itself demands organization in order to function, and the environment it creates in turn calls forth organization in order for men to function within it.

ROBERT L. HEILBRONER,
quoted in *The American Male*
by Myron Brenton

But where organizing an effort is concerned it is sometimes better to have mediocre talent than a bunch of creative individuals who disturb the situation by questioning everything.

ALAN HARRINGTON,
Life in the Crystal Palace

One of the many reasons for the bewildering and tragic character of human existence is the fact that social organization is at once necessary and fatal. Men are forever creating such organizations for their own convenience and forever finding themselves the victims of their homemade monsters.

ALDOUS HUXLEY,
Collected Essays

Two essential qualities in a good organizer are a thorough and constant perception of the end in view, and a power of dealing with masses of details, never forgetting that they are details, and not becoming their slave.

SIR ARTHUR HELPS,
Organization in Daily Life

All good organization tends to simplicity: and, when a wise method is proposed, people are ready to say how self-evident it is. But, without the few men who perceive these self-evident things, the business of the world would go on even worse than it does.

SIR ARTHUR HELPS,
Organization in Daily Life

While the Gestapo used mainly physical and psychological pressure to achieve its goals, the prisoners tried to counteract with organizational defenses, and more subtle psychological ones. But often their efforts to defend themselves found them deeper enmeshed in the system. Just as the SS' desire for efficient workshops led to areas of common interest between SS and prisoners, so the prisoners' efforts to defend themselves through prisoner organizations forced them to cooperate with the SS. The resulting contradiction was that the more effective the organization, the better it also served the SS.

BRUNO BETTELHEIM,
The Informed Heart

ORIGINALITY

Originality wells out from sources subconscious and somewhat mysterious. You must let the subterranean waters accumulate. A too strenuous life will dry them up.
CHARLES HORTON COOLEY,
Life and the Student

Originality begins in our reaction to the necessary events of life, to things that come up hard against us. . . . If you are destined to do anything original there is some germ of it growing in you now, and you first need to discover and cherish that.
CHARLES HORTON COOLEY,
Life and the Student

When there is an original sound in the world it makes a hundred echoes.
JOHN A. SHEDD,
Salt from My Attic

There is nothing mysterious about originality, nothing fantastic. Originality is merely the step beyond.
LOUIS DANZ,
Dynamic Dissonance

It is a wonderful thing as I was saying and as I am now repeating, it is a wonderful thing how much a thing needs to be in one as a desire in them how much courage anyone must have in them to be doing anything if they are a first one.
GERTRUDE STEIN,
The Making of Americans

Orginality: Don't worry about your originality. You could not get rid of it even if you wanted to. It will stick to you and show up for better or worse in spite of all you or anyone else can do.
ROBERT HENRI,
The Art Spirit

ORTHODOXY

Orthodoxy of all kinds in every period and place where it was powerful enough to do as it pleased has driven to madness or frustration valuable human beings whose personalities did not fit the prevailing style. Anybody can see this when he is not looking at his own orthodoxy.
DOROTHY CANFIELD FISHER,
Harper's Magazine, December 1932

OTHERS

One does not get a headache from what other people have drunk.
RUSSIAN PROVERB

We grow by love. It is said why live for others? But others are our nutriment.
WILLIAM ELLERY CHANNING,
Dr. Channing's Note-book

It is well to remember, my son, that the entire population of the universe, with one trifling exception, is composed of others.
JOHN ANDREW HOLMES,
Wisdom in Small Doses

To see ourselves as others see us is a most salutary gift. Hardly less important is the capacity to see others as they see themselves.
ALDOUS HUXLEY,
The Doors of Perception

PAIN

If the pleasures that an age offers are insipid, passionate souls will seek pain.
BRENDAN FRANCIS

Pain may be caused by many things which, if their advantageous aspect had been considered, might have given rise to satisfaction.

BALTASAR GRACIAN,
The Oracle

We know well enough that pain conduces more to a realisation of existence and to unity than does pleasure.

JEAN GUITTON,
Essay on Human Love

To render ourselves insensible to pain we must forfeit also the possibility of happiness.

SIR JOHN LUBBOCK,
The Pleasures of Life

The sensation of being cut by a skilful surgeon would not, I think, be pain, if one could keep one's imagination out of it.

J. A. SPENDER,
The Comments of Bagshot, Second Series

Behind joy and laughter there may be a temperament, coarse, hard and callous. But behind sorrow there is always sorrow. Pain, unlike pleasure, wears no mask.

OSCAR WILDE,
De Profundis

PARENTS

Parents may fairly be criticized for anything, with one exception—their children's behavior.

BRENDAN FRANCIS

We, the children, are so full of repressed resentments against the tyrannies inflicted upon us by our parents, and so full of repressed shame at the slavery to which we subjected them, that we cannot bear a word against them. The sentimentality with which we regard the home is an exact measure of the secret grudge we actually bear against it.

FLOYD DELL,
Were You Ever a Child?

There is no misreading of life that avenges itself so piteously on men and women as the notion that in their children they can bring to fruition their own seedling dreams. And it is just as unjust to the child, to be born and reared as the "crea-

tion" of the parents. He is *himself,* and it is within reason that he may be the very antithesis of them both.—No, it is wisdom in motherhood as in wifehood to have one's own individual world of effort and creation.

RUTH BENEDICT,
An Anthropologist at Work
by Margaret Mead

[Parents'] influence is inevitable and continuous: they cannot be passive if they would. You cannot really *neglect* your children, you can *destroy* them.

FREDERICK W. FABER,
Notes on Doctrinal and Spiritual Subjects,
Vol. II

Parenthood: that state of being better chaperoned than you were before marriage.

MARCELENE COX,
Ladies' Home Journal, February 1944

One reason why corporal punishment is popular is that a big person can hit a little person with relative safety. Many parents, it seems, give up corporal punishment when their children are old enough to make a stiff defense or counter-attack.

ARTHUR T. JERSILD,
Educational Psychology,
edited by Charles E. Skinner

From the complaints which everybody brings against everybody in the matter of the management of children, one might be led to suppose that such a thing as good management of them did not exist amongst mankind.

SIR HENRY TAYLOR,
Notes from Life

The schoolmaster learns to know people as "parents" and in this respect, I say it without hesitation, they are all more or less insane.

STEPHEN LEACOCK,
Essays and Literary Studies

And my parents, a somewhat distant warmth, like a good fire in a room—that warmth that I knew I could go to if I needed, but which was formless and with-

out a life of its own.
FRANÇOISE MALLET-JORIS,
A Letter to Myself

The secret cruelties that parents visit upon their children are past belief.
DR. KARL MENNINGER,
A Psychiatrist's World

Don't parents often get blamed too much for over-influencing their children, when the blame should mostly lie on the children for not kicking more strenuously against their influence? I can see already that it will be almost impossible not to try to propel the kiddies in directions (professional, etc.) that interest me, but I pray that they may be armed against me with contumacy when the right time comes.
C. E. MONTAGUE,
The Right Place

Too many parents, maybe, are holding fast to youth by vicariously reliving it through their children. Popularity and belledom are the golden goals; and the young are being trained for it as athletes are trained for the Olympics.
PHYLLIS MCGINLEY,
The Province of the Heart

Out of some forty families I have been able to observe, I know hardly four in which the parents do not act in such a way that nothing would be more desirable for the child than to escape their influence.
ANDRÉ GIDE,
Pretexts

There are so many disciplines in being a parent besides the obvious ones like getting up in the night and putting up with the noise during the day. And almost the hardest of all is learning to be a well of affection and not a fountain, to show them we love then, not when *we* feel like it, but when they do.
NAN FAIRBROTHER,
An English Year

PARIS

When one has Paris around one for the first time, one must let it act more like a bath, without trying to do too much about

it oneself: save to feel and let it happen.
RAINER MARIA RILKE,
Letters of Rainer Maria Rilke 1892–1910

When spring comes to Paris the humblest mortal alive must feel that he dwells in paradise.
HENRY MILLER,
The Tropic of Cancer

Paris, France is exciting and peaceful.
GERTRUDE STEIN,
quoted in *Gertrude Stein:
Her Life and Her Work* by Elizabeth Sprigge

PARODY

I remember once reading a parody of Ruskin in which he was made to say, "But a sewer is an entirely holy thing." I always thought parody, there, had spoken wisdom.
STEPHEN MACKENNA,
Journal and Letters of Stephen Mackenna

PARTY

When we are merriest, it is best to leave and drive home.
CZECH PROVERB

There must be some good in the cocktail party to account for its immense vogue among otherwise sane people.
EVELYN WAUGH,
Wine in Peace and War

Even though the hour is late, it takes more determination than I've got to walk away from a party that is going well.
WILLIAM FEATHER,
The Business of Life

A small boy, who was a stickler for the literal truth, once said to me that it was wrong to say "Good-bye" when you had not enjoyed yourself at a party. I inquired what should be substituted for it. He suggested "Bad-bye." I have never tried this.
ARTHUR PONSONBY,
Casual Observations

I delight in the idea of a party but find no pleasure in the reality. The result is that I can neither keep away from parties nor enjoy them.

J. B. PRIESTLEY,
All About Ourselves and Other Essays

Only the bravest of stay-at-homes asks the ticklish question: "Did anybody ask where I was?"

ANONYMOUS (HENRY S. HASKINS),
Meditations in Wall Street

There are few more melancholy spectacles than the litter of a room after the last guest has said "Good-bye."

ALEC WAUGH,
On Doing What One Likes

PASSION

Passion has as much conscience as a worm entering a luscious apple.

PAUL ELDRIDGE,
Horns of Glass

Interests are always ready to compound, passions never. You can always discuss figures, haggle over prices, ask a hundred and accept eighty-five. But you cannot discuss hatred, nor haggle over contradictory vanities and prejudices, nor ask for blood and accept a soft answer.

ALDOUS HUXLEY,
Beyond the Mexique Bay

If we resist our passions, it is more because of their weakness than our strength.

LA ROCHEFOUCAULD,
Maxims

Be still when you have nothing to say; when genuine passion moves you, say what you've got to say, and say it hot.

D. H. LAWRENCE,
Selected Essays

This, indeed, is one of the eternal paradoxes of both life and literature—that without passion little gets done; yet, without control of that passion, its effects are largely ill or null.

F. L. LUCAS,
Style

Quarry the granite rock with razors, or moor the vessel with a thread of silk; then you may hope with such keen and delicate instruments as human knowledge and human reason to contend against those giants, the passion and the pride of man.

JOHN HENRY CARDINAL NEWMAN,
The Idea of a University

Passion is of course designed by nature to be transitory,—a paroxysm, not a state.

SIR HENRY TAYLOR,
Notes from Life

PASSIVE

It is a great fault when anything is presented to us to twist it into a mere illustration of something we already are or know. We ought to divest ourselves of ourselves in looking at it; lie passive and bare to it.

MARK RUTHERFORD,
Last Pages from a Journal

Most things worth anything ... are more passive than active.

JANET ERSKINE STUART,
Life and Letters of Janet Erskine Stuart
by Maud Monahan

For the ordinary man is passive. Within a narrow circle (home life, and perhaps the trade union or local politics) he feels himself master of his fate, but against major events he is as helpless as against the elements. So far from endeavouring to influence the future, he simply lies down and lets things happen to him.

GEORGE ORWELL,
A Collection of Essays

I was like a sailor who drops his oars and lets himself drift; at last he takes the time to look at the shores; while he was rowing he saw nothing. My will, so constantly stretched taut, relaxed at present without any function. ... This was the great rest after the long fever; my former anxieties became incomprehensible to me. I was amazed that nature was so beautiful, and I called everything nature.

ANDRÉ GIDE,
The Journals of André Gide, Vol. I

Prisoners ... who came to feel that their environment was one over which they could exercise no influence whatsoever, these prisoners were, in a literal sense, walking corpses. . . .They were people who were so deprived of affect, self-esteem, and every form of stimulation, so totally exhausted, both physically and emotionally, that they had given the environment total power over them. They did this when they gave up trying to exercise any further influence over their life or environment.

> BRUNO BETTELHEIM,
> *The Informed Heart*

Ten years ago, Negroes seemed almost invisible to the larger society, and the facts of their harsh lives were unknown to the majority of the nation. . . .

In this decade of change the Negro stood up and confronted his oppressor—he faced the bullies and the guns, the dogs and the tear gas, he put himself squarely before the vicious mobs and moved with strength and dignity toward them and decisively defeated them.

> MARTIN LUTHER KING, JR.,
> *Where Do We Go from Here:*
> *Chaos or Community?*

PAST

The past is not a package one can lay away.

> EMILY DICKINSON,
> *Selected Poems and Letters of Emily Dickinson*

History has never allowed man to return to the past in any total sense. And our psychological problems cannot be solved by a regression to a past state in which they not had yet been brought into being.

> WILLIAM BARRETT,
> *Irrational Man*

It is unhealthy and undesirable to live so much in the past, and yet, God forgive me, how I do it. And one cannot bring it back, and one would probably not like it, if one could.

> GAMALIEL BRADFORD,
> *The Letters of Gamaliel Bradford*

Well. I have not only hopes for the future. I have hopes for the present and hopes for the past. I mean by that that I have hopes the past will be found to have been all right for what it was.

> ROBERT FROST,
> *Wisdom,* edited by James Nelson

All the past can help you.

> ROBERT HENRI,
> *The Art Spirit*

We think in generalities, but we live in detail. To make the past live, we must perceive it in detail in addition to thinking of it in generalities.

> ALFRED NORTH WHITEHEAD,
> *Essays in Science and Philosophy*

I will not grieve over the past—for why grieve? I will work on with energy and not waste time grieving, like the man caught in the quicksands who began by calculating how far down he had already sunk, forgetting that all the while he was sinking still deeper. I will hurry along the path I have discovered, greeting those whom I meet on my way, not looking back as did Lot's wife, but remembering that it is a hill up which we have to struggle.

> SØREN KIERKEGAARD,
> *The Journals of Søren Kierkegaard*

Do not be afraid of the past. If people tell you that it is irrevocable, do not believe them.

> OSCAR WILDE,
> *De Profundis*

PATIENCE

Patience is needed with everyone, but first of all with ourselves.

> SAINT FRANCIS DE SALES,
> *Saint Francis de Sales in His Letters*

The first virtue: patience. Nothing to do with simple waiting. It is more like obstinacy.

> ANDRÉ GIDE,
> *The Fruits of the Earth*

I am managing more and more to make use of that long patience you taught me by your tenacious example; that patience which, disproportionate to everyday life that seems to bid us haste, puts us in touch with all that surpasses us.

> RAINER MARIA RILKE,
> *Letters of Rainer Maria Rilke 1892–1910*

PATRIOTISM

Patriotism has served, at different times, as widely different ends as a razor, which ought to be used to keep your face clean and yet may be used to cut your own throat or that of some innocent person.

> C. E. MONTAGUE,
> *The Right Place*

A man cannot always be in a battle mood about his country. There is some fun to be had at her expense.

> FRANK MOORE COLBY,
> *The Colby Essays,* Vol. 2

Patriotism lies in the nature of man and is something so self-evident that any exaggeration or emphasis is only painful or ridiculous, and smothers it instead of sustaining it.

> THEODOR HAECKER,
> *Journal in the Night*

To love is ... the real duty of patriotism, whereas, in the mouths of many of its noisiest professors, the point would rather seem to be to hate.

> JOHN AYSCOUGH,
> *Levia-Pondera*

Men and women who would shrink from doing anything dishonorable in the sphere of personal relationships are ready to lie and swindle, to steal and even murder when they are representing their country.

> ALDOUS HUXLEY,
> *War: An Anthology,* edited by Edward Huberman and Elizabeth Huberman

PEACE

You can imagine what a bitter blow it is to me that all my long struggle to win peace has failed. Yet I cannot believe that there is anything more or anything different that I could have done and that would have been more successful.

> NEVILLE CHAMBERLAIN,
> *The Taste of Courage,* edited by Desmond Flower and James Reeves

A bad peace is better than a good war.

> RUSSIAN PROVERB

A man seeks to control and harmonize his life so that he may be at peace. But nature, perhaps, is not ready to round off so small a piece of creation, and he finds himself swept into conflict by impulses that are part of some larger whole. There are greater issues than his comfort.

> CHARLES HORTON COOLEY,
> *Life and the Student*

All men love peace in their armchairs after dinner; but they disbelieve the other nation's professions, rightly measuring its sincerity by their own.

> OSCAR W. FIRKINS,
> *Oscar Firkins: Memoirs and Letters,*
> edited by Ina Ten Eyck

It takes two to make peace.

> JOHN F. KENNEDY,
> quoted in the *New York Times,*
> June 3, 1961

It is not pleasant to be at war with society, but sometimes it is the only way of preserving one's peace of soul, which is peace with the living, struggling, *real* mankind. And this latter one cannot afford to lose.

> D. H. LAWRENCE,
> *Selected Essays*

But then peace, peace! I am so mistrustful of it: so much afraid that it means a sort of weakness and giving in.

> D. H. LAWRENCE,
> *Selected Letters of D. H. Lawrence*

I cannot forget that the Nobel Prize for Peace was also a commission—a commission to work harder than I had ever worked before for "the brotherhood of man." This is a calling which takes me beyond national allegiances, but even if it were not present, I would yet have to live with the meaning of my commitment to the ministry of Jesus Christ. To me the relationship of this ministry to the making of peace is so obvious that I sometimes marvel at those who ask me why I am speaking against the war.

MARTIN LUTHER KING, JR.,
The Trumpet of Conscience

Yes, we love peace, but we are not willing to take wounds for it, as we are for war.

JOHN ANDREW HOLMES,
Wisdom in Small Doses

To me it is a strange and dismal thing that in a world of such need, such opportunity, and such variety as ours, the search for an illusory peace of mind should be so zealously pursued and defended, while truth goes languishing. ... A querulous search for a premature, permanent "peace" seems to me a thinly disguised wish to die.

DR. KARL MENNINGER,
A Psychiatrist's World

PEACOCK

I do not believe that any peacock envies another peacock his tail, because every peacock is persuaded that his own tail is the finest in the world. The consequence of this is that peacocks are peaceable birds. Imagine how unhappy the life of a peacock would be if he had been taught that it is wicked to have a good opinion of oneself.

BERTRAND RUSSELL,
The Conquest of Happiness

PEOPLE

Doesn't it seem some days as though other people were put in the world for no other reason than to aggravate you?

E. W. HOWE,
Country Town Sayings

I constantly find myself driving in the road down here, and everywhere in the road there are people wanting to be picked up. My inclination is to pass them by. I want to remain sunk in my own thoughts. I have to force myself to make each new contact, but every time I do

there is a kind of reward.

SHERWOOD ANDERSON,
Letters of Sherwood Anderson

PERCEPTION

Systematic reasoning is something we could not, as a species or as individuals, possibly do without. But neither, if we are to remain sane, can we possibly do without direct perception, the more unsystematic the better, of the inner and outer world into which we have been born.

ALDOUS HUXLEY,
The Doors of Perception

The subtlest and most pervasive of influences are those which create and maintain the repertory of stereotypes. We are told about the world before we see it. We imagine most things before we experience them. And those preconceptions, unless education has made us acutely aware, govern deeply the whole process of perception.

WALTER LIPPMANN,
Public Opinion

Rightly to perceive a thing, in all the fulness of its qualities, is really to create it.

C. E. MONTAGUE,
The Right Place

The first requirement for the growth of the individual is that the person remain in touch with his own perceptions. No matter how different one's experience is from that of others, he must trust in the validity of his own senses if he is to evolve as a unique human being. Only the person can fully know what he sees, what he hears, and what he feels to be fundamentally true.

CLARK MOUSTAKAS,
Creativity and Conformity

To be able to make one's own observations and to draw pertinent conclusions from them is where independent existence begins. To forbid oneself to make observations, and take only the observations of others in their stead, is relegating to nonuse one's own powers of reasoning, and the even more basic power of perception. Not observing where it counts most, not knowing where one wants so much to know, all this is most destructive to the functioning of one's personality.

BRUNO BETTELHEIM,
The Informed Heart

PERFECTION

Perfection never exists in reality but only in our dreams and, if we are foolish enough to think so, in the past. But the notion of perfection is very real and has tremendous power in disparaging whatever is actually at hand.

DR. RUDOLF DREIKURS,
Ladies' Home Journal, October 1946

I think that unless in one thing or another we are straining towards perfection we have forfeited our manhood. Our perfection is in being imperfect. in something whose perfection is to us the highest thing in life.

STEPHEN MACKENNA,
Journal and Letters of Stephen Mackenna

Perfection in kind—even though the kind be bad—is something.

BARRETT WENDELL,
Barrett Wendell and His Letters
by M. A. DeWolfe Howe

Try as hard as we may for perfection, the net result of our labors is an amazing variety of imperfectness. We are surprised at our own versatility in being able to fail in so many different ways.

SAMUEL MCCHORD CROTHERS,
The Gentle Reader

Perfectionism is slow death. If everything were to turn out just like I would want it to, then I would never experience anything new; my life would be an endless repetition of stale successes. When I make a mistake I experience something unexpected.

HUGH PRATHER,
Notes to Myself

PERFUME

When all is said and done, perfume is the only ally on which a woman can fully count. It permits her to attract without losing her reserve, to unveil herself while keeping her modesty, to impose herself without importuning, to insist without wearying, and, above all, to express herself without giving away any of her mystery.

CHARLES-DAMIAN BOULOGNE,
My Friends the Senses

A woman who uses too much perfume is only calling attention to her need for it.

SYDNEY J. HARRIS,
Strictly Personal

PERPLEXITY

It is something to be capable of perplexity.

ANONYMOUS (HENRY S. HASKINS),
Meditations in Wall Street

Yes, our perplexity has borne a part, and let us be bolder than Wordsworth, *bears* a part, a "needful" part in the making up of our calm,—and not only our perplexity, but our very fever.

CHARLES DU BOS,
What Is Literature?

Where perplexity comes in is where nothing has been decided on.

GEORGE PORTER,
The Letters of the Late Father George Porter, S.J.

PERSECUTION

To flee persecution implies no fault in him who flees but in him who persecutes.

SAINT BERNARD OF CLAIRVAUX,
Letters

The positions we have abandoned constitute a danger to the positions we have taken up. Many of the world's fiercest persecutors have but persecuted their old selves; and there seems to be a psychological necessity for such an attitude.

HAVELOCK ELLIS,
Selected Essays

I feel wicked sleeping in a warm bed, while my dearest friends have been knocked down or have fallen into a gutter somewhere out in the cold night. I get frightened when I think of close friends who have now been delivered into the hands of the cruelest brutes that walk the earth. And all because they are Jews!

ANNE FRANK,
Anne Frank: The Diary of a Young Girl

PERSEVERANCE

To become a champion, fight one more round.

JAMES J. CORBETT,
quoted in *Irish Digest,* June 1954

Perseverance is not a long race; it is many short races one after another.

WALTER ELLIOTT,
The Spiritual Life

Before you begin a thing remind yourself that difficulties and delays quite impossible to foresee are ahead. If you could see them clearly, naturally you could do a great deal to get rid of them but you can't. You can only see one thing clearly and that is your goal. Form a mental vision of that and cling to it through thick and thin.

KATHLEEN NORRIS,
Hands Full of Living

The man who gives up accomplishes nothing and is only a hindrance. The man who does *not* give up can move mountains.

ERNEST HELLO,
Life, Science, and Art

The great thing and the hard thing is to stick to things when you have outlived the first interest, and not yet got the second which comes with a sort of mastery.

JANET ERSKINE STUART,
Life and Letters of Janet Erskine Stuart
by Maud Monahan

For me at least there came moments when faith wavered. But there is the great lesson and the great triumph if you keep the fire burning until, by and by, out of the mass of sordid details there comes some result, be it some new generalization or be it a

transcending spiritual repose.

OLIVER WENDELL HOLMES, JR.,
The Mind and Faith of Justice Holmes,
edited by Max Lerner

PERSONALITY

A cultivation of the powers of one's personality is one of the greatest needs of life, too little realized even in these assertive days, and the exercise of the personality makes for its most durable satisfactions.

RANDOLPH BOURNE,
Youth and Life

Personality is born out of pain. It is the fire shut up in the flint.

J. B. YEATS,
Letters to His Son, W. B. Yeats and Others

Personality to my mind is human nature when undergoing a passion for self-expression.

J. B. YEATS,
Letters to His Son, W. B. Yeats and Others

Man's main task in life is to give birth to himself, to become what he potentially is. The most important product of his effort is his own personality.

ERICH FROMM,
Man for Himself

How stupid it is to talk of a dual personality! You and I could tackle a dual personality. What we have to deal with is a multiple personality—an army of Jekylls and Hydes, Ormzuds and Ahrimans, all strangers within the gates of the mind.

JAMES DOUGLAS,
Down Shoe Lane

To confront with your personality all the other personalities of the earth.

WALT WHITMAN,
"A Song of Joys," *Leaves of Grass*

I once met at a sleepy boarding-house near the British Museum, in London, a weird, old sea-captain. ... He had never known, he assured me, anybody brave enough to go to a lonely place at night by himself, to call his own name out loud three times. Realizing one's own personality in that way, no matter how simple, he thought was beyond human endurance.

ERNEST DIMNET,
What We Live By

I think it is not well for any of us to allow another personality to submerge in any way our own.

OLIVE SCHREINER,
The Letters of Olive Schreiner

Perhaps, after all, personality reveals itself when we act not so much because of ourselves as by ourselves; when we are so interested in the thing we do, or the life we live, that self is forgotten.

HOLBROOK JACKSON,
Southward Ho! and Other Essays

I had to find out what was inside any one, and by any one I mean every one. I had to find out inside every one what was in them that was intrinsically exciting and I had to find out not by what they said, not by what they did, not by how much or how little they resembled any other one, but I had to find out by the intensity of movement that there was inside any one of them.

GERTRUDE STEIN,
quoted in *The Third Rose*
by John Malcolm Brinnin

Every man needs to develop the sides of his personality which he has neglected.

ALEXIS CARREL,
Reflections on Life

A man should not strive to eliminate his complexes but to get into accord with them: they are legitimately what directs his conduct in the world.

SIGMUND FREUD,
quoted in *The Life and Work of Sigmund Freud*, Vol. II, by Ernest Jones

Your letter reminded me that I am the same person who picked papyrus in Syracuse, had a scuffle with the railway staff in Naples, and bought antiques in Rome. The identity has been reestablished. It is strange how easily one gives in to the tendency to isolate parts of one's personality.

SIGMUND FREUD,
The Letters of Sigmund Freud

Any kindergarten recognition of the psychology of personality must force down our throats that in every family the most loving meddling with other people's personalities is still meddling and [is] rewarded as meddling always is, by frustration; wasteful, in that at that point the dignity of robust personality has been denied.

RUTH BENEDICT,
An Anthropologist at Work
by Margaret Mead

Yet, sometimes at night I get a feeling of claustrophobia; of being smothered by my own personality, of choking through being in the world. During these moments the universe seems a prison wherein I lie fettered by the chains of my senses and blinded through being myself. . . .

In those moments it seems that there must be a way out, and that through sloughing off the personality alone can it be taken.

CYRIL CONNOLLY,
The Unquiet Grave

To live is the rarest thing in the world. Most people exist. . . . Have we ever seen the full expression of a personality? . . . A perfect man is one who develops under perfect conditions; one who is not wounded, or worried, or maimed, or in danger. Most personalities have been obliged to be rebels. Half their strength has been wasted in friction . . . and these battles do not always intensify strength, they often exaggerate weakness. . . . The note of the perfect personality is not rebellion but peace.

OSCAR WILDE,
quoted in *The Note Books of a Woman Alone*,
edited by M. G. Ostle

Real personality is achieved only by dint of deliberate impersonality and by self-renunciation in the search for it, and an influence that is widespread and in that sense impersonal is acquired only by virtue of this personality.

HENRI DE LUBAC,
Paradoxes

It is by no means certain that our individual personality is the single inhabitant of these our corporeal frames. ... We all do things both awake and asleep which surprise us. Perhaps we have cotenants in this house we live in.

OLIVER WENDELL HOLMES,
The Guardian Angel

A man cannot get rid of himself in favor of an artificial personality without punishment. Even the attempt to do so brings on, in all ordinary cases, unconscious reactions in the form of bad moods, affects, phobias, compulsive ideas, backslidings, vices, etc.

C. G. JUNG,
Two Essays in Analytical Psychology

PERSUASION

If one word does not succeed, ten thousand are of no avail.

CHINESE PROVERB

To persuade is more trouble than to dominate, and the powerful seldom take this trouble if they can avoid it.

CHARLES HORTON COOLEY,
Life and the Student

The man who is easily persuaded finds himself discomfited later on.

BALTASAR GRACIAN,
The Oracle

I dearly love to persuade people. There can hardly be a greater pleasure (of a selfish kind) than to feel you have brought another person around to your way of thinking.

JAMES HINTON,
Life and Letters

PESSIMISM

Much pessimism is caused by ascribing to others the feelings you would feel if you were in their place.

W. SOMERSET MAUGHAM,
The Summing Up

The most prolific period of pessimism comes at twenty-one, or thereabouts, when the first attempt is made to translate dreams into reality.

HEYWOOD BROUN,
Pieces of Hate

The originator of a depressing mental view, mood, or idea is less permanently affected by its contemplation than are those who imbibe it from him at second hand. Jeremiah probably retired to rest at night and slept soundly long before the listeners to his fearful words closed their eyes, even though the miseries he spoke of would affect him no less than themselves.

THOMAS HARDY,
Thomas Hardy's Notebooks

There have always been many pessimists whenever there have been many people whose income has diminished.

BERTRAND RUSSELL,
The Conquest of Happiness

PHILOSOPHER

Philosophers may be divided into seers on the one hand, and into gropers on the other.

WALTER BAGEHOT,
Literary Studies, Vol. III

Philosophers fight like other men. ... They had rather thump an opponent than explain him; and quite right, too, and most fortunate for us outsiders, for a thump is clearer than an explanation.

FRANK MOORE COLBY,
The Colby Essays, Vol. 1

Language justly preserves the difference between the philosopher and sophist. It is no more possible to eliminate love and generation from the definition of the thinker than it is to eliminate thought and limits from the conception of the artist. It is interest, concern, caring, which makes the one as it makes the other.

JOHN DEWEY,
Characters and Events, Vol. I

Once philosophers have written their principal works, they not infrequently simply become their own disciples.

THEODOR HAECKER,
Journal in the Night

It is not easy for him to shout, or address a crowd: he must be silent for long seasons; for he is watching stars that move slowly and in courses that it is possible though difficult to foresee; and he is crushing all things in his heart as in a winepress until his life and their secret flow out together.

GEORGE SANTAYANA,
Character and Opinion in the United States

Positive gifts of imagination and moral heroism are requisite to make a great philosopher, gifts which come from the gods and not from circumstances.

GEORGE SANTAYANA,
Character and Opinion in the United States

If there is some deep and settled need in the heart of man, to give direction to his efforts, what else should a philosopher do but discover and announce what that need is?

GEORGE SANTAYANA,
Character and Opinion in the United States

No gentleman can be a philosopher and no philosopher a gentleman: To the philosopher everything is fluid—even himself. The gentleman is a little God over against the Cosmos.

OLIVER WENDELL HOLMES, JR.,
Holmes-Pollock Letters, Vol. II

None can call himself a philosopher whose own days are not made more intense and dramatic by his philosophizing. Even if his vision of things be bitter and grim, his world is made more interesting by his pondering upon it, not more commonplace or tedious.

JOHN COWPER POWYS,
The Meaning of Culture

A philosopher of imposing stature doesn't think in a vacuum. Even his most abstract ideas are, to some extent, conditioned by what is or is not known in the time when he lives.

ALFRED NORTH WHITEHEAD,
Dialogues of Alfred North Whitehead

PHILOSOPHY

About eleven o'clock we were out in the street walking along, and an American lady said, "How is it, Dr. Suzuki? We spend the evening asking you questions and nothing is decided." Dr. Suzuki smiled and said, "That's why I love philosophy: no one wins."

JOHN CAGE,
Silence

Every philosopher ... is inescapably a product of his own age and culture, and every philosophy is an historical phenomenon to be understood adequately only in its historical context.

THEODORE MEYER GREENE,
The Meaning of the Humanities

Philosophy is of a prophetic as well as historic spirit. Before facts emerge from the deep womb of Nature she knows and foretells their appearance.

BRONSON ALCOTT,
The Journals of Bronson Alcott

Everyone should study at least enough philosophy and *belles lettres* to make his sexual experience more delectable.

GEORG C. LICHTENBERG,
The Lichtenberg Reader

Philosophy which is "not harsh and crabbed as dull fools suppose, but musical as is Apollo's lute and a perpetual feast of nectared sweets" is born of like parentage with poetry.

J. B. YEATS,
Letters to His Son, W. B. Yeats and Others

It is strictly impossible to be a human being and not to have views of some kind about the universe at large, very difficult to be a human being and not to express those views, at any rate by implication.

ALDOUS HUXLEY,
Collected Essays

It is easy to disparage science, it is easy to laugh at philosophy. . . . Face to face with the supreme question concerning the right ordering of life they seem ludicrously insufficient. But, after all, science means only knowledge,—philosophy, only love of wisdom, only the essay at reaching the meaning of this experience of ours. I cannot believe that the attempt to know truth, to grasp the meaning of experience, is remote from conduct, from the ideals and aspirations of life.

> JOHN DEWEY,
> *Characters and Events,* Vol. I

Any genuine philosophy leads to action and from action back again to wonder, to the enduring fact of mystery.

> HENRY MILLER,
> *The Wisdom of the Heart*

There is an enormous need for philosophies to be rethought in the light of the changing conditions of mankind.

> ALFRED NORTH WHITEHEAD,
> *Dialogues of Alfred North Whitehead*

The very nature of a philosophy, to me, is speculative. It must be ever on the hunt.

> THOMAS WOLFE,
> *The Letters of Thomas Wolfe*

The hell with the philosophy of the great of this world! All eminent sages are as despotic as generals, as discourteous and lacking in delicacy as generals, because they know they are safe from punishment.

> ANTON CHEKHOV,
> *The Selected Letters of Anton Chekhov*

I can't take the teaching of philosophy seriously in itself, either as a means of being a philosopher or of teaching the young anything solid: they merely flirt with that for a year or two instead of flirting with something else.

> GEORGE SANTAYANA,
> *The Letters of George Santayana*

Some philosophers have imagined that to start an inquiry it was only necessary to utter a question, whether orally or by setting it down upon paper, and have even recommended to us to begin our studies with questioning everything! But the mere putting of a proposition into the interrogative form does not stimulate the mind to any struggle after belief. There must be a real and living doubt, and without this all discussion is idle.

> CHARLES SANDERS PEIRCE,
> *Collected Papers of Charles Sanders Peirce,*
> Vol. V

PHOTOGRAPH

A great photograph is a full expression of what one feels about what is being photographed in the deepest sense, and is, thereby, a true expression of what one feels about life in its entirety.

> ANSEL ADAMS,
> *Photographers on Photography,*
> edited by Nathan Lyons

A photograph is not an accident—it is a concept. It exists at, or before, the moment of exposure of the negative.

> ANSEL ADAMS,
> *Photographers on Photography,*
> edited by Nathan Lyons

It is the unexpected, hit-or-miss, instant impulse, these strange accidents, this surrealistic serendipity, out of which great photographs are born.

> CAROLYN KENMORE,
> *Mannequin: My Life as a Model*

I go back now, to Pennsylvania, and on one of the walls of the house in which my parents now live there hangs a photograph of myself as a boy. I am smiling and staring with clear eyes at something in the corner of the room. I stand before that photograph, and am disappointed to receive no flicker, not the shadow of a flicker, of approval, of gratitude. The boy continues to smile at the corner of the room, beyond me. That boy is not a ghost to me, he is real to me; it is I who am a ghost to him.

> JOHN UPDIKE,
> *Assorted Prose*

Every successful photograph, except for lucky shots, begins with an idea and a plan. The more precisely a photographer knows what it is he wishes to do, the better the chances are that he will do it.

ANDREAS FEININGER,
The Complete Photographer

Your desire to possess my photograph makes me express a similar request, which is probably easier to fulfill. I have not willingly sat for a photograph for fifteen years, because I am so vain I can't quite face the physical deterioration.

SIGMUND FREUD,
The Letters of Sigmund Freud (to C. G. Jung)

It must have happened to you now and again to have had the photograph of your friend's beloved produced for your inspection and opinion. It is a terrible moment. If she does happen to be a really pretty girl—heavens! What a relief. You praise her with almost hysterical gratitude.

RICHARD LE GALLIENNE,
Prose Fancies

The rarest thing in the world is a woman who is pleased with photographs of herself.

ELIZABETH METCALF,
Ladies' Home Journal, July 1946

Photographs have the kind of authority over imagination today, which the printed word had yesterday, and the spoken word before that. They seem utterly real. They come, we imagine, directly to us without human meddling, and they are the most effortless food for the mind conceivable.

WALTER LIPPMANN,
Public Opinion

I send you for your very own . . . one of the pictures I had to have taken to go on my passport. In some ways I think it is one of the most remarkable photographs I have ever seen,—no retouching, no shadows, no flattery—just stark me.

ANNE MORROW LINDBERGH,
Bring Me a Unicorn

PHOTOGRAPHY

I know personally several unusually creative photographers who have only the most rudimentary understanding of photographic techniques and who would not think of developing films or making prints.

ANDREAS FEININGER,
The Complete Photographer

As an amateur, you have an advantage over other photographers—you can do as you wish. You have no boss. No one to tell you what is wanted; nor to suggest how it might be done. This should make amateurs the happiest of photographers.

Unfortunately, this is rarely true. Very few amateurs realize their unique position and take advantage of it. Most of them are indecisive, lacking in both purpose and goal. To compensate for a lack of direction they look desperately for guidance.

ANDREAS FEININGER,
The Complete Photographer

I would like to be a photographer if the camera could work the way fingers work. I like to capture an instant. A picture is a one-second thing—it's a fragile moment in time. I try to do it with words.

ANNE SEXTON,
The Craft of Poetry,
edited by William Packard

It is very easy to say what is the least gratifying aspect of portrait photography, and that is when I have *not* been able to please a person with his own likeness, and I assure that in sixty-nine years I have a great collection.

IMOGEN CUNNINGHAM,
Open Secrets by Barbaralee Diamonstein

The possibilities of natural light are so infinitely great they can never be exhausted. In a lifetime you could hardly exhaust all the light-possibilities for a single subject.

EDWARD WESTON,
quoted in *The Amateur Photographer's Handbook* by Aaron Sussman

I have often thought that if photography were *difficult* in the true sense of the term—meaning that the creation of a simple photograph would entail as much time and effort as the production of a good water-color or etching—there would be a vast improvement in total output. The sheer ease with which we can produce a superficial image often leads to creative disaster.

ANSEL ADAMS,
Photographers on Photography,
edited by Nathan Lyons

The beauty of a photograph by Weston does not lie in the assortment of facts about negative, material, papers, developers—it lies in the realization of his *vision.*

ANSEL ADAMS,
Photographers on Photography,
edited by Nathan Lyons

Among the things that I did was the photographing of a cup and saucer, a white cup and saucer on a white ground, with what photographers call a gray scale in front of it.

I photographed that throughout one entire summer. When the summer was over, just for the heck of it, I started counting the negatives. When I got to a thousand, I stopped counting. ... The knowledge I gained of photography then became like something in my bloodstream.

EDWARD STEICHEN,
Wisdom, edited by James Nelson

The thing that makes photography wonderful is, if the photographer succeeds in getting his models—I am talking about studio work now—to forget themselves for an instant and be themselves—forget the camera situation for an instant.

EDWARD STEICHEN,
Wisdom, edited by James Nelson

Pick up any magazine. Turn on your TV set. So often the picture is a fancy side-stepping of excitement rather than involvement. You don't send an assault team out to capture a delicate emotion. Photography will be destroyed if it continues in its present state of superficiality.

W. EUGENE SMITH,
quoted in the *New York Times,*
February 15, 1971

PABLO PICASSO

As soon as Picasso was back in Paris he painted in the head of Gertrude Stein before seeing her and presented her with the portrait. ... Nobody liked the picture except the painter and the painted and there are many anecdotes about it, including that of Picasso's answer, when somebody said Gertrude Stein did not look like the painting, "Never mind, she will."

ELIZABETH SPRIGGE,
Gertrude Stein: Her Life and Her Work

PITY

Justice seeks out the merits of the case, but pity only regards the need.

SAINT BERNARD OF CLAIRVAUX,
Letters

Men may pity others under exquisite torment, when yet they would have been grieved if they had seen their prosperity.

JONATHAN EDWARDS,
The Nature of True Virtue

I seem to be the only person in the world who doesn't mind being pitied. If you love me, pity me. The human state is pitiable: born to die, capable of so much, accomplishing so little; killing instead of creating, destroying instead of building, hating instead of loving. Pitiful, pitiful.

JESSAMYN WEST,
Hide and Seek

Verily, I like them not, the merciful ones, whose bliss is in their pity: too destitute are they of bashfulness.

FRIEDRICH NIETZSCHE,
Thus Spake Zarathustra

But pity is not love. ... Pity is only pity.

J. B. YEATS,
Letters to His Son, W. B. Yeats and Others

Why does the struggle to come at truth take away our pity, and the struggle to overcome our passions restore it again?

W. B. YEATS,
Autobiography

PLACE

It is difficult to return to the places of one's early happiness. The young girls in the flower of their youth still laugh and chatter on the seashore, but he who watches them gradually loses his right to love them, just as those he loved lose the power to be loved.

ALBERT CAMUS,
The Rebel

Deterioration is contagious, and places are destroyed or renovated by the spirit of the people who go to them.

HOLBROOK JACKSON,
Southward Ho! and Other Essays

You can fall in love at first sight with a place as with a person.

ALEC WAUGH,
Hot Countries

All that most of us can know about any place, or portion of space, that we pass through is that it stirs in us some emotion or other, which we have no means of comparing closely with any emotion in any one else. The moment that we attempt to describe it, we offer something which may be descriptive of it, but is more certainly descriptive of ourselves.

C. E. MONTAGUE,
The Right Place

How hard it is to escape from places. However carefully one goes they hold you—you leave little bits of yourself fluttering on the fences—little rags and shreds of your very life.

KATHERINE MANSFIELD,
quoted in *Katherine Mansfield Memories of L M*

The spot of ground on which a man has stood is forever interesting to him.

ALEXANDER SMITH,
Dreamthorp

Some places speak distinctly. Certain dank gardens cry aloud for a murder; certain old houses demand to be haunted; certain coasts are set apart for shipwrecks.

ROBERT LOUIS STEVENSON,
quoted in *Reader's Digest*, January 1935

PLAGIARISM

Everyone is a thief in his own craft.

DUTCH PROVERB

PLAN

Plans—as if it were any use to have "plans" in such an unaccountable world as this! There are no plans any more—only events.

GEORGE E. WOODBERRY,
Selected Letters of George Edward Woodberry

Thinking always ahead, thinking always of trying to do more, brings a state of mind in which nothing seems impossible.

HENRY FORD,
365 of Henry Ford's Sayings

One cannot plan too carefully, but it is well to do this disinterestedly, as if you were planning for someone else, not committing yourself to execution nor drawing in advance upon that fund of emotion which you will need when you come to act. There are no such wastes as those of the anticipative imagination.

CHARLES HORTON COOLEY,
Life and the Student

PLANT

We go into the woods and bring out wild flowers, taking them up by the roots, the soil clinging. We bring them here to plant on our creek bank. Some will live, some die.

You get the notion of pain, of death in plants. It gets down into your own being.

SHERWOOD ANDERSON,
Letters of Sherwood Anderson

I remember my consternation at Cuverville, when pruning and cleaning out a peony plant, I noticed that a branch I had just removed because it seemed to me dead was still full of sap.

ANDRÉ GIDE,
The Journals of André Gide, Vol. I

Plants stand so patiently in the fields that we are accustomed to think that they are calm and immovable, whereas there is a feverish activity going on at all times.

ALFRED CARL HOTTES,
Garden Facts and Fancies

Today there breathes no man who can master more than a little portion of the plant world.... Sir Joseph Dalton Hooker, in his prime, could recognize on sight ten thousand species, because he had collected and identified everywhere.... A fair-to-middling student is glad to recognize on sight two thousand kinds of plants, and he easily goes rusty without constant practice.

DONALD CULROSS PEATTIE,
The Flowering Earth

PLATITUDE

A man who has the courage of his platitudes is always a successful man.

VAN WYCK BROOKS,
A Chilmark Miscellany

It is strange how we rebel against a platitude until suddenly in a different lingo it looms up again as the only verity.

RUTH BENEDICT,
An Anthropologist at Work
by Margaret Mead

The nearest approach to immortality for any truth is by its becoming a platitude.

PAUL ELDRIDGE,
Horns of Glass

The objection to most platitudes is not that they are obvious but that they are dishonest—that they pretend to be the expression of far deeper thought and experience than they are.

ROBERT LYND,
Solomon in All His Glory

Platitudes are, after all, only the neat packing of good sense so that it can be carried about: they are useless, like a portmanteau, until you put your own key to them; then by them you live and work.

STEPHEN MACKENNA,
Journal and Letters of Stephen Mackenna

PLAY

All work and no play dulls me. Company is not play, but many times hard work. To play, is for a man to do what he pleases, or to do nothing—to go about soothing his particular fancies.

CHARLES LAMB,
The Letters of Charles and Mary Lamb

Posing so purposefully to project breasts or buttocks, the last thing *Playboy's* playmates look is playful. Sex, it would seem, is a serious business, and there is no time for kidding around.

BRENDAN FRANCIS

Man only plays when in the full meaning of the word he is a man, and he is only completely a man when he plays.

J. C. F. SCHILLER,
quoted in *Life Against Death*
by Norman O. Brown

Play can easily vanish when people have to strain for competence.

DAVID RIESMAN,
The Lonely Crowd

We live to play: that is my slogan, under which we shall set about the real things of life, and be as busy, and in the same spirit, as is nature on a morning in spring.... We shall live proudly and exultingly and die in the same mood; so much interested in other things that we are no longer interested in ourselves.

J. B. YEATS,
Letters to His Son, W. B. Yeats and Others

When we are full of life, when each sense overflows with vitality, then we become prodigal, we scatter ourselves broadcast, we take chances, risk great odds, love, laugh, dance, write poems, paint pictures, romp with children; in short, we play. It is only the impotent who do not play. The people who play are the creators.

HOLBROOK JACKSON,
Southward Ho! and Other Essays

PLEASURE

It is nonsense to speak of "higher" and "lower" pleasures. To a hungry man it is, rightly, more important that he eat than that he philosophize.

W. H. AUDEN,
A Certain World

It's all right to have a good time. That's one of the most important messages of enlightenment.

THADDEUS GOLAS,
The Lazy Man's Guide to Enlightenment

Our pleasures are not lost, nor do they disappear; in another way, they mark us as much as our pains. The one among them which seemed to have vanished forever will save us from a crisis, will plead, unknown to us, against one of our disappointments, against some temptation to abdicate, to surrender.

E. M. CIORAN,
The Temptation to Exist

A sense of wrongdoing is an enhancement of pleasure.

OLIVER WENDELL HOLMES, JR.,
Holmes-Laski Letters

And now the innocent pleasures of life. One must admit they have but one fault, they are so innocent.

SØREN KIERKEGAARD,
Either/Or, Vol. I

Most men pursue pleasure with such breathless haste that they hurry past it.

SØREN KIERKEGAARD,
Either/Or, Vol. I

Whatever the formula, nothing can be more tiresome than the tireless, cheerless pursuit of pleasure.

ERNEST VAN DEN HAAG,
Man Alone,
edited by Eric Josephson
and Mary Josephson

I take it as a prime cause of the present confusion of society that it is too sickly and too doubtful to use pleasure frankly as a test of value.

REBECCA WEST,
quoted in *A Psychiatrist's World*
by Dr. Karl Menninger

Anxiety and remorse are the results of failing to advance spiritually. For this reason they follow close on pleasure, which is not necessarily harmful, but which, since it does not bring advancement with it, outrages that part of us which is concerned with growth. Such ways of making time fly past as chess, bridge, drink and motoring accumulate guilt.

CYRIL CONNOLLY,
The Unquiet Grave

There is something self-defeating in the too conscious pursuit of pleasure.

MAX EASTMAN,
Enjoyment of Living

Whenever you are sincerely pleased, you are nourished.

RALPH WALDO EMERSON,
"Considerations by the Way,"
Conduct of Life

I have finished my novel. What am I to do? ... There is pleasure, of course, but I like it only when it is stolen from my hours of work. When it is just a way of filling in leisure, it no longer amuses me.

JULIAN GREEN,
Julian Green: Diary 1928–1957

POET

If a poet demanded from the State the right to have a few bourgeois in his stable, people would be very much astonished, but if a bourgeois asked for some roast poet, people would think it quite natural.

CHARLES BAUDELAIRE,
Intimate Journals

I was in London last week, and read some poems to night-students of the university. I didn't like the people at all; some looked like lemons, and all spoke with the voices of puddings.

DYLAN THOMAS,
Letters to Vernon Watkins

A poet is one who endeavours to make the worst of both worlds. For he is thought seldom to make provision for himself in the next life, and 'tis odds if he gets any in this.

FRANCIS THOMPSON,
Works, Vol. III

You know, a fellow who has never written a line that anybody remembers is a woeful person, isn't he? Because poems are made up of lines; we remember some lines and not others.

MARK VAN DOREN,
*The Dialogues of Archibald MacLeish
and Mark Van Doren*

I wrote today to Laura Riding, with whom I carry on a slight correspondence, that her school was too thoughtful, reasonable & truthful, that poets were good liars who never forgot that the Muses were women who liked the embrace of gay warty lads. I wonder if she knows that warts are considered by the Irish peasantry a sign of sexual power?

> W. B. YEATS,
> *Letters on Poetry*
> *from W. B. Yeats to Dorothy Wellesley*

Two hours' idleness—because I have no excuse but to begin creative work, an intolerable toil. Little Sarojini of Hyderabad told me that in her father's garden one met an opium-eater who made poems in his dreams and wrote the title-pages when he awoke but forgot the rest. He was the only happy poet.

> W. B. YEATS,
> quoted in *W. B. Yeats Memoirs*,
> edited by Denis Donaghue

The tongue of the poet is always the last to be corrupted.

> ITALIAN PROVERB

Biographers of frail, unhappy poets are apt to harrow us up unnecessarily, for life is still strong in a man if he can curse his days beautifully, and a good deal of pleasure has gone into the making of some very sad songs. Moreover, if you really shattered a good poet you would get out of him no melancholy music whatever, but sounds more nearly resembling a leading article in the London *Times*.

> FRANK MOORE COLBY,
> *The Colby Essays*, Vol. 2

Irresponsible poets who simulate inspiration trample down the flower of language as brutally as politician and journalist, with their slovenliness, blunt and enfeeble the common run of words.

> CYRIL CONNOLLY,
> *The Unquiet Grave*

Not to be second-rate is the poet's most private prayer.

> JOHN HOLMES,
> *The Poet's Work*

How willingly I would as a poet exchange some of this lumbering, ponderous, helpless knowledge of books for some experience of life and man.... But all this grumbling is a vile thing.

> ELIZABETH BARRETT BROWNING,
> quoted in *Ladies of Literature*
> by Laura L. Hinkley

If your daily life seems poor, do not blame it; blame yourself, tell yourself that you are not poet enough to call forth its riches; for to the creator there is no poverty and no poor indifferent place.

> RAINER MARIA RILKE,
> *Letters to a Young Poet*

Your favorite poem is always the one you just wrote.

> ERICA JONG,
> *The Craft of Poetry*,
> edited by William Packard

I was always lucky to have a couple of teachers who knew where I was going. And who encouraged me when my poetry began to take the inner direction. Mark Strand, for example, said at one point, when I showed him my early poems, "You haven't really been fucked by poetry yet." I don't know if he would remember having used that phrase, but I've never forgotten it.

> ERICA JONG,
> *The Craft of Poetry*,
> edited by William Packard

The poet is trying honestly and exactly to describe a world that has perhaps no existence for one particular person at one particular moment. And the more sincere he is in keeping to the precise outline of the roses and cabbages of his private universe, the more he puzzles us who have agreed in a lazy spirit of compromise to see roses and cabbages as they are seen, more or less, by the twenty-six passengers on the outside of an omnibus.

> VIRGINIA WOOLF,
> *A Letter to a Young Poet*

Poets don't seem to have fun any more. What troubles me more than anything else these days is to see the seriousness with which they approach everything.

BLAISE CENDRARS,
Writers at Work, Third Series,
edited by George Plimpton

No honest poet can ever feel quite sure of the permanent value of what he has written: he may have wasted his time and messed up his life for nothing.

T. S. ELIOT,
The Writer on His Art,
edited by Walter Allen

The poet's voice need not merely be the record of man, it can be one of the props, the pillars to help him endure and prevail.

WILLIAM FAULKNER,
"Man Will Prevail," *The Faulkner Reader*

I like punctuation very much. It is breathing. I had a rubber stamp made—"Please believe the punctuation." I have needed that very much in dealing with printers. It has saved me a great deal of everything.

MURIEL RUKEYSER,
The Craft of Poetry,
edited by William Packard

The act of composition is not one of communication between the poet and his public but an intercommunication of different selves within him.

ROBERT GRAVES,
The Common Asphodel

The poet produces the beautiful by fixing his attention on something real.

SIMONE WEIL,
Gravity and Grace

It is the poet who lives locally, and whose senses are applied no way else than locally to particulars, who is the agent and the maker of all culture. It is the poet's job and the poet lives on the job, on the location.

WILLIAM CARLOS WILLIAMS,
Selected Letters of William Carlos Williams

POETRY

It would seem as if the most natural and fruitful impulse in the growth of a sensi-

tive mind, as far as poetry is concerned, is to plunge into a temporary obsession for one poet's style and one poet's vision, one after another.

JOHN COWPER POWYS,
The Meaning of Culture

In poetry everything which *must* be said is almost impossible to say well.

PAUL VALÉRY,
quoted in *A Certain World* by W. H. Auden

My trouble is that if I read modern poetry intently it disturbs my own verse.

W. B. YEATS,
*Letters on Poetry
from W. B. Yeats to Dorothy Wellesley*

When attempting to judge a poem I read it at three different times of day and in different moods--the melancholy, the heroic, the gay, the craven, the sluggish, the well-fed, the under-fed, the bitter.

W. B. YEATS,
*Letters on Poetry
from W. B. Yeats to Dorothy Wellesley*

The fear of poetry is an indication that we are cut off from our own reality.

MURIEL RUKEYSER,
The Life of Poetry

Of course "The Night Before" is purely objective, and may be called anything from pessimism to rot. I must confess that I haven't the slightest idea whether it is good for anything or not. I printed it to find out; but the opinions I have received are so conflicting that I am not much better off than I was before.

EDWIN ARLINGTON ROBINSON,
Untriangulated Stars

Poetry too readily understood is commonly dispensed with altogether, like conversation after marriage.

FRANK MOORE COLBY,
The Colby Essays, Vol. 2

Every force in the world which today presses with threats against poetry, tomorrow threatens any prose which, by reasons of intensity and integrity, is comparable to it.

JOHN PEALE BISHOP,
The Collected Essays of John Peale Bishop

Carlyle once said of Tennyson: "Alfred is always carrying a bit of chaos around with him, and turning it into a cosmos." Well, that is poetry's job, and it is amazingly like the enterprise of life.

JOHN LIVINGSTONE LOWES,
Convention and Revolt in Poetry

Most people do not believe in anything very much and our greatest poetry is given to us by those who do.

CYRIL CONNOLLY,
quoted in *The Making of a Poem*
by Stephen Spender

I think one likes to feel as one reads a poem that the world is shut out and that the world will end when the poem is completed.

OSCAR W. FIRKINS,
quoted in *Inward Ho*
by Christopher Morley

I hearken to my poems that still want to go into the *Book of Pictures*. Slowly I listen to each one and let it die away into its farthest echo. Few will stand up in the stillness in which I place them, several will recast themselves, of many only a piece will be left and will wait until, one day perhaps, something joins it.

RAINER MARIA RILKE,
Letters of Rainer Maria Rilke 1892–1910

The briefest poem may contain a sort of philosophic scheme of the entire creation.

JOSIAH ROYCE,
The Spirit of Modern Philosophy

Poetry is innocent, not wise. It does not learn from experience, because each poetic experience is unique.

KARL SHAPIRO,
Beyond Criticism

Poetry ought to make one live, in one's own way, and these poems, like all your poems, make me live in my own way.

EDITH SITWELL,
Edith Sitwell: Selected Letters 1916–1964

I have to pull myself together, and get my notes on poetry ready for the publishers. It is a terrific job, because some are rather abstruse—or would be to persons who do not habitually read poetry. They seem to me clear as daylight, but the publishers always want one to explain the unexplainable.

EDITH SITWELL,
Edith Sitwell: Selected Letters 1916–1964

I believe we are all asses (I first and foremost) when we publish our poems. Yet the doing so eases our souls—for some inscrutable reason; and if we can afford the consolation, and expect nothing from the public in return for our gifts, I suppose there is no reason to be urged against it.

JOHN ADDINGTON SYMONDS,
Letters and Papers of John Addington Symonds

POLICE

The dependence of the average citizen on the police is evident daily. Let almost anything happen that is out of the ordinary and their first reaction is "Call a cop!"

BURR W. LEYSON,
Fighting Crime

There is no question that the police are misunderstood, looked down upon, unfairly treated, ridiculed, criticized, overburdened, underestimated, and generally given a bad go of it in America.

DR. KARL MENNINGER,
A Psychiatrist's World

The policeman on post is in all truth the court of first instance; he is a *de facto* judge just as truly as any ermined magistrate, and a wise policeman can be guide, philosopher and friend as he carries on his daily, hourly court.

ARTHUR WOODS
(former Police Commissioner
of New York City),
Policeman and Public

The police cannot give efficient service unless they are backed up by their superior officers and know that their conscientious efforts will receive the hearty and earnest cooperation of the magistrates and judges.

JOHN F. HYLAN
Remarks of the mayor at a dinner-conference of the law-enforcing departments of the City of New York, October 6, 1920

I recall once in South America that I complained to the police that a camera had been stolen and they ended up arresting me. I hadn't registered or something. In other words, once you get them on the scene they really start nosing around. Once the law starts asking questions, there's no stopping them.

WILLIAM BURROUGHS,
Writers at Work, Third Series,
edited by George Plimpton

No police department can remain free of corruption in a community where bribery flourishes in public office and private enterprise; a corrupt police department in an otherwise corruption-free society is a contradiction in terms.

ORLANDO W. WILSON,
quoted in *The Trouble with Cops*
by Albert Deutsch

POLITICIAN

The pleasure politicians take in their limelight pleases me with a sort of pleasure I get when I see a child's eyes gleam over a new toy.

HILAIRE BELLOC,
A Conversation with a Cat

The politician is now assailed by half a dozen competing interests within his own state or region; and his party affiliation, his own political philosophy, may give him no help in making up his mind as to what is going to be good for the public and even for himself.

D. W. BROGAN,
The American Character

Politicians speak for their parties, and parties never are, never have been, never will be wrong.

WALTER DWIGHT,
The Saving Sense

The professional politician is one of the mysteries of American life, a bundle of paradoxes, shrewd as a fox, naïve as a schoolboy. He has great respect for the people yet treats them like boobs, and is constitutionally unable to keep his mouth shut.

JAMES RESTON,
New York Times, October 2, 1955

If we meet an honest and intelligent politician, a dozen, a hundred, we say they aren't like politicians at all, and our category of politicians stays unchanged; we know what politicians are like.

RANDALL JARRELL,
Mademoiselle,

I'll tell you what I really think about politicians. The other night I watched some politicians on television talking about Viet Nam. I wanted very much to burst through the screen with a flame thrower and burn their eyes out and their balls off and then inquire from them how they would assess this action from a political point of view.

HAROLD PINTER,
Writers at Work, Third Series,
edited by George Plimpton

The professional politician woos the fickle public more as a man engaged than married, for his is a contract that must be renewed every few years, and the memory of the public is short.

J. T. SALTER,
Boss Rule

Of course, in my country most political leaders are really, well, I suppose I think of them as being, well, not gangsters but more or less the same kind of thing, no? I mean—people who go in for getting elected. What can you expect of a man like that?

JORGE LUIS BORGES,
quoted in the *New York Times,*
April 6, 1971

Politicians, like prostitutes, are held in contempt, but what man does not run to them when he requires their services?

BRENDAN FRANCIS

Politics unfortunately abounds in shams that must be treated reverentially by every politician who would succeed. If you are the sort of man whose stomach revolts against treating shams reverentially, you will be well advised to stay out of politics altogether and set up as a prophet: your prophecies may perhaps sow some good for some future harvest. But as a politician you would be impotent. ... A wise politician will never grudge a genuflexion or a rapture if it is expected of him by the prevalent opinion.

F. S. OLIVER,
Politics and Politicians

To the politician we are something of a dark horse. He does not know what we want; he wishes he did. Do we know ourselves? Vaguely we know that we don't want the politician.

ROSE MACAULAY,
A Casual Commentary

POLITICS

Politics, and the fate of mankind, are shaped by men without ideals and without greatness. Men who have greatness within them don't go in for politics.

ALBERT CAMUS,
Notebooks 1935–1942

Politically, what we need is government in which a man offers himself as a candidate because he has a new program that he wants to effectuate, and we choose him because we want that good, and judge that he is the best man to effectuate it.

PAUL GOODMAN,
Growing Up Absurd

Our national politics has become a competition for images or between images, rather than between ideals.

DANIEL J. BOORSTIN,
The Image

The disagreement among American political parties, with only a few exceptions, has been over the practical question of how to secure the agreed objective, while conciliating different interests, rather than over ultimate values or over what interest is paramount.

DANIEL J. BOORSTIN,
The Genius of American Politics

The excitement of politics got into my veins. ... I knew how to say "no," but seldom could bring myself to say it. A woman and a politician must say that word often, and mean it—or else.

JAMES J. WALKER,
quoted in *Beau James* by Gene Fowler

All the politics-as-usual of today seems so terribly antiquated; it lags so sadly behind the actual situation of man—and behind even our present knowledge of man.

WILLIAM BARRETT,
Irrational Man

It was but the other day that a man sent me a letter asking what matter one should put into a political speech. To which I answered, having an expert knowledge in this, that the whole art of a political speech is to put *nothing* into it. It is much more difficult than it sounds.

HILAIRE BELLOC,
A Conversation with an Angel

Politics are like a labyrinth, from the inner intricacies of which it is even more difficult to find the way of escape, than it was to find the way into them.

WILLIAM E. GLADSTONE,
quoted in "Politics," *Encyclopedia of Social Sciences*

American politics is not, as is that of Europe, "a prelude to civil war"; it cannot become either entirely irresponsible or entirely dogmatic; and it must not try to be logical. It is a rocking sea of checks and balances in which uncompromising absolutes must drown.

ERIK H. ERIKSON,
Childhood and Society

The media, far from being a conspiracy to dull the political sense of the people, could be viewed as a conspiracy to disguise the extent of political indifference.

DAVID RIESMAN,
The Lonely Crowd

Political language—and with variations this is true of all political parties, from Conservatives to Anarchists—is designed to make lies sound truthful, and to give an appearance of solidity to pure wind.

GEORGE ORWELL,
A Collection of Essays

If the conscience of an honest man lays down stern rules, so also does the art of politics.

F. S. OLIVER,
Politics and Politicians

With all the temptations and degradations that beset it, politics is still the noblest career that any man can choose.

F. S. OLIVER,
Politics and Politicians

There are no political panaceas, except in the imagination of political quacks.

FRANCIS PARKMAN,
Francis Parkman: Representative Selections,
edited by Wilbur L. Schramm

Those of you who regard my profession of political life with some disdain should remember that it made it possible for me to move from being an obscure lieutenant in the United States Navy to Commander-in-Chief in fourteen years with very little technical competence.

JOHN F. KENNEDY,
The Kennedy Wit, edited by Bill Adler

My observation about politics in many countries is that its practitioners fall into these two groups. The boys in politics are those individuals who want position in order to *be* something; the men are those who want position in order to *do* something.

ERIC SEVAREID,
Candidates 1960

The attempt to turn a complex problem of the head into a simple moral question for the heart to answer, is of course a necessary part of all political discussions.

FRANK MOORE COLBY,
The Colby Essays, Vol. 2

It may turn out eventually that men and women have similar degrees of aggressiveness, but for the next fifty years or so, until the sex roles are humanized and reformed,

women will be a good and peaceful influence in politics.

GLORIA STEINEM,
Open Secrets by Barbaralee Diamonstein

PORNOGRAPHY

An individual's becoming aroused by perusing or reading pornographic sex material is certainly one of the most common of all sex acts; and, in our puritanical society, which places a premium on open displays of sexuality precisely by banning them, any person who shows a reasonable degree of interest in pornographic representations is certainly normal and non-deviated.

ALBERT ELLIS,
The Art and Science of Love

Pornography is a malady to be diagnosed and an occasion for judgment. It's something one is for or against. And taking sides about pornography is hardly like being for or against aleatoric music or Pop Art, but quite a bit like being for or against legalized abortion or federal aid to parochial schools.

SUSAN SONTAG,
Perspectives on Pornography,
edited by Douglas A. Hughes

What pornographic literature does is precisely to drive a wedge between one's existence as a full human being and one's existence as a sexual being—while in ordinary life one hopes to prevent such a wedge from being driven. Normally we don't experience, at least don't want to experience, our sexual fulfillment as distinct from or opposed to our personal fulfillment. But perhaps in part they are distinct, whether we like it or not.

SUSAN SONTAG,
Perspectives on Pornography,
edited by Douglas A. Hughes

If all the men who enjoy pornography were to "come out of the closet," there'd be no males, under ten, left in the house.

BRENDAN FRANCIS

It'll be a sad day for sexual liberation

when the pornography addict has to settle for the real thing.

BRENDAN FRANCIS

I mean: what's wrong with a naked body that you shouldn't look at a photograph of one? You deceive yourself, I used to say to myself—you're just pretending; you only want such things to gloat over them. No, but honestly, I used to reply to myself, it's true, it's true—those things *are* good things and suppose I am gloating, well, what's wrong with gloating if it comes to that? Can't I do a bit of gloating without going to the devil?

ERIC GILL,
Autobiography

It seems that every epoch and society has the pornography which it deserves. If much of what meets the eye on the American or Western world (including the European) market of "hard core obscenity" is artistically worthless and often aesthetically offensive, we may have to look for the causes of this in our censorial, sex-suppressive attitudes.

DRS. EBERHARD and
PHYLLIS KRONHAUSEN,
Pornography and the Law

POSSESSION

The American does not enjoy his possessions because sensory enjoyment was not his object, and he lives sparely and thinly among them, in the monastic discipline of Scarsdale or the barracks of Stuyvesant Town. Only among certain groups where franchise, socially speaking, has not been achieved, do pleasure and material splendor constitute a life-object and an occupation.

MARY McCARTHY,
On the Contrary

What she dreaded was to be possessed and still excluded.

ROBERT SPEAIGHT,
The Unbroken Heart

Possession kills desire; realization slays fantasy and transforms the wonderful into the commonplace.

DR. WILHELM STEKHEL,
The Depths of the Soul

I don't care much for furniture, for tables and chairs and lamps and rugs and things—perhaps because in my opulent childhood I was taught to regard with amused contempt any too-earnest attachment to material wealth, which is why I felt no regret and no bitterness when the Revolution abolished that wealth.

VLADIMIR NABOKOV,
Strong Opinions

There is no doubt that the acquisitive impulse is especially damaging to human felicity. As soon as it becomes a predominating obsession, evil and misery are everywhere present.

LLEWELYN POWYS,
Earth Memories

To pretend to satisfy one's desires by possession is like using straw to put out a fire.

CHINESE PROVERB

The pleasure of possession, whether we possess trinkets or offspring—or possibly books, or chessmen, or postage stamps—lies in showing these things to friends who are experiencing no immediate urge to look at them.

AGNES REPPLIER,
Times and Tendencies

To accumulate possessions is to deliver pieces of oneself to dead things. Possessions can absorb an emotional cathexis, but unlike personal relationships they feed nothing back.

PHILIP SLATER,
The Pursuit of Loneliness

All that we possess is qualified by what we are.

JOHN LANCASTER SPALDING,
Education and the Higher Life

One ought never to buy anything except with love. Anyone whatever, anything whatsoever, ought to belong to the person who loves it best.

ANDRÉ GIDE.
The Journals of André Gide, Vol. I

Love like that is so rare in the world to-day; all ties except the ties of material possessions seem to have grown so brittle.

ELLEN GLASGOW,
Letters of Ellen Glasgow

So often we think in a superior and lordly manner of our possessions, when, as a matter of fact, we do not really possess them, they possess us.

DAVID GRAYSON,
The Friendly Road

A man can hope for satisfaction and fulfillment only in what he does not yet possess; he cannot find pleasure in something of which he has already too much.

C. G. JUNG,
Modern Man in Search of a Soul

POSSIBILITY

Might-have-beens can never be measured or verified; and yet sometimes it cannot be doubted that possibilities never realized were actual possibilities once.

HENRY JAMES,
Introduction,
The Letters of William James, Vol. II

I cannot discover that anyone knows enough to say definitely what is and what is not possible.

HENRY FORD,
365 of Henry Ford's Sayings

To my mind, the possible and the future are one. I believe that all that is possible is striving to come into being; and all that can will be, if man helps.

ANDRÉ GIDE,
The Fruits of the Earth

A guy goes on a rampage. Kills a dozen people. His neighbors say, "I can't believe it! He was such a nice man." True, but he had other possibilities, and revealed one of them.

BRENDAN FRANCIS

People are so apt to think that there are but two ways in which a thing can terminate. They are ignorant of the number of combinations which even a few circumstances admit of.

SIR ARTHUR HELPS,
Essays Written in Intervals of Business

What may be may not be.

SCOTCH PROVERB

What after all has maintained the human race on this old globe despite all the calamities of nature and all the tragic failings of mankind, if not faith in new possibilities and courage to advocate them?

JANE ADDAMS,
Jane Addams Speaks,
compiled by Leonard S. Kenworthy

Of all the inventions of casuistry with which man for ages has in various ways manacled himself, and stayed his own advance, there is none equally potent with the supposition that nothing more is possible.... It is the most deadly—the most fatal poison of the mind.

RICHARD JEFFERIES,
The Story of My Heart

If I were to wish for anything, I should not wish for wealth and power, but for the passionate sense of the potential, for the eye which, ever young and ardent, sees the possible. Pleasure disappoints, possibility never. And what wine is so sparkling, what so fragrant, what so intoxicating, as possibility!

SØREN KIERKEGAARD,
Either/Or, Vol. I

Our minds are finite, and yet even in these circumstances of finitude we are surrounded by possibilities that are finite, and the purpose of human life is to grasp as much as we can out of that infinitude. I wish I could convey this sense I have of the infinity of the possibilities that confront humanity—the limitless variations of choice, the possibility of novel and untried combinations, the happy turns of experiment, the endless horizons opening out.

ALFRED NORTH WHITEHEAD,
Dialogues of Alfred North Whitehead

POSTERITY

Posterity is as likely to be wrong as anybody else.
HEYWOOD BROUN,
Collected Edition of Heywood Broun

People often speak of correcting the judgment of the time by that of posterity. I think it is quite as true to say that we must correct the judgment of posterity by that of the time.
OLIVER WENDELL HOLMES, JR.,
The Mind and Faith of Justice Holmes,
edited by Max Lerner

POVERTY

When the sea turned into honey, the poor man lost his spoon.
BULGARIAN PROVERB

That is one of the bitter curses of poverty; it leaves no right to be generous.
GEORGE GISSING,
The Private Papers of Henry Ryecroft

If a free society cannot help the many who are poor, it cannot save the few who are rich.
JOHN F. KENNEDY,
quoted in the *New York Times,*
January 21, 1961

They who have little are thought to have no right to anything.
JOHN LANCASTER SPALDING,
Means and Ends of Education

It is insulting to offer the consolations of philosophy to people who are cold and hungry. Food and coal are what they need.
ANDRÉ MAUROIS,
The Art of Living

Many a defect is seen in the poor man.
IRISH PROVERB

Poverty is an awful, eventually a degrading thing, and it is rare that anything good comes from it. We rise, old friend, in spite of adversity, not because of it.
THOMAS WOLFE,
The Letters of Thomas Wolfe

Clothes make the poor invisible too: America has the best-dressed poverty the world has ever known.... It is much easier in the United States to be decently dressed than it is to be decently housed, fed, or doctored. Even people with terribly depressed incomes can look prosperous.
MICHAEL HARRINGTON,
The Other America

It is a blow to reform and the political hopes of the poor that the middle class no longer understands that poverty exists. But, perhaps more important, the poor are losing their links with the great world.... They are not seen and because of that they themselves cannot see. Their horizon has become more and more restricted; they see one another, and that means they see little reason to hope.
MICHAEL HARRINGTON,
The Other America

Poverty humiliates because it argues incapacity: none so incapable as the poor.
JOSEPH RICKABY,
Waters That Go Softly

The shallow rich talk much of the turbulence of the poor and their tendency to agitate. It is the patience of the poor which most strikes those who know them.
J. A. SPENDER,
The Comments of Bagshot, Second Series

POWER

I love power. But it is as an artist that I love it. I love it as a musician loves his violin, to draw out its sounds and chords and harmonies. I love it as an artist.
NAPOLEON BONAPARTE,
quoted in *The Dance of Life*
by Havelock Ellis

Better to have a handful of might than a sack of justice.
CZECH PROVERB

It is so difficult, if you are made to stand out a bit from the mass, not to assure yourself that it is all due to some special virtue in yourself. All power of money or place therefore brings a kind of corruption almost inevitably.

SHERWOOD ANDERSON,
Letters of Sherwood Anderson

The only prize much cared for by the powerful is power. The prize of the general is not a bigger tent, but command.

OLIVER WENDELL HOLMES, JR.,
The Mind and Faith of Justice Holmes,
edited by Max Lerner

Life is action, the use of one's powers. As to use them to their height is our joy and duty, so it is the one end that justifies itself.

OLIVER WENDELL HOLMES, JR.,
The Mind and Faith of Justice Holmes,
edited by Max Lerner

The sense of power is an essential element in all pleasure, as consciousness of defeat is always painful.

JOHN LANCASTER SPALDING,
Things of the Mind

I have found power where people do not look for it, in simple, gentle and obliging men without the least desire to domineer—and conversely the inclination to domineer has often appeared to me as an inner sign of weakness; they fear the slavish soul and cast a king's mantle about it.

FRIEDRICH NIETZSCHE,
Thus Spake Zarathustra

PRAISE

When I was praised I lost my time, for instantly I turned around to look at the work I had thought slightly of, and that day I made nothing new.

RALPH WALDO EMERSON,
Journals of Ralph Waldo Emerson

What is the use of saying one is indifferent to reviews when positive praise, though mingled with blame, gives one such a start on, that instead of feeling dried up, one feels, on the contrary, flooded with ideas?

VIRGINIA WOOLF,
A Writer's Diary

I never yet knew a man so *blasé* that his face did not change when he heard that some action or creation of his had been praised; yes, even when that praise came from men most insignificant.

HILAIRE BELLOC,
The Silence of the Sea

If one man praises you, a thousand will repeat the praise.

JAPANESE PROVERB

I have always said that if I were a rich man I would employ a professional praiser.

SIR OSBERT SITWELL,
Wisdom, edited by James Nelson

It is essential to condemn what must be condemned, but swiftly and firmly. On the other hand, one should praise at length what still deserves to be praised. After all, that is why I am an artist, because even the work that negates still affirms something and does homage to the wretched and magnificent life that is ours.

ALBERT CAMUS,
Resistance, Rebellion, and Death

He who does without the praise of the crowd will not deny himself an opportunity to be his own adherent.

KARL KRAUS,
Karl Kraus by Harry Zohn

Most people like praise. . . . Many people have an unreasonable fear of administering it; it is part of the puritanical dislike for anything that is agreeable—to others. When it is really deserved, most people expand under it into richer and better selves.

JOSEPH FARRELL,
Lectures of a Certain Professor

Always when I see a man fond of praise I always think it is because he is an affectionate man craving for affection.

J. B. YEATS,
Letters to His Son, W. B. Yeats and Others

Imagine how delighted I am at receiving your post-card this morning, the first real *praise* that I have yet had for this work, and from such a quarter. . . . What my

friend Howison said is true: "What your genuine philosopher most craves is *praise*, rank, coarse praise."
WILLIAM JAMES,
The Thought and Character of William James
by Ralph Barton Perry

It's hard to focus the mind on praise, one thinks too much of the holes in the cheese or the slice of cheese, of the emptiness that goes with all good.
WILLIAM CARLOS WILLIAMS,
Selected Letters of William Carlos Williams

A man desires praise that he may be reassured, that he may be quit of his doubting of himself; he is indifferent to applause when he is confident of success.
ALEC WAUGH,
On Doing What One Likes

PRAYER

What I dislike least in my former self are the moments of prayer.
ANDRÉ GIDE,
The Journals of André Gide, Vol. I

I pray like a robber asking alms at the door of a farmhouse to which he is ready to set fire.
LEON BLOY,
quoted in *Rectitude*
by Antonin G. Sertillanges

Scream at God if that's the only thing that will get results.
BRENDAN FRANCIS

You pray in your distress and in your need; would that you might also pray in the fullness of your joy and in your days of abundance.
KAHLIL GIBRAN,
The Prophet

The exercise of prayer, in those who habitually exert it, must be regarded by us doctors as the most adequate and normal of all the pacifiers of the mind and calmers of the nerves.
WILLIAM JAMES,
"The Energies of Men,"
Essays on Faith and Morals

Ordinarily when a man in difficulty turns to prayer, he has already tried every other means of escape.
AUSTIN O'MALLEY,
Keystones of Thought

I am sure it is no easier to pray than it is to create music or write a poem; it must be as hard to do as it is to build a bridge, or to discover a great scientific principle, or to heal the sick, or to understand another human being. It is surely as important as these to man in his search for his role in the universal scheme of things.
LILLIAN SMITH,
The Journey

He who prays for his neighbors will be heard for himself.
TALMUD

I am used to praying when I am alone, thank God. But when I come together with other people, when I need more than ever to pray, I still cannot get used to it.
LEO TOLSTOY,
Last Diaries

Some people think that prayer just means asking for things, and if they fail to receive exactly what they asked for, they think the whole thing is a fraud.
GERALD VANN,
The Heart of Man

We, one and all of us, have an instinct to pray; and this fact constitutes an invitation from God to pray.
CHARLES SANDERS PEIRCE,
Collected Papers of Charles Sanders Peirce,
Vol. VI

Incense is prayer
That drives no bargain.
Child, learn from incense
How best to pray.
ALFRED BARRETT,
"Incense," *Mint by Night*

It is not well for a man to pray cream and live skim-milk.
HENRY WARD BEECHER,
quoted in *The Might and Mirth of Literature*
by John W. Macbeth

Our rages, daughters of despair, creep and squirm like worms. Prayer is the only form of revolt which remains upright.

GEORGES BERNANOS,
A Diary of My Times

Prayer always has an effect even if it is not the effect we desire.

ALEXIS CARREL,
Reflections on Life

PREACHING

That we should practise what we preach is generally admitted; but anyone who preaches what he and his hearers practise must incur the gravest moral disapprobation.

LOGAN PEARSALL SMITH,
Afterthoughts

In the long run, it is not what a preacher says in the pulpit, but what he thinks and feels in his daily, private hours that constitutes his real message to the world.

DR. FRANK CRANE,
Essays

It is very important to live your faith by confessing it, and one of the best ways to confess it is to preach it.

THOMAS MERTON,
The Sign of Jonas

Among provocatives, the next best thing to good preaching is bad preaching. I have even more thoughts during or enduring it than at other times.

RALPH WALDO EMERSON,
Journals of Ralph Waldo Emerson

Avoid showing, if you can help it, any sign of displeasure when you are preaching, or at least anger, as I did one day when they rang the bell before I had finished.

SAINT FRANCIS DE SALES,
Saint Francis de Sales in His Letters

PRECEDENT

If you're strong enough, there *are* no precedents.

F. SCOTT FITZGERALD,
The Crack-up

PREJUDICE

Prejudices subsist in people's imagination long after they have been destroyed by their experience.

ERNEST DIMNET,
What We Live By

We like to know where we are, and that depends upon our knowing where everybody else is.... A prejudice that we can allow for is much more dependable than a suspension of judgment that we cannot.

J. MIDDLETON MURRY,
Pencillings

Our prejudices are like physical infirmities—we cannot do what they prevent us from doing.

JOHN LANCASTER SPALDING,
Aphorisms and Reflections

PRESENT

Our faith in the present dies out long before our faith in the future.

RUTH BENEDICT,
An Anthropologist at Work
by Margaret Mead

If one cannot see any virtue in the present, at least one can firmly resolve never to put any mortgage on a future which may perhaps be more significant—never to allow any boredom to throw away a chance for friendship, nor any bitterness to wreck the carrying out of a plan one has reckoned good.

RUTH BENEDICT,
An Anthropologist at Work
by Margaret Mead

The present is always worse than the past; and why? Because our excitability has one specific quality: it quickly gives way to exhaustion.

ANTON CHEKHOV
The Selected Letters of Anton Chekhov

Man is formed to be a member of a social whole embracing not only the men of his lifetime but those past and to come. To live in the present only is as unnatural as to live in solitude.

CHARLES HORTON COOLEY,
Life and the Student

One's own time is always the obscurest epoch.

VAN WYCK BROOKS,
The Writer in America

There is something about the present which we would not exchange, though we were offered a choice of all past ages to live in.

VIRGINIA WOOLF,
The Common Reader, First Series

The present moment is significant, not as the bridge between past and future, but by reason of its contents, which can fill our emptiness and become ours, if we are capable of receiving them.

DAG HAMMARSKJÖLD,
Markings

I think that, as life is action and passion, it is required of a man that he should share the passion and action of his time at peril of being judged not to have lived.

OLIVER WENDELL HOLMES, JR.,
The Mind and Faith of Justice Holmes,
edited by Max Lerner

Work accomplished means little. It is in the past. What we all want is the glorious and living present.

SHERWOOD ANDERSON,
Letters of Sherwood Anderson

The vanishing, volatile froth of the Present, which any shadow will alter, any thought blow away, any event annihilate, is every moment converted into the Adamantine Record of the Past.

RALPH WALDO EMERSON,
Journals of Ralph Waldo Emerson

Do not let yourself be disturbed by what is to come; rather, be in that which is still around you and which enters with an immeasurable past into the present that is yours.

RAINER MARIA RILKE,
Letters of Rainer Maria Rilke 1892–1910

People do not live in the present always, at one with it. They live at all kinds of and manners of distance from it, as difficult to measure as the course of planets. Fears and traumas make their journeys slanted, peripheral, uneven, evasive.

ANAÏS NIN,
The Diaries of Anaïs Nin, Vol. IV

The less one is conscious of himself as the one who acts, that is, the more unfree and automatic he is, the less he will be aware of the immediate present.

ROLLO MAY,
Man's Search for Himself

As for the Present instant, it is so inscrutable that I wonder whether no sceptic has ever attacked its reality.

CHARLES SANDERS PEIRCE,
Collected Papers of Charles Sanders Peirce,
Vol. VI

The present moment is creative, creating with an unheard of intensity.

LE CORBUSIER,
When the Cathedrals Were White

PRESIDENCY

Sometimes I wish I just had a summer job here.

JOHN F. KENNEDY
(to students working in Washington),
The Kennedy Wit, edited by Bill Adler

There's some folks standing behind the President that ought to get around to where he can watch them.

KIN HUBBARD
Abe Martin on Things in General

Wisdom is essential in a President, the appearance of wisdom will do in a candidate.

ERIC SEVAREID,
Candidates 1960

To the best of my knowledge, no gentleman of the press has ever risen to scold the President for an unsatisfactory answer and to push him for a better one. Indeed, the first gentleman to do it will probably be the last.

CLINTON ROSSITER,
The American Presidency

The Presidency is a standing reproach to those petty doctrinaires who insist that executive power is inherently undemocratic; for, to the exact contrary, it has been more responsive to the needs and dreams of giant democracy than any other office or institution in the whole mosaic of American life.

CLINTON ROSSITER,
The American Presidency

The American people do not appreciate administrative capacity in the presidency to anything like the degree that they appreciate a sense of human contact with the President: that he is, par excellence, their voice, their spokesman, their friend.

FREDERICK M. DAVENPORT,
The People, Politics, and the Politician
by Asher Christensen
and Evron M. Kirkpatrick

The poor President, what with preserving his popularity and doing his duty, does not know what to do.

HENRY DAVID THOREAU,
Journal

I can't make a damn thing out of this tax problem. I listen to one side and they seem right—and then I talk to the other side and they seem just as right, and here I am where I started. God, what a job!

WARREN G. HARDING,
quoted in the *New York Times*,
October 5, 1952

One can never be sure that when a man becomes the President of the United States his sense of power and of purpose and his own source of self-confidence will show him how to help himself enhance his personal influence. But there is every reason to believe that he will be shown nothing of the sort if he has made the White House his first venture into politics. The Presidency is no place for amateurs.

RICHARD E. NEUSTADT,
Presidential Power

Truman is quite right when he declares that presidential power is the power to persuade. Command is but a method of persuasion, not a substitute, and not a method suitable for everyday employment.

RICHARD E. NEUSTADT,
Presidential Power

More important than what we think of the Presidential candidate is what we think of his "public image." We vote for him because his is the kind of public image we want to see in the White House.

DANIEL J. BOORSTIN,
The Image

Greatness in the Presidential chair is largely an illusion of the people.

HARRY M. DAUGHERTY,
quoted in *Candidates 1960* by Eric Sevareid

The inaugural speech [of Franklin Delano Roosevelt], beamed directly to the people, so roused the country that 460,000 persons sat down to write the new President a congratulatory letter. Ever since that historic day the postman has been a vital link in the decision-making process of a President-centered democracy.

ROBERT RIENOW
and LEONA TRAIN RIENOW,
The Lonely Quest

PRESSURE

Under the pressure of trial and responsibility we are often stronger than where there is no pressure. Many a man will acknowledge that in difficulty he has surprised himself by a resource and coolness which he never suspected before.

MARK RUTHERFORD,
The Deliverance of Mark Rutherford

However strange it is to be never at rest, and never satisfied, and ever trying after something that is never reached, and to be always laden with plot and plan and care and worry, how clear it is that it must be, and that one is driven by an irresistible might until the journey is worked out! It is much better to go on and fret, than to stop and fret. As to repose—for some men there's no such thing.

CHARLES DICKENS,
quoted in *Dickens* by Hesketh Pearson

PRIDE

It is perhaps because nature made me a gregarious man, going hither and thither looking for conversation, and ready to deny from fear or favour his dearest conviction, that I love proud and lonely things.

W. B. YEATS,
Autobiography

Many a man is praised for his reserve and so-called shyness when he is simply too proud to risk making a fool of himself.

J. B. PRIESTLEY,
All About Ourselves and Other Essays

Intellectual pride inflicts itself upon everybody. Where it dwells there can be no other opinion in the house.

HENRY CARDINAL MANNING,
Pastime Papers

The just estimate of ourselves at the moment of triumph is the most eminent renunciation of pride.

WILLIAM ELLERY CHANNING,
Dr. Channing's Note-book

PRINCIPLE

Principles always become a matter of vehement discussion when practice is at an ebb.

GEORGE GISSING,
The Private Papers of Henry Ryecroft

Known principles are the barbed-wire entanglements around the detention-camps where our intuitions are restrained from going into warfare.

ANONYMOUS (HENRY S. HASKINS),
Meditations in Wall Street

I find that men talk of principles; and mean, when you come to inquire, rules connected with certain systems.

SIR ARTHUR HELPS,
Companions of My Solitude

Many people have their principles all bad and their practice all good.

C. E. MONTAGUE,
A Writer's Notes on His Trade

I never allow principles to carry me far enough. I do not think that in this I am peculiar. I notice that in the gardens of most men are nothing but arrested buds. How rare it is to see the fully developed flower!

MARK RUTHERFORD,
Last Pages from a Journal

PRISON

A day in prison on which one does not weep is a day on which one's heart is hard, not a day on which one's heart is happy.

OSCAR WILDE,
De Profundis

The poor are wiser, more charitable, more kind, more sensitive than we are. In their eyes, prison is a tragedy in a man's life, a misfortune, a casualty, something that calls for sympathy in others. They speak of one who is in prison as of one who is "in trouble" simply. It is the phrase they always use, and the expression has the perfect wisdom of love in it.

OSCAR WILDE,
De Profundis

A prisoner has no sex. He is God's own private eunuch.

HENRY MILLER,
The Air-Conditioned Nightmare

I want to devote my time to reading and writing, with everything else secondary, but I can't do that in prison. I have to keep my eyes open at all times or I won't make it. There is always some madness going on, and whether you like it or not you're involved.

ELDRIDGE CLEAVER,
Soul on Ice

Black men born in the U.S. and fortunate enough to live past the age of eighteen are conditioned to accept the inevitability of prison. For most of us, it simply looms as the next phase in a sequence of humiliations. . . . I was prepared for prison. It required only minor psychic adjustments.

GEORGE JACKSON,
Soledad Brother

These prisons have always borne a certain resemblance to Dachau and Buchenwald, places for the bad niggers, Mexicans, and poor whites.

GEORGE JACKSON,
Soledad Brother

Change is a rare occasion in prison—sameness is the law. The same people with the same crime, the same colored clothes with the same stripe, the same brown-suited guards with the same orders, the same food on the same day, the same disciplinary slips with the same verdicts (guilty), the same bed in the same cell night after night after night.

ANONYMOUS PRISON INMATE,
quoted in the *New York Times,*
February 28, 1971

Any person who claims to have deep feeling for other human beings should think a long, long time before he votes to have other men kept behind bars—caged. I am not saying there shouldn't be prisons, but there shouldn't be bars. Behind bars, a man never reforms. He will never forget. He never will get completely over the memory of the bars.

MALCOLM X,
Autobiography

PRIVACY

Love your neighbors, but don't pull down the fence.

CHINESE PROVERB

One way to get away from it all without being thought queer is to go to the bathroom and lock the door.

WILLIAM FEATHER,
The Business of Life

The human animal needs a freedom seldom mentioned, freedom from intrusion. He needs a little privacy quite as much as he wants understanding or vitamins or exercise or praise.

PHYLLIS McGINLEY,
The Province of the Heart

I have a great deal of company in my house; especially in the morning, when nobody calls.

HENRY DAVID THOREAU,
Walden

PROBLEM

You often get a better hold upon a problem by going away from it for a time and dismissing it from your mind altogether.

DR. FRANK CRANE,
Essays

The best way to escape from a problem is to solve it.

BRENDAN FRANCIS

The biblical fall of man presents the dawn of consciousness as a curse. And as a matter of fact it is in this light that we first look upon every problem that forces us to greater consciousness and separates us even further from the paradise of unconscious childhood.

C. G. JUNG,
Psychological Reflections,
edited by Jolande Jacobi and R. F. Hull

A great man is one who seizes the vital issue in a complex question, what we might call the "jugular vein" of the whole organism,—and spends his energies upon that.

JOSEPH RICKABY,
An Old Man's Jottings

I do not believe that the deeper problems of living ever can be answered by the processes of thought. I believe that life itself teaches us either patience with regard to them, or reveals to us possible solutions when our hearts are pressed close against duties and sorrows and experiences of all kinds.

HAMILTON WRIGHT MABIE,
My Study Fire

PROCRASTINATION

The effect of my procrastination is that, always busy with the preliminaries and antecedents, I am never able to begin to produce.

HENRI FRÉDÉRIC AMIEL,
The Private Journal of Henri Frédéric Amiel

Why always "Not yet"? Do flowers in spring say "Not yet"?

NORMAN DOUGLAS,
An Almanac

One ought not to be shadowed by anything one feels one ought to do.

A. C. BENSON,
Excerpts from the Letters of Dr. A. C. Benson to M. E. A.

"Never put off until tomorrow what you can do today." Under the influence of this pestilent morality, I am forever letting tomorrow's work slop backwards into today's and doing painfully and nervously today what I could do quickly and easily tomorrow.

J. A. SPENDER,
The Comments of Bagshot, Second Series

In putting off what one has to do, one runs the risk of never being able to do it.

CHARLES BAUDELAIRE,
Intimate Journals

Tomorrow is often the busiest day of the week.

SPANISH PROVERB

PROMISE

From the promise to the deed is a day's journey.

BULGARIAN PROVERB

Giving yourself your word to do something ought to be no less sacred than giving your word to others.

ANDRÉ GIDE,
The Journals of André Gide, Vol. I

We promise according to our hopes, and perform according to our fears.

LA ROCHEFOUCAULD,
Maxims

Promises hold men more securely than benefits; for them hope is a cable, gratitude only a thread.

J. PETIT-SENN,
Conceits and Caprices

PROSTITUTE

Shy men of extreme sensibility are the born victims of the prostitute.

CHRISTOPHER ISHERWOOD,
Preface, *Intimate Journals*
by Charles Baudelaire

Since time immemorial, prostitutes have been the reward of men of action—soldiers, sailors, cowboys, gangsters—because whores are, above all else, women of action. Talk is not their stock in trade.

BRENDAN FRANCIS

I've only hated men at those moments when I realized that I was doing all the giving and they the taking. At least when I was a prostitute, it was all honest and up front. No illusions and no lies about the relationships, which made it easier for both parties and made it possible for both parties to have a lot of fun—when they both liked what they were doing.

XAVIERA HOLLANDER,
Xaviera!

I've always had great respect for whores. The many I've known were kind and generous.... I never knew a prostitute who did harm to anyone but herself. I except, of course, the whores who are real criminals and use knockout drops and bring men to their rooms to be robbed, beaten, and blackmailed.

ETHEL WATERS,
His Eye Is on the Sparrow

The work of the prostitute can be as routine and as boring as that in any other occupation.

CHARLES WINICK AND PAUL M. KINSIE,
The Lively Commerce

PROTEST

One must be very naïve to believe that it will do any good to cry out and shout in the world, as if that would change one's fate. Better take things as they come, and make no fuss.

SØREN KIERKEGAARD,
Either/Or, Vol. I

I will protest all my life. I am willing to. But I'm a person who makes, much more than a person who protests, and I think we are that, and I have decided that whenever I protest from now on, and a number of people are doing this too now, I will make something—I will make poems, plant, feed children, build, but not ever protest without making something. I think the whole thing must be made again.

MURIEL RUKEYSER,
The Craft of Poetry,
edited by William Packard

PROVERB

Don't quote your proverb until you bring your ship into port.

GAELIC PROVERB

Proverbs are not merely decorations on life. They have life itself in them. They are the bedrock substance of living, built up, by many people and many years. They are the beginnings of all literature, the first metaphors and similes, the first comedies and tragedies. They are the first poetry we have.

ROBERT PETER TRISTRAM COFFIN,
Kennebec, Cradle of Americans

Proverbs are always platitudes until you have personally experienced the truth of them.

ALDOUS HUXLEY,
Jesting Pilate

PROVIDENCE

The well of Providence is deep. It's the buckets we bring to it that are small.

MARY WEBB,
quoted in *Ladies' Home Journal*,
February 1946

Playing Providence is a game at which one is very apt to burn one's fingers.

THOMAS HENRY HUXLEY,
Aphorisms and Reflections

There is nothing more agreeable than to find that Providence dislikes the same peo-

ple that we do. It adds to our good opinion of Providence.

FRANK MOORE COLBY,
The Colby Essays, Vol. 2

Providence has a thousand means to raise the fallen and support the prostrate. Sometimes our fate resembles a fruit tree in winter. Who would think at beholding so sad a sight that these rigid branches, these jagged twigs, would turn green again in the spring and blossom and bear fruit? But we hope it, we know it!

GOETHE,
Wisdom and Experience

Love and trust, and live in the great mansion that is your home, the Providence of God.

JANET ERSKINE STUART,
Life and Letters of Janet Erskine Stuart
by Maud Monahan

What is absorbingly interesting is the extraordinary ingenuity of Providence in utilizing the paltriest instruments for the greatest "shoves."

ALICE JAMES,
The Diary of Alice James

By going a few minutes sooner or later, by stopping to speak with a friend on the corner, by meeting this man or that, or by turning down this street instead of the other, we may let slip some impending evil, by which the whole current of our lives would have been changed. There is no possible solution in the dark enigma but the one word, "Providence."

HENRY WADSWORTH LONGFELLOW

PRUDENCE

We can easily become as much slaves to precaution as we can to fear. Although we can never rivet our fortune so tight as to make it impregnable, we may by our excessive prudence squeeze out of the life that we are guarding so anxiously all the adventurous quality that makes it worth living.

RANDOLPH BOURNE,
Youth and Life

There is always much to be said for not attempting more than you can do, and for making a certainty of what you try. But this principle, like others in life, has its exceptions.

SIR WINSTON CHURCHILL,
A Churchill Reader,
edited by Colin R. Coote

Prudence and compromise are necessary means, but every man should have an impudent end which he will not compromise.

CHARLES HORTON COOLEY,
Life and the Student

How far is prudence authoritative? Clearly against rashness, against stupor, against blindness, against parsimony, in a word, against all the forms and occasions of imprudence. But against probity, against justice, against devotion, in the presence of any deep moral obligation or high moral privilege, prudence has a claim to a hearing—nothing more. All the great virtues are indiscretions, notably courage, the most widely cherished of them all— and it is precisely this element of indiscretion that affirms and almost constitutes the virtue.

OSCAR W. FIRKINS,
Oscar Firkins: Memoirs and Letters,
edited by Ina Ten Eyck

The man who would truly love, and know to the full what it means, will beware of that timid limping thing which sometimes parades, and hides its littleness, under the name of prudence.

ALBAN GOODIER,
The School of Love

Prudent people are very happy; 'tis an exceeding fine thing, that's certain, but I was born without it, and shall retain to my day of Death the Humour of saying what I think.

LADY MARY WORTLEY MONTAGU,
*The Complete Letters of
Lady Mary Wortley Montagu*

PSYCHIATRY

Many a patient, after countless sessions, has quit therapy, because he could detect no perceptible improvement in his shrink's condition.

BRENDAN FRANCIS

Voyager, what seas,
What oceans have you sailed?
And what strange shores,
Cliff-guarded, ringed with foam,
And inaccessible, have you set foot upon?
Into what quiet bays
And through what seething maelstroms has your craft
Ventured its way; and what the Polar Star
For your phantastic navigation?
O conqueror of the sea—
Canst conquer me?

EITHNE TABOR,
"Psychiatrist," *The Cliff's Edge*

To get the most out of your psychiatrist don't assume that he can read your mind. He can't.

DR. DAVID S. VISCOTT,
The Making of a Psychiatrist

One of the lovely things about becoming a psychiatrist is you learn everybody has all kinds of thoughts, fantasies, and wishes and that having them doesn't mean very much—certainly not nearly as much (or awful) as too many people think.... You can have perverted, twisted, kinky, obnoxious, selfish, stupid, childish, obsessive, and violent thoughts. The presence of all these thoughts is only another proof of the fact that you are human and have feelings.

DR. DAVID S. VISCOTT,
The Making of a Psychiatrist

The less a man is able to solve inner conflicts, or those between his desires and what the environment demands, the more he relies on society for the answers to any new challenge it may offer. And here it makes little difference whether he gets his answers from the editorial writer, the advertisements, or the psychiatrist. The more he accepts their answers as his own, the less he can meet the next challenge independently and the more solutions must come from the outside.

BRUNO BETTELHEIM,
The Informed Heart

Psychoanalysis is yet another method of learning how to endure the loneliness produced by culture.

PHILIP RIEFF,
The Triumph of the Therapeutic

The other thing ... was psychoanalysis. Artists tend to be afraid of it. They think they'll lose their creativity. But what analysis teaches you is how to surrender yourself to your fantasies. How to dive down into those fantasies.

ERICA JONG,
The Craft of Poetry,
edited by William Packard

Psychoanalysis is that mental illness for which it regards itself as therapy.

KARL KRAUS,
Karl Kraus by Harry Zohn

Psychoanalysis has terrified educated parents with the fear of the harm they may unwittingly do their children.

BERTRAND RUSSELL,
The Conquest of Happiness

The ordeal itself is much too silly and disgusting to be contemplated even as a joke. Freudianism and all it has tainted with its grotesque implications and methods appears to me to be one of the vilest deceits practiced by people on themselves and on others.

VLADIMIR NABOKOV,
Strong Opinions

Psychotherapy seeks to conserve everything. It does not want to "stamp out" that which appears destructive, because when the whole is seen, nothing is destructive.

ROBERT C. MURPHY,
Psychotherapy Based on Human Longing

The life of an analyst is tragic. A country doctor, a physical doctor, can be human, fallible. He can be loved for what he is outside his profession. An analyst does not exist in the mind of his patient except as a figure in his own drama.

ANAÏS NIN,
The Diaries of Anaïs Nin, Vol. II

But the really decisive moments in psychotherapy, as every patient or therapist who has ever experienced them knows, are unpredictable, unique, unforgettable, always unrepeatable and often indescribable.

R. D. LAING,
The Politics of Experience

PUBLISHER

Their business is not literature, but to sell things made up as books to the illiterate.

JOHN AYSCOUGH,
Levia-Pondera

Times have changed since a certain author was executed for murdering his publisher. They say that when the author was on the scaffold he said good-bye to the minister and to the reporters, and then he saw some publishers sitting in the front row below, and to them he did not say good-bye. He said instead, "I'll see you again."

SIR JAMES BARRIE,
quoted in *The Second Book of He and She*,
edited by James Moffatt

The publisher is a being slow to move, slow to take in changed conditions, always two generations, at least, behind his authors.

RICHARD LE GALLIENNE,
Prose Fancies

PURITY

Purity is the power to contemplate defilement.

SIMONE WEIL,
Gravity and Grace

PURPOSE

I have seen so much of ugly, meaningless, drifting men that I have come to love the men I feel definitely at work.

SHERWOOD ANDERSON,
Letters of Sherwood Anderson

Everything in life must be intentional, and the will constantly taut like a muscle.

ANDRÉ GIDE,
The Journals of André Gide, Vol. I

So many men in this world are going nowhere in particular that when one comes along ... who is really and passionately going somewhere, what a stir he communicates to a dull world! We catch sparks of electricity from the very friction of his passage.   DAVID GRAYSON,
The Friendly Road

To have no set purpose in one's life is the harlotry of the will.

STEPHEN MACKENNA,
Journal and Letters of Stephen Mackenna

Continuity of purpose is one of the most essential ingredients of happiness in the long run, and for most men this comes chiefly through their work.

BERTRAND RUSSELL,
The Conquest of Happiness

QUARREL

Most of the mighty quarrels that have sent men to battle and the stake might have been appeased had each side recognized that both were right in their affirmations, both wrong in their denials.

HAVELOCK ELLIS,
Selected Essays

Most quarrels are inevitable at the time; incredible afterwards.

E. M. FORSTER

Why do grownups quarrel so easily, so much, and over the most idiotic things? Up till now I thought that only children squabbled and that that wore off as you grew up. Of course, there is sometimes a real reason for a quarrel, but this is just plain bickering.

ANNE FRANK,
Anne Frank: The Diary of a Young Girl

A somewhat careful investigation of every quarrel easily brings the conviction that it is invariably the secret, unconscious emotions that bring about the conflict of opinions. Where this deep resonance of the unconscious is lacking we playfully pass over differences.

DR. WILHELM STEKHEL,
The Depths of the Soul

For souls in growth, great quarrels are great emancipators.

LOGAN PEARSALL SMITH,
Afterthoughts

It is a good rule never to start an argument just before breakfast or enter into a quarrel just before supper. A quarrel that is unavoidable then is likely to be less bitter if the battlers hold off long enough to take a bite of food.

ARTHUR T. JERSILD,
Educational Psychology,
edited by Charles E. Skinner

In real life it takes only one to make a quarrel.

OGDEN NASH,
Ogden Nash Pocket Book

QUESTION

He who asks a question is a fool for five minutes; he who does not ask a question remains a fool forever.

CHINESE PROVERB

You ask great questions accidentally. To answer them would be events.

EMILY DICKINSON,
Letters of Emily Dickinson

Better ask ten times than go astray once.

YIDDISH PROVERB

The best way to find out things, if you come to think of it, is not to ask questions at all. If you fire off a question, it is like firing off a gun; bang it goes, and everything takes flight and runs for shelter. But if you sit still and pretend not to be looking, all the little facts will come and peck round your feet, situations will venture forth from thickets and intentions will creep out and sun themselves on a stone.

LETTICE,
quoted in *The Flame Trees of Thika*
by Elspeth Huxley

QUOTATION

It is the little writer rather than the great writer who never seems to quote, and the reason is that he is never really doing anything else.

HAVELOCK ELLIS,
quoted in *Any Number Can Play*
by Clifton Fadiman

A writer with a knack of remembering the best things that have been said about everything of which he treats lays us all under an obligation that we can only repay by gratitude.

JOHN AYSCOUGH,
Levia-Pondera

The power of quotation is as dreadful a weapon as any which the human intellect can forge.

JOHN JAY CHAPMAN

To be amused by what you read—that is the great spring of happy quotations.

C. E. MONTAGUE,
A Writer's Notes on His Trade

I am reminded of the professor who, in his declining hours, was asked by his devoted pupils for his final counsel. He replied, "Verify your quotations."

SIR WINSTON CHURCHILL,
A Churchill Reader,
edited by Colin R. Coote

The quotation habit is generally a vicious one, often it has not even so worthy a design as to borrow from stronger and greater people an energy and clearness that we do not have, but rather serves as a sort of diploma to certify our culture—said culture consisting in our ability to quote scraps from Lamb, Dickens, John Keats, Browning, Doctor Johnson, and Matthew Arnold.

THOMAS WOLFE,
Of Time and the River

Next to the originator of a good sentence is the first quoter of it.

RALPH WALDO EMERSON,
"Quotation and Originality,"
Letters and Social Aims

The moment we quote a man to prove our sanity, we give up all. No authority can establish it, and if I have lost confidence in myself I have the Universe against me.

RALPH WALDO EMERSON,
Journals of Ralph Waldo Emerson

Have you ever observed that we pay much more attention to a wise passage when it is quoted than when we read it in the original author?

PHILIP G. HAMERTON,
The Intellectual Life

A quotation in a speech, article or book is like a rifle in the hands of an infantryman. It speaks with authority.

BRENDAN FRANCIS

We prefer to believe that the absence of inverted commas guarantees the originality of a thought, whereas it may be merely that the utterer has forgotten its source.

CLIFTON FADIMAN,
Any Number Can Play

I have suffered a good deal from writers who have quoted this or that sentence of mine either out of its context or in juxtaposition to some incongruous matter which quite distorted my meaning, or destroyed it altogether.

ALFRED NORTH WHITEHEAD,
Dialogues of Alfred North Whitehead

Most public speakers talk so badly that a sudden quotation from a poet appears in their babble like a lady in a slum.

AUSTIN O'MALLEY,
Keystones of Thought

How easy it is to quote. I think one could get an available line from a column of advertisements if one were put to it.

OLIVER WENDELL HOLMES, JR.,
Holmes-Pollock Letters, Vol. II

RAIN

It always seems to be raining harder than it really is when you look at the weather through the window.

SIR JOHN LUBBOCK,
The Pleasures of Life

I think rain is as necessary to the mind as to vegetation. My very thoughts become thirsty, and crave the moisture.

JOHN BURROUGHS,
quoted in *The Author's Kalendar, 1916,*
compiled by Anna C. Woodford

Washing your car and polishing it all up is a never failing sign of rain.

KIN HUBBARD,
Abe Martin on Things in General

One year the long rains failed.

That is a terrible experience, and the farmer who has lived through it will never forget it. Years afterwards, away from Africa, in the wet climate of a Northern country, he will start up at night, at the sound of a sudden shower of rain, and cry, "At last, at last."

ISAK DINESEN,
Out of Africa

When the gardeners are praying for rain the picnickers are praying for sunshine, so what is the poor Lord to do?

WILLIAM FEATHER,
The Business of Life

Rain is much nicer than snow because you don't have rain plows piling up rain in six-foot piles exactly where you want to go.

OGDEN NASH,
Ogden Nash Pocket Book

RAINBOW

The rainbow is more beautiful than the pot at the end of it, because the rainbow is now. And the pot never turns out to be quite what I expected.

HUGH PRATHER,
Notes to Myself

READING

Reading is a solitary pleasure, and shuts one up, and hedges one off, and has not the sweet unending charm of human companionship which is what really gives all games and sports their enduring hold on men.

GAMALIEL BRADFORD,
The Letters of Gamaliel Bradford

There are times when I think that the reading I have done in the past has had no effect except to cloud my mind and make me indecisive.

ROBERTSON DAVIES,
The Table Talk of Samuel Marchbanks

In the next few years, I put aside most other books for Marx and Engels, Lenin, Saint-Simon, Hegel, Feuerbach. Certainly I did not study with the dedication of a scholar, but I did read with the attention of a good student, and Marx as a man and Engels and his Mary became, for a while, more real to me than my friends.

LILLIAN HELLMAN,
An Unfinished Woman

Many persons read and like fiction. It does not tax the intelligence, and the intelligence of most of us can so ill afford taxation that we rightly welcome any reading matter which avoids this.

ROSE MACAULAY,
A Casual Commentary

Any method is right, every method is right, that expresses what we wish to express, if we are writers; that brings us closer to the novelist's intention if we are readers.

VIRGINIA WOOLF,
The Common Reader, First Series

What I mean by reading is not skimming, not being able to say as the world saith, "Oh, yes, I've read that!," but reading again and again, in all sorts of moods, with an increase of delight every time, till the thing read has become a part of your system and goes forth along with you to meet any new experience you may have.

C. E. MONTAGUE,
A Writer's Notes on His Trade

As far as possible I only read what I am

hungry for at that moment when I have an appetite for it, and then I do not read, I *eat.*

SIMONE WEIL,
Waiting for God

People say that life is the thing, but I prefer reading.

LOGAN PEARSALL SMITH,
Afterthoughts

REALITY

Some people are still unaware that reality contains unparalleled beauties. The fantastic and unexpected, the ever-changing and renewing is nowhere so exemplified as in real life itself.

BERENICE ABBOTT,
Photographers on Photography,
edited by Nathan Lyons

A man might pass for insane who should see things as they are.

WILLIAM ELLERY CHANNING,
Dr. Channing's Note-book

What an absurd amount of energy I have been wasting all my life trying to figure out how things "really are," when all the time they weren't.

HUGH PRATHER,
Notes to Myself

And through the children especially she comes in contact with reality and learns involuntarily. Books and reality and art are for me alike. One who has stood outside real life would bore me, but one who is right in it knows and feels naturally.

VINCENT VAN GOGH,
Dear Theo:
An Autobiography of Vincent Van Gogh

Reality, union with reality, is the true state of the soul when confident and healthy.... Unreality is what keeps us from ourselves, and most pleasures are unreal.

CYRIL CONNOLLY,
The Unquiet Grave

Reality is pretty brutal, pretty filthy, when you come to grips with it. Yet it's glorious all the same. It's so real and satisfactory.

GEORGE BERNARD SHAW,
Fanny's First Play

A test of what is real is that it is hard and rough. Joys are found in it, not pleasure. What is pleasant belongs to dreams.

SIMONE WEIL,
Gravity and Grace

The importance and the endurance of poetry, as of all art, are its hold upon reality. We hear much, on this side and that, of realism. Well, we may let realism go, but we cannot let go reality.

JOHN DEWEY,
Characters and Events, Vol. I

The stupendous fact that we stand in the midst of reality will always be something far more wonderful than anything we do.

ERICH GUTKIND,
quoted in *The Wisdom of the Heart*
by Henry Miller

It is a very rare matter when any of us at any time sees things as they are at the moment.

JOHN JAY CHAPMAN,
John Jay Chapman and His Letters
by M. A. DeWolfe Howe

But do not imagine that I am suffering from disappointment here—quite the contrary. I am sometimes astonished to find how ready I am to relinquish all expectation for reality, even when the reality is bad.

My God, if any of it could be shared! But would it *exist* then, would it *exist?* No, it is possible only at the price of solitude.

RAINER MARIA RILKE,
The Journal of My Other Self

How hard it is, sometimes, to trust the evidence of one's senses! How reluctantly the mind consents to reality!

NORMAN DOUGLAS,
An Almanac

The touch of reality is salvation for the man who smothers amid forms and shadows. A blind man would rejoice in sight though his eyes opened on the carnage of a battlefield.

OSCAR W. FIRKINS,
Oscar Firkins: Memoirs and Letters,
edited by Ina Ten Eyck

The question is not whether to adjust or to rebel against reality but, rather, how to discriminate between those realities that must be recognized as unalterable and those that we should continue to try to change however unyielding that may appear.

HELEN MERRELL LYND,
On Shame and the Search for Identity

REASON

Just as love is an orientation which refers to all objects and is incompatible with the restriction to one object, so is reason a human faculty which must embrace the whole of the world with which man is confronted.

ERICH FROMM,
The Sane Society

Reason, or the exercise of reason, is a living spontaneous energy within, not an art.

JOHN HENRY CARDINAL NEWMAN,
Oxford University Sermons

All men have a reason, but not all men can give a reason.

JOHN HENRY CARDINAL NEWMAN,
Oxford University Sermons

Reason is developed by going against habits and repetition; by following a legitimate whim; by not doing as others do.

A. R. ORAGE,
Essays and Aphorisms

Reason means truth and those who are not governed by it take the chance that some day the sunken fact will rip the bottom out of their boat.

OLIVER WENDELL HOLMES, JR.,
The Mind and Faith of Justice Holmes,
edited by Max Lerner

Truly, that reason upon which we so plume ourselves, though it may answer for little things, yet for great decisions is hardly surer than a toss-up.

CHARLES SANDERS PEIRCE,
Collected Papers of Charles Sanders Peirce,
Vol. I

A reason is generally a very curious thing; if I apprehend it with the total intensity of my passion, then it grows up into a huge necessity which can move heaven and earth. But if I lack passion, I look down upon it with scorn.

SØREN KIERKEGAARD,
Either/Or, Vol. I

REFORM AND REFORMER

It is no use to talk about Reform. Society will be very obedient when the myriad personalities that compose it have, and are aware that they have, an object in living. . . . The stench of atrophied personality.

RUTH BENEDICT,
An Anthropologist at Work
by Margaret Mead

Reformatory measures are hailed as cure-alls by people who have a happy confidence in the perfectibility of human nature, and no discouraging acquaintance with history to dim it.

AGNES REPPLIER,
Times and Tendencies

Reform often seems only the dislike of the blasé for the people with animal spirits.

FRANK MOORE COLBY,
The Colby Essays, Vol. 2

It is very insulting to attempt to reform people. When you behead a person, you leave him his soul as it is. But when you reform him, you change his soul, and it is a dangerous thing to tamper with human souls.

DON MARQUIS,
The Almost Perfect State

It is the genuine reformer who is seeking to right great wrongs who most needs the capacity to distinguish between grave evils and peccadillos. A measure of good-humored tolerance for human weakness is a part of his equipment for effective work. Lacking in this, he is doomed to perpetual irritation and disappointment.

SAMUEL MCCHORD CROTHERS,
The Gentle Reader

Like all other zealous reformers we do what we do because we like doing it better than anything else.

DON MARQUIS,
The Almost Perfect State

Reformers, as a group, are not a very attractive group of people. As you get older you recognize that. They are too self-righteous. They feel that they have the call.

ROBERT MOSES,
Wisdom for Our Time,
edited by James Nelson

All Reformers, however strict their social conscience, live in houses just as big as they can pay for.

LOGAN PEARSALL SMITH,
Afterthoughts

If we like a man's dream, we call him a reformer; if we don't like his dream, we call him a crank.

WILLIAM DEAN HOWELLS,
quoted in *The Author's Kalendar, 1914,*
compiled by Anna C. Woodford

It seems to me more and more clear that the only honest people are artists, and that these social reformers and philanthropists get so out of hand and harbour so many discreditable desires under the disguise of loving their kind, that in the end there's more to find fault in them than in us. But if I were one of them?

VIRGINIA WOOLF,
A Writer's Diary

REFUSAL

Remember that in giving any reason at all for refusing, you lay some foundation for a future request.

SIR ARTHUR HELPS,
Essays Written in Intervals of Business

If you would have the good-will of all men, take heed that, when anything is asked of you, you don't refuse it point-blank, but answer in generalities.

FRANCESCO GUICCIARDINI,
Counsels and Reflections

We prize more the egg refused us than the ox which is given us.

J. PETIT-SENN,
Conceits and Caprices

REGRET

Regret for the things we did can be tempered by time; it is regret for the things we did not do that is inconsolable.

SYDNEY J. HARRIS,
Strictly Personal

I have always found that each step we take in life is to be regretted—if we once begin to wonder how many other steps might have been possible.

JOHN OLIVER HOBBES,
The Herb-Moon

Make the most of your regrets; never smother your sorrow but tend and cherish it till it come to have a separate and integral interest. To regret deeply is to live afresh.

HENRY DAVID THOREAU,
Journal

Regrets are idle; yet history is one long regret. Everything might have turned out so differently.

CHARLES DUDLEY WARNER,
My Summer in a Garden

We should have no regrets. We should never look back. The past is finished. There is nothing to be gained by going over it. Whatever it gave us in the experiences it brought us was something we had to know.

REBECCA BEARD,
Everyman's Search

RELATIONSHIP

I do not believe that a beautiful relationship has to always end in carnage. I do not believe that we have to be fraudulent and pretentious, because that is the source of future difficulties and ultimate failure. If we project fraudulent, pretentious images, or if we fantasize each other into distorted caricatures of what we really are, then, when we awake from the trance and see beyond the sham and front, all will dissolve, all will die and transform into bitterness and hate.

ELDRIDGE CLEAVER,
Soul on Ice

It takes time and deeds, and this involves trust, it involves making ourselves vulnerable to each other, to strip ourselves naked, to become sitting ducks for each other—and if one of the ducks is shamming, then the sincere duck will pay in pain—but the deceitful duck, I feel, will be the loser.

ELDRIDGE CLEAVER,
Soul on Ice

What an awesome thing it is to feel oneself on the verge of the possibility of really knowing another person. Can it ever happen? I'm not sure. I don't know that any two people can really strip themselves that naked in front of each other. We're so filled with fears of rejection and pretenses that we scarcely know whether we're being fraudulent or real ourselves.

BEVERLY AXELROD,
Soul on Ice by Eldridge Cleaver

In a distracted world how close and dear human relationships may become.

ELLEN GLASGOW,
Letters of Ellen Glasgow

I have often wondered why it is that men should be so fearful of new ventures in social relationships. . . . Most of us fear, actually fear, people who differ from ourselves, either up or down the scale.

DAVID GRAYSON,
The Friendly Road

Relationship *is* life, and this relationship is a constant movement, a constant change.

J. KRISHNAMURTI,
You Are the World

Time necessarily brings changes in any re-

lation, and one must be prepared to recognize these changes and to grow and to change with time. But if one can believe that it is possible for the greater knowledge that two persons may acquire of each other in the course of time to bring also greater respect and love, then—beyond the inevitabilities of human life cycles—one need not fear time.

HELEN MERRELL LYND,
On Shame and the Search for Identity

We hope to share the experience of a relationship, but the only honest beginning, or even end, may be to share the experience of its absence.

R. D. LAING,
The Politics of Experience

Relationships are things that have their good times and bad times. I try to cope with the bad times by projecting myself into the character of the other person—to consider how that person feels, and try to imagine myself in that person's position. It's not a painful process—it helps you. I think if you can manage to do that, at least you don't run into terrible trouble with people.

TENNESSEE WILLIAMS,
Close-up by John Gruen

What a fear of relationship there is here. No talk. Drinking together. Blurring all feeling and senses. No sense of richness, fullness, expansion. Terrified of intimacy. And consequently alienated. Lonely.

ANAÏS NIN,
The Diaries of Anaïs Nin

When I left Olga today, I became aware of an admiration for woman which is quite distinct from my admiration of man. I felt that woman offers more in relationship, sacrifices more, cares more.

ANAÏS NIN,
The Diaries of Anaïs Nin, Vol. IV

A good relationship has a pattern like a dance. . . . To touch heavily would be to arrest the pattern and freeze the movement, to check the endlessly changing beauty of its unfolding. There is no place here for the possessive clutch, the clinging arm, the heavy hand; only the barest touch in passing.

ANNE MORROW LINDBERGH,
Gift from the Sea

No matter how genuine a relationship may be, there will always be stresses and storms, to bring unexpected words, to make one impotent and afraid, to make one feel the terribleness of not being able to count on the other person, to create the despairing feeling that breaks in love can never be repaired. But one lives and loves, and suffers and forgets, and begins again— perhaps even thinking that this time, this new time, is to be permanent. But man is not permanent and man is not predictable.

CLARK MOUSTAKAS,
Creativity and Conformity

RELIGION

What keeps me from talking about religion is the fact that in me there lies a fanatic dozing ever so lightly whom I particularly do not wish to rouse.

JULIAN GREEN,
Julian Green: Diary 1928–1957

What a strange underground power religion is, how difficult for us to estimate its strength.

LLEWELYN POWYS,
Letters

I think the most important quality in a person concerned with religion is absolute devotion to the truth.

ALBERT SCHWEITZER,
Out of My Life and Thought

What a superstition it is which forbids people who really think to talk to one another on religious matters! Not a soul has said a word·to me for years about God.

MARK RUTHERFORD,
Last Pages from a Journal

I know that a community of God-seekers is a great shelter for man. But directly this grows into an Institution it is apt to give ready access to the Devil by its back-door.

RABINDRANATH TAGORE,
Letters to a Friend

In religion our exclusions are nearly always wrong, and our inclusions, however inconsistent, nearly always right.

EVELYN UNDERHILL,
The Letters of Evelyn Underhill

Do—*do* try and be more objective in your religion. Try to see yourself less as a complex individual, and more as a quite ordinary scrap of the universe.

EVELYN UNDERHILL,
The Letters of Evelyn Underhill

There is something in religion which can only be expressed through conduct.

JOHN JAY CHAPMAN,
Memories and Milestones

Agnosticism should have its ritual no less than faith. It has sown its martyrs, it should reap its saints, and praise God daily for having hidden Himself from man.

OSCAR WILDE,
De Profundis

The religious man pretends that every aspect of life has meaning for him, but in practice he constantly minimizes the noisier and vivider elements.

RANDOLPH BOURNE,
Youth and Life

Light your lamp first at home and afterward at the mosque.

MOSLEM PROVERB

It is a fine thing to establish one's own religion in one's heart, not to be dependent on tradition and second-hand ideals. Life will seem to you, later, not a lesser, but a greater thing.

D. H. LAWRENCE,
Selected Letters of D. H. Lawrence

A man can no more possess a private religion than he can possess a private sun and moon.

G. K. CHESTERTON,
Introduction, *Book of Job*

Religion is of all subjects in the world the most elusive, the most dangerous, the most important, the most far-reaching and the most all embracing. To talk or read about religion to a child is the most responsible and the most anxious thing a grown-up could possibly have to do.

GEORGE BERNARD SHAW,
Letters to a Young Actress

One thing is certain: the religions are obsolete when the reforms do not proceed from them.

RALPH WALDO EMERSON,
Journals of Ralph Waldo Emerson

Religious talk is a very feast to self-deceit.

FREDERICK W. FABER,
Spiritual Conferences

It increases the value of the whole man; it deepens love, it exalts the stature, and adds force to every faculty. When it ceases to make us wiser and more passionate, when it does not confer greatness, it is a mere accretion.

WILLIAM HALE WHITE,
quoted in *William Hale White*
by Irvin Stock

The almost infinite meanings which may be given to the word religion make it difficult to express myself, but my point is that religion, anyway nowadays, is an inferior manifestation of religion, if you understand what I mean.

FREDERICK GOODYEAR,
Letters and Remains

Religion is always revolutionary, far more revolutionary than bread-and-butter philosophies.

HENRY MILLER,
The Air-Conditioned Nightmare

Nothing is so easy as to be religious on paper.

JOHN HENRY CARDINAL NEWMAN,
Oxford University Sermons

Universal good, then, the whole of that to which all things aspire, is something merely potential; and if we wish to make a religion of love ... we must take universal good, not universal power, for the object of our religion.... There would not be a universe worshipped, but a universe praying; and the flame of the whole fire, the whole seminal and generative movement of nature, would be the love of God. This love would be erotic; it would be really love and not something wingless called by that name.

GEORGE SANTAYANA,
Obiter Scripta

What a travesty to think religion means saving my little soul through my little good deeds and the rest of the world go hang.

GERALD VANN,
The Heart of Man

The fact of the religious vision and its history of persistent expansion, is our one ground for optimism. Apart from it, human life is a flash of occasional enjoyments lighting up a mass of pain and misery, a bagatelle of transient experience.

ALFRED NORTH WHITEHEAD,
Science and the Modern World

The problem of religion is to link finitude with infinitude. It is significant that people no longer believe in heaven.

ALFRED NORTH WHITEHEAD,
Dialogues of Alfred North Whitehead

REPUTATION

The one thing I detest, because it makes me feel detestable, is preaching or being wise man or seer.

The whole secret lies in the fact that it is also my problem to be "just the man, walking along, seeing, smelling." Could it not be that the more fool reputation a man gets the harder the job?

SHERWOOD ANDERSON,
Letters of Sherwood Anderson

Really great reputations have a vitality which enables them to survive that on which they were originally grounded.

JOHN AYSCOUGH,
Levia-Pondera

It is difficult to make a reputation, but it is even more difficult to mar a reputation once properly made—so faithful is the public.

ARNOLD BENNETT,
The Arnold Bennett Calendar,
compiled by Frank Bennett

Reputation is like credit—it enables one to venture on enterprises which else it were rash to undertake.

JOHN LANCASTER SPALDING,
Aphorisms and Reflections

RESIGNATION

Let us be resigned to everything, even to happiness.

HENRI FRÉDÉRIC AMIEL,
The Private Journal of Henri Frédéric Amiel

There seem times when one can neither help oneself nor anyone else to find what we are all in search of, and it seems impossible to submit or acquiesce. I, as you know, have been in this frame of mind, and can only say that one does go on, though it seems impossible. The only way, I think, is to do whatever comes to one, as quietly and fully as one can.

A. C. BENSON,
Excerpts from the Letters of Dr. A. C. Benson to M. E. A.

I do not like the idea of helplessly suffering one's misfortunes, of passively bearing one's lot. The Stoics depress me. I do not want to look on my life as an eternal making the best of a bad bargain.

RANDOLPH BOURNE,
Youth and Life

Those prisoners who blocked out neither heart nor reason, neither feelings nor perception, but kept informed of their inner attitudes even when they could hardly ever afford to act on them, those prisoners survived and came to understand the conditions they lived under. They came also to realize what they had not perceived before; that they still retained the last, if not the greatest, of the human freedoms: to choose their own attitude in any given circumstance.

BRUNO BETTELHEIM,
The Informed Heart

RESISTANCE

Without resistance you can do nothing.

JEAN COCTEAU,
Writers at Work, Third Series,
edited by George Plimpton

Nothing strong, nothing new, nothing urgent penetrates man's mind without crossing resistance.

HENRI DE LUBAC,
Paradoxes

RESOLUTION

Just as soon as we make a good resolution we get into a situation which makes its observance unbearable.

WILLIAM FEATHER,
The Business of Life

Empty pieties and good resolutions are part of the natural equipment of every proper man. They were never meant to be performed or fulfilled, but in the scheme of things they serve their purpose.

HOLBROOK JACKSON,
Southward Ho! and Other Essays

I believe that the resolutions less likely to be kept are those more likely to be made—the high that proved too high, the heroic for earth too hard.

ROSE MACAULAY,
A Casual Commentary

You are not going to have the laugh on me by luring me into resolutions. I know my weaknesses. . . . I shall continue to be pleasant to insurance agents, from sheer lack of manhood; and to keep library books out over the date and so incur a fine. My only hope, you see, is resolutely to determine to persist in these failings. Then, by sheer perversity, I may grow out of them.

CHRISTOPHER MORLEY,
Mince Pie

We always, it seems, do better with resolutions if we tell others, for we fear their mockery more than the prickings of our conscience.

GORHAM MUNSON,
The Writer's Workshop

RESPONSIBILITY

The great thought, the great concern, the great anxiety of men is to restrict, as much as possible, the limits of their own respon-

sibility.
GIOSUÈ BORSI,
A Soldier's Confidences with God

To be a man is, precisely, to be responsible.
ANTOINE DE SAINT-EXUPÉRY,
Airman's Odyssey

Today responsibility is often meant to denote duty, something imposed upon one another from the outside. But responsibility, in its true sense, is an entirely voluntary act; it is my response to the needs, expressed or unexpressed, of another human being.
ERICH FROMM,
The Art of Loving

Few things help an individual more than to place responsibility upon him, and to let him know that you trust him.
BOOKER T. WASHINGTON,
Up from Slavery

If men did not put their responsibilities above everything else, the bulk of lovemaking would not be done at night.
ANONYMOUS (HENRY S. HASKINS),
Meditations in Wall Street

Your responsibility ends when you have made sure that you are honest in will and intention, and are doing your best. There are no unbearable responsibilities in this world but those of our own seeking.
EVELYN UNDERHILL,
The Letters of Evelyn Underhill

We know, we affirm, I know and I affirm that at the very core of our being, of my being, there is the fact of responsibility.
ERIC GILL,
Modern Christian Revolutionaries
by Donald Attwater

To what extent is any given man morally responsible for any given act? We do not know.
ALEXIS CARREL,
Reflections on Life

REST

A good rest is half the work.
YUGOSLAV PROVERB

We should rest and amuse ourselves in such a way that rest and amusement do not become an additional fatigue or a total waste of time.
ALEXIS CARREL,
Reflections on Life

My thoughts seek you as waves seek the shore,
And when I think of you, I am at rest.
SARA TEASDALE,
"To E.," *Collected Poems of Sara Teasdale*

To work is simple enough; but to rest, there is the difficulty.
ERNEST HELLO,
Life, Science, and Art

Let your rest be perfect in its season, like the rest of waters that are still.
PHILIP G. HAMERTON,
The Intellectual Life

I find I haven't the art of rest. When I'm too tired to work at something which must be done but is distasteful, I give it up and work just as hard and long at something else: I take a defeat of the will instead of the frank brief rest that would make the distasteful work possible. Probably the great workers of the world have been the great masters of the art of resting.
STEPHEN MACKENNA,
Journal and Letters of Stephen Mackenna,

And one thing more with reference to the thoughts of recovery. There are here, in among the field-kingdoms, spots of dark, untilled land. . . . I asked what these dark strips of land were all about. They told me *c'est de la terre en repos*. So beautiful, you see, can resting be, and that is how it looks alongside work. Not disquieting, but such that one acquires a deep trust and the feeling of a big time.
RAINER MARIA RILKE,
Letters of Rainer Maria Rilke 1892–1910

RESTLESS

When we are restless we raise dust all about us and we forget the supreme truth that "we are."
RABINDRANATH TAGORE,
Letters to a Friend

Restlessness is, I think, inseparable from our mortal life; and the longing that it shall be otherwise is, I have sometimes thought, the first thing that will be satisfied by death.

A. C. BENSON,
*Excerpts from the Letters of
Dr. A. C. Benson to M. E. A.*

RESULT

I don't live in a laboratory. I have no way of knowing what results my actions will have. To live my life for results would be to sentence myself to continuous frustration and to hang over my head the threat that death may at any moment make my having lived a waste. My only sure reward is *in* my actions and not from them. The quality of my reward is in the depth of my response, the centralness of the part of me I act from.

HUGH PRATHER,
Notes to Myself

I can only say that it has become almost axiomatic with me to look for a person's overriding motive, his wider purpose, his deepest plan, in his achieved results rather than in the eloquent avowals that he makes to himself and others. The outer trend confirms the inner pattern.

LAURENS VAN DER POST,
Venture to the Interior

To work independently of *results;* this is perfect work.

AUGUSTUS DIGNAM,
Conferences

How often we hear it said, had this been done or that left undone, this or the other result would have followed. And, yet, were it possible to test these opinions, we should find them false.

FRANCESCO GUICCIARDINI,
Counsels and Reflections

RETIRE

Retiring must not mean just vegetating. I don't think anybody can do that.

EDWARD STEICHEN,
Wisdom, edited by James Nelson

When you've been used to doing things, and they've been taken away from you, it's as if your hands had been cut off.

GEORGE ELIOT,
Felix Holt

Most people perform essentially meaningless work. When they retire, that truth is borne in upon them.   BRENDAN FRANCIS

Don't simply retire *from* something; have something to retire *to.*

HARRY EMERSON FOSDICK,
Wisdom for Our Time,
edited by James Nelson

It is a good thing for a man to know when he has done his work. . . . There are very few men who know how to quit any great office, or to divest themselves of any robe of power.   SIR ARTHUR HELPS,
Companions of My Solitude

REVENGE

Revenge holds the cup to the lips of another but drinks the dregs itself.

JOSH BILLINGS,
His Works Complete

Development of the psychology and the moral of hitting back when you have been hit—something *active* is *necessary* after something passive—something to balance the having "been hit." One must *hit*—but this is not considered good by modern nice people. Still, one gets all poisoned if the passive experience is not answered by an active one. . . . Therefore, after an injury, one must *do* something, not to the person who injured you, but make an *action* as strong as the action which injured you and proving your strength as much as retaliation would. Creative, if possible, but anyway active. Then you will be all right, without any poison.

KATHARINE BUTLER HATHAWAY,
Journals and Letters of the Little Locksmith

Ordinary men—and, above all, peculiarly little men—experience a certain charm, a certain pleasure, in attacking great men. There is much of the spirit of revenge mixed up with this.

ERNEST HELLO,
Life, Science, and Art

Perhaps because our passions are less strong, perhaps even because the teaching of Christ has at last penetrated our thick heads, we look upon revenge as discreditable.

W. SOMERSET MAUGHAM,
The Summing Up

REVOLT

Most of us are on the verge of revolt a good deal of the time, but we don't do anything because we're too tightly harnessed.

WILLIAM FEATHER,
The Business of Life

REVOLUTION

It is very rarely that a country expects a revolution at a given time; indeed, it is perhaps not common for ordinary persons in any country to anticipate a revolution at all; though profound people may speculate, the mass will ever expect tomorrow to be as this day at least, if not more abundant.

WALTER BAGEHOT,
Literary Studies, Vol. III

The great revolution of the future will be Nature's revolt against man.

HOLBROOK JACKSON,
Platitudes in the Making

I know too well that man can only change himself psychologically, and that fear and greed make him inhuman, and it is only a change of roles we attain with each revolution, just a change of men in power, that is all. The evil remains.

ANAÏS NIN,
The Diaries of Anaïs Nin, Vol. II

Most revolutionaries are potential Tories, because they imagine that everything can be put right by altering the *shape* of society; once that change is effected, as it sometimes is, they see no need for any other.

GEORGE ORWELL,
A Collection of Essays

RIGHT

Being in the right does not depend on having a loud voice.   CHINESE PROVERB

It is a universal maxim worthy of all acceptation that a man may have that allowance which he takes. Take the place and attitude to which you see your unquestionable right, and all men acquiesce.

RALPH WALDO EMERSON,
Journals of Ralph Waldo Emerson

Act as if all were right and all will be right.

GEORGE PORTER,
*The Letters of
the Late Father George Porter, S. J.*

Human beings are perhaps never more frightening than when they are convinced beyond doubt that they are right.

LAURENS VAN DER POST,
The Lost World of the Kalahari

RIGHTS

When men say they have rights, they generally mean that they are suffering wrongs.

J. A. SPENDER,
The Comments of Bagshot, Second Series

Man first becomes formidable in action when he conceives his ideals as rights.

J. A. SPENDER,
The Comments of Bagshot, Second Series

It is in the concrete, and not in the abstract, that rights prevail in every sound and wholesome society.

FRANCIS PARKMAN,
Francis Parkman: Representative Selections,
edited by Wilber L. Schramm

Rights are something other people grant you after you've fought tooth-and-nail for them.
BRENDAN FRANCIS

Be as beneficent as the sun or the sea, but if your rights as a rational being are trenched on, die on the first inch of your territory.
RALPH WALDO EMERSON,
Journals of Ralph Waldo Emerson

RISK

The world belongs to Risk. The world will soon be a matching of risks, a scramble for the most daring.
GEORGES BERNANOS,
A Diary of My Times

An individual, like a people, like a continent, dies out when he shrinks from both rash plans and rash acts, when, instead of taking risks and hurling himself toward being, he cowers within it, takes refuge there: a metaphysics of regression, a retreat to the primordial!
E. M. CIORAN,
The Temptation to Exist

It is only by risking our persons from one hour to another that we live at all.
WILLIAM JAMES,
*The Will to Believe
and Other Essays in Popular Philosophy*

We are so constituted, that if we insist upon being as sure as is conceivable, in every step of our course, we must be content to creep along the ground, and can never soar.
JOHN HENRY CARDINAL NEWMAN,
Oxford University Sermons

The fishermen know that the sea is dangerous and the storm terrible, but they have never found these dangers sufficient reason for remaining ashore.
VINCENT VAN GOGH,
*Dear Theo:
An Autobiography of Vincent Van Gogh*

RIVER

The course of a river, or of a river tribu-

tary, suggests a journey of pleasure. Notice how it selects the choicest neighborhoods in its course, the richest fields, the suavest parts of the woods.
EDITH M. THOMAS,
The Round Year

The calm,
Cool face of the river
Asked me for a kiss.
LANGSTON HUGHES,
"Suicide's Note,"
Selected Poems of Langston Hughes

We are made to love the river and the meadow, as the wind to ripple the water.
HENRY DAVID THOREAU,
Journal

A river is the most human and companionable of all inanimate things. It has a life, a character, a voice of its own, and is as full of good fellowship as a sugar maple is of sap.
HENRY VAN DYKE,
The Friendly Year

A river without islands is like a woman without hair.
MARK TWAIN,
Mark Twain at Your Fingertips,
edited by Caroline T. Harnsberger

Darkened by our dumpings, thickened by our stains, rich, rank, beautiful, and unending as all life, all living, the river, the dark immortal river, full of strange tragic time is flowing by us—by us—by us—to the sea.
THOMAS WOLFE,
Of Time and the River

ROAD

The important thing to me about a road ... is not that it goes anywhere, but that it is liveable while it goes. For if I were to arrive ... I think I should be no happier than I am here.
DAVID GRAYSON,
The Friendly Road

The face of any old road is as visibly filled with expression and lined with experience as any old man's.

C. E. MONTAGUE,
The Right Place

He liked old shaded roads that wound away to quietness from driven glares of speed and concrete.

THOMAS WOLFE,
You Can't Go Home Again

ROGUE

A face shaped like lotus petals, a voice as cool as sandalwood, a heart like a pair of scissors, and excessive humility; these are the signs of a rogue.

SANSKRIT PROVERB

ROMANTIC

The curse of the romantic is a greed for dreams, an intensity of expectation that, in the end, diminishes the reality.

MARYA MANNES,
Out of My Time

ROME

The women of Rome, strangely enough, are beautiful even when they are ugly, and not many of them are that.

SIGMUND FREUD,
The Letters of Sigmund Freud

I have found the secret of my boredom in Rome: I do not find myself interesting here.

ANDRÉ GIDE,
The Journals of André Gide, Vol. I

I know of no city where you formulate an expression of like or dislike so quickly as in Rome. You are its friend or foe within five minutes after you leave its dingy railway station.

JAMES G. HUNEKER,
Steeplejack

Rome is the *imperator* who governs forces. She does not give up her secret; perhaps she has none. But she unveils yours for you. Whoever knows her, knows nothing of her, but discovers himself.

ROMAIN ROLLAND,
Journey Within

It is impossible for a stranger to say who may *not* beg in Rome. It seems to be a sudden madness that may seize anyone at the sight of a foreigner.

JAMES RUSSELL LOWELL,
Fireside Travels

One of the nice things about living in Rome is that you don't at all despise or avoid the things that the ordinary tourists do.

ALAN MOOREHEAD,
Holiday, August 1959

And here, about me is Rome ... Rome which is having its blossom time, with full hanging wisteria, with thousands of new roses daily, with all its beautiful fountains that are like eternal life, serenely new, without age, without exhaustion.

RAINER MARIA RILKE,
Letters of Rainer Maria Rilke 1892–1910

If Greece has taught us that marble bleeds, Rome shows us that dust flowers.

CECIL ROBERTS,
And So to Rome

ROSE

A rose sometimes falls to the lot of a monkey.

ARAB PROVERB

There is an old Persian parable about a king who loved roses and who desired to discover the loveliest rose in the world. He sent forth searchers for the rose of roses.

Then, after they had ransacked all the rose gardens on earth, the king found in a neglected corner of his own garden a rose that was more beautiful than all the others.

JAMES DOUGLAS,
Down Shoe Lane

The best rose-bush, after all, is not that which has the fewest thorns, but that which bears the finest roses.

HENRY VAN DYKE,
The Friendly Year

It was very still. . . . In bosses of ivory and in large splashed stars the roses gleamed on the darkness of foliage and stems and grass. Paul and Miriam stood close together, silent and watched. Point after point the steady roses shone out to them, seeming to kindle something in their souls. The dust came like smoke around, and still did not put out the roses.

D. H. LAWRENCE,
Sons and Lovers

The world is a rose; smell it and pass it to your friends.

PERSIAN PROVERB

If the rose puzzled its mind over the question how it grew, it would not have been the miracle it is.

J. B. YEATS,
Letters to His Son, W. B. Yeats and Others

ROUTINE

Routine is not organization, any more than paralysis is order.

SIR ARTHUR HELPS,
Organization in Daily Life

It is hard to do well the things that we are doing constantly.

FREDERICK W. FABER,
Spiritual Conferences

No sooner do we take a step out of our customary routine than a strange world surges about us.

J. B. PRIESTLEY,
All About Ourselves and Other Essays

RUSSIANS

The salient features of the Russian character are on the side of dream, pity and the quest of God.

MAURICE BARING,
Lost Lectures

If someone dies in a Russian's house, or

falls sick, or if somebody owes him money, or if he wants to make a loan—the Russian always feels a sense of guilt.

ANTON CHEKHOV,
Selected Letters of Anton Chekhov

Everybody has always underrated the Russians. They keep their own secrets alike from foe and friends.

SIR WINSTON CHURCHILL,
A Churchill Reader,
edited by Colin R. Coote

It is considered a political and social sin in Russia to print news about anybody's personal life. I don't know the origins of this taboo. . . . It is puzzling, however, because Russians gossip among themselves as people do everywhere, except they know more about each other than my neighbors on the tight little island of Martha's Vineyard.

LILLIAN HELLMAN,
An Unfinished Woman

SABBATH (*See also* RELIGION, SUNDAY)

He who ordained the Sabbath loves the poor.

JAMES RUSSELL LOWELL

Break down Sunday, close the churches, open the bars and the theatres on that day and where would values be? What was real estate worth in Sodom?

H. L. WAYLAND

The Sabbath is what you make of it—a holy day, a holiday, a rest day, a sports day—or, if you're not smart, another work day.

HERBERT L. GOLDSTEIN

SACRIFICE

Many men have sacrificed everything to errors, and I have always thought that heroism and sacrifice were not enough to justify a cause. Obstinacy alone is not a virtue.

ALBERT CAMUS,
Resistance, Rebellion, and Death

Without sacrifice there is no resurrection. Nothing grows and blooms save by giving. All you try to save in yourself wastes and perishes.

ANDRÉ GIDE,
The Fruits of the Earth

Sacrifice remains the solution of that which has no solution.

JEAN GUITTON,
Essay on Human Love

Many who have the courage to sacrifice themselves lack the courage to sacrifice others.

BRENDAN FRANCIS

Nothing is costly to one who does not count the cost.

ANTONIN G. SERTILLANGES,
Rectitude

SADNESS

As a rule, our minds are sad.

ABBÉ HUVELIN,
Some Spiritual Guides of the Seventeenth Century

I have taken life on the sad side, and it has helped me to understand many, many failures, many utter ruins.

ABBÉ HUVELIN,
Some Spiritual Guides of the Seventeenth Century

The saddest moment in a person's life comes only once.

BRENDAN FRANCIS

SAINT

The simplest and most effective way to sanctity is to disappear into the background of ordinary everyday routine.

THOMAS MERTON,
The Sign of Jonas

The saints' biographies display every sort of psychological background and previous history, but as far as I know none was covetous or cold.

IDA F. COUDENHOVE,
The Nature of Sanctity

I have met in my life two persons, one a

man, the other a woman, who convinced me that they were persons of sanctity. Utterly different in character, upbringing and interests as they were, their effect on me was the same. In their presence I felt myself to be ten times as nice, ten times as intelligent, ten times as good-looking as I really am.

W. H. AUDEN,
A Certain World

Still, in spite of their biographers, the saints have made their mark in the world.

THOMAS J. GERRARD,
A Challenge to the Time

The life of a saint is a struggle from one end to the other; the greatest saint is the one who at the end is the most vanquished.

PAUL CLAUDEL,
quoted in *The Journals of André Gide*, Vol. I

The sky is summered into trance,
The sea is caught up too,
And with what passion of amaze
Over their meeting
Blue broods into blue.

So might a saint in ecstasy
His heaven hot and bare,
Stumble upon another saint,
And with no greeting,
Kneel into his prayer.

EILEEN DUGGAN,
"Horizon," *Over the Bent World,*
edited by Sister Mary Louise, S.L.

Things are going well for me, like for a saint in this world.

YIDDISH PROVERB

Many people genuinely do not wish to be saints, and it is probable that some who achieve or aspire to sainthood have never felt much temptation to be human beings.

GEORGE ORWELL,
A Collection of Essays

Consult any one of those Saints whom the world calls mad. You will immediately be struck by the moderation and wisdom of his advice.... You will notice with astonishment that he understands human affairs a thousand times better than those do who spend their lives in transacting them. He knows the world a thousand times better than men of the world know it.

ERNEST HELLO,
Life, Science, and Art

To most, even good people, God is a belief. To the saints He is an embrace.

FRANCIS THOMPSON,
Works, Vol. III

The saint who works no miracles has few pilgrims.

ENGLISH PROVERB

To be a saint does not exclude fine dresses nor a beautiful house.

KATHERINE TYNAN HINKSON,
The Respectable Lady

There is something inexpressibly profound and which should be fathomed, through which the race of heroes and the race of saints stand in some inexpressibly deep contradiction.

CHARLES PÉGUY,
Men and Saints

SATISFACTION

The amount of satisfaction you get from life depends largely on *your* own ingenuity, self-sufficiency, and resourcefulness. People who wait around for life to supply their satisfaction usually find boredom instead.

DR. WILLIAM MENNINGER,
Self-Understanding

No man can be satisfied with his attainment, although he may be satisfied with his circumstances.

FRANK SWINNERTON,
Tokefield Papers

SCENERY

People ought to cultivate sensuality where scenery is concerned. One ought to touch it, to taste it, to embrace it, to eat it, to drink it, to make love to it.

JOHN COWPER POWYS,
The Meaning of Culture

SCHOLAR

It is not for nothing that the scholar invented the Ph.D. thesis as his principal contribution to literary form. The Ph.D. thesis is the perfect image of his world. It is work done for the sake of doing work—perfectly conscientious, perfectly laborious, perfectly irresponsible.

ARCHIBALD MACLEISH,
The Irresponsibles

That is the worst of erudition—that the next scholar sucks the few drops of honey that you have accumulated, sets right your blunders, and you are superseded.

A. C. BENSON,
From a College Window

To have one favourite study and live in it with happy familiarity, and cultivate every portion of it diligently and lovingly, as a small yeoman proprietor cultivates his own land, this, as to study at least, is the most enviable intellectual life.

PHILIP G. HAMERTON,
The Intellectual Life

SCIENCE

It is always observable that the physical and exact sciences are the last to suffer under despotisms.

RICHARD HENRY DANA,
quoted in *A Certain World*
by W. H. Auden

Every great advance in science has issued from a new audacity of imagination.

JOHN DEWEY,
The Quest for Certainty

The great tragedy of Science—the slaying of a beautiful hypothesis by an ugly fact.

THOMAS HENRY HUXLEY,
Aphorisms and Reflections

That man can interrogate as well as ob-

serve nature was a lesson slowly learned in his evolution.
SIR WILLIAM OSLER,
Aphorisms from His Bedside Teachings and Writings

There is one thing even more vital to science than intelligent methods; and that is, the sincere desire to find out the truth, whatever it may be.
CHARLES SANDERS PEIRCE,
Collected Papers of Charles Sanders Peirce,
Vol. V

The study of exact sciences ... is not so good a discipline as is commonly supposed for preparing the mind against inaccuracies of thought and expression in matters full of darkness and pitfalls. I have seen many illustrations of this in the arguments of mathematicians when out of their element.
CHAUNCEY WRIGHT,
Letters of Chauncey Wright

SEA

There is indeed, perhaps, no better way to hold communion with the sea than sitting in the sun on the veranda of a fisherman's café.
JOSEPH W. BEACH,
Meek Americans

I do not love the sea. The look of it is disquieting. There is something in the very sound of it that stirs the premonition felt while we listen to noble music; we become inexplicably troubled.
H. M. TOMLINSON,
The Face of the Earth

The attractions, fascinations there are in sea and shore! How one dwells on their simplicity, even vacuity! What is it in us, arous'd by those indirections and directions? That spread of waves and gray-white beach, salt, monotonous, senseless—such an entire absence of art, books, talk, elegance—so indescribably comforting, even this winter day—grim, yet so delicate-looking, so spiritual—striking emotional, impalpable depths, subtler than all the poems, paintings, music I have ever read, seen, heard. (Yet let me be fair, perhaps it is because I have read those poems and heard that music.)
WALT WHITMAN,
Specimen Days

I was born by the sea and I have noticed that all the great events of my life have taken place by the sea. My first idea of movement, of the dance, certainly came from the rhythm of the waves.
ISADORA DUNCAN,
My Life

I wish sometimes I were a seal. I would like to slip in and out of the water and have a glossy slippery coat. Swimming with nothing on gives you the feeling, too, it is delicious in warm water.
ANNE MORROW LINDBERGH,
Bring Me a Unicorn

To me there is something completely and satisfyingly restful in that stretch of sea and sand, sea and sand and sky—complete peace and complete fulfillment.
ANNE MORROW LINDBERGH,
Bring Me a Unicorn

I have observed, on board a steamer, how men and women easily give way to their instinct of flirtation, because water has the power of washing away our sense of responsibility, and those who on land resemble the oak in their firmness behave like floating seaweed when on the sea.
RABINDRANATH TAGORE,
Letters to a Friend

A poor woman from Manchester, on being taken to the seaside, is said to have expressed her delight on seeing for the first time something of which there was enough for everybody.
SIR JOHN LUBBOCK,
The Pleasures of Life

When anxious, uneasy and bad thoughts come, I go to the sea, and the sea drowns them out with its great wide sounds, cleanses me with its noise and imposes a rhythm upon everything in me that is bewildered and confused.
RAINER MARIA RILKE,
Letters of Rainer Maria Rilke 1892–1910

SECRET

Yea, as fascinating as a loose tooth is a secret to a young maid. For she knoweth not whether to spit it out or keep it safe; yet she cannot forget it.

GELETT BURGESS,
The Maxims of Methuselah

If you reveal your secrets to the wind you should not blame the wind for revealing them to the trees.

KAHLIL GIBRAN,
Sand and Foam

Impart to none what you would not have all know. For some men are moved to tattle by various motives—some through folly, some for gain, some from an empty desire to be thought knowing.

FRANCESCO GUICCIARDINI,
Counsels and Reflections

Honour makes men faithful in keeping secrets, and therefore unwilling to receive them, for secrets are like red-hot ploughshares. Only saints can walk safely between them.

HENRY CARDINAL MANNING,
Pastime Papers

SECRETARY

The corporation man sometimes emerges as much less than heroic to the one person in a real position to know—his secretary, on whom he often becomes markedly dependent.

MYRON BRENTON,
The American Male

Probably, but for the introduction of the lady secretary into the business man's office, the business man would have collapsed entirely by now. She calls up the sacred fire in her and she communicates it to her boss. He feels an added flow of energy and optimism, and—business flourishes.

D. H. LAWRENCE,
Assorted Articles

SEEING

I pray for a gift which perhaps would be miraculous: simply to be able to see that field of waving grass as I should see it if association and the "film of custom" did not obscure it.

MARK RUTHERFORD,
More Pages from a Journal

Actually, of course, few people in this world see what is going on about them. Nobody really sees until he understands, until he can create a pattern into which the helter-skelter of passing events fits and makes a significance. And for this sort of vision a personal death is required. . . . Nobody sees with his eyes alone; we see with our souls.

HENRY MILLER,
The Cosmological Eye

SELF

I'm tired of benevolence and eloquence and everything that's proper, and I'm going to cultivate myself and nobody else, and see what will come of that.

JOHN RUSKIN,
Letters of John Ruskin to Charles Eliot Norton,
Vol. I

At every single moment of one's life one is what one is going to be no less than what one has been.

OSCAR WILDE,
De Profundis

Nothing seems to me of the smallest value except what one gets out of oneself.

OSCAR WILDE,
De Profundis

It is only through the approval of others that self can tolerate the self.

KINGSLEY DAVIS,
Human Society

The true value of a human being is determined primarily by the measure and the sense in which he has attained liberation from the self.

ALBERT EINSTEIN,
Ideas and Opinions

Every man treats himself as society treats the criminal.

HARVEY FERGUSSON,
Modern Man

Every claim I make, every feeling I have, of power that is not my own, that is merely bought, is a cheating of the inner me.

SHERWOOD ANDERSON,
Perhaps Women

Heaven proceeds forever *from* me outward to all things, and not *to* me from coffee and custard.

RALPH WALDO EMERSON,
Journals of Ralph Waldo Emerson

In our own secret hearts we each and all of us feel, however poor our outward performances, and whatever the trivial and eradicable weaknesses of which we are conscious, superior to the rest of the world: or, if not superior, at least "different" with a difference that is very precious and beautiful to us, and the base of all our pride and perseverance.

SOLOMON EAGLE,
Essays at Large

We are all serving a life-sentence in the dungeon of self.

CYRIL CONNOLLY,
The Unquiet Grave

For me, it is a virtue to be self-centered; I am much better employed from every point of view, when I live solely for my own satisfaction, than when I begin to worry about the world. The world frightens me, and a frightened man is no good for anything.

GEORGE GISSING,
The Private Papers of Henry Ryecroft

Were it not for myself, I should get along quite well.

ALPHONSE KARR,
quoted in *Rectitude*
by Antonin G. Sertillanges

We project the unbearable self onto others, so that we can hate it in others and destroy it. These condemned elements are necessary to life. When you kill them, you kill life.

ANAÏS NIN,
The Diaries of Anaïs Nin, Vol. IV

One becomes typical by being to the utmost degree one's self.

HAVELOCK ELLIS,
The Dance of Life

Consciousness of self gives us the power to stand outside the rigid chain of stimulus and response, to pause, and by this pause to throw some weight on either side, to cast some decision about what the response will be.

ROLLO MAY,
Man's Search for Himself

For beyond the difficulty of communicating oneself, there is the supreme difficulty of being oneself. This soul, or life within us, by no means agrees with the life outside us. If one has the courage to ask her what she thinks, she is always saying the very opposite of what other people say.

VIRGINIA WOOLF,
The Common Reader, First Series

A man is not determined by what he does and still less by what he says. But in the deepest part of himself a being is determined solely by what he is.

CHARLES PÉGUY,
Men and Saints

I think we are well advised to keep on nodding terms with the people we used to be, whether we find them attractive company or not. Otherwise they turn up unannounced and surprise us, come hammering on the mind's door at 4 a.m. of a bad night and demand to know who deserted them, who betrayed them, who is going to make amends. We forget all too soon the things we thought we could never forget. We forget the loves and the betrayals alike, forget what we whispered and what we screamed, forget who we were.

JOAN DIDION,
Slouching Towards Bethlehem

Solitude is the best means of getting acquainted with one's self, but if one gets too well acquainted there is likely to be trouble. Sometimes we get sick of ourselves, and that's bad. . . . There's a good deal to live for, but a man has to go through hell really to find it out.

EDWIN ARLINGTON ROBINSON,
Untriangulated Stars

There are two sorts of truth about all of us. There is that which the world sees, and that which we know. Our deeds, which are known to all men, too often appear to us to be strange, inexplicable libels on ourselves.

DON MARQUIS,
Prefaces

Every being cries out silently to be read differently.

SIMONE WEIL,
Gravity and Grace

But can one actually find oneself in someone else? In someone else's love? Or even in the mirror someone else holds up for one? I believe that true identity is found, as Eckhart once said, "by going into one's own ground and knowing oneself." It is found in creative activity springing from within. It is found, paradoxically, when one loses oneself. One must lose one's life to find it.

ANNE MORROW LINDBERGH,
Gift from the Sea

It is only when we are misunderstood by others that we really understand ourselves.

VAN WYCK BROOKS,
A Chilmark Miscellany

To understand oneself is the classic form of consolation, to elude oneself is the romantic.

GEORGE SANTAYANA,
Words of Doctrine

The living self has one purpose only: to come into its own fullness of being, as a tree comes into full blossom, or a bird into spring beauty, or a tiger into lustre.

D. H. LAWRENCE,
Selected Essays

One ought to be a mystery, not only to others, but also to one's self. I study myself; when I am weary of this, then for a pastime I light a cigar and think: the Lord only knows what He meant by me, or what He would make out of me.

SØREN KIERKEGAARD,
Either/Or, Vol. I

SELF-ACCEPTANCE

One could say that the courage to be is the courage to accept oneself as accepted in spite of being unacceptable.

PAUL TILLICH,
The Courage to Be

One must be glad when as a great exception someone manages to get on terms with himself without any help.

SIGMUND FREUD,
The Life and Work of Sigmund Freud, Vol. II,
by Ernest Jones

Take yourself as you are, whole, and do not try to live by one part alone and starve the other.

JANET ERSKINE STUART,
Life and Letters of Janet Erskine Stuart
by Maud Monahan

First learn to love yourself, and then you can love me.

SAINT BERNARD OF CLAIRVAUX,
Letters

One must learn to love oneself—thus do I teach—with a wholesome and healthy love: that one may endure to be oneself, and not go roving about. . . . And verily, it is no commandment for today and tomorrow to *learn* to love oneself. Rather it is of all arts the finest, most subtle, last and most patient.

FRIEDRICH NIETZSCHE,
Thus Spake Zarathustra

To dare to listen to that inspiration from within which voices the ultimate reality of one's own being requires an act of faith which is rare indeed. When the conviction is borne in upon one that anything which is put together, or made up, has no ultimate reality and so is certain to disintegrate, one turns to one's own final reality in the faith that it and it alone can have any virtue or any value.

ESTHER HARDING,
Woman's Mysteries

Use all your intelligence and experience in managing your own life, employing the tenderness you would expect to find in a being of ideal kindness.

ABBE HENRI DE TOURVILLE,
Letters of Direction

Loving yourself is not a matter of building your ego. Egotism is proving you are worthwhile after you have sunk into hating yourself. Loving yourself will dissolve your ego: you will feel no need to prove you are superior.

THADDEUS GOLAS,
The Lazy Man's Guide to Enlightenment

Self-love is not opposed to the love of other people. You cannot really love yourself and do yourself a favor without doing other people a favor, and vice versa.

DR. KARL MENNINGER,
A Psychiatrist's World

SELF-ASSERTION

In our personal lives when we find signs that we are speaking in our own accent, speaking our own minds, living by our own opinions, we feel the pulse beat of our own personality coming to life again. We feel that in having discovered or arrived at ourselves, we have discovered a continent which is all our own.

IRWIN EDMAN,
The Uses of Philosophy,
edited by Charles Frankel

Risk! Risk anything! Care no more for the opinions of others, for those voices. Do the hardest thing on earth for you. Act for yourself.

KATHERINE MANSFIELD,
The Journal of Katherine Mansfield

The individual never asserts himself more than when he forgets himself. Whoever

thinks of himself stands in his own way.

ANDRÉ GIDE,
Pretexts

I hate a fellow whom pride or cowardice or laziness drives into a corner, and who does nothing when he is there, but sit and growl. Let him come out as I do and bark.

SAMUEL JOHNSON,
The Author's Kalendar, 1915,
compiled by Anna C. Woodford

To know oneself, one should assert oneself. Psychology is action, not thinking about oneself. We continue to shape our personality all our life. If we knew ourselves perfectly, we should die.

ALBERT CAMUS,
Notebooks 1935–1942

SELF-AWARENESS

The man who is aware of himself is henceforward independent; and he is never bored, and life is only too short, and he is steeped through and through with a profound yet temperate happiness. He alone lives, while other people, slaves of ceremony, let life slip past them in a kind of dream. Once conform, once do what other people do because they do it, and a lethargy steals over all the finer nerves and faculties of the soul. She becomes all outer show and inward emptiness; dull, callous, and indifferent.

VIRGINIA WOOLF,
The Common Reader, First Series

SELF-CONTROL

Holding-in creates horrid poisons which wear us out before our time. There are more deaths caused by ingrowing, suppurating self-control than the medical profession wots of.

ROBERTSON DAVIES,
The Table Talk of Samuel Marchbanks

SELF-DECEPTION

The worst of the idealistic education most of us have had under Christian authority is that it makes us so ashamed of our real feelings towards human beings that we indulge in a constant process of self-deception.

JOHN COWPER POWYS,
The Meaning of Culture

No is an affirmation of life just as *yes* is. Only falsehood is death. Lying to oneself, a defect of the spirit.

ROMAIN ROLLAND,
Journey Within

SELF-EXPRESSION

Creation is a better means of self-expression than possession; it is through creating, not possessing, that life is revealed.

VIDA D. SCUDDER,
The Privilege of Age

SELF-FULFILLMENT

There is at bottom only one problem in the world and this is its name. How does one break through? How does one get into the open? How does one burst the cocoon and become a butterfly?

THOMAS MANN,
Doctor Faustus

As long as anyone believes that his ideal and purpose is outside him, that it is above the clouds, in the past or in the future, he will go outside himself and seek fulfillment where it can not be found. He will look for solutions and answers at every point except the one where they can be found—in himself.

ERICH FROMM,
Man for Himself

Whatever he may think superficially, man can forgive himself everything except the sin of self-detention, nor can he ever forgive another for checking his highest aspirations; whereas everyone will accept, in his inmost being, the most severe suffering, if he feels assured that it is necessary for his proper development.

COUNT HERMANN KEYSERLING,
The Book of Marriage

Every human being is born to become what his original potentialities decree.... And every life must be chalked up at least a partial failure when it does not succeed in reaching its inherent destiny.

DR. SMILEY BLANTON,
Love or Perish

To be humble, submissive to the universe, selfless, yet make of one's self the poem, the lovely interpretation, medium for mysterious heightened sense of life—a flower—flexible—sensitive—*honest—true*. Always praying for simplicity—for receiving God.

KATHARINE BUTLER HATHAWAY,
*The Journals and Letters
of the Little Locksmith*

SELF-KNOWLEDGE

Know yourself, and your neighbor will not mistake you.

SCOTTISH PROVERB

Nothing, indeed, is so likely to shock us at first as the manifest revelation of ourselves.

HAVELOCK ELLIS,
The Dance of Life

My notion is that no man knows himself or can arrive at truth concerning himself except by what seems like indirection.

SHERWOOD ANDERSON,
Letters of Sherwood Anderson

I didn't know what he was playing up to—if he was playing up to anything at all—and I expect he did not know either; for it is my belief no man ever understands quite his own artful dodges to escape from the grim shadow of self-knowledge.

JOSEPH CONRAD,
Lord Jim

No man remains quite what he was when he recognizes himself.

THOMAS MANN,
Foreword, *Joseph and His Brothers*

A true knowledge of ourselves is knowledge of our power.

MARK RUTHERFORD,
Last Pages from a Journal

Know thyself. Ulysses showed his wisdom in not trusting himself. A Yale undergraduate left on his door a placard for the janitor on which was written, "Call me at 7 o'clock; it's absolutely necessary that I get up at seven. Make no mistake. Keep knocking until I answer." Under this he had written, "Try again at ten."

> WILLIAM LYONS PHELPS,
> *Essays on Things*

SELF-PITY

Do not confuse a man who pities himself with a man who is defeated: he still possesses energy enough to protect himself against the dangers which threaten him. Let him complain! That is his way of disguising his vitality. He asserts himself as best he can: his tears often conceal an aggressive intention.

> E. M. CIORAN,
> *The Temptation to Exist*

Life, I fancy, would very often be insupportable, but for the luxury of self-compassion; in cases numberless, this it must be that saves from suicide.

> GEORGE GISSING,
> *The Private Papers of Henry Ryecroft*

SELF-REJECTION

Blessed are they who heal us of self-despisings. Of all services which can be done to man, I know of none more precious.

> WILLIAM HALE WHITE,
> quoted in *The Note Books of a Woman Alone,*
> edited by M. G. Ostle

Our problem, wherever we work with people, is to try to release them from self-derogation.

> BONARO OVERSTREET,
> *Understanding Fear in Ourselves and Others*

It is very easy to get an audience these days if one preaches against conceit and pride in one's self, for most people feel so empty and convinced of their lack of worth anyway that they readily agree that the one who is condemning them must be right.

> ROLLO MAY,
> *Man's Search for Himself*

If you do not believe in yourself, do not blame others for lacking faith in you.

> BRENDAN FRANCIS

It would seem as if a self-destructive impulse waged constant battle with the will to live and took advantage of every opportunity to wreak its purpose upon its possessor.

> DR. KARL A. MENNINGER,
> *The Human Mind*

It is a very unhealthy frame of mind to get into to be always reproaching oneself for one's peccadilloes. I am sure the most cheerful people are those who confine their censures almost entirely to the lapses of their neighbours.

> ROBERT LYND,
> *The Peal of Bells*

It seems as if they purposely avoid the most serious, the most beautiful things; in short, that they voluntarily muzzle themselves and clip their own wings.

> VINCENT VAN GOGH,
> *Dear Theo:*
> *An Autobiography of Vincent Van Gogh*

People are never so ready to believe you as when you say things in dispraise of yourself; and you are never so much annoyed as when they take you at your word.

> W. SOMERSET MAUGHAM,
> *A Writer's Notebook*

To have that sense of one's intrinsic worth which constitutes self-respect is potentially to have everything: the ability to discriminate, to love and to remain indifferent. To lack it is to be locked within oneself, incapable of either love or indifference. If we do not respect ourselves, we are on the one hand forced to despise those who have so few resources as to consort with us, so little perception as to remain blind to our fatal weaknesses. On the other, we are peculiarly in thrall to everyone we see, curiously determined to live out—since our self-image is untenable—their false notions of us.

JOAN DIDION,
Slouching Towards Bethlehem

SELF-RELIANCE

Every now and then we discover in the seething mass of humanity round us a person who does not seem to need anybody else, and the contrast with ourselves is stinging.

ERNEST DIMNET,
What We Live By

Most people—one may say the best sort of people—greatly prefer to do things for themselves, however badly, than to have things done for them, however well.

ARTHUR PONSONBY,
Casual Observations

At bottom no one in life can help anyone else in life; this one experiences over and over in every conflict and every perplexity: that one is alone.
  That isn't as bad as it may at first glance appear; and again it is the best thing in life that each should have everything in himself: his fate, his future, his whole expanse and world.

RAINER MARIA RILKE,
Letters of Rainer Maria Rilke 1892–1910

Work out your own salvation. Do not depend on others.

BUDDHA

With begging and scrambling we find very little, but with being true to ourselves we find a great deal more than we desire.

RABINDRANATH TAGORE,
Letters to a Friend

The highest manifestation of life consists in this: that a being governs its own actions. A thing which is always subject to the direction of another is somewhat of a dead thing.

SAINT THOMAS AQUINAS,
quoted in *Modern Christian Revolutionaries*
by Donald Attwater

Taking everything into account only one solution becomes me—my own.

ANTONIN G. SERTILLANGES,
Rectitude

SENSUALITY

Man's brains have transformed the earth and the sea, but sensuality remains where it was before the flood. Women; wine; noise.

WILLIAM BOLITHO,
Camera Obscura

For all of my patients sensuality is a giving in to "the low side of their nature." Puritanism is powerful and distorts their life with a total anesthesia of the senses. If you atrophy one sense you also atrophy all the others, a sensuous and physical connection with nature, with art, with food, with other human beings.

ANAÏS NIN,
The Diaries of Anaïs Nin, Vol. II

Sensuality which used to show itself coarse, smiling, unmasked and unmistakable, is now serious, analytic, and so burdened with a sense of its responsibilities that it passes muster half the time as a new type of asceticism.

AGNES REPPLIER,
Points of View

SENTIMENTALITY

Sentimentality, the ostentatious parading of excessive and spurious emotion, is the mark of dishonesty, the inability to feel; the wet eyes of the sentimentalist betray his aversion to experience, his fear of life, his arid heart; and it is always, therefore, the signal of secret and violent inhumanity, the mask of cruelty.

JAMES BALDWIN,
Notes of a Native Son

The "sentimentalist fallacy" is to shed tears over abstract justice and generosity, beauty, etc., and never to know these qualities when you meet them in the street, because the circumstances make them vulgar.

WILLIAM JAMES,
Pragmatism

Sentimentality is a superstructure covering brutality.

C. G. JUNG,
Psychological Reflections,
edited by Jolande Jacobi and R. F. Hull

No one weeps more copiously than the hardened scoundrel, as was proved when a sentimental play was performed before a Chicago audience composed chiefly of gangsters, whose eyes were seen to be red and swollen on the rare occasions when they were not hidden by handkerchiefs.

HESKETH PEARSON,
Dickens

Never trust a sentimentalist. They are all alike, pretenders to virtue, at heart selfish frauds and sensualists.

J. B. YEATS,
Letters to His Son, W. B. Yeats and Others

SERENITY

The very moment everything looks serene, all hell breaks loose.

WILLIAM FEATHER,
The Business of Life

I lay in a meadow until the unwrinkled serenity entered into my bones, and made me into one with the browsing kine, the still greenery, the drifting clouds, and the swooping birds.

ALICE JAMES,
The Diary of Alice James

Whatever helps a person to use his resources productively and reduces his need to live up to a false image of strength and perfection is likely to add to his serenity and freedom from fear.

ARTHUR T. JERSILD,
Educational Psychology,
edited by Charles B. Skinner

We can make our lives so like still water that beings gather about us that they

might see, it may be, their own images, and so live for a moment with a clearer, perhaps even with a fiercer life, because of our quiet.

WILLIAM BUTLER YEATS,
quoted in *The Joys of Forgetting*
by Odell Shepard

SERMON

Every Monday morning I read what the ministers had said on Sunday, and it generally is that religion is needed.

FRANKLIN P. ADAMS,
Nods and Becks

A sermon is seldom as long as it seems.

SAMUEL MCCHORD CROTHERS,
The Gentle Reader

Five minutes of unbroken silence might make a great sermon.

BRENDAN FRANCIS

The sermon which I write inquisitive of truth is good a year after, but that which is written because a sermon must be writ is musty the next day.

RALPH WALDO EMERSON,
Journals of Ralph Waldo Emerson

The sermons I like best are those that have more love for one's neighbor than indignation against him.

SAINT FRANCIS DE SALES,
Saint Francis de Sales in Letters

One may sometimes attend church for a year, and hear excellent discourses on international peace, on industrial justice, on civil liberties, sex relations, social ethics in every phase; but rarely or never a word to help one's poor little soul in its effort to enter into commerce with the Eternal.

VIDA D. SCUDDER,
The Privilege of Age

Sunday. To Trinity Church, Dorchester. The rector in his sermon delivers himself of mean images in a sublime voice, and the effect is that of a glowing landscape in which clothes are hung out to dry.

THOMAS HARDY,
Thomas Hardy's Notebooks

We can bear hearing disagreeable truths spoken to a crowd or to a congregation—causticity has always been popular in preachers—because there are other heads than our own upon which to fit the cap.

AGNES REPPLIER,
Americans and Others

If the preacher is not gifted, remember that you can bring a large torch to a small taper and carry away a great blaze.

JOHN ANDREW HOLMES,
Wisdom in Small Doses

It requires great listening as well as great preaching to make a great sermon.

JOHN ANDREW HOLMES,
Wisdom in Small Doses

The Sunday sermon, and the leading editorial, are generally pieces of machine-work, as if you turned a crank and the discourse came out. It is not the man's real mind, his real experience. He does not know how to get at this; all is artificial . . . ; his ideas have no root, no succulency, no flavor. He speaks from art, from culture, from faculty, and not from inspiration.

JOHN BURROUGHS,
The Heart of Burroughs' Journals

SEX

Different though the sexes are, they intermix. In every human being a vacillation from one sex to the other takes place, and often it is only the clothes that keep the male or female likeness, while underneath the sex is the very opposite of what it is above.

VIRGINIA WOOLF,
Orlando

Making love, we are all more alike than we are when we are talking or acting. In the climax of the sexual act, moreover, we forget ourselves; that is commonly felt to be one of its recommendations. Sex annihilates identity, and the space given to sex in contemporary novels is an avowal of the absence of character.

MARY MCCARTHY,
On the Contrary

A maid that laughs is half taken.

ENGLISH PROVERB

Feminine virtue is nothing but a convenient masculine invention.

NINON DE LENCLOS,
The Compleat Lover,
edited by William Geoffrey

As in all other experiences, we always have the sexual experience we deserve, depending on our loving kindness towards ourselves and others.

THADDEUS GOLAS,
The Lazy Man's Guide to Enlightenment

Making love is one demonstration of how space relations ask us to surrender in love, and absorb the differences and imperfections and beauties of other human beings.

THADDEUS GOLAS,
The Lazy Man's Guide to Enlightenment

I still have a diary entry . . . asking myself whether talk about the size of the male organ isn't a homosexual preoccupation: if things aren't too bad in other ways I doubt if any woman cares very much.

LILLIAM HELLMAN,
Pentimento

Perhaps the most tragic of all human relationships are those which involve intense union at one point and abysmal separation at all others. The impassable barriers are brought more fully into consciousness by the union which exists in one aspect. Such tragedies are possible only in sex-relations, because the physiological basis is simple and universal, while the higher union of love is so intimate and personal.

EDWARD HOWARD GRIGGS,
A Book of Meditations

I don't know whether you've ever had a woman eat an apple while you were doing it. . . . Well you can imagine how that affects you.

HENRY MILLER,
Tropic of Capricorn

Today the emphasis is on sex, and very little on the beauty of sexual relationship. Contemporary books and films portray it

like a contest, which is absurd.
> HENRY MILLER,
> *Supertalk* by Digby Diehl

It is better to be silent than to say things at the wrong time that are too tender; what was appropriate ten seconds ago is so no longer, and hurts one's cause, rather than helps it.
> STENDHAL,
> *The Compleat Lover*,
> edited by William Geoffrey

I don't know what I am, dahling. I've tried several varieties of sex. The conventional position makes me claustrophobic. And the others either give me a stiff neck or lockjaw.
> TALLULAH BANKHEAD,
> quoted in *Miss Tallulah Bankhead*
> by Lee Israel

I am not promiscuous, you know. Promiscuity implies that attraction is not necessary.
> TALLULAH BANKHEAD,
> quoted in *Miss Tallulah Bankhead*
> by Lee Israel

Lust is more abstract than logic; it seeks (hope triumphing over experience) for some purely sexual, hence purely imaginary, conjunction of an impossible maleness with an impossible femaleness.
> C. S. LEWIS,
> *The Allegory of Love*

Like a fierce wind roaring high up in the bare branches of trees, a wave of passion came over me, aimless but surging. . . . I suppose it's lust but it's awful and holy like thunder and lightning and the wind.
> JOANNA FIELD,
> *A Life of One's Own*

Orgasm is the most obvious lie yet devised to thwart man. It can so thoroughly convince him of something which is unreal when he believes that the power of his excitement lies somewhere other than in his own physical apparatus.
> WILLIAM TALSMAN,
> *The Gaudy Image*

Woman . . . cannot be content with health and agility: she must make exorbitant efforts to appear something that never could exist without a diligent perversion of nature. Is it too much to ask that women be spared the daily struggle for superhuman beauty in order to offer it to the caresses of a subhumanly ugly mate?
> GERMAINE GREER,
> *The Female Eunuch*

Do not wonder at the man who runs after a heartless coquette, but keep your wonder for the man who does not.
> GEORG GRODDECK,
> *The Book of the It*

It is not at all simple to find that one-night stand. It is commonly said, for instance, that most people who begin an evening alone in a singles bar end up going home alone without a companion for the night. . . . The notion, propagated by the media, that sex is available on almost every street corner is demonstrably false. But the idea does make those who are unable to find sex feel that there is something terribly wrong with them. If sex is so available, they ask themselves, what's wrong with me?
> SUZANNE GORDON,
> *Lonely in America*

To be truly free and yet social means to cultivate detachment, as opposed to alienation. The therapeutic, even in erotic action, can do without attachment—indeed, he can do with and do without it, simultaneously, for relations that are too near and too fixed may lead to symptoms that destroy the capacity of an individual to live out his own life in ways of his own choosing.
> PHILIP RIEFF,
> *The Triumph of the Therapeutic*

However muted its present appearance may be, sexual dominion obtains nevertheless as perhaps the most pervasive ideology of our culture and provides its most fundamental concept of power.
> KATE MILLET,
> *Sexual Politics*

In fact, eroticism often arrives as a late guest at its own banquet. A high degree of affection or rapport between two people, especially if they see each other across an otherwise unbridgeable barrier of age or status, can easily generate sexual feelings.

C. A. TRIPP,
The Homosexual Matrix

We rarely talk of sex the way men do, in terms of I've had this one, I've had that one. There's a friend I've known for 19 years and all I've known of her private life is what I've heard from others. And yet our relation is very profound; if she dies, I die.

JEANNE MOREAU,
New York Times, June 30, 1976

Sex as an institution, sex as a general notion, sex as a problem, sex as a platitude—all this is something I find too tedious for words. Let us skip sex.

VLADIMIR NABOKOV,
Strong Opinions

I sometimes sleep with other girls
in boudoir or cheap joint,
with energy and tenderness
trying not to disappoint.
So do not think of helpful whores
as aberrational blots;
I could not love you half so well
without my practice shots.

JAMES SIMMONS,
"Cavalier Lyric," *Poems One Line
and Longer,*
edited by William Cole

The big difference between sex for money and sex for free is that sex for money usually costs a lot less.

BRENDAN FRANCIS

Women in the street. The warm beast of desire that lies curled up in our loins and stretches itself with a fierce gentleness.

ALBERT CAMUS,
Notebooks 1935–1942

Sex may be a hallowing and renewing experience, but more often it will be distracting, coercive, playful, frivolous, discouraging, dutiful and even boring.

LESLIE H. FARBER,
The Ways of the Will

A woman occasionally is quite a serviceable substitute for masturbation. It takes an abundance of imagination, to be sure.

KARL KRAUS,
Karl Kraus by Harry Zohn

The reason a mutilated body is more acceptable than a whole one is that it is only in mutilated form that the sexual impulse can exist in America. In pure form it would dissolve our culture and assign its machinery to rust and ruin, leaving a lot of embarrassed people alone with each other.

PHILIP SLATER,
The Pursuit of Loneliness

SHAKESPEARE

In reading Shakespeare lately I have been softly overcome with a peculiar peace and repose. Controversy ceases, artificial difficulties lose their importance, anxiety disappears. I am as a child in the arms of a man who knows but who smiles at my terrors.

MARK RUTHERFORD,
Last Pages from a Journal

I don't bother about responsibilities or outside matters but take a drive, walk a very little, lie upon a lounge and read Shakespeare. I try to do it free from religion which he is to most who speak English.

OLIVER WENDELL HOLMES, JR.,
Holmes-Pollock Letters, Vol. I

Among the many reasons which make me glad to have been born in England, one of the first is that I read Shakespeare in my mother tongue.

GEORGE GISSING,
The Private Papers of Henry Ryecroft

SHAME (*See also* CONSCIENCE)

Shame is the stirring of conscience after the act.

MARIA EDGEWORTH

Shame may restrain what the law does not prohibit.

SENECA

Shame can be good for you. It may lead to decency.
BEN HECHT

"You ought to be ashamed!" "Well, I am ashamed."
BEN HECHT

SHARE

When we can share—that is poetry in the prose of life.
SIGMUND FREUD,
The Letters of Sigmund Freud

Those who have much are often greedy; those who have little always share.
OSCAR WILDE,
De Profundis

It is impossible to share what fundamentally belongs to us.
ANONYMOUS (HENRY S. HASKINS),
Meditations in Wall Street

It is hard to believe that anything is worthwhile, unless there is some eye to kindle in common with our own, some brief word uttered now and then to imply that what is infinitely precious to us is precious alike to another mind.
GEORGE ELIOT

GEORGE BERNARD SHAW

Mr. Bernard Shaw has no enemies but is intensely disliked by all his friends.
OSCAR WILDE,
quoted in *Autobiography* by W. B. Yeats

SHOPPING

The quickest way to know a woman is to go shopping with her.
MARCELENE COX,
Ladies' Home Journal, March 1944

Why does a window dresser always turn the price tags so we can't read them?
KIN HUBBARD,
Abe Martin on Things in General

A woman may set out to buy a house-dress and come home with a cocktail suit.
JANET WOLFF,
What Makes Women Buy

SHYNESS

Ah, what a case can be made for vanity in the shy.
LILLIAN HELLMAN,
An Unfinished Woman

As children, we are made to feel we will only be loved if we are good (in the parents' terms). As soon as we begin to affirm our real selves, parents begin to reject us. We grow up with the idea that if we are ourselves we will be rejected. So, as artists, in our work we express our real self. But we keep the fear of not being loved for this real self. And timidity and shyness are the symptoms. A timidity we can overcome with those who understand and accept us.
ANAÏS NIN,
The Diaries of Anaïs Nin, Vol. IV

The shy man usually finds that he has been shy without a cause, and that, in practice, no one takes the slightest notice of him.
ROBERT LYND,
The Blue Lion

Other people are very like ourselves. They are shy and well meaning. They wish to be liked in spite of their failings. They want to please and to be pleased.
FRANK SWINNERTON,
Tokefield Papers

I put my best in books and letters and am more myself there than in *personal* relations, which always seem *less* real to me—because, like all shy people, I tend to adapt myself too much to my company.
A. C. BENSON,
*Excerpts from the Letters of
Dr. A. C. Benson to M. E. A.*

SILENCE

Accustomed to the veneer of noise, to the shibboleths of promotion, public relations and market research, society is suspicious of those who value silence.
JOHN LAHR,
Up Against the Fourth Wall

With silence one irritates the devil.
BULGARIAN PROVERB

The art of our time is noisy with appeals to silence.

SUSAN SONTAG,
Styles of Radical Will

Everyone has experienced how, when punctuated by long silences, words weigh more; they become almost palpable. Or how, when one talks less, one begins feeling more fully one's physical presence.

SUSAN SONTAG,
Styles of Radical Will

Be silent about great things; let them grow inside you. Never discuss them: discussion is so limiting and distracting. It makes things grow smaller. You think you swallow things when they ought to swallow you. Before all greatness, be silent—in art, in music, in religion: silence.

BARON FRIEDRICH VON HÜGEL,
Letters from Baron Friedrich Von Hügel to a Niece

There is no such thing as silence. Something is always happening that makes a sound.

JOHN CAGE,
Silence

I have noticed that every man, even those who are shy by nature, or timid by birth or upbringing, is, in a given case, far more likely to talk where he ought to keep silent, rather than to keep silent where talking would be in place.

THEODOR HAECKER,
Journal in the Night

There are two silences. One when no word is spoken. The other when perhaps a torrent of language is employed.... When true silence falls we are still left with an echo but are nearer nakedness. One way of looking at speech is to say it is a constant stratagem to cover nakedness.

HAROLD PINTER,
Up Against the Fourth Wall by John Lahr

Silence, if deliberate, is artificial and irritating; but silence that is unconscious gives human companionship without human boredom.

STEPHEN LEACOCK,
Last Leaves

Silence is necessary. I have never ceased to mount guard around my silence. I have defended it against my enemies—(that is nothing); I have defended it especially against my friends.

ROMAIN ROLLAND,
Journey Within

People go to take sun baths, why have so few had the idea of taking baths of silence?

PAUL CLAUDEL,
Lord, Teach Us to Pray

SIMPLICITY

There is more simplicity in the man who eats caviar on impulse than in the man who eats grape-nuts on principle.

G. K. CHESTERTON,
Heretics

I have no doubt we all appear simple and unsophisticated enough to superior beings.

SIR ARTHUR HELPS,
Companions of My Solitude

The real drawback to "the simple life" is that it is not simple. If you are living it, you positively can do nothing else. There is not time.

KATHERINE FULLERTON GEROULD,
Modes and Morals

As a rule, it is the simplifiers who are the most dangerous and the most mischievous seducers of men. God and the good are simple, but the world and the good things of the world are not.

THEODOR HAECKER,
Journal in the Night

He had not the good breeding to see that simplicity and naturalness are the truest marks of distinction.

W. SOMERSET MAUGHAM,
The Summing Up

But I know life is simple, however complex the organism may be; and everything goes to pieces when the living truth of the central simplicity is lost.

RABINDRANATH TAGORE,
Letters to a Friend

SIN

Certain sins manifest themselves as their mirror opposites which the sinner is able to persuade himself are virtues. Thus Gluttony can manifest itself as Daintiness, Lust as Prudery, Sloth as Senseless Industry, Envy as Hero Worship.

W. H. AUDEN,
A Certain World

A man is always capable of a sin which he thinks another is capable of, or which he himself is capable of imputing to another.

FREDERICK W. FABER,
Spiritual Conferences

Should we all confess our sins to one another we would all laugh at one another for our lack of originality.

KAHLIL GIBRAN,
Sand and Foam

Modern man's loss of a sense of being sinful doesn't spring from a feeling that he is inherently good. Rather, it springs from his feeling of being inherently ineffectual.

BRENDAN FRANCIS

All sins are attempts to fill voids.

SIMONE WEIL,
quoted in *A Certain World* by W. H. Auden

For sin is just this, what man cannot by its very nature do with his whole being; it is possible to silence the conflict in the soul, but it is not possible to uproot it.

MARTIN BUBER,
Hasidism

The manufacture of sin is so easy a manufacture, that I am convinced man could readily be persuaded that it was wicked to use the left leg as much as the right; whole congregations would only permit themselves to hop.

SIR ARTHUR HELPS,
Companions of My Solitude

Sin is the refusal to submit to the order of things.

ALEXIS CARREL,
Reflections on Life

What an unbearable creature he must have been in those days—and yet in those days he had been comparatively innocent. That was another mystery: it sometimes seemed to him that venial sins—impatience, an unimportant lie, pride, a neglected opportunity—cut you off from grace more completely than the worst sins of all. Then, in his innocence, he had felt no love for anyone: now in his corruption he had learnt.

GRAHAM GREENE,
The Power and the Glory

SINCERITY

The people you can be absolutely sincere with—sincere to be truest you—are the ones I am happiest with.

ANNE MORROW LINDBERGH,
Bring Me a Unicorn

A mugger is among the most sincere of men—sincere in his desire to rob you and, perhaps, to maim or kill you.

BRENDAN FRANCIS

I know not from what nonsense world the notion came first: that there is some connection between being sincere and being semi-articulate.

G. K. CHESTERTON,
Autobiography

Frank sincerity is a quality much extolled among men and pleasing to everyone, while simulation, on the contrary, is detested and condemned. Yet for a man's self, simulation is of the two by far the most useful; sincerity tending rather to the interest of others.

FRANCESCO GUICCIARDINI,
Counsels and Reflections

Show me in the world the sincere man. . . . The child is sincere, and the man when he is alone, if he be not a writer; but on the entrance of the second person, hypocrisy begins.

RALPH WALDO EMERSON,
Journals of Ralph Waldo Emerson

While the audience which uses the term sincerity thinks that it is escaping, in its tolerant mood, from the difficulty of judging skills, it is actually moving into a domain of considerably greater complexity. Just because such a premium is put on sincerity, a premium is put on faking it.

DAVID RIESMAN,
The Lonely Crowd

It is possible by long-continued practice, not merely in lying, but in talking on subjects in which we have no real interest, not to know when we are sincere and when we are not.

MARK RUTHERFORD,
Last Pages from a Journal

Be suspicious of your sincerity when you are the advocate of that upon which your livelihood depends.

JOHN LANCASTER SPALDING,
Thoughts and Theories of Life and Education

Why is it that human sincerity always excites love? Can it be as the poets suggest, that in the ultimate analysis it is itself love?

J. B. YEATS,
Letters to His Son, W. B. Yeats and Others

SINNER

It is only the great sinner who can do the two things of hating the sin and loving the sinner—the other sort only *hate the sinner.*

J. B. YEATS,
Letters to His Son, W. B. Yeats and Others

SKILL

Skill and assurance are an invincible combination.

DUTCH PROVERB

Every sort of mastery is an increase of one's freedom.

HENRI FRÉDÉRIC AMIEL,
The Private Journal of Henri Frédéric Amiel

Without any practical taste or skill myself, I always look with admiration, almost reverence, on the man who has it and uses it even for his own sake.

STEPHEN MACKENNA,
Journal and Letters of Stephen Mackenna

The men of real skill are almost always men who earn their living by their skill.

PHILIP G. HAMERTON,
The Intellectual Life

SKY

The sky is not less blue because the blind man does not see it.

DANISH PROVERB

For rich people, the sky is just an extra, a gift of nature. The poor, on the other hand, can see it as it really is: an infinite grace.

ALBERT CAMUS,
Notebooks 1935–1942

The man is blessed who every day is permitted to behold anything so pure and serene as the western sky at sunset, while revolutions vex the world.

HENRY DAVID THOREAU,
Journal

SLANG

Slang is ... vigorous and apt. Probably most of our vital words were once slang; one by one timidly made sacrosanct in spite of ecclesiastical and other wraths.

JOHN GALSWORTHY,
Castles in Spain and Other Screeds

SLEEP

If I sleep, I sleep for myself; if I work, I know not for whom.

ITALIAN PROVERB

Those no-sooner-have-I-touched-the-pillow people are past my comprehension. There is something suspiciously bovine about them.

J. B. PRIESTLEY,
All About Ourselves and Other Essays

Insomnia is a gross feeder. It will nourish itself on any kind of thinking, including thinking about thinking.

CLIFTON FADIMAN,
Any Number Can Play

Sleep is often the only occasion in which man cannot silence his conscience; but the tragedy of it is that when we do hear our conscience speak in sleep we cannot act, and that, when able to act, we forget what we knew in our dream.
ERICH FROMM,
Man for Himself

I swear they are all beautiful,
Every one that sleeps is beautiful.
WALT WHITMAN,
"The Sleepers," *Leaves of Grass*

Sleep frightens me, for it takes away all that I possess of others.
CHARLES-DAMIAN BOULOGNE,
My Friends the Senses

Early risers, as a rule, are a notably arrogant set.
WALTER DWIGHT,
The Saving Sense

A sleeping person induces respect, almost as much as a dead one. So that even the Greek gods, when they eavesdropped on naked girls asleep, dared at the most, a kiss.
EMIL LUDWIG,
Of Life and Love

Sleeping in a bed—it is, apparently, of immense importance. Against those who sleep, from choice or necessity, elsewhere society feels righteously hostile. It is not done. It is disorderly, anarchical.
ROSE MACAULAY,
A Casual Commentary

The horror of getting up is unparalleled, and I am filled with amazement every morning when I find that I have done it.
LYTTON STRACHEY,
Virginia Woolf and Lytton Strachey Letters

The busiest man needs no more hours of rest than the idler.
WILLIAM JAMES,
"The Energies of Men,"
Essays on Faith and Morals

I wish we could be unconscious for more of the time, to be really conscious for the rest of it—vital periods. But this semi-conscious stage! If only I could sleep from now to spring—hearing nothing, not the wind especially—and then wake keenly alive.
ANNE MORROW LINDBERGH,
Bring Me a Unicorn

No human being believes that any other human being has a right to be in bed when he himself is up.
ROBERT LYND,
Rain, Rain, Go to Spain

If you once turn on your side after the hour at which you ought to rise, it is all over. Bolt up at once.
SIR WALTER SCOTT,
Sir Walter Scott's Journal (1825-1832)

Sleep faster, we need the pillows.
YIDDISH PROVERB

SMART

It's hard to be so smart that the next minute can't fool you.
LEO STEIN,
quoted in *The Third Rose*
by John Malcolm Brinnin

SMELL

Every man likes the smell of his own farts.
ICELANDIC PROVERB

SMILE

What a blessed piece of hypocrisy it is to smile when one does not feel like it!
JOHN ANDREW HOLMES,
Wisdom in Small Doses

London. Saw a lady, who, when she smiled, smiled all over her face and chin, round to her ears and up among her hair, so that you were surfeited with smiling and felt you would never smile any more.
THOMAS HARDY,
Thomas Hardy's Notebooks

I had gone to a hospital for the severely wounded and was making the handshaking, false-smile clown-sounds that healthy people make when they are faced with the permanently injured, when suddenly a man came into the room. I think he was in his late twenties, I think he was blond, I think he was tall and thin. But I know that most of his face had been shot off. He had one eye, the left side of a piece of nose and no bottom lip. He tried to smile at me. It was in the next few hours that I felt a kind of exaltation I had never known before.

LILLIAN HELLMAN,
An Unfinished Woman

We do not completely love those at whom we cannot smile.

ANDRÉ MAUROIS,
The Art of Living

When people smile to themselves in the street, when I see the face of an ugly man or uninteresting woman light up ... I wonder from what visions within those smiles are reflected; from what footlights, what gay and incredible scenes they gleam of glory and triumph.

LOGAN PEARSALL SMITH,
More Trivia

SMOKING

It is better to be without a wife for a bit than without tobacco for an hour.

ESTONIAN PROVERB

[Sir Walter Raleigh] took a pipe of tobacco a little before he went to the scaffold which some formal persons were scandalized at, but I thinke twas well and properly donne, to settle his spirits.

JOHN AUBREY,
Brief Lives

Tobacco, when one is not smoking it, fills the thoughts, and, in order not to think about it, one goes on smoking it.

ROBERT LYND,
The Blue Lion

Women who dislike, or affect to dislike smoking, because they think it is the correct thing, can have no idea how they drive their husbands away from home. If a man may not smoke in his own house he will smoke in some other house, in preference to a lonely puff in the street: and that is worth a thought.

LADY ISABEL BURTON,
Smoke Rings and Roundelays,
selected by Wilfred Partington

I want all hellions to quit puffing that hell fume in God's clean air.

CARRY NATION,
(after snatching cigars from the mouths of smokers), quoted in *Charmers and Cranks*
by Ishbel Ross

If you see a man on a street corner smoking a corncob pipe, it will be safe to ask him to watch the baby while you slip around the corner. You would even be safe in asking him to lend you a five. He will be safe, too, because he won't have it.

CHRISTOPHER MORLEY,
Mince Pie

Nobody can be so revoltingly smug as the man who has just given up smoking.

SYDNEY J. HARRIS,
Strictly Personal

Cigarettes smell so awful to you when you have a nose that can truly smell.

ERNEST HEMINGWAY,
quoted in *Portrait of Hemingway*
by Lillian Ross

Smoke your pipe and be silent; there's only wind and smoke in the world.

IRISH PROVERB

I have only to be given one of those enormous and very expensive cigars by means of which companies are merged and dividends declared, and immediately I find myself turning into a different person. . . . I feel rich, powerful, rather than cynical and sensual, one who looks with narrowed eyes at the poor virtuous fools of this world.

J. B. PRIESTLEY,
All About Ourselves and Other Essays

SOBER

I was rather drunk with what I had done. And I am always one to prefer being sober. I must be sober. It is so much more exciting to be sober, to be exact and concentrated and sober.

GERTRUDE STEIN,
quoted in *The Third Rose*
by John Malcolm Brinnin

SOCIETY

The first duty of society is the preservation of society.

WALTER BAGEHOT,
Literary Studies, Vol. III

Society is one vast conspiracy for carving one into the kind of a statue it likes, and then placing it in the most convenient niche it has.

RANDOLPH BOURNE,
Youth and Life

Society has always seemed to demand a little more from human beings than it will get in practice.

GEORGE ORWELL,
A Collection of Essays

I think societal instinct much deeper than sex instinct—and societal repression much more devastating.

D. H. LAWRENCE,
Selected Letters of D. H. Lawrence

Our individual lives cannot, generally, be works of art unless the social order is also.

CHARLES HORTON COOLEY,
Life and the Student

Man's solution to his human needs is exceedingly complex, it depends on many factors and last, not least, on the way his society is organized and how this organization determines the human relations within it.

ERICH FROMM,
The Sane Society

The first duty of society is to give each of its members the possibility of fulfilling his destiny. When it becomes incapable of performing this duty it must be transformed.

ALEXIS CARREL,
Reflections on Life

Society must be made to rest upon justice and love, without which it is but organized wrong.

JOHN LANCASTER SPALDING,
Education and the Higher Life

The intelligence of man has created a social structure that presses heavily upon him, inhibiting and sometimes deforming his deep biological drives. To harmonize the pressures exerted by society and by the individual's drives is the greatest single problem of human life.

ABRAHAM MEYERSON,
Speaking of Man

I have always believed that the character of a society is largely shaped and unified by its great creative works, that a society is molded upon its epics, and that it imagines in terms of its created things—its cathedrals, its works of art, its musical treasures, its literary and philosophic works. One might say that a public may be so unified because the highly personal experience is held in common by the many individual members of the public.

BEN SHAHN,
The Shape of Content

SOLDIER

That a man can take pleasure in marching in fours to the strains of a band is enough to make me despise him.

ALBERT EINSTEIN,
Ideas and Opinions

Pass, pass, ye proud brigades, with your
    tramping sinewy legs,
With your shoulders young and strong,
    with your knapsacks and your muskets;
How elate I stood and watch'd you,
    where starting off you march'd.

WALT WHITMAN,
"The Return of the Heroes,"
Leaves of Grass

German prisoners, asked to assess their various enemies, have said that the British attacked singing, and the French attacked shouting, but that the American attacked in silence. They liked better the men who attacked singing or shouting than the grimly silent men who kept coming on stubbornly without a sound.

JAMES JONES,
WW II

The aim of military training is not just to prepare men for battle, but to make them long for it.

LOUIS SIMPSON,
"The Making of a Soldier USA,"
War: An Anthology, edited by Edward Huberman and Elizabeth Huberman

If it moves, salute it.
If it doesn't move, pick it up.
If you can't pick it up, paint it.
"The Soldier's Catechism,"
The Taste of Courage, edited by Desmond Flower and James Reeves

Three-quarters of a soldier's life is spent in aimlessly waiting about.

EUGEN ROSENSTOCK-HUESSY,
quoted in *A Certain World* by W. H. Auden

Although the American soldier has generally given a good account of himself in combat, he is extremely unlikely to voice patriotic rhetoric or overt political sentiments. Indeed, anti-ideology is itself an integral part of the soldier's belief system.

CHARLES E. MOSKOS, JR.,
"A Sociologist Appraises the G.I.,"
War: An Anthology, edited by Edward Huberman and Elizabeth Huberman

SOLITARY

After a debauch, one feels oneself always to be more solitary, more abandoned.

CHARLES BAUDELAIRE,
Intimate Journals

I am convinced this summer that I must never let myself slip completely out of the stream. It is so easy to do, such a frightful temptation, to get along with just a few chosen people—or *the lack of them!* To cherish the lack of them to the exclusion of all other people. Never, *never* give in to it (Aunt Annie said). It gets harder and harder, and one is always glad when one breaks through the shell of solitariness, to find the stimulation of people—different people.

ANNE MORROW LINDBERGH,
Bring Me a Unicorn

The more I see of life the more I perceive that only through solitary communion with nature can one gain an idea of its richness and meaning. I know that in such contemplation lies my true personality, and yet I live in an age when on all sides I am told exactly the opposite and asked to believe that the social and cooperative activity of humanity is the one way through which life can be developed. Am I an exception, a herd-outcast? There are also solitary bees, and is it not claimed that they are biologically inferior?

CYRIL CONNOLLY,
The Unquiet Grave

SOLITUDE

When I got to school, I ran away again in desperation for my ration of solitude, without which I cannot operate as a teacher, mother, wife or lover. I'm nullified without it. Like water from a creek to a vagabond, it is necessary to me.

SYLVIA ASHTON-WARNER,
Myself

It is known to many that we need solitude to find ourselves. Perhaps it is not so well known that we need solitude to find our fellows. Even the Saviour is described as reaching mankind through the wilderness.

HAVELOCK ELLIS,
Selected Essays

I am no good except when alone. In a group it's not so much the others that bore and annoy me; it's myself.

ANDRÉ GIDE,
The Journals of André Gide, Vol. I

Solitude is a wonderful thing when one is at peace with oneself and when there is a definite task to be accomplished.

GOETHE,
quoted in *The Art of Living*
by André Maurois

Another thing, I was too much in Solitude, and consequently was obliged to be in continual burning of thought as an only resource.

JOHN KEATS,
The Selected Letters of John Keats

He who does not enjoy solitude will not love freedom.

ARTHUR SCHOPENHAUER,
quoted in *A Certain World* by W. H. Auden

I have tasted to the full this summer the philosophic sweets of solitude but I find it not an unmixed blessing. It is something one enjoys, I think, when one has friends to run from; but when enforced, it loses much of its charm.

THOMAS WOLFE,
The Letters of Thomas Wolfe

The cure for all the illness of life is stored in the inner depth of life itself, the access to which becomes possible when we are alone. This solitude is a world in itself, full of wonders and resources unthought of. It is absurdly near; yet so unapproachably distant.

RABINDRANATH TAGORE,
Letters to a Friend

I am counting every moment until Nov. 29 when my boat sails. The very fact that I am going with a man whose mind I touch on only one point, means peace. I can live in my own mind and write poetry; can go into a dream and stay there.

W. B. YEATS,
*Letters on Poetry
from W. B. Yeats to Dorothy Wellesley*

The solitude which is really injurious is the severance from all who are capable of understanding us.

PHILIP G. HAMERTON,
The Intellectual Life

It might easily happen that one might look back on one's solitude as terribly precious because next to being with one particular person, or one particular friend, it's the best there is. Imagine the people one might have to live with!

KATHARINE BUTLER HATHAWAY,
The Journals and Letters of the Little Locksmith

It is this horror of solitude, this need to lose his *ego* in exterior flesh, which man calls grandly *the need for love.*

CHARLES BAUDELAIRE,
Intimate Journals

A solitude; even between husband and wife a gulf; and that one must respect, thought Clarissa, watching him open the door; for one would not part with it oneself, or take it, against his will, from one's husband, without losing one's independence, one's self-respect—something, after all, priceless.

VIRGINIA WOOLF,
Mrs. Dalloway

SOLUTION

It is often wonderful how putting down on paper a clear statement of a case helps one to see, not perhaps the way out, but the way in.

A. C. BENSON,
*Excerpts from the Letters of
Dr. A. C. Benson to M. E. A.*

SONG

"Blue Heaven" and other popular songs, the atmosphere they convey and what they mean . . . to those dumb, anonymous, dark crowds in movie theatres. Wistful desire for a sweetness in life, charm, delight, and something very personal, your own difference, your own feeling and situation.

KATHARINE BUTLER HATHAWAY,
Journals and Letters of the Little Locksmith

SORROW

No one can keep his griefs in their prime; they use themselves up.

E. M. CIORAN,
The Temptation to Exist

The sorrows which are worth the name are very rare.

AUGUSTUS DIGNAM,
Conferences

Were it possible for us to see further than our knowledge reaches, and yet a little way beyond the outworks of our divination, perhaps we would then endure our sorrows with greater confidence than our joys. For they are the moments when something new has entered into us, something unknown; our feelings grow mute in shy perplexity, everything in us withdraws, a stillness comes, and the new, which no one knows, stands in the midst of it and is silent.

RAINER MARIA RILKE,
Letters to a Young Poet

The pleasure that is in sorrow is sweeter than the pleasure of pleasure itself.

PERCY BYSSHE SHELLEY,
A Defence of Poetry

Grief is a matter of relativity; the sorrow should be estimated by its proportion to the sorrower; a gash is as painful to one as an amputation to another.

FRANCIS THOMPSON,
Works, Vol. III

There are times when sorrow seems to be the only truth.

OSCAR WILDE,
De Profundis

Every man is a solitary in his griefs. One soon finds that out.

NORMAN DOUGLAS,
An Almanac

Sorrow makes us all children again—destroys all differences of intellect. The wisest know nothing.

RALPH WALDO EMERSON,
Journals of Ralph Waldo Emerson

This, like our other ups and downs, is but for a little while in world history, but the moment has its right to sorrow, however much one may look beyond.

OLIVER WENDELL HOLMES, JR.,
The Mind and Faith of Justice Holmes,
edited by Max Lerner

Sorrow you can hold, however desolating, if nobody speaks to you. If they speak, you break down.

BEDE JARRETT,
The House of Gold

The groundwork of life is sorrow. But that once established, one can start to build. And until that is established, one can build nothing: no life of any sort.

D. H. LAWRENCE,
Selected Letters of D. H. Lawrence

SOUL

Who would ever think that so much can go on in the soul of a young girl?

ANNE FRANK,
Anne Frank: The Diary of a Young Girl

Only suckers worry about saving their souls. Who the hell should care about saving his soul when it is a man's duty to lose it intelligently, the way you would sell a position you were defending, if you could not hold it, as expensively as possible, trying to make it the most expensive position that was ever sold.

ERNEST HEMINGWAY,
quoted in *Portrait of Hemingway*
by Lillian Ross

One should stick by one's soul, and by nothing else. In one's soul, one knows the truth from the untruth, and life from death. And if one betrays one's own soul-knowledge one is the worst of traitors.

D. H. LAWRENCE,
Selected Letters of D. H. Lawrence

It is with the soul that we grasp the essence of another human being, not with the mind, not even with the heart.

HENRY MILLER,
The Books in My Life

The soul has its time and seasons and will not be forced: that which is its beatitude becomes its bunkum, and bunkum is seen to be beatitude the next day but one.

STEPHEN MACKENNA,
Journal and Letters of Stephen Mackenna

We are very strange creatures, so strange

that, in my opinion at least, not a philosopher of them all has written the first sentence in the book of the soul.

W. MACNEILE DIXON,
The Human Situation

To think about the soul, to think about it at least once in the confusion of every crowded day, is indeed the beginning of salvation.

GEORGES DUHAMEL,
The Heart's Domain

With all due reverence for the soul's dark night, one need not apologize for preferring the soul's golden dawn.

BRENDAN FRANCIS

SOUND

All sounds have been as music to my
    listening:
Pacific lamentations of slow bells,
The crunch of boots on blue snow rosy-
    glistening,
Shuffle of autumn leaves; and all
    farewells.

WILFRED OWEN,
"All Sounds Have Been as Music,"
Poems of Wilfred Owen

SOUTH

One isn't long in the Southern states without realizing that the land, the rivers, even the cities belong to the blacks and that all the whites are outsiders there.

SHERWOOD ANDERSON,
Letters of Sherwood Anderson

SPECIALIST

It seems to me that one of the foolishest ideas is people's habit of constantly looking for a *complete man,* a kind of nonsense handed down from Goethe. What we want is incomplete men. I like all qualities to be in excess, or rather that each person should be a specialist.

J. B. YEATS,
Letters to His Son, W. B. Yeats and Others

The incessant concentration of thought upon one subject, however interesting, tethers a man's mind in a narrow field.

SIR WILLIAM OSLER,
*Aphorisms from His Bedside Teachings
and Writings*

SPEECH

We all indulge in the strange, pleasant process called thinking, but when it comes to saying, even to someone opposite, what we think, then how little we are able to convey! The phantom is through the mind and out of the window before we can lay salt on its tail, or slowly sinking and returning to the profound darkness which it has lit up momentarily with a wandering light.

VIRGINIA WOOLF,
The Common Reader, First Series

Speech is the Mother, not the handmaid, of Thought.

KARL KRAUS,
quoted in *A Certain World* by W. H. Auden

Speech was the essential medium of his power, not only over his audiences but over his own temperament. Hitler talked incessantly, often using words less to communicate his thoughts than to release the hidden spring of his own and others' emotions, whipping himself and his audience into anger or exaltation by the sound of his voice. Talk had another function, too. "Words," he once said, "build bridges into unexplored regions." As he talked conviction would grow until certainty came and the problem was solved.

ALAN BULLOCK,
Hitler: A Study in Tyranny

I like people who refuse to speak until they are ready to speak.

LILLIAN HELLMAN,
An Unfinished Woman

There is something strange in the acts of writing and speaking. The ridiculous and amazing mistake people make is to believe they use words in relation to things. They are unaware of the nature of language—

which is to be its own and only concern, making it so fertile and splendid a mystery. When someone talks just for the sake of talking he is saying the most original and truthful thing he can say.

NOVALIS,
quoted in *Styles of Radical Will*
by Susan Sontag

Speech is conveniently located midway between thought and action, where it often substitutes for both.

JOHN ANDREW HOLMES,
Wisdom in Small Doses

SPIRITUAL

Every man has two journeys to make through life. There is the outer journey, with its various incidents and the milestones. . . . There is also an inner journey, a spiritual Odyssey, with a secret history of its own.

DEAN WILLIAM R. INGE,
More Lay Thoughts of a Dean

It is not by meticulous care in avoiding all contaminations that we can keep our spirit clean and give it grace, but by urging it to give vigorous expression to its inner life in the very midst of all the dust and heat.

RABINDRANATH TAGORE,
Letters to a Friend

A man's spiritual kin are his nearest relations.

HOLBROOK JACKSON,
Platitudes in the Making

The spiritual life is a continuous creation: to the extent that it gives way, materialistic explanations prevail against it.

HENRI DE LUBAC,
Paradoxes

Spiritual rose bushes are not like natural rose bushes; with these latter the thorns remain but the roses pass, with the former the thorns pass and the roses remain.

SAINT FRANCIS DE SALES,
Saint Francis de Sales in His Letters

SPONTANEITY

So, too, our whole life is an attempt to discover when our spontaneity is whimsical, sentimental irresponsibility and when it is a valid expression of our deepest desires and values.

HELEN MERRELL LYND,
On Shame and the Search for Identity

SPRING

Spring is sooner recognized by plants than by men.

CHINESE PROVERB

In the spring a young man's fancy lightly turns to love, but a family man's duties turn heavily towards the household chores that need doing but never get done.

MAX LERNER,
The Unfinished Country

Today I went out. It smelled, it felt, it sensed spring. I had for the first time faith—not intellectual belief, but a sudden feeling of turning tide. "Yes, there *will be* spring."

ANNE MORROW LINDBERGH,
Bring Me a Unicorn

The morning is like a nude woman veiled by her own hair. April is in heat; she is pairing with the Sun. She yields herself to his embraces all day.

JOHN BURROUGHS,
The Heart of Burroughs' Journals

Of course everything is blooming most recklessly: if it were voices instead of colors, there would be an unbelievable shrieking into the heart of the night.

RAINER MARIA RILKE,
Letters of Rainer Maria Rilke 1892–1910

Spring is here,—and I could be very happy, except that I am broke.

EDNA ST. VINCENT MILLAY,
Letters of Edna St. Vincent Millay

For the urban population spring is heralded by less celestial signs—not a wedge of geese in the sky, but a span of new plucked terriers on the Avenue, or a potted hyacinth groomed for April.

E. B. WHITE,
Every Day Is Saturday

Spring has no language but a cry.

THOMAS WOLFE,
Of Time and the River

Every year, back Spring comes, with nasty little birds yapping their fool heads off, and the ground all mucked up with arbutus.

DOROTHY PARKER,
An Omnibus of American Humor,
compiled by Robert N. Linscott

I almost picked the crocuses, you told them so sincerely. Spring's first conviction is a wealth beyond its whole experience.

EMILY DICKINSON,
Selected Poems and Letters of Emily Dickinson

Now it is really a strange hot day—sudden spring. One's consciousness seems to come suddenly out of its sheath—like a bud buried in a stalk that suddenly comes out and there is a flower—wide open.

KATHARINE BUTLER HATHAWAY,
*Journal and Letters
of the Little Locksmith*

STARS

I lay down on a camp bed in the farmyard under the open sky. The stars twinkled and I wanted to weep from joy at being alive and breathing those sweet-smelling grasses and seeing those stars above me.

SVETLANA ALLILUYEVA,
Twenty Letters to a Friend

There was a flurry of premature snow in the air and the stars looked cold. Staring up at them, he saw that they were his stars as always—symbols of ambition, struggle and glory.

F. SCOTT FITZGERALD,
The Crack-up

The sky minted into golden sequins.

GERARD MANLEY HOPKINS,
Notebooks and Papers

Should you ask me my comprehension of a starlight night, awe were my only reply.

EMILY DICKINSON,
Selected Poems and Letters of Emily Dickinson

Last night the stars were magnificent—Pegasus and Andromeda faced me brilliantly when I lifted my shade, so I went down and had a friendly reunion with the constellations. . . . I get a wonderful peace and the most exquisite pleasure from my friendship with the stars.

ELLEN GLASGOW,
Letters of Ellen Glasgow

Even a small star shines in the darkness.

DANISH PROVERB

We walk up the beach under the stars. And when we are tired of walking, we lie flat on the sand under a bowl of stars. We feel stretched, expanded to take in their compass. They pour into us until we are filled with stars, up to the brim.

ANNE MORROW LINDBERGH,
Gift from the Sea

When I look at the stars, nothing which the astronomers have said attaches to them, they are so simple and remote.

HENRY DAVID THOREAU,
Journal

Across
The Harlem roof-tops
Moon is shining
Night sky is blue.
Stars are great drops
Of golden dew.

LANGSTON HUGHES,
"Harlem Night Song,"
Selected Poems of Langston Hughes

It is so strange that there are times when I feel the stars are not at all *solemn:* they are secretly gay.

KATHERINE MANSFIELD,
The Journal of Katherine Mansfield

Why am I so lonely? Not long ago I strolled through the moshav one evening. It was a fabulous, starry night. Small lights glittered in the lanes, and in the middle of the wide lane. Sounds of music, songs, conversation, and laughter came from all around; and far, far in the distance I heard the barking of dogs. The houses seemed so distant; only the stars were near.

HANNAH SENESH,
Revelations: Diaries of Women, edited by
Mary Jane Moffat and Charlotte Painter

The great beauty of astronomy is not what is incomprehensible in it, but its comprehensibility—its geometrical exactitude.

WILLIAM HALE WHITE,
quoted in *Religion and Art of
William Hale White* by Wilfred Stone

STATISTICS

Statistics is the art of lying by means of figures.

DR. WILHELM STEKHEL,
Marriage at the Crossroads

Statistics are the triumph of the quantitative method, and the quantitative method is the victory of sterility and death.

HILAIRE BELLOC,
The Silence of the Sea

GERTRUDE STEIN

You would be surprised to know just how altogether American I found you.

SHERWOOD ANDERSON,
Letters of Sherwood Anderson

She knew that she was the object of derision to many and to some extent the knowledge fortified her. ... Yet it is very moving to learn that on one occasion when a friend asked her what a writer most wanted, she replied, throwing up her hands and laughing, "Oh, praise, praise, praise!"

THORNTON WILDER,
'47 Magazine of the Year, October 1947

Einstein was the creative philosophic mind of the century and I have been the creative literary mind of the century.

GERTRUDE STEIN,
quoted in *The Third Rose*
by John Malcolm Brinnin

STINGINESS

Stinginess becomes a game whose devotees can obtain extraordinary delights by gradually eliminating all reasons for spending.

ANDRÉ MAUROIS,
The Art of Living

STRANGE

If anyone tells you something strange about the world, something you have never heard before, do not laugh but listen attentively; make him repeat it, make him explain it; no doubt there is something there worth taking hold of.

GEORGES DUHAMEL,
The Heart's Domain

STRENGTH

There are few of us who have not a strong propensity to diminish our present strength by entertaining fears of future weakness.

CHARLES B. FAIRBANKS,
My Unknown Chum

It is not good to see people who have been pretending strength all their lives lose it even for a minute.

LILLIAN HELLMAN,
Pentimento

The using up of strength is in a certain sense still an increase of strength; for fundamentally it is only a matter of a wide circle: all the strength we give away comes back over us again, experienced and transformed.

RAINER MARIA RILKE,
Letters of Rainer Maria Rilke 1892–1910

We deceive ourselves when we fancy that only weakness needs support. Strength needs it far more.

MADAME SWETCHINE,
The Writings of Madame Swetchine

I felt invincible. My strength was that of a giant. God was certainly standing by me. I smashed five saloons with rocks before I ever took a hatchet.

CARRY NATION,
quoted in *Charmers and Cranks*
by Ishbel Ross

Strenuousness is the open foe of attainment. The strength that wins is calm and has an exhaustless source in its passive depth.

RABINDRANATH TAGORE,
Letters to a Friend

STRUGGLE

One day in retrospect the years of struggle will strike you as the most beautiful.

SIGMUND FREUD,
The Letters of Sigmund Freud

It is the devil to be struggling forward, like a man in the mire, and making not an inch by your exertions, and such seems to be my fate.

SIR WALTER SCOTT,
Sir Walter Scott's Journal (1825–1832)

Everything is bound to take up room and to shove other things aside in some measure: the question is to understand justly what hold each thing has normally in nature and in human nature, and how great is the ascension or flowering of life that it is capable of producing.

GEORGE SANTAYANA,
The Letters of George Santayana

Sweat and effort, human nature strained to its uttermost and on the rack, yet getting through alive, and then turning its back on its success to pursue another more rare and arduous still—this is the sort of thing the presence of which inspires us.

WILLIAM JAMES,
Talks to Teachers

If you stop struggling, then you stop life.

HUEY NEWTON,
Supertalk by Digby Diehl

STUBBORN

Hard heads suffer much.

ALBANIAN PROVERB

STUDENT

He wants to feel that the instructor is not simply passing on dead knowledge in the form that it was passed on to him, but that he has assimilated it and has read his own experience into it, so that it has come to mean more to him than almost anything in the world.

RANDOLPH BOURNE,
Youth and Life

The student who is worrying about his future, anxious over the examinations, doubting his fitness for the profession, is certain not to do so well as the man who cares for nothing but the matter in hand, and who knows not whither he is going.

SIR WILLIAM OSLER,
Aphorisms from His Bedside Teachings and Writings

Students who store themselves so amply with literature or science, that no room is left for determining the respective relations which exist between their acquisitions, one by one, are rather said to load their minds than to enlarge them.

JOHN HENRY CARDINAL NEWMAN,
Oxford University Sermons

I have heard a student censured for working out his own idea before learning all that others had done on the subject. But he was right; one may know too much, especially at first. The time for exhaustive reading is when you have worked out your own ideas with some fulness and in a spirit of discovery.

CHARLES HORTON COOLEY,
Life and the Student

STUPIDITY

Stupidity is an elemental force for which no earthquake is a match.

KARL KRAUS,
Karl Kraus by Harry Zohn

In fact, what we opprobriously call stupidity, though not an enlivening quality in common society, is Nature's favourite resource for preserving steadiness of conduct and consistency of opinion.

WALTER BAGEHOT,
Literary Studies, Vol. III

SUBWAY

Even in times of such outrageous contact, when humanity is squeezed into a paste and loses even individuality of body for the length of the journey, it is possible for those who live to enjoy life.

WILLIAM BOLITHO,
Camera Obscura

The warm wedlock of the rush hours.

CHRISTOPHER MORLEY,
Essays

You get a lot of horrible things said to you. Like, a man in a discotheque came up to me and said, "You're Miss Subways; how big is *your* tunnel?"

CAROL BROWN,
(former "Miss Subways"),
New York magazine, March 29, 1976

There are men in New York who ride the subways but do not want it generally known. ... The impulse is that the subways are for proles and the people of status travel only by cab, or perhaps once in a great while by bus.

TOM WOLFE,
*The Kandy-Kolored
Tangerine-Flake Streamline Baby*

SUCCESS

For a woman to apologize for success is as pointless as for a man to apologize for failure. One is as one is, and the love that can't encompass both is a poor sort of love.

MARYA MANNES,
Out of My Time

All you need in this life is ignorance and confidence; then success is sure.

MARK TWAIN,
Mark Twain at Your Fingertips,
edited by Caroline T. Harnsberger

The prospect of success in achieving our most cherished dream is not without its terrors. Who is more deprived and alone than the man who has achieved his dream?

BRENDAN FRANCIS

Many times I think of our talks in the old days. We both wanted to be writers. I got there. You didn't. To tell you the truth, old man, I can't see much difference.

SHERWOOD ANDERSON,
Letters of Sherwood Anderson

It's hard to tell which gets knocked the most, the success or the failure, but it's mighty close.

KIN HUBBARD,
Abe Martin on Things in General

Whoever wrote "to win success we must deserve it" must have been the same fellow who gave out the statement that two can live as cheaply as one.

KIN HUBBARD,
Abe Martin on Things in General

Success, which is something so simple in the end, is made up of thousands of things, we never fully know what.

RAINER MARIA RILKE,
Letters of Rainer Maria Rilke 1892–1910

It's damn pleasant. I think, abstractly, it adds to one's ability to act and to tackle *any* job, whether related to one's field or not. This is both helpful and dangerous, but in general, I would say that unless one has enough success at something to trust oneself ... one is poorly off.

ELIZABETH JANEWAY,
Open Secrets by Barbaralee Diamonstein

Most of the trouble with most people in America who become successful is that they can really and truly get by on bullshit alone. They can survive on it.

SAMMY DAVIS, JR.,
Showcase by Roy Newquist

Men are better companions before their success than after it, for they have so much more leisure.

GEORGE GISSING,
Commonplace Book

"Success" is never merely final or terminal. Something else succeeds it. ... The world does not stop when the successful person pulls out his plum; nor does he stop, and the kind of success he obtains,

and his attitude towards it, is a factor in what comes afterwards.
JOHN DEWEY,
Human Nature and Conduct

A successful man is he who received a great deal more from his fellow-men, usually incomparably more than corresponds to his service to them.
ALBERT EINSTEIN,
quoted in *Success*
by Robert E. Shafer and Verlene C. Bernd

I confess I do not like them overmuch, these very successful men. Their manner seems to bristle with comparisons unfavorable to their less fortunate fellows.
JOSEPH FARRELL,
Lectures of a Certain Professor

Since modern man experiences himself both as the seller and as the commodity to be sold on the market, his self-esteem depends on conditions beyond his control. If he is "successful," he is valuable; if he is not, he is worthless.
ERICH FROMM,
Man for Himself

There is nothing in the world that will take the chip off one's shoulder like a feeling of success.
THOMAS WOLFE,
You Can't Go Home Again

The common idea that success spoils people by making them vain, egotistic and self-complacent is erroneous; on the contrary it makes them, for the most part, humble, tolerant and kind.
W. SOMERSET MAUGHAM,
The Summing Up

Virtue we still consider the best goal for others: but for ourselves, success.
E. V. LUCAS,
365 Days and One More

What depresses me is the inevitable way the second rate forges ahead and the deserving is left behind. I shouldn't mind it if I saw the admirable sweep on to success, or immortality, but always it seems to be the ordinary, the vulgar, and the average,

or the lower average, that triumphs.
ELLEN GLASGOW,
Letters of Ellen Glasgow

I've often thought that success comes to her by the spirit in her that dares and defies her idea not to prove the right one. One has seen it so again and again, in the face of everything, become the right one.
HENRY JAMES,
The Wings of the Dove

The only success worth one's powder was success in the line of one's idiosyncrasy. Consistency was itself distinction, and what was talent but the art of being completely whatever it was that one happened to be? One's things were characteristic or were nothing.
HENRY JAMES,
The Next Time

SUFFERING

To be attached to what you don't want to be attached to is suffering, and to be detached from what you want to be attached to is suffering.
R. D. LAING,
Supertalk by Digby Diehl

So long as one is able to pose one has still much to learn about suffering.
ELLEN GLASGOW,
Letters of Ellen Glasgow

It is quite surprising, you know, how much steel one's heart can hold; a good twelve inches is driven in, you break off six of them that stick out, the rest is grown over, and you go on quite nicely, thank you.
THOMAS WOLFE,
The Letters of Thomas Wolfe

One does not get crucified, one crucifies oneself.
BULGARIAN PROVERB,

I misinterpret myself whenever I suffer over anything. That sounds rather false to you, probably, as if I were deserting the ship that we are all floating in. But, really, I do begin to think that we can step out of the door like the hummingbird. It's open all the time. Why cling to something that isn't good? ... We seem to resist the vitality of healing—we really wish to suffer.

KATHARINE BUTLER HATHAWAY,
Journal and Letters
of the Little Locksmith

I wonder why we suffer so strangely—to bring out something in us, I try to believe, which can't be brought out in any other way.

A. C. BENSON,
Excerpts from the Letters
of Dr. A. C. Benson to M.E.A.

He who has come through the fire will not fade in the sun.

HINDU PROVERB

What does it indicate that we pass suffering in the streets without noticing it,—see human misery, destitution, degradation, and not heed it?

WILLIAM ELLERY CHANNING,
Dr. Channing's Note-book

It is one thing to see others suffer, but it is a very different thing to suffer oneself. The arguments and sympathy which we give to others in the hours of trial seem poor and inadequate in our own case.

BASIL W. MATURIN,
Laws of the Spiritual Life

While to propose to be a better man is a piece of unscientific cant, to have become a deeper man is the privilege of those who have suffered.

OSCAR WILDE,
De Profundis

Masochism is less well repressed than sadism because less blame attaches to it, and there are many who exploit the role of martyr, little realizing how much they enjoy the suffering they mournfully display to the world.

DR. KARL A. MENNINGER,
The Human Mind

However much concerned I was at the problem of the misery in the world, I never let myself get lost in broodings over it; I always held firmly to the thought that each one of us can do a little to bring some portion of it to an end. Thus I came gradually to rest content in the knowledge that there is only one thing we can understand about the problem, and that is that each of us has to go his own way, but as one who means to help to bring about deliverance.

ALBERT SCHWEITZER,
Out of My Life and Thought

Even the most innocent of men's affairs seem doomed to cause suffering. Pushing the lawnmower through tall wet grass, and enjoying the strong aroma of the morning, I found that the blades had cut a frog in half. I have not forgotten his eyes.

CHRISTOPHER MORLEY,
Inward Ho

As deeply as a man looketh into life, so deeply also doth he look into suffering.

FRIEDRICH NIETZSCHE,
Thus Spake Zarathustra

SUGGESTION

It is well known that we are susceptible only to those suggestions with which we are already secretly in accord.

C. G. JUNG,
Modern Man in Search of a Soul

SUICIDE

As the lights in the penitentiary grow dim when the current is switched on for the electric chair, so we quiver in our hearts at a suicide, for there is no suicide for which all society is not responsible.

CYRIL CONNOLLY,
The Unquiet Grave

The perfect type of the man of action is the suicide.

WILLIAM CARLOS WILLIAMS,
Selected Essays

Many a man has decided to stay alive not because of the will to live but because of the determination not to give assorted surviving bastards the satisfaction of his death.

BRENDAN FRANCIS

The decision to remain alive or to die is probably a supreme example of self-determination.

BRUNO BETTELHEIM,
The Informed Heart

SUMMER

This is summer, unmistakably. One can always tell when one sees schoolteachers hanging about the streets idly, looking like cannibals during a shortage of missionaries.

ROBERTSON DAVIES,
The Tabletalk of Samuel Marchbanks

Is there anything more soothing than the quiet whir of a lawnmower on a summer afternoon?

F. SCOTT FITZGERALD,
The Crack-up

The exceeding beauty of the earth, in her splendour of life, yields a new thought with every petal. ... These are the only hours that are not wasted—these hours that absorb the soul and fill it with beauty. This is real life, and all else is illusion, or mere endurance.

RICHARD JEFFERIES,
The Pageant of Summer

The suggestiveness of summer!—a word that is so weighted with the fullness of existence—means more to me than any other word in the language, I think.

EDWARD MARTIN TABER,
A Book of Days,
compiled by Christopher Morley

Now it is summer, and as usual, life fills me with transport and I forget to work. This year I have struggled for a long time, but the beauty of the world has conquered me.

LEO TOLSTOY,
quoted in *The Writing Art,* selected by
Bertha W. Smith and Virginia C. Lincoln

Here is another dreadful warm day, fit for nobody but the flies. And then one is confined to town.

SIR WALTER SCOTT,
Sir Walter Scott's Journal (1825–1832)

SUNDAY

The boredom of Sunday afternoons, which drove De Quincey to opium, also gave birth to surrealism: hours propitious for making bombs.

CYRIL CONNOLLY,
The Unquiet Grave

Why is Sunday such an empty day, anywhere, city or country?

KATHARINE BUTLER HATHAWAY,
*Journal and Letters
of the Little Locksmith*

Some keep the Sabbath going to church;
I keep it staying at home,
With a bobolink for a chorister,
And an orchard for a dome.

EMILY DICKINSON,
Selected Poems and Letters of Emily Dickinson

An endless, dreary Sunday afternoon . . . its every hour a year. By turns walked despairingly down empty streets and lay quietly on the couch. Occasionally astonished by the leaden, meaningless clouds almost uninterruptedly drifting by. "You are reserved for a great Monday!" Fine, but Sunday will never end.

FRANZ KAFKA,
The Diaries of Franz Kafka 1914–1923

SUPERIORITY

If one is really a superior person, the fact is likely to leak out without too much assistance.

JOHN ANDREW HOLMES,
Wisdom in Small Doses

It is this setting ourselves up as in any way superior to the lowest man or woman in the world that brings evil into the world.

SHERWOOD ANDERSON,
Letters of Sherwood Anderson

It would be a colorless world if each individual did not secretly believe himself superior to almost everyone else.

DON MARQUIS,
The Almost Perfect State

Some cannot endure the presence of those who are, in any way, higher than their own intellectual or moral stature. They are restless till they can escape into the society of those who do not dwarf them.

HENRY CARDINAL MANNING,
Pastime Papers

Superiority has to face so many obstacles and to endure so much suffering, that the man who fulfills the mission of talent with patience and gentleness is a great man.

GEORGE SAND,
quoted in *Rectitude*
by Antonin G. Sertillanges

SUPPORT

It is strange but the only kind of support that means anything comes from those who believe in you to the hilt. The ones who go the whole hog. Let there be the slightest wavering, the slightest doubt, the slightest defection, and your would-be supporter turns into your worst enemy.

HENRY MILLER,
The Books in My Life

SURPRISE

Truly nothing is to be expected but the unexpected!

ALICE JAMES,
The Diary of Alice James

It is by surprises that experience teaches all she deigns to teach us.

CHARLES SANDERS PEIRCE,
Collected Papers of Charles Sanders Peirce,
Vol. V

Nearly all the best things that came to me in life have been unexpected, unplanned by me.

CARL SANDBURG,
New York Times, September 11, 1960

SUSPENSE

I don't know anything worse than *suspense,* being face to face with a crisis which doesn't arrive. But there's something tough inside us which doesn't give way.

A. C. BENSON,
Excerpts from the Letters of Dr. A. C. Benson to M. E. A.

SWEAR

Some days I just swear inside. A farmer whose field had washed away in a rain said to me, "Take God Almighty up one side and down the other, and he does about as much harm as he does good."

That goes for me too. I want to be as nice as a horse or a dog, and can't.

SHERWOOD ANDERSON,
Letters of Sherwood Anderson

SWIMMING

I swam, and what is more delicious than swimming? It is exercise and luxury at once.

RICHARD JEFFERIES,
The Story of My Heart

Then exercise—one must have some. I take it in the most condensed form—swimming. It is so cold that you exercise long after you come out just getting warm. Then it makes you feel both like a holy martyr and a god.

ANNE MORROW LINDBERGH,
Bring Me a Unicorn

SYMPATHY

And whoever walks a furlong without sympathy walks to his own funeral drest in his shroud.

WALT WHITMAN,
"Song of Myself," *Leaves of Grass*

The world has no sympathy with any but positive griefs. It will pity you for what you lose; never for what you lack.

MADAME SWETCHINE,
The Writings of Madame Swetchine

My need for sympathy has often induced me to seek it from people who, instead of strengthening me, unnerved me.

VINCENT VAN GOGH,
Dear Theo:
An Autobiography of Vincent Van Gogh

Sympathy is the one emotion which seems most perfect as it becomes most animal: in its human aspect it too often lapses into the moralizing grandmother.

JOHN OLIVER HOBBES,
Some Emotions and a Moral

We discover, perhaps to our astonishment, that our greatest moments come when we find that we are not unique, when we come upon another self that is very like our own. The discovery of a continent is mere idle folly compared with this discovery of a sympathetic other-self, a friend or a lover.

J. B. PRIESTLEY,
All About Ourselves and Other Essays

A man without sympathies for all that is rude, undeveloped, upheaving, struggling, suffering, man-making, as well as for what has been shaken to the top and is out of the pressure, is not a full, and must be an unhappy man.

JOHN BOYLE O'REILLY,
Watchwords

I think I feel rather differently about sympathy to what seems the normal view. I like just to feel it is there, but not always expressed.

A. C. BENSON,
Excerpts from the Letters of
Dr. A. C. Benson to M.E.A.

I believe sympathy is one of the most helpful helps one can bestow upon one's fellow creatures; and it seems a great pity that so many people feel it is their duty to criticize rather than sympathize.

HANNAH WHITALL SMITH,
Philadelphia Quaker
by Logan Pearsall Smith

Nothing is more salutary for those who are in affliction than to become consolers.

MAURICE HULST,
The Way of the Heart

TABOO

Life is livable because we know that wherever we go most of the people we meet will be restrained in their actions towards us by an almost instinctive network of taboos.

HAVELOCK ELLIS,
Selected Essays

TALENT

Everyone has a talent, what is rare is the courage to follow the talent to the dark place where it leads.

ERICA JONG,
The Craft of Poetry
edited by William Packard

Thousands of people have enough talent to become famous. It is the *need* to use it which is lacking.

KATHARINE BUTLER HATHAWAY,
Journal and Letters
of the Little Locksmith

One can never really explain a man or track talent to its lair; and all attempts to do so are works of the imagination.

JOHN JAY CHAPMAN,
Memories and Milestones

The buried talent is the sunken rock on which most lives strike and founder.

FREDERICK W. FABER,
Notes on Doctrinal and Spiritual Subjects,
Vol. II

A man who is born with a great share of some special talent is probably less deeply affected by nurture than one whose ability is generalized. His gift is his fate, and he follows a predestined course, from which no ordinary power can deflect him.

ALDOUS HUXLEY,
Collected Essays

Great talents are the most lovely and often the most dangerous fruits on the tree of humanity. They hang upon the most slender twigs that are easily snapped off.

C. G. JUNG,
Psychological Reflections,
edited by Jolande Jacobi and R. F. Hull

If a man has a talent and cannot use it, he has failed. If he has a talent and uses only half of it, he has partly failed. If he has a talent and learns somehow to use the whole of it, he has gloriously succeeded, and won a satisfaction and a triumph that few men ever know.

THOMAS WOLFE,
The Web and the Rock

No man can discover his own talents.

BRENDAN FRANCIS

If there is anything that a man can do and do well, I say let him do it. Give him a chance.

ABRAHAM LINCOLN,
quoted in *Abraham Lincoln*
by Benjamin P. Thomas

Timing and arrogance are decisive factors in the use of talent. The first is a matter of instinct, the second part carapace and part self-hypnosis, the shell that protects, the ego that assumes, without question, that the talent possessed is not only unique but important, the particular vision demanding to be shared.

MARYA MANNES,
Out of My Time

A talent somewhat above mediocrity, shrewd and not too sensitive, is more likely to rise in the world than genius, which is apt to be perturbable and to wear itself out before fruition.

CHARLES HORTON COOLEY,
Life and the Student

When a man can do anything well, and is entrusted to do it, he has generally an impulse to action which is as strong and as abiding as can be found among human motives, and which will even surpass the love of gain.

SIR ARTHUR HELPS,
Organization in Daily Life

Where talent is a dwarf, self-esteem is a giant.

J. PETIT-SENN,
Conceits and Caprices

TASTE

It is good taste in good taste not to make

too much of itself. Taste is a little prone to be arrogant, intolerant, contemptuous; to that extent it ceases to be taste. We should be stern for ourselves but lenient for others; the true taste is to be at once generous and humble.

OSCAR W. FIRKINS,
Oscar Firkins: Memoirs and Letters,
edited by Ina Ten Eyck

Mathers is much troubled by ladies who seek spiritual advice, and one has called to ask his help against phantoms who have the appearance of decayed corpses, and try to get in bed with her at night. He has driven her away with one furious sentence, "Very bad taste on both sides."

W. B. YEATS,
Autobiography

We talk of acquired tastes, but all tastes really are acquired, and it is doubtful whether we are any better off for having acquired them, better in the sense that through them our enjoyment of life is rendered any more intense.

ALEC WAUGH,
On Doing What One Likes

You see, the kind of people who always go on about whether a thing is in good taste invariably have very bad taste.

JOE ORTON,
Behind the Scenes,
edited by Joseph F. McCrindle

Every man's road in life is marked by the graves of his personal likings.

ALEXANDER SMITH,
Dreamthorp

Taste is never leaving money in an envelope under the flower pot when you're sharing an apartment with a man who's temporarily between jobs. It's saying, "Look, I'm going to pay the bills for a while and I don't want any arguments from you."

HELEN GURLEY BROWN,
Sunday News Magazine, May 15, 1977

TEACHERS AND TEACHING

Teachers at all levels encourage the idea that you have to talk about things in order to understand them, because they wouldn't have jobs, otherwise. But it's phony, you know.

DENISE LEVERTOV,
The Craft of Poetry,
edited by William Packard

I am sure it is one's duty as a teacher to try to show boys that no opinions, no tastes, no emotions are worth much unless they are one's own. I suffered acutely as a boy from the lack of being shown this.

A. C. BENSON,
The Upton Letters

Everyone who remembers his own educational experience remembers teachers, not methods and techniques. The teacher is the kingpin of the educational situation. He makes and breaks programs.

SIDNEY HOOK,
Education for Modern Man

A very wise old teacher once said: "I consider a day's teaching is wasted if we do not all have one hearty laugh." He meant that when people laugh together, they cease to be young and old, master and pupils, workers and driver, jailer and prisoners, they become a single group of human beings enjoying its existence.

GILBERT HIGHET,
The Art of Teaching

A schoolmaster should have an atmosphere of awe, and walk wonderingly, as if he was amazed at being himself.

WALTER BAGEHOT,
Literary Studies, Vol. I

No other job in the world could possibly dispossess one so completely as this job of teaching. You could stand all day in a laundry, for instance, still in possession of your mind. But this teaching utterly obliterates you. It cuts right into your being: essentially, it takes over your spirit. It drags it out from where it would hide.

SYLVIA ASHTON-WARNER,
Spinster

Benevolence alone will not make a teacher, nor will learning alone do it. The gift of teaching is a peculiar talent, and implies a need and a craving in the teacher himself.

JOHN JAY CHAPMAN,
Memories and Milestones

Is education of the young the whole of life? I hate the young—I'm worn out with them. They absorb you and suck you dry and are vampires and selfish brutes at best. Give me some good old rumsoaked club men—who *can't* be improved and make no moral claims—and let me play chequers with them and look out of the Club window and think about what I'll have for dinner.

JOHN JAY CHAPMAN,
John Jay Chapman and His Letters
edited by M. A. DeWolfe Howe

One might as well say he has sold when no one has bought as to say he has taught when no one has learned.

JOHN DEWEY,
quoted in *Readings in the History of Education*
edited by Edward A. Fitzpatrick

When will the public cease to insult the teacher's calling with empty flattery? When will men who would never for a moment encourage their own sons to enter the work of the public schools cease to tell us that education is the greatest and noblest of all human callings?

WILLIAM C. BAGLEY,
Craftsmanship in Teaching

I have sometimes wondered whether my pupils realized the intensity of feeling which underlay a decorous classroom manner of dealing with certain books and men. Perhaps I gave myself away when I read poetry aloud.

BLISS PERRY,
And Gladly Teach

Teaching may hasten learning; it may also block it or kill it outright, or sometimes just render it comatose for years.

JAMES HARVEY ROBINSON,
The Human Comedy

She said the younger teachers naturally felt the strain of the life most keenly; the older ones had a more satisfying interest in their work. "What is it?" I asked her. "Perhaps I can grow into it."—"Oh, no," she answered quickly and soberly, "I wouldn't want you to. We narrow our interests until we grow fossilized, as—as I am. And then we have to make our teaching fill our lives. We have to, to live. I want you to have many interests. You have much to expect of life."

RUTH BENEDICT,
An Anthropologist at Work
by Margaret Mead

The teacher should never lose his temper in the presence of the class. If a man, he may take refuge in profane soliloquies; if a woman, she may follow the example of one sweet-faced and apparently tranquil girl—go out in the yard and gnaw a post.

WILLIAM LYON PHELPS,
Teaching in School and College

A good teacher feels his way, looking for response.

PAUL GOODMAN,
Growing Up Absurd

My belief is that the last thing a good teacher wants to do is to teach outside the classroom; certainly my own vision of bliss halfway through a term is solitary confinement in a soundproof cell.

JACQUES BARZUN,
Teacher in America

Take away paradox from the thinker and you have the professor.

SØREN KIERKEGAARD,
quoted in *The University
and the Modern World* by Arnold S. Nash

I was, but am no more, thank God—a school teacher—I dreamed last night I was teaching again—that's the only bad dream that ever afflicts my sturdy conscience.

D. H. LAWRENCE,
Selected Letters of D. H. Lawrence

Teachers are overworked and underpaid. True, it is an exacting and exhausting business, this damming up the flood of human potentialities.

GEORGE B. LEONARD,
Education and Ecstasy

TELEVISION

Television, if unchecked, may carry us back to a pre-tribal state of social development, when the family was the largest conversational unit.

A. J. LIEBLING,
The Sweet Science

What compels you [Americans] to stare, night after night, at all the glittering hokum that has been deliberately put together for you?

J. B. PRIESTLEY,
'47 Magazine of the Year, October 1947

Children who have been taught, or conditioned, to listen passively most of the day to the warm verbal communications coming from the TV screen, to the deep emotional appeal of the so-called TV personality, are often unable to respond to real persons because they arouse so much less feeling than the skilled actor.

BRUNO BETTELHEIM,
The Informed Heart

There is much talk these days that Big Brother dominates most phases of our life. It is said that now it is proposed that brainwashing will be added to his demonic devices, and that Federal subsidies for television will automatically bring about some measure of Federal control. . . .

The danger, it seems to me, is not Big Brother but Small Sister, who will never raise her voice or suggest any action to meet the constantly growing number of new challenges.

LESTER MARKEL,
Sight, Sound, and Society,
edited by David Manning White
and Richard Averson

TEMPTATION

There are several good protections against temptations but the surest is cowardice.

MARK TWAIN,
Mark Twain at Your Fingertips,
edited by Caroline T. Harnsberger

We cannot go about, unfortunately, telling everybody about the temptations we have resisted. As a result, people judge us exclusively by the temptations to which we yield.

ROBERT LYND,
The Peal of Bells

Many people are quite pitiless towards those whose temptations are not their own.

BASIL W. MATURIN,
Laws of the Spiritual Life

TENNIS

I'm learning to use others' weaknesses. I don't hammer a man's soft spot constantly, because he may strengthen it. I just save it as a trump up my sleeve for moments when I really need a point.

ARTHUR ASHE, JR.,
Advantage Ashe

Instead of being used to commence a rally, the serve is now being used to abort a rally. It is an instrument of destruction in its own right.

EUGENE SCOTT,
Tennis: Game of Motion

Speed in tennis is a strange mixture of intuition, guesswork, footwork and hair-trigger reflexes. Many of the players famed for quickness on the court would finish dead last in a field of schoolgirls in a race any distance more than 10 yards.

EUGENE SCOTT,
Tennis: Game of Motion

Be bold. If you're going to make an error, make a doozy, and don't be afraid to hit the ball.

BILLIE JEAN KING,
Tennis to Win

By the way, what a polite game tennis is. The chief word in it seems to be "sorry" and admiration of each other's play crosses the net as frequently as the ball.

J. M. BARRIE,
quoted in *J. M. Barrie:
The Man Behind the Image* by Janet Dunbar

The good chances don't come that frequently, and the killer knocks them off surely when presented with them. The killer doesn't let up or ease off when he gets a good lead. This can be learned. Make sure of the easy shots—concentrate extra hard on those. Everybody has problems with difficult shots, but the killer gets his edge because he is meticulous with the setups.

ROD LAVER,
The Education of a Tennis Player

Don't compose eulogies to yourself when you get ahead. Concentrate on staying there.

ROD LAVER,
The Education of a Tennis Player

You can intimidate an opponent, disrupt his equanimity, destroy his confidence, shatter his nerves, and make him fly into a blind rage by the way you keep score.

REX LARDNER,
*The Underhanded Serve:
Or How to Play Dirty Tennis*

I will always be grateful for my public-park beginning in tennis. One learned many bad habits in tennis, but one learned to play against all kinds of players and against all odds.

ALICE MARBLE,
The Road to Wimbledon

Never change a winning game; always change a losing one.

BILL TILDEN,
quoted in *American Tennis*
by Parke Cummings

I cannot too strongly urge young players to attempt the impossible in recoveries. At least 75 percent of the shots considered impossible are actually recoverable if the effort is made for them.

BILL TILDEN,
The Fireside Book of Tennis

Although most players realize that watching the ball is the most important task at all levels of play, relatively few of them actually do it. One moment we are watching the ball like a hawk; the next our minds have wandered off and are thinking about something else entirely.

W. TIMOTHY GALLWEY,
Inner Tennis: Playing the Game

"Covering court" can be achieved partly by skipping, partly by anticipating the flight of the ball, and partly by that slow action which seems often to get there, called "padding." Desperate situations require desperate measures, though, and *sometimes* running is absolutely necessary.

HELEN WILLS,
Fifteen-Thirty

In sports, you simply aren't considered a real champion until you have defended your title successfully. Winning it once can be a fluke; winning it twice proves you are the best.

ALTHEA GIBSON,
I Always Wanted to Be Somebody

Behind every tennis player there is another tennis player.

JOHN MCPHEE,
Levels of the Game

I find it far easier to concentrate on a stadium court than on an outside court. The undivided attention of the spectators stimulates my ambition to win whether they support me or my opponent. Their tribute to the game in attending the matches helps to imbue tennis with the significance which I so acutely feel it has in a championship match.

HELEN HULL JACOBS,
Beyond the Game

THEATRE

I divide all productions into two categories: those I like and those I don't like. I have no other criterion.

ANTON CHEKHOV,
The Selected Letters of Anton Chekhov

The serious theatre can be uncomfortable. How often we go to a play with high expectations which, as the evening wears on, turn into a kind of impatient discomfort.

... But sometimes we go to a play and after the curtain has been up five minutes we have a sense of being able to settle back in the arms of the playwright. Instinctively we know that the playwright knows his business.

ANTON CHEKHOV,
The Selected Letters of Anton Chekhov

I've never seen sex handled in a real way on stage, even the world of a whore—especially the world of a whore. What is thought of as explicit and frank is crafted as if done by Busby Berkeley. It's boring or entertaining, but it has nothing to do with what's true.

JULES FEIFFER,
Behind the Scenes,
edited by Joseph F. McCrindle

I have had great benefits from the theatre, liked and enjoyed many people in it, count a few of them as my close friends, had pleasure in success and excitement even in failure, but I have wandered through it as if I were a kind of stranger.

LILLIAN HELLMAN,
An Unfinished Woman

I've gone through none of this awful business that all movies about playwrights persist in showing—of playwrights putting the third act where the first one was, and rewriting overnight in Boston.

EDWARD ALBEE,
quoted in *Showcase* by Roy Newquist

Everyone who goes to the theater has a right to his own opinion, but he doesn't have a right to have it taken seriously.

TYRONE GUTHRIE,
quoted in *Showcase* by Roy Newquist

One can dare anything in the theatre, and it is the place where one dares the least.

EUGENE IONESCO,
quoted in *Theatre of the Absurd*
by Martin Esslin

I am quite familiar with the fact that every fool who is connected with a theatre, from the call boy to the manager, thinks he knows better than an author how to make a play popular and successful. Tell them, with my compliments, that I know all about that; . . . that I know my business and theirs as well.

> GEORGE BERNARD SHAW,
> quoted in *George Bernard Shaw*
> by Archibald Henderson

I can't really work in the theater of the absurd. I can work in fantasy—in romantic fantasy—and I can work in very far-out plays. But I could never just make a joke out of human existence.

> TENNESSEE WILLIAMS,
> quoted in *Close-up* by John Gruen

The Russian dramatist is one who, walking through a cemetery, does not see the flowers on the graves. The American dramatist . . . does not see the graves under the flowers.

> GEORGE JEAN NATHAN,
> *The World of George Jean Nathan,*
> edited by Charles Angoff

I don't think the playwright has much right to expect anything from an audience, except possibly to give the play its attention for five minutes. Then, he has to earn it. Certainly, I don't think he has a right to expect them to find anything subtle.

> HOWARD LINDSAY,
> *Wisdom for Our Time,*
> edited by James Nelson

THINGS

Life is in inanimate things, you see, too. Men and women are touching, touching, touching.

> SHERWOOD ANDERSON,
> *Letters of Sherwood Anderson*

Things exist in their own right; it is a lesson that escapes us except as they hold us in awe.

> HENRY G. BUGBEE, JR.,
> *The Inward Morning*

One can get just as much exultation in losing oneself in a little thing as in a big thing.

It is nice to think how one can be recklessly lost in a daisy.

> ANNE MORROW LINDBERGH,
> *Bring Me a Unicorn*

Unless you refresh the mind from time to time you cannot always remember or believe how deep the inscape in things is.

> GERARD MANLEY HOPKINS,
> *Notebooks and Papers*

We all know the man whom children or dogs love instinctively. It is a rare gift to be able to inspire this affection. The Fates have been kind to him. But to inspire the affection of inanimate things is something greater. The man to whom a collar or a window sash takes instinctively is a man who may truly be said to have luck on his side.

> A. A. MILNE,
> *Not That It Matters*

The little place is the most curious mixture of sadness with delight. The sadness of *things*—things every one of which was done either by our hands or by our planning, old furniture renovated, there isn't an object in the house that isn't associated with past life, old summers, dead people, people who will never come again, etc., and the way it catches you round the heart when you first come and open the house from its long winter sleep is most extraordinary.

> WILLIAM JAMES,
> *The Letters of William James,* Vol. II

HENRY DAVID THOREAU

Who is there who would not rejoice to be reminded of the days when Thoreau and Emerson came into the imagination like sons of the morning and filled him with longing to be at once a loafer and a god?

> ROBERT LYND,
> *Solomon in All His Glory*

I have been trying to read Thoreau, but after the subtlety, wisdom and beauty of the writings of Pater and his school I find the grave didactic style of that old Puritan backwoodsman very slow and barren.

LLEWELYN POWYS,
Letters

THOUGHT

I am thinking of so much now, and the practical jostles with the limitless in me as in dreams sometimes. Everything that insists on being thought of and attended to, and all the rest that wants to be beside some sea and wants to sing, days on end, nights on end.

RAINER MARIA RILKE,
Letters of Rainer Maria Rilke 1892–1910

One thing above all gives charm to men's thoughts, and this is unrest. A mind that is not uneasy irritates and bores me.

ANATOLE FRANCE,
quoted in *The Journals of André Gide,* Vol. I

Men fear thought as they fear nothing else on earth—more than ruin, more even than death.

BERTRAND RUSSELL,
"Education," *Selected Papers*

Thinking is more interesting than knowing, but less interesting than looking.

GOETHE,
quoted in *A Certain World* by W. H. Auden

Full well aware that all has failed, yet, side by side with the sadness of that knowledge, there lives on in me an unquenchable belief, thought burning like the sun, that there is yet something to be found, something real, something to give each separate personality sunshine and flowers in its own existence now. ... It must be dragged forth by might of thought from the immense forces of the universe.

RICHARD JEFFERIES,
The Story of My Heart

One thought succeeds another; just as one is thought and I want to write it down, comes a new one—hold on, catch it—madness—insanity!

SØREN KIERKEGAARD,
The Journals of Søren Kirkegaard

When we ask the ultimate questions, whether about the direction of our own lives, or about the meaning of existence, the outcome of thinking is not an answer but a transformed way of thinking, not propositions to assent to but heightened power of apprehension.

HELEN MERRELL LYND,
On Shame and the Search for Identity

What, oh what, oh what is thought? It is the only thing—and yet nothing.

JOHN ADDINGTON SYMONDS,
Letters and Papers of John Addington Symonds

No amount of energy will take the place of thought. A strenuous life with its eyes shut is a kind of wild insanity.

HENRY VAN DYKE,
quoted in *The Author's Kalendar, 1914,*
compiled by Anna C. Woodford

Our inward thoughts, do they ever show outwardly? There may be a great fire in our soul, and no one ever comes to warm himself at it; the passers-by see only a little bit of smoke coming through the chimney, and pass on their way.

VINCENT VAN GOGH,
*Dear Theo:
An Autobiography of Vincent Van Gogh*

Thinking is a process that I hold in horror. I have thought for fifty years, with the most ghastly and disastrous results, mostly thoughts of my own, and if I attempt to superpose the thoughts of other people, I find my mental equipment utterly inadequate to the strain.

GAMALIEL BRADFORD,
The Letters of Gamaliel Bradford

Man is a thought-adventurer. But by thought we mean, of course, discovery. We don't mean this telling himself stale facts and drawing false conclusions, which usually passes as thought. Thought is an adventure, not a trick.

D. H. LAWRENCE,
Selected Essays

In the realm of thought every person performs innumerable abortions each minute of the waking day.

BRENDAN FRANCIS

You would be surprised how hard it often is to translate an action into thought.

KARL KRAUS,
quoted in *Karl Kraus* by Harry Zohn

Thought is so rare an essence that wherever we discover a manifestation of it we not only relish it but are tempted to approve of it.

HENRI DE LUBAC,
Paradoxes

I like to think of thoughts as living blossoms borne by the human tree.

JAMES DOUGLAS,
Down Shoe Lane

The glorification of affection and aspiration at the expense of thought is a survival of romantic optimism. It assumes a preestablished harmony between natural impulse and natural objects. Only such a harmony justifies the belief that generous feeling will find its way illuminated by the sheer nobility of its own quality.

JOHN DEWEY,
Human Nature and Conduct

The number of substitutes for fine and clean thinking the world provides positively gnaws at one's vitals.

HAROLD J. LASKI,
Holmes-Laski Letters, Vol. I

Today we overrate the rational values and behave as if thinking were a substitute for living. We have forgotten that thought and the intuition that feeds it only become whole if the deed grows out of it as fruit grows from the pollen on a tree, and so everywhere in our civilized world there tends to be a terrible cleavage between thinking and doing.

LAURENS VAN DER POST,
The Lost World of the Kalahari

TIME

If you realize too acutely how heavenly valuable time is, you are too paralyzed to do anything.

KATHARINE BUTLER HATHAWAY,
*Journal and Letters
of the Little Locksmith*

Stimulation is the indispensable requisite for pleasure in an experience, and the feeling of bare time is the least stimulating experience we can have.

WILLIAM JAMES,
Principles of Psychology, Vol. I

We spend, I am very certain, the half of our time among people that we do not particularly like and on things that do not particularly amuse us, and consequently have no time for the people and things that do really matter to us.

ALEC WAUGH,
On Doing What One Likes

Time is a storm in which we are all lost.

WILLIAM CARLOS WILLIAMS,
Selected Essays

When you are deeply absorbed in what you're doing, time gives itself to you like a warm and willing lover.

BRENDAN FRANCIS

Note . . . that it is so interminable and exasperating to watch the hand turn for five minutes on a clock face that it is almost impossible to do so.

ALBERT CAMUS,
Notebooks 1935–1942

If what we are accustomed to consider lost time could be removed, as to its effects at least, from the sun of our existence, it is certain that we should suffer from a great intellectual impoverishment.

PHILIP G. HAMERTON,
The Intellectual Life

Time always moves on. One can take a step back in space, and in other similar things: but never in time. One deceives oneself easily, in great and small, over this curious fact.

THEODOR HAECKER,
Journal in the Night

Natives dislike speed, as we dislike noise, it

is to them, at the best, hard to bear. They are also on friendly terms with time, and the plan of beguiling or killing it does not come into their heads. In fact the more time you can give them, the happier they are, and if you commission a Kikuyu to hold your horse while you make a visit, you can see by his face that he hopes you will be a long, long time about it. He does not try to pass the time then, but sits down and lives.

ISAK DINESEN,
Out of Africa

Regular, one, undifferentiated, time goes sliding on beneath and through all life, beneath and through its various pains and pleasures, its boredoms and enlightenments and seemingly timeless ecstasies— always the same mysterious dark lapse into nothing.

ALDOUS HUXLEY,
Beyond the Mexique Bay

An inch of time cannot be bought by an inch of gold.

CHINESE PROVERB

When time is endlessly killed, one lives in an endless present until time ends without ever having passed, leaving a person who never lived to exclaim, "I wasted time and now time doth waste me."

ERNEST VAN DEN HAAG,
Man Alone, edited by
Eric Josephson and Mary Josephson

One can always trust to time. Insert a wedge of time, and nearly everything straightens itself out.

NORMAN DOUGLAS,
An Almanac

We doubt that we could live with a clock that was always right, any more than with a person who was always right.

E. B. WHITE,
Every Day Is Saturday

Time is a very strange thing.
So long as one takes it for granted, it is
  nothing at all.
But then, all of a sudden, one is aware of
  nothing else.

HUGO VON HOFMANNSTHAL,
quoted in *A Certain World* by W. H. Auden

Men hate having anything to do. But men also hate having nothing to do. The human race therefore has always been fertile in the invention of things to do which are equivalent to nothing—things which will pass the time.

FRANK SHEED,
A Century of the Catholic Essay,
edited by Raphael H. Gross

Ordinary people merely think how they shall *spend* their time; a man of talent tries to *use* it.

ARTHUR SCHOPENHAUER,
quoted in *Ladies' Home Journal,*
November 1948

The more a person is able to direct his life consciously, the more he can use time for constructive benefits.

ROLLO MAY,
Man's Search for Himself

TODAY

Today never hands me the same thing twice and I believe that for most everyone else life is also a mixture of unsolved problems, ambiguous victories and vague defeats—with very few moments of clear peace. I never do seem to quite be on top of it. My struggle with today is worthwhile, but it is a struggle nonetheless and one I will never finish.

HUGH PRATHER,
Notes to Myself

No yesterdays are ever wasted for those who give themselves to today.

BRENDAN FRANCIS

TOLERANCE

By hook, by crook, by hair of head,
  By scruff of neck and seat of pants,
Our stubborn infants shall be led
  Along the path of tolerance.

PHYLLIS MCGINLEY,
"Primary Education," *A Pocketful of Wry*

Once people can become accustomed to tolerance, they can use it to help them grow, rather than as an Alice-in-Wonderland drink with which they shrink themselves to the size of others.

DAVID RIESMAN,
The Lonely Crowd

TRADITION

Tradition means giving votes to the most obscure of all classes—our ancestors. It is the democracy of the dead. Tradition refuses to submit to the small and arrogant oligarchy of those who merely happen to be walking around.

G. K. CHESTERTON,
quoted in *A Certain World* by W. H. Auden

Tradition is a guide and not a jailer.

W. SOMERSET MAUGHAM,
The Summing Up

It is the persons who are weak in the sense of their own personal identity who are overcome by the power of tradition, who cannot stand in its presence, and who therefore either capitulate to it, cut themselves off from it, or rebel against it. ... One of the distinguishing marks of strength as a self is the capacity to immerse one's self in tradition and at the same time be one's own unique self.

ROLLO MAY,
Man's Search for Himself

So that the river of tradition may come down to us we must continually dredge its bed.

HENRI DE LUBAC,
Paradoxes

TRAGEDY

The climax of every tragedy lies in the deafness of its heroes.

ALBERT CAMUS,
The Rebel

There is no suffering, no torture anywhere in the world which does not affect our everyday lives. ... Today, tragedy is collective.

ALBERT CAMUS,
"Neither Victims Nor Executioners,"
The Worlds of Existentialism,
edited by Maurice Friedman

The temper of mind that sees tragedy in life has not for its opposite the temper that sees joy. The opposite pole to the tragic view of life is the sordid view. When humanity is seen as devoid of dignity and significance, trivial, mean and sunk in dreary hopelessness, then the spirit of tragedy departs.

EDITH HAMILTON,
The Great Age of Greek Literature

We begin to live when we have conceived life as tragedy.

W. B. YEATS,
Autobiography

TRAINING

But doctors can't pass a street accident, nor dips an open handbag, coppers can't pass a door with a broken lock, Jesuits can't pass sin in the making, everyone falls prey to their training.

LEN DEIGHTON,
Spy Story

TRANQUILLITY

I don't want that tranquillity of heart which springs from within. Too much at my own expense. I want a bit of a good time—can't sit supping forever at these inside Baden-Baden cure-springs.

D. H. LAWRENCE,
Selected Letters of D.H. Lawrence

In all epochs one who would write something tranquil and considerate must resist the spirit of the time, since, whatever the spirit of the time may be, it is never that.

CHARLES HORTON COOLEY,
Life and the Student

TRANSLATION

The best translation is not that which is most like the original but that which is the most different from it.

GAMALIEL BRADFORD,
The Letters of Gamaliel Bradford

I can't bear to think of putting any Plotinus forth that is not quite as noble, as lucid, as generally readable as the best mind in me can, under its best inspiration, produce.

STEPHEN MACKENNA,
Journal and Letters of Stephen Mackenna

I say to him "Think like a wise man but express yourself like the common people" and the result is that he will make the first great translation of the *Upanishads*.

W. B. YEATS,
*Letters on Poetry
from W. B. Yeats to Dorothy Wellesley*

TRAVEL

Men travel faster now, but I do not know if they go to better things.

WILLA CATHER,
Death Comes for the Archbishop

It is such a bewildered, scared feeling to go for the first time to a place and not know where to call out to the driver to stop.

KATHARINE BUTLER HATHAWAY,
*Journal and Letters
of the Little Locksmith*

The true delight of travel, the one that is going to print itself unaccountably and indelibly on you, seems to prefer to come as a thief in the night, and not at the hours you specially fix for its entertainment.

C. E. MONTAGUE,
The Right Place

If you go only once round the room, you are wiser than he who sits still.

ESTONIAN PROVERB

I realize that the only thing that has hitherto kept us going has been that remaining sense of obligation to identify—Baedeker in hand—new regions, museums, palaces and ruins; since this obligation does not exist here I am simply drowning in a life of ease.

SIGMUND FREUD,
The Letters of Sigmund Freud

One of the main troubles about going to Europe is that no one wants to hear about your trip when you get back home. Your friends and relatives are rife with jealousy and are not only sorry you went to Europe, but deeply regret that you came back.

ART BUCHWALD,
Vogue, April 1, 1954

No one has yet fathomed just what constitutes happiness. It is never the present, always the future. A trip is a journey into the future, a hunting after happiness.

DR. WILHELM STEKHEL,
The Depths of the Soul

There is no moment of delight in any pilgrimage like the beginning of it, when the traveller is settled simply as to his destination, and commits himself to his unknown fate and all the anticipations of adventure before him.

CHARLES DUDLEY WARNER,
Baddeck and That Sort of Thing

A voyage to a destination, wherever it may be, is also a voyage inside oneself; even as a cyclone carries along with it the centre in which it must ultimately come to rest.

LAURENS VAN DER POST,
Venture to the Interior

If you reject the food, ignore the customs, fear the religion and avoid the people, you might better stay home. You are like a pebble thrown into water; you become wet on the surface but you are never a part of the water.

JAMES A. MICHENER,
Holiday, March 1956

How often persons who have traveled around the world tell you so earnestly that they found a place in Venice where they served American ham and eggs.

ALFRED CARL HOTTES,
Garden Facts and Fancies

I think that travel comes from some deep urge to see the world, like the urge that brings up a worm in an Irish bog to see the moon when it is full.

LORD DUNSANY,
Holiday, March 1951

What gives value to travel is fear. It is a fact that, at a certain moment, when we are so far from our own country . . . we are seized by a vague fear, and an instinctive desire to go back to the protection of old habits. This is the most obvious benefit of travel. . . . There is no pleasure in traveling, and I look upon it more as an occasion for spiritual testing.

ALBERT CAMUS,
Notebooks 1935–1942

The tourist may complain of other tourists; but he would be lost without them.

AGNES REPPLIER,
Times and Tendencies

There is no denying that most of us, when we arrive at a place, immediately begin to think of other places to which we may go from it.

ROBERT LYND,
The Blue Lion

The heaviest baggage for a traveller is an empty purse.

GERMAN PROVERB

To drink in the spirit of a place you should be not only alone but not hurried.

GEORGE SANTAYANA,
The Letters of George Santayana

Traveling with anyone is a very ticklish business. . . . What is your thrill may be my bore. . . . I cannot imagine what fire and pillage I would commit if anyone were in a position to keep me looking at things longer than I wanted to look.

CORNELIA STRATTON PARKER,
English Summer

Of course world travel isn't as good as it seems, it's only after you've come back that you forget to get bugged and remember the weird scenes you saw.

JACK KEROUAC,
Lonesome Traveler

If you look like your passport photo, then in all probability you need the journey.

EARL WILSON,
quoted in *Ladies' Home Journal*,
January 1961

TREASON

If this be treason make the most of it.

PATRICK HENRY

Treason can never win. If it wins it isn't treason. It is called courage, heroism, foresight, wisdom or whatever.

A. KURKIBA

TREES

I never knew how soothing trees are—many trees and patches of open sunlight, and tree-presences—it is almost like having another being.

D. H. LAWRENCE,
Selected Letters of D. H. Lawrence

He who plants trees loves others beside himself.

ENGLISH PROVERB

All these trees bloom white, which makes them startlingly like brides in their wedding dresses: white frocks, white flowers and a look of innocence, as though they were ashamed to have people stare at them.

ANTON CHEKHOV,
The Selected Letters of Anton Chekhov

A stricken tree, a living thing, so beautiful, so dignified, so admirable in its potential longevity, is, next to man, perhaps the most touching of wounded objects.

EDNA FERBER,
A Kind of Magic

There are trees that are all a-strain upward like a prayer; there are trees that rise only to flow eternally downwards, drooping like death; there are trees that are all a-twist, an agony of contortion, writhing, serpenting now towards earth and now towards sky, inwards and outwards, upwards and downwards, tortured uncertain lives, very dreadful and very beautiful: but in all the trees there is beauty, and the birds of God rest and nest and sing in all.

STEPHEN MACKENNA,
Journal and Letters of Stephen Mackenna

The little locust tree by the corner of the wall has died and spilled all the fragments of its white flowers over the ground until that part of the garden looks like a picture by Seurat.

THOMAS MERTON,
Sign of Jonas

Why are there trees I never walk under but large and melodious thoughts descend upon me?

WALT WHITMAN,
"Song of the Open Road," *Leaves of Grass*

Many savage nations worship trees, and I really think my first feeling would be one of delight and interest rather than of surprise, if some day when I am alone in the woods one of the trees were to speak to me.

SIR JOHN LUBBOCK,
The Pleasures of Life

Trees seem very human to me. ... The sight of the felling of great trees, which seems to thrill the average movie audience, arouses in me only the most unpleasant sensations, similar to those more conventionally experienced when the hero of a story finally loses his life.

DR. KARL MENNINGER,
A Psychiatrist's World

Trees are your best antiques.

ALEXANDER SMITH,
Dreamthorp

Ancestral Sequoias grew here before the Sierra was uplifted. Today they look down upon the plains of men. No one has ever known a Sequoia to die a natural death. Neither insects nor fungi can corrupt them. Lightning may smite them at the crown and break it; no fire gets to the heart of them. They simply have no old age, and the only down trees are felled trees.

DONALD CULROSS PEATTIE,
The Flowering Earth

Trees in the mass can be almost terrible.

ALDOUS HUXLEY,
Collected Essays

We complain and complain, but we have lived and seen the blossom—apple, pear, cherry, plum, almond blossom—in the sun; and the best among us cannot pretend they deserve—or could contrive—anything better.

J. B. PRIESTLEY,
Delight

TRIFLE

A hole is nothing at all, but you can break your neck in it.

AUSTIN O'MALLEY,
Keystones of Thought

One of the most serious thoughts that life provokes is the reflection that we can never tell, at the time, whether a word, a look, a touch, an occurrence of any kind, is trivial or important.

E. V. LUCAS,
365 Days and One More

Sensitive people realize that often it happens to them to be revived, kindled, strengthened to a degree which they could not describe by some little thing,—some word of praise, some token of remembrance, some proof of affection or recognition.

HELEN HUNT JACKSON,
quoted in *A Year of Ideals for Everyday Living,*
compiled by Delia L. Porter

Let us not take it for granted that life exists more fully in what is commonly thought big than in what is commonly thought small.

VIRGINIA WOOLF,
The Common Reader, First Series

What have you done with your gift of sex? It was a failure, in the end that is all that they will say. But it might easily have succeeded. A mere trifle, indeed so small as not to be perceived, decided between its failure and success. Why are you surprised? So it was with the greatest battles in the history of the world. Trifles decide trifles.

FRANZ KAFKA,
The Diaries of Franz Kafka 1914–1923

It is the small things that irritate and so embitter one's life. I can gladly fight against a storm so that the blood almost bursts from my veins; but the wind that blows a grain of dust into my eye can annoy me to such an extent that I stamp with rage.

SØREN KIERKEGAARD,
The Journals of Søren Kierkegaard

There was once a Hindu sage, who sat down on the banks of the Ganges and thought for seventy years about the millennium. Just as he arrived at the solution and was putting it into verse, a mosquito stung him and he forgot it again at once.

DON MARQUIS,
The Almost Perfect State

TROUBLE

Nothing can be accomplished by denying that man is an essentially troubled being, except to make more trouble.

WILLIAM BARRETT,
Irrational Man

People with great troubles talk about little ones, and the man who complains of the crumpled rose leaf very often has his flesh full of thorns.

G. K. CHESTERTON,
Tremendous Trifles

Telling someone else about it is an ancient form of relief based upon the principle that verbalizing our feelings enables us to objectify them.

DR. KARL A. MENNINGER,
The Human Mind

At present my domestic affairs are so ill, I want spirits to look abroad. I have got a cold that disables my eyes and disorders me every other way. Mr. Mason has ordered me blooding, which I have submitted to after long contestation. For how stupid I am; I entertain you with discourses of Physic, but I have the oddest Jumble of disagreeable things in my head that ever plagu'd poor mortals: a great cold, a bad peace, people I love in disgrace, sore eyes, the horrid prospect of a

civil war, and the filthy thought of a potion to take—I believe no body ever had such a melange before.

LADY MARY WORTLEY MONTAGU,
The Complete Letters of
Lady Mary Wortley Montagu, Vol. I

Trouble will rain on those who are already wet.

SPANISH PROVERB

It still remains true that the troubles men undergo are the forces that lead them to project pictures of a better state of things.

JOHN DEWEY,
Reconstruction in Philosophy

If we examine the sources of our troubles and agitations, we find that they almost invariably spring from a desire of appreciation or a fear of contempt.

JAMES CARDINAL GIBBONS,
The Ambassador of Christ

When one has an insatiable appetite for trouble all sorts will serve.

KATHLEEN NORRIS,
Hands Full of Living

There were no troubles in my own life, except the troubles inseparable from being a spirit living in the flesh.

GEORGE SANTAYANA,
The Letters of George Santayana

Don't borrow trouble; borrow money, and trouble will come of its own accord.

MAURICE SWITZER,
quoted in *Ladies' Home Journal,*
September 1949

Bygone troubles are good to tell.

YIDDISH PROVERB

The usual excuse of those who cause others trouble is that they wish them well.

VAUVENARGUES,
Maxims and Reflections

TRUST

I prefer to have too much confidence, and thereby be deceived, than to be always mistrustful. For, in the first case, I suffer for a moment at being deceived and, in the second, I suffer constantly.

PAUL GAUGUIN,
quoted in *Gauguin* by Henri Perruchot

TRUTH

It is only by lying to the limit one can come at the truth.

SHERWOOD ANDERSON,
Letters of Sherwood Anderson

"Preaching the truth" has an air of the grotesque. What is not truth?

LIONEL JOHNSON,
Some Winchester Letters of Lionel Johnson

You seek truth as if it were the opposite of yourself.

J. KRISHNAMURTI,
quoted in *The Books in My Life*
by Henry Miller

Speak the truth but leave immediately after.

YUGOSLAV PROVERB

If anything is worthy of a man's best and hardest effort, that thing is the utterance of what he believes to be the truth.

EDWIN ARLINGTON ROBINSON,
Untriangulated Stars

We taste and feel and see the truth. We do not reason ourselves into it.

W. B. YEATS,
quoted in *W. B. Yeats Memoirs,*
edited by Denis Donaghue

I have remembered today that the Brahmin Mohini said to me, "When I was young I was happy. I thought truth was something that could be conveyed from one man's mind to another. I now know that it is a state of mind."

W. B. YEATS,
Autobiography

One thinks different things about the same thing in the morning and in the evening. But where is truth, in the night thought or in the spirit of midday? Two replies, two races of men.

ALBERT CAMUS,
Notebooks 1935–1942

I have never believed in the power of truth in itself. But it is at least worth knowing that when expressed forcefully truth wins out over falsehood.

ALBERT CAMUS,
Resistance, Rebellion, and Death

Your thought is obscure—lightning flashes darting gleams—but that is the way truth is.

WILLIAM JAMES,
The Letters of William James, Vol. II

We have unquestionably a great cloud-bank of ancestral blindness weighing down upon us, only transiently riven here and there by fitful revelations of the truth.

WILLIAM JAMES,
Talks to Teachers

Telling the truth is a pretty hard thing.

THOMAS WOLFE,
You Can't Go Home Again

It is always a relief to believe what is pleasant, but it is more important to believe what is true.

HILAIRE BELLOC,
The Silence of the Sea

The truth is incontrovertible. Panic may resent it; ignorance may deride it; malice may distort it, but there it is.

SIR WINSTON CHURCHILL,
A Churchill Reader,
edited by Colin R. Coote

Every action is good or bad in the sense that it is fruitful or sterile, according to whether or not it is a true action. Examples of untrue action, society, etc., caused mostly by what people will think. Amiability, kind deeds, devotion to parents, husbands or wives, or children—confused with the extraordinary beauty of these when they are true.

KATHARINE BUTLER HATHAWAY,
*Journal and Letters
of the Little Locksmith*

It is obvious that to be in earnest in seeking the truth is an indispensable requisite for finding it.

JOHN HENRY CARDINAL NEWMAN,
Oxford University Sermons

Men ardently pursue truth, assuming it will be the angel's bread when found.

W. MACNEILE DIXON,
The Human Situation

Every involuntary repulsion that arises in your mind give heed unto. It is the surface of a central truth.

RALPH WALDO EMERSON,
Journals of Ralph Waldo Emerson

When I say that a thing is true, I mean that I cannot help believing it. I am stating an experience as to which there is no choice.

OLIVER WENDELL HOLMES, JR.,
The Mind and Faith of Justice Holmes,
edited by Max Lerner

Whatever view of reality deepens our sense of the tremendous issues of life in the world wherein we move is *for us* nearer the truth than any view which diminishes that sense.

DEAN WILLIAM R. INGE,
Christian Mysticism

All truth—and real living is the only truth—has in it elements of battle and repudiation. *Nothing is wholesale.* The problem of truth is: How can we most deeply live? And the answer is different in every case.

D. H. LAWRENCE,
Selected Letters of D. H. Lawrence

Truth has one fatal defect. When she was launched upon the world, a group of gods gave her every grace, every charm, every virtue, and every strength; but one envious god, unable to take away what other gods had given her, made her forever unprofitable.

ALGERNON S. LOGAN,
Views from the Stream, Vol. II

Truth is always exciting. Speak it, then. Life is dull without it.

PEARL BUCK,
To My Daughters, with Love

UGLY

It's nothing to be born ugly. Sensibly, the ugly woman comes to terms with her ugli-

ness and exploits it as a grace of nature. To become ugly means the beginning of a calamity, self-willed most of the time.

COLETTE,
Journey for Myself

It is comparatively easy to imagine a kinship with the perfect and divine essence if we are forever handling and seeing and reading beautiful things, but we're put to it to find this relation in that which outwardly, at least, is ugly.

THOMAS WOLFE,
The Letters of Thomas Wolfe

What is there but ugliness in any relation between two beings which doesn't work to soften their hearts and open their minds to their kind?

ALICE JAMES,
The Diary of Alice James

Ugliness is a point of view: an ulcer is wonderful to a pathologist.

AUSTIN O'MALLEY,
Keystones of Thought

UNCONSCIOUS

Psychoanalysis has taught us that every person bears within himself his underworld: it is merely a question whether he has the underworld or it has him.

DR. WILHELM STEKHEL,
Marriage at the Crossroads

The doctrine of the unconscious, properly understood, is a doctrine of the falseness of all worlds, taken literally, at their face value, at the level of consciousness. The true psychic reality, which is the unconscious, cannot be put into words, cannot ever be translated by the silence into words. The unconscious is and will remain forever ineffable.

NORMAN O. BROWN,
Love's Body

The unconscious is not a demonic monster but a thing of nature that is perfectly neutral as far as moral sense, aesthetic taste, and intellectual judgment go. It is dangerous only when our conscious attitude towards it becomes hopelessly false. And this danger grows in the measure that we practise repressions.

C. G. JUNG,
Psychological Reflections,
edited by Jolande Jacobi and R. F. Hull

The more one sees of human fate and the more one examines its secret springs of action, the more one is impressed by the strength of unconscious motives and by the limitations of free choice.

C. G. JUNG,
quoted in *The Inner World of Choice*
by Frances G. Wickes

Your conscious probably hasn't much use for my unconscious. But I have implicit faith in my unconscious; it will be able to cope with your conscious.

KARL KRAUS,
Karl Kraus by Harry Zohn

We never really know what we are doing. Either we are materialistic instruments . . . or we move in the gesture of creation, from our deepest self, usually unconscious. We are only the actors, we are never wholly the authors of our own deeds and works. IT is the author, the unknown inside us or outside us. The best we can do is to try to hold ourselves in unison with the deeps which are inside us. And the worst we can do is to try to have things our own way, when we run counter to IT, and in the long run get our knuckles rapped for our presumption.

D. H. LAWRENCE,
Selected Essays

UNDERSTANDING

Of course, *understanding* of our fellow-beings is important. But this understanding becomes fruitful only when it is sustained by sympathetic feeling in joy and sorrow.

ALBERT EINSTEIN,
Ideas and Opinions

When a man does not understand a thing, he feels discord within himself: he seeks causes for this dissonance not in himself, as he should, but outside himself, and the result is war with something he does not understand.

ANTON CHEKHOV,
The Selected Letters of Anton Chekhov

People don't want to be understood—I mean not completely. It's too destructive. Then they haven't anything left. They don't want complete sympathy or complete understanding. They want to be treated carelessly and taken for granted lots of times.

ANNE MORROW LINDBERGH,
Bring Me a Unicorn

If one is master of one thing and understands one thing well, one has at the same time insight into and understanding of many things.

VINCENT VAN GOGH,
Dear Theo:
An Autobiography of Vincent Van Gogh

To me, if I can see things through and through, I get uneasy—I feel it's a fake. I know I have left something out, I've made some mistake.

BARON FRIEDRICH VON HÜGEL,
Letters from Baron Friedrich Von Hügel
to a Niece

We rarely gain a high or larger view except as it is forced upon us through struggles which we would have avoided if we could.

CHARLES HORTON COOLEY,
Life and the Student

Can we understand at all, ever, where we do not love?

SHERWOOD ANDERSON,
Letter of Sherwood Anderson

To understand any living thing, you must, so to say, creep within and feel the beating of its heart.

W. MACNEILE DIXON,
The Human Situation

For I always have the impression of being much further away from a thing I "understand" than when I don't understand.

THEODOR HAECKER,
Journal in the Night

Sometimes almost more important than sexual love or money to live on is, I think, somebody who can accompany you in your mind's experiences.

KATHARINE BUTLER HATHAWAY,
*Journal and Letters
of the Little Locksmith*

To understand a matter properly, a man must dominate it, instead of allowing it to dominate him.

ERNEST HELLO,
Life, Science, and Art

When you want to recognize and understand what takes place in the minds of others, you have first to look into yourself.

DR. THEODOR REIK,
Listening with the Third Ear

To understand a man is to afford him immense satisfaction. The moment he is understood he begins to feel comforted.

JEAN GUIBERT,
On Kindness

When we talk about understanding, surely it takes place only when the mind listens completely—the mind being your heart, your nerves, your ears—when you give your whole attention to it.

J. KRISHNAMURTI,
You Are the World

People who do not understand themselves have a craving for understanding.

DR. WILHELM STEKHEL,
Marriage at the Crossroads

Understanding is the beginning of approving. To negate with conviction one must never have looked at what one negates.

ANDRÉ GIDE,
The Journals of André Gide

It cannot be denied that though a concentrated awareness is what we must aim at, there are many lovely and magical flashes of illumination which come sideways and indirectly.

JOHN COWPER POWYS,
The Meaning of Culture

Understanding a person does not mean condoning; it only means that one does not accuse him as if one were God or a judge placed above him.

ERICH FROMM,
Man for Himself

UNEXPECTED

Never do I hesitate to look squarely at the unexpected face that every passing hour unveils to us, and to sacrifice the false images of it formed in advance, however dear they may be.

ROMAIN ROLLAND,
Journey Within

UNHAPPINESS

By becoming more unhappy, we sometimes learn how to be less so.

MADAME SWETCHINE,
The Writings of Madame Swetchine

I believe half the unhappiness in life comes from people being afraid to go straight at things.

WILLIAM J. LOCKE,
Simon the Jester

No sooner is it a little calmer with me than it is almost too calm. As though I have the true feeling of myself only when I am unbearably unhappy. That is probably true too.

FRANZ KAFKA,
The Diaries of Franz Kafka 1914–1923

Ah! Those strange people who have the courage to be unhappy! *Are* they unhappy, by-the-way!

ALICE JAMES,
The Diary of Alice James

O Lord! unhappy is the man whom man can make unhappy.

RALPH WALDO EMERSON,
Journals of Ralph Waldo Emerson

Those who are unhappy have no need for anything in this world but people capable of giving them their attention.

SIMONE WEIL,
Waiting for God

Now that I seem to have attained a temporary calm, I understand how valuable unhappiness can be; melancholy and re-morse form the deep leaden keel which enables us to sail into the wind of reality; we run aground sooner than the flat-bottomed pleasure-lovers, but we venture out in weather that would sink them, and we choose our direction.

CYRIL CONNOLLY,
The Unquiet Grave

When you are unhappy or dissatisfied, is there anything in the world more maddening than to be told that you should be contented with your lot?

KATHLEEN NORRIS,
Hands Full of Living

UNITY

I don't know why in the West 13 is considered an unlucky number, but in the East 2 is considered the unlucky number because it marks the first departure from 1, unity.

JOE FRANKEL

UNIQUENESS

If we want to know the true value, the real purpose, the exact quality of anything, we must discover what it possesses that separates it from other things—what faculty, or function, or principle, or law pertains to it alone, and by which it may be distinguished.

OLIVER BELL BUNCE,
Bachelor Bluff

In every concrete individual, there is a uniqueness that defies all formulation. We can feel the touch of it and recognize its taste, so to speak, relishing or disliking, as the case may be, but we can give no ultimate account of it, and we have in the end simply to admire the Creator.

WILLIAM JAMES,
Memories and Studies

Every individual has some qualities and ways of experiencing that are his own, and it is this fact as well as things that can be called common, shared human characteristics that make him a member of humanity. It is in part the very uniqueness of every individual that makes him, not only a member of a family, race, nation, or class, but a human being.

HELEN MERRELL LYND,
On Shame and the Search for Identity

It's pretty damn hard to bring your uniqueness into actual being if you're always doing the same things as a lot of other people.

BRENDAN FRANCIS

That man is created in the capacity for uniqueness of character is shown by the human face, which is never at all alike in any two persons, and of which the peculiarity is nothing but an expression of the latent inherent difference which it is the proper work of life to bring into actuality.

COVENTRY PATMORE,
The Rod, the Root, and the Flower

UNIVERSE

In the depths of the world, of the sky, there's a rhythm that must be listened to. Anybody can. One day . . . that beat may seep down from your wrist to your pen. Like blood—which has no ultimate sex. *One must give back the stare of the universe.* Anybody can.

HORTENSE CALISHER,
Herself

Not unfortunately the universe is wild,—game-flavored as a hawk's wing.

B. P. BLOOD,
quoted in *The Will to Believe*
by William James

The universe is to be valued because there is truth in it and beauty in it; and we live to discover the truth and beauty no less than to do what is right. Indeed, we cannot attain to that state of mind in which we shall naturally do what is right unless we are aware of the truth and the beauty of the universe.

A. CLUTTON BROCK,
The Ultimate Belief

The conflict of forces and the struggle of opposing wills are of the essence of our universe and alone hold it together.

HAVELOCK ELLIS,
Selected Essays

I discover everywhere in the smallest things, that omnipotent hand which supports the heavens and the earth, and which seems as it were in sport while it conducts the universe.

FRANÇOIS FÉNELON,
Reflections and Meditations

The rankest pessimist has a strong practical trust in the universe, and no less certainly a shrewd practical dread of the universe is the inner coat, the lining, of the most robust assertions of the divinity of nature and the beneficence of God.

OSCAR W. FIRKINS,
Oscar Firkins: Memoirs and Letters,
edited by Ina Ten Eyck

As life draws near to the end (one never quite believes it) I think rather more than ever that man has respected himself too much and the universe too little. He has thought himself a god and has despised "brute matter," instead of thinking his importance to be all of a piece with the rest.

OLIVER WENDELL HOLMES, JR.,
Holmes-Pollock Letters, Vol. II

The universe is not on the side of frugality: the stars were hurled broadcast from the hand of a spendthrift God.

DON MARQUIS,
Prefaces

I can be genuinely in love with the community only in case I have somehow fallen in love with the universe. JOSIAH ROYCE,
The Problem of Christianity, Vol. II

The universe is built on a plan the profound symmetry of which is somehow present in the inner structure of our intellect.

PAUL VALÉRY,
quoted in *Rectitude*
by Antonin G. Sertillanges

The children of God should not have any other country here below but the universe itself, with the totality of all the reasoning creatures it has ever contained, contains, or ever will contain. That is the native city to which we owe our love.

SIMONE WEIL,
Waiting for God

URBANITY

Urbanity is a good thing, but it ought to be spontaneous, and if so you may expect occasional lapses, especially when one is more concerned about the truth than about the impression he is making.

CHARLES HORTON COOLEY,
Life and the Student

URGE

Do the things you have the urge to do. Go forth expectant and put the little urge into great action.

REBECCA BEARD,
Everyman's Search

USEFUL

To be loved is the best way of being useful.

FRENCH PROVERB

Do not have too great care about being useful to others, but be greatly concerned about being useful to yourself.

BROTHER GILES OF ASSISI,
Golden Sayings

To be a useful person has always appeared to me to be something particularly horrible.

CHARLES BAUDELAIRE,
Intimate Journals

The cultivation of usefulness produces an enormous amount of failure, simply because in our avidity we sow seeds too closely.

RABINDRANATH TAGORE,
Letters to a Friend

USELESS

The sense of uselessness is the severest

shock which our system can sustain.

THOMAS HENRY HUXLEY,
quoted in *No Easy Victories,*
edited by Helen Rowan

How good and excellent a thing it is to feel quite useless, like an old boiled rag, and to know ourselves.

BERTRAND WILBERFORCE,
The Life and Letters of
Father Bertrand Wilberforce by H. M. Capes

UTOPIA

I went [to Chautauqua] in curiosity for a day. I stayed a week, held spellbound by the charm and ease of everything, by the middle-class paradise, without a blot, without a tear.

And yet what was my own astonishment, on emerging into the dark and wicked world again, to catch myself quite unexpectedly and involuntarily saying: "Ouf! what a relief!" Now for something primordial and savage, even though it were as bad as an Armenian massacre, to set the balance straight again.

WILLIAM JAMES,
"What Makes a Life Significant?"
Talks to Teachers

VACATION

A vacation frequently means that the family goes away for a rest, accompanied by mother, who sees that the others get it.

MARCELENE COX,
Ladies' Home Journal, August 1942

Nearly everybody underestimates the price of a vacation.

WILLIAM FEATHER,
quoted in the *New York Times,*
August 20, 1952

Men, as a rule, are not so successful as women in their holiday partnerships. You seldom find two men who can hit it off for more than one holiday together.

JAMES DOUGLAS,
Down Shoe Lane

To go away with your family is, in a great many instances, nothing but an elaborate contrivance for staying at home.

HOLBROOK JACKSON,
Southward Ho! and Other Essays

Vacations, no matter how long they last, always seem too short.

JEAN GAUTIER,
A Priest and His Dog

I am getting the vacation feeling—I have nearly washed out the ever imminent sense that I am neglecting some legal or spiritual duty to others or myself when I am idle.

OLIVER WENDELL HOLMES, JR.,
Holmes-Pollock Letters, Vol. II

A good vacation is over when you begin to yearn for your work.

DR. MORRIS FISHBEIN,
Holiday, March 1946

'Tis a sad but sober fact, that most men lead flat and virtuous lives, departing annually with their family to some flat and virtuous place, there to disport themselves in a manner that is decent, orderly, wholly uninteresting, vacant of every buxom stimulus. To such as these a suggestion, in all friendliness: why not try crime?

KENNETH GRAHAM,
Pagan Papers

The release of vacations cannot make up for deep frustrations at work. As a matter of fact, the reliance on vacations to accomplish that often destroys them; by expecting too much, one gets less from the holiday than otherwise. Only an emotionally satisfying life, even within a hard-working existence, is enriched by vacations which are then equally though differently satisfying.

BRUNO BETTELHEIM,
The Informed Heart

All of us, from time to time, need a plunge into freedom and novelty, after which routine and discipline will seem delightful by contrast.

ANDRÉ MAUROIS,
The Art of Living

It is true that romance comes easier when you're on vacation. But there's one type of resort where all the natural advantages are virtually canceled out—a place in which you find, say, 16 women to every man.

LOUISE LEVITAS,
Coronet, July 1951

Holidays are often overrated disturbances of routine, costly and uncomfortable, and they usually need another holiday to correct their ravages.

E. V. LUCAS,
365 Days and One More

The most important thing about a vacation for many people is the fact that they can brag about having been on one.

BRENDAN FRANCIS

The choice and nature of our holidays is more perhaps than anything in our lives an expression of ourselves.

ALEC WAUGH,
On Doing What One Likes

Staying home, you might for once in your life get through a vacation without vastly exceeding your vacation pay. You'd be facing facts and living within your income—a thing as admirable as it is out of character.

ROBERT M. YODER,
Saturday Evening Post, June 27, 1953

I am feeling strong and well having lived in wild mountains among peasants for a fortnight, but now with perversity begin to look forward to all the things that exhaust me in civilized life.

DOROTHY WELLESLEY,
*Letters on Poetry
from W. B. Yeats to Dorothy Wellesley*

VALUES

Instead of lamenting, as a threat, the disintegration of many traditional values and the lack of clear definition with which our historical period presents us, we may attempt to understand and to use the very conflicts and ambiguities of the time to open the way for realization of new possibilities.

HELEN MERRELL LYND,
On Shame and the Search for Identity

No values are effective, in a person or a society, except as there exists in the person the prior capacity to do the valuing, that is, the capacity actively to choose and affirm the values by which he lives.

ROLLO MAY,
Man's Search for Himself

False values and fatuous words: these are the worst monsters for mortals—long slumbereth and waiteth the fate that is in them.

But at last it cometh and awaketh and devoureth and engulfeth whatever hath built tabernacles upon it.

FRIEDRICH NIETZSCHE,
Thus Spake Zarathustra

VINCENT VAN GOGH

It may be a point of pride to have a Van Gogh on the living room wall, but the prospect of having Van Gogh himself in the living room would put a good many devoted art lovers to rout.

BEN SHAHN,
The Shape of Content

Van Gogh is something else, something inexorably obsessed with expression that bends painting to its will. With him the never before painted came in, but with Manet everything paintable. (That sounds strange; for by the meaning of painting everything actually must be paintable; yes, but it isn't yet, and Van Gogh wanted it to be, to be, to be.)

RAINER MARIA RILKE,
Letters of Rainer Maria Rilke 1892–1910

VANITY

When a man gets talking about himself he seldom fails to be eloquent and often reaches the sublime.

JOSH BILLINGS,
His Works Complete

Vanity and conceit are qualities that exist in people quite independently of their gifts and graces. The ugly and stupid are perhaps more often conceited than the beautiful or the clever.

RICHARD LE GALLIENNE,
Prose Fancies

All is vanity, and discovering it—the greatest vanity.

JOHN OLIVER HOBBES,
The Sinner's Comedy

Vanity, like sexual impulse, gives rise to needless self-reproach. Why be ashamed of anything so human? What, indeed, should we be without it?

CHARLES HORTON COOLEY,
Life and the Student

She is a peacock in everything but beauty.

OSCAR WILDE,
The Picture of Dorian Gray

and he said: you pretty full of yourself
   ain't chu
so she replied: show me someone not full
   of herself
and i'll show you a hungry person

NIKKI GIOVANNI,
"Poems for a Lady Whose Voice I Like,"
The Women and the Men

As for things that have influenced me, I believe hard work, love of justice and of beauty, good nature and great vanity, have done all of me that was worth doing.

JOHN RUSKIN,
Letters of John Ruskin to Charles Eliot Norton

Most of us would be far enough from vanity if we heard all the things that are said of us.

JOSEPH RICKABY,
Waters That Go Softly

Most of us retain enough of the theological attitude to think that we are little gods.

OLIVER WENDELL HOLMES, JR.,
The Mind and Faith of Justice Holmes,
edited by Max Lerner

Don't you think there is something touching about a vain man? He is all one ache for your praise, would sell his soul for it.— Of course you cannot trust a man who will sell himself for a compliment.

J. B. YEATS,
Letters to His Son, W. B. Yeats and Others

A man receives the shocks of life on the buffer of his vanity. Vanity acts as his second and bottleholder in the world's prize-ring, and it fights him well, bringing him smilingly up to time after the fiercest knock-down blows.

ALEXANDER SMITH,
Dreamthorp

VARIETY

Men only resemble each other when sophisticated by sordid or fashionable life; whatever is natural admits of variety.

MADAME DE STAËL,
quoted in *Men in Epigram,*
compiled by Frederick W. Morton

Sour, sweet, bitter, pungent, all must be tasted.

CHINESE PROVERB

The longer one lives, the more one realizes that nothing is a dish for every day.

NORMAN DOUGLAS,
An Almanac

If a man could go home to a strange woman every night for a month it might brighten up his day a bit.

BRENDAN FRANCIS

It is good to vary in order that you may frustrate the curious, especially those who envy you.

BALTASAR GRACIAN,
The Oracle

VICE

There is more than a morsel of truth in the saying, "He who hates vice hates mankind."

W. MACNEILE DIXON,
The Human Situation

Ingenuity is required even for the practice of vice.

HINDU PROVERB

There is a capacity of virtue in us, and there is a capacity of vice to make your blood creep.

> RALPH WALDO EMERSON,
> *Journals of Ralph Waldo Emerson*

It is the restrictions placed on vice by our social code which make its pursuit so peculiarly agreeable.

> KENNETH GRAHAME,
> *Pagan Papers*

We seek a thousand reasons to accuse vice in poverty, but two thousand to excuse it in prosperity.

> J. PETIT-SENN,
> *Conceits and Caprices*

If the practice of virtue eludes you, then give yourself up to vice with such saintly dedication that eventually you will become one of the elect.

> BRENDAN FRANCIS

Most vices demand considerable self-sacrifices. There is no greater mistake then to suppose that a vicious life is a life of uninterrupted pleasure. It is a life almost as wearisome and painful—if strenuously led—as Christian's in *The Pilgrim's Progress.*

> ALDOUS HUXLEY,
> *On the Road*

The incompensable value of giving free rein to one's vices consists in this, that they rise into view in all their strength and size, even if, in the excitement of indulgence, one catches only a faint glimpse of them. One doesn't learn to be a sailor by exercising in a puddle, though too much training in a puddle can probably render one unfit to be a sailor.

> FRANZ KAFKA,
> *The Diaries of Franz Kafka 1914–1923*

Vice and ambition are such absorbing motives that under their influence one grows completely oblivious of the rarer qualities of others. It is as though one were passing through a field of the rarest flowers and grasses with one's head so insanely obsessed by some amorous design or some business encounter that one might as well be plodding through arid sand.

> JOHN COWPER POWYS,
> *The Meaning of Culture*

VICTIM

This above all, to refuse to be a victim. Unless I can do that I can do nothing. I have to recant, give up the old belief that I am powerless and because of it nothing I can do will ever hurt anyone. A lie which was always more disastrous than the truth would have been.

> MARGARET ATWOOD,
> *Surfacing*

It is a terrible, an inexorable, law that one cannot deny the humanity of another without diminishing one's own: in the face of one's victim, one sees oneself.

> JAMES BALDWIN,
> *Man Alone,* edited by
> Eric Josephson and Mary Josephson

It would perhaps be pleasant to be alternately victim and executioner.

> CHARLES BAUDELAIRE,
> *Intimate Journals*

Victims have a beauty of their own, a beauty not the less touching because it is for the most part dumb.

> FREDERICK W. FABER,
> *Bethlehem*

Seized by the collar, dragged through the streets, pushed through the door. In abstract, that is how it is; in reality, there are counterforces, only a trifle less violent than the forces they oppose—the trifle that keeps life and torment alive. I am the victim of both.

> FRANZ KAFKA,
> *The Diaries of Franz Kafka 1914–1923*

VILLAIN

You should think and deal with every man as a villain, without calling him so, or flying from him, or valuing him less. This is an old true lesson.

> JONATHAN SWIFT,
> quoted in *The Second Book of He and She,*
> edited by James Moffatt

By an unfailing coincidence, the man who wrongs us is a villain, and the man who does us a kindness is a saint.

ANONYMOUS (HENRY H. HASKINS),
Meditations in Wall Street

VIOLENCE

We are all shot through with enough motives to make a massacre, any day of the week that we want to give them their head.

J. BRONOWSKI,
The Face of Violence

Who has not hoped
To outrage an enemy's dignity?
Who has not been swept
By the wish to hurt?
And who has not thought that the
    impersonal world
Deserves no better than to be destroyed
By one fabulous sign of his displeasure?

J. BRONOWSKI,
The Face of Violence

A bestial and violent man will go so far as to kill because he is under the influence of drink, exasperated, or driven by rage and alcohol. He is paltry. He does not know the pleasure of killing, the charity of bestowing death like a caress, of linking it with the play of the noble wild beasts: every cat, every tiger, embraces its prey and licks it even while it destroys it.

COLETTE,
Journey for Myself

Violence commands both literature and life, and violence is always crude and distorted.

ELLEN GLASGOW,
Letters of Ellen Glasgow

Love and violence, properly speaking, are polar opposites. Love lets the other be, but with affection and concern. Violence attempts to constrain the other's freedom, to force him to act in the way we desire, but with ultimate lack of concern, with indifference to the other's own existence or destiny.

We are effectively destroying ourselves by violence masquerading as love.

R. D. LAING,
The Politics of Experience

For violence, like Achilles' lance, can heal the wounds it has inflicted.

FRANTZ FANON,
The Wretched of the Earth

The limitation of riots, moral questions aside, is that they cannot win and their participants know it. Hence, rioting is not revolutionary but reactionary because it invites defeat. It involves an emotional catharsis, but it must be followed by a sense of futility.

MARTIN LUTHER KING, JR.,
The Trumpet of Conscience

A social structure shakes with violence and shivers with fears of violence not merely when that structure is callously unjust, but also when its members must stimulate themselves to feverish activity in order to demonstrate how alive they are. That there are colonies of the violent among us, devoid of any stable sense of communal purpose, best describes, I think, our present temporarily schizoid existence in two cultures—vacillating between dead purposes and deadly devices to escape boredom.

PHILIP RIEFF,
The Triumph of the Therapeutic

VIRTUE

Virtues are generally fashioned (more or less elegantly, according to the skill of the moral couturier) out of necessities.

ALDOUS HUXLEY,
Collected Essays

Virtue is not the absence of vices or the avoidance of moral dangers; virtue is a vivid and separate thing, like pain or a particular smell.

G. K. CHESTERTON,
Tremendous Trifles

Virtuous people are simply those who have either not been tempted sufficiently, because they live in a vegetative state, or because their purposes are so concentrated in one direction that they have not had leisure to glance around them.

ISADORA DUNCAN,
My Life

It is a revenge the devil sometimes takes upon the virtuous, that he entraps them by the force of the very passion they have suppressed and think themselves superior to.

GEORGE SANTAYANA,
The Letters of George Santayana

Nature does not loathe virtue: it is unaware of its existence.

FRANÇOISE MALLET-JORIS,
A Letter to Myself

Man cannot be uplifted; he must be seduced into virtue.

DON MARQUIS,
The Almost Perfect State

And be on thy guard against the good and the just! They would fain crucify those who devise their own virtue—they hate the lonesome ones.

FRIEDRICH NIETZSCHE,
Thus Spake Zarathustra

We are more inclined to regret our virtues than our vices; but only the very honest will admit this.

HOLBROOK JACKSON,
Platitudes in the Making

The gods are strange. It is not our vices only they make instruments to scourge us. They bring us to ruin through what in us is good, gentle, humane, loving.

OSCAR WILDE,
De Profundis

VISION

It's true that people see things very much in terms of what others have seen. It's simply a question of the originality of a person's vision, which is to see, for example, and *really* to see, a landscape instead of seeing a Pissarro. That's not as easy as it

sounds, either.

ALBERTO GIACOMETTI,
quoted in *A Giacometti Portrait*
by James Lord

An eternal trait of men is the need for vision and the readiness to follow it; and if men are not given the right vision, they will follow wandering fires.

SIR RICHARD LIVINGSTONE,
On Education

Who is narrow of vision cannot be big of heart.

CHINESE PROVERB

Man thirsts for clarity of vision. The sensual desires it in some body. The moral in some law. The intellectual in some definition. The religious in some creed or beatific insight. How shall beings, as complex as we, expect to find this clarity in the mixed quantities that make our wandering life?

JOHN ADDINGTON SYMONDS,
Letters and Papers of John Addington Symonds

By this way you know vision: that it is not what you expected, or even what you could have imagined, and that it is never repeated.

COVENTRY PATMORE,
The Rod, the Root, and the Flower

Reason may fail you. If you are going to do anything with life, you have sometimes to move away from it, beyond all measurements. You must follow sometimes visions and dreams.

BEDE JARRETT,
The House of Gold

Now, this state of "spiritual unrest" can never bring you to a state of vision, of which the essential is peace. And struggling to see does not help one to see. The light comes, when it does come, rather suddenly and strangely I think. It is just like falling in love; a thing that never happens to those who are always trying to do it.

EVELYN UNDERHILL,
The Letters of Evelyn Underhill

VITALITY

I am a slow-thinking man, and it occurred to me simultaneously that of all natural forces, vitality is the incommunicable one. In days when juice came into one as an article without duty, one tried to distribute it—but always without success; to further mix metaphors, vitality never "takes." You have it or you haven't it, like health or brown eyes or honor or a baritone voice.

F. Scott Fitzgerald,
The Crack-up

Vitality shows not only in the ability to persist but the ability to start over.

F. Scott Fitzgerald,
The Crack-up

VOCATION

Always the higher a life is, the more it is beautiful in its place, and can be beautiful nowhere else.

Phillips Brooks,
Visions and Tasks

A man who is not in his place is like a dislocated bone; he suffers and he causes suffering.

Joseph Roux,
Meditations of a Parish Priest

Only God knows what is one's real work.

Anton Chekhov,
Uncle Vanya

To suffer for doing what one ought is a beautiful destiny. But, beautiful or ugly, it is fate.

Romain Rolland,
Journey Within

Looking at the masses of humanity, driven this way and that way, the Christian teaching is apt to be forgotten that for each individual soul there is a vocation as real as if that soul were alone upon the planet. Yet it is a fact.

Mark Rutherford,
The Deliverance of Mark Rutherford

VOICE

I would rather be kicked with a foot than be overcome by a loud voice speaking cruel words.

Elizabeth Barrett Browning,
quoted in *Ladies of Literature*
by Laura L. Hinkley

O what is it that makes me tremble so at voices?
Surely whoever speaks to me in the right voice, him or her I shall follow.

Walt Whitman,
"Vocalism," *Leaves of Grass*

Voices—I think they must go deeper into us than other things. I have often fancied heaven might be made of voices.

George Eliot

To expect to rule others by assuming a loud tone is like thinking oneself tall by putting on high heels.

J. Petit-Senn,
Conceits and Caprices

Do you hate a fashionable voice?—I remember, once, asking a now deceased cousin of mine for a description of some woman. He replied: "Oh, an empty sardine tin on a sandy shore!" It fits this person, too.

Edith Sitwell,
Edith Sitwell: Selected Letters 1919–1964

VOLUPTUOUSNESS

Voluptuousness: only to the withered a sweet poison; to the lion-willed, however, the great cordial, and the reverently saved wine of wines.

Friedrich Nietzsche,
Thus Spake Zarathustra

VOW

The memory that an oath or vow has been made will nerve one to abstinences and efforts otherwise impossible.

William James,
"The Energies of Men,"
Essays on Faith and Morals

VULGAR

In every greatest king, in every loveliest flowery princess, in every poet most refined, every best dressed dandy, every holiest and most spiritual teacher, there lurks, waiting, waiting for the moment to emerge, an outcaste of the outcastes, a dung carrier, a dog, lower than the lowest, bottomlessly vulgar.
ALDOUS HUXLEY,
Collected Essays

WAITING

People count up the faults of those who keep them waiting.   FRENCH PROVERB

To keep someone waiting or to be kept waiting is a cause of Angst which is out of all proportion to the minor fault of unpunctuality. Therefore we may assume that we keep people waiting symbolically because we do not wish to see them and that our anxiety is due not to being late, but to our having to see them at all.
CYRIL CONNOLLY,
The Unquiet Grave

To him that waits all things reveal themselves, provided that he has the courage not to deny, in the darkness, what he has seen in the light.   COVENTRY PATMORE

The future belongs to him who knows how to wait.   RUSSIAN PROVERB

We do not obtain the most precious gifts by going in search of them but by waiting for them. Man cannot discover them by his own powers, and if he sets out to seek for them he will find in their place counterfeits of which he will be unable to discern the falsity.
SIMONE WEIL,
Waiting for God

WALKING

So fresh and exciting this walk up the road with haversack on my back. . . . Off all the wife, the mother, the lover, the teacher, and the violent artist takes over. I am alone. I belong to no one but myself. I mate with no one but the spirit. I own no land, have no kind, no friend or enemy. I have no road but this one.
SYLVIA ASHTON-WARNER,
Myself

The experience of strolling by one's self through the vast multitudes of a strange city is one of the most wonderful in life. I suppose there is nothing quite like it this side of heaven.
GAMALIEL BRADFORD,
The Letters of Gamaliel Bradford

It is solved by walking.
LATIN PROVERB

We are unwilling walkers. We are not innocent and simple-hearted enough to enjoy a walk. We have fallen from that state of grace which capacity to enjoy a walk implies.
JOHN BURROUGHS,
quoted in *A Year of Sunshine,*
selected by Kate Sanborn

Glory to your feet.
ALBANIAN ROAD GREETING

Walking companions, like heroes, are difficult to pluck out of the crowd of acquaintances. Good dispositions, ready wit, friendly conversation serve well enough by the fireside but they prove insufficient in the field. For there you need transcendentalists—nothing less; you need poets, sages, humorists and natural philosophers.
BROOKS ATKINSON,
The Art of Walking,
edited by Edwin V. Mitchell

A pedestrian ought to be legally allowed to toss at least one hand grenade at a motorist every day.
BRENDAN FRANCIS

I'm worried about things. I think I'll walk & grieve and scowl at the unmitigated birds—the first adjective, of any kind, I cd think of.
DYLAN THOMAS,
Letters to Vernon Watkins

In our entrancement with the motorcar, we have forgotten how much more efficient and how much more flexible the footwalker is.

LEWIS MUMFORD,
quoted in *The Magic of Walking*
by Aaron Sussman and Ruth Goode

Walkers are not intelligent, and do not think ahead; they walk themselves weary and develop all manner of ailments in the process. A good walk, you say, is worth them all? Very true.

ROSE MACAULAY,
Personal Pleasures

Long walks with a pack on one's back are necessary in time of war, but I do not see why a man should go on marching in times of peace.

ROBERT LYND,
The Blue Lion

Along the Champs-Elysées, ideas pouring from me like sweat. I ought to be rich enough to have a secretary to whom I could dictate as I walk, because my best thoughts always come to me when I am away from the machine.

HENRY MILLER,
The Tropic of Cancer

The [English] literary movement at the end of the eighteenth century was obviously due in great part, if not mainly, to the renewed practice of walking.

LESLIE STEPHEN,
The Art of Walking,
edited by Edwin V. Mitchell

WAR

War makes strange giant creatures out of us little routine men who inhabit the earth.

ERNIE PYLE,
Here Is Your War

The story goes that during World War I a Guards officer was on leave. "Do tell us," said his clubmates, "what war is like?"

"Awful!" he replied, "The noise! And the *people!*"

W. H. AUDEN,
A Certain World

There is nothing that war has ever achieved we could not better achieve without it.

HAVELOCK ELLIS,
Selected Essays

How vile and despicable war seems to me! I would rather be hacked in pieces than take part in such an abominable business.

ALBERT EINSTEIN,
Ideas and Opinions

I love war and responsibility and excitement. Peace is going to be hell on me.

GEORGE S. PATTON,
quoted in *Patton: Ordeal and Triumph*
by Ladislas Farago

Men are at war with one another because each man is at war with himself.

FRANCIS MEEHAN,
The Temple of the Spirit

In war more than anywhere else in the world things happen differently from what we had expected, and look differently when near from what they did at a distance.

KARL VON CLAUSEWITZ,
On War

When you are winning a war almost everything that happens can be claimed to be right and wise.

SIR WINSTON CHURCHILL,
A Churchill Reader,
edited by Colin R. Coote

Those who do not go to war roar like lions.

KURDISH PROVERB

Anybody who thinks that war is pleasant ... you know, the old veteran stuff. You know, "War is great stuff." Well, it's great for the survivors—not great for the people who are killed in it.

BERNARD B. FALL,
Last Reflections on a War

We are all familiar with the argument: Make war dreadful enough, and there will be no war. And we none of us believe it.

JOHN GALSWORTHY,
Castles in Spain and Other Screeds

Get in a tight spot in combat, and some guy will risk his ass to help you. Get in a tight spot in peacetime, and you go it all alone.

BRENDAN FRANCIS

When nuclear dust has extinguished their betters,
Will the turtles surviving wear people-neck sweaters?

E. Y. HARBURG,
"Fission Fashion," *War: An Anthology,*
edited by Edward Huberman
and Elizabeth Huberman

What a country calls its vital economic interests are not the things which enable its citizens to live, but the things which enable it to make war. Gasoline is much more likely than wheat to be a cause of international conflict.

SIMONE WEIL,
quoted in *A Certain World* by W. H. Auden

There is hardly such a thing as a war in which it makes no difference who wins. Nearly always one side stands more or less for progress, the other side more or less for reaction.

GEORGE ORWELL,
A Collection of Essays

The army taught me some great lessons—to be prepared for catastrophe—to endure being bored—and to know that however fine [a] fellow I thought myself in my usual routine there were other situations in which I was inferior to men that I might have looked down upon had not experience taught me to look up.

OLIVER WENDELL HOLMES, JR.,
Holmes-Laski Letters, Vol. II

These wars make men so violent scarce that these good ladies take up with the shadows of them.

LADY MARY WORTLEY MONTAGU,
*The Complete Letters of
Lady Mary Wortley Montague,* Vol. I

He has only two interests, war and woman, and that keeps him vital. It is curious that those two interests have always gone together.

W. B. YEATS,
*Letters on Poetry
from W. B. Yeats to Dorothy Wellesley*

WARNING

It seems all the average fellow needs to make him take a chance is a warning.

KIN HUBBARD,
Abe Martin on Things in General

WASTE

Waste, yes, that is ... what spoils for me an evening like yesterday's. Waste of time, of money, or strength—and for what a petty pleasure!

ANDRÉ GIDE,
The Journals of André Gide, Vol. I

Most everyone seems to waste his life in false attempts: a show of fine energy foully misplaced.

THOMAS WOLFE,
The Letters of Thomas Wolfe

WATER

No honey or spice can make wine so sweet, as real thirst makes cold water.

SAINT AILRED OF RIEVAULX,
Christian Friendship

Two leaps the water from its race
  Made to the brook below,
The first leap it was curving glass,
  The second bounding snow.

WILLIAM ALLINGHAM,
"A Mill," quoted in *A Certain World*
by W. H. Auden

The water that bears the ship is the same that engulfs it.

CHINESE PROVERB

If there is magic on this planet, it is contained in water. Its least stir even, as now in a rain pond on a flat roof opposite my office, is enough to bring me searching to the window. A wind ripple may be translating itself into life. I have a constant feeling that sometime I may witness that momentous miracle on a city roof, see life veritably and suddenly boiling out of a heap of rusted pipes and old television aerials.

LOREN EISLEY,
The Immense Journey

WAY

The way for me to live is to have no way. My only habit should be to have none. Because I did it this way before is sufficient reason not to do it this way today.

HUGH PRATHER,
Notes to Myself

"This—is now *my way,*—where is yours?" Thus did I answer those who asked me "the way." For *the* way—it doth not exist!

FRIEDRICH NIETZSCHE,
Thus Spake Zarathustra

WEAKNESS

We like to know the weakness of eminent men; it consoles us for our inferiority.

MADAME DE LAMBERT,
quoted in *Men in Epigram,*
compiled by Frederick W. Morton

You cannot have force in two places at the same time; and you must know a man's weakness before you truly know his strength. It is often in the "weakness"—as the valet-moralist counts weakness—that the source of the hero's strength lies, the weakness which, as Hinton used to put it, was the path of least resistance through which the aboriginal energy of Nature passed into the man.

HAVELOCK ELLIS,
Selected Essays

Human nature is such that the spectacle of another's weakness awakens even in the best of us a feeling of power which con-

tains along with the sincerest pity, an almost imperceptible mingling of pleasure.

ANDRÉ MAUROIS,
The Art of Living

I think the weak—if they are not just pusillanimous—are compelled to have more strength than those who are overtly strong. They wouldn't survive at all unless they had this inner strength. They may suffer a great deal for it—and I suppose they do. But I've always felt that Blanche was stronger than Stanley Kowalski.

TENNESSEE WILLIAMS,
quoted in *Close-up* by John Gruen

WEATHER

The sun came out brilliantly this morning. To be sure, there was a chilliness in the air; but if you walked about with vigour, and said it was a charming morning, it gradually became so. An eccentric friend of mine, of the Johnsonian school, maintains that all kinds of weather may be treated in a similar manner.

SIR ARTHUR HELPS,
Companions of My Solitude

For the man sound in body and serene of mind there is no such thing as bad weather; every sky has its beauty, and storms which whip the blood do but make it pulse more vigorously.

GEORGE GISSING,
The Private Papers of Henry Ryecroft

Strange what a difference a glorious day can make! How one revels in life, in being, in poetry, in the holy ridiculousness of things!

LIONEL JOHNSON,
Some Winchester Letters of Lionel Johnson

One way to help the weather make up its mind is to hang out a washing.

MARCELENE COX,
Ladies' Home Journal, April 1949

Whenever people talk to me about the weather, I always feel certain that they mean something else.

OSCAR WILDE,
The Importance of Being Earnest

WELCOME

I appreciate your welcome. As the cow said to the Maine farmer, "Thank you for a warm hand on a cold morning."

JOHN F. KENNEDY,
The Kennedy Wit, edited by Bill Adler

WHISPER

The whisper of a pretty girl can be heard further than the roar of a lion.

ARAB PROVERB

WHITE

White is not a mere absence of colour; it is a shining and affirmative thing, as fierce as red, as definite as black.

G. K. CHESTERTON,
Tremendous Trifles

There are so many lovely white things, clouds and gulls and daisies and the white caps of waves—I saw them all from your garden.

ANNE MORROW LINDBERGH,
Bring Me a Unicorn

WALT WHITMAN

A lofty, sturdy wind blows through his poems. There is a healing quality to his vision.

HENRY MILLER,
The Books in My Life

Always wanting to merge himself into the womb of something or other.

D. H. LAWRENCE,
Selected Essays

Whitman like a strange, modern, American Moses. Fearfully mistaken. And yet the great leader.

D. H. LAWRENCE,
Selected Essays

Whitman seems to me to have been one of the few very great poets that have ever lived.

ALFRED NORTH WHITEHEAD,
Dialogues of Alfred North Whitehead

WIFE

If you want peace in the house, do what your wife wants.

AFRICAN PROVERB

What is instinct? It is the natural tendency in one when filled to dismay to turn to his wife.

FINLEY PETER DUNNE,
quoted in *A Book of Days*
by Winifred Gordon

If a woman's husband gets on her nerves, she should fly at him. If she thinks him too sweet and smarmy with other people, she should let him have it to his nose, straight out. She should lead him a dog's life, and never swallow her bile.

D. H. LAWRENCE,
Fantasia of the Unconscious

Wives, don't love your husbands nor your children nor anybody. Sit still, and say Hush! . . . And when your husband comes in and says he's afraid he's got a cold and is going to have double pneumonia, say quietly: "Surely not." And if he wants the ammoniated quinine, give it to him if he can't get it for himself. But don't let him drive you out of your solitude, your singleness within yourself.

D. H. LAWRENCE,
Fantasia of the Unconscious

He that has lost a wife and sixpence has lost sixpence.

SCOTCH PROVERB

If you haven't seen your wife smile at a traffic cop, you haven't seen her smile at her prettiest.

KIN HUBBARD,
Abe Martin on Things in General

I saw men whom thirty years had changed but slightly; but their wives had grown old. These were good women; it is very wearing to be good.

MARK TWAIN,
Mark Twain at Your Fingertips,
edited by Caroline T. Harnsberger

Women are not gamblers even to the small extent that men are. Wives tend to limit their husband's enterprise, especially if it involves risks, and consequently the opportunities for achievement, delight and surprise are limited.

GERMAINE GREER,
The Female Eunuch

WILL

We glorify rugged wills; but the greatest things are done by timid people who work with simple trust.

JOHN LA FARGE,
Wisdom for Our Time,
edited by James Nelson

And so you have not done something and not had something which you thought it impossible not to do and not to have. It was, you see, possible. The imagination is often the most stubborn antagonist of a better will.

THEODOR HAECKER,
Journal in the Night

He who can follow his own will is a king.

IRISH PROVERB

All *feeling* suffereth in me, and is in prison: but my *willing* ever cometh to me as mine emancipator and comforter.

FRIEDRICH NIETZSCHE,
Thus Spake Zarathustra

I can will knowledge, but not wisdom; going to bed, but not sleeping; eating, but not hunger; meekness, but not humility; scrupulosity, but not virtue; self-assertion or bravado, but not courage; lust, but not love; commiseration, but not sympathy; congratulations, but not admiration; religiosity, but not faith; reading, but not understanding.

LESLIE H. FARBER,
The Ways of the Will

The will is the strong blind man who carries on his shoulders the lame man who can see.

ARTHUR SCHOPENHAUER,
quoted in *The Unquiet Grave*
by Cyril Connolly

I don't think anything happens in this universe except by some power—or individual—making it happen. Nothing happens of itself. I believe all events are produced by will.

WILLIAM BURROUGHS,
Writers at Work, Third Series,
edited by George Plimpton

If it's *got* to be a battle of wills, I'll fight the devil himself, as long as the necessity lasts. But it's not my idea of life.

D. H. LAWRENCE,
Selected Letters of D. H. Lawrence

Great things are not done by impulse, but by a series of small things brought together. And great things are not something accidental, but must certainly be *willed.*

VINCENT VAN GOGH,
Dear Theo:
An Autobiography of Vincent Van Gogh

WIND

Frightful, wonderful squall all night long. My mind seems to be lifted up by the wind—carried off like a kite—a kite on the end of a rubber band.

ANDRÉ GIDE,
The Journals of André Gide, Vol. I

There is nothing more satisfying than to lie in bed at night, secure and warm, with a whistling wind outside.

CLARE LEIGHTON,
Four Hedges

A tremendous wind from the north; day like a raving maniac bent on demolishing the world. It almost blows the hair off a dog.

JOHN BURROUGHS,
The Heart of Burroughs' Journals

And wind moving through grass so that the grass quivers. This moves me with an emotion I don't ever understand.

KATHERINE MANSFIELD,
The Journal of Katherine Mansfield

WINE

Good wine praises itself.
ARAB PROVERB

The wines that one remembers best are not necessarily the finest that one has tasted, and the highest quality may fail to delight so much as some far more humble beverage drunk in more favourable surroundings.
H. WARNER ALLEN,
A Contemplation of Wine

Wine is a bride who brings a great dowry to the man who woos her persistently and gracefully; she turns her back on a rough approach.
EVELYN WAUGH,
Wine in Peace and War

It is difficult to enjoy a good wine in a bad glass.
EVELYN WAUGH,
Wine in Peace and War

A glass of good wine is a gracious creature, and reconciles poor mortality to itself, and that is what few things can do.
SIR WALTER SCOTT,
Sir Walter Scott's Journal (1825–1832)

When the head is under the influence of wine, many a thing swims out of the heart.
YUGOSLAV PROVERB

It was golden in colour, suave and yet virile, as if a breeze of the sea had swept the grape and the ghost of its tang still clung and mingled with the bloom.
D. B. WYNDHAM LEWIS,
On Straw and Other Conceits

The drinking of wine seems to have a moral edge over many pleasures and hobbies in that it promotes love of one's neighbor. As a general thing it is not a lone occupation. A bottle of wine begs to be shared; I have never met a miserly wine lover.
CLIFTON FADIMAN,
Any Number Can Play

No draught of wine amid the old tombs under the violet sky but made me for the time a better man, larger of brain, more courageous, more gentle. 'Twas a revelry whereon came no repentance. Could I but live for ever in thoughts and feelings such as those born to me in the shadow of the Italian vine!
GEORGE GISSING,
The Private Papers of Henry Ryecroft

Wine is a precarious aphrodisiac, and its fumes have blighted many a mating.
NORMAN DOUGLAS,
An Almanac

WINNER

I'd rather be a poor winner than any kind of loser.
GEORGE S. KAUFMAN,
quoted in George S. Kaufman
by Howard Teichman

Pray God that you will always be found on the winning side; for that way you get credit even for things in which you had no part; whereas he who stands with the losers has endless offences imputed to him of which he is wholly guiltless.
FRANCESCO GUICCIARDINI,
Counsels and Reflections

WINTER

The hardest thing any man can do is to fall down on the ice when it's slippery, and get up and praise the Lord.
JOSH BILLINGS,
His Works Complete

January, month of empty pockets! ... Let us endure this evil month, anxious as a theatrical producer's forehead.
COLETTE,
Journey for Myself

In a winter landscape—especially in a wood—there is the same kind of purity that the Greeks saw in the unclad human form; it is like a young athlete, ready for racing, with his flowing garments flung aside. It is an education in restraint; after seeing it, one cannot forget the fine severity beneath all natural beauty.

MARY WEBB,
The Spring of Joy

The fire is winter's fruit.

ARAB PROVERB

There's a certain slant of light
On winter afternoons,
That oppresses like the weight
Of cathedral tunes.

EMILY DICKINSON,
Selected Poems and Letters of Emily Dickinson

In good health, the air is a cordial of incredible virtue. Crossing a bare common, in snow puddles, at twilight, under a clouded sky, without having in my thoughts any occurrence of special good fortune, I have enjoyed a perfect exhilaration. I am glad to the brink of fear.

RALPH WALDO EMERSON,
Journals of Ralph Waldo Emerson

We wonder every winter that women do not freeze their legs off at the ankles.

E. W. HOWE,
Country Town Sayings

We sometimes wonder why the City Government tilts so vigorously at the snow. The first flake has hardly fluttered down when every infernal machine in town is rushing to do battle.... Is snow such poisonous stuff? Our own feeling is that it is something to be honored and preserved— and we would like to see all citizens provided with little tinkling bells so that they would make merry sounds as they plodded about their business, in high rubber boots.

E. B. WHITE,
Every Day Is Saturday

It's almost too cold to hold a pen this morning. I've lost a toe since breakfast, my nose is on its last nostril. I've four sweaters on (including yours), two pairs of trousers & socks, a leather coat & a dressing gown. Who was the French poet who had alphabetically lettered underpants, & wore every one up to H on a cold morning?

DYLAN THOMAS,
Letters to Vernon Watkins

Snow is what you are up to your neck in when people send you post cards from Florida saying they wish you were there, and I wish they might sit on a burr.

OGDEN NASH,
Ogden Nash Pocket Book

The first fall of snow is not only an event but it is a magical event. You go to bed in one kind of a world and wake up to find yourself in another quite different, and if this is not enchantment, then where is it to be found?

J. B. PRIESTLEY,
Apes and Angels

WISDOM

Everyone is wise until he speaks.

IRISH PROVERB

Almost all wise men, while they can easily solve the difficulties of others, are apt to be doubtful and anxious about their own and place far greater confidence in the judgment of others.

SAINT BERNARD OF CLAIRVAUX,
Letters

The art of being wise is the art of knowing what to overlook.

WILLIAM JAMES,
Principles of Psychology, Vol. II

There are some people to whom it is impossible to speak wisdom even if you should wish to. No spirit of kindly philosophy speaks out of their eyes. You find yourself automatically saying peevish or futile things that you do not in the least believe.

CHRISTOPHER MORLEY,
Mince Pie

The days that make us happy make us wise.

JOHN MASEFIELD,
"Biography," *Poems*

A wise man among the ignorant is as a beautiful girl in the company of blind men.

SAADI,
quoted in *Ladies' Home Journal*,
March 1949

If one is too lazy to think, too vain to do a thing badly, too cowardly to admit it, one will never attain wisdom.
CYRIL CONNOLLY,
The Unquiet Grave

Not by constraint or severity shall you have access to true wisdom, but by abandonment, and childlike mirthfulness. If you would know aught, be gay before it.
HENRY DAVID THOREAU,
Journal

Cleverness and stupidity are generally in the same boat against wisdom.
J. A. SPENDER,
The Comments of Bagshot, Second Series

The attempt to combine wisdom and power has only rarely been successful and then only for a short while.
ALBERT EINSTEIN,
Ideas and Opinions

Growth in wisdom may be exactly measured by decrease in bitterness.
FRIEDRICH NIETZSCHE,
quoted in *Selected Essays* by Havelock Ellis

WISHING

The fox that waited for the chickens to fall off their perch died of hunger.
GREEK PROVERB

If all our wishes were gratified, most of our pleasures would be destroyed.
RICHARD WHATELY,
quoted in *Ladies' Home Journal,*
October 1944

We are all kings and conquerors in the silent empire of our fantasies.
DR. SMILEY BLANTON,
Love or Perish

I ask myself whether fulfillment really has anything to do with wishes. Yes, as long as the wish is weak, it is like a half and needs to be fulfilled like a second half, in order to be something independent. But wishes can grow so wonderfully into something whole, full, sound that permits of no further completion whatever, that goes on growing only out of itself and forms and fills itself.
RAINER MARIA RILKE,
Letters of Rainer Maria Rilke 1892–1910

A man has more fun wishing for the things he hasn't got than enjoying the things he has got.
FINLEY PETER DUNNE,
quoted in *A Book of Days*
by Winifred Gordon

WIT

Though we use all our wit for blame, we know that we shall not be civilized until we can praise wittily. That would seem to us the civilization of the angels—or of God Himself. For then laughter would not be a weapon at all, but the very voice of delighted recognition.
A. CLUTTON BROCK,
Essays on Life

No doubt, it is not necessary to have an amount of wit or imagination; but it is indispensable that we should not think we have it when we don't.
FÉLIX A. DUPANLOUP,
The Child

When our wit brightens, it may be the effect of cocktails; sometimes it flares up at another's challenge; again it may be fired from a flame of incalculable distance and unknowable source.
ANONYMOUS (HENRY S. HASKINS),
Meditations in Wall Street

Wit: a form of sex display.
A. R. ORAGE,
Essays and Aphorisms

There's a hell of a distance between wisecracking and wit. Wit has truth in it; wisecracking is simply calisthenics with words.
DOROTHY PARKER,
Writers at Work,
edited by Malcolm Cowley

WITCH

Of course popular mythology would have it that we witches are a licentious lot, forever running around half-naked under the light of the moon making weird mad-dog noises, with the Devil as a perpetual playmate ready to help us in all sorts of nefarious goings-on. It's nice material for a movie but far removed from the real thing.

SYBIL LEEK,
Diary of a Witch

WOMAN

Whenever women do anything new it is always said they are about to lose their femininity. Society is constantly alarmed about this, as though femininity were important but fugitive. It may be so. Society seems almost to fear that if women were left to themselves they would cease to be women. This too may be true. It certainly looks as though women had a tendency to escape from the role assigned them, and now no one can say what that role is.

FLORIDA SCOTT-MAXWELL,
Women, and Sometimes Men

Woman has for long dealt with the untidy side of life, affording in private the relief of being natural. It is usual for her to concern herself with the things that should not be seen, and that give away our incorrigible humanity. Yet she is also the show piece, the orchid in the buttonhole, the final flourish of decoration.

FLORIDA SCOTT-MAXWELL,
Women, and Sometimes Men

It sometimes seems as though woman would not be woman unless man insisted upon it, since she tends so markedly to be just a human being when away from men, and only on their approach does she begin to play her required role.

FLORIDA SCOTT-MAXWELL,
Women, and Sometimes Men

Woman's basic fear is that she will lose love.

SIGMUND FREUD,
Civilization and Its Discontents

Well, you can't make women happy, that's a kind of fundamental law of the universe. You try and make them happy and they'll never forgive you for revealing to them that they can't be.

LEN DEIGHTON,
Spy Story

I hate women because they always know where things are.

JAMES THURBER,
Men Against Women,
edited by Charles Neider

When three women join together the stars come out in broad daylight.

TALUGU PROVERB

More and more women are coming to use men as "mere sex objects," which is a welcome switch for both sexes.

BRENDAN FRANCIS

A great many men, who are sane and reasonable in other matters, allow themselves, on the slightest provocation, to be worked up into a fever over the aspirations of women.

ROBERT GRANT,
The Art of Living

When every unkind word about women has been said, we have still to admit ... that they are nicer than men. They are more devoted, more unselfish, and more emotionally sincere.

CYRIL CONNOLLY,
The Unquiet Grave

Spiritually a woman is better off if she cannot be taken for granted.

GERMAINE GREER,
The Female Eunuch

Pretty women are never unaware that they are aging, even if the process has hardly begun.

GERMAINE GREER,
The Female Eunuch

The efforts made to eradicate all smell from the female body are part of the same suppression of fancied animality.

GERMAINE GREER,
The Female Eunuch

Nobody wants a girl whose beauty is imperceptible to all but him; and so men welcome the stereotype because it directs their taste into the most commonly recognized areas of value, although they may protest because some aspects of it do not tally with their fetishes. There is scope in the stereotype's variety for most fetishes. The leg man may follow miniskirts, the tit man can encourage see-through blouses and plunging necklines, although the man who likes fat women may feel constrained to enjoy them in secret.

GERMAINE GREER,
The Female Eunuch

No man, as a general rule, shows his soul to another man; he shows it only to a woman.

LAFCADIO HEARN,
Lafcadio Hearn: Life and Letters,
edited by Elizabeth Bisland

The widely extended impatience of women under the present conditions of things is nothing but an unconscious protest against the diminished manliness of men.

COVENTRY PATMORE,
Religio, Poetae, Etc.

Adam must have an Eve to blame for his faults.

ITALIAN PROVERB

Women are at last becoming persons first and wives second, and that is as it should be.

MAY SARTON,
Journal of a Solitude

Two different things wanteth the true man: danger and diversion. Therefore wanteth he woman, as the most dangerous plaything.

FRIEDRICH NIETZSCHE,
Thus Spake Zarathustra

Whenever you catch yourself thinking that women are saints and angels, be sure you take a blue pill.

NORMAN DOUGLAS,
An Almanac

There is no doubt that the world is kept

young by women of all ages. They mitigate the incurable solemnity of men.

JAMES DOUGLAS,
Down Shoe Lane

Married and unmarried women waste a great deal of time in feeling sorry for each other.

MYRTLE REED,
The Spinster Book

Our life is so dependent on our relations with women—and the opposite, of course, is also true—that it seems to me one must never think lightly of them.

VINCENT VAN GOGH,
Dear Theo:
An Autobiography of Vincent Van Gogh

The wind is not swifter than a woman's choice between two men.

IRISH PROVERB

Ah, but what is "herself"? I mean, what is a woman? I assure you, I do not know. I do not believe that you know. I do not believe that anybody can know until she has expressed herself in all the arts and professions open to human skill.

VIRGINIA WOOLF,
quoted in *Virginia Woolf*
by Monique Nathan

They are tann'd in the face by shining
   suns and blowing winds,
Their flesh has the old divine suppleness
   and strength,
They know how to swim, row, ride,
   wrestle, shoot, run, strike, retreat,
   advance, resist, defend themselves,
They are ultimate in their own right—
   they are calm, clear, well-possessed of
   themselves.

WALT WHITMAN,
"A Woman Waits for Me," *Leaves of Grass*

The real paradox is that the men who make, materially, the biggest sacrifices for their women should do the least for them ideally and romantically.

EDITH WHARTON,
The Custom of the Country

Basically, society has to get rid of that myth of the dominant male and the submissive female. When both sexes realize that either one can be on top, we're all going to enjoy our relationships a lot more.

GLORIA STEINEM,
Supertalk by Digby Diehl

Most women's magazines simply try to mold women into bigger and better consumers in the capitalist market.

GLORIA STEINEM,
Supertalk by Digby Diehl

I said that the standards for brides are so low that a man wouldn't marry a woman he'd hire to work in his office. Because he's only been taught to look for a housekeeper and a mistress.

GLORIA STEINEM,
Supertalk by Digby Diehl

Our lives, she thought, summing up her sex in general, are an immolation; theirs, summing up his, are an escape.

ROBERT SPEAIGHT,
The Unbroken Heart

Women in bulk are chastening. Great droves of the most enticing beings in the world do not entice.

FRANK MOORE COLBY,
The Colby Essays, Vol. 1

All women say that they do not cry very much, but I don't because I learned long ago that I do it at the wrong time and in front of the wrong people.

LILLIAN HELLMAN,
An Unfinished Woman

If a woman hasn't got a tiny streak of the harlot in her, she's a dry stick as a rule.

D. H. LAWRENCE,
Pornography and Obscenity

The most sympathetic of men never fully comprehend woman's concrete situation.

SIMONE DE BEAUVOIR,
The Second Sex

It is precisely in the field of conversation, where women's intuition is richest and most stimulating, that men are the least interested in it.

DAVID L. COHN,
Love in America

WONDER

Let others wrangle, I will wonder.

SAINT AUGUSTINE,
quoted in *The Pleasures of Life*
by John Lubbock

The world will never starve for want of wonders; but only for want of wonder.

G. K. CHESTERTON,
Tremendous Trifles

Wonder . . . is essentially an "opening" attitude—an awareness that there is more to life than one has yet fathomed, an experience of new vistas in life to be explored as well as new profundities to be plumbed.

ROLLO MAY,
Man's Search for Himself

Anyone hurt or twisted by life, to find the wonder in them.

SHERWOOD ANDERSON,
Letters of Sherwood Anderson

Wonder is the qualitative distance which God placed between man and truth. It enables man to find the truth.

THEODOR HAECKER,
Journal in the Night

WORDS

You can stroke people with words.

F. SCOTT FITZGERALD,
The Crack-up

There was an enquiry about the derivation of the word C—t when while two parsons and Grammarians were sitting together and settling the matter Wm Squibs interrupting them said a very good thing— Gentleman says he I have always understood it to be a Root and not a Derivative!

JOHN KEATS,
quoted in *Mrs. Grundy* by Peter Fryer

There are those whom words frighten more than the things they express.

JOHN LANCASTER SPALDING,
Aphorisms and Reflections

They cannot be remote from reality when they create reality.

JOHN COWPER POWYS,
The Meaning of Culture

The words in our aging vocabularies are like very sick people. Some may be able to survive, others are incurable.

ARTHUR ADAMOV,
quoted in *The Theatre of the Absurd*
by Martin Esslin

Better one word before than two after.

WELSH PROVERB

There is no means by which men so powerfully elude their ignorance, disguise it from themselves and from others as by words.

GAMALIEL BRADFORD,
The Letters of Gamaliel Bradford

Censorship and oppression prove that the word is enough to make the tyrant tremble—but only if the word is backed up by sacrifice. For only the word fed by blood and heart can unite men, whereas the silence of tyrannies separates them.

ALBERT CAMUS,
Resistance, Rebellion, and Death

Men no longer test words to see what truth is in them. The majority are only interested in knowing what their effect will be.

THEODOR HAECKER,
Journal in the Night

Something is always lost in generalisations. A railway leaves out all the gaps of dirt between. Generalisations are only means of getting about.

Cf. the words love, sex, nude, with the actual details.

T. E. HULME,
Speculations

Oh, words are action good enough, if they're the right words.

D. H. LAWRENCE,
Selected Letters of D. H. Lawrence

Almost all words do have color and nothing is more pleasant than to utter a pink word and see someone's eyes light up and know it is a pink word for him or her too.

GLADYS TABER,
Stillmeadow Daybook

Words are sometimes sensitive instruments of precision with which delicate operations may be performed and swift, elusive truths may be touched; often they are clumsy tools with which we grope in the dark toward truths more inaccessible but no less significant.

HELEN MERRELL LYND,
On Shame and the Search for Identity

In many souls, a hunger and thirst exists which can only be satisfied by printed words.

ERNEST HELLO,
Life, Science, and Art

I think that words are an around-the-world, ox-cart way of doing things, awkward instruments, and they will be laid aside eventually, probably sooner than we think. This is something that will happen in the space age.

WILLIAM BURROUGHS,
Writers at Work, Third Series,
edited by George Plimpton

The right word spoken at the right time sometimes achieves miracles.

JOSEF GOEBBELS,
The Goebbels Diaries

The closer the look one takes at a word, the greater the distance from which it looks back.

KARL KRAUS,
Karl Kraus by Harry Zohn

To move among this bright, strange, often fabulous herd of beings, to summon them at my will, to fasten them on to paper like flies, that they may decorate it, this is the pleasure of writing.

ROSE MACAULAY,
Personal Pleasures

WORK

Whether I'm any good or not, what I want is to work. The eternal quibbling about the purposes of art, its drift, etc., gets on my nerves, knocks me flat.

SHERWOOD ANDERSON,
Letters of Sherwood Anderson

Work should abound in small beginnings and small ends; they console us for the deadliness of middles.

> OSCAR W. FIRKINS,
> *Oscar Firkins: Memoirs and Letters,*
> edited by Ina Ten Eyck

Well, I must put on my old duds and clear the ashes out of the cellar. I used to think I was out of my sphere when doing that kind of work but now I think differently. Such things do a man a world of good if he can only bring himself to think so.

> EDWIN ARLINGTON ROBINSON,
> *Untriangulated Stars*

Next to doing a good job yourself the greatest joy is in having someone else do a first-class job under your direction.

> WILLIAM FEATHER,
> *The Business of Life*

Work and play are words used to describe the same thing under differing conditions.

> MARK TWAIN,
> *Mark Twain at Your Fingertips,*
> edited by Caroline T. Harnsberger

If one is chosen for a work, it generally means one can do it, and it is a better guide than private diffidence.

> A. C. BENSON,
> *Excerpts from the Letters of*
> *Dr. A. C. Benson to M. E. A.*

Men may suffer terribly from the death of a loved one, the breakup of a marriage, or some other personal tragedy. But what brings them to the point of immobilization most often is the loss of their job.

> MYRON BRENTON,
> *The American Male*

All the best work is done the way ants do things—by tiny but untiring and regular additions.

> LAFCADIO HEARN,
> *Lafcadio Hearn: Life and Letters,*
> edited by Elizabeth Bisland

Without doubt half the ethical rules they din into our ears are designed to keep us at work.

> LLEWELYN POWYS,
> *Book of Days of Llewelyn Powys*

The admonition to work has its origin in humanity's instinct of self-preservation. It does not spring from one's own needs but only from the needs of others. Apparently we all work for ourselves, but in reality we are always working for others.

> DR. WILHELM STEKHEL,
> *The Depths of the Soul*

No one who has much to do ought ever to say to themselves how much I have to do, and how little time to do it in, because as the old women in the Midlands say, it "vapours them," and then they can do nothing.

> JANET ERSKINE STUART,
> *Life and Letters of Janet Erskine Stuart*
> by Maud Monahan

The one thing that's saving me—saving me, I mean, not from any melodramatic issues but just from sheer unhappiness—is lots and lots of work.

> DYLAN THOMAS,
> *Letters to Vernon Watkins*

We ought really to think much more of our work and of what comes next to our hands to do day after day than of our affections and the proportions in which they are distributed.

> JOHN ADDINGTON SYMONDS,
> *Letters and Papers of John Addington Symonds*

I never forget that work is a curse—which is why I've never made it a habit.

> BLAISE CENDRARS,
> *Writers at Work,* Third Series,
> edited by George Plimpton

If there is one thing better than the thrill of looking forward, it is the exhilaration that follows the finishing of a long and exacting piece of work.

> ALEC WAUGH,
> *On Doing What One Likes*

I think of personnel specialists as tailors. Instead of fitting a suit to a man, they tailor a man into a slot. No alterations are permitted. If his talents bulge out of the slot here and there, or if it seems that he may rattle about in it, out he goes.

> ALAN HARRINGTON,
> *Life in the Crystal Palace*

One thing must be said for idleness: it keeps people from doing the Devil's work. The great villains of history were busy men, since great crimes and slaughters require great industry and dedication.

PHILIP SLATER,
The Pursuit of Loneliness

Work is needed to express what is true: also to receive what is true. We can express and receive what is false, or at least what is superficial, without any work.

SIMONE WEIL,
Gravity and Grace

One becomes more interested in a job of work after the first impulse to drop it has been overcome.

FULTON J. SHEEN,
Way to Happiness

All one's work might have been done better; but this is the sort of reflection a worker must put aside courageously if he doesn't mean every one of his conceptions to remain forever a private vision, an evanescent reverie.

JOSEPH CONRAD,
A Book of Days,
compiled by Christopher Morley

WORLD

The world is a sure teacher, but it requires a fat fee.

FINNISH PROVERB

In the evening, the gentleness of the world on the bay. There are days when the world lies, days when it tells the truth. It is telling the truth this evening—with what sad and insistent beauty.

ALBERT CAMUS,
Notebooks 1935–1942

The world is the world, and teaches all of us, more or less, one lesson.

OSCAR W. FIRKINS,
Oscar Firkins: Memoirs and Letters,
edited by Ina Ten Eyck

Enlightenment is not for the Quietists and Puritans who, in their different ways, deny the world, but for those who have learned to accept and transfigure it.

ALDOUS HUXLEY,
Collected Essays

The world is getting better every day— then worse again in the evening.

KIN HUBBARD,
Abe Martin on Things in General

The world is more exacting than God himself.

YIDDISH PROVERB

A day like today I realize what I've told you a hundred different times—that there's nothing wrong with the world. What's wrong is our way of looking at it.

HENRY MILLER,
A Devil in Paradise

At almost any point in the world's history, people could have said that the world was in such terrible shape that it was immoral to bring children into it. I would not have liked to have had denied me the chance to live in these exciting times.

CORETTA SCOTT KING,
Open Secrets by Barbaralee Diamonstein

What one thinks, what one feels, the agony, the suffering, the ambition, the envy, the extraordinary confusion one is in, that is the world.

J. KRISHNAMURTI,
You Are the World

It really is a beautiful world to play in, if one only had the time for it, and the money!

MICHAEL MONAHAN,
Palms of Papyrus

Forcing the world to adjust to oneself has always seemed to me an honorable life work. . . . That one fails in the end is irrelevant.

GORE VIDAL,
Behind the Scenes,
edited by Joseph F. McCrindle

The world pays us what it owes us oftener than we pay what we owe the world.

JOSH BILLINGS,
His Works Complete

And yet to be worldly, to hold to the world's simple creed and believe in its heaven, must surely stagger at times the faith of its firmest believer.

LOGAN PEARSALL SMITH,
Afterthoughts

My own habitual feeling is that the world is so extremely odd, and everything in it so surprising. Why *should* there be green grass and liquid water, and *why* have I got hands and feet?

DOM JOHN CHAPMAN,
The Spiritual Letters of Dom John Chapman

He who wants a new world must first buy the old.

DUTCH PROVERB

One belongs to the world as long as one is more ashamed of a *faux pas,* a display of ignorance, a wrong turn of phrase, a misquotation than of an unloving action.

THEODOR HAECKER,
Journal in the Night

Man does not come to know the world by that which he extorts from it, but rather by that which he adds to it: himself.

PAUL CLAUDEL,
Poetic Art

Remoteness from the world gives an inward distinction; but immersion, on the other hand, awakens all that is human in selfhood. The former demands self-discipline; but the latter is love.

KARL JASPERS,
Man in the Modern Age

WORRY

People get so in the habit of worry that if you save them from drowning and put them on a bank to dry in the sun with hot chocolate and muffins they wonder whether they are catching cold.

JOHN JAY CHAPMAN,
John Jay Chapman and His Letters
by M. A. DeWolfe Howe

You must not worry about me or say you do or don't. It's exactly as though you took a piece of my flesh and gnawed it. It helps neither you nor me. *Worry* is a waste of energy.

KATHERINE MANSFIELD,
quoted in *Katherine Mansfield*
by Antony Alpers

Worry is impatience.

AUSTIN O'MALLEY,
Keystones of Thought

Every faculty and virtue I possess can be used as an instrument wherewith to worry myself.

MARK RUTHERFORD,
Last Pages from a Journal

A great many worries can be diminished by realizing the unimportance of the matter which is causing anxiety. . . . Our doings are not so important as we naturally suppose; our successes and failures do not after all matter very much.

BERTRAND RUSSELL,
The Conquest of Happiness

WORST

The worst of partialities is to withhold oneself, the worst ignorance is not to act, the worst lie is to steal away.

CHARLES PÉGUY,
Basic Verities

WORTH

Who is really worth anything to anybody? Husband and wife to each other—sometimes; child to parent—often; parent to child—almost never; in other relations, the utmost readiness of forgetfulness and substitutions. I believe it is easier to give one's life for a friend than to remember him often and vividly three years after his death.

OSCAR W. FIRKINS,
Oscar Firkins: Memoirs and Letters,
edited by Ina Ten Eyck

It is a piece of great good luck to deal with someone who values you at your true worth.

BALTASAR GRACIAN,
The Oracle

In quite a few years we may have seemed to have counted for nothing more than the invisible cause of a place polished smooth on the back of a chair. And yet the stores of the race may have been minutely enriched if we have not returned ... unexperienced to our graves.

C. E. MONTAGUE,
The Right Place

WRITERS AND WRITING

There is no denying the fact that writers should be read but not seen. Rarely are they a winsome sight.

EDNA FERBER,
A Kind of Magic

They can't yank novelist like they can pitcher. Novelist has to go the full nine, even if it kills him.

ERNEST HEMINGWAY,
quoted in *Portrait of Hemingway*
by Lillian Ross

After you finish a book, you know, you're dead. . . . But no one knows you're dead. All they see is the irresponsibility that comes in after the terrible responsibility of writing.

ERNEST HEMINGWAY,
quoted in *Portrait of Hemingway*
by Lillian Ross

I'm not sure that it's the responsibility of a writer to give answers, especially to questions that have no answers.

EDWARD ALBEE,
Behind the Scenes,
edited by Joseph F. McCrindle

Writing is one of the few professions left where you take all the responsibility for what you do. It's really dangerous and ultimately destroys you as a writer if you start thinking about responses to your work or what your audience needs.

ERICA JONG,
The Craft of Poetry,
edited by William Packard

I've always felt strongly that a writer shouldn't be engaged with other writers, or with people who make books, or even with people who read them. I think the farther you get away from the literary traffic, the closer you are to sources. I mean, a writer doesn't really *live,* he observes.

NELSON ALGREN,
Writers at Work,
edited by Malcolm Cowley

No one in the modern world is more lonely than the writer with a literary conscience.

ELLEN GLASGOW,
Letters of Ellen Glasgow

Nothing would astonish me, after all these years, except to be understood.

ELLEN GLASGOW,
Letters of Ellen Glasgow

The mind craves nothing so much as a closed system, and the writer's mind is no exception; and yet he should, at whatever cost of violence, constantly set against any system which at the moment is approved the spontaneity and variety of life.

JOHN PEALE BISHOP,
The Collected Essays of John Peale Bishop

A writer's manner is conditioned physiologically; he possesses a rhythm of his own, urgent and irreducible.

E. M. CIORAN,
The Temptation to Exist

Most writers, you know, are awful sticks to talk with.

SHERWOOD ANDERSON,
Letters of Sherwood Anderson

The fact that many people should be shocked by what he writes practically imposes it as a duty upon the writer to go on shocking them.

ALDOUS HUXLEY,
Collected Essays

You never *see* the effect of your thinking on your readers; they live and die far away from you, a few write letters of praise or criticism, the thousands give no sign.

PHILIP G. HAMERTON,
The Intellectual Life

No wonder the really powerful men in our society, whether politicians or scientists, hold writers and poets in contempt. They do it because they get no evidence from modern literature that anybody is thinking about any significant question.

SAUL BELLOW,
Writers at Work, Third Series,
edited by George Plimpton

The secret of popular writing is never to put more on a given page than the common reader can lap off it with no strain WHATSOEVER on his habitually slack attention.

EZRA POUND,
A B C of Reading

Some American writers who have known each other for years have never met in the daytime or when both were sober.

JAMES THURBER,
Thurber Country

Most writers are in a state of gloom a good deal of the time; they need perpetual reassurance.

JOHN HALL WHEELOCK,
Editor to Author

A note: despair at the badness of the book: can't think how I could ever write such stuff—and with such excitement: that's yesterday: today I think it good again. A note, by the way of advising other Virginias with other books that this is the way of the thing: up down up down—and Lord knows the truth.

VIRGINIA WOOLF,
A Writer's Diary

On the day when a young writer corrects his first proof-sheet he is as proud as a schoolboy who has just gotten his first dose of the pox.

CHARLES BAUDELAIRE,
Intimate Journals

Success comes to a writer, as a rule, so gradually that it is always something of a shock to him to look back and realize the heights to which he has climbed.

P. G. WODEHOUSE,
Louder and Funnier

I do think that the quality which makes a man want to write and be read is essentially a desire for self-exposure and is masochistic. Like one of those guys who has a compulsion to take his thing out and show it on the street.

JAMES JONES,
Writers at Work, Third Series,
edited by George Plimpton

It often takes a new and orginal writer longer to reach his public than a facile and familiar one. But not because of his obscurity. It is his clarity which stands in the way.

J. MIDDLETON MURRY,
Pencillings

When one says that a writer is fashionable one practically always means that he is admired by people under thirty.

GEORGE ORWELL,
A Collection of Essays

Only ambitious nonentities and hearty mediocrities exhibit their rough drafts. It is like passing around samples of one's sputum.

VLADIMIR NABOKOV,
Strong Opinions

We do the best we can and hope for the best, knowing that "the best," so far as selling goes, is a matter of chance. The only thing that is not chance is what one asks of oneself and how well or how badly one meets one's own standards.

MAY SARTON,
Journal of a Solitude

I have bought Chekhov's stories: how delightful they are! You buy them, too.

ANTON CHEKHOV,
The Selected Letters of Anton Chekhov

I never saw an author in my life, saving perhaps one, that did not purr as audibly as a full-grown domestic cat on having his fur smoothed the right way by a skilful hand.

OLIVER WENDELL HOLMES,
The Autocrat of the Breakfast-Table, Vol. III

I am a great admirer of my own stuff while it's new, but after a while I'm not gone on it—like the true maternal instinct, that kicks off an offspring as soon as it can go on its own legs.

D. H. LAWRENCE,
D. H. Lawrence: Selected Literary Criticism,
edited by Anthony Beal

Almost anyone can be an author; the business is to collect money and fame from this state of being.

A. A. MILNE,
Not That It Matters

The praise given an author is, in his eyes, never worth that which is refused him.

J. PETIT-SENN,
Conceits and Caprices

One's astonishment, half tragic, half comic, at coming across a good sentence that one has completely forgotten having written. Poverty and wealth!

THEODOR HAECKER,
Journal in the Night

My idiotically low state of spirits is owing mainly to the evident utter failure of my two books of verse, a failure which I foresaw perfectly well, but it cuts just the same. . . . What fools we are, or I am, to set our hearts on such things. How much better it would be to plant cabbages, as Anatole France says, though I notice he has kept on writing books.

GAMALIEL BRADFORD,
The Letters of Gamaliel Bradford

Instead of marvelling with Johnson, how anything but profit should incite men to literary labour, I am rather surprised that mere emolument should induce them to labour so well.

THOMAS GREEN,
Extracts from the Diary of a Lover of Literature

A second chance—that's the delusion. There never was to be one. We work in the dark—we do what we can—we give what we have. Our doubt is our passion, and our passion is our task. The rest is the madness of art.

HENRY JAMES,
The Middle Years.

Every book is like a purge; at the end of it one is empty . . . like a dry shell on the beach, waiting for the tide to come in again.

DAPHNE DU MAURIER,
Ladies' Home Journal, November 1956

A bad book is as much of a labor to write as a good one; it comes as sincerely from the author's soul.

ALDOUS HUXLEY

Unlike the architect, an author often discards his blueprint in the process of erecting his edifice. To the writer a book is something to be lived through, an experience, not a plan to be executed in accordance with laws and specifications.

HENRY MILLER,
The Books in My Life

We shall probably have nothing to say, but we intend to say it at great length.

DON MARQUIS,
The Almost Perfect State

It is a fact that few novelists enjoy the creative labour, though most enjoy thinking about the creative labour.

ARNOLD BENNETT

Only a small minority of authors overwrite themselves. Most of the good and the tolerable ones do not write enough.

ARNOLD BENNETT

Looking back, I imagine I was always writing. Twaddle it was, too. But better far write twaddle or anything, anything, than nothing at all.

KATHERINE MANSFIELD,
The Journal of Katherine Mansfield

For several days after my first book was published I carried it about in my pocket, and took surreptitious peeps at it to make sure the ink had not faded.

SIR JAMES M. BARRIE,
A Reader for Writers
by Gorham Munson

Yes, I learned long ago that the only satisfaction of authorship lies in finding the very few who understand what we mean. As for outside rewards, there is not one that I have ever discovered.

> ELLEN GLASGOW,
> *Letters of Ellen Glasgow*

I suppose I am a born novelist, for the things I imagine are more vital and vivid to me than the things I remember.

> ELLEN GLASGOW,
> *Letters of Ellen Glasgow*

For a dyed-in-the-wool author nothing is as dead as a book once it is written. . . . She is rather like a cat whose kittens have grown up.

> RUMER GODDEN,
> *New York Times*, December 1, 1963

A unanimous chorus of approval is not an assurance of survival; authors who please everyone at once are quickly exhausted.

> ANDRÉ GIDE,
> *Pretexts*

If I have been discriminated against, however, it has mainly been by women—women reporters and interviewers. Even the supposedly intelligent ones cannot resist decribing me in terms of my physical appearance—they seem annoyed that I am not quite as heavy as they are—and it is unthinkable that they would describe a male author in such a way.

> JOYCE CAROL OATES,
> *Open Secrets* by Barbaralee Diamonstein

It is advantageous to an author, that his book should be attacked as well as praised. Fame is a shuttlecock. If it be struck at only one end of the room, it will soon fall to the ground. To keep it up, it must be struck at both ends.

> SAMUEL JOHNSON

An author should be more than content if he finds he has made a difference to a handful of people, or given innocent pleasure to a small company.

> A. C. BENSON,
> *From a College Window*

Writing a long and substantial book is like having a friend and companion at your side, to whom you can always turn for comfort and amusement, and whose so-

ciety becomes more attractive as a new and widening field of interest is lighted in the mind.

> SIR WINSTON CHURCHILL,
> *A Churchill Reader,*
> edited by Colin R. Coote

If I could I would always work in silence and obscurity, and let my efforts be known by their results.

> EMILY BRONTË,
> *The Writing Art,* selected by
> Bertha W. Smith and Virginia C. Lincoln

When a man publishes a book, there are so many stupid things said that he declares he'll never do it again. The praise is almost always worse than the criticism.

> SHERWOOD ANDERSON,
> *Letters of Sherwood Anderson*

We're infected by publicity. It's really ignoble. There's nothing to do but a *job* and shut up. That's all. The public looks at it, doesn't look at it, reads it, or doesn't read it, and that's its business. The author has only to disappear.

> LOUIS-FERDINAND CÉLINE,
> *Writers at Work,* Third Series
> edited by George Plimpton

I have never met an author who admitted that people did not buy his book because it was dull.

> W. SOMERSET MAUGHAM,
> *The Summing Up*

A person who publishes a book willfully appears before the populace with his pants down. . . . If it is a good book nothing can hurt him. If it is a bad book, nothing can help him.

> EDNA ST. VINCENT MILLAY,
> *Letters of Edna St. Vincent Millay*

Literary success of any enduring kind is made by refusing to do what publishers want, by refusing to write what the public wants, by refusing to accept any popular standard, by refusing to write anything to order.

> LAFCADIO HEARN,
> *Lafcadio Hearn: Life and Letters,*
> edited by Elizabeth Bisland

Don't forget that the race is only struggling out of its dumbness, and that it is only in moments of inspiration that we get out a sentence. All the rest is padding.

GEORGE BERNARD SHAW

No author is a man of genius to his publisher.

HEINRICH HEINE,
Works

It is the part of prudence to thank an author for his book before reading it, so as to avoid the necessity of lying about it afterwards.

GEORGE SANTAYANA,
The Letters of George Santayana

The power of writing one fine line transcends all the Able-Editor ability in the ably-edited Universe.

EDWARD FITZGERALD,
Letters

Every author's fairy godmother should provide him not only with a pen but also with a blue pencil.

F. L. LUCAS,
Style

The man of letters loves not only to be read but to be seen. Happy to be by himself, he would be happier still if people knew that he was happy to be by himself, working in solitude at night under his lamp.

REMY DE GOURMONT,
The Epigrams of Remy de Gourmont

I am very foolish over my own book. I have a copy which I constantly read and find very illuminating. Swift confesses to something of the sort with his own compositions.

J. B. YEATS,
Letters to His Son, W. B. Yeats and Others

To write a book, to send it forth to the world and its critics, is to a sensitive person like plunging mother-naked into tropic waters where sharks abound.

ALEXANDER SMITH,
Dreamthorp

Tell B[ernard] B[erenson] that my most successful book [The Christian's Secret] was written so to speak at the point of the bayonet, without one ray of enthusiasm, and hating to do it all the time. So he may be encouraged.

HANNAH WHITALL SMITH,
Philadelphia Quaker
by Logan Pearsall Smith

The literary beauty of my work has no other significance for me than that found by a workman who is aware of having performed his task well; I simply did my best; but, had I been a carpenter, I should have been just as conscientious in planing a plank properly as I have been in writing properly.

PAUL CLAUDEL,
quoted in The Journals of André Gide, Vol. I

What I like in a good author is not what he says, but what he whispers.

LOGAN PEARSALL SMITH,
All Trivia

What an author likes to write most is his signature on the back of a check.

BRENDAN FRANCIS

An author should consult his genius, rather than his interest, if he cannot reconcile them.

JOHN GAY,
Life and Letters

If you are getting the worst of it in an argument with a literary man, always attack his style. That'll touch him if nothing else will.

J. A. SPENDER,
The Comments of Bagshot, Second Series

An author ought to write for the youth of his own generation, the critics of the next, and the schoolmasters of ever afterwards.

F. SCOTT FITZGERALD,
quoted in the Guardian,
November 13, 1964

There's no doubt that I have found out how to begin [at 40] to say something in my own voice; and that interests me so that I feel I can go ahead without praise.

VIRGINIA WOOLF,
A Writer's Diary

When I first saw that a literary profession was to be my fate, I endeavored by all efforts of Stoicism to divest myself of that irritable degree of sensibility—or, to speak plainly, vanity—which makes the poetical race miserable and ridiculous.

SIR WALTER SCOTT,
Sir Walter Scott's Journal (1825–1832)

I like to know how what I write impresses anybody who takes the trouble to read it.

BARRETT WENDELL,
Barrett Wendell and His Letters
by M. A. DeWolfe Howe

Writing is a dog's life, but the only life worth living.

GUSTAVE FLAUBERT

If we should ever inaugurate a hall of fame, it would be reserved exclusively and hopefully for authors who, having written four best-sellers, *still refrained* from starting out on a lecture tour.

E. B. WHITE,
Every Day Is Saturday

Every author really wants to have letters printed in the papers. Unable to make the grade, he drops down a rung of the ladder and writes novels.

P. G. WODEHOUSE,
Louder and Funnier

A man really writes for an audience of about ten persons. Of course if others like it, that is clear gain. But if those ten are satisfied, he is content.

ALFRED NORTH WHITEHEAD,
Dialogues of Alfred North Whitehead

I want to write beautifully, create beautifully, not outside but in this thing in which I am born, in this place where, in the midst of ugly towns, cities, Fords, moving pictures, I have always lived, must always live. I do not want . . . even those old monks at Chartres, building their Cathedral, to be at bottom any purer than myself.

SHERWOOD ANDERSON,
Letters of Sherwood Anderson

It is bad to go out and look at things if you wish to write about them. You must let them look at you.

HENRY WARD BEECHER,
Eyes and Ears

All authentic writing comes from an individual; but a final judgment of it will depend, not on how much individuality it contains, but how much of common humanity.

JOHN PEALE BISHOP,
The Collected Essays of John Peale Bishop

I just think it's bad to talk about one's present work, for it spoils something at the root of the creative act. It discharges the tension.

NORMAN MAILER,
Writers at Work, Third Series,
edited by George Plimpton

The writer's intention hasn't anything to do with what he achieves. The intent to earn money or the intent to be famous or the intent to be great doesn't matter in the end. Just what comes out.

LILLIAN HELLMAN,
Writers at Work, Third Series,
edited by George Plimpton

The man who writes always wants to conclude something instead of being content to lay it bare.

JOHN JAY CHAPMAN,
Memories and Milestones

The writer's real dishonesty is to give an easy paraphrase of the hard truth.

RANDALL JARRELL,
Poetry and the Age

I went for years not finishing anything. Because, of course, when you finish something you can be judged. . . . I had poems which were rewritten so many times that I suspect it was just a way of avoiding sending them out.

ERICA JONG,
The Craft of Poetry,
edited by William Packard

You can't fake it. Bad writing is a gift.

RICHARD LE GALLIENNE,
quoted in *Pieces of Hate*
by Heywood Broun

What release to write so that one forgets oneself, forgets one's companion, forgets where one is or what one is going to do next—to be drenched in work as one is drenched in sleep or in the sea. Pencils and pads and curling blue sheets alive with letters heap up on the desk.

ANNE MORROW LINDBERGH,
Gift from the Sea

Which, of all defects, has been the one most fatal to a good style? The not knowing when to come to an end.

SIR ARTHUR HELPS,
Companions of My Solitude

I have rewritten—often several times—every word I have ever published. My pencils outlast their erasers.

VLADIMIR NABOKOV,
Strong Opinions

The great enemy of clear language is insincerity. When there is a gap between one's real and one's declared aims, one turns as it were instinctively to long words and exhausted idioms, like a cuttlefish squirting out ink.

GEORGE ORWELL,
A Collection of Essays

My own experience has been that the tools I need for my trade are paper, tobacco, food, and a little whisky.

WILLIAM FAULKNER,
Writers At Work,
edited by Malcolm Cowley

The only human value of anything, writing included, is intense vision of the facts.

WILLIAM CARLOS WILLIAMS,
Selected Essays

As for my next book, I am going to hold myself from writing it till I have it impending in me: grown heavy in my mind like a ripe pear; pendant, gravid, asking to be cut or it will fall.

VIRGINIA WOOLF,
A Writer's Diary

I tell him prose and verse are alike in one thing—the best is that to which went the hardest thoughts. This also is the secret of originality, also the secret of sincerity.

J. B. YEATS,
Letters to His Son, W. B. Yeats and Others

Writing is a solitary occupation. Family, friends, and society are the natural enemies of the writer. He must be alone, uninterrupted, and slightly savage if he is to sustain and complete an undertaking.

LAWRENCE CLARK POWELL,
quoted in *Hide and Seek* by Jessamyn West

In any work that is truly creative, I believe, the writer cannot be omniscient in advance about the effects that he proposes to produce. The suspense in a novel is not only in the reader, but in the novelist himself, who is intensely curious about what will happen to the hero.

MARY McCARTHY,
On the Contrary

The ideal view for daily writing, hour on hour, is the blank brick wall of a cold-storage warehouse. Failing this, a stretch of sky will do, cloudless if possible.

EDNA FERBER,
A Kind of Magic

The problem is neither to write like everyone else nor to write differently. Both are relatively easy. The problem is to write like everyone else and yet to write differently.

OSCAR W. FIRKINS,
Oscar Firkins: Memoirs and Letters,
edited by Ina Ten Eyck

People do not deserve to have good writing, they are so pleased with bad.

RALPH WALDO EMERSON,
Journals of Ralph Waldo Emerson

You don't write because you want to say something; you write because you've got something to say.

F. SCOTT FITZGERALD,
The Crack-up

When I stepped from hard manual work to writing, I just stepped from one kind of hard work to another.

SEAN O'CASEY,
Selected Plays of Sean O'Casey

YOUTH

I never felt that there was anything enviable in youth. I cannot recall that any of us, as youths, admired our condition to excess or had a desire to prolong it.

BERNARD BERENSON,
Rumor and Reflection

We tend to look upon the advice that we give to young people as something that should disillusion them.

WILLIAM C. BAGLEY,
Craftsmanship in Teaching

Praise youth and it will prosper.

IRISH PROVERB

Age and youth are great flatterers. Brooding on each other's obvious psychology neither dares tell the other outright what manifestly is the truth: your world is poison.

WILLIAM CARLOS WILLIAMS,
Selected Essays

Of all virtues the virtue of patience is most foreign to youth.

JOHN JAY CHAPMAN,
Memories and Milestones

Youth doesn't necessarily mean much. I'm very young, whereas all my contemporaries in Stampa are old men, because they've accepted old age. Their lives are already in the past. But mine is still in the future. It's only now that I can envisage the possibility of trying to start on my life's work.

ALBERTO GIACOMETTI,
quoted in *A Giacometti Portrait*
by James Lord

It is one of the surprising things about youth that it can so easily be the most conservative of all ages.

RANDOLPH BOURNE,
Youth and Life

To keep one's reactions warm and true, is to have found the secret of perpetual youth, and perpetual youth is salvation.

RANDOLPH BOURNE,
Youth and Life

Elderly people and those in authority cannot always be relied upon to take enlightened and comprehending views of what they call the indiscretions of youth.

SIR WINSTON CHURCHILL,
A Churchill Reader,
edited by Colin R. Coote

I hate to hear people saying, "He is young, he must wait; he will get plenty of chances." How do they know? Could Keats have waited, or Shelley, or Byron, or Burns?

J. A. SPENDER,
The Comments of Bagshot, Second Series

Being young is a fault which improves daily.

SWEDISH PROVERB

Those theorists who deny female sexuality ought to have seen as many pop concerts as I have, when thousands of girls between the ages of twelve and sixteen respond savagely to the stimulus of music and male exhibitionism. It is a commonplace in the music industry that the stars stuff their crotches, and that the girls wet the seat covers. The savagery and hysteria of the phenomenon is in direct relation to its rarity.

GERMAINE GREER,
The Female Eunuch

It is typically the most intelligent and sensitive of the young who become revolutionaries, destroyers.

JOYCE CARY,
Art and Reality

When one is young and has little money, it is prudent to spend that little on the unnecessary, the emotional dividends being higher.

CLIFTON FADIMAN,
Any Number Can Play

All youth is bound to be "mis-spent"; there is something in its very nature that makes it so, and that is why all men regret it.

THOMAS WOLFE,
Of Time and the River

The denunciation of the young is a necessary part of the hygiene of older people, and greatly assists the circulation of the blood.

LOGAN PEARSALL SMITH,
All Trivia

The presence of the young lightens the world and changes it from an oppressive, definitive, solidified one to a fluid, potentially marvellous, malleable, variable, as-yet-to-be-created world. I call them the transparent children.

ANAÏS NIN,
The Diaries of Anaïs Nin, Vol. IV

When I was a child, a boy, a young man adolescent, I felt at no time I had any right or place in the world: now it seems to me that only for such is the kingdom of earth, for those that are filled with the life of youth, and for all things that show no beginning of morose decay.

STEPHEN MACKENNA,
Journal and Letters of Stephen Mackenna

ZIEGFELD FOLLIES

Here is human beauty, underivatively admirable as a sunset, uncomplicated by costume, literature, with only its own prestige. I cannot imagine why its contemplation ... is not as culturally esteemed as visiting the Metropolitan.

WILLIAM BOLITHO,
Camera Obscura

INDEX

AUTHOR INDEX

Abbott, Berenice, 502
Abbott, Lyman, 100
Abzug, Bella S., 156
Acton, Lord, 153
Adam, Adolphe, 443
Adam, Karl, 122
Adamov, Arthur, 326, 589
Adams, Ansel, 191, 446, 473–474
Adams, Franklin P., 19, 525
Adams, Henry, 232
Adamson, Elizabeth I., 70
Addams, Jane, 184, 237, 331, 486
Adler, Alfred, 24, 133, 226, 421
African proverb, 97, 581
Albanian proverb, 448, 543
Albee, Edward, 69, 191, 554, 593
Albert, Ramona C., 220
Alcott, Bronson, 363, 472
Alfred of Rievaulx, Saint, 132, 305,
    310, 323, 579
Algren, Nelson, 195, 593
Allen, Fred, 116
Allen, H. Warner, 583
Alliluyeva, Svetlana, 85, 202, 266,
    397, 541
Allingham, William, 579
Allport, Gordon W., 133
Ambrose, Saint, 110, 122, 459
Amiel, Henri Fréderic, 7, 21, 45,
    166, 200, 207–208, 211, 217, 253,
    254, 300, 316, 348, 437, 443, 495,
    508, 532
Anderson, Judith, 10
Anderson, Marian, 394
Anderson, Sherwood, 32, 37, 42,
    51, 57, 65, 68, 100, 155, 162, 168,
    178, 186, 195–196, 223, 240, 245,
    268, 271, 278, 284, 291–292, 301,
    305, 310, 346, 351, 369, 377, 380,
    390, 397, 407, 409–410, 414, 433–
    434, 442, 446–448, 451, 453, 467,
    476, 488, 491, 499, 507, 519, 539,
    542, 544, 547–548, 555, 564, 566,
    586, 588, 589, 598
Angell, Roger, 73
Anonymous, 3, 14, 16, 41, 46, 65,
    79, 85, 89, 96, 107, 117, 131, 151,
    168, 171–172, 184, 189–190, 200–
    201, 204, 213–214, 219–220, 224,
    234, 247, 249, 253, 255–256, 264,
    267, 269, 278, 310, 313, 331, 337,
    339, 342, 354, 370, 389, 410, 425,
    437, 458, 464, 468, 493–494, 509,
    529, 574, 585
Aquinas, Saint Thomas, 39, 325,
    524
Arab proverb, 28, 133, 177, 346,
    370, 449, 458, 460, 513, 581, 583
Arcaro, Eddie, 355
Ariès, Philippe, 132
Arliss, George, 8
Armenian proverb, 117, 434
Arnold, Matthew, 119
Aron, Raymond, 29
Ashby-Sterry, J., 146, 286
Ashe, Arthur, Jr., 553
Ashton-Warner, Sylvia, 236, 369,
    536, 551, 577

Astor, Lady, 227
Atkinson, Brooks, 220, 577
Atkinson, Lydia B., 71
Atwood, Margaret, 285, 573
Aubrey, John, 534
Auden, W. H., 142, 150, 209, 220,
    374, 407, 417, 477, 515, 531, 578
Auerback, Red, 76
Augustine, Saint, 71, 143, 204, 213,
    224, 306, 326, 588
Austen, Jane, 25, 155, 204, 277
Axelrod, Beverly, 505
Ayscough, John, 21, 24, 29, 38, 87,
    101, 112, 271, 276, 466, 498, 500,
    507

Bacharach, Burt, 443
Bacon, Francis, 107, 299, 306
Bagehot, Walter, 11, 24, 104, 128,
    168, 172, 228, 234, 250, 300, 383,
    396, 429, 471, 511, 535, 543, 551
Bagley, William C., 551, 600
Bailey, Pearl, 28, 404, 433
Baker, Francis A., 64, 92, 184
Baldwin, Hanson W., 77
Baldwin, James, 28, 58, 278, 345,
    390, 524, 573
Balzac, Honoré de, 60, 64, 306,
    347, 362
Bankhead, Tallulah, 28, 138, 527
Barber, Red, 73
Baring, Maurice, 130, 218, 323, 514
Barkow, Al, 329
Barr, Charles, 318
Barrett, Alfred, 81, 94, 489
Barrett, William, 36, 152, 168, 465,
    483, 563
Barrie, Sir James, 498, 553, 595
Barry, Rick, 76
Barrymore, Ethel, 8
Barth, John, 206
Barzun, Jacques, 235, 296, 443, 552
Bashkirtseff, Marie, 220
Basil, Saint, 161, 202, 253, 254, 331
Basque proverb, 326
Baudelaire, Charles, 51, 87–88,
    115, 119, 177, 196, 213, 300, 335,
    378, 413, 424, 434, 449, 456, 478,
    495, 536–537, 569, 573, 594
Baum, Vicki, 385
Beach, Joseph W., 199, 316, 517
Beard, Rebecca, 97, 299, 504, 569
Beckett, Samuel, 364
Beecher, Henry Ward, 22, 25, 89,
    102, 110, 118, 126, 158, 186, 275,
    282, 289–290, 293, 356, 489, 598
Beerbohm, Max, 236, 265
Behan, Brendan, 38
Belgian proverb, 82
Bell, Clive, 179
Bell, Daniel, 72
Belli, Melvin, 392
Belloc, Hilaire, 66, 100, 170, 178–
    179, 184, 212, 214, 219, 271,
    275, 351, 363, 374, 392, 482, 483,
    488, 542, 564
Bellow, Saul, 49, 594
Bellows, George, 61

Benchley, Robert, 32, 48, 74, 221,
    227, 292–293, 339, 438
Benedict, Ruth, 63, 100, 124, 256,
    270, 314, 320, 340, 408, 437, 462,
    470, 477, 490, 503, 552
Ben-Gurion, David, 92
Bennett, Arnold, 4, 96, 111, 125,
    133, 364, 372, 424, 430, 455, 507,
    595
Benson, A. C., 1, 11, 39, 47, 54, 62,
    66, 83, 93, 96, 101, 110, 112, 118,
    120, 126–127, 134, 149, 159, 168,
    181, 185, 189, 193, 195, 197, 205,
    215, 217, 228, 235, 240, 244, 247,
    258, 261, 265, 282, 286, 306, 310,
    313, 317, 327, 349, 377, 381, 388,
    403, 415, 444, 448, 455, 460, 495,
    508, 510, 516, 529, 537, 546, 548–
    549, 551, 590, 596
Benson, E. F., 343
Benson, Robert Hugh, 11, 39, 65,
    143, 166, 229, 408
Berdyaev, Nicholas, 284
Berenson, Bernard, 18, 333, 600
Berg, Charles, 219
Berg, Patty, 329
Berger, John, 161
Berger, Mayer, 451
Bergson, Henri, 65, 161, 391, 445
Bernanos, Georges, 284–285, 490,
    512
Bernard of Clairvaux, Saint, 5, 15,
    89, 172, 254, 307, 328, 409, 468,
    475, 520, 584
Bernhardt, S., 10
Berry, Ray, 297
Bettelheim, Bruno, 111, 275, 350,
    385, 427, 434, 461, 465, 468, 498,
    508, 547, 552, 570
Bhagavad-Gita, 167, 371
Bibesco, Elizabeth, 258, 362
Billings, 15, 66, 112, 125, 135, 169,
    198, 250, 255, 261, 292, 346, 386,
    510, 571, 583, 591
Birkett, Lord, 459
Bishop, Claire Hutchet, 145
Bishop, John Peale, 56, 162, 195,
    480, 593, 598
Blackstone, Sir William, 27
Blake, William, 84
Blanton, Smiley, 21, 24, 41, 43,
    115, 117, 135, 139, 198, 221, 340,
    345–346, 411, 424, 522, 585
Blau, Herbert, 9
Blessington, Lady Marguerite, 28,
    39, 45, 97
Blitzstein, Marc, 456
Blood, B. P., 568
Bloy, Leon, 12, 44, 266, 489
Bogardus, Emory S., 394
Bogart, Humphrey, 227
Bogdanovich, Peter, 443
Bolitho, William, 34, 85–86, 150,
    300, 354, 415, 427, 524, 544, 601
Bonaparte, Napoleon, 487
Boorstin, Daniel J., 483, 492
Booth, Gotthard, 140
Booth, Shirley, 159

SUBJECT INDEX

Bold face refers to main entries.

Abandonment, wisdom and, 585
Ability, **1**
  experience and, 260
  interest and, 381
  success and, 544
  See also Mastery; Skill; Talent
Abnegation, 1
  See also Giving up; Renunciation
Abnormality, 1
  See also Eccentric; Idiosyncracy;
    Odd
Abortion, 1–2
Absence, **2**
  See also Emptiness
Absolute, the, in America, 34
Abstention, innocence and, 378
Abstinence:
  sexual, of Irish young people,
    383
  vow of, 576
Abstraction, art versus, 54
Abstractness (abstract ideas or
    thinking):
  of Americans, 34, 36
  of architecture, 47
  influence in proportion to power
    of, 376
  of lust, 527
  philosopher and, 472
  sentimentality and, 524–25
Abstract painting, 49
  by monkey, 50–51
Absurd(ity), **2**
  meaning and, 425
  of truth, 119
  See also Irrational
Abuse:
  of actors, 9
  applause as beginning of, 46
Acceptance, **2**
  of barbarity, 72
  contentment and, 177
  of death by sheep, 42
  of limitations, 403
  of oneself, 520–21 (*See also* Self-
    acceptance)
  of the world, 591
  See also Tolerance
Accident:
  great things not an, 582
  photographs and, 473
Accomplishment, 3
Accumulation of possessions, 485
Achievement, **3**
  diminution of personality and,
    19
  dissatisfaction with one's, 516
  without love, 115
  success and, 544
  writers' intention versus, 598
Acquaintance, 4
  with books, 105
  with one's self, 519-20
Acquisitiveness, felicity damaged
    by, 485

Act (in the theater or movies), **4–5,**
    442–43
  with confidence, 169
  See also Actors and Acting
Action, **5–7**
  alienation and, 25–26
  in American life, 30
  being and, 89
  belief and, 90
  certainty and, 124, 125
  character and, 129
  of children, 133
  Christianity and, 146
  consequences of, 174–75
  dreams and, 226
  expectation and, 258
  expression and, 263
  faith and, 270
  good and bad mingled in every,
    23
  heroism and, 349
  hope and, 354
  humility and men of, 359
  imperfection and, 371
  impulse to, 550
  after injury, 510
  inspiration and, 378
  knowledge and, 390
  learning and, 396
  less planning and more, 4
  by older persons, 23
  philosophy and, 473
  prostitutes as reward of men of,
    495
  result of, 510
  reward in and not from, 510
  speech and, 540
  sterile versus fruitful, 564
  suicide as perfect type of the
    man of, 546
  thought and, 557
  true, 564
  See also Doing
Activity, 7
  boredom and, 108
  ignorance and, 367
  insight and, 378
  masculine attitude and, 417
  See also Busy
Actors and acting, **7–10**
  television, 552
  See also Act
Actualization, self-, *see* Self-
    actualization
Adam and Eve, 126
  Eve blamed for Adam's faults,
    587
  fishing and, 287–88
  gardens and, 317
Adapt, 11
Adaptability of Americans, 33
Adaptation:
  to environment, 249
  to necessity, 447
Addiction to drugs, 228

Adjustment, happiness and, 343
Administrator, 11
Admiration, **11–12**
  by acquaintances, 4
  of babies, 71
  of boys for girls their own age,
    111
  clothes used to attract, 156
  between tennis players, 553
  See also Adoration; Idealization
Adolescence, **12–13**
  middle age as second, 20
  See also Young people; Youth
Adoption, 13
Adoration, **13**
  See also Admiration; Idolatry;
    Worship
Adult(hood), 13
  adolescents and, 12
  childhood versus, 130
  children's view of, 130–31
  faces of, 266
  habits of, 339
  physical awareness lost by, 99
  See also Age, middle; Age, old;
    Elders; Growing up; Maturity
Advantage, 13
Adventure, **13–14**
  art and, 55
  future, 315
  imagination and, 370
  as meaning of life, 366
  old age as, 22
  sharing and, 26
  thought as an, 556
Adversary, **14**
  opinion of, 457
  See also Enemy; Opposition
Adversity, 14
  See also Difficulty; Misfortune;
    Obstacles; Trouble
Advertising, **14–15**
  See also Publicity
Advice, **15–17**
  artists' rejection of, 59
  following, 255
  friendship and, 307, 311
  night as mother of, 453
  of saints, 515
  spiritual, 550
  to young people, 600
  See also Guidance; Suggestion;
    Warning
Aesthetic emotion of work of art,
    50
Aesthetics, *see* Art; Taste
Affectation, boys' ability to discern,
    109
Affection, **17**
  Americans' hungering for, 407
  cats and, 121
  Christmas and, 147
  complaining about lack of, 166
  after determination to marry,
    422, 423

of cats, 120, 121
conversation and, 182
of man and woman, 411
men prefer each other's, 420
silence and, 530
success and, 544
travel and, 561
walking and, 577
Comparison, **165**
of books with books, 101
of friends, 311
success and unfavorable, 545
Compassion, 165
toward babies, 71
See also Charitableness;
Empathy; Pity; Sympathy
Compensation, **165**
Competence, play and, 477
Competition, **166**
amusements and, 39
in battle, 78
See also Rivalry
Competitiveness, conformity and,
171
Complaint (complaining), **166**
to acquaintances, 4
of husband or wife, 422
about troubles, 563
Complaisance, follies committed
out of, 291
Completeness, **166–67**
beauty and, 81
desire to be, 56
incomplete men preferred to, 540
males lacking sense of, 418, 419
Completion, *see* End (completion);
Finishing
Complex, personality and, 470
Complication:
French passion for, 300
particular instances as, 379
Compliment, **167**
See also Flattery; Praise
Comprehension:
belief and, 89
See also Insight; Understanding
Compromise, prudence and, 497
Compulsion:
children and, 133
education and, 238
freedom and, 302, 303
work as, 303
See also Coercion; Forcing; Urge
Compulsoriness, in America, 32
Concealment:
of America's interests, 29
of feelings, 244
nothing to be gained by, 117
See also Hiding
Conceit:
of ugly and stupid, 572
See also Vanity
Concentration, **167–68**
of animals, 43
of basketball player, 76
maturity and, 424
See also Attention
Conception, **168**
of ideas, 364, 365
photograph as, 473
See also Idea; Thought

Conceptualization, architecture
and, 48
Concerts:
attendance at baseball games
and, 74
pop, sexuality and, 600
Conclusion, **168**
awareness and, 70
precedes premises, 431
talking and, 184
writers and, 598
Concreteness:
of action, 5
American desire to get away
from, 36
Condemnation:
acceptance vs., 2
See also Censure; Disapproval
Conditions, actions and, 6
Condolences, **168–69**
Conduct, **169**
cleanliness and, 153
experience and, 259
religion and, 506
See also Courtesy; Manners;
Politeness
Conference, **169**
Confession, **169**
need for friends and, 308
Confidence, **169**
faces as inspiring, 265
success and, 544
See also Assurance; Self-
confidence; Trust
Confiding, **170**
difficulty of, 244
Conflict, **170**
anxiety as signifying, 44
as essence of universe, 569
happiness in, 342
marriage and, 420
personality and, 470
psychiatry and, 497–98
in soul, sin and, 531
See also Argument;
Contradiction; Discord;
Dispute; Fight; Quarrel;
Struggle
Conformity, **170–71**
education and, 234–35
See also Conservative;
Conventionality
Confusion, 172
order and, 460
See also Chaos;
Misunderstanding; Perplexity
Connection:
among Americans, 34
See also Bond; Relatedness;
Relationship; Ties
Connoisseurs, aesthetic game of, 81
Conscience, **172**
American, 38
in artistic work, 60
of artists, 62
democratic, 207
literary, 593
passion and, 464
shame as stirring of, 528
sleep and, 533
Consciousness, **173–74**

anxiety and, 44–45
of being, 89
censors' hatred of, 123
the commonplace and, 163
community and, 165
as a curse, 494
dreams and, 225–26
existence and, 402
experience and, 262
freedom and, 303
growth of, 430
meditation and, 426
modern, 432
of moment, 433
of one's capabilities, 117
spring and, 540
unconscious and, 565
See also Awareness; Mind
Consequences, **174–75**
See also Result
Conservative, 175
youth as, 600
See also Reactionary; Tories
Consideration, 175
Consistency, **175**
success and, 545
Consolation, **175–76**
in action, 5
of Christianity, 144–45
in creating, 192
eluding oneself as, 520
of friends, 306
self-understanding as, 520
weakness of eminent men as, 580
Consolers, salutary for afflicted
ones to become, 549
Conspiracy against artists, 58
Constitution, U.S., free thought
and, 303
Constraint:
wisdom and, 585
See also Limit; Limitation;
Restraint
Consumer, 176
mother as, 441
women's magazines and, 588
Contemplation, **176**
art and, 52
of experience, 262
Contempt, 177
flattery as politeness of, 288
for humanity, 358–59
for joys offered freely, 386
troubles originate in fear of, 563
for writers and poets, 594
See also Despise; Hate
Contentment, **177**
not to be an artist, 56
See also Satisfaction
Continuity, of hate, 344
Contraception, abortion and, 1
Contradiction, 178
argument and, 49
ideas and, 364
life as, 23
See also Paradox
Control, as language's function,
390
Controversy, **178**
See also Argument
Conventionality, **178**

mystery and, 444
metaphysics and, 427
old age and, 21
place and, 476
See also Feeling; Passion;
    Sentiment; Sentimentality;
    and specific emotions
Emotional maturity, 424
Emotional problems, authority
    and, 66
Emotional security, family life and,
    274
Empathy:
    in relationships, 505
    understanding and, 566
    See also Compassion
Emptiness:
    of anxiety, 44
    the present can fill our, 491
    of Sunday, 547
    after writing book, 595
    See also Nothingness
Encouragement, **244**
    See also Support
End (completion):
    beginning and, 88
    of our story, 258
    of work, 590
    writer's style and knowing when
        to, 599
    See also Finishing
End (goal or purpose):
    art as, 55
    freedom not an, 304
    means and, 425
Endurance, **244–45**
    of gardens, 316
    growth and, 338
    of memories, 426
    See also Immortality
Enemy, **245**
    in battle, 77
    career and, 118
    change and, 127
    father and son as, 281
    forgiving an, 299
    hatred of, 346
    silence defended against, 530
    See also Adversary
Energy, **245–46**
    aggressive, 24
    of America, 30
    concentration of, 167, 168
    enthusiasm and, 249
    love as exchange of psychic, 411
    marriage and, 423
    reason as inner spontaneous, 503
    worry as waste of, 592
    See also Aliveness; Power;
        Vitality
Engels, Friedrich, 501
England and the English, **200,
    246–48**
    Biblical morality and, 93
    children in films in, 131
    conversation in America and in,
        182
    the country in, 187
    Frenchmen compared to, 301
    houses in, 31

literary movement at the end of
    the eighteenth century, 578
merchants, 115
Enjoyment, **248–49**
    in action, 7
    in America, 36
    Americans' insistence on, 35–36
    of autumn, 68
    of children by adults, 134
    of the imperfect, humor as, 361
    of life, 400
    old age and, 22
    of possessions, 485
    of suffering, 546 *(See also*
        Masochism)
    tastes and, 550
    of walking, 577
    wishing and, 585
    See also Amusement;
        Appreciation; Fun;
        Gratification; Pleasure
Enlightenment, **249**
    accepting and transfiguring the
        world and, 591
    of art, 55
    consciousness and, 173
    having a good time and, 477
    old age and, 20
    See also Illumination; Wisdom
Ennui, *see* Boredom
Entertainers on city streets, 150
Entertainment, *see* Amusement;
    Fun
Enthusiasm, **249**
Environment, **249–50**
    adapting to one's, 11
    See also Land; Landscape;
        Nature; Surroundings
Envy, **250**
    fame and, 271
    of horses' and cattle's life, 42
    infants', 71
    unconscious, 177
Epigram, **251**
Equality, **251**
    feeling of, 113
    materialism and, 207
    of Negroes in America, 30
    See also Egalitarianism
Equivocation, nothing to be gained
    by, 117
Eros, Christianity and, 144
Eroticism:
    collecting and, 160
    as late guest at its own banquet,
        528
    See also Sensuality; Sex
Error, **252**
    in freedom, better than right in
        chains, 301
    See also Mistake
Erudition:
    scholars and, 516
    See also Knowledge
Escape:
    gardens as, 316
    men's lives as, 588
    from places, 476
    from self-knowledge, 522
Essay, **252**

Essence of another human being,
    grasped by soul, 538
Establishment art as flouting, 55
Estrangement, *see* Alienation
Eternity:
    of freedom, 303
    See also Immortality
Ethics:
    grub comes before, 294
    work and, 590
    See also Morality
Etiquette, *see* Courtesy; Manners;
    Politeness
Eton school, 234
Eunuch, prisoner as, 493
Europe:
    America compared to, 38
    travel to, 560
Europeans, Americans compared
    to, 34
Evasion:
    of communication, 163
    conversation as, 180
    of oneself, as consolation, 520
Eve, *see* Adam and Eve
Evening, *see* Night
Event, **252**
    great men and great, 336
    happiness not a matter of, 342
    heart magnifies, 347
    produced by will, 582
Everyday life, *see* Commonplace;
    Daily life; Routine
Evil, **252–54**
    anti-Semitism and, 385
    attention and, 64
    character and, 128
    Christianity and, 145–46
    dullness and, 228
    excitement of fighting against,
        256
    good and, 330, 331
    good lost through fear of, 286
    innocence and, 378
    revolution does not get rid of,
        511
    superiority as cause of, 547
    underlying causes of, 123
    See also Devil; Villain
Exaggeration:
    ignorance and, 367
    of love, 412
    mistrust of, 230
Example, **254–55**
    moves the world, 6
    setting a good, 19, 254
Excellence, **255–56**
    envy and, 250
    loyalty to whatever makes
        possible, 334
Excess, **256**
    greatness and, 336
    weight, beauty and absence of,
        81
Excitement, **256**
    dogs as wanting, 221
    faith and, 270
    of the French, 300
    search for, 243
    See also Stimulation

and, 159
Intellectuals:
  baseball and, 75
  in London, 406
  See also Scholar
Intelligence, **380–81**
  advertising and, 14
  beauty preferred to, 85
  of children, 110, 139
  comic's appeal to, 161
  common, and culture, 198
  Emerson's work as hymn to, 241
  feeling of, 69
  mankind's use of, 415
  reading fiction does not tax the,
    501
  See also Cleverness; Smart
Intelligentsia, see Intellectuals
Intensity:
  of animals, 43
  of vision of facts, 599
  See also Vitality
Intention, **381**
  good, in art, 53
  writers', 598
  See also Aim; Goal; Purpose
Interest, **381**
  agreeableness and taking an, 24
  of artists, 62
  conviction and, 184
  play and, 477
  in war and women go together,
    579
  in work, 591
  See also Attention
Interpretation:
  of art, 54
  emotional crisis and, 243
  love and, 46
Interruption, **381–82**
  by husband and wife, 423
  mothers and, 439
Intimidation by pure style, 156
Italian opera, 456
Intolerance:
  for bigots, 93
  brotherhood and, 113
  See also Bigot
Intoxication:
  conversation as, 182
  See also Drugs, 227
Introduction, beauty as letter of, 87
Introspection, **382**
  middle-class, 428
  Puritan ancestry and, 181
Intrusion, advertising as, 15
Intuition, **382**
  desire and, 210
  genius and, 321
  of great men, 334
  Miller, Henry and, 429
  woman's, 588
Involvement, action and, 6
I.Q. of black children, 238
Ireland and the Irish, **382–83**
Irrational(ity):
  neurosis and, 134
  See also Absurd
Irresolution, **383**
  as means to an end, 425
  See also Indecision

Irritation of adults by children, 139
Islands, river without, 512
Isolation:
  diary and, 215
  See also Alone; Solitary
Israel, Irish as lost tribes of, 383
Istra, 84–85
Italy, kindness in, 31

Jail, see Prison; Prisoner
James, William, 260–61, **383–84**
January, 583
Jaspers, Karl, 37
Jazz, **384**
  painting and, 58
Jealousy, **40**¹, **384–85**
Jeremiah, 471
Jesters, folly of, 291
Jesus Christ, see Christ
Jew, **385**
  American, 38
  persecution of, 469
  See also Anti-Semitism
Job:
  failure at one's, 269
  interest in, 591
  loss of, 590
  money and, 434
  See also Career; Vocation;
    Occupation; Work
Jockeys, 355
Johnson, Samuel, 121
Joking:
  by artists, 59
  See also Comic; Funny; Humor;
    Laugh; Wise-cracking; Wit
Journalese, 450
Journalism, see Newspaper; Press
Journalist, the President and, 491
Journey:
  beginning, 88
  spiritual, 540
  See also Travel; Journey
Joy, **385–86**
  as adoration, 13
  of clothes, 158
  creative emotion and, 191
  enjoyment versus, 248
  friends increase, 306
  of God, 325
  marriage and, 423
  of painters, 57
  reality and, 502
  thankfulness and, 333
  See also Ecstasy; Exhilaration;
    Exaltation; Happiness
Juan, Don, collector as
  unconscious, 160
Judges:
  alimony and, 26
  inexperienced, 392
  police and cooperation of, 481
  policemen as, 481
Judging:
  ability, 1
  by appearances, 46
  by examples, 255
  See also Criticism
Judgment, **386–87**
  of artist, 57
  of children, 140

destiny and, 212
  of editors, 230
  of posterity, 487
Just, the: death and, 202
Just anger, 40
Justice, **387**
  communism and, 164
  in England, 246
  judgment and, 386
  law and, 393
  liberty and, 302
  for Negroes in America, 30
  pity and, 475
  society and, 535
  See also Injustice; Law

Kafka, Franz, 59
Kennedy, Robert, 394
Killing:
  fear of, in combat, 77
  by laughter, 391
  pleasure of, 574
  See also Homicide; Hunting;
    Murder
Kin:
  spiritual, 540
  See also Family; Kinship
Kindness, **388-89**
  in America, 31
  toward animals, 41
  argument versus, 48
  of artists, 59
  toward children, 139
  complaining about lack of, 166
  of friends, 308, 309
  in leaders, 395
  for men, 419
  sexual experience and, 526
  success and, 545
  See also Benevolence;
    Charitableness; Charity;
    Courtesy
Kinship, with animals, 41
Kiss, **389**
  children and, 135
Kitchen utensils, 198
Knowledge, **389-90**
  age and, 19
  American desire for, 34, 38
  in aphorisms, 45
  children and, 135
  conviction and, 184
  courage and, 188
  criticism and, 195
  doing, feeling, and, 223
  doubt and, 224
  dreams and, 225
  education and, 235
  of excellence, 255
  experience and, 261
  faith and, 271
  fantasy and, 274
  of future, 314
  genius and, 319-20
  of God through love, 327
  of great men, 334
  imagination and, 370
  intuitive, see Intuition
  of limitations, 403
  pleasures of ignorance and of,
    368

genius and, 320
habits better than, 339
of politics, 484
principles confused with, 493
See also Golden rule
Rush:
of American life, 36–37
See also Hurry
Rush hour, 544
traffic in, 66
Ruskin, John: parody of, 463
Russian revolutionaries, faces of, 266
Russians, **514**
Ruthlessness:
aloneness and, 26
of great men, 335

Sabbath, 514
See also Sunday
Sacrament, female beauty as, 86
Sacrifice, **514–15**
actors and, 9
choice and, 142
for infants, 71
old age and, 21, 23
self-, and fulfillment, 313
See also Giving up;
Relinquishing; Renunciation
Sadism:
art versus, 51
destiny and, 213
masochism less well repressed than, 546
See also Brutality; Cruelty
Sadness, **515**
beauty and, 84
of boys, 110
of Christian, 144
of Christmas season, 147
at flowers' fate, 289
of William James, 383
See also Depression; Gloom;
Melancholy; Unhappiness
Safety:
in beauty, 85
See also Security
Sagacity in business, 115
Sage:
mind in repose, 176
See also Wise men
Saint, **515–16**
as happiest people, 343
as merriest people, 392
women as, 587
Salad, skill of mixing, 292
Salaries of baseball players, 75
Salesmen, writers as, 62
Salvation:
artists and, 58
through brotherhood, 113
education as road to, 34
intelligence and, 381
painting as, 57
perpetual youth as, 600
of the soul, 538
thinking about soul as beginning of, 539
working out one's own, 524
Same(ness):

boredom and, 107
waking up the, as boring, 107
Sanity:
attribution of, 415
confining one's neighbor not a proof of one's, 415
Santa Claus (Father Christmas), 146–47
Satan, *see* Devil
Satanic, commerce as, 115
Satisfaction, **516**
death and, 201
in Heaven, 348
sensual love extinguished after, 411
understanding someone affords him, 567
See also Contentment;
Fulfillment; Gratification;
Happiness
Savage:
aloneness disliked by, 26
American mind and mind of, 36
Savagery:
for causes, 123
politeness as, 189
Saving:
the soul, 538
See also Salvation
Scandal, talk and, 183
Scarcity of excellence, 255, 256
Scenery, **516**
See also Landscape
Scholar, **516**
Schools:
ghetto, 238
mothers and, 140
mutilation in, 238–39
psychological realities at, 238
report cards from, 140
restrictiveness of, 140
See also Education; Homework;
Teachers; Teaching
Schubert, Franz, 443
Science, **516–17**
experience and, 260–61
philosophy and, 473
Scripture, *see* Bible; New Testament
Scruples of man of action, 6
Sculpture, *see* Statues
Sea, 517
battle at, 78
See also Waves
Seagulls, flying, 95
Seal, wishing to be a, 517
Seaside, happiness to be alone at the, 343
Seasons:
soul has its, 538
See also Autumn; Spring;
Summer; Winter
Secrecy:
belonging and, 91
See also Hiding
Secret, **518**
Rome unveils your, 513
of Russians, 514
Secretary, **518**
Security:
children's sense of, 137

emotional, and family life, 274
life and, 402
See also Safety; Stability
Sedative:
nature as, 447
See also Opiate; Tranquilizer
Seduction:
fashion and, 275
into virtue, 575
Seeing, **518**
in art, 51
artists' relation to, 57
beauty, 81, 82, 84
believing in, 270
drawing what one must make others see, 56
expressing versus, 53
flowers, 290
See also Looking; Vision;
Watching
Seeking:
gifts, 577
truth, 564–65
See also Pursuit
Seem:
ambition to, 28
See also Appearance; Impression
Seers, philosophers as, 471
Self, **518–20**
artists', 59, 62
change of, 125, 126
experience of, 262
forcing the world to adjust to one's, 591
friendship with, 311
genius and, 321
giving of one's, 324, 325
happiness in getting out of one's, 340
happiness in rebirth as another, 342
loneliness and union with one's, 407
personality and, 470
psychological history of mankind within, 302
simulation as most useful to, 531
tradition and, 559
usefulness to one's, 569
war among men because of war with one's, 578
withholding one's, 592
See also Ego; Egotism; Identity;
Individual; Inner self;
Personality
Self-acceptance, **520–21**
fear and, 285
Self-actualization:
creativity as, 192
as only purpose of self, 520
See also Self-fulfillment
Self-assertion, 521
children rejected for, 529
Self-assurance:
of young man, 18
See also Self-confidence
Self-awareness, **521**
anxiety and, 44–45
artists and, 56
of sincerity or lack of it, 532
See also Self-knowledge; Self-